JUSTICE ADMINISTRATION LEGAL SERIES

JOHN C. KLOTTER, B.A., J.D.
Professor Emeritus and Former Dean
School of Justice Administration
University of Louisville

JACQUELINE R. KANOVITZ, B.A., J.D.
Professor of Law and Associate Dean
University of Louisville

CONSTITUTIONAL LAW

KLOTTER / KANOVITZ

Sixth Edition

anderson publishing co.
2035 reading road
cincinnati, ohio 45202
(513) 421-4142

CONSTITUTIONAL LAW, SIXTH EDITION

ISBN 0-87084-496-2
Library of Congress Catalog Number 90-81067

Kelly Humble *Managing Editor* *Project Editor*—Elisabeth Roszmann

PREFACE

More than twenty years have passed since the first edition of this book was published. Our goal was then, and continues to be, presenting up-to-date analysis of critical constitutional issues affecting justice personnel. While the sixth edition follows the approach and structure of earlier editions, changes in constitutional focus and interpretation have created the need for what in some instances amounts to major revisions in content.

Criminal justice employees have traditionally been subjected to extensive restrictions on personal liberty, restrictions that other employees are not. These restrictions extend to height, weight and grooming, to the holding of outside employment and to other seemingly private matters. We live today in a litigious era and employment rights litigation has become a thriving industry. Chapter 12 was added in 1985 to address the constitutional status of commonplace justice agency employment restrictions. This chapter also covers employment protection under federal laws which prohibit discrimination on account of race, sex or age in hiring, promotion and other personnel decisions.

On the whole, constitutional trends during the Rehnquist Court era have been favorable to law enforcement agencies. Many former, and often unworkable, restrictions have been tempered. For example, the exclusionary rule has been modified, enforcement personnel now have more options in seizing evidence from vehicles, and several exceptions to the *Miranda* requirements have been recognized. The Supreme Court, in reviewing cases, has focused upon the "totality of circumstances," "public safety," "balancing effect," and similar flexible review standards.

The existence of more flexible review standards does not imply that criminal justice personnel are free to violate constitutional rights. They are liable in damages and criminally accountable for their unconstitutional behavior. Excess and abuses of authority, furthermore, could prompt courts again to tighten the rules.

Louisville, Kentucky
July 1990

John C. Klotter
Jacqueline R. Kanovitz

PREFACE TO FIRST EDITION

> Decency, security, and liberty alike demand that governmental officials shall be subjected to the same rules of conduct that are commands to the citizen. In a government of laws, existence of the government will be imperiled if it fails to observe the law scrupulously. Our government is the potent, the omnipresent teacher. For good or for ill, it teaches the whole people by its example. Crime is contagious. If the government becomes a lawbreaker, it breeds contempt for the law; it invites every man to become a law unto himself; it invites anarchy. To declare that in the administration of the criminal law the end justifies the means—to declare that the government may commit crimes in order to secure the conviction of a private criminal—would bring terrible retribution. Against that pernicious doctrine this court should resolutely set its face.

This philosophy, that government agents should be subjected to certain restrictions in enforcing laws was summarized by Supreme Court Justice Louis D. Brandeis in the case of *Olmstead v. United States.*[1]

Today, more than ever before, those who have been entrusted with the challenging but rewarding responsibility of protecting life and property must thoroughly understand the principles of state and federal constitutions and the duties which flow from their application.

The constitutions of the original thirteen states were written during a period in history when the people were keenly aware of their rights and of the possibility that a strong government might deprive them of these rights. The Constitution of the United States, which was written only a few years after the Declaration of Independence, was framed by men who had lived during a period of strict control and later during a period of too little control. As a result it was the intention of these dedicated men that the new government established under the United States Constitution protect both the rights of the individual and the rights of society.

One abiding principle which has endured since the adoption of the Constitution and the Bill of Rights is that which recognizes the dignity and worth of the individual human being. Even those who have violated the codes of civilized human behavior are entitled to certain minimum protections.

While maintaining a system which assures adequate respect for the rights and dignity of those charged with crime is a fundamen-

[1] 277 U.S. 438, 72 L.Ed. 944, 48 S.Ct. 564 (1928).

tal goal of our society, it is certainly not the only goal. Those who do not violate the law, the great majority, the producers, also have rights. They have the right to use the streets of this nation free from the fear of bodily harm, the right to protection from the rapist, the thief, and even from automobile drivers who operate their vehicles without regard for the lives and safety of others. And perhaps most of all society has the right to establish reasonable procedures to solve the crime problems. There are some who feel that the Supreme Court has erred too much on the side of the law-breaker and has made the task of enforcement impossible. It is not the purpose of this book either to praise or condemn the Court for its record in recent years. In an area of enforcement where certainty is vital, it is more important that the dictates of the law be understood than that consensus be reached as to the wisdom or necessity of an announced rule.

In preparing this book the authors have emphasized the provisions of the Constitution which directly relate to the powers of both federal and state law enforcement officers and prosecutors and limitations on these officers. Inasmuch as the constitutional provisions draw their meaning from judicial interpretation, selected cases have been included along with the textual analysis.

The synthesis of constitutional decisions is not a mechanical process. Inescapably some degree of interpretation is involved. The authors have not always agreed on the interpretations to be given the court decisions nor on the extent to which these court rulings should be projected. They consider this diversity in views prevents a "one-sided" interpretation of the law and provides a stimulus which should be utilized by the instructor where the book is employed as a text. While there has been a great deal of consultation and mutual interchange of ideas, in the interest of intellectual integrity, the authors have documented the chapters for which each assumes primary responsibility.

Chapter 1 of Part I deals with the development of the Federal Constitution and the history of the Bill of Rights. The remaining chapters in Part I discuss in depth the substantive content of the first eight Amendments and corresponding state provisions with emphasis on recent court interpretations and trends. These are of primary concern to police agencies and prosecutors.

In Part II of the book leading decisions handed down by the Supreme Court have been included in order to give the reader an understanding not only of what the law says but of the processes used by the Court in reaching its conclusions. The cases are included in Part II rather than immediately following the related discussions because many of them have broader application than the subject matter of any one chapter. The decisions should be studied carefully by the student or reader in order to develop a richer understanding of the policies and reasons underlying the rules which have been devised by the courts.

The book is prepared primarily for those who are engaged in the immense task of enforcing the criminal laws of the fifty states and of the United States. No effort has been made to use the local laws of any particular jurisdiction. Therefore, it is necessary and even imperative that the student familiarize himself with the constitutional, statutory and decisional law of his own state.

The trend has been toward an ever increasing uniformity in state and federal laws in the area of criminal procedure. This is attributable in part to the voluntary adoption of uniform standards by state legislators and judges, but mostly to the force of Supreme Court interpretation. Insofar as there are differences between local laws and the rules announced by the Supreme Court, it bears repeated mention that the Federal Constitution as construed by the highest tribunal in the land takes precedence over any conflicting state constitutional or statutory provisions. In other words, the Federal Constitution establishes the minimum protection which the states can and must afford to their citizens. Beyond this, however, the states are at liberty to formulate stricter requirements by legislative action or court decision.

Where this book is used as a text it is strongly recommended that the student be required to brief the cases in Part II as well as any additional cases which the instructor feels are of current importance. The law is constantly changing and the necessity of keeping up-to-date can be accomplished only by a reading of the latest pronouncements.

We express our sincere gratitude to Professor David A. McCandless, Director of the Southern Police Institute; to Professor Lawrence W. Knowles, Professor of Constitutional Law at the University of Louisville Law School; and to Mrs. Pearl W. Von Allmen, Librarian, University of Louisville Law School for their valuable assistance in preparing the manuscript.

Louisville, Kentucky
October, 1967

John C. Klotter
Jacqueline R. Kanovitz

CONTENTS

Part I
AN ANALYSIS OF CONSTITUTIONAL PROVISIONS AND COURT DECISIONS

Part II
JUDICIAL DECISIONS RELATING TO PART II 631

Part III
APPENDIX

Chapter 1
HISTORY
AND GENERAL APPLICATION
OF THE
CONSTITUTIONAL PROVISIONS*

We the People of the United States, in Order to form a more perfect Union, establish Justice, insure domestic Tranquility, provide for the common defence, promote the general Welfare, and secure the Blessings of Liberty to ourselves and our Posterity, do ordain and establish this Constitution for the United States of America.

Preamble to the United States Constitution

Section

---

* *by John C. Klotter*

§ 1.1 Foundations of American constitutional government

The men who met in Philadelphia in 1787 had ample precedent for the establishment of a written constitution. Americans had been living under colonial charters for over a hundred years. When ties with England were severed in 1776, the Continental Congress had issued a resolution recommending that the thirteen colonies adopt constitutions in preparation for statehood. New Hampshire was first to respond to the call on January 5, 1776.[1] By 1779, all thirteen of the former colonies had framed local constitutions. These early documents drew heavily from the colonial institutions of government and from English political traditions. Nearly all of the original state constitutions provided for bicameral legislatures which would be responsible for selecting the governor. This pattern closely resembled the English parliamentary system.

§ 1.2 – Early steps toward national unity

The federal union, consummated by the adoption of the Constitution in 1788-1789, was not the first attempt at alliance among the colonies. As early as 1643, an alliance called the New England Confederacy had been formed among the four colonies of Massachusetts, New Plymouth, Connecticut and New Haven for their mutual defense against the Dutch and the Indians. Because the colonists were reluctant from the outset to confer sovereign powers on a central government, the delegation was a gradual process.

The Revolutionary War provided the first real impetus for unity. Coordination of the war effort required something more than thirteen independent nations fighting separately for a common goal. When the First Continental Congress assembled in Philadelphia in 1774, all of the colonies except Georgia sent delegates.[2] Americans, however, were not yet ready to give their irrevocable and permanent allegiance to a new central governing body. They were throwing off the yoke of an oppressive monarch and were jealous of their independence. Consequently, the powers given to the Continental Congress were only those that were strictly necessary for the immediate purpose of winning the war. The states retained their sovereignty and the Continental Congress functioned purely in a representative capacity as the agent of the several states.

---

1 ERIKSSON, AMERICAN CONSTITUTIONAL HISTORY, ch. 7 (1933).

2 EVANS, CASES ON CONSTITUTIONAL LAW, ch. 1 (1933).

§ 1.3 Articles of Confederation

It soon became apparent that a stronger central government was necessary in order to carry on the war and conduct the common affairs of the nation. A committee was appointed in 1776 to study the problem and to draw up articles of union. This committee wrote the Articles of Confederation, which were adopted and became effective in March, 1781. While the Articles of Confederation set up a national government, its powers over domestic affairs were so limited that the new government was doomed to fail even before its short career was launched. Fearing a strong central government, the states refused to give the newly formed Congress the vital powers to levy taxes, regulate commerce or enforce its laws.[3] The Union established under the Articles of Confederation was nothing more than a loosely joined league of sovereign and independent states. The chief function of the national government was to represent the league of states in foreign affairs. It possessed no authority to pass laws affecting private citizens at home.

After the War of Independence was won and the colonists obtained the liberty they were struggling for, they found that the government, which they had so hastily set up, was not workable. The period immediately following the war was one of too little political control rather than too much. Fortunately, the leaders of this period were capable men who were able to work out a solution to the problem without further bloodshed, or without a dictatorship, which often follows a revolution.

§ 1.4 Drafting the Constitution of the United States

In February of 1787, the Congress, established under the Articles of Confederation, adopted a resolution recommending the calling of a convention to revise the Articles of Confederation. On May 25, 1787, the delegates assembled in Philadelphia and made George Washington their unanimous choice for president. Fifty-five delegates, representing all of the states except Rhode Island, attending during the session, which lasted nearly four months.

The most immediate question to be decided by the convention was whether the Articles of Confederation could be salvaged or whether the delegates should begin anew. It was James Madison's proposal to incorporate the best feature of the Articles of Confederation -- its provision for the *separation of power* into three branches of government -- into the new Constitu-

---

3 ERIKSSON, *supra* note 1.

tion. After much debate and compromise on such issues as the amount and kind of power that should be granted to the central government, the basis for representation in the national Congress, and the relation of the nation to the states, the convention submitted a finished document which bore very little resemblance to the instrument which they had been called upon to "revise." The new Constitution conferred a vast range of new powers on all branches of the central government and provided for corresponding limitations on the powers of the states.

This draft of a constitution proposed to give to the three million people and their descendants the framework for a legal and political system which would insure freedom and independence. Never before had a people been given such an opportunity for individual and collective development.

§ 1.5 –Ratification by the states

Although much effort went into preparing the proposed Constitution, the important task still remained. When the Congress called for a convention in February, 1787, the members did not anticipate drafting a new constitution; however, when the draft was submitted, the Congress neither approved nor disapproved it, but instead, passed it on to the state legislatures. After much debate, the state legislatures submitted the document to state conventions (as recommended by the Constitutional Convention) with a proviso that if nine states ratified this new Constitution, it would supersede the Articles of Confederation.

Many people bitterly opposed the adoption of the Constitution, while others argued that only by adopting it could the states work together toward a common goal. James Madison, Alexander Hamilton and John Jay undertook the task of selling the new Constitution to the people. In their famous *The Federalist Papers*, the authors urged the need for a strong national government to provide for political stability and national security. Their opponents argued that:

(1) the taxing powers of Congress were too great,
(2) the Constitution lacked procedural safeguards which would insure an impartial trial,
(3) the Constitution contained no Bill of Rights, and
(4) excessive power was concentrated in the central government, with the result that the individual states would be swallowed up and lose their sovereignty.

On September 28, 1787, the Constitution was submitted to the people by way of state conventions, but it did not receive the necessary nine-state ratification until June 21, 1788, when New Hampshire ratified it. This was sufficient to make the Constitution operative for those nine states. However, the advocates of the Constitution were aware that in order to have a workable government, the states of New York and Virginia -- neither of which had ratified the Constitution -- must be included in the new Union. Finally, on June 25, 1788, by a margin of ten votes in a convention of 168 members, Virginia (number ten) ratified the Constitution over the objection of such delegates as George Mason and Patrick Henry. On July 2, 1788, the president of the Confederation of Congress announced that the new instrument of government had been duly ratified. New York (eleven) ratified the Constitution on July 26, 1788.

It is interesting to note that North Carolina (twelve) did not ratify the Constitution until November 21, 1789; nor did Rhode Island (thirteen) until May 29, 1790.[4] These two states existed as sovereign states outside of the Union for many months. One of the events that encouraged them to become a part of the United States was the passage by Congress of a tariff on foreign imports, including those imported from North Carolina and Rhode Island.

On September 13, 1788, after the two additional states of New York and Virginia had ratified the Constitution, the Continental Congress, which was meeting irregularly, passed a resolution to put the new Constitution into operation. The first Wednesday of January, 1789, was set as the date for choosing presidential electors, the first Wednesday of February for the meeting of electors, and the first Wednesday of March for the opening session of the new Congress. Because of several delays, Congress was late in assembling, and it was not until April 30, 1789, that George Washington was inaugurated as the first president of the United States.[5] Thus, within a period of 25 years, two major victories had occurred -- the War of Independence was won and a firm and stable government was established for the thirteen states.

---

4 The dates that the individual states ratified the Constitution are as follows: Delaware - December 7, 1787; Pennsylvania - December 11, 1787; New Jersey - December 18, 1787; Georgia - January 2, 1788; Connecticut - January 9, 1788; Massachusetts - February 6, 1788; Maryland - April 26, 1788; South Carolina - May 23, 1788; New Hampshire - June 21, 1788; Virginia - June 25, 1788; New York - July 26, 1788; North Carolina - November 21, 1789; Rhode Island - May 29, 1790.

5 THE CONSTITUTION OF THE UNITED STATES OF AMERICA, ANALYSIS AND INTERPRETATION U.S. Government Printing Office, 1964.

§ 1.6 Structure of the Constitution

The United States Constitution, as drafted, was a relatively brief document and was not expected to cover every point that might arise in the future. The original document is divided into seven parts or articles.[6]

ARTICLE I. The first article of the Constitution sets out the structure and functions of Congress. It provides that the legislative powers of the United States shall be vested in Congress, which shall consist of two chambers -- the Senate and the House of Representatives. Sections 2 through 7 of this article provide for the number of representatives in each chamber, the qualifications for membership, the methods of selecting such members, the procedures to be followed in enacting legislation, and the manner of impeachment. Section 8 outlines the powers of Congress in domestic and foreign affairs; sections 9 and 10 deal with specific limitations on the powers of Congress and the states.

ARTICLE II. The second article sets up the executive branch of government. It provides that the executive powers of the United States shall be vested in the president. The remainder of this article deals with the qualifications of the president and vice president, the manner of election, the oath of office, the method and grounds for removal, and the powers and duties of the chief executive.

ARTICLE III. The third article vests the judicial power of the United States in the Supreme Court and in such inferior courts as Congress should see fit to establish. It defines in general terms the scope of the judicial power and outlines those cases in which the Supreme Court is to have original and appellate jurisdiction. The third article also contains a definition of treason and the requirements for a conviction.

---

6 The Constitution is reprinted in Part III of this book. It should be studied carefully for a more complete understanding of its contents.

ARTICLE IV. The fourth article spells out some of the duties which the states owe to each other, including the duties of extending full faith and credit to the laws of sister states, of granting equal privileges and immunities to citizens of other states, and of interstate extradition. This article also contains provisions for the admission of new states, grants Congress plenary power to govern territorial possessions of the United States, and assures each state a republican form of government. Finally, it guarantees the states protection against external invasion, as well as federal assistance in quelling internal violence and uprising.

ARTICLE V. The fifth article defines two procedures for amending the Constitution. First, it may be amended when two-thirds of both Houses shall propose amendments and these proposed amendments are ratified by the state legislatures of three-fourths of the states or by state conventions in three-fourths of the states. Second, the constitution may be amended when, by the application of the legislatures of two-thirds of the states, Congress shall call a convention for proposing amendments which shall be valid when ratified by the legislatures of three-fourths of the states, or by conventions in three-fourths of the states.

ARTICLE VI. The sixth article contains the "supremacy" clause which provides that the Constitution, laws and treaties of the United States shall be the supreme law of the land and that state judges are to be bound by it regardless of what their state constitutions and laws provide to the contrary. It also provides that all legislative, executive and judicial officers, both of the United States and of the several states, must take an oath of office to support the Constitution.

ARTICLE VII. The seventh article is of historic importance only. This article provides that the Constitution shall become effective when ratified by nine states and shall be operative for those states which ratify it.

The first three divisions of the Constitution are commonly referred to as the "*separation of power*" articles because they separate the essential powers of the national government into three coordinate branches -- legislative, executive and judicial. From the very beginning courts and scholars have disagreed concerning the powers of these branches. In 1983 the United States Supreme Court struck down as unconstitutional the "legislative veto," the technique that Congress has used for years to limit the powers of the President and federal administrative agencies acting under the President. Although article 1 of the Constitution vests legislative powers in Congress, and article 2 vests executive powers in the President, Congress has enacted laws giving the executive branch qualified authority to act, subject to the later disapproval of one or both Houses of Congress. Such legislative-veto clauses were attached to measures on subjects ranging from presidential war powers, foreign aid and arms sales, health and safety bills, energy regulations and the budget.[7]

In the *Chadha* case, Chief Justice Warren Burger, writing for the majority, explained that the legislative veto provision violates the principles of separation of powers and the system of checks and balances embodied in the Constitution. Specifically, the Supreme Court decided that the section of the Immigration Act authorizing one House of Congress, by resolution to invalidate decisions of the executive branch to allow a particular deportable alien to remain in the United States is unconstitutional. The reason cited was that action by the House, pursuant to that section, is essentially legislation and thus subject to the constitutional requirements of passage by majority of both Houses and presentation to the President. The effect of the decision goes far beyond the specific situation, however, as it reaffirms the principles of separation of powers and the system of checks and balances embodied in the Constitution.

One of the reasons why this great document has proven workable for almost two hundred years is that the governmental powers have been diversified to that too much power is not given to any one branch of government. The division of power among the three branches of government has, at least up to the present time, prevented the development of an autocracy which might result in a dictatorship.

---

[7] INS v. Chadha, 462 U.S. 919, 103 S. Ct. 2764, 77 L. Ed. 2d 317 (1983). *See also* Alaska Airlines, Inc. v. Brock, ___ U.S. ___, 107 S. Ct. 1476, 94 L. Ed. 2d 661 (1987) which held that the first-hire provisions of the employee protection program in the Airline Deregulation Act was unconstitutional because of the provision authorizing a one-house legislative veto of regulations adopted thereunder. This alters the balance of power between the legislative and executive branches.

§ 1.7 Nature of the federal union

In order to appreciate the nature and problems of the state-federal government in the United States, it is necessary to review the history of the American colonists' relationships with England and the events which led to the Constitution. For many years prior to the Declaration of Independence in 1776, a controversy existed regarding the sovereign powers of the colonies. The individuals who drafted the Declaration did not recognize the parliament of Great Britain as having any sovereign authority over the states.[8]

After the Declaration of Independence, each sovereignty resided in each of the several states. Each state had its own constitution and each functioned as an autonomous local unit. Even under the Articles of Confederation, the states retained their sovereignty. As a necessary condition to formulation of a federal union, however, the new states yielded a portion of their sovereign powers to the planned national or federal government which was created by the Constitution.

There was no precedent for the dual (state-federal) system of government which the Americans established in 1789. Consequently, it remained for the subsequent course of history to define and redefine the precise nature of the federal union and the relationship between the nation and the states. The original understanding was that the federal government was to be one of enumerated or delegated powers, and that all powers not expressly delegated to it were reserved to the states. In other words, the federal government was said to possess only such powers as were expressly granted to it by the states. Those powers not delegated remained in the states, where they originally resided, or were retained by the people. Once a state had joined the Union and had ceded a portion of its sovereignty, the relationship would be permanent.[9] The Civil War put to the test whether a state could disassociate itself by its own voluntary act of secession. The indestructible nature of the federal union was reaffirmed on the battlefields.

§ 1.8 Powers granted to the federal government

The enumerated powers granted to the federal government are found primarily in article I, section 8 of the Constitution. Although the powers are stated specifically and succinctly in these clauses, their interpretation has been a matter of debate for almost two centuries. The remainder of this sec-

---

8 BENNETT, AMERICAN THEORIES OF FEDERALISM (1963).

9 Texas v. White, 74 U.S. (7 Wall.) 700, 19 L. Ed. 227 (1868).

tion will be devoted to a discussion of those powers, with emphasis on those which are most important in the criminal justice process.

a. The power to levy and collect taxes, duties, imposts and excises, and the power to provide for the common defense and general welfare.

The power to tax is essential to the existence of a strong government. Without a source of revenue, no government can survive. One of the chief shortcomings of the government established under the Articles of Confederation was the lack of independent financial powers.

The power to tax is also the power to regulate. Therefore, within limitations as determined by the courts, Congress, under the taxing power, may regulate an activity indirectly by taxation if Congress has the power under the Constitution to regulate that activity directly. For example, the Supreme Court has upheld a tax on coal producers, even though the tax was designed for penalty and control purposes rather than for revenue purposes, on the theory that under the "commerce" clause, Congress may regulate the production and distribution of coal.[10]

Using the power to tax, Congress has regulated narcotics dealers by imposing a special tax upon such dealers and has regulated the distribution of firearms by placing a tax on dealers in firearms. Such taxes have been upheld as having a reasonable relation to revenue raising.[11]

b. The authority to borrow money on the credit of the United States.

In the event that taxes are inadequate, the power to borrow money provides a second important source of funds to meet the operating expenses of the federal government. Relying in part on this clause, the United States Supreme Court has approved the authority of Congress to issue Treasury notes and to make them legal tender for satisfaction of debts.[12]

c. The power to regulate interstate and foreign commerce.

Through Supreme Court interpretation, the power to regulate interstate and foreign commerce has become the most singularly potent of all the specifically enumerated powers. Any activity, interstate or purely local in

---

[10] Sunshine Anthracite Coal Co. v. Adkins, 310 U.S. 381, 60 S. Ct. 907, 84 L. Ed. 1263 (1940).

[11] United States v. Doremus, 249 U.S. 86, 39 S. Ct. 214, 63 L. Ed. 493 (1919) and Sonzinsky v. United States, 300 U.S. 506, 57 S. Ct. 554, 81 L. Ed. 772 (1937).

[12] Knox v. Lee, 79 U.S. (12 Wall.) 457, 20 L. Ed. 287 (1871).

character, is potentially within the reach of the regulatory powers of Congress if it has an appreciable effect upon the flow of interstate commerce, regardless of whether the effect is direct or indirect. Exercising this power, Congress has prescribed safety standards in transportation and industry, labor legislation, crop restriction programs, anti-trust laws, and even civil rights legislation, such as the 1964 Public Accommodations Law.[13] There is a whole body of federal criminal statutes built around the commerce powers, including the Mann Act, making it a federal offense to transport women across state lines for an immoral purpose; the National Motor Vehicle Theft Act, making it an offense to transport stolen vehicles in interstate commerce; and the Federal Kidnapping Act, imposing penalties for kidnapping an individual and carrying him across state lines. The authority granted to the United States under this "commerce" clause, used in conjunction with the "necessary and proper" clause (article I, section 8, clause 18) serves as the basis for the establishment of federal law enforcement agencies such as the Federal Bureau of Investigation.

This power to regulate commerce not only vests vast powers in the federal government, but also, with the possible exception of the "due process" clause, is the most important imitation imposed by the Constitution on the exercise of state power. The distribution of power by national and state governments is predicated to a great extent upon the implications of the commerce clause. Under the police power, the state may regulate matters of local concern; however, if the state laws, even under the police power, are deemed to impede substantially the free flow of commerce from state to state, these may be declared invalid under the authority of the commerce clause of the Constitution.[14] For example, if a state trespass law is applied in such a way as to come in conflict with the Civil Rights Act (based in part on the commerce clause), the trespass law cannot stand.[15]

Congress' powers under the interstate commerce clause are broad and deep. In a five to four decision the Supreme Court determined that Congress acted constitutionally when in 1974 it extended the definition of "employer" as used in the Equal Employment Opportunity Act to include state and local governments. In that decision the court held that the extension of the Age Discrimination and Employment Act to cover state and local governments was a valid exercise of Congress' powers under the commerce clause. In enforcing the Act, the Court determined that the mandatory retirement of a Wyoming game warden at age 55 based on age alone was in violation of the

---

13 Heart of Atlanta Motel, Inc. v. United States, 379 U.S. 241, 85 S. Ct. 348, 13 L. Ed. 2d 258 (1964).

14 California v. Thompson, 313 U.S. 109, 61 S. Ct. 930, 85 L. Ed. 1219 (1941).

15 Hamm v. City of Rock Hill, 379 U.S. 306, 85 S. Ct. 384, 13 L. Ed. 2d 300 (1964).

Act.[16] The four dissenting judges in this case criticized the majority for extending the commerce clause beyond its reasonable scope. Nevertheless, the commerce clause of the first article of the Constitution, as interpreted by the federal courts, has given many powers to Congress and the federal Government.

d. The right to establish rules of naturalization and laws relating to bankruptcies.

Based on this clause, Congress has enacted the Immigration and Nationality Act. The states have no authority whatsoever regarding naturalization, as this is the exclusive power of Congress.

Under this authority, Congress has enacted uniform laws on the subject of bankruptcies. States may enact laws relating to payments of debts, but any state law which is in conflict with the national bankruptcy laws enacted under this provision is invalid.[17]

e. The authority to coin money, to regulate the value thereof, and to fix the standards of weights and measures.

Congress has the exclusive authority to regulate every aspect of currency. Congress also has the power to designate the medium of exchange, to forbid defacement, melting, or exportation of money, and to establish agencies to enforce these laws.

f. The power to provide for the punishment of counterfeiting the securities and current coin of the United States.

Relying on this provision and the "necessary and proper" clause, Congress has established a federal agency to enforce the counterfeiting laws. The Supreme Court has sustained federal statutes penalizing the importation or circulation of counterfeit coins.[18]

g. The authority to establish post offices and post roads.

This provision gives Congress the authority to enact legislation regarding theft from the mails and to establish federal agencies to enforce these laws.

---

16 Equal Employment Opportunity Commission v. Wyoming, 460 U.S. 226, 103 S. Ct. 1054, 75 L. Ed. 2d 18 (1983).

17 International Shoe Co. v. Pinkus, 278 U.S. 261, 49 S. Ct. 108, 73 L. Ed. 316 (1929).

18 Baender v. Barnett, 255 U.S. 224, 41 S. Ct. 271, 65 L. Ed. 597 (1921).

While states have the authority to regulate the use of vehicles that carry mail, such as mail trains, the Supreme Court has held that the state cannot punish a person for operating a mail truck on its highways without procuring a driver's license from state authorities.[19]

h. The jurisdiction to secure to authors and inventors the exclusive right to their respective writings and discoveries.

This clause is the foundation upon which the national patent and copyright laws are based. The history of this provision traces back to the English statute of 1710 which procured to authors of books the right of publishing them for designated periods. A state may not pass a law which conflicts with federal laws based upon this clause.[20] However, a state may prescribe reasonable regulations to protect its citizens from fraud.

i. The prerogative of establishing judicial tribunals inferior to the Supreme Court.

Under the authority of this provision, Congress has established inferior federal courts. The Judiciary Act of 1789 provided for thirteen district courts, which were to have four sessions annually, and three circuit courts. Consistent with the provisions of this act, Congress has established the federal circuit courts, the federal district courts, the court of claims, the court of customs and appeals, and various tax courts. Not only may Congress establish courts, it may vest in these courts nonjudicial functions as well as judicial functions and can limit the powers of the courts established.[21]

j. The right to make and enforce laws related to piracies and felonies committed on the high seas and offenses against the laws of nations.

Congress has the power to define crimes that may be committed on United States vessels while on the high seas. An act punishing "the crime of piracy as defined by the laws of nations" was held to be an appropriate exercise of the constitutional authority to define and punish the offense.[22]

---

19 Johnson v. Maryland, 254 U.S. 51, 41 S. Ct. 16, 65 L. Ed. 126 (1920).

20 Wheaton v. Peters, 33 U.S. (3 Pet.) 591, 8 L. Ed. 1055 (1834).

21 Lurk v. United States, 370 U.S. 530, 82 S. Ct. 1459, 8 L. Ed. 2d 671 (1962).

22 United States v. The Cargo of the Brig Malek Adhel, 43 U.S. (2 How.) 210, 11 L. Ed. 239 (1844).

k. The power and responsibility for declaring war and making rules concerning captures on land and water.

This provision gives Congress the power to declare war. In addition, it has been interpreted to vest in Congress the authority to regulate rents during wartime and to establish other extensive wartime controls on the use of economic resources.[23]

l. The responsibility to raise and support armies.

Under this clause, Congress alone can raise and provide for the support of armies. Also under this authority, Congress may establish laws for the drafting of citizens to serve in the armed forces and may even suppress "houses of ill fame" in the vicinity of the places where forces are stationed.[24]

m. The power to provide and maintain a navy.

This provision, as the preceding one, was inserted for the purpose of designating Congress as the department of government which should exercise these powers. Generally, the court interpretations concerning the power to raise and support armies also apply to the navy.

n. The authority to make rules for the government and regulation of the land and naval forces.

This provision gives Congress the authority to establish the Code of Military Justice and to designate rules relating to trials by court-martial.

o. Power to provide for calling forth the militia to execute the laws of the Union, suppress insurrection, and repel invasions.

Based on this power Congress has enacted laws delegating to the president the authority to call forth the militia. Not only is this authority granted in the event of rebellion, but the militia may also be called to carry out the orders of the Supreme Court.

---

[23] United States v. Central Eureka Mining Co., 357 U.S. 155, 78 S. Ct. 1097, 2 L. Ed. 1228 (1958).

[24] McKinley v. United States, 249 U.S. 397, 39 S. Ct. 324, 63 L. Ed. 668 (1919).

p. Limited authority to organize, arm, discipline and train the militia.

This provision was interpreted as giving the Congress power to bring the militia under the control of the national government. In 1916, Congress re-organized the National Guard and authorized the president in emergencies to draft into military service members of the National Guard who thereupon should "stand discharged from the militia."

q. The exercise of exclusive legislative control over the seat of government in Washington and other federal installations.

Since Congress possesses legislative power over the District of Columbia, it may enact legislative provisions for the government of that District. Congress also has jurisdiction over certain lands within the states which have been ceded to the United States.

r. The power to make all laws necessary and proper for carrying into execution all of the above specifically enumerated powers.

This final broad grant of power has provided the necessary flexibility to enable the Constitution to be a living instrument and to endure for more than 200 years. By virtue of this "necessary and proper" clause, Congress can adopt measures for carrying out the enumerated powers appropriate to the times.

Although the powers granted to Congress were stated in the Constitution, the question arose early and still remains regarding the scope of this power. For example, in 1819 a controversy arose as to whether Congress had the power to charter a national bank. There was certainly no authorization for this within the powers specifically written in the Constitution. Nevertheless, Mr. Chief Justice Marshall in the celebrated case of *M'Culloch v. Maryland*[25] affirmed the power to exist and declared:

> Let the end be legitimate, let it be within the scope of the Constitution, and all means which are appropriate, which are plainly adapted to that end, which are not prohibited, but consist within the letter and spirit of the Constitution, are constitutional.

---

25 17 U.S. (4 Wheat.) 316, 4 L. Ed. 579 (1819). *See* case in Part II.

This broad interpretation of the necessary and proper clause has remained and has formed the basis of the implied powers doctrine. Since the New Deal era, the trend has been toward an even greater expansion of federal powers.

§ 1.9 Limitations on state powers

The powers granted to the federal government and discussed in the previous section are enumerated in the Constitution in positive terms. To further define the state-federal relationship, express limitations were placed on the states. Among the powers which the Constitution *prohibits* the states from exercising are the following:[26]

a. To enter into treaties, alliances, or confederations.

The power to make treaties lies exclusively in the hands of the federal government; states may not make treaties with other countries. Nor may states, once they have given powers to the federal government, withdraw from that government and bind themselves by confederations with other states or countries.

b. To coin money, emit bills of credit, or to make anything other than gold or silver coin legal tender in payment of debts.

As Congress has the authority to coin money, it would be confusing if the states had similar powers. Therefore, the Supreme Court declared that a law in Missouri authorizing the issuance of interest-bearing certificates was banned by this provision.[27]

c. To pass a bill of attainder.

A bill of attainder is a legislative act which inflicts punishment without trial. A Missouri statute which required persons to take an oath stating they had never given aid to the Confederacy was held invalid under this section as being a "bill of attainder."[28]

---

[26] U.S. CONST, art. I, §10.

[27] Byrne v. Missouri, 33 U.S. (8 Pet.) 40, 8 L. Ed. 859 (1834).

[28] Cummings v. Missouri, 71 U.S. (4 Wall.) 277, 18 L. Ed. 356 (1867).

d. To enact ex post facto laws.

Ex post facto means "after the fact" and as used in the Constitution signifies a law which:

(a) makes an act, innocent when committed, a crime,
(b) stipulates a greater punishment than was attached to the crime when it was committed, or
(c) alters the situation of the accused to his disadvantage.

e. To lay imposts or duties on imports or exports without the consent of Congress.

This restriction is a necessary concomitant of the exclusive power of Congress to regulate interstate commerce.

f. To keep troops or ships of war in times of peace.

This provision was intended to prevent the states from embroiling the nation in a way by their unilateral acts. The declaration of war as well as the conduct of the war are in the exclusive control of the federal government.

In addition to these explicit limitations, certain other restrictions on state governmental powers are implied from the nature of the federal union. The proposition that a state may not tax a federal agency is an example of such an implied limitation. Finally, there are those limitations which have been applied indirectly to the states by means of the "due process" clause of the Fourteenth Amendment. More will be said about these latter restrictions in future sections.

§ 1.10 Powers retained by the states

While the Constitution of the United States enumerates the powers granted to the federal government by the Constitution and limits the powers of the states, it is quite clear that the states, in granting specific powers to the federal government, intended to retain most of their inherent powers. Despite the broad interpretations of the powers granted to the federal government, the states assumed the major responsibility for government for the first eighty years after the adoption of the Constitution. Since the Civil War, and especially in the twentieth century, there has existed some tension between the states and the national government as more centralization has threatened the sovereignty of the individual states. The likelihood of this situation had been anticipated much earlier, and an attempt was made in 1791 to remove all doubt by the adoption of the Tenth Amendment. This amendment states that the powers not delegated to the United States by the Constitution, nor prohibited by it to the states, are reserved to the states respectively, or to the people.

It is interesting to note that some ten years after the adoption of the Constitution, the Kentucky and Virginia legislatures adopted resolutions concerning the rights retained by the states. In the Kentucky resolution adopted on November 19, 1798, it was resolved:[29]

> That the several states composing the United States of America are not united on the principle of unlimited submission to their general government; but that, by compact, under the style and title of the Constitution for the United States, and of amendments thereto, they constitute a general government for special purposes, delegate to that government certain definite powers, reserving, each state to itself, the residuary mass of rights to their own self-government; and that whenever the general government assumes undelegated powers, its acts are unauthorized, void, and of no force.

Notwithstanding such resolutions, powers assumed by the federal government have been extended and powers remaining in the states have diminished. However, the primary responsibility for the protection of the health, welfare and morals of the people remains with the state.

The courts have agreed that the *police power* of the state is inherent in the government of the state and that this is a power which the state did not surrender by becoming a member of the Union.[30] The police power of the state comprehends all those general laws and internal regulations necessary to secure the peace, good order, health and prosperity of the people, and the regulation and protection of property rights. In the case of the *District of Columbia v. Brooke*[31] the Court stated this is one of the most essential powers, at times the most insistent, and always one of the least limitable of the powers of government. Under this power, the states have passed laws defining crimes, regulating traffic, and providing for criminal procedural rules.

Strictly speaking, the federal government has no police power. However, Congress may exercise a similar power as incident to powers expressly conferred upon it by the Constitution.[32] Therefore, the validity of any statute

---

29 ERIKSSON, *supra* note 1, at 455.

30 Jacobson v. Massachusetts, 197 U.S. 11, 25 S. Ct. 358, 49 L. Ed. 643 (1904).

31 214 U.S. 138, 29 S. Ct. 560, 53 L.Ed. 941 (1909).

32 United States v. Dewitt, 76 U.S. (9 Wall.) 41, 19 L. Ed. 593 (1869).

so enacted depends on whether it directly relates to one of the powers delegated to the federal government.

§ 1.11 The Bill of Rights

During the battle over ratification of the Constitution, the anti-Federalists in the thirteen states strongly objected to the fact that the Constitution did not contain a bill of rights.[33] Although the Federalists argued that such a bill was unnecessary inasmuch as the powers granted to Congress were expressed powers and therefore had no need of limitation, many of the states refused to accept the Constitution without a promise that a bill of rights would be added. In Massachusetts, for example, the Federalists agreed to a list of nine proposed amendments in order to secure the ratification of the Constitution in that state. These amendments were not made a condition of ratification but were submitted as recommendations to be acted on after the new government should become operative. All of the states which ratified after Massachusetts followed this example and submitted recommended amendments to the Constitution.

Partly because seven of the thirteen original states which finally ratified the Constitution proposed amendments concerning the Bill of Rights, James Madison, during the first session of Congress, introduced twenty amendments which he had formulated after a careful study of the over two hundred amendments suggested by the ratifying conventions. After much discussion, the number was reduced to twelve and, of these, ten were ratified by three-fourths of the states and became the first ten amendments to the Constitution. These amendments are known as our Bill of Rights. This Bill of Rights was not intended to establish any novel principles of government but simply to embody certain guarantees and immunities which the colonists had inherited from their English ancestors and which had from time immemorial been subject to certain well-recognized exceptions arising from the necessities of the case.

At the time of its adoption, the Bill of Rights was intended to operation as a restriction only upon the national government. At this point in history, the states had given some of their sovereign powers to a strong central government and the people wished to insure that this strong government would not abridge those individual rights stated in the first ten amendments. The first ten amendments -- more strictly speaking the first eight amendments -- do not themselves restrict the states in any respect.

---

33 ERIKSSON, *supra* note 1, at 220.

The amendments which made some of the provisions of the Bill of Rights applicable to the states will be discussed in a later section. The restrictions placed upon the federal government by the Bill of Rights are discussed here briefly. Much of the remaining part of this book will be devoted to a careful analysis of the individual protections afforded by the Bill of Rights and the manner in which these are applied.

The specific provisions of the Bill of Rights lay down only a broad framework; they would mean little without court interpretation. Here each of the ten amendments that make up the Bill of Rights are briefly explained.[34] As most of these amendments -- the first, fourth, fifth, sixth and eighth -- are discussed thoroughly in the chapters that follow, no cases will be cited in reference to these sections. Those that are not discussed in future chapters are more fully explained here.

1 The First Amendment prohibits Congress from making any law concerning the establishment of religion or prohibiting the free exercise thereof or abridging the freedom of speech or of the press or the right of the people peaceably to assemble and to petition the government for redress of grievances.

2 The Second Amendment provides that "a well regulated Militia, being necessary to the security of a free State, the right of the people to keep and bear Arms, shall not be infringed." Early cases interpreted this provision to mean only that *Congress* may not infringe upon the right of the citizens to bear arms. Therefore, a state statute prohibiting regulation of the use of firearms was constitutional. The majority of the Seventh Circuit Court in 1982 approved the lower courts conclusion that the city of Morton Grove's ordinance to regulate handgun possession within the city limits did not violate the Second Amendment to the United States Constitution.[35] The Court, citing *Presser v. Illinois*,[36] held that the Second Amendment restricts only the federal government and therefore a city ordinance which does not conflict with the state constitution is enforceable. There is a difference of opinion as to whether this right to bear arms, as protected by the Second Amendment, is related to a well-regulated militia. In deciding whether the

---

34 The specific provisions of the Bill of Rights (first Ten Amendments) are reprinted in Part III of this book.

35 Quilici v. Village of Morton Grove, 532 F. Supp. 1169 (N.D. Ill. 1969).

36 Presser v. Illinois, 116 U.S. 252, 6 S. Ct. 580, 29 L. Ed. 615 (1886).

National Firearms Act violates this provision, the U.S. Supreme Court answered that in the absence of evidence tending to show that possession or use of a shotgun having a barrel of less than 18 inches in length has some reasonable relationship to the preservation or efficiency of a well-regulated militia, a law prohibiting transportation of unregistered shotguns in interstate commerce is not unconstitutional.[37]

3 The Third Amendment provides, "No Soldier shall, in time of peace, be quartered in any house without the consent of the Owner, nor in time of war, but in a manner to be prescribed by law." This amendment was included because the people remembered the outrages occasioned by the thrusting of armed troops into their homes by the British.

4 Because the homes of the people had been invaded indiscriminately by the British prior to the revolution, the Bill of Rights, in which the Fourth Amendment was inserted, provided generally against "unreasonable searches and seizures." This amendment has been carefully interpreted by the courts. One chapter in this book will be devoted to detention and arrest and another to search and seizure.

5 The Fifth Amendment enumerates safeguards for persons accused of crime. It provides:

(a) that the government shall not require a person to be held to answer for a capital or otherwise infamous crime unless on a presentment or indictment of a grand jury;
(b) that no person shall be subject for the same offense to be twice put in jeopardy of life or limb;
(c) that no person shall be compelled in any criminal case to be witness against himself;
(d) that no person shall be deprived of life, liberty, or property without due process of law; and
(e) that no person shall be deprived of his property for public use without just compensation.

6 The Sixth Amendment assures that in criminal prosecutions the accused shall enjoy the right to a speedy and public trial by an impartial jury of the state and district wherein the crime

---

37 United States v. Miller, 307 U.S. 174, 59 S. Ct. 816, 83 L. Ed. 1206 (1939).

shall have been committed; the right to be informed of the nature and cause of the accusation; the right to be confronted with the witness against him; the right to have compulsory process for attaining witnesses in his favor; and the right to have the assistance of counsel for his defense.

7 The Seventh Amendment is included primarily as a safeguard of property rights. It provides that "In Suits at common law where the value in controversy shall exceed twenty dollars, the right of trial by jury shall be preserved, and no fact tried by a jury, shall be otherwise reexamined in any Court of the United States, than according to the rules of the common law." Although it has been held that this amendment is not a limitation on the states and does not affect litigation in the state courts, each state has provisions in its constitution to secure generally the right to trial by jury in common law actions.

8 The Eighth Amendment restricts both the legislative and judicial branches of government and guarantees certain rights to the individual. This amendment guarantees that excessive bail shall not be required, excessive fines shall not be imposed, and unusual punishment shall not be inflicted. These rights were guaranteed under the unwritten English constitution and those who ratified the Constitution felt that they should be added specifically to the Bill of Rights.

9 The Ninth Amendment states, "The enumeration in the Constitution, of certain rights, shall not be construed to deny or disparage others retained by the people." This means only that, even though some of the rights of the people are not specifically mentioned in the Constitution and Bill of Rights, these rights will be retained by the people.

10 The Tenth Amendment states, "The powers not delegated to the United States by the Constitution, nor prohibited by it to the States, are reserved to the States respectively, or to the people."

The Tenth Amendment to the Constitution was added by the framers of the Constitution to make certain that the federal government would not assume powers not granted by the Constitution. As stated in the case of *National League of Cities v. Usery*, the ultimate purpose of the Amendment is to insure that the states enjoy a separate and independent existence and that

Congress may not exercise power in a fashion that impairs the States' integrity or their ability to function effectively in a federal system.[38]

In the case of *National League of Cities v. Usery*, the United States Supreme Court considered the Tenth Amendment statement that powers not delegated were to remain in the states or the people and the scope of the Interstate Commerce Clause. In a sharply divided vote, the majority agreed that the Commerce Clause does not empower Congress to enforce the minimum-wage and overtime provisions of the Fair Labor Standards Act against the states in "areas of traditional governmental functions." There, the majority of the Court reasoned that our federal system of government imposes definite limitations upon the authority of Congress to regulate the activities of the states as states by means of the Commerce power. The Court noted that this limitation is founded in the Tenth Amendment to the Constitution.

However, in the case of *Garcia v. San Antonio Metropolitan Transit Authority* in 1985, the majority rejected the *National League of Cities*' reasoning and held that Congress contravened no affirmative limit on its power under the Commerce Clause in enforcing the wage and hour provisions against the San Antonio Metropolitan Transit Authority.[39] In specifically overruling the *National League of Cities* case, the Court noted that any attempt to draw the boundaries of state regulatory immunity in terms of "traditional governmental functions" is not only unworkable but is inconsistent with established principles of federalism and, indeed, with those very federalism principles on which the *National League of Cities* purported to rest.

In reversing previous cases and holding that Congress does have authority to require municipalities to follow the provisions of the Fair Labor Standards Act, the Court commented:

> We perceive nothing in the overtime and minimum-wage requirements of the FLSA as applied to SAMTA, that is destructive of state sovereignty or violative of any constitutional provisions.

In reaching its decision in the *Garcia* case, the Court, in effect, applied the provisions of the Fair Labor Standards Act to state and local governmental agencies. This Act, among other things, requires the state and local governments to compensate employees for all overtime hours worked -- at the rate of time and one-half.[40]

---

38 426 U.S. 833, 96 S. Ct. 2465, 49 L. Ed. 2d 245 (1976).

39 Garcia v. San Antonio Metropolitan Transit Authority, 469 U.S. 528, 105 S. Ct. 1005, 83 L. Ed. 2d 1016 (1985).

40 Public Law 99-150, signed on November 15, 1985 by President Reagan, amended the Fair Labor Standards Act so as to allow state and local governments to con-

In response to complaints from local officials, Congress amended the FLSA in 1985. This amendment did not overrule the *Garcia* holding but did give states and local governments some additional authority in establishing working hours. It should be recognized, however, that Congress made it clear that the powers granted by the Constitution would not be overlooked as the new law contains a very stringent discrimination provision that holds employers accountable for penalizing or retaliating in any way against an employee who asserts his or her rights under the FLSA. The new law also clearly establishes guidelines that must be followed by state and local governments, notwithstanding provisions of the Tenth Amendment.

Even prior to the *Garcia* case, the United States Supreme Court indicated that the provisions of the Tenth Amendment do not prohibit Congress from regulating the activities of local and state governments. In 1983, in the case of *Equal Employment Opportunity Commission v. Wyoming*, the Court made it clear that the extension of the Age Discrimination in Employment Act to cover state and local governments is a valid exercise of Congress' powers under the Commerce Clause and is not precluded by virtue of external constraints imposed upon Congress' powers by the Tenth Amendment.[41]

In the *EEOC v. Wyoming* decision, the Supreme Court held that the Age Discrimination and Employment Act was applicable to state agencies and declared that the involuntary retirement of a Wyoming state warden at age 55 was in violation of the Act even though the warden was a state employee.

In view of these decisions, it is doubtful that those who prepared and approved the Tenth Amendment to the Constitution achieved the intended purpose.

§ 1.12 "Due process of law" – provisions and definitions

When the first Congress established by the Constitution convened, hundreds of amendments to the Constitution were considered by that body. Among these was the proposal that an amendment be adopted providing that "no person shall be deprived of life, liberty, or property, without due process of law." The amendments, which were ratified in 1791 and became known as

---

tinue offering employees compensatory time off in lieu of overtime pay, but with definite restrictions.

41 Equal Employment Opportunity Commission v. Wyoming, 460 U.S. 226, 103 S.Ct. 1054, 75 L.Ed. 2d 18, (1983). (*Also see* further discussion of *EEOC v. Wyoming* and other cases in Chapter 12 of this book.)

the Bill of Rights, included this provision which was tucked away as part of the Fifth Amendment to the Constitution.

The first step in comprehending the application of the "due process" provision of the Constitution is to recognize that this provision, as it appears in the Fifth Amendment, is a restraint upon the federal government only. This provision was adopted in 1791 because there was a fear of a strong central government and it was inserted at the insistence of the representatives of the various states.

It was not until 1868 that a federal Constitutional provision concerning due process became applicable to the states. In that year the Fourteenth Amendment was ratified. Part of that amendment was:

> Nor shall any *State* deprive any person of life, liberty, or property, without due process of law. (Emphasis added.)

This latter provision specifically applies to states and not to the federal government. Therefore, if a due process violation is claimed in a state case, the applicable due process provision is the Fourteenth Amendment clause and not the Fifth.

From the time of adoption, efforts have been made to define these clauses. No phrase has been the subject of greater controversy than the provision that no person shall "be deprived of life, liberty, or property, without due process of law." One reason for the confusion is that the Supreme Court of the United States has consistently declined to give a comprehensive definition. This is intentional because such a definition would limit the Court in future cases which could involve situations not presently anticipated. State courts, too, have refused to be pinned down to a specific and exact definition of due process.

Even though the courts have refused to give a specific definition, piecemeal definitions can be gleaned from the cases. For example, in the case of *Twining v. New Jersey*[42] the Court held:

> What is due process of law may be ascertained by an examination of those settled usages and modes of proceedings existing in the common law and statute law of England before the emigration of our ancestors, and shown not to have been unsuited to their civil and political condition by having been acted on by them after the settlement of this country.

---

42 211 U.S. 78, 29 S. Ct. 14, 53 L. Ed. 97 (1908).

In the case of *Murray v. Hoboken Land and Improvement Company*,[43] the Supreme Court made this statement:

> The Constitution contains no description of those processes which it was intended to allow or forbid. It does not even declare what principles are to be applied to ascertain whether it be due process. It is manifest that it was not left to the legislative power to enact any process which might be devised. The article is a restraint on the legislative as well as on the executive and judicial powers of the government, and cannot be so construed as to leave congress free to make any process "due process of law," by its mere will.

In his dissenting opinion in the case of *In re Winship*,[44] Justice Black stated that the four words -- *due process of law* -- have been the center of substantial legal debate over the years. He explained, however, that the words lose some of their ambiguity when viewed in the light of history. In the opinion he makes this oft-quoted comment:

> "Due process of law" was originally used as a shorthand expression for governmental proceedings according to the "law of the land" as it existed at the time of those proceedings. Both phrases are derived from the laws of England and have traditionally been regarded as meaning the same thing.

In arguing his view that some members of the Court had unjustifiably used the due process clause as a means of expanding the power of the Supreme Court, Mr. Justice Black continued with these words:

> In my view both Mr. Justice Curtis and Mr. Justice Moody gave "due process of law" an unjustifiably broad interpretation. For me the only correct meaning of that phrase is that our government must proceed according to the "law of the land" -- that is, according to the written constitutional and statutory provisions as interpreted by court decisions. The Due Process Clause, in both the Fifth and Fourteenth Amendments, in and of itself does not add to these provisions, but in effect states that our governments are governments of laws and constitutionally bound to act only according to law.

---

43 59 U.S. (18 How.) 272, 15 L. Ed. 372 (1856).

44 379 U.S. 358, 90 S. Ct. 1068, 25 L. Ed. 368 (1970). This case should be studied for a comprehensive discussion of the history of the due process clause.

The United States Supreme Court in 1979 more specifically placed some boundaries on the rights protected by the due process clause. There the Court, in reversing the lower court, held that the due process clause of the Fourteenth Amendment does not require a pre-suspension hearing prior to suspending driver's licenses for refusing to take a Breathalyzer test upon arrest for operating a motor vehicle while under the influence of intoxicating liquor. The majority explained that:

> [T]he due process clause has never been construed to require that the procedures used to guard against an erroneous deprivation of a protected "property" or "liberty" interest be so comprehensive as to preclude any possibility of error. The due process clause simply does not mandate that all government decision-making comply with standards that assure perfect, error-free determinations.[45]

Even more recently, in 1983, Justice Rehnquist in speaking for the majority, warned that "the requirements imposed by the clause, are, of course, flexible and variable dependent upon the particular situation being examined." In reversing a lower court decision, the Supreme Court ruled that an inmate, confined to administrative segregation after a prison riot, received due process because he received notices of charges against him, a hearing committee reviewed evidence of his participation in the riot, and he acknowledged that he had an opportunity to have his version of the events reported. The Court in its decision made several pertinent observations. One was:

> While no state "may deprive any person of life, liberty, or property, without due process of law," it is well settled that only a limited range of interest fall within this provision.[46]

In this case the Supreme Court reviewed other cases concerning the due process rights of prisoners.

---

45 Mackey v. Montrym, 443 U.S. 1, 99 S. Ct. 2612, 61 L. Ed. 2d 321 (1979). *See* Part II for portions of this case and § 7.17 for a discussion of the use of blood, breath and urine samples and further discussion of this case.

46 Hewitt v. Helms, 459 U.S. 460, 103 S. Ct. 864, 74 L. Ed. 2d 675 (1983). *But see* City of Akron v. Akron Center for Reproductive Health, 462 U.S. 416, 103 S. Ct. 2481, 76 L. Ed. 2d 687 (1983), which held that an ordinance requiring a physician performing abortions to insure that the remains of the unborn child are disposed of in a "humane and sanitary manner" is unconstitutional under the due process clause in that it fails to give a physician fair notice that his contemplated conduct is forbidden.

Despite these comments indicating that due process does not mean all things to all people, it is quite clear that the provisions have been broadly interpreted so as to protect many rights not contemplated by those who drafted the two clauses.

§ 1.13 General scope of the Fourteenth Amendment due process clause

It is important to note that when the Fourteenth Amendment was written and ratified it did not embrace those specific rights which are enumerated in the Bill of Rights. For example, it did not say that "the accused shall have the assistance of counsel for his defense." Soon after the Fourteenth Amendment was ratified, the Supreme Court faced the difficult task of determining whether the due process clause of the Fourteenth Amendment protected those individual rights against the state in the same manner that the Bill of Rights protected them against the federal government. Was, for example, the search and seizure provision of the Fourth Amendment made applicable to the states by the Fourteenth Amendment due process clause? This doctrine, later to be referred to as the "shorthand" doctrine, was considered in the case of *Hurtado v. California*.[47]

In the *Hurtado* case the defendant was charged with murder upon information filed by the district attorney. He was later tried by a jury, convicted, and sentenced to be hanged. The defendant appealed to the United States Supreme Court on the ground that the due process clause of the Fourteenth Amendment had been violated, as he had been held to answer for the crime upon information and without presentment or indictment by a grand jury. The defendant argued that the express provision of the Fifth Amendment requiring "presentment or indictment of a grand jury" was made applicable to the states by the due process clause of the Fourteenth Amendment. In denying this claim in the *Hurtado* case, the Court stated:

> If in the adoption of that amendment [Fourteenth Amendment] it had been part of its purpose to perpetuate the institution of the grand jury in all states, it would have embodied, as did the Fifth Amendment, express declarations to that effect.

Notwithstanding this statement in the *Hurtado* case, the argument persisted that as the Bill of Rights enumerated fundamental rights, they should be guaranteed against state infringement through the Fourteenth Amend-

---

47 110 U.S. 516, 4 S. Ct. 111, 28 L. Ed. 232 (1884).

ment due process clause. Although some of the judges of the Supreme Court and the various state and lower federal courts argued that those protections enumerated in the first eight amendments should be made applicable to the states by way of the Fourteenth Amendment, the majority of the judges found it difficult to read this into the Fourteenth Amendment.

As late as 1947 the Supreme Court, by a five to four decision, refused to give such broad meaning to the due process clause of the Fourteenth Amendment. In the case of *Adamson v. California*,[48] the defendant was convicted of murder in the first degree in the Superior Court of California. In accordance with the provisions of the California Penal Code, a district attorney for the state commented upon the failure of the defendant to testify at the trial. Defendant appealed the case under the Fourteenth Amendment due process clause, arguing that this penal code or this action under the code violated the federal Constitution.

The majority in *Adamson* agreed that such comment would infringe upon defendant's privilege against self-incrimination protected by the Fifth Amendment if this were a trial in a court of the United States, but refused to make this standard applicable to the states, saying:

> It is settled law that the clause of the Fifth Amendment, protecting a person against being compelled to be a witness against himself, is not made effective by the Fourteenth Amendment as a protection against state action on the ground that freedom from testimonial compulsion is a right of national citizenship, or because it is a personal privilege for immunity secured by the Federal Constitution as one of the rights of man that are listed in the Bill of Rights.

The majority went on to explain that the due process clause of the Fourteenth Amendment does not draw all of the rights of the federal Bill of Rights under its protection. Mr. Justice Frankfurter, concurring with the majority in discussing the history of this theory, made this additional statement:

> Of all these judges, only one, who may respectfully be called an eccentric exception, ever indicated the belief that the Fourteenth Amendment was a shorthand summary of the first eight Amendments theretofore limiting only the Federal Government, and that due process incorporated those eight Amendments as restrictions upon the powers of the States.

---

[48] 332 U.S. 46, 67 S. Ct. 1672, 91 L. Ed. 1903 (1947).

Notwithstanding the strong words by the majority in the *Adamson* case, Mr. Justice Black, perhaps indicating some of the reasoning of the courts which were to make future decisions, made this comment:

> In my judgment, history conclusively demonstrates that the language of the first section of the Fourteenth Amendment, taken as a whole, was thought by those responsible for its submission to the people, and by those who opposed its submission, sufficiently explicit to guarantee that thereafter no state could deprive its citizens of the privileges and protections of the Bill of Rights.

A broad interpretation of the due process clause of the Fourteenth Amendment vests great powers in the United States Supreme Court and conversely limits the powers of the state courts. Many of the state court justices resent this and have felt impelled to voice disagreement with what the Utah Supreme Court considers the almost unbelievable "arrogation of power by and to the federal government."[49] Expressing doubt that the Fourteenth Amendment was properly adopted in the first place, the majority of the Utah Supreme Court argued that even if the Fourteenth Amendment were adopted properly, there is nothing in the language to justify the application of the rights of the first ten amendments to the states by way of the Fourteenth Amendment. After commenting that the Fourteenth Amendment has been used to distort and nullify in some measure the purposes of the first ten amendments, the majority of the Utah court continues:

> The foregoing is said in awareness of the proliferations that have occurred on the first ten amendments, and particularly by the use of the Fourteenth Amendment, to extend and engraft upon the sovereign states, limitations intended only for the federal government. This has resulted in a constant and seemingly endless process of arrogating to the federal government more and more of the powers, not only not granted to it, but expressly forbidden to it, and in disparagement of the powers properly belonging to the sovereign states and the people. This development is a clear vindication of the forebodings of the founding fathers and their fears of centralization of power.

---

49 State v. Phillips, 540 P.2d 936 (Utah 1975).

§ 1.14 Federalization of specific protections via the due process clause

In the early decisions of the Supreme Court the judges reasoned that certain rights, such as free speech, were so fundamental that they must be protected against abuse by state officials. These judges, in applying the "fundamental rights" theory, justified making these rights applicable to the states by way of the Fourteenth Amendment due process clause on the basis that they were so fundamental that a state, in violating these rights, failed to comply with the demands of the Fourteenth Amendment. The reasoning was that they were made applicable to the states not merely because they were a part of the Bill of Rights but because they were fundamental rights that the citizens of the United States were entitled to have protected, against state or federal action. Although the shadow of the "fundamental rights" rationale remains, the courts apparently no longer rely on this reasoning in making those rights which are enumerated in the first amendments applicable to the states.

Because the federal courts were slow to make the specific provisions of the Bill of Rights applicable to the states, one set of standards was applied in federal courts and a separate set of standards applied when the federal courts were reviewing state court decisions. Gradually the reluctance on the part of the Supreme Court and other federal courts to apply federal standards in state cases faded. A brief discussion of the federalization of the specific provisions of the Bill of Rights will help demonstrate the rapid acceleration of this process.

Because freedom of speech and the other rights protected by the First Amendment are clearly fundamental, they were made applicable to the states by the Fourteenth Amendment at an early date. After some confusing decisions, all doubt was removed in 1925 when the Supreme Court in the case of *Gitlow v. New York*[50] expressed the opinion:

> For present purposes we may and do assume that freedom of speech and of the press -- which are protected by the First Amendment from abridgement by Congress -- are among the fundamental personal rights and liberties protected by the Due Process Clause of the Fourteenth Amendment from impairment by the states. We do not regard the incidental statement in *Prudential Insurance Company v. Cheek*, 259 U.S. 530 [66 L.Ed. 1044, 42 S.Ct. 516], that the Fourteenth Amendment imposes no restrictions on

---

50 268 U.S. 652, 45 S. Ct. 625, 69 L. Ed. 1138 (1925).

the states concerning freedom of speech, as determinative of this question.

Although the "shorthand" rationale gradually became more palatable to the judges sitting on the Supreme Court,[51] it was not until the 1960s that this doctrine, if not adopted in principle, was widely applied. In a landmark decision in 1961,[52] the Supreme Court of the United States made it clear that the protections of the Fourth Amendment would be applicable to the states and that the federal courts would establish minimum standards in determining the legality of searches and seizures. In 1963 the "right to counsel" protection of the Sixth Amendment was made applicable to the states.[53] Having opened the door, the courts found little difficulty in 1965 in including the "self-incrimination" protection of the Fifth Amendment as one of the rights which would apply to state agents.[54]

Continuing this trend, the United States Supreme Court in 1968 rejected what it called dicta in prior decisions and held that the Fourteenth Amendment guaranteed a right to a jury trial in all criminal cases which -- were they to be tried in a federal court -- would come within the Sixth Amendment's guarantee.[55] In the *Duncan* case, the Court acknowledged that the protections of the Bill of Rights were being made applicable to the states by the Fourteenth Amendment, commenting:

> In resolving conflicting claims concerning the meaning of this specious language (the Fourteenth Amendment) the Court has looked increasingly to the Bill of Rights for guidance; many of the rights guaranteed by the first eight amendments to the Constitution have been held to be protected against state action by the Due Process Clause of the Fourteenth Amendment.

However, acceptance of this reasoning was not unanimous. Justice Harlan viewed the decision as an uneasy and illogical compromise, commenting:

> I believe I am correct in saying that every member of the Court for at least the last 135 years has agreed that our founders did not con-

---

51 Powell v. Alabama, 287 U.S. 45, 53 S. Ct. 55, 77 L. Ed. 158 (1932).

52 Mapp v. Ohio, 367 U.S. 643, 81 S. Ct. 1684, 6 L. Ed. 2d 1081 (1961).

53 Gideon v. Wainwright, 372 U.S. 335, 83 S. Ct. 792, 9 L. Ed. 2d 799 (1963).

54 Malloy v. Hogan, 378 U.S. 1, 84 S. Ct. 1489, 12 L. Ed. 2d 653 (1964).

55 Duncan v. Louisiana, 391 U.S. 145, 88 S. Ct. 1444, 20 L. Ed. 2d 491 (1968).

sider the requirements of the Bill of Rights so fundamental that they should operate directly against the states.

Apparently disregarding Justice Harlan's views, the Supreme Court near the end of the 1960s reversed previous specific decisions and added the "double jeopardy" protection of the Fifth Amendment to those made applicable to the states by the Fourteenth Amendment.[56] The Court stated that "on the merits we hold that the double jeopardy clause of the Fifth Amendment is applicable to the states through the Fourteenth."

There are still a few of the protections of the Bill of Rights which have not been specifically made applicable to the states by the Fourteenth. For example, the protections of the Second and Third Amendments and the grand jury provisions of the Fifth Amendment have not yet been brought completely under the "due process" umbrella. There is little likelihood that the protections of the Third Amendment will be brought before the Supreme Court, but it will be interesting to see how that court handles the grand jury provisions of the Fifth Amendment if brought before the court in a proper case.[57]

As there are so few rights of the first ten amendments that have not been made applicable to the states by the Fourteenth Amendment due process clause, there is a valid argument for abandoning the past confusing and contradictory rationale and admitting that the Fourteenth Amendment, by implication, makes those rights applicable to the states. Until this is judicially recognized, the piecemeal method of determining what specific provisions of the Bill of Rights are enforceable against state action will continue.

§ 1.15 Effects of broadening the scope of the Fourteenth Amendment due process clause

With the broadening in scope of the due process clause of the Fourteenth Amendment, the powers of the Supreme Court and other federal courts have been enlarged. Where state officials previously looked primarily to the state court cases to determine standards in protecting the individual rights, they must now look as well to the Supreme Court decisions. For example, only a few years ago the states were free to formulate their own policies in multiple prosecution situations, as the double jeopardy provision of the Bill of Rights did not superimpose the whole body of federal double

---

[56] Benton v. Maryland, 395 U.S. 784, 89 S. Ct. 2056, 23 L. Ed. 2d 707 (1969).

[57] These provisions of the Constitution will be discussed more thoroughly in future chapters.

jeopardy law upon the states. Since the decision in the *Benton* case[58] in 1969, however, federal cases must be examined to determine the federal standards in double jeopardy situations.

As indicated in the previous paragraph, the states may require more strict standards by interpreting the state constitution to impose conditions not required by the federal courts. An interesting case decided in 1975, however, mandates that the states, in requiring stricter standards, must do so by way of their own state constitutional provisions and not by way of the federal constitutional provisions.[59]

In the *Hass* case, the Supreme Court held that a state may not impose greater restrictions than the federal courts as a matter of federal constitutional law when the Supreme Court specifically refrains from imposing them. For example, if the United States Supreme Court finds that the Fifth Amendment self-incrimination provision does not prohibit the use of statements for impeachment purposes when made without the *Miranda*[60] warnings, the *state* cannot then interpret the self-incrimination protection of the federal Constitution as prohibiting the use of such confessions for impeachment purposes. By way of its *own* self-incrimination provision, the state may so limit the use of the confession, but it may not refer to the Fifth Amendment self-incrimination provision for that purpose.

Because both federal and state courts may, by court interpretation of constitutional provisions, limit police action, state officials must be familiar not only with the state statutes and court decisions but with federal laws and especially federal court decisions which to a great extent determine police procedures.

§ 1.16 Adjudication of constitutional questions

When studying cases, especially federal cases, which limit police procedures while investigating crimes, some criminal justice personnel and lay people are confused by the judicial process. For example, in the *Mapp* case[61] -- fully discussed later in the book -- the police were acting under a state law and following procedures established by the Supreme Court of the State of Ohio. But when the decision declaring the evidence inadmissible was handed down, it was done so by the Supreme Court of the United States. How does

---

58 Benton v. Maryland, 395 U.S. 784, 89 S. Ct. 2056, 23 L. Ed. 2d 707 (1969).

59 Oregon v. Hass, 420 U.S. 784, 95 S. Ct. 1215, 43 L. Ed. 2d 570 (1975). *See* case in Part II.

60 Miranda v. Arizona, 384 U.S. 436, 86 S. Ct. 1602, 16 L. Ed. 2d 694 (1966).

61 Mapp v. Ohio, 367 U.S. 643, 81 S. Ct. 1684, 6 L. Ed. 2d 1081 (1961).

a question involving the enforcement of a state statute by state officers ever get to the United States Supreme Court?

In article III of the Constitution, the Supreme Court is given original jurisdiction in all cases affecting ambassadors, other public ministers and consuls, and those in which a state shall be a party. That article also provides that the Supreme Court shall have appellate jurisdiction over cases and controversies arising under the Constitution, the laws of the United States, treaties, etc., subject to regulation by Congress. The Constitution does not expressly provide for the power of the Supreme Court to determine the constitutionality of acts of Congress or state statutes. Neither does this article provide for the power of the Supreme Court to review decisions of the state courts.

Other provisions of the Constitution which have been interpreted to give additional powers to the Supreme Court are the amendments and the supremacy clause (article VI, section 2) which provides that the Constitution and those acts of Congress made in pursuance thereof shall be the supreme law of the land. Probably the most far-reaching provision and the one that has given the Supreme Court and other federal courts the authority to act in "police power" cases is the Fourteenth Amendment. Had it not been for the Fourteenth Amendment due process clause and the Fourteenth Amendment equal protection clause, the Supreme Court could not have reviewed state decisions relating to search and seizure, self-incrimination, right to counsel, and other Bill of Rights protections. Had it not been for the Fourteenth Amendment, the Supreme Court could not have demanded that state officers abide by the requirements of the *Miranda* case.

To better understand the process, the reader should look for the review procedure followed in each case. If the case is a federal case, i.e., the person is charged with violating a federal statute, he will be tried first in the federal district court. He may then appeal to the federal circuit court of appeals and, finally, to the United States Supreme Court.

If he is accused of violating a state statute, the procedure is generally as follows (although the states differ as to the procedure followed and the designation of courts). In a felony case, after a preliminary hearing in a lower court, the trial is in a felony court, often called a circuit court. If convicted, the defendant may appeal to a state court of appeals and to the supreme court of the state. Then, on constitutional questions, he may appeal directly to the Supreme Court of the United States.

Neither the supreme court of the state nor the Supreme Court of the United States is required to hear all cases and to do so would be impossible. The United States Code (28 U.S.C. § 1257) provides some guidelines as to which cases will be reviewed by the United States Supreme Court. In essence, a review is granted only when there is a substantial federal question involved.

In addition to review by appeal, state cases reach the federal courts by way of the *writ of habeas corpus*. This was used very sparingly in earlier cases but in the last twenty years has been used more frequently, especially in reviewing constitutional claims. The Code, at 28 U.S.C. § 2241, provides that persons convicted of crimes in state courts may seek review by habeas corpus proceedings in federal courts on the issue of whether they were afforded their fair, full, constitutional rights and safeguards in the state proceedings. As an example, in the case of *Gideon v. Wainwright*,[62] Gideon sought habeas corpus relief after he had served some time in the state reformatory, claiming that his constitutional guarantee of the assistance of counsel was not properly granted at the state court trial. In a habeas corpus proceeding, the action is brought against the person or persons who are responsible for the custody of the person requesting relief.

§ 1.17 Summary

The Constitution of the United States is the political foundation of the United States Government. It was written and adopted after careful consideration and after experiments had been made with other forms of alliances among the colonies.

The United States Constitution is composed of seven articles, the first three of which separate the powers of government. Amendments have been adopted in accordance with the terms of the Constitution. These amendments, when adopted, became a part of the Constitution and have the same binding effect as the original Constitution.

The people of the thirteen states relinquished, by way of the Constitution, certain enumerated powers to the federal government established by the Constitution. These powers once delegated cannot be withdrawn. The extent to which powers were granted continues to be the subject of debate and court interpretation reaching from the time the Constitution was ratified by the states to the present.

Although certain powers are delegated to the federal government, many powers, including the police power, remain primarily in the states. However, limitations in exercising these powers have been placed on the states by the specific provisions of the Constitution and by court decisions.

---

62 372 U.S. 335, 83 S. Ct. 792, 9 L. Ed. 2d 799 (1963).

The first ten amendments to the Constitution, known as the Bill of Rights, were adopted and became effective in 1791, two years after the Constitution was ratified. These forbid the abridgment of individual rights by Congress and other agents of the United States Government. When adopted, they did not apply to the states. Today, most of the provisions of the Bill of Rights are now made applicable to the states through the Fourteenth Amendment.

The due process clause of the Fifth Amendment is a part of the Bill of Rights and applies to agents of the United States Government. The due process clause under which the federal courts review the actions of state agents is a part of the Fourteenth Amendment which was adopted in 1868.

Because of the broad interpretation of the Fourteenth Amendment due process clause by the Supreme Court, state officials as well as federal officials must look to the United States Supreme Court for decisions clarifying constitutional standards. States may, through legislative acts or court decisions, require more strict standards, but the states cannot establish standards which do not meet the minimum standards established by the federal courts or federal legislation.

Chapter 2
SPEECH, PRESS AND ASSEMBLY*

Congress shall make no law...abridging the freedom of speech, or of the press; or the right of the people peaceably to assemble, and to petition the Government for a redress of grievances.

First Amendment

Section

---

* *by Jacqueline R. Kanovitz*

§ 2.1 Introduction

Many portions of our Bill of Rights have antecedents traceable to the Magna Charta or the centuries-old English common law tradition. This is not so with the First Amendment. Freedom of speech, press, religion, and assembly is a legal concept pioneered on American soil.[1] The merger of Church and State in England furnished a fertile ground for religious and political repression. Censorship of the press through licensing originated with the efforts of the Church to suppress heretical writings. By virtue of a decree issued by the Court of the Star Chamber in 1585, no book could be printed or published in England until reviewed and licensed by the Archbishop or a delegate. The function of licensing was to weed out all printed materials containing unorthodox religious thought or criticism of the Crown.[2] The history of this period is replete with instances of books being burned, printing presses being destroyed, and authors being carted off to prison. Licensing laws came to an end in 1694.[3] But the lifting of licensing laws did not usher in an era of intellectual freedom. Political dissent was later stifled by means of rigorous enforcement of seditious libel laws. The offense of seditious libel consisted of merely speaking out against public officials. During the heyday of repression, a man could be punished for the crime of seditious libel if he read objectionable material, heard it read and laughed at it, or repeated it to another.[4]

The framing of a Bill of Rights was the first order of business facing the Congress that met after the ratification of the Constitution. The foundations for a strong central government had been laid. Now curbs were required to assure that the repressive English experience would never be repeated in the United States. In delineating the rights of free citizens in their relations with government, it was no coincidence that the freedoms of speech, press, religion, and assembly were positioned first. Our colonial forefathers had the vision to realize that without these freedoms, no other freedoms would be secure. Through the First Amendment, they sought to carve out a zone of intellectual liberty removed from federal control. With the adoption of the Fourteenth Amendment, which provides, among other things, that no state shall deprive any person of liberty without due process of law, First Amendment limitations were made binding on the states.[5]

---

1 BRYANT, THE BILL OF RIGHTS 81 (1965).

2 *Id.* at 98-100.

3 *Id.* at 94.

4 *Id.* at 115.

5 Gitlow v. New York, 268 U.S. 652, 45 S. Ct. 625, 69 L. Ed. 1138 (1925).

The nation has now experienced two centuries of internal stability under one Constitution. When viewed from the perspective of world history, this is a remarkable accomplishment. The First Amendment has been a singularly important factor. When citizens can openly criticize their government and advocate changes, changes can be made through an orderly political process. In every age, dissident groups have existed. Yet the presence of these vocal minorities furnishes evidence that democracy is working. Although public protest may have an unsettling flavor, experience has shown that when the channels of peaceful debate are closed, discontent will ultimately find expression in socially less acceptable forms. When grievances exist, they must be aired -- if not through the press and on speakers' platforms, then by riots upon the streets. The First Amendment provides a safety valve through which the pressures and frustrations of a heterogeneous society can be ventilated. Professor Emerson has identified yet another vital function that free speech serves in the life of a democracy:

> [F]reedom of expression is an essential process for advancing knowledge and discovering truth. An individual who seeks knowledge and truth must hear all sides of the question, consider all alternatives, test his judgment by exposing it to opposition, and make full use of different minds....The reasons which make open discussion essential for an intelligent individual judgment likewise make it imperative for rational social judgment.[6]

In a society which remains committed to the freedoms expressed in the First Amendment, a working knowledge of the First Amendment is essential for those who enforce the nation's laws.

§ 2.2 Overview of Chapter 2

The First Amendment reads "Congress shall make no law...abridging the freedom of speech...." As an initial step in First Amendment analysis, a determination must be made whether "speech" is involved. Is live "interpretive dancing" speech? What of burning a draft card as an act of political protest? These and related issues are explored in Section 2.3.

A conclusion that speech is involved begins rather than ends the constitutional inquiry. The court, as its next step in constitutional analysis, must determine whether the challenged restriction constitutes an *abridgment of free speech*. In conducting this inquiry, laws which regulate speech because of its

---

6 EMERSON, THE SYSTEM OF FREEDOM OF EXPRESSION 6-7 (1969).

content-based communicative aspects (i.e., ideas, viewpoints or message) must be distinguished from those which regulate its noncommunicative aspects (i.e., time, place or manner in which the speech privilege may be exercised). Restrictions on the communicative aspects of speech strike at the core of the First Amendment and will be permitted only in limited instances. The constitutionality of restrictions on the communicative aspects of speech furnishes the subject of Sections 2.4-2.12.

From here, Chapter 2 proceeds to look at regulations focusing on the noncommunicative effects of speech. Freedom of speech cannot be maintained without some cost to society: Parades disrupt traffic, billboards are aesthetically unpleasant and handbills produce litter. These effects recur regardless of the topic addressed. Under what circumstances may governments regulate the noncommunicative aspects of speech? This answer is normally approached through a technique known as "interest-balancing," under which the court weighs the burden on free expression against the importance of the government's regulatory interest. "Interest balancing" is covered in Section 2.13.

Upon the conclusion of Section 2.13 the student should have a sound grasp of First Amendment theory. From here, Chapter 2 shifts its focus to some commonplace problems encountered in law enforcement. To what extent does the First Amendment guarantee would-be speakers access to public property for speech-related uses? Under what circumstances are laws requiring permits valid? What is the officer's duty in an open-air gathering where the audience is intolerant and threatens to get out of hand? These and related issues are covered in Sections 2.14-2.21.

§ 2.3 Is speech involved?

The First Amendment notion of speech spans broad boundaries. Because a system of free expression is built on intellectual liberty, free speech must also embrace the freedom not to speak or the right to remain silent. The government has no more power to force citizens to voice public adherence to ideological beliefs they find unacceptable[7] than it has to compel newspapers to print stories they are unwilling to print.[8] In *West Virginia State*

---

7 West Virginia State Bd. of Educ. v. Barnette, 319 U.S. 624, 63 S. Ct. 1178, 87 L. Ed. 1628 (1943); Wooley v. Maynard, 430 U.S. 705, 97 S. Ct. 1428, 51 L. Ed. 2d 752 (1977).

8 First Nat'l Bank of Boston v. Belotti, 435 U.S. 765, 98 S. Ct. 1407, 55 L. Ed. 2d 707 (1978); Pacific Gas & Elec. Co. v. Public Utilities Comm'n of Cal., 475 U.S. 1, 106 S. Ct. 903, 89 L. Ed. 2d 1 (1986).

Board of Education v. Barnette,[9] the Supreme Court struck down a state statute requiring school children to pledge their allegiance to and salute the flag, stating:

> If there is any fixed star in our constitutional constellation it is that no official, high or petty, can prescribe what shall be orthodox in politics, nationalism, religion, or other matters of opinion or force citizens to confess by word or act their faith therein. If there are any circumstances which permit of an exception, they do not now occur to us.[10]

By the same token, public schools may not set aside time for silent prayer and meditation.[11] Speech for First Amendment purposes thus includes ideologically grounded silence.

Communication of ideas and information unquestionably entails speech. There are countless methods for communicating ideas, methods which stretch the limits of human creativity. Public speaking, writing, canvassing, and distributing leaflets by no means exhaust the possibilities. The Supreme Court has held that the following activities, among others, constitute speech: politically-motivated business boycotts,[12] parades, pickets, and outdoor demonstrations,[13] letter writing,[14] membership solicitation,[15] electronic media broadcasting, and live entertainment, including non-obscene nude dancing.[16]

Though most communicative endeavors combine language with behavior, language is not a constitutionally indispensable ingredient of speech. On several occasions the Supreme Court, under the rubric of "symbolic speech," has extended First Amendment protection to mute expressive acts. For in-

---

9 *Supra* note 7.

10 *Id.* at 642, 63 S. Ct. at 1187, 87 L. Ed. at 1639.

11 Wallace v. Jeffries, 472 U.S. 38, 105 S. Ct. 2749, 86 L. Ed. 2d 29 (1985).

12 NAACP v. Claiborne Hardware Co., 458 U.S. 886, 102 S. Ct. 3409, 73 L. Ed. 2d 1215 (1982).

13 Thornhill v. Alabama, 310 U.S. 88, 60 S. Ct. 736, 84 L. Ed. 1093 (1940); Edwards v. South Carolina, 372 U.S. 229, 83 S. Ct. 680, 9 L. Ed. 2d 697 (1963).

14 Procunier v. Martinez, 416 U.S. 396, 94 S. Ct. 1800, 40 L. Ed. 2d 224 (1974), *partially overruled*, Thornburgh v. Abbott, __ U.S. __, 109 S. C.t 1874, 104 L. Ed. 2d 459 (1989).

15 Thomas v. Collins, 323 U.S. 516, 65 S. Ct. 315, 89 L. Ed. 430 (1945).

16 Schad v. Borough of Mount Ephraim, 452 U.S. 61, 101 S. Ct. 2176, 68 L. Ed. 2d 671 (1981).

stance, the refusal, on reasons of conscience, to salute the American flag,[17] the displaying of a red flag as a symbol of opposition to organized government,[18] the sitting in segregated public facilities to protest segregation,[19] and the wearing of a black arm band as an act of political dissent[20] are examples of "symbolic speech" conduct.

Expressive *conduct*, however, enjoys less First Amendment protection than expressive language. In *United States v. O'Brien*,[21] the Supreme Court affirmed the conviction of an anti-war protester who had publicly burned his draft card to dramatize his opposition to war. A federal statute made the knowing destruction or mutilation of draft cards an offense. In holding that the application of this regulation to O'Brien did not abridge his freedom of expression, the Court laid down a three-pronged test for when individuals can be prosecuted for conduct employed by them as a symbolic substitute for words. Governments can prosecute symbolic speakers for their *conduct* if:

(1) the government has a substantial interest in regulating the noncommunicative aspects of the conduct;
(2) the governmental interest is unrelated to suppressing the message accompanying that conduct; and
(3) the means selected by the government to promote its interest are no more restrictive than necessary.

The government could punish O'Brien for his conduct of burning his draft card because the regulatory concern of this statute centered on the need for preserving draft cards to effectively administer the draft, not on O'Brien's anti-war message.

The line the Supreme Court drew in *O'Brien* makes sense. The killing of a public official is not protected by the First Amendment simply because the wrongdoer found this act the most effective way to communicate his opposition to the dead man's policies. In *Clark v. Community for Creative Non-Violence*,[22] the Supreme Court, relying on the *O'Brien* test, held that the District of Columbia could apply a park regulation to forbid a group from holding a mass wintertime sleep-in demonstration in a park in the heart of Washington

---

17 West Virginia State Bd. of Educ. v. Barnette, 319 U.S. 624, 63 S. Ct. 1178, 87 L. Ed. 1628 (1943).

18 Stromberg v. California, 283 U.S. 359, 51 S. Ct. 532, 75 L. Ed. 1117 (1931).

19 Brown v. Louisiana, 383 U.S. 131, 86 S. Ct. 719, 15 L. Ed. 2d 637 (1966).

20 Tinker v. Des Moines Independent School Dist., 393 U.S. 503, 89 S. Ct. 733, 21 L. Ed. 2d 731 (1969).

21 391 U.S. 367, 88 S. Ct. 1673, 20 L. Ed. 2d 672 (1968).

22 468 U.S. 288, 104 S. Ct. 3065, 82 L. Ed. 2d 221 (1984).

D.C. to protest the plight of the nation's poor and homeless. Here, as in *O'Brien*, the government's regulatory concern, protection of parks, centered only on the speaker's conduct and was unconcerned with the message. But in *Schacht v. United States*,[23] the Supreme Court reached an opposite result. At issue was the constitutionality of a federal statute banning the wearing of military uniforms in dramatic productions only when worn under circumstances tending to discredit the armed forces. Here, unlike in *O'Brien* and *Clark*, the government's primary target was the unpatriotic message conveyed by the conduct.

It was against this background that the Supreme Court recently decided *Texas v. Johnson*,[24] the controversial flag burning case. Johnson had participated in a political demonstration in Texas during the 1984 Republican National Convention. During the demonstration, Johnson doused an American flag with kerosene and set it on fire while protestors chanted, "America, the red, white, and blue, we spit on you." He was convicted for violating a statute making it an offense to intentionally desecrate the national flag. The Supreme Court overturned his conviction on the grounds that the challenged statute failed the *O'Brien* test. With flag desecration, the speech and non-speech elements are inseparable. Since a person's treatment of the American flag invariably reveals his attitudes toward the flag and those things it symbolizes, flag desecration involves symbolic speech conduct. The Texas government's claimed interest in regulating flag handling, the interest in "preserving the flag as a symbol of nationhood and national unity," was inseparable from the message that accompanies the act of desecration. The Supreme Court wrote:

> If there is a bedrock principle underlying the First Amendment, it is that the Government may not prohibit the expression of an idea simply because society finds the idea itself offensive or disagreeable.
>
> We have not recognized an exception to this principle even when our flag has been involved....'[T]he constitutionally guaranteed freedom to be intellectually...diverse or even contrary, and the right to differ as to things that touch the heart of the existing order, encompass the freedom to express publicly one's opinions about our flag, including those opinions which are defiant and contemptuous.' Nor

---

23 398 U.S. 58, 90 S. Ct. 1555, 26 L. Ed. 2d 44 (1970).

24 ___ U.S. ___, 109 S. Ct. 2533, 105 L. Ed. 2d 342 (1989). *Texas v. Johnson* is reproduced in Part II.

> may the Government...compel conduct that would evince respect for the flag.[25]

While *Texas v. Johnson*, on its surface, is not a patriotic case and has sparked public controversy, the Supreme Court wisely cautioned: "We do not consecrate the flag by punishing its desecration, for in doing so we dilute the freedom that this cherished emblem represents."[26]

The student should be cautioned against concluding that this discussion represents an exhaustive treatment of all possible forms of speech covered by the First Amendment. Only a sampling has been given. The determination that "speech" is involved constitutes the first step in the far more complicated inquiry of when regulatory measures restricting that endeavor constitute *abridgments of free speech*. Even First Amendment rights are not absolute and illimitable. In assessing the constitutionality of speech restrictions, a basic and critical distinction must be drawn between measures that are concerned with speech content or message and those focusing on regulatory concerns unrelated to message.[27] A prohibition on picketing near school property during school hours,[28] or on using loudspeakers in residential neighborhoods,[29] seeks to regulate effects from speech that are unrelated to its message, whereas one prohibiting advocacy of the violent overthrow of government strikes at its communicative content. Judicial responses to each of these forms of regulation are covered in the sections that follow. As might be expected, the government possesses broader power to regulate the noncommunicative effects of speech than to regulate its content.

§ 2.4 Regulation of speech content

The First Amendment sharply curtails the government's power to legislate which ideas, issues or viewpoints can be aired in public. The following passage from *Cohen v. California*[30] summarizes the philosophical premises upon which the First Amendment rests:

---

25 *Id.* at ___, 109 S. Ct. at 2544-2545, 105 L. Ed. 2d at 360 (citations omitted).

26 Id. at ___, 109 S. Ct. at 2547-2548, 109 L. Ed. 2d 364.

27 L. TRIBE, AMERICAN CONSTITUTIONAL LAW §§ 12-2, 12-8 and 12-20.

28 Grayned v. City of Rockford, 408 U.S. 104, 92 S. Ct. 2294, 33 L. Ed. 2d 222 (1972).

29 Kovacs v. Cooper, 336 U.S. 77, 69 S. Ct. 448, 93 L. Ed. 513 (1949); Ward v. Rock Against Racism, ___ U.S. ___, 109 S. Ct. 2746, 105 L. Ed. 2d 109 (1989).

30 403 U.S. 15, 24, 91 S. Ct. 1780, 1787-88, 29 L. Ed. 2d 284, 293 (1971).

> The constitutional right of free expression is powerful medicine in a society as diverse and populous as ours. It is designed and intended to remove governmental restraints from the arena of public discussion, putting the decision as to what views shall be voiced largely into the hands of each of us, in the hope that use of such freedom will ultimately produce a more capable citizenry and more perfect polity and in the belief that no other approach would comport with the premise of individual dignity and choice upon which our political system rests.

Under traditional First Amendment analysis, the government may not restrict *protected* expression because of its content, message, viewpoint, or topic unless the government establishes a *compelling regulatory interest*.[31] A handful of speech subjects have, nevertheless, been excluded from First Amendment protection. For instance, obscenity, violence incitement, threats, and fighting words fall outside the First Amendment and therefore may be regulated freely. But on the other hand, when dealing with constitutionally protected speech, the Supreme Court has repeatedly emphasized that there is an "equality of status in the field of ideas," and that the "government must afford all points of view an equal opportunity to be heard."[32] The government's constitutional obligation to stay out of the marketplace of ideas is often referred to as the *content-neutrality* principle.

Cases applying the First Amendment to strike down measures regulating speech content are legion. In *Linmark Associates Inc. v. Township of Willingboro*,[33] the Supreme Court invalidated an ordinance banning the use of "for sale" and "sold" signs in residential neighborhoods. The measure had been enacted to stem what the township perceived as panic selling to escape racial integration. The Court ruled that the government's efforts to suppress truthful commercial information because it feared the consequences that might result if the public was well informed violated the First Amendment. The choice "between the dangers of suppressing information, and the dangers

---

31 Consolidated Edison Co. v. Public Service Comm'n, 447 U.S. 530, 100 S. Ct. 2326, 65 L. Ed. 2d 319 (1980); Carey v. Brown, 447 U.S. 455, 100 S. Ct. 2286, 65 L. Ed. 263 (1980); Schad v. Borough of Mount Ephraim, 452 U.S. 61, 101 S. Ct. 2176, 68 L. Ed. 671 (1981); Widmar v. Vincent, 454 U.S. 263, 102 S. Ct. 269, 70 L. Ed. 2d 440 (1981); Brown v. Hartlage, 456 U.S. 45, 102 S. Ct. 1523, 71 L. Ed. 2d 732 (1982); FCC v. League of Women Voters, 468 U.S. 364, 104 S. Ct. 3106, 82 L. Ed. 2d 278 (1984).

32 Police Dept. of Chicago v. Mosley, 408 U.S. 92, 96, 92 S. Ct. 2286, 2290, 33 L. Ed. 2d 212, 217 (1972).

33 431 U.S. 85, 97 S. Ct. 1614, 52 L. Ed. 2d 155 (1977).

of its misuse if it is freely available," the Court observed, is one that "the First Amendment makes for us."[34] In *Brown v. Hartlage*,[35] the Court ruled that a statute designed to prevent election corruption could not be applied to a political candidate for promising that if elected his first official act would be to reduce his salary. Mr. Justice Brennan there wrote:

> In barring certain public statements..., the State ban runs directly contrary to the fundamental premises underlying the First Amendment....That Amendment embodies our trust in the free exchange of ideas as the means by which the people are to choose between good ideas and bad, and between candidates for political office. The State's fear that voters might make an ill-advised choice does not provide the State with a compelling justification for limiting speech. It is not the function of government to 'select which issues are worth discussing or debating,'...in the course of a political campaign.[36]

Judicial hostility toward laws attempting to channel the content of public discourse is particularly strong when freedom of the press is involved. Several years ago, Florida enacted a "right of reply" statute requiring newspapers that had assailed the good character or public record of a political candidate to afford the candidate an opportunity to respond free of charge. The statute's purpose was to assure full and unbiased news coverage on vital election matters. The Supreme Court, in what was one of the rare cases in modern times to command unanimous agreement, voted to strike down the statute on the ground that "no government agency -- local, state, or federal -- can tell a newspaper in advance what it can print and what it cannot." Chief Justice Burger wrote:

> The choice of materials to go into a newspaper and decisions made as to...content of the paper, and treatment of public issues and public officials -- whether fair or unfair -- constitutes the exercise of editorial control and judgment. It has yet to be demonstrated how government regulation of this critical process can be exercised consistent with First Amendment guarantees....[37]

---

34 *Id*. at 97, 97 S. Ct. at 1620, 52 L. Ed. 2d at 164.

35 456 U.S. 45, 102 S. Ct. 1523, 71 L. Ed. 2d 732 (1982).

36 *Id*. at 60, 102 S. Ct. at 1532, 71 L. Ed. 2d at ___.

37 Miami Herald Publishing Co. v. Tornillo, 418 U.S. 241, 258, 94 S. Ct. 2831, 2840, 41 L. Ed. 2d 730 (1974). *See also* FCC v. League of Women Voters, 468 U.S. 364, 104 S. Ct. 3106, 82 L. Ed. 2d 278 (1984).

The principle that government must stay out of the ideological marketplace was again applied in *First National Bank of Boston v. Bellotti*,[38] where the Court struck down a state statute prohibiting corporations from seeking to influence voter referendums through expenditures where the issues did not directly affect the corporation's business. Mr. Justice Powell there wrote:

> In the realm of protected speech, the legislature is constitutionally disqualified from dictating the subjects about which persons may speak and the speakers who may address a public issue....If a legislature may direct business corporations to 'stick to business,' it also may limit other corporations -- religious, charitable, or civic -- to their respective 'business' when addressing the public. Such power in government to channel the expression of views is unacceptable under the First Amendment.[39]

The content-neutrality principle has, on a number of occasions, been used by the Supreme Court to invalidate statutes which make content-based distinctions in regulating the use of public facilities for expressive purposes.[40] *Boos v. Barry*[41] furnishes an illustration. The Court struck down a District of Columbia statute prohibiting the display within 500 feet of a foreign embassy of any sign *designed to bring any foreign government into public disrepute*. Because of the italicized language, this statute made the right to display signs near embassies depend on the speaker's topic and viewpoint. The Court held that the government is without power to dictate what subjects can be discussed on city sidewalks.

Peace officers are representatives of the government and share its burden of First Amendment neutrality. They must accordingly take care that their own ideological beliefs do not influence their regulatory decisions.

Notwithstanding the content-neutrality principle, there remains a handful of subject areas where First Amendment protection has been withdrawn. Obscenity, fighting words, violence incitement, and threats represent the most important of the unprotected speech categories. The Supreme Court has offered the following justification for withdrawing First Amendment protection from speech falling in these categories:

---

38 435 U.S. 765, 98 S. Ct. 1407, 55 L. Ed. 2d 707 (1978).

39 *Id*. at 784-785, 98 S. Ct. at 1420, 55 L. Ed. 2d at 723.

40 Police Dept. of Chicago v. Mosley, 408 U.S. 92, 92 S. Ct. 2286, 33 L. Ed. 2d 212 (1972); Carey v. Brown, 447 U.S. 455, 100 S. Ct. 2286, 65 L. Ed. 2d 263 (1980).

41 485 U.S. 312, 108 S. Ct. 1157, 99 L. Ed. 2d 333 (1988).

> [S]uch utterances are no essential part of any exposition of ideas, and are of such slight social value as a step to truth that any benefit that may be derived from them is clearly outweighed by the social interest in order and morality.[42]

Because legislatures are at liberty to punish unprotected speech solely because of its content, peace officers must be familiar with the boundaries of the unprotected speech categories in order to effectively enforce such laws.

§ 2.5 – Obscene speech

In *Roth v. United States*,[43] decided in 1957, the Supreme Court announced that obscenity was not constitutionally protected free speech. For the next fifteen years, the Court struggled to formulate a legal definition for obscenity that could command the approval of a majority of its members. The current test derives from *Miller v. United States*.[44] Under the *Miller* test, before literary works can be stripped of First Amendment protection on grounds of obscenity, the trier of fact must make all three of the following findings:

1. The average person, applying contemporary community standards, would find that the work, taken as a whole, appeals to the prurient interests.
2. The work depicts "hard-core" sexual acts, specifically defined by state law, in a patently offensive way.
3. The work, taken as a whole, lacks serious literary, artistic, political or scientific value.

Contemporary local community standards are applied to determine whether the work appeals to prurient interests, whereas national standards control whether it possesses serious literary or other value.[45] "Prurient" does not mean lust-provoking. States may not ban works that do no more than

---

42 Chaplinsky v. New Hampshire, 315 U.S. 568, 572, 62 S. Ct. 766, 769, 86 L. Ed. 1031 (1942).

43 345 U.S. 476, 77 S. Ct. 1304, 1 L. Ed. 2d 1498 (1957), *overruled*, Miller v. California, 413 U.S. 15. 93 S. Ct. 2607, 37 L. Ed. 2d 419 (1973).

44 413 U.S. 15, 93 S. Ct. 2607, 37 L. Ed. 2d 419 (1973).

45 Pope v. Illinois, 481 U.S. 497, 107 S. Ct. 1918, 95 L. Ed. 2d 439 (1987).

arouse normal, healthy sexual desire.[46] Prurient means a shameful or morbid interest in sex. The determination of whether a work violates the *Miller* standard must be made on the basis of the work as a whole rather than from isolated pictures or passages.

The "hard-core" sexual matter that state obscenity laws can cover may include patently offensive verbal or visual depictions of ultimate sexual acts (normal or perverted, real or simulated); masturbation; lewd exhibition of genitals; sadomasochistic and violent sexual behavior; and bestiality and perversions generally.[47]

States remain free to water down the *Miller* test where the interests of children are involved. For example, to protect children from sexual exploitation and abuse, states may treat live and photographic reproductions of children engaged in sexual acts as obscene without considering whether the work, as a whole, appeals to prurient interest or is patently offensive.[48] Conversely, the states may shelter children from exposure to sexually explicit materials believed to be harmful to children even though the works are not obscene and would receive First Amendment protection if distribution was restricted to adults.[49]

Though obscene material lacks substantive First Amendment protection, the Supreme Court has erected rigorous procedural safeguards governing the conduct of searches and seizures in the enforcement of obscenity laws. This seeming contradiction disappears once one appreciates that the *Miller* line between obscene and non-obscene is not so sharp that a police officer casually perusing an adult bookstore can tell at a momentary glance on which side of the line a particular work falls. To assure that protected materials are not inadvertently seized, the Supreme Court has adopted specialized rules for the conduct of searches and seizures. The following rules are designed to minimize opportunities for law enforcement officers to make discretionary judgments in enforcing obscenity laws:

---

46 Brockett v. Spokane Arcades, Inc., 472 U.S. 491, 105 S. Ct. 2794, 86 L. Ed. 2d 394 (1985).

47 Ward v. Illinois, 431 U.S. 767, 97 S. Ct. 2085, 52 L. Ed. 2d 738 (1977),

48 New York v. Ferber, 458 U.S. 747, 102 S. Ct. 3348, 73 L. Ed. 2d 1113 (1982).

49 Ginsberg v. New York, 390 U.S. 629, 88 S. Ct. 1274, 20 L. Ed. 2d 195 (1968); FCC v. Pacifica Foundation, 438 U.S. 726, 98 S. Ct. 3026, 57 L. Ed. 2d 1073 (1978). *See also* Bethel School District v. Fraser, 478 U.S. 675, 106 S. Ct. 3159, 92 L. Ed. 2d 549 (1986).

1. Warrantless searches and seizures are not permitted in the enforcement of obscenity laws.[50] Before a police officer can *seize* literary works, he must secure a preliminary determination by a judge that there is probable cause to believe that the works are obscene. The undercover purchase of obscene works offered for public sale, however, is not regarded as a search and seizure. Purchased material, therefore, can be used in evidence.[51]

2. Where the object of the search is literary materials, a higher degree of specificity is required both for the affidavit to secure the warrant and for the warrant itself. Ideally the judge should view the materials personally. Where this is not feasible, the officer in his affidavit should include concrete factual data regarding the types of hard-core sexual acts, their quantitative and qualitative aspects, and their relationship to the plot, if any. His conclusory assertions that the work is obscene will not suffice; the responsibility for evaluating the data in light of the legal standards rests with the magistrate.[52]

3. The Fourth Amendment requirement that search warrants particularly describe the "things to be seized" is rigorously applied to obscenity search warrants. General language authorizing the officer to seize "all obscene publications" found at a particular location is a constitutionally inadequate description because it attempts to delegate to the executing officer the power to make on-the-spot determinations of obscenity. This determination under our system may be made by a judicial officer alone.[53]

4. Only one copy of each book or film described in the warrant may be seized and taken for evidence. Law enforcement offi-

---

[50] Roaden v. Kentucky, 413 U.S. 496, 93 S. Ct. 2796, 37 L. Ed. 2d 757 (1973); Walter v. United States, 447 U.S. 649, 100 S. Ct. 2395, 65 L. Ed. 2d 410 (1983).

[51] Maryland v. Macon, 472 U.S. 463, 105 S. Ct. 2778, 86 L. Ed. 2d 370 (1985).

[52] Roaden v. Kentucky, *supra* note 50. Heller v. New York, 413 U.S. 483, 93 S. Ct. 2789, 37 L. Ed. 2d 745 (1973), *cert. denied, sub. nom.*, Buckley v. New York, 418 U.S. 944, 94 S. Ct. 3231, 41 L. Ed. 2d 1175 (1974).

[53] Marcus v. Search Warrant, 367 U.S. 717, 81 S. Ct. 1708, 6 L. Ed. 2d 1127 (1961); A Quantity of Copies of Books v. Kansas, 378 U.S. 205, 84 S. Ct. 1723, 12 L. Ed. 2d 809 (1964).

cers may not seize all copies and halt sales until after a judge has pronounced the works obscene in adversary proceedings.[54]

5. State law must also afford the seller, on request and promptly after the seizure, an opportunity to secure a judicial determination of obscenity in an adversary proceeding.

§ 2.6 – Fighting words

In *Chaplinsky v. New Hampshire*,[55] a man was convicted for addressing the following insult to a city marshal in a face-to-face confrontation on a city street: "You are a God damned racketeer" and a "damned Fascist." Previously, the Supreme Court had observed that "resort to epithets or personal abuse is not in any proper sense communication of information safeguarded by the Constitution...."[56] But *Chaplinsky* was the first case to apply this dicta and affirm a conviction for what the Court styled "fighting words."

Subsequent cases have reaffirmed the holding in *Chaplinsky* that "fighting words" fall outside the perimeter of free speech protection and have sought to clarify the scope and content of this exclusion. It is not enough that the words used are offensive to the hearer or that they may in fact provoke a violent retaliation.[57] If the listener's reaction were the sole determining factor, no one could safely articulate any unpopular or controversial beliefs since every such idea is likely to antagonize at least some members of the public. The "fighting words" exception does not measure the speaker's right to express his ideas by the boiling point of his audience. Indeed, this exclusion is not concerned with the communication of ideas or information at all. The only messages falling within the speech category carved out by *Chaplinsky* are verbal insults and direct personal abuse.

The *Chaplinsky* definition of "fighting words," as refined by subsequent decisions, is composed of two aspects -- one dealing with speech content and

---

[54] Fort Wayne Books, Inc. v. Indiana, ___ U.S. ___, 109 S. Ct. 916, 103 L. Ed. 2d 34 (1989); Marcus v. Search Warrant, 367 U.S. 717, 81 S. Ct. 1708, 6 L. Ed. 2d 1127 (1961); Heller v. New York, 413 U.S. 483, 93 S. Ct. 2789, 37 L. Ed. 2d 745 (1973), *cert. denied, sub. nom.*,

[55] 315 U.S. 568, 62 S. Ct. 766, 86 L. Ed. 1031 (1942).

[56] Cantwell v. Connecticut, 310 U.S. 296, 309-310, 60 S. Ct. 900, 84 L. Ed. 1221 (1940) (dicta).

[57] Edwards v. South Carolina, 372 U.S. 229, 83 S. Ct. 680, 9 L. Ed. 2d 697 (1963); Cox v. Louisiana, 379 U.S. 536, 85 S. Ct. 453, 13 L. Ed. 2d 471 (1965); Street v. New York, 394 U.S. 576, 89 S. Ct. 1354, 22 L. Ed. 2d 572 (1969); Bachellar v. Maryland, 397 U.S. 564, 90 S. Ct. 1312, 25 L.Ed. 2d 570 (1970).

the other with the circumstances under which the speech is uttered. Fighting words are:

(1) personally abusive, insulting or derisive remarks,
(2) addressed at another to his face under circumstances inherently likely to provoke an immediate and violent response.[58]

Verbal abuse invariably tends to offend the listener, but the tendency to offend by itself is not a quality that causes a loss of free speech protection. It is the likelihood that abusive language will trigger an immediate and violent response that causes loss of free speech protection and permits the speaker to be punished. This likelihood can be known only by examining the actual words used against the background in which they are uttered. The same insults may constitute "fighting words" in one context and protected speech in another.

The "fighting words" exception has been narrowly applied when the insults are directed against police officers.[59] Police officers are expected to have higher-than-normal boiling points and to exercise restraint in the face of verbal provocations and taunts that might antagonize an ordinary citizen and cause him to respond with violence.[60] In *Lewis v. City of New Orleans*,[61] an officer arrested a woman under a statute making it a crime to "curse or revile or to use...opprobrious language toward or with reference to any member of the city police while in the actual performance of his duty." The woman had cursed and yelled obscenities at the officer for asking her husband to produce his driver's license. The Supreme Court found this statute unconstitutionally broad because it made abusive language *per se* punishable when spoken to a police officer. As the Court pointed out, insulting utterances cease claim to First Amendment protection only when spoken under circumstances likely to provoke the listener into an immediate and violent response. The fact that the speaker may be a feeble old lady and the listener a well-trained police officer are factors that reduce the likelihood that provocations and insults will precipitate a physical confrontation. Because this statute gave police officers the unqualified right to arrest *any* person who cursed or insulted them, it was unconstitutionally broad. Police officers should be hesitant to invoke statutes

---

58 Lewis v. New Orleans, 415 U.S. 130, 94 S. Ct. 970, 39 L. Ed. 2d 214 (1974); Gooding v. Wilson, 405 U.S. 518, 92 S. Ct. 1103, 31 L. Ed. 2d 408 (1972); City of Houston v. Hill, 482 U.S. 451, 107 S. Ct. 2502, 96 L. Ed. 2d 398, *cert. denied*, 483 U.S. 1001, 107 S. Ct. 3222, 97 L. Ed. 2d 729 (1987).

59 *See* cases note 58 *supra*.

60 City of Houston v. Hill, *supra* note 58.

61 415 U.S. 130, 94 S. Ct. 970, 39 L. Ed. 2d 214 (1974).

which give them *carte blanche* to arrest anyone who criticizes them or who challenges their actions.

City of Houston v. Hill[62] confirms this. The Court there observed that the First Amendment protects a significant amount of verbal criticism and challenges directed at police officers. The Court also noted that the "freedom of individuals verbally to oppose or challenge police actions without thereby risking arrest is one of the principal characteristics by which we distinguish a free nation from a police state." Police, therefore, should be slow to arrest or issue citations simply because proper respect was not shown.

§ 2.7 – Offensive speech

Crude and offensive forms of expression are protected in some contexts but not in others. In *Cohen v. California*,[63] the Supreme Court ruled that crude and offensive language may not be punished when it is used by an adult speaker in the context of emphasizing a point. Cohen had been arrested under a statute making it an offense to "willfully disturb the peace or quiet...by offensive conduct" when he entered a courtroom wearing a jacket with the message "Fuck the Draft!" boldly displayed across the front. The Supreme Court noted that Cohen's language, while crude and tasteless, amounted neither to obscenity nor to "fighting words." Having eliminated those categories of speech where it had previously allowed censorship, the Supreme Court addressed the question of whether the First Amendment permits governments to make the use of offensive and vulgar language in public a crime. The Court concluded that the First Amendment strips the government of the power to "cleanse public debate to the point where it is grammatically palatable" by establishing what language is orthodox and acceptable for adults to use.

However, in *Bethel School District v. Fraser*,[64] the Supreme Court refused to grant public school students the same freedom to engage in vulgar speech that *Cohen v. California* had granted adults. A high school student disciplined for employing inappropriately offensive and lewd language while addressing a high school assembly, claimed that the school had abridged his freedom of expression. The Supreme Court ruled that the role of public schools included teaching by example the boundaries of appropriate behav-

---

62 482 U.S. 451, 107 S. Ct. 2502, 96 L. Ed. 2d 398 (1987). *City of Houston v. Hill* is reproduced in Part II.

63 403 U.S. 15, 91 S. Ct. 1780, 29 L. Ed. 2d 284 (1971).

64 478 U.S. 675, 106 S. Ct. 3159, 92 L. Ed. 2d 549 (1986).

ior. Schools, therefore, could discipline students for using language that adults are privileged to use. By the same token, the government may protect minors from exposure to some constitutionally protected materials that adults have a First Amendment privilege to view. In *FCC v. Pacifica Foundation*,[65] the Supreme Court upheld a Federal Communications Commission ban on the broadcasting of indecent but not obscene programs at times when children were likely to be in the listening audience.

Erznoznik v. City of Jacksonville[66] represented the high-water mark of Supreme Court protection for offensive speech. The City of Jacksonville had enacted an ordinance declaring it a public nuisance for drive-in theaters to show films revealing nude breasts, buttocks or pubic areas if their screens were visible to public streets. The city conceded that this ordinance was not confined to obscene films but argued that it represented a valid exercise of police power to protect members of the public from involuntary exposure to views that might offend them. Mr. Justice Powell, writing for the majority, disagreed. He observed:

> Much that we encounter offends our esthetic, if not our political and moral, sensibilities. Nevertheless, the Constitution does not permit government to decide what types of otherwise protected speech are sufficiently offensive to require protection for the unwilling listener or viewer.[67]

Constitutional protection for offensive speech, nevertheless, began to unravel in *Young v. American Mini Theatres, Inc.*,[68] where the Supreme Court upheld an ordinance regulating the location of adult movie theaters. Mr. Justice Stephens, speaking for a plurality of the Court, stated: "Even though the First Amendment protects communication in this area from total suppression, the State may legitimately use the content of these materials as a basis for placing them in a different classification...."[69] *Young v. American Mini Theatres, Inc.* was followed in *City of Renton v. Playtime Theatres, Inc.*,[70]

---

[65] 438 U.S. 726, 98 S. Ct. 3026, 57 L. Ed. 2d 1073 (1978). But see, Sable Communications of Cal. v. FCC, ___ U.S. ___, 109 S. Ct. 2829, 106 L. Ed. 2d 93 (1989).

[66] 422 U.S. 205, 95 S. Ct. 2268, 45 L. Ed. 2d 125 (1975).

[67] *Id.* at 210, 95 S. Ct. at 2273, 49 L. Ed. 2d at 326.

[68] 427 U.S. 50, 96 S. Ct. 2440, 49 L. Ed. 2d 310 (1976). The Constitutional implications of the trend began with *Young v. American Mini Theatres, Inc.* are considered in § 2.11 *infra*.

[69] 427 U.S. at 70-71, 96 S. Ct. at 2452.

[70] 475 U.S. 41, 106 S. Ct. 925, 89 L. Ed. 2d 29 (1986).

where the Court upheld a zoning ordinance prohibiting adult motion picture theaters from locating within 1,000 feet of any residence, church or park. According to the Supreme Court, the zoning ordinance did not abridge freedom of expression because its regulatory focus was the *secondary effect* of adult movie houses on the surrounding neighborhood rather than the *content* of the films shown in these establishments. The Court ruled that local governments may take the undesirable secondary effects produced by adult movie theaters into account and may regulate those effects under its zoning laws.

In summation, modern cases place "offensive speech" in a borderline free speech category that enjoys a lesser degree of First Amendment protection. As a result, regulations impacting "offensive speech" receive only moderate judicial scrutiny.

§ 2.8 – Threats

First Amendment protection does not extend to threats of crime or wrongful injury. Therefore, a person can be punished for threatening utterances -- but only if a genuine threat is made. In *Watts v. United States*,[71] a young man took the floor at an anti-war rally and spoke:

> They always holler at us to get an education. And now I have already received my draft classification as 1-A and I have got to report for my physical this Monday morning. I am not going. If they ever make me carry a rifle the first man to get in my sights is L.B.J. They are not going to make me kill my black brothers.

"L.B.J." was Lyndon Baines Johnson, then President of the United States. Watts was indicted and convicted under a federal statute making it a crime to "knowingly and willfully...[make] any threat to take the life of or to inflict bodily harm upon the President...." The Court found that Watts' oratory, viewed in context and considering its conditional nature, amounted to nothing more than a "very crude offensive method of stating a political opposition to the President," rather than a threat on the President's life. Political criticism is not taken outside the First Amendment because it is tasteless, caustic or hyperbolic.

---

71 394 U.S. 705, 89 S. Ct. 1399, 22 L. Ed. 2d 664 (1969).

§ 2.9 – Speech posing a clear and present danger

The Supreme Court's major First Amendment preoccupation during the early part of this century centered upon identifying the point at which government can halt speech which threatens the local or national security. Speech is a potent force in impelling action. When does advocacy of the overthrow of government, violence or other lawless action exceed the free speech privilege? The answer given by Mr. Justice Holmes in *Schenck v. United States*,[72] the 1919 landmark case, made an imprint on First Amendment theory that few other cases can claim.

Schenck had been convicted under the Espionage Act for distributing circulars to inductees that criticized the war effort and urged resistance to conscription. At the time of his appeal, the nation had not yet recovered a peacetime mentality. Mr. Justice Oliver Wendell Holmes, writing for the Court, affirmed Schenck's conviction and issued an opinion with four words in it that would dominate First Amendment analysis for years to come -- "clear and present danger." Holmes wrote:

> We admit that in many places and in ordinary times the defendants in saying all that was said in the circular would have been within their constitutional rights. But the character of every act depends upon the circumstances in which it is done....The question in every case is whether the words used are used in such circumstances and are of such a nature to create a *clear and present danger* that they will bring about the substantive evils that Congress has a right to prevent.[73] (Emphasis added.)

Holmes, however, affirmed Schenck's conviction without searching inquiry into whether Schenck's utterances posed any real danger to the war effort. In so doing, Holmes made a questionable application of his new doctrine, an application he later came to regret. During the years that followed, the Supreme Court's mainstream majority, reflecting the anti-Communist hysteria of the post-war era, mechanically applied the doctrine to punish harmless political dissidents. Mr. Justice Holmes' voice was now heard primarily in dissenting opinions where he sought to clarify the role he conceived for the danger test. In his *Abrams v. United States*[74] dissent, Holmes argued that government could suppress speech advocating the government's overthrow or other unlawful ends only as a last-ditch effort -- when conditions were so critical that no time remained to avert the threatened evil through

---

72 249 U.S. 47, 39 S. Ct. 247, 63 L. Ed. 470 (1919).

73 *Id*. at 52, 39 S. Ct. at 249, 63 L. Ed. at 473-474.

74 250 U.S. 616, 40 S. Ct. 17, 63 L. Ed. 1173 (1919).

counterargument. And in *Whitney v. California*,[75] joined by Mr. Justice Brandeis, Holmes wrote:

> Fear of serious injury cannot alone justify suppression of free speech and assembly. Men feared witches and burnt women. It is the function of speech to free men from the bondage of irrational fears. To justify suppression of free speech there must be reasonable ground to fear that serious evil will result if free speech is practiced. There must be reasonable ground to believe that the danger apprehended is imminent. There must be reasonable ground to believe that the evil to be prevented is a serious one....[E]ven advocacy of violation [of the law], however reprehensible morally, is not a justification for denying free speech where...there is nothing to indicate that the advocacy would be immediately acted on....
>
> Those who won our independence by revolution were not cowards. They did not fear political change. They did not exalt order at the cost of liberty. To courageous, self-reliant men, with confidence in the power of free and fearless reasoning applied through the processes of popular government, no danger flowing from speech can be deemed clear and present, unless the incidence of the evil apprehended is so imminent that it may befall before there is an opportunity for full discussion. If there be time to expose through discussion the falsehood and fallacies, to avert the evil by the processes of education, the remedy to be applied is more speech, not enforced silence. Only an emergency can justify repression.[76]

In *American Communications Ass'n C.I.O. v. Douds*,[77] a majority of the Court gave at least a formal endorsement to the Holmes-Brandeis interpretation of the meaning of the danger test. But the endorsement came too late. McCarthyism had already swept the nation. The time for the greatest test of the danger doctrine had arrived. In *Dennis v. United States*,[78] top echelon American Communist Party leaders appealed their conviction of conspiring to violate the Smith Act by teaching and advocating, along with organizing the party to teach and advocate, the overthrow of the U.S. government. (In his dissenting opinion, Mr. Justice Douglas pointed out that the prosecution

---

[75] 274 U.S. 357, 47 S. Ct. 641, 71 L. Ed. 1095 (1927), *overruled*, Brandenburg v. Ohio, 395 U.S. 444, 89 S. Ct. 1827, 23 L. Ed. 2d 430 (1969).

[76] *Id*. at 376-377, 47 S. Ct. at 648-49, 71 L. Ed. at 1106.

[77] 339 U.S. 382, 70 S. Ct. 674, 94 L. Ed. 925 (1950).

[78] 341 U.S. 494, 71 S. Ct. 857, 95 L. Ed. 1137 (1951).

mustered no evidence to establish the strength and tactical position of the Communist Party in the United States.) The trial judge, nevertheless, instructed the jury that it should bring back a guilty verdict if it found that the defendants had the intent to "overthrow...the Government of the United States by force and violence as speedily as circumstances would permit." The Supreme Court voted six to two to affirm the conviction on a record wholly devoid of proof that the Communist Party, as then constituted, posed any clear, present or immediate danger to the nation, or that the doctrines propagandized constituted a present threat. The majority rejected the requirement that the danger must be both *clear* and *present* in all cases before speech control measures can be applied. They restated the clear and present danger test so as to make the seriousness of the threatened harm a factor that could offset its lack of immediacy. Mr. Chief Justice Vinson quoted Judge Learned Hand:

> In each case [courts] must ask whether the *gravity of the 'evil,' discounted by its improbability*, justifies such invasion of free speech as is necessary to avoid the danger.[79] (Emphasis added.)

Having watered down the danger doctrine, the majority applied this new formulation and determined that when "a group aiming at [the government's] overthrow is attempting to indoctrinate its members and to commit them to a course whereby they will strike when the leaders feel the circumstances permit," the extreme seriousness of the threatened harm compensated for its lack of immediacy. The government could thus take action to crush such a conspiracy "even though doomed from the outset because of inadequate numbers."

This watered down version of the danger doctrine gave too little protection to politically controversial speech and was soon discarded by the Court. When the *Dennis* reformulation of the danger doctrine was abandoned, the clear and present danger standard was carried down with it. Within a few short years Holmes' famous phrase would all but pass into legal oblivion. In the context of incitive utterances, the area of the doctrine's most important application, *Brandenburg v. Ohio*[80] emerged in 1969 as the contemporarily controlling test determining when advocacy of violence or other lawless behavior can be stopped.

In *Brandenburg*, a Ku Klux Klan leader was convicted under the Ohio Criminal Syndicalism statute for delivering a speech at a Klan rally wherein he stated that "if our President, our Congress, our Supreme Court, continues

---

79 *Id*. at 510, 71 S. Ct. at 868, 95 L. Ed. 2d at 1153.

80 395 U.S. 444, 89 S. Ct. 1827, 23 L. Ed. 2d 430 (1960). *See also* § 2.21 *infra*.

to suppress the White Caucasian race, it's possible that there might be some revengeance taken." He further opined that "the nigger should be returned to Africa, the Jew returned to Israel." The Ohio statute made it a crime to advocate "the duty, necessity, or propriety of crime, sabotage, violence, or unlawful methods of terrorism as a means of accomplishing...political reform...."

The Supreme Court, echoing the philosophy but not the language of the Holmes-Brandeis test, ruled that advocacy of force or violence is punishable under our Constitution only where the advocacy is both

(1) directed toward inciting or producing *imminent* lawless action, and
(2) is likely to incite or produce such action.

The first half of the *Brandenburg* test focuses on the speaker's words, while the second half examines the context in which the words are uttered. The requirement that the harm be immediately threatened before utterances can be punished smacks of Holmes. The Court's curious failure to cite the classic formulation, while adopting a strikingly similar test appears a move to reinstate the doctrine's philosophical core while at the same time to disassociate the Court from questionable applications made of this doctrine during periods of national emergency. It was, after all, the watering down of the clear and present danger doctrine that had cast it into disrepute.

Brandenburg v. Ohio signals a return to greater national tolerance for radical doctrines and political creeds. But it does more than this. On the local level, *Brandenburg* identifies when police officers can interrupt a speech gathering and arrest the speaker for incendiary speech. Police officers may not arrest a First Amendment actor because of the incitive nature of his speech unless

(1) he intends to incite his audience to action,
(2) he urges them to perform *immediate* concrete acts of violence or other unlawful behavior, and
(3) the danger of an outbreak appears imminent.

In *Hess v. Indiana*,[81] the only case to apply the *Brandenburg* test to a crowd-control situation, the Supreme Court determined that the police officers at the scene had improperly assessed the situation's urgency. During a campus anti-war demonstration, while the police were attempting to remove a reluctant crowd of about 150 spectators off the street and onto the sidewalk, Gregory Hess, while facing the group that had already moved off the street, was heard to utter in a loud voice, "We'll take the fucking street later (or again)," the final words of his sentence being muffled by other noise. He

---

81 414 U.S. 105, 94 S. Ct. 326, 38 L. Ed. 2d 303 (1976).

was immediately arrested and charged with disorderly conduct. The Supreme Court gave two separate reasons for reversing his conviction. First, Hess's statement did not appear to be addressed to any particular person or group. Consequently, it could not be said that "he was *advocating*, in the normal sense, any action." And second, even if Hess could have been regarded as exhorting the crowd to take some action, his message, as the Court read it, urged future action ("We'll take the fucking street later"). It thus lacked the quality of immediacy required under the *Brandenburg* test. Absent proof that Hess's language was both intended to, and was likely to, produce an imminent disorder, he was not subject to arrest for his words.

§ 2.10 – Commercial speech

Commercial speech occupies a novel status within the First Amendment scheme. In *Virginia State Board of Pharmacy v. Virginia Citizens Consumer Council Inc.*,[82] the Supreme Court, observing that the consumer's interest in information about goods and services might well be keener than his interest in political debate, overruled an earlier case that had placed commercial speech outside the First Amendment. Mr. Justice Blackmun, author of the Court's opinion, nevertheless, appended a controversial footnote to this case that the Court may someday come to regret. In footnote 24 he wrote:

> In concluding that commercial speech enjoys First Amendment protection, we have not held that it is wholly undifferentiable from other forms. There are commonsense differences between speech that does 'no more than propose a commercial transaction'...and other varieties. Even if the differences do not justify the conclusion that commercial speech is valueless, and thus subject to complete suppression by the State, they nonetheless suggest that a different degree of protection is necessary....[83]

We have seen from earlier sections that several speech categories (i.e., obscenity, fighting words, etc.) have been wholly excluded from First Amendment protection. *Virginia State Board of Pharmacy*, however, represents the first case to suggest that the Amendment creates *variable degrees* of constitutional protection for protected speech.[84] Two years later, the Court elaborated upon why commercial speech, though no longer excluded from

---

82 425 U.S. 748, 96 S. Ct. 1817, 48 L. Ed. 2d 346 (1976).

83 *Id*. at 771 n. 24, 96 S. Ct. at 1830 n. 24, 48 L. Ed. 2d at 364 n. 24.

84 Roberts, *Toward a General Theory of Commercial Speech and the First Amendment*, 40 OHIO ST. L.J. 115, 131 n. 111 (1979).

the First Amendment, was entitled to less protection than speech on other topics:

> To require a parity of constitutional protection for commercial and noncommercial speech alike could invite dilution, simply by a leveling process, of the force of the Amendment's guarantee with respect to the latter kind of speech. Rather than subject the First Amendment to such a devitalization, we instead have afforded commercial speech a limited measure of protection commensurate with its *subordinate position in the scale of First Amendment values*, while allowing modes of regulation that might be impermissible in the realm of noncommercial expression.[85]

Commercial speech could be accorded a *lesser degree* of free speech protection because it was *less valuable* than ideological speech. No one took issue with this explanation for differential treatment because, in the limited context of commercial speech, the explanation seemed unassailable. Its disconcerting implications for First Amendment theory in general will be addressed in the next section.

Commercial speech enjoys First Amendment protection only when it relates to lawful activity and is not misleading.[86] However, because commercial speech occupies only a second-class status within the First Amendment scheme, the government may impose restrictions and make content-based distinctions which would be wholly impermissible in other protected speech areas.[87] The Supreme Court will subject restrictions on commercial speech to a three-part inquiry and will uphold them if:

(1) the government has a substantial regulatory interest,
(2) the measure directly advances that interest, and
(3) the measure is no broader than necessary.[88]

---

85 Ohralik v. Ohio State Bar Ass'n, 436 U.S. 447, 456, 98 S. Ct. 1912, 1918, 56 L. Ed. 2d 444 (1978) (emphasis added).

86 Friedman v. Rogers, 440 U.S. 1, 99 S. Ct. 887, 59 L. Ed. 2d 100 (1979); Pittsburg Press Co. v. Pittsburg Human Relations Comm'n, 413 U.S. 376, 93 S. Ct. 2553, 37 L. Ed. 2d 669 (1973).

87 Metromedia, Inc. v. City of San Diego, 453 U.S. 490, 101 S. Ct. 2882, 69 L. Ed. 2d 800 (1981); Bolger v. Youngs Drug Products Corp., 463 U.S. 60, 103 S. Ct. 2875, 77 L. Ed. 2d 469 (1983).

88 Central Hudson Gas v. Public Service Comm'n of N.Y., 447 U.S. 557, 100 S. Ct. 2343, 65 L. Ed. 2d 341 (1980).

The government may, for example, promote outdoor beautification and traffic safety at the expense of all commercial billboard advertising.[89] A comparable ban would be of questionable validity if directed at ideological speech.[90]

§ 2.11 – Recent trends

Under traditional free speech analysis, expression was either wholly within or wholly without the boundaries of the First Amendment. Obscenity, fighting words, violence incitement and the like were placed outside. Governments were and are free to regulate this *unprotected* speech solely because of its content. For expression falling inside the First Amendment's boundaries, however, the rule was otherwise. With rare exceptions, it was illegitimate for governments to consider content in enacting laws that affected *protected* speech. Moreover, no topics were more valuable or less valuable, more protected or less protected than any of the others. The Supreme Court had proclaimed an "equality of status" in the marketplace of ideas and the government was told to stay out of that marketplace.[91]

This simple two-level scheme of analysis -- protected versus unprotected -- broke apart with the commercial speech cases. Commercial speech, though placed inside the constitutional boundary line, was determined to be "less protected" than other varieties of protected expression, because it was less valuable.[92] The novel proposition that there are variable degrees of speech protection, depending on the value the court assigns to the underlying subject matter, has recently made an appearance outside the commercial speech arena. In *Young v. American Mini Theatres, Inc.*[93] a plurality of the Court adopted this rationale as the basis for upholding a zoning restriction on the location of adult movie houses exhibiting sexually explicit (but not obscene) films. Mr. Justice Stevens, author of the plurality opinion, wrote:

> [E]ven though we recognize that the First Amendment will not tolerate the total suppression of erotic materials that have some arguably artistic value, it is manifest that society's interest in protecting this type of expression is of...different, and lesser, magnitude

---

89 Metromedia, Inc. v. City of San Diego, *supra* note 87.

90 Schad v. Borough of Mount Ephraim, 452 U.S. 61, 101 S. Ct. 2176, 68 L. Ed. 2d 671 (1981). *But see* Members of City Council v. Taxpayers for Vincent , 466 U.S. 789, 104 S. Ct. 2118, 80 L. Ed. 2d 772 (1984).

91 § 2.4 *infra*.

92 Ohralik v. Ohio State Bar Ass'n, *supra* note 85.

93 427 U.S. 50, 96 S. Ct. 2440, 49 L. Ed. 2d 310 (1976).

> than the interest in untrammeled political debate....Whether political oratory or philosophical discussion moves us to applaud or to despise what is said, every schoolchild can understand why our duty to defend the right to speak remains the same. But few of us would march our sons and daughters off to war to preserve the citizen's right to see "Specified Sexual Activities" exhibited in the theaters of our choice. Even though the First Amendment protects communication in this area from total suppression, we hold that the State may legitimately use the content of these materials as the basis for placing them in a different classification from other motion pictures.[94]

If Mr. Justice Stevens' assessment of the comparative worthlessness of sexually explicit materials were offered as a value judgment by an ordinary citizen, most of us would agree with it. Yet, as a constitutional pronouncement coming from the Supreme Court and imprinted on the First Amendment, his views are alarming. It was never the design of the First Amendment to allow legislators, administrative officials or even Supreme Court judges to make subjective judgments about the relative value of speech topics and to adjust First Amendment protection in accordance with their personal value systems.[95]

Five judges in *Young* disassociated themselves from Mr. Justice Stevens' efforts to introduce new accordion-like features into the First Amendment. Responding to Stevens' view that non-obscene erotic speech could be treated differently than other discourse because it was less valuable, Mr. Justice Stewart wrote:

> [T]he Court invokes a concept wholly alien to the First Amendment. Since 'few of us would march our sons and daughters off to war to preserve the citizen's right to see "Specified Sexual Activities" exhibited in the theatres of our choice,'...the Court implies that these films are not entitled to the full protection of the Constitution....[I]f the guarantees of the First Amendment were reserved for expression that more than a 'few of us' would take up arms to defend, then the right of free expression would be defined and circumscribed by current popular opinion. The guarantees of the Bill

---

94 *Id*. at 70-71, 96 S. Ct. at 2452, 49 L. Ed. 2d at 326.

95 For criticism of Mr. Justice Stevens' views, see Roberts, *Toward a General Theory of Commercial Speech and the First Amendment*, 40 OHIO STATE L.J. 115 (1979); Goldman, *A Doctrine of Worthier Speech: Young v. American Mini Theatres, Inc.*, 21 ST. LOUIS U.L.J. 281 (1977); *Case Comments*, 40 OHIO STATE L.J. 155 (1979).

of Rights were designed to protect against precisely such majoritarian limitations on individual liberty.[96]

Two years later in *FCC v. Pacifica Foundation*,[97] Mr. Justice Stevens, in an opinion joined by Chief Justice Burger and Mr. Justice Rehnquist, again took occasion to expand on his new sliding-scale approach to First Amendment issues. Finding offensive language to be of marginal social value, he here voted to affirm the threat of Federal Communication Commission sanctions against a radio station for airing a satiric humorist's monologue that contained distasteful language. As in the *Young* case, the perceive *value* of the speech determined the *degree* of free speech protection. Mr. Justice Powell, who had endorsed a similar approach in the context of commercial speech,[98] now wrote:

> ...I do not subscribe to the theory that the Justices of this Court are free generally to decide on the basis of its content which speech protected by the First Amendment is most 'valuable' and hence deserving of the most protection, and which is less 'valuable' and hence deserving of less protection....In my view, the result in this case does not turn on whether Carlin's monologue, viewed as a whole, or the words that constitute it, have more or less 'value' than a candidate's campaign speech. This is a judgment for each person to make, not one for the judges to impose upon him.[99]

Though Mr. Justice Stevens' approach to First Amendment analysis has been roundly criticized by legal scholars,[100] a majority of the current Supreme Court appear now to endorse his views. In *Bethel School District v. Fraser*,[101] a high school student was disciplined for giving an indecent, lewd and offensive speech during a school assembly. The Court sided with the school authorities. The Court's rationale turned, in part, on its assessment that offensive speech lacks sufficient social worth to warrant full-scale First Amendment protection.

---

[96] Young v. American Mini Theatres, Inc., 427 U.S. 50, 86, 96 S. Ct. 2440, 2460, 49 L. Ed. 2d 310, 335-336 (1976) (Dissent).

[97] 438 U.S. 726, 89 S. Ct. 3026, 57 L. Ed. 2d 1073 (1978).

[98] Ohralik v. Ohio State Bar Ass'n, *supra* note 85.

[99] FCC v. Pacifica Foundation, 438 U.S. 726, 761, 98 S. Ct. 3026, 3046-3047, 57 L. Ed. 2d 1073 (1978).

[100] Roberts, *supra* note 95; Goldman, *supra* note 95; L. TRIBE, AMERICAN CONSTITUTIONAL LAW § 12-18.

[101] 478 U.S. 675, 106 S. Ct. 3156, 92 L. Ed. 2d 459 (1986).

§ 2.12 – Summary

Under orthodox First Amendment analysis, the government may restrict expression because of its content, subject-matter or viewpoint only where it falls on the unprotected side of the constitutional dividing line. The following speech subjects have been excluded from First Amendment protection: obscenity, fighting words, threats, speech posing a clear and present danger, and speech falling under the *Brandenburg* incitive utterances test, the danger doctrine's modern successor.

Prior to the recent commercial speech cases, virtually all other speech -- unorthodox, offensive and controversial no less than highly esteemed -- had an equal claim to First Amendment protection. To have suggested during the Warren Court era that legislators, administrative officials or even judges could assess some speech subjects to be of sufficiently low social value as to warrant a reduced measure of First Amendment protection would have been regarded as heresy. This simple two-level approach, however, began to develop cracks in the commercial speech cases. When commercial speech was admitted into the First Amendment, it was given second-class citizenship. Commercial speech was said to enjoy less protection than ideological speech because it made a "less valuable" contribution to the marketplace of ideas. More recently, lewd, indecent and offensive speech was also relegated to the new less value/less protected speech category. There appears, however, little impetus toward expanding the low valued speech category beyond commercial and offensive speech. The Court should refrain from concerning itself with the social value of the speech in determining how much First Amendment protection it will receive. Freedom of expression contemplates that judgments about the worth of an idea should be made in the marketplace rather than the courtroom.

§ 2.13 Regulation of the noncommunicative aspects of expression

Freedom of expression has its social and private costs. Parades invariably disrupt normal traffic flows, to say nothing of the burden they place on the community's police, sanitation and parking resources. Billboards are esthetically displeasing and may turn into traffic hazards. When canvassers, picketers and marchers invade residential neighborhoods, a measure of privacy and tranquility is lost. Traffic congestion, noise, litter, and inconvenience are standard accompaniments to free speech in the local community and produce injurious effects irrespective of the speech's content or message. Professor Lawrence H. Tribe has coined the phrase "noncommunicative impact" to describe such injurious effects.[102]

The First Amendment does not eliminate the power of local governments to protect the quality of life in the local community. Where the government's regulatory concern in limiting expressive activity is directed toward its noncommunicative impact, a different approach to First Amendment dispute resolution will be employed than when the focal point is its thematic content or message.[103] A passage from *Metromedia, Inc. v. City of San Diego*[104] underscores this distinction:

> Billboards, then, like other media of communication, combine communicative and noncommunicative aspects. As with other media, the government has legitimate interests in controlling the noncommunicative aspects of the medium,...but the First and Fourteenth Amendments foreclose a similar interest in controlling the communicative aspects.

How does the court determine whether the government can prohibit loudspeakers in residential neighborhoods, ban billboards or halt distribution of handbills as a means of combating litter?

Where a restriction on expressive activity is directed at its noncommunicative effects, the constitutional inquiry will be conducted through an approach known as "interest balancing."[105] Under this approach, the court will assess the degree of the interference with First Amendment interests and values and will then weigh the seriousness of this encroachment against the strength of the government's regulatory interest.[106] Where a measure substantially limits expressive activities or seriously interferes with First Amendment values, the government bears a heavier burden of justification than where the measure impinges on freedom of expression only incidentally or infrequently.[107] For more serious interferences, the government must

---

102 L. TRIBE, AMERICAN CONSTITUTIONAL LAW §§ 12-2, 12-20.

103 *Id.*

104 453 U.S. 490, 502, 101 S. Ct. 2882, 2890, 69 L. Ed. 2d 800 (1981).

105 TRIBE, *supra* note 102.

106 Metromedia Inc. v. City of San Diego, *supra* note 87.

107 Schad v. Borough of Mount Ephraim, *supra* note 90; Young v. American Mini-Theatres, Inc., *supra* note 96.

demonstrate a *compelling regulatory interest*;[108] on the other hand, a less pressing regulatory need will suffice where the impact on First Amendment interests is slight.[109]

A comparison of *Schad v. Borough of Mount Ephraim*[110] and *Young v. American Mini Theatres, Inc.*[111] demonstrates the relationship between the extensiveness of the restriction's First Amendment impact and the government's burden of justification. At stake in *Young* was an anti-skid row ordinance prohibiting "adult" theatres from locating within 1000 feet of any two adult theatres, hotels, pool halls or bars. Observing that this ordinance did not greatly restrict permissible locations, the Court ruled that the government's interest in preventing neighborhood deterioration accompanying the growth of red light districts furnished a sufficient regulatory justification for its minor interference with freedom of expression. In *Schad*, on the other hand, the zoning ordinance altogether banned live entertainment establishments from the borough's commercial districts. The Supreme Court ruled that the government had not established a sufficiently compelling justification for its more substantial interference with protected speech, particularly when other commercial uses no less taxing on the borough's police, parking and sanitation resources were allowed under its zoning laws. A stronger regulatory justification was required in *Schad* because the zoning ordinance had a more devastating First Amendment impact.

The heavy burden placed on the government to justify measures that seriously impinge on expressive activity is a natural correlative of the exalted position that free speech holds in our society. In *Schneider v. Town of Irvington*,[112] the Supreme Court ruled that the government's interest in keeping its streets free from litter was too trivial to justify imposing a ban on the public distribution of handbills. But in *Metromedia Inc. v. City of San Diego*,[113] in contrast, the Court upheld a measure banning all off-site commercial billboard advertising. Here the government's regulatory interest extended beyond esthetic considerations; distracting billboard signs create potential traffic hazards. And in *Grayned v. City of Rockford*,[114] the Court ruled that the

---

108 Smith v. Daily Mail Publishing Co., 443 U.S. 97, 99 S. Ct. 2667, 61 L. Ed. 2d 399 (1979); Schad v. Borough of Mount Ephraim, *supra* note 90.

109 Young v. American Mini-Theatres, Inc., *supra* note 96.

110 452 U.S. 61, 101 S. Ct. 2440, 68 L. Ed. 2d 671 (1981).

111 427 U.S. 50, 96 S. Ct. 2440, 49 L. Ed. 2d 310 (1976).

112 308 U.S. 147, 60 S. Ct. 146, 84 L. Ed. 2d 155 (1939).

113 453 U.S. 490, 101 S. Ct. 2882, 69 L. Ed. 2d 800 (1981). *See also* City Council of Los Angeles v. Taxpayers for Vincent, 466 U.S. 789, 104 S. Ct. 2118, 80 L. Ed. 2d 772 (1984).

114 408 U.S. 104, 92 S. Ct. 2294, 33 L. Ed. 2d 222 (1972).

government's interest in providing a proper learning environment furnished a sufficient regulatory justification for an anti-noise ordinance prohibiting disturbances on grounds adjacent to schools while classes were in session.

Cases employing interest-balancing techniques in First Amendment dispute resolution could be cited endlessly. They illustrate considerations involved in the constitutional analysis of regulatory measures dealing with the noncommunicative effects of speech.[115] (Interest balancing is rarely employed where the challenged measure is aimed at communicative content or message.)[116]

Even when the government has a substantial regulatory interest, restrictions on expression will not be countenanced where alternatives less destructive of First Amendment interests would equally serve the government's ends.[117] The requirement that laws operating in First Amendment settings be narrowly drawn so as to cause no unnecessary interference with freedom of expression is often referred to as the "doctrine of the least restrictive alternative." *Village of Schaumburg v. Citizens for a Better Environment*,[118] illustrates this doctrine. The city, in an effort to protect its inhabitants from fraud, enacted an ordinance prohibiting public solicitation by charitable organizations that did not use at least 75 percent of their proceeds for charitable purposes. The Supreme Court, after finding that the city had a sufficiently compelling interest to justify regulating charitable solicitations, invalidated the ordinance on the ground that the city had not selected the least drastic means for protecting its citizens from fraudulent practices. Penal laws should have been enacted punishing persons guilty of fraudulent charitable solicitations while leaving honest organizations free to solicit funds.

The doctrine of the least restrictive alternative serves as a reminder that the government may not enact sweeping restrictions designed to curb freedom of expression where other choices remain available.

§ 2.14 First Amendment right of access to government property: concept of the public forum

The constitutional guarantee of freedom of expression would be of limited importance if it did not carry with it some assurance of the availability of

---

115 L. TRIBE, AMERICAN CONSTITUTIONAL LAW §§ 12-2, 12-20.

116 *Id.*

117 Village of Schaumberg v. Citizens for a Better Environment, 444 U.S. 620, 199 S. Ct. 826, 63 L. Ed. 2d 73 (1980); Globe Newspaper Co. v. Superior Court, 457 U.S. 596, 102 S. Ct. 2613, 73 L. Ed. 2d 248 (1981).

118 444 U.S. 620, 100 S. Ct. 826, 63 L. Ed. 2d 73 (1980).

means to reach a suitable audience. For those championing poorly financed causes who lack funds to rent private meeting halls or to buy newspaper space and television time, government-owned facilities often constitute the only suitable locations for communicating with large numbers of people. The Supreme Court has employed public forum analysis to ascertain when members of the public have a First Amendment right of access to government property.

A "forum," in the context of First Amendment analysis, denotes some particular government-controlled location, facility or channel of communication to which a First Amendment actor seeks access. The "forum" may variously be a place such as a street or public building, a government-operated communications facility like a government newspaper, or an intangible instrumentality that lacks physical situs, such as an interschool mail system or an official government fund-raising network.

The First Amendment does not guarantee speech access to property simply because it is owned or controlled by the government.[119] For free speech purposes, there are two classifications of government-owned property -- *public forums* and *nonpublic forums*. The extent to which the government can control speech access depends on which type of forum is involved. In *Cornelius v. NAACP Legal Defense and Educational Fund, Inc.*,[120] the Supreme Court explained the role of public forum analysis as follows:

> Nothing in the Constitution requires the Government freely to grant access to all who wish to exercise their right to free speech on every type of government property without regard to the nature of the property or to the disruption that might be caused by the speaker's activities....Recognizing that the Government 'no less than a private owner of property, has power to preserve the property under its control for the use to which it is lawfully dedicated,'...the Court has adopted a forum analysis as a means of determining when the Government's interest in limiting the use of its property to its intended purpose outweighs the interest of those wishing to use the property for other purposes. Accordingly, the extent to which the Government can control access depends on the nature of the relevant forum. Because a principal purpose of traditional public fora is the free exchange of ideas, speakers can be excluded from a public forum only when the exclusion is necessary to serve a compelling government interest and the exclusion is narrowly drawn to

119 United States Postal Service v. Council of Greenburgh Civic Ass'n, 453 U.S. 114, 130, 101 S. Ct. 2676, 2685, 69 L. Ed. 2d 517 (1981).

120 473 U.S. 788, 105 S. Ct. 3439, 87 L. Ed. 2d 567 (1985).

> achieve that interest....Access to a nonpublic forum, however, can be restricted as long as the restrictions are reasonable and [are] not an effort to suppress expression merely because public officials oppose the speaker's views.[121]

Public forum analysis of limitations on the use of public property for expressive purposes entails a two-step process. When a restriction on the First Amendment use of a public facility is challenged, the court will first classify the location as a public or a nonpublic forum. Once classification is accomplished, the court will assess whether the government's regulatory justification satisfies First Amendment standards applicable to forums of the type involved.

§ 2.15 – Criteria for differentiating public forums from nonpublic forums

Streets, sidewalks and parks are areas that have historically been available to members of the public for speech and assembly. Because of longstanding traditions of First Amendment use, these locations have been referred to as quintessential examples of *traditional public forums*.[122] Streets and sidewalks do not cease to be public forums because they are located in front of public buildings[123] or in quiet residential areas.[124] In *United States v. Grace*,[125] a citizen picketed on the sidewalks outside the Supreme Court, carrying a sign with the text of the First Amendment on it. He participated in this strange venture to test the constitutionality of a District of Columbia ordinance which prohibited picketing in front of the Supreme Court courthouse. He was arrested and eventually carried his case to the Supreme Court. The Court ruled that the public streets and sidewalks in front of its courthouse were not constitutionally different from any other street or sidewalk and that Congress could not declare them off limits for peaceful First Amendment activity.

---

121 *Id.*, 373 U.S. at 799-800, 105 S. Ct. at 3439.

122 Perry Education Ass'n v. Perry Local Educators Ass'n, 460 U.S. 37, 46, 103 S. Ct. 948, 955, 74 L. Ed. 2d 794 (1983).

123 United States v. Grace, 461 U.S. 171, 179, 103 S. Ct. 1702, 1703, 75 L. Ed. 2d 736 (1983); Frisby v. Schultz, ___ U.S. ___, 108 S. Ct. 2495, 2500, 101 L. Ed. 2d 420 (1988).

124 Frisby v. Schultz, *supra* note 123.

125 461 U.S. 171, 103 S. Ct. 1702, 75 L. Ed. 2d 736 (1983). This case is reproduced in Part II.

Streets, sidewalks and parks have acquired public forum status through long-standing traditions of First Amendment use by members of the public and are therefore called *traditional public forums*. But public forum status can be acquired in a second way: When the government *intentionally* opens nontraditional facilities and makes them available for speech and assembly, a *public forum by designation* or, as it is sometimes called, a *limited public forum* results. It bears emphasis that the government is not constitutionally obliged to make facilities other than streets, parks and sidewalks available for expressive use by members of the public, even if the facility is highly suitable or specially designed for communication.[126] For instance, while fire hydrants and similar public fixtures may appear to be ideal, cost-free locations for hanging signs and posters, the government is under no constitutional compulsion to allow free speech uses.[127] Similarly, if the government establishes an interschool mail facility for official communications within the school system, the government is not constitutionally required to make this facility available to outsiders wanting to communicate with teachers.[128] Moreover, public property does not automatically become a public forum by designation simply because members of the public are welcome to visit. For instance, the streets of military reservations,[129] as well as the interiors of government workplaces,[130] hospitals, libraries and similar buildings remain nonpublic forums even though members of the public are free to come and go at will. Something more is required.

Property other than streets, sidewalks and parks become public forums through designation only if the government *intends* this result.[131] The government's intent, however, need not be expressed. Courts will infer this intent from the combined effects of the nature of the facility, its compatibility with expressive activity and the government's past policies and practices of making that facility available for expressive use by outsiders.[132] Where the

---

126 Lehman v. City of Shaker Heights, 418 U.S. 298, 94 S. Ct. 2714, 41 L. Ed. 2d 770 (1974); United States Postal Service v. Council of Greenburgh Civic Ass'n, *supra* note 119; Perry Education Ass'n v. Perry Local Educators' Ass'n, *supra* note 122; Members of City Council v. Taxpayers for Vincent, 466 U.S. 789, 104 S. Ct. 2118, 80 L. Ed. 2d 772 (1984); Hazelwood School Dist. v. Kuhlmeier, 484 U.S. 260, 108 S. Ct. 562, 98 L. Ed. 2d 592 (1988).

127 Members of City Council v. Taxpayers for Vincent, *supra* note 126.

128 Perry Education Ass'n v. Perry Local Educators' Ass'n, *supra* note 122.

129 Greer v. Spock, 424 U.S. 828, 96 S. Ct. 1211, 47 L. Ed. 2d 505 (1976); United States v. Albertini, 472 U.S. 675, 105 S. Ct. 2897, 86 L. Ed. 2d 536 (1985).

130 Cornelius v. NAACP Legal Defense & Educational Fund, *supra* note 120.

131 *Id.*

132 *Id.*

government routinely makes a meeting hall, auditorium or other facility that is especially suited to speech available to members of the public, the government's conduct operates to designate this facility as a public forum. In consequence of this designation, the government loses its freedom to turn other groups away for reasons relating to intended subject matter, viewpoint or speaker identity.[133] The government, on the other hand, does not designate its facilities as public forums by allowing outsiders to make occasional communicative use of them,[134] particularly when the permitted use advances the government's purpose or is related to the forum's official business.[135] In *Perry Education Association v. Perry Local Educators' Association*,[136] the Supreme Court held that school mail facilities were not transformed into a public forum merely because the school had occasionally permitted civic and church organizations to use the facility or because it had permitted unrestricted use by the union selected by teachers as their exclusive bargaining agent. In another case, the Court ruled that a federal military reservation continued to be a nonpublic forum even though civilian speakers and entertainers had occasionally been invited there to address and entertain military personnel.[137] In both of these cases, the First Amendment uses by nonaffiliated individuals were either sporadic and limited rather than indiscriminate and routine or, in the case of the teacher's union, were related to official business conducted in the forum.

Courts most certainly will not find that a public forum has been established where the government has maintained a consistent practice of controlling speech access by outsiders,[138] or where expressive activity would disrupt the forum's normal business routines.[139] Federal workplaces,[140] schools,[141]

---

133 Southeastern Promotions, Ltd. v. Conrad, 420 U.S. 546, 95 S. Ct. 1239, 43 L. Ed. 2d 448 (1975); Widmar v. Vincent, 454 U.S. 263, 102 S. Ct. 269, 70 L. Ed. 2d 440 (1981); Concerned Women for America Education & Legal Defense Foundation v. Lafayette County & Oxford Public Library, 699 F. Supp. 95 (S.D. Miss. 1988), *aff'd*, 883 F.2d 32 (5th Cir. 1989).

134 Perry Education Ass'n v. Perry Local Educator's Ass'n, *supra* note 122; Greer v. Spock, *supra* note 129.

135 Perry Education Ass'n v. Perry Local Educator's Ass'n, *supra* note 122.

136 *Id.*

137 Greer v. Spock, *supra* note 129.

138 Hazelwood School Dist. v. Kuhlmeier, *supra* note 126; Greer v. Spock, *supra* note 129.

139 Cornelius v. NAACP Legal Defense & Educational Fund, *supra* note 120; Jones v. North Carolina Prisoner's Labor Union, 433 U.S. 119, 97 S. Ct. 2532, 53 L. Ed. 2d 629 (1977).

140 Cornelius v. NAACP Legal Defense & Educational Fund, *supra* note 120.

military bases,[142] and similar government-operated facilities serve important nonspeech uses. Courts have refused to find the existence of a public forum by designation where communicative activity would be incompatible with the efficient performance of the governmental function which the forum at issue performs.

As we have seen, the First Amendment does not guarantee speech access to property simply because it is owned or controlled by government. Government property which is neither by tradition nor designation a public forum remains *nonpublic forum* property. The government, no less than a private landowner, has the power to preserve its nonforum property for the government's intended use and may restrict access to those who participate in the forum's official business.[143]

§ 2.16 – Constitutionality of restrictions on public forum access

When a regulation which restricts the First Amendment use of government property is challenged, the court will first classify the location as a public forum or a nonpublic forum. Having made the classification, the court will then determine whether the regulation satisfies First Amendment standards applicable to forums of the type involved. The determination that the location constitutes a public forum means that the restrictions on First Amendment uses will be judged by stringent standards.[144] Courts have tolerated of narrow, focused restrictions known as time, place and manner restrictions.[145] Where, however, the government seeks to flatly prohibit speech uses[146] or to make distinctions among would-be forum users based on speech subject matter or speaker identity,[147] a compelling regulatory interest is nec-

---

141 Hazelwood School Dist. v. Kuhlmeier, *supra* note 126.

142 Greer v. Spock, *supra* note 129.

143 Perry Education Ass'n v. Perry Local Educators Ass'n, *supra* note 122.

144 United States v. Grace, *supra* note 123; Boos v. Barry, 485 U.S. 312, 108 S. Ct. 1157, 99 L. Ed. 2d 333 (1988).

145 Heffron v. International Soc'y for Krishna Consciousness, 452 U.S. 640, 101 S. Ct. 2559, 69 L. Ed. 2d 298 (1981); Clark v. Community for Creative Non-Violence, 468 U.S. 288, 104 S. Ct. 3065, 82 L. Ed. 2d 221 (1984); Frisby v. Schultz, *supra* note 123.

146 United States v. Grace, *supra* note 123.

147 Boos v. Barry, *supra* note 144; Widmar v. Vincent, 454 U.S. 263, 102 S. Ct. 269, 70 L. Ed. 2d 440 (1981).

essary. As the next section reveals, the government has much broader managerial discretion when regulating expressive uses of nonpublic forums.[148]

Content-neutral time, place, and manner restrictions

The government may enact content-neutral[149] time, place or manner restrictions on the First Amendment use of public forums if the measure:

(1) advances a *significant government interest*,
(2) is *narrowly drawn*, and
(3) leaves would-be forum users ample *alternative outlets for communicating* their views.

The government can tone down the intrusive aspects of speech by regulating its *manner*, such as restricting the use of sound trucks and other artificial sound amplification equipment,[150] or by regulating the *time* and *place*, such as prohibiting noisy activities in front of schools, hospitals and similar locations during times when noisy activity would be disruptive and unwelcome.[151] To protect the safety and convenience of others using heavily congested facilities, the government can ban solicitation and leafleting in densely trafficked areas.[152] Two parades cannot march on the same street at the same time. To assure that this does not happen, a municipality can control their times and locations by requiring First Amendment actors to secure a permit before holding a parade or other outdoor demonstration.[153] The government, moreover, has a substantial regulatory interest in protecting residential dwellers from unwelcome speech intrusion into the sanctity and tranquility of their homes. Anti-picketing ordinances can be enacted which prohibit picketing focused at individual residences.[154]

A valid time, place and manner restriction, however, must be narrowly tailored so as to suppress no more speech than is necessary to correct the evil that the government seeks to eradicate.[155] In *Board of Airport Commission-*

148 *See* § 2.17 *infra*.

149 A content-neutral restriction is one that is justified without reference to the speaker's message. *See* § 2.4 *supra*.

150 Ward v. Rock Against Racism, ___ U.S. ___, 109 S. Ct. 2746, 105 L. Ed. 2d 661 (1989); Kovacs v. Cooper, 336 U.S. 77, 69 S. Ct. 448, 93 L. Ed. 513 (1941).

151 Grayned v. City of Rockford, 408 U.S. 104, 92 S. Ct. 2294, 33 L. Ed. 2d 222 (1972).

152 Heffron v. International Soc'y for Krishna Consciousness, *supra* note 145.

153 Cox v. New Hampshire, 312 U.S. 569, 61 S. Ct. 762, 85 L. Ed. 1049 (1941).

154 Frisby v. Schultz, *supra* note 123.

155 *Id.*

ers v. Jews for Jesus, Inc.,[156] the Supreme Court invalidated a regulation that banned "all First Amendment activities" within the central terminal area of the Los Angeles International Airport. Pointing out that a ban on *all* First Amendment activities extended to wearing campaign buttons, talking and reading and not merely to behavior that might create congestions or inconvenience other forum users, the Supreme Court pronounced this regulation unconstitutional under the doctrine of First Amendment overbreadth.

Finally, a valid time, place and manner restriction must leave would-be forum users ample alternative channels for communicating their views. A measure that fails to leave available alternatives for reaching the desired audience seriously encroaches on First Amendment values and is subject to more rigorous constitutional standards than are applied to time, place and manner restrictions. In *Linmark Associates v. Town of Willingboro*,[157] the Supreme Court declined to uphold an ordinance prohibiting the display of real estate "for sale" and "sold" signs on residences as a valid time, place, and manner restriction on communicative activity, among other reasons, because this regulation failed to leave the speaker with adequate alternatives for communicating this message. The Court observed:

> Although in theory sellers remain free to employ a number of different alternatives, in practice realty is not marketed through leaflets, sound trucks, demonstrations, or the like. The options to which sellers realistically are relegated -- primarily newspaper advertising and listing with real estate agents -- involve more cost and less autonomy than 'For Sale' signs; are less likely to reach persons not deliberately seeking sales information; and may be less effective media for communicating the message than is conveyed by a 'For Sale' sign in front of the house to be sold...The alternatives, then, are far from satisfactory.[158]

Absolute prohibition on speech in a public forum

Stricter scrutiny is applied to regulations which flatly prohibit expressive activity in a public forum than for less sweeping time, place or manner restrictions. To justify broadly banning particular modes of protected expression from public forums, the government must establish that the regulation is narrowly drawn to advance a *compelling government interest* and represents

---

156 482 U.S. 569, 107 S. Ct. 2568, 96 L. Ed. 2d 500 (1987).
157 431 U.S. 85, 97 S. Ct. 1614, 52 L. Ed. 2d 155 (1977).
158 *Id*. 431 U.S. at 93, 97 S. Ct. at 1618, 52 L. Ed. 2d at 162.

the *least burdensome alternative* for promoting that interest.[159] In *Schaumburg v. Citizens for a Better Environment*,[160] the Supreme Court struck down an ordinance that prohibited door-to-door or on-street solicitation of contributions by charitable organizations that did not use at least 75 percent of their proceeds for charitable purposes. This ordinance went far beyond regulating the time, place or manner for conducting charitable solicitations; it absolutely prohibited certain charitable organizations from engaging at all in specified expressive activities (i.e., door-to-door and on-street solicitations). While conceding that fraud prevention is a legitimate regulatory interest, the Supreme Court ruled that the government had not selected the least intrusive means for promoting this end. To avoid unnecessarily restricting protected expression, the government should have enacted legislation punishing charitable organizations which practiced fraud, rather than forbidding all organizations not using at least 75 percent of their proceeds for charitable purposes -- honest and dishonest alike -- from engaging in First Amendment activity.

Content-based restrictions on public forum access

A content-based regulation is a regulation which favors or disfavors First Amendment activity because of the speaker's choice of subject matter, viewpoint or the speaker's identity.[161] An ordinance prohibiting *any person* from picketing in front of another's residence is content-neutral.[162] A similar ordinance which prohibits *labor picketing* in residential areas or conversely, *all picketing except picketing concerning labor disputes* is content-based because in one case it favors and in the other case, disfavors speech on the basis of subject matter.[163]

The Supreme Court has employed a stricter standard of review for content-based restrictions on public forum access than for content-neutral ones. Content-based restrictions are much more likely to pose risks of improper motivations and dangers that public debate will be distorted than content-neutral regulations.[164] For this reason, government may enforce a content-based exclusion from a public forum only if "the regulation is necessary to serve a *compelling state interest* and...is *narrowly drawn* to achieve that

---

159 Schaumberg v. Citizens for a Better Environment, 444 U.S. 620, 100 S. Ct. 826, 63 L. Ed. 2d 73 (1980).

160 *Id.*

161 Leeds, *Pigeonholes in the Public Forum*, 20 U. RICH. L. REV. 449, 506 (1986).

162 Frisby v. Schultz, *supra* note 123.

163 Carey v. Brown, 447 U.S. 455, 100 S. Ct. 2286, 65 L. Ed. 2d 263 (1980).

164 Stone, *Content-Neutral Restrictions*, 54 U. CHI. L. REV. 46, 55-56 (1987).

end."[165] The Supreme Court recently overturned a District of Columbia ordinance prohibiting any person from displaying a sign within 500 feet of a foreign embassy if the sign *tended to bring the foreign embassy's government into disrepute* because the measure was content-based and, in the Court's opinion, was not carefully drawn.[166]

Content-discrimination in violation of the First Amendment can also result from unwritten government policies and practices. If the government allows diverse nonaffiliated organizations to use its meeting halls, communication facilities and similar property for speech-related purposes, the practice of permitting indiscriminate use may cause the facility to become a public forum by designation.[167] Should this occur, the government forfeits its discretion to make distinctions between would-be forum users based on the subject matter of their speech, viewpoint or speaker identity.[168]

§ 2.17 – Constitutionality of restrictions on nonpublic forum access

Restrictions on expressive activity in *nonpublic forums* are subject to less stringent First Amendment standards than apply in *public forums*. The government, like a private property owner, has broad managerial discretion to limit expressive uses of nonpublic forums and may make distinctions[169] or impose limitations on access[170] that would be constitutionally impermissible had the speech occurred in a public forum. In *United States v. Grace*,[171] the Supreme Court observed:

> We have regularly rejected the assertion that people who wish 'to propagandize protests or views have a constitutional right to do so whenever and however and wherever they please.'...There is little doubt that in some circumstances the government can ban the entry on to public property that is not a 'public forum' of all persons except those who have legitimate business on the premises. The gov-

---

165 Perry Education Ass'n v. Perry Local Educators' Ass'n, 460 U.S. 37, 45, 103 S. Ct. 948, 954, 74 L. Ed. 2d 794 (1983).

166 Boos v. Barry, *supra* note 144.

167 *See* § 2.15 *supra*.

168 Widmar v. Vincent, 454 U.S. 262, 102 S. Ct. 262, 70 L. Ed. 2d 440 (1981).

169 Lehman v. City of Shaker Heights, 418 U.S. 296, 94 S. Ct. 2714, 41 L. Ed. 2d 770 (1974).

170 Members of City Council v. Taxpayers for Vincent, *supra* note 126.

171 461 U.S. 171, 177-178, 103 S. Ct. 1702, 1707, 75 L. Ed. 2d 736 (1983).

ernment, 'no less than a private owner of property, has the power to preserve the property under its control for the use to which it is lawfully dedicated.'

The government's proprietary control over nonpublic forums allows it to make distinctions based on speech subject matter and speaker identity that would violate the First Amendment if established for public forums. The Supreme Court has in several cases sanctioned content-discrimination. In *Lehman v. City of Shaker Heights*,[172] the Court on observing that the card advertising spaces on city buses were neither by tradition nor designation public forums, bowed to the municipal transit authority's managerial discretion to refuse advertisements from political candidates while accepting them from civic, public service and commercial organizations. In *Jones v. North Carolina Prisoner's Labor Union*,[173] the Supreme Court ruled that since prisons were nonpublic forums, prison authorities could refuse an inmate labor union's request for bulk mailing privileges and meeting rights which other organizations such as Alcoholics Anonymous and Jaycees enjoyed. In *Perry Education Association v. Perry Local Educators' Association*,[174] the Supreme Court observed:

> Implicit in the concept of the nonpublic forum is the right to make distinctions in access on the basis of subject matter and speaker identity. These distinctions may be impermissible in a public forum but are inherent and inescapable in the process of limiting a nonpublic forum to activities compatible with the intended purpose of the property.

Even though the government has broad managerial discretion to control speech access to nonpublic forums, the Constitution does not allow the government to exercise this discretion arbitrarily. In nonpublic forums, courts will review First Amendment access policies to assure that they are:

(1) viewpoint neutral, and
(2) reasonable in light of the function that the forum in controversy serves.[175]

---

172 418 U.S. 296, 94 S. Ct. 2714, 41 L. Ed. 2d (1974).

173 433 U.S. 119, 97 S. Ct. 2532, 53 L. Ed. 2d 629 (1977).

174 460 U.S. 37, 103 S. Ct. 948, 957, 74 L. Ed. 2d 794 (1983).

175 Perry Education Ass'n v. Perry Local Educator's Ass'n, *supra* note 165; Cornelius v. NAACP Legal Defense & Educational Fund, 473 U.S. 788, 105 S. Ct. 3439, 87 L. Ed. 2d 567 (1985).

The government's decision to ban some or all speech in nonpublic forums must be properly motivated and reasonable.

The Supreme Court applied this standard in *Perry Education Association v. Perry Local Educators' Association*,[176] where a rival teacher's union challenged the school district's preferential treatment in permitting another union, elected by district school teachers as their exclusive bargaining agent, to use the interschool mail system to communicate with teachers while denying them a similar privilege. The Supreme Court classified the interschool mail system as a nonpublic forum and then ruled that the school district's distinction between the exclusive bargaining agent and rival unions satisfied the two-pronged constitutional standard applicable to nonpublic forums. Preferential treatment for the union elected by the teachers as their exclusive bargaining agent was based on its status rather than viewpoint favoritism. Moreover, it was inherently reasonable for the school district to restrict the use of its mail facilities to the union having operational responsibilities within the school system. The Court concluded that "when government property is not dedicated to open communication the government may -- without further justification -- restrict use to those who participate in the forum's official business."[177]

In *Cornelius v. NAACP Legal Defense and Educational Fund, Inc.*,[178] the Supreme Court again ruled that the existence of reasonable grounds for differentiating between those granted and those denied speech access to nonpublic forums is enough to justify viewpoint-neutral distinctions. The government is not required to further demonstrate that its choice was the most reasonable or that the excluded speech was incompatible with the normal operation of that forum. The constitutional burdens placed on the government in regulating speech access to nonpublic forums -- that it behave rationally and for motives other than disapproval of the speaker's views -- are minimal in comparison to the standards the government is held to when it makes content-based distinctions in regulating speech access to public forums. In public forums, the government must demonstrate that its preferential access policies are narrowly tailored to serve a compelling government interest.[179]

---

176 *Supra* note 165.

177 *Id*. 460 U.S. at 53, 103 S. Ct. at 959.

178 473 U.S. 788, 105 S. Ct. 3439, 87 L. Ed. 2d 567 (1985).

179 *See* § 2.16 *supra*. *See also* Perry Education Ass'n v. Perry Local Educators' Ass'n, *supra* note 165.

§ 2.18 – Private property and the First Amendment

The First Amendment prohibits Congress from abridging the freedom of speech. When the Fourteenth Amendment was adopted, the First Amendment became binding on lower levels of government. However, neither the First Amendment nor any other portion of the United States Constitution imposes comparable restraints on private citizens.

Ownership of private property carries with it the right of the owner to exclude unwelcome visitors. The Constitution does not give a First Amendment actor the right to invade an unwilling listener's property for purposes of expressing his views. A trespass is nonetheless a trespass even though committed in the misguided belief that the First Amendment privileges the entry.

In *Central Hardware Co. v. N.L.R.B.*,[180] police arrested a union organizer for trespassing on the privately owned parking lot of a retail hardware store. The union argued that because the store's parking lot was "open to the public," it had acquired the characteristic of a municipal parking facility and though privately owned, was subject to the commands of the First Amendment. The Court rejected this position, stating that a similar argument could be made with respect to almost every retail store and service establishment and that to accept such an argument would constitute an unwarranted infringement on age-old property notions. In *Lloyd Corp. v. Tanner*,[181] decided the same day as *Central Hardware*, security guards threatened to arrest persons distributing handbills on the property of a privately owned shopping center for criminal trespass. The leaflet distributors claimed that because a shopping center includes sidewalks, streets and parking areas, it serves the same function as a municipal business district. They argued that as a result, members of the public have the same free-speech rights on shopping center premises as they do on city streets. The Supreme Court disagreed. The streets, pedestrian walks and parking facilities of shopping center complexes, though they may serve a purpose similar to those found in downtown business districts, are private property for First Amendment purposes. The fact that the public is invited to use these facilities in conjunction with the owner's business does not convert them into public free-speech forums. Consequently, corporate proprietors of shopping centers are free to absolutely exclude or enforce any restrictions they so desire on the expressive use of their facilities.

A word of caution, however, is in order. First Amendment actors should not be arrested solely because they are located on private property unless the

---

180 407 U.S. 539, 92 S. Ct. 2238 (1976).

181 407 U.S. 551, 92 S. Ct. 2219, 33 L. Ed. 131 (1972). *See also* Hudgens v. NLRB, 424 U.S. 507, 96 S. Ct. 1029, 47 L. Ed. 2d 196 (1975).

owner has requested them to leave. If the owner is willing to receive them, there is no trespass. When a police officer, without solicitation, interrupts speech activity on private property that is not objectionable to the property owner, the officer violates freedom of expression between the speaker and his willing listener.

§ 2.19 – Permit controls

Advance notice of parades and other outdoor demonstrations is crucial if local governments are to assure adequate policing of these events. Furthermore, government involvement in scheduling and routing decisions is useful to minimize public inconvenience. Permits are the device most commonly used to secure these benefits. The requirement that First Amendment actors secure a permit in advance of holding a parade, outdoor demonstration or similar open-air gathering is constitutionally valid if the statute contains narrow, objective and definite standards to guide the licensing authority's decisions and if the licensor's discretion does not extend beyond resource allocation, routes, scheduling and traffic considerations.[182] The Supreme Court has repeatedly invalidated permit statutes that lack clear standards or allow for subjective judgments because such measures create a serious risk of abuse.[183] Licensing officials may not be given a free hand to determine in advance what subjects can be discussed or viewpoints aired on city streets and sidewalks. Ordinances that allow the administrator to consider the applicant's character or the nature of his organization,[184] his past intemperate speech,[185] the parade's effect upon the health, safety, peace, welfare, decency, morals, convenience, or good order of the community,[186] or the likelihood of riots and disorders are unconstitutional.[187]

For those schooled in peacekeeping, these decisions may seem wrong. Mr. Justice Blackmun, however, has summed up why issuance of permits may not depend on the discretion of an administrator:

---

182 Cox v. New Hampshire, 312 U.S. 569, 61 S. Ct. 762, 85 L. Ed. 1049 (1941).

183 Lovell v. Griffin, 303 U.S. 444, 58 S. Ct. 666, 82 L. Ed. 949 (1938); Kunz v. New York, 340 U.S. 290, 71 S. Ct. 312, 95 L. Ed. 280 (1951); Niemotko v. Maryland, 340 U.S. 268, 71 S. Ct. 325, 95 L. Ed. 267 (1951); City of Lakewood v. Plain Dealer Publ. Co., ___ U.S. ___, 108 S. Ct. 2138, 100 L. Ed. 2d 771 (1988).

184 Staub v. Baxley, 355 U.S. 313, 78 S. Ct. 277, 2 L. Ed. 2d 302 (1958).

185 Kunz v. New York, *supra* note 183.

186 Shuttlesworth v. City of Birmingham, 394 U.S. 147, 89 S. Ct. 935, 22 L. Ed. 2d 162 (1969).

187 Hague v. CIO, 307 U.S. 496, 59 S. Ct. 954, 83 L. Ed. 1423 (1939).

> [A] free society prefers to punish the few who abuse rights of free speech *after* they break the law than to throttle them and all others beforehand. It is always difficult to know in advance what an individual will say, and the line between legitimate and illegitimate speech is often so finely drawn that the risks of freewheeling censorship are formidable.[188]

Standardless discretion is also objectionable in permit ordinances because such measures lend themselves too readily to arbitrary and erratic applications against persons or organizations whose viewpoints, lifestyles, or causes are unacceptable to the administrator in charge.[189]

Where the permit law is unconstitutional, would-be paraders or marchers may ignore it and engage in the desired free-speech activity with impunity.

§ 2.20 – Need for precision in regulating

The problem just pointed out in connection with permit ordinances brings up a subject of general First Amendment importance -- namely, the need for legislative precision in drafting laws that affect speech. Vague statutes are objectionable on several scores. The first objection grows out of the basic due process notion of "fair notice." As the Supreme Court has observed:

> [B]ecause we assume that man is free to steer between lawful and unlawful conduct, we insist that laws give the person of ordinary intelligence a reasonable opportunity to know what is prohibited so that he may act accordingly. Vague laws may trap the innocent by not providing fair warning.[190]

Notice to would-be actors of what conduct is condemned is certainly not the only, and probably not the most serious, infirmity. In a nation of laws and not men, legislatures may not delegate to police officers, judges or other

---

188 Southeastern Promotions, Ltd. v. Conrad, 420 U.S. 546, 559, 95 S. Ct. 1239, 1246-1247, 43 L. Ed. 2d 448 (1975).

189 Shuttlesworth v. City of Birmingham, 394 U.S. 147, 89 S. Ct. 935, 22 L. Ed. 2d 162 (1969).

190 Grayned v. City of Rockford, 408 U.S. 104, 108, 92 S. Ct. 2294, 2299, 33 L. Ed. 2d 222 (1972).

public officials the power to determine on an *ad hoc* and subjective basis what behavior will be visited with criminal sanctions. Clear standards must be provided for those who enforce our laws if arbitrary, inconsistent and discriminatory applications are to be avoided.[191]

Finally, vague laws with potential First Amendment application produce an inhibiting or "chilling" effect on protected liberties. Cautious persons faced with laws of uncertain meaning would prefer to forego assertion of their rights rather than risk arrest or prosecution even if they are certain the law is unconstitutional and that they will ultimately be vindicated on appeal.[192] Because of this, the Supreme Court has imposed more stringent standards for evaluating statutory vagueness when free speech interests are at risk than for evaluating criminal statutes generally.[193] Furthermore, a litigant will in some instances be permitted to raise a First Amendment vagueness challenge even though he was not engaged in protected activity and could have been penalized for his behavior had the law been drawn with the requisite narrow specificity.[194]

It is not the purpose of this section to make the reader an expert in detecting when statutes are unconstitutionally vague. This is a function for courts. Nevertheless, a sampling of several cases finding statutes unconstitutionally vague may be useful, first, to explain why in some cases an offender may escape punishment for behavior that could have been criminalized under a properly drafted law, and second, to illustrate the wisdom of invoking laws that set forth objective criteria describing what conduct is condemned, rather than those calling for discretionary judgments or subjective assessments of facts, when the choice presents itself.

Statutes which empower an officer to arrest unconventional or suspicious-looking persons for behavior that would go unnoticed if engaged in by more respectable members of our society are extremely vulnerable to a vagueness challenge. In *Papachristou v. City of Jacksonville*,[195] the Supreme Court nullified a vagrancy measure that made it a crime, amongst other things, to "wander or stroll about from place to place without any lawful purpose or object." The features found objectionable in the Jacksonville ordi-

---

[191] *Id.*

[192] *Id.*

[193] Smith v. California, 361 U.S. 147, 148, 80 S. Ct. 215, 4 L. Ed. 2d 205 (1959); Village of Hoffman Estates v. Flipside, Hoffman Estates, Inc. 455 U.S. 489, 102 S. Ct. 1186, 71 L. Ed. 2d 362 (1982).

[194] Coates v. City of Cincinnati, 402 U.S. 611, 91 S. Ct. 1686, 29 L. Ed. 2d 214 (1971) (White concurring); Gooding v. Wilson, 405 U.S. 518, 92 S. Ct. 1103, 31 L. Ed. 2d 408 (1972).

[195] 405 U.S. 156, 92 S. Ct. 839, 31 L. Ed. 2d 110 (1972).

nance are inherent in vagrancy and loitering statutes generally and it would be naive to suppose *Papachristou's* impact was intended by the Court to be confined to the measure before it. More recently, the Supreme Court invalidated a California statute requiring persons who loiter or wander on streets to provide "credible and reliable" identification and to account for their presence when requested by a police officer.[196] Here, too, the excessive subjectivity that goes into a determination of whether a suspect's identification is "credible and reliable" creates a risk of arbitrary and discriminatory enforcement. Legislatures must provide law enforcement officers with criteria more concrete and objective than these statutes did to govern their arrest decisions.

Where the statute creates a potential for misapplications against First Amendment actors, an even higher degree of statutory precision and clarity will be required. In *Coates v. City of Cincinnati*,[197] an ordinance making it unlawful for "three or more persons to assemble...on any sidewalks, and there conduct themselves in a manner annoying to persons passing by," was declared vague. But in *Cameron v. Johnson*,[198] a measure making it unlawful for "any person, singly or in concert with others, to engage in picketing or mass demonstrations in such a manner as to obstruct or unreasonably interfere with free ingress and egress to or from" any public building was found to furnish sufficient guidelines. A comparison of these two statutes is instructive and points out features that increase the risk of a successful First Amendment vagueness challenge.

Both statutes were designed to promote the convenience of other street users. The *Cameron* obstruction-of-public-passages measure, however, focused the officer's attention on objectively observable physical events (whether ingress or egress had been obstructed) and did not allow him to consider the picketer's message in making his arrest decision. The *Coates* ordinance, on the other hand, required the officer to make a subjective assessment whether the street assemblants' *message* or behavior had *annoyed* those passing by.

There is a vast difference between "obstruct" and "annoy" as the determining factor in an arrest. *Annoyance* is an emotional response that varies from person to person, and the officer could, at best, guess how persons in the vicinity were reacting. Even a conscientious officer would be hard-pressed to segregate his own feelings of annoyance from the subjective assessment the statute required him to make about the reactions of others. More important, the *Coates* ordinance allowed the officer to arrest the assemblants for "annoying" ideas and messages as well as for "annoying" physi-

---

196 Kolender v. Lawson, 461 U.S. 352, 103 S. Ct. 1855, 75 L. Ed. 2d 903 (1983).

197 *Supra* note 194.

198 390 U.S. 611, 88 S. Ct. 1335, 20 L. Ed. 2d 182 (1968).

cal behavior. It is clearly beyond the legislature's power to make it a crime to speak on subjects that annoy other citizens or, worse yet, that annoy a policeman.

The lesson to be learned from a comparison of these cases is that statutes which authorize a law enforcement officer to consider the speaker's message as a factor in an arrest decision are far more risky than those which confine the officer to observable physical events or behavior. The void-for-vagueness doctrine is primarily concerned with laws that invite too much subjectivity and could too easily be susceptible to improper applications, particularly when speech is involved.

§ 2.21 – Policing of open-air gatherings

Even when the police are at the scene of an open-air free speech gathering, occasional disruptions occur. When does regulatory intervention into ongoing speech become constitutionally appropriate? Before undertaking discussion of this matter, a word of caution is necessary.

Prior to halting First Amendment activity, the officer should carefully scrutinize his motives. If he is undertaking the arrest because the speaker is a Communist or a minority group representative or because he is espousing views the officer finds offensive, the conviction will not stand. A police officer must put aside his own ideological beliefs and focus entirely upon the speaker's conduct on this particular occasion. There are few practices that will alienate disaffected groups more completely or jeopardize convictions more certainly than selective enforcement of laws against First Amendment actors. Even though there may be a narrowly drawn statute prohibiting individuals from demonstrating in the exact location, the conviction will not stand if the rules have been waived for other, more favored groups.[199] In his official conduct, the officer must be able to put aside his personal prejudices and enforce one law for all groups alike.

Mention has already been made of the various legal controls available to local communities for regulating public assemblies. If there is an ordinance requiring a permit, an anti-noise law, a precise and narrowly drawn statute forbidding picketing in certain locales, or a similar regulatory measure making specific conduct illegal, the officer unquestionably has authority to invoke the law and halt the prohibited activity without waiting for further disruptions. Traffic control measures of general application may also be enforced against participants in a demonstration. Concerning this, the Supreme Court has stated:

---

[199] Cox v. Louisiana, 379 U.S. 536, 85 S. Ct. 453, 13 L. Ed. 2d 471 (1965).

> One would not be justified in ignoring the familiar red light because this was thought to be a means of social protest. Nor could one, contrary to traffic regulations, insist upon a street meeting in the middle of Times Square at the rush hour as a form of freedom of speech or assembly. Governmental authorities have the duty and responsibility to keep their streets open and available for movement. A group of demonstrators could not insist upon the right to cordon off a street, or entrance to a public or private building, and allow no one to pass who did not agree to listen to their exhortations.[200]

Many communities have statutes against obstructing public passages. The following measure is typical:

> No person shall willfully obstruct the free...use of any public sidewalk, street, highway, bridge, alley, road or other passageway, or the entrance, corridor, or passage of any public building...by impeding, hindering, stifling, retarding or restraining traffic or passage thereon or therein.[201]

A carefully drawn statute like this is a constitutionally valid exercise of police power. If applied equally to all groups, such a measure would support a conviction of demonstrators who force pedestrians off the public sidewalks by walking several abreast, who obstruct ingress or egress to buildings, or who otherwise interfere with normal traffic patterns.[202] The chief threat to convictions for obstructing public passage is past enforcement patterns. These measures are rarely enforced in a consistent and uniform manner against all groups. If local authorities have tolerated some demonstrations that disrupt normal street uses, First Amendment equal protection will make conviction of others for similar behavior difficult.[203]

Where First Amendment actors have complied with all noise, traffic permit and similar regulatory measures, but their open-air speech gathering threatens to get out of hand, law enforcement officers have typically relied upon disorderly conduct, breach of the peace and "failure to move on" statutes. Application of such measures against First Amendment actors

---

200 *Id.* at 554-555, 85 S. Ct. at 464, 13 L. Ed. 2d at 484.

201 LA. REV. STAT. ANN. § 14:100-1 (Cum. Supp. 1962).

202 Cameron v. Johnson, *supra* note 198.

203 Cox v. Louisiana, *supra* note 199; Flower v. United States, 407 U.S. 197, 92 S. Ct. 1842, 32 L. Ed. 2d 635 (1972).

raises two distinct concerns. First, the officer should consider whether the invoked statute furnishes sufficiently concrete and objective guidelines to withstand a void-for-vagueness challenge. Second, the officer must assess whether the situation has reached the point where the First Amendment permits him to interrupt ongoing speech.

1. *Refusal to move on*

Statutes authorizing the police to arrest individuals for disobeying their orders to "move on" should be used with extreme caution as speech control measures. Unless the statute specifically sets forth the circumstances under which an officer may issue such an order, the statute will not pass void-for-vagueness standards. Legislatures may not delegate to police officers discretion to issue on-the-spot orders halting demonstrations, coupled with the authority to arrest those who disobey. An ordinance that leaves the terms and conditions upon which citizens can use the streets for speech-related purposes to the unfettered discretion of a police officer could easily be bent into a vehicle for arresting persons whose ideologies or physical appearances offend the officer. Even though the officer may be acting solely in the interest of keeping peace, a valid conviction cannot result if the statute violates due process vagueness standards.

Shuttlesworth v. City of Birmingham[204] is the leading case on point. Shuttlesworth, a civil rights leader, and several companions were standing outside a department store during a protest boycott. An officer approached the group and told them to move on and clear the sidewalk. The others left, but Shuttlesworth stayed behind. When he questioned the officer's authority to clear the sidewalk, he was arrested under an ordinance which made it an offense, among other things, to "stand...upon any street or sidewalk of the city after having been requested by any police officer to move on." The Supreme Court, with no hesitation, reversed the conviction. The thrust of the Court's ruling was that legislatures may not delegate to police officers authority to arrest those who disobey their orders to disperse while failing to furnish them with objective standards or guidelines as to when such orders may issue. The reason for the ruling was explained by Mr. Justice Black in a different case:

> [U]nder our democratic system of government, lawmaking is not entrusted to the moment-to-moment judgment of the policeman on his beat. Laws, that is valid laws, are to be made by representatives chosen to make laws for the future, not by police officers whose

---

[204] 382 U.S. 87, 86 S. Ct. 211, 15 L. Ed. 2d 176 (1965).

> duty is to enforce laws already enacted and to make arrests only for conduct already made criminal....To let a policeman's command become equivalent to a criminal statute comes dangerously near making our government one of men rather than of laws.[205]

Statutes making it an offense to disobey an order are not constitutionally objectionable if coupled with articulated standards to control when an order may be made. Had the Birmingham ordinance made it an offense to "*obstruct the free passage upon any public street and remain after having been requested by an officer to move on*," the vagueness objection would have been removed.[206] There is a critical difference between this statute and the Birmingham ordinance. This statute requires the officer to observe specific acts declared unlawful by the legislature (e.g., obstructing the public passage) before issuing an order, the violation of which becomes grounds for arrest.

The point of this discussion is that law enforcement officers have no inherent authority to issue arrest-triggering orders at will and no legislature can give them this power. But since law enforcement officers have no way of judging the constitutionality of the laws they enforce, this simple rule of thumb may avoid problems:

> If the demonstrators are in a place where they have a legal right to be and are conducting themselves in a peaceful and lawful manner, an officer cannot make their conduct a criminal offense by ordering them to disperse and arresting them if they refuse.[207]

2. *Disorderly conduct and breach of peace*

A group of protesters march two abreast from city hall to the mayor's residence to press for reforms. As they walk, they chant and sing songs. Residents begin coming out of their homes and a large crowd congregates on the sidewalks. The police officers assigned to the march attempt to keep the two groups separate. As the crowd swells, some rough language is heard. Jeers and insults are followed by rocks and eggs. The police dodge these missiles and attempt to catch those persons in the crowd who are throwing

---

205 Gregory v. City of Chicago, 394 U.S. 111, 120, 89 S. Ct. 946, 951, 22 L. Ed. 2d 134 (1969).

206 Shuttlesworth v. City of Birmingham, *supra* note 204. *See also* Boos v. Barry, 485 U.S. 312, 108 S. Ct. 1157, 99 L. Ed. 2d 333 (1988).

207 Brown v. Louisiana, 383 U.S. 131, 86 S. Ct. 719, 15 L. ED. 2d 637 (1966); Wright v. Georgia, 373 U.S. 284, 83 S. Ct. 1240, 10 L. Ed. 2d 349 (1963).

them. Though the demonstrators maintain their decorum in the face of all of this, the spectators are dangerously close to a riot. What are the police to do now?

Unfortunately, this scenario has been played in virtually every community. Though the theme of the protest may vary from time to time and from place to place, when hotly-contested issues are debated in a public forum, a spark may sometimes ignite. At what point may the police halt speech in the interest of averting local violence and disorder?

At the outset, a distinction must be made between those cases where the free speech claimants are boisterous, intemperate, antagonistic or disorderly, and those cases where the threat to the public peace arises out of hostile audience-reaction to the theme of an orderly First Amendment gathering. The latter situation is frequently referred to as the problem of "mob censorship" or the "heckler's veto." Different regulatory responses are called for in each situation.

The propriety of arresting a speaker or group of demonstrators, on charges of disorderly conduct or for causing a breach of the peace, depends upon three primary considerations:

(1) the conduct of the speaker or group engaged in First Amendment behavior,
(2) the reaction of the audience, and
(3) the availability of police manpower at the scene to avert a possible crisis situation.

These factors are interrelated. Their interplay can be seen by a comparison of the two leading cases of *Feiner v. New York*[208] and *Cox v. Louisiana*.[209]

In the *Feiner* case, a university student delivered a soapbox oratory to a racially mixed crowd of about eighty persons on a busy street in downtown Syracuse, New York. The audience filled the sidewalks and spread out into the street. Pedestrians were inconvenienced and were forced to walk in traffic. In the course of his speech, Feiner, in a loud, high-pitched voice, attacked the mayor of Syracuse as a "champagne-sipping bum," made derogatory remarks about President Truman and certain local political officials, and then urged the blacks in the audience to "rise up in arms and fight for their rights." The audience was restless; there was some pushing, shoving and angry muttering. At least one man indicated that if the police did not stop Feiner, he would do it himself. There were only two police officers present at

---

208 340 U.S. 315, 71 S. Ct. 303, 95 L. Ed. 295 (1951).

209 379 U.S. 536, 85 S. Ct. 453, 13 L. Ed. 2d 471, 95 L. Ed. at 300 (1965).

this time. Feiner was requested several times by the police to stop speaking, and when he continued he was arrested on a charge of disorderly conduct. In affirming his conviction, the Supreme Court said:

> We are well aware that the ordinary murmurings and objections of a hostile audience cannot be allowed to silence a speaker, and are also mindful of the possible danger of giving overzealous police officials complete discretion to break up otherwise lawful public meetings. 'A State may not unduly suppress free communication of views, religious or other, under the guise of conserving desirable conditions....' But we are not faced here with such a situation. It is one thing to say that the police cannot be used as an instrument for the suppression of unpopular views, and another to say that, *when as here the speaker passes the bounds of argument or persuasion and undertakes incitement to riot*, they are powerless to prevent a breach of the peace.[210]

The crucial factor in *Feiner* was that Feiner himself was intentionally provoking the situation. The audience was not reacting intolerantly or unreasonably to what Feiner was saying; he was intentionally inflaming them by urging them to "rise up in arms and fight." There were only two police officers available at the scene to keep the peace, and the audience was threatening to get out of hand. Under these circumstances, the police were justified in arresting Feiner without first attempting to cool down an angry mob that outnumbered them 40 to 1.

Cox v. Louisiana, the second case, presents a somewhat different situation. In *Cox*, 2,000 black university students assembled at the state capital and marched in an orderly fashion, two abreast and stopping for traffic lights, to the courthouse. The purpose of the demonstration was to protest the jailing of twenty-three fellow students who had been arrested on the previous day for picketing a segregated lunch counter. The students were at all times decorous and well-behaved. When the students reached the courthouse, they sang "God Bless America," pledged allegiance to the flag, prayed briefly, sang two "freedom songs," and then prepared to listen to a speech delivered by Cox, their advisor and a Field Secretary for CORE. The local authorities had been given advance notice of this demonstration the evening before, and seventy-five to eighty firemen and police officers had been stationed between the demonstrators and a crowd of 100 to 300 curious white spectators who had gathered on the sidewalk to watch. According to the Court, the mood of the demonstrators was never hostile, aggressive or unfriendly. Rather, they be-

---

210 340 U.S. at 320-321, 71 S. Ct. at 306.

haved in a polite and orderly manner throughout. As in *Feiner*, there was some grumbling and jeering on the part of the audience, but there was no showing that the police detachment at the scene was inadequate to control any possible outbreaks that might arise. At the end of his speech, Cox urged the students to go uptown and "sit in" at various segregated lunch counters. The sheriff, deeming the last appeal to be inflammatory, took a bullhorn and ordered the demonstrators to go home. When the order was ignored, the police began to shoot tear gas shells into the crowd of demonstrators; the group soon broke up. Cox was later arrested and charged with breach of the peace. On appeal, the Supreme Court reversed his conviction, holding that Cox and his supporters had not engaged in any conduct which the state of Louisiana could punish as a breach of the peace. Their singing and chanting, while it may have been loud, was not disorderly or riotous. The tension and angry muttering, grumbling and jeering from the onlookers, though probably of the same intensity as in *Feiner*, was not attributable to anything that Cox and his followers had said. If First Amendment rights are not to be sacrificed because of local hostilities to their assertion, the police, in a case like *Cox*, have a clear-cut duty to arrest the hecklers and not the speaker.

On the basis of *Feiner* and *Cox*, some guidelines for police action can be drawn. If the speaker is deliberately attempting either to incite or to antagonize his audience, the police may break up the assembly and arrest the speaker or group when the situation threatens to get out of hand. In the more modern terminology of the *Brandenburg* case,[211] the police may intervene to avert a disturbance the speaker is inciting when:

(1) the speech is directed toward producing *immediate* lawless action, and
(2) an uncontrollable outbreak is threatened.

On the other hand, if the speaker or group is not responsible for the hostile attitude of the listeners, aside from the fact that they are peacefully expressing unpopular views, the police have a clear obligation to do everything to keep the audience in line so that the meeting will be allowed to continue. A meeting held in a lawful manner does not lose its constitutional protection because an unsympathetic audience threatens to retaliate with violence.[212] If the police have adequate advance notice of the event, certainly there would

---

211 Brandenburg v. Ohio, 395 U.S. 444, 89 S. Ct. 1827, 23 L. Ed. 2d 430 (1969). Review § 2.9 *supra*.

212 Gregory v. City of Chicago, *supra* note 205.

be no excuse for depriving a group of its constitutional right to peaceful assembly by failing to provide adequate police protection.[213]

Occasionally, however, miscalculations can occur as to the strength of the peace-keeping force needed at the scene of a demonstration. Even in the face of what appears to be a manpower shortage, the police at the site should do everything within their power to contain the hecklers until reinforcements arrive. Only at the point when the situation appears wholly unmanageable, should thought be given to the possibility of halting protected speech as a means of peacekeeping. Unquestionably, in the face of an impending riot, the police would be justified in enlisting the voluntary cooperation of the demonstrators in averting a crisis, even though the crisis was not of their own making. In the event that this request is refused, a difficult decision must be reached -- a decision for which no authoritative guidance exists. The Supreme Court has never clarified whether the police may arrest orderly protest demonstrators who refuse to stop speaking when requested to do so in the face of an impending riot. *Gregory v. City of Chicago*[214] posed this question but the Court's holding fell short of answering it. Comedian Dick Gregory led a group of civil rights demonstrators on an orderly protest march through a Chicago residential area. Approximately one hundred Chicago police officers had been assigned to accompany them. As they marched, the Gregory group was met by a crowd of approximately 1,000 hostile spectators. The police made a commendable effort to keep the two groups separate, but the onlookers became increasingly more unruly and began hurling rocks, eggs and bottles at the marchers. The demonstrators, nevertheless, maintained their decorum and made no effort to retaliate. Fearful that the situation was rapidly becoming riotous, the police five times requested Gregory and his group to leave the area, offering an escort and protection. Some of the marchers left. Those who remained were arrested and charged with disorderly conduct. The Supreme Court, in a sparse one-page opinion written by Mr. Chief Justice Warren, reversed the conviction, stating that there was no evidence in the record to indicate that the marchers had at any time behaved in a disorderly manner.

Granting that peaceful demonstrators are not vicariously responsible for the lack of restraint shown by spectators and thus cannot be charged with *disorderly conduct* because spectators threaten to riot, the case leaves unanswered whether peaceful demonstrators may be arrested on some other grounds if, in the face of a threatened civil disorder, they refuse to obey a po-

---

213 Williams v. Wallace, 240 F. Supp. 100 (M.D. Ala. 1965); Cottonreader v. Johnson, 252 F. Supp. 492 (M.D. Ala. 1966).

214 394 U.S. 111, 89 S. Ct. 946, 22 L. Ed. 2d 134 (1969).

lice request to stop demonstrating. Until this question is resolved, the solution lies in "protective custody." Where all reasonable efforts to pacify a hostile crowd of spectators have failed and the police are no longer able to maintain order, the police should ask the demonstrators to cooperate voluntarily in stopping their protest; if cooperation is not forthcoming, the only alternative is to take them into custody for their own protection but without preferring charges.

Since the Constitution protects the right to engage in peaceful protest, but not the right to disrupt meetings, consideration should never be given to halting speech before a conscientious attempt has been made to arrest those who are directly responsible for causing the disturbance. Even though arresting the speaker or demonstrators who have attracted the crowd may appear the most expedient way to maintain order on the streets, suppressing free speech is a high price to pay for averting minor disturbances. Where it is the hostile reception and not the speech itself that menaces the public peace, peace-keeping efforts should be focused upon the crowd in an effort to protect free speech, unless it becomes impossible for the speech to continue because the necessary order no longer exists.

§ 2.22 Summary and practical suggestions

The First Amendment reads "Congress shall make no law...abridging the freedom of speech...." Speech for constitutional purposes can take many forms, including silent symbolic behavior. Picketing, demonstrating, and open-air gatherings represent forms of expression most likely to give rise to regulatory problems for police.

The determination that speech is involved begins, rather than ends, the constitutional inquiry of whether laws inhibiting the particular activity constitute *abridgments of free speech*. Restrictions regulating what can be said (i.e., communicative impact) are far more likely to abridge free speech than those regulating noncommunicative features such as excessive noise, disruptions of normal traffic patterns, or other harms unrelated to the speaker's message.

Under traditional First Amendment analysis, restrictions on speech content are unconstitutional unless the regulated speech falls on the unprotected side of the line or unless the measure is supported by considerations of overriding public necessity. Obscenity, fighting words, violence incitement and threats represent the most important speech categories that have been excluded from First Amendment protection. Commercial and offensive speech have received only an intermediate level of free speech protection.

Virtually all other speech topics are fully and equally protected by the free speech privilege.

Where restrictions on expressive activity seek to regulate features other than message, constitutional inquiries into their validity incorporate a technique known as "interest balancing." The court will assess the degree of interference with free speech interest and will weigh the magnitude of this encroachment against the strength of the government's regulatory interest. Only a compelling interest can serve to justify measures that seriously interfere with freedom of expression. Even then restriction of speech will not be allowed if alternatives less injurious to First Amendment values would serve the government's ends equally well.

The extent to which the First Amendment guarantees the public a right of access to government property for speech-related purposes depends on whether the chosen location is a public forum or a nonpublic forum. The streets, sidewalks and parks of the community are *traditional public forums*. Other government facilities can become *public forums by designation* if the policies and practices of the government indicate an intent to dedicate the facility to speech uses. The Constitution does not guarantee speech access to property simply because the government owns or controls it. Government property which is neither by tradition nor designation a public forum remains a *nonpublic forum*.

The government's ability to restrict First Amendment activity in public forums is narrowly circumscribed. While the government can impose reasonable, content-neutral time, place and manner restrictions on public forum speech uses, the government must establish a compelling regulatory interest when it entirely excludes protected expression from a public forum or when it adopts access policies that make distinctions based on speech subject matter or speaker identity. In nonpublic forums, the government managerial discretion is broader; it may ban speech or make access distinctions based on speech content or speaker identity if the distinctions are viewpoint neutral and reasonable in light of the function that the forum in dispute serves.

The First Amendment does not guarantee any right of access to private property; those engaged in expression are not privileged to trespass on private property contrary to the owner's wishes.

All criminal laws, and particularly those capable of being applied to speech, must, to withstand constitutional challenge under the void-for-vagueness doctrine, contain sufficiently clear, precise and objective guidelines to enable officers to distinguish between innocent and unlawful conduct. Laws authorizing arrest for vagrancy, loitering, or failure to move on, and laws permitting the officer to consider speech-content in making an arrest decision are particularly vulnerable. Whenever a choice exists between invoking a narrow statute covering specific conduct (such as obstructing the public passage or picketing in a school zone) or a more general statute (such as one criminalizing failure to move on, disorderly conduct or breach of peace), the officer should choose the former; such measures are far less likely to be found unconstitutionally vague.

In policing public assemblies, officers should bear in mind that ordinances purporting to authorize arrests for disobeying their commands are of questionable constitutionality and that, in any event, if the First Amendment actors are in a place where they have a legal right to be and are conducting themselves in a peaceful manner, an officer cannot criminalize their behavior by ordering them to disperse and arresting them if they disobey.

Before halting an open-air speech gathering to keep the public peace, an officer should keep three precepts in mind. First, the officer must guard against even an appearance of prejudice and concentrate solely on the speaker's or group's behavior, disregarding any personal animosity he may harbor because of their appearance, lifestyle or viewpoint. Second, the speaker or group can be arrested for breach of the peace or disorderly conduct only when they are deliberately goading or stirring the crowd and an outbreak appears imminent. Third, where free speech participants do not exceed their rights under the First Amendment, but a hostile audience threatens to get out of hand, the police should utilize whatever crowd control techniques that may be at their disposal at the time. Only when their efforts to maintain order have failed should they request that First Amendment activities be suspended. Should their request be refused, protective custody, rather than arrest, is the appropriate manner of proceeding.

Chapter 3
AUTHORITY TO DETAIN AND ARREST*

The right of the people to be secure in their persons, houses, papers, and effects, against unreasonable searches and seizures, shall not be violated, and no Warrants shall issue, but upon probable cause, supported by Oath or affirmation, and particularly describing the place to be searched, and the persons or things to be seized.

Fourth Amendment, 1791

Section

---

* *by John C. Klotter*

§ 3.1 Historical development of the law of arrest – England

Under English common law, sheriffs and constables appointed by the Crown were the only designated peace officers. These sheriffs and constables had the authority to call upon ordinary citizens to form a *posse comitatus* and to assist in making an arrest. As the duty to protect society was largely the responsibility of the private citizen, the citizen, as well as designated peace officers, had the power of arrest. Unlike the statutory authority possessed by the private citizen today, under common law the private citizen had power that was equal in nearly all respects to that of the appointed sheriff or constable. Sheriffs, constables, and private individuals had a duty and responsibility to carry out without delay the command of a warrant issued by a judicial officer. Where no warrant was obtained, a distinction was drawn in the law of arrest between felonies and misdemeanors.

Great latitude was given the officer or citizen in making an arrest for a felony. In the case of a felony, an officer or a private citizen acting without a warrant could make an arrest if a felony were committed in his presence or view, or if he had reasonable grounds to believe that the person to be arrested had committed the felony. Under this common law interpretation, a peace officer or private person who had reasonable grounds to believe that a felony had been committed could make an arrest even though the crime in fact was not committed in his presence and even though the person suspected might later prove to be innocent.

At common law, an arrest for an offense less than a felony could not be made without a warrant unless it involved a breach of the peace. Although actual personal violence was not an essential element of a breach of the peace, there must have been some violation of public order or public decorum. For example, shooting, hollering, cursing or using vile and obscene language was considered a breach of the peace, while mere drunkenness without any other disturbance was not considered a breach of the peace to justify an arrest without a warrant.

Many of the arrest practices developed in England prior to the adoption of our Constitution were brought to this country by the colonists and form a part of our legal tradition. Due to necessity and changing conditions, most states, by statute, have modified and deleted some of the more technical requirements of the common law of arrest. For example, most states have deleted the requirement that a misdemeanor be a breach of the peace in order for the police to make a warrantless arrest. Nonetheless, the fundamental and substantive protections developed under the common law for those suspected of having committed a crime remain unchanged today and are embodied in the philosophy of the Fourth Amendment. Referring to this historical basis in *Henry v. United States*,[1] Mr. Justice Douglas observed:

> The requirement of probable cause has roots that are deep in our history. The general warrant, in which the name of the person to be arrested was left blank, and the writ of assistance, against which James Otis inveighed, both perpetuated the oppressive practice of allowing the police to arrest and search on suspicion....And as the early American decisions both before and immediately after its [the Fourth Amendment] adoption show, common rumor or report, suspicion or even "strong reason to suspect" was not adequate to support a warrant for arrest.

History has played a large role in molding our legal institutions. The decisions of the Supreme Court of the United States today are to a great extent the result of the development and refinement of common-law concepts and practices followed several centuries ago.

§ 3.2 Constitutional provisions

The Constitution of the United States and the constitutions of all of the respective states have provisions concerning arrest, search and seizure. The Fourth Amendment to the Constitution, which was adopted in 1791, provides as follows:

> The right of the people to be secure in their *persons*, houses, papers, and effects, against unreasonable searches and seizures, shall not be violated, and no Warrants shall issue, but upon probable cause, supported by Oath or affirmation, and particularly describing the place to be searched, and the *persons* or things *to be seized*. (Emphasis added.)

Although this section is often referred to as the search-and-seizure provision of the Constitution, it also protects individuals from illegal seizures of their persons -- i.e., arrests. Both the express terminology of the amendment and the historical context of its adoption lead to this conclusion. In the 1959 *Henry* case the Supreme Court dispelled any uncertainty which might previously have existed as to the status of illegal arrest under the Fourth Amendment in the following language:

---

1 361 U.S. 98, 80 S. Ct. 168, 4 L. Ed. 2d 134 (1959).

> [I]t is the command of the Fourth Amendment that no warrants either for searchers or *arrests* shall issue except upon "probable cause...." (Emphasis added.)

In *Payton v. New York*[2] in 1980, the United States Supreme Court reiterated that:

> The simple language of the amendment applies equally to seizures of persons and to seizures of property.

There the Court specifically left no doubt that:

> The Fourth Amendment to the United States Constitution, made applicable to the States by the Fourteenth Amendment...prohibits the police from making a warrantless and nonconsensual entry into a suspect's home in order to make a routine felony arrest.

Prior to 1962, federal arrests, searches and seizures were governed by the standards embodied in the Fourth Amendment, while similar state procedures were judged by a more flexible standard embraced in the due process clause of the Fourteenth Amendment. In 1963, however, the Supreme Court of the United States in *Ker v. California*[3] held that arrests by state and local police officers are to be judged by the same constitutional standards as apply to the federal government. Hence, in order for an arrest to be valid today, the police must comply with the provisions of the Fourth Amendment as well as their own state constitutions and statutes.

§ 3.3 "Arrest" defined

Each state has a statute or code authorizing a peace officer to make an arrest. The authority to detain and arrest varies from state to state and from time to time. For purposes of comparison, two examples of state statutes are included.

The Kentucky Revised Statutes provides that:[4]

---

2 445 U.S. 573, 100 S. Ct. 1371, 63 L. Ed. 2d 639 (1980). *See* Part II for portions of this case.

3 374 U.S. 23, 83 S. Ct. 1623, 10 L. Ed. 2d 726 (1963).

4 KY. REV. STAT. § 431.005 (Michie/Bobbs-Merrill 1985 & Supp. 1988)

431.005 Arrest by peace officers; by private persons

(1) A peace officer may make an arrest:

(a) In obedience to a warrant; or

(b) Without a warrant when a felony is committed in his presence; or

(c) Without a warrant when he has probable cause to believe that the person being arrested has committed a felony; or

(d) Without a warrant when a misdemeanor, as defined in KRS 431.060, has been committed in his presence; or

(e) Without a warrant when a violation of KRS 189.290, 189.393, 189.520, 189.580, 511.080, or 525.070 has been committed in his presence [except that a violation of KRS 189A.010 need not be committed in his presence in order to make an arrest without a warrant if the officer has probable cause to believe that the person has violated KRS 189A.010.][5]

(2) Any peace officer may arrest without warrant when he has probable cause to believe that if the person is not arrested he will present a danger or threat of danger to others if not immediately restrained and in addition he has probable cause for believing that said person has intentionally or wantonly caused physical injury to his spouse, former spouse, parent, grandparent, child, stepchild or, if said person is a party of an unmarried couple which has a child in common, the other party of the couple. Within twelve (12) hours following apprehension and booking of a person arrested under this section, an officer shall return to the abused person, if the abused person is an adult, and request that a signed, written statement be made by the abused person stating that an abuse occurred and the person who committed it. If the abused person refuses to sign the statement, the charges shall be summarily dismissed and the defendant released from custody.

(4) A private person may make an arrest when a felony has been committed in fact and he has probable cause to believe that the person being arrested has committed it.

---

5 189.290 Operator of vehicle to drive carefully; 189.393 Complying with traffic officer's signal; 189.520 Operating vehicle while under influence of intoxicants or drugs; 189.580 Duty in case of accident; 511.080 Criminal trespass in the third degree; 525.070 Harassment.

In accordance with the Kentucky Code a peace officer may make an arrest without a warrant when a felony has been committed in his presence or he has reasonable grounds to believe the person being arrested has committed a felony. Barring the specific exceptions, an arrest may be made for a misdemeanor offense only if the misdemeanor has been committed in his presence or a warrant has been obtained.

The Illinois code conveys more authority to the peace officer to make an arrest. The code provides:[6]

107-2. Arrest by peace officer.
S107-2.

(1) Arrest by Peace Officer. A peace officer may arrest a person when:

  (a) He has a warrant commanding that such person be arrested; or
  (b) He has reasonable grounds to believe that a warrant for the person's arrest has been issued in this State or in another jurisdiction; or
  (c) He has reasonable grounds to believe that the person is committing or has committed an offense.

(2) Whenever a peace officer arrests a person, the officer shall question the arrestee as to whether he or she has any children under the age of 18 living with him or her who may be neglected as a result of the arrest or otherwise. The peace officer shall assist the arrestee in the placement of the children with a relative or other responsible person designated by the arrestee. If the peace officer has reasonable cause to believe that a child may be a neglected child as defined in the Abused and Neglected Child Reporting Act, he shall report it immediately to the Department of Children and Family Services as provided in that Act.

In Illinois an arrest may be made with a warrant or without a warrant for a misdemeanor or a felony when the officer has reasonable grounds to believe the person is committing, or has committed, either. An "offense" as used in that statute includes both misdemeanors and felonies.[7]

Although the state and federal statutes and codes include provisions specifying when a peace officer may make an arrest with or without a war-

---

[6] ILL. REV. STAT., ch. 38, 107.2 (1982 & Supp. 1983-84).

[7] ILL. REV. STAT., ch. 38, 102-155 (1981).

rant, few of these statutes attempt to define arrest. One exception is the Illinois Code, which defines arrest as follows:

"Arrest" means the taking of a person into custody.[8]

Because most of the statutes fail to define arrest, it is necessary to look to court decisions, treatises and encyclopedias for definitions. Some of the more common definitions include the following:

(a) The term 'arrest' has a technical meaning, applicable in legal proceedings. It implies that a person is thereby restrained of his liberty by some officer or agent of the law, armed with lawful process, authorizing and requiring the arrest be made. It is intended to serve, and does serve, the end of bringing the person arrested personally within the custody and control of the law, for the purpose specified in, or contemplated by, the process.[9]

(b) An arrest is the taking of another into custody for the actual or purported purpose of bringing the other before a court or of otherwise securing the administration of the law.[10]

(c) An arrest is the taking, seizing, or detaining of the person of another,
   (1) by touching or putting hands on him; or
   (2) by any act that indicates an intention to take him into custody and that subjects him to the actual control and will of the person making the arrest; or
   (3) by the consent of the person to be arrested.[11]

(d) The assertion of authority, with intent to arrest, and restraint of the person arrested.[12]

Arrest has also been judicially defined as the taking, seizing or detaining of the person of another, by touching or by putting hands upon him, in the execution of process or any act indicating an intention to arrest.

None of these definitions is entirely satisfactory. Arrest is a term which eludes precise definition. Basically, it is a legal conclusion used to describe the complex series of events which have in fact taken place. The law defines

---

8 Ill. Rev. Stat., ch. 38, 102.5 (1975).

9 Hadley v. Tinnin, 170 N.C. 84, 86 S.E. 1017 (1915), quoting *Lawrence v. Buxton*, 102 N.C. 131, 8 S.E. 774 (1889).

10 RESTATEMENT (SECOND) OF TORTS § 112 (1965).

11 5 AM. JUR. 2D *Arrest* § 11 (1962).

12 People v. Jackson, 52 Ill. Dec. 514, 96 Ill. App. 3d 1057, 422 N.E.2d 195 (1981).

the elements necessary to constitute an arrest. Whether or not all of these elements are present in a given situation depends upon the facts of each case, including the mental attitude of the officer, the circumstances under which he confronts the person, the reasonable reaction of that person to the officer's action and a multitude of other actions which cannot be conveyed by a bland definition.[13]

Even with the many attempts to define the term "arrest," the courts are still struggling with the distinction between a "detention," which is based on something less than probable cause, and an "arrest," which requires an arrest warrant or probable cause to arrest without a warrant. For example, in the case of *Hayes v. Florida* in 1985 the United States Supreme Court was asked to determine the line between a detention and activity which amounts to an arrest.[14] In the *Hayes* case when the suspect was requested to accompany the police officers to the station in order to take fingerprints, he indicated his reluctance to do so. One of the officers then said that they would arrest him if he did not agree to go with them to the station, at which time he replied that he would rather go to the station than be arrested. The trial court denied his pretrial motion to suppress the fingerprint evidence and he was convicted.

While recognizing that there may be a brief detention in the field for the purpose of fingerprinting when there is only reasonable suspicion not amounting to probable cause, the United States Supreme Court indicated that, in this case, the officer's conduct amounted to more than a detention as explained in *Terry v. Ohio*.[15] The Court explained that at some point in this investigative process, police procedures can qualitatively and quantitatively be so intrusive with respect to the suspect's freedom of movement and privacy as to trigger the full protection of the Fourth and Fourteenth Amendments. The Court continued by stating:

> And our view continues to be that the line is crossed when the police, without probable cause or a warrant, forcibly remove a person from his home or other place in which he is entitled to be and transport him to the police station, where he is detained, although briefly, for investigative purposes. We adhere to the view that such seizures, at least where not under judicial supervision, are sufficiently like arrests to invoke the traditional rule that arrest may constitutionally be made only on probable cause.

---

13 United States v. Rodgers, 246 F. Supp. 405 (E.D. Mo. 1965).

14 Hayes v. Florida, 470 U.S. 811, 105 S. Ct. 1643, 84 L. Ed. 2d 705 (1985).

15 Terry v. Ohio, 392 U.S. 1, 88 S. Ct. 1868, 20 L. Ed. 2d 889 (1968). The detention authority is discussed in another section of this chapter.

While the *Hayes* case clearly indicates that the activities of the officer in that instance were such as to invoke the traditional rule that arrest may constitutionally be made on probable cause, it still did not clearly define what elements are necessary to constitute an arrest. The Court did render two advisory opinions concerning the Fourth Amendment implications of a police practice. First, the Court indicated that the opinion does not imply that a brief detention in the field for the purpose of fingerprinting, where there is only reasonable suspicion not amounting to probable cause, is necessarily impermissible under the Fourth Amendment. Secondly, the Court cautioned that "neither reasonable suspicion nor probable cause would suffice to permit the officers to make a warrantless entry into a person's home for the purpose of obtaining fingerprint identification."

An illegal arrest does not deprive the court of jurisdiction to try an offender.[16] An indictment may be returned even though the arrest was illegal. On the other hand, the determination as to whether the officer's actions amount to a legal arrest becomes very important in some cases. Frequently, the success or failure of the state in its prosecution of a case will depend entirely upon the legality of the officer's arrest.

For example, the determination as to whether the arrest was legal becomes very important where the court is considering a motion to suppress evidence. If an arrest is illegal, the search incident to that arrest is not authorized and any evidence secured thereby will not be admissible in court. In some instances this suppression of evidence will have the same effect as depriving the court of jurisdiction to try the offender. If the only evidence which the state has to convict an armed robbery suspect is a gun, stocking, and large roll of bills taken from his person during a search incident to an illegal arrest, the offender will go free. Therefore, it is imperative that justice personnel thoroughly understand the meaning of the word "arrest."

§ 3.4 Elements necessary to constitute an arrest

Although it is difficult, if not impossible, to frame a definition of an arrest which will apply in all circumstances, the following common elements must be considered in order to understand the court's reasoning in determining when the acts of the officer are considered an arrest.

---

[16] Frisbie v. Collins, 342 U.S. 519, 72 S. Ct. 509, 96 L. Ed. 541 (1952).

1. *Real or assumed legal authority*

To constitute an "arrest" as the term is used in criminal law, the restraint on the liberty of the individual must be either under actual authority of an officer or under assumed authority of an office. An officer is exercising assumed authority when he acts under a void warrant or makes an arrest for a misdemeanor not committed in his presence, where such is not authorized by the statutes of his state. In *District of Columbia v. Perry*,[17] a Maryland state trooper pursued a speeder across the state line into the District of Columbia where he ultimately halted the car. While the Maryland trooper was checking the motorist's license, a member of the District of Columbia police force arrived at the scene. Upon being informed by the Maryland officer that the motorist was driving in excess of the local speed limit and was believed to be intoxicated, the District of Columbia officer arrested him. The court held that the arrest was illegal since the Maryland officer had no authority to make an arrest in the District. The District of Columbia officer was likewise without authority to make a valid arrest because neither the speeding nor the driving while intoxicated, both misdemeanors, were committed in his presence. There was an arrest in fact when the District of Columbia officer took the speeding motorist into custody under assumed legal authority, but the arrest was illegal because it was not in compliance with local statutes.

2. *Intention*

The intention of the arresting officer to take a person into custody is one of the basic elements which distinguishes an arrest from lesser forms of detention. Although the intent of the officer is an important factor in every arrest, specific or actual intent is not necessary. For example, under certain circumstances a court may infer from the officer's conduct an intent to take a person into custody, when in fact no such intention existed. Hence, in a false arrest case, the officer cannot escape liability by stating that he did not intend to make the arrest, if the circumstances indicated that the officer did in fact take the person into custody.

In an Illinois case, an appeals court determined that an "arrest" occurs when police inform the suspect of a violation, he submits to their control, and it is clearly shown that the officers intended to effectuate the arrest and the defendant so understood them.[18] In the *Sanders* case the court noted that absence of a threatening presence of several officers, display of a weapon, a

---

[17] 215 A.2d 845 (D.C. 1966).

[18] People v. Sanders, 431 N.E.2d 1145 (Ill. App. Ct. 1981).

physical touching, use of language or tone of voice which indicates that compliance with the officer's request might be compelled, permits the conclusion that no seizure of the person has taken place.

3. *Custody and control*

To constitute a technical arrest, the arrested party must come within the actual custody and control of the officer. The person to be arrested may come within the custody and control of the law

(1) by submission, or
(2) by a manual caption as evidenced by some touching of the body.[19]

If the person submits voluntarily to the control of the officer, he is under arrest as much as if the officer had subdued and handcuffed him. It is not necessary that there be an application of actual force, manual touching, or physical restraint visible to the eye, so long as the person arrested understands that he is in the power of the one arresting him and submits to his control. In fact, mere words on the part of the officer can constitute an arrest if they are coupled with an intent on behalf of the officer to restrain and if they in fact cause a person to be restrained of his liberty. However, it is not necessary that specific words be used. As explained in one case, "arrest" occurs where a defendant clearly understands that he is not free to go, and no "magic words" such as, "I place you under arrest," are required.[20]

In 1988 the Supreme Court considered a test to be applied in determining whether a person is in the custody and control of the arresting officer.[21] In the *Chesternut* case officers on routine patrol observed the defendant running when he noticed the patrol car. After catching up with the defendant and driving alongside him for a short distance, the defendant began to run and discarded a number of packets. Surmising that the pills subsequently discovered in the packets contained codeine, the police arrested him and, after a search of his person revealed other drugs and a hypodermic needle, charged him with possession of controlled substances. At a preliminary hearing, a magistrate dismissed the charges on the grounds that the defendant had been unlawfully seized at the time he discarded the packets and that

---

19 Bankers Ass'n v. Cassady, 264 Ky. 378, 94 S.W.2d 622 (1936); State v. Durivan, 217 Mo. App. 584, 269 S.W. 415 (1925).

20 State v. Ortiz, 662 P.2d 514 (Haw. App. 1983).

21 Michigan v. Chesternut, ___ U.S. ___, 108 S. Ct. 1975, 100 L. Ed. 2d 565 (1988).

any "investigatory pursuit" amounts to a seizure since the defendant's freedom is restricted as soon as the officers begin their pursuit. The Michigan Court of Appeals upheld the decision of the magistrate and the state appealed to the United States Supreme Court.

The question for the Court was whether the officer's pursuit of the defendant constituted a seizure implicating Fourth Amendment protections. The United States Supreme Court ruled that a mere pursuit of the defendant did not constitute a "seizure" and that the charges against him were improperly dismissed. While the Court agreed that there was no "bright line" rule applicable, the majority noted that the test as applied in previous cases is that:

> The police can be said to have seized an individual "only if, in view of all of the circumstances surrounding the incident, a reasonable person would have believed that he was not free to leave."

The Court explained that what constitutes a restraint on liberty prompting a person to believe he is not free to "leave" will vary, not only with the particular police conduct at issue, but also with the setting in which the conduct occurs. The Court was of the opinion that the "reasonable person" standard allows the police to determine in advance whether the conduct contemplated will implicate the Fourth Amendment, and that this standard ensures that the scope of the Fourth Amendment protection does not vary with the state of mind of the particular individual being approached.

Applying the reasonable person standard test to this case, the Court concluded that the defendant was not seized by the police before he discarded the packets containing the controlled substance. Because the defendant was not in the custody and control of the police at the time of the initial pursuit, he was not unlawfully seized and the lower court improperly dismissed the charge against the defendant.

One court has explained "custody and control" by stating that no actual force is necessary to constitute an arrest if the arresting officer intends to take the person into custody and supports his intention by an unequivocal act, such as keeping the arrested person in sight and controlling his actions. However, the court continued,

> [O]ne person can no more arrest another by simply telling him to "consider himself under arrest" and then turning on his heel and leaving that person free to go his own way, than one can commit a homicide by merely telling another to consider himself dead.[22]

---

[22] Berry v. Bass, 157 La. 81, 102 So. 76 (1924).

Some writers have argued that an intention to submit on the part of the arrestee is essential to constitute an arrest. If this were true in all situations, a person who was unconscious or intoxicated could not be placed under arrest. A person may be arrested for intoxication where there is actual seizure and restraint even though he does not understand or intend to be arrested.

Even with the definitions and guidelines obtained from various cases it is often difficult to determine whether an arrest has been consummated. Depending as it does on the intention of the officer making the arrest and the person arrested in some instances, the determination is often a question to be resolved by a jury.

§ 3.5 Arrest under the authority of a warrant

The primary and most basic source of authority to arrest, recognized under the common law and under modern statutes, is that of a warrant. This is the only authority expressly sanctioned by the Constitution of the United States. The Fourth Amendment sets forth the standards under which a warrant may be issued:

> [N]o warrant shall issue but upon probable cause, supported by Oath or affirmation, and particularly describing...the persons or things to be seized.

Most state statutes or codes have provisions to the effect that a peace officer may arrest where he has a warrant commanding him to make such an arrest. For example, the Illinois Code provides:

> A peace officer may arrest a person when: (a) He has a warrant commanding that such person be arrested;...[23]

Similarly, the California statute states: "A peace officer may make an arrest in obedience to a warrant...."[24] Even without such statutory authorization, this right would exist by virtue of the common law.

The function of an arrest warrant is to protect private citizens from the harassment of unjustified arrests, incarcerations and criminal prosecutions. At common law it was expected that most arrests would be made under a warrant, and only in exceptional situations was authority extended to permit

---

23 ILL. REV. STAT. ch. 38, § 107-2(a) (1982 & Supp. 1988-89).
24 CAL. PENAL CODE § 836 (West or Deering 1970).

an arrest without it. The common-law preference for arrests made under the authority of a warrant is embodied in the Fourth Amendment. The chief objection to the warrantless arrest is that it bypasses

> ...the safeguards provided by an objective predetermination of probable cause, and substitutes instead the far less reliable procedure of an after-the-event justification for the arrest or search, too likely to be subtly influenced by the familiar shortcomings of hindsight judgment.[25]

Wherever it is at all practicable, the officer should obtain a warrant before acting. The Supreme Court has indicated that in doubtful or marginal cases where probable cause for an arrest is not clearly made out, action under a warrant will be sustained where one without it will fail. The Court stated:

> "[T]he informed and deliberate determinations of magistrates empowered to issue warrants...are to be preferred over the hurried action of officers...."[26]

In most instances, if the warrant is proper on its face and the officer does not abuse his authority in executing the warrant, he will be protected against civil liability for false arrest or false imprisonment. However, if the officer's activity indicates gross incompetence or neglect of duty in presenting supporting affidavits to justify the issuance of an arrest warrant, he is not entitled to rely on the judicial officer's judgment in issuing the warrant.[27] In the case of *Malley v. Briggs*, the Supreme Court noted that under the rule of qualified immunity, a police officer cannot avoid civil rights liability for causing an unconstitutional arrest by presenting the judicial officer with a complaint and a supporting affidavit which failed to establish probable cause.

Notwithstanding the fact the court may look behind the warrant to determine liability on the part of the officer who has furnished information for the warrant, it is preferable to obtain a warrant based on probable cause rather than to make the arrest without a warrant.

---

25 Beck v. Ohio, 379 U.S. 89, 85 S. Ct. 223, 13 L. Ed. 2d 142 (1964).

26 United States v. Ventresca, 380 U.S. 102, 85 S. Ct. 741, 13 L. Ed. 2d 684 (1965), quoting *United States v. Lefkowitz*, 285 U.S. 452, 52 S. Ct. 420, 76 L. Ed. 877 (1932).

27 Malley v. Briggs, 475 U.S. 335, 106 S. Ct. 1092, 89 L. Ed. 2d 271 (1986).

§ 3.6 Requirements for a valid arrest warrant

To be valid and executable, the warrant must comply with definite standards or requirements. Some of these requirements are constitutional requirements, while others are either statutory or judicially determined. If any one of the requirements is lacking, the warrant is invalid, and an arrest made under that warrant, as well as the search incidental to that arrest, is unauthorized. The most common requirements for a valid arrest warrant are discussed below.

1. The warrant must be supported by "probable cause."

Probably the most important requirement is the Fourth Amendment direction that "no warrant shall issue but upon probable cause...." the Supreme Court of the United States has defined probable cause as follows:

> Probable cause exists where "the facts and circumstances within [the arresting officers'] knowledge and of which they had reasonably trustworthy information [are] sufficient in themselves to warrant a man of reasonable caution in the belief that" an offense has been or is being committed. [Citation omitted.][28]

This probable cause must be found to exist by a magistrate or other judicial officer. In order for the warrant to serve the protective function which it was designed to achieve, the magistrate, in issuing the warrant, must

(1) evaluate the evidence presented against the person suspected of having committed a crime, and
(2) determine whether, in his impartial judgment, the charges against the individual are sufficiently supported to justify placing him in custody.

In the case of *Baker v. McCollan*,[29] the Court reiterated that the probable cause determination must be made by a judicial officer. The Court also found, however, that an adversary hearing is not required and that "A person arrested pursuant to a warrant issued by a magistrate on a showing of probable cause is not constitutionally entitled to a separate judicial determination that there is probable cause to detain him pending trial."

---

28 Draper v. United States, 358 U.S. 307, 79 S. Ct. 329, 3 L. Ed. 2d 327 (1959).

29 443 U.S. 137, 99 S. Ct. 2689, 61 L. Ed. 2d 433 (1979).

The officer who requests an arrest warrant has some responsibility in assuring that probable cause for the warrant exists even if a magistrate issues the warrant. If the warrant application is so lacking in indicia of probable cause as to render official belief in its existence unreasonable, the officer's shield of immunity will be lost. In placing this burden on the officer, the United States Supreme Court explained:[30]

> The question is whether a reasonably well trained officer in petitioner's position would have known that his affidavit failed to establish probable cause and that he should have not applied for the warrant.

In placing this responsibility on the police officer, the court noted that:

> We find it reasonable to require the officer applying for the warrant to minimize the danger by exercising reasonable professional judgment.

Requiring the police officer to determine whether there is probable cause to seek a search warrant makes it even more important that the officer develop an understanding as to what constitutes probable cause. Unfortunately, this has never been reduced to a set formula of facts and circumstances. As the term indicates, it is not necessary that there be absolute certainty but only probability that a crime has been committed and that the defendant probably committed that offense. Probable cause is less than guilt beyond a reasonable doubt but is more than mere suspicion.

(a) Sufficiency of information

As the magistrate must make this determination on the basis of the evidence presented to him in the complaint, he must be supplied with sufficient information to support an independent judgment that probable cause exists to justify the issuance of an arrest warrant. Although the peace officer is not required to furnish evidence sufficient to establish guilt beyond a reasonable doubt, he must supply more than mere suspicions or conclusions. The complaint must indicate in detail some of the reasons and facts that support the officer's conclusion that a crime has in fact been committed and that the person to be arrested did in fact commit the crime.

---

[30] Malley v. Briggs, 475 U.S. 335, 106 S. Ct. 1092, 89 L. Ed. 2d 271 (1986).

For example, in the case of *Whiteley v. Warden*,[31] the arrest and the incidental search were held invalid because nothing more than the peace officer's conclusion that a crime had been committed was given to the magistrate. The basis for the arrest warrant issued by the justice of the peace was a complaint which stated:

> "I, C.W. Ogburn, do solemnly swear that on or about the 23 day of November, A.D., 1964, in the County of Carbon and State of Wyoming, the said Harold Whitely and Jack Daley, defendants, did then and there unlawfully break and enter a locked and sealed building...."

In reversing the conviction, the Supreme Court of the United States pointed out that the complaint consisted of nothing more than the complainant's conclusion that the individuals named perpetrated the offenses described in the complaint. Although the officers in this case had more information at their disposal, they did not furnish it to the magistrate who issued the warrant. The Court reaffirmed the reasoning that the magistrate must base his decision on the information he has available when the warrant is issued.

The amount of pre-arrest information necessary to obtain a warrant is no greater than that required to make an arrest without a warrant. In fact, there has been some indication in recent Supreme Court decisions that the "probable cause" requirement for a warrant may be even less exacting than the "reasonable grounds" for making an arrest without a warrant.[32] The Supreme Court has recognized that affidavits are drafted by nonlawyers in the midst of criminal investigations. If the constitutional requirement of probable cause were given an overly technical construction by magistrates and judges, a principal incentive now existing for the procurement of arrest warrants would be destroyed.[33]

In *Spinelli v. United States*,[34] the Court summarized the standards to be applied in determining probable cause:

---

31 401 U.S. 560, 91 S. Ct. 1031, 28 L. Ed. 2d 306 (1971).

32 Aguilar v. Texas, 378 U.S. 108, 84 S. Ct. 1509, 12 L. Ed. 2d 723 (1964).

33 United States v. Ventresca, 380 U.S. 102, 85 S. Ct. 741, 13 L. Ed. 2d 684 (1965). Also see rule 4 (b) of the Federal Rules of Criminal Procedure which provides that "The finding of probable cause may be based upon hearsay evidence in whole or in part."

34 393 U.S. 410, 89 S. Ct. 584, 21 L. Ed. 2d 637 (1969).

> In holding as we have done, we do not retreat from the established propositions that only the probability, and not a prima facie showing, of criminal activity is the standard of probable cause...; that affidavits of probable cause are tested by much less rigorous standards than those governing the admissibility of evidence at trial...; that in judging probable cause issuing magistrates are not to be confined by niggardly limitations or by restrictions on the use of their common sense...; and that their determination of probable cause should be paid great deference by reviewing courts....

In the case of *Illinois v. Gates* in 1983, the Supreme Court, in modifying its decision in *Aguilar* and *Spinelli*, applied the "totality of circumstances" test in determining if probable cause exists.[35] Here the court noted that the task of the issuing magistrate is to make a practical, common sense decision whether, given all the circumstances set out in the affidavit before him...there is a fair probability that contraband or evidence of the crime will be found in a particular place. The court again admonished, however, that a mere conclusion on the part of the officer is insufficient to establish probable cause. For example, an officer's statement that "affiants have received reliable information from a creditable person and believe" that heroin is stored in the home is inadequate. However, the *Gates* court reiterated that probable cause is a lesser standard than "proof beyond a reasonable doubt" or "the preponderance of the evidence."

The *Gates* analysis applies to both arrest and search warrant, as both are governed by the Fourth Amendment warrant clause. Although probable cause is a fluid concept turning on an assessment of probabilities in a given factual context and is not readily reduced to a specific set of legal rules, excerpts from cases can furnish some reasonably clear guidelines. In obtaining and presenting evidence which will support a probable cause decision, justice personnel are cautioned that an effort will be made to impeach the reliability of the information. However, there is rebuttable presumption that the warrant is based on valid probable cause and the burden is on the defendant to show that there were not sufficient facts to support the probable cause finding.

(b) Use of informants

In recent years there have been many court decisions concerning the propriety of using hearsay evidence in determining if probable cause exists. Closely related is the legality of using information to support the probable

---

35 Illinois v. Gates, 462 U.S. 213, 103 S. Ct. 2317, 76 L. Ed. 2d 527 (1983).

cause determination without disclosing the informant who supplied the information to the officer.

In the case of *Aguilar v. Texas*,[36] the United States Supreme Court reaffirmed previous decisions stating that the affidavit for the arrest warrant may be based on hearsay information and need not reflect the direct personal observation of the affiant. The Court, however, went on to explain that the magistrate must be informed of some of the underlying circumstances from which the informant concluded that a crime had in fact been committed. In 1965, in *United States v. Ventresca*,[37] the Court again placed the stamp of approval on the use of undisclosed informants, but cautioned that recital of some of the underlying circumstances in the affidavit is essential if the magistrate is to perform his function.

The Supreme Court in *Spinelli v. United States*[38] warned that information from unnamed informants could be used in determining probable cause only if two requirements were met. There the Court indicated the affiant must establish

(1) that the informant is reliable and
(2) that the information from the informant is credible.

However, in 1983 the same Court indicated those conditions are not required but that the "totality of circumstances" approach is the proper one. The opinion includes this statement:[39]

> For all these reasons, we conclude that it is wiser to abandon the "two-pronged test" established by our decisions in *Aguilar* and *Spinelli*. In its place we reaffirm the totality of the circumstances analysis that traditionally has informed probable cause determinations. The task of the issuing magistrate is simply to make a practical, common-sense decision whether, given all the circumstances set forth in the affidavit before him, including the "veracity" and "basis of knowledge" of persons supplying hearsay information, there is a fair probability that contraband or evidence of a crime will be found in a particular place. And the duty of a reviewing court is simply to ensure that the magistrate had a "substantial basis for...conclud[ing]" that probable cause existed.

---

36 378 U.S. 108, 84 S. Ct. 1509, 12 L. Ed. 2d 723 (1964).

37 380 U.S. 102, 85 S. Ct. 741, 13 L. Ed. 2d (1965).

38 393 U.S. 410, 89 S. Ct. 584, 21 L. Ed. 2d 637 (1969).

39 Illinois v. Gates, 462 U.S. 213, 103 S. Ct. 2317, 76 L. Ed. 2d 557 (1983). *See* § 4.7 (Search and Seizure) for a discussion of the facts in the *Gates* case.

2. *The affidavit for the warrant must be supported by oath or affirmation.*

This Fourth Amendment requirement is a prerequisite to conferring jurisdiction on the magistrate over the person of the defendant. Some person must swear to the facts and circumstances which are described in the affidavit. Although it is the responsibility of the magistrate or other judicial officer to make certain that the affidavit is given under oath, it is advisable that the police officer who is submitting the affidavit, if necessary, remind the magistrate of this requirement. Although the officer would probably not be held liable if he executed the warrant which was not given under oath, any evidence obtained as a result of this arrest warrant and an incidental search would be inadmissible if the defense could show that the oath was not given.

3. *The person to be seized must be particularly described.*

A third requirement included in the Fourth Amendment is that the person to be seized must be particularly described. As stated by the American Law Institute:

> An arrest under a warrant is not privileged unless the person arrested (a) is a person sufficiently named or otherwise described in the warrant and is, or is reasonably believed by the actor to be, the person intended, or (b) although not such person, has knowingly caused the actor to believe him to be so.[40]

The usual method of designating the person to be arrested is to insert his name in the warrant. Although the name on the warrant does not necessarily have to be spelled exactly as the true name is spelled, so long as it identifies the person to be arrested, it must at least be similar. For example, the Supreme Court has held that a warrant that authorized the arrest of the person designated as "James West" without providing any further designation or description would not justify the arrest of "Vandy M. West" who had never been known by the name appearing on the warrant, and who in no way caused the mistake, irrespective of the fact that "Vandy West" was the intended subject of the warrant.[41] A warrant which leaves a blank for the arresting officer to fill in the name violates the Fourteenth Amendment standards of particularity. If the name is not known, the warrant must include a

---

40 RESTATEMENT (SECOND) OF TORTS § 125 (1965).

41 West v. Cabell, 153 U.S. 78, 14 S. Ct. 752, 38 L. Ed. 643 (1894).

description which is sufficient to identify with reasonable certainty the person to be arrested. This may be done by describing his occupation, his personal appearance, peculiarities, place of residence, or other means of identification.[42]

There has been much unnecessary confusion concerning the use of the "John Doe" warrants. A warrant that authorizes the arrest of "John Doe," without any further description or identification of the person to be arrested, is a nullity. It is obvious that such a warrrant does not particularly describe "the person to be seized." A warrant is valid, however, if it is drafted to authorize the arrest of "John Doe," and provides an adequate description which will identify the person to be arrested. For example, the California Court of Appeals in the *Montoya* case agreed that:

> The weight of authority holds that to meet the constitutionals requirements, a "John Doe" warrant must describe the person to be seized with reasonable particularity.

The court in that case went on to find that the description of the defendant as a "white male about 30 to 35 years, 5'10", 175 pounds, dark hair, medium build," did not meet the constitutional requirements of reasonable particularity.

On the other hand, where the warrant directed officers to arrest "John Doe, a white male with black wavy hair and stocky build observed using a telephone in apartment 4C 1806 Patricia Lane, East McKeesport Pennsylvania," the Third Circuit Court of Appeals held that there was sufficient physical description coupled with precise location at which the person could be found to make the John Doe warrant valid.[43] The court in so holding explained that "the technical requirements of elaborate specificity once exacted under common law pleadings have no place in this area."

The best procedure is to make every effort to determine the name and/or alias of the person to be arrested. If this is not possible and a John Doe arrest warrant is issued, the peace officer should try to include all identifying information, especially that information which is peculiar to the individual to be arrested.

4. *The warrant must state the nature of the offense.*

Judicial and legislative decisions have added requirements not specifically enumerated in the Constitution. One of these is that the warrant must

---

42 People v. Montoya, 255 Cal. App. 2d 137, 63 Cal. Rptr. 73 (1967).

43 United States v. Ferrone, 438 F. 2d 381 (3d Cir. 1971).

state the nature of the offense. The offense need not be stated in the same detail as would be necessary in the indictment or information, but the warrant must include language specifying the nature of the offense with sufficient clarity to advise the subject of the accusation.

5. *The warrant must designate the officer or class of officers who are directed to comply with the order of the court.*

Generally the warrant may be directed to a specific officer or to a class of officers. Some statutes require that the warrant be directed to all peace officers in the state. For example, the Illinois Code states:

> The warrant shall be directed to all peace officers in the State. It shall be executed by the peace officer, or by a private person specially named therein, and may be executed in any county in the State.[44]

It is preferable to have such a provision in the warrant so that all officers within the class have authority to execute the warrant.

An arrest warrant may also be addressed to a specific private person unless there is a statute which prohibits this. This person must be expressly named on the warrant because he does not fall within the class of officers authorized by statute to execute a warrant.

6. *The warrant must be issued in the name of the state or United States.*

Although certain powers are delegated to *local* officials by the state constitution or statute, the police power rests primarily with the state. Thus, the name of the state must appear on the warrant, even if the warrant is issued by a county or city official. A warrant issued by a federal official must have "United States" on it.

7. *The warrant must be issued and signed by a neutral and detached judicial officer.*

An arrest warrant must be issued by a neutral and detached judicial official. The United States Supreme Court has determined that an attorney gen-

---

44 ILL. REV. STAT. ch. 38, § 107-9(e) (1988).

eral is not neutral and detached, and a warrant issued by the attorney general, even though he is authorized by statute to do so, is not valid.[45]

In *Coolidge*, the Court made it quite clear that neither law enforcement officers nor prosecutors may issue warrants, noting:

> Without disrespect to the state law enforcement agent here involved, the whole point of the basic rule so well expressed by Mr. Justice Jackson is that prosecutors and policemen simply cannot be asked to maintain the requisite neutrality with regard to their own investigations -- the "competitive enterprise" that must rightly engage their single-minded attention.

Although some law enforcement officers, with special permission, still issue warrants in a few states, this practice is clearly condemned.

There is still doubt concerning the authority of a court clerk to issue an arrest warrant. The majority of the Justices of the United States Supreme Court in the case of *Shadwick v. City of Tampa*[46] agreed that a court clerk was a neutral and detached person and was authorized to issue an arrest warrant for the arrest of persons charged with breach of a municipal ordinance. This reasoning, however, has not received full support from the states. Justice Powell, writing for the majority in the *Shadwick* case, explained that when the clerk is an employee of the judicial branch of the city and disassociated from the role of law enforcement, he may issue an arrest warrant for a violation of the municipal ordinance even though he is not a judge or an attorney.

This decision should be considered with caution as the Court emphasized that the clerk's neutrality had not been impeached and was in fact not questioned. Also, the capability of the clerk to determine "probable cause" was not questioned. The door was left open to challenge a clerk's ability to determine whether probable cause exists for a requested arrest or search.

The best procedure is for a person who is "neutral and detached" and who is qualified by education and experience to issue the arrest warrant. The whole purpose of requiring a judicial officer to issue the warrant is to be certain that a disinterested and qualified person makes this important decision. If the issuance of a warrant is only a ministerial act to be performed by an untrained clerk, the purpose is defeated.

Not only must the warrant be issued by a judicial officer, it must also be signed *after* it has been completed. A warrant signed and later filled in is in fact a "traveling warrant," which was condemned by the framers of the Con-

---

45 Coolidge v. New Hampshire, 403 U.S. 443, 91 S. Ct. 2022, 29 L. Ed. 2d 564 (1971).

46 407 U.S. 345, 92 S. Ct. 2119, 32 L. Ed. 2d 783 (1972).

stitution. In some states, the warrant must include the name of the issuing official and also the title of his office.

8. *Additional state requirements*

In addition to the preceding requirement, states may have other requirements. For example, some states require that the warrant itself must state the date when issued and the municipality or county where issued; others require that the amount of bail be inserted on the warrant itself. Because statutes in some states require additional information to be on the warrant, it is essential that the peace officer consult the applicable statutes of his state.

§ 3.7 Execution of the warrant

The general rule is that if the warrant appears regular on its face and is properly executed, it is the duty of the arrested person to comply with the warrant until other judicial processes determine that the warrant is not valid. According to the North Carolina Court of Appeals, even though the warrant issued by a magistrate which appeared regular on its face may not have in fact stated a crime, the determination of whether a crime was in fact charged is to be made by the courts and not through private violence.[47] Most courts have taken the position that if the warrant is executed without illegal entry and without excessive force, and if the warrant appears regular on its face, the arrestee must comply with the warrant. The court in the *Truzy* case explained that it would be bad public policy to jeopardize the safety of police officers because they cannot determine the strict legal sufficiency of each warrant they must execute.

Even though the warrant has been properly issued on a showing of probable cause, and sufficiently describes the person to be arrested, the arrest will not be legal unless the warrant is properly executed. Some of the requirements to be met in executing the warrant are listed below. In addition, the local statutes must be consulted to determine the authority and duties of the arresting officer. If all the requirements under state and federal law are complied with, the arrest will be legal, the officer will be protected, and the evidence secured incident to the arrest will generally be admissible.

---

47 State v. Truzy, 44 N.C. App. 53, 260 S.E.2d 113 (1979).

1. The executing officer must be specifically named or come within the class designated on the warrant.

A warrant addressed to a particular officer by name or designation of his officer must be served by such officer or his duly authorized deputy. If the warrant is addressed to a particular class of peace officers, it must be served by an officer who falls within that class. If an arrest warrant is addressed to a private person, he must execute the warrant and may not appoint someone to execute the warrant for him.

Today, the common practice is to issue an arrest warrant to "all peace officers in the state." Such a warrant can be executed by anyone within that class. If, however, as was the earlier practice and still the practice in some areas, a warrant is issued to a sheriff, he, being the highest peace officer within the jurisdiction, may deputize others to execute it, or his regular deputies may execute the warrant on the theory that they are acting through the sheriff.[48]

2. The warrant must be executed within the jurisdictional limits.

The validity of an arrest under a warrant depends on the territorial jurisdiction of the issuing official. Most modern statutes contain provisions authorizing the execution of a warrant in any county of the state, even though it was issued by a magistrate in another county. In the absence of a statute conferring statewide authority on issuing magistrates, a warrant may not be executed outside the county of its origin.

Under our federal system, the issuing state is powerless to authorize an arrest outside its territorial jurisdiction. A warrant for arrest issued in one state has by statute conferred validity on out-of-state warrants. A warrant issued in one state may, however, *indirectly* serve as the basis for an arrest in the second state even in the absence of special legislation. For example, knowledge that a warrant has been issued for John Smith's arrest in state *A* may furnish reasonable grounds for a police officer in state *B* to believe that a felony has been committed and to justify Smith's arrest in state *B*. In such a case, it is not the warrant but the reasonable inference which a police officer in the second state may properly draw from the fact of its issuance that forms the basis of the arrest. In addition, an out-of-state warrant may serve as the basis for issuing a fugitive warrant in another state.

You must have the compliance of the other states.

48 Ex parte Rhodes, 48 La. App. 1363, 20 So. 894 (1896).

3. *The arresting officer should make known his purpose.*

As a general rule, the arresting officer should make known his purpose and the cause of the arrest. Some states have statutes requiring the officer to inform the person to be arrested of the cause of the arrest and the fact that a warrant has been issued. If possible, the officer should make it clear that he is making an arrest and that he has authority to do so. This is particularly important if the officer is not in uniform.

There are logical exceptions to this rule. If the person to be arrested flees or forcibly resists before the officer has an opportunity to advise him or if the giving of such information will imperil the arrest, such notice is not required. Also, if the person to be arrested purposely makes it impossible for the officer to make known his purpose -- for example, by fleeing to another part of the house to hide -- he cannot complain that the officer did not inform him of the intended arrest. Where a police officer had attempted unsuccessfully to advise the suspect by phone from an adjoining apartment, and the suspect hid under a bed when the officers knocked on the door, "it was not unreasonable to dispense with an announcement of presence and purpose."[49]

4. *The officer usually must show the arrest warrant or advise the arrestee that the warrant has been issued.*

Under the common law rule which has been adopted in a number of states, a warrant must be in the possession of the arresting officer and shown to the person arrested if so demanded. The officer does not have to show the warrant before the arrest, especially if the officer reasonably believes that showing the warrant would be dangerous to him or others or would imperil the making of the arrest. For example, where the arrestee resists arrest at the outset and there is danger of his escape, the officer is not bound to exhibit the warrant until the prisoner is secured.[50] In such a case, after the person has submitted to the arrest, the officer, if requested, should acquaint the arrestee with the cause of the arrest either by stating the substance of the warrant or by reading it to him.

Because of the need for quick action in our highly mobile society, there has been a trend in recent years to relax the common-law requirement re-

---

49 Kirvelaitis v. Gray, 513 F.2d 213, (6th Cir. 1975). *See also* United States v. Guyon, 717 F.2d 1536 (1983); Hernandez v. State, 663 S.W.2d 5 (Tex. 1983) where the courts determined that a "rush" entry was justified by exigent circumstances.

50 Crosswhite v. Barnes, 139 Va. 471, 124 S.E. 242 (1924).

garding the display of the warrant. The federal rules[51] and most modern state codes contain provisions to the effect that the officer need not have the warrant in his possession at the time of the arrest, but after the arrest, if the person arrested so requests, the warrant shall be shown to him as soon as practicable. The Kentucky Code, which is similar to most modern codes, provides:

> A warrant of arrest may be executed by any peace officer. The officer need not have the warrant in his possession at the time of arrest. In any event, he shall inform the defendant of the offense charged and the fact that a warrant has been issued.[52]

5. *Absent "Exigent Circumstances" or "Consent" the arrest warrant may not be executed in the home of a third party.*

In 1981 the United States Supreme Court placed limitations on the execution of an arrest warrant even when the warrant is valid.[53] In the case of *Steagald v. United States* enforcement agents had an arrest warrant for a person named Ricky Lyons. The agents received a call from an informant indicating that Lyons could be reached during the next 24 hours at a certain number in Atlanta. The agents checked with the telephone company, secured the address, and entered the home of the petitioner in this case, Gary Keith Steagald, in search of Lyons. Ricky Lyons was not found but during the search of the house the agents observed cocaine. At this point one of the agents obtained a search warrant for the search of the house and found additional cocaine and arrested Steagald. Prior to the trial, the petitioner moved to suppress all evidence uncovered during the various searches on the ground that it was illegally obtained because the agents had entered the house in search of Lyons and did not have a search warrant.

The United States Supreme Court reversed the decision of the Court of Appeals and held that entry of the home of the third party (Steagald) absent consent or exigent circumstances violated the Fourth Amendment. The Court reasoned that the arrest warrant for Lyons protected his interest but did not protect the interest of Steagald. In effect, the majority of the Supreme Court placed additional limitations on the authority of officers to

---

51 FED. R. CRIM. P. 4(d)(3).

52 KY. R. CRIM. P. 2.10(1) (1988).

53 Steagald v. United States, 451 U.S. 204, 101 S. Ct. 1642, 68 L. Ed. 2d 38 (1981); *See* § 3.11 of this chapter for guidelines in determining what is meant by exigent circumstances.

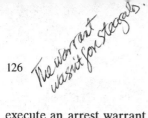

execute an arrest warrant, determining that absent exigent circumstances or consent, law enforcement officers cannot legally search for the subject of the arrest warrant in the home of the third party without first obtaining a search warrant.

The problem here, as indicated in a critical dissenting opinion by Justice Rehnquist, is that placing the burden on law enforcement officers to obtain a separate search warrant before entering the dwelling of the third party carries with it the high possibility that the fugitive named in the arrest warrant will escape apprehension. While there is some indication in the majority opinion as to what amounts to exigent circumstances, the definition is certainly not comprehensive. Citing other cases, the majority justifies placing this burden on the police officer by explaining that the subject of the arrest warrant can be readily seized before entering or after leaving the home of the third party. The opinion also contains these sentences concerning the exigent circumstance justification.

> Finally, the exigent circumstances doctrine significantly limits the situations in which a search warrant would be needed. For example, a warrantless entry of the home would be justified if the police were in "hot pursuit" of a fugitive....Thus to the extent that searches for persons pose special problems, we believe that the exigent circumstances doctrine is adequate to accommodate legitimate law enforcement needs.

Although this example of exigent circumstances is helpful, it leaves many questions unanswered and requires that one look to other cases in determining the scope of the exigent circumstances doctrine.

§ 3.8 Arrest without a warrant

Neither the Fourth Amendment to the Constitution nor the constitutional provisions of the various states contains any express reference to the right to arrest without a warrant. But it was recognized early in the common law that under certain circumstances it was impractical, if not impossible, to obtain a warrant. The common law attempted to strike a balance between the interests of the community in protecting itself and the rights of citizens to be free from unjustified arrests, and in certain situations authority was extended to permit arrest without a warrant.

The exceptions to the rule requiring a warrant were based on the strictest necessity. The common law permitted a peace officer to make an arrest for a felony committed in his presence. In addition, because of the social importance of apprehending a felon while he was then available, an officer was allowed to make an arrest if he had reasonable grounds to believe that a felony had been committed and that the person to be arrested had committed it. The right to make an arrest without warrant for a misdemeanor was narrowly confined to those circumstances in which prompt action on the part of the peace officer or private citizen was necessary to prevent a breach of the peace or to maintain public order. Before an arrest was authorized, the law required that the person making the arrest actually witness the commission of a misdemeanor amounting to a breach of the peace.

In 1975 the United States Supreme Court reemphasized and restated the reason for authorizing an arrest without a warrant in these terms:

> Maximum protection of individual rights could be assured by requiring a magistrate's review of the factual justification prior to any arrest, but such a requirement would constitute an intolerable handicap for legitimate law enforcement. Thus, while the Court has expressed a preference for the use of arrest warrants when feasible, . . . it has never invalidated an arrest supported by probable cause solely because the officers failed to secure a warrant. [Citations omitted.][54]

The common-law distinction between felony and misdemeanor arrests is preserved in most states today, and the legality of an arrest without a warrant, in many instances, may turn upon the issue of whether the offense for which the arrest was made constitutes a felony or a misdemeanor.

§ 3.9 Arrest without a warrant in felony situations

1. Definition of a felony

The statute of each state defines the authority to arrest for a felony and, in some states, classifies the various crimes into felonies or misdemeanors. Thus, a police officer, especially one who operates in a state which distinguishes felonies and misdemeanors for arrest purposes, should acquaint himself with the statutes of his state.

The Uniform Arrest Act defines a felony as any crime which is or may be punished by death or imprisonment in a state prison. As the laws in most states do not provide for imprisonment in a state institution unless the term is at least one year, it is generally agreed that an offense is a felony if the

---

54 Gerstein v. Pugh, 420 U.S. 103, 95 S. Ct. 854, 43 L. Ed. 2d 54 (1975).

penalty attached is at least one year and the incarceration is in a state institution rather than a local jail. An offense, however, may be designated by statute as a felony even though it does not carry a year's incarceration. Thus an offense is considered a felony when

(1) the statute provides that it is a felony, or
(2) there is no such designation, but the offense is punishable by imprisonment in a state prison.

Although there is apparent consensus in the technical definition of a felony and misdemeanor, all semblance of uniformity disappears when these terms are used or applied to concrete areas of criminal conduct. What may be regarded as a felony in one state may constitute a misdemeanor in another. Except for the crimes of murder, robbery and rape, generalizations in the area are unreliable. Therefore, the legislative designations in the particular jurisdiction must be carefully examined. If the state statute does not specifically enumerate the felonies, justice personnel should go through the statutes and codes and designate the felonies as such.

2. *Authority to arrest*

The states are uniform in authorizing, by statute or judicial decision, a peace officer to arrest without a warrant when he has reasonable grounds to believe that a felony has been committed and that the person to be arrested has committed it. A small number of states add an additional requirement limiting this authority to those situations where it is impractical to obtain a warrant before making the arrest. For example, the Texas Code provides that:

> Where it is shown by satisfactory proof to a peace officer, upon the representation of a credible person, that a felony has been committed, and that the offender is about to escape, so that there is not time to procure a warrant, such peace officer may, without warrant, pursue and arrest the accused.[55]

The code provisions authorizing warrantless arrests for felonies do not spell out what is meant by "reasonable grounds to believe." The term "reasonable grounds" does not appear in the Fourth Amendment but is often used interchangeably with the term "probable cause." Technically, "probable

---

[55] TEX. CODE CRIM. PROC. ANN. art. 14.04 (Vernon 1977).

cause" refers to the minimum knowledge that a judicial officer must have before issuing an arrest warrant, and "reasonable grounds" refers to the knowledge that an officer must possess prior to making a valid arrest without a warrant. Nevertheless, the courts have often referred to "probable cause" when defining the minimum knowledge that an officer must possess to make a constitutionally valid arrest without a warrant, and the reader should not be confused by this usage.

In requiring that the arresting officer possess reasonable grounds to believe in the guilt of a suspect, the Constitution seeks to safeguard citizens from unfounded charges of crime. At the same time, its standards are intended to be sufficiently flexible to permit efficient law enforcement. Because of the need to compromise between these two opposing interests, the Constitution does not demand infallibility from the arresting officer.

"Reasonable grounds" lies somewhere on the evidentiary scale between good faith suspicion and proof beyond a reasonable doubt. The rule of "probable cause" or "reasonable grounds" makes allowances for some mistakes on the part of an arresting officer. The fact that subsequent events and information may prove that the person arrested has not actually committed a felony makes no difference as long as appearances at the time of the arrest are such as to lead a police officer reasonably to conclude that a felony has been committed, and that the person he is about to arrest is responsible for the felony.

3. *Determining "reasonable grounds"*

"Reasonable grounds" depends on the facts and circumstances of each case. In determining whether an officer has reasonable grounds for an arrest, the information to be considered is that which is available to him at the time of the arrest. An arrest cannot be justified by what a subsequent search produces, but must stand or fall solely on the basis of the facts possessed by the officer at the precise moment of the arrest. According to the *Restatement of Torts*, the nature of the crime, the chance of escape, and the harm to others if the suspect escapes are all relevant factors to be considered by an officer in determining whether grounds for a warrantless arrest exist.[56]

A completely satisfactory definition of what constitutes "reasonable" is impossible to formulate. One court has characterized reasonable grounds as "the sum total of layers of information and the synthesis of what the police have heard, what they know and what they observe as trained officers." In determining whether reasonable cause exists in a particular case, the test

---

56 RESTATEMENT (SECOND) OF TORTS § 119 comment j (1965).

most frequently employed in the federal courts is that set forth by the Supreme Court in *Draper v. United States*:[57]

> Probable cause exists where "the facts and circumstances within [the arresting officers'] knowledge and of which they had reasonably trustworthy information [are] sufficient in themselves to warrant a man of reasonable caution in the belief that" an offense has been or is being committed.

Judge Warren Burger, while serving as a member of the District of Columbia Circuit Court, went a little further and indicated that the police officers may call on their experience in determining if reasonable grounds exist.

However, the best guidelines for police action are found not in the legal definitions given by the courts, but in the factual situations where probable cause has been found to exist. In making a felony arrest, a police officer may rely on information from a wide variety of sources. The most common sources include the officer's personal observations, informants' tips, reports from other officers or law enforcement agencies, leads furnished by the victim of the crime, physical evidence found at the scene of the crime, and past criminal records of suspects.[58] Reliable information may be obtained from many other sources. The more information obtained from whatever source, the better the officer's chances are of showing that reasonable grounds for the felony arrest exist.

In determining if there is sufficient "reasonable ground" or "probable cause" to make a warrantless arrest, the officer need not rely upon any single source.[59] As one case indicated, probable cause to make a warrantless arrest exists where, considering the totality of the circumstances, the police possess reasonable trustworthy information which would warrant a prudent person in believing that the suspect has committed an offense.[60] Probable cause may be based on the collective knowledge of all the officers involved.[61]

In the paragraphs which follow some of the most common sources of trustworthy information on which an officer may determine probable cause for a warrantless arrest are considered.

---

57 358 U.S. 307, 79 S. Ct. 329, 3 L. Ed. 2d 327 (1959).

58 LAFAVE, ARREST: THE DECISION TO TAKE A SUSPECT INTO CUSTODY, 265-299 (1965).

59 United States v. Briley, 726 F.2d 1301 (8th Cir. 1984).

60 United States v. Wallraff, 705 F.2d 980 (8th Cir. 1983).

61 United States v. Rose, 541 F.2d 750 (8th Cir. 1976), *cert. denied*, 430 U.S. 908, 97 S. Ct. 1178, 51 L. Ed. 2d 584 (1977).

(a) Personal observations of the arresting officer

When a police officer observes the actual commission of a felony there is no question whether he has adequate grounds to arrest without a warrant. But criminals seldom commit crimes in the presence of law enforcement officers. Frequently the police officer only observes acts which are suspicious. For example, he might observe a car with a motor running in an industrial complex, and, as he approaches, the car moves on. Or he might observe a man running down the street late at night carrying a bag. In instances such as these the officer does not have probable cause or reasonable grounds to believe that a felony has been committed or that these individuals have committed or are intending to commit a felony. Therefore, an arrest under these circumstances would be illegal as the Constitution does not permit an arrest on suspicion only.

Nevertheless, an officer would be lax in his duties if he allowed suspicious circumstances such as these to pass without further inquiry or investigation. Where circumstances justify it, further inquiry may produce sufficient additional information to justify an arrest.[62] Where the totality of the circumstances -- which could include the time of the day or night, the area, attempted flight by the suspect, the known record of the suspect and other factors known to the officer -- collectively lead the officer in light of his experience to reasonably believe a felony has been committed, the arrest is justified.[63]

Consider the following example of reasonable grounds based upon the personal observation of the arresting officer. A District of Columbia officer observed three persons standing in the shadow of a building "passing and changing" packages. As the area was considered by the police to be high in narcotics traffic, the officer decided to investigate. When he told the men that he would like to talk with them for a minute, one of the men shouted, "Fuck you," and ran. The officer gave chase. About a block away, the suspect tried to crawl underneath a Volkswagen parked at the curb. After the second command to come out, the suspect emerged from under the Volkswagen and, as he did so, the police officer observed a bag of heroin lying in plain view under the suspect. The defendant claimed that there were no reasonable grounds for his arrest for disorderly conduct and, therefore, the heroin had been obtained by an illegal search and seizure.

The United States Court of Appeals for the District of Columbia Circuit held that there were reasonable grounds for the arrest, adding:

---

[62] *See* § 3.14 *infra*, concerning police authority to detain.

[63] Green v. United States, 259 F.2d 180 (D.C. Cir. 1972), *cert. denied*, 359 U.S. 917, 79 S. Ct. 594, 3 L. Ed. 2d 578 (1959)

> We reiterate that we are not deciding that defendant was guilty of disorderly conduct, a decision that would require a determination concerning community standards. The standard that governs arrest does not require proof enough to convict. The police officer's probable cause for arrest may stand even though the prosecutor needs additional evidence for the preliminary hearing or the trial.[64]

(b) Informers' tips

Tips received from informers frequently afford an invaluable source of pre-arrest information, especially in the vice areas where a premium is put on secrecy. Without the leads furnished by confidential informants, many crimes would go undetected. The Supreme Court has expressly sanctioned the use of this type of information in making a warrantless arrest.[65] As a safeguard against lying or inaccurate informers, the police should make an independent investigation whenever feasible to substantiate the report before making an arrest.

Where the arrest is based in whole or in part on an informer's word, an important factor is the reliability of the source. Some considerations relevant to the question of reliability are the length of time the officer has known or dealt with the informer, his general character and reputation, the number of tips received from him in the past, the accuracy of the information previously given, and whether the informer is a volunteer or is paid for his knowledge.[66] The Supreme Court has held that detailed information from a paid informant who had a past history of supplying reliable tips regarding violations of narcotics laws was sufficient in itself to furnish probable cause for an arrest without a warrant.[67]

Although it is preferable to have an informer who has given correct information in the past and to corroborate this information, there are times

---

[64] Von Sleichter v. United States, 472 F.2d 1244 (D.C. Cir. 1972). *But see* State v. Cross, 535 So. 2d 282 (Fla. App. 1988), which held that the possession of a package about the size of a baseball and wrapped in brown paper did not give the officer reasonable grounds to arrest for drug trafficking. Here, there was no information in the record suggesting that use of such containers gives rise to probable cause of illegal drug possession.

[65] Draper v. United States, 358 U.S. 307, 79 S. Ct. 329, 3 L. Ed. 2d 327 (1959).

[66] Comment, *Informer's Word as the Basis for Probable Cause in the Federal Courts*, 53 CAL. L. REV. 840 (1965).

[67] Draper v. United States, 358 U.S. 307, 79 S. Ct. 329, 3 L. Ed. 2d 327 (1959).

when the arresting officer must rely solely on an unknown informer's tip. If the circumstances justify it, the officer may rely upon an informant even if the informant's identity is not known to the officer. For example, where an FBI officer was assaulted and his gun, money and credentials were stolen, an elderly male, who told the police officers that he did not want to get involved, said that he saw the offender on the second floor of a certain house. The anonymous informant did not state that he had seen the offense being committed nor that he had seen the youth fleeing the scene. Following the informant's lead, the officers made the arrest and retrieved the gun taken from the agent.

At the trial the defendant moved to suppress the gun and other evidence found in the apartment on the grounds that the police did not have probable cause for arrest, primarily because the officers were not justified in relying on information received from an informant who was not known to the officers. In upholding the arrest, the majority of the justices of the Seventh Circuit followed this rationale:

> The fact that one of the neighbors was willing to supply this information, albeit in a guarded manner, thus raises a presumption of reliability on which the police properly could and did rely.
>
> ...In view of the exigencies of the situation and considering the practical aspects of obtaining any information at all in the particular neighborhood, the police had probable cause [reasonable grounds] to make the arrest.[68]

On the other hand, the officer cannot always depend on the informer's tip alone supplying information for probable cause. For example, information obtained from unsworn statements of a jail prisoner, a first-time informer whose reliability has not been established, or an anonymous tip received over the telephone would probably require some independent investigation and corroboration before an arrest could be made. Corroborating data might come from the suspect's prior record of arrest or convictions for the same type of offense, his association with known violators, furtive conduct such as flight when approached by police officers, the receipt by the officer of similar reports from others, or a combination of these elements.

In the case of *Illinois v. Gates*, discussed in a previous section, the United States Supreme Court reviewed a magistrate's finding of probable cause and his accompanying decision to issue a warrant. In that case the court discarded the previously utilized "two-prong" test of the reliability of informants' tips and instead adopted a "totality of circumstances" approach.

---

68 United States v. Ganter, 436 F.2d 364 (7th Cir. 1970).

The discussion related to the reliability of an informant's tip when obtaining a warrant, however, at least some courts have upheld the application of the same test where information from an informant is used to make an arrest without a warrant.[69]

The standards applicable to the factual basis supporting the officer's probable cause assessment at the time of the arrest are at least as stringent as the standards applied with respect to the magistrate's assessment. The difference is that the officer must present evidence to justify a probable cause arrest without an arrest warrant *after* the arrest takes place rather than presenting this evidence to a magistrate before an arrest warrant is issued.

In the case of *United States v. Fixen*, an undisclosed informant gave information to the police which lead them to observe the activities of the defendant. These activities included a meeting between the defendant and his source of supply of drugs and a transfer of an attache case and brown bag from the supplier's car to the defendant's car. When the police intercepted the defendant's car, they seized the cocaine and the defendant was charged with possession with intent to distribute cocaine.

In comparing the information available to the officers in this case with the *Gates* case where the information from the undisclosed informant was used to obtain a warrant, a reviewing court agreed there was sufficient information to justify probable cause for an arrest and search incidental to that arrest and that the police were not required to disclose their confidential informant. The reviewing court, after enumerating the information the police officers had before making the stop, commented:

> The record here presents verified predictions and observed suspicious activity. Although the information which was verified would alone appear innocent, a police officer's special training and experience may enable him reasonably to suspect that criminal activity is afoot from observing what might appear innocuous to uninitiated....
>
> True, the government does not assert that this informant had previously proven himself reliable or accurate. Therefore, his "reliability" and "veracity" were subject to question. However, the police corroboration "reduced the chances of a reckless or prevaricating tale, thus providing a substantial basis for crediting the hearsay."

What if probable cause (or reasonable grounds) is based on a tip which is ultimately proved untrue? In a 1974 case a defendant, convicted of interstate transportation of stolen securities, claimed that evidence seized after his

---

69 United States v. Fixen, 780 F.2d 1434 (9th Cir. 1986).

arrest was inadmissible because the arresting FBI agent acted solely on the basis of information from his supervisor who, in turn, had received the informer's false statement.[70] The informer had advised the supervisor that he had personally observed stolen securities in the defendant's possession but the informer admitted at trial that he had never seen the defendant before. The FBI officer was not aware that the informant had lied, and the defense counsel conceded that the facts related in the affidavit attached to the post-arrest complaint form supported a finding of probable cause if true.

In upholding the arrest and resulting search, a majority of the court explained that:

> The discrepancy between what the informer may have told the FBI and what was actually proved at trial may not now be used to invalidate an arrest, absent any showing of fraud or deceit on the part of the law enforcement officials involved. [Citation omitted.] "[P]robable cause is not defeated because an informant is later proved to have lied, as long as the affiant accurately represents what was told him."

If the FBI officer had any inkling that the informer was giving false information or even if he should have known from the circumstances that the evidence was questionable, not only would the evidence be inadmissible but also, the officer would be subject to civil or criminal action.

The question often arises whether it is necessary to disclose the informant who has supplied the reasonable grounds necessary to make a felony arrest. Following the rationale of the probable cause cases, the Supreme Court decided in at least one case that the officer need not disclose the identity of the informant "if the trial judge is convinced, by evidence submitted in open court...that the officers did rely in good faith upon credible information supplied by a reliable informant."[71]

(c) Information from other officers or law enforcement agencies

The police department of a large metropolis operates as a closely coordinated unit in which fast and accurate dissemination of information is essential to efficient law enforcement. Frequently, an officer receives a message over the police radio, directing him to go to a certain place and arrest a certain person without informing the officer of any reasons for the arrest. Certainly, no one would seriously contend that this officer had probable

70 United States v. Garofalo, 496 F.2d 510 (8th Cir. 1974).

71 McCray v. Illinois, 386 U.S. 300, 87 S. Ct. 1056, 18 L. Ed. 2d 62 (1967).

cause to believe in the guilt of the person arrested. Nevertheless, the Constitution does not require that the arresting officer personally, independent of his police colleagues, have knowledge of all the facts necessary to constitute probable cause.[72]

Probable cause in such a circumstance must be evaluated on the basis of the collective information of the police rather than that of the officer who performs the act of arrest.[73] Where words heard over a police radio form the basis of the arresting officer's probable cause, the sending officer must have reasonable grounds on which to base his message. A contrary rule would permit the police to do indirectly what the Constitution forbids them from doing directly, by publishing a report on the police radio.

In the case of *Whiteley v. Warden*,[74] an arrest warrant which was issued without probable cause was the basis for a bulletin sent to an officer in another county. The officer in the other county, relying upon the radio message that a warrant was outstanding, made the arrest and incidental search. The state claimed that even though the warrant was invalid since it was not supported by probable cause, the police officer who relied upon the radio bulletin in making the arrest nevertheless made a legal arrest and resulting search. The Supreme Court held that if the initial warrant is defective, an arrest made by another officer solely on the basis of a radio message stating the warrant has been issued is also defective. The Court agreed, however, that the arresting officers who relied upon the information received over the police radio were certainly protected from civil and criminal liability. The Court explained:

> We do not, of course, question that the Laramie police were entitled to act on the strength of the radio bulletin. Certainly police officers called upon to aid other officers in executing arrest warrants are entitled to assume that the officers requesting aid offered the magistrate the information requisite to support an independent judicial assessment of probable cause. Where, however, the contrary turns out to be true, an otherwise illegal arrest cannot be insulated from challenge by the decision of the instigating officer to rely on fellow officers to make the arrest.

---

72 Draper v. United States, 359 U.S. 307, 79 S. Ct. 329, 3 L. Ed. 2d 327 (1959).

73 Smith v. United States, 358 F.2d 833 (D.C. Cir. 1966).

74 401 U.S. 560, 91 S. Ct. 1031, 28 L. Ed. 2d 306 (1971).

The same reasoning was applied in the case of *United States v. Impson*[75] where the arrest was made by a Wichita Falls, Texas, police agent at the telephonic request of a U.S. Secret Service agent. Here there was no arrest warrant. The court reiterated that there is no question that the arresting officer in another area can act on the basis of information which has been relayed to him by police transmission facilities; however, the prosecution must show that the officer who made the telephonic request himself had reasonable grounds for the arrest.

(d) Past criminal record of a suspect

The past criminal record of a suspect standing alone can never constitute probable cause for an arrest.[76] Any other rule would deprive all ex-convicts of the protections of the Fourth Amendment and subject them to arrest at will. Nevertheless, a police officer may properly consider a suspect's record in conjunction with other information in deciding whether there are adequate grounds for arrest.

(e) Physical evidence found at the scene of a crime

Whether physical evidence found at the scene of a crime, standing alone, can justify an arrest depends upon the type of evidence involved. For example, a handkerchief bearing the initials "JS" found a few inches from a murder victim would not furnish reasonable cause for a felony arrest of a "John Smith" in the absence of some stronger evidence to implicate him in the crime. On the other hand, fingerprints taken from the shattered window of a burglarized jewelry store, which had been washed just prior to closing, if they matched with a set of prints on file with the police, would furnish sufficient cause to make an arrest.[77]

In a case where a tavern proprietor reported that a burglar tried to pry open the side door of the tavern with a screwdriver and that another burglar wore gloves, the use, as evidence, of a screwdriver and gloves found in a field where the suspect had been running was admitted as justifying the arrest.[78]

Another example of the court's approval of the use of evidence found at the scene to justify probable cause for an arrest, is the North Carolina case of

---

[75] 482 F.2d 197 (5th Cir. 1973); United States v. Hensley, 469 U.S. 221, 105 S. Ct. 675, 83 L. Ed. 2d 604 (1985).

[76] Beck v. Ohio, 379 U.S. 89, 85 S. Ct. 223, 13 L. Ed. 2d 142 (1964).

[77] State v. Callas, 68 Wash. 2d 542, 413 P.2d 962 (1966).

[78] People v. Allen, 17 Ill. 2d 55, 160 N.E.2d 818 (1959). *See* KLOTTER, CRIMINAL EVIDENCE, § 14.4(b) (1984).

State v. Reynolds.[79] In the *Reynolds* case the defendant had reported to the police that a neighbor was unconscious or dead in her house. In justifying the probable cause to arrest the defendant who made the report, the court indicated that during the investigation the officers found the suspect was not wearing shoes, and bare footprints were found in and around the house, he was shirtless and a bloodstained T-shirt was found in the house, the defendant was scratched about his face and there was evidence of a vigorous struggle, and the only unsecured entrance to the house was a window that the defendant had said he used to break into the house to check on the woman. Here the evidence found at the scene together with the officer's observations was sufficient to justify probable cause for the defendant's arrest.

In determining if the police have reasonable grounds or probable cause to make the arrest, the court will consider the total information that the officer has gathered, including the information from the scene of the crime and his personal observations. It is, therefore, important that the information be documented in order to present this to the court when the determination of probable cause is being considered.

Other examples of evidence which have been considered sufficient to furnish reasonable grounds are a billfold found at the scene of the crime with the victim's name, and a description of the car observed at the scene of the crime, including the license number, make, and color.

(f) Reports of victims or eyewitnesses

It is seldom that the police catch a criminal in the act of committing a crime. The license number of a car used in a hold-up, the physical description of an assailant, or the victim's identification of a picture taken from the rogue's gallery are frequently the best and only leads which the police may have into an unsolved crime. Victims and eyewitness observers may, and do in many instances, furnish reliable information. For example, in *United States v. Masini*,[80] a bookstore proprietor who had been alerted by the police that passers of counterfeit $20 bills were active in the area became suspicious when a man entered his store and purchased two paperback books using a $20 bill which did not look or feel right. He immediately telephoned the police and accompanied them on a search for the man. The suspect was found in a hotel lobby and, upon being identified by the proprietor, was placed under arrest. The arrest was upheld.

---

[79] State v. Reynolds, 298 N.C. 380, 259 S.E.2d 843 (1979).

[80] 358 F.2d 100 (6th Cir. 1966).

§ 3.10 Arrest without a warrant in misdemeanor situations

At common law, a breach of the peace was the only non-felony for which a warrantless arrest was authorized. The common law developed in an agrarian society where the problems of law enforcement were relatively simple. But modern experience in urban areas with heavy crime rates has demonstrated the need for reconsideration of the rule. Efforts of law enforcement agencies in apprehending, for example, petty thieves and others who had committed misdemeanors not amounting to a breach of the peace, were being unduly hampered by the strictness of the common-law rule.

In response to the changing needs of the community, most states either by statute or judicial decision have enlarged the powers of the police to make warrantless arrests for misdemeanors. In most states it is no longer required that the offense for which the arrest is made constitute a breach of the peace. The statutes generally provide that a peace officer may arrest without a warrant any person who has committed a misdemeanor in his presence.

Unlike a felony arrest, the common statutory law and the law in most states today leave no room for a reasonable mistake on the part of an officer making a warrantless arrest for a misdemeanor. The common law distinction between felonies and misdemeanors and the requirement that the misdemeanor be actually committed in the presence of the officer have been criticized in recent years as demanding of a police officer a decision which even judges find difficult.

A growing number of states have enlarged the powers of the police officer to make arrests without warrants for misdemeanors.[81] For example, the Illinois Code provides that:

A peace officer may arrest a person when:

(a) He has a warrant commanding that such person be arrested; or
(b) He has reasonable grounds to believe that a warrant for the person's arrest has been issued in this State or in another jurisdiction; or

---

81 These are among the state statutes authorizing misdemeanor arrests even if the offense is not committed in the officer's presence:
ARIZ. REV. STAT. ANN. § 13-3883 (Supp. 1988).
HAW. REV. STAT. § 803-5 (1988).
IOWA CODE ANN. § 804.7(2)(3) (1988).
LA. CODE. CRIM. PROC. ANN. art. 213(a) (West Supp. 1989).
N.Y. CRIM. PROC. LAW § 140.10 (McKinney 1989).
WIS. STAT. § 968.07(1)(d) (1971).

(c) He has reasonable grounds to believe that the person is committing or has committed an offense.[82]

The term "offense" is defined as the violation of any penal statute of the state or ordinance of a political subdivision of the state. This statute and the statutes of approximately a half-dozen other states make it possible for police officers to make an arrest for a misdemeanor upon reasonable grounds or probable cause even if the misdemeanor is not committed in their presence.

In addition to these, some states authorize peace officers to make warrantless arrests for misdemeanors not committed in their presence under certain special conditions such as: "the offender will flee if not immediately apprehended"; "he will destroy or conceal evidence of the commission of the offense if not apprehended immediately"; or "he may cause injury to himself or others or damage to property if not apprehended."[83]

Other states authorize warrantless arrests for misdemeanors not committed in the officer's presence only for certain specified misdemeanors or classes of misdemeanors.[84] An example is the Oregon statute which authorizes an arrest on probable cause for a Class A misdemeanor.[85]

Although there is a recognizable trend toward broadening a peace officer's misdemeanor arrest powers, the majority of states still require that the misdemeanor be actually committed in his presence and that the arrest take place immediately or in close pursuit. Any deviation must be by statutory enactment.

If the state statutes allow an officer to make a warrantless misdemeanor arrest where the violation is out of his presence under specific conditions then, of course, these conditions must be apparent at the time the arrest is made. For example, the North Carolina statute authorizes a police officer to make an arrest when he has probable cause to believe that the person to be arrested has committed a misdemeanor in his presence *or* when he has probable cause to believe the person to be arrested has committed a misde-

---

82 ILL. REV. STAT. ch. 38, § 107-2 (1982 & Supp. 1988-89).

83 KAN. STAT. ANN. § 22-2401(c)(2) (1989).
NEB. REV. STAT. § 29-404.02(2) (1986).
N.C. GEN. STAT. § 15A-401(b)(2) (1988).
UTAH CODE ANN. § 77-7-2(3) (1988)
WYO. STAT. ANN. § 7-2-103(4) (1988).

84 D.C. CODE ANN. § 23-581 (1988).
MD. ANN. CODE art. 27, § 594B(d)(e) (1988).
WASH. REV. CODE ANN. § 10.31.100 (Supp. 1988).

85 OR. REV. STAT. § 133.310(1)(a) (1987).

meanor out of his presence and also has probable cause to believe that one of the following conditions exist:

(a) the person to be arrested will not be apprehended unless immediately arrested, or
(b) the person to be arrested may cause physical injury to himself or others unless immediately arrested, or
(c) the person to be arrested may damage property unless immediately arrested.[86]

To justify an arrest under this statute, the officer must be able to produce evidence to reasonably demonstrate one of the conditions did, in fact, exist. For example, if the defendant is known to the officer and lives in or near the community where the crime occurred, it is unlikely that the warrantless misdemeanor arrest would be justified for the reasons "that he will not be apprehended unless immediately arrested."[87]

1. "Misdemeanor" defined

The Uniform Arrest Act defines a misdemeanor as "any crime or violation of a municipal ordinance which is not classified as a felony." Unless the offense is defined as a felony, or unless it is punishable by at least one year in the penitentiary, the offense must be treated as a misdemeanor. Many states by statute specifically set out which crimes are felonies so that there will be no doubt as to the procedure to be followed; however, in many instances the officer must determine on the spot whether the offense is a felony or a misdemeanor. If in doubt, the offense should be treated as a misdemeanor for the purposes of arrest and search. Since the arrest privileges for misdemeanors are generally more restricted than those for felonies, the officer will be protected if he mistakenly employs the misdemeanor procedure for what later turns out to be a felony.

2. "In the officer's presence" defined

Determining the precise meaning of the phrase "in the officer's presence" has caused the courts considerable difficulty. In *Miles v. State*,[88] the Oklahoma court said:

---

86 N.C. GEN. STAT. § 15A-401(b) (1985).

87 In re Pinyatello, 36 N.C. App. 542, 245 S.E.2d 185 (1978).

88 30 Okla. Crim. 302, 236 P. 57 (1925).

> An offense is committed in the presence of an officer, within the meaning of the statute authorizing an arrest without a warrant, only when he sees it with his eyes or sees one or more of a series of acts constituting the offense, and is aided by his other senses. An offense is likewise deemed committed in the presence of the officer where the offense is continuing, or has not been fully consummated at the time the arrest is made.

In order for an offense to be considered to have taken place within the presence of the arresting officer, he must be made aware of its commission through one or more of his senses. He must perceive the acts which make up the offense while they take place and not merely learn of the event at a later date. The offense must still be in progress when the officer reaches the scene in order for him to make a warrantless arrest for a misdemeanor in most states. If the offense has terminated before he arrives, under the usual statute the officer would be required to obtain a warrant before making the arrest. The officer need not witness the entire misdemeanor; if any part of the offense is still in progress when he reaches the scene, the arrest may be made.

For example, in *People v. Foster*,[89] the defendant allegedly assaulted a shopkeeper who retreated into her store, bolted the door and called the police. When the police arrived at the store, the defendant was kicking at the shop door and screaming insults and threats at those inside. The shopkeeper emerged with blood still streaming from her nose and told the police that the defendant had attacked her. The defendant violently resisted arrest, kicking and scratching. It required five officers to finally subdue her and to place her under arrest. In commenting on the legality of the arrest, the court stated,

> It would be a strange law that would hold such an arrest illegal on the ground that the underlying assault had not been perpetrated in the officer's presence. A more reasonable view is that the affray was still in progress when the police came. Blood was flowing, a mob had gathered, the accused was kicking at the door to get another crack at her victim. What has the statutory requirement of sworn information and warrant to do with all this? To prevent irresponsible arrests of presumably innocent citizens, the statute demands that the officer, unless the misdemeanor be committed in his presence, have assurance in the form of a sworn complaint. None of us would strike from the law that reasonable requirement. But the requirement and its purpose are satisfied when as here the visi-

---

89 10 N.Y.2d 99, 176 N.E.2d 397 (1961).

ble signs of a continuing assault are right in front of the policeman's eyes. Here there was presented to his consciousness adequate information that what he saw was the last phase of an assault.

If the entire offense has been completed before the police officer arrives on the scene, and order has been restored, under most state statutes the officer would have to procure a warrant before making an arrest.

3. *Necessity for quick action*

In addition to witnessing the misdemeanor for which the arrest is made, most states require that the officer make the arrest immediately or after close pursuit. If for some reason the officer is delayed or unable to make the arrest until a later time, he must obtain a warrant. For example, frequently a patrolman pursues a speeder who manages to avoid him by crossing the state line. If on the following day, or even a few hours later, the patrolman catches the speeder again within the state, no arrest can be made unless the officer has taken steps in the meantime to obtain a warrant, or unless the speeder is again violating the law.

§ 3.11 Authority to enter premises to make an arrest without a warrant

An entry into one's home to make an arrest unless there is a clear need to do so is prohibited. While the concept appears in English and American cases, there has existed much confusion as to the authority of governmental officials to enter the home to make an arrest.[90]

Until 1980, when the case of *Payton v. New York*[91] was decided, the exact authority to enter a person's home to make a warrantless arrest for a felony was in doubt. Even with the Supreme Court's decision there is still some confusion, but of a somewhat different nature. At the time this case was decided, according to the majority, 24 states permitted warrantless and nonconsensual entry into a suspect's home in order to make a routine felony arrest; 15 states prohibited such entries; and 11 states had apparently taken no position on the question. Due to these conflicting decisions by the various state courts, officers in some states were authorized to enter premises to

---

90 Agnello v. United States, 269 U.S. 20, 46 S. Ct. 4, 70 L. Ed. 145 (1925).

91 Payton v. New York, 445 U.S. 573, 100 S. Ct. 1371, 63 L. Ed. 2d 639 (1980). *See* case in Part II.

make arrests, even in the absence of exigent circumstances, while officers in other states were not authorized to do so.

Recognizing this conflict, the United States Supreme Court in *Payton* rendered a decision which in effect declared a New York statute authorizing police officers to enter private residences without a warrant and with force if necessary to make routine felony arrests to be unconstitutional as inconsistent with the Fourth Amendment. In the two New York cases which reached the Supreme Court, police officers acting with probable cause but without warrants had gone to the appellants' residences to arrest the appellants on felony charges and had entered the premises without the consent of the occupant. In each case the New York trial judge had held that the warrantless entry was authorized by New York statutes and refused to suppress evidence that was seized upon entry. In both instances the cases were treated as involving routine arrests in which there was ample time to obtain a warrant and no exigent circumstances were claimed.

First the Supreme Court of the United States narrowed the scope of this case by pointing out that they had no occasion to consider:

(1) the authority to enter premises to make an arrest where *exigent* circumstances existed;
(2) the right of the police officers to enter a third party's home;
(3) the question of probable cause to believe that the suspect was home when the officers entered; or
(4) whether consent was given by anyone on the premises.

In answer to the narrow question as to whether a statute authorizing police officers to enter a home of a suspect without consent to make a routine felony arrest is constitutional, the Supreme Court in distinguishing between arrest in public places and entry into places of residence concluded:

> In terms that apply equally to seizures of property and seizure of persons, the Fourth Amendment has drawn a firm line at the entrance to the house. Absent exigent circumstances, that threshold may not reasonably be crossed without a warrant.

The holding of the Supreme Court, succinctly stated, comes from the case itself:

> We now reverse the New York Court of Appeals and hold that the Fourth Amendment to the United States Constitution made applicable to the states by the Fourteenth Amendment . . . prohibits

the police from making a warrantless and non-consensual entry into a suspect's home in order to make a routine felony arrest.

Mr. Justice White with whom Mr. Justice Rehnquist joins, logically points out the confusion that could result from this rule with the warning that the "policeman on his beat must now make subtle discriminations that perplex even judges in their chambers." Mr. Justice White explained that the uncertainty inherent in the exigent circumstances determination burdens the judicial system. He elaborates with these words:

> Today's decision, therefore, sweeps away any possibility that warrantless home entries might be permitted in some limited situations other than those in which exigent circumstances are present. The Court substitutes, in one sweeping decision, a rigid constitutional rule in place of the common-law approach, evolved over hundreds of years, which achieved a flexible accommodation between the demands of personal privacy and the legitimate needs of law enforcement.

Unfortunately, the majority of the court does not define what is meant by "exigent circumstances." The only light shed on this question is in the dissenting opinion where the dissenting justices caution that:

> Under today's decision, whenever the police have made a warrantless home arrest there will be the possibility of "endless litigation with respect to the existence of exigent circumstances, whether it was practicable to get a warrant, whether the suspect was about to flee, and the like...."

Reiterating the decision it made in the *Payton* case, the Supreme Court in 1984 again declared an entry into a home to make an arrest without a warrant to be in violation of the Fourth Amendment.[92] In the case of *Welch v. Wisconsin*, the defendant had run off the road and abandoned his car on the side of the road. Investigating officers learned from witnesses that the defendant was either intoxicated or ill. They then checked the car registration and learned that the defendant lived close by and, without obtaining a warrant, went to the home to arrest him.

Although it turned out that the defendant's driver's license had been suspended and that previously he had been charged with being intoxicated, the officers did not know this at the time they entered the home to make the

---

92 Welch v. Wisconsin, 466 U.S. 470, 104 S. Ct. 2091, 80 L. Ed. 2d 732 (1984).

arrest. The state claimed that the arrest in the home was justified as there were exigent circumstances in that the alcohol content of the blood would have dissipated had the arrest been delayed.

The Wisconsin Supreme Court upheld the action of the officers, indicating there were exigent circumstances, that the officers were in "hot pursuit," that there was a need to prevent physical harm to the suspect, and that the public need to prevent destruction of evidence of intoxication justified the entry.

The majority of the Supreme Court, with Justice Blackmun as the spokesman, pointed out that there was no immediate pursuit of the defendant from the scene, nor was there a need to protect either the public or the defendant inasmuch as he had abandoned the vehicle and was home sleeping. The Justices explained that the need to protect evidence does not justify the warrantless intrusion, that there were no exigent circumstances as required in the *Payton* case. The Court again cautioned that before government agents may invade the sanctity of the home, the burden is on the government to demonstrate exigent circumstances that overcome the presumption of unreasonableness that attaches to all warrantless home searches.

The Court emphasized that an entry of the suspect's premises without a warrant is *per se* unreasonable, unless the police can show the presence of exigent circumstances. While the Court did not define exigent circumstances, it did shed some light on what is considered in determining exigent circumstances. The Court mentioned these examples:

(1) hot pursuit of a fleeing felon,
(2) possible destruction of evidence, and
(3) an ongoing fire.

The Court also, in citing other cases, indicated that in determining exigency one must consider the gravity of the underlying offense thought to be in progress, whether life or security is endangered, the time of the offense, the time of the arrest, and if there is any threat to public safety.

A North Carolina Court of Appeals was unwilling to find the warrantless arrest in a hotel room illegal when the officers had probable cause to arrest the defendants for participation in more than one serious offense and the defendant was about to check out of the motel and leave the area. These factors constituted "exigent circumstances" to justify entry into the motel room.[93]

To summarize the decisions of the Supreme Court relating to the entry into a home to make an arrest without a warrant, this is the current rule:

---

93 State v. Wallace, 71 N.C. App. 681, 323 S.E.2d 403 (1985).

Without an arrest warrant, an officer may not enter the home of a suspect to make an arrest even on probable cause unless there are exigent circumstances or consent is given to enter by someone in authority. Also without an arrest warrant the officer may not legally enter the home of a third party to make an arrest of the suspect unless a search warrant for the home of the third party has been issued, he has consent of one in charge of the premises, or exigent circumstances exist.

§ 3.12 The citation and summons in law enforcement

The making and completion of an arrest consume many hours of police time. When a physical arrest is made, the person charged with an offense must be taken to the station or holdover, a complaint must be filed, he must be booked, and finally, provision must be made for his release on bail or on his own recognizance. Frequently, the needs of adequate law enforcement may be met by issuing a citation rather than physically arresting every minor lawbreaker.

Although the term "citation" was used in Roman law, the issuance of citations in this country is of relatively recent origin. Recognizing the practicalities of the citation, the practice was first sanctioned in this country when traffic citations were issued. Even when the practice became recognized by statute, the citation was issued primarily in traffic cases until relatively recently.

Some of the advantages of a citation over a physical arrest are that it:

(1) saves the officer the considerable time and trouble in taking an individual to a place where he can be detained,

(2) does not impose the unnecessary indignity of bodily arrest upon those who are not criminals in any real or serious sense, and

(3) will help to elevate the public image of law enforcement officers by lessening the antagonism between the public and the police.

While the earlier statutes authorized the use of a citation only in traffic cases, the more recent statutes have recognized the advantages of the citation and extended their use to other misdemeanor offenses. Where the facts indicate that there is a high probability that the offender will honor the citation and appear in court, issuance of the citation is the preferable procedure to follow.

While the purpose to be served by issuing a citation is recognized in practically all states, the procedures differ from state to state. Some examples of state statutes will underscore these similarities and differences. The Ohio Revised Code provides that:[94]

> (A) Notwithstanding any other provision of the Revised Code, when a law enforcement officer is otherwise authorized to arrest a person for the commission of a minor misdemeanor, the officer shall not arrest the person, but shall issue a citation, unless one of the following applies:
>
> (1) The offender requires medical care or is unable to provide for his own safety.
> (2) The offender cannot or will not offer satisfactory evidence of his identity.
> (3) The offender refuses to sign the citation.
> (4) The offender has previously been issued a citation for the commission of that misdemeanor and has failed to do one of the following:
>
> (a) Appear at the time and place stated in the citation;
> (b) Comply with division (C) of this section.
>
> (B) The citation shall contain all of the following:
>
> (1) The name and address of the offender;
> (2) A description of the offense and the numerical designation of the applicable statute or ordinance;
> (3) The name of the person issuing the citation;
> (4) An order for the offender to appear at a stated time and place;
> (5) A notice that the offender may comply with division (C) of this section in lieu of appearing at the stated time and place;
> (6) A notice that the offender is required to do one of the following and that he may be arrested if he fails to do one of them:
>
> (a) Appear at the time and place stated in the citation;
> (b) Comply with division (C) of this section.

[94] OHIO REV. STAT. ANN. § 2935.26 (Anderson 1988).

(C) In lieu of appearing at the time and place stated in the citation, the offender may, within seven days after the date of issuance of the citation, do either of the following:

(1) Appear in person at the office of the clerk of the court stated in the citation, sign a plea of guilty and a waiver of trial provision that is on the citation, and pay the total amount of the fine and costs;

(2) Sign the guilty plea and waiver of trial provision of the citation, and mail the citation and a check or money order for the total amount of the fine and costs to the office of the clerk of the court stated in the citation.

Remittance by mail of the fine and costs to the office of the clerk of the court stated in the citation constitutes a guilty plea and waiver of trial whether or not the guilty plea and waiver of trial provision of the citation are signed by the defendant.

(D) A law enforcement officer who issues a citation shall complete and sign a citation form, serve a copy of the completed form upon the offender and, without unnecessary delay, file the original citation with the court having jurisdiction over the offense.

(E) Each court shall establish a fine schedule that shall list the fine for each minor misdemeanor, and state the court costs. The fine schedule shall be prominently posted in the place where minor misdemeanor fines are paid.

(F) If an offender fails to appear and does not comply with division (C) of this section, the court may issue a supplemental citation, or a summons or warrant for the arrest of the offender pursuant to the Criminal Rules. Supplemental citations shall be in the form prescribed by division (B) of this section, but shall be issued and signed by the clerk of the court at which the citation directed the offender to appear and shall be served in the same manner as a summons.

As indicated in this statute and in the title, a citation is used *rather* than an arrest but provides that the offender may be arrested if he fails to comply with the terms of the statute. The statute gives preference to the use of a citation in misdemeanor cases unless certain specific conditions exist. It also requires that the officer include, among other things, a description of the offense and the numerical designation of the applicable statute or ordinance.

In interpreting this provision the Ohio court has affirmed that a uniform traffic ticket properly charges the defendant with the offense when it describes the nature of the offense as "DWI" and makes reference to the ordinance that gives rise to the offense, even if it does not indicate the substance that caused the defendant to be intoxicated.[95]

A somewhat different statute is that of North Carolina. It provides:[96]

§ 15A-302. Citation.

(a) Definition. -- A citation is a directive, issued by a law enforcement officer or other person authorized by statute, that a person appear in court and answer a misdemeanor or infraction charge or charges.

(b) When Issued. -- An officer may issue a citation to any person who he has probable cause to believe has committed a misdemeanor or infraction.

(c) Contents. -- The citation must:

(1) Identify the crime charged, including the date, and where material, identify the property and other persons involved,
(2) Contain the name and address of the person cited, or other identification if that cannot be ascertained,
(3) Identify the officer issuing the citation, and
(4) Cite the person to whom issued to appear in a designated court, at a designated time and date.

(d) Service. -- A copy of the citation shall be delivered to the person cited who may sign a receipt on the original which shall thereafter be filed with the clerk by the officer. If the cited person refuses to sign, the officer shall certify delivery of the citation by signing the original, which shall thereafter be filed with the clerk. Failure of the person cited to sign the citation shall not constitute grounds for his arrest or the requirement that he post a bond.

(e) Dismissal by Prosecutor. -- If the prosecutor finds that no crime or infraction is charged in the citation, or that there is insufficient evidence to warrant prosecution, he may dismiss the charge and so notify the person cited. An appropriate entry must be made in the records of the clerk. It is not neces-

---

95 478 N.E.2d 803 (Ohio 1985).

96 N.C. GEN. STAT. § 15A-302 (1985).

sary to enter the dismissal in open court or to obtain consent of the judge.

(f) Citation No Bar to Criminal Summons or Warrant. -- If the offense is a misdemeanor, a criminal summons or a warrant may issue notwithstanding the prior issuance of a citation for the same offense.

The issuance of the citation is not an arrest; however, an arrest warrant or criminal summons may be issued if the person fails to appear in court at the time stated on the citation. It is noted in the official commentary that follows the North Carolina statute that, as the citation is issued by a law enforcement officer, contempt of court may not be used to enforce obedience to its direction to appear, "thus other criminal process may be issued if the defendant does not appear."

Another statute which authorizes the use of the citation is that of Kentucky. It provides:[97]

431.450 Uniform citation.

(1) The department of state police in consultation with the transportation cabinet shall design, print, and distribute to all law enforcement agencies in the Commonwealth a uniform citation.

(2) The citation shall:

(a) Be approved by the Supreme Court;
(b) Consist of an original document and five (5) copies;
(c) Be serially numbered in such a manner that the year of issue and the individual citation number may be readily ascertained; and
(d) Contain such other information as may be required by the Supreme Court.

(3) The circuit court clerk shall maintain a system of accountability for all citations issued in accordance with rules and regulations issued by the Supreme Court to assure that citations are not wrongfully destroyed, tampered with, or otherwise compromised in any manner.

---

97 KY. REV. STAT. ANN. § 431.450 (Michie/Bobbs-Merrill 1985 & Supp. 1988).

(4) All peace officers in the Commonwealth shall use the uniform citation for all violations of the traffic laws and for all felonies, misdemeanors and violations.

The Kentucky statute does not include specific directions concerning the use of citations but allows the State Police, with the Transportation Cabinet and with the approval of the Supreme Court, the authority to prepare and distribute a Uniform Citation Form.

As a general rule, the use of the citation does not enlarge the officer's authority to make an arrest without a warrant. For example, the Ohio statute provides that the officer may issue a citation when he is otherwise authorized to arrest a person for commission of a minor misdemeanor. However, in some states the statute provides for the issuance of a citation where a physical arrest would not be authorized. In fact, in North Carolina "failure of the person cited to sign the citation shall not constitute grounds for arrest or the requirement that he post a bond."

As previously indicated, the citation has a definite place in the criminal justice process and should be used when practical, even in minor felony situations. However, it is essential that criminal justice personnel be familiar with the statutes of the states in which they practice and comply with the provisions of the respective statutes.

§ 3.13 Fresh pursuit as extending the power of arrest

As a general rule, the peace officer has no official power to apprehend offenders beyond the boundaries of the county or district for which he has been appointed. However, both the common law and most statutes recognize a limited exception to this rule when an officer is in "fresh" or "hot" pursuit of a suspect who is fleeing to avoid apprehension. The doctrine of fresh pursuit arose out of necessity; and the instances of its application are becoming more frequent today as the means of rapid transportation improve.

Fresh pursuit has been defined as "pursuit without unreasonable interruption" or "the immediate pursuit of a person who is endeavoring to avoid arrest." At common law the doctrine of fresh pursuit applied only to felony cases. Although a few states retain the common-law limitation, the majority of the states recognize the right of a peace officer to pursue one who has committed any offense, including a misdemeanor, across corporate or county lines anywhere *within* the state if the pursuit is immediate and continuous.

Because of the nature of our federal system, no state can confer on its officers any power which is effective in another state. Before a peace officer can act as an officer of another state, there must be a statute existing in the second state which confers authority on an officer entering that state in fresh pursuit.

In recent years there has been a trend among the states toward increased cooperation in the area of law enforcement. Many states have adopted the Uniform Fresh Pursuit Act or similar legislation permitting law enforcement officers from other states who enter their state in fresh pursuit to make an arrest. For example, the Iowa Code provides:

> Any member of a duly organized state, county, or municipal law-enforcing unit of another state of the United States who enters this state in fresh pursuit, and continues within this state in such fresh pursuit, of a person in order to arrest him on the ground that he is believed to have committed a felony in such other state, shall have the same authority to arrest and hold such person in custody, as has any member of any duly organized state, county, or municipal law enforcing unit of this state, to arrest and hold in custody a person on the ground that he is believed to have committed a felony in this state.[98]

A few states extend the privilege to out-of-state officers to make an arrest in fresh pursuit only on a reciprocity basis. An officer entering one of these states can make an arrest only if his own state has adopted similar legislation which would permit an officer from the second state to make an arrest in fresh pursuit there. To understand the exact territorial limits of his authority, an officer should be familiar not only with his local statutes, but with the fresh pursuit statutes of all neighboring states.

The right of fresh pursuit across state boundary lines is generally confined by statute to felonies. An officer pursuing a fleeing misdemeanant must end his pursuit at the state line. Illinois is one of the few states which permits out-of-state law enforcement officers in fresh pursuit to cross its borders in order to make an arrest for a misdemeanor. There seems to be no logical reason why other states should not authorize fresh pursuit arrests for misdemeanors as well as felonies.

Because of the differences in the laws of the various states, the officer who might have the opportunity to follow a suspect into another state on fresh pursuit must know the laws of the surrounding states. The fact that the officer's own state authorizes officers from other states to come into that state in fresh pursuit and make either felony or misdemeanor arrests does not mean that the other bordering states reciprocate. For example, although a peace officer from the states surrounding the state of Illinois may enter Illi-

---

98 IOWA CODE ANN. § 806 (1988).

nois and make an arrest for a misdemeanor, officers from Illinois do not have that same privilege in the surrounding states. A police officer from Illinois entering Kentucky on fresh pursuit has very little protection because the Commonwealth of Kentucky has not adopted any uniform fresh pursuit act. Therefore, in Kentucky, the Illinois officer has only the authority to arrest as a private citizen, and as a private citizen he may make an arrest only when a felony in fact has been committed. In this situation, the officer entering the neighboring state while in fresh pursuit of a speeder is merely another speeder.

§ 3.14 Use of force in making an arrest

In determining the amount of force justified, the arresting officer considers all of the circumstances such as the type of offense, the accused's reputation, his words or actions, and whether he is armed. The United States Supreme Court has made it clear that the reasonableness of a seizure of the person depends not only on when the seizure is made, but also how it is carried out.[99]

In arriving at some general principles concerning the use of force, courts have applied a balancing process to determine whether the circumstances justify a particular arrest or seizure of the person. It is apparent that more force will be justified in making an arrest for a serious felony than would be authorized to consummate an arrest for a minor misdemeanor. As was noted in the case of *Tennessee v. Garner* which is discussed in the following paragraphs:[100]

> One other aspect of the common law rule bears emphasis. It forbids the use of deadly force to apprehend a misdemeanant, condemning such action as disproportionately severe.

In 1985, the Supreme Court handed down a landmark decision regarding the use of force in making an arrest. Prior to 1985 many states followed the common law rule relating to the use of deadly force which allowed the use of whatever force was necessary to effect the arrest of a fleeing felon. Some states followed the modified common law rule which generally allowed the use of deadly force to make an arrest for a felony only if:

---

99 United States v. Ortiz, 422 U.S. 891, 95 S. Ct. 2590, 45 L. Ed. 2d 630 (1975).

100 Tennessee v. Garner, 471 U.S. 1, 105 S. Ct. 1694, 95 L. Ed. 2d 1 (1985). *See* case in Part II.

(1) the suspect was attempting to escape by use of deadly force,
(2) the suspect indicated that he would endanger human life, or
(3) the suspect had committed a dangerous or atrocious felony.

A third group of states had followed the Model Penal Code which justified the use of deadly force to effect a felony arrest only when:

(1) the officer believes that the force employed creates no substantial risk of injury to innocent persons, and
(2) the officer believes the crime for which the arrest is made involves conduct, including the use of threatened use of deadly force, or the officer believes there is a substantial risk that the person to be arrested would cause death or serious bodily harm if his apprehension is delayed.

In the *Garner* case, the state court found the use of deadly force was justified under the Tennessee statute which followed the common law rule. This state statute provided that, "If, after notice of the intention to arrest the defendant, he either flees or forcibly resists, the officer may use all the necessary means to effect the arrest." Both the Tennessee statute and the department policy allowed the use of deadly force in making a burglary arrest.

The facts of the Tennessee case indicate that a Memphis police officer shot and killed Garner after he was told to halt and after the fleeing suspect, at night, climbed over a fence in the backyard of a house he was suspected of burglarizing. The officer testified that he saw no signs of a weapon and, though not certain, was "reasonably sure" and "figured" that Garner was unarmed. Here there was little doubt as to the fact that the burglary actually occurred, as a purse taken from the house was found on the body of the suspect. However, there was also no indication that the officer's life or anyone else's life was in danger.

In rejecting the reasoning that the common law rule should still apply, the Supreme Court made this comment:

> The use of deadly force to prevent the escape of all felony suspects, whatever the circumstances, is constitutionally unreasonable. It is not better that all felony suspects die than that they escape. When a suspect poses no immediate threat to the officer and no threat to others, the harm resulting from failing to apprehend him does not justify the use of deadly force to do so. It is no doubt unfortunate when a suspect who is in sight escapes, but the fact that the police arrive a little late or are a little slower afoot does not always justify

> killing the suspect. A police officer may not seize an unarmed, non-dangerous suspect by shooting him dead.

In the *Garner* case, the Court handed down a decision which must be followed in all states. This means that some states must modify their laws to conform with the decision. The Court did not hold the Tennessee statute unconstitutional as written but unconstitutional as applied in this case. In positively stating what can be done, the Court made this comment:

> Thus, if the suspect threatens the officer with a weapon, or there is probable cause to believe that he has committed a crime involving the infliction or threatened infliction of serious physical harm, deadly force may be used, if necessary, to prevent escape, and, if where feasible, some warning has been given.

In applying the *Garner* rule, a Federal Court agreed that a police officer had probable cause to fire upon a fleeing felon, even though the officer could not actually see the felon's gun, where the officer observed the employees inside of a bank holding their hands above their heads during the commission of an offense, as the felon posed a threat to the entire community.[101] In this case the federal court quoted the paragraph stated above and reasoned that when the officer responded to a radio dispatch reporting a robbery in progress at the First National Bank and upon arriving at the scene, observed the suspect in a stocking mask threatening the institution's employees, he was justified in using deadly force to apprehend the suspect.

§ 3.15 Police authority to detain

1. *General concepts*

For many years police administrators and judges have been wrestling with the question surrounding the right of the police officer to stop a suspect under circumstances where there were not sufficient grounds for an actual arrest. Although it was common practice for police officers to stop and question a suspect under such circumstances, the courts and legal writers were, until recently, sharply divided as to whether such a right in fact existed and, if it did exist, its precise limitations. There is still much confusion in this area, but police officers today can act with substantial authority. In the case

---

101 Ford v. Childers, 650 F. Supp. 110 (C.D. Ill. 1986).

of *Terry v. Ohio*,[102] the Court squarely faced this problem and laid down some general rules.

The facts of the *Terry* case are very similar to those of thousands of other cases where police officers are confronted with situations which require that they take some action. Here, while patrolling the streets in downtown Cleveland, the officer observed three men "casing a job, a stick-up." The activities of the suspects -- looking in the store window, walking a short distance, turning back, peering in the same store window and returning to confer -- caused the officer to determine that a further inquiry was justified. He therefore approached the three men, identified himself as a police officer and asked their names. When the men mumbled something in response to his inquiry, the officer grabbed the petitioner, spun him around, and patted down the outside of his clothing. Feeling a pistol in the pocket of Terry's overcoat, the officer reached inside the overcoat but was unable to remove the gun. He ordered Terry to remove the overcoat and then retrieved a .38-caliber revolver. He testified that he only patted the men down to see whether they had weapons.

The Court acknowledged that the question before them was a difficult and troublesome one. In approving the detention of the suspects, the majority of the Court held:

> A police officer may in appropriate circumstances and in an appropriate manner approach a person for purposes of investigating possibly criminal behavior even though there is no probable cause to make an arrest.

Thus, the Supreme Court has upheld the authority of the police officer to stop or detain a person when he observes unusual conduct which leads him reasonably to conclude in light of his experience that criminal activity may be afoot. The Court went on to explain that if he has this right to detain, he must necessarily have the right to protect himself and others while conducting a carefully limited search of the outer clothing in an attempt to discover weapons which may be used to assault him.

This does not authorize a police officer to detain anyone on mere suspicion. The officer must be able to articulate the reasons for his belief that criminal activity was being planned or was in the process of being executed. The Court did say, however, that the officer could give weight to his experience, and to the reasonable inference which he is entitled to draw from the facts, in light of that experience.

---

102 392 U.S. 1, 88 S. Ct. 1868, 20 L. Ed. 2d 889 (1968). *See* case in Part II.

Reaffirming that the police may rely upon their experience and the experience of other enforcement personnel, the Supreme Court in 1989 approved the detention of a suspected drug carrier at the Honolulu International Airport.[103] In this case the officers had information that the suspect had:

(1) paid $2,100 for two airplane tickets from a roll of twenty-dollar bills;
(2) traveled under a name that did not match the name under which the telephone number was listed;
(3) gave his original destination as Miami, a source for illegal drugs;
(4) stayed in Miami for only 48 hours, even though a round trip from Honolulu to Miami takes twenty hours;
(5) appeared nervous during this trip; and
(6) checked none of his luggage.

The Supreme Court was called upon to determine whether the agents had a reasonable suspicion that the respondent was engaged in wrongdoing when they encountered him along the sidewalk so as to bring the case within the purview of *Terry v. Ohio*.

While again emphasizing that the officer must be able to articulate something more than an "inchoate or unparticularized suspicion or hunch" the court agreed that the level of suspicion required for a *Terry* stop is obviously less demanding than that for probable cause. Also, the level of suspicion required to detain is considerably less than proof of wrongdoing by a preponderance of the evidence. Applying the "totality of circumstances" -- the whole picture -- test, the Court noted that while none of the circumstances standing alone may have justified the *Terry*-type stop in this case, considered together they amount to reasonable suspicion.

In discussing the drug courier profiles, the court explained that the decision approving the detention was not somehow changed by the agent's belief that his behavior was consistent with one of the DEA's "drug courier profiles" while the existence of reasonable suspicion requires the agent to articulate the factors leading to his conclusions, the fact that these factors may be set forth in a "profile" does not somehow detract from the evidentiary significance as seen by a trained agent. Applying the reasoning to this case the court concluded that:

---

[103] United States v. Sokolow, ___ U.S. ___, 109 S. Ct. 1581, ___ L. Ed. 2d ___ (1989). *See* case in Part II.

> We hold that the agents had a reasonable basis to suspect that the respondent was transporting illegal drugs on these facts.

The authority to detain as explained in the *Terry* case is not based upon any state statute or constitutional provision as such. The Court explained that this was in fact a stop and seizure within the meaning of the Fourth Amendment, but that such detention in the circumstances that existed here was "reasonable."[104]

Since the *Terry* case was decided by the Supreme Court, many lower courts have rendered decisions interpreting this case. In some instances the lower courts have found that officers have abused the privilege to detain as discussed in the *Terry* case, while others have recognized practical necessities and have approved stopping motorists as well as pedestrians under the *Terry* reasoning.

The *Terry* rationale and the general authority to arrest on reasonable grounds can often be combined to give the officer authority to stop and then arrest. In certain circumstances, the suspicion of the officer may be aroused, but he does not have the authority to make an arrest because he doesn't have the required reasonable grounds. Often, however, he does have the authority as defined in the *Terry* case to detain the suspect. If during the period of detention, additional facts are uncovered which supply reasonable grounds or probable cause to arrest, the arrest, of course, can be consummated.

The officer who is well acquainted with the authority to ask questions as explained in the *Terry* case and the authority to arrest can, in the vast majority of the cases, reasonably determine if the proper procedure is to detain, arrest, or take no immediate action.

Although the detention in the *Terry* case involved a pedestrian on the street, there is no reason why the same rationale could not be applied where the detention is to be in a building. The Bronx County Supreme Court in New York has logically reasoned that the "stop and frisk" rationale must also apply within private living quarters.[105] The court in this case explained that the dangers in a closed apartment are even greater than they are on a sidewalk. Again, the court pointed out that the officers must, of course, be able to point to specific facts upon which to base their belief that criminal activity was afoot.

The Supreme Court in 1980 reviewed the authority to stop a person as discussed in the *Terry* case and further explained the point at which a person is "seized." The majority adhered to the view that a person is "seized" only

---

104 The scope of the frisk doctrine is discussed in Chapter 4 which deals with search and seizure (at § 4.16).

105 People v. Henry, Bronx County Supreme Court, N.Y., decided Oct. 20, 1968.

when, by means of physical force or a show of authority, his freedom of movement is restrained. The reasoning is that:

> The purpose of the Fourth Amendment is not to eliminate all contact between the police and the citizenry, but to prevent arbitrary and oppressive interference by enforcement officers with the privacy and personal security of individuals.[106]

The Court restated the proposition that there is nothing in the Constitution which prevents a policeman from addressing questions to anyone on the street even without the authority to stop, as expressed in the *Terry* case. It cautioned, however, that the person addressed has an equal right to ignore his interrogator and walk away unless there is authority to detain or arrest.

Recent cases have removed some of the doubt concerning the authority of a police officer to detain without making an arrest. Nevertheless, the officer is still limited not only as to the initial detention but as to the length of the detention. In any event, he must act reasonably and not overstep his authority.

In 1983 the United States Supreme Court elaborated on the "street identification requirement" standards. In the case of *Kolender v. Lawson*, the defendant challenged a California Penal Code section, which provided that:

> Every person...is guilty of disorderly conduct, a misdemeanor...who loiters or wanders upon the streets or from place to place without apparent reason or business and who refuses to identify himself and to account for his presence when requested by any police officer to do so, if the surrounding circumstances are such as to indicate to a reasonable man that the public safety demands such identification.[107]

The Court found that the statute was unconstitutional as in violation of the due process clause as a vested virtually complete discretion in the hands of the police to determine whether the statute had been violated. While, according to the courts, the stop might be justified if the requirements of the *Terry* case were met, requiring the suspect to comply with the identification requirements went too far.

---

[106] United States v. Mendenhall, 446 U.S. 554, 100 S. Ct. 1870, 64 L. Ed. 2d 497 (1980).

[107] Kolender v. Lawson, 461 U.S. 352, 103 S. Ct. 1855, 75 L. Ed. 903 (1983).

2. Legislation concerning detention

In an attempt to add clarity to an area fraught with confusion, a few states had, prior to the *Terry* decision, adopted legislation defining and limiting the right to stop and question. Since the decision in *Terry v. Ohio*, additional states have adopted legislation clarifying the right of the officer to detain and to frisk. Two examples of such legislation are here discussed.

(a) The Uniform Arrest Act

The Uniform Arrest Act adopted by the Interstate Commission on Crime contains the following provisions concerning detention:

> I. A peace officer may stop any person abroad whom he has reasonable ground to suspect is committing, has committed or is about to commit a crime, and may demand of him his name, address, business abroad and whither he is going.
>
> II. Any person so questioned who fails to identify himself or explain his actions to the satisfaction of the officer stopping him may be detained and further questioned and investigated.
>
> III. The total period of detention provided for by this section shall not exceed two hours. Such detention is not an arrest and shall not be recorded as an arrest in any official record. At the end of the detention period the person so detained shall be released unless arrested and charged with a crime.

This type of statute has been adopted by Rhode Island, New Hampshire and Delaware. The constitutionality of the detention provisions of the Uniform Arrest Act has been upheld by the Supreme Courts of both Delaware and Rhode Island, but the Supreme Court of the United States has not reviewed a case in which this issue was presented. The Delaware and Rhode Island courts, in construing the statute, attempted to distinguish the procedures authorized by the act from the technical arrest. They explained that the detention is not recorded as an arrest and the person is not formally charged with a crime.

Although this provision has not been specifically upheld by the Supreme Court of the United States, the stopping which is authorized by this act was upheld in the *Terry* case discussed in the previous section. However, the Supreme Court did not approve the two-hour detention period and the constitutionality of this section of the act remains open to speculation.

(b) The "Stop and Frisk" Act

In response to demands of law enforcement agencies for a greater measure of certainty in the area of permissible investigatory conduct, the New York Legislature in 1964 enacted a statute which is commonly referred to as the "Stop and Frisk" Act. This act authorizes a police officer to stop a suspect when he reasonably suspects such person is committing or will commit a certain crime.

Provisions of the Stop and Frisk Act do not permit an officer to stop and question on mere caprice or whim. The test employed under the act is "reasonable suspicion." An officer is justified in detaining one whom he "reasonably suspects" is committing, has committed, or is about to commit certain specified crimes.

In the case of *Sibron v. New York*,[108] the Supreme Court of the United States discussed the New York Stop and Frisk Act. The Court acknowledged that the state is free to develop its own law to meet the needs of local law enforcement and may call the standards it employs by any name it may choose. But the Court went on to explain that the state may not authorize police conduct which violates Fourth Amendment rights regardless of the labels which it attaches to such conduct. Applying this reasoning, the Supreme Court refused to make any pronouncement on the facial constitutionality of the New York Stop and Frisk Act but did not find that it was unconstitutional as applied in this particular case. In upholding the stop, the Court stated in *Sibron*:

> We have held today in *Terry v. Ohio*...that police conduct of the sort with which section 180-a deals must be judged under the Reasonable Search and Seizure Clause of the Fourteenth Amendment.

In a concurring opinion Mr. Justice Harlan stated that the statute is certainly not unconstitutional on its face.

It is clear from the cases that states may enact legislation setting out the standards to be followed by police officers when stopping persons for investigation purposes. But if a statute is written which authorizes detention, the statute must comply with the rules as established by the Supreme Court. One statute was challenged as not meeting these standards. It provided:

---

108 392 U.S. 40, 88 S. Ct. 1889, 20 L. Ed. 2d 917 (1968).

> A person commits an offense if he intentionally refuses to report or gives a false report of his name and residence to a peace officer who has lawfully stopped him and requested the information.[109]

This statute, which was used by a Texas officer as authority to stop a person and ascertain his identity, was declared unconstitutional as applied.[110] The court cautioned that, notwithstanding the statute, before a person can be stopped as provided in *Terry v. Ohio*, there must be a reasonable, articulable suspicion that a crime had just been, was being, or was about to be committed. Detaining the appellant and requiring him to identify himself violated the Fourth Amendment because the officers lacked any reasonable suspicion to believe appellant was engaged or had engaged in criminal conduct. The court concluded:

> Accordingly, appellant may not be punished for refusing to identify himself, and the conviction is reversed.

What if the officer detains a person based on the authority of a statute or ordinance which is later declared unconstitutional? Is he criminally or civilly liable? The United States Supreme Court in 1979 rendered a decision which gives some needed protection to criminal justice personnel. There the Court held that even though the statute is declared unconstitutional at a later date on vagueness grounds, the officer, who acts in good faith under the statute, is protected.[111] In this case the Court made a statement which should give criminal justice personnel some protection. The exact wording is:

> Police are charged to enforce laws until and unless they are declared unconstitutional. The enactment of a law forecloses speculation by enforcement officers concerning its constitutionality -- with the possible exception of a law so grossly and flagrantly unconstitutional that any person of reasonable prudence would be bound to see its flaws. Society would be ill-served if its police officers took it upon themselves to determine which laws are and which are not constitutionally entitled to enforcement.

While police officers are generally not subject to liability for enforcing laws that have not been declared unconstitutional, they may be civilly or criminally liable for taking action when the laws under which they justify their

---

109 TEX. PENAL CODE ANN. § 38.02 (Vernon 1989)

110 Brown v. Texas, 443 U.S. 47, 99 S. Ct. 2637, 61 L. Ed. 2d 357 (1979).

111 Michigan v. DeFillipo, 443 U.S. 31, 99 S. Ct. 2627, 61 L. Ed. 2d 313 (1979).

action have been declared unconstitutional. To avoid criminal liability, civil liability and the exclusion of evidence, officers should be familiar with the changing laws and compile contemporaneous and detailed records which can later be used in articulating justification for an arrest or a detention.

3. *Authority to detain motorists*

Because automobiles are frequently used both as a means for perpetrating crime and as an instrument of escape, the courts in recent years have had to reckon with the special problems involved in the detention of motorists. Strictly speaking, stopping a moving vehicle comes closer to the definition of arrest than does a casual approach to a pedestrian on the street. When a pedestrian is confronted by a police officer who wants to ask a few questions, he can generally continue on his course during the conversation. On the other hand, when the driver of a motor vehicle is forced off the road or directed to stop by a siren, his freedom of locomotion has been impeded without his consent for the duration of the interview.

There is no doubt that a police officer may arrest the driver of an automobile under the same authority that he can make an arrest of a pedestrian -- that is, if he has a warrant of arrest; if he has reasonable grounds to believe that a felony has been committed; or if a misdemeanor is committed in his presence. But in many instances it is desirable to have the right to stop an automobile for the purpose of asking questions on grounds which might not amount to a basis for arrest.

(a) Reasonable suspicion of criminal activity

Although the facts in the case of *Terry v. Ohio*[112] concerned the detention of a pedestrian on a street, there seems to be no valid reason why this same reasoning cannot be applied in an automobile situation. Agreeing that stopping automobiles intruded upon the privacy of individuals, the Supreme Court nevertheless acknowledged the necessity of such intrusion in the case of *United States v. Cortez.*[113] In the *Cortez* case the officers stopped a pickup truck which..., in view of their experience and investigation, they believed was carrying illegal aliens. After the stop, the suspect Cortez voluntarily opened the door of the camper and the officers then discovered the illegal aliens. Prior to trial on charges of transporting illegal aliens, the defendants sought to suppress the evidence of the presence of the aliens discovered as the result

---

[112] 392 U.S. 1, 88 S. Ct. 1868, 20 L. Ed. 2d 889 (1968).

[113] 449 U.S. 411, 101 S. Ct. 690, 66 L. Ed. 2d 621 (1981).

of the stopping of the vehicle, contending that the officers did not have cause to make the investigative stop. The district court denied the motion and the respondents were convicted but the Court of Appeals reversed, holding the officers lacked a sufficient basis to justify stopping the vehicle.

In approving the detention of the vehicle, the Supreme Court made some significant observations that are of special importance to criminal justice personnel. First, the court reasoned that the investigatory stop as explained in the case of *Terry v. Ohio* does apply in automobile situations. As to the quantum and quality of evidence required to justify the investigatory stop, the court made this comment:

> Courts have used a variety of terms to capture the elusive concept of what cause is sufficient to authorize police to stop a person. Terms like "articulable reasons" and "founded suspicion" are not self-defining; they fall short of providing clear guidance dispositive of the myriad factual situations that arise. But the essence of all that has been written is that the totality of circumstances -- the whole picture -- must be taken into account. Based upon that whole picture the detaining officer must have a particularized and objective basis for suspecting the particular person stopped of criminal activity.

What the court said is that in order to make a *Terry*-type stop, the officer must make an assessment of the situation based upon all circumstances. From this assessment the trained officer may then draw inferences and make deductions. However, in making these deductions, the evidence collected may be weighed not in terms of library analyses by scholars, but as understood by those versed in the field of law enforcement.

One part of the opinion places the Court's stamp of approval on the ability of trained enforcement officers to assess facts differently from the untrained layperson, using these words:

> It implicates all of the principles just discussed -- especially the imperative of recognizing that, when used by trained law enforcement officers, objective facts, meaningless to the untrained, can be combined with permissible deductions from such facts to form legitimate basis for suspicion of a particular person and for action on that suspicion.

Having recognized the necessity to investigate criminal activity and having applied the *Terry* rule to automobile situations, the Supreme Court in 1985 considered the authority of police officers to detain a vehicle on the authority of a "wanted flier" issued by another department in another state.[114] In the *Hensley* case a police officer in a Cincinnati suburb issued a wanted flyer to other departments in the area based on reasonable and reliable information that the automobile described was involved in a robbery. The flyer stated that the suspect was wanted for investigation, described the suspect, and gave the date and location of robbery. The bulletin asked other departments to pick up and detain the suspect for the department that issued the flyer.

Subsequently, on the basis of the flyer, without a warrant for the defendant's arrest, police officers in Covington, Kentucky, stopped the automobile and, upon observing a revolver butt under the passenger seat, arrested the passenger and later the defendant. Following the detention, the officer seized evidence that was later introduced at trial and the defendant complained that the initial stop was illegal; therefore, the use of evidence was in violation of the Constitution and the Exclusionary Rule.

In upholding the stop and detention, the Court recognized that the law enforcement interests at stake in these circumstances outweigh the individual's interests to be free of a stop and detention that is no more extensive than permissible in the investigation of imminent or ongoing crimes. The Court indicated that when police have reasonable suspicion, grounded in specific and articulable facts, that a person he may encounter was involved in or is wanted in connection with a completed felony, then a *Terry* stop may be made to investigate that suspicion.

In the second case decided in 1985, the Supreme Court was asked to determine if a 20-minute detention is too long.[115] In the *Sharpe* case the Supreme Court found reasonable a 20-minute detention of a truck camper and its driver, based upon reasonable suspicion that the camper was loaded with marijuana. Here, after following two vehicles traveling in tandem for about 20 miles, a DEA agent decided to make an "investigative stop" and radioed the South Carolina Highway Patrol for assistance. When the DEA agent attempted to stop the two vehicles, one vehicle pulled over to the side of the road, but the other continued on, pursued by the state officer. The agent, who had left the local police with the first vehicle, arrived at the scene where the second vehicle was stopped about fifteen minutes after the truck had been stopped. After smelling marijuana, the agent opened the rear door and seized the marijuana which was later used in evidence.

The District Court denied the defendant's motion to suppress the contraband, but the Court of Appeals reversed, holding that because the investigative stop failed to meet the Fourth Amendment's requirement of brevity,

---

114 United States v. Hensley, 469 U.S. 221, 105 S. Ct. 675, 83 L. Ed. 2d 604 (1985).

115 United States v. Sharpe, 470 U.S. 675, 105 S. Ct. 1568, 84 L. Ed. 2d 605 (1985).

the marijuana should have been suppressed as a fruit of an unlawful seizure. The United States Supreme Court disagreed. The majority noted that in evaluating the reasonableness of an investigative stop, the Court examines "whether the officer's action was justified at its inception and whether it was reasonably related in scope to the circumstances which justified the interference in the first place." As to the length of the stop or detention, the spokesman indicated that the Court must consider the purposes to be served by a stop as well as the time reasonably needed to effectuate those purposes. Here the Court agreed with the trial court that the detention for 20 minutes was not too long under the circumstances. The majority explained that, in this case, the DEA agent had diligently pursued his investigation and clearly no delay unnecessary to the investigation was involved.

It should be noted that had the circumstances been different, the 20 minutes may have been too long. On the other hand, had the circumstances justified a more time-consuming investigation as, for example, to check whether the car was a stolen vehicle, more than 20 minutes would not necessarily have been too long.

In determining how long a detention may continue, the courts will look at the purpose of the stop and determine whether the police have diligently pursued the investigation to confirm or dispel their suspicions.

This series of cases following the *Terry v. Ohio* case in 1968 justifies the conclusion that most vehicle stops will be upheld if the officer can justify his actions based on his experience and the information available to him at the time he decided to stop a particular vehicle. Once the vehicle is stopped, he may require the defendant to get out of the vehicle even if there are no particular facts for suspicions of danger to justify this intrusion.[116]

(b) License and registration checks

One issue that has been repeatedly brought to the attention of the courts involves the right of a police officer to stop a motor vehicle to check the driver's license or the car's registration, mechanical condition or weight. Does the law allow a police officer to stop a motor vehicle on less reasonable grounds than those required to stop a pedestrian? Does the fact that a motorist is using the highway lessen the rights guaranteed to him under the Fourth Amendment?

Although many state courts had rendered decisions concerning the authority of the police officer to stop a motor vehicle to check the driver's license or the car's registration, the Supreme Court of the United States had

---

116 Pennsylvania v. Mimms, 434 U.S. 106, 98 S. Ct. 330, 54 L. Ed. 2d 331 (1977).

not acted in this matter until 1979. In the case of *Delaware v. Prouse*,[117] the Supreme Court addressed the issue of routine police "stops" for the purpose of checking the driver's license or registration certificates. A patrolman in a police cruiser had stopped an automobile occupied by the respondent and seized marijuana in plain view on the car floor. At the hearing on the respondent's motion to suppress the marijuana, the patrolman testified that prior to stopping the vehicle he had observed neither traffic nor equipment violation nor any suspicious activity and that he made the stop only in order to check the driver's license and the car's registration. The Court pointed out that the patrolman was not acting pursuant to any standards, guidelines, or procedures pertaining to document spot checks promulgated by either his department or the State Attorney General.

Recognizing that the states have a vital interest in insuring that only those qualified to do so are permitted to operate motor vehicles and that these vehicles are fit for safe operation, the Court nevertheless questioned that these important ends justify the intrusion upon Fourth Amendment interests which such stops entail. The Court then summarized its decision with these words:

> We hold that except in those situations in which there is at least articulable and reasonable suspicion that a motorist is unlicensed or that an automobile is not registered, or that either the vehicle or the occupant is otherwise subject to seizure for violation of the law, stopping an automobile and detaining the driver in order to check his driver's license and registration of the automobile are unreasonable under the Fourth Amendment. This holding does not preclude the state of Delaware or other states from developing methods for spot checks that involve less intrusion or that do not involve the unrestrained exercise of discretion.

The court volunteered that roadblock-type stops are one possible alternative, reasoning that at traffic checkpoints the motorist can see that the other vehicles are being stopped. The rationale for the roadblock stop is that the driver can see visible signs of the officer's authority and he is much less likely to be frightened or annoyed by the intrusion.

Referring to the case of *Terry v. Ohio*,[118] the majority stated that when there is probable cause to believe that a driver is violating any one of a multitude of applicable traffic or equipment regulations or other articulable facts justifying a reasonable suspicion that the driver is unlicensed or his vehicle

---

117 440 U.S. 648, 99 S. Ct. 1391, 59 L. Ed. 2d 660 (1979).

118 *Supra* note 90.

unregistered, stopping the vehicle would not violate the Fourth Amendment. The Court also left open the opportunity for states to establish compliance of the licensing and registration laws by developing methods that do not involve the "unconstrained exercise of discretion."

Two lower court cases decided after the case of *Delaware v. Prouse* indicate that the lower court justices have taken the Supreme Court at its word and have approved the establishment of roadblocks to check driver's license and registration of motorists. In the case of *United States v. Pritchard*, the U.S. Court of Appeals for the Tenth Circuit approved the use of a roadblock on an interstate highway to check the license and registration of every motorist that passed by.[119] Although conceding that evidence indicated that police had planned to enforce the law if they observed evidence of other crimes while checking license and registration, the Court refused to condemn the practice, pointing out that the Supreme Court in *Prouse* specifically stated that the holding did not preclude the state from developing methods for spot checks that involved less intrusion or that do not involve the unconstitutional exercise of discretion.

In a second case the New York Court of Appeals ruled that vehicle stops as part of a roving roadblock procedure in a heavily burglarized area, conducted in a uniform, nonarbitrary and nondiscriminatory manner, for the purpose of ascertaining identities and gathering information about the crimes did not violate the Constitutional proscription against unreasonable searches and seizures.[120]

§ 3.16 Summary

The outcome of a case may often depend on how the officer handles the arrest. If the officer oversteps his authority, the exclusionary rule (which will be discussed in the following chapter) may preclude the use of all evidence gained as a result of the arrest in any subsequent trial.

As a general rule, an officer may make an arrest under the authority of an arrest warrant, or without a warrant if an offense is committed in his presence and, in the case of a felony, if he has reasonable grounds to believe that the person whom he is about to arrest has committed the crime. The preferable method of making an arrest is by the authority of an arrest warrant. To be valid, the warrant must meet the constitutional and statutory requirements. The United States Constitution specifically requires that the warrant:

---

119 United States v. Pritchard, 645 F.2d 854 (10th Cir. 1981).

120 People v. John, 564 N.Y.2d 48, 438 N.E.2d 864, 453 N.Y.S.2d 158 (1982).

(1) be issued upon probable cause,
(2) be supported by oath or affirmation, and
(3) particularly describe the persons to be seized.

Other requirements have been added by legislation or case decisions.

Although the Constitution contains no exceptions, the courts have recognized the necessity of making arrests without warrants. Generally, an arrest without a warrant will be found valid in a felony case if the officer can show that he had reasonable grounds to believe that a felony was committed and that the person he arrested committed the felony. In determining such reasonable grounds, he may use facts obtained from his personal observation, certain informers' information, information from other departments or other agencies, the past criminal record of the suspect, and physical evidence.

In the usual misdemeanor case, the officer cannot make the arrest unless the misdemeanor is committed in his presence. In order for the offense to be considered as taking place within the presence of the officer, he must be made aware of its commission through one or more of his senses. Some state legislation has extended the authority to arrest without a warrant in misdemeanor situations to make it possible for the officer to arrest validly if he has reasonable grounds to believe that a misdemeanor has been committed.

To conserve the time of the police as well as of the person who has violated a law, the legislatures and courts have sanctioned the use of the citation and summons. Although the statutes differ in wording, a citation is not considered an arrest, but an alternative to an arrest. The citation is used primarily in traffic cases, but it should be used whenever possible to bring those accused of other minor violations before the courts.

Because a state cannot confer any official power which would be effective in another state, fresh pursuit of an offender is usually authorized within the state, but into another state only if approved by the host state. The right of fresh pursuit across state boundary lines is generally confined by statutes to felonies. There are, however, a few states that authorize out-of-state law enforcement officers to cross state borders in order to make an arrest for a misdemeanor. Most states still do not have fresh pursuit legislation, and, absent such legislative authority, an officer from another state making an arrest acts only in the capacity of a private citizen.

In some instances the officer does not have the authority to arrest, but does have the authority to detain. In a few states, the authority to detain has been granted by statute, but even without a statute, such a detention is justified under recent court decisions when the officer observes unusual conduct which leads him reasonably to conclude, in light of his experience, that criminal activity may be afoot.

A police officer may arrest the driver of an automobile under the same authority that he can make an arrest of a pedestrian. And an officer may detain a driver as he may detain a pedestrian under the *Terry* reasoning.

While an officer may not routinely stop a motorist solely for the purpose of checking his driver's license or registration certificate, he may detain if he has articulable suspicion that the driver is unlicensed. And under the *Terry* rule the driver of a car may be detained on the authority of a "wanted flier" issued by another department. The length of such detention is determined by the circumstances, but the Supreme Court agreed that a 20-minute detention was not too long where the officer had diligently pursued the investigation.

Chapter 4
SEARCH AND SEIZURE*

The right of the people to be secure in their persons, houses, papers, and effects, against unreasonable searches and seizures, shall not be violated, and no Warrants shall issue, but upon probable cause, supported by Oath or affirmation, and particularly describing the place to be searched, and the persons or things to be seized.

Fourth Amendment, 1791

Section

---

* *by John C. Klotter*

§ 4.1 Historical development of search and seizure laws

In order to understand our present constitutional provisions and the interpretations made by the various courts concerning search and seizure, the history of this protection must carefully be studied. As the laws concerning search and seizure were greatly influenced by the laws and customs of England, both the English background and the American background are necessarily included in this study.

Although the use of search warrants appears not to have been known in early English common law, the use of the search warrant gradually crept into the administration of the English government to the point that, until 1766, the person, property and premises of the individual were subject to practically unlimited searches and seizures. At first the use of search warrants was confined to stolen goods; but it came to be used indiscriminately for other types of evidence. In 1766 the English House of Commons passed resolutions condemning the use of "general warrants."

The United States Supreme Court, in an early case referring to the general warrant and the condemnation of such warrants by the English Parliament, stated:

> It was welcomed and applauded by the lovers of liberty in the colonies as well as in the mother country. It is regarded as one of the permanent monuments of the British Constitution, and is quoted as such by the English authorities on that subject down to the present time.[1]

As this rule was being developed in England, events were taking place in this country which, to a great extent, determined the future of search and seizure laws. Five years prior to the condemnation of the general warrant by the House of Commons, an incident took place in America which brought the necessity for *specific provisions* for the protection of an individual's security, personal liberty and private property to the attention of those who would later write our Constitution.

In a crowded Boston courtroom in February, 1761, a group of merchants denounced the general warrants which gave the English soldiers authority to search any ship, store or house. The issue before the court was the admissibility of evidence obtained by the Crown through a writ of assistance or general warrant, a device frequently employed by the authorities to search for smuggled goods. At that time writs of assistance, as they were called, were

---

1 Boyd v. United States, 116 U.S. 616, 6 S. Ct. 524, 29 L. Ed. 746 (1886).

issued with little restraint. They empowered the authorities to search virtually any house or any other building on a mere suspicion that goods subject to seizure might be found there. No showing of probable cause was required.

James Otis, an attorney who had previously served as attorney general for the Colony of Massachusetts, represented the merchants. He called the writ of assistance "the worst instrument of arbitrary power, the most destructive of English liberty, and the fundamental principles of law, that was ever found in an English law book." John Adams, who heard the arguments in the case, said later, after he had become President of the United States, "Every man of the crowded audience appeared to me to go away as I did, ready to take up arms against the writs of assistance. Then and there was the first scene of the first act of opposition to the arbitrary claims of Great Britain. Then and there the child of independence was born."[2]

Fifteen years after this case the colonies declared their independence. In 1789 the Constitution was ratified, and in 1791 the Fourth Amendment was adopted to ensure that the personal security and private property of the individual would be protected against invasion by the federal government.

§ 4.2 Constitutional provisions

Even prior to the adoption of the Constitution many of those who objected to its ratification criticized the absence of a provision protecting the people against unreasonable searches and seizures. This was understandable as the writs of assistance were fresh in the minds of those who advocated the inclusion of a Bill of Rights. Led by James Madison, the First Congress initiated legislation to protect the people against unreasonable searches and seizures. After ratification in 1791, this became the Fourth Amendment to the Constitution and provided that:

> The right of the people to be secure in their persons, houses, papers, and effects against unreasonable searches and seizures, shall not be violated, and no Warrants shall issue, but upon probable cause, supported by Oath or affirmation, and particularly describing the place to be searched, and the persons or things to be seized.

Like other provisions of the Bill of Rights, the Fourth Amendment would have little meaning without judicial interpretation. For example, the word "unreasonable" as used in the Amendment could allow many searches or could restrict searches to those with warrants only. Other terms which

---

2 WORKS OF JOHN ADAMS, Vol. II, App. A, pp. 523-525.

must be interpreted before the provision will have meaning include "persons," "houses," "papers," "effects," "probable cause," "particularly describing" and even the word "searched." In hundreds and even thousands of cases the courts have attempted to define the meaning of these terms as used in this section of the Constitution, and thereby define the scope of this protection.[3] To make this protection more understandable, a few of the more important cases are included in Part II of this book.

The constitutions of the several states uniformly imposed the United States Constitution. For example, the constitution of Texas has the following provision:

> The people shall be secure in their persons, houses, papers and possessions, from all unreasonable searches or seizures, and no warrant to search any place, or to seize any person or thing, shall issue without describing them as near as may be, nor without probable cause, supported by oath or affirmation.[4]

The state constitutions would also have very little meaning without judicial interpretation. The state courts have often disagreed among themselves as to the scope and application of the constitutional provisions; and the state courts have likewise disagreed with the federal courts. However, as will be indicated in future paragraphs, where there is such disagreement the interpretation by the Supreme Court of the United States will prevail and this will be binding insofar as minimum standards are applied to the states.

The federal constitutional provisions place limitations on the federal officials and, by way of the Fourteenth Amendment, on state officials. In addition, the state constitutions as interpreted by the state courts place limitations on the powers of the state officials. However, neither the federal provisions nor the state provisions are applicable to searches and seizures by private persons, as these are limitations upon governmental rather than private activities.

---

[3] In interpreting the term "people" as used in the Fourth Amendment, the United States Supreme Court held that the term refers to a class of persons who are a part of a national community or who have otherwise developed a sufficient connection to the United States to be considered part of the community. Thus, the Fourth Amendment was intended to protect people of the United States against arbitrary action by their own government, rather than to restrain action of the federal government against aliens outside of the United States territory. United States v. Verdugo-Urquidez, __ U.S. __, 110 S. Ct. 1056, __ L. Ed. 2d __ (1990).

[4] TEX. CONST. art. I, § 9.

§ 4.3 The exclusionary rule

1. Statement of the rule

The Exclusionary Rule simply stated is, "Evidence obtained by an unreasonable search and seizure in violation of the Fourth Amendment to the Constitution will not be admitted as evidence in court." This rule is not a provision of the Fourth Amendment itself, but is a rule that has been framed by the courts. The Exclusionary Rule, especially as it relates to search and seizure, is a product of United States Courts, and is not followed in England or in other nations whose system of law is based on Anglo-Saxon sources.

2. Reason for adoption of the rule by the court

Justice Murphy, in his dissenting opinion in the case of *Wolf v. Colorado*, argued there are only three ways by which the Fourth Amendment search and seizure protection may be enforced. His statement in that case is:

> If we would attempt the enforcement of the search and seizure clause in the ordinary case today, we are limited to three devices: judicial exclusion of illegally obtained evidence; criminal prosecution of violators; and civil action against violators in the action of trespass.[5]

Justice Murphy goes on to explain that only one of these is effective judicial exclusion of illegally obtained evidence. In other cases, the judges and attorneys have rested the reason for the Exclusionary Rule on two enunciated judicial bases:

(1) the "imperative of judicial integrity" requires the exclusion of tainted evidence, and
(2) the exclusion of illegally seized evidence will deter unlawful police conduct.[6]

Those who favor the Exclusionary Rule explain that for the courts to authorize the use of evidence obtained in violation of one of the amendments of the Constitution would place the courts in the position of approving viola-

---

5 338 U.S. 25, 69 S. Ct. 1359, 93 L. Ed. 1782 (1949).

6 United States v. Peltier, 422 U.S. 531, 95 S. Ct. 2313, 45 L. Ed. 2d 374 (1975).

tions of the Constitution. The rationale for the second foundation is that if police officers and the prosecutors realize that evidence obtained in violation of the Fourth Amendment will be inadmissible, they will be instilled with the necessity of taking a greater degree of care toward the rights of an accused, and will make greater efforts to learn and apply the laws relating to search and seizure.

3. Arguments opposing the exclusionary rule

English courts and other nations whose system of law is based on Anglo-Saxon sources have rejected the Exclusionary Rule. The reason for the common law or English rule has been succinctly stated by English judges as follows:

> I think it would be a dangerous obstacle to the administration of justice if we were to hold (that) because evidence was obtained by illegal means, it could not be used against a party charged with an offense...It, therefore, seems to me that the interest of the State must excuse the seizure of documents, which seizure would otherwise be unlawful, if it appears in fact that such documents are evidence of a crime committed by anyone.[7]

Many legal scholars have argued that the Exclusionary Rule has not proved workable and has done more harm than good. Professor John H. Wigmore, for example, has criticized the wisdom of the rule, pointing out the illogic of the rule which reprimands the police officer by freeing the lawbreaker.[8]

The argument for not adopting the Exclusionary Rule was succinctly stated by Justice Cardozo of the New York Court of Appeals, when he commented, "The criminal is to go free because the constable has blundered."[9]

§ 4.4 –Adoption of rule by federal courts in *Weeks v. United States*

For many years the American courts followed the common law doctrine in all cases and authorized the use of evidence even though it was obtained in

---

7 Elias v. Pasmore, 2 K.B. 164, ___ All E.R. 380 (1934).

8 8 WIGMORE, EVIDENCE, § 2184a, 3d ed. (1961).

9 People v. DeFore, 242 N.Y. 13, 150 N.E. 585 (1926).

Barrs the use illegally obtained.

violation of the search and seizure provisions. But in 1914, the Supreme Court, in *Weeks v. United States*,[10] unequivocally rejected the common law rule, and specifically held that evidence obtained by unreasonable search and seizure would be excluded in the federal courts.

In the *Weeks* case, a United States marshal, working with local police officers, seized from the defendant's home some letters and envelopes which were subsequently used as evidence against the defendant. The defendant was found guilty on a federal charge of using the mails to defraud. On appeal, the Supreme Court held that in a federal prosecution, the Fourth Amendment barred the use of evidence secured through illegal search and seizure.

The *Weeks* decision, however, did not prohibit the use in federal courts of evidence illegally obtained by *state* officers. But, in extending the application of the exclusionary rule, the Court, in 1920, held that if a federal officer seized documents illegally, his knowledge acquired in that action could not be used in obtaining other evidence.[11] And finally, in 1960, the door was closed to the use of *all* such illegally obtained evidence in federal courts when the court ruled that evidence obtained by state officers in violation of the Fourth Amendment could not be used in federal courts.[12]

As late as 1949, the Supreme Court refused to apply the exclusionary rule to the states. In *Wolf v. Colorado*,[13] the Court stated:

> We have no hesitation in saying that were a State affirmatively to sanction such police incursion into privacy it would run counter to the guarantee of the Fourteenth Amendment. But the ways of enforcing such a basic right raise questions of a different order. How such arbitrary conduct should be checked, what remedies against it should be afforded, [and] the means by which the right should be made effective, are all questions that are not to be so dogmatically answered as to preclude varying solutions which spring from an allowable range of judgment on issues not susceptible of quantitative solutions.

In the *Wolf* case the Court reviewed the actions taken by the various state courts and summarized their positions. In the summary, the Court noted that of the forty-seven states which had passed on the exclusionary

---

[10] 232 U.S. 383, 34 S. Ct. 341, 58 L. Ed. 652 (1914).

[11] Silverthorne Lumber Co. v. United States, 251 U.S. 385, 40 S. Ct. 182, 64 L. Ed. 319 (1920).

[12] Elkins v. United States, 364 U.S. 206, 80 S. Ct. 1437, 4 L. Ed. 2d 1669 (1960).

[13] 338 U.S. 25, 69 S. Ct. 1359, 93 L. Ed. 1782 (1949).

rule, thirty-one rejected the rule and sixteen states were in agreement with it. The Court also pointed out that of ten jurisdictions within the United Kingdom and the British Commonwealth of Nations, none had held evidence obtained by illegal search and seizure inadmissible. The concluding paragraph of the majority opinion in *Wolf* summarized the holding with:

> We hold, therefore, that in a prosecution in a State court for a State crime the Fourteenth Amendment does not forbid the admission of evidence obtained by unreasonable search and seizure.

§ 4.5 – Extension of rule to all courts in *Mapp v. Ohio*

In 1961, two centuries after James Otis made his denunciation of the writs of assistance, the exclusionary rule reached maturity when the Supreme Court extended the rule to every court and law enforcement officer in the nation.[14] By the decision in *Mapp v. Ohio*, the Supreme Court made it clear that henceforth evidence obtained by procedures which violated Fourth Amendment standards would no longer be admissible in state or federal courts against the party whose rights were violated.

On May 23, 1957, three Cleveland police officers arrived at Dollree Mapp's residence in the City of Cleveland, pursuant to information that a person who was wanted for questioning in connection with a recent bombing was hiding in Miss Mapp's home, and that there was a large amount of obscene paraphernalia hidden there also. After telephoning her attorney, Dollree Mapp refused to admit the officers without a search warrant. Three hours later, the officers returned with reinforcements and again sought entrance. When she did not come to the door, one of the doors was forcibly opened and the policemen gained entry. Miss Mapp demanded to see the search warrant, and a paper, claimed to be the warrant, was held up by one of the officers. She grabbed the paper and placed it in her bosom. A struggle ensued in which the officers recovered the piece of paper and handcuffed Miss Mapp. A search was conducted of the entire apartment, including the bedroom, living room, kitchen, dinette, and basement of the building. The obscene materials, for the possession of which the defendant was ultimately convicted, were discovered as a result of that widespread search.

The state contended that even if the search were made without authority or otherwise unreasonably, it was not prevented from using the unconstitutionally seized evidence at the trial because *Wolf v. Colorado*, *supra*, had au-

---

14 Mapp v. Ohio, 367 U.S. 643, 81 S. Ct. 1684, 6 L. Ed. 2d 1081 (1961). *See* case in Part II.

thorized the admission of such evidence in a state court and also that the state of Ohio did not follow the exclusionary rule. After a discussion of other applicable cases, the Court flatly declared the application of the exclusionary rule to all the states, saying:

> Today we once again examine *Wolf's* constitutional documentation of the right to privacy free from unreasonable state intrusion, and, after its dozen years on our books, are led by it to close the only courtroom door remaining open to evidence secured by official lawlessness in flagrant abuse of that basic right, reserved to all persons as a specific guarantee against that very same unlawful conduct. We hold that all evidence obtained by searches and seizures in violation of the Constitution is, by that same authority, inadmissible in a state court.

The exclusionary rule, defined in the *Weeks* case as a matter of judicial implication, was made applicable in the federal courts in 1914. Between the years 1914 and 1961, the Supreme Court said the rule was not applicable to the states by reason of the Fourteenth Amendment, and then reversed itself and said the rule was to be made effective against the states.

The decision in the *Mapp* case in 1961 left no doubt that the exclusionary rule prohibited the use of evidence obtained in violation of the Fourth Amendment in both federal and state courts. This ruling, together with previous decisions of the Supreme Court, made it mandatory that state officials comply with the search and seizure standards as enunciated by the United States Supreme Court and, in some instances, federal district courts. In addition, state and local officers must comply with decisions of state courts where these limitations are greater than those imposed by the federal courts.

This ruling should not be interpreted to mean that all searches are unreasonable. However, because of the inability of state and federal courts to clearly announce rules concerning search and seizure, and the failure of officers, knowingly or unknowingly, to follow even those rules that are clear, thousands of cases have been disposed of without even reaching the stage where guilt or innocence is considered.

§ 4.6 Effects of the rule and approaches to modification

1. Effects of the rule

Although there is disagreement as to the impact of the Exclusionary Rule, there is no disagreement that the application of the rule does result in the release of guilty criminals. Supporters of the Exclusionary Rule argue that the rule deters police from acting illegally while opponents argue that there is no convincing evidence to verify the factual premise of deterrence upon which the rule is based or to determine the limits of its effectiveness. Proponents rely upon a 1978 study by the general accounting office which found that evidence was actually suppressed at trial because of the Exclusionary Rule in only 1.3 percent of the federal criminal cases.[15] However, this study was based on data collected only over a six-week period, and considered only federal cases. According to a National Institute of Justice study, the impact of the Exclusionary Rule in California shows that a significant number of felony cases declined for prosecution were rejected because of search and seizure problems.[16] This study indicated that 4.8 percent of all felony arrests declined for prosecution in California from 1976 through 1979 were rejected because of search and seizure related issues.

In the case of *Illinois v. Gates*, the United States Supreme Court considered modifying the Exclusionary Rule but did not address the issue directly because the lower Illinois courts never specifically addressed the question.[17] However, in that case, Justice White, in a concurring opinion, weighed the cost and benefits of applying the rule. Several paragraphs of this decision succinctly express his argument.

These cases reflect that the exclusion of evidence is not a personal constitutional right but a remedy, which, like all remedies, must be sensitive to the costs and benefits of its imposition. The trend and direction of our exclusionary rule decisions indicate not a lesser concern with safeguarding the Fourth Amendment but a fuller appreciation of the high costs incurred when probative, reliable evidence is barred because of investigative error. The primary cost, of course, is that the exclusionary rule interferes with the truth-seeking function of a criminal trial by barring relevant and trustworthy evidence. We will never know how many guilty defendants go free as a result of the rule's operation. But any rule of evidence that denies the jury access to clearly probative and reliable evidence must bear a heavy burden of justification, and must be carefully limited to the circumstances in which it will pay its way by deterring official lawlessness. I do not presume that modification of

---

15 Address of the Honorable William French Smith, Attorney General of the United States, presented to state directors of law enforcement training at St. Anselm College, May 24, 1983.

16 Vol. 9, International Association of Chiefs of Police Newsletter, April, 1983.

17 Illinois v. Gates, 462 U.S. 213, 103 S. Ct. 2317, 76 L. Ed. 2d 257 (1983). *See* case in Part II for comprehensive discussion of the development of the exclusionary rule.

the exclusionary rule will, by itself, significantly reduce the crime rate -- but that is no excuse for indiscriminate application of the rule.

The suppression doctrine entails other costs as well. It would be surprising if the suppression of evidence garnered in good faith, but by means later found to violate the Fourth Amendment, did not deter legitimate, as well as unlawful, police activities. To the extent the rule operates to discourage police from reasonable and proper investigative actions, it hinders the solution and even the prevention of crime. A tremendous burden is also placed on the state and federal judicial systems. One study reveals that one-third of federal defendants going to trial file Fourth Amendment suppression motions, and 70 percent to 90 percent of these involve formal hearings. Comptroller General of the United States, Impact of the Exclusionary Rule on Federal Criminal Prosecutions 10 (1979).

The rule also exacts a heavy price in undermining public confidence in the reasonableness of the standards that govern the criminal justice system. "(A)lthough the (exclusionary) rule is thought to deter unlawful police activity in part through the nurturing of respect for Fourth Amendment values, if applied indiscriminately it may well have the opposite effect of generating disrespect for the law and the administration of justice."

2. *Approaches to modifications*

Supporters of modification are advocating what has become known as the "good faith exception." Under this approach, evidence would be admissible when an officer either obtains a warrant or conducts a search without a warrant but with a reasonable, good faith belief that he is acting in accordance with the Fourth Amendment. The test of good faith would not be whether the police officer merely believed his search was legal, but whether his belief was objectively reasonable. Justice White, in the *Gates* decision, indicates that the standard would be an objective one. He compares the test he proposed to the "closely related good faith test which governs civil suits under 42 U.S.C. 1983." Under this interpretation, there would be no premium on ignorance. On the contrary, this would encourage police departments to insure proper training and establish rules for search and seizure cases.

Proponents of modification of the Exclusionary Rule in various articles and cases have advanced reasons for modifying the Exclusionary Rule. These can be summarized as follows:

(1) There is no provision in the Constitution or the Fourth Amendment which requires or indicates that evidence should

be excluded merely because it has been obtained in violation of the court standards. This is a judicial rule. It is not required by the Constitution and is not followed in other countries whose laws are based on the Anglo-Saxon model.

(2) Society and the law-abiding citizen are denied the protection of the law. The price paid for the exclusionary rule is much too high; the right to be protected from criminal attack should be considered along with the protection of the rights of the person accused of crime.

(3) The laws relating to search and seizure are so complex that the officer not trained in law cannot comprehend them. If the police officer is to be deterred from violating the search and seizure protections, they must be made clear enough so that the average person can understand them. This is not the case, however; the laws are so complex and fraught with such variables, depending on the factual situations, that even judges cannot understand them. Often there are conflicts between concurring and dissenting judges in a single opinion and the federal reviewing courts do not agree with the state courts.

(4) Police officers are more informed today and the harsh methods for "policing the officer" are no longer justified. Today more than four hundred schools in the United States offer education to police officers and other criminal justice personnel. Although no amount of formal police training will make the policeman an expert in the law of search and seizure, the training for police officers, not only in the technicalities regarding search and seizure, but also regarding the rights of individuals in general, is at least as comprehensive as that given to members of other professions. To continue to use the argument that the exclusionary rule "polices the policeman" no longer has merit.

Arguments advanced by Mr. Justice White in the case of *Illinois v. Gates* and arguments made by others who advocate modification of the Exclusionary Rule were given weight by the majority of the Supreme Court in two decisions rendered on July 17, 1984. Both of these cases dealt with the admissibility of evidence gathered by police after obtaining search warrants from detached and neutral magistrates. In neither case did the Court face the question whether a good faith exception to the Exclusionary Rule should be recognized where officers act without a warrant.

In the case of *United States v. Leon* a confidential informant of unproven reliability informed an officer of the Burbank Police Department that named individuals were selling controlled substances from a specific residence.[18] On the basis of this information police initiated an extensive investigation focusing on the residence named and later two other residences as well. Based on an affidavit summarizing the police officers' observations, an application for a warrant to search the three residences and the defendants' automobiles was prepared, reviewed by the Deputy District Attorney and submitted to the judge. The judge, after evaluating the evidence, issued a facially valid search warrant which, when executed by the officers, produced large quantities of drugs.

The defendants were indicted by a grand jury and charged with conspiracy to possess and distribute cocaine, and a variety of substantive counts. After a motion was filed by the respondents to suppress the evidence, the District Court granted the motion to suppress in part, concluding that the affidavit was insufficient to establish probable cause because the informant's creditability was not sufficiently established and some of the information was "stale." The Court of Appeals refused the government's invitation to recognize a good faith exception to the Fourth Amendment Exclusionary Rule and the government petitioned for certiorari. The prosecution expressly declined to seek review of the lower court's determination that the search warrant was unsupported by probable cause and presented only the question "whether the Fourth Amendment's Exclusionary Rule should be modified so as not to bar the admission of evidence seized in reasonable, good faith reliance on a search warrant that is subsequently held to be defective."

After reviewing the scope of the Fourth Amendment Exclusionary Rule and reiterating some of the arguments as to why the rule should be modified, the United States Supreme Court reversed the judgment of the Court of Appeals. The majority found that the officers' reliance on the judge's determination of probable cause was objectively reasonable, and that the application of the extreme sanction of exclusion is inappropriate.

In concluding that, in this case, the evidence should be admitted, but warning not all evidence will be admitted, the court used these terms:

> We conclude that the marginal or nonexistent benefits produced by suppressing evidence obtained in objectively reasonable reliance on a subsequently invalidated search warrant cannot justify the substantial cost of exclusion. We do not suggest, however, that exclusion is always inappropriate in cases where an officer has obtained a warrant and abided by its terms...Nevertheless, the officer's reliance

---

[18] 468 U.S. 897, 104 S. Ct. 3415, 82 L. Ed. 2d 677 (1984).

> on the magistrate's probable cause determination and on the technical sufficiency of the warrant he issued must be objectively reasonable,...and it is clear that in some circumstances the officer will have no reasonable grounds for believing that the warrant was properly issued.

In the second case, *Massachusetts v. Shepherd*, the facts were different but the legal issue was almost identical.[19] Here a police detective drafted an affidavit to support an application for a search warrant authorizing the search of Shepherd's residence. The affidavit was reviewed and approved by the District Attorney and the detective began his search for a warrant form to be taken to the judge. As this occurred on Sunday, the local court was closed and the detective finally found a warrant form previously used in another district to search for a controlled substance. After making some changes on the form, the detective presented it and the affidavit to a judge at his residence, informing him that the warrant might need to be changed further. Concluding that the affidavit established probable cause to search the respondent's residence and telling the detective that the necessary changes in the warrant form would be made, the judge made some changes, but did not change the substantive portion, which continued to authorize a search for a controlled substance, nor did he alter the form so as to incorporate the affidavit.

When the judge returned the warrant to the officer he advised that the warrant was sufficient authority in form and content to carry out the requested search. The ensuing search of the respondent's residence by the detective and other police officers was limited to the items listed on the affidavit and several incriminating pieces of evidence were discovered. The respondent was charged with first degree murder. Evidence located by the police included a pair of bloodstained boots, blood stains on the concrete floor, a woman's earring with blood stains on it, a bloodstained envelope, a pair of man's jockey shorts, a woman's leotards with blood on them, three types of wire, and a woman's hairpiece.

At a pre-trial suppression hearing, the trial judge concluded that the warrant failed to conform to the commands of the Fourth Amendment because it did not particularly describe the items to be seized. The judge ruled, however, that the evidence should be admitted notwithstanding the defect in the warrant because the police had acted in good faith in executing what they reasonably thought was a valid warrant. At the subsequent trial, Shepherd was convicted of murder.

---

[19] 468 U.S. 981, 104 S. Ct. 3424, 82 L. Ed. 2d 737 (1984).

The Supreme Judicial Court of Massachusetts concluded that although the police conducted the search in a good faith belief, reasonably held, that the search was lawful and authorized by the warrant issued by the judge, the evidence had to be excluded because the United States Supreme Court had not recognized a good faith exception to the Exclusionary Rule.

The United States Supreme Court disagreed. The majority concluded that an officer is not required to disbelieve a judge who has just advised him, by word and by action, that the warrant he possesses authorizes him to conduct the search he has requested. In considering the purpose of the Exclusionary Rule, the Supreme Court majority agreed that suppressing evidence because the judge failed to make all the necessary clerical corrections will not serve the deterrent function that the Exclusionary Rule was designed to achieve.

It is again emphasized that these two cases modify the Exclusionary Rule but do not reverse it. First, both cases deal with situations where search warrants were issued by judicial officers and the police officers acted in good faith in executing what they believed to be valid warrants. Secondly, the Court made it clear that while normally the warrant issued by a magistrate is sufficient to establish that a law enforcement officer has acted in good faith in conducting the search, the officers' reliance on the magistrates' probable cause determination and on the technical sufficiency of the warrant must be objectively reasonable. If it is clear that the warrant was improperly issued, then the good faith exception will not apply.

In both the *Leon* case and the *Shepherd* case, police officers executed what they believed to be valid warrants. Soon after these cases were decided, the question arose as to whether the "good faith" rationale would be applied in situations where the officers acted without a warrant. The "good faith" issue did reach the Supreme Court again in 1987 but in a case that has very limited application.[20] In the *Krull* case officers, acting pursuant to a statute, made an inspection of an automobile wrecking yard and discovered several stolen cars. The state statute, as those in many other states, regulated the business of buying and selling motor vehicles, parts, and scrap metal. The day after the search, a federal court ruled that such a statute was unconstitutional, and at the trial a motion was made to exclude the evidence obtained by the police who acted in good faith under the statute.

The lower court decision was that the evidence was inadmissible even though the detective had acted in good faith reliance on the state statute in making the search. The United States Supreme Court reversed the lower court decision, explaining that the evidence should have been admitted, as the application of the Exclusionary Rule in these circumstances would have little

20 Illinois v. Krull, 475 U.S. 868, 107 S. Ct. 1160, 94 L. Ed. 2d 364 (1987).

deterrent effect on police conduct, which is the basic purpose of the Exclusionary Rule.

The court removed some of the burden on the officer by explaining that if a statute is not clearly unconstitutional, officers cannot be expected to question the judgment of the legislature that passed the law. Although the court in the *Krull* case did not extend the "good faith" exception to a considerable extent, it did clarify the reasoning by commenting:

> Application of the Exclusionary Rule "is neither intended nor able to cure the invasion of the defendant's rights which he has already suffered" . . . Rather, the rule "operates as a judicially created remedy designed to safeguard Fourth Amendment rights generally through its deterrent effect, rather than as a personal constitutional right of the party aggrieved"...as with any remedial device, application of the Exclusionary Rule properly has been restricted to those situations in which its remedial purpose is effectively advanced. Thus, in various circumstances, the court has examined whether the Rule's deterrent effect will be achieved, and has weighed the likelihood of such deterrence against the cost of withholding reliable information from the truth seeking process.

Yet to be considered are the other situations where the officer acts without a warrant but acts in good faith. If the reasoning of the court in the two cases mentioned is carried to a logical conclusion, such evidence will be admitted. It is anticipated, however, that the courts will be very careful in establishing an overall "good faith" rule or exception. They will be even more careful in applying the exception in individual cases.

Even though evidence is obtained illegally it may, according to court decisions, be used for some purposes. The Supreme Court did not "close the door" to the use of illegally seized evidence as indicated in the *Mapp* case. Some cases noting these exceptions to the exclusion of such evidence follow.

In what Mr. Justice Brennan termed as "yet another element in the trend to depreciate the constitutional protections guaranteed the criminally accused," the majority of the Supreme Court justices in the case of *United States v. Havens*[21] determined that illegally seized evidence may sometimes be used for impeachment purposes if the defendant takes the stand. In this case, a customs officer found cocaine sewn into a makeshift pocket in a T-shirt worn by a companion of the defendant, a Mr. McLeroth. The defendant's companion implicated the defendant and his bag was searched. In the search, the customs officer found a T-shirt from which pieces had been cut

---

21 446 U.S. 620, 100 S. Ct. 1912, 64 L. Ed. 2d 559 (1980).

that matched the pieces that were sewn to McLeroth's T-shirt. This evidence was not introduced when the prosecution was presenting its case in chief, but was used on a rebuttal after the defendant had stated on the stand that to his knowledge the T-shirt was not in his luggage. The government introduced the evidence after the jury was instructed that the rebuttal evidence was to be considered only for impeaching the defendant's credibility.

The Supreme Court referred to a case decided in 1954 which held that the use of evidence obtained in an illegal search was admissible to impeach when statements were made by the defendant in the course of his *direct* testimony.[22] Here, however, the prosecution introduced the evidence for impeachment purposes to discredit the testimony given by the defendant on cross-examination by the prosecution. To allow this, then, would extend the exception to the exclusionary rule a step further. Nevertheless, the majority of the Supreme Court determined that, in this instance where the cross-examination grew directly and logically from the defendant's direct testimony, the introduction of the evidence was proper. The Court compared this to cases where evidence obtained as a result of a confession without the *Miranda* warnings was admissible for impeachment purposes.[23] Part of the rationale there as here, according to the Court, is that arriving at the truth in a criminal case is the fundamental goal of our legal system. The Court reiterated what it had said in other cases that:

> We have repeatedly insisted that when defendants testify, they must testify truthfully or suffer the consequences....It is essential therefore to the proper functioning of the adversary system that when a defendant takes the stand, the government be permitted proper and effective cross-examination in an attempt to elicit the truth.

In another case the Supreme Court refused to allow a grand jury witness to invoke the exclusionary rule, indicating that this would unduly interfere with the effective and expeditious discharge of the grand jury's duties.[24] In this case the majority of the Supreme Court indicated some disillusionment with the exclusionary rule in their conclusions that:

> In sum, the rule is a judicially created remedy designed to safeguard Fourth Amendment rights generally through its deterrent effect, rather than a personal constitutional right of the party aggrieved.

---

22 Walder v. United States, 347 U.S. 62, 74 S. Ct. 354, 98 L. Ed. 503 (1954).

23 Oregon v. Hass, 420 U.S. 714, 95 S. Ct. 1215, 43 L. Ed. 2d 570 (1975).

24 United States v. Calandra, 414 U.S. 338, 94 S. Ct. 613, 38 L. Ed. 2d 561 (1974).

> Despite its broad deterrent purpose, the exclusionary rule has never been interpreted to proscribe the use of illegally seized evidence in all proceedings or against all persons. As with any remedial device, the application of the rule has been restricted to those areas where its remedial objectives are thought most efficaciously served.

In yet another case the majority found that the judicially created exclusionary rule should not be extended to forbid in civil proceedings of one sovereign (here, the federal government) the use of evidence seized by a criminal law enforcement agent in another sovereign (here, the state government), since the likelihood of deterring law enforcement conduct through such a rule is not sufficient to outweigh the societal cost imposed by the exclusion.[25]

One reason the exclusionary rule was adopted was to prevent officials -- purposely or negligently -- from violating rights protected by the Fourth Amendment. If the exclusionary rule is further modified or its application further restricted, law enforcement officers must continue to make every effort to understand thoroughly the rules regarding search and seizure and to apply them in a professional manner. Failure to do so will most certainly result in a return to the strict application of the rule.

The various methods by which evidence may be legally seized are discussed in the sections which follow.

§ 4.7 Search with a valid search warrant

One method of making a search which is universally recognized as legal is to search with a valid warrant. Both the United States Constitution and the constitutions of the various states describe the circumstances under which search warrants may be issued. They generally provide, "No warrants shall issue, but upon probable cause, supported by oath or affirmation, and particularly describing the place to be searched and the persons or things to be seized." No other means of making a search is mentioned in the Constitution.

When it is practicable, the best method of making a search is with a search warrant. Generally speaking, an officer who proceeds under the authority of a warrant regular and valid upon its face is protected against both civil and criminal liability.

---

[25] United States v. Janis, 429 U.S. 874, 96 S. Ct. 3021, 49 L. Ed. 2d 1046 (1976).

1. *Definition of a search warrant*

A search warrant has been defined as an order in writing in the name of the state, signed by a judicial officer in the proper exercise of his authority, directing a peace officer to search for personal property and to bring it before the court.

2. *Requirements for a search warrant*

A search warrant cannot be issued unless it meets the requirements as set forth in the Constitution. Also, search warrants must meet other requirements as determined by the courts in order for the search warrant to be legal and the evidence seized thereunder to be admissible in the court.

For a warrant to be valid:

(a) The proper official must issue the warrant

Provisions of state statutes specifically authorize the use of a warrant and designate the officials who may issue the warrant. The warrants must be issued by a "neutral and detached" official in order to meet the Fourth Amendment standards.[26]

The issuance of a search warrant is a function of the judicial branch of government. Therefore, a practice whereby a member of the police department or a district attorney has the authority to issue a search warrant is probably improper.[27] Where a judicial officer has *limited* authority under the statute to issue warrants in *restricted* cases, obviously a warrant issued by such official for searches which would be outside his authority would not be legal and the evidence secured thereunder would be inadmissible.

Although the Supreme Court has justified the issuance of an arrest warrant by a clerk when the arrest is for a violation of the municipal ordinance, there is no such authority for the issuance of a search warrant by a clerk.[28] And where the statute provides that a search warrant may be issued by a district court judge or a supreme court judge, a warrant signed by the clerk of the court rather than the judge is invalid.[29]

Apparently in a few jurisdictions, prosecuting attorneys and even police officers have been authorized to issue search warrants. This practice was

---

[26] Lo-Ji Sales, Inc. v. New York, 442 U.S. 319, 99 S. Ct. 319, 60 L. Ed. 2d 920 (1979).

[27] In *White v. Simpson*, 28 Wis. 2d 590, 137 N.W.2d 391 (1965), a statute permitting the district attorney to issue arrest warrants was declared unconstitutional.

[28] *See* § 3.6 and cases cited under subdivision 7.

[29] State v. Cochrane, 84 S.D. 538, 173 N.W.2d 495 (1970).

found improper in a 1971 case.[30] In that case warrants were signed and issued by the attorney general acting as a justice of the peace. The majority of the court agreed with the petitioner's claim that the warrant was invalid as not being issued by a "neutral and detached magistrate." The Court emphasized the reason for the rule that the warrant must be issued by a "neutral and detached magistrate" with this statement:

> Without disrespect to the state law enforcement agent here involved, the whole point of the basic rule...is that prosecutors and policemen simply cannot be asked to maintain the requisite neutrality with regard to their own investigations....

In a move to speed up the process of securing search warrants, the state of California and a few other states have enacted legislation giving peace officers authority to sign the judge's name to search warrants after obtaining judicial permission over the telephone. In such case, the same degree of proof must be presented by telephone to the judge as is required in a face-to-face request by police for search warrants.

(b) A warrant may be issued only for authorized objects

There is nothing in the Constitution which limits the type of evidence that can be seized under a warrant. However, the United States Supreme Court, in several early cases, adopted what came to be called the "mere evidence" rule. One of these cases, *Gouled v. United States*,[31] held that searches for and seizures of items to be used as "mere evidence" of crime would not be authorized unless the government could assert some superior right to the property. From this grew the rule which was later codified in the Federal Rules of Criminal Procedure, that warrants could be issued only for stolen or embezzled property, property used as a means of committing a crime, or contraband goods.

The "mere evidence" rule was challenged and expressly overruled in the case of *Warden v. Hayden*.[32] In that case, Mr. Justice Brennan, speaking for the majority, rejected the proposition that the Constitution limits searches and seizures to fruits of the crime, weapons by which escape of the person arrested might be effected, and property, the possession of which is a crime. The majority explained:

---

30 Coolidge v. New Hampshire, 403 U.S. 443, 91 S. Ct. 2022, 29 L. Ed. 2d 564 (1971).

31 255 U.S. 298, 41 S. Ct. 261, 65 L. Ed. 647 (1921).

32 387 U.S. 294, 87 S. Ct. 1642, 18 L. Ed. 2d 782 (1967).

> We come, then, to the question whether, even though the search was lawful, the Court of Appeals was correct in holding that the seizure and introduction of the items of clothing violated the Fourth Amendment because they are "mere evidence." The distinction made by some of our cases between seizure of items of evidential value only and seizure of instrumentalities, fruits, or contraband has been criticized by courts and commentators. The Court of Appeals, however, felt "obligated to adhere to it."...We today reject the distinction as based on premises no longer accepted as rules governing the application of the Fourth Amendment.

Following this decision, Congress amended the Federal Code by inserting this language:

> In addition to the grounds for issuing a warrant in section 3103 of this title, a warrant may be issued to search for and seize any property that constitutes evidence of a criminal offense in violation of the laws of the United States.[33]

With this amendment, federal warrants may now be issued for "mere evidence" in addition to the other articles previously mentioned.

Some state legislatures, recognizing the arbitrary distinction of types of evidence which could be seized, broadened the authority by statute even before the *Warden* case. For example, in Illinois a statute was enacted which provides that the search warrant may be issued for seizure of..."any instruments, articles or things which have been used in the commission of, or which may constitute *evidence* of, the offense in connection with which the warrant is issued."[34] (Emphasis added.)

Some states still have provisions which limit the type of evidence which can be seized under a warrant. If the state still has these limitations, they must be followed.

(c) The warrant must be issued "on probable cause"

(i) Definition and explanation

The Fourth Amendment to the Constitution and the state constitutions provide that no warrant shall issue but upon "probable cause." Many efforts

---

33 18 U.S.C. § 3103(a) (1970). See New Jersey v. T.L.O., 469 U.S. 325, 105 S. Ct. 733, 83 L. Ed. 2d 720 (1985) which cites *Warden v. Hayden*. The seizure was justified despite the fact that the evidence constituted "mere evidence" of a violation.

34 Ill. Rev. Stat. ch. 38, § 108-3(a) (1988).

have been made to define probable cause as required by this provision of the Constitution and many cases have been decided determining not only the meaning of probable cause, but the evidence necessary in order for the judicial officer to determine that probable cause exists.

The Supreme Court, in the case of *Dumbra v. United States*,[35] made this statement concerning the probable cause requirements:

> [I]f the apparent facts set out in the affidavit are such that a reasonably discreet and prudent man would be led to believe that there was a commission of the offense charged, there is probable cause justifying the issuance of a warrant.

As a general rule the application for a search warrant must contain a statement of facts which indicate that there is probable cause to believe that the evidence being sought is in the place designated to be searched. The issuing magistrate or judge, before determining that probable cause exists, must have facts that go beyond mere suspicion but which need not constitute "beyond a reasonable doubt" evidence. While some states authorize the issuing official to consider information that is not written in the affidavit to support the warrant, other states required that the information used to establish probable cause be either stated in the application or summarized in writing or recorded when the warrant is issued.[36] In an Illinois case the court noted that evaluation as to whether probable cause exists for the issuance of a search warrant must be made by a "neutral and detached" judicial officer and not the police officer; and the determination must be made from sworn statements or affidavits presented to the judicial judge.[37]

If a statute requires the information used to establish probable cause be stated or summarized in writing or recorded when the warrant is issued, then other information cannot be considered when the warrant is challenged.

In the usual case, the affiant is a police officer or an agent, but information may be furnished to the issuing official by a private citizen. For example, the affidavit of a police officer, even though insufficient in itself, when supported by the sworn testimony of a landlord was adequate in one case to establish probable cause.[38]

The affidavit to support probable cause may be challenged if the defense makes a substantial preliminary showing that a false statement was made

---

[35] 268 U.S. 435, 45 S. Ct. 546, 69 L. Ed. 1032 (1925).

[36] N.C. GEN. STAT. § 15A-245 (1988); State v. Hicks, 60 N.C. App. 116, 298 S.E.2d 180 (1982).

[37] People v. Greer, 57 Ill. Dec. 607, 429 N.E.2d 505 (1981).

[38] State v. Valde, 225 N.W.2d 313 (Iowa 1975).

knowingly and intelligently and in bad faith. In a case that reached the U.S. Supreme Court,[39] the use of items of clothing and a knife found in the search of the defendant's apartment was challenged because the affidavit supporting the search warrant contained substantial misstatements. The Supreme Court of Delaware had held that the defendant under no circumstances may challenge the veracity of a sworn statement used by the police to procure a search warrant. The defendant had requested the right to call witnesses who would testify that statements attributed to them and included in the affidavit were, in fact, not made by them. The state's attorney argued that the defense could not "go behind the warrant affidavit in any way."

The Supreme Court acknowledged that there is a presumption that the affidavit supporting the warrant is valid and that the warrant itself is valid. The Court also acknowledged that the challenger's attack to the warrant or the affidavit must be more than conclusory and must be supported by more than a mere desire to cross-examine. Furthermore, the Court agreed that allegations of negligence or innocent mistake are insufficient and that if there remains sufficient content in the affidavit to support a finding of probable cause, no hearing to challenge the warrant will be entertained.

However, if, after a hearing, the defendant establishes by the preponderance of the evidence that the false statement was included in the affidavit by the affiant knowingly and intelligently, or with reckless disregard for the truth, and the false statement was necessary to the finding of probable cause, then the search warrant must be voided and the fruits of the search excluded from the trial to the same extent as if probable cause was lacking on the face of the affidavit.

As was indicated in the section relating to probable cause for an arrest warrant, probable cause is a fluid concept and depends upon the probabilities that the evidence can be found in the place described. Although the definition cannot be reduced to specific terms, the cases shed some light on the meaning of probable cause. "Probable" does not mean beyond a reasonable doubt but as was noted in the case of *Illinois v. Gates*, the magistrate should determine that there is "a fair probability" that evidence of the crime will be found in the particular place described.

The probable cause requirement of the Fourth Amendment received additional attention from the Supreme Court in 1986.[40] The defendant in an obscenity case presented the novel argument that the probable cause standard for an application for a warrant authorizing the seizure of materials presumably protected by the First Amendment must be of a higher degree than

---

39 Franks v. Delaware, 438 U.S. 154, 98 S. Ct. 2674, 57 L. Ed. 2d 667 (1978).

40 New York v. P.J. Video, Inc., 475 U.S. 868, 106 S. Ct. 1610, 89 L. Ed. 2d 871 (1986).

that required for other tangible articles. The New York Court of Appeals was swayed by this argument and reversed a conviction of a defendant in an obscenity case, agreeing with the defendant that there was a higher probable cause standard for issuing warrants to seize such things as books and movies than for warrants for seizure of such things as weapons or drugs.

The United States Supreme Court admonished the trial court; pointing out that the Supreme Court had never held or said that such a higher standard is required where searches are for articles protected by the First Amendment. Specifically, the Supreme Court noted that:

> We think, and accordingly hold, that an application for a warrant authorizing the seizure of material presumptively protected by the First Amendment should be evaluated under the same standards of probable cause used to review warrant applications generally.

As to the probable cause standard, the Court, in citing other cases, noted that:

> The term "probable cause"...means less than evidence which would justify condemnation...It imports a seizure made under circumstances which warrants suspicion...Finely tuned standards such as proof beyond a reasonable doubt or by the preponderance of the evidence, useful in formal trials, have no place in the magistrate's decision.

The court ended the decision with this comment:

> We believe that the analysis and conclusion expressed by the dissenting judge are completely consistent with our statement in *Gates* that "probable cause requires only a probability or substantial chance of criminal activity, not an actual showing of such activity."

The standard of proof required is discussed in the following paragraphs.

(ii) Standard of proof

There are many issues relative to the probable cause requirement. Two have received particular attention over the years. One of these concerns the standard or degree of proof necessary to support a finding of probable cause. This is discussed here. The other matter concerns the use of informants, both disclosed and undisclosed, and will be discussed in the next subsection.

Probable cause is just what it says. That is, there must be sufficient facts to indicate that the articles described are *probably* located at the place described. Absolute certainty is not required in determining probable cause. Something less than "beyond a reasonable doubt" is necessary, but more than mere suspicion is required. In the case of *Brinegar v. United States*,[41] the Supreme Court stated that there is a large difference between the two things to be proved (guilt and probable cause), as well as the tribunals which determine them. This Court also made it clear that a lesser quanta of proof is required to establish probable cause than to establish proof beyond a reasonable doubt.

Though proof beyond a reasonable doubt is not the necessary standard of proof for probable cause, a clearly conclusory statement by the affiant is not sufficient. For example, where the sole support for a warrant was the sworn statement of a sheriff that the defendant "did then and there lawfully break and enter a locked and sealed building" the warrant was invalid.[42] The conviction was set aside because the affidavit stated a mere conclusion of the officer. The Supreme Court made this comment concerning probable cause in the *Whiteley* case:

> The decisions of this Court concerning Fourth Amendment probable cause requirements before a warrant for either arrest or search can issue require that the judicial officer issuing such a warrant be supplied with sufficient information to support an independent judgment that probable cause exists for the warrant.

Although some earlier cases held that no opinions or hearsay could be the basis of issuing a search warrant, modern decisions have approved complaints that have been based in part on hearsay information.[43]

(iii) Use of informants

Much of the information to support probable cause comes from informants and is, therefore, hearsay. Although such hearsay may be used, the officer or affiant must establish that the hearsay information is sufficient to insure a substantial basis for concluding that probable cause exists. The issuing official will also evaluate the information in view of his own experience

---

41 338 U.S. 160, 69 S. Ct. 1302, 93 L. Ed. 1879 (1949).

42 Whiteley v. Warden, 401 U.S. 560, 91 S. Ct. 1051, 28 L. Ed. 2d 306 (1971).

43 People v. Elias, 316 Ill. 376, 147 N.E. 2d 472 (1975); People v. Jackson, 22 Ill. 2d 382, 176 N.E.2d 803 (1961); Jones v. United States, 362 U.S. 257, 80 S. Ct. 725, 4 L. Ed. 2d 697 (1960); United States v. Ventresca, 380 U.S. 102, 85 S. Ct. 7441, 13 L. Ed. 2d 684 (1965).

and judgment. He will take into consideration the corroborative information furnished by the police officer and compare the specific allegations with the circumstances surrounding the alleged offense.

There are many varieties and types of informants. Despite the fact that much attention has been devoted to the use of undisclosed informants, in many instances the information to support probable cause is from reputable lay citizens, public officials or other law enforcement officials.

In the case of *Aguilar v. Texas*, decided in 1964, the United States Supreme Court approved the use of information from an undisclosed informant in determining probable cause, but warned that the magistrate must be informed of the underlying circumstances from which the informant concluded that the information was reliable and the informant creditable.[44] In that case, the Court laid down a two-pronged standard for testing the credibility of an informant's tip upon which a magistrate is asked to rely:

(1) the magistrate must be given some of the underlying circumstances from which the affiant concluded that the information was creditable, or that his information was reliable; and
(2) he must be given some of the underlying circumstances from which the informant reached the conclusion conveyed in the tip.[45]

In 1969, the Supreme Court set aside a conviction because the underlying circumstances were not explained in enough detail. There the Court warned that if the informant's tip is not corroborated, the issuing official must be given sufficient information for him to reach an independent conclusion that the informant was creditable and his information reliable.[46] Unless these two prongs were both approved, evidence from an undisclosed informant was not admissible to show probable cause. As pointed out by one court, the dual requirements represented by the two-pronged test are analytically severable and an overkill on one prong will not carry over to make up for a deficit on the other prong.[47]

After much confusion and many cases attempting to interpret the requirements, the Supreme Court was, in 1983, again requested to verify the requirements for probable cause.[48]

---

44 Aguilar v. Texas, 378 U.S. 108, 84 S. Ct. 1509, 12 L. Ed. 2d 723 (1964).

45 United States v. Cummings, 507 F.2d 524 (8th Cir. 1974).

46 Spinelli v. United States, 393 U.S. 410, 89 S. Ct. 584, 21 L. Ed. 2d 637 (1969).

47 Stanley v. State, 19 Md. App. 507, 313 A.2d 847 (1974).

48 Illinois v. Gates, 462 U.S. 213, 103 S. Ct. 2317, 76 L. Ed. 2d 527 (1983).

In the *Gates* case, the police had received an anonymous letter including statements that Gates and his wife were engaged in selling drugs, that the wife would be driving a car loaded with drugs on a certain date, and that the suspects had over $100,000 worth of drugs in their basement. Acting on this information, a police officer, with assistance from the Drug Enforcement Administration agent, verified that the husband, Gates, took a flight as stated in the anonymous letter and met a woman driving a car bearing an Illinois license plate issued to the husband. A search warrant for the residence and automobile was obtained based on the affidavit setting forth the foregoing facts and a copy of the anonymous letter.

The trial court ordered that the evidence obtained as a result of the warrant be suppressed and the Illinois Appellate Court affirmed. The Illinois Supreme Court also affirmed, holding that the letter and affidavit were inadequate to sustain a determination of probable cause for issuance of the search warrant under *Aguilar v. Texas*. The prosecution appealed.

The question before the United States Supreme Court was whether the rigid "two pronged" test under *Aguilar* and *Spinelli* for determining whether an informant's tip establishes probable cause for issuance of a warrant should be modified and the "totality of circumstances" approach that traditionally has informed probable cause determinations is to be substituted in its place. The United States Supreme Court, by a narrow five to four decision, held that the issuing judge had a substantial basis for concluding that probable cause to search respondent's home and car existed. The Supreme Court agreed with the Illinois Supreme Court that an informant's veracity, reliability, and basis of knowledge are all highly relevant in determining the value of a report concerning an informant. However, the Supreme Court did not agree that these elements should be understood as entirely separate and independent requirements, to be rigidly exacted in every case.

Recognizing that informants' tips come in many shapes and sizes and from many different types of persons, the Court indicated that the "totality of circumstances" approach is far more consistent with the court's prior treatment of probable cause and would be the test to be applied by reviewing courts.

The test, according to the *Gates* case, in determining if an informant's tip plus other information is sufficient to justify the issuance of a search warrant, is the "totality of circumstances" approach that traditionally has informed probable cause determinations. Although this still leaves some doubt, the Supreme Court made it clear that:

> The task of the issuing magistrate is simply to make a practical, common-sense decision whether, given all of the circumstances set forth in the affidavit before him, including the "veracity" and "basis

> of knowledge" of persons supplying hearsay information, there is a fair probability that contraband or evidence of a crime will be found in a particular place, and the duty of the reviewing court is simply to insure that the magistrate had a "substantial basis for concluding" that probable cause existed.

The effect of this decision is to give more authority to issuing magistrates in determining if probable cause exists after considering all of the circumstances, including the use of evidence from an undisclosed informant. The Supreme Court again admonished the lower courts that a grudging or negative attitude by reviewing courts toward warrants is inconsistent with the Fourth Amendment's strong preference for searches conducted pursuant to a warrant.[49]

It is obvious that information from disclosed informants may also be used in determining probable cause. Even before the *Gates* case relaxed the requirements for using the information from an undisclosed informant, the courts agreed that the rationale behind requiring a showing of credibility and reliability is to prevent searches based upon an unknown informant's tip that may not reflect anything more than idle rumor or irresponsible conjecture. This danger of the use of unreliable evidence is not as likely when a disclosed informant gives the information to support the warrant.

Frequently there is misunderstanding regarding the disclosure of informants. There are, of course, instances where the informer must be disclosed if it is necessary for a fair defense. This is quite different from disclosing the informer who has not participated in a crime but only gives information on which probable cause for the search warrant is based. In the case of *Nutter v. State*,[50] the state court defined the circumstances under which the informer must be disclosed. The court explained that the state has a privilege to withhold from disclosure the identity of persons who furnish information to police concerning the commission of crimes. However:

> On the issue of guilt or innocence and upon demand by the defendant, the trial court may, in the exercise of its judicial discretion,

---

49 United States v. Ventresca, 380 U.S. 102, 84 S. Ct. 741, 13 L. Ed. 2d 684 (1965); See Massachusetts v. Upton, 466 U.S. 727, 104 S. Ct. 2085, 80 L. Ed. 2d 721 (1984) which reaffirmed the *Gates* opinion and in which the U.S. Supreme Court criticized the Massachusetts court for failing to abandon the two-pronged test of *Aguilar*. The Supreme Court of the United States made it quite clear that the two-pronged test is dead and the proper test is the "totality of circumstances" analysis.

50 8 Md. App. 635, 262 A.2d 80 (1970).

> compel such disclosure upon determination that it is necessary and relevant to a fair defense. Factors to be considered in ascertaining whether such disclosure is necessary and relevant to a fair defense include the nature of the crime charged; the importance of the informer's identity to a determination of innocence, as for example whether or not the informer was an integral part of the illegal transaction and the possible significance of his testimony; and the possible defenses. Whether the privilege must yield depends upon the facts and circumstances of the particular case. But if the informer testifies for the state, the privilege may not be invoked by it.

According to the United States Supreme Court there is no fixed rule with respect to the disclosure of an informer in criminal prosecutions. The problem is one that calls for balancing the public interest in protecting the flow of information against an individual's right to prepare his defense. Whether a proper balance renders nondisclosure erroneous must depend on the particular circumstances of each case, taking into consideration the crime charged, possible defenses, the possible significance of the informer's testimony, and other relevant factors.[51]

In this case where the informer was the only witness in a position to amplify or contradict testimony of the government witnesses, and a government witness testified that the informer had denied knowing the accused or ever having seen him before, it was prejudicial error to deny disclosure of the informant. However, it is again noted that if the informant merely gives information concerning probable cause for the warrant and is not involved in the activity, his identity need not be disclosed.

A North Carolina court made it clear that there is a difference between disclosing the informant who furnishes probable cause for a search warrant and the informant who participates in the alleged crime and is a material witness who might be helpful to the defense.[52] In the *Hodges* case the defendant sought disclosure of the name of the informant alleging that the informant participated in the sale of narcotics to the undercover police officer and was the only person at the scene except the officer when the transaction took place. The reviewing court recognized at the outset of the review that the court was not concerned with probable cause for a search warrant, but "instead we are involved with guilt or innocence, the right of the defendant to know the identity of a participating informant in advance of trial so that the defendant may properly prepare his defense."

---

51 Roviaro v. United States, 353 U.S. 53, 77 S. Ct. 623, 1 L. Ed. 2d 639 (1957).

52 State v. Hodges, 275 S.E.2d 533 (N.C. App. 1981).

While acknowledging that both state and federal cases protected the informer's privilege and that there is no fixed rule with respect to the disclosure of informants, the Court noted that the problem is one that calls for a balancing of public interest in protecting the flow of information against the individual's right to prepare his defense. The court explained that the issue in this case was not whether the confidential informant who gave information for a search warrant should be disclosed but whether the testimony is highly relevant and might be helpful to the defense. Disclosure is required when the informant participated in the alleged crime and is thus a material witness.

(d) The warrant must be "supported by oath or affirmation"

The Fourth Amendment to the Constitution includes a requirement that the warrant be supported by oath or affirmation. Although this responsibility is placed upon the issuing official, it is often necessary that the official be reminded of this requirement. If this requirement is not met, the evidence obtained under the warrant will not be admitted into court. Therefore, not only the police officer but the prosecutor should make certain that this provision is carried out. Unless the affidavit on which the search warrant is based is supported by oath or affirmation, the warrant is issued unlawfully and the search conducted thereunder is unlawful.[53]

There is a presumption that the warrant is supported by oath and affirmation. However, this presumption is rebuttable and the defense may introduce evidence showing that no oath was administered.

(e) The place to be searched and the things to be seized must be "particularly" described

The Fourth Amendment to the Constitution and the various state constitutional provisions include a requirement that not only the place to be searched be particularly described, but also that the property to be seized be particularly described. The Constitution does not define the word "particularly" and again it is necessary to review the cases for an interpretation.

It is not necessary to have a legal description such as would be required on a deed of conveyance. The Constitution requires that the premises be defined with practical accuracy. However, the description must be sufficiently definite so as to clearly distinguish the premises from all others. It must be such that the officer executing the warrant can, with reasonable effort, identify the exact place to the distinction of all others. The name of the owner of

---

53 Rose v. State, 171 Ind. 662, 87 N.E. 103 (1909).

the house is not necessary, unless this is needed to identify the particular house.

Describing the house as a certain number on a certain street is usually sufficient but is not necessarily required, if the premises are otherwise so described that they can be readily identified. Where there are two streets in the same city bearing identical names and numbers, or more than one building at the designated street number, a description giving only the number and street would not be sufficient, as it would not exclude others. Obviously, a search warrant directing officers to search all places would be clearly illegal, and a search warrant with the description of the premises left blank, to be filled in by the officer making the search, is illegal. It is this type of general warrant that the Fourth Amendment was designed to prohibit.

Some courts are very technical in requiring that the description be specific. For example, the United States District Court for the Eastern District of Michigan found a warrant invalid because it failed to sufficiently identify the place to be searched in that it did not indicate that the building was a two-family dwelling.[54]

While some courts are very strict in applying the "particular description" requirement, the trend apparently is to apply a more practical test. For example, in the case of *Maryland v. Garrison* the Supreme Court made allowances for mistakes by police officers in approving a search of a second apartment on the third floor of a building where the officers mistakenly believed there was only one apartment.[55]

When the Baltimore police officers requested a warrant for controlled substances and related paraphernalia, they reasonably believed that there was only one apartment on the third floor of the premises, but in fact the third floor was divided into two apartments. Before they became aware they were in the wrong apartment, the officers discovered the contraband that provided the basis for the conviction for violating Maryland's Controlled Substance Act. The trial court denied the defendant's motion to suppress the evidence, but the Maryland Court of Appeals reversed.

The majority of the United States Supreme Court, agreeing that the officers made a reasonable effort to ascertain and identify the place intended to be searched, reasoned that the discovery after the execution of the warrant of facts demonstrating that the warrant was unnecessarily broad, does not retroactively invalidate the warrant. The Court included this comment:

> But we must judge the constitutionality of their conduct in light of the information available to them at the time they acted. Those

---

54 United States v. Estes, 336 F. Supp. 214 (E.D. Mich. 1972).

55 Maryland v. Garrison, ___ U.S. ___, 107 S. Ct. 1013, 94 L. Ed. 2d 72 (1987).

> items of evidence that emerge after the warrant is issued have no bearing on whether or not a warrant was validly issued...the validity of the warrant must be assessed on the basis of the information that the officers disclosed, or had a duty to discover and to disclose, to the issuing magistrate.

The Court cautioned that officers in preparing affidavits for a search warrant must make a reasonable effort to find all of the facts. But the majority recognized the need to allow some latitude for honest mistakes that are made by officers in the "dangerous and difficult process of making arrests and executing search warrants."

The constitutional provisions require that the "places" must be described and that the "things" to be seized must also be described. If the warrant fails to adequately describe the property to be seized, any seizure made under the warrant will be inadmissible.[56] The officer must, therefore, obtain as specific a description of the goods as is reasonably possible under the circumstances.

The purpose of the description of "things" requirement is to prevent the seizure of articles that are not subject to seizure and to identify the property to the extent that even an officer who is unfamiliar with the case can read the description and know what items should be seized. Generally greater detail in the description is required when the property to be seized can be possessed lawfully than is required when the property can never be lawfully possessed, such as controlled substances. While it is preferable to state the drug to be seized specifically, some cases have upheld the seizure of "controlled substances" especially when the statement of probable cause in the affidavit describes the specific drug.

In condemning the seizure of evidence not particularly described, the United States Supreme Court made this comment:

> Nor does the Fourth Amendment countenance open-ended warrants, to be completed while a search is being conducted and items seized or after the seizure has been carried out.[57]

In 1985 a United States Court of Appeals reviewed the "description" requirements discussed in previous cases.[58] The affidavit for the warrant and supporting exhibits attached to the warrant detailed the nature of the tax

---

56 Giles v. United States, 284 F. 208 (D.N.H. 1922).

57 Lo-Ji Sales, Inc. v. New York, 442 U.S. 319, 99 S. Ct. 2319, 60 L. Ed. 2d 920 (1979).

58 United States v. Cantu, 774 F.2d 1305 (5th Cir. 1985).

fraud investigation and identified specific documents, typewriters used in preparation of false federal income tax claims, and "all other property that constitutes evidence of the preparation and filing of false income tax refund claims." In this case, the reviewing court agreed that the description of materials specified in the warrant clearly identified the documents subject to seizure and the items actually seized fell squarely within the scope of the warrant.

A North Carolina court in reviewing the particularity of the description noted that warrants which do not specify items to be searched or persons to be arrested and which are not supported by a showing of probable cause that a particular crime has been committed are general warrants banned by the Fourth Amendment.[59] In making references to the description of "things" as used in the Constitution, the court noted that:

> A warrant describes items with sufficient particularity when it enables the officer executing the warrant reasonably to ascertain and identify the items to be seized...However, the degree to which a warrant must particularly describe the items to be seized depends on the nature of the items.

The court explained that where the case involves a complex scheme and numerous records, the investigators executing a search warrant will have to exercise some discretion in separating innocuous material from incriminating evidence and that the Fourth Amendment does not require that the warrant enumerate each individual paper.

In order to avoid having the search declared illegal and the evidence obtained thereunder rendered inadmissible, the officer should take care to specifically designate the exact premises to be searched, including the area within the premises. He should also obtain as nearly as possible the description of the things to be seized therefrom.

Some state statutes include additional requirements. For example, the state of Illinois requires that the warrant shall state the time and date of issuance. The officer must be familiar with the state codes concerning the requirements for a search warrant. Obviously, another requirement is that the signature of the issuing official be on the warrant. The warrant is not complete until signed and it cannot be amended once the signature has been affixed to the warrant. The magistrate cannot by his subsequent signing of the warrant legalize the search made under the unsigned warrant.

---

59 State v. Kornegay, 326 S.E.2d 881 (N.C. 1985).

3. *Execution of the search warrant*

When the warrant has been properly issued by the issuing official, the police officer has no choice but to execute the warrant. In executing the warrant and in proceeding in the manner in which the warrant directs, the officer is carrying out the orders of the court. If the warrant is valid on its face, has been issued by the proper official, and is executed properly, the officer is protected from civil liability as well as criminal prosecution.

Even *with* the warrant, the officer must follow certain procedures in order for the execution to be lawful and the evidence to be admissible in court. These procedures are set out below:

(a) The warrant must be executed by an officer so commanded

As the warrant is an order of the court it can only be executed by the person designated by name or class. If, as is true in the usual case, the warrant is issued to a class of officers, it may be executed by any officer in that class. Many statutes now provide that the warrant shall be directed for execution to all peace officers of the state. If the warrant is directed for execution to a certain peace officer, other officers may assist in the execution.

(b) The warrant must be executed within time limitations

In absence of statute, the constitutional guarantees are violated where the warrant is not executed within a reasonable time. The term "reasonable" has not been specifically defined, however. Obviously the warrant must be executed while there is still probable cause that the items to be sought are on the described premises. If there is evidence that the described property has been removed from the premises, then the search warrant may not be used as a weapon or form of coercion upon the person or premises against whom it is directed.

To avoid unnecessary confusion and litigation, many of the states by legislative action have designated the time within which a warrant may be executed. For example, the Illinois criminal code provides that the warrant shall be executed within ninety-six hours from the time of issuance. Rule 41 of the Federal Rules provides that the warrant shall command the officer to search forthwith the place named for the property specified and that the warrant may be executed and returned only within ten days after its date. A warrant not executed within the time limitations as provided by the statute, or not executed within a reasonable time, is void. If the statutes limit the execution of the warrant to the daytime, unless certain conditions are met, a warrant executed in violation of the state statute would be illegally executed and the evidence obtained thereunder inadmissible.

A federal case held that a search initiated in the daytime under a daytime search warrant may continue into the nighttime for so long as reasonably necessary for completion.[60]

(c) Only necessary force may be used in executing a warrant

By common law and under the statutes, the officer is justified in using necessary force to execute the warrant. The United States Code provides that in executing a warrant an officer has the authority to break both outer and inner doors if, after giving notice of his authority and purpose and demanding entrance, he is refused admittance.[61] If the occupant denies admittance to the premises, the officer may use such force as is reasonably necessary to gain entry. Denial of admission does not have to be specific but may be inferred from the surrounding circumstances, as when a person known to be inside refuses to come to the door. Once inside, the searching officer may use such force as is necessary to gain entrance into closets, rooms or other places. In such case the force should be used only if the occupant refuses to provide access to the place to be searched.

The courts have placed more importance on life and safety than on the execution of the search warrant. Therefore, deadly force or force which may cause serious bodily injury is not reasonable nor authorized. If, however, the person in charge of the premises or the person who is described in the search warrant threatens the officer with deadly force, the officer may use such force to seize the person and search him. If the offense involved is a misdemeanor, the officer would find it extremely difficult to justify the use of deadly force merely to execute the search warrant.

If no one is in charge of the premises, the officer may nevertheless carry out the instructions of the court in searching the premises described. In some instances where there is no need for prompt action, it is advisable to seek entrance from a neighbor or delay until the occupant can admit the police officers. Although this is apparently not a legal requirement, it might be preferable to breaking down doors unnecessarily.

(d) Prior notice and demand should usually precede forcible entry

Some statutes require that prior notice and demand be given before entry, while other statutes are silent on the subject. Even where there is no statute, most courts by case law require that prior notice be given unless an exception exists. The purpose of the entry announcement, or as some courts call it the "knock and announce" rule, is to protect the privacy of the individ-

---

60 United States v. Joseph, 278 F.2d 504 (3d Cir. 1960).

61 18 U.S.C. § 3109 (1970).

ual, to avoid needless destruction of property of occupants who are willing to voluntarily admit the police, and to shield the officers from attack by surprised residents.[62] Notwithstanding the fact that notice of entry is generally preferable and often required, case law has recognized the anachronism of the notice rule in an era of indoor plumbing. The experienced officer recognizes that it takes only a few seconds for a person to destroy evidence. And the danger of giving the person accused of a serious crime the time to injure the officer is readily recognized.[63]

Acknowledging the need to make a speedy entrance, especially in drug cases, several states have enacted what is known as "no-knock" provisions in their statutes. The Federal Drug Abuse, Prevention, and Control Act of 1970 included such legislation, but this was repealed in 1974 due, in part, to apparent abuse by enforcement officers. The passing of the 1970 Act and the later amendment to that Act caused some unnecessary confusion in the minds of many officers. First, this Act applied only to federal officers, and the repeal, therefore, did not affect the vast majority of officers. Secondly, case law existed prior to the Act and has been reemphasized since the amendment.

In the case of *Miller v. United States*,[64] an exception for exigent circumstances such as immediate physical danger, flight, or destruction of evidence was discussed. And in 1956, the California Supreme Court, in the case of *People v. Maddox*,[65] allowed unannounced entry despite a provision in the state statute which provided that notice be given.

Some states, such as Nebraska, have statutes authorizing the issuance of no-knock warrants where evidence exists showing the necessity. The statute provides:

> The judge or magistrate may so direct only upon proof under oath, to his satisfaction, that the property sought may be easily or quickly destroyed or disposed of, or that danger to the life or limb of the officer or another may result, if such notice be given;...[66]

---

[62] United States v. Beale, 436 F.2d 573 (5th Cir. 1971) and Sabbath v. United States, 391 U.S. 585, 88 S. Ct. 1755, 20 L. Ed. 2d 828 (1968).

[63] Jackson v. United States, 354 F.2d 980 (1st Cir. 1965). A thirty-second wait between notice and forcible entry was reasonable in a North Carolina case where the warrant directed the officers to search an apartment for cocaine. State v. Edwards, 70 N.C. App. 317, 319 S.E.2d 613 (1984).

[64] 357 U.S. 301, 78 S. Ct. 1190, 2 L. Ed. 2d 1332 (1958).

[65] 46 Cal. 2d 301, 294 P.2d 6 (1956).

[66] NEB. REV. STAT. § 29-411 (1975).

If a no-knock warrant is obtained, information must be included in the affidavit in order to justify the court in issuing this type of warrant.[67] Such a state statutory "knock and announce" rule was satisfied where the police, armed with a search warrant, knocked on the defendant's door, the defendant asked from inside "who is there?", the police answered by calling the defendant's name, and the defendant responded by saying "come on in" which the police immediately did.[68] The Court in this case explained that the main purpose of the rule, to guarantee peaceful surrender of premises for the service of warrants, had, in effect, been satisfied by the scenario. In applying that reasoning to the case, the Court determined that the entry was made without injury to persons or property, hence the purpose of the rule in preventing violence to persons and damages to property was fulfilled. Concluding that an announcement of the purpose, prior to the entry under these circumstances so as to afford the occupant the opportunity to surrender the premises peacefully would have been a "futile gesture" as appellee had already surrendered the premises, the majority agreed that the entry met the constitutional mandate.

In a 1974 case, the Second Circuit Court of Appeals listed three exceptions to the requirement that the officer must knock, announce his authority and purpose, and be refused admittance before he can break in.[69] There the Circuit Court stated that the United States Supreme Court has acknowledged the three exceptions, namely:

(1) where persons within already know of the officer's authority and purpose;
(2) where the officers are justified in the belief that persons within are in imminent peril of bodily harm; or
(3) where those within, made aware of the presence of someone outside, are then engaged in activity which justifies the officers' belief that an escape or the destruction of evidence is being attempted.

The court justified the "entry without a knock" under the exigent circumstance rule on the grounds that the agents had reasonable grounds to believe, and did believe, that the defendant was likely to be armed, and the fact that the officers knocked loudly, paused for three seconds, and entered. This was sufficient notice, where the suspect was an experienced narcotics violator and obviously would be aware of the authority and purpose.

---

67 State v. Daniels, 294 Minn. 323, 200 N.W.2d 403 (1972).

68 Commonwealth v. Morgan, 534 A.2d 1054 (Pa. 1987).

69 United States v. Artieri, 491 F.2d 440 (2d Cir. 1974).

(e) Only the property described may be seized

The warrant particularly describes things to be seized. Only those things described can be seized under the authority of a warrant. If other property is seized, the authority for such seizure must be found elsewhere. The right of the police officer to seize property not described in the warrant will be discussed in a later section.

Many statutes and codes require that agents executing a search warrant serve a copy of the warrant on the person in charge of the premises. The question that arises is that if the warrant is not left with the person in charge, does this make the seizure illegal and the evidence inadmissible? At least one federal circuit court has decided this question. In the case of *United States v. McKenzie*[70] the Sixth Circuit Court of Appeals found that the defendant's argument that the search was fatally defective because he was not served with a copy of the warrant until the day after the search was without merit.

In addition to the requirements mentioned for executing the search warrant, other requirements may be included in the statutes or code of the state. Therefore, the officer should be acquainted with all the statutory provisions in his state concerning execution of the warrant.

4. *Search of person on premises*

From previous paragraphs it can be deduced that if the officer is aware that a person is on the premises and the personal property sought can be hidden on the premises, that person should be described in the warrant. In some instances, however, the officer does not know who will be on the premises and cannot describe him in the warrant. This often poses a problem for the executing officer -- to fail to search the person on the premises could place the officer's personal safety in jeopardy or result in the concealment of the sought-after items.

To give some statutory protection to officers in such situations, several states have enacted legislation specifically providing that the person executing the warrant may reasonably detain and search a person on the premises to protect the officer or to prevent the disposal or concealment of items particularly described in the warrant.[71] However, the Illinois statute which granted such authority was challenged and declared unconstitutional as applied.[72]

---

[70] 446 F.2d 949 (6th Cir. 1971).

[71] Wis. Stat. Ann. § 968.16 (1970); Ill. Rev. Stat. ch. 38, §§ 108-109 (1980).

[72] Ybarra v. Illinois, 444 U.S. 85, 100 S. Ct. 338, 62 L. Ed. 2d 238 (1979).

In this case the Illinois officers, on the strength of a complaint, obtained a search warrant authorizing the search of a tavern and the person of the bartender for "evidence of the offense of possession of a controlled substance." Upon entering the tavern to execute the warrant, the officers announced their purpose to conduct a cursory search of the 9 to 13 customers present in the tavern. In frisking one of the patrons, Ventura Ybarra, in front of the bar, the officer felt what he described as a cigarette pack with objects in it. He did not seize this the first time but after all of the patrons had been searched he went back and retrieved the cigarette pack from Ybarra's pants pocket. Inside the packet he found six tinfoil packets containing a brown powdery substance which later was discovered to be heroin. Although the complaint did not allege that the bar was frequented by persons illegally purchasing drugs and did not state that the informant had seen a patron purchase drugs from the operator, the Illinois Appellate Court found that the Illinois statute authorizing the detention and search of persons on the premises was not unconstitutional. This decision was upheld by the Illinois Supreme Court and the case went to the United States Supreme Court on *certiorari*.

The United States Supreme Court, with three judges dissenting, determined that the search of Ybarra was unconstitutional and, therefore, the seizure of narcotics should have been excluded. The reasoning of the majority was that:

> Where the standard is probable cause, a search or seizure of a person must be supported by probable cause particularized with respect to that person. This requirement cannot be undercut or avoided by simply pointing to the fact that coincidentally there exists probable cause to search or seize another or to search the premises where the person may happen to be. The Fourth and Fourteenth Amendments protect the legitimate expectations of privacy.

In the *Ybarra* case the state argued that even if the search could not be made under the Illinois statute it should have been upheld under the doctrine of *Terry v. Ohio*.[73] The majority, although admitting that in some instances the *Terry* doctrine would apply, pointed out that in this case there was no evidence introduced to support a reasonable belief that Ybarra was armed and presently dangerous; that there was no claim on which to predicate a pat-down for weapons under *Terry v. Ohio* and *Adams v. Williams*.[74] The three

---

73 Terry v. Ohio, 392 U.S. 1, 88 S. Ct. 1868, 20 L. Ed. 2d 889 (1968).

74 Id.; Adams v. Williams, 407 U.S. 143, 92 S. Ct. 1921, 32 L. Ed. 2d 612 (1972).

dissenting justices, Chief Justice Burger, Mr. Justice Blackmun, and Mr. Justice Rehnquist, were of the opinion that this frisk was clearly within the guidelines of *Terry v. Ohio* and that the majority's opinion unjustifiably narrowed the scope of the *Terry* rule. Chief Justice Burger with whom Mr. Justice Blackmun and Mr. Justice Rehnquist joined, made this comment:

> The Court's holding is but another manifestation of the practical poverty of the judge-made exclusionary rule....Here the Court's holding operates as but a further hindrance on the already difficult effort to police the narcotics traffic which takes a terrible toll on human beings.

In most instances an important decision such as Ybarra is followed by other decisions to interpret the holding. One court has determined that a warrant authorizing the search of a house and "any person present" was properly issued to law enforcement officers who had reason to believe that a robbery suspect had hidden the proceeds of the crime inside the house prior to his arrest.[75] In this case the defendant relied on *Ybarra*, but the court determined there was a factual distinction between this case and the Ybarra case. Here the warrant itself authorized the search of unnamed persons in the place and was supported by probable cause to believe that these persons might be harboring contraband. The court noted that such a warrant is constitutionally satisfactory, pointing out that to require greater specificity as to the identity of the persons would "excessively impede law efforts and invite criminal defiance of the law."

Following like reasoning a state court upheld the search under a warrant permitting search of all occupants at a particular premises where there was little likelihood that an innocent person might be on the premises.[76] This court approved the use of an "all occupants" warrant, noting that cocaine could easily be secreted on the persons.

In another case, the United States Supreme Court approved the detention of the resident of a house during execution of a search warrant where the officers had no probable cause to arrest or search the residence at the time the detention began. In this case Justice Stevens, joined by five other justices, concluded that the brief detention of a resident was a limited additional burden attending a search authorized by a search warrant.[77] The Court did not justify the detention of the resident on the basis of the search warrant as there was no description in the warrant. However, the Court

---

[75] United States v. Graham, 563 F. Supp. 149 (D.C.N.Y. 1983).

[76] Commonwealth v. Heidelberg, 535 A.2d 611 (Pa. 1987).

[77] Michigan v. Summers, 452 U.S. 692, 101 S. Ct. 2587, 69 L. Ed. 340 (1981).

found it was reasonable to detain the person who occupied the premises and even to conduct a search of that person for the protection of the officer.

However, a search of a person who simply knocked on the door of the house where the officers were executing a search warrant was improper according to U.S. Court of Appeals for the Eighth Circuit.[78] The court pointed out that the sergeant who stopped and frisked the person who knocked on the door had no factual data about the appellant that would have given rise to probability of illegal activity. The court, in quoting other cases, made this comment:

> Thus, the facts here do not distinguish appellant from anyone else who may have approached the house. The Fourth Amendment does not authorize the detention and search of all persons who may be present...or of all persons who may enter premises during the time of the warrant's execution.

It is noted that in this case it was indicated that the police could have denied the defendant entry on to the premises while the search was being conducted.

In summary, persons on the premises who are not included in the warrant cannot be searched under the warrant. However, if persons are described in the warrant or in some instances even if the warrant contains directions to search "any person present" they may be detained and searched. Also, the person in charge of the house while the search warrant is being executed may be detained during the search and arrested if evidence indicates probable cause he has committed or is committing a crime. If there is not sufficient information or reasonable grounds to justify an arrest of the person present when the warrant is being executed, there may be sufficient reasonable cause to believe that criminal activity is afoot justifying a stop and frisk. If proper preparations are made prior to the search so that the warrant is properly written, there is a good chance that a constitutional challenge at a later time will be avoided.

6. *Return of the warrant*

An officer who acts under a search warrant and seizes property must make return of all things which he seizes. The federal code provides that the warrant may be executed and returned within ten days after its date. Although there is some indication that failure to comply strictly with the statute may not make the warrant void, certainly this requirement should be fol-

---

78 United States v. Clay, 640 F.2d 157 (8th Cir. 1981).

lowed. An example of a statute which gives clear instructions as to the procedure to be followed is that of Illinois:

> A return of all instruments, articles or things seized shall be made without unnecessary delay before the judge issuing the warrant or before any judge named in the warrant or before any court of competent jurisdiction. An inventory of any instruments, articles or things seized shall be filed with the return and signed under oath by the officer or person executing the warrant. The judge shall upon request deliver a copy of the inventory to the person from whom or from whose premises the instruments, article or things were taken and to the applicant for the warrant.[79]

6. *Advantages in searching with the search warrant*

The first part of the Fourth Amendment prohibits unreasonable searches and seizures, and it goes on to set out the requirements for a search warrant. In the early discussion of this provision it was argued that no search would be justified without a warrant as there was no provision in the Constitution for a search without a warrant. Although in exceptional cases the courts have recognized the necessity of allowing searches *without a warrant*, this is not the preferred method.

Advantages of a search with a warrant include:

(a) Evidence obtained under a warrant is more likely to be admitted than evidence obtained by a search incident to arrest

There is a definite indication, especially in the more recent cases, that the courts are encouraging the use of search warrants in preference to searches without the warrant. In *United States v. Ventresca*,[80] the Court made this comment concerning the search warrant:

> In *Johnson v. United States* and *Chapman v. United States*, the Court, in condemning searches by officers who invaded premises without a warrant, plainly intimated that had the proper course of obtaining a warrant from a magistrate been followed and had the magistrate on the same evidence available to the police made a finding of probable cause, the search under the warrant would have been sustained.

---

79 Ill. Rev. Stat. ch. 38, § 108-10 (1988).

80 380 U.S. 102, 85 S. Ct. 741, 13 L. Ed. 2d 684 (1965).

In indicating the encouragement given the officers to use the warrant, the Court stated:

> A grudging or negative attitude by reviewing courts toward warrants will tend to discourage police officers from submitting their evidence to a judicial officer before acting.

The courts are recognizing that one of the reasons that warrants are not requested by enforcement agents is the reluctance of judicial officers to issue warrants in fear of a reversal by a higher court and the frequency of the courts declaring the search warrant invalid at the trial of the case. Officers who have had such experience recognize that, in many instances, search warrants have been found invalid because of some technicality, and the evidence obtained thereunder has been held inadmissible in the trial of the case. Much of this appears to be due to the failure of the issuing official to follow proper procedures in issuing the warrant. These recent Supreme Court cases, however, would tend to encourage a more positive attitude concerning the recognition of the validity of the search warrant by the courts. The encouragement to use the search warrant has also been evidenced by some provisions of the state codes. For example one state statute directs: "No warrant shall be quashed or evidence suppressed because of technical irregularities not affecting the substantial rights of the accused."[81]

(b) The officer is more likely to be protected when the search is with a warrant

Generally, the officer acting under a search warrant is protected from criminal and civil liability if the warrant is proper on its face and the officer does not abuse his authority in executing a warrant. This does not mean that the officer is always entitled to rely on the judicial officer's judgment in issuing the warrant. In the case of *Malley v. Briggs* which dealt with an arrest warrant, the Supreme Court ruled that a police officer cannot avoid civil rights liability for causing an unconstitutional arrest by presenting the judicial officer with a complaint and a supporting affidavit which failed to establish probable cause.[82]

The Supreme Court indicated the police officer was entitled only to qualified immunity, not absolute immunity, from liability from damages under Title 42, § 1983 of the United States Code when presenting a judicial officer with a complaint which fails to establish probable cause. In determining

---

81 Ill. Rev. Stat. ch. 38, § 108-14 (1988).

82 Malley v. Briggs, 475 U.S. 335, 106 S. Ct. 1092, 89 L. Ed. 2d 271 (1986).

liability, the question is whether a reasonably well-trained officer would have known that his affidavit failed to establish probable cause and that he should not have applied for the warrant. Notwithstanding the possibility of civil liability as explained in *Malley v. Briggs*, it is still preferable to obtain a warrant based on probable cause rather than make the search without a warrant.

§ 4.8 Search incident to a lawful arrest

1. *Rationale for exceptions*

Although the search under the search warrant is preferred and there are no specific exceptions in the Fourth Amendment or in the constitutions of the various states, the law has long recognized the power of an arresting officer to search the person of the arrestee and the surrounding premises that are under his control. This search incident to a lawful arrest is one of the exceptions to the rule that the search must be made with a search warrant. As a matter of fact, more searches are made under this authority than under any other authority. There is no question but that such a search must be authorized if the law is to be enforced, as it is impractical to obtain warrants in all instances.

This right to make the search incident to the lawful arrest has been repeatedly recognized by all the courts including the Supreme Court of the United States. In the case of *United States v. Rabinowitz*,[83] the Court specifically recognized the authority to search incident to a lawful arrest. In this case, the defendant was convicted of selling, possessing and concealing forged and altered obligations of the United States with intent to defraud. Armed with valid warrants for arrest, the government officers, accompanied by two stamp experts, went to the defendant's place of business, a one-room office open to the public. The officers thereupon arrested the defendant under the authority of the arrest warrant and, over his objections, searched the desk, safe, and file cabinets located in the office for an hour and a half. They found and seized 573 stamps with overprints forged, along with some other stamps which were subsequently returned to the defendant. In upholding the search for and seizure of the stamps, the Supreme Court stated:

> It is unreasonable searches that are prohibited by the Fourth Amendment. [Citation omitted.] It was recognized by the framers of the Constitution that there were reasonable searches for which no warrant was required. The right of the "people to be secure in

[83] 339 U.S. 56, 70 S. Ct. 430, 94 L. Ed. 653 (1950).

their persons" was certainly of as much concern to the framers of the Constitution as the property of the person. Yet no one questions the right, without a search warrant, to search the person after a valid arrest. The right to search a person incident to arrest always has been recognized in this country and in England.

If the reason for this exception to the general rule is understood, it is much less difficult to apply the rule. The reason for the rule was explained by Justice Frankfurter in the dissenting opinion of *Rabinowitz*. Justice Frankfurter stated:

> What, then, is the exception to the prohibition of the Fourth Amendment of search without a warrant in case of a legal arrest, whether the arrest is on a warrant or based on the historic right of arrest without a warrant if a crime is committed in the presence of the arrester? The exception may in part be a surviving incident of the historic role of "hue and cry" in early Anglo-Saxon law. [Citation omitted.] Its basic roots, however, lie in necessity. What is the necessity? Why is search of the arrested person permitted? For two reasons: first, in order to protect the arresting officer and to deprive the prisoner of potential means of escape,...and, secondly, to avoid destruction of evidence by the arrested person.

In recognizing this necessity, the courts have approved searches where the searches are necessary to protect the officer and to avoid destruction of the evidence.

2. *Requirements*

Although the courts have uniformly adopted the rule which allows a search incident to a lawful arrest, they have established specific requirements. These requirements are discussed here.

(a) The arrest must be lawful

The first and most important requirement is that the arrest itself must be a lawful arrest. If the arrest is not lawful, then the resulting search is not lawful and the evidence so obtained is inadmissible.

If the arrest and resulting search incident to that arrest is to be upheld, all of the legal requirements discussed in the previous chapter regarding arrest must be met. The officer can expect that the defense attorney, if possible, will show that the arrest was illegal and thus destroy all lawful basis for the search.

(b) Only certain articles may be seized

As is the case of the search with a warrant, there are limitations as to the type of article which can be seized without a warrant as an incident to a lawful arrest. Because of recent decisions, restrictions on the types of articles which can be seized have been relaxed. As explained in the previous section, in the case of *Warden v. Hayden*, the United States Supreme Court reversed previous decisions and held that there was no constitutional prohibition concerning the seizure of "mere evidence." Prior to that time, the federal courts and state courts had followed the rule that only fruits of the crime, means of committing the crime, and weapons to effect an escape could be seized. Since that decision "mere evidence" as well as fruits of the crime, the means of committing the crime, and weapons may be seized as an incident to an arrest by federal officers.

Because state statutes and some state court decisions are not consistent, there is still conflict as to the type of evidence which may be seized by state officers for use in state courts. Some states by statute have provided for the seizure of specific items when the search is made incident to an arrest. For example, the Illinois Code provides that:

> When a lawful arrest is effected a peace officer may reasonably search the person arrested and the area within such person's immediate presence for the purpose of:
> (a) Protecting the officer from attack; or
> (b) Preventing the person from escaping; or
> (c) Discovering the fruits of the crime; or
> (d) Discovering any instruments, articles, or things which may have been used in the commission of, or which may constitute evidence of, an offense.[84]

Under such a statute, "mere evidence" as well as the fruits of the crime and instruments used in the commission of the crime may be seized. And the *Hayden* decision makes it clear that such seizure does not violate constitutional provisions.

Notwithstanding the *Hayden* rule, some states by statute or court decision still restrict the seizure to fruits of the crime, means by which it was committed, and weapons to effect an escape. Unless such statutes or state court decisions are changed, the search for "mere evidence" would be unau-

---

84 Ill. Rev. Stat. ch. 38, § 108-1 (1988).

thorized. As pointed out by the U.S. Supreme Court, there is no rational reason for such rule, but some states, because of negligence or lack of understanding, have failed to take action which would remove these restrictions. As a result where such state statutes and court decisions exist, the seizure is limited. The state officer must therefore look to the state statutes and state decisions to determine if there are any additional restrictions as to the articles which can be seized incident to a lawful arrest.

(c) The search must be made contemporaneously with the arrest

If the reasons for the search incident to a lawful arrest are studied, a requirement that the search be made contemporaneously with the arrest is understandable. When the arrest takes place the officer has the authority to search the person arrested and the immediate area in order to protect himself and to deprive the prisoner of the means of escape. After the prisoner is safely in his jail cell, the search cannot be justified, as the necessity no longer exists. The second reason for justifying the search is to avoid destruction of the evidence by the persons arrested. If the arrestee is safely behind bars, there is no danger of this. A search warrant can be obtained for searching for that evidence.

The federal and state courts, especially in the recent decade, have struggled with the term "contemporaneous." A strict interpretation would require that the search which is justified by the legal arrest be made at the very time of the arrest. However, in recognizing practicalities, the courts have not required such strict compliance. For example, the search of the defendant's carry-on luggage after she had been taken to a drug agent's office was permissible as a search incident to arrest, even though she was arrested on the way to the office.[85] And a delay from the time the driver was arrested to the time his vehicle was searched while he was handcuffed did not negate the search made incident to a lawful arrest.[86] In the *Williams* case the court resolved that "contemporaneous" is not the same as "simultaneous." All that is required, according to that court, is that the search of the vehicle take place during the "same time period" as the arrest. The time period is measured by the time reasonably necessary to perform a law enforcement officer's duties attendant upon arrest.

While the United States Supreme Court has left no doubt that a search of the person incident to the arrest may occur before the actual arrest if the

---

85 United States v. Porter, 738 F.2d 622 (4th Cir.), *cert. denied*, 469 U.S. 983, 105 S. Ct. 389, 83 L. Ed. 2d 323 (1984).

86 State v. Williams, 516 So. 2d 1081 (Fla. Dist. Ct. App. 1987).

arrest occurs contemporaneously with the search, it is preferable to advise the person apprehended that he is being arrested.[87] In the case of *Smith v. Ohio*, the United States Supreme Court was asked to answer the single question of "whether a warrantless search that provides probable cause for an arrest can nonetheless be justified as an incident of that arrest."[88] Here, the defendant, when asked by an officer to "come here a minute" threw onto the hood of his car a paper grocery sack that he was carrying. The officer, *before* making an arrest, pushed the defendant's hand away and opened the bag, which contained drug paraphernalia.

As the defendant was not arrested until *after* the contraband was discovered, the contraband cannot serve as part of his justification. The Court concluded that:

> The exception for searches incident to arrest permits the police to search a lawfully arrested person and areas within his immediate control...it does not permit police to search any citizen without a warrant or probable cause so long as an arrest immediately follows.

(d) The arrest upon which the search is based must be in good faith

If the arrest in fact is a sham or subterfuge, even though it is supported by probable cause or an arrest warrant, and is executed merely as an expedient to further the chief aim of searching the premises for evidence, the search will not be upheld. A good example of this is the case of *United States v. Pampinella*.[89] Here the federal officers, knowing that the defendant was leaving town, arrested his wife on a warrant charging husband and wife with harboring a criminal. After the arrest of the wife under an arrest warrant, the officers found a machine gun in a locked suitcase in the closet. The court, even though recognizing that the arrest was lawful, held the search was unreasonable because the arrest was a pretext to search for some sort of evidence against the defendant. In reaching the conclusion that this arrest was a hoax or subterfuge in order to make a search, the court noted the fact that several days after the search the defendant was charged with illegal possession of the gun, and the harboring charges against both the defendant and the wife had been dropped.

---

87 Rawlings v. Kentucky, 448 U.S. 98, 100 S. Ct. 2556, 65 L. Ed. 2d 633 (1980).

88 Smith v. Ohio, __ U.S. __. 110 S. Ct. 1288, __ L. Ed. 2d __ (1990).

89 131 F. Supp. 595 (N.D. Ill. 1955).

3. *Area of search*

A difficult problem is presented when the search is made incident to a lawful arrest. Here, neither the place to be searched nor the things to be seized are particularly described. The courts have recognized that the search incident to arrests made, under appropriate circumstances, extend beyond the person of the one arrested to include the premises under his immediate control. The question then arises: what does the term immediate control mean? Does this mean the entire house? Does it mean the automobile driven by a person who has been arrested? Does this mean the house and all of the outbuildings when the arrest has taken place in the yard? In the following paragraphs, each of these situations will be discussed.

(a) Person arrested

In *United States v. Robinson* and a companion case,[90] the United States Supreme Court held that a full search incident to a lawful custodial arrest is authorized and no further justification is needed. In approving the search incident to a lawful arrest the Supreme Court affirmed that:

> It is well settled that a search incident to a lawful arrest is a traditional exception to the warrant requirements of the Fourth Amendment. This general exception has historically been formulated into two distinct propositions. The first is that a search may be made of the person of the arrestee by virtue of the lawful arrest. The second is that a search may be made of the area within the control of the arrestee.

The majority rejected the argument that the search incident to the lawful arrest depends upon the probability of discovering fruits or further evidence of the particular crime for which the arrest is made. They explained that the justification for the authority to search incident to a lawful arrest rests quite as much on the need to disarm the suspect in order to take him into custody as it does on the need to preserve evidence on his person for later use at trial.

Despite the ruling in *United States v. Robinson*, some state courts have restricted the search of the person incident to a lawful arrest. By a four to three majority, the California Supreme Court held that a full warrantless search of the person incident to an arrest for a minor offense cannot be justi-

---

[90] United States v. Robinson, 414 U.S. 218, 94 S. Ct. 467, 38 L. Ed. 2d 427 (1973). *See also* Gustafson v. Florida, 414 U.S. 260, 94 S. Ct. 488, 38 L. Ed. 2d 456 (1973).

fied.[91] The Hawaii Supreme Court also found unreasonable a search incident to a minor offense arrest that would have been proper under the *Robinson* and *Gustafson* rule.[92] The Oregon Court, after first refusing to go along with the *Robinson* ruling, later abandoned its own rule that such searches can be no broader than necessary and agreed to follow the *Robinson* rule in order to "avoid further confusion."[93]

In spite of some decisions to the contrary, the majority rule which now exists is that an officer who has proper authority to make an arrest may make a full search of the arrestee and seize evidence, even though such evidence has no direct connection with the arrest.

(b) Premises where arrest made

Prior to the case of *Chimel v. California* in 1969,[94] there was some confusion concerning the scope of the search where the arrest was made on the premises. In the case of *Harris v. United States*,[95] the Supreme Court, quoting from a previous case, held that the search of a dwelling place was justified as an incident to arrest. In the *Harris* case the petitioner was arrested in the living room and a search was made of the entire apartment. During the search, which continued for five hours, illegally possessed draft classification cards were obtained. Though it was conceded that this evidence was in no way related to the crime for which petitioner was initially arrested, he was convicted and the conviction was upheld. There, the court reasoned that the petitioner was in exclusive possession of a four-room apartment, and his control extended to the bedroom in which the draft cards were found.

Mr. Justice Murphy, in his dissenting opinion in the *Harris* case, condemned the search of the full apartment as an incident to the lawful arrest, arguing that this was not the intent of the courts in authorizing the search without a search warrant. Also, some state courts refused to go along with the *Harris* decision and limited the search incident to a lawful arrest to the immediate area of the arrest.[96]

Probably one of the most far-reaching decisions of the United States Supreme Court during the 1968-1969 term was the decision in *Chimel v. California, supra*. In the *Chimel* case, police officers arrested the petitioner with

---

91 People v. Brisendine, 13 Cal. 3d 528, 531 P.2d 1099, 119 Cal. Rptr. 315 (1975); People v. Longwill, 538 P.2d 753, 123 Cal. Rptr. 297 (1975).

92 State v. Kaluna, 55 Haw. Stat. 361, 520 P.2d 51 (1974).

93 State v. Florance, 270 Or. 169, 527 P.2d 1202 (1974).

94 395 U.S. 752, 89 S. Ct. 2034, 23 L. Ed. 2d 685 (1969). *See* case in Part II.

95 331 U.S. 145, 67 S. Ct. 1098, 91 L. Ed. 1399, 67 S. Ct. 1098 (1947) quoting *Agnello v. United States*, 269 U.S. 20, 46 S. Ct. 4, 70 L. Ed. 145 (1925).

96 Benge v. Commonwealth, 321 S.W.2d 247 (Ky. 1959).

an arrest warrant and, incident to this arrest for burglary, made a physical search of the entire residence. The facts in the case were very similar to the facts of the *Harris* case, where FBI agents made a search of the entire apartment on the basis of a lawful arrest. In this *Chimel* case, the Supreme Court reviewed and discussed the *Harris* and other cases and specifically reversed prior decision stating, "It is time, for reasons we have stated, to hold that on their own facts, and insofar as the principles they stand for are inconsistent with those that we have endorsed today, they are no longer to be followed."

The Court did not state that a search cannot be made as an incident to a lawful arrest, but merely limited the scope of such a search. The Supreme Court, in setting out the proper extent of a search incident to an arrest, noted:

> When an arrest is made, it is reasonable for the arresting officer to search the *person* arrested in order to remove any weapons that the latter might seek to use in order to resist arrest or effect his escape. [Emphasis added.]

Besides authorizing the search of the person arrested, the Court approved a limited search for evidence.

> In addition, it is entirely reasonable for the arresting officer to search for and seize any evidence on the arrestee's person in order to prevent its concealment or destruction. And the area into which arrestee might reach in order to grab a weapon or evidentiary items must, of course, be governed by a like rule.

In this *Chimel* case the Court also defined the term "immediate control" which had been used loosely in other cases. In defining this term the Court said:

> There is ample justification, therefore, for a search of the arrestee's person and the area "within his immediate control" -- construing that phrase to mean the area from which he might gain possession of a weapon or destructible evidence.

The United States Supreme Court in 1978 reiterated the rule that an arrest in an apartment does not justify the search of the whole apartment incident to that arrest.[97] In this case an undercover police officer was shot and

---

97 Mincey v. Arizona, 437 U.S. 385, 98 S. Ct. 2408, 57 L. Ed. 2d 290 (1978). *See* Thompson v. Louisiana, 469 U.S. 17, 105 S. Ct. 409, 83 L. Ed. 2d 246 (1984). In

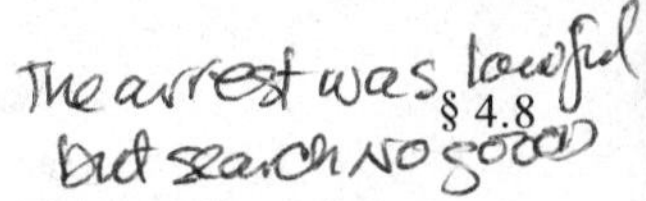

killed during a narcotics raid on the defendant's apartment. The officers arrested the defendant and searched the apartment for four days during which time the entire apartment was searched, photographed, and diagrammed. They opened drawers, closets, cupboards, and inspected their contents; they emptied clothing pockets; they dug bullet fragments out of the walls and floors; and they pulled up sections of the carpet and removed them for examination. No warrant was obtained but the evidence including bullets and shell casings, guns, narcotics, and narcotic paraphernalia was used at the trial. The defendant was found guilty of murder, assault, and narcotics violations.

The state sought to justify the search because of "exigent circumstances" and the fact that the search of the scene of a homicide should be recognized as an additional exception to the rule. The Supreme Court's opinion on the emergency issue is:

> We do not question the right of police to respond to emergency situations. Numerous state and federal cases have recognized that the Fourth Amendment does not bar police officers from making warrantless entries and searches when they reasonably believe that a person within is in need of immediate aid. Similarly, when police come upon the scene of a homicide they may make a prompt warrantless search of the area to see if there are other victims or if the killer is still on the premises...And the police may seize any evidence that is in plain view during the course of their legitimate emergency activities.

The Court insisted, however, there was no indication in this case that evidence would be lost, destroyed, or removed during the time required to obtain a search warrant and there was no suggestion that a search warrant could not easily and conveniently be obtained. The Court then concluded:

> In sum, we hold that the "murder scene exception" created by the Arizona Supreme Court is inconsistent with the Fourth and Fourteenth Amendments -- that the warrantless search of Mincey's apartment was not constitutionally permissible simply because a homicide had recently occurred there.

1990 the United States Supreme Court held that the Fourth Amendment permits a properly limited protective sweep in conjunction with an in-home arrest when the searching officer possess a reasonable belief based on specific and articulable facts that the area to be swept harbors an individual posing a danger to those on the arrest scene. Maryland v. Buie, __ U.S. __, 110 S. Ct. 1093, __ L. Ed. 2d __ (1990).

To summarize, the Supreme Court has determined that when a legal arrest is made, the arresting officer or officers may search the *person* of the defendant for weapons or evidence and in addition may search the area into which the defendant might reach *to obtain a weapon* or *to destroy evidence*.

In an August, 1969, case,[98] the Maryland Court of Special Appeals was faced with making a determination as to the area which could be searched without violating the "reach" provisions of the *Chimel* case. The court rejected the "arm's length" restrictions which had been advocated by some judges and defense attorneys and held that the area is not limited to an arm's length radius encircling the arrestee at the moment of his arrest. Specifically, the court commented:

> But as the search is tested by its reasonableness and its scope is justified by the need to protect the arresting officer and to prevent the destruction of evidence, we cannot construe *Chimel [v. California]* to mean that the area is confined to that precise spot which is at arm length from the arrestee at the moment of his arrest. He may well lunge forward or move backward or to the side and thus into an area in which he *might* grab a weapon or evidentiary items then within his reach before the officer could, by the exercise of reasonable diligence, restrain him. We think that *Chimel* requires that the State show that the search was conducted and items were seized in an area "within the reach" of the arrestee in this concept, as for example, by evidence as to the location of the items with respect to the whereabouts of the arrestee, the accessibility of the items and their nature.

The Maryland court made it clear, however, that the search would not reasonably extend to a locked drawer explaining:

> It would seem that a seizure of a weapon or destructible evidence in a locked drawer in the immediate presence of the arrestee in the literal sense would be beyond the permissible scope of a search.

According to at least one court, then, the area of search incident to a lawful arrest extends to the area where the arrestee might lunge in order to

---

98 Scott v. State, 7 Md. App. 505, 256 A.2d 384 (1969).

reach a weapon or destroy evidence. Obviously, the scope of the search will depend on the facts of each case.[99]

(c) Automobile

This discussion concerns the search of an automobile as an incident to the lawful arrest. Further justification for the search of the automobile will be discussed in other sections.

The search of an automobile *incident to an arrest* is justified on the same grounds as the search of the premises. That is, the search incident to the arrest is justified for two reasons. First, in order to protect the arresting officer and to deprive the prisoner of means of escape, and secondly, to avoid destruction of evidence by the arrested person. As pointed out, the search incident to arrest is limited to the area within the immediate control of the arrestee. But what is the immediate control? When a person is operating a motor vehicle, the whole thing is apparently under his control or within his possession. Interpreting this very liberally, some early decisions held that the entire automobile may be searched as an incident to a lawful arrest.

It is generally recognized that the arresting officer may protect himself and, when conditions justify, search the person of the driver when a traffic arrest is made. Even under earlier decisions, however, he could not generally search the entire car in the usual *traffic* situation.

Following the *Chimel* case, there was disagreement among the courts as to the application of the rule in the *Chimel* rule to automobiles. After many conflicting decisions by the lower courts, the Supreme Court in 1981 addressed the issues of the extent, time, and place associated with a search of an automobile incident to a lawful arrest.[100]

In this case an automobile in which the respondent was one of the occupants was stopped by a New York State policeman for traveling at an excessive rate of speed. In the process of discovering that none of the occupants owned the car or were related to the owner, the policeman smelled burnt marijuana and saw, on the floor of the car, an envelope suspected of containing marijuana. He directed the occupants to get out of the car and arrested them for unlawful possession of marijuana. After searching each of the occupants, he searched the passenger compartment of the car. There he found a jacket belonging to respondent, unzipped the pockets, and discovered cocaine. The trial court denied defendant's motion to suppress the cocaine seized from the jacket. The Appellate Division of the New York Supreme

---

99 *See also United States v. Melville*, 309 F. Supp. 829 (S.D.N.Y. 1970), in which the court found that "special circumstances" would justify a search beyond the "lunge" area.

100 New York v. Belton, 453 U.S. 454, 101 S. Ct. 2860, 69 L. Ed. 2d 768 (1981).

Court upheld the constitutionality of the search but the New York Court of Appeals reversed.

A majority of the members of the U.S. Supreme Court disagreed with the New York Supreme Court and ruled that the search was justified. After reiterating that it is essential that police officers have a familiar standard in determining the scope of search, the U.S. Supreme Court made these comments:

> Accordingly we hold that when a policeman has made a lawful custodial arrest of the occupant of an automobile, he may, as a contemporaneous incident of that arrest, search the passenger compartment of that automobile.

As to the search of the contents of containers, the Court continued with this sentence:

> The police may also examine the contents of any containers found within the passenger compartment, for if the passenger compartment is within reach of the arrestee, so also will be containers in it be within his reach.

The *Belton* rule is that the police may search the passenger compartment of the car as an incident to a lawful arrest and may examine the contents of any container found in the passenger compartment whether it be opened or closed. It does *not* justify a search of the trunk of the car as an incident to a lawful arrest.

As was expected, the *Belton* case spawned many cases by lower courts. For example, the First Circuit Court of Appeals upheld a warrantless search of the interior of an automobile on the basis of *New York v. Belton*, reasoning that the defendant could easily have reached into the passenger compartment to seize a weapon or destroy contraband.[101] And in a state case a North Carolina court interpreted the *Belton* rule to justify the search of a locked glove compartment after the arrest of the defendant in his car.[102] However, a federal court of appeals placed some limitation on the authority to search the passenger compartment of the vehicle when the search is justified as an incident to the lawful arrest.[103] In this case the court ruled that if the occupant of the car has been totally immobilized, removed from the vehicle, and the search takes place 30 to 45 minutes after the arrest there is no justifica-

---

101 United States v. Bautista, 731 F.2d 97 (1st Cir. 1984).

102 State v. Massenburg, 66 N.C. App. 127, 310 S.E.2d 619 (1984).

103 United States v. Vassey, 834 F.2d 782 (1987).

tion for the search as an incident to the arrest. Here the occupant had been rendered absolutely incapable of getting into the passenger compartment as he was handcuffed and placed in a patrol car at the time of the search.

The discussion under this subsection relates to a search of an automobile incident to a lawful arrest. As is explained in later sections, the search may be justified under other exceptions, such as the moving vehicle exception, but justice personnel must be prepared to articulate the facts which justified the particular exception.

(d) Area other than where arrest made

If the arrest takes place outside the residence, the house usually cannot be the subject of an incidental search. In the case of *Vale v. Louisiana*[104] the defendant was arrested on the front steps of his house. In this case, the Supreme Court held that the warrantless search of the inside of the house could not be justified as an incident to the arrest. The Court said that even if the *Chimel* case is not accorded retroactive effect, no precedent of the Court could sustain the constitutional validity of the search in this case.

Where the arrest is made outside the residence, the search of the person is authorized to protect the officer and to prevent destruction of the evidence. Additionally, the search can extend to the area into which the arrestee may reach. Under the more recent decisions, however, the search of out-buildings generally would not be justified unless they were within the immediate reach of the arrestee.

An interesting case concerning a search incident to an arrest was the case of *United States v. Alberti*.[105] The defendant was located in the garage and then lured by misrepresentation into his apartment so that the arrest could be made and search could be made of the premises. The court here held that, under the circumstances, the search was unreasonable and the evidence must be excluded.

(e) Arrestee's clothing and containers

For some time, a practical question has been posed by police who make an arrest and then search the clothing of the arrestee after he is lodged in the jail. In a 1974 case the United States Supreme Court again expressed the view that the Fourth Amendment prohibits only unreasonable searches and approved a search of clothing of the person after he has been arrested and put in jail.[106]

---

104 399 U.S. 30, 90 S. Ct. 1969, 26 L. Ed. 2d 409 (1970).

105 120 F. Supp. 171 (S.D.N.Y. 1954).

106 United States v. Edwards, 415 U.S. 800, 94 S. Ct. 1234, 39 L. Ed. 2d 771 (1974).

In this case, the defendant was arrested shortly after 11 p.m., and immediately taken to jail. The next morning new clothes were purchased for him, and his clothing was taken and held as evidence. An examination of the clothing revealed paint chips matching the samples that had been taken at the scene of the break-in. The defendant objected to the introduction of the evidence claiming that neither the clothing nor the results of the examination were admissible because the warrantless seizure of the clothing was invalid under the Fourth Amendment. The trial judge did not agree. He admitted the evidence and the defendant was found guilty.

The Court of Appeals reversed and disallowed the admission of this evidence because the warrantless seizure of the defendant's clothing was after the administrative process and mechanics of arrest had come to a halt. The Supreme Court of the United States, reversing the Court of Appeals, held that the search and seizure of the clothing did not violate the Fourth Amendment, and explained that:

> [O]nce the accused is lawfully arrested and is in custody, the effects in his possession at the place of detention that were subject to search at the time and place of his arrest may lawfully be searched and seized without a warrant even though a substantial period of time has elapsed between the arrest and subsequent administrative processing, on the one hand, and the taking of the property for use as evidence, on the other.

The Court cautioned that there is, of course, a time when the Fourth Amendment would prohibit post-arrest seizures of the effects of the arrestee. But in this case the seizure of the clothes had been reasonable under the circumstances.

Justices Stewart, Brennan, and Marshall dissented, arguing that the search which occurred ten hours after the arrest, at a time when the administrative processing and mechanics of arrest had come to an end, was unconstitutional under the Fourth Amendment.

Relying heavily on the case of *New York v. Belton*,[107] the Florida Supreme Court approved searches incident to arrest of closed containers the arrestee was carrying at the time of arrest. The Court reasoned that as long as the arrestee was carrying the item when he was arrested, the police may open it, incident to the arrest, and seize its contents.[108] The majority of the

---

107 453 U.S. 454, 101 S. Ct. 2860, 69 L. Ed. 768 (1981).

108 Savoie v. State, 422 So. 2d 308 (Fla. 1982). *See* United States v. Torres, 740 F.2d 122 (2d Cir. 1984) where a search of a bag the defendant was carrying when arrested was permissible as a search incident to a lawful arrest and United States

Court found that the defendant's claim that his attache case could not be searched without a warrant after it had been seized was illogical and unreasonable. The Court said, "in our view, the law is now clear that when there is a lawful arrest, it is a reasonable intrusion incident to that arrest to search the person and any container that person is carrying."

§ 4.9 Waiver of constitutional rights

In accord with the general principle which allows a person to waive his constitutional rights, the rights protected by the Fourth Amendment to the federal Constitution and the state provisions concerning search and seizure may be waived. However, these constitutional rights are considered to be waived only after careful evaluation. The cases are not in complete agreement as to what amounts to a consent, but some definite rules have been developed. Federal courts have taken the approach that every reasonable presumption against waiver of the fundamental constitutional rights will be taken.

Recognizing that a search may be conducted with the consent of the individual concerned, the following principles must be kept in mind.

1. The consent must be voluntary

To be constitutionally adequate, the consent must be given without force, duress or compulsion of any kind.[109] The government has the burden of proving that the consent was voluntary and the proof must be clear and positive. Mere submission to authority is not voluntary consent. For example, if the officer says, "You don't mind if I conduct a search of your premises, do you?", and the owner of the premises makes no answer, this is not a voluntary consent.

In determining if the consent to the search is in fact voluntary or the product of duress or coercion, expressed or implied, the courts look to the totality of the circumstances. For example, when a Drug Enforcement Administration agent asked a 22-year-old suspect if she would accompany him to the DEA office at the airport for further questions and at the office asked the suspect if she would allow a search of her person and handbag and at that time told her she had the right to decline the search if she desired, her re-

---

v. Litman, 739 F.2d 137 (4th Cir. 1984) where the court upheld the search of a shoulder bag incident to an arrest.

109 United States v. Fowler, 17 F.R.D. 499 (S.D. Cal. 1955)

sponse, "Go ahead" was consent under the circumstances.[110] At the trial the defense attorney argued that the fact that the respondent was 22 years old, had not graduated from high school and was a Negro accosted by white officers amounted to coercion. The Court agreed that these factors should be considered in determining if a waiver were in fact voluntary but they were not controlling.

Lower courts have warned that the decision in the *Mendenhall* case is not without limits. For example, the U.S. Court of Appeals for the Fifth Circuit observed that consent will not be easily proved.[111] The court went on to caution that "only exceptionally clear evidence of consent should overcome a presumption that a person requested to accompany an agent to an office no longer would feel free to leave and that silently following an officer would rarely constitute sufficient evidence of consent."

In a 1973 case,[112] the defense very persuasively argued that if warnings, such as the *Miranda* warnings, must be given before a person can waive his Fifth Amendment rights, the same reasoning should apply in regard to the waiver of Fourth Amendment rights. The specific case before the Supreme Court of the United States concerned the admissibility of three stolen checks obtained from the trunk of an automobile by officers who asked the driver if they could search the trunk. Without any advice from the police that he did not have to waive his Fourth Amendment rights, the driver said, "Sure, go ahead."

The defendant moved to suppress the introduction of the evidence on the ground that the material had been acquired through an unconstitutional search and seizure. The Federal District Court reasoned that the State was under an obligation to demonstrate not only that the consent was uncoerced but that it was given with an understanding it could be freely and effectively withheld. On appeal by the prosecution, the Supreme Court of the United States reversed the Circuit Court of Appeals decision and held in effect that the *Miranda*-type of warning is not required in a search and seizure situation.

The majority in *Schneckloth* reaffirmed the rule that the consent must be voluntary, but included the following statement regarding the warning:

---

110 United States v. Mendenhall, 446 U.S. 544, 100 S. Ct. 1870, 64 L. Ed. 2d (1980).

111 United States v. Berry, 670 F.2d 583 (5th Cir. 1982). *See also* United States v. Elsoffer 671 F.2d 1294 (11th Cir. 1982).

112 Schneckloth v. Bustamonte, 412 U.S. 218, 93 S. Ct. 2041, 36 L. Ed. 2d 854 (1973). *See* United States v. Watson, 423 U.S. 411, 96 S. Ct. 820, 46 L. Ed. 2d 598 (1976), where the majority of the United States Supreme Court again held that defendant did not have to know that he could have withheld his consent to a search.

> Our decision today is a narrow one. We hold only that when the subject of a search is not in custody and the State attempts to justify a search on the basis of his consent, the Fourth and Fourteenth Amendments require that it demonstrate that the consent was in fact voluntarily given, and not the result of duress or coercion, express or implied. Voluntariness is a question of fact to be determined from all the circumstances, and while the subject's knowledge of a right to refuse is a factor to be taken into account, the prosecution is *not* required to demonstrate such knowledge as a prerequisite to establishing a voluntary consent. [Emphasis added.]

The warning that the police officer must look to *state* as well as federal rules bears repeating. The New Jersey Supreme Court rejected the consent principles set forth in the *Schneckloth* case, claiming this new test a "drastic departure" from previous decisions.[113] In New Jersey the state must show that the person involved *knew* that he had a right to refuse to accede to the request for the consent search. Officers are again cautioned that, if the state has, by statute or court decision, required stiffer restrictions, those restrictions must be adhered to if based on the state constitutional provision.

There is still some conflict among authorities concerning the validity of a waiver where the officer advises the person in charge of the premises that a warrant will be applied for if permission to search is not granted. One federal court has indicated that it is not coercion if the officer only points out that he will apply for a warrant if the consent to search is denied.[114] The view of the majority was that the advice given by the law enforcement agent was well-founded since he could in fact apply for a warrant. This should be distinguished from the situation where the officer claims he *has* a warrant and will use it if consent to search is not given, when in fact he does *not* have a warrant or has a warrant that is unserviceable.[115] To avoid the risk of later challenge, the officer should not even mention the search warrant unless he in fact has one.

2. *Extensiveness of search is limited to exact words of consent*

Since the officers are acting under a waiver of constitutional rights, the court requires that they carefully observe any limitations placed upon the

---

113 State v. Johnson, 68 N.J. 349, 346 A.2d 66 (1975).

114 United States v. Faruolo, 506 F.2d 490 (2d Cir. 1974).

115 Middleton v. Commonwealth, 502 S.W.2d 517 (Ky. 1973); Bumper v. North Carolina, 391 U.S. 543, 88 S. Ct. 1788, 20 L. Ed. 2d 797 (1968).

consent either directly or by inference. Therefore, a consent to search a portion of one's premises is not a consent to search other portions.

The question also arises as to the withdrawal of the consent. Some authorities have argued that after the commencement of the search by voluntary consent, the consent may not be withdrawn. But in the case of *Strong v. United States*,[116] the court found that the defendant may revoke his consent during the process of the search.

If the person giving consent agrees to allow officers to search his house for one item, this does not convey the consent to search for other items. For example, consent by a resident for officers to search his house for narcotics does not authorize examination of bookkeeping ledgers in the house. The judges of the Seventh Circuit agreed with the defendant that a "consent search" may be limited by the person giving consent, and the limitations must be observed. Also, this was not a situation where evidence of a different crime was discovered in plain view, as the ledgers had to be opened before there was any indication of a violation.[117]

It has been argued that where the person authorizes the search and later withdraws this consent, the officer is placed in the position of being led into making the search without a warrant, when he possibly would have made efforts to obtain the warrant had he not been authorized to search without it. This argument is persuasive but the apparent trend is to the contrary. In recent cases concerning the waiver of constitutional rights (as, for example, in the self-incrimination situation), the courts have allowed the consentor to withdraw his consent at any time. In view of these decisions, it would seem that the search must be discontinued when the consent is withdrawn, unless the search can be justified on other grounds.

3. *The person giving the consent must have the capacity to consent*

The most serious problem confronting the officer who is contemplating the consent search is whether the person who gives consent is legally qualified to do so. This situation arises in the case of landlords, joint tenants, partners, spouses or agents.

The general rule is that the consent of one who possesses common authority over the premises or effects is valid against the absent, non-consenting person with whom the authority is shared.[118] In the *Matlock* case the major-

116 46 F.2d 257 (1st Cir. 1931).

117 United States v. Dichiarinte, 445 F.2d 126 (7th Cir. 1971).

118 United States v. Matlock, 415 U.S. 164, 94 S. Ct. 988, 39 L. Ed. 2d 242 (1974).

ity of the United States Supreme Court ruled that people who share premises have their own right to consent and each person assumes the risk that the other may consent to a search. Although the United States Supreme Court had not decided whether a refusal by one who possesses common authority prevents a valid consent by the other person who is on the premises at the time the search is considered, some lower courts have indicated that such a consent is valid. These cases hold that where two persons jointly possess property, as for example by husband and wife or joint tenants, one may permit a search even after the other has refused to give consent.[119]

After considering other cases and relying primarily on the *Matlock* rule, the New York Court of Appeals reasoned that a person who shared space with others has the authority to permit police to search the residence even over the objection of the other inhabitants.[120]

In explaining their decision, the New York Court concluded:

> We are led to the conclusion that an individual who possesses the requisite degree of control over specific premises is vested in his own right with the authority to permit an official inspection of such premises and that this authority is not circumscribed by any reasonable expectation of privacy belonging to co-occupants.

The law relating to the third party consent was clearly explained in the case of *United States v. Buettner-Janusch* where the Second Circuit Court of Appeals held that an undergraduate research assistant of the defendant and a fellow professor had authority to consent to a warrantless search of the defendant's laboratory by DEA agents.[121] Here the student and fellow professor not only had access to the laboratory, but had an express or implied permission to use the laboratory.

The third party consent does not involve the vicarious waiver of the defendant's constitutional rights but validates a search when the defendant can be said to have assumed the risk that someone having authority over the area to be searched would permit the government intrusion in his own right. In the *Buettner-Janusch* situation the defendant forfeited any reasonable expectation of privacy in the enclosed area of his laboratory at the University, such as the cabinets, cold room, and freezers, by granting permission to use the area to an undergraduate research assistant, a fellow professor, and at least eight other persons.

---

[119] United States v. Baldwin, 644 F.2d 381 (5th Cir. 1981); United States v. Hendrix, 549 F. Supp. 1225 (E.D. Cal. 1986).

[120] People v. Cosme, 397 N.E.2d 1319 (N.Y. 1979).

[121] United States v. Buettner-Janusch, 646 F.2d 759 (2d Cir. 1981).

The immediate and present right to possess premises may or may not coincide with the legal right to pass title to the property, but in any event, the constitutional right to be free from unreasonable searches and seizures protects the possessory right, not the legal title. As a result, the landlord lacks the legal capacity to authorize a consent search that would be valid against a tenant of the leased premises. Even a boarder in a roominghouse is a tenant under this rule, and only he can give consent. This includes the tenant at sufferance who has not paid his room rent, but is still allowed to stay in the room.

The same reasoning appears to be true concerning business partners. In the case of *United States v. Sferas*,[122] the court held:

> [T]he rule seems to be well established that where two persons have equal right to the use or occupancy of premises, either may give consent to a search, and the evidence thus disclosed can be used....

The consent of one probably would not extend to a desk or other facility reserved exclusively for the use and control of another partner.

It is quite common for the officer to arrive at the residence of the suspect and find that the suspect is not home. He often is advised, however, that a member of the family is present. The question then arises as to whether the member of the family, whether it be the wife, a child, or a parent, can waive the constitutional protection and consent to the search of the residence of the suspect. The decisions of the various courts have not been in agreement, especially as to the authority of the wife to consent to the search. From the decisions, however, we can come to some general conclusions.

(a) Consent by the spouse

Although some courts are still holding to the contrary, the "modern authority" as mentioned in one case is that the wife is in the same position as a tenant in common and can consent to the search of the premises occupied by both. In the case of *United States v. Thompson*,[123] the United States Court of Appeals for the Fifth Circuit stated that it was abandoning the 40-year-old rule that a wife cannot consent to the search of the couple's apartment, and authorized such a search. The court went on to say, however,

> Our holding that a wife can consent to a search of the premises she shares with her husband is limited to those premises under mutual control. The issue of whether a wife can consent to the search of premises reserved exclusively for the husband is not before us.

---

122 210 F.2d 69 (7th Cir. 1954).

123 421 F.2d 373 (5th Cir. 1970)

The Oregon Court of Appeals determined that it did not make any difference if the consenting spouse was not at home when the search was made and the fact that the non-consenting husband was at home when the officers advised him that his wife had consented to the search still did not make any difference.[124] In this case when the officers advised the husband that his wife had consented to the search, the defendant husband said nothing, but when asked if he would assist stated "he would rather not say anything or do anything." The appeals court concluded that the silence of the husband did not amount to a waiver but that he assumed the risk that the wife might consent to a search of the common areas and, therefore, had no legitimate expectation of privacy with respect to those areas.

Even those states which have been reluctant to abandon the rule that the wife alone may not give a valid consent to search the house when the search is directed to the absent spouse, have recently accepted the "modern authority."[125] Recognizing the trend toward equalization of the rights and obligations of men and women, the spouses who jointly occupy premises are now generally considered as tenants in common.

Even if the consenting party is not the spouse, but only acting in this capacity, a consent to the search of her paramour's room is valid, according to the Tenth Circuit Court of Appeals.[126] Here, the woman who claimed she was the defendant's wife consented to a search of the hotel room where the officers found a zipper bag containing contraband. The defendant claimed that since the woman was not his wife, although she had lived with him for three years, she had no authority to permit the search of the room. The court said:

> We believe that the rule that a wife may give consent to search premises that she has a right to use and occupy equal to that of her husband,...extends to the present circumstances and is equally applicable to the search of the zipper bag.

There remains confusion concerning the authority of the wife (or husband) to consent to a search of the part of the premises used *exclusively* by the other. One court decided that a wife cannot consent to the search of a rented garage which was leased entirely by the husband and not jointly occupied.[127] On the other hand, where the husband and wife had mutual use of

---

124 State v. Frame, 45 Or. 723, 609 P.2d 830 (1980).

125 Commonwealth v. Sebastian, 500 S.W.2d 417 (Ky. 1973); Yuma Co. Attorney v. McGuire, 111 Ariz. 437, 532 P.2d 157 (1975).

126 White v. United States, 444 F.2d 724 (10th Cir. 1971).

127 United States ex rel. Cabey v. Mazurkiewicz, 312 F. Supp. 11 (E.D. Pa. 1969).

the bedroom and the wife had access to the dresser drawer located in the room, the wife's consent to take evidence from the dresser drawer was upheld.[128] If the facts indicate that one spouse has *exclusive* control over a portion of the premises or a particular container, reliance on consent by the other spouse may jeopardize the seizure. To be certain the evidence will be admissible, consent should be obtained from the party who has control, or the area should be guarded by an officer until a search warrant is obtained.

(b) Consent by the parent

The general rule is that a minor child's possessory right in the family home is only that which he derives from the parent, and that the parent may authorize the consent search valid against the child. Where a room was occupied jointly by the defendant and his two younger brothers, the First Circuit Court of Appeals had no difficulty in finding that the mother could give consent to search the room.[129] In the *Peterson* case, the majority found that even though the minor child considered a room exclusively his, the mother had access and complete control over the entire premises and, therefore, had the authority to consent.

This rule was affirmed by the Pennsylvania Supreme Court in 1982. In the case of *Commonwealth v. Lowery*, the Court reiterated that a parent may consent to the search of the child's room even if that child is contributing toward his room and board.[130] Here the son lived at home with his parents and paid them $100 a month for room and board. However, he never locked his bedroom door or forbade family members from entering the room. In fact, the mother often entered the room to tidy up or drop off clean laundry. When the police arrived one evening while the son was taking a nap in the basement, the mother consented to a search of the room for LSD. The Court indicated that the mother could consent to the search even though the son paid for his room and board. The justices considered several factors in reaching the decision:

(1) The son had access to the whole house, not just the one room,
(2) he never objectively manifested an expectation of privacy in his room, and
(3) the son and the mother had joint access and control over the room.

---

128 People v. Stacey, 58 Ill. 2d 83, 317 N.E.2d 24 (1974).

129 United States v. Peterson, 524 F.2d 167 (4th Cir. 1975).

130 Commonwealth v. Lowery, 451 A.2d 245 (Pa. 1982).

The majority rule is that adult children who live in the house and have exclusive use of a particular room are treated as tenants in common as to the area used by all. Also, the parent, or anyone else who has common access to an area of the home may consent to a search of that area.[131]

(c) Consent by a minor child

An officer cannot rely on a consent given by a minor child. First, it would be very difficult to prove that the child understood the fact that he did not have to give consent, and secondly, the minor child's interest in the property is not that of a tenant in common. It would seem, however, that an adult child who has the status of a joint tenant or resident does have authority to consent to the search of the area used jointly.

(d) Consent by school authorities

The question as to whether the principal or police administrator of a school can consent to the search of a student's locker or personal belongings has not been specifically answered, depending as it does on the many factors. In one case the reviewing court upheld the lower court's conclusion that the locker belonged to the school and that the student had no right to exclusive dominion over it.[132] In this case the court pointed out that the principal, as a representative of the municipal owner of the locker, has a duty to inspect it whenever a suspicion of illegal use arises. While this same conclusion was reached in a Kansas case, it appears that to some extent the question turns on whether the lockers used by the students, as well as the locks to secure these lockers are owned by the municipality or school board.[133] If the principal or one in charge has made it clear by written posters or rules and regulations that the lockers are subject to be inspected, then the students' expectation of privacy would be diminished and the courts would more likely recognize that the principal can consent to the search or make the search himself.

In the case of *New Jersey v. T.L.O.*, the Supreme Court considered the reasonableness of a search of a student's purse by a school official.[134] In this case the court held that under ordinary circumstances the search of a student or a student's purse by a teacher or other school official will be justified if there are reasonable grounds for suspecting that the search will turn up evidence that the student has violated or is violating the law or rules of the

---

131 People v. Bunker, 22 Mich. App. 396, 177 N.W. 2d 644 (1970).

132 People v. Overton, 24 N.Y.2d 522, 249 N.E.2d 366 (1969).

133 State v. Stein, 203 Kan. 638, 452 P.2d 1 (1969), *cert. denied*, 397 U.S. 947, 90 S. Ct. 966, 25 L. Ed. 2d 128 (1970).

134 New Jersey v. T.L.O., 469 U.S. 325, 105 S. Ct. 733, 83 L. Ed. 2d 720 (1985).

school. The majority struck a balance between the student's legitimate expectation of privacy and the school's equally legitimate need to maintain an environment in which learning can take place. The Supreme Court indicated that the Fourth Amendment standard, which requires probable cause, would not be applied in the school situation. Rather, the legality of the search of a student should depend simply on the reasonableness, under all of the circumstances, of the search.[135]

This case does not present the question of the appropriate standard for assessing the legality of searches conducted by school officials in conjunction with, or on behalf of, a law enforcement agency. The Court expressed no opinion on that question. It would seem, however, that if the principal or school administrator has a reasonable suspicion that a student's locker contains evidence of a crime or of a violation of a school rule, a search may be made of that locker if made without involving law enforcement officers. The evidence may be turned over to an officer for use in a criminal trial. However, if the officer instigates the action or is involved in the action, then the probable cause standard as required by the Fourth Amendment must be met.

Before leaving the consent searches, it should be mentioned that when someone leaves articles in another's house or in another's care, the person who has custody of such article may consent to a search for that article.[136]

As the burden of proof is on the prosecution to show that the consent was given voluntarily, this consent should be obtained in writing when possible and should be witnessed by more than one person. If forms are used, they should be readily available at all times.

The law enforcement officer should recognize that the courts will give weight to the fact that the consent was given by the very young or the very old person or by one who has difficulty in understanding the English language. In such cases, the courts will be less ready to accept the consent to search.

§ 4.10 Search of movable vehicles and objects

The guarantee of freedom from unreasonable searches and seizures recognizes a necessary difference between the search of a dwelling house, for which a warrant may readily obtain, and the search of a ship, boat, wagon, airplane or other movable object, where it is not practical to secure a warrant, because the object may be quickly moved out of the jurisdiction in which the warrant must be sought. The most often-quoted case which stated

---

135 *See* § 4.12, *Search by a Private Individual*, for further discussion of the New Jersey v. T.L.O. case.

136 Marshall v. United States, 352 F.2d 1013 (9th Cir. 1965).

what has become known as the "moving vehicle" rule is *Carroll v. United States*.[137]

Following this decision and some contemporaneous decisions which distinguished between search of a vehicle and search of a house or other permanent structure, there was some doubt, especially in lower courts, about the moving vehicle doctrine.[138] Much of this doubt was laid to rest when the Supreme Court, in 1970, reaffirmed the right of officers to search a vehicle which is moving or about to be moved out of the jurisdiction, provided that there is probable cause to believe that the vehicle contains articles the officers are entitled to seize.

In the case of *Chambers v. Maroney*,[139] the police officers received a report that a filling station had been robbed. After receiving a description of the getaway car and a partial description of suspects who had been seen in the area, they stopped a station wagon answering the description of the car about two miles from the holdup site and arrested the occupants. During the course of the search of the car, the police found concealed, in a compartment under the dashboard, two .38-caliber revolvers and, in the right-hand glove compartment, an amount of small change and cards bearing the name of the attendant of another station which had been reported robbed at an earlier time.

At the trial, the materials taken from the station wagon were introduced over the objection of petitioner's counsel. Because the search was made some time after the arrest, the court quickly disposed of the search incident to the lawful arrest, saying that such a search was in violation of the Constitution. The Supreme Court, however, pointed out that there were other alternative grounds for the search in this case.

Relying heavily upon the *Carroll* case, the Supreme Court stated that the government recognized a necessary difference between a search of a store, dwelling house or other structure, in respect of which a proper official warrant may readily be obtained, and a search of a ship, motorboat, wagon or automobile for contraband goods where it is not practical to secure a warrant. The following paragraph taken from the case explains the "probable cause-moving vehicle" doctrine:

> In enforcing the Fourth Amendment's prohibition against unreasonable searches and seizures, the Court has insisted upon probable cause as a minimum requirement for a reasonable search permitted by the Constitution. As a general rule, it has also required the judgment of a magistrate on the probable-cause issue and the is-

137 267 U.S. 132, 45 S. Ct. 280, 69 L. Ed. 543 (1925).

138 Husty v. United States, 282 U.S. 694, 51 S. Ct. 240, 75 L. Ed. 629 (1931).

139 399 U.S. 42, 90 S. Ct. 1975, 26 L. Ed. 2d 419 (1970).

> suance of a warrant before a search is made. Only in exigent circumstances will the judgment of the police as to probable cause serve as sufficient authorization for a search. *Carroll* holds a search warrant unnecessary where there is probable cause to search an automobile stopped on the highway; the car is movable, the occupants are alerted, and the car's contents may never be found again if a warrant must be obtained. Hence an immediate search is constitutionally permissible.

The United States Supreme Court in December, 1975, affirmed the action it took in the *Chambers* case on facts which were very similar to those in that earlier case. In *Texas v. White*,[140] officers searched the automobile after the suspect had been arrested and the car driven by an officer to the station house. The Texas Court of Criminal Appeals, in a 3-2 decision, reversed the conviction on the ground that the evidence of four checks was obtained without a warrant in violation of the defendant's Fourth Amendment rights. The United States Supreme Court, however, with two justices dissenting, disagreed in these terms:

> In *Chambers v. Maroney* we held that police officers with probable cause to search an automobile on the scene where it was stopped could constitutionally do so later at the station house, without first obtaining a warrant. There, as here, "the probable-cause factor" that developed on the scene "still obtained at the station house."...The Court of Criminal Appeals erroneously excluded the evidence seized from the search at the station house in the light of the trial judge's finding...that there was probable cause to search [the defendant's] car.

The justification for this exception to the requirement that a search warrant must be obtained is that, because the vehicle is moving, or about to be moved, from the jurisdiction, there is no possibility of getting a search warrant even if probable cause for the warrant exists. Therefore, there are three requirements which must be met if the search is to be justified under this exception:

1. The officer must have probable cause which would justify a search warrant if one could be obtained.
2. The vehicle must be moving or about to be moved.
3. The facts must indicate that a warrant may not be readily obtained.

---

140 423 U.S. 67, 96 S. Ct. 304, 46 L. Ed. 2d 209 (1975).

At a minimum, the officer must have facts or information which would authorize the issuance of a search warrant, had application been made for one. Although the officer need not go before the judicial officer and prove probable cause before the search, he must have facts or information which would warrant a person of reasonable caution to believe that an offense had been, or was being, committed, and that articles which are subject to seizure were in the vehicle to be searched.

The doctrine is generally applied when an automobile is searched without a warrant; however, the same rationale may justify the search of a boat, plane, tractor-trailer or mobile home. The Eighth Circuit Court of Appeals found little difference between the search of an automobile and the search of a trailer where exigent circumstances existed. Cautioning that exigent circumstances must exist, and that there must be a pressing need for a prompt search, the justices of the Eighth Circuit nevertheless approved the search of a tractor-trailer.[141] If exigent circumstances are present and probable cause exists, there is no reason why a search of aircraft is not constitutionally permissible.[142]

Although the *Carroll* doctrine has been frequently referred to as the "automobile exception," some lower federal courts and state courts found the "moving vehicle" logic persuasive when considering the reasonableness of seizing other movable objects. Here the courts reasoned that exigent circumstances plus the fact that the object was about to be moved from the jurisdiction justified the warrantless search. Some examples include: a package being shipped by air freight,[143] a duffel bag in transit,[144] and purses from the desk of a manager of a credit union office who had admitted juggling accounts.[145]

For several years the United States Supreme Court struggled with the legality of searches of containers such as suitcases taken from occupied vehicles. In the case of *United States v. Chadwick*, the Court found a difference between vehicles and movable objects such as footlockers that were placed in vehicles. There the Court stated "the answer lies in the diminished expectation of privacy which surrounds the automobile."[146] In the *Chadwick* case the

---

141 United States v. Bozada, 473 F.2d 389 (8th Cir. 1973). *See also* Lederer v. Tehan, 441 F.2d 295 (6th Cir. 1971), where the court approved the search of a "U-Haul" truck.

142 United States v. Sigal, 500 F.2d 1118 (10th Cir. 1974).

143 People v. McKinnon, 7 Cal. 3d 399, 500 P.2d 1007, 103 Cal. Rptr. 897 (1972).

144 United States v. Wilson, 524 F.2d 595 (8th Cir. 1975).

145 United States v. Hand, 516 F.2d 472 (5th Cir. 1975).

146 433 U.S. 1, 538 S. Ct. 2476, 53 L. Ed. 2d 97 (1977).

officers had been alerted that the suspects were drug traffickers and observed them taking a double-locked footlocker from the train station and loading it in the trunk of the automobile. The Court disallowed the use of this evidence reasoning that there was no exigency to support the need for an immediate search.

During the 1980-1981 term of the Supreme Court the majority again disallowed the use of evidence from a container in an occupied vehicle.[147]

One of the major decisions of the United States Supreme Court in 1982 related to containers found in an automobile. By a 6-3 vote the Court concluded that police acting under the automobile exception to the Fourth Amendment warrant requirement may search every part of the vehicle being searched, including closed containers that might conceal the contraband for which they are looking.[148]

This decision specifically overruled the holding in *Robbins* that a warrantless search of two opaquely wrapped packages found in the trunk of a lawfully searched automobile violated the Fourth Amendment. It also discredited that portion of the opinion in *Arkansas v. Sanders* that had suggested warrantless container searches could never be sustained on the grounds of the automobile exception. In the *Ross* case the court held in effect that if an officer has probable cause to search an occupied vehicle for a particular type of evidence, for example, contraband or stolen goods, he is entitled to conduct a warrantless search of all compartments or closed containers within the vehicle in which the evidence sought may reasonably be found. Again explaining the rationale for the automobile exception the court noted:

> The scope of a warrantless search based on probable cause is no narrower -- and no broader -- than the scope of a search authorized by a warrant supported by probable cause. Only the prior approval of the magistrate is waived; the search otherwise is as the magistrate could authorize.

It should be noted that the *Ross* decision did not completely overrule *Chadwick*. *Chadwick* is still the prevailing law where the police focus is aimed at a particular "known container." If, as in the *Chadwick* case, a search is directed toward a particular container in an automobile, it will be necessary to seize the container and get a warrant prior to its opening.

---

147 Robbins v. California, 453 U.S. 420, 101 S. Ct. 2841, 69 L. Ed. 2d (1981). *See also* Arkansas v. Sanders, 442 U.S. 753, 99 S. Ct. 2586 (1979).

148 United States v. Ross, 456 U.S. 798, 102 S. Ct. 2157, 72 L. Ed. 2d 572 (1982) and cases cited.

It is interesting to note that Justice Blackmun, who dissented in the *Chadwick*, *Sanders*, and *Robbins* cases, reiterates his dissatisfaction with the court's vacillation regarding the search of containers in automobiles. In joining the majority opinion, he indicated that the decision in the *Ross* case should provide an "authoritative ruling."

In previous cases relating to the moving vehicle/probable cause doctrine which justifies the search of a vehicle moving or about to be moved, the Supreme Court has indicated that the exception applies to automobiles, boats, and airplanes. In a more recent case, the Supreme Court considered the legality of the search of a motor home temporarily parked in a downtown parking lot.[149]

In the *Carney* case, DEA agents had information that the defendant's mobile home was being used as a location to exchange marijuana for sex. The agents observed the defendant approach a youth who accompanied the defendant to a motor home which was parked in a lot in downtown San Diego. When the youth emerged from the motor home the agents convinced him to return and ask the defendant to come out, which the boy did. When the defendant stepped out, an agent entered the home without a warrant and found marijuana lying on the table.

The defendant was charged with possession of marijuana for sale and made a motion to suppress the evidence discovered in the motor home. After this motion was denied, a California Court convicted the defendant on a plea of *nolo contendere*. The California Supreme Court reversed the conviction, determining that the search of the motor home was unreasonable and that the motor vehicle exception to the warrant requirements did not apply because of the expectations of privacy of occupants of a motor home.

The Chief Justice, writing for the United States Supreme Court, pointed out that privacy expectations are reduced in automobiles not only because some parts of the vehicle are open to plain view, but also because motor vehicles are heavily regulated. The majority reasoned that since the vehicle is readily mobile and there is a reduced expectation of privacy stemming from its use as a licensed motor vehicle subject to regulation, it may be searched if located in a place not regularly used for residential purposes. The Court used these terms in part of its decision:

> When a vehicle is being used on the highway, or if it is readily capable of such use and is found stationary in a place not regularly used for residential purposes...the two justifications for the vehicle exception come into play. First, the vehicle is obviously readily mobile...Second, there is a reduced expectation of privacy stemming

---

149 California v. Carney, 471 U.S. 386, 105 S. Ct. 2066, 85 L. Ed. 2d 406 (1985).

> from its use as a licensed motor vehicle subject to a range of police regulations inapplicable to a fixed dwelling.

One other point before leaving the search of moving vehicles and containers in moving vehicles: this relates to the authority to delay the search of the container or the vehicle. In the case of *Michigan v. Thomas*, a majority of the U.S. Supreme Court reaffirmed that "the officer may conduct a warrantless search of a vehicle, even after it has been impounded and in police custody."[150] These justices indicated that once probable cause exists for a car search, the legality of that search does not depend on whether the car has been immobilized, or on the likelihood that the car or its contents will be tampered with.

§ 4.11 Seizure without a search (plain view)

Provisions of the Fourth Amendment to the federal Constitution and the provisions of the state constitutions protect persons against unreasonable searches and seizures. Therefore, where there is no search required, the constitutional guarantee is not applicable. The guarantee applies only in those instances where the seizure is assisted by a necessary search. A series of federal and state cases has affirmed the rule that a seizure of contraband or instrumentalities of the crime in plain view is not a violation of the Fourth Amendment where the officers are on the premises lawfully. This exception to the rule that the officer must have a warrant was well stated in the case of *United States v. McDaniel*.[151] In this case the court made the following comment:

> [I]f, without a search and without an unlawful entry into the premises, a contraband article or an article which is needed by the police, is seen in the premises, the police are not required to close their eyes and need not walk out and leave the article where they

---

150 Michigan v. Thomas, 458 U.S. 259, 102 S. Ct. 3079, 73 L. Ed. 2d 750 (1982). The Court in United States v. Johns, 469 U.S. 78, 105 S. Ct. 881, 83 L. Ed. 2d 890 (1985) held that the search of a vehicle under the probable cause-moving vehicle may be as thorough as a search under a warrant. The Court also held that a search of containers from the vehicle three days after the vehicle search does not violate the Fourth Amendment.

151 154 F. Supp. 1 (D.D.C. 1957). *See also* Coolidge v. New Hampshire, 403 U.S. 443, 91 S. Ct. 2022, 29 L. Ed. 2d 564 (1971).

> saw it. Any other principle might lead to an absurd result and at times perhaps even defeat the ends of justice.

Although the rule is clear that it is not a search for an officer to seize what is open and visible to the eye when seen from a place where the officer is entitled to be, there is some question as to the lawfulness of the officer's presence on the premises. An officer lawfully present may use the evidence which is seized where he sees the objects by looking through an open door, an open window, or an open transom. In the *Harris* case,[152] the Court approved the seizure of draft cards when a search was made incident to a lawful arrest and the object of the search was canceled checks, commenting:

> Nor is it a significant consideration that the draft cards which were seized were not related to the crimes for which petitioner was arrested. Here during the course of a valid search the agents came upon property of the United States in the illegal custody of the petitioner. It was property to which the Government was entitled to possession....Nothing in the decisions of this Court gives support to the suggestion that under such circumstances the law enforcement officials must impotently stand aside and refrain from seizing such contraband material.

Such seizures are authorized where the officer is on the premises lawfully or if he can observe the contraband or illegally possessed goods from a position where he is not a trespasser, but if the officer does become a trespasser on property which is under the protection of the Fourth Amendment, his action then amounts to an illegal search and seizure. He cannot use information so obtained to procure a warrant, nor can he seize the evidence without a warrant.

In 1982 the United States Supreme Court approved the seizure of evidence by an officer who observed contraband from a doorway.[153] In this case

---

152 Harris v. United States, 331 U.S. 145, 67 S. Ct. 1098, 91 L. Ed. 1399 (1947). *See also* State v. Bagley, 286 Minn. 180, 175 N.W.2d 448 (1970), quoting Abel v. United States, 362 U.S. 217, 80 S. Ct. 683, 4 L. Ed. 2d 668 (1960), where seizure of goods not described in the warrant was approved, the Court emphasizing, "When an article subject to lawful seizure properly comes into the officer's possession in the course of a lawful search it would be entirely without reason to say he must return it because it was not one of those things it was his business to look for." For another case authorizing seizure of marijuana "in plain sight," see United States v. Lozaw, 427 F.2d 911 (2d Cir. 1970).

153 Washington v. Chrisman, 455 U.S. 1, 102 S. Ct. 812, 70 L. Ed. 2d 778 (1982).

a University police department officer placed the defendant's roommate under lawful arrest for possession of alcoholic beverages. The arrestee asked the officer to accompany him to his dormitory room to obtain identification. The officer, standing in the open doorway of the room while the arrestee searched for his identification, observed marijuana and a pipe on a desk in the room. The officer then entered the room, confirmed that the seeds were marijuana, and determined that the pipe smelled of marijuana. He then informed the roommate, the defendant in this case, of his rights under *Miranda* and asked if there were any other drugs in the room. The defendant orally and in writing agreed to a search of the room which yielded more marijuana and another controlled substance.

The defendant (the roommate of the arrestee) was later charged with two counts of possessing controlled substances. The Washington Court of Appeals affirmed the use of the evidence seized by the police but the Washington Supreme Court reversed. The United States Supreme Court disagreed with the Washington Supreme Court and declared that the police officer "had a right to remain literally at Overdahl's elbow at all times." After confirming that the officer had a right to accompany the arrestee, the Court made this comment:

> We hold, therefore, that it is not "unreasonable" under the Fourth Amendment for a police officer, as a matter of routine, to monitor the movements of an arrested person as his judgment indicates following the arrest. The officer's need to insure his own safety -- as well as the integrity of the arrest -- is compelling.

The Supreme Court again verified the plain view exception in these terms:

> The "plain view" exception to the Fourth Amendment warrant requirement permits a law enforcement officer to seize what clearly is incriminating evidence or contraband when it is discovered in the place where the officer has right to be.

Citing this as a classic example of the plain view doctrine, the Court confirmed that the Fourth Amendment does not prohibit seizure of evidence of criminal conduct found in these circumstances. Justice White, writing for the dissenters in the *Chrisman* case, argued that the plain view doctrine does not authorize one to raid a dwelling to seize contraband merely because the contraband is visible from outside the dwelling. He contended that unless the officer is actually inside the dwelling legally at the time he observes the contraband, the further intrusion to actually seize the contraband must be justified by a warrant or by a different exception to the warrant requirements. Applying this concept to the case, the dissenters would not have authorized the use of the evidence seized as the officer was outside the room when he saw the contraband and should have obtained a warrant to actually seize the narcotics.

In another Supreme Court decision the focus was on the requirement that the officer recognize the articles seized as contraband before the plain view doctrine will be accepted.[154] The question was whether the officer must "know" that certain items are contraband or evidence of the crime before the seizure is justified under the plain view approach. In this case the officer validly stopped the automobile at a routine driver's license checkpoint. He shined his flashlight into the car and saw an opaque green party balloon knotted near the top fall from the respondent's hand to the seat beside him. Based on his experience in drug offense arrests, the officer was aware that narcotics frequently were packed in such balloons and while the respondent was searching in the glove compartment for his license, the officer shifted his position to obtain a better view and noticed a small plastic vial, loose white powder, and an opened bag of party balloons in the glove compartment. These articles were seized by the officer under the plain view authority and used as evidence at the trial.

The trial court approved the use of the evidence but the Texas Court of Criminal Appeals reversed, holding that the evidence should have been suppressed because it was obtained in violation of the Fourth Amendment. The Texas Court of Criminal Appeals reasoned that for the doctrine to apply, not only must the officer be legitimately in a position to view the object but it also must be "immediately apparent" to the police that they have evidence before them and thus the officers here had to "know" that incriminating evidence was before them when they seized the balloon. The United States Supreme Court disagreed with the Texas court and determined that absolute certainty was not a requirement, only probable cause. The Court agreed that the officer possessed probable cause to believe that the balloon in the suspect's possession contained an illegally possessed substance.

Utilizing the plain view doctrine, the Supreme Court in 1986 announced that officers were justified in seizing a gun observed under the seat of a car while attempting to get the vehicle identification number (VIN).[155] In the *Class* case, two officers observed the defendant driving above the speed limit in a car with a cracked windshield, both traffic violations under the New York law. When one of the officers attempted to see the vehicle identification number (VIN), he noticed that some papers obscured the area on the dashboard where the number is located. In attempting to see the number, the officer reached into the interior of the car to remove the papers. In doing so,

---

154 Texas v. Brown, 460 U.S. 730, 103 S. Ct. 1535, 75 L. Ed. 2d 502 (1983).

155 New York v. Class, 475 U.S. 106, 106 S. Ct. 960, 89 L. Ed. 2d 81 (1986).

he saw the handle of a gun protruding from underneath the driver's seat and seized the gun. The defendant was then arrested and later convicted of criminal possession of a weapon. He appealed, claiming that the seizure of the gun was in violation of the Constitution.

The New York Court of Appeals reversed, holding that in the absence of any justification for the search of the respondent's car besides the traffic violation, the search was prohibited and the gun must accordingly be excluded from evidence.

The United States Supreme Court disagreed. Citing the important interests served by the use of motor vehicle identification numbers and requiring the placement in an area ordinarily in plain view from outside the passenger compartment, the Supreme Court noted that the intrusion was not in violation of the Fourth Amendment. The Court cautioned, however, that "our holding today does not authorize police officers to enter a vehicle to obtain a dashboard-mounted VIN when the VIN is visible from outside the automobile."

Justice O'Connor, writing for the five-Justice majority, explained that the entry into the car was a "search" but it was reasonable and not prohibited by the Constitution. The majority reasoned that had the defendant remained in the car, the police could have asked him to move the papers. Once he got out, the officers had two alternatives: moving the papers themselves or allowing the driver to return to the car to move them. The second alternative would have exposed them to possible danger from a concealed weapon. In view of this danger, the minimal nature of the intrusion, the lack of privacy expectation in the VIN, and the officer's own witnessing of the defendant's traffic offenses, the police action was reasonable.

As revealed in the previous paragraphs, in order for the plain view exception to apply, an officer must be legitimately in a position to view the article that will ultimately be seized. This requirement is interpreted as meaning that the officer must be legitimately on the premises or near enough to observe what is taking place on the premises without violating the rights of the person who has the right to claim protection of the Constitution. Does this apply to an area open to view from the air? According to the United States Supreme Court, a naked eye viewing of a backyard from a public airspace is not a Fourth Amendment search even if it results from "focused observation" rather than a casual overflight.[156]

In the *Ciraolo* case, the officers had received a tip that the defendant was growing marijuana in his backyard, which was completely fenced. The police, for the express purpose of flying over the property, took an airplane flight over the yard and, without visual assistance, observed and photographed what

---

[156] California v. Giraolo, 476 U.S. 267, 106 S. Ct. 1809, 90 L. Ed. 2d 210 (1986).

legitimate Plain View

appeared to be marijuana under cultivation. This resulted in the issuance of a search warrant and seizure of the plants.

The California Court of Appeals reversed the marijuana conviction on the ground that the defendant had a reasonable expectation of privacy, placing emphasis on the fact that the police had taken the flight for the specific purpose of observing the enclosed curtilage. The United States Supreme Court acknowledged that the enclosed yard was within the curtilage of the residence, but added that this fact in itself does not prohibit all police observation. Pointing out that the police followed the aircraft regulations and that anyone flying through the same airspace could have seen everything the officers saw, the Court concluded that the expectation of privacy was unreasonable. Relying upon decisions made in an earlier case, the Court commented:

> The Fourth Amendment protection of the home has never been extended to require law enforcement officers to shield their eyes when passing by a home on public thoroughfares. Nor does the mere fact that an individual has taken measures to restrict some view of his activities preclude an officer's observations from the public vantage point where he has a right to be and which renders the activities clearly visible.

Four dissenting justices in the *Ciraolo* case took a very different view, arguing that the single fact that airspace is generally open to anyone for travel does not deprive citizens of their privacy interests in outdoor activities in an enclosed curtilage.

As indicated, for the plain view exception to apply, there must be a seizure without a search. That is, the officer must be legitimately in a position to view the article that will be seized and near enough to observe that the article is contraband or otherwise subject to seizure. If a "search" is required in order to determine if the article is stolen merchandise, then the seizure without a search doctrine will not apply.[157] In the *Hicks* case, the officers were in the apartment of the suspect legally as they were investigating a report that a bullet was fired through the floor of the respondent's apartment, injuring a man on the floor below. While in the apartment of the suspect, searching for the person who fired the weapon as well as other victims and for weapons, they seized three weapons and discovered a stocking mask. While there, one of the officers noticed two sets of expensive stereo components and, suspecting that they were stolen, read and recorded their serial numbers, moving some of them, including a turntable, to do so.

---

157 Arizona v. Hicks, ___ U.S. ___. 107 S. Ct. 1149, 94 L. Ed. 2d 347 (1987). *See* case in Part II.

Here the officer's only justification for checking the serial numbers was the fact that the expensive stereo components seemed out of place in this otherwise ill-appointed four-room apartment. His suspicions were confirmed, but only after he had moved the equipment to determine the serial numbers of the equipment and had called headquarters, where he was advised that a turntable had been taken in an armed robbery.

While the *Texas v. Brown* case offered the rule that the officer need not be near, certain that the evidence seized was contraband, the Court in that case indicated that there must be probable cause to believe that the article to be seized was possessed in violation of the law. In the *Hicks* case, the Court indicated that the search was invalid because the police had only a "reasonable suspicion" (less than probable cause to believe) that the stereo equipment was stolen.

In making it clear that probable cause is the standard, the Court made this comment:

> We now hold that probable cause is required. To say otherwise would be to cut the "plain view doctrine" loose from its theoretical and practical moorings...

The Court continued with this explanation:

> No reason is apparent why an object should routinely be seizable on lesser grounds, during an unrelated search and seizure, than would have been needed to obtain a warrant for that same object if it had been known to be on the premises.

To summarize, the requirements for the application of the "plain view exception" are:

(1) the officer must be legitimately in a position to view the object, and
(2) he must have probable cause to associate the property with criminal activity.

Often the question arises as to the use of field glasses, telescopes or flashlights in observing the objects that are ultimately seized under the plain view doctrine. In a 1952 opinion, the United States Supreme Court held that the use of binoculars or telescopes did not amount to a trespass.[158] Also the fact that the property is hidden by the darkness of night and is revealed only by the use of a flashlight does not necessarily mean the property was found

---

158 On Lee v. United States, 343 U.S. 747, 72 S. Ct. 967, 96 L. Ed. 1270 (1952).

by a search. Stating this more dramatically, the Fifth Circuit Court in 1971 commented: "the plain view rule does not go into hibernation at sunset."[159] There the justices agreed that the aid of a flashlight did not transform a night time observation into a search. Although some of the lower courts have argued that the use of a telescope or other artificial device to enhance observation of objects and activities offend the Fourth Amendment,[160] the Supreme Court decisions have indicated that the use of such devices does not violate the Constitution. In the *Texas v. Brown* case, the Supreme Court made this comment:

> It is likewise beyond dispute that Maples' action in shining his flashlight to illuminate the interior of Brown's car trenched upon no right secured to the latter by the Fourth Amendment....The use of a search light is comparable to the use of a marine glass or field glass. It is not prohibited by the Constitution. Numerous other courts have agreed that the use of artificial means to illuminate a darkened area simply does not constitute a search, and thus triggers no Fourth Amendment protection.[161]

§ 4.12 Search by a private individual

You cannot
be working for the police

The constitutional prohibitions against unreasonable searches operate against official action. Therefore, where evidence has been unlawfully seized by a private person with no official knowledge or without collusion, the evidence may generally be used by the prosecution. A private person who unlawfully enters the premises may be subject to civil suit or even criminal action, but the evidence may nevertheless be used. According to the decisions, such a search and seizure is outside the scope of constitutional protection. Obviously, should the court find that a law enforcement officer participated in the search in any way or had knowledge that the search was to be made, the evidence would not be admissible.[162] Even if the police "stand idly by"

---

159 Walker v. Beto, 437 F.2d 1018 (5th Cir. 1971).

160 United States v. Taborda, 635 F.2d 131 (2d Cir. 1980).

161 Texas v. Brown, *supra*, lists the decisions that have upheld the use of artificial means to observe evidence subject to seizure. *See also* Wheeler, Guyne & White v. State (decided 7/12/82) Tex. Ct. App., which held that the use of binoculars to see marijuana plants growing in a greenhouse was not in violation of the Fourth Amendment.

162 Lustig v. United States, 338 U.S. 74, 69 S. Ct. 137, 93 L. Ed. 1819 (1949). *See* Coolidge v. New Hampshire, 403 U.S. 443, 91 S. Ct. 2022, 29 L. Ed. 2d 564 (1971)

while a private person acts and the police have knowledge of the action, there is a good possibility that the exclusionary rule will apply.[163]

However, in one case, the Seventh Circuit Court of Appeals pointed out that the inspection by a carrier (airline) official, without the participation of state or federal authority is not a government search.[164] But where the agent had already called the Drug Enforcement Administration and was told that agents would be there shortly, there was too much government participation, and the exclusionary rule was enforced.[165]

In 1980 case the United States Supreme Court was presented with what was called by the Court a "bizarre case."[166] The question to be decided was whether the fact that a private individual had opened the package thereby disclosing the illegal contents justify law enforcement officers in conducting a further search of the packages. The "bizarre facts" were that sealed packages containing 871 boxes of film depicting homosexual activities were shipped by private carrier from St. Petersburg, Florida, to Atlanta, Georgia. The shipment was addressed to "Leggs, Inc." but was mistakenly delivered to "L'Eggs Products, Inc." Employees of the latter company opened each of the packages and found that on the side of each film container was an explicit description of the contents. The employees attempted, without success, to view portions of the film by holding it up to the light. They then turned the film over to the FBI. The FBI agents further examined the film and viewed the film with a projector.

The petitioners were indicted on obscenity charges relating to the interstate transportation of 5 of the 871 films in the shipment. A motion to suppress was denied in the District Court and the suspects were found guilty. The Court of Appeals affirmed and the United States Supreme Court granted certiorari. Five justices of the United States Supreme Court agreed that the film should not have been admitted and reversed. However, no more than two agreed on the reasoning. Two of the justices reasoned that although the FBI agents were lawfully in possession of the boxes of film, they did not have authority to search the contents any further than the private party had already searched them. They explained that as the private party had not reviewed the films, neither could the FBI. These two concluded that:

> Since the additional search conducted by the FBI -- the screening of the films -- was not supported by any justification, it violated that amendment [Fourth Amendment].

---

163 Stapleton v. Superior Ct., 73 Cal. Rptr. 575, 447 P.2d 967 (1968).

164 United States v. Issod, 508 F.2d 990 (7th Cir. 1975).

165 United States v. Newton, 510 F.2d 1149 (7th Cir. 1975).

166 Walter v. United States, 447 U.S. 649, 100 S. Ct. 2395, 65 L. Ed. 2d 410 (1980).

Two other justices agreed with the result but disagreed with the reasoning. These two apparently felt that the expectation of privacy continued even though a private person had opened the films originally. They, in effect, held that the Fourth Amendment applies to private persons as well as public agents. A fifth justice concurred in the result without opinion.

Four justices of the Supreme Court would have upheld the seizure. The dissenting judges first expressed their appreciation that at least the majority preserves the integrity of the rule to the effect that the Fourth Amendment proscribes only governmental action and:

> [D]oes not apply to a search or seizure, even an unreasonable one, effected by a private individual not acting as an agent of the Government or with the participation or knowledge of any governmental official.

The dissenters were of the opinion that, after the packages had been opened by a private individual by the time the FBI received the films, the petitioners had no remaining expectation of privacy in their contents. They, therefore, would have allowed the films to be used as evidence. In the concluding paragraph of the dissenters' opinion, they expressed their concern about the technicalities with these words:

> We tend occasionally to strain credulity and to spin the thread of argument so thin that we depart from the common-sense approach to an obvious fact situation. It seems to me to be beyond the limits of sound precedent to exclude the evidence of petitioners' crimes in the face of the "bizarre" developments that transpired here, developments that petitioners brought upon themselves.

As explained by the dissent, this case is a peculiar one and the margin for reversal was narrow.

The one conclusion that can be drawn after looking at the decisions of the various justices is that most of the justices still hold to the rule that the Fourth Amendment proscribes only governmental action and does not apply to search and seizure effected by private individuals not acting as agents of the government or with the knowledge of any governmental official.

This conclusion is justified by the decision in *United States v. Jacobson*.[167] In this case the Court held that employees of a private freight carrier were not government agents and seizure of white powdery substance from a

---

[167] 466 U.S. 109, 104 S. Ct. 1652, 80 L. Ed. 2d 85 (1984).

damaged package did not constitute a search within the meaning of the Fourth Amendment.

Even though the DEA agents took part of the powdery substance and conducted a field test and exceeded the scope of the private search, the seizure and test was not an unlawful "search" and "seizure."

In another case, the court conceded that the question was a close one but approved the seizure of a sawed-off shotgun from a motel room by the motel manager after the 2 p.m. check-out time had passed, and the defendant had been arrested by police officers on another charge.[168] Before action of a private individual can be attributed to the government, some degree of government instigation or knowledge must be shown.[169]

There seems to be no question that the exclusionary rule does not apply where a private person without any official authority makes the search. An issue which has been becoming more difficult, however, is whether the exclusionary rule should be applied where railroad police, private contract police, investigators or school authorities make the search.

Airline agents are not -- according to the Nebraska Supreme Court -- law enforcement officers. Therefore, a senior passenger agent who seized marijuana from baggage in the baggage room did not violate the Constitution and the evidence was admissible. The court said the constitutional provisions against unreasonable searches and seizures apply only to governmental agents and not to private persons.[170]

The U.S. Court of Appeals for the Sixth Circuit reaffirmed that a private carrier agent, in this case Federal Express, was not a government agent when he opened a damaged package.[171] Here the company's security manager, suspecting contraband, opened the package and found four bottles labeled "Methaqualone," a drug that, while controlled, may also be legally possessed. The agent called the DEA who took the pills for testing. The court reasoned that even though a memo circulated to the employees urging cooperation in detecting illegal drugs had been prepared with the cooperation of the DEA,

---

168 United States v. Parizo, 514 F.2d 52 (2d Cir. 1975).

169 United States v. Luciow, 518 F.2d 298 (8th Cir. 1975).

170 State v. Skonberg, 194 Neb. 554, 233 N.W.2d 919 (1975). *See* New Jersey v. T.L.O., 469 U.S. 325, 105 S.Ct. 733, 83 L. Ed. 2d 720 (1985), which held that the Fourth Amendment applies to searches conducted by public school officials but under ordinary circumstances the search of a student by a school official will be justified at its inception where there are reasonable grounds for suspecting that the search will turn up evidence that the student has violated or is violating either the law or rules of the school.

171 United States v. Barry, 673 F.2d 912 (6th Cir. 1982).

the initial opening of the package was nothing more than a private search, which the Fourth Amendment does not cover.

While the cases are consistent in determining that airline agents and private carrier agents are not public police for purposes of applying the exclusionary rule, the cases are not so clear regarding private security police. In determining if such personnel act as private citizens or officials, each case will be scrutinized. If personnel who make investigations and seize property are licensed by the state, there is a good possibility that such licensed personnel will be considered "official" and the exclusionary rule will apply. If, on the other hand, guard personnel are employed without any official sanction, the probability is that they are not acting in the official capacity so as to bring them within the purview of the Fourth Amendment.

Before the case of *New Jersey v. T.L.O.* the lower courts were divided in determining whether action by school officials was to be held state action rendering the Fourth Amendment applicable.[172] In the *T.L.O.* case the Supreme Court determined that action by school officials was "state action" rendering the Fourth Amendment applicable where marijuana was seized from a high school student. Here a high school teacher, upon discovering that the student was smoking cigarettes in a school lavatory, took the student to the principal's office. The assistant vice principal opened the student's purse and found a pack of cigarettes, some marijuana, a pipe, plastic bags, and a substantial amount of money as well as an index card containing a list of students who owed the defendant money. The New Jersey Supreme Court ordered the suppression of the evidence as the search of the purse was unreasonable.

The United States Supreme Court reached a compromise decision, agreeing that school officials were "public officials" but refusing to apply the strict rules that limit searches by public authorities. In establishing the guidelines, the Court included these comments:

> We hold today that officials need not obtain a warrant before searching a student who is under their authority.
>
> School officials need not be held subject to the requirement that searches be based on probable cause to believe that the subject of the search has violated or is violating the law.
>
> Rather, the legality of the search of students should depend simply on the reasonableness, under all of the circumstances, of the search.

Applying this standard, the search of the student's purse was justified.

---

[172] New Jersey v. T.L.O., 469 U.S. 325, 105 S. Ct. 733, 83 L. Ed. 2d 720 (1985).

The search and seizure rule, as it relates to school officials, is that school officials are public officials for purposes of the Fourth Amendment, but a search of the student by the teacher or other school official will be justified "if there are reasonable grounds for suspecting that the search will turn up evidence that the student has violated or is violating either the law or the rules of the school." A search warrant is not required prior to the search. The applicable test is "reasonable grounds for suspicion" in making the search without a warrant rather than "probable cause" as is required for law enforcement officials.

As in the case of school authorities, the United States Supreme Court has established different search standards where parole or probation officers initiate the search. There is no doubt that probation and parole officers are government agents for purposes of the Fourth Amendment; however, this does not necessarily mean that the probation officer must follow the same probable cause requirements as are required by police officers. According to the majority of the members of the Supreme Court, supervision of probationers is a "special need" of the state that may justify departure from the usual warrant and probable cause requirements as are required for police officers.[173] In the *Griffin* case the probation officers, after receiving information from a police detective that there were or might be guns in the probationer's apartment, searched the apartment and found a handgun. Under Wisconsin law and regulations established by the department under the statutes, probation officers may search a probationer's home without a warrant if there are "reasonable grounds" to believe that there is the presence of contraband. This standard of reasonable grounds is less than probable cause which is normally required for a search warrant.

In justifying this departure from the "probable cause" standard, the Court included these comments:

> We think the probation regime would also be unduly disrupted by a requirement of probable cause.
>
> The probation agency must be able to act based upon a lesser degree of certainty [than the Fourth Amendment would otherwise require] in order to intervene before a probationer damages himself or society.

In the *Griffin* case the search on less than probable cause was carried out pursuant to a state regulation and, according to the Court, satisfied the Fourth Amendment's reasonableness requirement. In the discussion the Court compared this to searches by school officials as authorized in *New Jer-*

---

173 Griffin v. Wisconsin, ___ U.S. ___, 107 S. Ct. 3164, 97 L. Ed. 2d 709 (1987).

sey v. T.L.O. Left unanswered is the legality of the search of a probationer's home without probable cause where the search is not conducted pursuant to a valid state regulation governing probationers.

§ 4.13 Premises protected by the Fourth Amendment

The Fourth Amendment and the provisions of the various state constitutions protect the right of the people to be secure in their persons, houses, papers and effects. Courts have been called upon in many instances to define what premises and areas are protected by this provision. The term "houses" has been interpreted very broadly to include any dwelling, whether it be a mansion, a small house, apartment, or hotel room. The house is protected even though it is temporarily unoccupied as in the case of a summer or weekend home. However, once a dwelling has been vacated, as when a tenant checks out of a hotel, it is not protected. The protection also extends to a place of business.[174]

Not only does the protection extend to the house itself, but also to the curtilage. The curtilage has been defined as the open space situated within a common enclosure and belonging to the dwelling house. It has also been defined as the space which is necessary and convenient and is habitually used for family purposes, including a yard, a garden, or even a field which is near to and used in connection with the dwelling. It is often difficult to define the area included within the curtilage, but certainly the yard around the house is included and protected under the Fourth Amendment and the state provisions.

The United States Supreme Court in the case of *United States v. Dunn* set out some guidelines to be used in determining if an area is within the curtilage for Fourth Amendment purposes.[175] The Court enumerated four factors to be considered in determining the extent-of-curtilage questions.

(1) The proximity of the area to the home;
(2) Whether the area is within an enclosure surrounding the home;
(3) The nature and uses to which the area is put; and
(4) The steps taken by the resident to protect the area from observation by passers-by.

---

174 United States v. Rabinowitz, 339 U.S. 56, 70 S. Ct. 430, 94 L. Ed. 653 (1950).

175 United States v. Dunn, ___ U.S. ___, 107 S. Ct. 1134, 94 L. Ed. 2d 326 (1987).

Applying these criteria, the Court ruled that a barn which was located 60 yards from the home and which was not within the area enclosed by a fence surrounding the house was not within the curtilage of the home, although the ranch was completely encircled by a perimeter fence and contained several interior barbed-wire fences, including one around the house approximately 50 yards from the barn, and a wooden fence enclosing the front of the barn. Without a warrant, the officer crossed the perimeter fence, several barbed-wire fences, and the wooden fence in front of the barn. They did not enter the barn but observed what they believed to be a drug laboratory within the barn. With this information and confirming evidence observed at a later date, they obtained a search warrant and executed it, arresting the defendant and seizing chemicals and equipment.

In upholding the seizure, the Supreme Court indicated that the government's intrusion upon open fields is not an unreasonable search, and that the erection of fences on an open field -- at least of the type involved here -- does not create a constitutionally protected interest.

After comprehensively reviewing previous cases, including the case of *Hester v. United States* which established the rule that "open fields" are not protected by the Constitution, and *Katz v. United States* which created some doubt concerning the open fields doctrine, the Court in 1984 confirmed that the "open fields doctrine" still has legal life, and approved the warrantless discovery and seizure of marijuana one mile from the defendant's home.[176] Here the officers, after arriving at the farm, drove past the house to a locked gate with a "no trespassing" sign but with a foot path around one side. The agents walked around the gate and along the road and found a field of marijuana over a mile from the defendant's house. The defendant was arrested and indicted for manufacturing a controlled substance in violation of a federal statute. Citing the *Katz* case, the Court explained that the Fourth Amendment does not protect the merely subjective expectation of privacy, but only those "expectations" that society is prepared to recognize as "reasonable." In the syllabus of this case, it is noted that:

> Moreover, the common law, by implying only the land immediately surrounding and associated with the home warrants the Fourth Amendment protections that attach to the home, conversely implies that no expectation of privacy legitimately attaches to open fields.

---

176 Hester v. United States, 265 U.S. 57, 44 S. Ct. 445, 68 L. Ed. 898 (1924); Katz v. United States, 389 U.S. 347, 88 S. Ct. 507, 19 L. Ed. 2d 576 (1967); Oliver v. United States, 466 U.S. 170, 104 S. Ct. 1735, 80 L. Ed. 2d 214 (1984).

After a long debate in the lower courts, the United States Supreme Court in 1988 concluded that the Fourth Amendment does not prohibit the warrantless search and seizure of garbage left for collection outside of the curtilage of the home.[177] In this case, investigators obtained evidence of narcotics violations from garbage bags left on the curb in front of the defendant's house. The majority first found that the curb was not part of the curtilage, and, secondly, that residents of the house could have no reasonable expectation of privacy in the items which they discarded. In regard to the expectation of privacy principle, the court resolved that:

> An expectation of privacy does not give rise to Fourth Amendment protection, however, unless society is prepared to accept that expectation as objectively reasonable.

§ 4.14 Standing to challenge the search

Although the *Mapp* court said that the only courtroom door remaining open to evidence secured by illegal search has been closed, it seems there are still several cracks which have not, as yet, been closed. If the premises are searched and the evidence is incriminating against a party who does not have standing to challenge the search, the evidence may be used against him. The reasoning is that the defendant's rights have not been violated and he may therefore not complain of the unreasonable searches and seizure or prevent the fruits thereof from being used against him. There is no doubt that the person whose rights were violated may complain, but the party who had no substantial possessory interest in the premises searched may not complain.

In the case of *Jones v. United States*,[178] the Court expressed the rule in this paragraph:

> In order to qualify as a "person aggrieved by an unlawful search and seizure" one must have been a victim of a search or seizure, one against whom the search was directed, as distinguished from one who claims prejudice only through the use of evidence gathered as a consequence of a search or seizure directed at someone else.

The courts have not been consistent in determining who is a person "aggrieved." In the *Jones* case the Court held that the defendant had standing

---

177 California v. Greenwood, ___ U.S. ___, 108 S. Ct. 1625, 100 L. Ed. 2d 30 (1988). *See* the case for a review of lower court decisions.

178 362 U.S. 257, 80 S. Ct. 725, 4 L. Ed. 2d 697 (1960).

to suppress, even though he testified that his home was elsewhere, that the paid nothing for the use of the apartment where the narcotics were found, and that he had been allowed to use the apartment as a friend of the tenant of the apartment.

But in 1963 the United States Supreme Court approved the admission into evidence of narcotics obtained as a result of an illegal arrest and search. The Court approved the use of the evidence because the right to privacy of the person complaining was not invaded.[179]

This "no standing" doctrine was followed where the search was of another person. In the case of *State v. McConoughey*,[180] the Minnesota Supreme Court refused to reverse a decision where such a search was challenged. The court pointed out that when the search is made of another person, the defendant has no standing to object to the search.

This same reasoning was applied where a car in which the defendant was not riding was searched. Although a money order machine found in the car was used in evidence against the defendant, he could not be heard to complain, the court explaining:

> The record is devoid of evidence indicating any interest, ownership, or otherwise, of [defendant in the car] such as to afford him standing to complain of its search. Only one whose Fourth Amendment right of privacy has been violated may object to the introduction of the fruits of an illegal search.[181]

This line of reasoning was followed in *Rakas v. Illinois*[182] where evidence was used against a passenger in an automobile. The majority of the Court refused to suppress evidence against petitioners who asserted neither a property nor a possessory interest in the automobile searched nor an interest in the property seized.

After receiving a robbery report, the police stopped the suspected getaway car in which the petitioners were passengers. Upon searching the car, the police found a box of rifle shells in the glove compartment and a sawed-off rifle in the front passenger seat and arrested petitioners. The petitioners conceded that they did not own the automobile and were simply passengers, the owner of the car having been the driver of the vehicle. Nor did they as-

---

179 Wong Sun v. United States, 371 U.S. 471, 83 S. Ct. 407, 9 L. Ed. 2d 441 (1963).

180 282 Minn. 161, 163 N.W.2d 568 (1968).

181 Cassady v. United States, 410 F.2d 379 (5th Cir. 1969). *See also* State v. McFarland, 195 Neb. 395, 238 N.W.2d 237 (1976), which held that a thief in possession of a stolen car had no standing to object to a search of the car.

182 439 U.S. 128, 99 S. Ct. 421, 58 L. Ed. 2d (1978).

sert that they owned the rifle or the shells that were seized. The Supreme Court reiterated its previous findings in other cases and again stated that Fourth Amendment rights are personal rights which may not be asserted vicariously. Only those who have constitutional standing can challenge the admissibility of the evidence.

Applying the "no standing rule" the Court of Appeals of Texas agreed that the defendant lacked standing as a mere passenger in a car noting that:

> Appellant, a passenger, has standing to challenge the search of the automobile in which he is riding *if* the search resulted from an infringement, such as an illegal detention, of the *passenger's* Fourth Amendment right.[183]

The court explained that even assuming arguendo that the search of the vehicle was illegal, the search of the driver's vehicle did not infringe upon the rights of the passenger.

In a 1980 Supreme Court decision, seven of the justices even more strongly supported the "standing" reasoning in concluding that a defendant charged with unlawful possession of stolen mail cannot challenge the seizure of 12 stolen checks seized by police during the search of an apartment rented by one of the defendants' mothers.[184] The Court determined that the fact that the defendants were charged with "possession" would not give them any standing to challenge the constitutionality of the search. The Court stated the rule in these terms:

> Today we hold that defendants charged with crimes of possession may only claim the benefits of the exclusionary rule if their own Fourth Amendment rights have in fact been violated. The automatic standing rule of *Jones v. United States*,...is therefore overruled.

The same court that decided the *Salvucci* case determined that a defendant had no expectation of privacy in an acquaintance's purse into which he had placed his own drugs.[185] The fact that the defendant owned the drugs did not give him automatic standing to challenge the search of the purse.

---

183 Harris v. State, 713 S.W.2d 773 (Tex. App. 1986).

184 United States v. Salvucci, 448 U.S. 83, 100 S. Ct. 2547, 65 L. Ed. 2d 619 (1980). *But see* Minnesota v. Olson, __ U.S. __, 110 S. Ct. 1684, __ L. Ed. 2d __ (1990), whichi held that an overnight guest had standing to challenge a warrantless entry and search.

185 Rawlings v. Kentucky, 448 U.S. 98, 100 S. Ct. 2556, 65 L. Ed. 2d 633 (1980).

Other examples of instances where courts have admitted evidence when the defendant was unable to show that he had a property right or possessory interest in the place being searched, assist in understanding this exception. In a Kentucky case, the Court of Appeals upheld the seizure of a revolver from the hallway of another person's home where the defendant did not show any property rights or possessory interests in the house from which the revolver was seized.[186] Nor did the U.S. Court of Appeals for the Tenth Circuit find any legal obstacle to the admission of narcotics against the defendant when the narcotics were seized from the defendant's sister's automobile.[187]

It must be noted that even though the evidence is admitted as to the party who has no standing to suppress, the search is nevertheless illegal under the Constitution.

§ 4.15 Search after lawful impoundment

Often the police officer has the duty and responsibility to impound a car that has been abandoned, is blocking traffic, is illegally parked, or for some other reason.[188] In such instances the officer is usually required, either by law or by regulation, to search the vehicle and make a list of the contents of the vehicle before impounding it. The question then arises as to the use of the contents as evidence where the possession of such contents constitutes a crime.

The rationale for the seizure of contraband or other articles from an impounded car is sound. Such a seizure is justified on the ground that the officer who has the duty of impounding the car for his own protection and for the protection of the owner should inventory the contents to safeguard the owner and protect against false claims of loss. As pointed out by the Nebraska Supreme Court in *State v. Wallen*,[189] if during a proper inventory of the contents of an impounded vehicle, evidence of crime is discovered, such evidence may be used to support a charge for the crime indicated.

The courts have cautioned that the seizure of evidence on the impounded car theory is only legitimate if the car is in fact legally impounded. It is preferable to impound the car under the authority of a state or federal law. If there is no such law, then a departmental order defining the circumstances under which the car should be impounded often can be relied upon.

---

186 Geary v. Commonwealth, 503 S.W.2d 505 (Ky. 1972).

187 United States v. Galvez, 465 F.2d 681 (10th Cir. 1972).

188 *E.g.*, Dist. Colum. Traf. & Veh. Reg. § 91.

189 185 Neb. 44, 173 N.W.2d 372 (1970).

The court, in the case of *Heffley v. State*,[190] warned that: "If, however, the policing conduct indicates that the intention is exploratory rather than [for an] inventory, the fruits of that search are forbidden."

The Nebraska court in the *Wallen* case compared the seizure of articles from an impounded car with a seizure without a search. The court explained that the taking of the inventory, a reasonable precaution, did not constitute an unreasonable seizure any more than in any other case where the police stumble on the evidence of crime in the pursuance of duty.

One of the most often quoted cases concerning the authority to seize articles from an impounded car is the case of *Cooper v. California*.[191] In that case the defendant was arrested for violation of the narcotics laws and his automobile was seized by police officers pursuant to the California statute authorizing state officers to seize vehicles used unlawfully to transport narcotics. The Supreme Court approved the search of the car a week after the arrest, even though there was no search warrant. Where the car is seized and impounded pending forfeiture proceedings, it would be unreasonable, according to the majority, to hold that the police, having to retain the car in their garage for such a length of time, had no right, even for their own protection, to search it.

In the *Cooper* case the state law specifically provided for forfeiture of the car to the state if the car was used for unlawful transportation of narcotics. The Ninth Circuit Court of Appeals refused to apply this doctrine when the officers were not under a mandatory duty to hold the car.[192] Most courts, however, do not require that the impoundment be under state law.[193]

Probably because of the wide differences in the opinions of lower courts concerning the seizure of articles from an impounded car, the Supreme Court in 1976 finally acted and placed a limited stamp of approval on this procedure.[194] In the *Opperman* case, an automobile was towed to the city impound lot after it had been parked illegally overnight. From outside the car, the police officer observed a watch on the dashboard and some items of personal property located in the back seat. At his direction, the car was unlocked and a standard inventory form was used to inventory the contents. From the glove compartment, which was unlocked, marijuana was seized and used in evidence. After conviction in the lower court, the Supreme Court of South Dakota reversed the conviction, concluding that the evidence had been

---

190 Heffley v. State, 83 Nev. 100, 423 P.2d 666 (1967).

191 386 U.S. 58, 87 S. Ct. 788, 17 L. Ed. 2d 730 (1968).

192 Ramon v. Cupp, 423 F.2d 248 (9th Cir. 1970).

193 State v. Montague, 73 Wash.2d 381, 438 P.2d 571 (1968).

194 South Dakota v. Opperman, 428 U.S. 364, 96 S. Ct. 3092, 49 L. Ed. 2d 1000 (1976).

obtained in violation of the Fourth Amendment as made applicable to the states by the Fourteenth Amendment.

The United States Supreme Court reversed the decision of the South Dakota Supreme Court and held that the evidence was properly admitted. In approving this procedure in limited circumstances, the Court first distinguished between automobiles and homes or offices in relation to the Fourth Amendment protections, and then approved the seizure of evidence from an impounded car under the facts of the case. The majority pointed out that the police were indisputably engaged in a caretaker search of the lawfully impounded automobile, and there was no suggestion of investigatory motive on the part of the police. In the concluding paragraph, these words were used:

> On this record we conclude that in following standard police procedures, prevailing throughout the country and approved by the overwhelming majority of courts, the conduct of the police was not "unreasonable" under the Fourth Amendment.

Following the decision in *South Dakota v. Opperman*, several lower courts considered the legality of using evidence from containers found in vehicles taken into police custody.[195] The reasonableness of the inventory seizure again reached the Supreme Court of the United States in the case of *Colorado v. Bertine* in 1987.[196]

In the *Bertine* case, a Boulder, Colorado, police officer arrested the defendant for driving his van while under the influence of alcohol. After the defendant was taken into custody and before a tow truck arrived to take the van to an impoundment lot, another officer, acting in accordance with local police procedures, inventoried the van's contents, opening a closed backpack in which he found various containers holding controlled substances, cocaine paraphernalia, and a large amount of cash. The United States Supreme Court first acknowledged that the case is controlled by the principles governing inventory searches of automobiles and of arrestee's personal effects as set forth in *South Dakota v. Opperman*. In approving the opening of the closed backpack and the use of the evidence, it was reasoned that the police were potentially responsible for the property taken into their custody and that

---

195 United States v. Griffin, 729 F.2d 475 (7th Cir. 1984); United States v. Bloomfield, 594 F.2d 1200 (8th Cir. 1979); People v. Brasch, 122 Ill. App. 3d 747, 461 N.E.2d 651 (1984).

196 Colorado v. Bertine, ___ U.S. ___, 107 S. Ct. 738, 93 L. Ed. 2d 739 (1987). *See* Florida v. Wells __ U.S. __, 110 S. Ct. 1632, __ L. Ed. 2d __ (1990), where the United States Supreme Court discusses the necessity of having a departmental policy regarding inventory searches.

the government interests were served by the inventory searches. In the closing paragraphs of the majority decision, the discussion centered on the exercise of police discretion. In approving the good faith inventory procedures by police, the Court commented:

> Here, the discretion afforded the Boulder Police was exercised in light of standardized criteria, related to the feasibility and appropriateness of parking and locking a vehicle rather than impounding it. There was no showing that the police chose to impound Bertine's van in order to investigate suspected criminal activity.

Two caveats are appropriate:

(1) neither the *Opperman* decision nor the *Bertine* decision give officers *carte blanche* authority to search all stopped or impounded cars. The decisions are limited to the facts of the cases.

(2) The respective states, under their own constitutional authority, may prescribe additional limitations. For example, even in the *Colorado v. Bertine* case, had the Colorado Supreme Court premised its ruling on its own constitutional provisions, the evidence would not have been admitted in that state. And some states have limited the inventory search and hold that evidence from closed compartments or containers within the vehicle may not be removed.[197]

The "inventory" exception to the warrant requirement is not a new principle but merely an application of the accepted rule that the officer may seize evidence coming to his attention when he is in a position legally to observe it. Therefore, the impoundment doctrine does not justify a search into all parts of the car, including the hubcaps and upholstered part of the car, which are not normally inventoried, as the officer does not view the evidence without a search.

---

197 City of Danville v. Dawson, 528 S.W.2d 687 (Ky. 1975); State v. McDougall, 68 Wis. 2d 399, 228 N.W.2d 671 (1975). However, the Illinois Court of Appeals in *People v. Cain*, 171 Ill. App. 3d 468, 525 N.E.2d 1194 (1988) held that the arrestee's personal property obtained pursuant to an inventory search may be examined at a later date without a warrant. Once the police have properly inventoried a defendant's property and viewed objects that are placed in an inventory envelope, the defendant retains no reasonable expectation of privacy in the objects.

§ 4.16 Stop and frisk seizures

A new chapter was written into the complicated search and seizure law in 1968 when the Supreme Court decided the case of *Terry v. Ohio*.[198] For many years there had been doubt as to whether a police officer could stop a suspicious person on the street and ask questions without making a formal arrest. Even more uncertain was the authority to frisk the suspect for weapons. In the *Terry* case, which has been discussed more thoroughly in a previous section, a police officer stopped a suspect on a downtown Cleveland, Ohio, street when he observed the suspect and two other men casing a store. Without putting the suspect under arrest, the police officer patted down the outside clothing of the suspect for weapons and later removed a pistol from the suspect's overcoat pocket. After holding that the detention was justified under the circumstances, the Court concluded that the revolver seized from *Terry* was properly admitted into evidence against him. The Court was careful to distinguish this from a search incident to a lawful arrest, explaining:

> Suffice it to note that such a search, unlike a search without a warrant incident to a lawful arrest, is not justified by any need to prevent the disappearance or destruction of evidence of crime....The sole justification of the search in the present situation is the protection of the police officer and others nearby, and it must therefore be confined in scope to an intrusion reasonably designed to discover guns, knives, clubs, or other hidden instruments for the assault of the police officer.

It is emphasized that the frisk authorized in the detention situation is only for the protection of the officer and is limited to a patting down rather than a full-scale search. In a companion case to the *Terry* case,[199] the United States Supreme Court refused to extend the frisk doctrine to a small package of narcotics found by an officer when he patted down the suspect. The Court reasoned that where there is a self-protective search for weapons, the officer must be able to point to particular facts from which he reasonably inferred the individual was armed and dangerous. Also, the patting down for weapons was distinguished from a patting down for small items such as packages containing narcotics.

---

198 392 U.S. 1, 88 S. Ct. 1868, 20 L. Ed. 2d 889 (1968). This case is discussed in §3.14 as it relates to the authority to detain without making an arrest.

199 Sibron v. New York, 392 U.S. 40, 88 S. Ct. 1889, 20 L. Ed. 2d 917 (1968).

As was inevitable, the lower courts have been called upon to further interpret the *Terry* ruling. One of the questions left unanswered by *Terry* was whether an article which did not feel like a knife or a club, but could be a dangerous weapon, could be seized. A second question was whether the officer, while in the process of seizing a weapon, could seize other articles which were not dangerous. In the case of *People v. Collins,*[200] the California Supreme Court was able to lay down a rule as to one of these questions. In holding that in some instances the officer can pat down the suspect for a "sap" (such as a bag of sand) which could be used as a weapon, the court explained the test thusly:

> Accordingly, we hold that an officer who exceeds a pat-down without first discovering an object which feels reasonably like a knife, gun, or club must be able to point to specific and articulable facts which reasonably support a suspicion that the particular suspect is armed with an atypical weapon which would feel like the object felt during the pat-down.

In that case the court referred the matter back to the lower court, so that the prosecution could meet the burden of pointing to specific and articulable facts to justify the intrusion.

There is some evidence to indicate that if the officer, in good faith, pats down a suspect and discovers some object which feels like a weapon, and in order to protect himself reaches into the suspect's pocket to obtain the weapon, but in addition or instead of a weapon finds other contraband, the use of such contraband would be legitimate.[201] For example, the California Supreme Court[202] held that a watch found by police officers in the pocket of the suspect was admissible where the officers honestly believed that the watch might have been a knife. The majority of the court agreed that the seizure of the watch did not violate the principles of *Terry v. Ohio*.

In a North Carolina case, the Supreme Court of that state approved the conduct of the officer in grabbing an automobile passenger's hand and removing it from his pants pocket. The Court also found proper the seizing of a bag of white powdery substance discovered when the officer grabbed the defendant's hand and removed it from his pocket.[203]

In the landmark *Terry* case, the officers observed conduct on the street which justified the stop and frisk for weapons. There, a pistol was seized. In

---

[200] People v. Collins, 1 Cal. 3d 658, 83 Cal. Rptr. 179, 463 P.2d 403, (1970).

[201] People v. Woods, 6 Cal. App. 3d 832, 86 Cal. Rptr. 264 (1970).

[202] People v. Mosher, 1 Cal. 3d 379, 82 Cal. Rptr. 379, 461 P.2d 659 (1969).

[203] State v. Peck, 305 N.C. 734, 291 S.E.2d 637 (1982).

the later *Adams* case,[204] a gun was seized from the waistband of a suspect while the suspect was sitting in his car. Lower courts have been required to determine if the stop and frisk rule applies in other specific situations such as stopping automobiles.

The majority members of the Ninth Circuit Court of Appeals agreed that under certain circumstances officers are justified in stopping vehicles even though they do not have probable cause to make an arrest.[205] In the *Untermeyer* case, the police officer was patrolling in a residential area in which burglaries had been recently committed. He observed a suspect walk from a darkened home to a foreign car that was parked nearby, enter the passenger side, and drive a short distance before the headlights were turned on. The court concluded that "the unusual circumstances and [defendant's] unusual conduct were such as to lead the local police officer 'reasonably to conclude in light of his experience that criminal activity may be afoot,'" and affirmed the marijuana possession conviction.

Following like reasoning, the Fifth Circuit Court, specifically referring to the *Terry* and *Adams* cases, approved the stopping of a car where an armed robbery victim told police that one of the attackers was wearing a "bush" or "jungle" hat and further described the attackers, and where the officers saw passengers meeting the descriptions in a car which exceeded the speed limit and failed to stop at an intersection. The court found that even if the officer could not search the occupants of the car following the issuance of a traffic citation, he could frisk these occupants under the "stop and frisk" authority.[206]

A question that has perplexed police officers for some time, was whether police can order a person out of an automobile and frisk or pat down the outer clothing for the protection of the officer where the purpose of the stop of the vehicle is only to issue a traffic summons or citation and no arrest takes place. This question was answered in the case of *Pennsylvania v. Mimms*.[207] In this case two Philadelphia police officers stopped a vehicle with an expired license plate for the purpose of issuing a traffic summons. One of the officers approached the vehicle and asked the driver to step out of the car and produce his owner's card and operator's license. When the driver stepped out of the car the officer noticed a large bulge under the respondent's sports jacket and fearing that the bulge might be a weapon, frisked the respondent and discovered a .38-caliber revolver loaded with five rounds of ammunition.

---

204 Adams v. Williams, 407 U.S. 143, 92 S. Ct. 1921, 32 L. Ed. 2d 612 (1972).

205 Untermyer v. Hellbush, 472 F.2d 156 (9th Cir. 1973).

206 United States v. Edwards, 469 F.2d 1362 (5th Cir. 1972).

207 434 U.S. 106, 98 S. Ct. 330, 54 L. Ed. 2d (1977).

The Supreme Court of Pennsylvania found that the revolver was seized contrary to the guarantees found in the Fourth Amendment and should have been suppressed. The majority of the United States Supreme Court did not agree. They explained, "that the touchstone of our analysis under the Fourth Amendment is always the reasonableness in all circumstances of the particular governmental invasion of a citizen's personal security." In upholding the right of the officer to order the driver out of the car under the circumstances, the Supreme Court said:

> We think it too plain for argument that the State's proffered justification -- the safety of the officer -- is both legitimate and weighty. Certainly it would be unreasonable to require that police officers take unnecessary risks in the performance of their duties.

As to the second question -- the propriety of the search of the jacket -- the court concluded:

> The bulge in the jacket permitted the officer to conclude that Mimms was armed and thus posed a serious and present danger to the safety of the officer. In these circumstances, any man of "reasonable caution" would likely have conducted the pat-down.

Relying upon the majority opinion in the *Mimms* case, the South Dakota Supreme Court upheld the investigatory stop of a motorist and the search of a paper bag located in his car.[208] The majority of the justices of that court agreed that the previous decisions from the Supreme Court do not require an arrest as a condition precedent to a search for weapons to protect the safety of the investigating officer.

In 1983 the United States Supreme Court, in an opinion by Judge O'Connor, approved the search for weapons in the passenger compartment of a car after an investigatory stop.[209] There the automobile was stopped after it swerved into a ditch. The driver met the officers at the rear of the car but then began walking toward the open door of the car. Shining his flashlight into the car the officer saw something under the armrest, and upon lifting the armrest saw an open pouch that contained what appeared to be marijuana. The Court reasoned that the protective search of the passenger compartment was reasonable under the principle articulated in *Terry*.

From this and other cases it can be concluded that if, as in the case described in the preceding paragraph, an officer stops a car to issue a traffic citation, he may, for his protection, order the driver to step out of the car. And

---

208 State v. Luxem, 324 N.W. 2d 273 (S.D. 1982).

209 Michigan v. Long, 463 U.S. 1032, 103 S. Ct. 3469, 77 L. Ed. 2d 1201 (1983).

if the facts available warrant a man of reasonable caution to conclude that the person is armed and poses a serious and present danger to the safety of the officer, a pat down or frisk for weapons is justified.

Mere curiosity, however, does not equate with reasonable suspicion that criminal activity may be afoot. Not every car may be stopped and the occupants frisked -- even at three o'clock in the morning. Thus, where the record disclosed nothing to indicate the officer had any reason to believe there was danger to anyone's safety when he ordered the occupant of the backseat of a car to get out, and the officer then frisked him, the frisk and seizure of counterfeit bills were illegal.[210]

In an interesting application of the "stop and frisk" rule, Justice O'Connor, writing for the majority in a 1983 case, held that law enforcement agents may temporarily detain luggage on suspicion amounting to less than probable cause that it contains narcotics.[211] In the *Place* case, agents in New York received information from officers in Miami indicating that the suspects would arrive at LaGuardia with the narcotics. When the defendant arrived at LaGuardia, he was allowed to go but the agents took his bags to Kennedy Airport for inspection by a trained narcotics detection dog. The inspection took place about 90 minutes after the seizure of the luggage. On the basis of the dog's response, the agents retained the luggage over the weekend and obtained a search warrant for one of the bags which turned out to be cocaine.

Applying the reasoning of the *Terry* and other cases relating to stop and frisk, the majority expounded that if an officer's observation leads him reasonably to believe that a traveler is carrying luggage that contains narcotics, then the officer may detain the luggage briefly to investigate the circumstances that aroused his suspicion, provided investigative detention is properly limited in scope. After stating that the luggage exposure to the trained dog was not a search and indicating that the stop and frisk theory may be used in detaining luggage, the court then decided that the 90-minute time span between the luggage seizure and its exposure to the dog was unreasonable. The effect of the *Grace* case is to make the *Terry* principles applicable to seizures of personal property on the basis of reasonable, articulable suspicion, premised on objective facts, that luggage contained contraband or evidence of a crime.

Although the *Terry* type of seizure of evidence has been approved in many cases, some justices are becoming critical of overzealous police activity.[212] As pointed out in previous paragraphs, the United States Supreme Court's approval of the *Terry* stop and frisk has been very helpful to police

---

210 United States v. Johnson, 463 F.2d 70 (10th Cir. 1972).

211 United States v. Place, 462 U.S. 696, 103 S. Ct. 2637, 77 L. Ed. 2d 110 (1983).

212 United States v. Thomas, 314 A.2d 464 (D.C. 1974).

officers. Before this case, there was much confusion regarding the right of the police to stop without probable cause. If this type of police practice is to continue to receive court approval, the officer must constantly be cautious that he does not overstep the line and use this procedure as a subterfuge for making an illegal search. Obviously, if the detention and frisk are a subterfuge, evidence obtained will be properly excluded.

§ 4.17 "Administrative" and "compelling government interest" searches

While the Fourth Amendment protection of privacy interest shields persons and places from unreasonable searches, the courts have recognized that warrantless searches may be necessary where there is a "compelling government interest" which outweighs privacy concerns. For example, some courts have recognized that warrants are not required when inspections are made on property where regulated businesses are conducted, for routine searches of persons and effects at international borders, prior to airline passenger service to prevent the boarding of vessels by passengers intent on piracy, and for drug and alcohol tests where the intrusion serves special governmental needs beyond the normal need for law enforcement. In these cases the courts have explained the necessity to balance the individual privacy expectation against the government's interest in protecting the individual's health and safety.

1. *Searches and inspections of regulated businesses*

With the decision of the United States Supreme Court in the case of *United States v. Biswell*, the Court approved the inspectional searches of regulated businesses.[213] In this case a treasury agent, acting under the authority of the Gun Control Act, requested entry into a locked gun storeroom and was admitted after showing the owner of the premises a copy of the Act. This Act authorizes entry during business hours into premises for the purpose of inspecting or examining records and documents required to be kept on firearms or ammunition stored by the dealer at such premises. The Circuit Court of Appeals reversed the lower court decision which allowed the admission into evidence of two sawed-off rifles which the owner was not licensed to possess. The United States Supreme Court reversed the holding of the Court of Appeals, explaining that close scrutiny of the traffic in firearms is justified and that this limited threat to the dealer's expectation of privacy is reasonable. The Court commented:

213 406 U.S. 311, 92 S. Ct. 1593, 32 L. Ed. 2d 87 (1972).

> When a dealer chooses to engage in this type of pervasively regulated business and to accept a federal license, he does so with the knowledge that his business records, firearms and ammunition will be subject to effective inspection.

In the case of *Donovan v. Dewey*, the Court concluded that where Congress has made a reasonable determination that a system of warrantless inspections is necessary to enforce a regulation purpose, and where the federal regulatory presence is sufficiently comprehensive and defined that the owner of commercial property cannot help but be aware that his property will be subject to periodic inspection, warrantless inspections may be permitted.[214] In this case, in view of the substantial federal interest in improving the health and safety conditions in mines, and of Congress' awareness that the mining industry is among the most hazardous, and that this industry's poor health and safety record has significant deleterious effects on interstate commerce, Congress could reasonable determine that a system of warrantless inspections was necessary "if the law is to be properly enforced and inspection made effective." Inspections of commercial property may be unreasonable if they are not authorized by law or are unnecessary for furtherance of federal or state interests. Privacy interests must be balanced against the need for a warrantless search but there can be no ready test for determining reasonableness other than balancing the need to search against the invasion which the search entails.

Where the statute fails to tailor the scope and frequency of administration inspections to the particular health and safety concerns addressed by this statute, then the inspection will be unconstitutional.[215] In the *Marshall* case, the Supreme Court found that the regulation which allowed OSHA (Occupational Safety and Health Act) employees to make warrantless inspections of business premises and to "roam at will" throughout an industrial establishment to look for a myriad of health and safety violations constituted an unreasonable intrusion into the proprietor's Fourth Amendment rights.

2. *Border searches*

Since the founding of our Republic, Congress has granted officers plenary authority to conduct routine searches and seizures at the border without probable cause or a warrant in order to regulate the collection of duties and to prevent contraband from entering the United States.[216] Notwithstanding

---

214 Donovan v. Dewey, 452 U.S. 594, 101 S. Ct. 2534, 69 L. Ed. 2d 262 (1981).

215 Marshall v. Barlow's, Inc., 436 U.S. 307, 98 S. Ct. 1816, 56 L. Ed. 2d 305 (1978).

216 United States v. Ramsey, 431 U.S. 606, 97 S. Ct. 1972, 52 L. Ed. 2d 617 (1977).

this exception to the warrant requirements, the defendant challenged the seizure of 88 cocaine-filled balloons taken from her alimentary canal after she was detained by customs officials on arrival at the Los Angeles Airport on a flight from Bogota, Colombia.[217] The Supreme Court, in approving the use of the evidence, noted that the Fourth Amendment's balance of reasonableness is qualitatively different at the international border than in the interior. The court commented:

> These cases reflect longstanding concern for the protection of the integrity of the border. This concern is, if anything, heightened by the veritable national crisis in law enforcement caused by smuggling of illicit narcotics...
>
> The Fourth Amendment balance between the interests of Government and the privacy right of the individual is also struck more favorably to the Government at the border.

3. *Airport searches*

Stating that "nothing in the history of the Amendment remotely suggests that the framers would have wished to prohibit reasonable measures to prevent the boarding of vessels by passengers intent on piracy," the United States Court of Appeals for the Second Circuit approved the use of evidence seized from the bag of an airline passenger.[218] In this case the Deputy United States Marshall examined the beach bag as the defendant was preparing to board an Eastern Airlines plane. During the examination he found a total of 1,664 glassine envelopes, each containing a white powder which later was determined to be heroin.

The reasonableness of airport searches depends, as many of the airport search opinions have stated, "on balancing the need for a search against the offensiveness of the intrusion." To brand such a search as unreasonable would go beyond any fair interpretation of the Fourth Amendment.

After reviewing other cases, the *Edwards* Court summarized:

> Although no one could reconcile all of the views expressed in the opinions of the various circuits or, indeed, of this circuit alone, a consensus does seem to be emerging that an airport search is not to be condemned as violating the Fourth Amendment simply because it does not precisely fit into one of the previously recognized cate-

---

217 United States v. Montoya de Hernandez, 473 U.S. 531, 105 S. Ct. 3304, 87 L. Ed. 2d 381 (1985).

218 United States v. Edwards, 498 F.2d 496 (2d Cir. 1974).

gories for dispensing with a search warrant, but only if the search is "unreasonable" on the facts.

This and other cases illustrated that the government has a compelling interest in dispensing with the search warrant requirement in making airport searches when the risk is jeopardy to hundreds of human lives and millions of dollars of property interests. However, if the government is abusing this authority in using an airport search, not for the purpose intended but as a general means for enforcing the criminal laws, then the evidence seized will be inadmissible unless the procedure complies with the general rules concerning searches.

4. *Drug and alcohol testing*

Regulations requiring employees to submit to drug screening have been challenged on several constitutional issues including due process, self- incrimination, and the Fourth Amendment search and seizure provisions. Does the compelling government interest served by such regulations outweigh the employee's privacy concerns?[219]

Does the Fourth Amendment demand that the government obtain a warrant before requiring employees to produce urine samples to be analyzed for evidence of illegal drug use? This was one of the questions that was presented to the Supreme Court in the case of *National Treasury Employees Union v. Von Raab*.[220] This case reached the courts when the United States Customs Service implemented a drug-screening program requiring urinalysis tests from service employees seeking transfer or promotion to positions having a direct involvement in drug interdiction or requiring the incumbent to carry firearms or to handle "classified" materials. The program mandates that the applicant be notified that his selection is contingent upon successful completion of drug screening and it provides that the test results may not be turned over to any other agency, including criminal prosecutors, without the employee's written consent. The Federal Employees Union and one of its officials filed suit on behalf of the Service Employees alleging that the drug testing program violated the Fourth Amendment. The Court of Appeals held that such searches are reasonable in light of their limited scope and the Service's strong interest in detecting drug use among employees in covered positions.

---

219 *See* Chapter 12 of this text for further discussion of departmental regulations relating to drug testing.

220 National Treasury Employees Union v. Von Raab, ___ U.S. ___, 109 S. Ct. 1384, 103 L. Ed. 2d 685 (1989). *See* case in Part II.

The United States Supreme Court agreed that this requirement to furnish samples is a search that must meet the reasonableness requirement of the Fourth Amendment, but reasoned that the public interest in the program must be balanced against the individual's privacy concerns. Applying this test, the Court indicated that a search warrant is not required.

The testing requirement, according to the majority of the Supreme Court, is reasonable despite the absence of a requirement of probable cause or some level of individualized suspicion. In justifying this invasion of the privacy, the Court commented:

> It is readily apparent that the government has a compelling interest in ensuring that front-line interdiction personnel are physically fit and have unimpeachable integrity and judgment. Indeed, the government's interest here is at least as important as its interest in searching travelers entering the country.

Applying the "compelling government interest" reasoning, the Supreme Court also upheld regulations which require rail employees who are involved in train accidents to be tested for drug or alcohol abuse.[221] While agreeing that the test in question cannot be viewed as private action outside the reach of the Fourth Amendment, the Court nevertheless approved the drug and alcohol test mandated or authorized by the FRA as reasonable even if there is no warrant requirement or "reasonable suspicion" that any particular employee may be impaired. Compelling government interests served by the regulation outweigh the employee's privacy concerns.

§ 4.18 Summary and practical suggestions

The events of history make it clear that searches must be restricted if we are to enjoy individual freedom and the right of privacy. On the other hand, the courts have recognized the necessity of seeking out and prosecuting the violators of the laws of the states and the nation. Although the courts have revised and reversed their decisions over a period of time, they do agree in certain instances. In interpreting the Constitution, the courts have established certain rules of procedure that must be followed by justice personnel. Those who know and understand the rules and the reasons for these rules will be more successful in their profession.

---

221 Skinner v. Railway Labor Executives Association, ___ U.S. ___, 109 S. Ct. 1402, 103 L. Ed. 2d 639 (1989).

In summary, then, the courts have established certain procedural rules, some of which are as follows:

a. Evidence is generally excluded if the search is illegal (some exceptions).

b. The preferred method of search is with a valid search warrant. The courts have indicated that preference will be given to searches under a valid search warrant.

c. Some searches are "reasonable" without a warrant. Among these are:

   (1) A search incident to a lawful arrest;
   (2) A search where a legal waiver has been voluntarily given;
   (3) A search of a moving vehicle or other movable object where exigent circumstances exist;
   (4) A search made in an area or under circumstances which the courts have found not to be within the scope of the constitutional protection.

d. In some cases evidence may be seized when no search is required. If the officer is legally in a position where contraband or illegally possessed articles are in plain view, these articles may be seized. This sometimes includes seizure of articles from impounded automobiles.

e. In order to challenge the search the party must have standing to suppress, i.e., he must have a substantial possessory interest in the property searched to justify his challenge.

f. As the constitutional prohibitions limit official action, articles seized by private individuals with no official knowledge may be admitted into evidence even if the search is illegal or would violate the Fourth Amendment if carried out by an officer.

g. Under the proper circumstances an officer may stop and frisk a suspect for weapons. Evidence legitimately obtained in this manner is usually admitted into evidence.

h. In limited circumstances, searches are considered constitutionally "reasonable" where a compelling government interest outweighs privacy concerns. In this category are inspections of regulated businesses, international border searches, boarding airline passenger searches, and selective testing for illegal use of drugs and alcohol.

Over the years the courts and legislatures have placed many restrictions on the seizure of evidence, whether it be under a search warrant or by way of one of the exceptions. The officer who seizes articles which are to be used in evidence should be so familiar with the specific rules and requirements that he can select and articulate the grounds for making the search at the time he makes it. It is very dangerous to conduct the search and seize articles and then look for a peg to hang the seizure on. Recognizing that the seizure will be challenged, he must be prepared to justify the search and/or seizure when it is challenged in court.

Chapter 5
WIRETAPPING AND EAVESDROPPING*

To safeguard the privacy of innocent persons, the interception of wire or oral communications where none of the parties to the communication has consented to the interception should be allowed only when authorized by a court of competent jurisdiction and should remain under the control and supervision of the authorizing court. Interception of wire and oral communications should further be limited to certain major types of offenses and specific categories of crime with assurances that the interception is justified and that the information obtained thereby will not be misused.

Congressional Findings,
Omnibus Crime Control
and Safe Streets Act of 1968

---

* *by John C. Klotter*

§ 5.1 Introductory remarks

The problems relating to the admissibility of evidence obtained by way of wiretapping and eavesdropping are of relatively recent origin when compared to constitutional protections such as that against self-incrimination or the right to counsel. Decisions and legislation of the last three decades have so changed the law concerning wiretapping and eavesdropping that the law prior to that time has little more than historical significance. However, without a study of that history it would be difficult to understand the provisions of the federal and state statutes and the rationale for the Supreme Court decisions interpreting the statutes.

In order to interpret the laws relating to wiretapping and eavesdropping, it is essential that the search and seizure laws be researched first. Before Congress enacted the 1968 legislation relating to wiretapping and electronic surveillance,[1] the Supreme Court handed down decisions which mandated

---

1 Title III of the Omnibus Crime Control and Safe Streets Act of 1968, part of which was codified at 18 U.S.C. ch. 119, §§ 2510-2520 and amended in 1970, 1971, 1978, and 1980. Hereafter cited as the Crime Control Act or as 18 U.S.C. § 2510-2520. *See* Part II of this book for a complete reprint of Title III.

specific safeguards. These decisions were based on the Fourth Amendment search and seizure provisions and, in effect, require that any legislation be compatible with constitutional safeguards enunciated in all previous search and seizure decisions.

Although current federal and state statutes set out in detail the procedures for legal wiretapping and eavesdropping, a study of earlier court decisions and statutes is necessary for an understanding of the present laws. After reviewing the history of wiretapping and eavesdropping, the federal statutes are examined and interpreted. The chapter is concluded with a summary of the decisions which interpret the statutes and the decisions relating to permissible listening.

§ 5.2 Electronic listening devices

To our colonial forefathers, a search and seizure meant an actual physical intrusion into their homes and a ransacking of their private papers and effects by law enforcement officers. Modern invention and technology have produced far more refined and sophisticated techniques for gaining access to information relating to criminal activity. The twentieth century has witnessed the development of electronic listening and surveillance devices which have revolutionized law enforcement. No longer is it necessary for the police to stand under windows or physically enter homes to learn about the activities which transpire inside.

Although newspapers have printed accounts of wireless transmitters the size of sugar cubes or smaller, which can be disguised as martini olives to pick up and transmit sound by means of their toothpick aerials, and other sophisticated means that have been utilized to intercept communication, there are indications that in practical situations their use is often very limited. Even if the devices are successfully installed, they are often ineffective. The transmission may be inaudible, or too much background noise may be transmitted, making the conversation difficult to understand. Most "bugs" must be located relatively close to the speaker in order to be overheard and there is often difficulty in installing the bugs on the premises. Also, bugs are subject to malfunction and discovery, especially as sophisticated antibug devices have been developed. Nevertheless, law enforcement agents have been successful in utilizing electronic surveillance for the purpose of discovering criminal activity and identifying violators.

The extent to which wiretap and other electronic surveillance equipment has been employed by law enforcement agencies in crime detection activity was largely undetermined until 1976. Section 2519 of the Report of the National Commission for the review of federal and state laws relating to wiretapping and electronic surveillance,[2] United States Code, requires that annual reports be submitted to the Director of the Administrative Office of the United States Courts each year. These reports indicate that 4,334 court orders authorizing electronic surveillance were issued for the period 1968 to 1974.[3] The report made in 1983 points out that 578 authorized intercepts were officially reported for the year 1982. A telephone wiretap was the electronic surveillance device used in 86 percent of the installed intercepts. These figures do not, of course, include instances where wiretap and eavesdrop equipment was used to overhear and/or record communications where one party to the communications gave consent.[4]

Because of Title III of the Crime Control Act's prohibition against the manufacture, sale and advertising of devices for other than official use, there has been a noticeable drop in the manufacture and marketing of such devices.[5] The act does not prohibit the sale of surveillance devices to authorized agencies, and sophisticated equipment is available for law enforcement official use.

§ 5.3 Ethics of interception of wire and oral communications

Electronic eavesdropping and surveillance, even when employed for legitimate law enforcement ends, involve a considerable danger to individual privacy and security of the innocent as well as the guilty. There has yet to be invented a listening device that will distinguish between criminals and innocent citizens, or which will tune off during private conversations and pick up only those pertaining to illegal schemes.

The ethics of law enforcement listening in crime detection has received vigorous debate and comment from legislators, judges, professors and those engaged in the daily business of police work. On the side of those who champion individual liberty, these modern investigatory techniques have been likened to the Nazi Gestapo and the Red Police. Mr. Justice Holmes, one of

---

2 In 1976, the National Commission for the Review of Federal and State Laws Relating to Wiretapping and Electronic Surveillance (hereinafter cited as the Commission) submitted a report of its findings and recommendations, entitled *Electronic Surveillance Report*, published by the U.S. Government Printing Office. The Publication will be referred to as the NWC report.

3 NWC Rep. 1976, Page 226.

4 Report of Applications for Orders Authorizing or Approving the Interception of Wire or Oral Communications for the Period January 1, 1982 to December 31, 1982, U.S. Government Printing Office.

5 *Id.* at 23.

the early leading critics of law enforcement wiretapping on the Supreme Court bench, characterized the practice as a "dirty business" and expressed the opinion that "it is a less evil that some criminals should escape than that the government should play an ignoble part."[6] In the view of Mr. Justice Douglas, the techniques of electronic investigations are more serious and objectionable than the writs of assistance, which came under attack in colonial days, since the victim is never aware that the police are delving into the intimacies of his private life.[7] Even Mr. Justice Frankfurter, who was one of the staunch "conservatives" on the Court, on occasion found cause for alarm. In one of his dissenting opinions he cautioned that crime detection was becoming a dirty game in which the "dirty business" of criminals is outwitted by the "dirty business" of law officers, and he predicted that the use of electronic short-cuts in crime investigation would breed disrespect for the law, encourage lazy, immoral conduct on the part of the police, and in the long run undermine effective law enforcement in this country.[8]

Proponents of liberal investigatory policies, on the other hand, have stressed the fact that crime in the United States is on the increase, that the security of society is at stake, and that electronic tools of investigation are necessary, perhaps indispensable, weapons in the arsenal of the police. Crime generally takes place in secrecy and behind closed doors. The jet-age criminal is an extremely shrewd, crafty and evasive fellow. Particularly in the areas of organized crime and threats against the national security, detection would be virtually impossible without the gifts of modern science. It would be unrealistic to deprive the police of electronic investigatory apparatus and tie them to eighteenth century methods of crime detection.

In the "findings" of a congressional committee report included in Title III of the 1968 act, this statement is included:

> (c) Organized criminals make extensive use of wire and oral communications in their criminal activities. The interception of such communications to obtain evidence of the commission of crimes or to prevent their commission is an indispensable aid to law enforcement and the administration of justice.[9]

---

6 Olmstead v. United States, 277 U.S. 438, 48 S. Ct. 564, 72 L. Ed. 944 (1928) (Holmes, J., dissent).

7 DOUGLAS, THE RIGHT OF THE PEOPLE 151 (1958).

8 On Lee v. United States, 343 U.S. 747, 760-61, 72 S. Ct. 967, 96 L. Ed. 1270 (1952).

9 PUB L. NO. 90-351 § 801. This statement was reaffirmed by a majority of the Commission. NWC REPORT, p. 3.

In the opinion of many professional police administrators there is no available substitute for wiretapping and electronic listening in combatting crime in metropolitan areas.

Although some judges have indicated that there is a need for extra vigilance in the supervision of electronic eavesdropping, the rights protected are those enumerated in the Fourth and Fifth Amendments, and if the safeguards surrounding those rights are carefully honored, there is no constitutional reason why law enforcement personnel should not be authorized to use electronic devices in carrying out their responsibilities.

§ 5.4 History of wiretapping

As the use of wire as a means of communication is of relatively recent origin, one does not have to go too far back in history to trace the developments of the use of electronic listening devices to intercept wire communications. When the use of such devices did become a problem both the courts and legislative bodies were called upon to make and interpret laws relating to wiretapping.

Legislation was introduced in Congress in 1929 and again in 1931 which would have made wiretapping illegal. This proposed legislation did not receive congressional approval but Congress in 1934, under its broad powers to regulate interstate and foreign commerce, passed the Federal Communications Act of 1934.[10] The primary purpose of the law was to transfer jurisdiction over wire and oral communications to the newly formed Federal Communications Commission, and there is considerable evidence that Congress was not thinking in terms of law enforcement wiretapping at all. However, the bill did pass and, included within it was the following provision:

> No person not being authorized by the sender shall intercept any communication and divulge or publish the existence, contents, substance, purport, effect, or meaning of such intercepted communications to any person.

Section 501 of the same act imposed a fine not exceeding $10,000 or a prison term not exceeding one year, or both, for a willful or knowing violation of Section 605.

In addition to the federal statute relating to wiretapping which was enacted in 1934, some states enacted their own legislation which prohibited wiretapping under certain conditions. There was little uniformity in the re-

---

[10] Codified at title 47 of the UNITED STATES CODE.

sulting rules for the states. Not only did the state statutes differ, but the court decisions in the states differed in interpretation of the statutes. According to a hearing held before a congressional committee in 1961, six states authorized wiretapping by statute, 33 states imposed total bans on wiretapping, and 11 states had no definite statute on the subject. To demonstrate examples of extremes, a Pennsylvania statute is compared with the statute in effect in New York.

The Pennsylvania statute provided that no communications by telephone or telegraph could be intercepted without permission of both parties.[11] This Pennsylvania statute also specifically prohibited such interception by public officials and provided that evidence obtained could not be used in court.

In contrast, the lawmakers in New York, recognizing the need for legal wiretapping, authorized wiretapping and eavesdropping by statute.[12] This statute required that the order authorizing wiretapping must specify the duration of the wiretap and must identify the particular telephone number before the message could be interpreted. The aim of the New York law was to allow court-ordered wiretapping but to have safeguards similar to those required in search and seizure situations.[13] Other states, including Oregon, Maryland, Nevada, and Massachusetts, enacted similar laws which authorized court-ordered wiretapping.

It is difficult to summarize the law concerning the use of wiretap evidence in state courts prior to the case of *Berger v. New York* in 1967.[14] Briefly the situation was this: in some states wiretapping was prohibited and the use of such evidence in court was prohibited by statutes; in some states wiretapping was prohibited, but evidence obtained thereby was admissible in state courts; and in a third group of states wiretapping was authorized by statute when procedural safeguards were complied with. If the state court authorized the use of wiretap evidence, the U.S. Supreme Court would not reverse the decision.

Early court decisions also were not consistent. The constitutional legality of wiretapping first reached the Supreme Court in the landmark case of *Olmstead v. United States*.[15] This case involved a large organization headed by Olmstead who was the ringleader of a multi-million dollar conspiracy to violate the National Prohibition Act. The evidence used by the prosecution was obtained almost entirely by tapping the telephone wires leading to the

---

11 Former PA. STAT. ANN. tit. 18, § 3742 (1957).

12 Former N.Y. CRIM. P. § 813A (1942).

13 The New York Statute was found to be constitutional by the New York State Supreme Court in 1962. People v. Dinan, 11 N.Y.2d 350, 183 N.E.2d 689 (1962).

14 388 U.S. 41, 87 S. Ct. 1873, 18 L. Ed. 2d 1040 (1967).

15 277 U.S. 438, 48 S. Ct. 564, 72 L. Ed. 944 (1928).

homes and offices of some of the key figures. Olmstead was convicted and the Supreme Court by a narrow 5 to 4 decision affirmed his conviction. The Supreme Court reasoned that the Fifth Amendment was not violated as the defendant had not been compelled to talk over the telephone. Although having more difficulty with the Fourth Amendment, the Supreme Court concluded that the proscription of the Fourth Amendment was limited to searches and seizures of *material* things -- the person, his house, his papers, and his effects. Nothing of tangible physical nature was taken here; therefore the Fourth Amendment was not violated.

The *Olmstead* decision was not effectively overruled until a series of cases was handed down in 1967. In *Berger v. New York*, the Supreme Court overruled *Olmstead* and held that "conversation" was within the Fourteenth Amendment protection and the use of electronic devices to capture conversation was a "search" within the meaning of the amendment.[16]

As late as 1961, the United States Supreme Court refused to make the wiretapping exclusionary rule applicable to the states.[17] However, by way of the decisions in *Berger v. New York* and *Katz v. United States*, the Supreme Court made it clear that its past decisions holding that wiretapping is not within the purview of the Fourth Amendment were no longer applicable.[18] In accordance with the restrictions of those two Supreme Court decisions, any state statute which authorizes the use of wiretap evidence must be so drafted as to comply with all of the requirements of the Fourth Amendment as interpreted by the Supreme Court of the United States.

§ 5.5 History of eavesdropping

The law relating to eavesdropping developed along much different lines than that relating to wiretapping. While the wiretapping law is an outgrowth of the twentieth century development of electronic listening and surveillance devices, eavesdropping is as old as man himself. In fact, eavesdropping was a common law crime, the essence of which consisted of listening under walls, windows, or eaves in order to vex or annoy another by spreading slanderous rumors against him.[19] Modern science has provided the eavesdropper with more dignified and sensitive tools.

---

16 Berger v. New York, 388 U.S. 41, 87 S. Ct. 1873, 18 L. Ed. 2d 1040 (1967). *See* Part II for portions of the case.

17 Pugach v. Dollinger, 365 U.S. 458, 81 S. Ct. 650, 5 L. Ed. 2d 678 (1961).

18 Katz v. United States, 389 U.S. 347, 88 S. Ct. 507, 19 L. Ed. 2d 576 (1976).

19 4 BLACKSTONE, COMMENTARIES, ch. 13, § 5.

By means of microphones, wireless radio transmitters, and other electronic listening devices, private conversations can be picked up and monitored miles away from where they are spoken. While the Federal Communications Act of 1934 limited wiretapping, it did not apply to eavesdropping. Eavesdropping protection has grown up primarily around an expanding interpretation of the Fourth Amendment. As these decisions have provided guidelines for recent legislation, they are briefly discussed and summarized.

Some of the distinctions the result of technical rules, serve to point out the confusion that existed prior to the 1968 act. For example, in 1928 in the case of *Goldman v. United States*, the United States Supreme Court determined that placing a sensitive detectaphone against a partition wall and listening to the conversation did not violate the Fourth Amendment.[20] The Court reasoned that as there was no physical trespass by the police into the defendant's home or office, there was no Fourth Amendment invasion.

On the other hand, the same court held that where a microphone with a foot-long spike was driven through a common wall until the spike made contact with the heating duct in the premises occupied by the defendant, this was an invasion of his constitutional rights.[21] Here the spiked mike actually penetrated the wall of the defendant's office. The Court held this was a physical trespass into the constitutionally protected area and, therefore, distinguishable from the *Goldman* situation.

This line of demarcation was rejected in the case of *Katz v. United States* where agents attached an electronic listening and recording device to the outside of a telephone booth from which the defendant placed his calls.[22] Though the government urged that its agents relied upon the decisions in the *Goldman* case and argued there was no technical trespass as was condemned in the *Silverman* case, the Supreme Court refused to heed the arguments. In rejecting the old physical trespass distinction, the Court held in *Katz*:

> We conclude that the underpinnings of *Olmstead* and *Goldman* have been so eroded by our subsequent decisions that the "trespass" doctrine there enumerated can no longer be regarded as controlling.

Since the decision in the *Katz* case, there is no question but the Supreme Court considers eavesdropping by electronic devices, or bugging, to fall within the ambit of the Fourth Amendment. Therefore, all of the safeguards

---

20 Goldman v. United States, 316 U.S. 129, 62 S. Ct. 993, 86 L. Ed. 1322 (1942).

21 Silverman v. United States, 365 U.S. 505, 81 S. Ct. 679, 5 L. Ed. 2d 734 (1961).

22 Katz v. United States, 389 U.S. 347, 88 S. Ct. 507, 19 L. Ed. 2d 576 (1967).

which apply when the search is of tangible goods will apply when the search is of verbal evidence.

Recognizing the need for law enforcement surveillance prior to the time that Congress recognized this need, some states enacted legislation which attempted to bring eavesdropping under judicial supervision through a system of court orders.[23] The New York law was found to be unconstitutional by the United States Supreme Court as it did not comply with the requirements of the Fourth Amendment as made applicable to the states by the Fourteenth. In the case of *Berger v. New York*, the Supreme Court of the United States implied that state statutes could be enacted authorizing eavesdropping but that such statutes must provide safeguards as are required by the Fourth Amendment.[24]

§ 5.6 Objectives of the 1968 wiretapping and electronic surveillance statutes and the 1986 Electronic Communications Privacy Act

Soon after *Olmstead v. United States*[25] where the Supreme Court decided that wiretapping did not violate the provisions of the Fourth Amendment, efforts were made to enact legislation to regulate wiretapping on a national level. Such legislation was introduced in 1929 and 1931 and finally became a part of the Federal Communications Act in 1934.[26] From the beginning the 1934 act resulted in legal chaos. Much of the confusion was caused by the fact that the act did not have a provision which specifically excluded evidence obtained in violation of the statute and the fact that the act did not specifically apply to enforcement officers. Further confusion was brought about when the Supreme Court decided that evidence obtained in violation of the act would be inadmissible in federal courts but not state courts.

Because of a series of state cases, the rules regarding wiretapping and the use of wiretap evidence varied from state to state. And evidence which could be admitted in some states could not be admitted in federal courts. In order to clarify the rules concerning the use of wiretap and eavesdrop evidence, several states enacted legislation which authorized wiretapping and eavesdropping under court order. However, the Supreme Court in the *Berger* case decided that the New York statute was too broad, resulting in a trespas-

---

23 MASS. GEN. LAWS ANN. ch. 272, § 99 (1959).

24 Berger v. New York, 388 U.S. 41, 87 S. Ct. 1873, 18 L. Ed. 2d 1040 (1967). *See* Part II for portions of case.

25 277 U.S. 438, 48 S. Ct. 564, 72 L. Ed. 944 (1928).

26 Codified at title 47 of the United States Code.

sory intrusion into constitutionally protected areas and, therefore, in violation of the Fourth and Fourteenth Amendments. The Court, however, after pointing out in what respects the Fourth Amendment was infringed, implied that a statute could be drawn to meet the Fourth Amendment requirements.

It was evident that the only solution was for Congress to enact a comprehensive law designed to regulate wiretapping and eavesdropping on a uniform nationwide basis. In drafting this legislation it was necessary to incorporate all of the safeguards referred to in the Supreme Court decisions. For that reason the law is replete with requirements which are designed to make it constitutionally sound.

The various sections of Title III of the 1968 Crime Control Act are discussed in detail in the following sections. Briefly, it was anticipated that the following purposes would be accomplished by the Act:[27]

a. Prohibit nonconsensual private wiretapping and bugging (with some exceptions).

b. Permit private intercepts with the consent of one party to the conversation if not done to commit a tort or crime and not prohibited by state law.

c. Permit interceptions by communications common carriers (including firms which conduct major portions of their business by telephone) if necessarily incident to the rendition of services or the protection of rights or property of the communications common carrier.

d. Set up a federal court order system for wiretapping or bugging to obtain evidence of specified offenses.

e. Set similar standards for an optional state court order system for wiretapping or bugging.

f. Prohibit federal nonconsensual law enforcement wiretapping and bugging except under court order.

g. Prohibit state nonconsensual law enforcement wiretapping and bugging unless authorized under a state statute providing a court order system at least as restrictive as the federal system.

h. Permit federal law enforcement intercepts with the consent of one party to the conversation.

i. Permit state law enforcement intercepts with the consent of one party to the conversation unless prohibited by state law.

---

27 NWC REPORT, p. 40.

j. Expressly disclaim any intent to regulate federal wiretapping or bugging in security cases.

k. Authorize recovery of civil damages for unauthorized wiretapping or bugging.

l. Require annual reports for federal and state court-ordered wiretapping and bugging.

It is significant that the 1968 law does not confer an absolute right to privacy from wiretapping and eavesdropping. Implicit in the command of the Fourth Amendment, according to the courts, is a recognition that the individual citizen's rights are subject to limited curtailment in carefully scrutinized situations. Basically, what the law does is to extend the conventional warrant system to electronic investigations. Because of the unique method of seizing evidence, however, it was necessary that Congress spell out the procedure to be followed in obtaining a wiretap or eavesdropping order.

In 1986 Congress enacted the Electronic Communications Privacy Act which amended Title III of the Omnibus Crime Control and Safe Streets Act of 1968.[28] According to the Committee on the Judiciary of the United States Senate, the purpose of this act is "to protect against the unauthorized interception of electronic communications," and to amend the 1968 law to "update and clarify Federal privacy protections and standards in light of dramatic changes in new computer and telecommunications technologies."[29]

These extraordinary changes in the communications field since 1968 have necessitated clarifications and additions to the 1968 act which established criteria for conducting surveillance. The Senate Judiciary Committee report points out that the law existing in 1968 has not kept up with the development of communications and computer technology. Nor has it kept pace with changes in the structure of the telecommunications industry. In explaining the need for amendments to the 1968 Act, the Senate Judiciary Committee commented:

> Today we have large-scale electronic mail operations, computer-to-computer data transmissions, cellular and cordless telephones, paging devices, and video teleconferencing. A phone call can be carried by wire, by microwave, or fiber optics. It can be transmitted in the forms of digitized voice, data or video. Since the divestiture of AT&T and deregulation, many different companies, not just common carriers, offer a wide variety of telephone and other communications services. It does not make sense that a phone call

---

28 PUB. L NO. 99-508, 18 U.S.C. § 2510, *et seq*.

29 Senate Report (Judiciary Committee) 99-541, Act. 17 (1986).

transmitted via common carrier is protected by the current federal wiretap statute, while the same phone call transmitted via private telephone network such as those used by major U.S. corporations today, would not be covered by the statute.

The 1986 Act is designed to address privacy concerns relating to the use of certain devices. While cellular communications, whether between two cellular telephones or between a cellular telephone and a "landline" telephone are covered by this statute, the statute specifically excludes from its coverage the radio portion of a cordless telephone communication transmitted between the handset and the base unit. As there is little expectation of privacy concerning the radio portion of the cordless telephone communication, Congress felt it inappropriate to bring such communications under Title III of the 1986 Act. However, since communications between the base unit and the telephone called are carried over wire, these communications remain protected and a court order is necessary to tap into this communication. The amended act also includes provisions relating to the installation and use of pen registers and contains procedural requirements for orders to use "trap and trace" devices.[30]

To clarify some of the problems concerning the use of wiretap orders, the 1986 law expands the list of felonies for which a wiretap may be issued. It also expands the list of justice department officials who may apply for a court order to place the wiretap. The specific provisions of the Act are included in the sections that follow.

§ 5.7 Interception and disclosure of wire, oral, or electronic communications[31]

Section 2511 of the United States Code as amended in 1986 prohibits the interception and disclosure of wire, oral, or electronic communications, but has specific exceptions.[32] Section 2511(1) in effect prohibits the intentional interception or use of any wire, oral, or electronic communication except when in compliance with a detailed statutory procedure. The addition of "electronic communications" to the law in 1986 increased the coverage of the statute to "any transfer of signs, signals, writing, images, sounds, data, or intelligence of any nature transmitted in whole or in part by a wire, radio, electromagnetic, photoelectronic, or a photooptical system that affects foreign or interstate commerce.

---

30 18 U.S.C. § 3121-3126

31 18 U.S.C. § 2511.

32 *See* Part II of this book for a full statement of the Act.

According to the report of the House and Senate Judiciary Committees, "As a general rule, a communication is an electronic communication protected by the wiretap law if it is not carried by sound waves and cannot fairly be characterized as containing the human voice."[33] Included in the prohibition are electronic mail, digitized transmissions, and video teleconferences.

The 1986 Amendment to the Act uses the term "intentionally" to replace "willfully" which was used in the 1968 Act. This change in terminology was to avoid the confusion and uncertainty which was reflected in decisions prior to the 1986 Act. Failure to comply with the provisions of this section of the act subjects the violator to a fine or imprisonment of not more than five years or both. However, exceptions are set out where lower fines are applicable if the violation applies to certain radio communications. In addition, § 2511(5) allows for injunctive relief which is distinct from the criminal penalties.[34]

After stating that the interception of certain communications is generally prohibited, the law makes some specific exceptions. Section 2511(2)(a) provides that it shall not be unlawful for an operator of a switchboard or an officer, employee, or agent of a provider of wire or electronic communications service, whose facilities are used in the transmission of a wire communication, to intercept, disclose, or use that communication in the normal course of his employment.

The law also provides that it shall not be unlawful for an officer, employee, or agent of the Federal Communications Commission, in the normal course of his employment, to intercept a communication or to disclose the information thereby obtained.

The section which is most important to criminal justice personnel is section 2511(2)(c). This provides that:

> It shall not be unlawful under this chapter for a person acting under color of law to intercept a wire, oral, or electronic communication, where such person is a party to the communication or one of the parties to the communication has given prior consent to such interception.

---

33 Senate Report (Judiciary Committee) 99-541, Oct. 17, 1986.

34 According to the Judiciary Committee report, the term "intentional" is narrower than the dictionary definition of "intentional." In the context of this Act it means more than one voluntarily engaged in conduct or caused a result. Such conduct or the causing of the result must have been the person's conscious objective. And "intentional" state of mind means that one's state of mind is intentional as to one's conduct or the result of one's conduct if such conduct or result is one's conscious objective. House Report (Judiciary Committee) 99-647, June 19, 1986.

This clear statement of the authority for law enforcement officers to intercept wire, oral, or electronic communications makes it possible for the officer to act with more certainty. In intercepting communications with the consent of one party, it is not necessary that a judge approve the interception.

If the interceptor was a party to the communication, it is not necessary that the government prove that other parties to the tape-recorded telephone conversation consented to the interception.[35] Also, a police officer was one party to the communication when he attached a suction cup of an induction coil to the back of a receiver of the telephone and inserted the other end of the induction coil into a microphone jack of a tape recorder.[36] This interception did not violate the Federal Act or the New Jersey Wiretap Statute, as the officer's acquisition of the telephone communication resulted from answering the telephone when it rang and as the officer could legally receive the incoming calls. As a party thereto, he could also tape record the conversation.

In interpreting the provisions relating to "acting under color of law," a federal court has held that an informer who acted under supervision of the government investigator was acting under color of law within the meaning of this section.[37]

Another exception provides that it shall not be unlawful for a person not acting under the color of law to intercept a wire, oral, or electronic communication where such other person is a party to the communication or where one of the parties to the communication has given prior consent, provided the interception is not for the purpose of committing any criminal or tortious act in violation of the Constitution or laws of the United States or of any state. A federal court of appeals interpreted this to mean that the statute prohibiting unauthorized wiretapping did not apply to an interspousal wiretap used in preparation for a divorce litigation where the alleged violator attached a recording device to her own telephone and recorded a conversation to which she was a party.[38] On the other hand, the federal wiretap statute prohibits the use of a taped conversation in a matrimonial action where the wiretapper is not a party to the conversation and does not have consent of either party to the conversation.[39]

---

[35] United States v. Truglio, 731 F.2d 1123 (4th Cir. 1984), *cert. denied*, 469 U.S. 862, 105 S. Ct. 197, 83 L. Ed. 2d 130, (1984).

[36] State v. Vizzini, 278 A.2d 235 (N.J. 1971).

[37] United States v. Marcello, 703 F.2d 805 (5th Cir. 1981) *reh'g denied*, 708 F.2d 720 (5th Cir.), *cert. denied*, 104 S. Ct. 341, 464 U.S. 935, 78 L. Ed. 2d 309 (1983).

[38] Platt v. Platt, 685 F. Supp. 208 (E.D. Mo. 1988).

[39] Ex parte O'Daniel, 515 So.2d 1250 (Ala. 1987), *on remand*, 515 So.2d 1253 (1987).

To make clear the authority of agents of the United States, § 2511 includes an exception which makes it clear that it is not unlawful for an officer, employee, or agent of the United States, in the normal course of his official duties, to conduct electronic surveillance as defined in Section 101 of the Foreign Intelligence Surveillance Act of 1978.

In summary, Section 2511 generally prohibits the intentional interception of any wire, oral, or electronic communication as defined in the Act except certain specific activities as clearly stated in the Act. The exception which is of most importance to criminal justice personnel is that which allows interceptions where the person intercepting is a party to the communication or one of the parties to the communication has given prior consent to such interception.

§ 5.8 Manufacture, distribution, possession and advertising of wire, oral or electronic communication interception devices

As a means of preventing violations of the law, 18 U.S.C. § 2512 provides for a maximum fine of $10,000 or imprisonment of not more than five years, or both, to any person who manufactures, assembles, possesses, sells or advertises for sale any device, knowing or having reason to know that the design of such device renders it primarily useful for the purpose of surreptitious interception of wire or oral communications. This provision is only effective, however, if the manufacturer, assembler, possessor or seller knows or has reason to know that such device will be sent through the mail or transported in interstate or foreign commerce.[40]

A necessary exception is included in this section which authorizes manufacture, assembly, or sale of such devices where they are for lawful use to agents or employees of the United States, a state, or a political subdivision thereof.

§ 5.9 Confiscation of wire, oral, or electronic communication interception devices

To make it more unprofitable to violate the law, Section 2513 provides for the confiscation by the government of electronic, mechanical, or other devices used, sent, carried, manufactured, assembled, possessed, sold or adver-

---

40 The Commission conclude that "Title III's prohibition against the manufacture, sale, and advertising, etc., of devices primarily useful for surreptitious electronic surveillance has resulted in a notable drop in the manufacture and marketing of such devices." NWC REPORT, p. 23.

tised in violation of the law. This section provides that such confiscation shall be by such officers, agents or other persons as authorized or designated by the Attorney General.

§ 5.10 Immunity of witnesses

Section 2514 provided that a court, at the request of a United States Attorney and with the approval of the Attorney General, could give immunity to persons testifying concerning violations enumerated in section 2516. When such immunity was given, under the provisions of law, the judge could then require the person to testify and hold him in contempt of court for failure to comply with this order. This section was held to be constitutional.[41]

In 1970, however, Congress saw fit to repeal this section of the statute, the effective date of the repeal to be four years following the sixtieth day after the date of enactment (Oct. 15, 1970). The repeal did not affect any immunity to which any individual was entitled under the section by reason of any statement or other information given before such date. The subject matter concerning the immunity of witnesses is now covered under 18 U.S.C. § 6002 and § 6003.

§ 5.11 Prohibition of use of evidence of intercepted wire or oral communications

The failure of Congress to specify in previous legislation that evidence obtained in violation of the law would be inadmissible in court led to untold confusion. As the drafters of Title III of the Crime Control Act were familiar with this confusion, they included a provision which prohibits the use of direct evidence or derivative evidence if the provisions of the act are violated. Specifically, the law states:

> Whenever any wire or oral communication has been intercepted, no part of the contents of such communication and no evidence derived therefrom may be received in evidence in any trial, hearing, or other proceeding in or before any court, grand jury, department, officer, agency, regulatory body, legislative committee, or other authority of the United States, a State, or a political subdivision thereof if the disclosure of that information would be in violation of this chapter.[42]

---

41 In re Dec., 1968 Grand Jury v. United States, 420 F.2d 1201 (7th Cir. 1970).

42 18 U.S.C. § 2515 (1986).

This makes it clear that no evidence obtained directly or indirectly as a result of an intercepted wire or oral communication in violation of the provisions of the chapter may be used in any proceeding in any court or hearing. This applies to evidence obtained by federal, state or local officers and in federal, state and local courts.

This exclusionary remedy enacted by Title III exceeds Fourth Amendment requirements in several relevant particulars. First, it encompasses proceedings for which exclusion is not required under the Fourth Amendment. In *United States v. Calandra*,[43] the Supreme Court held that the Fourth Amendment does not require suppression of unlawfully seized evidence from grand jury proceedings, and that, therefore, a witness ordered to testify could not refuse on the grounds that the inquiry was derived from evidence obtained in the course of an unlawful search and seizure. But because grand jury proceedings are specifically mentioned in the enumeration of prohibited uses under section 2515, a contrary resolution was reached when the same question arose in connection with illegally intercepted conversations.[44]

A second difference hinges upon the types of transgressions that lead to the imposition of evidentiary sanctions. The Act contains a detailed array of procedural requirements governing the procurement and execution of listening orders, some of which were drafted to satisfy the constitutional mandate of *Katz* and others of which go beyond. In *United States v. Giordano*[45] the Supreme Court categorically rejected the argument that the Title III exclusionary remedy was limited to cases in which the government fails to observe a procedural requirement founded on the Constitution.

In ruling that evidentiary sanctions may be invoked in some cases where the omitted requirement is purely statutory in origin, the Court stated the test to be whether the requirement constituted a "central safeguard" in the prevention of abuses. For example, the statutory requirement that all applications for intercept orders initiate with the personal approval of the Attorney General, or of an assistant attorney general specially designated by him, was held to be such a safeguard, whereas the directive that all wiretap applications correctly identify the authorizing official was held not to be "central."[46]

As the Act makes clear that evidence obtained as a result of an illegal interception will be excluded in a criminal trial, the burden is on the government to prove that the law was not violated in obtaining such evidence.[47] However, such proof need not consist of testimonial evidence as the burden

---

43 414 U.S. 338, 94 S. Ct. 613, 38 L. Ed. 2d 561 (1974).

44 Gelbard v. United States, 408 U.S. 41, 92 S. Ct. 2357, 33 L. Ed. 2d 179 (1972).

45 416 U.S. 505, 94 S. Ct. 1820. 40 L. Ed. 2d 341 (1974).

46 United States v. Chavez, 416 U.S. 562, 94 S. Ct. 1849, 40 L. Ed. 2d 380 (1974).

47 United States v. David, 799 F.2d 1490 (11th Cir. 1986).

can be met by circumstantial evidence. For example, in the case of *United States v. Davis*, the court held that the burden on the government is met when it is shown by circumstantial evidence that an informant placed a telephone call knowing that call would be recorded.

§ 5.12 Authorization for interception of wire, oral, or electronic communications

Subsection (1), Section 2516 sets out the procedures by which a federal investigative agency may apply for an order authorizing the wire or oral communication interceptions. This section provides that the Attorney General, Deputy Attorney General, Associate Attorney General, or any Assistant Attorney General, any acting Assistant Attorney General, or any Deputy Assistant Attorney General in the Criminal Division specially designated, may authorize an application to a Federal Judge for an order authorizing or approving the interception of wire or oral communications.[48]

According to the provision of the statute, applications can be made only if the interception could provide evidence of a violation of specific laws. Generally, a federal officer may apply for a court order to authorize interception if there is probable cause to believe that there is a violation of:

(a) the national security laws;
(b) the serious felony statutes which are punishable by death or imprisonment for more than one year;
(c) laws relating to organized crime and gambling;
(d) narcotics laws, counterfeiting laws, or other laws specified in the statute.[49]

The Electronic Communications Act of 1986 amended the previous laws so as to add to the list of felonies for which the wiretap or bugging order may be obtained.

---

48 The 1986 Act increases the number of persons that are authorized to apply for a court order. Under the 1986 Act only the Attorney General or an Assistant Attorney General specifically designated by the Attorney General could authorize such application. This lead to much confusion and resulted in eavesdropping evidence being admissible in hundreds of federal cases. United States v. Giordano, 416 U.S. 505, 94 S. Ct. 1820, 40 L. Ed. 2d 341 (1974). *See also* the 1976 Report of the National Commission for the Review of Federal and State laws Relating to Wiretapping published by the U.S. Government Printing Office.

49 *See* 18, § 2516(1) for a comprehensive enumeration of the laws for which an application may be made.

In addition to authorizing designated federal officials to apply for a court order, section 2516 states that "the principal prosecuting attorney of any State, or the principal prosecuting attorney of any political subdivision thereof, if such attorney is authorized by a statute of that State to make application to a State court judge of competent jurisdiction...may apply to such judge for, and such judge may grant in conformity with section 2518 of this chapter and with the applicable State statute, an order authorizing an interception..."

It is noted that the state prosecutor can authorize application only if the state statute so provides. If there is no enabling state statute, prosecuting attorneys cannot authorize the application for a court order which would grant authority to wiretap or eavesdrop. However, federal officers are authorized to wiretap under this section regardless of the provisions of the state law; it is only wiretapping by state officers under this section that requires further authorization by state statute.[50]

While a state may adopt standards for wiretapping which are more stringent than the requirements of federal law, thus excluding from state courts evidence that would be admissible in federal courts,[51] a state may not adopt standards that are less restrictive than federal requirements.

One of the subsections of Section 2516 provides that designated state prosecutors may make application for a court order for wiretapping or eavesdropping only if the interception may provide evidence of certain crimes. The offenses designated in the statute include murder, kidnapping, gambling, robbery, bribery, extortion, dealing in narcotic drugs, marijuana or other dangerous drugs, or other crimes dangerous to life or property and punishable by imprisonment for more than one year.[52]

In states where there is no enabling legislation, a state officer who intercepts communication is subject to penalty the same as any other "person" as defined in Section 2510 and evidence obtained in violation of the Act is not admissible in state court.

---

50 United States v. Hall, 543 F.2d 1229 (9th Cir. 1976), *cert. denied*, 429 U.S. 1075, 97 S. Ct. 814, 50 L. Ed. 2d 973 (1976).

51 Commonwealth v. Vitello, 327 N.E.2d 819 (Mass. 1975); State v. Willis, 643 P.2d 1112 (Kan. 1982).

52 By the end of 1982 a total of 27 states and the District of Columbia had statutory provisions for court-approved electronic surveillance. Some states, however, prohibit such surveillance even though the federal statute authorizes it. *See* the Report of the Applications for Orders Authorizing or Approving the Interception of Wire or Oral Communications for the period ending 1982, U.S. Government Printing Office.

§ 5.13 Authorization for disclosure and use of intercepted wire, oral, or electronic communications

Section 2517 was included to make it clear that law enforcement officers who obtain evidence in accordance with the provisions of the act may legally disclose the information and use the evidence to the extent appropriate to the proper performance of their official duties. This section also makes abundantly clear that derivative evidence obtained as a result of the legal interception can be used during the investigation and in any criminal proceeding.

The section goes even further and provides that the officer is not limited to the use of evidence described in the order authorizing the interception but may use other evidence incidentally obtained during the authorized interception. As an example, if the officer obtains an order authorizing the interception of a wiretap communication for the purpose of obtaining evidence of narcotics violations, but during that authorized interception obtains evidence of a kidnapping, this may be used when authorized or approved by a judge of competent jurisdiction. Such use can be compared with the seizure of tangible evidence not described in the search warrant but observed by the police officer who is executing a legitimate search warrant.

When an enforcement officer, while engaged in intercepting a communication in the manner authorized by the state statute, intercepts communications relating to offenses other than those specified in the order of authorization, he nonetheless may disclose or use this evidence, provided he makes application to the judge and the judge approves such use. For example, even though a warrant issued for electronic surveillance did not list "obstruction of justice" as a possible violation, such evidence could be used, where the judge who authorized the surveillance was made aware of the facts, clearly relating to other offenses, in the application for its continuance.[53]

§ 5.14 Procedure for interception of wire, oral, or electronic communications

Section 2518[54] designates the procedures which must be followed in obtaining an order authorizing the interception of wire or oral communications. Because it is necessary to protect the constitutional rights of individuals, the procedure for obtaining an order is detailed and comprehensive. The proce-

---

53 United States v. Ardito, 982 F.2d 358 (2d Cir. 1986), *cert. denied*, 475 U.S. 1141, 106 S. Ct. 1972, 90 L. Ed. 2d 338 (1986).

54 18 U.S.C. § 2518 (1990).

dures closely resemble those which have been traditionally employed for obtaining the conventional search warrant.

1. Application for interception order

All applications for orders permitting the interception of wire or oral communications must be authorized by the Attorney General, the Deputy Attorney General, the Associate Attorney General or other officer as designated in Section 2516 in the case of federal investigations, or by the principal prosecuting officer of the state or of its political subdivisions in the case of state and local investigations. It must be made in writing upon an oath or affirmation before the appropriate federal or state judge, as the case may be, and must include the following information:

(a) the identity of the law enforcement officer making the application, and the officer authorizing it;

(b) a statement of the facts relied upon by the applicant warranting the issuance of an order, including details as to the particular offense which has been, is being, or is about to be committed; a particular description of the nature and location of the facilities from which or the place where the communication is to be intercepted, the identity of the persons whose communications are to be overheard or recorded; and a description of the types of communications sought;

(c) facts concerning whether or not other investigative procedures have been tried and failed or why they appear unlikely to succeed if tried or would be too dangerous; and

(d) the anticipated period of time for which the interception is required to be maintained;

(e) facts concerning all previous applications involving any of the same persons, facilities or place and the action taken by the judge on the same.

This section has generated as much litigation as any section mentioned in the chapter. The law requires that the identity of the person, if known, committing the offense and whose communications are to be intercepted be included in the application. Searching for means to challenge wiretap orders, attorneys have claimed that:

(a) if a person is not named in the application, evidence obtained as a result of the order will not be admissible against him, and

(b) failure to include the name of a known offender whose communication is expected to be overheard renders the intercepted conversations inadmissible at the trial.

In *United States v. Kahn*[55] the Supreme Court construed the statutory requirement that the application and order identify the persons, if known, who are committing the offense and whose communications are to be intercepted. Federal authorities, having probable cause to believe that one Irving Kahn was using specified telephones to conduct an illegal gambling business, secured a court order authorizing the interception of "wire communications of Irving Kahn and others as yet unknown." In the course of executing the order, the agents overheard several conversations between Kahn's wife and known gambling figures, implicating her in the illegal operation. Indictments were obtained against both Kahns. On behalf of Mrs. Kahn, it was urged that the conversations in which she participated should be suppressed because the government could have discovered her complicity and named her in the application had it made a thorough investigation prior to applying for the listening order. The Supreme Court ruled that a full investigation, in advance of seeking an order, into the possibility that all likely users of a particular telephone were engaging in criminal activities was unnecessary.

The statute requires the naming of particular individuals in the application and order only when law enforcement authorities have probable cause to believe that that person is committing the offense for which wiretap authority is sought. Since the government had no reason to suspect Mrs. Kahn of complicity until after the interception had been conducted, the failure to name her in the application was not an error. The Court further held that, when a wiretap order is properly issued, intercept authority is not limited to conversations in which the person specifically named in the order is a party. Conversations between Mrs. Kahn and others whose identities were unknown in advance of interception were properly admissible into evidence under the language of the order and under section 2518.

The Fifth Circuit Court of Appeals agreed that failure to name specific persons not known to be involved at the time of the surveillance application should not lead to the suppression of the evidence against them.[56] On the other hand, the Fourth Circuit Court of Appeals, referring to the strict interpretation of the statute mentioned in *Giordano*, decided that FBI agents' failure to include in a wiretap application the name of a *known* offender whose communications they *expected* to overhear rendered the offender's in-

---

55 415 U.S. 143, 94 S. Ct. 977, 39 L. Ed. 2d 225 (1974).

56 United States v. Doolittle, 507 F.2d 1368 (5th Cir. 1975).

tercepted conversations inadmissible at the trial.[57] Here the court explained that compliance with the identification requirements contained in 18 U.S.C. § 2518(1)(b)(iv) assist both the Executive and Judicial branches to carry out their oversight and review functions.

Section 2518(c) requires that the application contain a full and complete statement as to whether or not other investigative procedures have been tried and failed or why they reasonably appear to be unlikely to succeed or to be too dangerous. While the earlier cases appear to apply this requirement strictly, more recent cases have held that there is no requirement that any particular investigative procedure be exhausted before a wiretap is authorized.[58] In a 1987 case the Court agreed that the government made a sufficient showing that it undertook an antecedent investigatory procedure by less intrusive means to warrant authorization for telephone wiretaps in a narcotics case, where the government introduced evidence that confidential informants were used extensively, to a limited effect, access to federal witness protection program was offered and rejected, agents were assigned to the case in adequate numbers, visual surveillance was tried but proved inconclusive, pen registers were utilized and telephone toll records were analyzed.[59]

In another recent case the Court noted that the authorities are not required to exhaust all conceivable investigative procedures before resorting to wiretapping.[60] Notwithstanding the fact that many cases have upheld the use of wiretap where law enforcement agents have introduced evidence to show other investigatory procedures have been tried and failed or reasonably appear to be unlikely to succeed if tried, the burden is still on the prosecution to show that this provision of the statute is complied with. Merely stating that a wiretap is regularly used for this type of case, or a conclusory statement that a wiretap is the best investigative method, does not comply with the mandates of this part of the statute.[61]

---

57 United States v. Bernstein, 509 F.2d 996 (4th Cir. 1975).

58 United States v. Kalustian, 529 F.2d 585 (9th Cir. 1975); United States v. Young, 822 F. 2d 1234 (2d Cir. 1987).

59 United States v. Hoffman, 832 F.2d 1299 (1st Cir. 1987)

60 United States v. Apodaca, 820 F.2d 348 (1st Cir.), *cert. denied*, __U.S.__, 108 S. Ct. 245, 98 L. Ed. 2d 202 (1987).

61 United States v. Clements, 588 F.2d 1030 (5th Cir.), *cert. denied*, 441 U.S. 936, 99 S. Ct. 2062, 60 L. Ed. 2d 666 (1979).

2. *Determination of judge*

According to section 2518(3) the judge to whom the application is submitted may issue an *ex parte* order authorizing or approving the interception if he determines on the basis of the facts submitted[62] that there is probable cause to believe that:

(a) an individual has committed, is committing, or is about to commit one of the enumerated offenses;

(b) communications concerning that offense will be obtained through such interception;

(c) normal investigative procedures have been tried and have failed or reasonably appear unlikely to succeed if tried or would be too dangerous; and

(d) the facilities from which, or the place where, the interception will occur are being used in connection with the commission of such offense, or are leased to, listed in the name of, or commonly used by such person.

Congress, according to the Third Circuit Court of Appeals, did not intend to require a higher degree of probable cause for a wiretap than that ordinarily required for a search warrant.[63] The court held that the facts contained in the wiretap application met the standards for what constitutes probable cause.

In the case of *United States v. Harvey* in 1982, a Federal District Court in Florida emphasized that the same probable cause standard which exists for a search warrant is applicable to wiretaps. Applying this definition, the Court held that "probable cause exists where facts and circumstances within the affiant's knowledge, and of which he has reasonable trustworthy information, are sufficient unto themselves to warrant a man of reasonable caution to believe that an offense is being committed, has been committed, or is about to

---

62 In discussing the issuance of an *ex parte* order, the Commission commented that, "There has been no evidence heard to contradict the finding of the drafters of Title III that vital differences between ordinary searches by electronic surveillance devices require that wiretap applications be reviewed by higher-level judges rather than judges of limited jurisdiction who normally issue ordinary search warrants." NWC REPORT, p. 12.

63 United States v. Falcone, 505 F.2d 478 (3d Cir. 1974). The Eighth Circuit reached a similar conclusion in United States v. Brick, 502 F.2d 291 (8th Cir. 1974).

be committed.[64] However, the test for probable cause when naming a specific party as an authorized interceptee is not whether the party is guilty or involved in the underlying offense, but whether it is reasonably probable that evidence of the crime will be obtained by listening to such a party.[65]

3. *Specifications in order*

The order must specify:

(a) the identity of the individual, if known, whose communications are to be intercepted;
(b) the nature and location of the communications facilities or place where authority to intercept is granted;
(c) a description of the type of communication sought to be intercepted and the particular offense to which it relates;
(d) the identity of the agency authorized to intercept and the person authorizing the application; and
(e) the period of time during which such interception is authorized.[66]

4. *Duration and minimization*

The listening order may not remain in effect any longer than is necessary to achieve the objectives of the authorization and in any event no longer than *thirty days*. It should be promptly executed and the interception should be conducted in such a manner as to minimize the interception of communications not otherwise subject to interception. There is no limit on the number of extensions which can be granted, but each extension requires the same information and showing of probable cause as the original application. The order and any extensions thereof automatically terminate upon the attainment of the authorized objective.[67]

In several cases the courts have attempted to interpret what is meant by "minimization" of the interception of communications not otherwise subject to interception. Apparently there is no hard and fast formula for minimization, and the requirement is satisfied if the court, in reviewing the government procedures, concludes that on the whole the agents have shown a high

---

64 United States v. Harvey, 560 F. Supp. 1040 (S.D. Fla. 1982)
65 United States v. Dorfman, 542 F. Supp. 345 (D.C. Ill. 1982).
66 18 U.S.C. § 2518 (4).
67 18 U.S.C. § 2518(5).

regard for the right of privacy and have done all they reasonably could to avoid unnecessary intrusions.[68]

According to one court, the factors to be considered in determining whether investigators have complied with the section limiting wiretap intrusion into conversations, and in determining if the minimization requirements have been followed, include:

(1) the scope of the criminal enterprise,
(2) the government's reasonable expectation of the content of the particular calls,
(3) the extent of judicial supervision,
(4) the length of the call,
(5) whether the call was a one-time only call,
(6) whether the call originated from a pay or residential telephone, and
(7) whether the callers used ambiguous or coded language.[69]

5. *Emergency interceptions*

Congress contemplated that situations may occasionally arise where the time factor is such as to make it impossible or impracticable for the investigating officer to make application for an order prior to engaging in listening. He cannot always anticipate in advance where or when a conversation will occur and once the sound waves dissipate, the evidence is lost forever. The concession, made for emergency situations, is nevertheless a limited one.

To prevent abuse of the privilege where no necessity exists, the responsible officer must make a reasonable determination that:

(a) an emergency exists with respect to immediate danger or death or serious injury to any person to conspiratorial activities characteristic of organized crime or threatening the national secu-

---

68 United States v. Bynum, 485 F.2d 490 (2d Cir. 1973); United States v. James, 494 F.2d 1007 (D.C. Cir. 1974); and United States v. Armocida, 515 F.2d 29 (3d Cir. 1975). The Commission, after reviewing many cases, recommended that "no hard and fast minimization guidelines can be drafted, nor is there a need to do so." NWC REPORT, p. 12.

69 United States v. Garcia, 785 F.2d 214 (8th Cir. 1986), *cert. denied*, 475 U.S. 1143, 106 S. Ct. 1797, 90 L. Ed. 2d 342 (1986). *See* U.S.C.A., Note 31 for a comprehensive digest of cases interpreting this section.

rity, requiring that an interception be made before an authorization can be obtained, and that
(b) there are grounds upon which such an order could be entered in accordance with the standards set out in the federal statute.

If these two conditions are satisfied, the listening may be conducted in the absence of an order, provided that the officer makes application for an order approving what has transpired within *forty-eight* hours thereafter. In the event that no application is sought or the application for an approval order is denied, all overheard or recorded communications will be treated as having been obtained in violation of the law for purposes of admissibility.[70]

6. *Recording of communications to assure authenticity*

Although not mandatory under the law, section 2518(8) does provide as a rule of policy that recordings should be made of every intercepted communication, if possible. The purpose of this requirement is to assure completeness and accuracy and to safeguard against error. The recording, moreover, must be made in such a way as to protect it from editing or other alterations. Immediately upon the expiration of the period of the order or any extensions thereof, the recording must be transmitted to the judge issuing the order and sealed under his direction. Custody of the recordings shall be wherever the judge orders. The presence of the seal on the recording, or a satisfactory explanation for its absence, is a prerequisite for its introduction into evidence at a trial. But since the police are not required to make a recording in every case, the absence of a seal on a recording would probably not foreclose an officer from testifying in court on the basis of his own recollection of what he directly heard. The only consequence is the forfeiture of the ability to utilize the recording itself as evidence. The advantage of having this testimony in recorded form and of being able to utilize it in court lies in the fact that it is a more cogent and convincing mode of presenting the evidence.

7. *Pre-use notice*

Before the contents of any intercepted wire or oral communication, or any evidence derived therefrom, may be received into evidence at any trial,

---

[70] 18 U.S.C. § 2518(7). The majority members of the Commission determined that this emergency provision had not been used in very many cases. Nevertheless they recommended that it be left in the law and, in fact, enlarged so as to allow electronic surveillance in other cases, such as hijacking or kidnapping, as a means of preventing death or serious bodily harm. NWC REPORT, p. 15.

hearing or other proceeding in a federal or state court, each party must be furnished, at least *ten days* in advance, unless waived by the judge, with copies of the records of the communications, the court order and accompanying application.[71] Once this disclosure has been made, the party will be in a better position to raise such objections to its receipt as are authorized by law. Essentially, this requirement amounts to a mandatory form of discovery.

8. *Motion to suppress*

On the basis of the information disclosed to him by virtue of the pre-use notice requirement, a party aggrieved by the interception may move to suppress the communications themselves and all evidentiary fruits flowing therefrom on the grounds that:

(i) the communication was unlawfully intercepted;
(ii) the order of authorization or approval under which it was intercepted is insufficient on its face; or
(iii) the interception was not made in conformity with the order of authorization or approval.[72]

The motion should be made before the trial, hearing or proceeding unless there is no opportunity to make it or the person was unaware of the grounds of the motion. If the motion is granted, the evidence will be excluded from the proceeding.

A final provision of section 2518 authorizes the United States to appeal from an order granting a motion to suppress the use of evidence. This appeal must be made within 30 days after the date the order was entered and must be diligently prosecuted. This provision is a unique provision but should prove worthwhile as far as the prosecutor is concerned. Because the prosecutor has the specific authority to appeal, a judge might be more inclined to evaluate the facts more carefully before denying the use of the evidence.

Section 2518 was modified so as to authorize an application for an interception without giving a particular description of the nature and location of the facilities from which the communication is to be intercepted, if the application contains a full and complete statement as to why such specification is not practical and identifies the person committing the offense and whose communications are to be intercepted. This exception is authorized only if the judge finds that such specification is not practical and the applicant

---

[71] 18 U.S.C. § 2518(9). The ten days' requirement may be waived by the judge if the party will not be prejudiced by the delay.

[72] 18 U.S.C. § 2518(10).

makes a showing of a purpose, on the part of the person, to thwart interception by changing facilities.

This provision which was added in 1986 authorizes the judge to issue an order for "roving taps." According to the Committee that considered the provisions for the Act, this was necessary to cover circumstances under which law enforcement officials may not know, until shortly before the communication, which telephone line would be used by the person under surveillance. In the case of both oral and wire communications, only a limited list of federal officials can apply for a special order seeking relief under this provision.

Section 2518(12) which was also added in 1986 placed limitations on the use of the "roving tap." This provides that actual interception cannot begin until the facility from which the communication is to be intercepted is ascertained. This places the burden on the investigating agency to ascertain when and where the interception is to take place.

§ 5.15 Reports concerning intercepted wire, oral, or electronic communications

Another unique feature of the wiretap legislation is that it requires reports concerning the activities governed by it. Because of the controversy concerning intercepted communications, an effort is apparently being made to determine if such interceptions are in fact necessary and effective.

Section 2519 requires that the judge who issued or denied the order shall make a report for the Administrative Office of the United States Courts concerning orders issued under the act. This report must be submitted within 30 days after the expiration of the order and must include in addition to the fact that the order was issued, the offense, the identity of the investigative agency, the nature of the facilities, and other pertinent information concerning the order.

In addition, the Attorney General and the prosecuting attorneys of the states and political subdivisions must submit a report once each year to the Administrative Office of United States Courts. This report must include in addition to a summary of previously reported information, the number of arrests resulting from interceptions, the number of trials, the number of convictions, and a general assessment of the importance of the interceptions.

The report that is submitted, in accordance with the provisions of the law, includes a comprehensive tabulation of the number of applications for interceptions which were granted, as well as the number of authorizations where interception devices were installed as reported by the prosecuting officials. It is noted, however, that the report does not include statistics concerning interceptions made with the consent of one of the parties to the communication. As provided by the Electronic Communication Act of 1986, the Attorney General is required to file a separate report annually with Congress indicating the number of pen registers and trap and trace devices applied for by law enforcement agencies of the Department of Justice.

The Report on Applications for Orders Authorizing or Approving the Interception of Wire, Oral, or Electronic Communications (Wiretap Report) for the period January 1, 1988, through December 31, 1988, as published by the Administrative Office of the U.S. Courts[73] announced that 738 applications submitted for the authorization of wire, oral, or electronic surveillance in 1988 were granted; 293 by federal judges and 445 by state judges. These figures indicate a 24 percent increase in federal authorizations over the previous year and a 2 percent increase in state applications. Most state applications were approved by judges in New York, New Jersey, Maryland, Florida and Pennsylvania.[74] A total of 2,486 persons were arrested as a result of electronic surveillance activity during 1988. Of these, 543 were convicted during 1988.[75]

Although the use of court-ordered interceptions is an effective tool in combatting crime, it is not without cost. According to the 1989 report, the average cost per intercept report during 1988 was $49,284; this was an increase over the $36,904 cost per wiretap in 1987. The average cost for the 282 federal wiretaps reported was $70,761 while state wiretaps average $32,915. It is interesting to note that the highest cost for single state intercept authorization was reported by the New York State Attorney General. Here the intercept lasted for 122 days and cost $752,720. As one might expect, most of the approved intercepts involved narcotics violations.

On the positive side regarding costs, some examples indicate the feasibility of the use of wiretap as a way to gain evidence of drug trafficking without exposing undercover agents to dangerous contacts with drug dealers. An example of a successful operation was where a phone tap was placed on a single family house in Florida. This assisted prosecutors in a narcotics investigation which resulted in 61 arrests and 30 convictions. In addition, law enforcement officials seized over three million dollars in real property,

---

[73] Statistical Analysis and Reports Div., Administrative Office of the U.S. Courts, Washington, DC 20544 (1989).

[74] As of the end of 1988, 34 states had enacted legislation which authorized state officers to intercept communications in accordance with the federal act. *See* Table 1, the Report on Applications for Orders Authorizing or Approving the Interception of Wire, Oral, or Electronic Communications published by the Statistical Analysis and Reports Div. of the Administrative Office of the U.S. Courts.

[75] Some criminal cases which involve the use of electronic surveillance were still active investigations at the time the report was written and results from many of the intercepts concluded in 1988 had not been reported.

weapons, and vehicles. Another federal wiretap in the Northern District of Illinois resulted in the seizure of $100,000 in cash and jewelry, 20 vehicles valued at $225,000, and forfeiture of over 4.5 million dollars in real estate.

§ 5.16 Recovery of civil damages

In addition to the criminal sanctions and the exclusion of evidence obtained in violation of the law, a third mode of enforcement is incorporated into the law. Section 2520 authorizes the commencement of a civil suit if the law is violated but includes some exceptions. Under the provisions of the Act, appropriate relief includes preliminary or declaratory relief as may be appropriate, actual and punitive damages, and reasonable attorney fees and litigation costs. The court may assess damages consisting of whichever is the greater of

(a) the sum of the plaintiff's actual damages and any profits the violator made as to the result of the violation; or
(b) money damages of whichever is the greater of $100 per day or $10,000.

Section 2520(d) provides a good faith defense for those who rely on court orders or warrants, a grand jury subpoena, a legislative authorization, or a statutory authorization. There is also a good faith defense if an investigating officer acts under section 2518-7 which concerns emergency situations. As used in the subsections, the term "good faith" includes the receipt of a facially valid court order.

The statute also includes a statute of limitations for actions brought under this section. Actions may not be commenced later than two years after the date upon which claimant first has a reasonable opportunity to discover the violation.

§ 5.17 Constitutionality of Title III of the 1968 Crime Control Act as amended

It was inevitable that Title III provisions of the Crime Control Act authorizing the interception of communications would be challenged. The courts have almost unanimously agreed that federal legislation and state laws modeled on it comply with the requirements of the Fourth Amendment. Title III has successfully run the gauntlet of constitutional attack in the United States Courts of Appeals, after having been challenged in many Federal District Courts.[76] Discussion of some of these cases will dispel most doubt as to the constitutional status of the enactment as amended.

In the case of *Dalia v. United States*,[77] the authority of agents to break into a residence or a business premise to install an eavesdropping device as authorized under Title III of the 1968 Omnibus Crime Control and Safe Streets Act was challenged.

The defendant claimed that the Fourth Amendment ban on illegal searches forbade police from entering a home to install a bug unless a search warrant is issued by a judicial officer. The government argued that an order under Title III met the requirements of the warrant clause. The government argued too that the entry was a necessary aspect of executing the order, and it was implicitly authorized just as an entry necessary to execute a conventional search warrant is authorized.

By a 5-4 decision the Supreme Court held that the surreptitious entries were implicitly authorized by the 1968 Omnibus Crime Control and Safe Streets Act which gave the law enforcement officials authority to wiretap and bug. The justices rejected a claim that the Fourth Amendment's ban on illegal searches forbade police from breaking into a home or office to install a bug. They also decided that the judges need not specifically approve the break-in when they issued a surveillance order.

In the case of *United States v. Kail* in 1979 as amended in 1980, the majority of the Ninth Circuit Court again reiterated that the procedures specified in the Omnibus Crime Control and Safe Streets Act for obtaining a wiretap are not unconstitutional.[78]

In the *Kail* case the defendants who had been indicted for conducting a gambling business moved to suppress the evidence obtained by wiretaps, claiming that a two year and three month delay between authorization to intercept the wire communications and return of gambling indictment violated the due process clause. The Circuit Court determined that the delay was not in violation of the due process clause but in addition indicated that the procedures specified in the Crime Control and Safe Streets Act were not uncon-

---

[76] United States v. Tortorello, 480 F.2d 764 (2d Cir. 1973); United States v. Cafero, 473 F.2d 489 (3d Cir. 1973); United States v. Bobo, 477 F.2d 974 (4th Cir. 1973); United States v. Harris, 460 F.2d 1041 (5th Cir. 1972); United States v. Martinez, 498 F.2d 464 (6th Cir. 1974); United States v. Cox, 462 F.2d 1293 (8th Cir. 1972); United States v. Cox, 449 F.2d 679 (10th Cir. 1971); United States v. James, 494 F.2d 1007 (D.C. Cir. 1974). *See also* NWC REPORT, p. 6

[77] 441 U.S. 238, 99 S. Ct. 1682, 60 L. Ed. 2d 177 (1979).

[78] 612 F.2d 443 (9th Cir. 1979). The chapter was held to be constitutional in United States v. Bailey, 607 2d 237 (9th Cir. 1979), *cert. denied*, 445 U.S. 934, 100 S. Ct. 327, 63 L. Ed. 2d 769 (1979).

stitutional and that once a valid wiretap order has been issued there need not be a separate authorization for use of a pen register. As to the requirement that other procedures have been tried, the court indicated that an affidavit seeking a wiretap authorization must be viewed as a whole in determining whether it shows that other investigative procedures have been tried and failed or why they reasonably appear unlikely to succeed.

The Fourth Amendment to the Constitution is not violated even though the person who is the target of the investigation is not specifically named in the order where the investigation is directed at a widespread narcotics conspiracy. In the case of *United States v. Figueroa* the judge, after being furnished probable cause to believe an inmate of a United States Penitentiary was controlling the narcotics traffic within the prison, as well as conducting narcotics business outside the prison over ATU telephones, issued an order naming seven individuals as possible interceptees. The order included a provision that the interception shall continue until communications are intercepted which fully reveal the names of others "yet unknown."[79] The Court agreed that the mere fact that the order allowed interception of conversations of "others as yet unknown" does not render the statute unconstitutional on its face as authorizing a general warrant in violation of the Fourth Amendment.[80]

The fact that the courts have generally upheld the statute as constitutional does not settle the issue forever. In the lower federal courts the major issues concerning court-authorized electronic surveillance have centered around minimization and suppression. These issues will no doubt be brought up again. Also, there has been criticism concerning consensual electronic surveillance. It is anticipated that this, too, will be challenged in future cases. However, as of the date of this printing, the legislation has not been declared unconstitutional.

§ 5.18 Listening with the consent of one party

Prior to and following the *Katz* and *Berger* cases, enforcement officers used recorders and small microphones to overhear and record conversations between officers and suspects or between informers and suspects. This pro-

---

[79] United States v. Figueroa, 757 F.2d 466 (2d Cir. 1985), *cert. denied*, 474 U.S. 840, 106 S. Ct. 122, 88 L. Ed. 2d 100 (1985).

[80] For other cases concerning the constitutionality of Title 18, §§ 2510-2529, *see* United States v. Bailey, 607 F.2d 237 (9th Cir. 1979), *cert. denied*, 444 U.S. 934, 100 S. Ct. 327, 63 L. Ed. 2d 769 (1979); United States v. Feldman, 535 F.2d 1175 (9th Cir. 1976) *cert. denied*, 429 U.S. 940, 97 S. Ct. 354, 50 L. Ed. 2d 309 (9th Cir. 1976).

cedure has been challenged repeatedly, but it has been uniformly upheld. Several cases are discussed in order for the reader to have a better understanding of the law as it applies in different situations.

In an early case in 1952, the United States Supreme Court set out the rationale which served as a guide for the important cases that followed. In *On Lee v. United States*,[81] a Narcotics Bureau undercover agent wearing a small microphone and an antenna concealed in his overcoat entered the laundry of an old acquaintance. Unknown to the suspect, a second narcotics agent was stationed outside with a radio receiver set tuned in to that conversation. At the trial, the second agent was permitted to testify as to matters overheard. This procedure was challenged on the ground that it was an illegal search and seizure in violation of the Fourth Amendment. The United States Supreme Court rejected this argument. The rationale for admitting the evidence was that since the agent with the transmitter had entered the place of business with the consent, if not the implied invitation, of the petitioner, the petitioner could not complain when the agent arranged for transmission of the conversation he could not have related personally. The fact that the transmitter was concealed did not bring the situation within the ban of the Fourth Amendment.

In the 1963 case of *Lopez v. United States*,[82] the Supreme Court reconsidered its holdings in *On Lee*. The facts of the *Lopez*case were similar to those in *On Lee* except that only one officer was involved, and the conversation was taped rather than transmitted by way of a microphone. An Internal Revenue agent who had been offered a bribe was instructed by his superior officers to "play along." Outfitted with a miniature tape recorder, the agent went to the defendant's office and obtained incriminating evidence which was subsequently used to convict the defendant. On appeal, the United States Supreme Court affirmed the conviction, explaining that the petitioner took the risk that the officer would accurately reproduce the comments in court, whether by a faultless memory or mechanical recording.

Many similar decisions were handed down by the United States Supreme Court and lower courts prior to the 1968 wiretapping and electronic surveillance statutes. In 1966, the United States Supreme Court upheld the use of recordings of conversations between a police officer and a Mr. Osborn, one of James Hoffa's attorneys.[83] In this case, two federal district court judges had authorized the Federal Bureau of Investigation to conceal a recorder on the local police officer's person in order to get evidence con-

81 343 U.S. 747, 72 S. Ct. 967, 96 L. Ed. 1270 (1952).

82 373 U.S. 427, 83 S. Ct. 1381, 10 L. Ed. 2d 462 (1963).

83 Osborn v. United States, 385 U.S. 323, 87 S. Ct. 429, 17 L. Ed. 2d 394 (1966).

cerning an attempt to bribe a member of the jury panel in the James Hoffa trial.

And in 1968, the United States Court of Appeals for the Tenth Circuit approved the recording of an airport conversation between the suspect and an informer who had a transmitter hidden in his clothing.[84] Relying heavily on Mr. Justice White's concurring opinion in the *Katz* case, the majority of the judges reasoned that to allow a person to record a conversation between himself and another does not violate any Fourth Amendment protection.[85] Decisions similar to these were handed down by the United States Court of Appeals for the Fifth Circuit in *Dancy v. United States*[86] and by the Washington Supreme Court in *State v. Wright*.[87]

Following the passage of the 1968 Crime Control Act, the constitutionality of using information obtained from an informant who had a concealed transmitter on his person when talking with the suspect was again challenged.[88] In the *White* case the suspect was convicted of narcotic law violations. At the trial, evidence of incriminating statements made by the defendant and recorded by government agents was admitted. A government informant had consented to have a transmitter fixed to his person prior to talking with the defendant. One agent had the informant's consent to be in the kitchen closet where he heard the conversation. A second agent recorded the conversation from outside the house by means of a radio receiver. Although the prosecution was unable to locate and produce the informant at

---

84 Holt v. United States, 404 F.2d 914 (10th Cir. 1968).

85 *See* Katz v. United States, 389 U.S. 347, 88 S. Ct. 507, 19 L. Ed. 2d 576 (1976), in which Mr. Justice White added a footnote to his concurring opinion stating: "In previous cases, which are undisturbed by today's decision, the court has upheld as reasonable under the Fourth Amendment, admission at trial of evidence obtained (1) by an undercover police agent to whom a defendant speaks without knowledge that he is in the employ of the police, *Hoffa v. United States*, 385 U.S. 293; (2) by a recording device hidden on the person of such informant, *Lopez v. United States*, 373 U.S. 427; and (3) by a policeman listening to the secret microwave transmissions of an agent conversing with the defendant in another location, *On Lee v. United States*, 343 U.S 747. When one man speaks to another he takes all of the risks ordinarily inherent in so doing, including the risk that the man to whom he speaks will make public what he has heard....It is but a logical and reasonable extension of this principle that a man takes the risk that his hearer, free to memorize what he hears for later verbatim repetitions, is instead recording it or transmitting it to another."

86 390 F.2d 370 (5th Cir. 1968).

87 74 Wash. 2d 355, 444 P.2d 676 (1968).

88 United States v. White, 401 U.S. 745, 91 S. Ct. 1122, 28 L. Ed. 2d 453 (1971).

the trial, the trial court accepted testimony of the two agents. The defendant was found guilty in the lower court, but the Circuit Court of Appeals held that the testimony of the agents was impermissible under the Fourth Amendment and reversed the conviction.

Mr. Justice White wrote the majority opinion for the United States Supreme Court which concluded that this procedure did not violate the Fourth Amendment, reversing the Court of Appeals. The Court again explained the reasoning for such a holding, stating:

For constitutional purposes, no different result is required if the agent, instead of immediately reporting and transcribing his conversation with the defendant, either:

(1) simultaneously records them with electronic equipment which he is carrying on his person...
(2) or carries radio equipment which simultaneously transmits the conversations either to recording equipment located elsewhere or to other agents monitoring the transmitting frequency.

In April, 1979, the United States Supreme Court again affirmed its rule of the *Lopez* and *White* cases that consensual monitoring and recording by means of a transmitter concealed on an informant's person is not a violation of the Fourth Amendment even though the defendant did not know that he was speaking with a government agent.[89] The Court went further in this case by stating that evidence so acquired is admissible even if obtained in violation of the Internal Revenue Service regulations which prohibit such recordings unless approved by certain named authorities in the Internal Revenue Service. Since the Internal Revenue agents acted in good faith in permitting the eavesdropping, neither the violation of the rule nor the electronic eavesdropping itself violated due process, equal protection or the Fourth Amendment.

The Court also held that for constitutional purposes it makes no difference if the informer is unavailable for trial. This may raise evidentiary problems or pose issues of prosecutorial misconduct but does not present Fourth Amendment issues.

In 1988 the judges of the Second Federal Court of Appeals considered the legality of recording and monitoring telephone conversations between persons inside a correctional institution and a party on the outside.[90] In this case two inmates of the New York Metropolitan Correctional Center, who

---

89 United States v. Caceres, 440 U.S. 741, 99 S. Ct. 1465, 59 L. Ed. 2d 733 (1979).

90 United States v. Willoughby, 860 F.2d 15 (2d Cir. 1988). *See* Part II for portions of this case.

were awaiting trial, made calls to the defendant concerning the silencing of a witness who was to testify against the two inmates. The defendants were indicted in a five-count indictment in which they were charged with conspiracy to tamper with witnesses and to obstruct justice. Prior to the trial, the defense moved to suppress the tape recordings on the grounds that the taping of the conversation violated their rights under Title III of U.S.C. §§ 2510-2520 as amended in 1986.

Acknowledging that Title III of the Act generally prohibits the intentional interception of wire communications in the absence of authorization by court order, the Court nevertheless reiterated that the prohibition does not apply when "one of the parties to the communication has given prior consent to such interception." The Court further noted that the consent may be either express or implied; that the institution had advised inmates that their telephone calls would be monitored and such notice was prominently posted. Therefore, the inmates' use of the telephone constituted implied consent to the monitoring within the meaning of Title III.[91]

Based on the foregoing cases it is safe to state that there is no federal constitutional objection to the use of electronically recorded or transmitted conversations with others, whether accomplished by a police agent or a paid informant, if one party to the conversation is aware of and agrees to the recording. Nor does this practice violate the terms of Title III of the 1968 Crime Control Act. This practice is nothing more than recording what the hearer could memorize for later verbatim repetition.

But, even if the use of electronic surveillance equipment is permitted under the federal law, a state statute or constitutional provision may prohibit this use. For example, a majority of the Michigan Supreme Court held that the warrantless police monitoring of conversations between the defendant and an informer, by way of a radio transmitter concealed on the informer's person, violated the *state's* constitutional prohibition against unreasonable searches and seizures.[92] That state court acknowledged that while the United States Supreme Court found no Fourth Amendment prohibition against similar conduct in the *White* case, it placed a more restrictive interpretation on this practice under the Michigan Constitution.

Some states place additional requirements. For example, in Montana, the Supreme Court concluded that the use of all electronics for eavesdropping in the state must come to a halt, including the consent eavesdropping.[93]

---

91 *See also*, United States v. Amen, 831 F.2d 373 (2d Cir. 1987), *cert. denied*, __U.S.__, 108 S. Ct. 1573, 99 L. Ed. 2d 889 (1988) for a discussion of "consent" cases.

92 People v. Beavers, 393 Mich. 554, 227 N.W.2d 511 (1975).

93 State v. Hanley, 37 Mont. 427, 608 P.2d 104 (1980).

Also various interpretations of the Florida courts indicate that a warrant is required for consent surveillance especially where the conversation occurs inside the suspect's home.[94] Also, some state statutes such as Pennsylvania have amended their law to prohibit wiring informants.[95] Due to the state statutes and decisions limiting one party consent listening, it is necessary that the state statutes and decisions be reviewed.

§ 5.19 Other permissible warrantless listening interceptions and recordings

Federal wiretapping and electronic surveillance legislation have provided law enforcement agencies with sources of crime information which had been previously unavailable. Although the law condemns some electronic surveillance, it does not condemn all warrantless listening. Some of the statutorily approved exceptions have been mentioned previously. The purpose of this section is to bring together and examine those other instances where listening, recording or using electronic devices without first obtaining a warrant still remains permissible.

1. Listening not involving the interception of any wire or oral communication

Application for a court order authorizing listening is required under 18 U.S.C. § 2516(1) only where *"an interception of a wire or oral communication"* is contemplated. Excluded from statutory coverage are those instances where listening is accomplished without the aid of any sound amplifying or bugging apparatus.

In *United States v. McLeod,*[96] a government agent on four separate occasions stood a few feet from the defendant while she was placing a call at a public telephone and, without the aid of any listening device, overheard her give out sports-wagering information. The defendant objected to the use of this information on the ground that the government had failed to obtain an order authorizing interception of her communications. The Seventh Circuit, observing that no "interception" had taken place, ruled that a listening order was unnecessary. A similar result was reached in *United States v. Sin Nagh*

---

[94] Odom v. State, 403 So. 2d 936 (Fla. 1981); State v. Sarmiento, 397 S.2d 643 (Fla. 1981).

[95] PA. STAT. ANN. tit. 18, § 5705 (A) (Purdon Supp. 1978).

[96] 493 F.2d 1186 (7th Cir. 1974).

Fong[97] where agents staked out in an adjoining motel room and heard the defendant's conversation next door without the aid of any artificial voice magnifying equipment.

It would appear from these cases that where an agent is standing in a place where he has a lawful right to be at the time, he need not procure a warrant to eavesdrop on conversations audible to him without electronic or mechanical assistance.

2. *Pen registers*

A pen register is a device which records on paper all outgoing telephone numbers dialed from a particular phone and then cuts off without determining whether the call has been completed and without monitoring the actual conversation. Prior to the 1986 Electronic Communication Privacy Act, the use of a pen register did not violate chapter 119 of Title 18 of the United States Code. Both federal and state courts had held that as the device did not record any conversation but merely ascertained the number dialed from the defendant's phone, no court order was required.[98] Also the Supreme Court has clearly indicated the use of the pen register does not violate the Fourth Amendment.[99] In fact, the Court went a step further and ruled that an individual has no reasonable expectation of privacy with respect to dialed telephone numbers, therefore, the Fourth Amendment requirements do not apply.[100]

Nevertheless the 1986 Act prohibits the use of pen registers without a court order and establishes procedures for obtaining such an order.[101]

The 1986 Act relating to pen registers and trap and trace devices provides:

> Except as provided in this section, no person may install or use a pen register or trap and trace device without first obtaining a court order under Section 31123 of this Title or under the Foreign Intelligence Surveillance Act of 1978.

---

97 490 F.2d 527 (9th Cir. 1974).

98 People v. Smith, 31 Ill. App. 3d 423, 333 N.E.2d 241 (1975), *quoting* Bubit v. United States, 382 F.2d 607 (10th Cir. 1967).

99 United States v. New York Telephone Co., 434 U.S. 159, 98 S. Ct. 364, 54 L. Ed. 2d 376 (1977).

100 Smith v. Maryland, 442 U.S. 735, 99 S. Ct. 2577, 61 L. Ed. 2d 220 (1979).

101 18 U.S.C. §§ 3121-3126.

Under the terms of the Act, an attorney for the government or a law enforcement officer may make application for an order to a court of competent jurisdiction. The agent making the application must identify the law enforcement agency conducting the investigation and also must certify that the information likely to be obtained is relevant to an ongoing criminal investigation being conducted by that agency.

When an application is received, the court shall enter an ex parte order authorizing the installation and use of a pen register or a trap and trace device. The order must include the identity of the person upon whose telephone line the pen register or trap-and-trace device is to be attached, the identity, if known, of the person who is the subject of the investigation, the number of the telephone to which the pen register device is to be attached, and a statement of the offense to which the information relates. One favorable and positive aspect of the law is that the provider of the wire or electronic communications service as well as landlords, custodians, and other persons are required to cooperate with law enforcement agents in accomplishing the installation of the pen register.[102]

3. *Trap-and-trace devices*

Prior to the Electronic Communication Privacy Act of 1986, the United States Supreme Court ruled that placing a device which transmitted beeper signals inside a container which was sold to a person suspected of manufacturing illegal drugs, did not invade any legitimate expectation of privacy.[103] However, in *United States v. Karo* in 1984 the Court cautioned that such monitoring is within the parameters of the Fourth Amendment where the monitoring includes a beeper signal from a private residence as the defendants had a justifiable privacy interest.[104]

The Electronic Communication Privacy Act of 1986 amended Title 18 of the United States Code by inserting Chapter 206 which regulates the use of pen registers and trap-and-trace devices. The new section provides that "except as provided in that section, no person shall install or use a...trap or trace device without first obtaining a court order under section 3123 of this Title...This amended Act requires an application for an order for a trap and trace device similar to the order required for a pen register. Issuance of the order is justified if the court finds that the attorney for the government or in-

---

102 18 U.S.C. § 3124.

103 United States v. Knotts, 460 U.S. 276, 103 S. Ct. 1081, 75 L. Ed. 2d 55 (1983).

104 468 U.S. 705, 104 S. Ct. 3296, 82 L. Ed. 2d 530 (1984).

vestigating officer certifies to the court that the information likely to be obtained by such installation is relevant to an ongoing criminal investigation.[105]

As in the case of the pen register, the effect of the 1986 Amendment to the law is to require a court order or warrant for the use of beepers and other such devices even though such use does not violate the Fourth Amendment.

§ 5.20 Summary

Statutory provisions and cases governing the admissibility of evidence obtained by wiretapping, eavesdropping, and other electronic communication devices are of relatively recent origin when compared to other constitutional protections. The legal restrictions on electronic communications are closely related to laws restricting searches and seizures.

After several conflicting decisions and attempts by states to enact statutes that would permit wiretapping and eavesdropping, the Supreme Court of the United States decided that a New York statute which authorized the interception of communications when approved by judicial authority was invalid since it did not meet the requirements of the Fourth Amendment.

To bring some uniformity out of the confusion, Congress enacted Title III of the Omnibus Crime Control Act of 1968 which was codified as 18 U.S.C. §§ 2510-2520. After some modifications, the Electronic Communication Privacy Act of 1986 amended, updated and clarified the 1968 Act. This carefully drawn legislation generally prohibits interception of wire, oral, and other electronic communications, as defined in the Act, but makes some specific exceptions. It authorizes interception of wire, oral, or other communications by enforcement officers if:

(a) one party consents;
(b) a judicial officer by an *ex parte* order authorizes interception; or
(c) an officer determines that an emergency situation relating to national security or organized crime exists, provided he obtains judicial approval later.

---

105 § 3126 of the Act defines the term "trap and trace" device as a device which captures incoming electronic or other impulses which identify the originating number of an instrument or device from which a wire or electronic communication was transmitted.

The federal statute authorizes state officers to proceed under a state court order only if a state statute so provides. The federal statute does not make such an interception legal in those jurisdictions which have clearly statutory mandates forbidding the same. To make it possible for officers to make full use of the law, the state must enact measures to safeguard individual rights under a system of court orders which comply with the guidelines established by the federal law. In the absence of such state legislation, all wiretapping and eavesdropping and other communication interception, as defined by the statute, by state investigative individuals, except by consent of one party, is illegal, and the fruits thereof tainted beyond use in any state proceeding.

The comprehensive federal law provides that evidence obtained in accordance with the mandates of the Act will be admissible in court, while evidence obtained in violation of the provisions will not be admissible. In addition to criminal penalties, the law further authorizes the recovery of civil damages by a person whose communications have been unlawfully intercepted.

Neither the state statutes nor the Fourth Amendment prohibits listening with the consent of one party. However, some states by statute or court decision limit one party consent listening.

Although the courts have held that the warrantless use of pen registers and beepers do not violate the federal constitution, the Electronic Communication Privacy Act of 1986 prohibits such use unless a court order is obtained, provided, however, that this prohibition does not apply with respect to the use of a pen register or trap and trace device by a provider of electronic or wire communication services under certain specified conditions.

Although criminal justice personnel are restricted in obtaining evidence by the interception of communications, certain evidence obtained in this manner may be used if the laws are strictly observed. Reports submitted to the Administrative Office of the United States Courts indicate that electronic surveillance evidence has been valuable in apprehending and convicting violators, especially when used in the investigation of drug related crimes. To make the most effective use of this law enforcement tool, justice personnel should be thoroughly familiar with state and federal statutes. To utilize this legal method of obtaining evidence, state legislation should be enacted and procedures for obtaining orders should be established with the cooperation of prosecuting attorneys and judicial officers.

Chapter 6
INTERROGATIONS AND CONFESSIONS*

A confession is voluntary in law if, and only if, it was, in fact, voluntarily made....But a confession obtained by compulsion must be excluded whatever may have been the character of the compulsion, and whether the compulsion was applied in the judicial proceeding or otherwise.

Mr. Justice Brandeis
Ziang Sung Wan v. United States
266 US 1, 14 (1924)

Section

---

* *by John C. Klotter*

§ 6.1 Introductory remarks

The law concerning interrogations and confessions is not set out in any precise point in the Constitution, but derives from a mixture and fusing of several different provisions, with primary emphasis today on the Fifth Amendment privilege against self-incrimination and the Sixth Amendment guarantee of the right to counsel. As a means of enforcing the rights and privileges protected by the Fourth, Fifth, and Sixth Amendments, confessions are excluded from criminal prosecutions if obtained in violation of the rules which the courts have established.

The traditional approach to confessions and interrogations stressed the aspect of voluntariness and trustworthiness. When confessions were thrown out, it was traditionally because the court found that the confession was not freely and voluntarily made. Coercion and duress made the statements inherently suspect, and for this reason due process of law required exclusion.

A confession must pass at least five hurdles before it may be received as evidence in a court of law. First, it must pass the traditional test of voluntariness and trustworthiness. Secondly, it must meet those requirements established by the Supreme Court in the cases of *McNabb v. United States* and *Mallory v. United States*,[1] the so-called "delay in arraignment" test. More recently the Supreme Court has established additional requirements known as the *Miranda v. Arizona* requirements.[2] The courts have decided that a confession may be tainted by an illegal arrest or an illegal search. And failure to provide counsel may make the confession inadmissible. Each of these will be discussed in the sections that follow.[3]

These strict requirements limit the use of confessions, but questioning is a valuable technique in investigating offenses when used properly. Contrary to what some attorneys claim, statements from suspects are admissible. In fact, the Supreme Court in the *Miranda* case specifically pointed out that under certain conditions, statements may be obtained and used as evidence.[4]

---

1 McNabb v. United States, 318 U.S. 332, 63 S. Ct. 608, 87 L. Ed. 819 (1943); Mallory v. United States, 354 U.S. 449, 77 S. Ct. 1356, 1 L. Ed. 2d 1479 (1957), which is reprinted in Part II of this book.

2 *See generally* Miranda v. Arizona, 384 U.S. 436, 86 S. Ct. 1602, 16 L. Ed. 2d 694 (1966).

3 In *Miranda* the Court required that the accused be advised as to both his Fifth Amendment right against self-incrimination and his Sixth Amendment right to counsel. 384 U.S. at 467-73. The Sixth Amendment right to counsel is discussed in more detail in Chapter 8, *infra*.

4 *Id*. at 478. The portions of the text of this case included in Part II of this book should be carefully read.

Everyone involved in the criminal justice process should be thoroughly familiar not only with the restrictions placed upon questioning by officials, but also the reason for these restrictions. To protect society as well as the rights of the accused, criminal justice personnel also must be able to determine when questioning is proper and when it is preferable not to use it as an investigatory tool.

§ 6.2 The free and voluntary rule

At early common law an admission or confession was nonetheless admissible as evidence of guilt despite the fact that it was the product of force or duress. As a result, enforcement officers, rather than conducting a thorough investigation to establish guilt, resorted to torture in order to extract a confession from the accused. As society became more humane, these methods fell into disrepute. Given sufficient torture, even an innocent man might confess to a crime he had not committed. It was this risk that led to the ultimate abandonment of the common-law rule and the substitution both in England and the United States of what came to be known as the "free and voluntary" rule.

1. Statement of the rule

The free and voluntary rule is generally stated to be as follows:

> A confession of a person accused of crime is admissible in evidence against the accused only if it was freely and voluntarily made, without duress, fear, or compulsion in its inducement and with full knowledge of the nature and consequences of the confession.[5]

An Illinois case in 1926 gave this formulation of the rule:

> Confessions are competent evidence only when they are voluntarily made....Generally speaking, a confession is regarded as voluntary when it is made of the free will and accord of the accused, without fear or any threat of harm, or without promise or inducement by hope of reward.[6]

---

5 20 AM. JUR. *Evidence* § 482 (1939).

6 People v. Fox, 319 Ill. 606, 150 N.E. 347 (1926).

2. *Reasons for the rule*

The historic justification for the rule was that only voluntary confessions could be relied on as trustworthy. After the adoption of the Fifth Amendment with its provisions regarding self-incrimination, the courts began to express disagreement with the traditional rationale. In the 1897 case of *Bram v. United States*,[7] the Supreme Court stated that the competency of a confession as evidence was controlled by the self-incrimination clause of the Fifth Amendment. The following quotation is found in the opinion:

> In criminal trials, in the courts of the United States, whenever a question arises whether a confession is incompetent because [it is] not voluntary, the issue is controlled by that portion of the Fifth Amendment...commanding that no person "shall be compelled in any criminal case to be a witness against himself."[8]

This approach was approved by the majority in the *Miranda* case as the proper test to be employed in reviewing confessions from state courts as well, but there were four dissenters. Mr. Justice White, joined in his dissent by Justices Harlan and Stewart, stated that the rule announced by the majority was without support either in history or in the language of the Fifth Amendment. According to their views, the privilege against self-incrimination, as developed at common law, prohibited only compelled *judicial* interrogations. They found no authority for extending the privilege to out-of-court confessions and felt that the test of voluntariness should be maintained.

The free and voluntary rule advocated by the dissenters in *Miranda* is a more flexible approach than the position taken by the majority. Nevertheless, regardless of whether the courts adopt the traditional rationale or the view that ties the confession in with the protection against self-incrimination, voluntariness is still a crucial factor bearing on its competency as evidence.

3. *Factors to consider in determining whether a confession is voluntary*

Standards of voluntariness have been developed on a case-by-case basis without any attempt to formulate an all-inclusive definition. Such factors as the characteristics of the suspect, including his ability to resist various inducements, the length of the interrogation, and the techniques employed have been considered relevant by the courts in their inquiry.

---

7 168 U.S. 532, 18 S. Ct. 183, 42 L. Ed. 568 (1897).

8 *Id*. at 542.

Some of the factors which have been considered relevant by the courts in determining if the confessions are voluntary include the following:

(a) Use of force

Instances of physical brutality and the use of third degree methods to obtain a confession are rare, but unfortunately they still occur. These are the cases that reach the courts and reflect poorly on law enforcement. The majority in the *Miranda* case cited a recent incident in New York where a witness under interrogation was kicked and burned with a lighted cigarette butt. Such conduct will render a confession inadmissible even though independent evidence exists which substantiates the truth of the confession.[9] It is regrettable that conduct like this, though undoubtedly an exception today, is responsible for tightening the rules on interrogation in general.

(b) Threats or promises

Not only will actual physical force make a confession inadmissible, but threats of bodily harm or other threats that would cause a suspect to make statements against his will may also make a confession incompetent. In the case of *Payne v. Arkansas*[10] the United States Supreme Court reversed the conviction of a 19-year-old boy accused of murder because he had been held incommunicado for three days and was told that a mob was outside the jail to "get him."

In another case a threat by police officers to bring the accused's invalid wife to headquarters for questioning which prompted the accused to confess to murder was grounds for reversal.[11] And even a threat to a public employee that he could be removed from office if he did not cooperate made a confession inadmissible.[12]

The investigator must also be careful about making promises of leniency. A promise by the officer or the prosecutor to reduce or to drop the charge may result in a confession being inadmissible as involuntary.

(c) Psychological coercion

Although all courts have recognized that physical force will taint a confession and make it involuntary, there has been less harmony in the past concerning the use of trickery or psychological coercion in obtaining a confes-

9 Brown v. Mississippi, 297 U.S. 278, 56 S. Ct. 461, 80 L. Ed. 682 (1936).

10 356 U.S. 560, 78 S. Ct. 844, 2 L. Ed. 2d (1958).

11 Rogers v. Richmond, 365 U.S. 534, 81 S. Ct. 735, 5 L. Ed. 2d 760 (1961).

12 Garrity v. New Jersey, 385 U.S. 493, 87 S. Ct. 616, 17 L. Ed. 2d 562 (1967).

sion. In the *Miranda* case,[13] Mr. Chief Justice Warren observed that coercion can be mental as well as physical, and that the interrogation can become unconstitutional through the use of sufficient psychological pressure as well as physical duress. Warren cited, with disapproval, certain practices recommended in various police manuals and texts as contributing to the success of interrogations. Specifically he referred to techniques which are designed to put the subject in a psychological state where his story is but an elaboration of what the interrogator purports to know already -- namely, that the suspect is guilty. In condemning these procedures, the Chief Justice warned:

> It is obvious that such an interrogation environment is created for no purpose other than to subjugate the individual to the will of his examiner. This atmosphere carries its own badge of intimidation. To be sure, this is not physical intimidation, but it is equally destructive of human dignity....Unless adequate protective devices are employed to dispel the compulsion inherent in custodial surroundings, no statement obtained from the defendant can truly be the product of his free choice.[14]

While psychological coercion may make a confession involuntary and inadmissible, a confession resulting from hallucinations that interfere with the suspect's ability to make free and rational choices is admissible. By a 7-2 decision the Supreme Court ruled that a coercive police activity is required before a finding can be made that a confession is not voluntary within the meaning of the due process clause.[15] Therefore, it is not a violation of due process to admit into evidence a confession made by a person who walks up to a police officer and tells him he wishes to confess to a murder even if he has been "ordered by God" to make the confession.

Where the psychological coercion is combined with force and prolonged questioning, the confession may be inadmissible under the "totality of circumstances" test. In this regard the United States Court of Appeals for the Eighth Circuit determined that the confession of a murder defendant who had been questioned without nourishment about 25 times while handcuffed in a small hot room in the presence of six officers was involuntary under this test.[16] The majority, while admitting that the defendant was not a model prisoner and that there was substantial testimony indicating that he partici-

---

13 Miranda v. Arizona, 384 U.S. at 448.

14 *Id.* at 457-58.

15 Colorado v. Connelly, 107 U.S.515, 107 S. Ct. 515, 93 L. Ed. 2d 473 (1986).

16 Stidham v. Swenson, 506 F.2d 478 (8th Cir. 1974).

pated in a brutal killing in the penitentiary, still refused to justify the admission of the confession stating:

> We remain a government of laws, and those charged with law enforcement have a special responsibility to see that the guilty as well as the innocent are given the protection of the Constitution. If we depart from this principle, we deal the administration of justice a heavy blow.[17]

(d) Application of the free and voluntary rule to the states through the Fourteenth Amendment

If the highest court of a state upholds a confession as having been freely and voluntarily given, can the Supreme Court of the United States review this decision? This question was answered affirmatively in *Brown v. Mississippi* in 1936.[18]

In the *Brown* case the defendant and two other Negroes were charged with murder and offered pleas of "not guilty." During the investigation, the deputy sheriff and several other men accused the defendant of the crime. When he denied his guilt they seized him and twice hanged him by a rope to a limb of a tree. When he was let down the second time, he still protested his innocence and was tied to a tree and whipped. Finally he was released. A day or two later, the deputy and another person severely whipped the defendant again; declaring that the would continue to whip him until the defendant confessed. The defendant then agreed to confess to such a statement as the deputy would dictate and he did so, after which he was delivered to jail. Notwithstanding the fact that the whippings were admitted, the confessions were held to be admissible and the defendant was found guilty.

In reversing the decision of the state court, the United States Supreme Court stated the question as follows:

> The question in this case is whether convictions, which rest solely upon confessions shown to have been extorted by officers of the state by brutality and violence, are consistent with the due process of law required by the Fourteenth Amendment of the Constitution of the United States.[19]

---

17 *Id.* at 482.

18 297 U.S. 278, 56 S. Ct. 461, 80 L. Ed. 682 (1936).

19 *Id.* at 279.

The Court answered the question in the negative saying that confessions obtained in this manner were not freely and voluntarily given and a conviction based upon such a confession could not stand. The Court added:

> The state is free to regulate the procedure of its courts in accordance with its own conceptions of policy, unless in so doing it offends some principle of justice so rooted in the traditions and conscience of our people to be ranked as fundamental....The rack and torture chamber may not be substituted for the witness stand. The state may not permit an accused to be hurried to conviction under mob domination -- where the whole proceeding is but a mask -- without supplying corrective process.[20]

The United States Supreme Court in 1985 reaffirmed its authority to review confession cases, noting that the voluntariness of a confession is a matter that is subject to review by Federal Courts.[21] Although in this case the New Jersey Supreme Court had determined that the petitioner's confession was voluntary, the Supreme Court announced that it is not bound by a state court voluntariness finding, and that it is the historic duty of the United States Supreme Court to make an independent evaluation where the voluntariness of a confession is an issue.

Under the authority of the Fourteenth Amendment, the Supreme Court will review the facts surrounding a confession taken by state officers, and will reverse a decision based upon a confession if the standards do not comply with those established by that Court.

(e) Standards of proof

The Supreme Court has, on many occasions, reiterated the rule that only voluntary confessions may be admitted at the trial to determine guilt or innocence. A question which until recently had been left in doubt, however, concerned the standard of proof required in determining if a confession is voluntary. Quite a bit of light was shed on this question in the recent case, *Lego v. Twomey.*[22]

In this case a pre-trial suppression hearing was conducted to determine if instructions given in the lower court met the voluntariness standards. The judge in the lower court had not found the confession voluntary "beyond a reasonable doubt" and the defendant argued that this made the admissibility of the confession erroneous. The Supreme Court, however, disagreed. The

---

20 *Id.* at 285-86.

21 Miller v. Fenton, 474 U.S. 104, 106 S. Ct. 445, 88 L. Ed. 2d (1985).

22 404 U.S. 477, 92 S. Ct. 619, 30 L. Ed. 2d 618 (1972).

majority spokesman explained that the defendant is presumed innocent, and the burden falls on the prosecution to prove guilt beyond a reasonable doubt; but, the Court continued, "This is not the same burden that applies in determining the admissibility of a confession." In clearly stating the rule the Supreme Court commented:

> When a confession challenged as involuntary is sought to be used against a criminal defendant at the trial, he is entitled to a reliable and clearcut determination that the confession was in fact voluntarily rendered. Thus the prosecution must prove at least by a *preponderance of the evidence* that the confession was voluntary. (Emphasis added.)[23]

The Court resolved that the states are free, pursuant to their own law, to adopt higher standards such as the "beyond a reasonable doubt" standard, but that such a strict standard is not required by the Constitution.

Although state courts may require a higher standard than the preponderance of evidence test put forth by the Supreme Court in *Lego*, a Federal Court of Appeals cannot apply a tougher confession voluntariness standard.[24]

After discussing the ruling in the *Lego* case, the majority of the justices of the Fourth Circuit interpreted the mandate as follows:

> Upon this reading of *Lego*, the directions of *Inman* must be revised to admit those confessions into evidence where voluntariness is demonstrated by a preponderance of the evidence rather than the higher degree of proof.[25]

§ 6.3 The delay in arraignment rule

1. *Statement and discussion of rule*

In addition to the free and voluntary rule, the federal courts and some of the state courts have rejected confessions even though obtained freely and voluntarily where there was a delay in taking the person apprehended before a judicial officer as required by statute. Every state, as well as the United States, has a statute or code provision which provides that the person ar-

---

23 *Id.* at 489.

24 United States v. Johnson, 495 F.2d 378 (4th Cir. 1974). *See also* United States v. Cox, 485 F.2d 669 (5th Cir. 1973).

25 495 F.2d at 383.

rested must be taken "without unnecessary delay" or "forthwith" before the nearest available commissioner or other committing officer.

Prior to 1943, the fact that there had been delay in taking the accused before a committing magistrate did not in and of itself render the confession invalid. This delay was merely one of many factors which the courts would take into account in determining whether the confession was in fact freely and voluntarily given.

In the 1943 case of *McNabb v. United States*,[26] the Supreme Court for the first time began to insist on a strict and literal compliance with the federal rule requiring that prisoners be taken before a magistrate without undue delay. The case involved the murder of federal officers who were investigating a ring of bootleggers in Tennessee. Following the shooting, several members of the McNabb family were arrested by federal officers and later jailed. They were questioned intermittently over a period of several days and finally made incriminating statements. During the period of the questioning, they were not, so far as the record showed, taken before a United States commissioner or judge as required by the federal code. The Supreme Court, in reversing the conviction, rested its holding purely on the ground that evidence secured through a disregard of procedures established by Congress could not be allowed to stand.

Apparently the *McNabb* rule was somewhat forgotten, for in 1957 there was, to put it mildly, an expression of surprise when a rape conviction was set aside because the accused had not been brought before the judicial officer as required by the federal code. In the case of *Mallory v. United States*,[27] the Supreme Court vigorously reaffirmed the *McNabb* rule and dispelled all doubt regarding its future application in the federal courts. The complaining witness in the *Mallory* case had gone to the basement of her apartment house to wash some laundry. Having difficulty in detaching a hose, she sought help from the janitor, who lived in a basement apartment with his wife, two grown nephews, a younger son, and the petitioner, his 19-year-old half-brother. The janitor was not at home but the petitioner, who was alone in the apartment at the time, detached the hose and returned to his quarters. Shortly thereafter, a masked man, whose general features were identified to resemble those of the petitioner and his two grown nephews, attacked the woman.

The petitioner and one of his grown nephews disappeared from the apartment house shortly after this rape was committed. The petitioner was apprehended between 2:00 and 2:30 p.m. the following afternoon along with his older nephews who were also suspects. After questioning by the police, the three suspects were asked to submit to lie detector tests at about 4:00

---

[26] 318 U.S. 332, 68 S. Ct. 608, 87 L. Ed. 819 (1943).

[27] 354 U.S. 449, 77 S. Ct. 1356, 1 L. Ed. 2d 1479 (1957).

p.m. The operator of the polygraph was not located for about two hours during which time the suspects received food and drink. The petitioner was questioned starting about 8:00 p.m., and about one and one-half hours later he stated that he might have done it. An attempt was made to reach the United States Commissioner after 10:00 p.m., but when the commissioner was not located Mallory was requested to repeat the confession, which he did. Between 11:30 p.m. and 12:30 a.m., he dictated the confession to a typist. He was not brought before the United States Commissioner until the next morning.

Notwithstanding this delay the confession was admitted into court, Mallory was found guilty of rape, and the jury imposed the death sentence. In reversing the conviction, the Court said:

> We cannot sanction this extended delay, resulting in confession, without subordinating the general rule of prompt arraignment to the discretion of arresting officers in finding exceptional circumstances for its disregard. In every case where the police resort to interrogation of an arrested person and secure a confession, they may well claim, and quite sincerely, that they were merely trying to check the information given by him....It is not the function of the police to arrest, as it were, at large and to use an interrogation process at police headquarters in order to determine whom they should charge before a committing magistrate on "probable cause."[28]

Here the Court did not even consider the free and voluntary rule but reversed the confession merely because there had been a delay in bringing the accused before the United States Commissioner.[29]

2. *Application in federal courts*

The *McNabb* rule of 1943 was the result of a federal case involving the murder of a federal officer. Mallory was charged with rape, but because the alleged crime occurred in the District of Columbia, it was tried in federal court and the Federal Rules were followed. The statute which required that persons arrested be taken without unnecessary delay before the United

---

28 *Id.* at 455-56.

29 It is interesting to note that Mallory was not prosecuted on this charge since there was little evidence without the confession. However, in May, 1960, he was prosecuted in Philadelphia on a charge of rape and burglary, found guilty of burglary and aggravated assault. He was sentenced to serve 20 years on the burglary charge and 18 months on the assault count, with sentences to run consecutively.

States Commissioner applied only to federal courts. Therefore, the *McNabb-Mallory* rule, that in federal courts and in federal procedures a confession will not be admissible if obtained during that period when the arrested person should, according to federal law, have been brought before a federal judicial officer, as originally published, was limited to federal courts and did not apply in state courts.

3. *Application to the states*

Prior to *Miranda* the Supreme Court of the United States had not reversed a state court decision solely on the ground that the confession was obtained during a delay in arraignment. However, in the case of *Culombe v. Connecticut*,[30] one of the factors considered by the Supreme Court in reversing a state decision was the delay in arraignment.

The wording of the *Miranda* case mandates that the "delay in arraignment" rule be applied to state court proceedings. Justice Warren, writing for the majority, asserted that the *McNabb-Mallory* rule had received little consideration in the past quarter of a century, but that:

> These supervisory rules, requiring production of an arrested person before a commissioner without unnecessary delay and excluding evidence obtained in default of that statutory obligation, were nonetheless responsive to the same considerations of the Fifth Amendment policy that face us now as to the States.[31]

Tying this rule with the decision in a previously decided case, Justice Warren continued:

> Our decision in *Malloy v. Hogan*...necessitates an examination of the scope of the privilege in state cases as well. In *Malloy*, we squarely held the privilege applicable to the States, and held that the substantive standards underlying the privilege applied with full force to the state court proceedings.[32]

This answered the question which many police officials, prosecutors and judges had been considering: that is, when would the *McNabb - Mallory* rule be made applicable to the states? Although there has been no decision specifically concerning this issue since *Miranda*, and there may not be one

---

30 367 U.S. 568, 81 S. Ct. 1860, 6 L. Ed. 2d 1073 (1961). *See* Part II for portions of this case.

31 Miranda v. Arizona, 384 U.S. at 463.

32 *Id*. at 463-64.

because of the other requirements of the *Miranda* case, it is anticipated that if a state case reaches the Supreme Court on the delay in arraignment rule exclusively, this rule will be made applicable to the states through the Fourteenth Amendment.

4. *Determining "without unnecessary delay"*

Because the *Mallory*[33] case did not state or define what was an "unnecessary delay," hundreds of cases have been decided in an attempt to reach a definition. In *Mallory* the petitioner was apprehended at about 2:30 p.m. but no attempt was made to reach the United States Commissioner until after 10 p.m. This delay was too long, but there were some factors which aggravated the situation. One was the fact that the Commissioner was in the same building as the federal agents who apprehended and interviewed the suspect and was readily available.

The Supreme Court has determined that it is not an unnecessary delay if the suspect voluntarily confesses while the police are awaiting the time when the Commissioner's office will be open. This is a *necessary* delay and would not affect the admissibility of the confession. Also, if the delay occurs after the confession, the delay will not make the confession inadmissible if the confession were made voluntarily and the other safeguards met.[34]

Congress, recognizing that the *Mallory* rule was not only ambiguous but placed an unnecessary burden on law enforcement officers, enacted legislation in 1968 which modified the *McNabb-Mallory* requirements. The part of that act which deals with the problem is as follows:

> In any criminal prosecution by the United States or by the District of Columbia, a confession made or given by a person who is a defendant therein, while such person was under arrest or other detention in the custody of any law-enforcement officer or law-enforcement agency, shall not be inadmissible solely because of delay in bringing such person before a commissioner or other officer empowered to commit persons charged with offenses against the laws of the United States or of the District of Columbia if such confession is found by the trial judge to have been made voluntarily and if the weight to be given the confession is left to the jury and if such confession was made or given by such person within *six hours* immediately following his arrest or other detention: *provided*, That the time limitation contained in this subsection shall not apply in any

---

33 Mallory v. United States, 354 U.S. at 450-51. *See* Part II for portions of this case.

34 United States v. Mitchell, 322 U.S. 65, 64 S. Ct. 896, 88 L. Ed. 1140 (1944).

> case in which the delay in bringing such person before such commissioner or other officer beyond such six-hour period is found by the trial judge to be reasonable considering the means of transportation and the distance to be traveled to the nearest available such commissioner or other officer.[35]

This in effect states that a confession shall not be inadmissible in a federal court solely because the confession was obtained during the delay in arraignment. The act establishes the time as six hours between arrest and the making of the confession but gives the judge discretion to admit the confession even if more than six hours have elapsed if the judge finds the delay reasonable.

Because of the six hours mentioned in the Omnibus Crime Control Act, some attorneys representing defendants who gave voluntary statements claimed that if a person is detained more than six hours, a confession after that time is inadmissible for that reason. Two United States Courts of Appeals have disagreed.[36] A majority of the members of each court indicated that the six-hour period as established by Congress was a period in which a confession can be obtained and not be challenged solely because of delay in bringing the person before a magistrate. But if a longer delay occurs, it merely constitutes another factor to be considered by the trial judge in determining voluntariness.

While a number of delays for law enforcement purposes, including fingerprinting and other processing, are "necessary" delays within the meaning of the statute,[37] an unexplained 43-hour delay between arrest and arraignment is unreasonable,[38] and a confession obtained during this unnecessary delay is not admissible.

A state court, the Indiana Court of Appeals for the First District, agrees that a delay of more than six hours (26 hours in this case) should not by itself render a confession obtained during that period inadmissible.[39] In interpreting the state law, which is identical to the federal law, the Indiana court confirmed that the delay is but one factor to be considered in determining the admissibility of a confession taken more than six hours after the defendant's arrest.

---

35 Omnibus Crime Control and Safe Streets Act of 1968 § 701(c), 82 Stat. 210. This section of the Act is found in 18 U.S.C. § 3501(c) (1970).

36 United States v. Hathorn, 451 F.2d 1337 (5th Cir. 1971); United States v. Halbert, 436 F.2d 1226 (9th Cir. 1970).

37 United States v. Rondon, 614 F. Supp. 667 (D.C.N.Y. 1985).

38 United States v. Khan, 625 F. Supp. 868 (S.D.N.Y. 1986).

39 Apple v. State, 304 N.E.2d 321 (Ind. 1974).

"Unnecessary delay" depends upon the facts and circumstances of each case. If, as in the *Mallory* case, the judicial officer is readily available, the arrest is made during the office hours of the judicial officer, and there is no justification for not taking the person arrested before him for a hearing, the delay will probably be considered an unnecessary delay. On the other hand, if the arrest is made in the evening when no judicial officer is available, or if the arrest is made some distance from the judicial officer so that it is not practical to take the person arrested before the officer within the six-hour period, the delay will probably be considered necessary, and a confession, even if obtained during the period of delay, will be admitted if other requirements are met.

§ 6.4 Warning and waiver requirements (Miranda rule)

Up to this point two rules relating to the admissibility of confessions have been discussed: (1) The traditional "free and voluntary" rule, and (2) the later "delay in arraignment" rule. In 1966 the Supreme Court of the United States, by way of judicial decision, established further requirements which must be met before a confession is admissible into evidence.[40]

1. *Statement and discussion of warning and waiver requirements*

In the *Miranda* case the Supreme Court not only reversed the decision of a lower court which had upheld the use of a confession, but affirmatively enumerated warnings that must be given by enforcement officials. In summarizing the many points discussed in the case, the majority concluded that when an individual is taken into custody or otherwise deprived of his freedom by the authorities and is subject to questioning, he must be given the following warnings:

(1) "You have the right to remain silent and say nothing."
(2) "If you do make a statement, anything you say can and will be used against you in court."
(3) "You have the right to have an attorney present or to consult with an attorney."
(4) "If you cannot afford an attorney, one will be appointed for you prior to any questioning if you so desire."[41]

---

40 Miranda v. Arizona, 384 U.S. 436, 86 S. Ct. 1602, 16 L. Ed. 2d 694 (1966). *See* Part II for portions of case.

41 *Id.* at 444. The Supreme Court left the door open for an exception when it stated: "However, unless we are shown other procedures which are at least as effective in

Not only must these warnings be given initially, but opportunity to exercise these rights must be afforded throughout the questioning. If the accused indicates at any stage of the questioning that he does not wish to be interrogated or that he wishes to consult an attorney, the questioning must stop.

The rights may be waived, but the waiver must be made voluntarily, knowingly and intelligently. However, a valid waiver will not be presumed simply from the silence of the accused after the warnings are given. Also, a waiver will not be considered as voluntary if there is valid evidence that the accused was threatened, tricked or cajoled.

Although the case in which these requirements were established is known as the *Miranda* case, there were in fact four cases incorporated into the decision. The confessions in the case of *Miranda v. Arizona* and each of the three companion cases, *Vignera v. New York*, *Westover v. United States* and *California v. Stewart*, were declared inadmissible by the United States Supreme Court. In *Miranda* and *Vignera*, the decisions of the state courts were reversed because the accused had not been effectively warned of his right to remain silent and of his right to have counsel. In *Westover* the confessions were inadmissible even though the defendant had been warned of his rights by the FBI agents prior to the taking of the statements, because the federal authorities were the beneficiaries of the pressures applied during the local in-custody interrogation, where no warnings were given. And in the *Stewart* case, the United States Supreme Court affirmed the action of the California Supreme Court which had rejected the confession because the warnings were not given.

To obtain a complete understanding of the case it should be read in its entirety, and all of the facts of the four cases studied. Here, only the facts relating to *Miranda* are stated and discussed. Ernesto Miranda was arrested on March 13 by Phoenix police officers and taken to the interrogation room where he was questioned by two police officers. He was not advised that he had a right to have an attorney present, but signed a statement that the confession was made voluntarily and was advised that the statement "may be used against him." After two hours he confessed to kidnapping and rape. The confession so obtained was admitted at the trial and he was sentenced to 20 to 30 years' imprisonment.

The Arizona Supreme Court affirmed the conviction, and appeal was taken to the United States Supreme Court. The United States Supreme Court reversed the Arizona Supreme Court decision and declared the confession inadmissible. That majority decided that Miranda was not apprised of

---

apprising accused persons of their right of silence and in assuring a continuous opportunity to exercise it, the...safeguards must be observed." *Id.* at 467.

his right to counsel nor effectively of his right not to be compelled to incriminate himself. Also, the fact that the typed statement indicating the confession was voluntary did not approach the knowing and intelligent waiver required to relinquish constitutional rights.

The format of the *Miranda* case is unusual. Ordinarily the facts of a case are stated at the beginning, with the reasoning coming after the facts, and the court decision coming last. The *Miranda* decision starts with a discussion of the rules, with page after page of an account of other cases, tactics used by police officers, police literature and rules to be followed in future cases, and ends with the facts of the four cases.

Although two constitutional questions -- the right to counsel and self- incrimination -- were both discussed throughout the case, the Supreme Court of the United States made it clear that the decision was predicated on the Fifth Amendment privilege against self-incrimination. Referring to the Fifth Amendment in at least a half-dozen places, the Court included this remark:

> In order to combat these pressures and to permit a full opportunity to exercise the *privilege against self-incrimination*, the accused must be adequately and effectively apprised of his rights and the exercise of those rights must be fully honored. [Emphasis added.][42]

2. *Judicial interpretation of "custodial interrogation"*

In several instances the majority in the *Miranda* case limited the warning and waiver requirements by prefixing these with such words as:

> ...the prosecution may not use statements, whether exculpatory or inculpatory, stemming from *custodial interrogation* of the defendant unless it demonstrates the use of procedural safeguards effective to secure the privilege against self-incrimination. [Emphasis added.][43]

And in another place the summary statement includes this conclusion:

> We hold that when an individual is taken into *custody* or otherwise deprived of his freedom by the authorities *and subjected to questioning*, the privilege against self-incrimination is jeopardized. [Emphasis added.][44]

---

42 *Id*. at 467.

43 *Id*. at 444.

44 *Id*. at 478.

In the case "custodial interrogation" is defined as:

> We mean *questioning* initiated by law enforcement officers after a person has been taken into *custody* or otherwise deprived of his freedom of action in any significant way. [Emphasis added.][45]

(a) Custody Defined

The definitions in the *Miranda* case do not clearly indicate the meaning of "custody" or "interrogation." A series of cases, however, has made it abundantly clear that unless the accused is in custody or otherwise deprived of his freedom in a significant way, the warnings are not required.

A fine line exists as to whether a suspect is in "custody" or is not in "custody" so as to make the *Miranda* advice necessary. Factors to consider in determining if the person being interviewed is in "custody" are:

(1) the environment,
(2) the number of officers present and their attitude toward the person being questioned,
(3) the stage of the investigation, that is, whether the investigation is still in an investigatory stage, and
(4) if the interviewee is free to leave. Some cases will help clarify this issue.

In one of the earlier cases which followed soon after the *Miranda* case, the United States Supreme Court decided that a statement taken at the home of the suspect without the *Miranda* warnings was not admissible.[46] In that case, however, four police officers arrived at the suspect's boarding house at 4:00 a.m., entered the bedroom and began to question the suspect. As, according to the officers' own testimony, petitioner was under arrest and not free to leave when he was questioned in his bedroom in the early hours of the morning, he was in custody for *Miranda* purposes.

On the other hand, an interrogation at the police station was not "in custody" where the person interviewed voluntarily reported to the police station, was informed that he was not under arrest, was interviewed for one half hour and left without hindrance.[47] In the case of *Oregon v. Mathiason* the suspect, after talking with the investigator on the phone, voluntarily arrived at the station, shook hands with the officer, and voluntarily accompanied the

---

45 *Id*. at 444.

46 Orozco v. Texas, 394 U.S. 324, 89 S. Ct. 1095, 22 L. Ed. 2d 311 (1969).

47 Oregon v. Mathiason, 492 U.S. 492, 97 S. Ct. 711, 50 L. Ed. 2d 714 (1977).

officer to his office. The defendant was told he was not under arrest and was not given the *Miranda* warnings. The officer advised the suspect that the police believed the defendant was involved in burglary and falsely stated that defendant's fingerprints were found at the scene. After considering this for a few minutes, the suspect said he had taken the property. At the end of the taped conversation, the officer told the defendant he was not arresting him at that time and the suspect was released to go about his job and return to his family.

The court distinguished this from the facts of *Orozco v. Texas*, but pointed out in this case that there was no indication that the questioning took place in a context where respondent's freedom to depart was restricted in any way. The Court commented that "it is clear from these facts that Mathiason was not in custody "or otherwise deprived of his freedom of action in any significant way." In explaining this was not a custodial situation the court remarked:

> Such a non-custodial situation is not converted to one in which *Miranda* applies simply because a reviewing court concludes that, even in the absence of any formal arrest or restraint on freedom of movement, the questioning took place in a "coercive environment." Any interview of one suspected of a crime by a police officer will have coercive aspects to it, simply by virtue of the fact that the police officer is a part of the law enforcement system which will ultimately cause the suspect to be charged with a crime. But police officers are not required to administer *Miranda* warnings to everyone whom they question. Nor is the requirement of warnings to be imposed simply because the questioning takes place in the station house, or because the questioned person is one whom the police suspect. *Miranda* warnings are required only where there has been such a restriction on a person's freedom as to render him "in custody." It was that sort of coercive environment to which *Miranda* by its terms was made applicable, and to which it is limited.

Is a person a subject of custodial interrogation when he is stopped on the road when suspected of a traffic offense? By an eight-to-one majority, the U.S. Supreme Court held that roadside questioning during a routine traffic stop does not constitute custodial interrogation unless the officer subjects the motorist to treatment that renders him in custody. When the freedom of action of the motorist is curtailed to a degree associated with formal arrest, *Miranda* becomes applicable.[48]

---

48 Berkemer v. McCarty, 468 U.S. 420, 104 S. Ct. 3138, 82 L. Ed. 2d 317 (1984).

In a *per curiam* opinion the Supreme Court in 1988 referred to the *Berkemer* reasoning in reversing a decision of the Superior Court of Pennsylvania because that Court had indicated that roadside questioning made the confession inadmissible.[49] Making reference to *Berkemer v. McCarty* the majority repeated that:

> ...the noncoercive aspect of ordinary traffic stops prompts us to hold that persons temporarily detained pursuant to such stops are not "in custody" for purposes of *Miranda*.

After making this comment, the Court found that accordingly, the person who was stopped for a traffic violation "was not entitled to a recitation of his constitutional rights prior to arrest, and his roadside responses to questioning were admissible."

The "custody question" has arisen in many arenas. Some of these are related to give a more thorough picture of the issue.

In a North Carolina case, the Court of Appeals indicated that a defendant who voluntarily takes a polygraph test administered by a state agent is not in custody during or after the test so as to be entitled to a full warning of Constitutional rights.[50] The court reasoned that a constitutional rights warning before questioning by an officer is not required when the person questioned is not in custody. Custody, the court continued, in turn depends upon whether or not a reasonable person confronting the officer would feel free to leave under all the circumstances.

The Texas Court of Criminal Appeals confirmed what other courts have decided on many occasions: that stopping a traffic offender is not necessarily taking "custody" of the person.[51] Since the traffic offender was not in custody, under the facts of this case, his response to the officer's question about possession of a weapon, as a traffic ticket was being written, was not the product of a custodial interrogation.

On the other hand a gambling suspect -- although not formally arrested -- who was surrounded at his place of business with 20 armed agents was in custody, and evidence obtained after he had been asked if he had any concealed weapons nearby was not admissible according to the Fifth Circuit Court of Appeals.[52]

The question has arisen as to whether a person who is on parole or probation or one who is incarcerated is "in custody" as to require the *Miranda*

---

49 Pennsylvania v. Bruder, __U.S.__, 109 S. Ct. 205, __L. Ed. 2d__ (1988).

50 State v. Jeffries, 55 N.C. App. 269, 285 S.E. 2d 307 (1982).

51 Wussow v. State, 507 S.W. 2d 792 (Tex. 1974).

52 United States v. Castellana, 488 F.2d 65 (5th Cir. 1974).

warnings. The courts have not agreed on an answer. In the case of *Childers v. Commonwealth*,[53] the Kentucky Court of Appeals concluded that *Miranda* warnings are not required in an interview between a probation officer and his client. Referring to a federal case the Kentucky Court pointed out the reasoning in making this finding is that the privilege against self-incrimination is fundamentally inconsistent with the acquisition and maintenance of probationary status.

But according to the Maryland Court of Appeals, while agreeing that as a general matter lawful detention or imprisonment necessarily makes many rights and privileges unavailable to an inmate, persons in custody are not deprived of their Fifth Amendment rights.[54] In determining that a jailed inmate must be given the *Miranda* warnings before he is questioned by jail officials about a gun he allegedly cached at the institution, the Maryland Court held that the defendant was in "custody." Distinguishing between the Fourth Amendment rights and the guarantees contained in the Fifth and Sixth Amendments, that Court found:

> Thus, the Fifth Amendment guarantee against compulsory self-incrimination, being different in nature from other constitutionally established individual liberties, should not, in our opinion, be diminished by the needs of penal administration to the extent that such statements may be utilized in a criminal prosecution.

The United States Supreme Court in 1984 considered the question of whether a probationer is in custody during court-ordered sessions with his probation officer.[55] After discussing the custody question, the Court agreed that this was not a custody situation, and the admonishment that the probationer be truthful in all matters did not amount to questioning.

(b) Questioning defined

Most of the cases decided since the *Miranda* warning have concerned the definition of "custody." But both "custody" and "interrogation" are elements that must be present in order to mandate the *Miranda* warnings.

In *Miranda* the Court elaborated that by "custodial interrogation, we mean questioning initiated by law enforcement officers." Does this mean there must be actual specific questions to constitute "interrogation" as used in the case? For almost 14 years this question concerned law enforcement per-

---

53 Childers v. Kentucky, 593 S.W. 2d 80 (Ky. 1979).

54 Whitfield v. State, 411 A.2d 415 (Md. 1980).

55 Minnesota v. Murphy, 465 U.S. 420, 104 S. Ct. 1136, 79 L. Ed. 2d 409 (1984).

sonnel and lower courts. In 1980, however, the Supreme Court for the first time faced the question as to what constitutes "interrogation."[56]

In the *Innis* case the defendant was arrested after a robbery victim identified his photograph. At the time he was arrested on the street, he was advised of his rights and was again twice advised of his rights when other police officers arrived at the arrest scene. The suspect was then placed into a police car to be driven to the central station in the custody of three officers who were instructed by a superior officer not to question respondent or to intimidate him in any way. While en route to the station, two of the officers engaged in a conversation between themselves concerning the missing shotgun. One of the officers stated that there were "a lot of handicapped children running around in this area and God forbid one of them might find a weapon with shells and they might hurt themselves." The statement was not directed to the suspect nor did the officers indicate that they expected an answer. However, the respondent interrupted the conversation, stating that the officers should turn the car around so that he could show them where the gun was located. Upon returning to the scene of the arrest where a search for the shotgun was in progress, the respondent was again advised of his *Miranda* rights. He replied he understood those rights, but that he "wanted to get the gun out of the way because of the kids in the area in the school." He then led the police to the shotgun.

Before the trial, the trial court denied the suspect's motion to suppress the shotgun and the statements he made to the police, holding that the respondent had waived his *Miranda* rights and respondent was subsequently convicted. The Rhode Island Supreme Court set aside the conviction and held the respondent was entitled to a new trial, concluding that he had invoked his *Miranda* rights and that the police officers had "interrogated" him without a valid waiver of rights.

The United States Supreme Court first stated the rule regarding the term "interrogation."

> We conclude that *Miranda* safeguards come into play whenever a person in custody is subjected to either express questioning or its functional equivalent. That is to say, the term "interrogation" under *Miranda* refers not only to express questioning, but also to any words or actions on the part of the police (other than those normally attendant to arrest and custody) that the police should know are reasonably likely to elicit an incriminating response from the suspect. The latter portion of this definition focuses primarily upon the perceptions of the suspect, rather than the intent of the police.

---

56 Rhode Island v. Innis, 446 U.S. 289, 100 S. Ct. 1682, 64 L. Ed. 2d 297 (1980).

> This focus reflects the fact that the *Miranda* safeguards were designed to vest a suspect in custody with an added measure of protection against coercive police practices, without regard to objective proof of the underlying intent of the police.

After framing this definition the Court applied the definition to the facts of the case. The Court in declining to hold that the dialogue between the two officers amounted to interrogation held rather that the conversation was at least in form "nothing more than a dialogue between the two officers to which no response from the respondent was invited."

Does this *Innis* decision clarify *Miranda* or only add additional questions? Chief Justice Burger, who concurred in the decision but not the reasoning, claimed the definition was not necessary. He indicated that he felt that the Court's opinion will not clarify the requirements of *Miranda* but will "...introduce new elements of uncertainty; under the Court's test, a police officer in the brief time available, apparently must evaluate the suggestibility and susceptibility of the accused." The final paragraph of Mr. Justice Burger's decision expresses his concern:

> Trial judges have enough difficulty discerning the boundaries and nuances flowing from post-*Miranda* opinions, and we do not clarify that situation today.

Applying the *Innis* rule, a majority of the District of Columbia Court of Appeals indicated that *Miranda* may be offended when officers continue to discuss the case by answering the suspect's questions about the evidence against him after the defendant has said, "I have nothing to say."[57] In the *Wilson* case the majority noted that the officers had agreed among themselves to reveal more of the knowledge about the crime, hoping that the defendant would change his mind and give them a statement. Following this strategy they identified the person who had implicated the defendant without asking questions of the defendant. The defendant then indicated that he was "flabbergasted" and agreed to make a statement. The reviewing court reasoned that these tactics come within the *Innis* definition of interrogation.

Does the *Innis* ruling require exclusion of a statement made where police allowed the defendant's wife to speak with the defendant in the presence of the officer and where the conversation was tape-recorded? In the case of *Arizona v. Mauro*, the defendant who was in custody for killing his son stated that he did not wish to answer any questions until a lawyer was present.[58] All

---

57 Wilson v. United States, 444 A.2d 25 (D.C. 1982).

58 Arizona v. Mauro, __U.S.__, 107 S. Ct. 1931, __L. Ed. 2d__ (1987).

questioning ceased and the respondent was placed in the police captain's office. In another room, the defendant's wife insisted that she be allowed to speak with her husband. The police reluctantly allowed the meeting in the office on the condition that an officer be present. Using a tape recorder placed in plain sight, the officer taped a brief conversation, during which the wife expressed despair and the defendant told her not to answer any questions until a lawyer was present. The prosecution used the tape to rebut the defendant's insanity defense, and the defendant was convicted and sentenced to death.

The Arizona Supreme Court, in reversing the decision of the lower court, held that the police had impermissibly interrogated the defendant within the meaning of *Miranda*. Referring to the case of *Rhode Island v. Innis*, the Arizona court indicated that the action on the part of the officers was the functional equivalent of interrogation after the suspect had requested counsel.

The Supreme Court ruled, however, that as long as police do not question suspects directly, or do not use subterfuge or "psychological ploy" to try to get suspects to say something incriminating, recording of their conversation does not violate the suspect's rights under the *Miranda* rule. Justice Powell, writing for the majority, explained that police departments need not adopt inflexible rules that would keep suspects from talking to each other at the station; the Court noted that:

> ...officers do not interrogate a suspect simply by hoping he will incriminate himself.

Thus, respondent's statements to his wife were voluntary, and their use at the trial was not prohibited under the Fifth and Fourteenth Amendments.

To summarize, if the suspect is in custody as discussed in previous paragraphs and is to be asked pertinent questions, the *Miranda* warnings must be administered. Also, if the suspect is in custody, and if the officer uses words or acts in such a way that he should know would reasonably be likely to elicit incriminating responses from the suspect, then here too the warnings must be given. The knowledge standard referred to includes anything the officers know or should know about the particular suspect, such as his current mental and emotional condition, which would trigger a response from the suspect.

3. *Adequacy of Warning*

In the *Miranda* case the majority of the Supreme Court, in referring to the warning required repeated, "he must be warned prior to any questioning" and then continued with some specific warnings that are required and which are stated in the previous paragraphs. In that same paragraph, however, the court indicated that unless other effective means are adopted to notify the person of his right to silence and to assure him that the exercise of these rights will be honored, the specific warnings must be administered.[59] The question then arises: "What if the suspect is warned of his rights, but the warnings are not in the specific terminology used in the *Miranda* case?" Although some courts soon after the *Miranda* decision demanded that the warnings be given in the exact words of *Miranda*, others gradually began to recognize the miscarriage of justice that resulted from such a rigid rule.[60] After some conflicting Court of Appeals decisions, the United States Supreme Court, in a per curiam opinion, directly faced the issue.[61] In the *Prysock* case the decision began with this question:

> This case presents the question whether the warnings given to respondent prior to a recorded conversation with a police officer satisfied the requirements of *Miranda v. Arizona*...

The Court of Appeals for the Fifth Appellate District reversed the respondent's conviction because the respondent had not been explicitly informed of his right to have an attorney appointed before further questioning.

The United States Supreme Court reversed and used these words to clarify the requirements:

> This Court has never indicated the "rigidity" of *Miranda* extends to the precise formulation of the warnings given a criminal defendant...This Court and others *have* stressed as one virtue of *Miranda* the fact that the giving of the warning obviates the need for a case-by-case inquiry into the actual voluntariness of the admissions of the accused...Nothing in these observations suggest any desirable rigidity in the *form* of the required warnings.

The United States Supreme Court explained that as the police had fully conveyed to the defendant his rights in substance, the court of appeals erred in holding that the warnings were inadequate simply because of the order in which they were given.

The adequacy of the warning again reached the Supreme Court in 1989 in the case of *Duckworth v. Eagan*.[62] In this case the defendant confessed to

---

59 Miranda v. Arizona, 384 U.S. 436, 86 S. Ct. 1602, 16 L. Ed. 2d 694 (1966).

60 United States ex rel. Williams v. Toomey, 467 F.2d 1248 (7th Cir. 1972).

61 California v. Prysock, 453 U.S. 355, 101 S. Ct. 2806, 69 L. Ed. 2d 696 (1981).

62 Duckworth v. Eagan, __U.S.__, 109 S. Ct. 2875, __L. Ed. 2d__ (1989). *See* Part II for portions of this case.

stabbing a woman nine times after she refused to have sexual relations with him, and he was convicted of attempted murder. Prior to a statement given by the defendant, the officer had advised him that:

> Before we ask you any questions, you must understand your rights. You have the right to remain silent. Anything you say can be used against you in court. You have the right to talk to a lawyer for advice before we ask you any questions, and to have him with you during questioning. You have the right to the presence of a lawyer even if you cannot afford to hire one. We have no way of giving you a lawyer, but one will be appointed for you, if you wish, if and when you go to court.

A divided United States Court of Appeals for the Seventh Circuit reversed, holding that the advice that counsel would be appointed "if and when you go to court" was constitutionally defective because it denies an accused a clear and unequivocal warning of the right to appointed counsel before any interrogation.

The United States Supreme Court disagreed with the Court of Appeals, the majority indicating that the warnings were sufficient to ensure that the right against compulsory self-incrimination is protected. Citing other cases, the Supreme Court noted that "The inquiry is simply whether the warnings reasonably convey to a suspect his rights as required by *Miranda*." In this case according to the majority they did.

In their concluding statement, the majority made this statement:

> We hold that the initial warnings given to respondent, in their totality, satisfied *Miranda*, and therefore that his first statement denied his involvement in the crime, as well as the knife and the clothing were all properly admitted into evidence.

The dissenting judges agreed with the lower court that the confession should not have been admitted as the *Miranda* rule was not complied with. These justices made the observation that:

> It poses no great burden on law enforcement officers to eradicate the confusion stemming from the "if and when" caveat. Deleting the sentence containing the offending language is all that needs to be done...Purged of this language, the warnings tell the suspect in a straightforward fashion that he has the right to the presence of a lawyer before and during questioning, and that a lawyer will be appointed if he cannot afford one.

This does not mean that the warnings may be given haphazardly. It is preferable to administer the warnings in the exact form that they are included in the *Miranda* case; however, if the warnings are not in the exact words or are not in the exact order, but the defendant is adequately informed of his rights, a verbatim recital of the words of *Miranda* is not required.

4. *Waiver after warning*

In *Miranda* the majority members of the Supreme Court included some definite statements about the waiver. Among these are the following:

> [A] valid waiver will not be presumed simply from the silence of the accused after warnings are given or simply from the fact that a confession was in fact eventually obtained....
>
> ....
>
> [A]ny evidence that the accused was threatened, tricked, or cajoled into a waiver will, of course, show that the defendant did not voluntarily waive his privilege....
>
> ....
>
> Opportunity to exercise these rights [self-incrimination and counsel rights] must be afforded to him throughout the interrogation. After such warnings have been given, and such opportunity afforded him, the individual may knowingly and intelligently waive these rights and agree to answer questions or make a statement....[63]

The Court goes on to explain that the prosecution must demonstrate that warnings and waiver have been given and that the statements made by the defendant were made voluntarily, knowingly and intelligently. A valid waiver will not be presumed simply from the silence of the accused after warnings are given, nor will a waiver be considered as voluntary if there is valid evidence that the accused was threatened, tricked or cajoled. Not only must the warnings be given initially, but opportunity to exercise these rights must be afforded throughout the questioning. If the accused indicates at any stage of the questioning that he does not wish to be interrogated, or that he wishes to consult with an attorney, the questioning must stop.

Few believed that the matter of waiver would end with the *Miranda* decision. Several questions have recurred frequently since the decision was

---

63 Miranda v. Arizona, 384 U.S. at 475, 476, 479.

handed down in 1966. One of these concerns the specificity of the waiver; that is, must the person interviewed specifically state he understands the meaning of the waiver and expressly waive his rights? A second question is whether or not the interrogation must cease forever once the person in custody indicates he wishes to remain silent or he wishes to have an attorney appointed. These will be discussed separately.

The majority in the *Miranda* case made it clear that a valid waiver will not be presumed simply from the silence of the accused and that the accused must knowingly and intelligently waive his rights after warning. However, the *Miranda* rule, according to a later decision, does not require that an "in custody" suspect make a "specific" written or oral waiver of the right to counsel.[64] In the *Butler* case, the accused was charged with kidnapping, armed robbery, and felonious assault. According to the uncontroverted testimony of the FBI agents, the suspect was advised of his rights and answered in the affirmative when he was asked if he understood his rights. He refused, however, to sign the waiver at the bottom of the form but stated "I will talk to you but I am not signing any form." He then made the inculpatory statements which were used by the prosecution. At the trial, the defendant moved to suppress the incriminating statements on the ground that he had not waived his right to assistance of counsel at the time the statements were made. The trial court found that the defendant had effectively waived his rights but the North Carolina Supreme Court reversed, finding that the statements had been admitted in violation of the requirements of *Miranda*. That Court determined that *Miranda* require that a waiver be "specifically" made.

The United States Supreme Court disagreed with the North Carolina Supreme Court, emphasizing that "*Miranda* did not hold that such an express statement is indispensable to finding of waiver." The Supreme Court explained that the question is not one of form, but rather whether the defendant, in fact, knowingly and voluntarily waived his rights delineated in the *Miranda* case. An *express waiver*, according to the United States Supreme Court, is not an essential requirement even when the right is fundamental, such as the right to counsel.

In one District of Columbia case, the Court of Appeals approved a waiver where the accused did not verbally waive his rights but nodded his head and made other nonverbal communications. The Court there said "appellant was not refusing to answer questions, he was listening to the detective's questions and communicated his understanding and responses through nonverbal means."[65] The Court indicated that by nodding responses

---

64 North Carolina v. Butler, 441 U.S. 369, 99 S. Ct 1755, 60 L. Ed. 2d 286. (1979).

65 Bliss v. United States, 445 A.2d 625 (D.C. 1982).

to questions and then by talking to the detectives a short time later, he waived his rights.

This does not mean, of course, that the silence of the accused will amount to a waiver nor does it mean that any time he nods his head a waiver will be assumed. The prosecution has the burden of showing that the defendant knowingly and voluntarily waived the rights delineated in the *Miranda* decision. Therefore the prosecution must offer some evidence to indicate that the suspect did knowingly and intelligently waive his rights.[66] In the *Tague* case, which reached the Supreme Court on the question of waiver, the arresting officer testified that he had read the petitioner his *Miranda* rights from a card but offered no other evidence to indicate the petitioner understood the rights read to him or any evidence that the defendant waived his rights. In distinguishing this case from the case of *North Carolina v. Butler*, this statement was included:

> In this case no evidence at all was introduced to prove the petitioner knowingly and intelligently waived his rights before making the inculpatory statement. The statement was therefore inadmissible.

In considering what amounts to a waiver after the *Miranda* warnings have been given, the Supreme Court was faced with the question of whether refusal to give a written statement contaminates an oral statement that was willingly given. In the case of *Connecticut v. Barrett*, the defendant, while in custody on suspicion of sexual assault, was three times advised by the police of his *Miranda* rights.[67] On each occasion, after signing and dating an acknowledgment that he had been given those rights, he indicated to the police that he would not make a *written* statement, but he was willing to talk about the incident that led to his arrest. The oral confession was introduced at the trial of the case, the trial court finding that the defendant had fully understood the *Miranda* warnings and had voluntarily waived his right to counsel even though he refused to make a written statement. The Connecticut Supreme Court, however, reasoned that his express desire for counsel before making a written statement constituted an invocation of his right to counsel for all purposes.

When the case reached the United States Supreme Court, the majority agreed with the trial court and not the Connecticut Supreme Court in holding that the Constitution does not require suppression of the incriminating oral statements as it was clear that the suspect had unequivocally expressed his

---

66 Tague v. Louisiana, 444 U.S. 469, 100 S. Ct. 652, 62 L. Ed. 2d 662 (1980).

67 Connecticut v. Barrett, __U.S.__, 107 S. Ct. 828, 93 L. Ed. 2d 920 (1987).

willingness to speak orally to police about the sexual assault. Referring to the reasons for the *Miranda* requirement, the Court indicated that there was no constitutional objective that would be served by suppressing the oral statement in this case. Although Barrett made limited requests for counsel, these were accompanied by affirmative announcements of his willingness to speak to the authorities. Succinctly stating the reasoning, the Court made this comment:

> The fact that officials took the opportunity provided by Barrett to obtain an oral confession is quite consistent with the Fifth Amendment. *Miranda* gives the defendant the right to choose between speech and silence, and Barrett chose to speak.

As in other constitutional situations, the accused may waive his constitutional rights if the waiver is voluntarily and intelligently made.

The second waiver issue -- the resumption of questioning after a suspect has exercised his right to remain silent -- is a difficult one and no satisfactory answer has been forthcoming as admitted by the members of the Supreme Court.

After some lower court decisions the Supreme Court in 1975 ruled that the police may resume questioning a suspect who has exercised his right to remain silent as long as they respect the suspect's right to stop answering questions at any time.[68] In the *Mosley* case, the defendant had indicated he did not want to answer any questions and his request was honored. Some two hours later, however, he was questioned by officers from the homicide bureau about a killing in an unrelated robbery in which he had not been charged. At the second questioning he was given fresh *Miranda* warnings and confessed to the second crime. On appeal, however, he claimed that he should not have been questioned the second time after he had exercised his right to remain silent. The majority found that the defendant's rights were fully protected and upheld the conviction. In Mr. Justice Stewart's opinion there is nothing in the *Miranda* decision which requires a police officer to cease questioning forever once a defendant expresses his wish to remain silent.

Some years later in 1981 the United States Supreme Court again considered the question of waiver where the defendant had invoked his right to counsel after the first interrogation.[69] The Supreme Court held that custo-

---

68 Michigan v. Mosley, 23 U.S. 96, 96 S. Ct. 321, 46 L. Ed. 2d 313 (1975).

69 Edwards v. Arizona, 451 U.S. 477, 101 S. Ct. 1880, 68 L. Ed. 2d 378 (1981). The *Edwards* rule was reaffirmed in 1984 in the case of Solem v. Stumes, 465 U.S. 638,

dial interrogation of an arrestee who had invoked his right to counsel must cease unless counsel has been provided or the suspect himself initiates further dialogue with the police. In this case the officers advised the suspect of his rights; the suspect said "I want an attorney before making a deal." Questioning ceased but two detectives who were colleagues of the officers who had interrogated Edwards the previous night came to the jail to see Edwards. After being told by a guard that he had to talk to the two officers, the officers again informed him of his *Miranda* rights and Edwards indicated he was willing to talk but that he first wanted to hear the taped statement of the alleged accomplice who had implicated him. He thereupon implicated himself in the crime. The trial court denied petitioner's motion to suppress his confession, finding the statement to be voluntary, and he was thereafter convicted. The Arizona Supreme Court held that he waived his right to remain silent and his right to counsel when he voluntarily gave his statement after again being informed of his rights.

The United States Supreme Court announced the holding in these terms:

> We further hold that an accused, such as Edwards, having expressed his desire to deal with police only through counsel, is not subject to further interrogation by the authorities until counsel has been made available to him, unless the accused himself initiates further communications, exchanges, or conversations with the police.

Edwards left some uncertainty about what the court means by "initiation." In 1983 the Supreme Court was given an opportunity to make this more clear but was unable to put together a majority decision regarding the test to be employed.[70] In this case a suspect in Oregon said he wanted a lawyer but soon afterwards asked an officer, "Well, what is going to happen to me now?" Four of the justices thought that this meant he had "initiated" a new conversation. The minority argued he had not because he was not offering to discuss the subject matter of the criminal investigation. Justice Powell cast the deciding vote in settling the defendant's fate ruling that the suspect had waived his rights without considering the "initiated" question. Justice Powell suggested that police and courts read the *Miranda* case, the *Edwards* case and this case for a clarification of the waiver rule. He indicated

---

104 S. Ct. 1338, 79 L. Ed. 2d 579 (1984). However, the Court refused to make the rule retroactive.

70 Oregon v. Bradshaw, 462 U.S 1039, 103 S. Ct. 2830, 77 L. Ed. 2d 405 (1983).

however that it was his hope that the case would have furnished an opportunity to clarify confusion, but that his hope had not been fully realized.

In 1986, the Court applied the *Edwards* reasoning to a case with a slightly different factual situation. In the case of *Michigan v. Jackson*, the defendant requested counsel at the arraignment.[71] Before the defendant had an opportunity to consult with his counsel, police officers, after advising the defendant of his *Miranda* rights, questioned him and obtained a confession.

In this case the defendant did not request counsel during the interrogation prior to arraignment but requested counsel at the arraignment. Nonetheless, the rationale that was framed in *Edwards v. Arizona* was applied when the Court held that if police initiate an interrogation after the defendant's assertion of his right to counsel at the arraignment or similar proceedings, any waiver of that right after police-initiated interrogation is invalid unless counsel is present.

To restate this, once a suspect has been arraigned and has claimed counsel at the arraignment or preliminary hearing, a police officer may not initiate questioning. Questioning, as in the *Edwards* case, may be initiated by the suspect, but the burden is on the prosecution to show that the suspect did, in fact, initiate further questioning.

However, the situation is quite different when police ask preliminary questions without giving the *Miranda* warnings and later continue the questioning after the full *Miranda* warnings have been administered. In the case of *Oregon v. Elstad*, the suspect was asked some preliminary questions at his home concerning a burglary and replied, "Yes, I was there."[72] No warnings had been given to the suspect at his home prior to the time he made the first incriminating statement. After the suspect had been transported to the sheriff's headquarters, approximately an hour later, he was advised for the first time of his *Miranda* rights with the officer reading the rights from a standard card. At this point the defendant waived his right to counsel as well as his rights under the Fifth Amendment and agreed to make a statement.

The Oregon Court of Appeals reversed the conviction, indicating that the impact of the first statement made by the defendant at his home had not dissipated at the time of the subsequent confession at headquarters. The Court of Appeals was of the opinion that the "cat was sufficiently out of the bag" to exert a coercive impact on the later admission.

The United States Supreme Court distinguished this from the *Edwards* situation, as here no *Miranda* warnings had been given and counsel had not been requested. The United States Supreme Court commented that:

---

71 Michigan v. Jackson, 475 U.S. 625, 106 S. Ct. 1404, 89 L. Ed. 2d 631 (1986).

72 Oregon v. Elstad, 470 U.S. 298, 105 S. Ct. 1285, 84 L. Ed. 2d 222 (1985).

> It is an unwarranted extension of *Miranda* to hold that a simple failure to administer the warnings, unaccompanied by any actual coercion or circumstances calculated to undermine the suspect's ability to exercise his free will, so taints the investigatory process that a subsequent, voluntary and informed waiver is ineffective.

In the *Oregon v. Elstad* decision the Court merely held that statements made by the defendant without the *Miranda* warnings do not necessarily contaminate later statements made after the warnings have been given. Emphasizing this point, the Court continued by stating that:

> Absent deliberate coercion or improper tactics in obtaining an unwarned statement, a careful and thorough administration of the *Miranda* warnings cures the condition that rendered the unwarned statement inadmissible.

As to waiver after first claiming the rights, the rule as it now stands is that a defendant who has asserted his rights may not be subjected to further interrogation without counsel unless he initiates further communication with the police. If the suspect affirmatively requests to discuss the matter with the police, there is no question about the initiation; however, there is quite a bit of uncertainty about an indirect waiver and certainly a confession obtained after the police have initiated the second questioning will not be admissible.

5. *Effect of legislative acts on Miranda requirements*

In an obvious attempt to negate some of the strict requirements placed on investigators by the Supreme Court, the United States Congress in 1968 added several sections to the Omnibus Crime Control Act. Paragraphs (a) and (b) from section 3501 of Title 18 of the United States Code, derived from the Omnibus Crime Act, relate directly to the warnings as required in the Miranda case. These provisions of the act are as follows:

> (a) In any criminal prosecution brought by the United States or by the District of Columbia, a confession, as defined in subsection (e) hereof, shall be admissible in evidence if it is voluntarily given. Before such confession is received in evidence, the trial judge shall, out of the presence of the jury, determine any issue as to voluntariness. If the trial judge determines that the confession was voluntarily made, it shall be admitted in evidence and the trial judge shall permit the jury to hear relevant evi-

dence on the issue of voluntariness and shall instruct the jury to give such weight to the confession as the jury feels it deserves under all the circumstances.

(b) The trial judge in determining the issue of voluntariness shall take into consideration all the circumstances surrounding the giving of the confession, including

(1) the time elapsing between arrest and arraignment of the defendant making the confession, if it was made after arrest and before arraignment,
(2) whether such defendant knew the nature of the offense with which he was charged or of which he was suspected at the time of making the confession,
(3) whether or not such defendant was advised or knew that he was not required to make any statement and that any such statement could be used against him,
(4) whether or not such defendant was advised prior to questioning of his right to the assistance of counsel, and
(5) whether or not such defendant was without the assistance of counsel when questioned and when giving such confession.

The presence or absence of any of the above-mentioned factors to be taken into consideration by the judge need not be conclusive on the issue of voluntariness of the confession.[73]

Paragraph (a) makes the traditional voluntary test the sole criterion of the admissibility of a confession in federal court. Paragraph (b) delineates the factors which shall be considered in determining the issue of voluntariness. The mandatory requirements of *Miranda* are to be considered by the trial judge but they "need not be conclusive on the issue of voluntariness of the confession." These paragraphs direct that the trial judge take all of these factors, as well as others, into consideration, but that they only be considered as they reflect on the voluntariness of the confession. A confession may therefore be admissible under this act even if the technical requirements of *Miranda* are not met.

The first question that comes to mind is whether or not the legislative body has the authority to change the requirements as established by the Supreme Court when those requirements are based upon a constitutional

---

73 Crime Control Act, *supra* note 33, § 701(a) & (b), *codified* at 18 USC § 3501(a) & (b) (1970).

provision. When this provision was added to the statutory laws of the United States, some legal authorities, including the criminal law committee of the Federal Bar Association, argued that this was squarely in conflict with the Supreme Court decision in *Miranda* and therefore unconstitutional. Other students of constitutional law disagree, arguing that the Supreme Court has criticized legislative bodies for not taking action to establish procedural guidelines.[74]

Those who argue that this provision is constitutional point out that in the *Miranda* case the majority encouraged legislative bodies to take action using this terminology:

> Congress and the States are free to develop their own safeguards for the privilege, so long as they are fully as effective as those described above in informing accused persons of the right of silence and in affording a continuous opportunity to exercise it.[75]

The Tenth Circuit Court of Appeals has considered this section and concluded that the trial judge properly relied on section 3501 in admitting the confession of a counterfeiting defendant who claimed that she was not advised of her right to counsel and that the police continued to interrogate her when she asked for a lawyer.[76] The ruling, which in effect re-establishes the voluntary test but enumerates some factors which the judge must consider in determining voluntariness, is not in violation of the Constitution.

Citing 18 U.S.C. § 3501, the Circuit Court in *United States v. McLernon* held that this section requires a specific voluntariness instruction if the issue of voluntariness has been placed before the jury.[77]

§ 6.5 Exclusion of confession as a means of enforcing the Fourth Amendment

Up to this point three avenues of challenging the admissibility of confessions have been discussed. To review:

(1) Confessions are inadmissible unless the prosecution can show that they are free, voluntary and trustworthy;

---

74 United States v. Wade, 388 U.S 218, 87 S. Ct. 1926, 18 L. Ed. 2d 1149 (1967).

75 Miranda v. Arizona, 384 U.S. at 490.

76 United States v. Crocker, 510 F.2d 1129 (10th Cir. 1975).

77 United States v. McLernon, 746 F.2d 1098 (6th Cir. 1984).

(2) if the defense can prove to the satisfaction of the court that the confession was obtained during an unnecessary delay in arraignment, the confession will not be admitted; and

(3) with some exceptions, the prosecution must demonstrate that the *Miranda* warnings (or equivalent) were administered, and that the defendant waived his rights before the evidence will be admissible in court.

This fourth avenue of challenge relies on the "fruit of the poisonous tree" doctrine or what is sometimes called the *Wong Sun* doctrine.[78] Simply stated, this rule provides that if the confession is derived immediately from an unlawful arrest or unlawful search, the confession is "tainted" and neither it nor its fruits may be used against the defendant whose Fourth Amendment rights were violated.

In the case of *Wong Sun v. United States*,[79] an oral statement implicating one of the accused was held inadmissible because of an unlawful entry and an unauthorized arrest. The facts of this case are complicated, and the entire case should be read to fully understand the significance. Because of the complicated facts and the complexity of the decision, it has earned the name of "The Chinese Puzzle Case." Over the objection of the accused, statements made orally by one of the petitioners in his bedroom at the time of the arrest and search were admitted into evidence at the trial.

The court found that the arrest was illegal, as not based upon probable cause, that the incidental search was therefore illegal, and that the oral confession made at the time was not admissible. The judge reasoned that such statements were fruits of the agents' unlawful action, and that the exclusionary prohibition relating to evidence obtained by illegal search extends to the indirect as well as the direct products of such invasions.

Although denying the use of a confession obtained immediately after an illegal arrest, the Supreme Court in the *Wong Sun* case allowed into evidence a second confession taken after the suspect had been released on his own recognizance. Here the United States Supreme Court said the taint had dissipated sufficiently so that the confession would be considered voluntary and admissible.

Many lower court decisions were rendered between 1963 when the *Wong Sun* case was handed down, and 1975. However, the United States Supreme Court did not again fully consider the doctrine until the case of *Brown v. Illi-*

---

[78] The name being derived from Wong Sun v. United States, 371 U.S. 471, 83 S. Ct. 407, 9 L. Ed. 2d 441 (1963).

[79] 371 U.S. 471, 83 S. Ct. 407, 9 L. Ed. 2d 441 (1963).

nois[80] in 1975. The question presented in the *Brown* case was whether an illegal arrest and search tainted the confession obtained after the warnings and procedures required by *Miranda* had been met. Here the defendant was arrested without probable cause in what the court defined as a clearly investigatory arrest. Prior to questioning, however, the officers properly advised him of his rights, and the accused voluntarily agreed to make statements to the police. The prosecution claimed that since the defendant had waived his rights voluntarily, the fact that there was an illegal arrest preceding the advice should not taint the confession.

Mr. Justice Blackmun, speaking for the majority, noted that there was a causal connection between the illegality of the arrest and the confession, and that giving the *Miranda* warnings by themselves does not attenuate the taint of an illegal arrest. The majority of the Court in effect agreed that the Fifth Amendment rights are protected by giving the *Miranda* warnings, but that this in itself does not protect the Fourth Amendment rights; that despite *Miranda* warnings the Fourth and Fourteenth Amendments require the exclusion from evidence of statements obtained as the fruits of an arrest which the arresting officer knows, or should have known, was without probable cause and unconstitutional.

Ever since the *Wong Sun* case was decided in 1963, courts have been struggling with the "causal connection" issue. In order for the illegal arrest and/or search to contaminate the confessions, there must be a causal connection between the illegality of the arrest or search and the confession which followed the arrest or search. This was one issue in the case of *Dunaway v. New York*, decided in 1979.[81] Here the court said if the causal connection between the statements and the illegal arrest is broken significantly to purge the primary taint of the illegal arrest, the confession will be admissible. In determining in that case that the police violated the Fourth and Fourteenth Amendments when they seized the defendant without probable cause, the question remained whether the connection between this unconstitutional police conduct and the incriminating statements and sketches obtained during the petitioner's illegal detention was nevertheless attenuated to permit the use at trial of the statements and sketches. In reversing the conviction, the minority indicated there was such a close connection, pointing out that:

> Where there is a close causal connection between the illegal seizure and the confession, not only is the exclusion of the evidence more likely to deter similar police conduct in the future, but the use of the evidence is more likely to compromise the integrity of the courts.

---

80 422 U.S. 590, 95 S. Ct. 2254, 45 L. Ed. 2d 416 (1975).

81 Dunaway v. New York, 442 U.S. 200, 99 S. Ct. 2248, 60 L. Ed. 2d 824 (1979).

In a 1982 case a five-Justice majority found that the facts in a similar case were indistinguishable from *Dunaway v. New York* and ruled that a robbery suspect's confession, six hours after his illegal arrest, was not sufficiently purged of the taint of that illegality to render it admissible in evidence.[82]

In these cases the confessions were held inadmissible because they derived immediately from an unlawful search or arrest and there was a causal connection between the illegal arrest or search and the confession. Although it is apparent that it is a difficult task to refute the presumption that there was a causal connection between the illegal arrest and the confession, it is not an impossible one. First it is noted that in the *Taylor* case four Justices were of the opinion that the taint of the illegal arrests had dissipated. Secondly, in one case the Supreme Court, in reviewing a lower court decision, held that the lower court had erred in holding that the degree of attenuation was not sufficient to dissipate the connection between the illegality and the testimony. There the testimony followed four months after the illegal search.[83]

A more recent case has reiterated the rule that a confession which follows immediately an illegal arrest or search will not be admissible in a criminal case if there is a causal connection between the illegality of the arrest and the statement. The case of *Lanier v. South Carolina* involved a defendant who was convicted of armed robbery.[84] He contended that his confession should have been suppressed because it was the product of an illegal arrest. However, the South Carolina Court of Appeals affirmed the trial court's rejection of the motion to suppress the confession, and he appealed to the United States Supreme Court.

The United States Supreme Court restated its holding in previous cases, pointing out that:

> Under well established precedent, "the fact that a confession may be voluntary for purposes of the Fifth Amendment, in the sense that *Miranda* warnings were given and understood, is not by itself sufficient to purge the taint of the illegal arrest."

The Court, in effect, noted that even if the *Miranda* warnings are given and understood, this is not sufficient to purge the taint of an illegal arrest where the confession follows the illegal arrest.

To summarize, the rule is that if the confession is derived immediately from an unlawful search or seizure, and there is a causal connection between the illegality of the arrest and the statement, the testimony or confession will

---

82 Taylor v. Alabama, 457 U.S. 687, 102 S. Ct. 2664, 73 L. Ed. 2d 314 (1982).

83 United States v. Ceccolini, 435 U.S. 268, 98 S. Ct. 1054, 55 L. Ed. 2d (1973).

84 Lanier v. South Carolina, 474 U.S. 25, 106 S. Ct. 297, 88 L. Ed. 2d 23 (1985).

not be admissible in a criminal case. But if the taint has attenuated (this might occur after an elapse of a substantial period of time) the testimony will not be contaminated and the evidence will be admissible unless challenged on other grounds.

§ 6.6 Corroboration

Under early English law, confessions were admissible even if there was no other evidence to prove guilt of the accused. According to the writers of the period, this led to some persons' being found guilty when in fact there was no crime. In this country the rule is generally adopted that if the state relies upon the confession, it must also have evidence independent of the confession to show the corpus delicti; that is, the fact that the crime charged has in fact been committed. This does not mean, as some seem to argue, that it is necessary to produce the body in a homicide case. It is sufficient if the outside proof together with the confession satisfies the jury beyond a reasonable doubt that a crime in fact has been committed. Some states have by statute codified this requirement and require that the corpus delicti be proved by independent proof.

The Texas Court of Appeals determined that this corroboration requirement had been met where, in addition to the appellant's confession, this state presented witnesses who testified that three persons were seen running from the car that had been stopped and that an individual, dead from a gunshot wound, was lying on the ground next to the vehicle. The court agreed that in this case the appellant's confession was corroborated by the testimony of the witnesses offered by the state to establish the corpus delicti.[85]

In the case of *Bruton v. United States*[86] decided in 1968, the Supreme Court determined that an admission of an extrajudicial confession of a codefendant who did not take the stand deprived the defendant of his rights under the Sixth Amendment confrontation clause. That Court cautioned that such codefendant's confession could not be used even if only for the purpose of corroborating statements made in the defendant's own confession.

The Supreme Court again considered the admissibility of a co-defendant's incriminating confession at a joint trial in the case of *Cruz v. New York* in 1987.[87] At the petitioner's and his brother's joint trial for the felony mur-

---

85 Adams v. Texas, 636 S.W.2d 447 (Tex. 1982).

86 391 U.S. 123, 88 S. Ct. 1620, 20 L. Ed. 2d 476 (1968).

87 Cruz v. New York, __U.S.__, 107 S. Ct. 1714, __L. Ed. 2d__ (1987). The majority in the *Cruz* case rejected the "harmless violation and reasoning of the plurality in

der of a gas station attendant, the trial court allowed the state to introduce the brother's videotaped confession. The United States Supreme Court reversed the conviction and remanded the case for further proceeding even though the petitioner's own confession was admitted properly into evidence. The court held that:

> Where a non-testifying co-defendant's confession incriminating the defendant is not directly admissible against the defendant...,the Confrontation Clause bars its admission at their joint trial, even if the jury is instructed not to consider it against the defendant, and even if the defendant's own confession is admitted against him.

§ 6.7 Derivative evidence

Many of the older state court decisions and a few state statutes authorized the use of evidence obtained as the result of an otherwise invalid confession. For example, if a confession were obtained from a murder suspect by the use of force and duress, and in the confession the suspect told where the murder weapon was hidden, the earlier cases allowed such evidence to be used at the trial. However, in 1962 the California Supreme Court equated evidence discovered as the result of an involuntary confession with evidence discovered as the result of an unreasonable search and seizure, and held that such evidence was not admissible. The court in the case of *People v. Ditson*[88] stated:

> It follows that the reason for the common law rule permitting the introduction of real evidence discovered by means of an involuntary confession -- that such evidence tends to prove the trustworthiness of the confession -- must now be deemed Constitutionally indefensible, and hence that the rule must be abandoned.

Since *Miranda*, the "fruit of the poisonous tree" doctrine unquestionably applies to real evidence obtained by means of an invalid confession. After

---

the case of Parker v. Randolph, 442 U.S. 62, 99 S. Ct. 2132, 60 L. Ed. 2d 713 (1979).

88 57 Cal. 2d 415, 20 Cal. Rptr. 165, 369 P.2d 714 (1962). *See also* Lee v. State, 428 S.W.2d 328 (Tex. 1968), which held that a license plate obtained indirectly by the illegal confession was not admissible into evidence.

discussing the warnings which must be given prior to questioning, the Court declared:

> But unless and until such warnings and waiver are demonstrated by the prosecution at trial, no evidence obtained as a result of interrogation can be used against him. [Emphasis added.][89]

Just how far does the fruit of the poisonous tree doctrine extend? For example, will the testimony of the witness be excluded when the identity of that witness has been disclosed by the illegally obtained confession? In an often misunderstood and misquoted decision, the United States Supreme Court in 1974 determined that the exclusionary rule which prohibits the admission of certain statements when the *Miranda* warning is not given, did not apply to the in-court testimony of a witness who was discovered as a result of no-warning questioning.[90] In this case the defendant was arrested for raping and severely beating a 43-year-old woman. Before the commencement of the interrogation, the police asked the defendant if he knew what crime he had been arrested for, if he wanted an attorney, and if he understood his constitutional rights. The defendant replied that he did understand the charge, that he did not want an attorney, and that he understood his rights. The police advised him further that any statements he might make could be used against him at a later date, but did not advise him that he would be furnished counsel free of charge if he could not pay for such services himself.

During the questioning, the defendant, in relating an alibi, stated that he was with a friend, one Robert Henderson, at the time of the crime. The police, however, elicited from Henderson information tending to incriminate the defendant.

Prior to the trial the defendant made a motion to exclude Henderson's testimony because the defendant had revealed Henderson's identity without receiving the full warnings mandated by the *Miranda* decision. This motion was denied and Henderson testified. Following the affirmance of the conviction, the defendant sought habeas corpus relief which the federal district court granted, finding that Henderson's testimony was inadmissible because of the *Miranda* violation. The United States Court of Appeals affirmed.

A majority of the members of the United States Supreme Court, in reversing the lower federal courts and approving the admission of the testimony, made these comments in relation to the testimony of the witness:

---

89 Miranda v. Arizona, 384 U.S. at 479.

90 Michigan v. Tucker, 417 U.S. 433, 94 S. Ct. 2357, 41 L. Ed. 2d 182 (1974).

> This Court said in *Miranda* that statements taken in violation of the *Miranda* principles must not be used to prove the prosecution's case at trial. That requirement was fully complied with by the state court here: respondent's statements, claiming that he was with Henderson and then asleep during the time period of the crime were not admitted against him at trial....
>
> Just as the law does not require that a defendant receive a perfect trial, only a fair one, it cannot realistically require that policemen investigating serious crimes make no errors whatsoever. The pressures of law enforcement and the vagaries of human nature would make such an expectation unrealistic. Before we penalize police error, therefore, we must consider whether the sanction serves a valid and useful purpose.[91]

Although the Court concluded that it would serve no useful purpose to apply the exclusionary rule to the testimony given by Henderson and held that Tucker had been properly convicted of rape, the Court did not go so far as to hold that it is not necessary to administer the *Miranda* warnings. The Supreme Court cautioned that if the *Miranda* warnings are not administered, or at least if compliance with the *Miranda* principles are not proved by the prosecutor, statements will not be admitted into evidence. On the other hand, if the failure to advise the suspect of his right to have appointed counsel, as in this case, has no bearing on the reliability of a witness, the testimony of the discovered witness should not be excluded.

In the *Tucker* case the Supreme Court made reference to the strong interest of our justice system in making available to the courts all relevant and trustworthy evidence and to the fact that society has an interest in effective prosecution of criminals. That Court also reminded that the case of *Harris v. New York*[92] held the failure to give the suspect the full *Miranda* warnings did not prevent use of his statements to impeach his testimony at trial, and that such failure does not make evidence inadmissible for all purposes. Nonetheless, unless the Supreme Court goes further, it is preferable to follow the rule which holds that tangible evidence obtained as a direct result of an illegal confession will not be admitted in court.

On the other hand, if the record clearly shows that the statements taken from the accused during the police interrogation were not involuntary, the use of a witness discovered by the police as a result of the accused's statements will be allowed.

---

91 *Id.* at 445-446.

92 401 U.S. 222, 91 S. Ct. 643, 28 L. Ed. 2d 1 (1971).

§ 6.8 Admissible statements

Too often the investigator, after reading the Supreme Court decisions, feels that all statements will be inadmissible. However, the Supreme Court in the *Miranda* case emphasized that it did not purport to find all confessions inadmissible. In making this point the Court remarked:

> Confessions remain a proper element in law enforcement. Any statement given freely and voluntarily without any compelling influence is, of course, admissible in evidence....There is no requirement that the police stop a person who enters a police station and states that he wishes to confess to a crime, or a person who calls the police to offer a confession or any other statement he desires to make. Volunteered statements of any kind are not barred by the Fifth Amendment and their admissibility is not affected by our holding today.[93]

The Court, in calling attention to specific instances where interrogation would be valid, held that when investigating crimes the officer may inquire of persons not under restraint. Also, on-the-scene questioning as to facts surrounding a crime or other general questioning of citizens in the fact-finding process is not affected by the holding. This type of questioning was distinguished from the questioning of a suspect, since in this situation the compelling atmosphere inherent in the process of in-custody interrogation is not necessarily present.

The *Miranda* case requires that warnings be given to a person in custody and who is to be subjected to interrogation. It does not require that a person be warned if he voluntarily makes a statement without interrogation or other compelling influences. Therefore, if a person who is not being questioned and who is not being otherwise influenced to make a statement voluntarily does so, there is no requirement that he be stopped and the warning be given.

This rule was reaffirmed in a 1976 case when the Supreme Court decided that it is not necessary to give the warnings called for in *Miranda* to a taxpayer who is under criminal tax investigation where the taxpayer is not in custody.[94] The petitioner in the *Beckwith* case argued that he was placed in a position which would be legally equivalent to that in the Miranda situation and, therefore, statements made should not have been admitted unless the *Miranda* warnings had been given. The Court was not persuaded by this ar-

---

93 Miranda v. Arizona, 384 U.S. at 478.

94 Beckwith v. United States, 425 U.S. 341, 96 S. Ct. 1612, 48 L. Ed. 2d 1 (1976).

gument since the questioning, even though of a criminal nature, was in the home of the defendant and the defendant was not in custody. The Court said:

> Although the "focus" of an investigation may indeed have been on Beckwith at the time of the interview in the sense that it was his tax liability which was under scrutiny, he hardly found himself in the custodial situation described by the *Miranda* Court as the basis for its holding.[95]

In an even more recent case,[96] the Supreme Court found that a person is not necessarily in custody even in a police environment. In admitting the confession the majority held:

> In the present case, however, there is no indication that the questioning took place in a context where respondent's freedom to depart was restricted in any way. He came voluntarily to the police station, where he was immediately informed that he was not under arrest. At the close of a one-half hour interview respondent did in fact leave the police station without hindrance. It is clear from these facts that Mathiason was not in custody "or otherwise deprived of his freedom of action in any significant way."

The Court warned that in some special circumstances a suspect's will may be overborne by law enforcement agents even when he is not in custody. When such a claim is advanced, the Court explained, the record should be examined to determine if the confession met the voluntariness requirements.

Empirical investigation has established that suspects do make statements even after the warnings have been administered. Questioning of suspects and witnesses remains a valuable tool in the effective prosecution of violators. Evidence also indicates that violators are successfully prosecuted without using the questioning techniques condemned in the *Miranda* case. Police officers and prosecutors have learned when to use the confession as an effective tool and when to rely upon other investigative measures.

In the sections that follow, other examples of situations where statements have been upheld as admissible are stated and discussed.

---

95 *Id*. at 347.

96 Oregon v. Mathiason, 429 U.S. 711, 97 S. Ct. 711, 50 L. Ed. 2d 714 (1977).

§ 6.9 "Public safety" exception

Although not reversing decisions that require that the *Miranda* warnings be given, the United States Supreme Court in 1984 recognized what the Court called a "narrow exception" to the *Miranda* rule. Briefly stated, the exception is that statements elicited from the defendant as well as real evidence resulting from such statements may be used in evidence even if the officers do not recite the *Miranda* warnings before asking the questions if the officers' safety or the safety of others is in jeopardy.[97]

As this rule has limited application, it is necessary that the facts be stated. The defendant was charged in the New York State court with criminal possession of a weapon. According to the testimony, a woman approached two police officers, told them that she had just been raped, described her assailant, advised them that the man had just entered a nearby supermarket and warned them that the assailant was carrying a gun. While one of the officers radioed for assistance, the other officer entered the store and spotted the respondent, who ran toward the rear of the store. One of the officers pursued him with a drawn gun and ordered him to stop and put his hands over his head. During the frisk the officer discovered that the suspect was wearing an empty shoulder holster, and after handcuffing him, asked him where the gun was. The suspect indicated that the gun was in some empty cartons and said "the gun is over there."

The trial court excluded the statement "the gun is over there" and the gun because the suspect had not been given the *Miranda* warnings. Other statements were also excluded because these other statements were tainted by the *Miranda* violation. Both the appellate division of the Supreme Court of New York and the New York Court of Appeals agreed with the lower court that the evidence should be excluded.

The United States Supreme Court disagreed. The Court held that there is an exception to the *Miranda* warning requirements with these terms:

> We hold that on these facts that there is a "public safety" exception to the requirement that *Miranda* warnings be given before a suspect's answers may be admitted into evidence, and that the availability of that exception does not depend upon the motivation of the individual officers involved.

As justification for the exception the majority of the Supreme Court reasoned that the police, in the very act of apprehending the suspect, were confronted with an immediate necessity of ascertaining the whereabouts of the

---

[97] New York v. Quarles, 467 U.S. 649, 104 S. Ct. 2626, 81 L. Ed. 2d 550 (1984).

gun which they had every reason to believe the suspect had just removed from his empty holster. The Court continued by stating that:

> So long as the gun was concealed somewhere in the supermarket with its actual whereabouts unknown, it obviously posed more than one danger to the public safety: an accomplice might make use of it, a customer or employee might later come upon it.

The Court pointed out that if the police are required to recite the *Miranda* warnings, the suspect might be deterred from responding immediately, posing a danger to the police and to others.

In recognizing the necessity for the exception the court made this comment:

> We conclude that the need for answers to questions in a situation posing a threat to the public safety outweighs the need for the prophylactic rule protecting the Fifth Amendment's privilege against self-incrimination. We decline to place officers such as Officer Kraft in the untenable position of having to consider, often in a matter of seconds, whether it best serves society for them to ask the necessary questions without the *Miranda* warnings and render whatever probative evidence they uncover inadmissible, or for them to give the warnings in order to preserve the admissibility of evidence they might uncover and possibly damage or destroy their ability to obtain that evidence and neutralize the volatile situation confronting them.

The dissenting judges argued that the ruling would create "chaos" for authorities interpreting the new doctrine and, worse, open the way for the use of coerced statements at trials. The majority recognized that the exception lessened the clarity of the *Miranda* rule; however, they pointed out that the exception will not be difficult for officers to apply because in each case it will be circumscribed by the exigency which justifies it. In concluding paragraphs of the case the majority explained that police officers can and will "distinguish almost instinctively between questions necessary to secure their safety or the safety of the public and questions designed solely to elicit testimonial evidence from the suspect."

Despite the decision of the majority that this rule will not be difficult to apply, there does seem to be some indication that other cases will have to be decided to determine the application of the exceptions to the rule. Nevertheless, the exceptions stated here indicate:

(1) that the Court is recognizing exceptions to the *Miranda* rule and
(2) that some evidence which would have been inadmissible without this exception will be admissible if the exception is applied scrupulously by knowledgeable officers.

§ 6.10 Use of confession for impeachment purposes

If a confession is found to be inadmissible to help establish the prosecutor's "case in chief" because the *Miranda* warnings were not administered, is that confession nevertheless admissible to impeach the credibility of the defendant if he takes the stand in his own behalf? This was the question presented to the United States Supreme Court in *Harris v. New York*[98] in 1971. In the *Harris* case the defendant was charged with selling heroin. Recognizing that the *Miranda* requirements were not met, the prosecutor did not offer statements allegedly made by the defendant to show defendant's guilt. However, when the defendant took the stand in his own defense and made statements contrary to the pretrial statements made to the police, the pretrial statements were offered in evidence to impeach the testimony of the defendant. The extrajudicial confession was admitted at the trial for the limited purpose of impeaching the in-court testimony of the defendant. The jury was instructed to use the statement only to assess the defendant's credibility and not as evidence of guilt.

Chief Justice Burger, speaking for the majority of the Supreme Court, used these words in approving the use of the confession for the limited impeachment purpose:

> Every criminal defendant is privileged to testify in his own defense or to refuse to do so. But that privilege cannot be construed to include the right to commit perjury....Having voluntarily taken the stand, petitioner was under an obligation to speak truthfully and accurately, and the prosecution here did no more than utilize the traditional truth-testing devices of the adversary process.[99]

The majority of the Supreme Court in 1975 reiterated its approval of the limited use of custodial statements for impeachment purposes.[100] Again the

---

98 401 U.S. 222, 91 S. Ct. 643, 28 L. Ed. 2d 1 (1971).

99 *Id.* at 225-26 (footnote omitted).

100 Oregon v. Hass, 420 U.S. 714, 91 S. Ct. 1215, 43 L. Ed. 2d 570 (1975).

Supreme Court approved the use of the confession by the prosecution when used for rebuttal purposes to impeach the credibility of the defendant who took the stand in his own behalf.

Carrying the "impeachment admission" rule one step further, the United State Supreme Court approved the use of a statement taken in violation of the *Jackson* rule when the statement is used only for impeachment purposes.[101] As noted in Section 6 of this chapter, the *Jackson* case reasserts the rule that once a criminal defendant invokes his Sixth Amendment right to counsel, a subsequent waiver of that right, even if voluntary, knowing, and intelligent under traditional standards, is presumed invalid if secured pursuant to a police-initiated conversation. However, according to the *Harvey* ruling, such statements may be used to impeach the defendant's false or inconsistent testimony if he elects to take the stand, even though the same statement may not be used as substantive evidence.

In making reference to previous decisions the Court explained:

> Both *Jackson* and *Edwards* establish prophylactic rules that render some otherwise valid waivers of constitutional rights invalid when they result from police-initiated interrogation, and in neither case should the shield provided be perverted into a license to use perjury by way of a defense, free from the risk of confrontation with prior inconsistent utterances.

The rules expressed in the case of *Harris v. New York* in 1971 and *Oregon v. Hass* in 1975 that a confession taken without the proper *Miranda* warnings may be used for impeachment purposes does not apply if the confession is obtained involuntarily. In the case of *Mincey v. Arizona*,[102] the United States Supreme Court held that statements made by a defendant in a hospital, while in great pain, while depressed almost to the point of a coma, and while he was encumbered by tubes, needles and breathing apparatus, were involuntary and could not be used against him even for impeachment purposes. The Court distinguished between using confessions without the *Miranda* warnings and the use of involuntary confessions for impeachment purposes. While the *Miranda*-less confession is admissible for impeachment purposes if trustworthy by established legal standards, an involuntary statement cannot be used in any way against a defendant at his trial.

While the United States Supreme Court has indicated approval of the use of *Miranda*-less confessions for impeachment purposes, that Court has left some ambiguity concerning the use of silence of the accused for im-

---

101 Michigan v. Harvey, __ U.S. __, 110 S. Ct. 1176, __ L. Ed. 2d __ (1990).

102 437 U.S. 385, 98 S. Ct. 2408, 57 L. Ed. 2d 290 (1978).

peachment purposes. In the case of *United States v. Hale*[103] in 1975, the Court held that the silence of the accused, after warning, may not be used for impeachment purposes; and in *Doyle v. Ohio*[104] in 1976, the Supreme Court found that impeachment by silence violated the Constitution. In the *Doyle* case a defendant received the *Miranda* warnings and at the time made no statements to the police. During the subsequent trial, however, he testified that he had been framed. The prosecutor impeached the defendant's credibility on cross-examination by revealing that the defendant remained silent after the arrest and the warnings had been given. Disallowing the use of evidence of the silence, the Court reasoned that:

> It does not comport with due process to permit the prosecution during the trial to call attention to his silence at the time of arrest and to insist that because he did not speak about the facts of the case at the time, as he was told he need not do, an unfavorable inference might be drawn as to the truth of his trial testimony.

In 1980 the Supreme Court determined that silence of the accused may be used for impeachment purposes if failure to speak occurred before the petitioner was taken into custody and before given *Miranda* warnings.[105] In this case the murder defendant who testified at the trial that he acted in self-defense was asked on cross-examination about his failure to make this claim during the two weeks between the crime and his arrest. Here the silence was not after the warnings had been given but consisted of his failure to come forth and claim self-defense during the two weeks between the commission of the crime and the time that the defendant was apprehended. In distinguishing between these two cases and summarizing the holding, the Supreme Court in the *Jenkins* case concluded:

> In this case, no governmental action induced the petitioner to remain silent before arrest. The failure to speak occurred before the petitioner was taken into custody and given *Miranda* warnings. Consequently, the fundamental unfairness present in *Doyle* is not present in this case. We hold that impeachment by use of pre-arrest silence does not violate the Fourteenth Amendment.

From these cases we can formulate a workable rule. If the accused remains silent after being given the *Miranda* warnings, evidence of that silence

---

[103] 422 U.S. 171, 99 S. Ct. 2133, 45 L. Ed. 2d 99 (1975).

[104] 426 U.S. 610, 96 S. Ct 2240, 49 L. Ed. 2d 91 (1976).

[105] Jenkins v. Anderson, 447 U.S. 231, 100 S. Ct. 2124, 65 L. Ed. 2d 86 (1980).

cannot be used against him at the trial for impeachment purposes; but, evidence of silence of the accused prior to such warnings where failure to state facts and circumstances which naturally would have been asserted, may be used to impeach the defendant's credibility.

§ 6.11 Use of statements made at grand jury hearings

Finding that judicial inquiries and custodial interrogations are not equivalents, the United States Supreme Court in 1976 refused to exclude incriminating statements made to a grand jury hearing even though the *Miranda* requirements were not met where the statements were used in a subsequent prosecution of the witness for perjury.[106]

During the course of a grand jury investigation into narcotics traffic, the witness, Mandujano, denied any knowledge of such traffic. He specifically denied discussing the purchase of heroin with money advanced to him by an undercover agent. The falsity of the statement was conceded but the defendant claimed that the testimony before the grand jury should be suppressed because the government failed to provide the warnings called for by *Miranda*. The district court granted his motion to suppress and the court of appeals affirmed. The government appealed to the United States Supreme Court, where the decision was reversed and remanded.

It is apparent that there is a reluctance on the part of the majority of the Supreme Court to extend the *Miranda* rationale. According to the Supreme Court, the lower courts "erroneously applied the standards fashioned by this Court in *Miranda*." The warnings enumerated in *Miranda*, in the Court's words, "were aimed at the evils seen by the Court as endemic to police interrogations of a person in custody." They need not be followed in other situations.

§ 6.12 Non-official questioning

The requirements of warning and waiver as established by the *Miranda* case are based on the Fifth Amendment self-incrimination protection. The constitutional prohibitions against self-incrimination only operate against official action. Therefore, in the absence of state involvement, volunteered

---

106 United States v. Mandujano, 425 U.S. 564, 96 S. Ct. 1768, 48 L. Ed. 2d 212 (1976).

statements made to private citizens are admissible even if no *Miranda* warnings are given.[107]

In Chapter 4, a series of cases holding that the Fourth Amendment prohibitions operate only against official action was discussed. The conclusion was that seizure of evidence by a private person is admissible even though the seizure would have been unreasonable if carried out by a law enforcement officer. The same reasoning applies where statements are made to a private individual.

Nevertheless, as the free and voluntary rule is based in part on a rule of evidence (the evidence must be trustworthy), the defendant would have grounds for challenge if force were used by a private citizen. On the other hand, if the challenge is predicated only on the *Miranda* rule or the delay in arraignment rule, the statements made to the private person would no doubt be admissible.

It is interesting to note that at the second trial of Ernesto A. Miranda, a confession made to his mistress was admitted. The Arizona Supreme Court found that the mistress was not obligated to administer the warnings as set out by the Supreme Court in the earlier *Miranda* case.[108]

Quite clearly, if there is any official involvement, the private citizen exception would not be applicable. It is apparent that the question of official involvement will be a recurring one, especially as private security people are licensed by state agencies.

§ 6.13 Standing to challenge admissibility

In the discussion relating to search and seizure, it was pointed out that a person whose Fourth Amendment rights are not violated cannot complain when illegally seized evidence is used against him. This general reasoning applies in regard to Fifth Amendment self-incrimination rights.

In an Illinois case police officers arrested A for robbery and questioned him about other persons involved in robberies in that area. After A implicated B, B was arrested, and without the *Miranda* warnings he told the police during the investigation that the defendant had committed crimes in that area. The defendant claims that the evidence against him should have been suppressed because it was obtained by unlawful interrogation of the two other suspects. The Supreme Court of Illinois disagreed and upheld the conviction. The basis of the court's reasoning was that the rights protected by

---

[107] United States v. Casteel, 476 F.2d 152 (10th Cir. 1973); Commonwealth v. Mahnke, 335 N.E.2d 660 (Mass. 1975), *cert. denied*, 425 U.S. 959 (1976).

[108] State v. Miranda, 104 Ariz. 174, 450 P.2d 364 (1969).

Miranda are violated only when evidence obtained without the required warnings and waiver is introduced against a person whose own questioning produced the evidence.[109]

§ 6.14 Admissibility of a second confession after an inadmissible first confession

Will a tainted first confession make a second confession inadmissible which has been obtained after all the safeguards have been complied with? This question was thoroughly discussed in the case of *Payne v. State*[110] in 1960. In this case the defendant was charged with first degree murder. He was denied a hearing before a magistrate, was not advised of his right to remain silent, was held for three days without counsel, advisor or friends, was denied food for long periods of time, and was finally told by the chief of police that 30 or 40 people wanted to get him. During the period he made a statement in which he admitted the crime. Later he was requested to reenact the crime, and in doing so he repeated in effect what he had said in the confession several hours before.

The question concerned the admissibility of the statements he made while reenacting the crime and testimony concerning this reenactment. The court, after considering the law in such a situation, held that if a confession is obtained by methods which would make it involuntary, subsequent confessions while the accused is under the operation of the same influence are also involuntary. The court went on to say that once a confession made under improper influence is obtained, the presumption arises that a subsequent confession of the same crime flows from the same influences, even though made to a different person than the one to whom the first was made. Of course, this presumption can be overcome, but the prosecution must have sufficient evidence to do so. If it can be shown by the prosecution that the influences operating when the first confession was made did not exist when the later confession was made, the second confession may be admissible. However, the evidence to rebut this presumption must be clear and convincing.

Would like reasoning apply if the second confession were made to another law enforcement agency? This is similar to the situation which occurred in the case of *Westover v. United States*, which was decided in the same opinion as *Miranda*. Here the FBI agents interrogated the accused after they

---

109 People v. Denham, 41 Ill. 2d 1, 241 N.E.2d 415 (1968).

110 231 Ark. 727, 332 S.W.2d 233 (1960).

had warned him of his right to remain silent and his right to have an attorney. However, prior to this interrogation, Westover had been in the custody of local police for over 14 hours and had been interrogated at length during that period. The Court declared that despite the fact that the FBI agents had given warning prior to their interview, from Westover's point of view the warning came at the end of the interrogation process, not at the beginning, and that under these circumstances an intelligent waiver of constitutional rights cannot be assumed.

But if at the first interview the defendant makes no incriminating statements or as one court put it, does not "let the cat out of the bag," the fact that improper procedures were followed at the first interview does not necessarily contaminate the second interview.[111] The New Jersey Supreme Court, citing other cases including the case of *Commonwealth v. Marabel*,[112] ruled that as the defendant said nothing damaging during the first interview where warnings were not given, the fact that there were no warnings did not taint a later confession where the proper warnings were given before the confession was made.[113]

A case that received much attention in 1985 relates to the question whether a first voluntary *Miranda*-less confession taints a second confession made after the warnings have been given.[114] In the *Elstad* case, officers first talked with the suspect at his home where the suspect stated, "Yes, I was there" prior to the giving of the *Miranda* warning. Later the warnings were given at the sheriff's office and the suspect gave a full statement. The U.S. Supreme Court's opinion included this statement.

> We hold today that a suspect who has once responded to unwarned yet uncoercive questioning is not thereby disabled from waiving his rights and confessing after he has been given the requisite *Miranda* warnings.

As a matter of correct practice the warning should be given prior to any interrogation. If police officers receive the suspect after he has been in the custody of another department, the interrogation should not proceed unless the accused knowingly and intelligently waives his rights.

---

[111] *See* United States v. Begay, 441 F.2d 1311 (5th Cir. 1970).

[112] 445 Pa. 435, 283 A.2d 285 (1971).

[113] State v. Melvin, 65 N.J. 1, 319 A.2d 450 (1974).

[114] Oregon v. Elstad, 47 U.S. 298, 105 S. Ct. 1285, 84 L. Ed. 2d 222 (1985).

§ 6.15 Summary and practical suggestions

In this chapter the historical development of the rule concerning free and voluntary confessions was discussed. This rule developed over a period of many years and is recognized in all state and federal courts, as well as in England. Of more recent origin is the so-called "delay in arraignment" rule, which was established by the *McNabb* and *Mallory* cases. This rule was rejected by most of the state courts. However, since the decision in *Miranda v. Arizona* the delay in arraignment rule is also applied to the state courts via the Fourteenth Amendment.

In 1966 the United States Supreme Court added additional requirements to those established by previous court decisions and statutory enactments.[115] In the *Miranda* case the Supreme Court held that unless other safeguards are adopted, the person in custody must be warned prior to questioning that he has a right to remain silent, that anything he says can and will be used against him in a court of law, that he has the right to the presence of an attorney, and that if he cannot afford an attorney, one will be appointed for him prior to any questioning if he so desires. Additionally, opportunity must be afforded the person questioned to exercise these rights. The Fifth Amendment self-incrimination rights may be waived but they must be knowingly and intelligently waived.

A confession is also considered incompetent and inadmissible if it immediately follows an illegal arrest or search, even if it meets the other requirements. In this regard, offering the *Miranda* warnings after an illegal arrest or search does not cure the Fourth Amendment violation. In addition, the courts have excluded confessions as a means of enforcing the Sixth Amendment "right to counsel" protection. This is discussed in the following chapters.

A confession standing alone will not form the judicial basis for a conviction. Additional outside proof must be introduced to satisfy the jury beyond a reasonable doubt that a crime has in fact been committed.

If a confession is found not to meet the required standards, not only will the confession often be inadmissible for the prosecution's case in chief, but real evidence derived from that confession will probably not be admitted either. However, a witness located as a result of an involuntary confession will probably be allowed to testify if his testimony otherwise meets the legal requirements.

---

115 *See* Miranda v. Arizona, 384 U.S. 436, 86 S. Ct. 1602, 16 L. Ed. 2d 694 (1966).

The *Miranda* decision and post-*Miranda* decisions have made it clear that warnings are not required in all cases. If the person is not in "custody" or is not "questioned," statements voluntarily given may be admitted even if no warning was given. And even though in-custody statements may be inadmissible under *Miranda*, for the prosecutor's case in chief, they may be used to impeach a testifying defendant's credibility when not claimed to be coerced. However, evidence that the defendant remained silent during police interrogation, and after warnings were given, may not be used to impeach the testifying defendant's credibility.

A confession may be found by the court to be inadmissible against the person whose rights were violated, but some courts have approved the introduction of evidence against persons other than those whose questioning produced the confession. And the *Miranda* requirements only apply where there is official action. If a confession is obtained by one acting solely in a non-official capacity, that statement may be admitted without the necessity of administering the *Miranda* warnings.

There is a presumption that a second confession, obtained after an involuntary first confession, was induced by the same forces which made the first confession inadmissible. However, this presumption in some instances can be overcome by the prosecution.

The courts have established strict rules concerning the admissibility of confessions, but these rules do not prohibit all interrogation, and the investigator should continue to use interrogation as an investigative device. Experience has demonstrated that a large percentage of the persons accused of crime will confess voluntarily, even after being warned as required by *Miranda*. Even though confessions have been admitted where the warnings have not been given in the exact *Miranda* terms, the investigator and administrator should make certain that the warning is given in detail to avoid challenge.

In many instances other methods can be used in conducting the investigation so that it will not be necessary to depend upon the interrogation and a confession. Where a case can be prosecuted without the confession, it is preferable to use the other means available. Despite these restrictions, interrogation is still a useful and legitimate tool in crime investigation.

Although the terms "interrogation" and "confession" have been used throughout this chapter, it is suggested that other terminology be substituted. The terms were used here since they are generally recognized by criminal justice personnel and prosecutors. However, apparently some members of the public, and especially some writers, associate these terms with force and duress. To avoid any misunderstanding it is preferable to "talk with" the suspect rather than to "interrogate" him. And it is better to refer to the disclosures as "statements," "remarks," or "comments."

under the due process clause + equal protection clause of the 14th Amend

Chapter 7
SELF-INCRIMINATION AND RELATED ISSUES*

No person...shall be compelled in any criminal case to be a witness against himself,...

Fifth Amendment, 1791

Section

* *by John C. Klotter*

§ 7.1 Pre-constitutional development of the self-incrimination privilege

The rule that a man shall not be compelled to furnish evidence against himself has a long history. Before the year 1236, the accused in a criminal case was required to be sworn, but there was no questioning by the judge. The act of taking the oath was a ritual, and the determination of guilt or innocence was determined not on what was said but on the correct pronunciation of the oath.

In the year 1236, the ecclesiastical courts adopted a new procedure which required that the accused who was under an oath to speak the truth, answer specific questions asked him by the judge. The Star Chamber Statute of 1487 sanctioned the examination of the accused under oath at his trial, and the practice of putting the suspect under oath without any formal charge against him was a favorite method in heresy and sedition trials.[1] However, after the abolition of the Star Chamber and the High Commission in seventeenth century England, all ecclesiastical courts were forbidden to administer any oath whereby a party might be obliged to accuse himself of any crime.

By the end of the reign of King Charles II, the claim that no man was bound to incriminate himself on any charge in any court was generally conceded by the English judges. But it was not until after 1700 that the privilege was fully recognized in England.

§ 7.2 Provisions of state constitutions and the Fifth Amendment to the United States Constitution

At the time of the formation of the Union, the principle that no person could be compelled to be a witness against himself had become entrenched in the common law. It was, therefore, understandable that as the original states developed their constitutions, this concept was preserved. In fact, five of the original thirteen states guarded this principle from legislative or judicial change by incorporating it into their constitutions. North Carolina, Pennsylvania, and Virginia included the provisions concerning self-incrimination in their constitutions in 1776. Massachusetts included the provision in its constitution in 1780, and New Hampshire in 1784. The remainder of the states extended this protection even though it was not specifically mentioned in their constitutions.[2]

---

1 8 WIGMORE, EVIDENCE § 2250 (1961).

2 *See* Twining v. New Jersey, 211 U.S. 78, 29 S. Ct. 14, 53 L. Ed. 97 (1908).

Although this privilege had been included in the constitutions of some of the original thirteen states, the privilege was not included in the Federal Constitution as originally adopted. It was made a part of the Constitution by inclusion in the Fifth Amendment in 1791. The part of the Amendment which specifically protects the privilege against self-incrimination reads as follows:

> [N]or shall [any person] be compelled in any criminal case to be a witness against himself,...

All of the states except New Jersey and Iowa have state constitutional provisions relating to self-incrimination. In most states the wording is like that in the federal Constitution, but in others the wording is somewhat different. For example, in Kentucky, the constitution provides that:

> In all criminal prosecutions the accused...cannot be compelled to give evidence against himself....[3]

Although the term "give evidence" could be interpreted to be broader in application than "be a witness," these terms have generally been interpreted to give the same protection against self-incrimination.

§ 7.3 Application of the Fifth Amendment privilege against self-incrimination to the states

The question arose early as to whether the privilege against self- incrimination was a right protected against state action by the Fourteenth Amendment. In other words, if the state courts determined that the self- incrimination privilege was not violated, did the federal courts have the authority to reverse the decision under the provisions of the Fifth Amendment as applied to the states through the Fourteenth? Early cases answered this with a definite "No."[4]

The United States Supreme Court, in rejecting the claim that this privilege is protected by the Fourteenth Amendment against abridgment by the states, remarked:

> [T]he exemption of compulsory self-incrimination is not a privilege or immunity of National citizenship guaranteed by this clause of the Fourteenth Amendment against abridgment by the States.

---

3 KY. CONST. § 11.

4 Twining v. New Jersey, 211 U.S. 78, 29 S. Ct. 14, 53 L. Ed. 97 (1908).

Even as late as 1947 the majority on the Court refused to apply the Fifth Amendment privilege against self-incrimination in state cases. The Court said in the case of *Adamson v. California*:[5]

> It is settled law that the clause of the Fifth Amendment, protecting a person against being compelled to be a witness against himself, is not made effective by the Fourteenth Amendment as a protection against state action on the ground that freedom from testimonial compulsion is a right of national citizenship, or because it is a personal privilege or immunity secured by the Federal Constitution as one of the rights of man that are listed in the Bill of Rights.

Four judges, Justices Black, Douglas, Murphy, and Rutledge dissented. Justice Black argued:

> [H]istory conclusively demonstrates that the language of the first section of the Fourteenth Amendment, taken as a whole, was thought by those responsible for its submission to the people, and by those who opposed its submission, sufficiently explicit to guarantee that thereafter no state could deprive its citizens of the privileges and protections of the Bill of Rights.

More than half a century after the *Twining* case, the Supreme Court completely reversed the *Twining* decision and, in *Malloy v. Hogan*,[6] held that the Fifth Amendment protection against self-incrimination is made applicable to the states through the Fourteenth Amendment. In 1959 the petitioner Malloy was arrested during a gambling raid in Hartford, Connecticut. He pleaded guilty to the crime of pool-selling, a misdemeanor, and was sentenced to one year in jail and fined $500. About sixteen months after his guilty plea, the petitioner was ordered to testify before a referee appointed by the Superior Court of Hartford County to conduct an inquiry into alleged gambling and other criminal activities in the county. He refused to answer any questions on the grounds that it would tend to incriminate him.

The Superior Court adjudged him in contempt and committed him to prison until he was willing to answer the questions. The Connecticut Supreme Court of Errors held that the Fifth Amendment privilege against self-incrimination was not available to a witness in a state proceeding. The Supreme Court of the United States reversed the decision, asserting:

---

5 Adamson v. California, 332 U.S. 46, 67 S. Ct. 1672, 91 L. Ed. 1903 (1947).

6 378 U.S. 1, 84 S. Ct. 1489, 12 L. Ed. 2d 653 (1964).

> We hold today that the Fifth Amendment's exception from compulsory self-incrimination is also protected by the Fourteenth Amendment against abridgment by the States.

To reinforce the holding in the *Malloy* case, the Supreme Court in 1965 reversed another conviction because the trial court commented upon the failure of the accused to testify on his own behalf.[7]

By making the self-incrimination guarantee of the Fifth Amendment applicable to the states by way of the Fourteenth, the Supreme Court also mandated that the standards to be applied are those as determined by the Supreme Court and other federal courts. State courts, in interpreting their own state constitutions, may establish additional, more restrictive requirements, but the state may not establish requirements that are less restrictive than those established by the Supreme Court of the United States via the Fifth Amendment.

§ 7.4 Expansion of the privilege to include pretrial situations

The Fifth Amendment provision concerning self-incrimination provides that no person shall be compelled in any criminal case to be a witness against himself. When interpreted literally this would mean only that a person shall not be required in a court proceeding in which he is a defendant to give evidence against himself. If this reasoning were followed, coerced confessions obtained prior to the trial of the case would not be considered as violating the self- incrimination privilege.

There has been much discussion concerning the relationship between the self-incrimination privilege and the confession rule. The late Dean Wigmore, in his treatise on evidence, made this statement regarding confessions and self-incrimination:

> The history of the two principles is wide apart, differing by one hundred years in origin, and derived through separate lines of precedents....If the privilege, fully established by 1680, had sufficed for both classes of cases there would have been no need in 1780 for creating a distinct rule about confessions....so far as concerns practice, the two doctrines have not the same boundaries. The privilege covers only disclosures made under legal compulsion; the confes-

---

7 Griffin v. California, 380 U.S. 609, 85 S. Ct. 1229, 14 L. Ed. 2d 106 (1965).

sion rule covers statements made anywhere, including statements made in court.[8]

Notwithstanding this reasoning, today the self-incrimination privilege does extend to out-of-court as well as in-court situations. All doubt concerning the application of the Fifth Amendment privilege against self-incrimination was laid to rest in the case of *Miranda v. Arizona*.[9] After discussing the development of the self-incrimination rule, Chief Justice Warren, speaking for the majority, stated:

> Today, then, there can be no doubt that the Fifth Amendment privilege is available outside of criminal court proceedings and serves to protect persons in all settings in which their freedom of action is curtailed...from being compelled to incriminate themselves.[10]

§ 7.5 Scope of the self-incrimination protection[11]

What can an accused person be compelled to do without violating the self-incrimination provisions? Does this protection extend to such practices as the taking of fingerprints and photographs? As the rule developed in England, the prohibition was against compelling an accused to disclose his guilt or to testify to facts subjecting him to punishment. The privilege was expressed in our constitutions by such words as "to be a witness against himself" or "to give evidence against oneself." Some authorities have argued that the protection extends only to testimonial compulsion and that no other compelled conduct, however unlawful or inadmissible on other grounds, is within the protection of the privilege. Most authorities, however, agree that the protection extends to documents and other evidence of a testimonial or communicative nature.

Traditionally, the self-incrimination protection extends to private papers, and the accused generally cannot be forced to bring private papers before the court. However, this does not apply to papers or books owned by the government or required to be maintained by government agencies. For example, passports are the property of the United States Government, and a defendant cannot refuse, on self-incrimination, grounds to make them available for use

---

8 8 WIGMORE, EVIDENCE § 2266 (1961).

9 384 U.S. 436, 86 S. Ct. 1602, 16 L. Ed. 2d 694 (1966).

10 *Id.* at 467.

11 *See* §§ 7.13 to 7.17 of this chapter for a discussion of additional restrictions predicated on the Due Process Clauses of the Constitution.

in court. The United States Court of Appeals for the Second Circuit defined the limits of the self- incrimination protection as it relates to books and papers in these terms:

> The Fifth Amendment can only be invoked to protect books or documents under certain circumstances. Simply stated, the privilege can be invoked to protect one's own books which are in one's own possession and which are self-incriminatory: The guaranty does not apply without this tripartite unity of ownership, possession and self-incrimination.[12]

If papers and documents are truly private, they are protected by the Fifth Amendment as well as the Fourth Amendment. On the other hand, if the papers, records or books are involved in a business, and others have knowledge of these records, they are not private within the meaning of the Constitution.[13] While personal diaries, letters, private writings made solely for personal use, or communications to a person occupying family or privileged relationships are protected by the Constitution, business records which the law requires to be maintained may be seized without violating the Fifth Amendment protection.[14]

Where the preparation of business records is voluntary, no compulsion is present.[15] Therefore, a subpoena that demands production of documents does not compel oral testimony, nor would it ordinarily compel a person to restate, repeat, or affirm the truth of documents sought.

In the *Doe* case, a federal grand jury was investigating corruption in the awarding of county and municipal contracts. Subpoenas were served on the defendant, who was the owner of a sole proprietorship, demanding production of business records of several of his companies. The District Court granted the defendant's motion to quash finding that the act of producing records would involve testimonial self-incrimination. The Court of Appeals affirmed, holding that the records were privileged and that the act of pro-

---

12 United States v. Falley, 489 F.2d 33 (2d Cir. 1973).

13 Fisher v. United States, 425 U.S. 391, 96 S. Ct. 1569, 48 L. Ed. 2d 39 (1976) held that a taxpayer's Fifth Amendment privilege against self-incrimination is not violated by the enforcement of a summons initiated by the Internal Revenue Service for the production of an accountant's work papers. This is true even though the papers prepared by the accountant were turned over to the taxpayer's attorney. *See also* United States v. Bennett, 409 F.2d 888 (2d Cir. 1969).

14 *Id.*

15 United States v. Doe, 465 U.S. 605, 104 S. Ct. 1237, 79 L. Ed. 2d 552 (1984).

ducing them also would have violated his Fifth Amendment privilege against self-incrimination.

On review by the Supreme Court of the United States, the majority decided that the contents of the subpoenaed records were not privileged under the Fifth Amendment, as that amendment only protects a person asserting the privilege, from compelled self-incrimination. As the preparation of the business records is voluntary, no compulsion is present. Therefore, as to the records themselves, according to the majority, the privilege does not apply if the preparation of the business records was not compelled.

On the other hand, the subpoena to produce the records is in violation of the Fifth Amendment, and the act of producing the subpoenaed documents cannot be compelled without a statutory grant of "use" immunity.

The concluding paragraph of the majority is as follows:

> We conclude that the Court of Appeals erred in holding that the contents of the subpoenaed documents were privileged under the Fifth Amendment. The act of producing the documents at issue in this case is privileged and cannot be compelled without a statutory grant of use immunity.

In the *Doe* case, Justice O'Connor wrote a separate concurring opinion to make it explicit that "The Fifth Amendment provides absolutely no protection for the contents of private papers of any kind."

Justice Marshall's dissenting opinion, however, does not agree with Justice O'Connor's determination that the Fifth Amendment offers no protection for the contents of private papers of any kind. The dissenting judges would have upheld the lower court's decision that the contents of private books and papers are protected by the Fifth Amendment as well as the act of producing the documents.

Professor McCormick, in discussing the scope of the privilege and commenting on the rule as expounded by Wigmore (widely accepted in recent opinions) concluded that:

> The accused without breach of the privilege may be fingerprinted and photographed, deprived of his papers and other objects in his possession, may be physically examined, may have his blood and other bodily fluids taken for test without his consent, may be required to give a specimen of his handwriting, may be compelled to assume positions taken by the perpetrator of the crime, and may be forced to participate in the police lineup, to stand up for identifica-

tion, put on articles of clothing, or display a scar or a limp. The list is illustrative, not exhaustive.[16]

Some of the specific situations which concern the police and prosecutor are discussed in the following paragraphs.

1. *Fingerprinting and photographing*

It has long been recognized that the taking of fingerprints and photographs for identification purposes does not violate the self-incrimination protections. The United States Court of Appeals for the District of Columbia said this was elementary when the person is in lawful custody. The exact words of the court were:

> We find no error in the admission of the palm print of Smith taken the day before trial for purposes of comparison with the palm print on the victim's credit cards. Unlike the situation in *Bynum v. United States*, appellant here was in lawful custody at the time the prints were recorded. And it is elementary that a person in lawful custody may be required to submit to photographing and fingerprinting as part of routine identification processes. [Citations omitted.][17]

There are indications that the taking of fingerprints by force would not be permissible unless there is a valid arrest. And only necessary force may be used. If there is unusual resistance, it is preferable to obtain a court order before taking the prints.

2. *The police lineup and other confrontations for identification*

The police lineup and "confrontation for identification" prior to trial have been challenged on at least three constitutional grounds. Although the courts have generally agreed that this procedure does not violate the self-incrimination provisions of the Fifth Amendment, the majority of the Supreme Court decided that a post-indictment criminal lineup is a critical stage in a

---

16 MCCORMICK, EVIDENCE § 126 (1954).

17 Smith v. United States, 324 F.2d 879 (D.C. Cir. 1963).

criminal proceeding and that, therefore, counsel may be required.[18] But the lineup or other confrontation does not violate self-incrimination protections. In the *Wade* case Justice Brennan, speaking for the majority, stated:

> We have no doubt that compelling the accused merely to exhibit his person for observations by a prosecution witness prior to trial involves no compulsion of the accused to give evidence having testimonial significance.

In *Caldwell v. United States*[19] the court explained why the lineup and confrontation for identification do not violate self-incrimination provisions of the Fifth Amendment, commenting:

> The mere viewing of a suspect under arrest by eye witnesses does not violate this constitutional privilege because the prisoner is not required to be an unwilling witness against himself. There is a distinction between bodily view and requiring an accused to testify against himself.

Similar reasoning was followed by the United States District Court for Eastern District of Pennsylvania, in concluding that the self-incrimination protection was not violated when a suspect was required to have a dental examination.[20] In this case, at the prosecutor's request, the court allowed an examination to determine whether or not the defendant was missing a tooth in the area of his mouth pinpointed by one of the witnesses. According to the majority, the examination was not testimonial or communicative in nature and did not violate either the Fourth or Fifth Amendments.

It has long been held that the compelled display of identifiable, physical characteristics infringes no interest protected by the privilege against compulsory self-incrimination.

---

18 Stovall v. Denno, 388 U.S. 293, 87 S. Ct. 1969, 18 L. Ed. 2d 1199 (1967); Gilbert v. California, 388 U.S. 263, 87 S. Ct. 1951, 18 L. Ed. 2d 1178 (1967); United States v. Wade, 388 U.S. 218, 87 S. Ct. 1926, 18 L. Ed. 2d 1149 (1967). *See* Chapter 8, *infra*.
See United States v. Crews, 445 U.S. 463, 100 S. Ct. 1244, 63 L. Ed. 2d 537 (1980), where the Supreme Court indicated that under some circumstances the use of photographs and the conduct of a lineup after an *illegal arrest* could contaminate the in-court identification if the pretrial identification procedures were suggestive.

19 338 F.2d 385 (8th Cir. 1964).

20 United States v. Holland, 378 F. Supp. 144 (E.D. Pa. 1974).

3. *Use of blood, urine and breath samples for determining alcohol content of the blood*

For many years there has been much discussion concerning the use of breath, urine or blood tests to determine the alcohol content of the blood. One of the first cases to consider the constitutionality of forcibly taking blood from a person who has been arrested was *Breithaupt v. Abram*.[21] Here a conviction was upheld, the Court holding that under the circumstances, the withdrawal of blood following an arrest for operation of a motor vehicle while under the influence of alcohol did not offend a sense of justice, and that the withdrawal of the blood and the admission of the blood for analysis did not violate the Fifth Amendment privilege against self-incrimination. The Court reasoned that the protection of the Fourteenth Amendment did not embrace the Fifth Amendment privilege; therefore, this protection did not apply in state proceedings.

The question again arose in the case of *Schmerber v. California*.[22] This case very definitely clarified the issue. Schmerber was arrested at the hospital for driving an automobile while under the influence of intoxicating liquor. With the advice of counsel, Schmerber objected to the taking of the blood sample, but it was taken by a physician at the request of a police officer over Schmerber's objection. This evidence was used in the criminal court, and the defendant was convicted of the criminal offense of driving an automobile while under the influence of intoxicating liquor. In appealing his conviction, the defendant asserted, among other things, that his rights were violated, contending that the admission of the analysis as evidence denied him due process of law under the Fourteenth Amendment as well as his privilege against self-incrimination under the Fifth Amendment as made applicable to the states through the Fourteenth Amendment.

The Supreme Court of the United States upheld the conviction and again emphasized that the taking of the blood sample was not a violation of the privilege against self-incrimination and explained that the privilege protects an accused only from being compelled to testify against himself or otherwise to provide the state with evidence of a testimonial or communicative nature. Although reaffirming the rule established in the *Malloy* case, that the Fourteenth Amendment secures against state invasion the same privileges that the Fifth Amendment guarantees against federal infringement, the Court continued with the statement:

---

21 352 U.S. 432, 77 S. Ct. 408, 1 L. Ed. 2d 448 (1957).

22 384 U.S. 757, 86 S. Ct. 1826, 16 L. Ed. 2d 908 (1966). *See* Part II for a reprint of this case.

> We hold that the privilege protects an accused only from being compelled to testify against himself, or otherwise provide the state with evidence of a *testimonial* or *communicative* nature, and that the withdrawal of blood and use of analysis in question in this case did not involve compulsion to these ends. [Emphasis added.]

The Court cautioned that the decision was limited to the facts of the case where the blood sample was taken by medical personnel in a medical environment.

It is interesting to note the Court also upheld the test as not being a violation of the Fourth Amendment because the blood sample was taken after arrest and there was no time to secure a warrant. The majority reasoned that the evidence of the blood alcohol content in this case might have dissipated had the officer been required to take the time to obtain a warrant.

Making reference to the *Schmerber* case, the Supreme Court in 1983 determined that the admission into evidence of a defendant's refusal to submit to a blood-alcohol test does not offend the privilege against self-incrimination.[23] The court reasoned that as no impermissible coercion is involved when the suspect refuses to submit to the test, there is no violation regardless of the form of the refusal.

In the *South Dakota v. Neville* case, the South Dakota trial court had granted the defendant's motion to suppress all evidence relating to his refusal to take the blood-alcohol test and this action was affirmed by the South Dakota Supreme Court. The United States Supreme Court disagreed with the South Dakota court's reasoning and remanded the case. The Supreme Court of the United States pointed out that South Dakota's "implied consent" law, declaring that any person operating a vehicle in South Dakota is deemed to have consented to the chemical test of the alcoholic content of his blood if arrested for driving while intoxicated, was not offensive to the Constitution. The court reiterated that the privilege bars the state only from compelling communications and testimony and since a blood test was "physical" or "real" evidence rather than testimonial evidence, such evidence is unprotected by the Fifth Amendment privilege. The Court in the *Neville* case, after first stating that the respondent conceded that the state court could legitimately compel the suspect against his will to take the test, continued with this comment:

> Given, then, that the offer of taking a blood-alcohol test is clearly legitimate, the action becomes no less legitimate when the state of-

---

23 South Dakota v. Neville, 459 U.S. 553, 103 S. Ct. 916, 25 L. Ed. 2d 748 (1983).

fers a second option of refusing the test, with the attendant penalties for making that choice.

Summarizing their opinion, the court held:

> We hold, therefore, that a refusal to take a blood-alcohol test, after a police officer had lawfully requested it, is not an act coerced by the officer, and thus is not protected by the privilege against self-incrimination.[24]

4. *Handwriting specimens*

Although there is still some disagreement, most authorities logically reason that the Fifth Amendment does not cover compulsory handwriting, especially where the writing is for identification purposes. In an Oregon case, the highest court of that state affirmed a conviction where handwriting specimens were taken at the police station.[25] The court refused to include this in the protection of the Fifth Amendment. It equated handwriting specimens with fingerprints and photographs, commenting:

> It seems now to be a well accepted fact that handwriting is almost as individualistic and identifying as are fingerprints.
> ...[W]e are unable to find a valid reason for holding that a person whose handwriting has been secured for comparison has had his constitutional right to counsel and privilege against self-incrimination invaded.

In 1973, the United States Supreme Court reiterated its previous announcement that the Fifth Amendment self-incrimination provision does not prohibit compelled display of identifiable, physical characteristics; nor did it prevent the grand jury from subpoenaing handwriting exemplars for identification purposes.[26]

Again in 1980 the United States Supreme Court found that no constitutional privilege is violated by legislation authorizing the Secretary of Trea-

---

24 *But see* State v. Audreus, 297 Minn. 260, 212 N.W.2d 863 (1973), where the State Supreme Court of Minnesota found that evidence of the defendant's refusal to submit to a chemical test may *not* be admitted.

25 State v. Fisher, 242 Or. 419, 410 P.2d 216 (1966).

26 United States v. Mara, 410 U.S. 19, 93 S. Ct. 777, 35 L. Ed. 2d 67 (1973). *See also* Trimble v. Hedman, 291 Minn. 442, 192 N.W.2d 432 (1971).

sury, and the Internal Revenue Service as his designate, power to compel handwriting exemplars.[27] Upholding the rationale of previous cases, the Court reiterated that:

> Compulsion of handwriting exemplars is neither a search nor seizure subject to the Fourth Amendment protections...nor testimonial evidence protected by the Fifth Amendment privilege against self-incrimination....The compulsion of handwriting exemplars has been the subject of far less protection than compulsion of testimony and documents.

Although the courts are agreed that the use of handwriting specimens for comparison purposes does not violate the Fifth Amendment self-incrimination privilege, a practical question arises as to how one can be forced to give handwriting specimens. One method approved in the case of *United States v. Doe*[28] is the use of a court order. In this case, when the defendant persisted in his refusal to give a handwriting exemplar, the court held him in civil contempt and ordered that he be held for 30 days or until such time as he purged himself of this contempt by furnishing the required handwriting exemplar. The court further stated that the suspect could be requested to furnish an exemplar consisting of the reproduction of the very instrument (a postal money order in this case) that he was accused of stealing.

Since one can be required by the court order to furnish a sample of the handwriting for comparison purposes, a fortiori, it is not a violation of the privilege to use handwriting specimens obtained from suspects by subterfuge. Therefore, the courts have upheld the use of handwriting specimens obtained from fingerprint cards, police booking forms, and questionnaires.[29]

5. *Voice exemplars for identification purposes*

Many courts now accept spectrograph evidence to prove identity in criminal cases.[30] The constitutional question is whether compulsion to produce voice exemplars for such comparison violates the Fifth Amendment privilege against self-incrimination. This was the issue before the Supreme

---

27 United States v. Euge, 444 U.S. 707, 100 S. Ct. 874, 63 L. Ed. 2d 141, *reh'g denied*, 446 U.S. 913, 100 S. Ct. 1845, 64 L. Ed. 2d 267 (1980).

28 405 F.2d 436 (2d Cir. 1968).

29 Duncan v. United States, 357 F.2d 195 (5th Cir. 1966); Sutton v. Maryland, 4 Md. App. 70, 241 A.2d 145 (1968).

30 *See* KLOTTER, CRIMINAL EVIDENCE § 13.19 (4th ed. 1987).

Court in 1973 in the case of *United States v. Dionisio*.[31] In this case the grand jury had subpoenaed about twenty persons, including the respondent, to give voice exemplars for identification purposes. The respondent refused to comply on the basis that this violated his Fifth and Fourteenth Amendment rights. The United States Supreme Court, however, approved the compelled production of voice exemplars, agreeing that since they were to be used for identification purposes and not for the testimonial or communicative content, this procedure did not violate the Fifth Amendment against self-incrimination. It is obvious that a person could not be required to say anything that would be incriminating. On the other hand, if he is required only to say words which are not testimonial or communicative, the Fifth Amendment is not violated.

6. *Footprint comparisons and body examinations*

At one time, some courts interpreted the self-incrimination provision as prohibiting the police from requiring a suspect to place his foot in a footprint cast. Since the *Schmerber* case, this is no longer considered a violation of the Fifth Amendment as there is no testimony or communication involved.

Also applying the *Schmerber* rationale, the courts find no self-incrimination problem with examining a suspect's body for traces of blood,[32] or taking penis scrapings and saliva samples from a suspect.[33]

7. *Removal of bullet from body for comparison purposes*

Commenting that the appropriate framework for an analysis of surgical intrusions to remove a bullet from a suspect is provided in the case of *Schmerber v. California*, the majority of the Supreme Court agreed that such an intrusion is unconstitutional in some cases.[34] Basing their decision primarily on the Fourth Amendment, which was also discussed in *Schmerber*, the Court held that the proposed surgery in the case being considered would violate the suspect's right to be secure in his person and that the search would be "unreasonable" under the Fourth Amendment.

In this case, a shopkeeper wounded his assailant during an attempted robbery. The assailant was taken to the hospital where he was identified by

---

[31] 410 U.S. 1, 93 S. Ct. 764, 35 L. Ed. 2d 67 (1973).

[32] McFarland v. United States, 150 F.2d 593 (D.C. Cir. 1945).

[33] Brent v. White, 276 F. Supp. 386 (E.D. La 1967).

[34] Winston v. Lee, 470 U.S. 753, 105 S. Ct. 1611, 84 L. Ed. 2d 662 (1985).

the shopkeeper. The Commonwealth moved for an order directing the suspect to undergo surgery to remove a bullet lodged near his left collarbone, asserting that the bullet would provide evidence of respondent's guilt or innocence. When the Virginia Supreme Court refused to intervene, the federal district court, after an evidentiary hearing, enjoined the threatened surgery. The federal court of appeals affirmed.

The United States Supreme Court, making reference to the *Schmerber* case, indicated that the reasonableness of surgical intrusions beneath the skin depends on a case-by-case approach in which the individual's interest in privacy and security are weighed against society's interest in obtaining evidence for fairly determining guilt or innocence. Here the threats to respondent's safety posed by the surgery were the subject of sharp dispute, and there was conflict in testimony concerning the nature and scope of the operation. The Court also took into consideration the fact that the Commonwealth's assertion of a compelling need to intrude into the body to retrieve the bullet was not persuasive, as the Commonwealth had available substantial additional evidence that the respondent was the individual who accosted the victim.

Weighing these factors, the Supreme Court indicated that, in this case, it would be a violation of the Constitution to require the defendant to submit to surgical intrusion beneath the skin to recover the bullet. It is noted, however, that the door was left open for intrusions into the body where the threats to the suspect's health are minor and other evidence of guilt is lacking.

§ 7.6 Claiming the privilege

In a criminal case the ordinary witness claims the privilege at the trial as each question is asked. This is a personal privilege and must be claimed by the witness who may be incriminated if he answers the question. The privilege is claimed by the witness stating: "I refuse to answer on the grounds that it might incriminate me."

The defense attorney cannot claim the privilege on behalf of his client when the witness is asked a question which, if answered, would incriminate the witness or the client. The witness must claim the privilege himself although he may have an attorney present to advise him when the privilege may be claimed.

The defendant, on the other hand, in effect claims the privilege by refusing to take the stand in a criminal case. If the defendant takes the stand, he waives the privilege as to questions relating to the offense charged.

The defendant may not invoke the privilege for a third party. But a witness other than the defendant may invoke the privilege on his own behalf and refuse to answer questions which might tend to incriminate him. On the other hand, if that witness does not himself invoke the privilege, neither the defendant nor the defendant's attorney may complain.[35]

The privilege may be claimed outside of court when the person questioned refuses to answer questions asked of him by an official. It may be claimed by expressing an intention not to reply or by remaining mute when a question is asked.

In court the judge, not the person claiming the privilege, must decide whether the witness may invoke the privilege and decline to answer the question on the grounds of possible self-incrimination. In the case of *State v. Robbins*,[36] the Maine Supreme Judicial Court, after citing federal cases including United States Supreme Court cases, reiterated the standards to be applied:

> 'To sustain the privilege, it need only be evident from the implications of the question, in the setting in which it is asked, that a responsive answer to the question or an explanation of why it cannot be answered might be dangerous because the injurious disclosure could result.'

The judge must decide after he has obtained all the facts and, in some instances, after he has interrogated the witness outside the hearing of the jury, whether the answer would in fact incriminate the witness. The judge in his discretion, may direct the witness to answer some questions which would not be incriminating, and not to answer other questions which could be of an incriminating nature.

Often the judge has the difficult task of reconciling the conflict between the defendant's right to testimony in his defense and the witness's claim of privilege of silence. In the *Robbins* case, for example, the State Supreme Court found that the judge had abused his discretion by failing to require the recalcitrant witness to answer questions which presented no real threat of incriminating her, where the answers would have contradicted and incriminated the key prosecuting witness. If, on the other hand, the witness's answer would in fact incriminate him, he will not be required to answer even if the evidence is important to a defendant.

---

[35] United States v. Nobles, 422 U.S. 225, 95 S. Ct. 2160, 45 L. Ed. 2d 141 (1975).

[36] 318 A.2d 51 (Me. 1974), *quoting* Hoffman v. United States, 341 U.S. 479, 71 S. Ct. 814, 95 L. Ed. 1118 (1951).

§ 7.7 Waiver of the privilege

Although the guarantee of immunity from compulsory incrimination is a personal privilege, it may be waived. Where the accused acts voluntarily he may waive his privilege protected by the self-incrimination provisions, either in court or outside of court. The burden is on the prosecution to show that the defendant knowingly and intelligently waived the privilege.

At the trial itself, both the accused and the ordinary witness may waive the rights protected by the self-incrimination provisions. However, the procedure in waiving the right differs between the ordinary witness and the defendant.

1. Waiver by the defendant at trial

The accused has the option under the criminal procedure provisions in this country to remain off the stand altogether or to testify. However, by volunteering to become a witness he waives his right as it concerns relevant inquiries about the charges against him.[37] With few exceptions the defendant cannot take the stand and testify in his own behalf and then refuse to answer relevant inquiries on cross-examination. Even at the trial the accused must be made aware that he is waiving his rights and this waiver must be made intelligently and knowingly.

Many states, including Tennessee, had statutes which required that a defendant desiring to testify in a criminal case do so before any other testimony for the defense was heard by the court trying the case. When this procedure is followed, if the defendant refuses to take the stand prior to the time other testimony for the defense is heard, he waives his right to testify in his own behalf.

This requirement that the defendant take the stand first has been challenged.[38] In the case of *Brooks v. Tennessee* the trial court refused to allow defendant to testify after the defense had called two other witnesses. Appeal was made to the Tennessee Supreme Court which refused to reverse the conviction. In the appeal to the Supreme Court of the United States, the defendant claimed that requiring a defendant to testify first or lose his right to testify violates the federal Constitution.

The Supreme Court reversed the lower court, deciding that this requirement violates both the self-incrimination protection of the Fifth Amendment and the due process protection of the Fourteenth Amendment.

---

[37] Johnson v. United States, 318 U.S. 189, 63 S. Ct. 549, 87 L. Ed. 704 (1943).

[38] Brooks v. Tennessee, 406 U.S. 605, 92 S. Ct. 1891, 32 L. Ed. 2d 358 (1972).

As to the Fifth Amendment protection the Court said, "This rule cuts down on the privilege to remain silent by making its assertion costly." After explaining that the penalty for not testifying first is to keep the defendant off the stand entirely, even though as a matter of professional judgement his lawyer might want to call him later in the trial, the Court concluded by saying: "Petitioner, then, was deprived of his constitutional rights when the trial court excluded him from the stand for failing to testify first."

By this *Brooks* decision the Supreme Court has declared that a procedure requiring the defendant to take the stand before any other testimony for the defense is heard, whether it be state statute or by the rules of the court, is unenforceable as in violation of the Fifth and Fourteenth Amendments.

2. *Waiver by the ordinary witness at trial*

Unlike the accused, the ordinary witness has no privilege to decline altogether to testify. On the other hand, by taking the stand he waives nothing. He makes the choice as each question is asked. However, when the witness has testified to an incriminating fact, he is considered to have waived his privilege as to all further questions relevant to the same transaction.

The decision of the witness not to answer questions on the grounds it may incriminate him is not conclusive, of course. Although the judge should give the claim careful consideration, he makes the final decision as to whether the witness will be required to answer the question.

3. *Waiver outside of court*

In an out-of-court situation, if the witness or accused refuses to answer questions, neither the police nor the prosecutor can force him to do so. But if the statement is made after waiver and is made knowingly and intelligently, it may be used in court.[39]

§ 7.8 Comment on the failure to testify

Most state legislatures recognized that authorizing the prosecutor to make comments concerning the accused's failure to testify would discourage the exercise of the privilege against self-incrimination and traditionally for-

39 *See* Chapter 6, *supra*, concerning interrogations and confessions for the waiver requirement.

bade the counsel for the state to comment on the failure of the accused to testify. However, a few states, including the state of California, at one time by statute authorized such comment when the accused did not take the stand in his own behalf. In 1947 the Supreme Court refused to set aside a conviction in a case where the prosecutor, under the California law, had commented on the failure of the accused to testify.[40]

In spite of this decision, all questions concerning the authority of the prosecutor to comment on the failure of the accused to testify were resolved in the case of *Griffin v. California*.[41] Here the Court held that the trial court and prosecutor were precluded from commenting before the jury upon the defendant's failure to testify in his own behalf. The decision was not surprising as it reiterated the decision of *Malloy* which held that the Fourteenth Amendment secured against state invasion the protections of the Fifth Amendment concerning self-incrimination.

In light of these decisions it is clear that the prosecutor now does not have the right to comment on the defendant's failure to testify, even though such right might be specifically authorized in a state statute.

Although the prosecutor does not have the right to comment on the defendant's failure to testify, a state trial judge has a constitutional obligation, upon proper request, to give the instruction that "the defendant is not compelled to testify and the fact that he does not cannot be used as an inference of guilt and should not prejudice him in any way."[42] In the *Carter* case the defendant did not testify for himself and asked the judge to give evidentiary weight to his failure to testify. The lower court and the Kentucky Supreme Court rejected the argument that the Fifth and Fourteenth Amendments require the trial judge to give the requested instruction, holding that such instruction would have required the judge to "comment upon" the petitioner's failure to testify in violation of the Kentucky Statute prohibiting such a comment and the *Griffin v. California* rule.

The United States Supreme Court reaffirmed the *Griffin* decision but reasoned that even without adverse comment, a jury, unless instructed otherwise, may well draw adverse inferences from the defendant's silence. The court went on to indicate that while no judge may prevent jurors from speculating about why a defendant stands mute in the fact of a criminal accusation, a judge can, and must, if requested to do so, use the unique power of the jury instruction to reduce the speculation to a minimum.

Again making reference to the *Griffin* decision, the United States Supreme Court in 1988 explained that in *Griffin v. California* that court had

---

40 Adamson v. California, 332 U.S. 46, 67 S. Ct. 1672, 91 L. Ed. 1903 (1947).

41 380 U.S. 609, 85 S. Ct. 1229, 14 L. Ed. 2d 106 (1965).

42 Carter v. Kentucky, 408 U.S. 288, 101 S. Ct. 1112, 67 L. Ed. 2d 241 (1981).

established the rule that where the prosecutor on his own initiative asks the jury to draw an adverse inference from the defendant's silence, or to treat the defendant's silence as substantive evidence of guilt, the privilege against compulsory self-incrimination is violated.[43] However, where the defense counsel urged in his closing arguments that the government had now allowed the defendant to explain his side of the story, and had unfairly denied the defendant the opportunity to explain his actions, the prosecutor's reference to the defendant's opportunity and failure to testify is not a violation of the privilege.

From these cases the rule can be formulated that generally the prosecutor is precluded from commenting on the failure of the defendant to testify at the trial. However, if the defendant's attorney makes reference to the fact that the defendant did not have an opportunity to testify on his own behalf, then the prosecutor is justified in making a fair response to this claim by his own comments.

§ 7.9 Immunity from criminal prosecution

No discussion concerning self-incrimination would be complete without a mention of the immunity statutes which have received so much attention in the last few years. The most publicized example of the value of the immunity statute was the use of this statute in making it possible to sentence the late Salvatore Giancana for contempt. Giancana, reputed to be one of the top men of Chicago's branch of the Cosa Nostra, was granted immunity from prosecution by a federal grand jury investigating the crime syndicate operations. Because he was granted immunity, he had no legal basis for pleading silence for fear of incriminating himself. Therefore, when he continued to refuse to testify, Judge Campbell committed Giancana for contempt, to the custody of the Attorney General.[44]

The immunity concept is not new. In 1892 the United States Supreme Court was called upon to decide the constitutional sufficiency of the federal immunity statute which provided only that the compelled testimony should not be given in evidence or used in any manner against the defendant in any criminal proceedings. The Court held that this was unconstitutional as it did not give the witness complete immunity; it did not prevent the use of testimony to search out other testimony which might be used against the accused.[45]

---

43 United States v. Robinson, __U.S.__, 108 S. Ct. 864, __L. Ed. 2d__ (1988).

44 In re Grand Jury Investigation of Giancana, 352 F.2d 921 (7th Cir. 1965).

45 Counselman v. Hitchcock, 142 U.S. 547, 12 S. Ct. 195, 35 L. Ed. 1110 (1892).

If the statute gives complete immunity, it is not considered to be unconstitutional. This seems to be a just and fair decision as the purpose of the privilege initially was to protect the individual so that he could not be compelled to be a witness against himself so as to subject him to criminal prosecution. If there can be no prosecution, then the reason for the self- incrimination protection no longer exists.

Because of our dual system of government, there has been some confusion concerning the authority of the federal courts to grant immunity from prosecution in the state court, and the corresponding authority of the state court to make a person immune from prosecution in the federal courts. This issue was presented in the case of *Murphy v. Waterfront Commission.*[46] Here the petitioner was subpoenaed by the commission and granted immunity from prosecution in either New York or New Jersey. He, however, persisted in his refusal to testify because there was a possibility that the evidence could be used in federal court. The Supreme Court of the United States held that neither a state nor the federal government may use testimony given after immunity was granted by either. The effect of the Supreme Court's holding is to leave unimpaired the immunity laws of the states and strengthen the hands of the prosecutors in obtaining valuable evidence, especially in organized crime situations.

The basic question which has been discussed frequently in the lower courts is whether a person can be required to testify after being given immunity by statute. A related question is whether such person must be given absolute immunity against any future prosecution. Although the first question has been answered affirmatively in past cases, the answer to the second has been in doubt. This question was considered by the Supreme Court in 1972. The majority agreed that absolute immunity is not required before a person can be ordered to testify under the provisions of immunity statutes.[47]

Here the petitioner was ordered to appear before a grand jury to answer questions after he had been granted immunity. Even after immunity had been granted, however, the petitioner refused to answer the questions claiming that the scope of the immunity provided by the statute was not coextensive with the scope of the self-incrimination privilege. He contended that the statute must, at a minimum, grant full "transactional immunity" in order to be

---

46 378 U.S. 52, 84 S. Ct. 1594, 12 L. Ed. 2d 678 (1964). *See also* In re Zicarelli, 55 N.J. 249, 261 A.2d 129 (1970), holding that a state immunity statute does not violate self-incrimination provisions.

47 Kastigar v. United States, 406 U.S. 441, 92 S. Ct. 1653, 32 L. Ed. 2d 212 (1972). This case contains an excellent discussion of the history of immunity statutes and of "transactional" and "use" immunity.

coexistent with the privilege, and that a statute which does not afford absolute "immunity from prosecution" is not transactional and not constitutional.

Mr. Justice Powell, speaking for the majority of the Court, refused to go along with this strict interpretation. In making clear that a statute prohibiting the use in any criminal case of compelled testimony, or any information directly or indirectly derived from such testimony, is consonant with the Fifth Amendment standards, this terminology was used:

> We hold that such immunity from use and derivative use is coexistent with the scope of the privilege against self incrimination, and therefore is sufficient to compel testimony over a claim of the privilege.

The Court held that this prohibition of use of testimony provides a comprehensive safeguard which bars the use not only of the compelled testimony itself, but also the use of any testimony to develop "leads." The case also provides that the prosecution has the affirmative duty to prove that evidence it proposes to use in a future case is derived from a legitimate source wholly independent of the compelled testimony.

In summary, the Kastigar case makes it clear that absolute immunity from all prosecution is not required, but for an immunity statute to be constitutional it must confer immunity from "use" of the compelled testimony and evidence derived therefrom. Furthermore, in a subsequent criminal prosecution the prosecutor has the burden of proving affirmatively that evidence proposed to be used is derived from a legitimate source wholly independent of the compelled testimony.

§ 7.10 Claiming the privilege in disciplinary situations

The Fifth Amendment of the United States Constitution and the state self-incrimination provisions provide that no person shall be compelled in any criminal case to be a witness against himself. Does this protection extend to a situation where public employees are asked to make statements or answer questions regarding job performance? Secondly, may an employee who refuses to waive self-incrimination rights be dismissed for that refusal?

On at least two occasions the United States Supreme Court has considered the question of whether a police officer can be required to choose between exerting his self-incrimination protection or being removed from office for failure to answer questions at a disciplinary hearing. In the case of *Gar-*

rity v. New Jersey,[48] police officers were required to answer questions relative to irregularities in handling cases in the municipal courts or be subject to removal from office. The appellant in that case answered the questions, and some of the answers were used in subsequent prosecution for conspiracy to obstruct the administration of the traffic laws. He appealed to the higher courts and finally to the United States Supreme Court on the grounds that statements coerced in this fashion should not be used against him in a criminal trial. The Court concluded:

> [T]he protection of the individual under the Fourteenth Amendment against coerced statements prohibits use in subsequent criminal proceedings of statements obtained under threat of removal from office, and that it extends to all, whether they are policemen or other members of the body politic.

In a similar case, a New York City police officer was fired because he refused to sign a waiver and refused to testify before a New York County grand jury which was investigating alleged bribery and corruption of police officers in connection with unlawful gambling operations.[49] The question, as stated by the Supreme Court in that case, was "whether a policeman who refuses to waive the protection which the privilege gives him may be dismissed from office because of that refusal."

Under the circumstances stated, the Supreme Court agreed with the previous *Garrity* ruling but explained that in that case the petitioner's testimony was demanded not solely for the purpose of securing an accounting of his performance of his public trust. The Court indicated that if the testimony is to be used exclusively for administrative purposes, and there is a clear indication that the testimony cannot be used for criminal prosecution, the officer can be required to answer questions. The Court expressed this in the following manner:

> If appellant, a policeman, had refused to answer questions specifically, directly, and narrowly relating to the performance of his official duties, without being required to waive his immunity with respect to the use of his answers or the fruits thereof in a criminal prosecution of himself,...the privilege against self-incrimination would not have been a bar to his dismissal.

---

48 385 U.S. 493, 87 S. Ct. 616, 17 L. Ed. 2d (1967).

49 Gardner v. Broderick, 392 U.S. 273, 88 S. Ct. 1913, 20 L. Ed. 2d 1082 (1968).

Relying on the wording of the *Gardner* case, the Massachusetts Supreme Court found that Boston police officers who were allegedly involved in unseemly antics during off-duty hours must respond to a police department questionnaire concerning their conduct.[50] In that case, affidavits alleged that fifteen or twenty Boston police officers, while in Newport, Rhode Island, to participate in a Law Day celebration, swam and played in the nude in a swimming pool at the Ramada Inn, struck a customer with a cue stick, broke into the hotel liquor cabinet, used foul and opprobrious language, and left without paying for breakfast.

A deputy superintendent of the Boston Police Department was placed in charge of the investigation. He prepared a questionnaire which required the officers to file a narrative report of the events based upon fifteen questions set forth in the questionnaire. The questionnaire also provided that the officers' answers could not be used in evidence in a criminal prosecution against them. The officers urged that the questionnaires violated their rights guaranteed by the state and federal constitutions and sought injunctive relief. The highest court of the state of Massachusetts quoted the words of the *Gardner* case and refused to grant injunctive relief to the officers. According to that court, requiring the officers to answer the inquiries directed to the activities in Rhode Island does not infringe their Fifth Amendment rights when the evidence is being used in relation to the performance of official duties and not for criminal prosecution.

Making reference to the case of *Garrity v. New Jersey*, the United States District Court for the Southern District of Alabama found that the Fifth Amendment rights of state employees were violated when they were discharged for pleading the Fifth Amendment before a state grand jury.[51] In this *Sawyer* case state employees were fired for refusing to testify before a grand jury after being given an order to do so. Although there was some indication that the evidence would not be used against the employees in a criminal trial, there was no definite assurance of immunity. In deciding for the employees the court concluded that:

> Since the employees were threatened with termination should they refuse to submit to testing, they were entitled to rest on the Fifth Amendment until and unless they received affirmative assurances of immunity from prosecution.

---

50 Broderick v. Police Comm'r, 330 N.E.2d 199 (Mass. 1975), *cert. denied*, 423 U.S. 1048 (1976).

51 Sawyer v. Alabama, 693 F. Supp. 1036 (S.D. Ala. 1988).

Succinctly stated, the rule is that where the employee's testimony is demanded solely and exclusively for administrative purposes and the testimony cannot be used for criminal prosecution, the employee can be required to answer the questions and this does not violate the self-incrimination provisions. But an employee cannot be required to choose between exerting his self-incrimination protection or being removed from office for failure to answer questions if the answers or fruits thereof can be used in a criminal trial.

§ 7.11 Implied consent statutes

Recognizing that a high percentage of fatal automobile accidents involve drivers who have been drinking, state legislators, prosecutors and police have attempted to find some valid means of determining if drivers have been operating vehicles under the influence of intoxicants. In 1953 New York enacted the first implied consent statute. Since that time at least twenty-five other states have enacted legislation similar to the New York statute.[52] This law provides that anyone, whether licensed locally, unlicensed, or licensed in another state, is deemed to have given his consent, in return for the driving privilege, to submit to an alcohol test, if there are reasonable grounds to believe that he has been driving while intoxicated. Under the provisions of this statute, if the individual refuses to take the test, his license may be suspended for a period of six months.

Implied consent statutes have been challenged in various states as violating the self-incrimination provisions of the state and federal constitutions, the search and seizure provisions, the equal protection provisions, and due process of law. To date, these laws have been held to be constitutional. In upholding its statute, the Kansas Supreme Court noted that the only question concerns the power of the state first to suspend and later revoke a driver's license of the licensee upon being arrested on a charge of driving a motor vehicle while under the influence of intoxicating liquor, when the driver refuses to submit to one of the statutory tests.[53] The court repeated that this was not a violation of due process, that it was not an act that would shock the conscience, and was not inherently brutal and offensive. The court also held that it did not violate the self-incrimination provisions of either the federal or state constitutions.

The implied consent law was challenged before the highest court in Nebraska in 1966.[54] That court also upheld the validity of the law, stating:

---

52 *See, e.g.*, N.Y. VEH. & TRAF. LAW § 1194 (Supp. 1976).

53 Lee v. State, 187 Kan. 566, 358 P.2d 765 (1961).

54 State v. Oleson, 180 Neb. 546, 143 N.W.2d 917 (1966).

> We conclude that the validity of a sample of blood or urine under the implied consent law is not impaired by a request for legal counsel, or the failure of defendant's counsel to appear before the sample is taken. We do not, by this opinion, intend to impair the right of a defendant to counsel for the purpose of protecting his rights. Our holding, simply stated, is that a defendant loses no rights subject to protection by legal counsel when he is requested to and furnishes a sample of blood or urine for chemical analysis to be used as evidence against him under the implied consent law.

The implied consent and related statutes have also been challenged on the ground that a comment on the failure to take the blood alcohol test violates the self-incrimination privilege. For example, in the case of *Newhouse v. Misterly*,[55] the defendant, after being arrested for drunken driving, refused to take the breath test or perform other acts as requested by the enforcement officers. At the trial the prosecution introduced evidence of the defendant's refusal to take the test and argued that the refusal showed the defendant was conscious of the fact that the test would indicate use of alcohol. In refusing to invalidate the defendant's conviction, the reviewing court held that the prosecutor and judge could properly comment at the trial on defendant's refusal to submit to the test. The same reasoning was followed in the Louisiana court which held that since bodily evidence itself violates no privilege against self-incrimination, neither does testimony concerning the refusal to give the bodily evidence.[56]

In the case of *South Dakota v. Neville* the United States Supreme Court in approving the admission of evidence of defendant's refusal to submit to a blood-alcohol test mentioned the implied consent law of South Dakota.[57] In that case the Supreme Court indicated that South Dakota, as part of its program to deter drinkers from driving, had enacted an "implied consent" law. Although the Supreme Court did not specifically say that the implied consent law is constitutional, it left no doubt that the South Dakota statute, which declares that any person operating a vehicle in the state is deemed to have consented to a chemical test of the alcoholic content of his blood if arrested for driving while intoxicated, did not violate the Constitution. In referring to the case of *Schmerber v. California* and in discussing the implied consent law in relation to that decision, the Court concluded part of the decision with this comment:

---

55 415 F.2d 514 (9th Cir. 1969).

56 State v. Pugas, 252 La. 345, 211 So. 2d 285 (1968).

57 South Dakota v. Neville, 459 U.S. 553, 103 S. Ct. 916, 74 L. Ed. 2d 748 (1983).

> Since a blood test was "physical or real" evidence rather than testimonial evidence, we found it unprotected by the Fifth Amendment privilege.

In view of these decisions it is apparent that implied consent laws which declare that any person operating a motor vehicle is deemed to have consented to a chemical test of the alcohol content of his blood if arrested while intoxicated, or a statute authorizing evidence of refusal to take a blood- alcohol test to be introduced in court, does not violate the self-incrimination provisions of the Fifth Amendment.

§ 7.12 Compulsory registration as violation of the self-incrimination privilege

Starting with the case of *Marchetti v. United States*,[58] a series of convictions has been challenged under the self-incrimination provision because the defendants were required by law to register. In the *Marchetti* case the defendant was charged with failure to purchase a wagering stamp as required by federal statute. The defendant argued that when purchasing the stamp (which requires that he indicate whether he is engaged in gambling), and in posting the stamp, he is being required to incriminate himself. The United States Supreme Court, in reversing the lower court conviction, held that if the defendant claims the privilege, it is a complete defense in a criminal prosecution for violations of the federal tax statutes requiring him to register as a gambler. The Court made it clear that persons may be criminally punished for gambling, but that provisions which require persons engaged in wagering to register as such are not enforceable and that persons may not be criminally punished for failure to comply with the requirements if they properly assert the constitutional challenge.

The *Marchetti* reasoning was applied in another case in 1969. This case involved the infamous Dr. Timothy Leary, a former professor at Harvard University, who actively encouraged the use of LSD.[59] In this case the defendant was convicted in federal court of violating the federal statutes governing traffic in marijuana. One section of the law required that a tax be paid on all transfers of marijuana and that the required order form must show the name and address of the transferor and transferee. One of the questions to be decided in the case was whether petitioner's conviction for failure to com-

---

58 Marchetti v. United States, 390 U.S. 39, 88 S. Ct. 697, 19 L. Ed. 2d 889 (1968).

59 Leary v. United States, 395 U.S. 6, 89 S. Ct. 1532, 23 L. Ed. 2d 57 (1969).

ply with the transfer tax provisions of the Marijuana Tax Act violated his Fifth Amendment privilege against self-incrimination. The Supreme Court, following the reasoning of the *Marchetti* case, reversed the conviction after finding that the Marijuana Tax Act compelled the petitioner to expose himself to a real and appreciable risk of self-incrimination.

The Court went on to find that he did not in fact waive his privilege of self-incrimination but violated the statutes requiring registration because of fear of criminal prosecution under the state and federal laws. As in previous cases of this type, the Court pointed out that it did not intend to prohibit enforcement of laws prohibiting the importation of narcotics but only that a person could not be forced to register when such registration would subject him to state or federal prosecution.

§ 7.13 Due process considerations

In the previous sections of this chapter the discussion has centered primarily around the Fifth Amendment self-incrimination provision as it is made applicable to the states by the Fourteenth Amendment due process clause. The remainder of the chapter will be devoted to a discussion of "Due Process" issues.

In some instances police conduct and procedure is challenged as violating more than one provision of the Constitution. For example, the lineup and other pretrial confrontations for identification are challenged as violating the self-incrimination provision of the Fifth Amendment, the right-to-counsel provision of the Sixth Amendment, and in some instances the due process clauses of the Fifth or Fourteenth Amendments. The same applies to the use of photographs for identification purposes. The taking of blood or other body fluids for the purpose of making a chemical analysis is often challenged as violating the self-incrimination provision, the search and seizure provision, and the due process clauses as well as the right to counsel.

In *Rochin v. California*[60] (which is discussed in subsequent paragraphs), police conduct was challenged as violating the Fourth Amendment, the Fifth Amendment self-incrimination provision, and finally, the due process clause of the Fourteenth Amendment. Even if the court finds that the conduct of the police officer is not in violation of self-incrimination provisions, that conduct may be challenged because of a general "due process" violation. Some of these issues will be discussed in the following sections.

---

60 342 U.S. 165, 72 S. Ct. 205, 96 L. Ed. 2d 183 (1952).

§ 7.14 Pretrial confrontation for identification

If the lineup, showup, or other confrontation is so unnecessarily suggestive as to be conducive to irreparable mistaken identification, the procedure violates due process. For example, if the suspect in the lineup is of one race, and five other persons in the lineup are of a different race, this would, of course, make the procedure unfair and unconstitutional.

In the case of *Foster v. California*,[61] decided in 1969, a witness to an armed robbery was called to the police station to view a lineup. In the lineup there were three men, including the petitioner. The petitioner was six feet in height while the other two men in the lineup were about five feet, six inches tall. Also, only the petitioner wore a leather jacket which was similar to the one the witness had said he saw on the robber. At the first lineup the witness could not positively identify the robber and he was called to view a second lineup. At the second lineup there were five men in the lineup but petitioner was the only person in the second lineup who had appeared in the first lineup. This time the witness was convinced that petitioner was the man he saw at the scene of the robbery.

The Supreme Court reversed the conviction and condemned this procedure as a violation of the due process clause of the Fourteenth Amendment, saying:

> In the present case the pretrial confrontations clearly were so arranged as to make the resulting identifications virtually inevitable.

Lineup and confrontation situations were considered again by the Supreme Court in a more recent case.[62] In this case the defendant was convicted of rape and sentenced to twenty years' imprisonment. The state's evidence consisted in part of testimony concerning a stationhouse identification of the defendant by the victim. The victim on several occasions viewed suspects in her home or at the police station, some in lineups and others in showups, and was shown between thirty and forty photographs before she identified the defendant. The officers testified that they did not have a full lineup because they were unable to find other persons fitting the petitioner's unusual description, and that they therefore conducted a showup. This showup consisted of two detectives walking the defendant past the victim at

---

[61] 394 U.S. 440, 89 S. Ct. 1127, 22 L. Ed. 2d 402 (1969).

[62] Neil v. Biggers, 409 U.S. 188, 93 S. Ct. 375, 34 L. Ed. 2d 401 (1972). This case reviews the lineup and confrontation cases and their relation to due process; it is reprinted in Part II. *See also* Manson v. Brathwaite, 432 U.S. 98, 97 S. Ct. 2243, 53 L. Ed. 2d 140 (1977).

police headquarters. At the victim's request the police also directed the petitioner to say, "Shut up or I'll kill you," these words being used at the time of the rape.

Following the stationhouse showup as described, the victim positively identified the defendant and identified him again at the trial. The in-court identification of the defendant was challenged on the ground that the stationhouse identification was suggestive and therefore contaminated the in- court identification.

The Supreme Court by a four-to-four decision affirmed the conviction after reasserting some general guidelines relating to suggestiveness and misidentification. The four members of the Court agreed that the admission of evidence of an identification showup without more does not in itself violate due process. The Court again warned the lower courts not to lose sight of the reason for examining the lineup or showup, explaining that, "the primary evil to be avoided is a very substantial likelihood of irreparable misidentification." The danger, the Court pointed out, is that suggestive confrontations may increase the likelihood of misidentification at trial; but the central question is whether under "the totality of circumstances" the in-court identification was reliable even though the confrontation procedure may have been suggestive. Applying this test to the facts of this case, the affirming Justices agreed that even though the stationhouse identification may have been suggestive, there was "no substantial likelihood of misidentification."

Five factors were listed in *Biggers* to be considered in evaluating the likelihood of misidentification:

(1) the witness's opportunity to view the criminal during the crime;
(2) the witness's degree of attention;
(3) the accuracy of the witness's prior description of the criminal;
(4) the level of certainty demonstrated by the witness at the confrontation; and
(5) the length of time between the crime and the confrontation.

In making reference to the five factors which were formulated by the Court for evaluating the likelihood of misidentification because of pretrial identification procedures, the Texas Court of Appeals in 1982 commented that "it is settled that a one-on-one showup identification, conducted soon after the criminal activity has occurred...is not illegal per se."[63] In this case the victim in an attempted rape case identified her assailant as he was being

63 Ortega v. State, 628 S.W.2d 539 (Tex. 1982).

placed in the police car near the scene of the crime. However, she was unable to identify the suspect at the trial but did testify at the trial that the man in the patrol car on the night of the incident was her assailant. The police officers identified the defendant at the trial as the man in the patrol car. Authorizing this in-court identification, the members of the Texas Court of Appeals were satisfied that there was not a likelihood of irreparable misidentification and there was no violation of due process of law.

Apparently the Second Circuit Court of Appeals was inclined to agree that a woman witness may change her mind without making the showup unreliable.[64] That court refused to reverse the conviction of the defendant even though the witness had first identified another man but quickly changed her mind when she was shown the defendant. The court said the prior misidentification is only one factor to be considered and does not of itself render the identification unreliable. The dissenting judges were of the opinion that this was such a compelling case of likely misidentification that the appellant should have been granted a retrial at which the in-court identification by this witness would have been excluded.

It is obvious that much of this controversy can be avoided if care is taken to conduct the showup, lineup or other confrontation in such a way that there will be no possibility of unfairness or unreliability. If, in conducting the lineup or showup, the procedure could cause the witness to identify the wrong person, the court may find that this procedure violates the due process provisions of the Constitution and refuse to allow the witness to identify the defendant in court.

§ 7.15 Pretrial photographic identification

Closely related to the lineup is the identification by means of photographs. In the case of *Simmons v. United States*,[65] this type of pretrial identification by means of photographs was challenged as being suggestive and conducive to misidentification and therefore in violation of the due process clause. Snapshots of the suspect had been shown to the five bank employees who had witnessed a bank robbery, and each witness identified Simmons as one of the robbers. The Court refused to prohibit the employment of this technique but cautioned that each case must be decided on its own facts. The reasons stated were:

---

64 Lucas v. Regan, 503 F.2d 1 (2d Cir. 1974).

65 390 U.S 377, 88 S. Ct. 967, 19 L. Ed. 2d 1247 (1968).

> [C]onvictions based on eyewitness identification at trial following a pretrial identification by photograph will be set aside on that ground only if the photographic identification procedure was so impermissibly suggestive as to give rise to a very substantial likelihood of irreparable misidentification.

As in the case of the lineup, if the photographs are used in such a way as to suggest to the witness the identification of the suspect, there is a good possibility that the in-court identification at the trial will be contaminated.

Although the statement of the rule is clear, the line as to what is a suggestive photographic identification and what is not suggestive is a fine one. Perhaps some insight can be gleaned by comparing three similar cases. In one case a New York robbery victim observed his attackers before they sprayed a chemical in his eyes and robbed him of a gun.[66] A week later the victim picked out the suspect from a spread of eight photographs, but one of the photographs was different in that it had a date inscribed which was close to the date the victim's gun was recovered. After the victim stated at the trial that he paid no attention to the numbers or dates, the identification of the suspect at the trial was authorized. The use of the photograph was not "unduly suggestive" nor conducive to irreparable mistaken identification, and the identification was approved by the reviewing court.

In a second case, however, the United States Court of Appeals for the Sixth Circuit found that the use of a single photograph was suggestive and denied due process.[67] Here the victim looked at more than twenty mug shots at police headquarters without identifying anyone as the robber. However, after the suspect had been arrested, police showed the victim a single photo of the suspect and he identified that person as the robber. The court found that the use of the single photograph, even after the victim had not identified the suspect from the first twenty, denied due process as there was no compelling circumstance which justified using a single photo.

In a third case, witnesses were shown five photographs on one occasion and identified a suspect.[68] Two months later the same witnesses were shown six photographs. The defendant challenged the selection of his photograph by the witnesses at the second display because he was the only person pictured there who was also pictured in the first display. Recognizing the risk of misidentification, the court, however, thought the risk was reduced in this case due to the time factor and the fact that one photograph was in color and one in black and white. Because the court believed there was nothing im-

---

[66] United States v. Counts, 471 F.2d 422 (2d Cir. 1973).

[67] Workman v. Cardwell, 471 F.2d 909 (6th Cir. 1972).

[68] United States v. Bowie, 515 F.2d 3 (7th Cir. 1975).

properly suggestive in the initial showings to the three witnesses in the case, the defendant's attack on the later photographic display was not persuasive, and the in-court identification was authorized. They found that the in-court identification was not the product of a pretrial procedure so impermissibly suggestive as to give rise to a very substantial likelihood of irreparable misidentification.

A United States Supreme Court decision in 1980 put agents on notice that they must be careful about what photographs are used for pretrial identification.[69] In this case the defendant had been taken into custody, ostensibly as a suspected truant from school, and was detained at police headquarters where he was briefly questioned, photographed, and then released. The victim then identified the defendant's photograph that was taken following the illegal arrest. The defendant was then taken into custody and at a court-ordered lineup was personally identified by the victim. The defendant claimed that the procedure contaminated the in-court identification and, therefore, the in-court identification should have been suppressed as the fruit of the defendant's concededly unlawful arrest. The Supreme Court, in reversing the lower Appeals Court, determined that the illegal arrest did not affect the victim's ability to give accurate identification testimony at the trial. The Court went on to say that at the trial the victim made the identification based upon her observations at the time of the robbery and that the "fruit served at the trial was not poisoned." The majority cautioned, however, that in some cases the intervening photographic and lineup identifications could under certain circumstances affect the reliability of the in-court identification and render it inadmissible.

Applying the rule established by the Supreme Court, the Third Circuit Court decided that if suggestive identification procedures are used, the question becomes whether the suggestiveness creates a very substantial likelihood of misrepresentation.[70] The court continued by stating the question is to be answered with reference to the totality of circumstances, with particular attention paid to such relevant factors as the quality of the witnesses' original opportunity to view the criminal, the degree of attention, the level of certainty when confronted with a suspect or his image, and the length of time between the crime and the confrontation.

Adopting this test, the majority of the Court found that any possible suggestiveness in presenting photographs in successive photographic arrays did not render the pretrial photographic identification of the defendant by three different witnesses inadmissible. Explaining that as each witness had an ample opportunity to observe the defendant and to form an impression,

---

69 United States v. Crews, 445 U.S. 463, 100 S. Ct. 1244, 63 L. Ed. 2d 537 (1980).

70 United States v. Dowling, 855 F.2d 114 (3d Cir. 1988).

and that as the witnesses were presented with photo arrays soon after the robbery and all three witnesses identified the defendant's picture from the first array, the procedure was not unduly suggestive. Adding that there was no evidence that the police contributed in any way to the possible suggestiveness, the Court concluded that "we cannot say there was a very substantial likelihood of misidentification."

From these and other cases it is apparent that care should be taken in establishing identification procedures to avoid a successful challenge of the process.

§ 7.16 Conduct which "shocks the conscience"

As was pointed out in the first chapter, the scope of the due process clause is so broad that a clear-cut definition is impossible. If, for example, the procedure used by enforcement agents offends a "sense of justice," the conviction based upon evidence obtained after such procedures may be reversed by the Supreme Court using the due process clause of the Fourteenth Amendment as a vehicle. One of the best examples of reversal of a conviction on these grounds is stated in the case of *Rochin v. California*.[71] In that case, deputy sheriffs having information that the accused was selling narcotics, entered the open door of a dwelling house and forced open the door to the accused's bedroom. Observing two capsules on the nightstand next to the bed, the officers asked, "Whose stuff is this?" The accused seized the capsules and put them in his mouth. The officers then attempted to extract the capsules but being unable to obtain the capsules before the accused swallowed them, took the accused to the hospital. At the hospital and at the direction of the officers, a doctor forced an emetic solution through a tube into Rochin's stomach against his will, and this "stomach pumping" produced vomiting. Two capsules obtained in this manner were used against the defendant at the trial and he was found guilty of possessing a preparation of morphine.

After explaining the application of the due process clause, the Court said it was compelled to conclude that the procedure by which this conviction was obtained violates that clause. The Court went on to say:

> This is conduct that shocks the conscience. Illegally breaking into the privacy of the petitioner, the struggle to open his mouth and remove what was there, the forcible extraction of the stomach contents -- this course of proceeding by agents of government to obtain

---

71 342 U.S. 165, 72 S. Ct. 205, 96 L. Ed. 183 (1952).

> evidence is bound to offend even hardened sensibilities. They are methods too close to the rack and the screw to permit of constitutional differentiation.

This case was reversed, not on the self-incrimination grounds but solely under the authority of the due process clause of the Fourteenth Amendment.

§ 7.17 Use of blood, breath, and urine samples

As was noted earlier, the taking of blood from the body of the suspect for chemical analysis has been challenged as a violation of the Fifth Amendment as made applicable to the states by the Fourteenth Amendment. This procedure has also been challenged as a violation of the due process clause of the Fourteenth Amendment directly. In the *Schmerber* case, the Supreme Court considered the due process claim but the majority rejected it.[72] The Court distinguished this from the "stomach pumping" of the *Rochin* case. The Court said: "Under such circumstances the withdrawal of blood does not offend that sense of justice of which we spoke in *Rochin v. California*."

A District of Columbia court has reaffirmed the right of enforcement agents to take urine and blood.[73] In so doing the court explained:

> Such physical evidence obtained from the defendant's body has been excluded on constitutional grounds only where the conduct used to obtain evidence was outrageous, unreasonable and offensive to a sense of justice.

Also there is no deprivation of constitutional rights when a person charged with the offense of operating a motor vehicle while under the influence of intoxicating liquor submits to a drunkometer test unless unnecessary force is used.[74]

This is not to say that the taking of blood or urine from the human body will never be challenged as a violation of the due process clause. As was pointed out in the *Schmerber* case, if the test is administered by such methods as to invite an unjustified element of personal risk of infection and pain, this might be in violation of the due process clause of the Fourteenth Amendment.

---

72 Schmerber v. California, 384 U.S. 757, 86 S. Ct. 1826, 16 L. Ed. 2d 908 (1966).

73 Davis v. District of Columbia, 247 A.2d 417 (D.C. App. 1968).

74 Toledo v. Deitz, 3 Ohio St. 2d 30, 209 N.E.2d 127 (1965). *See* KLOTTER, CRIMINAL EVIDENCE § 13.12 (4th ed. 1987).

Recently the suspension of a driver's license for refusing to take a Breathalyzer test was challenged as violating due process. In the case of *Mackey v. Montrym*,[75] decided in 1979, the Supreme Court was asked to declare unconstitutional a Massachusetts statute which mandates suspension of a driver's license for refusing to take a Breathalyzer test upon arrest for operating a motor vehicle while under the influence of intoxicating liquor. The defendant claimed that suspension of his license after refusing to take a Breathalyzer test without first holding a hearing violated his right to due process and sought an order enjoining a suspension of his license, compensatory and punitive damages, and declaratory injunctive relief on behalf of all persons whose licenses had been suspended pursuant to the statute without a prior hearing. A three-judge District Court declared that the defendant was entitled as a matter of due process to some sort of pre-suspension hearing before the registrar to contest the allegation of his refusal to take the test. That court held the implied consent statute unconstitutional on its face as a violation of due process.

The U.S. Supreme Court reversed the lower court and held that a pre-suspension hearing is not required by the due process clause. The Court concluded with this paragraph:

> We conclude...that the compelling interest in highway safety justifies the Commonwealth in making a summary suspension effective pending the outcome of the prompt post-suspension hearing available.

It is interesting to note that the Court in this case emphasized that the lower court overstated the risk of error in the initial reliance on the corroborated affidavit of a law enforcement officer. The Court pointed out that:

> The officer whose report of refusal triggers a driver's suspension is a trained observer and investigator. He is, by reason of his training and experience, well suited for the role the statute accords him in the pre-suspension process. And, as he is personally subject to civil liability for an unlawful arrest and to criminal penalties for willful misrepresentation of the facts, he has every incentive to ascertain accurately and truthfully report the facts.

---

75 443 U.S. 1, 99 S. Ct. 2612, 61 L. Ed. 2d 321 (1979).

This places a great responsibility on the police officer to accurately and fairly report the facts. Failure to do so as specifically pointed out in this case subjects the officer to civil and criminal liabilities.

§ 7.18 Summary and practical suggestions

The privilege from self-incrimination had become embodied in the common law prior to the adoption of the United States Constitution and the Bill of Rights. To make certain that this privilege would be protected in the future, members of the First Congress included it as part of the Bill of Rights. In addition, provisions concerning self-incrimination are included in the constitutions of all but two of the states.

In the early decisions, courts determined that the privilege as stated in the Fifth Amendment was applicable to the federal agencies only and not to the states. However, after considerable discussion, it was determined in 1964 by the United States Supreme Court in the *Malloy* case that this self-incrimination protection was made applicable to the states through the Fourteenth Amendment, and that the minimum standards would be those stated by the federal courts.

The early decisions left some doubt as to the application of the self-incrimination provisions outside of court. However, in 1966, the *Miranda* decision of the United States Supreme Court made it abundantly clear that the self-incrimination protection would extend to out-of-court as well as in-court situations.

Although the rule prohibiting the admissibility of involuntary confessions developed differently from the rule concerning self-incrimination, the Supreme Court in the case of *Miranda* reiterated the rule that an out-of-court confession which was solicited without proper warning was inadmissible as violative of the Fifth Amendment, and that this protection would be made applicable to the states through the Fourteenth Amendment. This case held that self-incrimination protection may be waived in such out-of-court situations, but that it must be knowingly and intelligently waived.

It is generally agreed that the privilege protects an accused only from being compelled to provide the state with evidence of a testimonial or communicative nature. Therefore, the taking of photographs, fingerprints, blood tests, handwriting specimens and other such evidence from persons legally arrested does not ordinarily violate the self-incrimination protections.

The self-incrimination claim is no longer available if the witness is given immunity under a properly drawn and applied immunity statute. If he is given "use" and "derivative" immunity, he can be required to testify, but the evidence cannot be used against him directly or indirectly in any future court proceeding.

The implied consent statutes provide that a person who obtains a driver's license is deemed to give his consent to submit to an alcohol test if there are reasonable grounds to believe that he was driving while intoxicated. Such statutes do not violate the self-incrimination provisions of the federal or state constitutions.

Statutes which require persons to register where such registration subjects them to state or federal criminal prosecution have been held to be unconstitutional. However, these decisions make it clear that there is no intention to prohibit enforcement of criminal laws where the accused is not required to incriminate himself by such registration.

Some enforcement procedures, such as a confrontation for identification prior to trial, have been challenged as violating the "self-incrimination," the "right-to-counsel," and the "due process" provisions of the Constitution. If the lineup or other confrontation for identification is conducted in such a way as to be unduly suggestive, the in-court identification will be disallowed because of the due process considerations. Also, conduct such as pumping the stomach has been found to offend a sense of justice and has made evidence so obtained inadmissible.

When establishing and implementing departmental procedures, the administrator must take into consideration the Fifth Amendment self- incrimination protection as well as the due process protections as interpreted by the Supreme Court. Carefully established procedures for the use of the showup and photographs for identification purposes will avoid unnecessary challenges to the in-court identification of the defendant by witnesses.

Chapter 8
ASSISTANCE OF COUNSEL*

In all criminal prosecutions, the accused shall enjoy the right...to have the Assistance of Counsel for his defence.

Sixth Amendment, 1791

* *by John C. Klotter*

§ 8.1 Historical development of the right-to-counsel protection

The law relating to counsel for the criminal defendant has developed over a period of several centuries. This development has been influenced by events which transpired in England prior to the settlement of this country and by American colonial history before the Revolutionary War. Because inequities which existed in the mother country and the colonies were familiar to the framers of the United States Constitution, provisions to reduce abuses were included in the Constitution of the United States and the constitutions of the various states. One section provides for the assistance of counsel for those accused of crimes.

In England, prior to 1688, a person charged with treason or felony had no right to demand the assistance of counsel to aid him in preparing his defense. Strangely, during this period persons charged with misdemeanors and parties in civil cases were entitled to seek and obtain legal assistance in their behalf. The rule which allowed counsel in misdemeanors but denied it in more serious offenses was vigorously assailed by seventeenth century English statesmen and lawyers. Its apologists defended the practice on the ground that the court functioned in the place of counsel and provided ample safeguards for the accused. After the English Revolution of 1688, the rule denying counsel in treason cases was abolished, but existing restrictions on the right to counsel in other felony cases continued until as late as 1836, when Parliament granted a corresponding right with respect to felony offenses in general.[1]

The historical development of the right to counsel in America does not parallel the English experience. The necessity of legal assistance in criminal cases was recognized at a much earlier date. Following the Declaration of Independence in 1776, the constitutions of several of the thirteen original states incorporated provisions guaranteeing the right to counsel. There is some diversity with respect to the wording of the early constitutional provisions. For example, in Maryland and New York, where provisions were adopted in 1776 and 1777 respectively, the provisions were to the effect that a defendant accused of crime should be "allowed" counsel. In Pennsylvania, New Hampshire, Delaware and Connecticut the accused was accorded the "right to be heard by himself and by his counsel." And in Massachusetts the constitution provided that the defendant should have the "right to be heard by himself or his counsel at his election."[2]

---

1 Powell v. Alabama, 287 U.S. 45, 60, 53 S. Ct. 55, 77 L. Ed. 2d 158 (1932).

2 Betts v. Brady, 316 U.S. 455, 465, 62 S. Ct. 1252, 86 L. Ed. 1595 (1942).

Inasmuch as many of the men who were responsible for drafting the various state constitutional provisions were also involved in the writing of the United States Constitution, it is not surprising that the Bill of Rights, which was adopted by the first Congress, contained provisions concerning the right to counsel.

§ 8.2 Constitutional provisions concerning the right to counsel

Prior to the adoption of the United States Constitution, many who argued its merits recognized that the document did not include any specific provisions guaranteeing the right to counsel. This omission was considered serious because an inarticulate person might be unjustly convicted through a lack of legal skills in presenting his defense. Therefore, when the Bill of Rights was considered by the first Congress, the right to counsel was included in the draft as part of the Sixth Amendment. The Amendment reads in pertinent part:

> In all criminal prosecutions, the accused shall enjoy the right...to have the Assistance of Counsel for his defence.

Like the other provisions of the Bill of Rights, the portions of the Sixth Amendment on counsel were originally intended to apply only to the operations of the federal government. The Amendment was written in broad, general terms without any attempt to define the scope of its application. Consequently, it becomes necessary to examine case law interpretations to determine what the right to counsel means in modern perspective.

In addition to the guarantee contained in the Bill of Rights, forty-nine states have incorporated similar provisions in their own local constitutions. Although these provisions are worded differently, both in substance and application very little distinction exists. For example, article 2, section 9 of the Illinois Constitution states:

> In all criminal prosecutions the accused shall have the right to appear and defend in person and by counsel.

The state and federal constitutional provisions pertaining to counsel for the accused have not changed during the past half-century. However, due to statutory enactments, and more importantly to court decisions, the rights protected have been vastly expanded. The law is much clearer today than in the past. But many questions still remain unanswered.

§ 8.3 Effects of denial of right to counsel

In a previous chapter the statement is made that if counsel is not afforded as required by the Constitution, a confession obtained after counsel is denied will not be admissible. It is explained that the Sixth Amendment right-to-counsel provision is enforced by excluding the confession. In addition, if counsel is denied at the post-indictment lineup or in certain other confrontation-for-identification situations, such denial could contaminate the in-court identification of the accused by the witness.

If, at the preliminary hearing, the accused is not afforded the right to counsel when this is a "critical stage" of the proceeding, a plea of guilty will not be accepted at a future trial of the case. The same reasoning applies where the right-to-counsel requirements are not complied with at the arraignment. The right to assistance of counsel at the criminal trial itself is deemed so fundamental that failure properly to observe that right automatically vitiates any conviction resulting from that trial.[3] This is true even though there is no showing of prejudicial unfairness.

Legally, a conviction obtained without the proper representation by counsel is totally void. Evidence concerning the conviction cannot be admitted in a later "habitual criminal" proceeding (whereby penalties can be increased for subsequent offenses), nor can it be used to impeach the defendant's testimony in any later proceedings.[4]

As failure to follow statutory provisions and court decisions relating to the right to counsel might prohibit the use of a confession or otherwise vitiate a conviction, it is essential that the criminal justice representative be fully aware of the laws relating to the right to counsel, especially as they apply in pretrial situations.

§ 8.4 Right to counsel at trial in federal courts in felony cases

The provisions of the Sixth Amendment are clear in stating that the accused shall enjoy the right to have the assistance of counsel for his defense. But does this command impose an affirmative obligation on the part of the

---

3 Ferguson v. Georgia, 365 U.S. 570, 81 S. Ct. 756, 5 L. Ed. 2d 783 (1961). *See also* Cuyler v. Sullivan, 444 U.S. 823, 100 S. Ct. 1708, 64 L. Ed. 2d 333 (1980), which held that if there is inadequate assistance of counsel in a state court, the conviction will be set aside for non-compliance with the Sixth and Fourteenth Amendments.

4 Loper v. Beto, 450 U.S. 473, 92 S. Ct. 1014, 31 L. Ed. 2d 374 (1972).

court to appoint counsel where the accused does not request assistance or is unable to pay the legal expenses involved? For several decades lawyers debated whether counsel was "required" or only "permitted" and whether, assuming the right did exist, it extended to all felony cases or was limited to "capital" offenses.

The law remained in a state of confusion until 1938 when the Supreme Court partially clarified the rule with respect to federal prosecutions. In the case of *Johnson v. Zerbst*,[5] the Court ruled that in all federal trials of persons charged with crimes of a serious nature, counsel must be appointed for an indigent defendant unless he intelligently waives his right to counsel. The case involved the prosecution of two Marines who were arrested while on leave in Charleston, South Carolina and charged with passing counterfeit bills, a felony under the laws of the United States though not a capital offense. Both men were taken to jail to await action by the grand jury and were indicted some two months later. Although they were represented by counsel at the time of arrest, they were unable to secure counsel for the trial. One of them attempted to conduct his own defense, but no counsel was appointed during the trial. They were both found guilty and sentenced to four and one-half years in the penitentiary.

After serving part of the sentence and after the time for appeal had elapsed, one of the defendants, Johnson, brought habeas corpus proceedings in a federal district court. Upon denial of relief the case was appealed to the Supreme Court of the United States. His conviction was reversed and the case remanded to the district court for retrial in conformity with the views expressed by the Supreme Court in its opinion. In reaching the conclusion that the defendant had been deprived of his constitutional rights, the majority stated:

> Since the Sixth Amendment constitutionally entitles one charged with crime to the assistance of counsel, compliance with this constitutional mandate is an essential jurisdictional prerequisite to a federal court's authority to deprive an accused of his life or liberty. When this right is properly waived, the assistance of counsel is no longer a necessary element of the court's jurisdiction to proceed to conviction and sentence. If the accused, however, is not represented by counsel and has not competently and intelligently waived his constitutional right, the Sixth Amendment stands as a jurisdictional bar to a valid conviction and sentence depriving him of his life or his property.

---

5 304 U.S. 458, 58 S. Ct. 1019, 82 L. Ed. 1461 (1938).

This case established two important rules concerning the right to counsel during a criminal trial in the federal courts.

(1) Counsel must be appointed for an indigent defendant unless there has been a competent waiver.
(2) In order to waive counsel the defendant must make an intelligent and informed choice.

The mere failure to request counsel does not amount to a waiver. Moreover, since an intelligent waiver presupposes that the accused has knowledge of his rights, there is a duty on the part of the federal courts to fully advise the defendant of his rights.

§ 8.5 Right to counsel at trial in state courts in felony cases

State agents must abide by the dual requirements of their own separate constitutions and the Sixth Amendment of the Federal Bill of Rights. For many years, diversity existed among the states regarding trial counsel for the indigent defendant.[6] The differences today have largely disappeared as a result of federal judicial intervention in the field, but a discussion of state provisions is nonetheless warranted.

The first step toward the establishment of federal standards in the states came in *Powell v. Alabama*,[7] where the Supreme Court ruled that a defendant in a state criminal trial for a capital offense was denied due process of law as guaranteed by the Fourteenth Amendment by the failure of the trial court to assign him a court-appointed attorney. In holding that counsel must be appointed in all capital trials where the accused is unable to employ counsel and incapable of conducting his own defense, Mr. Justice Sutherland observed:

> The right to be heard would be, in many case, of little avail if it did not comprehend the right to be heard by counsel. Even the intelligent and educated layman has small and sometimes no skill in the science of law. If charged with crime, he is incapable, generally, of determining for himself whether the indictment is good or bad. He is unfamiliar with the rules of evidence. Left without the aid of counsel he may be put on trial without a proper charge, and convicted upon incompetent evidence, or evidence irrelevant to the is-

---

6 Betts v. Brady, 316 U.S. 455, 465, 62 S. Ct. 1252, 86 L. Ed. 1595 (1942).

7 287 U.S. 45, 53 S. Ct. 55, 77 L. Ed. 2d 158 (1932).

> sue or otherwise inadmissible. He lacks both the skill and knowledge adequately to prepare his defense, even though he [has] a perfect one. He requires the guiding hand of counsel....

The *Powell* holding was limited to the assistance of counsel in capital trials and was based on an interpretation of the due process clause of the Fourteenth Amendment.[8]

The next significant right-to-counsel case in state prosecutions was *Betts v. Brady*,[9] decided by the Supreme Court in 1942. The question presented was whether the *Powell* rationale should be expanded to include state felony trials in which life or death was not at issue. The defendant had been indicted in Maryland on robbery, a non-capital felony. He requested that an attorney be appointed at his trial but was advised by the court that counsel for the indigent was available only in prosecutions for murder and rape. The trial resulted in a conviction and the defendant appealed. The Supreme Court, with three justices dissenting, refused to reverse the Maryland court ruling, explaining:

> [W]e are unable to say that the concept of due process incorporated in the Fourteenth Amendment obligates the states, whatever may be their own views, to furnish counsel in every such case.

The *Betts* holding distinguished between state and federal prosecutions. While counsel was required under the Sixth Amendment in all federal trials where a felony was charged, the states under the Fourteenth Amendment were accorded greater leeway, counsel for the indigent being required only in capital crimes. *Betts* remained the settled law until 1963 when the state courts in Florida learned that they could not rely on past precedent in establishing procedural rules regarding the appointment of counsel in non-capital felony cases.

In 1963, often referred to as "the year of Gideon," the Supreme Court handed down the landmark case of *Gideon v. Wainwright*,[10] overruling *Betts v. Brady*. The facts of the case were very similar to the facts of *Betts*. Gideon was charged with breaking and entering a poolroom with intent to commit a misdemeanor, a felony under Florida law though not a capital offense. Because it was not a capital crime, the trial court refused his request for counsel and informed him that he would have to conduct his own defense. Gideon

---

8 The Due Process Clause of the Fourteenth Amendment provides "nor shall any *State* deprive any person of life, liberty, or property, without due process of law;..."

9 316 U.S. 455, 62 S. Ct. 1252, 86 L. Ed. 1595 (1942).

10 372 U.S. 335, 83 S. Ct. 792, 9 L. Ed. 2d 799 (1963).

was found guilty and sentenced to eight years' imprisonment. He later filed a petition of habeas corpus and the case ultimately reached the Supreme Court of the United States. Gideon challenged that he had been denied his rights under the Sixth and Fourteenth Amendments. The Supreme Court voted to reverse his conviction. Mr. Justice Black, who wrote the majority opinion, expressly overruled *Betts v. Brady*, declaring:

> The right of one charged with crime to counsel may not be deemed fundamental and essential to fair trials in some countries but it is in ours.

Therefore, it was settled once and for all that the states are henceforth required to furnish counsel to an indigent defendant in all felony trials regardless of whether or not capital punishment is at stake. Counsel during the trial is regarded as a fundamental right essential to procedural fairness. A conviction brought about where legal assistance has been denied is a violation of the Fourteenth Amendment and can be attacked by direct appeal or in habeas corpus proceedings.

It is interesting to note that at Gideon's second trial, with an attorney representing him, he was adjudged not guilty.

Because the *Gideon* case was given retroactive application, many prisoners in Florida and other states were released. The decision has also influenced the administration of justice in a more indirect way.

The question in one case was whether previous convictions obtained in violation of *Gideon* could be considered in determining the length of a convicted defendant's prison sentence. Here, the statute permitted a longer sentence after a second conviction. In the *Tucker* case,[11] the Supreme Court held that a conviction obtained without the proper appointment of counsel cannot be used to enhance punishment after a subsequent conviction.

In another case,[12] the defendant was charged with raping his eight-year-old stepdaughter. The defendant testified for himself, and during the process of impeaching his credibility, the prosecutor was permitted on cross-examination to interrogate him about his previous criminal record. The defendant challenged the use of such evidence to impeach his credibility because at least some of the previous convictions were constitutionally invalid. Specifically, he argued that since he was denied counsel at two previous trials, these convictions could not be used to impeach his credibility at this trial even though he had already served his time on these previous sentences.

---

11 United States v. Tucker, 404 U.S. 443, 92 S. Ct. 589, 30 L. Ed. 2d 592 (1972).

12 Loper v. Beto, 450 U.S. 473, 92 S. Ct. 1014, 31 L. Ed. 2d 374 (1972).

The Supreme Court agreed that previous convictions which are void because of failure to afford the defendant his right to counsel deprive a criminal defendant of due process of law where the prior convictions are used to impeach the credibility of the defendant's testimony at a future trial.

The effect of this decision is to require the prosecutor to review the record of previous convictions of defendants, and for that matter other witnesses, if he intends to use the previous conviction for impeachment purposes. If he finds that the defendant was improperly denied counsel or the conviction is constitutionally void for other reasons, such convictions cannot be used for impeachment purposes.

§ 8.6 Counsel at the arraignment

Once it was conceded that counsel was required during the criminal trial, the next question concerned whether an accused could insist upon the presence of counsel at state expense during the preliminary stages. Very little in the way of guidance was afforded by the language of the Sixth Amendment which specifies no more than that the accused should enjoy the right to counsel in all "criminal prosecutions." Does the term "prosecution" signify only the actual trial or can it be interpreted in its broader sense to include the prosecution from beginning to end?

The problem of counsel during the arraignment stage was met by the Supreme Court in the case of *Hamilton v. Alabama*.[13] An arraignment is the last official step before the trial. The accused is brought before the court, informed of the charges against him, and given an opportunity to enter a plea of guilty, not guilty, or *nolo contendere*. Under the Federal Rules of Criminal Procedure and under the practice in most states, the accused must be advised at the arraignment stage, if not before, that he has the right to counsel.

The *Hamilton* case raised the question whether the defendant is constitutionally entitled to representation by a court-appointed attorney during his arraignment. The defendant in that case had been charged with breaking and entering a dwelling house at night with the intent to ravish. Under Alabama law, an accused was required to enter a plea of insanity at the arraignment or be barred from raising the defense. The Supreme Court held that under these circumstances the arraignment was so critical a stage in Alabama criminal procedure that the denial of counsel at this stage was in itself a denial of due process of law.

The *Hamilton* decision has been cited for the proposition that counsel must be appointed in any arraignment which is a critical stage in the state

---

13 368 U.S. 52, 82 S. Ct. 157, 7 L. Ed. 2d 114 (1961).

Hamilton- He was not getting due process under the 14th Amendment.

proceeding. There remains, of course, the possibility that an accused may intelligently and knowingly waive his right, but absent such a waiver, the assistance of counsel is mandatory if crucial decisions must be made at the arraignment. Otherwise, valuable rights can be lost by failure to make a timely assertion.

Many courts have now adopted the reasoning that any arraignment is a critical stage in a felony case. For example, in the case of *Hessenauer v. People*[14] the court stated:

> It is by now well established that arraignment is a "critical stage" in a felony case and that the right to counsel attaches automatically before any plea is made or accepted. [Citations omitted.]

Unless it appears from the record that the trial judge specifically offered and the accused knowingly and understandably rejected the counsel, the finding of a waiver will not generally be made.

§ 8.7 Counsel at the preliminary hearing

Pushing the criminal process back another step, the preliminary hearing or examination is an earlier procedure followed in most states within a short period after the arrest. At the preliminary hearing, it is frequently required that the accused be advised of his right to counsel. The primary function of the preliminary hearing is to afford an opportunity for a judicial officer to pass upon the sufficiency of the evidence to hold the accused. If probable cause is lacking, the magistrate will order the suspect's release. On the other hand, if sufficient evidence to warrant further proceedings exists, the magistrate will set bail or otherwise dispose of the case.

In *White v. Maryland*[15] the Supreme Court addressed the question of the right to assigned counsel at the preliminary hearing. The defendant in that case had been arrested on charges of murder on May 27, 1960, and was brought before a magistrate for the first time on May 31. At the preliminary hearing and without the presence or advice of counsel, the accused entered a plea of guilty. When brought in for arraignment on September 8, 1960, counsel had still not been appointed, and the proceedings were postponed until an appointment could be made. He was finally arraigned with counsel on November 25, 1960, and entered a plea of not guilty by reason of insanity. At the trial, the defendant again entered a plea of not guilty. The guilty plea

---

14 45 Ill. 2d 63, 256 N.E.2d 791 (1970).

15 373 U.S. 59, 83 S. Ct. 1050, 10 L. Ed. 2d 193 (1963).

made during the preliminary hearing was introduced into evidence, and the defendant was convicted and sentenced to death. In reversing the decision, the Supreme Court compared White's predicament to the situation which occurred in the *Hamilton* case, noting the similarities. The Court observed:

> Whatever may be the normal function of the "preliminary hearing" under Maryland law, it was in this case as "critical" a stage as arraignment under Alabama law. For petitioner entered a plea before the magistrate and that plea was taken at a time when he had no counsel.
>
> We repeat what we said in *Hamilton v. Alabama*, that we do not stop to determine whether prejudice resulted: "Only the presence of counsel could have enabled this accused to know all the defenses available to him and to plead intelligently." We therefore hold that *Hamilton v. Alabama* governs and the judgment below must be and is reversed.

Although both the *Hamilton* and *White* cases involved capital offenses, it seems logical to conclude that the reasoning of *Gideon* would make the same rules applicable in other felony prosecutions where the arraignment or the preliminary hearing is a critical stage in the proceedings.

The Pennsylvania Supreme Court has refused to extend the "critical stage" to the prosecution "bring-up" questioning.[16] In a case before that court the majority of the justices decided that a statement made while the defendant was temporarily away from the prison and in the district attorney's office for questioning was admissible even though no attorney was present. This "bring-up" order was granted after the preliminary hearing was held and the defendant ordered committed to the county prison to await grand jury action. The defendant argued that the "bring-up" order proceeding was a critical stage in the prosecution process at which point he was entitled to be represented by counsel, and that the statement taken at this time could not be used against him. These words were used in explaining why this was not a critical stage of the proceeding:

> We view *White* and *Hamilton* as holding a judicial proceeding is a critical stage only in cases where lack of an attorney at the proceeding directly prejudices the accused. Hence, to come within the holding of these two cases the prejudice must have arisen *at* a judicial proceeding.

---

16 Commonwealth v. Broaddus, 458 Pa. 261, 317 A.2d 635 (1974).

Concluding that this was not a judicial proceeding, the Pennsylvania Court refused to extend the *Hamilton-White* guarantee to the "bring-up" situation.

§ 8.8 Right to counsel during the investigation – after indictment

Many prosecutors and police administrators expressed shock when the Supreme Court in 1964 reversed a state murder conviction because the accused was not permitted to consult with his attorney after his arrest and while he was being held in custody at the police station. This decision was only the culmination of a trend begun in *Powell v. Alabama*[17] and could have been predicted with a fair degree of accuracy on the basis of *Gideon v. Wainwright*[18] and later cases. In a period of less than twenty years, the right to counsel had been extended to the trial of all felony cases, then to the arraignment stage, and finally to the preliminary hearing. The "critical stage" approach logically carried this constitutional right back another step to the investigative stage, and it was only a matter of time until the rule would be formally announced by the Supreme Court.

Then came *Massiah v. United States*,[19] handed down by the Supreme Court late in the 1963-1964 term. The facts were that a defendant, who had been arrested, indicted and released on bail for violating the federal narcotics laws, placed his confidence in a codefendant who had agreed to assist the federal authorities in further investigation. With the cooperation of this man, the investigators listened to a conversation between him and the defendant which took place in a car which had been equipped with a radio transmitter. Incriminating statements overheard in this manner were admitted into evidence over the defendant's objection that its receipt violated his Sixth Amendment rights. On appeal the Supreme Court reversed the conviction, stating:

> We hold that the petitioner was denied the basic protections of that guarantee when there was used against him at his trial evidence of his own incriminating words, which federal agents had deliberately elicited from him after he had been indicted and in the absence of his counsel.

---

17 287 U.S. 45, 53 S. Ct. 55, 77 L. Ed. 2d 158 (1932).

18 372 U.S. 335, 83 S. Ct. 792, 9 L. Ed. 799 (1963).

19 377 U.S. 201, 84 S. Ct. 1199, 12 L. Ed. 2d 246 (1964).

However, the fact that the defendant's Sixth Amendment right to counsel comes into existence with the indictment does not necessarily preclude the police from questioning the defendant after indictment if the defendant knowingly and intelligently chooses to communicate with police without the assistance of counsel.[20] In the *Patterson* case the suspect, after being informed that he had been indicted for murder, while in police custody, twice indicated his willingness to discuss the crime during interviews with the authorities. On both occasions after he was read from a form advising him of his rights, he initialed each of the specific warnings on the form, and signed the form. These statements were used against him at the trial. The Supreme Court of Illinois rejected his contention that the warnings he received, while adequate to protect his Fifth Amendment rights, did not adequately inform him of his Sixth Amendment right to counsel, and affirmed his conviction.

The United States Supreme Court agrees that the postindictment questioning that produced the defendant's incriminating statements did not violate his Sixth Amendment right to counsel. The Court explained that:

> ...once an accused "knowingly and intelligently" elects to proceed without counsel, the uncounseled statements he then makes need not be excluded at the trial.

The Supreme Court majority noted that the United States Supreme Court has never adopted the suggestion that the Sixth Amendment right to counsel is "superior" to or "more difficult" to waive than its Fifth Amendment counterpart. The court continued by explaining that an accused's waiver is "knowing" and "intelligent" if he is made aware of the basic facts regarding his rights. The *Miranda* warnings are sufficient for this purpose in the post-indictment questioning context, because, at that stage, the role of the counsel is relatively simple and limited, and the dangers and disadvantages of self-representation are less substantial and more obvious to an accused than they are at the trial.

In summary, the indictment is a critical stage in the judicial process and the accused is entitled to counsel at this stage. However, the fact that a defendant's Sixth Amendment right to counsel comes into existence with his indictment does not necessarily preclude police from questioning the defendant, *if* defendant knowingly and intelligently chooses to communicate with police without the assistance of counsel. If defendant indicates at this stage that he wants counsel's assistance, questioning must cease unless he initiates further discussion.

---

20 Patterson v. Illinois, _U.S._, 108 S. Ct. 2389, _L. Ed. 2d_ (1988). *See* Part II for portions of this case.

In a case[21] similar to *Massiah*, the defendant, Williams, made incriminating statements and agreed to take detectives to find the body of the victim, after a warrant had been issued for his arrest in a Davenport courtroom. The statements were made after an attorney had been appointed in Davenport and the detectives agreed not to question Williams until he talked with an attorney in Des Moines where he was being taken by the detectives.

Although the officers did not question the suspect, one commented that "this little girl should be entitled to a Christian burial," and according to the Court, "deliberately and designedly set out to elicit information."

The United States Supreme Court found that there was no need to consider *Miranda v. Arizona* (based on the Fifth Amendment), but that Williams was entitled to the assistance of counsel guaranteed by the Sixth and Fourteenth Amendments. After determining that the defendant had not waived his right to counsel, the Supreme Court held the statements and evidence were not admissible and ordered a new trial.

At the new trial conducted in 1977, the prosecution did not offer Williams' statements into evidence nor did it seek to show that Williams had directed the police to the child's body. However, evidence of the condition of her body as it was found, articles and photographs of her clothing, and the results of post mortem medical and chemical tests of the body were admitted. Justification for the admission of this evidence was that the state had proved by a preponderance of the evidence that if the search had not been suspended and Williams had not led the police to the victim, her body would have been discovered within a very short time. The Supreme Court of Iowa affirmed and the defendant renewed his attack on the state-court conviction seeking a writ of habeas corpus in the United States District Court. The District Court denied Williams' petition for a hearing but the Court of Appeals reversed the district court's denial of habeas corpus relief. The United States Supreme Court granted the State's petition for certiorari.

The United States Supreme Court held that if the prosecution can establish by a preponderance of the evidence that the information ultimately or inevitably would have been discovered by lawful means, the fact that the defendant made a statement to the officers in the absence of counsel should not contaminate the evidence.[22] The Court indicated that "anything less would reject logic, experience, and common sense."

The defendant relied upon the Sixth Amendment Exclusionary Rule rather than the Fourth Amendment Exclusionary Rule in protesting the use of the evidence. The Court explained that the Sixth Amendment right to counsel protects against unfairness by preserving the adversary process in

---

21 Brewer v. Williams, 430 U.S. 387, 97 S. Ct. 1232, 51 L. Ed. 2d 424 (1977).

22 Nix v. Williams, 467 U.S. 264, 104 S. Ct. 2501, 81 L. Ed. 2d 377 (1984).

which the reliability of proffered evidence may be tested on cross-examination. But if the government can prove that the evidence would have been obtained inevitably and therefore would have been admitted regardless of any overreaching by the police, there is no rational basis to keep the evidence from the jury in order to ensure fairness of the trial proceedings.

To state this more succinctly, the rule is that if the Sixth Amendment right to counsel provisions are violated and this violation leads to evidence, usually the evidence will not be admitted at trial; but if the prosecution can establish by a preponderance of the evidence, that the evidence ultimately or inevitably would have been discovered by lawful means, the evidence is admissible. The prosecution is not required under this "inevitable discovery" exception to prove the absence of bad faith on the part of the government officer.

The United States Supreme Court cited the *Massiah* rule when deciding if a defendant's Sixth Amendment right to the assistance of counsel was violated by the admission at trial of incriminating statements made by the defendant to his cellmate, an undisclosed government informant, after indictment and while in custody.[23] In this case a government informant advised an FBI agent that he was sharing a cell with the defendant. The agent told the informant to be alert to any statements made but not to initiate any communication with or question the defendant. The defendant did in fact tell the informant details of the crime and the informant testified at the trial.

The United States Supreme Court, reasoning that confinement may bring into play subtle influences that will make a suspect particularly susceptible to the ploys of undercover agents, held that this practice violated right to counsel protections. In the last paragraph of the majority opinion this sentence is included:

> By intentionally creating a situation likely to induce Henry to make incriminating statements without the assistance of counsel, the government violated Henry's Sixth Amendment right to counsel.

In this case the defendant was in custody and had been indicted. Also the cellmate was a government informant. The Court indicated that it would be a different matter if the government used undercover agents to obtain incriminating statements from persons not in custody but suspected of criminal activity prior to the time charges are filed. Also, it would be a different matter if the cellmate was not a paid government informant and had not been contacted by government agents.

---

[23] United States v. Henry, 447 U.S. 264, 100 S. Ct. 2183, 65 L. Ed. 2d 115 (1980).

In 1986 the Supreme Court again considered the admissibility of statements made to a cellmate after the defendant had been arraigned.[24] In the *Kuhlman* case, the defendant was confined in a cell after he had been arraigned on charges arising from a robbery and murder. With him in the same cell was a prisoner who had previously agreed to act as a police informant. Here, however, the informant obeyed the police officer's instruction to only listen to the defendant for the purpose of identifying his confederates in the robbery and murder but not to question about the crimes. He was told to "keep his ears open" for names of the defendant's confederates. After several days of confinement, the defendant did tell the informant that he and two others had planned and carried out the robbery and had committed a murder. This evidence was used at the trial.

The Circuit Court, in a habeas review of the defendant's conviction, considered the situation to be equivalent to that in *United States v. Henry*. However, the United States Supreme Court disagreed. The majority distinguished this case from the *Henry* case, noting that the Sixth Amendment does not forbid admission of an accused's statement made to a jailhouse informant who is placed in close proximity to the defendant in a jail but who makes no effort to stimulate conversations about the crime with which the defendant is charged.

In this case the Court added that the defendant must demonstrate that the police and their informant took some action, beyond merely listening, that was designed deliberately to elicit incriminating remarks.

However, the Court was not so inclined to allow use of the confession where the codefendant became a government informant and agreed to wear a transmitter to a meeting with the defendant at which the two, without an attorney, were to discuss defense strategy on the pending charges.[25] The defendant and the informant had been indicted on theft charges. Some time after both were released on bail the codefendant informant advised authorities that the defendant had concocted a plan to kill one of the state's witnesses. The codefendant then agreed to wear a transmitter at the meeting with the defendant in which the two were to discuss strategy. The codefendant informant was instructed not to attempt to question the defendant; nonetheless, his profession of poor memory and invitations to reminisce about the pair's criminal activities led the defendant to make numerous incriminating statements about the pending charges.

The Maine Supreme Judicial Court ruled that the defendant's Sixth Amendment right to counsel had been infringed by introducing portions of the recording at the trial. The majority of the United States Supreme Court

---

[24] Kuhlmann v. Wilson, 477 U.S. 436, 106 S. Ct. 2616, 91 L. Ed. 2d 364 (1986).

[25] Maine v. Moulton, 474 U.S. 159, 106 S. Ct. 477, 88 L. Ed. 2d 481 (1985).

because

agreed that the evidence should have been inadmissible, comparing the case with the case of *United States v. Henry*. The Court said that once the defendant is formally charged he is entitled to "rely on counsel as a medium between him and the state." This guarantee includes the state's affirmative obligation not to act in a manner that circumvents the protections accorded the accused by invoking his right. In applying this rule, the Court reasoned that the police created such an opportunity when, knowing that the defendant was going to discuss defense strategy, they concealed the fact that the co-defendant was their agent.

Succinctly, the rule in this case is that when a defendant has been formally charged with a crime and has retained counsel, incriminating statements made to an undercover informant, *whose remarks prompted the statement*, are not admissible.

§ 8.9 Right to counsel during the investigation – before indictment

Mr. Justice White's predictions in *Massiah* that the same reasoning would apply in pre-indictment situations became a reality a few weeks later in the celebrated case of *Escobedo v. Illinois*.[26] In the *Escobedo* case the interrogation took place prior to the indictment. Very briefly, the facts were these: The defendant was arrested for the first time and released the same day on a writ of habeas corpus. He told the police nothing at this time. He was rearrested about eleven days later and before making any statement, requested an opportunity to consult with his attorney. His attorney likewise made repeated efforts to gain access to his client. Both men were told that they could not see the other until the police had finished with their interrogation. In the course of the questioning, the defendant stated that another person had committed the shooting, thereby admitting knowledge of the crime and implicating himself in it. At the trial, he moved to suppress the incriminating statements but his motion was denied.

The Supreme Court of Illinois upheld the trial court's ruling on the competency of the statements and the defendant appealed to the United States Supreme Court. The Supreme Court voted five to four to reverse the decision below. Mr. Justice Goldberg, who wrote the majority opinion, adopted the "critical stage" reasoning developed in the *White* and *Hamilton* cases. Stating that the post-arrest interrogation was the stage "when legal aid and advice were most critical" to a criminal accused, Justice Goldberg observed in *Escobedo*:

---

26 378 U.S. 478, 84 S. Ct. 1758, 12 L. Ed. 2d 977 (1964).

> In *Gideon v. Wainwright,* we held that every person accused of a crime, whether state or federal, is entitled to a lawyer at trial. The rule sought by the State here, however, would make the trial no more than an appeal from the interrogation; and the "right to use counsel at the formal trial [would be] a very hollow thing [if], for all practical purposes, the conviction is already assured by pre-trial examination." [Citation omitted.]

The precise point in the criminal process when the right to counsel attaches and the suspect must be *permitted* to consult with his attorney was stated as follows:

> We hold, therefore, that where, as here, the investigation is no longer a general inquiry into an unsolved crime but has begun to focus on a particular suspect, the suspect has been taken into police custody, the police carry out a process of interrogation that lends itself to eliciting incriminating statements, the suspect has requested and been denied an opportunity to consult with his lawyer, and the police have not effectively warned him of his absolute constitutional right to remain silent, the accused has been denied "the Assistance of Counsel" in violation of the Sixth Amendment to the Constitution as "made obligatory upon the States by the Fourteenth Amendment," and no statement elicited by the police during interrogation may be used against him at a criminal trial.

Clarifying this lengthy sentence, Justice Goldberg concluded with the admonition that:

> [W]hen the process shifts from investigatory to accusatory -- when its focus is on the accused and its purpose is to elicit a confession -- our adversary system begins to operate, and, under the circumstances here, the accused must be permitted to consult with his lawyer.

With *Escobedo*, the right to counsel has been extended to the earliest possible point in the criminal process. Many questions, nevertheless, were left unanswered. Escobedo had *requested* counsel during the interrogation and his request was denied. What if he had been ignorant of his rights and had not made demands on the police? Moreover, Escobedo had already retained his own attorney and was not asking for the assistance of assigned counsel. Would it have made any difference if he had requested the police to furnish him legal assistance at state expense? Finally, Escobedo was being interrogated about a felony. Would his rights have been identical if instead it had been a misdemeanor? These were just a few of the questions that were being asked after the *Escobedo* case.

Directly following the *Escobedo* decision, the state courts in a series of cases attempted to apply the rules developed, but with differing interpretations. In California, the highest court of the state refused to admit any confession where counsel was not granted and there was no warning given to the suspect that he had a right to remain silent or to have counsel present, despite the fact that defendant never indicated during the interrogation that he desired legal assistance.[27] In Illinois, on the other hand, the highest state court on precisely the same facts, reached the opposite conclusion, declining to hold a confession inadmissible in the absence of evidence that the accused had requested and been denied an attorney, even though the police had not effectively warned him concerning his constitutional rights.[28] *Escobedo* had created an intolerable situation, and the need for an authoritative clarification was obvious.

On June 13, 1966, the Supreme Court of the United States spoke. Almost everyone versed in the law could have predicted the result. Only the reasoning of the Court was surprising. In *Miranda v. Arizona*[29] and its three companion cases, four convictions were reversed because in each instance incriminating statements had been obtained from the defendants under circumstances which did not comport with the constitutional standards enunciated by the Court. The reversal was not made to hinge upon the Sixth Amendment right to counsel, but on the Fifth Amendment provisions concerning self-incrimination. The presence of counsel was held necessary as a means of enforcing the immunity against compulsory self-incrimination.

Because of the *Miranda* ruling, it is no longer necessary for the suspect to request counsel during the *custodial interrogation*. The burden is placed on the police to inform the suspect of his constitutional rights and to refrain from asking any further questions unless the accused knowingly waives his right to counsel and to remain silent. Chief Justice Warren, who wrote the majority opinion, summarized the Court's sweeping new mandate as follows:

> If, however, he indicates in any manner and at any stage of the process that he wishes to consult with an attorney before speaking there can be no questioning. Likewise, if the individual is alone and indicates in any manner that he does not wish to be interrogated, the police may not question him. The mere fact that he may have answered some questions or volunteered some statements on his

---

[27] People v. Dorado, 40 Cal. Rptr. 264, 394 P.2d 952 (1964).

[28] People v. Hartgraves, 31 Ill. 2d 375, 202 N.E.2d 33 (1964).

[29] 384 U.S. 436, 86 S. Ct. 1602, 16 L. Ed. 2d 694 (1966).

> own does not deprive him of the right to refrain from answering any further inquiries until he has consulted with an attorney and thereafter consents to be questioned.[30]

In determining when the warnings must be given and the suspect afforded an opportunity to consult with counsel, the *Escobedo* and *Miranda* cases must be read together. In *Escobedo* the Court stated that when the process shifts from the investigatory to the accusatory, when its *focus is on the accused* and its purpose to elicit a confession, the accused must be permitted to consult with counsel. In the *Miranda* case the Court explained what was meant by custodial interrogation:

> By custodial interrogation, we mean questioning initiated by law enforcement officers after a person has been taken into custody or otherwise deprived of his freedom of action in any significant way.[31]

Applying these two cases together, the following succinct rule relating to the assistance of counsel results: when a person is taken into custody *and* questioned, he must be *advised* of his right to counsel; when he is questioned with a view to obtaining incriminating statements although he is not in custody, he must be *permitted* to consult with counsel.

As indicated in Chapter 6 of this book, the suspect may waive the right to counsel provided the waiver is made voluntarily, knowingly and intelligently.[32] In the case of the *United States v. Edwards* in 1981 the United States Supreme Court declared that when the accused has expressed his desire to deal with police only through counsel, interrogation must cease until counsel had been made available to the accused unless the accused himself initiates further communications.[33] The *Edwards* case did not define what the court meant by "initiation" of further communications. Although this question is still not settled, the Supreme Court in 1983 threw some light on this requirement in the case of *Oregon v. Bradshaw*.[34] In this case the Supreme Court by a slim majority held that the defendant had initiated further communications by asking "well, what is going to happen to me now.?"

---

30 *Id.* at 445.

31 *Id.* at 444.

32 *See* Section 6.4 for a more comprehensive discussion of the waiver of rights after the *Miranda* warnings have been administered.

33 Edwards v. Arizona, 451 U.S. 477, 101 S. Ct. 1880, 68 L. Ed. 2d 378 (1981). *See* portions of case in Part II.

34 462 U.S. 1039, 103 S. Ct. 2830, 77 L. Ed. 2d 405 (1983).

Following the *Edwards* case, lower courts were confronted with the application of the rule where the police-initiated interrogation occurs in the context of a separate investigation. This question reached the Supreme Court in 1988 in a case where the suspect had requested counsel during one interrogation session and the questioning had ceased, but the suspect was later questioned by a different officer regarding a different crime; the second officer being unaware that the defendant had earlier requested counsel.[35]

After being arrested at the scene of a burglary, and being advised by the arresting officer of his right to counsel, the defendant replied that he "wanted a lawyer before answering any questions." Three days later, while the defendant was still in custody, a different officer, unaware that the defendant had earlier requested counsel who had not yet been provided, advised him of his rights and interrogated him about a different burglary, obtaining an incriminating statement. The State Supreme Court refused to distinguish *Edwards* with respect to a suspect who was reinterrogated about an unrelated offense after he had requested counsel, ruling that the fact that the further interrogation in *Edwards* had involved the same offense was not legally significant.

The United States Supreme Court agreed that the *Edwards* rule applies to bar police-initiated interrogation following a suspect's request for counsel in the context of a separate investigation. The fact that the officer who conducted the second interrogation did not know that defendant had requested counsel cannot justify the failure to honor that request, since *Edwards* focuses on the state of mind of the suspect and not of the police, and since the officer could have discovered the request simply by reading the arresting officer's report.

But even though a suspect is in custody, he has no right to the presence of counsel at a court-ordered psychiatric examination. The Texas Court of Criminal Appeals and the United States Court of Appeals for the Fifth Circuit agree that a psychiatric examination is not an adversary proceeding.[36] As its sole purpose is to enable an expert to form an opinion as to an accused's mental capacity to form a criminal intent, and not to establish facts showing that the accused committed certain acts which constitute the crime, no counsel is required.

The cases discussed indicate that when a person is taken into custody and questioned, he must be advised of his right to counsel. Is it necessary for police to advise the suspect in custody that an attorney has been retained by someone else to represent him? This was the question in the case of *Moran*

---

35 Arizona v. Roberson, __U.S.__, 108 S. Ct. 1093, __L. Ed. 2d__ (1988).

36 United States v. Williams, 456 F.2d 217 (5th Cir. 1972); Stultz v. State, 500 S.W.2d 853 (Tex. 1973).

v. Burbine.[37] In the *Moran* case, the Court was requested to declare a confession to police officers inadmissible because the suspect had not been advised that his sister had contacted a public defender who had agreed to represent him. The suspect, having been arrested and held on a breaking and entering charge, was also suspected of being responsible for a murder which occurred in another city. Unknown to the defendant, his sister, who was unaware that the suspect was under suspicion of murder, sought help from the public defender's office. The assistant public defender, after agreeing to represent the suspect, telephoned the detective division stating that she would act as the defendant's counsel and was informed that he would not be questioned until the next day. The defendant was not advised that counsel had been retained to represent him nor that counsel had contacted the detective.

Less than an hour after the investigators gave the public defender this information, the police from the second city began a series of interviews with the suspect and gave him the required warnings. The suspect did not request an attorney and validly waived his privilege against self-incrimination and his right to counsel. The confession given after the waiver was used in court, and the defendant was found guilty of murder.

In a habeas corpus proceeding, the defendant argued that the police conduct, in failing to inform him about the attorney's call and in conducting the interviews after telling the attorney there would be no interviews, tainted the waivers. The Federal Court of Appeals agreed, and the case went to the Supreme Court of the United States.

The majority of the U.S. Supreme Court held that the confession should be admitted following this reasoning:

> The police failure to inform respondent of the attorney's telephone call did not deprive him of information essential to his ability to knowingly waive his right to remain silent and to the presence of counsel.

The Court went on to explain that the suspect's decision not to rely on his right was not coerced, that at all times he knew that he could stand mute and request a lawyer, and that he was aware of the state's intention to use his statements to secure a conviction. In effect, the Court reasoned that as the suspect himself was aware of his right to counsel and his Fifth Amendment rights, the fact that he was not advised that counsel had been retained, and the fact that counsel had not been advised concerning the questioning, did not influence his ability to make this decision.

---

37 Moran v. Burbine, 475 U.S. 412, 106 S. Ct. 1135, 89 L. Ed. 2d 410 (1986).

Another caveat is in order here; had the suspect requested counsel or had he been denied permission to contact counsel before making the statements, the decision probably would have been different.

§ 8.10 Counsel at the lineup

Although the lineup is generally considered a part of the investigative stage, because of its importance it is discussed here as a separate section. In 1967 the Supreme Court of the United States extended the right to counsel to the police lineup and other exhibitions of the accused for identification purposes where this stage of the procedure is "critical."[38]

In previous chapters the cases relating to the lineup are reviewed to determine if the procedure violates the self-incrimination provisions of the Fifth Amendment or the due process provisions of the Fifth and Fourteenth Amendments. From that discussion it is apparent that the lineup and other identification confrontations are challenged on three constitutional grounds: self-incrimination, due process, and right to counsel. In this section the cases relating to right to counsel at the lineup or other identification confrontation are considered.[39]

In a decision in which the members of the United States Supreme Court had little consensus, the lineup was determined to be a critical stage of the proceeding if the in-court identification of the accused could be jeopardized.[40] The Court in this case quickly decided that the lineup does not violate the self-incrimination protections since the defendant is not being compelled to give evidence of a testimonial or communicative nature. As to the right-to-counsel challenge, the majority agreed that an attorney should generally be present at the lineup in order to get evidence to challenge the credibility of the witnesses' future courtroom identification. The reasoning is that if the procedure followed by the police is such as to suggest that a suspect is the one who committed the crime, the in-court identification may be influ-

---

[38] United States v. Wade, 388 U.S. 218, 87 S. Ct. 1926, 18 L. Ed. 2d 1149 (1967); Gilbert v. California, 388 U.S. 263, 87 S. Ct. 1951, 18 L. Ed. 2d 1178 (1967); Stovall v. Denno, 388 U.S. 293 (1967). This rule was not made retroactive beyond June 12, 1967.

[39] *See* United States v. Crews, 445 U.S. 463, 100 S. Ct. 1244, 63 L. Ed. 2d 537 (1980), which discusses the possible suppression of an in-court identification that is the product of an illegal arrest.

[40] United States v. Wade, 388 U.S. 218, 87 S. Ct. 1926, 18 L. Ed. 2d 1149 (1967). Seven of the nine justices dissented as to at least part of the primary opinion.

enced by this procedure so that there will be danger of misidentification at the trial.

Since the counsel's presence at the lineup is merely to equip him to attack the courtroom identification, he has no right to object to the fact that the lineup is being conducted. In fact, the Court specifically left the door open to the establishment of procedures whereby the counsel would not be required to attend the lineup, saying:

> Legislative or other regulations, such as those of local police departments, which eliminate the risks of abuse and unintentional suggestion at lineup proceedings and the impediments to meaningful confrontation at trial may also remove the basis for regarding the stage as "critical."

Contrary to common opinion, the Supreme Court did not hold that the in-court identification in this case would be excluded *per se*, but referred the case back to the lower court in order to give the government the opportunity to establish by clear and convincing evidence that the in-court identifications were based on observations of the suspect other than the lineup identification.

The holding in the *Wade* case also brought with it some unanswered questions. In *Wade*, the lineup was conducted after the indictment. Soon after that case was decided, the question arose as to whether the same rule would apply to a police station showup which took place before the defendant had been indicted or otherwise formally charged with any criminal offense. This question was considered by the Supreme Court in the case of *Kirby v. Illinois*.[41]

In the *Kirby* case the petitioner and a companion were stopped for investigation. When each produced items bearing the name "Shard," they were arrested and taken to the police station. There, the arresting officers learned of the robbery of a person named "Shard" two days earlier. Shard was called to the station and immediately identified petitioner and his companion as the robbers. At the time of this confrontation, the petitioner and his companion were not advised of their right to counsel, nor did either ask for or receive legal assistance. At the trial, after a pretrial motion to suppress his testimony had been overruled, Shard testified as to his previous identification of the petitioner and his companion and again identified them as the robbers. The defendants were found guilty, and the conviction was upheld on appeal. They appealed to the Supreme Court claiming that the preindictment confronta-

---

41 406 U.S. 682, 92 S. Ct. 1877, 32 L. Ed. 2d 411 (1972).

tion contaminated the in-court identification and that the *Wade* rule precluded the use of the identification.

Before discussing the constitutional right-to-counsel issue, the Court again reiterated its past decisions that this in no way violates the constitutional privilege against compulsory self-incrimination. As to the due process challenge to the lineup and confrontation, the Court said the due process clauses of the Fifth and Fourteenth Amendments forbid a lineup that is unnecessarily suggestive and conducive to irreparable mistaken identification, but that such was not the issue here. Also disallowing the right-to-counsel claim, the Court refused to extend the right-to-counsel protection of the Sixth Amendment to a pre-indictment identification such as the one at issue in this case. In the decision, Mr. Justice Stewart, speaking for the majority, announced:

> The initiation of judicial criminal proceedings is far from a mere formalism. It is the starting point of our whole system of adversary criminal justice. For it is only then that the government has committed itself to prosecute, and only then that the adverse positions of government and defendant have solidified....It is this point, therefore, that marks the commencement of the "criminal prosecutions" to which alone the explicit guarantees of the Sixth Amendment are applicable.

Applying these principles to lineup and confrontation situations, it is apparent that the attorney does not have to be advised when a lineup or confrontation is to be conducted prior to the indictment. However, such confrontation may still be challenged as being in violation of the due process protection, and in some instances it is advisable to have the attorney at the lineup to avoid any in-court challenge.

Following the important *Kirby* decision of 1972, many state and lower federal courts attempted to interpret the *Kirby* rule which states in general terms that there is no constitutional right to an attorney for a pre-indictment or pre-information lineup. In applying this rule, the United States Court of Appeals for the Fifth Circuit found that returning the arrested suspect, who was involved in an accident while driving a stolen car, to the scene for identification was not a violation of his constitutional rights.[42] The show-up identification without counsel present before formal charges are made against the defendant is not in violation of the Sixth Amendment right-to-counsel provisions according to recent decisions.

---

42 United States v. Abshire, 471 F.2d 116 (5th Cir. 1972).

Using similar reasoning, the United States Court of Appeals for the Ninth Circuit agreed that returning a suspected bank robber to the bank a short time after the robbery so that employees could observe and identify him was not in violation of the Sixth Amendment even though counsel was not present.[43] At the time of the show-up, no adversary proceeding had been started against the defendant and there were no unduly suggestive circumstances at the show-up.

In the case of *State v. Mason*,[44] the Missouri Court of Appeals was requested to determine if counsel is required at a lineup where the suspect is being held on another charge at the time he is placed in the lineup. In this case the defendant was being held on a charge of flourishing a deadly weapon and he was placed in a lineup for viewing by two boys who had seen the burglary committed. The defendant on appeal claimed that adversary proceedings had been initiated and that counsel should have been advised. The Missouri Court of Appeals disagreed. The Court reasoned that defendant was in custody on the flourishing charge but was not arrested for the burglary until after he was identified by the boys who saw the burglary. Referring to *Kirby v. Illinois*, the Court noted that the right to counsel attaches only after adversary proceedings have been initiated against the defendant. Here adversary proceedings had not been initiated on the burglary charge. Therefore, the Court concluded:

> Defendant was not arrested for the burglary until after he was identified by the Chaneys; he had no absolute right to counsel at the time of the second lineup in connection with the burglary.

But the Pennsylvania Supreme Court has adopted a standard of procedure that affords the accused a greater protection than the minimal safeguards provided in the *Kirby* case. In that state, the right to counsel attaches at the time of arrest in confrontation for identification situations.[45]

Apparently the California Supreme Court has joined a few other states in declaring that a criminal suspect has a right to counsel at a lineup occurring before formal proceedings have been initiated against him.[46] Other states that have apparently taken the same approach are Alaska and Michigan.[47]

---

43 United States v. Miramon, 470 F.2d 1362 (9th Cir. 1972).

44 588 S.W.2d 731 (Mo. App. 1979).

45 Commonwealth v. Richman, 458 Pa. 167, 320 A.2d 351 (1974).

46 People v. Bustamante, 634 P.2d 927 (Cal. 1981).

47 Blue v. State, 558 P.2d 636 (Alaska 1977); People v. Jackson, 217 N.W.2d 22 (Mich. 1979).

Because the state may, by a court decision or a statutory enactment, provide greater restrictions than established by the U.S. Supreme Court, those involved in the criminal justice process must be familiar with both.

By sifting out the pertinent parts of the *Wade*, *Gilbert*, *Stovall* and *Kirby* cases, some conclusions can be reached concerning the lineup and other identification confrontations:

(1) The lineup does not violate the self-incrimination provisions.

(2) The accused may waive the right to have counsel at the lineup if he does so voluntarily, knowingly and intelligently.

(3) Unless there is a state provision to the contrary, counsel does not have to be advised concerning a lineup or confrontation if this is conducted prior to the initiation of judicial criminal proceedings.

(4) Absent a knowing and intelligent waiver, the witness's in-court identification following a post-indictment lineup identification of the suspect may be excluded unless the prosecution can show an independent source for the in-court identification.

(5) The defense attorney has no right to participate in or control the conduct of the lineup.

(6) The lineup or the confrontation is still a valuable tool in law enforcement where the witness making the identification will not be called upon to identify the accused at trial, even if counsel is not present.

Another reminder is justified here. Even though counsel may not be required, as in the case of a pre-indictment confrontation or street confrontation, the in-court identification may still be contaminated if the procedure is so suggestive as to violate the due process provisions of the Constitution.

Advising counsel that a lineup is to be conducted will probably not impede legitimate law enforcement, and in fact, law enforcement may be assisted by preventing the infiltration of taint into the prosecution's identification evidence. Therefore, the best procedure is to make every effort to advise counsel when a lineup is to be conducted and to allow him to be present at the lineup. If a waiver is contemplated, the accused should be fully advised of his right to have counsel present.

A defendant's Sixth Amendment right to counsel also may be violated if the initial identification proceeding is conducted at the preliminary hearing rather than at an out-of-court lineup or show up. In the case of *Moore v. Illi-*

nois[48] the Supreme Court referred to the rationale of the *Wade* and *Gilbert* cases in holding that an uncounseled one-on-one corporeal identification at a preliminary hearing where the proper procedures were not followed adversely affected the in-court identification. In this case a rape victim was accompanied by a police officer to a preliminary hearing where the suspect was to appear to determine whether he should be bound over to the grand jury. The officer told her she was going to view a suspect and she should identify him if she could.

The victim had not seen the suspect since the rape occurred. While the victim was in the courtroom, the petitioner's name was called and he was led before the bench. The judge told the petitioner that he was charged with rape and deviant sexual behavior. The judge then called the victim and asked her whether she saw the assailant in the courtroom and she pointed to the petitioner. Counsel was not present at the first preliminary hearing but was appointed at a subsequent hearing at which time he moved to suppress the victim's identification of petitioner because it had been elicited at the earlier hearing through an unnecessarily suggestive procedure at which petitioner was not represented by counsel.

The Supreme Court of Illinois rejected the petitioner's argument that the victim's identification testimony should have been excluded on the ground that the prosecution had not shown an independent basis for the identification. The Federal District Court in a habeas corpus proceeding also denied the writ. The Court of Appeals for the Seventh Circuit affirmed this ruling.

The Supreme Court of the United States, however, in reversing the lower courts, made this finding:

> In view of the violation of petitioner's Sixth and Fourteenth Amendment right to counsel at the pre-trial corporeal identification, and of the prosecution's exploitation at trial of evidence derived directly from that violation, we reverse the judgment of the Court of Appeals and remand for a determination of whether the failure to exclude that evidence was harmless constitutional error....

It is apparent that a show up at the preliminary hearing can be just as suggestive as one conducted by enforcement officers. The *Moore* case also made it clear that the right to counsel attaches "at or after the initiation of adversary judicial proceedings" including proceedings instituted by way of a preliminary hearing.

---

48 434 U.S. 220, 98 S. Ct. 458, 54 L. Ed. 2d 424 (1977).

§ 8.11 Counsel for persons charged with misdemeanors

The Sixth Amendment provides that the accused shall enjoy the right to counsel in all criminal prosecutions. For many years this was interpreted to require the appointment of counsel for indigents only in *capital* cases. In 1963 the United States Supreme Court determined that the states must furnish counsel to indigent defendants in all *felony* cases regardless of whether or not capital punishment is at stake. Although some federal appeals courts and some state courts had ruled that the right to counsel existed during the trial of a misdemeanor case,[49] the United States Supreme Court did not take action until 1972. In the case of *Argersinger v. Hamlin*,[50] the United States Supreme Court acted on this question and established some specific guidelines as to the right to counsel in misdemeanor cases.

In the *Argersinger* case the petitioner, an indigent, was charged in Florida with carrying a concealed weapon, an offense punishable by a maximum of six months' imprisonment and a $1,000 fine. He was not represented by counsel at the trial where the judge ordered that he serve 90 days in jail. The Florida Supreme Court, following decisions in previous cases, upheld the conviction agreeing that the right to court-appointed counsel extends only to persons charged with offenses punishable by more than six months' imprisonment. The defendant appealed to the Supreme Court of the United States claiming that his Sixth Amendment right to counsel as applied to the states by the Fourteenth Amendment was violated.

The majority of the members of the United States Supreme Court stated that the problems associated with misdemeanors are often as complicated as felonies and require the presence of counsel to insure the accused a fair trial. Establishing the line where counsel is required if not waived, the Court concluded:

> We need not consider the requirements of the Sixth Amendment as regards the right to counsel where the loss of liberty is not involved,....
>
> and
>
> We hold, therefore, that absent a knowing and intelligent waiver, no person may be *imprisoned* for any offense, whether classified as petty, misdemeanor, or felony unless he was represented by counsel at his trial. [Emphasis added.]

---

49 *E.g.*, Harvey v. Mississippi, 340 F.2d 263 (5th Cir. 1965); People v. Mallory, 378 Mich. 538, 147 N.W.2d 66 (1967).

50 407 U.S. 25, 92 S. Ct. 2006, 32 L. Ed. 2d 530 (1972). *See* Part II for this case.

The Supreme Court in the *Argersinger* case answered some counsel questions, but created others. In that case the defendant actually had been ordered to serve ninety days in jail. According to some interpretations of the Supreme Court decision, the right to counsel at trial is guaranteed in a misdemeanor case where imprisonment is a *possibility*. Others follow the exact wording of the case which held that, absent a knowing and intelligent waiver, no person may be *imprisoned* for any offense unless he is represented by counsel at his trial.

In the case of *Scott v. Illinois*[51] the petitioner, an indigent, was convicted of shoplifting and fined $50.00. The statute, however, sets the maximum penalty for such an offense at $500.00 fine, one year in jail, or both. Thus, there was a possibility of imprisonment. Justice Rehnquist, writing for the majority, clarified the *Argersinger* decision by stating:

> We, therefore, hold that the Sixth and Fourteenth Amendments to the United States Constitution require only that no indigent criminal defendant be sentenced to a term of imprisonment unless the state has afforded him the right to assistance of counsel in his defense.

In a misdemeanor case, then, the state trial does not have to appoint counsel for an indigent criminal defendant who is charged with a statutory offense for which imprisonment upon conviction is authorized but not imposed. This would seem to indicate that the judge must determine before trial that no imprisonment will be imposed if the case is to be tried without counsel unless counsel is intelligently and competently waived.

§ 8.12 Juveniles' constitutional right to counsel

On May 15, 1967, the Supreme Court of the United States extended the right-to-counsel privilege to juveniles.[52] The facts of the case are briefly as follows: Gerald Francis Gault, a 15-year-old boy, was arrested and charged with being a delinquent minor after a verbal complaint concerning a telephone call made to a neighbor woman in which the neighbor claimed that Gault had made lewd and indecent remarks. He was not advised at the hearing of his right to counsel, right to confrontation, or privilege against

---

51 440 U.S. 367, 99 S. Ct. 1158, 59 L. Ed. 383 (1979).

52 In re Gault, 387 U.S. 1, 87 S. Ct. 1428, 18 L. Ed. 2d 527 (1967).

self-incrimination. Also, no one was sworn at the hearing, no transcript was made, and no record of the substance of the proceedings was prepared.

The youth was declared a delinquent and committed to the State Industrial School until he reached the age of 21 unless sooner discharged by due process of law. The Supreme Court of Arizona affirmed dismissal of a petition for a writ of habeas corpus and an appeal was made to the United States Supreme Court.

On the right-to-counsel issue the majority commented:

> We conclude that the Due Process Clause of the Fourteenth Amendment requires that in respect of proceedings to determine delinquency which may result in commitment to an institution in which the juvenile's freedom is curtailed, the child and his parent must be notified of the child's right to be represented by counsel retained by them, or if they are unable to afford counsel, that counsel will be appointed to represent the child.

This wording would seem to indicate that juveniles are guaranteed the right to counsel to the same degree as adults.

In holding that the self-incrimination provisions also apply to juveniles, the Court injected the right-to-counsel protection, stating:

> We conclude that the constitutional privilege against self-incrimination is applicable in the case of juveniles as it is with respect to adults.

Other comments in the case indicate that with few exceptions the constitutional guarantees afforded adults will also be given to juveniles.

Since the *Gault* decision, questions have arisen as to the waiver of the right to counsel in the case of a juvenile. In the *Gault* case the Court stated that the child and his parents must be notified of the child's right to be represented by counsel. In carrying out this demand the New York Supreme Court ruled that the parents as well as the child must be advised concerning the right to counsel. That court held that unless the juvenile is advised of all his rights in the presence of the parent or a lawyer, so the court can be sure the rights are understood, a juvenile's confession will not stand up in court.[53]

The rule requiring that both the parent and the juvenile be advised concerning the right to counsel has exceptions which have been applied in several courts. For example, a New Jersey juvenile domestic relations court decided that the capacity to waive one's right to counsel cannot be determined

---

[53] In re Aaron D., 30 App. Div. 2d 183, 290 N.Y.S.2d 527 (1967).

by age alone.[54] The court said that although it has been frequently argued that a juvenile is not competent to waive his right to counsel because of his young age, this proposition has been generally rejected by the weight of authority.

To avoid any possibility of taint, it is suggested that the requirements of the *Gault* decision be followed and that the accused juvenile be advised of his rights in the presence of his parents or an attorney.

§ 8.13 Right to counsel on appeal

Not only does the right to counsel protect persons accused of crime prior to trial, it has been expanded to protect the person who has been convicted in the trial court. Where an appeal is granted as a matter of right, it is unconstitutional for the state to refuse to appoint counsel for indigents.[55]

Having decided that counsel must be appointed for indigent state defendants on their first appeal where the appeal is a matter of right, the Supreme Court was requested in 1974 to expand that right and require counsel for discretionary state appeals and for appeals to the United States Supreme Court. In the case of *Ross v. Moffitt*[56] the respondent, an indigent, was represented by a court-appointed counsel at the trial and was convicted of forgery in two separate cases. He appealed as a matter of right to the North Carolina Court of Appeals and was again represented by court-appointed counsel. However, the court refused to appoint counsel for a discretionary review by the North Carolina Supreme Court, and he was denied the appointment of counsel to prepare a petition for certiorari to the United States Supreme Court.

Recognizing that the right to counsel had already been expanded greatly and that the Supreme Court had given extensive consideration to the rights of indigent persons on appeal, Mr. Justice Rehnquist, speaking for the majority, refused to extend that right to the described situation. This decision provides that the due process clause does not require a state to provide the respondent with counsel on his discretionary appeal to the state supreme court nor to the United States Supreme Court. The rationale is that on appeal, the defendant, not the state, initiates the appellate process, seeking not to fend off the efforts of the state's prosecutor but rather to overturn a finding of guilt made by a judge or a jury below.

---

54 In re R.M., 105 N.J. Super. 372, 252 A.2d 237 (1969).

55 Douglas v. California, 372 U.S. 353, 83 S. Ct. 814, 9 L. Ed. 2d 811 (1963).

56 417 U.S. 600, 94 S. Ct. 2437, 41 L. Ed. 2d 341 (1974).

Neither due process nor the guarantee of equal protection requires the state to appoint a lawyer for poor Death Row inmates seeking state habeas corpus relief.[57]

§ 8.14 Right to counsel at probation or parole revocation hearing

Of special interest to probation, parole and corrections personnel is the case of *Mempa v. Rhay*[58] in which the Supreme Court decided that a probationer is entitled to appointment of counsel at a combined probation revocation and delayed sentencing hearing. Mr. Justice Marshall, speaking for the Court, determined that where a defendant has been convicted and placed on probation, counsel must be appointed to represent him at the probation revocation hearing where the imposition of sentence is a possibility. This is a critical stage of the prosecution proceedings, and a lawyer must be afforded at such a *combined* hearing, whether it be labeled "revocation of probation" or "deferred sentencing." Applying the *Mempa* ruling, the Michigan Court of Appeals held that the accused is entitled to counsel at the probation revocation hearing where sentencing is to be adjudged in the event that the probation is revoked.[59]

In 1972 the United States Supreme Court was called on to determine if this right extended to parole revocation procedures in *Morrissey v. Brewer.*[60] The parole officer in the case had recommended that parole be revoked because of the parolee's continued violation of parole rules. The petitioner claimed that his due process rights as guaranteed by the Fourteenth Amendment were violated because he had received no hearing prior to revocation of the parole. The state responded by arguing that no hearing was required.

In a lengthy decision the Supreme Court of the United States specifically stated that it did not decide the question whether the parolee is entitled to the assistance of retained counsel or to appointed counsel if he is indigent,

---

57 Murray v. Giarratano, __U.S.__, 109 S. Ct. 2765, __L. Ed. 2d__ (1989).

58 389 U.S. 128, 88 S. Ct. 254, 19 L. Ed. 2d 336 (1967).

59 People v. Brown, 17 Mich. App. 396, 169 N.W.2d 522 (1969).

60 408 U.S. 471, 92 S. Ct. 2593, 33 L. Ed. 2d 484 (1972). Every probation and parole officer would read this case fully for an understanding of the function of probation and parole as viewed by the United States Supreme Court. *See* Baxter v. Palmigiani, 425 U.S. 308, 96 S. Ct. 1551, 47 L. Ed. 2d 810 (1976) for a decision denying right to counsel for prisoners charged with misconduct.

but did set out other requirements which must be met prior to a parole revocation. Among these are:

(a) written notice of the claimed violation;

(b) disclosure to the parolee of evidence against him;

(c) opportunity to be heard in person and to present witnesses and documentary evidence;

(d) the right to confront and cross-examine adverse witnesses;

(e) a neutral and detached hearing body such as a traditional parole board, members of which need not be judicial officers or lawyers; and

(f) a written statement by the factfinders as to the evidence relied on and reasons for revoking parole.

After setting out these requirements, the Court added that it had no intention of creating an inflexible structure for parole revocation procedures. The Court explained that these were only basic requirements and that the states could formalize their own procedures so long as they complied with these requirements.

The Supreme Court did not specifically require that counsel be authorized at the parole revocation since it did not consider such proceedings to be prosecutorial in nature. However, if the requirements as stated above are to be guaranteed, the parolee may well argue that only with counsel can he be certain that these requirements are met.

After the decision in the *Morrissey* case, the justices were again called upon to determine the necessity of appointing counsel at a probation revocation hearing -- this time, where the probationer had been sentenced *at trial*.[61] The Court declared that since the loss of probation, like the loss of parole, is a serious deprivation of liberty, due process must be afforded the probationer already sentenced at trial by entitling him to two hearings as set down in *Morrissey*:

(1) a preliminary hearing at the time of detention to determine whether probable cause exists to believe he has violated parole or probation; and

(2) a comprehensive hearing prior to any final revocation decision.

Addressing the question of whether indigents in parole or probation revocation hearings have a constitutional right to appointed counsel, the Court

---

[61] Gagnon v. Scarpelli, 411 U.S. 778, 93 S. Ct. 1756, 36 L. Ed. 2d 656 (1973).

considered the informal nature of such hearings, the advocacy of the parole or probation officer, and the "more limited due process rights" of those already convicted of crime, deciding that appointment of counsel in such situations should be decided on a case-by-case basis.

The Kentucky Court of Appeals, looking to the guidelines suggested in the two Supreme Court cases mentioned above, held that a reckless driver is not entitled to be discharged from custody merely because he was not represented by counsel at a revocation hearing.[62] In this Kentucky case an habitually reckless driver was given a 180-day contempt sentence for violating a no-driving injunction which was initially suspended. He had no right to counsel at the hearing on the prosecutor's motion to set aside the suspension order, the Kentucky Court explained, as the court was not reviewing an action independent of the original contempt proceeding. The reasoning of the judges was that in this habeas corpus proceeding where the action by the lower Kentucky Court was being challenged, there was not even a suggestion that the driver had not violated the terms of the probation or that there were any mitigating circumstances. He insisted that the mere fact that he was not represented by counsel at the revocation hearing entitled him to be discharged from custody. The court disagreed and refused to grant relief.

To summarize, the United States Supreme Court has interpreted the Constitution to require retained counsel, or appointed counsel for indigent persons, at hearings where deferred sentencing and probation revocation are combined. The Court neither required nor denied counsel at parole or probation revocation hearings where the probationer had been sentenced at trial, but held the presence of counsel at such hearings should be decided on a case-by-case basis. Due process requirements which the Court *did* specify could arguably be fulfilled only with the assistance of counsel in certain situations.

§ 8.15 Effective assistance of counsel

Although the right to counsel has been guaranteed by the federal Constitution since 1791, this right has been greatly extended in the last decade. Gradually, the right has been expanded to apply at trial in all felony and some misdemeanor cases, and at proceedings prior to and subsequent to the trial proceedings. Recently the quality of representation has been more effectively challenged. Although the Supreme Court has never enunciated any clear standards for courts to follow on claims of ineffectiveness of counsel, state supreme courts and federal circuit courts have groped for a prescription

---

62 Reeder v. Commonwealth, 507 S.W.2d 491 (Ky. 1973).

to apply in this situation. Over a period of time the courts have generally accepted a formula which came to be known as the "mockery of justice" standard. This standard has been defined in these words:

> [A] charge of inadequate representation can prevail "only if it can be said that what was or was not done by the defendant's attorney for his client made the proceedings a farce and a mockery of justice, shocking to the conscience of the Court."[63]

As the scope of the right-to-counsel under the provisions of both the state constitutions and the U.S. Constitution expanded, the demands to change the test to a more stringent one for the attorney have been forcefully urged. As a result some courts, including the Third, Fourth, Fifth, Sixth, Seventh, and District of Columbia Circuits,[64] have adopted a more objective standard known as the "reasonably competent" standard. Under this standard, if counsel does not exhibit the "normal and customary" degree of skill and knowledge possessed by attorneys who are reasonably knowledgeable of criminal law, the assistance is ineffective, and this fact will furnish grounds for reversal. Several states including Tennessee have also changed to the standard requiring that advice given and services rendered by an attorney be within the range of competence demanded of attorneys in criminal cases.[65] Georgia,[66] Iowa,[67] and Pennsylvania[68] also follow this standard.

An accused is entitled to be represented by counsel without conflicting interests. However, the court need not initiate an inquiry into the propriety of multiple representation when an accused is represented by counsel who also represents other defendants who were involved in the same incident.

In the case of *Cuyler v. Sullivan*,[69] the defendant appealed to the Supreme Court on the grounds that counsel representing him and two others, all of whom were charged with first degree murder, did not properly represent him as he had a conflict of interest. The facts were as follows. Two privately retained lawyers represented the respondent and two others who were charged with the same murders. The respondent who was tried first made no objection at the time to the multiple representation. The defense rested at

---

63 Cardarell v. United States, 375 F.2d 222 (8th Cir. 1967), *quoting* O'Malley v. United States, 285 F.2d 733, 734 (6th Cir. 1961).

64 Romero v. United States, 459 U.S. 926, 103 S. Ct. 236, 74 L. Ed. 187 (1983).

65 Hellard v. State, 629 S.W.2d 4 (Tenn. 1982).

66 Brown v. Ricketts, 233 Ga. 809, 213 S.E.2d 672 (1975).

67 Ogden v. State, 215 N.W.2d 335 (Iowa 1974).

68 Commonwealth v. Sullivan, 472 Pa. 129, 371 A.2d 468 (1977).

69 444 U.S. 823, 100 S. Ct. 1708, 64 L. Ed. 2d 333 (1980).

the close of the prosecutor's case and respondent was convicted. The two codefendants later were acquitted at separate trials. Respondent then sought habeas corpus relief alleging that he had not received effective assistance of counsel because his lawyer represented conflicting interests.

Although the Supreme Court of the United States agreed that facts established the existence of multiple representation, they found that multiple representation in itself does not necessarily mean a conflict of interest. The Court noted that the defendant did not allege that state officials knew or should have known that his lawyers had a conflict of interest. The majority of the Supreme Court concluded that:

> But nothing in our precedents suggests that the Sixth Amendment requires state courts in themselves to initiate inquiries into the propriety of multiple representation in every case. Defense counsel have an ethical obligation to avoid conflicting representations and to advise the court promptly when a conflict of interest arises during the course of a trial.

Even though in this case the Supreme Court denied relief, the Justices agreed that a lawyer forced to represent codefendants whose interests conflict cannot provide the adequate legal assistance required by the Sixth Amendment. The Court continued:

> In order to demonstrate a violation of his Sixth Amendment rights, a defendant must establish that an actual conflict of interest adversely affected his lawyer's performance.

Is the defendant denied effective assistance of counsel if counsel advises his client not to commit perjury while testifying in his own behalf? In the case of *Nix v. Whiteside*, the defendant, accused of the murder and stabbing death of a marijuana seller, told his counsel from the outset that he had believed the victim was going for a gun.[70] Initially, the defendant admitted he had not actually seen a weapon, but about a week before the trial the defendant told the lawyer for the first time that he would testify that, just before the stabbing, he had seen "something metallic" in the victim's hand.

Believing that such testimony would be perjury, the lawyer told the defendant that the existence of a gun was not necessary to establish a claim of self-defense and if the defendant so testified the lawyer would inform the court and seek withdrawal from representation. When the defendant testi-

---

[70] Nix v. Whiteside, 475 U.S. 157, 106 S. Ct. 988, 89 L. Ed. 2d 123 (1986).

fied, he did not mention that he had seen "something metallic" and was convicted. On federal habeas corpus review, the defendant convinced the Eighth Court that he had been denied effective assistance by his lawyer's refusal to testify as he had proposed.

Denying that the defendant had not been effectively represented, the Chief Justice thought that the lawyer's conduct fell well within accepted standards of professional conduct and the range of reasonable professional conduct acceptable under previously established rules. The majority indicated that all the attorney's action did in this case was to deprive the client of something to which he had no right at all -- his contemplated perjury. Therefore, there was not attorney error.

Expanding the right to effective counsel further, the United States Supreme Court in 1985 recognized for the first time a constitutional right to have effective counsel on appeal where the appeal is a matter of right.[71] Justice Brennan, speaking for the majority, ruled that the appellant's attorney had failed to follow a state procedural rule resulting in a conviction and that this was a denial of due process. The Court noted that appellate procedures are surrounded by constitutional protections and that the services of counsel are necessary to present an appeal in a manner likely to elicit meaningful review. During the appeal, as at trial, the accused faces an adversary proceeding "governed by intricate rules that to a lay person would be hopelessly forbidding." The majority continued by indicating that if the appellant does not have the effective assistance of counsel where the appeal was an "appeal as of right," the due process provisions are violated.

However, the accused is not deprived of the right of effective counsel by enforcement of the federal drug forfeiture law. In a pair of cases decided in 1989 the United States Supreme Court declared that the federal drug forfeiture act may be applied to property that a defendant wants to use in order to pay counsel of his choice.[72] The Court emphasized that there is no exemption for assets that a defendant wishes to use to retain an attorney.

§ 8.16 Right to freely communicate with counsel

The right to counsel encompasses the right to communicate with counsel in private. Several cases have established the duty of officers having custody of a suspect to afford him a reasonable opportunity to consult privately with his attorney. No officer has the right to be present and to hear what is said

---

71 Evitts, Lucey, 469 U.S. 387, 105 S. Ct. 830, 83 L. Ed. 2d 821 (1985).

72 United States v. Monsanto, __U.S.__, 109 S. Ct. 2657, __L. Ed. 2d__ (1989); Caplin v. Drysdale, __U.S.__, 109 S. Ct. 2646, __L. Ed. 2d__ (1989).

during the interview,[73] nor does the officer have the right to listen or record the conversations by means of "bugging" devices. Conversations between an attorney and his client are said to be "privileged."

In a 1963 decision the Supreme Court of the State of Washington was outspoken in its disapproval of practices which tend to interfere with the right of the accused to consult with counsel in private.[74] The defendant in this case was charged with lewdness and later with second degree burglary and larceny. Being unable to post bond, the defendant remained in the county jail from the time of his arrest until the end of the trial. A room had been provided in the county jail for consultations between prisoners and their attorneys. After several interviews between the defendant and his attorney, it was discovered that their conversations had been recorded by the use of a microphone which had been installed in the conference room. The trial judge refused to dismiss the case but advised that he would exclude any derivative evidence which had come to light as a result of the eavesdropping procedure. In reversing the defendant's conviction, the state Supreme Court stated that effective legal representation could not be obtained without privacy. After citing several cases on point, the court concluded:

> A defendant and his lawyer have a right to talk together by telephone or personal interview without their conversations being monitored by the prosecution through a secret mechanical device which they did not know was being used. We do not think that the granting of a new trial is an adequate remedy for the deprivation of the right to counsel where eavesdropping has occurred....It is our conclusion that the defendant is correct when he says that the shocking and unpardonable conduct of the sheriff's officers in eavesdropping upon the private consultations between the defendant and his attorney, thus depriving him of his right to effective counsel, violates the whole proceedings. The judgment and sentence must be set aside and the charges dismissed.

The cases are consistent in holding that the right to counsel includes the right to consult with counsel in private.

---

73 State ex rel. Tucker v. Davis, 9 Okla. Crim. 94, 130 P. 962 (1913). *See also*, 21 AM. JUR. 2d *Criminal Law* § 312 (1965).

74 State v. Cory, 62 Wash. 2d 371, 382 P.2d 1019 (1963).

§ 8.17 Self-representation rights

With so many decisions relating to the right-to-counsel provisions of the Constitutions, one would think that this matter had been fully litigated. However, it seems that questions are still arising concerning the interpretation of this Sixth Amendment provision. One of the important decisions of the 1974-75 term of the United States Supreme Court related to the defendant's right to serve as his own counsel. After reviewing the history of the right to counsel and the right of self-representation, and after examining the various statutory and state constitutional provisions, six members of the United States Supreme Court concluded that a defendant who truly wishes to defend himself should not be forced to accept the services of an attorney.[75] Some of the facts of this landmark decision will assist in understanding its implications.

Anthony Faretta was charged with grand theft in Los Angeles County, California. A Superior Court judge appointed the public defender to represent Faretta, but before the date of the trial Faretta requested that he be permitted to represent himself. After first ruling that Faretta would be authorized to conduct his own defense, the judge reversed his earlier ruling and again appointed the public defender to represent the accused. Throughout the trial, the judge required that Faretta's defense be conducted only through the appointed attorney. At the conclusion the jury found the defendant guilty as charged, and the judge sentenced him to prison. He appealed on the grounds that he had not been granted permission to represent himself. The Supreme Court agreed, pointing out that at the time the Sixth Amendment was adopted, the right of self-representation was recognized in the colonies as well as in England. Mr. Justice Stewart, who wrote the opinion, included this phrase:

> In sum, there is no evidence that the colonists and the Framers ever doubted the right of self-representation, or imagined that this right might be considered inferior to the right of assistance of counsel. To the contrary [they] always conceived of the right to counsel as an "assistance" for the accused, to be used at his option, in defending himself.

Apparently it does not make any difference if the defendant is equipped to represent himself or not. According to the Supreme Court:

---

[75] Faretta v. California, 422 U.S. 806, 95 S. Ct. 2525, 45 L. Ed. 2d 562 (1975).

> We need make no assessment of how well or how poorly Faretta had mastered the intricacies of the hearsay rule and the California code provisions that govern challenges of potential jurors on *voir dire*. For his technical legal knowledge, as such, was not relevant to an assessment of his knowing exercise of the right to defend himself.

Three justices, in dissenting to this conclusion, warned that the holding would raise a host of procedural problems. The warning of the minority has proved valid. The United States District Court for Southern New York was asked to determine if the defendant who has counsel also has a right to participate in his own trial as co-counsel. That court found that a defendant does not have a right to the best of two Sixth Amendment worlds -- he may have counsel appointed, or waive counsel and conduct his own defense; but he does not have the right to demand both.[76]

In another case,[77] the Court of Appeals for the Second Circuit reversed a conviction because the trial court had disqualified, without the consent of the defendant, an attorney who had indicated a potentially serious conflict of interest. That reviewing court found that the defendant may waive his right to have his retained counsel free from conflicts of interest. The court reasoned that if the defendant can insist on representing himself, as in the case of *Faretta*, he may insist on being represented by a particular attorney even though that attorney has a conflict of interest insofar as his effective representation of the defendant is concerned.

One can conclude from these cases that:

(1) the accused has an absolute right to defend himself at the trial even though he may not be qualified to do so;
(2) although he may represent himself, he *probably* cannot demand counsel and then choose to be his own co-counsel;
(3) the right to manage one's own defense includes the right to choose attorneys who face a serious conflict of interest.

There is no doubt that additional questions will arise. For example, will the Supreme Court allow a person to be put to death who so poorly represents himself as to be deprived of procedural and substantive "due process of law"? Such a question can only be answered in the future.

---

76 United States v. Swinton, 400 F. Supp. 805 (S.D.N.Y. 1975).

77 United States v. Armedo-Sarmiento, 524 F.2d 591 (2d Cir. 1975).

§ 8.18 Summary and practical suggestions

Under the English common law prior to 1688, there was no right to counsel in felony cases. From the year 1695 when counsel was allowed for the first time in trials for treason until the present there has been a progressive expansion of the right to counsel. This right was deemed to be of such importance that many of the states prior to the writing of the United States Constitution included guarantees in their state constitutions. With the adoption of the Sixth Amendment in 1791, the right to counsel became embodied in the Federal Constitution.

The provision of the Sixth Amendment that in all criminal prosecutions the accused shall have the assistance of counsel for his defense was originally interpreted to mean that an accused was entitled to counsel only during trials in the federal courts. However, after the Fourteenth Amendment was adopted in 1868, the courts began to consider the right to counsel as a fundamental right and, therefore, binding upon the states through the Fourteenth Amendment.

The Sixth Amendment is written in broad generalities. Over the years the courts have been called upon to interpret whether its requirements are satisfied by allowing the accused to employ counsel of his choice and whether the government must furnish counsel to indigents who are unable to retain their own. More pressing has been the question concerning the stage in the criminal process at which the right to counsel attaches. In 1938 the Supreme Court in the *Johnson* case made it clear that the accused must be represented by counsel during trials in the federal courts unless he intelligently and competently waives this right. For many years the Court refused to apply the identical rule to state prosecutions, but in the 1963 case of *Gideon v. Wainwright* the *Johnson* rule was made effective against the states also. The precise holding in *Gideon* was that counsel must be provided for indigent defendants in state felony trials unless the right is intelligently waived.

After some years of confusing lower court decisions, the United States Supreme Court in 1972 extended the right-to-counsel protection to trials in misdemeanor cases. This right to have counsel appointed for indigents in misdemeanor situations is limited to misdemeanors where imprisonment is a possibility. As in the case of felony offenses, the right to have counsel in a misdemeanor case may be knowingly and intelligently waived.

The right to have counsel appointed has been extended to the arraignment and to the preliminary hearing when these are critical stages in the criminal process. In 1964, a major stride was taken by the Supreme Court in *Escobedo v. Illinois* where the Court held that the right to counsel begins when the police carry out a process of interrogation that lends itself to eliciting incriminating statements. After this point the police can no longer refuse a suspect his request to see his attorney. The scope of the *Escobedo* holding was clarified two years later by the Supreme Court in the 1966 case of *Miranda v. Arizona*. Though the case hinged primarily on the privilege against self-incrimination, the Court made some very pertinent observations concerning the right to counsel and established the rule that an accused must be warned of his right to counsel after he is taken into custody and before interrogation, and that he must be informed of his right to appointed counsel if unable to employ his own. Waiver of the right cannot be predicated on the failure of the accused to request counsel.

In 1967 the Supreme Court extended the right to counsel to a lineup or other confrontation-for-identification situations. Here the Court said that because the pretrial identification may unduly influence the in-court identification at the trial, as a general rule the accused should have an attorney available at the lineup proceeding. It was explained, however, that this right may be knowingly and intelligently waived. Also the Court left the door open for the prosecution to show that the in-court identification was not contaminated by the pretrial identification procedure.

In 1972 the Supreme Court explained that the *Wade* requirements applied only in a post-indictment confrontation, but these rules do not apply to a police station show up which takes place before the defendant has been indicted or otherwise formally charged with a criminal offense.

One of the rights made applicable to juveniles by the *Gault* decision in 1967 was the right to have the assistance of counsel. The ruling of the majority of the Supreme Court in that case was that the child and his parent must be notified of the child's right to be represented by counsel. Some courts have reasoned, however, that a juvenile, especially an older juvenile, may in certain circumstances waive the right to counsel if he is informed and has average intelligence. The better practice is to advise both the juvenile and his representative concerning the right to counsel.

The right-to-counsel protection of the Sixth Amendment was first limited to counsel at the trial in felony cases in federal court. It has gradually extended to pretrial proceedings. The right has also been extended to post-trial proceedings involving deferred sentencing, and is to be decided on a case-by-case basis where the parolee or probationer was sentenced previously.

Not only is the accused entitled to have counsel, he is entitled to have at least "reasonably competent" counsel. The courts do not agree as to the standard that should be applied in determining the competency of counsel. Two standards which have been mentioned by various courts are the "mockery of justice" standard and the "within the range of competence demanded of attorneys in criminal cases" standard.

The fact that the accused is entitled to counsel does not mean that he must be assigned counsel against his will. In 1975 the Supreme Court determined that a state may not constitutionally refuse to allow a defendant to conduct his own defense.

Everyone studying the criminal justice system should be familiar with the cases and statutes describing the right to counsel. Investigators and police administrators should be especially familiar with the law relating to the right to counsel during the investigation.

In the *Escobedo* and *Miranda* cases, specific requirements were delineated. However, this should not discourage the use of information legitimately obtained from suspects prior to the formal indictment. Experience has demonstrated that valuable evidence can be obtained by proper questioning without violating the Sixth Amendment constitutional rights. Although the rules established by the courts limit the circumstances under which a confrontation for identification may take place, this investigative technique is proper and valuable when conducted by personnel who are familiar with the limitations.

The administrator should insure that procedures conform to the legal requirements of the *Escobedo* and *Miranda* cases, as well as to those of the *Wade* and *Kirby* cases.

Chapter 9
DOUBLE JEOPARDY*

[N]or shall any person be subject for the same offense to be twice put in jeopardy of life or limb....

Fifth Amendment, 1791

---

* *by Jacqueline R. Kanovitz*

§ 9.1 Introduction

The double jeopardy clause of the Fifth Amendment provides that no person shall "be subject for the same offense to be twice put in jeopardy of life or limb...." The historical genesis of this doctrine is not entirely clear. Although the Magna Charta makes no reference to double jeopardy, there is considerable evidence that the principle against twice trying a man for the same offense had gained recognition under the English common law by the thirteenth century, long before the American colonial period.[1] It was fully entrenched in English jurisprudence and was brought to this continent as part of the common law legal tradition. The earliest written formulation of the double jeopardy restraint in this country appeared in the *Massachusetts Body of Liberties* of 1641.[2] The Fifth Amendment prohibition against twice placing a man in jeopardy reflects the awareness by those responsible for drafting the Bill of Rights that a legal system which fails to limit the number of times the government may seek to establish a criminal accused's guilt on the same offense runs a serious risk of abuse.

Despite the central importance of the double jeopardy restraint, it was one of the last significant portions of the Bill of Rights to be made applicable to the states. This occurred in 1969 in the case of *Benton v. Maryland*.[3] In *Benton*, the Supreme Court announced that immunity from double jeopardy constituted a fundamental right and that, henceforth, state double jeopardy practices would be governed by established Fifth Amendment standards.

§ 9.2 Constitutional policies underlying double jeopardy restriction

The deceptively simple statement contained in the Fifth Amendment mandating that government shall not twice subject an accused to jeopardy for the same offense, masks what has been termed a "wilderness of legal complexity."[4] The Supreme Court's efforts to give coherent meaning and application to this limitation have been remarkably disappointing, as even mem-

---

1 Bartkus v. Illinois, 359 U.S. 121, 79 S. Ct. 676, 3 L. Ed. 2d 684 (1959) (Black, J., dissenting).

2 J.A. SIGLER, DOUBLE JEOPARDY, 22 (1969).

3 395 U.S. 784, 89 S. Ct. 2056, 23 L. Ed. 2d 707 (1969).

4 Fisher, *Double Jeopardy: Six Common Boners Summarized*, 15 U.C.L.A. L. REV. 81 (1967).

bers of the Court have come to realize.[5] Few portions of the Bill of Rights remain more poorly analyzed. Any attempt to comprehend double jeopardy jurisprudence must begin with an identification of the interests of an accused person that this restraint was designed to safeguard.

Limiting the number of times that the government may attempt to establish guilt protects several distinct interests. First, criminal trials represent a heavy strain, personal as well as financial. An acquittal would not end the accused's emotional ordeal if reprosecution remained permissible. The double jeopardy prohibition reflects society's concern that a man who has been tried once and either acquitted or convicted should be able to leave that phase of his life behind him forever and plan his future without fear that his ordeal will be repeated.[6] But more importantly, repetitive criminal prosecutions for the same offense give rise to a serious risk that innocent persons will be convicted because they have become too worn down, either psychologically or financially, to put forth an adequate defense.[7] Mr. Justice Black has summarized the constitutional policies underlying the double jeopardy restraint as follows:

> [T]he State with all its resources and power should not be allowed to make repeated attempts to convict an individual for an alleged offense, thereby subjecting him to embarrassment, expense and ordeal and compelling him to live in a continuing state of anxiety and insecurity, as well as enhancing the possibility that even though innocent he may be found guilty.[8]

§ 9.3 Double jeopardy overview

The Fifth Amendment directs that an accused should not be *twice put in jeopardy* for the same offense. It follows from this constitutional language that if the proceedings against an accused are dismissed or abandoned prior to the point when he has been placed in jeopardy for the first time, he gains no constitutional immunity from being compelled to face those charges at a later date. Our initial inquiry must, therefore, center on identifying the point

---

5 Burks v. United States, 437 U.S. 1, 9, 98 S. Ct. 2141, 2146, 57 L. Ed. 2d 1 (1978); Whalen v. United States, 445 U.S. 684, 701-702, 100 S. Ct. 1432, 1442, 63 L. Ed. 2d 715 (1980).

6 United States v. Candelaria, 131 F. Supp. 797 (S.D. Cal. 1955).

7 *See generally*, Note, *Twice in Jeopardy*, 75 YALE L.J. 262 (1965).

8 Green v. United States, 355 U.S. 184, 187-188, 78 S. Ct. 221, 2 L. Ed. 2d 199 (1957).

in the criminal proceedings when jeopardy attaches. Under settled doctrine, jeopardy attaches in jury trials when the jury is empaneled and sworn, and in bench trials (trials before a judge sitting without a jury) when the court has commenced taking testimony.[9] Criminal proceedings scuttled prior to this point carry no double jeopardy protection.

The fact that criminal proceedings reach the jeopardy attachment point once does not, on the other hand, guarantee that the accused's confrontation with society will end with the termination of that proceeding. Tension between the accused's interest in ending his ordeal after he has once been placed on trial and society's interest in seeing that the accused does not escape from the criminal process before the government has received a fair chance to present its case against him has led to the creation of a handful of exceptions where retrial is permissible despite the fact that the first trial progressed to the jeopardy attachment point. These exceptions depend on how the first trial terminates. The following represents a summary.

(1) Where the first trial ends in an *acquittal*, the accused gains absolute constitutional immunity against reprosecution for the same offense.[10]

(2) Where the first trial ends in a *conviction*, the accused gains constitutional immunity from reprosecution unless he elects to surrender this protection by appealing his conviction. A reversal on appeal for reasons other than a lack of sufficient evidence leaves the government free to retry him.[11]

(3) Where the first trial passes the jeopardy attachment point but *ends before a verdict has been reached*, the accused gains constitutional immunity against reprosecution for the same offense except in two important instances: (a) where the accused makes the choice to forego having the merits of the charges against him resolved by the tribunal empaneled to sit in judgment of him and seeks a mistrial or dismissal on grounds unrelated to his factual guilt or innocence, and (b) where a "manifest necessity" requires that the first trial be ended before a verdict has been reached.[12]

---

9 Discussed in § 9.4 *infra*.

10 Discussed in § 9.6 *infra*.

11 Discussed in §§ 9.6 and 9.7 *infra*.

12 Discussed in § 9.5 *infra*.

The Fifth Amendment prohibits the second jeopardy only when it is brought for the *same offense*. Determining when prosecutions brought for the same underlying criminal behavior under different sections of the penal code represent the *same offense* presents one of the most troublesome issues in double jeopardy law. This problem is explored in Sections 9.8, 9.9, and 9.10. The constitutionalization of the *collateral estoppel doctrine* has eliminated the need for reaching this determination in cases where (a) the accused is acquitted in an earlier proceeding, (b) the acquittal turned on the resolution in his favor of an ultimate fact issue, (c) that same issue is involved at his second trial on different charges, and (d) a contradictory determination would be required to convict him in the second proceeding.[13] The study of the collateral estoppel doctrine will conclude the investigation of double jeopardy law.

§ 9.4 Stage in the prosecution when jeopardy attaches

"Jeopardy" is the risk of conviction and punishment that an accused faces when he is placed on trial in a criminal action.[14] Although the constitutional language, "jeopardy of life or limb," suggests that this safeguard is reserved for serious criminal offenses only, this provision has been broadly construed and applies in all criminal prosecutions, including misdemeanor trials where no more than a fine is authorized, as well as in juvenile court proceedings.[15] The double jeopardy restraint does not, however, apply in civil proceedings even when the government is the instituting party.[16]

What the Constitution forbids is the second jeopardy. It follows that an accused must have formerly been placed in jeopardy before reprosecution immunity is gained. Under the English common law and in England today, jeopardy does not attach so as to bar reprosecution of an accused until a verdict has been reached in his case.[17] In the United States, an earlier attachment rule has been adopted. When an accused is tried before a jury, he is regarded as having been placed in jeopardy as soon as his first jury has been

---

13 Discussed in § 9.11 *infra*.

14 Breed v. Jones, 421 U.S. 519, 95 S. Ct. 1779, 44 L. Ed. 2d 346 (1975).

15 Breed v. Jones, *supra* note 14; Robinson v. Neil, 409 U.S. 505, 93 S. Ct. 876, 35 L. Ed. 2d 29 (1973).

16 One Lot Emerald Cut Stones and One Ring v. United States, 409 U.S. 232, 93 S. Ct. 489, 34 L. Ed. 2d 438 (1972).

17 Note, *Double Jeopardy: The Reprosecution Problem*, 77 HARV. L. REV. 1272, 1273 (1964).

empaneled and sworn.[18] In non-jury cases, this point is reached after the first witness has been sworn and the court has begun hearing evidence.[19] In the vast majority of cases, the prosecution will run its normal course and the trial will terminate in a verdict. The critical difference between the English and American attachment rules emerges only in those cases where the first proceeding is prematurely disrupted. In England, an accused is without legal protection where his first trial comes to a verdictless conclusion. In the United States, subject to the exceptions noted below, the rule is different. The act of placing an accused on trial, rather than the verdict, supplies the foundation for American reprosecution immunity.

The American attachment rule reflects the judgment that once a trial has started, the accused has a legitimate interest in proceeding with the first tribunal chosen so that his confrontation with society can be concluded once and for all. The commencement of the trial has thus been selected as the jeopardy attachment point. In fact, the federal time-of-attachment rule is regarded as such an integral part of the Fifth Amendment protection that it is binding on the states and cannot be altered. In *Crist v. Bretz*,[20] the Supreme Court held that a statute attempting to postpone the time of attachment in jury trials until after the first witness has been sworn violated the Fifth Amendment.

If the attachment of jeopardy were sufficient to bestow unqualified reprosecution immunity on the accused in all cases, the chapter on double jeopardy would now be finished. However, society's interest in resolving the merits of the charge stands in opposition to the accused's interest in ending his ordeal. Despite the attachment of jeopardy, society's interest is preferred and the accused can be retried:

(1) where the accused requests and is granted a termination of his first trial before the changes against him have been resolved;[21]
(2) where the trial judge prematurely halts the first trial for reasons of "manifest necessity,"[22] and
(3) where the accused's conviction is set aside on appeal because of trial court error.[23]

---

18 Illinois v. Somerville, 410 U.S. 458, 93 S. Ct. 1066, 35 L. Ed. 2d 425 (1973); Downum v. United States, 372 U.S. 734, 83 S. Ct. 1033, 10 L. Ed. 2d 100 (1963); Crist v. Bretz, 437 U.S. 28, 98 S. Ct. 2156, 57 L. Ed. 2d 24 (1978).

19 Serfass v. United States, 420 U.S. 377, 95 S. Ct. 1055, 43 L. Ed. 2d 265 (1975).

20 437 U.S. 28, 98 S. Ct. 2156, 57 L. Ed. 2d 24 (1978).

21 *See* § 9.5 *infra*.

22 *Id*.

23 *See* § 9.7 *infra*.

These exceptional situations where retrial is permitted will be explored at later points in this chapter.

None of the steps preliminary to placing the accused on trial constitutes jeopardy or affords protection against further criminal proceedings. The Fifth Amendment safeguard is not activated by an arrest. A suspect is, accordingly, not constitutionally immunized when he is released from custody following an arrest. The same holds true for a probable cause hearing before a magistrate. Because the accused is not placed in jeopardy at a preliminary hearing, a dismissal of the charges at this juncture carries no assurance of finality.[24] By the same token, the accused gains no reprosecution immunity from the pretrial dismissal of an indictment.[25] Although repeated arrests, indictments and arraignments on charges never brought to trial can be almost as taxing as repeated prosecutions, abuses like these are beyond the scope of the Fifth Amendment guarantee.

§ 9.5 Double jeopardy protection afforded by a verdictless trial

Under the American attachment rule, the accused is placed in jeopardy at the start of his first trial. He has a valuable interest in seeing that his ordeal is not prolonged beyond the original proceedings. Where, however, his first trial is terminated before a verdict is reached, his interest collides with society's interest in seeing that the guilty do not escape punishment. There are two instances where the accused's interest in the finality of a verdictless trial will be subordinated to society's interest in securing a determination of his guilt or innocence. Despite the fact that the first proceedings progressed beyond the jeopardy attachment point, reprosecution will be allowed where:

(1) a premature termination of the first proceeding was granted at the accused's request or with his consent, or
(2) the original proceedings were halted for reasons of "manifest necessity."

1. Verdictless terminations at the accused's initiative

If a criminal trial passes the jeopardy attachment point and the prosecution is willing to continue but the accused moves to have the proceedings

---

24 Collins v. Loisel, 262 U.S. 426, 43 S. Ct. 618, 67 L. Ed. 1062 (1922).

25 Serfass v. United States, 420 U.S. 377, 95 S. Ct. 1055, 43 L. Ed. 2d 265 (1975); Bassing v. Cady, 208 U.S. 386, 28 S. Ct. 392, 52 L. Ed. 540 (1908).

terminated for reasons unrelated to his factual guilt or innocence, the granting of a mistrial or dismissal on the accused's motion removes any constitutional barrier to reprosecution.[26] The rationale underlying this exception is that the accused, by seeking a verdictless termination of the proceedings, has made a "deliberate election...to forego his valued right to have his guilt or innocence determined before the first trier of fact,"[27] and therefore must shoulder the consequences. The accused's motion will lift the bar against reprosecution even if the prosecutor's errors occasioned the need for his request unless the prosecutor deliberately caused the need for a mistrial to obtain some tactical advantage.[28]

2. *Verdictless terminations founded on manifest necessity*

Entirely different considerations are met when the original proceedings are halted without the accused's consent. Exposing him to retrial here invades his interest in ending his confrontation with society once and for all. On the other hand, freeing the accused without a determination of guilt because a juror has died or the judge has become too ill to proceed ignores society's stake in criminal prosecutions. In *United States v. Perez*,[29] the Supreme Court adopted a middle ground position. Where the first trial ends in a dismissal or mistrial granted without the accused's consent, retrial is permissible under the *Perez* test where, taking all circumstances into consideration, there was a *manifest necessity* for prematurely halting the original proceedings.

The *Perez* "manifest necessity" test has been found satisfied where the judge,[30] a juror,[31] or the accused[32] becomes too ill to continue; where wartime exigencies make it impossible to complete the trial at the time and place set;[33] and where a deadlocked jury is unable to reach a verdict.[34] The

---

26 United States v. Dinitz, 424 U.S. 600, 96 S. Ct. 1075, 47 L. Ed. 2d 267 (1976); United States v. Scott, 437 U.S. 82, 98 S. Ct. 2187, 57 L. Ed. 2d 65 (1978).

27 United States v. Scott, *supra* note 26, 437 U.S. at 93, 98 S. Ct. at 2195.

28 Oregon v. Kennedy, 456 U.S. 667, 102 S. Ct. 2083, 72 L. Ed. 2d 416 (1982).

29 22 U.S. (9 Wheat.) 579, 6 L. Ed. 165 (1824).

30 Freeman v. United States, 237 F. 815 (2d Cir. 1916).

31 United States v. Potash, 118 F.2d 54 (2d Cir.), *cert. denied*, 313 U.S. 584, 61 S. Ct. 1103, 85 L. Ed. 1540 (1941).

32 United States v. Stein, 140 F. Supp. 761 (S.D.N.Y. 1956).

33 Wade v. Hunter, 336 U.S. 684, 69 S. Ct. 834, 93 L. Ed. 974 (1949).

34 Logan v. United States, 144 U.S. 263, 12 S. Ct. 617, 36 L. Ed. 429 (1892); Richardson v. United States, 468 U.S. 317, 104 S. Ct. 3081, 82 L. Ed. 2d 242 (1984).

fact that the government bears responsibility for the events requiring the mistrial does not necessarily foreclose application of the *Perez* test. In *Illinois v. Sommerville*,[35] the Supreme Court determined that a manifest necessity for ending the first trial existed where the government had drawn a defective indictment but the error was not discovered until the proceedings had gotten under way. However, if a mistrial is granted on the prosecutor's motion or by the trial court on its own initiative, and "there is reason to believe that the prosecutor is using the superior resources of the State to harass or to achieve a tactical advantage over the accused," retrial is foreclosed.[36] In sum, application of the manifest necessity test calls for a careful judicial balancing of the accused's interest in ending his ordeal in one trial and society's interest in securing a verdict on the merits. This balancing must be conducted in light of the circumstances that unfold at the trial rather than on the basis of mechanical rules.

§ 9.6 Double jeopardy consequences of a completed trial

An accused person who has been acquitted gains absolute constitutional immunity against reprosecution for the same offense.[37] It is irrelevant that the acquittal may have resulted from mistaken rulings on the admissibility of government evidence, on misinterpretations of criminal statutes, or on trial errors that seriously handicap the prosecution.[38] Regardless of the errors that may underlie the acquittal, retrial for the same offense following an acquittal is constitutionally foreclosed under any and all circumstances.

Should the accused be convicted at his first trial and acquiesce in the verdict, identical protection against reprosecution for the same offense is gained. If, however, the accused successfully challenges his conviction and has it set aside because of trial errors, different considerations are involved, as the next section shows.

---

35 410 U.S. 458, 93 S. Ct. 1066, 35 L. Ed. 2d 425 (1973).

36 Arizona v. Washington, 434 U.S. 497, 508, 98 S. Ct. 824, 832, 54 L. Ed. 2d 717 (1978).

37 Fong Foo v. United States, 369 U.S. 141, 82 S. Ct. 671, 7 L. Ed. 2d 629 (1962); Green v. United States, 355 U.S. 184, 78 S. Ct. 221, 2 L. Ed. 2d 199 (1957); Kepner v. United States, 195 U.S. 100, 24 S. Ct. 797, 49 L. Ed. 114 (1904); United States v. Ball, 163 U.S. 662, 16 S. Ct. 1192, 41 L. Ed. 300 (1896).

38 *See* cases cited in note 37 *supra*.

§ 9.7 Double jeopardy consequences of a successful appeal

An accused who seeks review of his conviction and succeeds in having it overturned forfeits the protection of his first jeopardy and may be retried.[39] In *United States v. Tateo*,[40] the Supreme Court ventured the following explanation:

> Corresponding to the right of an accused to be given a fair trial is the societal interest in punishing one whose guilt is clear after he has obtained such a trial. It would be a high price indeed for society to pay were every accused granted immunity from punishment because of any defect sufficient to constitute reversible error in proceedings leading to conviction. From the standpoint of a defendant, it is at least doubtful that appellate courts would be as zealous as they are now in protecting the effects of improprieties at the trial or pretrial stage if they knew that reversal of a conviction would put the accused irrevocably beyond the reach of further prosecution. In reality, therefore, the practice of retrial serves defendants' rights as well as society's interest.

There is, however, one sound and entirely logical exception to the rule that an accused can be retried in the event his conviction is later set aside. Where the accused's conviction is overturned because the evidence presented at the trial was, as a matter of law, insufficient to establish his guilt, reversal on appeal amounts in essence to an appellate court acquittal of the charges.[41] To remand the case for retrial after such a finding would run counter to the most fundamental principle of double jeopardy doctrine, i.e., that acquittals are final and end the accused's ordeal with society. It should be mentioned in passing, however, that the setting aside of a conviction because of insufficient evidence is extremely rare. When convictions are overturned, the far more

---

39 Green v. United States, 355 U.S. 184, 78 S. Ct. 221, 2 L. Ed. 2d 199 (1957); United States v. Tateo, 377 U.S. 463, 84 S. Ct. 1587, 12 L. Ed. 2d 448 (1964); Burks v. United States, 437 U.S. 1, 98 S. Ct. 2141, 57 L. Ed. 2d 1 (1978); Hudson v. Louisiana, 450 U.S. 40, 101 S. Ct. 970, 67 L. Ed. 2d 30 (1981); Tibbs v. Florida, 457 U.S. 31, 102 S. Ct. 2211, 72 L. Ed. 2d 652 (1982); Justices of Boston Municipal Court v. Lydon, 466 U.S. 294, 104 S. Ct. 1805, 80 L. Ed. 2d 311 (1984).

40 377 U.S. 463, 466, 84 S. Ct. 1587, 1589, 12 L. Ed. 2d 448 (1964).

41 Burks v. United States, *supra* note 39, Hudson v. Louisiana, *supra* note 39. *But see* Tibbs v. Florida, *supra* note 39; Justices of Boston Municipal Court v. Lydon, *supra* note 39.

common reason is trial court errors. Upsetting a conviction because of trial court errors, rather than because of a fatal weakness in the government's case, leaves the accused subject to retrial.

§ 9.8 Constitutional protection against successive prosecutions under overlapping criminal statutes: the problem of defining when offenses are the same

The text of the Fifth Amendment forbids placing an accused twice in jeopardy for the *same offense*. At the time the Constitution was adopted, the number of different crimes was relatively small and each crime category covered a broad spectrum of criminal behavior. As a result, when the government was discontented with the outcome of the first proceedings, little opportunity existed for trying the accused a second time for the same underlying criminal behavior, by varying the statutory charges. The situation in modern times is radically different. Contemporary penal codes are replete with overlapping statutes dealing with slightly different aspects of the same criminal behavior. In no area of double jeopardy jurisprudence has the Supreme Court's record been more disappointing than in its efforts to develop constitutional standards for determining when crimes charged at successive trials represent the same offense. The states, left largely without guidance, had essentially two focal points upon which to erect tests for determining offense-identity. The test could concentrate on the statutory definitions of crimes supplied by the legislature, on the criminal behavior, or on a combination of statutory offense and criminal behavior.

The overwhelming majority of state jurisdictions adopted the first approach. Utilizing the legislative definitions of crimes as their starting points, these courts developed what has become known as the "same evidence" test for determining when crimes charged at successive trials represent the *same offense*. A second group of states, viewing the criminal behavior as the constitutionally appropriate yardstick for determining how many times an accused can be tried, devised an approach known as the "same transaction" test for determining offense-identity. A third group opted for a hybrid approach that combines features blended from the other two. For want of a better name, we will call the third approach the "alleged conduct" test. These three approaches are explored below.

1. "Same evidence" test

The "same evidence" test approach for determining whether prosecutions brought under different portions of the penal code are actually brought for the *same offense* focuses on the definitions fixed by the legislature for each of the various crimes. Substantive crimes are composed of elements which the prosecutor must establish to obtain a conviction. A court applying the "same evidence" test will compare the statutes under which the accused has been charged at successive trials to ascertain the evidence required to obtain a conviction under each. If the elements necessary to obtain a conviction under the first statute would suffice to obtain a conviction under the second, a court applying this test will treat offenses created by both statutes as the same.[42] If, on the other hand, each violated statute requires proof of at least one element not shared by the other, the offenses are regarded as distinct for double jeopardy purposes, even though both violations arise out of the same underlying criminal behavior and even though there is substantial overlap in their required proof elements.

The "same evidence" test has been paraphrased in numerous ways, but the following explains the essence of the test:

> Where the same act or transaction constitutes a violation of two distinct statutory provisions, the test to be applied to determine whether there are two offenses or only one is whether each provision requires proof of an additional fact which the other does not....[43]

Because the "same evidence" test focuses on the proof required to obtain convictions under the several statutes, this test is sometimes referred to as the "required evidence" test.

Existing penal codes are replete with instances of duplicating and overlapping statutes dealing with slightly different aspects of the same general behavior. Because of this, the "same evidence" test for determining offense identity affords only minimal protection against repetitive criminal prosecutions. Sex crimes dramatically illustrate the proliferation of statutory offenses. An alleged act of forcible intercourse might, depending upon the statutory law of a given jurisdiction, generate ten or more "same evidence" test offenses. Though bizarre, it is conceivable under this test that an accused sex offender could be tried consecutively for assault and battery, rape, fornication, carnal knowledge, seduction, adultery, indecent exposure, lewd and lascivious behavior, and, depending upon the victim's age and relationship to the accused, child molesting, impairing the morals of a minor, contributing to

---

42 Gavieres v. United States, 220 U.S. 338, 31 S. Ct. 421, 55 L. Ed. 489 (1911). *See also* Note, *Twice in Jeopardy*, 75 YALE L. REV. 262 (1965).

43 Blockburger v. United States, 284 U.S. 299, 304, 52 S. Ct. 180, 182, 76 L. Ed. 306 (1932).

delinquency, and incest.[44] Since virtually all of these statutory violations require proof of at least one distinct element not shared by any of the others, multiple "same evidence" test offenses have allegedly been committed, and the accused can be tried separately for each.

Overlapping statutes dealing with slightly different aspects of the same underlying behavior are not the only instance where the "same evidence" test fails to function as an effective limitation on the prosecutor's ability to bring successive criminal prosecutions for the same underlying behavior. A single criminal act may produce multiple consequences as, for example, where an accused recklessly drives an automobile into a crowd of pedestrians, killing several,[45] or robs several individuals at the same time and place.[46] Where multiple wrongs of the same general type are committed simultaneously, the requirement that the prosecutor prove the death or injury of a distinct victim at each trial furnishes a sufficient variance in the required proof to satisfy the "same evidence" test and to allow the prosecutor to proceed separately on each injury.[47] Pushed to its limits, the "same evidence" test has been applied to sanction multiple prosecutions growing out of a single discharge of a gun where the bullet fragmented and struck two victims,[48] and where it entered the body of a pregnant woman, wounding her and killing her unborn child.[49]

The "included offense" doctrine, nevertheless, mitigates some of the harshness of the "same evidence" test. When two statutory offenses are so related that it is legally impossible to commit one without inevitably and simultaneously committing the other, the relationship between them creates included offenses.[50] The concept of an included offense can be illustrated as

---

44 United States *ex rel.* Brown v. Hendrick, 431 F.2d 436 (3d Cir.), *cert. denied*, 402 U.S. 976 (1971). *See also*, Note, 7 BROOKLYN L. REV. 79, 82 (1937).

45 Holder v. Fraser, 215 Ark. 67, 219 S.W.2d 625 (1949).

46 Gandy v. State, 42 Ala. App. 215, 159 So. 2d 71, *cert. denied*, 276 Ala. 704, 159 So. 2d 73 (1963); People v. Kelley, 168 Cal. App. 2d 387, 335 P.2d 955 (1959); Commonwealth v. Meyers, 193 Pa. Super. 531, 165 A.2d 400 (1960), *cert. denied*, 368 U.S. 860, 82 S. Ct. 102, 7 L. Ed. 2d 57 (1961); Morgan v. State, 220 Tenn. 247, 415 S.W.2d 879 (1967).

47 Holder v. Fraser, *supra* note 45; Murray v. Commonwealth, 289 S.W.2d 203 (Ky. 1956); State v. Whitley, 382 S.W.2d 665 (Mo. 1964); State v. Varner, 329 S.W.2d 623 (Mo. 1959), *cert. denied*, 365 U.S. 803, 81 S. Ct. 468, 5 L. Ed. 2d 460 (1961).

48 Commonwealth v. Browning, 146 Ky. 770, 143 S.W. 407 (1912); Berry v. State, 195 Miss. 899, 16 So. 2d 629 (1944).

49 State v. Shaw, 219 So. 2d 49 (Fla. Dist. Ct. App. 1969).

50 People v. Pater, 267 Cal. App. 2d 921, 73 Cal. Rptr. 823 (1968); People v. Krupa, 64 Cal. App. 2d 592, 149 P.2d 416 (1944); Johnson v. State, 217 Tenn. 234, 397 S.W.2d 170 (1965).

follows. Suppose that the legislature has defined two crimes, A and B. To procure a conviction for crime A, the prosecutor must establish the existence of three elements, X, Y, and Z, whereas crime B requires proof of X and Y alone. Since all of the elements of crime B are incorporated into crime A, and it is legally impossible to commit crime A without simultaneously committing crime B, crime B is an included offense. The most common examples of included offenses are crimes of different degrees such as first- and second-degree murder.[51] Larceny is an offense included in the crime of robbery though their relationship is not one of degrees. Robbery consists of the felonious taking of personal property from the owner's possession by force and fear. It is essentially a combination of two other crimes -- assault (putting the victim in fear) and larceny (taking and carrying off his property). Since it is legally impossible to commit robbery without simultaneously committing an assault plus larceny, the latter offenses are both included within the crime of robbery.

Even in "same evidence" test jurisdiction, the prosecutor is barred from trying included offenses separately.[52] A prosecution for the greater offense bars the state from later charging the accused on any lesser included crimes. Conversely, trial for the lesser included crime precludes reprosecution for the greater offense. The sequence in which the prosecutions are brought is immaterial.[53] The reason for this limitation inheres in the statement of the "same evidence" test: "unless *each* provision requires proof of an additional fact which the other does not," the offenses are the same. In the case of criminal statutes creating greater and lesser ingredient crimes, only one statute, the statute defining the greater offense, requires proof of a fact beyond that required for the other.

The included offense exception to the "same evidence" test, nevertheless, has no application where the greater offense has not yet been completed at the time the lesser offense is tried.[54] In *Diaz v. United States*,[55] the Supreme Court held that an accused could be tried for homicide following an earlier conviction of assault and battery growing out of the same incident and involving the same victim where the victim died subsequent to the first prosecution. The Court's rationale was that at the time of the first trial the ac-

---

51 Singleton v. United States, 294 F. 890 (5th Cir. 1923).

52 Brown v. Ohio, 432 U.S. 161, 97 S. Ct. 2221, 53 L. Ed. 2d 187 (1977); Harris v. Oklahoma, 433 U.S. 682, 97 S. Ct. 2912, 53 L. Ed. 2d 1054 (1977); Jeffers v. United States, 432 U.S. 137, 97 S. Ct. 2207, 53 L. Ed. 2d 168 (1977).

53 *See* cases cited in note 52 *supra*.

54 Garrett v. United States, 471 U.S. 773, 105 S. Ct. 2407, 85 L. Ed. 2d 764 (1985).

55 223 U.S. 442, 32 S. Ct. 250, 56 L. Ed. 500 (1912).

cused was not, and could not have been, placed in jeopardy of conviction for a homicide that had not yet occurred.[56]

2. "Same transaction" test

Concern over the "same evidence" test's potential for abusive applications has prompted a minority of state courts to search for a double jeopardy definition of "offense" more sensitive to the constitutional policies underlying the double jeopardy restraint. One approach, known as the "same transaction" test, measures the boundaries of an offense by the underlying criminal behavior. Each *criminal transaction* is regarded as a single unit for prosecution purposes even though multiple statutory violations are involved. The "same transaction" test does not require the prosecutor to elect among the various statutes that have been violated. He can charge the accused with all violations committed provided that he consolidates them for trial in one proceeding rather than tries them sequentially.[57] This result, endorsed by the American Law Institute Model Penal Code,[58] is widely acclaimed by legal scholars,[59] and is presently mandated in England.[60]

The "same transaction" test, though an improvement over the "same evidence" test in promoting the constitutional policies underlying the double jeopardy restraint, nonetheless suffers from its own shortcomings. The chief difficulty stems from the absence of any bright lines marking off the boundaries of a criminal act or transaction. Although the prosecutor is required to join for trial all charges growing out of the same criminal act or transaction, the question arises how are these concepts to be defined? Few endeavors consist of a single act. Even the discharge of a gun requires a series of separate motions -- transporting the weapon to the appropriate location, loading it, aiming it and ultimately firing it. It would be nonsense to suggest that each muscular exertion constitutes a separate criminal act or transaction for prosecution purposes. But what forges motions together to make them a unitary criminal transaction? The problem becomes more acute if additional facts are added. Suppose the firing of the weapon occurred while the accused was

---

56 *See also* Garrett v. United States, *supra* note 54.

57 Ashe v. Swenson, 397 U.S. 436, 90 S. Ct. 1189, 25 L. Ed. 2d 469 (1970) (Brennan, J., concurring); People v. White, 390 Mich. 245, 212 N.W.2d 222 (1973).

58 Model Penal Code § 1.07(2) (1985).

59 Carroway, *Persuasive Multiple Offense Problems - A Policy Analysis*, 1971 UTAH L. REV. (1975); Kirchheimer, *The Act, The Offense, and Double Jeopardy*, 58 YALE L.J. 513 (1949); Note, *Twice in Jeopardy*, 75 YALE L.J. 262 (1965).

60 Connelly v. Director of Public Prosecutions, (1964) 2 All E.R. 401, A.C. 1254.

attempting to flee the scene of a robbery just perpetrated by him; to further complicate matters, suppose in addition that the bullet ricochets, injuring one bystander and killing another. How many "criminal transactions" exist under the behaviorally-oriented test of offense-identity?

In a jurisdiction utilizing the "same evidence" test of an offense, the solution is simple although unsatisfactory in terms of double jeopardy policy. No less than three major substantive crimes were committed -- armed robbery, assault and battery, and homicide -- and since each violation requires proof of different elements, the accused can be prosecuted three separate times without violating his double jeopardy rights.[61] Determining the number of criminal acts or transactions for the sake of applying the behavior test of an offense is more complex. No pre-established legal standards exist for dividing a flow of events into discrete criminal transactions. When faced with this problem, courts applying the "same transaction" test have normally stressed the factors of continuity of time and singularity of motivating intent.[62] In *People v. White*,[63] the Supreme Court of Michigan, utilizing these criteria, determined that an accused who forced a woman into his car, kidnapped her, drove her some distance away, and ultimately feloniously assaulted and raped her, was guilty of a unitary criminal transaction for prosecution purposes, even though multiple statutory violations had been perpetrated. The controlling factor was that all violations had been committed in a continuous sequence and were the product of a singular criminal purpose, rape.

3. *"Alleged conduct" test*

The "same evidence" test and the "same transaction" test both have their shortcomings. The "same evidence" test with its emphasis on the distinct elements required to obtain convictions under several statutes violated in the course of a criminal enterprise often fails as an effective check on the prosecutor's power to bring successive criminal prosecutions for the same criminal behavior. The "same transaction" test, on the other hand, while attempting to solve this problem, suffers from uncertainties in defining when criminal behavior transgressing several statutes constitutes a single criminal transaction or unit for prosecution purposes. The "alleged conduct" test, while combining

---

61 State v. Moton, 476 S.W.2d 785 (Mo. 1972).

62 Neal v. State, 55 Cal. 2d 11, 357 P.2d 839 (1960), *cert. denied*, 365 U.S. 823, 81 S. Ct. 708, 5 L. Ed. 2d 700 (1961); State v. Corning, 289 Minn. 354, 184 N.W.2d 603 (1971); State v. Brown, 262 Or. 442, 497 P.2d 1191 (1972).

63 390 Mich. 245, 212 N.W.2d 222 (1973).

features from the other two approaches, attempts to shore up the problems encountered with each. Two or more statutory violations constitute the same offense under this approach if proof of the same conduct or behavior is in fact alleged to establish each violation.[64]

The "alleged conduct" test differs from the "same evidence" test in that it focuses on the *actual* proof the prosecutor offers to obtain convictions for two or more statutory violations tried separately and not simply the proof elements required by each statute. Assume, for example, that an ex-convict is arrested and tried consecutively for carrying a *concealed* weapon and being a *former convict* in possession of a deadly weapon. Both charges, though they grow out of the same criminal behavior, are not the same offense under the "same evidence" test because each statutory violation requires proof of a distinct element.[65] The first statute requires proof that the weapon was concealed while the second requires proof that the possessor was an ex-convict. Nevertheless, since the prosecutor must in fact allege the same act of carrying the weapon to prove both violations, the offenses are the same under the "alleged conduct" test.

The "alleged conduct" test shares with the "same transaction" test concern that the accused be spared the ordeal of being twice tried for the same underlying factual behavior. The "alleged conduct" approach, however, avoids the need to determine the scope of a "criminal transaction" since a second prosecution brought under a different section of the penal code is barred only when the identical acts are alleged.

§ 9.9 Supreme Court rulings defining when offenses charged at separate trials are the same

The Supreme Court has entertained only a handful of cases dealing with when offenses charged at separate trials are the same. The results of these cases are somewhat inconclusive. The Supreme Court has never approved the "same transaction" test, though this approach has occasionally been advocated in concurring and dissenting opinions.[66] In a case decided early in this century,[67] the Supreme Court applied the "same evidence" test to find that an accused could be separately tried for disorderly conduct and insulting a pub-

---

64 Illinois v. Vitale, 447 U.S. 410, 100 S. Ct. 2260, 65 L. Ed. 2d 228 (1980).

65 Bell v. Kansas, 452 F.2d 783 (10th Cir. 1971), *cert. denied*, 406 U.S. 974, 92 S. Ct. 2421, 32 L. Ed. 2d 674 (1972); State v. Brown, 262 Or. 442, 497 P. 2d 1191 (1972).

66 Ashe v. Swenson, 397 U.S. 436, 90 S. Ct. 1189, 25 L. Ed. 2d 469 (1970) (Brennan, J., concurring).

67 Gavieres v. United States, 220 U.S. 338, 31 S. Ct. 421, 55 L. Ed. 489 (1911).

lic official though both charges grow out of the same acts. More recent cases, however, suggest a two-stage analysis for determining offense identity. Two offenses are constitutionally the same for purposes of reprosecution either if:

(1) they are the same under the "same evidence" test, or
(2) the government would be forced to allege the identical factual behavior to support both convictions.[68]

Use of the "alleged conduct" test as supplementary to the "same evidence" test traces to *Illinois v. Vitale*.[69] The accused, while driving an automobile, struck and killed two children. A policeman at the scene issued a traffic citation for the violation of **failing to reduce speed** when necessary to avoid colliding with persons or vehicles. After the accused was tried, convicted and fined for this offense, the state indicted him for two counts of involuntary manslaughter under a statute that condemned the **taking of human life while recklessly driving** under circumstances likely to cause death or bodily injury. The case reached the Supreme Court on the question of whether the **failure to reduce speed** and the **taking of human life while recklessly driving** were the "same offense" for double jeopardy purposes.

The Supreme Court began its analysis by characterizing the "same evidence" as the "principal test" for determining when crimes charged at separate trials represent the same offense. The Court then, as the "same evidence" test requires, compared the proof elements necessary to obtain convictions under the two statutes and concluded that the **failure to reduce speed** and **involuntary manslaughter from reckless driving** were not the same offense under the "same evidence" test.

Significantly, however, the court did not stop with its "same evidence" offense-identity analysis. Although concluding that failure to reduce speed and involuntary manslaughter were not the same under this test, the Supreme Court indicated that if, on remand, the prosecutor in fact relied on Vitale's reckless failure to reduce speed rather than other acts of recklessness to establish the elements of manslaughter, the accused's double jeopardy rights would be violated. In the Court's words:

> [On remand] it may be that to sustain its manslaughter case the State may find it necessary to prove a failure to slow or to rely on conduct necessarily involving such failure; it may concede as much prior to trial. In that case, because Vitale has already been con-

68 Illinois v. Vitale, 447 U.S. 410, 100 S. Ct. 2260, 65 L. Ed. 2d 228 (1980).
69 *Id.*

> victed for conduct that is a necessary element of the more serious crime for which he has been charged, his claim of double jeopardy would be substantial....[70]

Under the *Illinois v. Vitale* analysis, the accused gets a double shot at establishing that crimes charged at successive trials represent the "same offense." The first shot entails a "same evidence" test facial examination of the several statutes involved to determine whether each statute requires proof of one or more distinct elements. If the offenses are the same under this test, the accused's double jeopardy defense must be accepted and the inquiry proceeds no further. If, however, the offenses are distinct, the court must next apply the "alleged conduct" test. This test enables the accused to establish a double jeopardy violation if the prosecutor at his second trial in fact relies, or will be forced to rely, on the same criminal conduct alleged at his earlier trial.

Had there been no multiple prosecution cases since *Illinois v. Vitale* this case could be viewed as a definitive statement of when offenses charged at separate trials are the same. Unfortunately, several Supreme Court cases since *Illinois v. Vitale* have placed the status of the "alleged conduct" test in doubt. These cases raise doubt as to whether an accused who is twice tried for the same behavior under different portions of the penal code can claim double jeopardy protection beyond that afforded by the "same evidence" test.[71]

§ 9.10 Constitutional protection against trial by several jurisdictions

The United States is comprised of the federal government and fifty separate sovereign states, each of which is separately endowed with power to try and punish crimes. Criminal enterprises may cross state lines or simultaneously violate federal and state law. Does a criminal act become more than one offense for double jeopardy purposes when identical laws of two separate political entities have been violated?

This problem differs from the one we encountered in the last two sections. There, the question of offense-identity was triggered by multiple statutory violations of the laws of a single jurisdiction. The "same evidence," "same transaction," and "alleged conduct" tests were used to resolve offense-identity issues. In dual sovereignty situations, a different approach applies.

---

70 *Id.* at 420, 100 S. Ct. at 2267, 65 L. Ed. 2d at 238.

71 Thomas, *The Prohibition of Successive Prosecutions for the Same Offense: In Search of a Definition*, 71 IOWA L. REV. 323, 382-397.

1. *Successive state and federal prosecutions*

The problem of successive prosecutions by a state and the federal government first reached the Supreme Court in *United States v. Lanza*.[72] Lanza was convicted by the State of Washington for manufacturing, transporting and selling liquor in violation of state law. Following his Washington conviction, Lanza was tried in a federal court under the Volstead Act for the same acts and was again convicted. The issue before the Supreme Court was whether the Double Jeopardy Clause of the Fifth Amendment barred federal court proceedings against an accused who had previously stood trial on identical charges before a state tribunal. A negative answer was given. The Supreme Court, in response to the double jeopardy argument, pointed out that under our federal union, the United States government and the states are separate entities, each separately endowed with the sovereign power to define what conduct amounts to an offense against its peace and dignity. An act denounced as a crime both by a state and the United States is, therefore, an offense against each. Treating a prior state court prosecution brought to vindicate its laws as a bar to federal enforcement proceedings would seriously encroach on the federal government's sovereignty. If an act simultaneously violates the laws of a state and the United States, state courts cannot immunize an accused against federal accountability for his behavior by apprehending and trying him first.

Though *Lanza* established that the federal government has constitutional power to try an accused following a state court prosecution for the same criminal behavior, the United States has adopted a policy of voluntary abstention from retrial except in extraordinary cases. In 1959, Attorney General William P. Rogers made a policy statement that no federal prosecution should be commenced following state criminal proceedings based on the same behavior "unless the reasons are compelling." He further indicated that the federal government should cooperate with state and local authorities to the end that a single prosecution would occur in the jurisdiction with the paramount interest.[73] The federal government's policy makes good sense.

Lanza tested the federal government's power to try an accused following a state prosecution on similar charges. In *Bartkus v. Illinois*[74] an identical ra-

---

72 260 U.S. 377, 43 S. Ct. 141, 67 L. Ed. 314 (1922).

73 Dept. of Justice Press Release, *New York Times*, April 6, 1959, *quoted* in Hall and Kamisar, MODERN CRIMINAL PROCEDURE 479 (1966). *See also* Rinaldi v. United States, 434 U.S. 22, 98 S. Ct. 81, 54 L. Ed. 2d 207 (1971).

74 359 U.S. 121, 79 S. Ct. 676, 3 L. Ed. 2d 684 (1959).

tionale was applied when the sequence of prosecutions was reversed. Illinois courts convicted an accused for bank robbery after he had previously been tried in a federal court for violating the National Bank Robbery Law. The Supreme Court, rejecting the accused's double jeopardy claim, applied the dual sovereignty rationale, i.e., an act denounced as a crime under the laws of separate sovereign political entities is an offense against each, and each may try and punish for the infraction of its laws.

2. *Successive state court prosecutions*

The dual sovereignty argument for permitting successive prosecutions rests on particularly strong grounds where a criminal transaction contravenes the laws of two or more states. There are, added to considerations of political sovereignty, considerations of territorial independence. Under our federal system, each state has sovereign power to prosecute for crimes committed within its borders. Therefore, criminal proceedings taken by one state have no double jeopardy impact on the powers of a sister state to prosecute for violations of its laws.[75]

3. *Successive prosecutions brought before state and local courts*

The dual sovereignty justification for allowing separate prosecutions when the same conduct offends the identical laws of two states, or of a state and the federal government, has no application when the prosecuting authorities are the state and one of its local political subdivisions. Local governmental units are territorial parts of the state, created to assist the state in discharging its government responsibilities, and are not separate sovereign entities. For this reason, a conviction or acquittal before a municipal court operates as a bar to state court proceedings brought for the same offense even though the same behavior is outlawed by both levels of government.[76] For double jeopardy purposes, only one prosecuting entity is involved.

In the next section we encounter the collateral estoppel doctrine. A review of the material on offense-identity coupled with a hypothetical will illustrate the relationship of the collateral estoppel doctrine to the material just covered. When successive prosecutions are brought against an accused, he may make several different arguments for double jeopardy immunity. First, he may argue that the second prosecution, though under a different

---

75 Heath v. Alabama, 474 U.S. 82, 106 S. Ct. 433, 88 L. Ed. 2d 387 (1985).

76 Waller v. Florida, 397 U.S. 387, 90 S. Ct. 1184, 25 L. Ed. 2d 435 (1970).

statute, in essence charges the *same offense*. This argument focuses the court's attention on the question of offense-identity. Losing this argument, an accused who is *acquitted* at his first trial may next seek to claim reprosecution immunity under the collateral estoppel doctrine.

Collateral estoppel is concerned with identity of *issues* involved in successive trials rather than identity of *offenses*. To successfully assert double jeopardy immunity based on collateral estoppel, the accused must demonstrate that his first trial resolved in his favor some factual issue that precludes his culpability of the offense charged at his second trial. Consider a man who is charged with raping and murdering the same victim at one time and place. Rape and murder are not the same offense under the "same evidence" and "alleged conduct" tests, though they might be under the "same transaction" test. If, however, the accused is tried and acquitted for one of these crimes and can demonstrate that the acquittal turned on his successful establishment of an alibi defense, he can then claim collateral estoppel protection against reprosecution for the other offense.

§ 9.11 Collateral estoppel

The collateral estoppel doctrine holds that where an ultimate factual issue has been raised and decided in a judicial proceeding, the matter is conclusively established between the parties and is binding in any subsequent litigation in which the identical issue may again be called into question.[77] The losing party may not relitigate the issue before a different judge or jury in the hopes of prevailing the second time around. In the hypothetical posed where an accused is acquitted at his first trial on the basis of an alibi defense, subsequent criminal proceedings are thereafter foreclosed because to prevail in the subsequent proceeding, the government would be forced to relitigate the issue of the accused's presence at the scene of the crime, thus disproving the original findings. If the accused was not present at the time of the rape, it follows that he was not there for the murder and vice versa.

The collateral estoppel doctrine is of ancient origin and is founded upon considerations of finality. In *Ashe v. Swenson*,[78] the Supreme Court constitutionalized this doctrine by incorporating it into the double jeopardy restraint. The accused's double jeopardy rights are violated under the doctrine

---

77 Ashe v. Swenson, 397 U.S. 436, 90 S. Ct. 1189, 25 L. Ed. 2d 469 (1970).

78 *Id.*

of collateral estoppel, even though he is retried for a different offense, if the following three conditions are met:

(1) He was acquitted at is first trial.
(2) His acquittal turned upon an adjudication in his favor of an ultimate fact common to both proceedings.
(3) A contradictory resolution of that fact would be required for the second tribunal to convict him.

§ 9.12 Summary

The double jeopardy restraint is primarily concerned with sparing an accused the emotional and financial ordeal of being forced repeatedly to muster his energies in his defense. To this end the Constitution directs that an accused may not twice be placed in jeopardy for the same offense. Identifying the point in the criminal proceedings when jeopardy attaches is important, because until this point is reached and the accused undergoes a "first jeopardy," he gains no prosecution immunity. Under settled interpretation, an accused is placed in jeopardy when the first jury is impaneled or, in bench trials, when the first witness is sworn. Criminal proceedings terminated before this point carry no constitutional protection against later resurrection of the charges.

The fact that the original proceeding passes beyond the jeopardy attachment point does not invariably mean that the accused's ordeal will end with the conclusion of the trial. Even though the accused has previously been placed in jeopardy for the identical offense, there are three exceptions under which reprosecution is allowable.

(1) *Defense motions halting the original proceedings*. Where the accused makes a deliberate choice to forego having the merits of the charges against him resolved by the original tribunal and requests a mistrial or dismissal on grounds unrelated to his culpability, protection of his first jeopardy is lost and he may be reprosecuted.

(2) *Verdictless terminations founded on manifest necessity*. Where there is manifest necessity for halting the first proceedings before a verdict is reached, the accused is subject to retrial even though he did not consent to the premature termination of the original proceedings.

(3) *Successful appeal from conviction*. Where a conviction obtained at the first trial is set aside at the accused's instance for

> reasons other than the legal insufficiency of the government's evidence against him, the government is free to retry him.

When the prosecution mounts a second prosecution for the same criminal behavior under a different section of the penal code, problems of offense-identity are met. For want of authoritative Supreme Court guidelines, state courts have evolved three separate standards. The "same evidence" test, currently employed by a majority of state courts, compares the proof elements required to obtain a conviction under each statute charged. If each statute violated requires proof of at least one different element, separate offenses are created; these charges may be consecutively tried even though all violations arise out of the same underlying factual incident. The "same evidence" test of offense-identity gives extremely narrow operation to the double jeopardy safeguard. An alternative approach, styled the "same transaction" test, focuses on the behavior of the accused and requires the prosecution to join for trial all statutory violations committed during a single criminal transaction. The "alleged conduct" test borrows elements from the other two; it protects an accused from being retried under different portions of the penal code for the same criminal conduct that was in fact alleged against him in an earlier criminal proceeding.

In *Illinois v. Vitale*, the Supreme Court indicated that offenses are constitutionally the same for reprosecution purposes if:

(1) they are the same under the "same evidence" test, or
(2) the prosecutor relies or intends to rely on the same criminal conduct alleged against the accused in an earlier proceeding.

More recent cases, however, cast doubt on whether an accused can claim protection in excess of that afforded by the "same evidence" test.

Where the same conduct violates the laws of two states, or of a state and the federal government, none of the offense-identity tests outlined above are applicable. Each sovereign political entity may separately try and punish any infractions of its laws. A state and its local subdivisions, however, do not constitute separate sovereign entities for double jeopardy purposes.

A determination that the offense charged at the second trial is different does not necessarily end the constitutional inquiry. Double jeopardy can occur under the collateral estoppel doctrine if a conviction for a different offense would require relitigation of some factual issue previously resolved in the accused's favor. The double jeopardy safeguard, as this chapter has outlined it, has been incorporated into the Fourteenth Amendment and applies in state proceedings as fully as it does in federal ones.

Chapter 10
FAIR AND JUST TRIAL AND HUMANE PUNISHMENT*

> *In all criminal prosecutions, the accused shall enjoy the right to a speedy and public trial, by an impartial jury of the State and district wherein the crime shall have been committed, which district shall have been previously ascertained by law, and to be informed of the nature and cause of the accusation; to be confronted with the witnesses against him; to have compulsory process for obtaining witnesses in his favor, and to have the Assistance of Counsel for his defense.*
>
> Sixth Amendment

Section

---

* *by Jacqueline R. Kanovitz*

§ 10.1 Introduction

An inscription on the walls of the Department of Justice reads: "The United States wins its points when justice is done its citizens in the courts." The criminal justice system, as we know it, did not, like Minerva, the goddess of wisdom, spring forth full-blown at a single moment in history. There was a time in the Western world when a man could be condemned without a trial,[1] and when the most barbaric and inhuman atrocities imaginable were performed in the name of criminal punishment.[2] The first major triumph in the evolution of the Anglo-American criminal justice system occurred at Runnymede in 1215, where King John was forced to capitulate to the demands of his insurgent barons and to sign the historic document known as the Magna Charta. The Magna Charta secured for Englishmen the guarantee that no free man would thenceforth be condemned to death or sent to prison "except by the legal judgment of his peers or by the law of the land."[3] This language echoes a familiar ring. It is the precursor of the due process principle that is enshrined in the Fifth and Fourteenth Amendments to the U.S. Constitution. Those who drafted our Constitution were not content, however, to rely upon this short-hand phrase alone as a means of constitutionalizing and perpetuating a number of specific procedural safeguards that had, over the centuries, come to be associated with the due process notion. In the Bill of Rights, they elaborated on what process was due. Several of the familiar constitutional safeguards surrounding the prosecution and trial of criminal cases will be canvassed in this chapter: the assurance of a speedy and public trial, the requirement that the tribunal assembled to pass judgment be an impartial one, the right to be tried before a petit jury, the right to confront and cross-examine adverse witnesses, and the assurance that the punishment inflicted will be neither cruel nor unusual. These limitations are designed to enhance the integrity and reliability of the guilt-determining process and to insure respect for human dignity in the realm of criminal justice.

§ 10.2 Speedy trial

The Sixth Amendment guarantee that "the accused shall enjoy the right to a speedy...trial" embodies a fundamental safeguard applicable in both fed-

---

1 DOUGLAS, WE THE JUDGES 354 (1956).

2 4 W. BLACKSTONE, COMMENTARIES *92.

3 MAGNA CHARTA, ch. 39, reprinted in R. PERRY & J. COOPER, SOURCES OF OUR LIBERTIES 17 (1959).

eral and state prosecutions.[4] Delays in the administration of justice jeopardize three distinct interests of the accused. The first interest, physical *freedom*, is implicated in cases where the accused cannot obtain bail release. Prolonged confinement under unwholesome and overcrowded jail conditions offers little of positive value. The disruption of job relationships and family life has an adverse impact on chances of rehabilitation, and is particularly unfortunate for those who are ultimately found not guilty.[5] However, quite apart from whether the accused is incarcerated pending trial, the existence of outstanding untried charges may have an injurious effect on his *psychological and emotional well-being.* Criminal accusations damage a man's reputation and standing in the community, curtail employment opportunities, and give rise to future uncertainties. The emotional trauma resulting from disruption of normal life patterns and relationships may produce symptoms of severe anxiety and depression, making the period between accusation and trial a mental nightmare.[6] Finally, delay in bringing an accused to trial can cause serious injury to his *capacity to prepare a meaningful defense.* When the wheels of justice grind too slowly, the integrity of the proceedings may be compromised by the intervening death or disappearance of defense witnesses and the general dulling of memories.[7] The erosive effects of delay are compounded when the accused is incarcerated pending trial. The special disadvantage of the pretrial detainee was noted in *Smith v. Hooey*,[8] where the U.S. Supreme Court said:

> [I]t is self-evident that "the possibilities that long delay will impair the ability of an accused to defend himself" are markedly increased when the accused is incarcerated....Confined in a prison,...his ability to confer with potential defense witnesses, or even to keep track of their whereabouts, is obviously impaired. And, while "evidence and witnesses disappear, memories fade, and events lose their perspective," a man isolated in prison is powerless to exert his own investigative efforts to mitigate these erosive effects of the passage of time.[9]

---

4 Klopfer v. North Carolina, 386 U.S. 213, 87 S. Ct. 988, 18 L. Ed. 2d 1 (1967).

5 Barker v. Wingo, 407 U.S. 514, 532-533, 92 S. Ct. 2182, 2193, 33 L. Ed. 2d 101 (1972).

6 *Id.*; Smith v. Hooey, 393 U.S. 374, 89 S. Ct. 575, 21 L. Ed. 2d 607 (1972); Klopfer v. North Carolina, 386 U.S. 213, 87 S. Ct. 988, 18 L. Ed. 2d 1 (1967).

7 *See* cases cited in note 6, *supra*.

8 393 U.S. 374, 89 S. Ct. 575, 21 L. Ed. 2d 607 (1969).

9 *Id*. at 379-380, 89 S. Ct. at 578, 21 L. Ed. 2d at 612 (footnote omitted).

The speedy trial guarantee is designed to protect an accused against:

(1) prolonged pretrial incarceration,
(2) heightened anxiety and concern, and
(3) damage to his ability to defend himself.[10]

Delay, however, is a double-edged sword; society also suffers when justice is delayed too long. The general availability and memory of prosecution witnesses are subject to the same time hazards as defense witnesses; the prosecution thus may be shorn of evidence to establish the defendant's guilt.[11] In *Barker v. Wingo*,[12] the Supreme Court elaborated upon the social consequences of tardy justice:

> [T]here is a societal interest in providing a speedy trial which exists separate from, and at times in opposition to, the interests of the accused. The inability of courts to provide a prompt trial has contributed to a large backload of cases in urban courts which, among other things, enables defendants to negotiate more effectively for pleas of guilty to lesser offenses and otherwise manipulate the system. In addition, persons released on bond for lengthy periods awaiting trial have an opportunity to commit other crimes....Moreover, the longer an accused is free awaiting trial, the more tempting becomes his opportunity to jump bail and escape. Finally, delay between arrest and punishment may have a detrimental effect on rehabilitation.[13]

When there are added social costs, measured in terms of lost wages and the public expense of maintaining pretrial detainees and providing support for their dependent families, every member of society suffers the consequences of delayed justice.

---

10 *See* cases cited in note 6, *supra*.

11 Dickey v. Florida, 398 U.S. 30, 42, 90 S. Ct. 1564, 1571, 26 L. Ed. 2d 26 (1970) (Brennan, J., concurring); *see also*, Ponzi v. Fessenden, 258 U.S. 254, 264, 42 S. Ct. 309, 312, 66 L. Ed. 2d 607 (1922).

12 407 U.S. 514, 92 S. Ct. 2182, 33 L. Ed. 2d 101 (1972).

13 *Id*. at 519-520, 92 S. Ct. at 2186-2187, 33 L. Ed. 2d at 110-111 (footnotes omitted).

§ 10.3 – Stage in criminal process when speedy trial guarantee attaches

Criminal trials are the culmination of a number of procedural phases commencing with the discovery of a crime and proceeding through detailed investigation, arrest, indictment, arraignment and various other pretrial events, both formal and informal. Problems can arise at each of these stages, and the ultimate result will be to retard the criminal trial.

In *United States v. Marion*,[14] the Supreme Court ruled that the Sixth Amendment speedy trial guarantee does not begin to run until after the government has constituted the putative suspect an "accused," either through an arrest, indictment, information or comparable method of proffering formal charges. In excluding delays occurring during the pre-accusatory period from the Sixth Amendment, the Supreme Court supported its position by reference to the Amendment's text, "In all criminal cases, the *accused* shall enjoy the right to a speedy...trial...." "Accused" is a technical term designating one who already has been charged with crime. Its use symbolized to the *Marion* Court a constitutional intent to postpone attachment of the speedy trial guarantee until after the point of accusation is reached.

Policy reasons also support a literal reading of the Sixth Amendment. The public interest, as well as that of the accused-to-be, is best served by a detailed and thorough investigation. Moreover, an accused already has two other forms of legal protection against delays in charging him. First, there are statutes of limitation which bar prosecution if charges are not brought within a fixed time after the crime is committed. Second, an accused-to-be can claim a due process deprivation if the authorities, after completing their investigation, either deliberately postpone charging him for the sake of obtaining some tactical advantage or recklessly disregarding a known and appreciable risk that their delay will handicap his defense.[15]

The speedy trial guarantee is activated only from the time formal charges are made and a suspect becomes an accused. If the charges are later dropped[16] or dismissed[17] and the accused is subject to no restraint on his liberty, the intervening period between dismissal of the original charges and any

---

14 404 U.S. 307, 92 S. Ct. 455, 30 L. Ed. 2d 468 (1971); *see also* United States v. MacDonald, 456 U.S. 1, 102 S. Ct. 1497, 71 L. Ed. 2d 696 (1982).

15 United States v. Lovasco, 431 U.S. 783, 97 S. Ct. 2044, 52 L. Ed. 2d 752 (1977) (dicta).

16 United States v. MacDonald, 456 U.S. 1, 102 S. Ct. 1497, 71 L. Ed. 2d 696 (1982).

17 United States v. Loud Hawk, 474 U.S. 302, 106 S. Ct. 648, 88 L. Ed. 2d 640 (1986).

later reactivation will be excluded in evaluating a speedy trial claim because during this period the defendant was not an *accused*.

§ 10.4 – Criteria for judging when speedy trial is denied

Barker v. Wingo[18] was the first case in which the Supreme Court devoted a serious effort toward establishing criteria for judging when the right to a speedy trial is denied. One option was to establish a specific time within which criminal defendants must be tried. This has in fact been done by a substantial number of legislatures,[19] as well as by courts pursuant to their supervisory rule-making powers. The Supreme Court declined this invitation. Had the drafters of our Constitution regarded passage of time the only relevant consideration, the Court reasoned, they would have fixed the period themselves. Alternatively, the Court could have adopted the "demand-waiver" doctrine prevalent in several circuits. Under this doctrine, the accused was treated as having waived his right to complain of any delay which occurred before he demanded that his case be tried. The Supreme Court in *Barker* agreed that the accused's timely efforts to secure a speedy trial were an important factor in determining whether his right to a speedy trial was denied, but the Court declined to make this the sole factor.

The Supreme Court ultimately adopted a four-pronged balancing test. The factors to be weighed in the balance are:

(1) the length of the delay,
(2) the reasons for it,
(3) the defendant's timely assertion of his rights, and
(4) whether he suffered prejudice.

1. Length of delay

The length of the delay is important, not for its own sake, but because it tends to indicate the likelihood of injury to one of the interests the right to a speedy trial protects. These interests include security against excessively long pretrial confinements, extended periods of anxiety, concern and public stigma, and erosion of the defensive capacity.[20] Thus, length of delay oper-

---

[18] 407 U.S. 514, 92 S. Ct. 2182, 33 L. Ed. 2d 101 (1972).

[19] KAMISAR, LAFAVE & ISRAEL, MODERN CRIMINAL PROCEDURE 1059-1060 (4th ed. 1974).

[20] Review § 10.2 *supra*.

ates primarily as a "triggering mechanism."[21] Unless the lapse of time between accusation and trial is "presumptively prejudicial,"[22] there is no need for extending the inquiry into the other three factors. What constitutes a sufficient delay to warrant further investigation is a relative matter; the primary considerations are the complexity of the case and the types of prosecutorial and defensive evidence entailed. A presumptively prejudicial delay in the case of an ordinary street crime, for example, would be considerably less than for a complex conspiracy,[23] both because less time is required for trial preparation and because eyewitness testimony grows stale more quickly than documentary evidence. The Supreme Court declined to establish a period that would automatically trigger scrutiny, but indicated that lower federal courts might do so, pursuant to supervisory rule-making powers. Several courts have done so. In the District of Columbia, a six month delay between accusation and trial will trigger an investigation.[24]

The first factor, delay, operates as a red flag signaling the need for a more detailed scrutiny of the record. If the delay has been sufficiently long that some prejudice can be presumed, the inquiry shifts to the problem of fixing responsibility.

2. *Reasons for delay*

In the second phase of the *Barker* analysis, the court must make a serious effort to locate responsibility. The Sixth Amendment does not protect an accused against self-inflicted delays.[25] Consequently, delays attributable to the accused, or to which he has consented, are disregarded in determining whether his right to a speedy trial has been violated.[26] The accused may not complain of lost time resulting from the government's inability to locate him

---

21 Barker v. Wingo, 407 U.S. 514, 530, 92 S. Ct. 2182, 2192, 33 L. Ed. 2d 101, 117 (1972).

22 *Id.*

23 *Id.* at 531, 92 S. Ct. at 2192, 33 L. Ed. 2d at 117.

24 United States v. West, 504 F.2d 253 (D.C. Cir. 1974).

25 United States v. Loud Hawk, 474 U.S. 302, 106 S. Ct. 648, 88 L. Ed. 2d 640 (1986); United States v. Lustman, 258 F.2d 475 (2d Cir.), *cert. denied*, 358 U.S. 880, 79 S. Ct. 118, 3 L. Ed. 2d 109 (1958).

26 Dickey v. Florida, 398 U.S. 30, 90 S. Ct. 1564, 26 L. Ed. 2d 26 (1970) (Brennan, J., concurring); United States v. Ferguson, 498 F.2d 1001 (D.C. Cir.), *cert. denied*, 419 U.S. 900, 95 S. Ct. 183, 42 L. Ed. 2d 145 (1974).

while he was a fugitive;[27] from trial postponements resulting from his own illness;[28] from defense motions reasonably acted upon;[29] nor for intervals during which he was mentally incompetent to stand trial.[30] For Sixth Amendment purposes, the only relevant delays are those attributable to the government. The government includes both the prosecutor and the court. The weight assignable to government-caused delays varies with the underlying reason. The Supreme Court admonished:

> A deliberate attempt to delay the trial in order to hamper the defense should be weighed more heavily against the government. A more neutral reason such as negligence or overcrowded courts should be weighed less heavily but nevertheless should be considered since the ultimate responsibility for such circumstances must rest with the government rather than with the defendant. Finally, a valid reason, such as a missing witness, should serve to justify appropriate delay.[31]

Formerly, some courts took the position that an accused serving out a sentence in another jurisdiction could not complain of the lack of a speedy trial. In voluntarily committing an act resulting in his imprisonment elsewhere, so the reasoning went, the delay was attributable to him. In *Smith v. Hooey*,[32] the Supreme Court took issue with this reasoning. Because extradition procedures exist for securing temporary custody of an out-of-state prisoner, when a prisoner requests a speedy trial but fails to receive it, the fault lies with the government.

The determination that there has been some unexcused delay attributable to the government does not end the inquiry. To evaluate whether

---

[27] United States v. Simmons, 338 F.2d 804 (2d Cir. 1964), *cert. denied*, 380 U.S. 983, 85 S. Ct. 1352, 14 L. Ed. 2d 276 (1965).

[28] Joy v. United States, 416 F.2d 962 (9th Cir. 1969).

[29] United States v. Jones, 524 F.2d 834, 850 (D.C. Cir. 1975).

[30] United States v. Cartano, 420 F.2d 362 (1st Cir.), *cert. denied*, 397 U.S. 1054, 90 S. Ct. 1398, 25 L. Ed. 2d 671 (1970); Nickens v. United States, 323 F.2d 808 (D.C. Cir. 1963), *cert. denied*, 379 U.S. 905, 85 S. Ct. 198, 13 L. Ed. 2d 178 (1964); United States v. Lustman, 258 F.2d 475 (2d Cir.), *cert. denied*, 358 U.S. 880, 79 S. Ct. 118, 8 L. Ed. 2d 109 (1958).

[31] Barker v. Wingo, 407 U.S. 514, 531, 92 S. Ct. 2182, 2192, 33 L. Ed. 2d 101, 117 (1972). *See also* United States v. Loud Hawk, 474 U.S. 302, 106 S. Ct. 648, 88 L. Ed. 2d 640 (1986).

[32] 393 U.S. 374, 89 S. Ct. 575, 21 L. Ed. 2d 607 (1969).

this delay violated the speedy trial guarantee, the court must focus upon the last two factors.

3. *Assertion of rights*

Prior to *Barker*, a majority of the lower federal courts adhered to the so-called "demand-waiver" doctrine, which required the court to disregard all delay which occurred before the accused demanded trial.[33] A defendant's silence while the delay continued was treated as a waiver. *Barker* acknowledged that the defendant's "assertion of or failure to assert his right to a speedy trial" was "one of the factors to be considered in an inquiry into the deprivation of the right,"[34] but declined to make this the sole factor. The Court added, however, that:

> [T]he failure to assert the right will make it difficult for a defendant to prove that he was denied a speedy trial.[35]

Where the accused is uncounseled and ignorant of his rights or where he is incarcerated pending trial, his failure to make a timely demand will be treated with greater leniency than where he welcomes the delay, hoping that the government will abandon its case against him.[36]

4. *Prejudice to defendant*

Whether the accused has been prejudiced by reason of the delay in trying him constitutes the final consideration. *Barker* instructs that, in evaluating this factor, consideration should be given to those interests which the speedy trial guarantee was designed to protect.[37]

Extended periods of pretrial incarceration are a serious matter, especially when the pretrial detainee is innocent. Consequently, where the accused is incarcerated pending trial, a comparatively shorter period may vio-

---

33 Barker v. Wingo, 407 U.S. 514, 524-525, 92 S. Ct. 2182, 2188-2189, 33 L. Ed. 2d 101, 114-115 (1972).

34 *Id.* at 528, 92 S. Ct. at 2191, 33 L. Ed. 2d at 116.

35 *Id.* at 531-532, 92 S. Ct. at 2192-2193, 33 L. Ed. 2d at 117-118.

36 United States v. Calloway, 505 F.2d 311 (D.C. Cir. 1974).

37 Review § 10.2 *supra*.

late the constitutional guarantee.[38] The District of Columbia Circuit has adopted an automatic rule requiring dismissal where the accused is confined for more than one year awaiting trial for a non-violent offense.[39]

Even when the accused remains at large, however, the period between arrest and trial may be a strained and abnormal time for him. Job opportunities may be closed; he may be shunned by his fellow citizens; apprehensiveness over the future may become psychologically immobilizing. Whether these consequences accompany delay in a given case becomes a relevant subject for inquiry.

The most serious time hazard is the risk that the accused will be handicapped in his ability to put forth an adequate defense. The likelihood that some defense witnesses will die, disappear, or that their testimony will be weakened by normal memory deterioration increases with the passage of time. If the accused is capable of documenting specific instances of evidentiary impairment, his claimed deprivation of a speedy trial will be carefully scrutinized. The Supreme Court has noted, moreover, that:

> Loss of memory...is not always reflected in the record because what has been forgotten can rarely be shown.[40]

On this basis, several lower federal courts have been willing to take judicial notice that after an excessive period of time, evidentiary deterioration will set in, and they are willing to presume prejudice, although the accused is unable to point to specific injuries. This presumption has the effect of shifting to the government the burden of establishing the absence of injury.[41]

Application of criteria

Having identified the four factors relevant in evaluating a speedy trial denial claim, the Supreme Court proceeded to develop guidelines for their application. It cautioned:

---

38 Petition of Provoo, 17 F.R.D. 183 (D. Md.), *aff'd sub nom.*, United States v. Provoo, 350 U.S. 857, 76 S. Ct. 101, 100 L. Ed. 761 (1955); United States ex rel. Von Cseh v. Fay, 313 F.2d 620 (2d Cir. 1963).

39 United States v. West, 504 F.2d 253 (D.C. Cir. 1974).

40 Barker v. Wingo, 407 U.S. 514, 532, 92 S. Ct. 2182, 2193, 33 L. Ed. 2d 101, 118 (1972).

41 Smith v. United States, 418 F.2d 1120 (D.C. Cir.), *cert. denied*, 396 U.S. 936, 90 S. Ct. 280, 24 L. Ed. 2d 235 (1969); Chism v. Koehler, 392 F. Supp. 659 (W.D. Mich. 1975), *aff'd*, 527 F.2d 612 (6th Cir. 1976), *cert. denied*, 425 U.S. 944, 96 S. Ct. 1686, 48 L. Ed. 2d 188 (1976); United States v. Chin, 306 F. Supp. 397 (S.D.N.Y. 1969).

> We regard none of the four factors identified above as either a necessary or sufficient condition to the finding of a deprivation of the right of speedy trial. Rather, they are related factors and must be considered together with such other circumstances as may be relevant. In sum, these factors have no talismanic qualities; courts must still engage in a difficult and sensitive balancing process.[42]

To illustrate the proper application of these criteria, the *Barker* Court labored over them in relation to the case before it. Barker was indicted for murder in 1958 but was not tried until five years later. During the intervening period, the prosecution obtained 16 separate continuances. (Most of these continuances had been sought to gain time to try an accomplice so that the government would be in a position to compel his testimony against Barker.) Barker raised no objection to the first 11 continuances, which consumed approximately 70 percent of the total five year delay. It was not until after his accomplice was convicted that Barker began actively pressuring for a speedy trial. The Supreme Court characterized this as a "close" case,[43] and proceeded to evaluate the factors. Five years between arrest and trial was an extraordinary period, certainly long enough to trigger a detailed scrutiny. The government's excuse, the desire to convict an accomplice and make him a government witness against Barker, might have justified an appropriate delay, but five years was inexcusably long. Counterbalancing the excessive and inexcused delay, however, was the fact that prejudice was minimal and Barker admitted, through counsel, that he was content to await the outcome of his accomplice's trial, gambling on the hope that if his accomplice were acquitted, the government would abandon its case against him. Barker's claim was denied. The most damaging aspect of his case was his complacency in the face of delay. The Supreme Court said:

> We do not hold that there may never be a situation in which an indictment may be dismissed on speedy-trial grounds where the defendant has failed to object to continuances. There may be a situation in which the defendant was represented by incompetent counsel, was severely prejudiced, or even cases in which the continuances were granted *ex parte*. But barring extraordinary circumstances, we would be reluctant indeed to rule that a defendant was

---

42 Barker v. Wingo, 407 U.S. 514, 533, 92 S. Ct. 2182, 2193, 33 L. Ed. 2d 101, 118 (1972).

43 *Id*. at 533, 92 S. Ct. at 2193, 33 L. Ed. 2d at 119.

> denied this constitutional right on a record that strongly indicates, as does this one, that the defendant did not want a speedy trial....[44]

When an accused has been subjected to an unconstitutional delay, the only remedy available is to dismiss the indictment and grant trial immunity. The government may not reimburse the accused for the time by subtracting the delay from any sentence ultimately imposed.[45] Discharging potentially guilty persons without a trial is serious business. This may account for characteristic judicial hesitation to find that the delay has exceeded constitutional bounds, even though the delay was appreciable. However, in spite of the risks that accompany this remedy, this alternative is preferable when the lack of a speedy trial puts a cloud over the reliability of the guilt-determining process.

§ 10.5 Public trial

The constitutional guarantee of a "public trial" is found in the Sixth Amendment, juxtaposed to the speedy trial requirement. Its precise origin is uncertain. Some have considered this guarantee to be a reaction to the infamous practices of the English Court of Star Chamber, while others have traced it beyond to the tyrannous closed-door sessions in Spain during the Inquisition.[46] Regardless of the historical evil that inspired this safeguard, the right of a criminal defendant to be tried in open court has come to be regarded as a fundamental ingredient of procedural due process.

The following advantages have been ascribed to public trials:[47]

(1) Opening the proceedings to public scrutiny operates as a check upon government excesses or abuses.

(2) The presence of an audience makes witnesses are more reluctant to give perjured testimony.

---

[44] *Id.* at 536, 92 S. Ct. at 2194, 33 L. Ed. 2d at 120.

[45] Strunk v. United States, 412 U.S. 434, 93 S. Ct. 2260, 37 L. Ed. 2d 56 (1973).

[46] In re Oliver, 333 U.S. 257, 266-269, 68 S. Ct. 499, 504-506, 92 L. Ed. 682, 690-692 (1948)

[47] Gannett Co. v. DePasquale, 443 U.S. 368, 99 S. Ct. 2898, 61 L. Ed. 2d 608 (1979); Globe Newspaper v. Superior Court, 457 U.S. 596, 102 S. Ct. 2613, 73 L. Ed. 2d 248 (1982); United States v. Kobli, 172 F.2d 919 (3d Cir. 1949); State v. Schmit, 273 Minn. 78, 139 N.W.2d 800 (1966); People v. Jelke, 308 N.Y. 56, 123 N.E.2d 769 (1954).

(3) Unknown persons possessing knowledge of the crime may be drawn to the trial as spectators and may come forward with their knowledge.

(4) Public trials afford citizens an opportunity to learn about the workings of their courts and to evaluate whether the judicial system is functioning adequately.

The last advantage is perhaps the most important one. Open trials enhance "both the basic fairness of the criminal trial and the appearance of fairness so essential to public confidence in the system."[48]

The public trial guarantee applies not only to the trial itself; it applies as well to ancillary pretrial proceedings, such as *voir dire* examinations of potential jurors[49] and hearings on motions to suppress evidence claimed to have been illegally seized.[50] In rare instances where the interests of fair administration of justice require, the Constitution allows the trial judge to close the courtroom and to bar spectators for limited periods of time. However, before the trial judge may close the proceedings over the accused's objection, the Sixth Amendment lays down four limitations.[51] First, before ordering closure, the trial judge must weigh the Sixth Amendment interests of the accused against the opposing claimed need for closure. He may close the courtroom only when closure is essential to preserve higher values. Second, the duration and scope of the closure order may be no broader than necessary to protect the interests that create the need for this order. Third, before ordering closure, the court must explore reasonable alternatives to this action. Finally, the judge must make written findings adequate to support his closure order.

The Supreme Court has rigorously applied these standards. A temporary closure might be justified under these standards to induce a youthful rape victim to testify without embarrassment or fright on painful matters.[52] However, even here, the judge must conduct a particularized inquiry into the necessity for closure before closing the proceedings to members of the pub-

---

48 Press-Enterprise Co. v. Superior Court, 464 U.S. 501, 508, 104 S. Ct. 819, 823, 78 L. Ed. 2d 629 (1984).

49 Press-Enterprise Co. v. Superior Court, *supra* note 48.

50 Waller v. Georgia, 467 U.S. 39, 104 S. Ct. 2210, 81 L. Ed. 2d 31 (1984).

51 Waller v. Georgia, *supra* note 50; Press-Enterprise Co. v. Superior Court, *supra* note 48.

52 People v. Jelke, 308 N.Y. 56, 123 N.E.2d 769 (1954).

lic. In *Globe Newspaper Company v. Superior Court,*[53] the Supreme Court invalidated a state statute that attempted to impose a *mandatory* rule requiring spectators to be excluded from the courtroom whenever minor victims of sex offenses were testifying on the witness stand. The Court explained that the Constitution requires the trial judge to conduct a focused inquiry into the facts of each case to determine whether this drastic action is necessary.

The Supreme Court has on several occasions considered legal issues growing out of the introduction of electronic recording and televising equipment in the courtroom. There is absolutely no Sixth Amendment requirement that the trial or any part of it be broadcast live or on tape for members of the public. The Sixth Amendment requirement is satisfied so long as members of the media and public are permitted to attend the trial in person. State courts are, nevertheless, free to permit live electronic coverage of criminal trials if limitations are imposed to assure that coverage does not adversely impact trial participants or otherwise jeopardize the fairness of the proceedings.[54] Should the trial become so "public" that its serene and dignified atmosphere is lost and the trial degenerates into a three-ring circus, the accused can complain of a deprivation of his due process rights.[55] The problem of excessive trial publicity will be met again in §10.13 *infra*.

The Sixth Amendment right to a public trial is a right which belongs to the accused and which he alone can assert.[56] The unwarranted exclusion from the courtroom of members of the public and media representatives may, however, trigger valid First Amendment claims upon the part of the excluded parties. In *Richmond Newspapers, Inc. v. Commonwealth of Virginia,*[57] the Supreme Court ruled that a criminal trial judge, even when acting on the accused's request, may not order members of the press and public to vacate the courtroom unless this action is required to protect the accused's right to a fair trial or to promote other overriding considerations. The basis for the Court's holding was the First Amendment right of the public to observe criminal trials as a means of learning about the workings of their government. Hence, even though the accused may wish to forego his Sixth Amendment right to a public trial, spectators may sometimes have standing to object.

---

53 457 U.S. 596, 102 S. Ct. 2613, 73 L. Ed. 2d 248 (1982) (decided under First Amendment).

54 Chandler v. Florida, 449 U.S. 560, 101 S. Ct. 802, 66 L. Ed. 2d 740 (1981).

55 Estes v. Texas, 381 U.S. 532, 85 S. Ct. 1628, 14 L. Ed. 2d 543 (1965).

56 Gannett Co. v. DePasquale, *supra* note 47.

57 448 U.S. 555, 100 S. Ct. 2814, 65 L. Ed. 2d 973 (1980). *See also* Globe Newspaper Company v. Superior Court, 457 U.S. 596, 102 S. Ct. 2613, 73 L. Ed. 2d 248 (1982).

§ 10.6 Right to trial by jury

The petit jury is an ancient and venerable institution. The Magna Charta of 1215 declared that no free man could be condemned to death or sent to prison "except by the legal judgment of his peers."[58] Historians have debated whether the Great Charter's reference to a judgment by peers established for Englishmen the right to trial by jury.[59] Though the foundations of the peer judgment concept may have been laid by the Magna Charta, there is little evidence of any institution even remotely resembling the modern petit jury until the fourteenth century.[60] For a time, the jury method of determining criminal guilt existed in competition with several older forms such as "trial by ordeal" and "trial by battle."[61] Gradually, these barbaric practices fell into disuse and the jury system gained preeminence. By the time it was transplanted to American soil, the common-law petit jury -- an impartial tribunal consisting of 12 laymen assembled to listen to evidence adduced in open court and to render a verdict by unanimous decision -- had a tradition dating back several centuries.

William Blackstone, writing in 1768, hailed the jury principle as the "glory of English law" and "the most transcendent privilege which any subject can enjoy or wish for."[62] While Blackstone's accolades may appear extravagant to the twentieth century reader, his sentiments typify eighteenth-century thinking. Those who drafted our Constitution were men of the times; they held the jury principle in such esteem that double precautionary measures were taken to safeguard it. Article III, section 2 of the 1787 Constitution ensured that "[t]he Trial of all Crimes, except in Cases of Impeachment, shall be by Jury...." Two years later, the Sixth Amendment added the further guarantee that "[i]n all criminal prosecutions, the accused shall enjoy the right to...trial, by an impartial jury...."

---

58 MAGNA CHARTA, ch. 39, reprinted in R. PERRY & J. COOPER, SOURCES OF OUR LIBERTIES 17 (1959).

59 *Id.* at 7-8; 1 F. POLLOCK & MAITLAND, THE HISTORY OF ENGLISH LAW BEFORE THE TIME OF EDWARD I, 173 n. 3 (2d ed. 1909); 2 J. STORY, COMMENTARIES ON THE CONSTITUTION OF THE UNITED STATES, 540-541 (4th ed. 1873); Frankfurter & Corcoran, *Petty Federal Offenses and the Constitutional Guaranty of Trial by Jury*, 39 HARV. L. REV. 917, 923 (1926).

60 *Id.*

61 Wells, *The Origin of the Petty Jury*, 27 L.Q. REV. 347, 357 (1911); *see also* CORNISH, THE JURY 10-12 (1968).

62 3 W. BLACKSTONE, COMMENTARIES *379.

The jury system offers several unique advantages over other methods of adjudicating criminal guilt. First, the jury is a democratic institution. It affords citizens an opportunity to participate in the administration of criminal justice, and through participation, to gain an insight into the workings of their judiciary. Shared responsibility enhances public trust in the integrity of criminal verdicts. Second, the jury, being drawn from a representative cross-section of the community, reflects the conscience of the community and its sense of justice and mercy. The jury thus interjects humanizing qualities into a depersonalized penal system. Finally, and most importantly, the jury constitutes a fundamental safeguard against miscarriages of justice. Mr. Justice White, writing in *Duncan v. Louisiana*,[63] summarized the protective function of the jury:

> A right to jury trial is granted to criminal defendants in order to prevent oppression by the Government. Those who wrote our constitutions knew from history and experience that it was necessary to protect against unfounded criminal charges brought to eliminate enemies and against judges too responsive to the voice of higher authority. The framers of the constitution strove to create an independent judiciary but insisted upon further protection against arbitrary action. Providing an accused with the right to be tried by a jury of his peers gave him an inestimable safeguard against the corrupt or overzealous prosecutor and against the complacent, biased, or eccentric judge. If the defendant preferred the common-sense judgment of a jury to the more tutored but perhaps less sympathetic reaction of the single judge, he was to have it....[64]

Despite the central role which the jury has occupied in the Anglo-American scheme of criminal justice for the past several centuries, it was not until 1968 that state criminal defendants acquired jury trial rights under the U.S. Constitution coextensive with those enjoyed in a federal court. In *Duncan v. Louisiana*,[65] the Supreme Court announced that the Sixth Amendment right to jury trial qualified for protection under the Fourteenth Amendment due process clause and that the states were obliged to furnish jury trials in all cases which, if tried in a federal court, would come within the Sixth Amendment guarantee.

63 391 U.S. 145, 88 S. Ct. 1444, 20 L. Ed. 2d 491 (1968).

64 *Id*. at 155-156, 88 S. Ct. at 1451, 20 L. Ed. 2d at 499-500 (footnote omitted).

65 391 U.S. 145, 88 S. Ct. 1444, 20 L. Ed. 2d 491 (1968).

The government may not make it prohibitively risky to assert the right to trial by jury. In *United States v. Jackson*,[66] the Supreme Court struck down the capital punishment provisions of the Federal Kidnapping Act. The Act authorized the jury, upon finding the defendant guilty, to impose the death penalty, but limited the maximum punishment inflictable at a non-jury trial to life imprisonment. The inevitable impact of such enhanced punishment was to discourage defendants from asserting their constitutional right to a jury trial. Legislatures are precluded from establishing one form of punishment applicable to those who assert their right to contest their guilt before a jury, and another less serious form available in other instances. Institutionalized deterrents to requesting trial by jury are offensive to the Sixth Amendment.

§ 10.7 – Offenses for which jury trials are not constitutionally required

At the time the Constitution was adopted, there existed under the English common law a limited number of instances where jury trials were unavailable.[67] The defendant had no right to a jury in cases of "petty offenses."[68] Similar exclusions were common throughout the colonies. But when the Constitution defined the jury trial rights of the accused, it did so in comprehensive language. Article III, section 2 jury-trial protection extended to the "Trial of all Crimes," while the Sixth Amendment mandate embraced "all criminal prosecutions."

Despite this broad and unequivocal language, the Supreme Court has consistently interpreted the Constitution as perpetuating the historical distinction between petty and serious offenses. The major controversies have centered, not on whether petty offenses are subject to a jury trial requirement, but on developing criteria for locating the Sixth Amendment boundary line. The felony-misdemeanor distinction was not a workable tool.[69] Some misdemeanor charges might be extremely serious, carrying significant penalties and causing measurable damage to reputations. In a series of cases, the Supreme Court wavered between an objective one-factor approach based upon punishment severity and a more particularized analysis.[70] In *Baldwin v.*

---

66 390 U.S. 570, 88 S. Ct. 1209, 20 L. Ed. 2d 138 (1968). *But see* Corbitt v. New Jersey, 439 U.S. 212, 99 S. Ct. 492, 58 L. Ed. 2d 466 (1980).

67 Frankfurter & Corcoran, *Petty Federal Offenses and the Constitutional Guaranty of Trial by Jury*, 39 HARV. L. REV. 917, 934 (1926).

68 *Id*.

69 Callan v. Wilson, 127 U.S. 540, 8 S. Ct. 1301, 32 L. Ed. 223 (1888).

70 Note, *The Petty Offender's Constitutional Right to a Jury Trial: The Denial in* Duncan v. Louisiana, 36 TENN. L. REV. 763 (1969).

New York,[71] the matter was finally settled. The Supreme Court held that the best index of how seriously society regards a crime is the punishment it authorizes for the offender. The boundary line between petty and serious offenses for jury trial purposes was fixed at six months' imprisonment. Where the accused faces possible incarceration for a longer period, he has a right to have a jury determine his guilt. The definition of a petty offense as one which carries no more than a six-month penalty was adopted as a rule of administrative convenience. Where the maximum sentence possible falls below the six-month limit, the advantages flowing from speedy and inexpensive non-jury adjudications were deemed sufficient to offset any possible hardship visited upon a petty offender of being tried without a jury.

Under the common law, there was no right to a jury trial on criminal contempt charges. Contempts were not regarded as crimes and could be tried summarily by the judge without regard to the penalty imposed. The common-law method of trying criminal contempts was deemed to be constitutionally permissible as late as 1968, and individuals were sometimes given long prison terms without the benefit of a jury decision.[72] This practice was doubly oppressive since it placed in the hands of the judge whose orders had been flaunted the power to sit as judge, jury and prosecutor in vindicating his own authority. It was partly for this reason that the Supreme Court in *Bloom v. Illinois*[73] expanded the jury trial guarantee to cover serious criminal contempts. Six months is now the maximum sentence that a judge may impose upon a conviction for criminal contempt without impaneling a jury.[74]

There is no right to a jury trial in proceedings before a military tribunal even when brought for serious charges.[75] Nor are jury trials available as a matter of constitutional right in juvenile court proceedings.[76]

§ 10.8 – Size of jury

The petit or trial jury, as it evolved at common law, consisted of 12 men who were selected at random from the community and whose function was to hear all the evidence in open court and reach a unanimous decision regarding the defendant's guilt or innocence of the charges leveled against him. When

---

71 399 U.S. 66, 90 S. Ct. 1886, 26 L. Ed. 2d 437 (1970). *See also* Blanton v. City of North Las Vegas, ___ U.S. ___, 109 S. Ct. 1289, 103 L. Ed. 2d 550 (1989).

72 Green v. United States, 356 U.S. 165, 78 S. Ct. 632, 2 L. Ed. 2d 672 (1958).

73 391 U.S. 194, 88 S. Ct. 1477, 20 L. Ed. 2d 522 (1968).

74 Frank v. United States, 395 U.S. 147, 89 S. Ct. 1503, 23 L. Ed. 2d 162 (1969).

75 Ex parte Milligan, 71 U.S. (4 Wall.) 2, 122, 18 L. Ed. 281, 296 (1886). *See also* Dennis, *Jury Trial and the Federal Constitution*, 6 COLUM. L. REV. 423 (1906).

76 McKeiver v. Pennsylvania, 403 U.S. 528, 91 S. Ct. 1976, 29 L. Ed. 2d 647 (1971).

the jury concept was brought to America, its common-law characteristics were maintained. This pattern still prevails in the federal courts and in most state systems.

Several decades ago, there was a reform movement to streamline judicial administration, and one suggestion was to reduce the size of petit juries. Several jurisdictions implemented the proposal. In Florida, Louisiana, South Carolina, Texas and Utah, less than 12-member juries were established for felonies, and in at least eight jurisdictions, misdemeanor juries were reduced below the traditional common-law size.[77] Until *Duncan v. Louisiana*,[78] which incorporated the Sixth Amendment jury trial guarantee into the Fourteenth Amendment and made it binding upon the states, these local experiments were not a matter of federal constitutional concern. But once the states became subject to Sixth Amendment jury trial mandates, the question was presented whether these reductions in jury size were offensive to the U.S. Constitution.

This issue was brought to a head in *Williams v. Florida*,[79] which challenged the constitutionality of the six-man felony jury provided for under Florida law. The Supreme Court was not writing on a clean slate. Earlier cases had suggested that the common-law jury blueprint was embedded within the Sixth Amendment.[80] In *Williams*, however, the Supreme Court reassessed the matter and determined that, history aside, the number "12" was not an immutable corollary of the Sixth Amendment right to a jury trial. Mr. Justice White, who wrote the majority opinion, stated that the relevant inquiry was not whether a particular feature was buttressed by centuries of tradition, but whether it was critical to the jury's constitutional role. Having cast the inquiry in this form, Mr. Justice White concluded:

> [T]he essential feature of a jury obviously lies in the interposition between the accused and his accuser of the commonsense judgment of a group of laymen, and in the community participation and shared responsibility that results [*sic*] from that group's determination of guilt or innocence. The performance of this role is not a function of the particular number of the body that makes up the jury. To be sure, the number should probably be large enough to

---

[77] Williams v. Florida, 399 U.S. 78, 99 n. 45, 90 S. Ct. 1893, 1905, n. 45, 26 L. Ed. 2d 446, 459, n. 45 (1970).

[78] 391 U.S. 145, 88 S. Ct. 1444, 20 L. Ed. 2d 491 (1968).

[79] 399 U.S. 78, 90 S. Ct. 1983, 26 L. Ed. 2d 446 (1970).

[80] Rassmussen v. United States, 197 U.S. 516, 25 S. Ct. 514, 49 L. Ed. 862 (1905); Maxwell v. Dow, 176 U.S. 581, 20 S. Ct. 448, 44 L. Ed. 597 (1900); Thompson v. Utah, 170 U.S. 343, 18 S. Ct. 620, 42 L. Ed. 1061 (1898).

> promote group deliberation, free from outside attempts at intimidation, and to provide a fair possibility for obtaining a representative cross-section of the community. But we find little reason to think that these goals are in any meaningful sense less likely to be achieved when the jury numbers six, than when it numbers 12....And, certainly the reliability of the jury as a factfinder hardly seems likely to be a function of its size.[81]

The six-member jury approved in *Williams v. Florida*, however, represents the minimum constitutionally acceptable size for juries. In *Ballew v. Georgia*,[82] the Supreme Court ruled that a state criminal defendant was deprived of his Sixth and Fourteenth Amendment rights when he was tried before a five-member jury for a nonpetty offense. A five-member panel was, in the Court's opinion, too small to achieve broad-based representation from the community and to assure the type of unbiased and thoroughgoing deliberation that is basic to the constitutional right to a jury trial.

§ 10.9 – Unanimous verdicts

Under the common law, the jury's decision had to represent the unanimous consensus of all its members. If the entire body was unable to agree on one of the two alternatives, a mistrial resulted. A hung jury operates neither as an acquittal nor a conviction; it leaves the door open for further criminal proceedings.

The practice of requiring unanimous verdicts in criminal cases was firmly entrenched in Anglo-American jurisprudence when the Constitution was drafted, and remains the prevailing practice throughout the nation today. Only two jurisdictions have dispensed with the common law unanimity requirement where there is at stake a possible punishment in excess of a year's imprisonment. In Louisiana, a three-fourths majority vote is sufficient to render a non-capital felony verdict,[83] while in Oregon the concurrence of five-sixths of the jurors is necessary.[84] Though several other jurisdictions have dispensed with the need for unanimity in misdemeanor trials, Louisiana and Oregon stand alone in authorizing majority verdicts in felony prosecutions. These local experiments were undertaken in an effort to reduce the

---

81 399 U.S. at 100-101, 90 S. Ct. at 1906, 26 L. Ed. 2d at 490 (1970).

82 435 U.S. 223, 98 S. Ct. 1029, 55 L. Ed. 2d 234 (1978).

83 LA. CODE CRIM. PROC. ANN. art. 782 (West 1966).

84 OR. CONST. art. I, § 11; OR. REV. STAT. §§ 136.330, 136.610 (1967).

frequency of hung juries, thereby eliminating some measure of the costs and delays attendant upon recurring mistrials.[85]

Adaptation of the jury to accommodate diverse local situations was unobjectionable prior to *Duncan v. Louisiana*,[86] since the states were under no federal constitutional compulsion to accord jury trials at all. But the 1968 ruling, applying Sixth Amendment jury trial standards to the states, triggered the need for a fresh look at state majority criminal verdict practices.

The opportunity was presented in *Apocado v. Oregon*,[87] challenging whether jury unanimity was indispensable to a constitutionally valid verdict. (Oregon, it should be recalled, is one of the two jurisdictions authorizing majority verdicts in felony prosecutions.) The Supreme Court split 5-4 in favor of upholding *state* criminal convictions based upon less-than-unanimous verdicts. Mr. Justice Powell provided the pivotal swing vote necessary to create a majority in favor of upholding the Oregon jury practice. He agreed that unanimous verdicts were an indispensable feature of the Sixth Amendment jury trial guarantee as it applied in *federal* proceedings, but rejected as unsound the premise that when a given procedural safeguard is incorporated into the Fourteenth Amendment and made binding upon state jurisdictions, identical state application is required. He saw no inconsistency in requiring different jury verdict standards in state and federal trials despite the Supreme Court's mandate four years before in *Duncan v. Louisiana*.[88] Mr. Justice Powell's vote carried the day. Thus, the Sixth Amendment requires a unanimous verdict to convict in a federal criminal proceeding, but is satisfied by less when the trial takes place in a state.

The Oregon statute under review in *Apodaca* provided for a 12-member panel with ten votes being sufficient to return a guilty verdict. In *Burch v. Louisiana*,[89] the Supreme Court was called upon to decide whether the states could combine less-than-unanimous verdicts with a substantial reduction in the jury's size. The challenged Louisiana law authorized trial by jury of six with the concurrence of five being sufficient to render a verdict. The Supreme Court ruled that a non-unanimous six-person jury presented a sufficient threat to the fairness of the proceedings and the proper functioning of the jury to draw the constitutional line. If a state elects to utilize six-member juries in trials of nonpetty offenses, the verdict must be unanimous.

---

85 Comment, *Should Jury Verdicts Be Unanimous in Criminal Cases?* 47 OR. L. REV. 417 (1968).

86 391 U.S. 145, 88 S. Ct. 1444, 20 L. Ed. 2d 491 (1968).

87 406 U.S. 404, 92 S. Ct. 1628, 32 L. Ed. 2d 184 (1972).

88 391 U.S. 145, 88 S. Ct. 1444, 20 L. Ed. 2d 491 (1968). *Duncan* is discussed in § 10.6 *supra*.

89 441 U.S. 130, 99 S. Ct. 1623, 60 L. Ed. 2d 96 (1979).

§ 10.10 – Composition of the jury

In order to be constituted in conformity with Sixth Amendment requirements, the petit jury must be drawn from a source fairly representative of the community.[90] The systematic exclusion of any cognizable group or class of qualified citizens from the pool of potential jurors is constitutionally offensive.[91] The reasons for the Sixth Amendment's fair cross-section requirement were explained by Mr. Justice Marshall in *Peters v. Kiff*,[92] a case challenging the racial composition of the jury pool:

> [A] State cannot, consistent with due process, subject a defendant to indictment or trial by a jury that has been selected in an arbitrary and discriminatory manner, in violation of the Constitution and laws of the United States. Illegal and unconstitutional jury selection procedures cast doubt on the integrity of the whole judicial process. They create the appearance of bias in the decision of individual cases, and they increase the risk of actual bias as well.
>
> [T]he exclusion from jury service of a substantial and identifiable class of citizens has a potential impact that is too subtle and too pervasive to admit of confinement to particular issues or particular cases....
>
> [W]e are unwilling to make the assumption that the exclusion of Negroes has relevance only for issues involving race. When any large and identifiable segment of the community is excluded from jury service, the effect is to remove from the jury room qualities of human nature and varieties of human experience, the range of which is unknown and perhaps unknowable. It is not necessary to assume that the excluded group will consistently vote as a class in order to conclude...that their exclusion deprives the jury of a perspective on human events that may have unsuspected importance in any case that may be presented.[93]

---

90 Taylor v. Louisiana, 419 U.S. 522, 95 S. Ct. 692, 42 L. Ed. 2d 690 (1975).

91 *Id.*

92 407 U.S. 493, 92 S. Ct. 2163, 33 L. Ed. 2d 83 (1972).

93 *Id.* at 502-504, 92 S. Ct. at 2168-2169, 33 L. Ed. 2d at 93-94 (footnotes omitted).

§ 10.11 –Waiver of right to jury trial

The Sixth Amendment provides that "[i]n all criminal prosecutions, the accused shall enjoy the right to a...trial by an impartial jury...." No mention is made of the right to waive a jury and plead one's case before a judge. Under the common law of England when our Constitution was adopted, this right was not recognized.[94] Although technically the "consent" of the accused was required before he could be subjected to a jury trial, if he initially was recalcitrant, he would be tortured until he submitted.[95] In 1772, England ceased torturing defendants who refused to consent to trial before a jury, but it was not until decades later that the concept of bench trials gained acceptance.[96] Though bench trials are provided for in the United States, many jurisdictions do not give the accused unrestricted control over whether his case is tried by a jury or a judge. His right to waive trial by jury may be conditioned upon the approval of the court, the prosecutor, or both.[97] In the federal system, waivers are governed by Rule 23(a) of the Federal Rules of Criminal Procedure:

> Cases required to be tried by jury shall be so tried unless the defendant waives a jury trial in writing with the approval of the court and the consent of the government.

In *Singer v. United States*,[98] a defendant, who was forced to undergo a jury trial because the prosecution refused its consent to his attempted waiver, challenged the constitutionality of Rule 23(a) insofar as it conditioned his right to forego trial by jury upon the government's approval. His theory essentially was that the Sixth Amendment guarantee of a jury trial implied the correlative right to forego the jury and have the case decided by the judge if the accused considered the latter mode of trial more advantageous. Reviewing historical evidence, the Supreme Court concluded that neither the common law nor the Constitution recognized the right to demand trial before a judge sitting without a jury. The Court then demolished the defendant's remaining arguments:

---

94 Singer v. United States, 380 U.S. 24, 27-28, 85 S. Ct. 783, 786, 13 L. Ed. 2d 630, 633-634 (1965).

95 *Id.*

96 *Id.*

97 Note, *Constitutional Law: Criminal Procedure: Waiver of Jury Trial:* Singer v. United States, 308 U.S. 24 (1965), 51 CORNELL L. REV. 339, 342-343 (1966).

98 380 U.S. 24, 85 S. Ct. 783, 13 L. Ed. 2d 630 (1965).

> In light of the Constitution's emphasis on jury trial, we find it difficult to understand how the petitioner can submit the bald proposition that to compel a defendant in a criminal case to undergo a jury trial against his will is contrary to his right to a fair trial or to due process. A defendant's only constitutional right concerning the method of trial is to an impartial trial by jury. We find no constitutional impediment to conditioning a waiver of this right on the consent of the prosecuting attorney and the trial judge when, if either refuses to consent, the result is simply that the defendant is subject to an impartial trial by jury -- the very thing that the Constitution guarantees him....[99]

§ 10.12 Fair and impartial trial

Whether the trial is before a judge or a jury, the accused is entitled to have his guilt determined by an impartial tribunal. The assurance of a fair and impartial trial is a basic ingredient of the due process of law guaranteed by the Fifth and Fourteenth Amendments. Concerning the presiding judge, due process requires that he be detached and disinterested in the outcome. In *Tumey v. Ohio*,[100] the Supreme Court set aside a criminal conviction because the judge who tried the case had a direct pecuniary interest in the outcome. (His salary was paid from fees and costs levied against those who were convicted.) This method of compensating the judge offered a potent inducement to resolve doubtful cases in favor of fee-generating guilty verdicts.

The accused is entitled to be tried before a neutral and unbiased judge even when he bears responsibility for the judge's ill-will. In *Mayberry v. Pennsylvania*,[101] the accused insisted upon representing himself and during the course of a lengthy trial, addressed numerous insulting and slanderous remarks to the judge. His excesses included calling the judge a "hatchet man for the state," a "dirty sonofabitch," a "tyrannical old dog," a "bum," a "nut," and a "fool." Mayberry repeatedly ignored rulings from the bench and voiced his displeasure when his motions were overruled by telling the judge to "shut up" and "go to hell." Toward the end of the trial, he became so insolent and abusive that the judge found it necessary to gag him and to remove him temporarily from the courtroom. After the jury had returned a verdict, the judge found the defendant guilty of multiple counts of contempt for his trial be-

---

[99] *Id*. at 36, 85 S. Ct. at 790, 13 L. Ed. 2d at 638.

[100] 273 U.S. 510, 47 S. Ct. 437, 71 L. Ed. 749 (1927); *see also* Ward v. Village of Monroeville, 409 U.S. 57, 93 S. Ct. 80, 34 L. Ed. 2d 267 (1972).

[101] 400 U.S. 455, 91 S. Ct. 499, 27 L. Ed. 2d 532 (1971).

havior and imposed an 11- to 22-year prison sentence. Though characterizing the accused's behavior as "a shock to those raised in the Western tradition,"[102] and "not befitting an American courtroom,"[103] the Supreme Court unanimously reversed his contempt convictions on the ground that a trial judge who has been the target of personal abuse should step down at the end of the trial and turn the contempt proceedings over to another judge, one who is "not bearing the sting of...slanderous remarks."[104] The accused does not forfeit his right to a fair trial before an impartial tribunal because he deliberately engages in conduct that provokes the prejudice he complains of.

When a case is tried before a jury, subtle influences, such as appearing before the jury in prison clothing, may tip the delicate balance against the accused. In *Estelle v. Williams*,[105] the Supreme Court held that the government may not compel a criminal defendant to stand trial before a jury while dressed in prison garments because this practice served no important governmental interest. Indeed, it might be taken by jurors as an indication of the defendant's guilt. The accused, however, cannot complain of every practice that singles him out from others in the courtroom or draws attention to him. The deployment of uniformed security personnel in the courtroom is not particularly likely to cause jurors to draw a negative inference about the accused's innocence but more important, is justified by considerations of public necessity.[106]

Central to the notion of a fair trial is the requirement that the defendant's guilt be established on the basis of evidence developed inside the courtroom and on the witness stand where the defendant is protected by counsel and has an opportunity for cross-examination.[107] Jury contacts with out-of-court information concerning the issues involved in a case may reach due process proportions if the exposure occurs under circumstances which create a substantial risk that the jurors' judgments may have been influenced. In *Turner v. Louisiana*,[108] the Supreme Court overturned a conviction in which two deputy sheriffs, who had been key prosecution witnesses, functioned as jury custodians during the three-day trial. Although there was no

---

102 *Id.* at 456, 91 S. Ct. at 500, 27 L. Ed. 2d at 535.

103 *Id.* at 462, 91 S. Ct. at 504, 27 L. Ed. 2d at 538.

104 *Id.* at 466, 91 S. Ct. at 505, 27 L. Ed. 2d at 540.

105 425 U.S. 501, 96 S. Ct. 1691, 48 L. Ed. 2d 126 (1976).

106 Holbrook v. Flynn, 475 U.S. 560, 106 S. Ct. 1340, 89 L. Ed. 2d 525 (1986).

107 Parker v. Gladden, 385 U.S. 363, 87 S. Ct. 468, 17 L. Ed. 2d 420 (1966).

108 379 U.S. 466, 85 S. Ct. 546, 13 L. Ed. 2d 424 (1965). *See also* Parker v. Gladden, *supra* note 107. *But see* Smith v. Phillips, 455 U.S. 209, 102 S. Ct. 940, 71 L. Ed. 2d 78 (1982); Rushen v. Spain, 464 U.S. 114, 104 S. Ct. 453, 78 L. Ed. 2d 267 (1983).

evidence that the deputies actually discussed the case outside the courtroom, the verdict depended, in large measure, upon whether or not the jury credited the testimony of these two witnesses on various disputed facts. Because the three-day period of close association between the jurors and these two witnesses might have had some impact upon the jury's assessment of their testimonial credibility, the integrity of the verdict was called into question and a new trial was required.

§ 10.13 – Prejudicial media coverage

The media has traditionally played an influential role in shaping public opinion. When the opinion thus molded relates to the guilt or innocence of an untried criminal defendant, there is a head-on collision between freedom of the press and the right to a fair trial. Mr. Justice Frankfurter identified the problem when he inquired:

> How can fallible men and women reach a disinterested verdict based exclusively on what they heard in court when, before they entered the jury box, their minds were saturated by press and radio for months preceding by matters designed to establish the guilt of the accused.[109]

Few cases have captivated public interest as intensely as the Dr. Samuel Sheppard murder trial of the fifties. Even before formal charges had been placed against Sheppard, the news media had proclaimed his guilt and were pressuring for "justice." For months, the headlines of local newspapers were saturated with stories of his lack of cooperation with the authorities, his refusal to take a lie detector test, his illicit love affairs, interviews with "bombshell witnesses," and other damaging disclosures. At Sheppard's trial, the courtroom was jammed with news media representatives. To facilitate more detailed coverage, the judge permitted broadcasting equipment to be installed in vacant courthouse rooms. Although media representatives were not permitted to take pictures inside the courtroom while the trial was in progress, the jurors and witnesses were rushed by photographers and reporters waiting in the corridors whenever they entered or left. Verbatim records of the trial proceedings along with editorialized comments and reactions were published daily by the newspapers. Newspaper clippings alone filled five volumes. Sheppard's trial was, in the words of the state appeals

---

109 Irvin v. Dowd, 366 U.S. 717, 729-730, 81 S. Ct. 1639, 1646, 6 L. Ed. 2d 751, 760 (1961) (Frankfurter, J., concurring).

court, "a 'Roman holiday' for the news media," and in the words of the U.S. Supreme Court, permeated by a "carnival atmosphere." Sam Sheppard ultimately won a reversal of his conviction.[110] Though his case was extreme, the underlying problem is a recurrent one.

The defendant's right to a fair trial before an impartial tribunal can be compromised by an irresponsible media. Where the community has been bombarded in advance of trial with prejudicial publicity, selecting a constitutionally acceptable jury may become close to impossible.[111]

1. *Constitutional standards*

In a nation where most citizens either read the newspaper or own radios or television, the facts associated with names like Jack Ruby, Watergate, or John DeLorean are likely to come to the attention of virtually all persons qualified for jury service. If media exposure to the facts of a pending criminal case were sufficient to disqualify prospective jurors, jury trials would be available in routine cases only. The due process standard for impartiality is not whether the prospective juror is entirely unfamiliar with the facts involved, or even whether he holds a "preconceived notion as to the guilt or innocence of the accused."[112] The standard is whether the "juror can lay aside his impression or opinion and render a verdict based on evidence presented in court."[113] A prospective juror's affirmations on *voir dire* examination that he is up to this task are not binding on a reviewing court. The following considerations are relevant in assessing whether the accused was in fact accorded a fair trial before an impartial jury.

(a) Substance of publicity

There is a tremendous difference between factual news reporting and an editorialized indictment. Even factual reporting, however, can be highly damaging when it leads to disclosure of incriminating items later ruled inad-

---

110 Sheppard v. Maxwell, 384 U.S. 333, 342, 86 S. Ct. 1507, 1512, 16 L. Ed. 2d 600, 608 (1966).

111 Rideau v. Louisiana, 373 U.S. 723, 83 S. Ct. 1417, 10 L. Ed. 2d 663 (1963); Irvin v. Dowd, 366 U.S. 717, 81 S. Ct. 1639, 6 L. Ed. 2d 751 (1961). *But see* Patton v. Yount, 467 U.S. 1025, 104 S. Ct. 2885, 81 L. Ed. 2d 847 (1984).

112 Irvin v. Dowd, *supra* note 111. *See also* Murphy v. Florida, 421 U.S. 794, 95 S. Ct. 2031, 44 L. Ed. 2d 589 (1975).

113 *See* cases cited in note 112, *supra*.

missible.[114] Few extrajudicial disclosures present greater potential for damage than news items relating to confessions. In *Rideau v. Louisiana*[115] the accused, during a televised interview from the jail, confessed to the details of a brutal rape-murder. The Supreme Court, skeptical of whether a fair trial was possible after this public disclosure, set aside his conviction.

(b) Extensiveness of publicity

The duration and intensity of publicity represents a second consideration that reviewing courts will weigh in assessing whether the constitutional requirement of an impartial jury has been satisfied.[116]

(c) Proximity to time of trial

The length of time between the damaging disclosures and the trial operates as a third consideration.[117] Because memories fade over time, where the case is not brought to trial until months or years later, the chances of finding an impartial jury are greatly increased.[118] Probably the most damaging disclosures are those which transpire while the trial is in progress.[119] Jury exposure to news accounts during the trial, nevertheless, can readily be avoided. When the case is likely to draw massive publicity, the court can sequester (isolate) jurors from public contacts while the trial is in progress.[120]

(d) Attitudes revealed on voir dire examination

Prospective jurors are subjected to *voir dire* examination. The attitudes revealed by jury candidates furnish an indicator of the depths of community prejudice. In *Murphy v. Florida*,[121] the Supreme Court observed:

> The length to which the trial judge must go in order to select jurors who appear to be impartial is...[a] factor relevant in evaluating

---

114 Rideau v. Louisiana, *supra* note 111.

115 *Id.*

116 Sheppard v. Maxwell, 384 U.S. 333, 86 S. Ct. 1507, 16 L. Ed. 2d 600 (1966).

117 Patton v. Yount, 467 U.S. 1025, 104 S. Ct. 2885, 81 L. Ed. 2d 847 (1984).

118 *Id.*

119 United States v. Concepcion Cueto, 515 F.2d 160, 164 (1st Cir. 1975); United States v. Bowe, 360 F.2d 1, 12 (2d Cir. 1966), *cert. denied*, 385 U.S. 961, 87 S. Ct. 401, 17 L. Ed. 2d 306 (1967).

120 Sheppard v. Maxwell, *supra* note 116.

121 421 U.S. 794, 95 S. Ct. 2031, 44 L. Ed. 2d 589 (1975).

> those jurors' assurances of impartiality. In a community where most veniremen will admit to a disqualifying prejudice, the reliability of the others' protestations may be drawn into question; for it is then more probable that they are part of a community deeply hostile to the accused, and more likely that they may unwittingly have been influenced by it.[122]

For six months preceding the trial in *Irvin v. Dowd*,[123] the media bombarded the community with headline stories relating the defendant's confession to six murders and 24 burglaries, his previous criminal record, his attorney's plea bargain attempts, and the prosecutor's determination to secure the death penalty, *ad nauseam*. The result of the *voir dire* revealed a community sentiment intensely hostile toward the defendant. By their own admission, 90 percent of all veniremen examined were uncertain of their ability to render an impartial verdict based upon the evidence adduced at the trial. Eight of the 12 jurors selected for the case indicated preconceived notions that the defendant was guilty but, despite this, affirmed their ability to act impartially. The Supreme Court reversed the conviction. The *voir dire* examination furnished the triggering factor. The Court said:

> Where so many, so many times, admitted prejudice, such a statement of impartiality [by the jurors actually selected] can be given little weight.[124]

2. *Traditional remedies for counteracting harmful publicity*

After a community has been exposed to prejudicial pre-trial publicity, several precautionary measures of varying degrees of efficacy are available. First, a probing *voir dire* examination can be conducted of each prospective juror in order to eliminate those who entertain a bias or prejudice that might color their verdict. But, as *Irvin v. Dowd* shows, where a community has been thoroughly saturated, *voir dire* examinations are unlikely to discover, let alone eliminate, deep-seated prejudices. In such cases, thought must be given to other corrective measures. One possible solution is to grant a trial continuance until community sentiments have softened. Though delay has antiseptic value, as a method for assuring a fair trial it suffers from one serious drawback: repairing the damage done to one constitutional right is effected at the

---

122 *Id*. at 803-804, 95 S. Ct. at 2037, 44 L. Ed. 2d at 597. *But see* Patton v. Yount, *supra* note 117.

123 366 U.S. 717, 81 S. Ct. 1639, 6 L. Ed. 2d 751 (1961).

124 *Id*. at 728, 81 S. Ct. at 1645, 6 L. Ed. 2d at 759.

cost of injury to another. By the time the case has lost its notoriety, it may no longer be possible to accord the accused a speedy criminal trial.[125] In the tradeoff, the accused has been forced to give up his right to a speedy trial in order to obtain an impartial tribunal which is no more than his constitutional due.

Where the publicity has been localized, changing the venue of the trial to some other community may afford an alternative to delay.[126] A change of venue is of dubious value, however, where the case has become a nationwide *cause celebre*. No community is so remote that names like John DeLorean are foreign. When contaminating disclosures have for months been spread across the nation's headlines and television screens, the defendant may be forced into the "Hobson's choice" of accepting a delayed trial or foregoing the jury entirely.

Contaminating disclosures *during the trial* are easier to control. Once the jury has been impaneled, the judge can issue cautionary instructions to the jurors to refrain from reading or listening to any extrajudicial discussions about the case, or where circumstances indicate that this might not be effective, he can isolate the jury from public contact for the duration of the trial, a remedy known as "sequestration." Even this remedy represents no panacea. If the jurors are kept from their friends and families for weeks, latent hostilities directed against the defendant may develop.

None of these measures for undoing harmful publicity is entirely satisfactory either alone or in combination. Probing *voir dire* examinations, trial continuances, changes of venue and sequestration of jurors are, at best, palliatives. Their utility in a given case can never be measured precisely, and their use is frequently accompanied by additional public costs, vexatious delays, or sacrifices of other constitutional rights. If remedial measures designed to undo damage caused by excessive publicity provide less than ideal solutions to the problem of protecting the accused's right to a fair trial, the question arises whether media contamination of criminal trials can be warded off in advance. This question raises delicate First Amendment issues.

3. *Restraining media excesses*

Criminal trial judges, in recent years, have demonstrated growing impatience with media irresponsibility and have designed new measures to keep

---

125 Speedy trial guarantee is discussed in §§ 10.2-10.4 *supra*.

126 Groppi v. Wisconsin, 400 U.S. 505, 510, 91 S. Ct. 490, 493, 27 L. Ed. 2d 571, 575-576 (1971). *See also* Sheppard v. Maxwell, 384 U.S. 333, 86 S. Ct. 1507, 16 L. Ed. 2d 600 (1966).

inflammatory disclosures out of print. The media's response has, of course, been an assertion of the First Amendment. Since 1976, several cases have reached the Supreme Court challenging trial court actions taken in an effort to stop prejudicial pretrial publicity.

(a) Pretrial gag orders

In *Nebraska Press Association v. Stuart*,[127] the Supreme Court was asked to decide whether a trial court may, consonant with the First Amendment, issue a pretrial order directing the media to withhold publication of damaging information in its possession. A few days after the accused was arrested in a small rural community for murdering six members of the same family, the trial judge, in an effort to ward off prejudicial disclosures, entered a pretrial order prohibiting the media from publishing the existence and contents of confessions, inculpatory statements or other "strongly implicative" details about the case. All nine Supreme Court justices concurred in the view that trial judges are without power under the First Amendment to order media representatives to refrain from reporting matters learned in open courtroom proceedings. They, nevertheless divided on whether the media could be restrained from publishing damaging information learned from extrajudicial news sources. Three Justices found press gag orders constitutionally intolerable under any and all circumstances. Five, however, would permit trial judges to halt publication of damaging news reports obtained from extrajudicial news sources in extreme cases when publicity had already reached the constitutional danger mark and no other measures existed for protecting the accused's right to a fair trial (i.e., trial continuances, changes of venue, etc.). However, when all the views expressed in *Nebraska Press Association* are read and analyzed, the conclusion is inescapable that of all the various maneuvers for protecting the accused's right to a fair trial, ordering the press to abstain from publishing lawfully obtained news ranks among the least acceptable under our Constitution.

After the holding in *Nebraska Press Association*, criminal trial judges, stripped of constitutional power to order media representatives to withhold publication of damaging information, began experimenting with pre-trial and trial closure orders. Members of the public and media representatives would be ordered to leave the courtroom during testimony that the judge decided should remain out of print. The inception of trial closure orders set the stage for a new round of constitutional litigation where the issue now centered on the media's claimed First Amendment right of access to all phases of criminal proceedings.

---

127 427 U.S. 539, 96 S. Ct. 2791, 49 L. Ed. 2d 683 (1976).

(b) Trial closure orders

Gannett Co. v. DePasquale[128] was the first of several closure challenges to reach the Supreme Court. The trial judge had, at the request of the prosecutor and accused, closed the courtroom to the public and media representatives during a *pretrial* hearing on a motion to suppress illegally obtained evidence. The Supreme Court ruled that the trial judge's action was constitutional. The Court rejected the media's argument that the First Amendment guarantees journalists an absolute right of access to pretrial judicial proceedings that can be asserted even in instances where their presence might undermine the accused's right to a fair trial. *Gannett Co. v. DePasquale* and subsequent cases[129] establish that the media can be excluded from *pretrial* hearings on motions to suppress or from other *pretrial* hearings if:

(1) there is a substantial probability that publicity from open proceedings will impinge on the accused's right to a fair trial and
(2) alternatives short of closure would be inadequate to protect the accused's rights.

In *Richmond Newspaper, Inc. v. Commonwealth of Virginia*,[130] decided the year after *Gannett v. DePasquales*, the Supreme Court faced the question of whether media representatives could be excluded from the courtroom during the trial itself. The trial judge there, at the accused's request, cleared all spectators and media representatives from the courtroom throughout the duration of the trial. The Supreme Court ruled that the judge's action in closing the trial was unconstitutional. The Supreme Court's post-*Richmond Newspaper* decisions make it abundantly clear that, except in the rarest of circumstances, trial judges lack power to exclude media representatives from the courtroom while the *trial itself* is in progress.[131] Media presence at the trial is different from media presence at pretrial hearings where there is the risk that the media representatives will learn about and publish information concerning evidence that is not admissible, or at least not admitted, at the

---

128 443 U.S. 368, 99 S. Ct. 2898, 61 L. Ed. 2d 608 (1979).

129 Press-Enterprise Co. (II) v. Superior Court, 478 U.S. 1, 106 S. Ct. 2735, 92 L. Ed. 2d 1 (1986).

130 448 U.S. 555, 100 S. Ct. 2814, 65 L. Ed. 2d 973 (1980).

131 Globe Newspaper v. Superior Court, 457 U.S. 596, 102 S. Ct. 2613, 73 L. Ed. 2d 248 (1982); Press-Enterprise Co. (I) v. Superior Court of California, 464 U.S. 501, 104 S. Ct. 819, 78 L. Ed. 2d 629 (1984); Waller v. Georgia, 467 U.S. 39, 104 S. Ct. 2210, 81 L. Ed. 2d 31 (1984). Related Sixth Amendment considerations are covered in § 10.5 *supra*.

trial. However, little damage is done to the accused's right to a fair trial if media representatives attend the trial itself and jurors the next day read about matters they have already heard in open court. For this reason, the constitutional balance has been struck in favor of the media's right to attend the actual trial.

Even if trial closure orders could be imposed constitutionally, trial closure would do little to protect the accused's right to a fair trial. The real danger to an accused stems not from the printing of trial testimony. The real danger is that jurors (actual and prospective) will read and be influenced by extrajudicial news stories and rumors. Since the First Amendment will not tolerate press gag orders silencing the media from publishing information lawfully obtained, public agencies and others involved in criminal proceedings must be circumspect about news releases.

(c) Monitoring extrajudicial press releases by attorneys, law enforcement agencies and potential witnesses

In the *Sheppard* case reviewed at the beginning of this section, the Supreme Court condemned official collaboration with media representatives to leak inadmissible incriminating evidence to the press, and suggested that trial judges possess the power to order prosecutors, defense attorneys, and prospective witnesses to refrain from discussing the case with media representatives.[132] Following this suggestion, journalistic organizations and legal associations around the country undertook studies of the problem. These studies led to the promulgation of voluntary self-imposed standards governing pretrial releases of information relating to pending criminal cases. The American Bar Association's (ABA) model standard establishes guidelines pointing out subjects appropriate for public comment and subjects which should be kept confidential. The standard deserves the attention of law enforcement agencies. During the investigatory phase and before formal charges have been lodged, the ABA standards would permit the release of "pertinent facts relating to the crime itself and to investigative procedures."[133] "The identity of a suspect prior to arrest and the results of investigative procedures," on the other hand, would not be discussable unless "necessary to aid in the investigation, to assist in the apprehension of the suspect, or to warn the public of any dangers."[134]

---

132 Sheppard v. Maxwell, 385 U.S. 333, 86 S. Ct. 1507, 16 L. Ed. 2d 600 (1966).

133 ABA STANDARDS, *Fair Trial and Free Press* § 2.1(a) (1968).

134 *Id.*

Between the lodging of formal charges and the final disposition of the case, law enforcement officers would be precluded from making public comments on six subjects:

(1) the defendant's prior criminal record;
(2) the existence or contents of inculpatory statements or confessions;
(3) the defendant's agreement to or refusal to submit to various laboratory tests and their outcome;
(4) the identity and/or probable testimony of any prospective witness;
(5) the possibility of a plea bargain; and
(6) the officer's opinion on the merits of the case or the strength of the government's evidence against the defendant.[135]

While the defendant is in custody, law enforcement officers would be required to refrain from posing him for photographs or from making him available to the media for a press conference unless, adequately counseled, he requests such exposure. On the other hand, law enforcement officers would be allowed to comment upon:

(1) the facts and circumstances surrounding the arrest, including any resistance encountered or weapons used;
(2) the nature of any evidence seized at the time of the arrest (other than a confession, admission or statement);
(3) the substance of the charges placed against the person arrested;
(4) the court records in the case;
(5) the scheduling or results of any stage in the criminal process;
(6) the fact that the accused denies the charges; and
(7) the need for public assistance in obtaining evidence.[136]

Violation of the American Bar Association standards would be grounds for disciplinary action.[137]

In 1966 the Justice Department adopted a body of guidelines for federal law enforcement officers very similar to the American Bar Association's pro-

---

135 *Id.* at § 2.1(c).

136 *Id.*

137 *Id.* at § 2.1(d).

posals except regarding the disclosure of criminal records.[138] The Justice Department rules condemn public disclosures of the existence and content of any inculpatory statements or confessions, expressions of opinion as to the suspect's guilt, the use of inflammatory labels like "mad dog sex killer" or "hoodlum," and disclosure of the existence or results of polygraph tests, ballistics reports, fingerprint analyses or other laboratory-developed evidence. On the matter of prior criminal records, however, the Justice Department has adopted the position that it will neither voluntarily release this information without solicitation nor decline to make it available in the face of a specific request.

Law enforcement agencies would do well to study the American Bar Association and Justice Department models. Since the printing of crime information cannot be halted once it lawfully comes into the hands of the media, courts and law enforcement agencies must begin monitoring inflammatory news leaks. There is no First Amendment duty to grant media representatives access to crime information not available to other members of the public.[139] If law enforcement agencies restrict press releases along the lines suggested above, significant strides will be made in promoting the right of an accused to receive a fair trial.

§ 10.14 Confrontation of adverse witnesses

The right of an accused to face his accusers in the presence of the tribunal assembled to pass judgment upon him finds its source in the Sixth Amendment:

> In all criminal prosecutions, the accused shall enjoy the right...to be confronted with the witnesses against him....

The Confrontation Clause affords criminal defendants two related rights:

(1) the right to meet face-to-face in open courtroom all witnesses who appear at his trial and offer evidence against him; and
(2) the right to conduct cross-examination.[140]

---

138 Address by Attorney General Nicholas Katzenbach to the American Society of Newspaper Editors, April 16, 1965, reprinted in HALL & KAMISAR, MODERN CRIMINAL PROCEDURE 413 (1966).

139 The Florida Star v. BJF, ___ U.S. ___, 109 S. Ct. 2603, 105 L. Ed. 2d 445 (1989); Houchins v. KQED, Inc., 438 U.S. 1, 98 S. Ct. 2588, 57 L. Ed. 2d 553 (1979).

140 Pennsylvania v. Ritchie, 480 U.S. 39, 107 S. Ct. 989, 998, 94 L. Ed. 2d 40 (1987).

An accused can waive the first right by voluntarily failing to show up for his trial[141] or by behaving so disruptively that it becomes necessary to remove him from the courtroom.[142] Short of such behavior, the accused's right to meet his accuser face-to-face is apparently absolute. In *Coy v. Iowa*,[143] the Supreme Court struck down a state statute conferring discretion on trial judges to order placement of a screen between a youthful complaining witness in a sex abuse case and the accused in order to spare the child-witness the trauma of observing his or her victimizer in the courtroom. The Court stated that the right to meet one's accusers face-to-face is part of the "irreducible literal meaning" of the confrontation clause and cannot be denied.

The Sixth Amendment entitles the defendant to confront adverse witnesses in open court on the witness stand because a courtroom confrontation enhances the reliability of the testimony in several different ways.[144] First, the witness is required to testify under oath and on pain of perjury if he deliberately gives false testimony. Second, the fact-finding tribunal has an opportunity to observe him as he testifies and to evaluate, on the basis of his demeanor, whether he is telling the truth. Finally and most important of all, when the witness gives incriminating testimony in a courtroom atmosphere, the defendant has an opportunity to cross-examine him. Cross-examination is a potent device for exposing testimonial weaknesses. The witness may have had an inadequate opportunity to observe the events to which he testified; his memory may be faulty; narrative imprecisions may have crept into his testimony; or his testimony may suffer from an underlying lack of candor or sincerity. Through cross-examination, the defendant may be able to bring to the jury's attention infirmities in the witness' cognitive, perceptual, recollective or narrative abilities, or to discredit his truthfulness.

Cross-examination is so central to the constitutional right of confrontation that the Supreme Court, in references to the confrontation clause, has repeatedly alluded to it as assuring the "right to confront and *cross-examine*" as if the latter term appeared in the constitutional text.[145] There would be little reason for guaranteeing the right to confront adverse witnesses if nothing more than a visual encounter were contemplated. Because confrontation

---

141 Taylor v. United States, 414 U.S. 17, 94 S. Ct. 194, 38 L. Ed. 2d 174 (1973).

142 Illinois v. Allen, 397 U.S. 337, 90 S. Ct. 1057, 25 L. Ed. 2d 353 (1970).

143 487 U.S. 1012, 108 S. Ct. 2798, 101 L. Ed. 2d 857 (1988).

144 Chambers v. Mississippi, 410 U.S. 284, 93 S. Ct. 1038, 35 L. Ed. 2d 297 (1973); California v. Green, 399 U.S. 149, 90 S. Ct. 1930, 26 L. Ed. 2d 489 (1970).

145 *See, e.g.*, Chambers v. Mississippi, 410 U.S. 284, 297-298, 93 S. Ct. 1038, 1047, 35 L. Ed. 2d 297, 310 (1973).

and cross-examination are fundamental mechanisms for testing the reliability of an adverse witness' testimony, this Sixth Amendment assurance is an element of due process and is obligatory on the states.[146]

§ 10.15 Prosecutor's constitutional disclosure obligations

Several decades ago, the Supreme Court observed that prosecutors occupy a unique position in our adversary system of criminal justice:

> The United States Attorney is the representative not of an ordinary party to a controversy, but of a sovereignty whose obligation to govern impartially is as compelling as its obligation to govern at all; and whose interest, therefore, in a criminal prosecution is not that it shall win a case, but that justice shall be done. As such, he is in a peculiar and very definite sense the servant of the law, the twofold aim of which is that guilt shall not escape or innocence suffer. He may prosecute with earnestness and vigor -- indeed, he should do so. But, while he may strike hard blows, he is not at liberty to strike foul ones. It is as much his duty to refrain from improper methods calculated to produce a wrongful conviction as it is to use every legitimate means to bring about a just one.[147]

In a series of cases, the Supreme Court has developed a constitutional access-to-evidence doctrine. This doctrine, which is designed to assure that the defendant is afforded a meaningful opportunity to present an adequate defense, originated in cases where the prosecutor had knowingly relied upon perjured evidence to secure a guilty verdict.[148] The wisdom and justice of setting aside a criminal conviction where the prosecutor has suborned perjury is self-evident. There are two separate considerations at stake, either of which standing alone can be sufficient to call for a reversal. First, the government's insufferable behavior needs to be deterred. Second, a conviction procured through perjured testimony is suspect. In *Mooney v. Holohan*[149] the Supreme Court said:

---

146 Pointer v. Texas, 380 U.S. 400, 85 S. Ct. 1065, 13 L. Ed. 2d 923 (1965).

147 Berger v. United States, 295 U.S. 78, 88, 55 S. Ct. 629, 633, 79 L. Ed. 1314, 1321 (1935).

148 Mooney v. Holohan, 294 U.S. 103, 55 S. Ct. 340, 79 L. Ed. 791 (1935).

149 *Supra* note 148.

> [Due process] is a requirement that cannot be deemed satisfied...if a state has contrived a conviction through the pretense of a trial which in truth is but used as a means of depriving a defendant of liberty through a deliberate deception of court and jury by the presentation of testimony known to be perjured. Such a contrivance by a state to procure the conviction and imprisonment of a defendant is as inconsistent with the rudimentary demands of justice as is the obtaining of a like result by intimidation.[150]

In *Alcorta v. Texas*,[151] the *Mooney* principle was extended to a situation where the prosecutor, while not instigating the false testimony, stood by in silence, knowing that a prosecution witness was committing perjury and made no effort to correct the misimpression. The Supreme Court reversed Alcorta's conviction on the ground that the prosecutor, by failing to correct testimony he knew to be false, became a participant in creating a "false impression" with respect to a material fact.

Alcorta was significant because it marked the beginning of a shift in emphasis. In reversing the conviction, the Supreme Court focused upon the verdict's integrity ("false impression") rather than the need for deterring misbehavior. *Alcorta* laid the foundations for the development of a broader disclosure rule. There is a remarkable similarity between a "false impression" resulting from perjured testimony and a "false impression" resulting from the suppression of any material evidence.

The transition from a specialized disclosure obligation operating in the realm of perjured testimony to a more generalized responsibility was accomplished in *Brady v. Maryland*.[152] Brady and a confederate were accused of perpetrating a murder during the course of a robbery. Brady was tried separately. At his trial, Brady admitted participating in the crime, but appealed to the jury to recommend a life sentence rather than death. He contended that it was his confederate, Boblit, who did the actual killing. Prior to the trial, Brady's attorney had requested the prosecutor to allow him to examine Boblit's extrajudicial statements. The prosecutor turned some of them over to Brady's counsel but withheld from him Boblit's statement in which he confessed to firing the fatal shot. Brady was sentenced to death. The Supreme Court reversed his conviction and issued the following proclamation:

150 *Id*. at 112, 55 S. Ct. at 342, 79 L. Ed. at 794.

151 355 U.S. 28, 78 S. Ct. 103, 2 L. Ed. 2d 9 (1957).

152 373 U.S. 83, 83 S. Ct. 1194, 10 L. Ed. 2d 215 (1963).

> We now hold that the suppression by the prosecution of evidence favorable to an accused upon request violates due process where the evidence is material either to guilt or to punishment, irrespective of the good faith or bad faith of the prosecution.
>
> The principle....is not punishment of society for misdeeds of a prosecutor but avoidance of an unfair trial to the accused....A prosecution that withholds evidence on demand of an accused which, if made available, would tend to exculpate him or reduce the penalty helps shape...a proceeding that does not comport with standards of justice, even though, as in the present case, his action is not "the result of guile,"...[153]

Brady divorced the government's disclosure obligations from a rationale based on misconduct and predicated its responsibilities on a broad recognition that when the government withholds significant evidence favorable to the accused, the integrity of the proceeding is compromised. Although the prosecutor's good faith or bad faith has ceased to be relevant, *Brady* does not eliminate the need for establishing government complicity in depriving the accused of a fair trial. A defendant's discovery after his trial that favorable evidence existed but was simply not presented or that a prosecution witness committed perjury, may be an occasion for sympathy but it does not rise to the level of a constitutional violation unless his failure to discover can be linked to the government.[154] The minimum link is notice.

1. *Imputed notice*

To secure relief under the *Brady* doctrine, the accused must prove that the government had notice of favorable evidence and failed to disclose it. The fatal knowledge, however, need not be present in the mind of the attorney assigned to prosecute the case. *Giglio v. United States*[155] determined that knowledge in the possession of any member of the prosecutor's staff would suffice. In *Giglio*, a crucial government witness testified on cross-examination that he received no promises of leniency from the government in return for testifying against his co-conspirator. The truth of the matter was that an associate in the U.S. Attorney's office had promised him leniency, but the promise was unknown to the government attorney who tried the case. The

---

153 *Id*. at 87-88, 83 S. Ct. 1196-1197, 10 L. Ed. 2d at 218-219.

154 Burks v. Egeler, 512 F.2d 221 (6th Cir.), *cert. denied*, 423 U.S. 937, 96 S. Ct. 297, 46 L. Ed. 2d 220 (1975).

155 405 U.S. 150, 92 S. Ct. 763, 31 L. Ed. 2d 104 (1972).

Supreme Court held that the breakdown of communications in the prosecutor's office did not exonerate the government from its obligation to expose testimony known to be false by any member of the prosecutor's staff. Mr. Chief Justice Burger offered the following analysis:

> [W]hether the nondisclosure was a result of negligence or design, it is the responsibility of the prosecutor. The prosecutor's office is an entity and as such it is the spokesman for the Government. A promise made by one attorney must be attributed, for these purposes, to the Government....To the extent this places a burden on the large prosecution offices, procedures and regulations can be established to carry that burden and to insure communication of all relevant information on each case to every lawyer who deals with it.[156]

Lower federal courts have expanded the imputed notice doctrine and have held that evidence in the possession of law enforcement officers in the prosecuting jurisdiction, whether or not revealed to the prosecutor or his staff, falls within the informational domain for which the prosecutor is responsible under the *Giglio* case.[157] In *Barbee v. Warden*,[158] the prosecutor introduced the defendant's revolver into evidence but failed to disclose that ballistics and fingerprint tests performed on it had been negative. Indeed, he was ignorant of this favorable defense evidence because the police, deeming the negative results to be useless to the prosecutor, had failed to pass the laboratory reports along. The Fourth Circuit ruled:

> The police are also part of the prosecution, and the taint on the trial is no less...[i]f the police allow the State's Attorney to produce evidence pointing to guilt without informing him of other [contradictory] evidence.[159]

The lesson to be learned from *Barbee* is that the police must keep detailed and accurate records of all investigatory results, whether positive or negative, and when the investigation is concluded, they should turn the complete file over to the prosecutor, unpruned of investigatory items which from

---

156 *Id.* at 154, 92 S. Ct. at 766, 31 L. Ed. 2d at 108 (citations omitted).

157 United States v. Morell, 524 F.2d 550 (2d Cir. 1975); Barbee v. Warden, 331 F.2d 842 (4th Cir. 1964); *see also*, Moore v. Illinois, 408 U.S. 786, 92 S. Ct. 2562, 33 L. Ed. 2d 706 (1972) (Marshall, J., dissenting).

158 331 F.2d 842 (4th Cir. 1964).

159 *Id.* at 846.

a law enforcement vantage point represent wasted efforts. There is no advantage in withholding from the prosecutor negative laboratory results, disappointing statements given by possible prosecution witnesses, and items of a similar nature. Keeping the prosecutor ignorant of weaknesses in the government's case will not make the case one bit stronger. To the contrary, ignorance may handicap the prosecutor in preparing to meet the defense's trial strategies, and even if the prosecution wins, the conviction may be vulnerable as a result of the prosecutor's inadvertent failure to discharge his *Brady* disclosure obligations.

2. *Materiality standard*

The *Brady* disclosure rule places a duty on the prosecutor to turn over evidence in his possession favorable to the accused when that evidence is *material* either to the defendant's guilt or punishment.[160] The disclosure duty grows out of the government's due process responsibility for assuring the accused a fair trial and applies whether or not defense counsel has requested this information.[161]

Central to the *Brady* obligation is the concept of *materiality*. The prosecutor is not required to turn over all information in his files. He must only disclose evidence that is *material*. In formulating a definition for materiality, the Supreme Court sought to adopt a test that would taint convictions for failure to disclose only when the nondisclosure casts doubts on the integrity of the defendant's conviction. The test for *materiality* requires the appeals court to assess the probable impact of the withheld information on the verdict. The withheld information will be regarded as *material* justifying reversal of the conviction only if "there is a reasonable probability that, had the evidence been disclosed to the defense, the result of the proceeding would have been different."[162] A reasonable probability is "a probability sufficient to undermine confidence in the outcome."[163]

The *Brady* disclosure rule applies both to exculpatory evidence and to evidence discrediting the government's witnesses.[164] Where the reliability of a government witness may be determinative of guilt or innocence, the prosecutor must advise defense counsel of all plea bargains, fee agreements,

---

160 United States v. Bagley, 473 U.S. 667, 105 S. Ct. 3375, 87 L. Ed. 2d 481 (1985).

161 *Id.*

162 *Id.* at 682, 105 S. Ct. at 3384, 87 L. Ed. 2d at 494.

163 *Id.*

164 Porretto v. Stalder, 834 F.2d 461 (5th Cir. 1987); Nixon v. United States, 703 F. Supp. 538 (S.D. Miss. 1988), *aff'd*, 881 F.2d 1305 (5th Cir. 1989).

promises and inducements, as well as information about the witness' criminal record.

3. *Problem of evidence destroyed in good faith*

In *California v. Trombetta*,[165] the prosecutor received a *Brady* production request for samples of the breath specimen the police had taken from the accused when he was arrested for drunk driving. After this sample had been subjected to an Intoxilyzer test, the police, following customary procedures, failed to preserve it (although it would have been technologically feasible for them to have done so). The results registered substantial intoxication. Following his conviction on drunk driving charges, the accused appealed. He took the position that the failure of the arresting officers to preserve the breath samples so that he too could run tests on them made the prosecution unfair. The Supreme Court stated the issue to be whether the government's constitutional disclosure obligation demands that it take *affirmative steps to preserve evidence* for the accused in anticipation that he may later demand to see this evidence. The Court in *Trombetta* recognized a limited duty to preserve evidence. This duty is triggered only when

(1) the evidence possesses an exculpatory value that is apparent before it is destroyed, and
(2) the information is of such a nature that the defendant will be unable to obtain comparable evidence by other reasonably available means.[166]

The Supreme Court found neither of these conditions met in *Trombetta*. As the Court pointed out, because Intoxilyzer tests are highly accurate and reliable, it was unlikely that the destroyed breath samples would have furnished exculpatory evidence to the accused. Moreover, the accused still had the ability , by calling expert witnesses, to challenge the test's reliability without the samples. The Court concluded that, under theses circumstances, the government's failure to preserve the breath samples for the accused was not a violation of its *Brady* duties.

In a case decided four years later, the Supreme Court appears to have departed from the *Trombetta* standard. In *Arizona v. Youngblood*, [167] the Supreme Court proclaimed that "unless a criminal defendant can show bad

---

165 467 U.S. 479, 104 S. Ct. 2528, 81 L. Ed. 2d 413 (1984).

166 *Id.* at 489, 104 S. Ct. at 2534, 81 L. Ed. 2d at 422.

167 __ U.S. __, 109 S. Ct. 333, 102 L. Ed. 2d 281 (1988).

faith on the part of the police, failure to preserve potentially useful evidence does not constitute a denial of due process of law."[168] *Arizona v. Youngblood* involved the investigation of a child molestation case in which the police had failed to refridgerate the victim's clothing or to run tests on the semen samples taken from him. The accused, who was taken into custody six weeks later and who was subsequently convicted, argued that his conviction should be set aside because had tests been conducted on the lost semen samples, the results might have exonerated him. The Supreme Court made no effort to apply the *Trombetta* test, but focused instead on the mental state of the police officers who had failed to preserve the semen samples. Since this failure had ocurred before the police had a suspect and at a time when the police had no way of knowing whether the evidence they failed to preserve would incriminate or exonerate the person later arrested, the Supreme Court concluded that the failure of these officers to preserve the semen samples represented a careless but good faith error. *Arizona v. Youngblood* suggests that a criminal defendants can establish bad faith and thus raise a due process claim only if he can show that the police knew, or at least suspected, that the evidence they failed to preserve would or might exonerate him.

The extent to which the *Trombetta* test retains validity after *Arizona v. Youngblood* remains unclear. However, until the Supreme Court expressly recants the duty recognized in *Trombetta*, police departments should incorporate the *Trombetta* doctrine into their operating procedures and should preserve any evidence that is not available through other sources if that evidence might have exculpatory value.

§ 10.16 Cruel and unusual punishment

There was a time in English history when a convicted criminal, as punishment for his offense, might be burned at the stake, boiled in oil, or have his hands or ears cropped off. Blackstone, in his *Commentaries on the Law of England* published in 1769, reported that for the crime of treason, an Englishman might be dragged to the gallows, hung, cut down, disemboweled while still living, and finally put to death by decapitation and quartering.[169] The Eighth Amendment erected a constitutional barrier against the infliction of "cruel and unusual punishments" by the federal government. This limitation is now equally binding on the states.[170]

---

168 *Id.* at ___, 109 S. Ct. at 337, 102 L. Ed. 2d at 289.

169 4 W. BLACKSTONE, COMMENTARIES *92.

170 Robinson v. California, 370 U.S. 660, 82 S. Ct. 1417, 8 L. Ed. 2d 758 (1962).

Notions regarding what constitutes cruel treatment in the realm of penal justice have varied over time. Public hangings, floggings and the cropping off of ears were punishments still in common practice when this nation was founded.[171] In 1779, Thomas Jefferson advocated the castration of any man found guilty of rape, polygamy or sodomy, and the facial mutilation of any woman found guilty of a comparable offense.[172] Judged by twentieth-century standards, Jefferson's proposal sounds fiendish and bizarre. But to decent thinking men of the eighteenth century, bodily mutilation was regarded as an acceptable punishment for certain types of crimes.[173] What would happen if some state legislature belatedly enacted Thomas Jefferson's proposal today? Should a court, in evaluating the statute's Eighth Amendment constitutionality, look backwards in history to the time of the Constitution's adoption to see how enlightened public opinion in 1791 would have reacted to this measure, or should the court make its assessments on the basis of contemporary penological thoughts and values? To ask this question is to answer it.

The Supreme Court has repeatedly emphasized the Eighth Amendment's "expansive and vital character"[174] and capacity for evolutionary growth.[175] What constitutes "cruel and unusual punishment" is not linked to eighteenth-century standards. The constitutional meaning of "cruelty" changes as "public opinion becomes enlightened by justice."[176] Should the time come when civilized standards have advanced to a point where the death penalty is no longer acceptable to the vast majority of Americans, these attitudes will become enshrined in the Eighth Amendment, and death will then be regarded as cruel and unusual punishment. As of this writing, however, that time is nowhere in sight.

The Eighth Amendment has been pressed into service in a wide variety of contexts. First, the constitutional prescription against cruelty operates to assure that inmates confined to prison will not be denied the minimum necessities for civilized existence or exposed to the wanton and unnecessary infliction of pain.[177] In *Hutto v. Finney*[178] the Supreme Court affirmed a fed-

---

171 Mr. Justice Brennan traced the history of the Eighth Amendment in his concurring opinion in *Furman v. Georgia*, 408 U.S. 238, 257, 92 S. Ct. 2726, 2736 33 L. Ed. 2d 346, 360 (1972).

172 VAN DEN HAAG, PUNISHING CRIMINALS 193-194 (1975).

173 *See* note 171, *supra*.

174 Weems v. United States, 217 U.S. 349, 377, 30 S. Ct. 544, 553, 54 L. Ed. 793, 802 (1910).

175 Trop v. Dulles, 356 U.S. 86, 78 S. Ct. 590, 2 L. Ed. 2d 630 (1958).

176 Weems v. United States, 217 U.S. 349, 378, 30 S. Ct. 544, 553, 54 L. Ed. 793 (1910).

177 Rhodes v. Chapman, 452 U.S. 337, 101 S. Ct. 2392, 69 L. Ed. 2d 59 (1981).

eral district court ruling which had found that punitive confinement of prisoners in filthy, overcrowded eight-by-ten-foot cells, where violence was rampant and where the prisoners' diet was confined to a paste called "grue" violated the Eighth Amendment when prolonged over extended periods of time. In another case, deliberate indifference upon the part of corrections officials to the known medical needs of a prisoner was held to fall below constitutional standards.[179] Society must observe civilized standards of decency even as it punishes those who have broken its laws. The infliction of unnecessary suffering in the administration of criminal punishments is repugnant to the Eighth Amendment.

The Eighth Amendment condemnation of cruel and unusual punishment does not, however, have as its primary concern the overseeing of corrections administration. Courts have been wisely reluctant to take on this task except in extreme instances.[180] Traditionally, the Eighth Amendment's primary focus has been directed to exercises of the legislative power to define and provide punishments for crime. The Eighth Amendment checks the legislature in several different ways.

First, the Eighth Amendment serves as a substantive limitation on what behavior legislatures can criminalize. Civilized societies reserve criminal sanctions for antisocial conduct. It is unconstitutionally cruel to brand a person a criminal and inflict punishment upon him because he suffers from drug addiction, alcoholism, or some other human affliction.[181] The Eighth Amendment confines criminal sanctions to overt antisocial behavior (trafficking in narcotics) and requires that conditions of human suffering (being an addict) be left unpunished.

Next, the Eighth Amendment restrains the legislature from imposing cruel forms of punishment. Though death is not *per se* cruel and unusual punishment,[182] the Eighth Amendment certainly would not tolerate crucifying a condemned man or burning him at the stake as a means of carrying his sentence into effect. The Constitution forbids any method of punishment that entails unnecessary pain and suffering. Fines, prison sentences, and the death penalty carried into effect by conventional means probably mark the limits of constitutionally inflictable punishments. In *Trop v. Dulles*,[183] the Supreme Court ruled that Congress may not authorize the stripping of a man's citizenship as punishment for wartime desertion. The Court regarded

---

178 437 U.S. 678, 98 S. Ct. 2565, 57 L. Ed. 2d 522 (1978).

179 Estelle v. Gamble, 429 U.S. 97, 97 S. Ct. 285, 50 L. Ed. 2d 251 (1976).

180 Rhodes v. Chapman, *supra* note 177.

181 Robinson v. California, 370 U.S. 660, 82 S. Ct. 1417, 8 L. Ed. 2d 758 (1962).

182 Furman v. Georgia, 408 U.S. 238, 92 S. Ct. 2726, 33 L. Ed. 2d 346 (1972).

183 356 U.S. 86, 78 S. Ct. 590, 2 L. Ed. 2d 630 (1958).

loss of citizenship as a cruelly degrading form of punishment, likely to cause acute mental torment and suffering.

Nevertheless, the two most important areas for application of the Eighth Amendment in recent years have been:

(1) overseeing that the death penalty is not arbitrarily or discriminatorily imposed, and
(2) assuring that punishments are not out of proportion to the crime for which imposed.

Each of these roles will be developed in greater detail in the discussion that follows.

§ 10.17 – Excessive punishments

Even widely accepted and familiar punishments such as fines, prison terms and the death penalty may become unconstitutionally cruel if they are excessively severe in relationship to the underlying offenses for which they are imposed. The Eighth Amendment incorporates notions of punishment-offense proportionality. This dimension of the cruelty clause was first recognized by the Supreme Court in *Weems v. United States*.[184] Weems, a government employee, was convicted of falsifying public documents. He was sentenced to 15 years' incarceration at hard labor in ankle chains, to an unusual loss of his civil rights, and to perpetual surveillance. The Supreme Court ruled that this amounted to cruel and unusual punishment. Though the Court might have contented itself with disposing of this case on the basis of the unnecessary physical and emotional torment accompanying the sentence, the Court did not do so. Instead it pointed out the lack of proportion between the crime and punishment and remarked:

> [I]t is a precept of justice that punishment for crimes should be graduated and proportioned to [the] offense [charged].[185]

Despite the Supreme Court's clear mandate for treating disproportionately severe punishments as unconstitutionally cruel, until quite recently, claims of Eighth Amendment excessiveness were routinely rejected by lower courts.[186] This reluctance was in some ways healthy. Except in extreme

---

184 217 U.S. 349, 30 S. Ct. 544, 54 L. Ed. 793 (1910).

185 *Id*. at 367, 30 S. Ct. at 549, 54 L. Ed. at 798.

186 *See, e.g.*, Donaldson v. Wyrick, 393 F. Supp. 1041 (W.D. Mo. 1974).

cases, courts should defer to the superior expertise of legislatures in determining the seriousness of the crime and the appropriate punishment.

The aspect of cruelty first recognized in *Weems* came of age in the post-*Furman v. Georgia*[187] capital punishment cases. Having failed in *Furman* to convince the Supreme Court that death was *per se* a cruel and unusual form of punishment, death row prisoners began flooding the courts with claims of Eighth Amendment excessiveness. In *Gregg v. Georgia*,[188] the first of many such cases, the Supreme Court ruled that death was not an unconstitutionally excessive punishment for the crime of murder. Mr. Justice Stewart, author of the *Gregg* opinion, wrote:

> [W]e are concerned here only with the imposition of capital punishment for the crime of murder, and when a life has been taken deliberately by the offender, we cannot say that the punishment is invariably disproportionate to the crime. It is an extreme sanction, suitable to the most extreme of crimes.[189]

In a footnote, however, Mr. Justice Stewart cautioned:

> We do not address here the question whether the taking of a criminal's life is a proportionate sanction where no victim has been deprived of life -- for example, when capital punishment is imposed for rape, kidnapping, or armed robbery that does not result in the death of any human being.[190]

The question reserved in *Gregg* was considered the following year in *Coker v. Georgia*.[191] A Georgia jury had imposed the death penalty upon an escaped convict who had raped an adult woman. The Supreme Court announced that judicial review of sentences challenged as excessive under the Eighth Amendment should be guided by public sentiment regarding the seriousness of the offense, as evidenced by the laws of other jurisdictions and sentences imposed by judges and juries on similar offenders. Utilizing these criteria, the Supreme Court ascertained that Georgia was the only state which authorized the death penalty for raping an adult victim, and that even Georgia juries rarely imposed this sanction. Thus finding, the Supreme Court pronounced death an unconstitutionally severe punishment for the crime of raping an adult. In light of the Court's reference to rape as the

---

187 408 U.S. 238, 92 S. Ct. 2726, 33 L. Ed. 2d 346 (1972).

188 428 U.S. 153, 96 S. Ct. 2909, 49 L. Ed. 2d 859 (1976).

189 *Id.* at 187, 96 S. Ct. at 2931-2932, 49 L. Ed. 2d 882 (footnotes omitted).

190 *Id.* at 187 n. 35, 96 S. Ct. at 2931-2932 n. 35, 49 L. Ed. 2d at 882 n. 35.

191 433 U.S. 584, 97 S. Ct. 2861, 53 L. Ed. 2d 982 (1977).

"ultimate violation of self," second only in gravity to murder, *Coker* implies that death is constitutionally unacceptable punishment for any nonhomicidal offense. Mr. Chief Justice Burger hammered away at this point in his dissenting opinion.

> This [holding] casts serious doubts upon the constitutional validity of statutes imposing the death penalty for a variety of conduct which, though dangerous, may not necessarily result in any immediate death, e.g., treason, airplane hijacking, and kidnapping. In that respect, today's holding does even more harm than is initially apparent.[192]

A decade after *Coker*, it still remains true that the Supreme Court has never approved the death penalty for any crime that did not result in the taking of human life. Indeed, the Supreme Court has ruled that death is unconstitutionally excessive punishment for a criminal defendant who participates in a felony in which human life is taken if the defendant was not responsible for the killing and did not anticipate that a killing would or might occur. In *Enmund v. Florida*,[193] the Court overturned a death sentence imposed on the driver of a getaway car who remained outside the house during an armed robbery in which his accomplice killed the robbery victim where the defendant was unaware that his accomplice intended to kill if necessary. This is not to say that the death penalty can never be imposed on an offender unless he personally pulls the trigger. The Supreme Court has ruled that death is not excessive punishment if the accused actively participates in a major felony knowing that an accomplice will or might take human life.[194]

The development of Eighth Amendment notions of punishment-offense proportionality in noncapital cases has been slower in coming. It was not until 73 years after *Weems* that the Court again found a noncapital sentence unconstitutionally severe.[195] In *Rommel v. Estelle*,[196] the Supreme Court explained why courts should tread gingerly when an Eighth Amendment challenge is aimed at the length of a prison sentence rather than the death penalty.

> [T]he 'seriousness' of an offense or pattern of offenses in modern society is not a line, but a plane. Once the death penalty and other punishments different in kind from fine or imprisonment have been

---

192 *Id.* at 621, 97 S. Ct. at 2881, 53 L. Ed. 2d. at 1007.

193 458 U.S. 782, 102 S. Ct. 3368, 73 L. Ed. 2d 1140 (1982).

194 481 U.S. 137, 107 S. Ct. 1676, 95 L. Ed. 2d 127 (1987).

195 Solem v. Helm, 463 U.S. 277, 103 S. Ct. 3001, 77 L. Ed. 2d 637 (1983).

196 445 U.S. 263, 100 S. Ct. 1133, 63 L. Ed. 2d 382 (1980).

> put to one side, there remains little in the way of objective standards for judging whether or not a life sentence imposed...for...felony convictions not involving 'violence' violates the cruel-and-unusual punishment prohibition of the Eighth Amendment....Whatever views may be entertained regarding severity of punishment, whether one believes in its efficacy or its futility,...these are peculiarly questions of legislative policy.[197]

In *Solem v. Helm*,[198] however, the Supreme Court found sufficient objective evidence to distinguish a South Dakota criminal recidivist statute from the laws of other jurisdictions. Unlike the laws elsewhere, South Dakota's statute imposed a *mandatory* life sentence to be served without parole on all multiple offenders. The Supreme Court ruled that this was constitutionally excessive punishment for an offender who had committed several nonviolent and relatively nonserious crimes.

There have been several recent cases questioning when particular characteristics of the offender which may diminish his moral culpability make death an inhuman and inappropriate punishment. The age of the offender has Eighth Amendment significance. In *Thompson v. Oklahoma*,[199] the Supreme Court ruled that the Constitution prohibits execution of youthful offenders who are *younger than* 16 at the time of their crimes, even if they commit brutal murders that would justify the death sentence had they been an adult. The Constitution, however, does not categorically forbid the execution of youthful offenders *over* 16 when they commit murder, though their youthfulness is a factor that the sentencer must be allowed to take into account in fixing the punishment.[200]

The Supreme Court has engaged in parallel Eighth Amendment line drawing concerning insane and mentally incompetent offenders. Civilized societies from time immemorial have recoiled from the practice of executing the insane. The Eighth Amendment condemnation of cruel and unusual punishments incorporates this moral taboo and prohibits the carrying into effect of the death sentence against a prisoner who becomes insane and who, because of his insanity, no longer has the capacity either to come to grips with his own conscience or to understand why he has been singled out to receive the death penalty.[201] The Supreme Court, however, has found insufficient evidence of a national consensus against executing mentally retarded

---

197 *Id*. at 283, 100 S. Ct. at 1143-1144 n. 27, 63 L. Ed. 2d at 396 n. 27.

198 *Supra* note 195.

199 487 U.S. 815, 108 S. Ct. 2687, 101 L. Ed. 2d 702 (1988).

200 Stanford v. Kentucky, ___ U.S. ___, 109 S. Ct. 2969, 106 L. Ed. 2d 306 (1989).

201 Ford v. Wainwright, 477 U.S. 399, 106 S. Ct. 2595, 91 L. Ed. 2d 335 (1986).

persons convicted of capital offenses to justify adopting a similar rule for them. In *Penry v. Lynaugh*,[202] the Court ruled that while the sentencing body must be allowed to take the offender's mental retardation into account as a possible factor mitigating against imposition of the death penalty, the Eighth Amendment does not categorically forbid executing mentally retarded persons unless they are legally insane. In *Penry*, the defendant, though he had the mental age of a six-and-a-half-year-old, was found legally sane.

§ 10.18 – Sentencing in capital punishment cases

In *Furman v. Georgia*,[203] handed down in 1972, the Supreme Court dealt capital punishment laws around the nation a fatal blow. The decision reflected the Court's disenchantment with capital punishment sentencing procedures then prevalent, rather than with the death penalty as such. Typically, sentencing judges and juries were given unguided discretion to select between a life sentence or death for serious felonies. The result was random and unequal justice, with the death penalty being reserved almost exclusively for minorities and the poor. This system was pronounced by the Supreme Court as being constitutionally unacceptable.

Furman led to a moratorium on the execution of death row prisoners. Chaos ensued as legislatures around the nation met for the purpose of remodeling their capital punishment laws. Since broad and unguided sentencing discretion had led to the death penalty's downfall, it was clear that this feature had to be excised from capital punishment sentencing procedures if the death penalty was to be salvaged. Legislatures had two choices. They could retain sentencing discretion but provide standards to guide the sentencing body in its determination to impose the death penalty, or, in the alternative, sentencing discretion could be eliminated and death made a mandatory punishment for specified offenses.

Between 1972 and 1976, the year when death penalty sentencing procedures were again considered, legislatures met and opted for one or the other solution. In 1976, the Supreme Court granted certiorari to review the post-*Furman* capital punishment sentencing procedures adopted by several states whose efforts to comply with the Court's mandate were representative of those nationwide.[204] The results were illuminating. Without attempting to

---

202 ___ U.S. ___, 109 S. Ct. 2934, 106 L. Ed. 2d 256 (1989).

203 *Supra* note 187.

204 Gregg v. Georgia, 428 U.S. 153, 96 S. Ct. 2909, 49 L. Ed. 2d 859 (1976); Proffitt v. Florida, 428 U.S. 242, 96 S. Ct. 2960, 49 L. Ed. 2d 913 (1976); Jurek v. Texas, 428 U.S. 262, 96 S. Ct. 2950, 49 L. Ed. 2d 929 (1976); Woodson v. North Car-

treat each case individually, it is possible to distill what features are required and what features are constitutionally impermissible in capital punishment sentencing.

First, where a person's life is at stake, the Eighth Amendment demands individualized sentencing discretion.[205] The Supreme Court invalidated several mandatory death penalty laws, citing the incompatibility of mandatory sentencing with contemporary penological goals and practices. But more importantly, by treating "all persons convicted of a designated offense, not as uniquely individual human beings, but as members of a faceless, undifferentiated mass to be subjected to the blind infliction of the [death] penalty,"[206] the mandatory approach offended the fundamental constitutional premise underlying the Eighth Amendment -- respect for human dignity. States may not make death a mandatory punishment even for such extreme offenses as the deliberate slaying of a policeman.[207]

Legislatures in those jurisdictions which had responded to *Furman* by enacting mandatory death penalty laws were sent back to the drawing board with instructions to design procedures which give the sentencing body an opportunity to consider all "relevant facets of the character and record of the individual offender [and] the circumstances of the particular offense."[208] The first requirement for a valid capital punishment sentencing system is that it afford the sentencing body discretionary power to withhold the death penalty and impose a prison sentence instead where it feels that mercy is justified.

Though the Eighth Amendment demands sentencing discretion, that discretion must be informed, guided and controlled. Hence the second requirement for a valid death penalty sentencing procedure is that the sentencing body must be provided with concrete, clear and objective guidelines focusing attention on those features that justify the imposition of the death penalty.[209] Third, and as a natural correlative, the sentencing body must be afforded an opportunity to hear and consider all relevant mitigating evidence bearing on the defendant's age, character, record, or other circumstances that might move it to be merciful and withhold the death sentence.[210]

---

olina, 428 U.S. 280, 96 S. Ct. 2978, 49 L. Ed. 2d 944 (1976); Roberts v. Louisiana, 428 U.S. 325, 96 S. Ct. 3001, 49 L. Ed. 2d 974 (1976).

205 Woodson v. North Carolina, *supra* note 204.

206 Woodson v. North Carolina, *supra* note 204, 428 U.S. at 304, 96 S. Ct. at 2991, 49 L. Ed. 2d at 961.

207 Roberts v. Louisiana, 431 U.S. 633, 97 S. Ct. 1993, 52 L. Ed. 2d 637 (1977); *see also* Sumner v. Shuman, 483 U.S. 66, 107 S. Ct. 2716, 97 L. Ed. 2d 56 (1987).

208 Woodson v. North Carolina, *supra* note 204.

209 Gregg v. Georgia, *supra* note 204.

210 *Id.*

In *Gregg v. Georgia*,[211] the Supreme Court approved the Georgia legislature's approach as complying with the Eighth Amendment. The Georgia approach has become a prototype for laws elsewhere. Georgia employs a bifurcated, or two-stage, proceeding in the trial of capital cases. During the first phase, guilt is ascertained in the usual fashion. In the event that a conviction results, a second and separate phase is held for sentencing. Bifurcation is constitutionally required because much evidence relevant to fixing the proper punishment, such as the accused's character and prior criminal record, is irrelevant to his guilt of the crimes for which he is on trial and would be highly prejudicial if introduced at the guilt phase of his trial. The Georgia statute, as required, lists a number of aggravating and mitigating circumstances that a sentencing body must consider during the second phase. The function of statutory aggravating circumstances is to "narrow the class of persons eligible for the death penalty and...reasonably justify the imposition of a more severe sentence" on certain offenders found guilty of the same crime.[212] The role of statutory mitigating circumstances, on the other hand, is to focus the sentencer's attention on those features of the crime or the offender which make mercy peculiarly appropriate. Among the aggravating circumstances listed in the Georgia statute are whether the defendant was previously convicted of a capital felony, whether he was serving out a life sentence when he escaped and committed murder, whether the murder victim was a peace officer, whether the crime was committed for pay, and whether the act endangered multiple lives. The sentencing body is required to make written findings documenting the existence of at least one statutory aggravating circumstance to justify its imposition of the death penalty.

Post-*Gregg* cases have continued to emphasize the need for clear, detailed and objective standards to guide the sentencing body's discretion in capital punishment cases. In *Godfrey v. Georgia*,[213] the Supreme Court ruled that a statutory aggravating factor authorizing imposition of the death penalty upon a finding that the murder "was outrageously or wantonly vile, horrible or inhuman in that it involved...depravity of mind, or an aggravated battery to the victim"[214] furnished an inadequate standard for differentiating between murderers who should be spared and those who deserved the death penalty. The Court observed that the listed factors normally accompany every intentional homicide. Hence, the statute failed to furnish the type of concrete

---

211 *Supra* note 204.

212 Zant v. Stephens, 462 U.S. 862, 103 S. Ct. 2733, 2742-2743, 77 L. Ed. 2d 235 (1983).

213 446 U.S. 420, 100 S. Ct. 1759, 64 L. Ed. 2d 398 (1980).

214 Lockett v. Ohio, 438 U.S. 586, 89 S. Ct. 2954, 57 L. Ed. 2d 973 (1978); Eddings v. Oklahoma, 455 U.S. 104, 102 S. Ct. 869, 71 L. Ed. 2d 1 (1982).

differentiating standards that the Constitution demands before an offender can be sentenced to death.

Insistence that sentencing bodies be permitted to hear and consider all relevant mitigating evidence concerning the background or character of the defendant, the circumstances of the offense or any other factor that might influence the sentencer to show mercy has been another constant theme in post-*Gregg* Supreme Court holdings. In *Lockett v. Ohio*,[215] the Supreme Court found Ohio's statute deficient for this reason. Under Ohio's scheme, the sentencing body was required to impose the death penalty if it found that the murder was accompanied by any of seven aggravating circumstances unless it also found that the victim had provoked the offense, the crime resulted from duress, or the accused was suffering from mental illness. The Supreme Court found that this statute unduly limited the sentencer's ability to show mercy. For a sentence to be valid under the Eighth Amendment, the sentencer must be permitted to hear and consider *all* possible mitigating evidence that the accused elects to offer in the hopes of escaping the death penalty.[216]

§ 10.19 – Capital punishment sentencing procedures revisited

In the years before *Furman*, the death penalty was imposed irrationally and unequally on the poor and on blacks. The Supreme Court's Eighth Amendment reforms of death penalty sentencing procedures were designed to eliminate arbitrary sentencing discretion in an effort to assure the existence of a rational basis for differentiating offenders who were selected to receive death sentences from those who were spared. The reforms have achieved a higher degree of rationality and fairness in sentencing, but it still remains true today that blacks and the poor are much more likely than others to receive the death penalty.

In *McCleskey v. Kemp*,[217] decided 15 years after the Supreme Court began its Eighth Amendment reforms in *Furman*, the Court received a devastating challenge to capital punishment sentencing. McCleskey, a black man sentenced to death by a Georgia jury for killing a white police officer during a robbery, used statistical evidence to demonstrate that, despite the Court's sentencing reforms, a significant disparity continued to exist in the frequency with which Georgia juries sentenced black defendants charged with killing white victims to death. His study showed that black defendants charged with

---

215 *Supra* note 214.

216 Eddings v. Oklahoma, *supra* note 214.

217 481 U.S. 279, 107 S. Ct. 1756, 95 L. Ed. 2d 262 (1987).

killing white victims were four times more likely than anyone else to receive a death sentence. McCleskey contended that these statistics demonstrated that racial considerations continued to play a role in Georgia's capital punishment sentencing and that, as a consequence, the Georgia system violated the Eighth Amendment. This was a serious challenge, a challenge which, as the Court recognized, extended to the very legitimacy of discretionary capital punishment sentencing by juries in a multiracial society. A sharply divided Court (5-4) voted to affirm McCleskey's sentence in an opinion which sadly and reluctantly concedes that the current system is still imperfect, but that it is the best a criminal justice system can do in a society firmly committed to the value of jury trials, where a majority of the members are white.

Mr. Justice Powell, who wrote the majority opinion, began his analysis by reviewing post-*Furman* sentencing reforms. These reforms had, in Justice Powell's opinion, narrowed and focused capital punishment sentencing discretion and had purged the system of arbitrary and irrational considerations, to the extent that it is legally possible to eliminate them. The Georgia capital punishment sentencing procedures had been pronounced in compliance with Eighth Amendment standards in *Gregg v. Georgia*[218] and had formed the pattern for death penalty reform statutes throughout this nation.

Mr. Justice Powell then addressed McCleskey's statistical study. He conceded that this study suggested the likelihood that racial considerations continued to enter into capital punishment sentencing decisions but noted that, under a system where sentencing discretion is required, sentencing disparities are inevitable. The risk that racial considerations may enter into capital punishment sentencing decisions was, in Justice Powell's estimate, not a constitutionally unacceptable one when that risk was assessed in light of the alternative of abolishing jury sentencing discretion in death penalty cases. After pointing out the values and benefits of jury sentencing, Powell proclaimed that there can be "no perfect procedure for deciding in which cases governmental authority should be used to impose death."[219] Since the existing system, despite its imperfections, had safeguards that made it as fair as possible, the choices were between declaring the system constitutionally adequate or junking jury sentencing in capital punishment cases. The majority opted for the former course.

---

218 428 U.S. 153, 96 S. Ct. 2909, 49 L. Ed. 2d 859 (1976).

219 McCleskey v. Kemp, *supra* note 217, 481 U.S. at 313, 107 S. Ct. at 1778, 95 L. Ed. 2d at 291.

§ 10.20 Summary

Under our criminal justice system, those charged with crime are entitled to receive their day in court and to enjoy various constitutional protections that have for centuries been considered indispensable to a fair and just trial. Included in the more significant procedural rights not discussed in earlier chapters are the Sixth Amendment right to a *speedy* and *public* trial before an *impartial* jury, the Sixth Amendment right to confront adverse witnesses, and the Eighth Amendment assurance that no punishment imposed will be either cruel or unusual.

1. Speedy trial

The constitutional guarantee of a speedy trial safeguards the accused's interest

(1) in being free from lengthy pretrial confinements where bail is unavailable,
(2) in avoiding extended periods of personal anxiety and public suspicion, and
(3) in being tried before time has destroyed his capacity to prepare a meaningful defense.

The Sixth Amendment says that the "*accused* shall enjoy the right to a speedy...trial." The Supreme Court has read this language literally and has ruled that the Sixth Amendment affords no protection against pre-accusatory delays.

The Sixth Amendment right to a speedy trial attaches from the time a suspect becomes an *accused*, either through his arrest, indictment, filing of an information, or other method utilized for lodging formal charges. There are four factors on which a court will focus in determining whether the delay between accusation and trial has violated the Sixth Amendment:

(1) the length of the delay,
(2) the reasons for the delay,
(3) the defendant's timely assertion of his rights, and
(4) whether he has been prejudiced.

The length of the delay is important as a triggering mechanism. Once there has been a presumptively prejudicial delay, the court is obliged to examine and weigh the other three factors.

2. *Public trial*

The guarantee of a *public* trial was designed as a check against official perversions of the justice system. Openness of the proceedings serves other interests as well (i.e., improves the quality of testimony, affords the public an opportunity to learn about government, etc.). The public trial guarantee is not absolute; the judge may clear the courtroom temporarily when, for example, it is necessary to enable a very young or timid witness to testify.

3. *Jury trial*

The Sixth Amendment guarantee of the right to a jury trial is available in state as well as federal prosecutions. Though the Constitution assures that jury trials will be available in "all criminal prosecutions," the Supreme Court has read the common law petty-offense exception into the Sixth Amendment. An offense is "petty," for purposes of dispensing with the constitutional obligation to grant a jury trial if it is punishable by no more than six months' imprisonment. The common-law jury was a body of 12 persons selected from the community and charged with responsibility for listening to evidence developed in open court and reaching a *unanimous* verdict. Although this pattern still prevails in federal courts and in most state jurisdictions, several states have by statute reduced the jury's size or have authorized less-than-unanimous criminal verdicts. Modifications of the jury's common law features are not offensive to the Sixth Amendment, provided that the substance of the jury trial safeguard is unimpaired. The Sixth Amendment requires that members of the jury be drawn from a source fairly representative of a cross section of the community.

4. *Fair and impartial trial*

The requirement of a fair and impartial trial precludes trying an accused before a judge who has a financial stake in the outcome or who harbors personal ill-will against the accused. Other irregularities that may prejudice the accused's right to a fair trial defy meaningful categorization, but two stand out and were given special coverage in this chapter:

(a) prejudicial pretrial publicity; and
(b) the prosecutor's failure to live up to his constitutional disclosure responsibilities.

(a) Prejudicial publicity

The Constitution does not require that the jurors selected be entirely unfamiliar with the case, but it does require that they approach their task with an open mind -- i.e., that they be capable of setting aside preconceived notions as to guilt and of rendering a verdict based upon evidence developed in the courtroom. When there has been massive pretrial publicity which gives reason for concern about the trial's integrity, corrective measures are required. Trial continuances and changes of venue are the two most common. The Supreme Court has resisted efforts to solve the pretrial publicity problem through gag orders limiting what the media can publish. Police departments should promulgate guidelines covering departmental press releases. By controlling the flow of information reaching media representatives, police departments can make a significant contribution toward safeguarding the accused's right to a fair trial.

(b) Prosecutor's disclosure obligation

The public prosecutor, as a representative of the government, has a duty to see that no one is unfairly convicted. This obligation includes the duty:

(1) to correct perjured testimony if the government knows it to be false, and
(2) to disclose to the accused favorable evidence in its possession that is material to the accused's guilt or punishment.

However, the failure of the police to preserve evidence potentially useful to the accused is grounds for complaint only if the evidence is destroyed in bad faith.

5. *Confrontation*

The Sixth Amendment right of an accused to confront adverse witnesses has been made binding upon the states through the Fourteenth Amendment. The right to confront adverse witnesses guarantees the accused the right to be present in the courtroom when testimony is taking place. The constitutional policy underlying the confrontation clause is concern for the trustworthiness of the testimony. When a witness testifies in court, he is under oath and subject to cross-examination, and the judge or jury, as the case may be, has an opportunity to listen to him, observe his demeanor and form an independent opinion as to his truthfulness.

6. *Cruel and unusual punishment*

The Eighth Amendment ban on cruel and unusual punishments, now binding on the states through the Fourteenth Amendment, precludes punishments that are:

(1) aimed at human afflictions rather than antisocial behavior,
(2) inflict wanton and unnecessary pain, and those that are
(3) excessively severe in relationship to the offense for which imposed.

In the case of capital punishment, the Eighth Amendment condemns sentencing schemes that are mandatory, on the one hand, or which fail to provide adequate standards to guide the sentencer's discretion, on the other. The central principle that unifies these diverse applications of the Eighth Amendment is respect for human dignity. Legislatures and prison administrators must never forget that even those convicted of the most atrocious crimes remain members of the human race and that society itself is debased when any of its members receive dehumanizing punishments.

Chapter 11
CIVIL RIGHTS
AND CIVIL RIGHTS LEGISLATION*

> *[I]n view of the Constitution, in the eye of the law, there is in this country no superior, dominant, ruling class of citizens. There is no caste here. Our Constitution is color-blind, and neither knows nor tolerates classes among citizens. In respect of civil rights, all citizens are equal before the law. The humblest is the peer of the most powerful. The law regards man as man, and takes no account of his surroundings or of his color when his civil rights as guaranteed by the supreme law of the land are involved.*
>
> Mr. Justice Harlan,
> dissenting in *Plessy v. Ferguson*,
> 163 U.S. 537, 559 (1896).

---
* *by Jacqueline R. Kanovitz*

§ 11.1 Historical background

In the pre-Civil War era, a Negro slave had no legal status. He was regarded as little more than a chattel or valued possession. He could not bring suit in a court of law, own property, make contracts, marry or enter into other normal legal relationships.[1] As a precaution against assisting runaway slaves, proprietors of inns and other public accommodations were, in most localities, prohibited by law from receiving persons of African descent.[2]

The institution of slavery found sanction in the Constitution of the United States. The property rights of the master were recognized and protected under Article IV, section 2, which guaranteed the return of fugitive slaves. The political consequences of slavery were treated in Article I, section 2, which provided that slaves were to be counted as three-fifths of a person for purposes of apportioning representatives to the lower house of Congress. On the eve of the Civil War, the Supreme Court placed its stamp of legitimacy on the institution of slavery. In the infamous *Dred Scott* decision,[3] Mr. Chief Justice Taney proclaimed that the dark race as a class was inferior and altogether unfit to associate with the white race, either in social or political relations;[4] and whether enslaved or emancipated, the Negro could not be a citizen of the United States or claim the rights and privileges guaranteed by the Constitution. This, then, was the legal status of the black man on the eve of the Civil War.

§ 11.2 –Reconstruction amendments and legislation

After the Civil War ended, Congress turned its attention to the tragic plight of the millions of black people who had been left homeless and jobless in bitter, war-ravaged communities. Emancipation of the former slaves was accomplished by the Thirteenth Amendment. Ratified in 1865, the Thirteenth Amendment proclaimed that "[n]either slavery nor involuntary servitude...shall exist within the United States, or any place subject to their jurisdiction," and authorized Congress to enact appropriate legislation to carry this constitutional proclamation into effect.

The blessings of freedom were not immediately realized by the emancipated slaves. Hostile Southern legislatures responded to the Thirteenth

---

1 Civil Rights Cases, 109 U.S. 3, 3 S. Ct. 18, 27 L. Ed. 835 (1883).

2 *Id.*

3 Dred Scott v. Sanford, 60 U.S. (19 How.) 393, 15 L. Ed. 691 (1856).

4 *Id.* at 407, 15 L. Ed. at 701.

Amendment by enacting Black Codes designed to compel the newly freed slaves to return to the services of their former masters. To accomplish this, Black Codes prohibited former slaves from holding, owning or leasing property, entering into contractual relationships, or engaging in any occupation.[5] A period of racial turbulence and violent unrest followed as terrorist organizations like the Ku Klux Klan and the Knights of the White Camellia sprang up in numerous local communities.

The Congress that met at the close of the Civil War faced some of the most difficult problems that have ever beset any nation. Military governments were set up in the former Confederate states, and traditions of self-government in the South gave way to a period of federal domination. In the decade that followed, two more constitutional amendments were ratified, and a host of federal civil rights statutes were hastily enacted.

The Fourteenth Amendment was ratified in 1868. Unlike the Thirteenth, whose mandate applies to all, the directives of the Fourteenth Amendment were addressed only to the states. The immediate object of the Fourteenth Amendment was to protect the newly freed slaves from arbitrary and unequal treatment at the hands of hostile state legislatures and local government officials. To this end, the Fourteenth Amendment first declared that all persons born within the United States were citizens and then provided:

> No State shall make or enforce any law which shall abridge the privileges or immunities of citizens of the United States; nor shall any State deprive any person of life, liberty, or property, without due process of law; nor deny to any person within its jurisdiction the equal protection of the laws.

By virtue of section 5, Congress was authorized to enact appropriate legislation to implement the Fourteenth Amendment. The process of amendment was completed in 1870 with the ratification of the Fifteenth Amendment, dealing with suffrage, and providing that the right of a citizen to vote could not be denied on account of "race, color, or previous condition of servitude."

In the winter of 1865-1866, a Joint Congressional Committee on Reconstruction was set up to investigate reports of racial mistreatment and turbulent conditions in the South.[6] The results of this investigation led to the adoption of the Civil Rights Act of 1866, the first of many federal civil rights

---

5 Slaughter-House Cases, 83 U.S. (16 Wall.) 36, 21 L. Ed. 394 (1973).

6 United States Commission on Civil Rights, LAW ENFORCEMENT: A REPORT OF EQUAL PROTECTION IN THE SOUTH 6-10 (1965).

laws to come out of the Reconstruction era. Section 1 of the Civil Rights Act of 1868 provided, among other things, that:

> citizens of every race and color, without regard to any previous condition of slavery or involuntary servitude,...shall have the same right, in every State and Territory in the United States, to make and enforce contracts, to sue, be parties, and give evidence, to inherit, purchase, lease, sell, hold, and convey real and personal property, and to full and equal benefit of all laws and proceedings for the security of person and property, as is enjoyed by white citizens.[7]

Section 2 of the Civil Rights Act of 1866 had, and continues to have, direct impact upon the professional conduct of law enforcement officers. Inspired by reports of racial mistreatment at the hands of local officials, section 2 made it a federal offense, punishable by a $1,000 fine, one year imprisonment, or both, for any person acting "under color of any law, statute, ordinance, regulation, or custom" of any state to deprive any inhabitant of the United States of certain enumerated rights.[8] Section 2, with a few changes and modifications, survives today as one of the two major federal criminal civil rights statutes. The text of the modern revision is presently codified at 18 U.S.C. §242. Its companion statute, 18 U.S.C. §241, is derived from the Civil Rights Act of 1870[9] and makes it a federal offense, punishable by fines up to $5,000, imprisonment for as much as 10 years, or both, to conspire to "injure, oppress, threaten, or intimidate any citizen in the free exercise or enjoyment of any right or privilege secured to him by the Constitution or laws of the United States."[10]

The Ku Klux Klan Act of 1871 was the last significant enactment of the Reconstruction period. Section 1 of the Ku Klux Klan Act,[11] which survives today as 42 U.S.C. § 1983, creates a civil cause of action, enforceable in fed-

---

7 Act of April 9, 1866, ch. 31, § 1, 14 Stat. 27, reenacted as 42 U.S.C. §§ 1981 and 1982. As a result of judicial misgivings about the constitutionality of § 1, (today 42 U.S.C. §§ 1981 and 1982) this statutue was allowed to gather dust for a full century after its enactment. In 1968, the Supreme Court resuscitated the 1866 law in *Jones v. Alfred H. Mayer Co.*, 392 U.S. 409, 88 S. Ct. 2186, 20 L. Ed. 2d 1189 (1968), and it is today a potent civil rights measure. The current interpretation of §§ 1981 and 1982 is discussed in § 11.4, *infra*.

8 Act of April 9, 1866, ch. 31, § 2, 14 Stat. 27.

9 Act of May 31, 1870, ch. 114, 16 Stat. 140, 144.

10 Since police are subject to criminal prosecution under §§ 241 and 242, these statutes are treated in fuller detail in §§ 11.12 and 11.13 *infra*.

11 Act of April 20, 1871, ch. 22, § 1, 17 Stat. 13.

eral courts, against any person, acting under color of state authority, who deprives another of any rights, privileges or immunities secured by the Constitution or laws of the United States. Section 1983 is the civil counterpart of 18 U.S.C. § 242. Since most action undertaken by a police officer is under color of his state authority, a law enforcement officer who abuses his official authority may find himself in federal court defending a section 242 criminal action or a section 1983 damage suit. More will be said about these Reconstruction era laws in the sections which follow.

For the present, it is enough to note that conservative early interpretations deprived these Reconstruction statutes of the full measure of their legal impact until almost a century after their enactment. Ironically, their resurrection came after the Congress of the United States had struggled in 1964 with the enactment of a public accommodations[12] and equal employment opportunities act,[13] and in 1968, with an open housing law.[14] In retrospect, the bitterly fought controversies in the 1960s as to whether this nation should have a public accommodations law, an equal employment opportunities act, and a fair housing law were tempests in a teapot. The black citizens of the nation had virtually all of these rights already and had had them for almost a century. The Reconstruction Congress had taken care of this. It remained only for the Supreme Court to interpret the Reconstruction laws as broadly as they read.[15]

---

12 Civil Rights Act of 1964, tit. II, § 201, 78 Stat. 243, 42 U.S.C. § 2000(a) *et seq.*, guarantees all persons the right to service in hotels, motels, restaurants, motion picture theaters and other places of public accomodation without regard to race, color, religion or national origin. The remedies provided for are civil.

13 Civil Rights Act of 1964, tit. VII, § 703, 78 Stat. 255, 42 U.S.C. § 2000(e) *et seq.*, makes it an unlawful employment practice for an employer to fail or refuse to hire or to discharge any individual or otherwise to discriminate against an individual with respect to his compensation, terms, conditions or privileges of employment because of his race, color, religion, sex or national origin. Similar types of restrictions are imposed upon employment agency and labor union practices. Title VII is not a criminal statute. The remedies for enforcement are civil. The impact of Title VII on police personnel practices is considered in Chapter 12.

14 Civil Rights Act of 1968, tit. VIII, 82 Stat. 81, 42 U.S.C. § 3601 *et seq.*, makes it unlawful to discriminate against any person in the sale or rental of real estate because of that person's race, color, religion or national origin. As with the other civil rights laws enacted during the 1960s, the remedies provided for the enforcement of the 1968 law are civil rather than criminal.

15 *See* § 11.4, *infra*.

§ 11.3 – Separate but equal

By 1877, the crusading zeal of the Northern liberals and radicals had run its course. The last of the federal troops were withdrawn from the South, and white rule was again restored. In 1883, the Supreme Court formally announced that the period of national wardship for the black man had come to an end, and the time had arrived for him to take up his own struggle for political equality.[16] The nation turned its attention to industrial expansion and the conquest of the West. For the next 70 years, the South would be left, without substantial interference by the Congress or the Supreme Court, to formulate its own solutions to racial issues. The solutions which the South proposed took the form of segregation codes, designed to cut off all social intercourse between the races. By the last decade of the nineteenth century, *Jim Crow* laws had begun their debut. State legislatures proceeded cautiously at first because doubts existed as to the constitutionality of these measures. The Supreme Court's endorsement came in the 1896 case of *Plessy v. Ferguson*.[17] Plessy, an individual of one-eighth Negro descent, had been criminally prosecuted for violating a state statute requiring racial segregation in public carriers. On appeal, he contended that the statute violated the Thirteenth and Fourteenth Amendments. Eight members of the Supreme Court disagreed. They proclaimed that there was no constitutional infirmity in state-compelled separation of the races provided that equal facilities were available to the members of each race. Mr. Justice Harlan alone dissented, sounding what would become the position of the Court in 1954:

> [I]n view of the Constitution, in the eye of the law there is in this country no superior, dominant, ruling class of citizens. There is no caste here. Our Constitution is color-blind, and neither knows nor tolerates classes among citizens. In respect of civil rights, all citizens are equal before the law. The humblest is the peer of the most powerful. The law regards man as man and takes no account of his surroundings or his color when his civil rights as guaranteed by the supreme law of the land are involved.[18]

§ 11.4 – The second Reconstruction

Plessy v. Ferguson provided a legal foundation for the segregation codes that flourished in the South for the next sixty years. In 1954, the Supreme

---

16 Civil Rights Cases, 109 U.S. 3, 3 S. Ct. 18, 27 L. Ed. 835 (1883).

17 163 U.S. 537, 16 S. Ct. 1138, 41 L. Ed. 256 (1896).

18 *Id*. at 559, 16 S. Ct. at 1164, 41 L. Ed. at 263-264 (Harlan, J., dissenting).

Court handed down the landmark decision of *Brown v. Board of Education*,[19] where it announced that "separate but equal" no longer satisfied the Constitution within the field of public education. It soon became apparent that *Brown* was not limited to the field of public education. The Fourteenth Amendment equal protection clause, as today construed, requires the government to treat citizens of all races equally. State and local governments cannot discriminate in public programs or in the use of public facilities,[20] nor can they compel or assist private individuals to engage in racially discriminatory practices.[21] The era of government-sponsored barriers to full racial equality was over.

Striking down state laws sanctioning or compelling separation of the races and eliminating discrimination in government-operated programs and facilities was not sufficient to integrate the black man into the "Great Society." Strong barriers of private prejudice remained as formidable obstacles to full racial equality. So long as private employment opportunities and private housing markets remained closed to the black man, he was destined to remain a second-class citizen. The focus of the 1960's civil rights movement shifted to this new frontier.

The big constitutional issue of the 1960s was whether Congress had the power to direct private individuals -- the nation's restaurant and hotel proprietors, employers, and real estate owners -- to lay aside their prejudice and treat all persons alike in their business and professional dealings. If such a power did exist, it was not to be found in the Fourteenth Amendment. Its directive, "No *State* shall...deny to any person within its jurisdiction the equal protection of the laws," had served the civil rights movement well in its drive to eliminate discriminatory government practices, but the focal point now was the private sector; by settled interpretation, the Fourteenth Amendment did not reach or operate upon discriminatory practices engaged in by private citizens.[22] The Thirteenth Amendment's command that "[n]either slavery nor involuntary servitude...shall exist within the United States...," was not similarly restricted, but it was originally passed over as a source of congressional power to eradicate private barriers to racial equality for an entirely different

---

19 347 U.S. 483, 74 S. Ct. 686, 98 L. Ed. 873 (1954).

20 *See e.g.*, Holmes v. City of Atlanta, 350 U.S. 879, 76 S. Ct. 141, 100 L. Ed. 776 (1955) (remanded); Simkins v. Moses H. Cone Mem'l Hosp., 323 F.2d 959 (4th Cir. 1963), *cert. denied*, 376 U.S. 938, 84 S. Ct. 793, 11 L. Ed. 2d 659 (1964); Kerr v. Enoch Pratt Free Library, 149 F.2d 212 (4th Cir.), *cert. denied*, 326 U.S. 721, 66 S. Ct. 26, 90 L. Ed. 2d 427 (1945).

21 Adickes v. S.H. Kress & Co., 398 U.S. 144, 90 S. Ct. 1598, 26 L. Ed. 2d 142 (1970); Shelley v. Kraemer, 334 U.S. 1, 68 S. Ct. 836, 92 L. Ed. 1161 (1948).

22 *Id.*

reason. Discrimination, without more, did not appear to constitute a reestablishment of slavery and, consequently, private discriminatory practices were thought to fall beyond the reach of Congress's power to implement the Thirteenth Amendment.

Despite this, several important race relations measures were enacted by Congress during the 1960s; the primary source of federal power relied upon was the Interstate Commerce Clause.[23] With a little imagination, discrimination in the operation of places of public accommodation, in the sale and rental of housing, and in employment practices could be linked to the free flow of goods and services across state lines.[24] During the 1960s, Congress drafted legislation to the limits of its interstate commerce powers. The first significant enactment came in 1964. Title II of the Civil Rights Act of 1964, known as the Public Accommodations Law,[25] guaranteed all persons the right to equal services in hotels, motels, restaurants, motion picture houses, and other privately-owned places of public accommodation, without regard to race, color, religion, or national origin. Title VII of the same enactment, known as the Equal Employment Opportunities Law,[26] afforded similarly broad protection against discriminatory practices upon the part of employers, employment agencies and labor unions. In 1968, Congress turned its attention to the housing problem and enacted the Fair Housing Law[27] which condemned discrimination in the sale and rental of private housing. The civil rights measures of the 1960s were not criminal statutes; they were and are enforced by means of civil sanctions. Was congressional reliance on the commerce powers well-founded? The Supreme Court's response was affirmative. In *Katzenbach v. McClung*,[28] it upheld the constitutionality of the Public Accommodations Law[29] as applied to a restaurant whose impact upon interstate commerce was marginal.

In 1968, while the ultimate reach of Congress's power to regulate private discrimination under the Commerce Clause was still unsettled, the Supreme

---

23 *See e.g.*, S. Rep. No. 872, 88th Cong., 2d Sess., 12-13.

24 Heart of Atlanta Motel v. United States, 379 U.S. 241, 85 S. Ct. 348, 13 L. Ed. 2d 258 (1964); Katzenbach v. McClung, 379 U.S. 294, 85 S. Ct. 377, 13 L. Ed. 2d 290 (1964).

25 Civil Rights Act of 1964, tit. II, § 201, 78 Stat. 243, 42 U.S.C. § 2000(e) *et seq.*

26 Civil Rights Act of 1964, tit. VII, § 703, 78 Stat. 243, 42 U.S.C. § 2000(e)-2 *et seq.* The impact of Title VII on police employment practices is covered in Chapter 12 of this book.

27 Civil Rights Act of 1968, tit. VIII, § 801, 82 Stat. 81, 42 U.S.C. § 3601 *et seq.*

28 379 U.S. 294, 85 S. Ct. 377, 13 L. Ed. 2d 290 (1964).

29 Civil Rights Act of 1964, tit. II, § 201, 78 Stat. 243, 42 U.S.C. § 2000(a) *et seq.*

Court decided *Jones v. Alfred H. Mayer Co.*[30] This case gave a revolutionary interpretation to the Thirteenth Amendment. Prior to the effective date of the 1968 Fair Housing Law, a housing dispute arose between Jones, a black man, and the Alfred H. Mayer Co. Jones claimed that Mayer's refusal to sell to him was racially motivated. His attorney found a musty Reconstruction-vintage statute, 42 U.S.C. § 1982,[31] dusted it off, and filed suit in a federal court asking for an injunction. The Supreme Court ruled that the Reconstruction Congress intended by this law to prohibit *all* racially motivated refusals to sell or rent housing, private as well as governmental and, more importantly, that Congress had the power to do this. The authority came from the enabling clause of the Thirteenth Amendment which, in the words of the Court, empowered Congress *"to pass all laws necessary and proper for abolishing all badges and incidents of slavery in the United States."*[32]

Jones v. Alfred H. Mayer Co. is a landmark on several different scores. First, it interpreted the enabling clause of the Thirteenth Amendment as a blanket authorization to Congress to "determine what are the badges and incidents of slavery, and...to translate that determination into effective legislation"[33] condemning racially discriminatory practices of private individuals. No longer would it be necessary for Congress to regulate private race relations under the guise of removing "impediments" to the free flow of interstate commerce. Congress has virtually unlimited power under the Thirteenth Amendment to legislate against racial discrimination -- private as well as public, federal as well as state. Equally important, *Jones* breathed new life into several Reconstruction civil rights measures which had lain dormant on the books for a century.

The civil rights laws enacted during the 1960s possessed some visible earmarks of political feasibility and compromise. In the Public Accommodations Act of 1964, for instance, Congress exempted the so-called "Mrs. Murphy's boarding houses," owner-occupied establishments having five or fewer rooms to let.[34] Furthermore, several important areas where racial discrimination continues to be practiced were left untouched by civil rights measures enacted during the 1960s. Discrimination in private school education provides one notable example. The Reconstruction statutes resurrected in *Jones*

---

30 392 U.S. 409, 88 S. Ct. 2186, 20 L. Ed. 2d 1189 (1968).

31 The text of 42 U.S.C. § 1982 provides: All citizens of the United States shall have the same right, in every State and Territory, as is enjoyed by white citizens thereof to inherit, purchase, lease, sell, hold, and convey real and personal property.

32 392 U.S. at 439, 88 S. Ct. at 2203, 20 L. Ed. 2d at 1207 (emphasis in original).

33 *Id.* at 440, 88 S. Ct. at 2203, 20 L. Ed. at 1207.

34 42 U.S.C. § 2000 (a)(b)(1).

provide machinery for legal redress in these areas. In *Runyon v. McCrary*,[35] the Supreme Court held that the refusal of a private, commercially operated, nonsectarian school to admit black children because of their race was actionable under 42 U.S.C. § 1981. (Section 1981[36] is another Reconstruction-era statute enacted by Congress pursuant to its powers to enforce the Thirteenth Amendment.) One hundred years after the Civil War was over, this country experienced what will probably be known to our grandchildren as the second Reconstruction, a period of reforms in race relations in which the courts were at least as instrumental as the legislature.

The remaining sections of this chapter will focus on federal civil and criminal remedies available for holding police officers constitutionally accountable for misbehavior while acting in their official capacity. Like the statutes considered above, these remedial statutes derive from the Reconstruction era. Though mistreatment of racial minorities at the hands of local public officials provided the original impetus for their enactment, these Reconstruction-era measures have broad application in modern times. Forty-two U.S.C. § 1983, 18 U.S.C. § 241, and 18 U.S.C. § 242 are not merely race-protection statutes. They protect the constitutional rights of all the nation's inhabitants.

§ 11.5 Federal civil remedies for official misconduct (42 U.S.C. § 1983)

Forty-two U.S.C. § 1983[37] creates a federal civil cause of action for the recovery of damages against any person who, while acting "under color of any [state] statute, ordinance, regulation, custom, or usage," deprives or causes another to be deprived of "rights, privileges, or immunities secured by the constitution and laws" of the United States. Originally enacted as Section 1 of the Ku Klux Klan Act of 1871,[38] Section 1983 is widely used today to hold police officers and other state officials accountable for their unconstitutional

---

[35] 427 U.S. 160, 96 S. Ct. 2586, 49 L. Ed. 2d 415 (1976).

[36] 42 U.S.C. § 1981 provides, in pertinent part, that "[a]ll persons...shall have the same right...to make and enforce contracts...as is enjoyed by white citizens...."

[37] The full text of 42 U.S.C. § 1983 reads: "Every person who, under color of any statute, ordinance, regulation, custom, or usage, of any State or Territory, subjects, or causes to be subjected, any citizen of the United States or other person within the jurisdiction thereof to the deprivation of any rights, privileges, or immunities secured by the Constitution and law, shall be liable to the party injured in an action at law, suit in equity, or other proper proceeding for redress."

[38] Act of April 20, 1871, ch. 22, § 1, 17 Stat. 13.

behavior. Between 1967 and 1971 alone, 13,000 federal damage suits were filed against police officers.[39] From appearances, the volume of litigation based on Section 1983 is still on the increase. The federal remedy created by Section 1983 is completely supplemental to state tort law remedies and an aggrieved party need not exhaust state judicial remedies before seeking damages under this section.[40]

To state a claim for damages under section 1983, the party suing must establish that:

> (1) the defendant acted "under color of" state law in performing the acts complained of, and
> (2) deprived or caused him to be deprived of some right, privilege or immunity guaranteed by the Constitution or laws of the United States.[41]

The mental state the defendant must possess for liability under section 1983 varies with the underlying constitutional violation alleged. For some constitutional violations a willful intent is necessary, while for others a mental state of reckless indifference or perhaps simple unreasonableness suffices.[42]

Police officers have a very important legal defense against section 1983 liability, known as the *qualified immunity defense*.[43] Even though a police officer may have behaved unconstitutionally, he is excused from damage liability under the qualified immunity defense if the illegality of his conduct was unclear when he acted, or if a reasonable officer, based on the facts and information in his possession, could have believed that he was acting lawfully.[44]

---

[39] Carmen, *An Overview of Civil and Criminal Liabilities of Police Officers and Departments,* 9 AM. J. CRIM. L. 33 (1981).

[40] Monroe v. Pape, 365 U.S. 167, 81 S. Ct. 473, 5 L. Ed. 2d 492 (1961), *overruled in part*, Monell v. Department of Social Serv., 436 U.S. 658, 98 S. Ct. 2018, 56 L. Ed. 2d 611 (1978); Haring v. Prosise, 462 U.S. 306, 103 S. Ct. 2368, 76 L. Ed. 2d 595 (1983).

[41] Gomez v. Toledo, 446 U.S. 635, 100 S. Ct. 1920, 64 L. Ed. 2d 572 (1980); Parratt v. Taylor, 451 U.S. 527, 101 S. Ct. 1980, 68 L. Ed. 2d 420 (1981).

[42] The state of mind a defendant must possess to incur liability under section 1983 is covered in § 11.9 *infra*.

[43] The qualified immunity defense is covered in § 11.10 *infra*.

[44] Harlow v. Fitzgerald, 457 U.S. 800, 102 S. Ct. 2727, 73 L. Ed. 2d 396 (1982); Anderson v. Creighton, 483 U.S. 635, 107 S. Ct. 3034, 97 L. Ed. 2d 523 (1987).

§ 11.6 – "Under color of" state law

Section 1983 is based upon the Fourteenth Amendment;[45] consequently, it reaches only "state action" or action taken "under color of" state law. Any official conduct engaged in by a law enforcement officer pursuant to some state law authorizing or requiring this action, satisfies the section 1983 "under color of" state law requirement. State law, however, rarely authorizes, let alone requires, an officer to violate federal constitutional or statutory rights. Can an officer be held liable under section 1983 for acts in excess of his state law authority?

1. *Officer's section 1983 liability for acts in excess of his state authority*

In *Monroe v. Pape*,[46] the Supreme Court faced the issue of whether a police officer could be regarded as acting "under color of" state law and, thus, be liable under section 1983 when he exceeds the lawful authority entrusted him by the state. Monroe brought suit against thirteen members of the Chicago police department, alleging that they had broken into his home without a warrant or probable cause, that they had ransacked the premises, had beaten and arrested him, and that ultimately they released him without charges. The officers defended against section 1983 liability on the grounds that the acts alleged were not authorized by state law and were in fact a violation of it; consequently, these acts could not be regarded as having been performed "under color of" state law. The Supreme Court disagreed and ruled that section 1983's "under color of" state law requirement did not require actual state legal authorization for the acts complained of; it was sufficient that the state had placed these officers in a position where they were able to assert a "colorable claim" or "pretense" of state authority for their conduct. In the course of its opinion, the Court uttered what has become the traditional definition of acting "under color of" state law:

> Misuse of power, possessed by virtue of state law and made possible only because the wrongdoer is clothed with the authority of state law, is action taken 'under color of' state law.[47]

---

[45] District of Columbia v. Carter, 409 U.S. 418, 93 S. Ct. 602, 34 L. Ed. 2d 613 (1973).

[46] 365 U.S. 167, 81 S. Ct. 473, 5 L. Ed. 2d 492 (1961).

[47] *Id.* at 184, 81 S. Ct. at 482, 5 L. Ed. 2d at 503 *quoting* United States v. Classic, 313 U.S. 299, 326 (1941).

It is significant that the *Monroe* defendants were purporting to act in the line of duty in performing their official responsibilities when they engaged in the unconstitutional behavior for which they were sued. The fact that the defendant is a police officer does not mean that every act he performs is "under color of" state law. When a police officer acts in a private capacity, his legal liability is no different than that of any other citizen. The line between behavior "under color of" legal authority and private acts, however, is not always an easy line to draw. To complicate matters, courts have consistently stated that whether the officer is in uniform or out of it, or whether he is on duty or off, is not controlling.[48] Where can the line between private misbehavior and misbehavior "under color of" a police officer's state legal authority be drawn?

Decisions holding an officer's conduct to be "under color of" his legal authority fall into two categories. The first category includes acts ostensibly undertaken in an official capacity. When an officer intends or purports to act in the line of duty, such as when he interrogates, conducts searches, makes arrests or engages in other investigatory or public safety functions, he is acting "under color of" law even when he oversteps the boundaries of his lawful authority. Concerning actions undertaken in the line of duty, it does not matter whether the officer is in uniform or "on duty" in the strict sense.[49] Courts have found police officers to be acting "under color of" their legal authority, even though they are off-duty and in civilian clothes, when they act within the ambit of their official duties. The reason is that whenever an officer is engaged in performing the responsibilities of his office, he is asserting at least a "colorable claim" or "pretense" of state legal authority for his actions. He is thus acting "under color of" state law as *Monroe v. Pape* defines this phase.

The second category involves misbehavior made possible only because the wrongdoer is a police officer. Even though an officer is not engaged in performing any actual or purported duties of his office, he will still be treated as acting "under color of" his state authority if his status as a police officer materially aids him in committing the wrongs for which he is sued. Unless the officer was ostensibly acting within the line of duty or unless his official position aided him in his wrongdoing, the wrongs represent private misbe-

---

48 Stengel v. Belcher, 522 F.2d 438 (6th Cir. 1975), *cert. granted*, 425 U.S. 910, 96 S. Ct.1505, 47 L. Ed. 2d 760, *cert. dismissed*, 429 U.S. 118, 97 S. Ct. 514, 50 L. Ed. 2d 269 (1976); Robinson v. Davis, 447 F.2d 753 (4th Cir. 1971), *cert. denied*, 405 U.S. 979, 92 S. Ct. 1204, 31 L. Ed. 2d 254 (1972); Rogers v. Fuller, 410 F. Supp. 187, 191 (N.D.N.C. 1976); Johnson v. Hackett, 284 F. Supp. 933, 937 (E.D. Pa. 1968).

49 Davis v. Murphy, 559 F.2d 1098 (7th Cir. 1977).

havior. An officer cannot be sued for private wrongs under § 1983, though he might be liable under the tort law of his state.

Stengel v. Belcher[50] illustrates action taken in the line of duty, though not in uniform. An off-duty, out-of-uniform police officer witnessed several patrons engage in a brawl in the tavern where he was drinking. Without identifying himself as a police officer, he intervened in an attempt to restore order; a scuffle followed; the officer drew his gun and fired. Two men were mortally wounded and a third was injured. Trial testimony established that, under departmental regulations, police officers were required to carry pistols and to halt criminal activity even when they were off duty. The court ruled that the officer was acting "under color of" his state authority and not as a private citizen when he used excessive force in attempting to quiet a disturbance. An officer who oversteps constitutional boundaries while acting in the line of duty, acts "under color of" his legal authority and is subject to a section 1983 suit.

Catlette v. United States[51] illustrates misbehavior made possible only because the wrongdoer is a police officer. A group of Jehovah's Witnesses sought legal protection from a gang of local ruffians who were threatening them with violence. When they reached the deputy sheriff's office, he detained them, telephoned the gang, and then joined with the gang in forcing these frightened men to drink castor oil and to submit to other indignities. Even though the deputy had removed his badge before engaging in sadistic behavior that was not even remotely related to the duties of his office, the court found the deputy's behavior to be "under color of" his legal authority. In *Crews v. United States*,[52] a town marshal bull-whipped a black man and forced him to leap to his death from a bridge. That court found the marshal's acts to be "under color of" state law because he had used his office to feign an arrest and to take the black man into custody so that he could victimize him.

Catlette and *Crews* are not examples of excesses committed in the line of duty since neither officer intended nor purported to perform anything his official duties permitted, let alone required him to do. These officers acted "under color of" their legal authority in the sense that their misconduct -- the ability to detain the victims in the one case and to take the victim into custody in the other -- was made possible only because "the wrongdoer [was] clothed with the authority of state law."[53]

---

50 *Supra* note 48.

51 132 F.2d 902 (4th Cir. 1943).

52 160 F.2d 746 (5th Cir. 1947).

53 Monroe v. Pape, *supra* notes 46 and 47.

Where the police officer engages in misbehavior that is neither related to his employment responsibilities nor facilitated by his badge, he acts as a private citizen and the injured party must look to state tort law remedies for his redress. In *Watkins v. Oaklawn Jockey Club*,[54] the court held that a police officer, working during his off-duty hours as a private guard at a race track, could not be sued under section 1983 for ordering the plaintiff to leave the track, where the officer made it clear that he was issuing this order on instruction of the track owners. In another case, the court refused to treat an off-duty, nonuniformed police officer's involvement in an altercation as conduct "under color of" his legal authority, even though the officer was driving in an undercover police vehicle, where the altercation was over a personal matter and the officer never identified himself as a police officer, showed his badge, made an arrest or in any other way indicated that he was acting in an official capacity.[55]

Occasionally acts committed while a uniformed police officer is on duty may fall outside the "color of" the officer's legal authority. In *Delcambre v. Delcambre*,[56] the court dismissed a section 1983 action against a local police chief who had assaulted his sister-in-law at the police station while he was on duty, where the altercation arose out of a family matter and the chief did not arrest, charge or take any other acts in the performance of his official duties. In *Johnson v. Hackett*,[57] a uniformed police officer, while on duty, yelled racial slurs at a pedestrian who was doing no wrong and challenged this man to fight. This court, too, refused to treat the officer's behavior as "under color of" his legal authority. Both cases were correctly decided because the misconduct of these officers bore no relation to their official duties; nor did their status as police officers aid them in perpetrating the acts for which they were sued.

In summation, state and local police officers act "under color" of their legal authority for purposes of Section 1983 actions whenever they intend or purport to be acting in an official capacity, or when their official position aids them in perpetuating the wrong.

---

[54] 183 F.2d 440 (8th Cir. 1950).

[55] Manning v. Jones, 696 F. Supp. 1231 (S.D. Ind. 1988).

[56] 635 F.2d 407 (5th Cir. 1981).

[57] 284 F. Supp. 933 (E.D. Pa. 1968).

2. *Section 1983 liability of federal law enforcement personnel*

Federal law enforcement agents are not subject to suit under section 1983 because they act under color of *federal* rather than *state* law.[58] This does not mean that aggrieved citizens lack redress against federal agents who invade their constitutional rights. It simply means that no action under section 1983 is available. Until relatively recently, however, the only recourse was a state civil suit under a tort law theory such as false arrest, false imprisonment, assault and battery, or invasion of privacy. While legal theories could be found to redress some of the constitutional wrongs for which Section 1983 provided a remedy, state tort law never purported to afford a remedy for all types of constitutional injuries.

This gap in section 1983 protection led to an anomalous situation. When a citizen was complaining of wrongs committed by a state law enforcement officer, he was assured of a federal forum and an effective remedy under section 1983, but the doors to federal court were closed to him when he suffered a comparable deprivation at the hands of federal enforcement personnel. The federal courts, thus, had broader powers of supervision over the conduct of state law enforcement officers than over federal agents. In *Bivens v. Six Unknown Named Agents of the Federal Bureau of Narcotics*,[59] the Supreme Court corrected this inequity. The Court there announced that federal courts, unaided by statute, could entertain private actions brought against federal agents to recover damages for an unreasonable search and seizure. The cause of action was held to arise directly out of the Fourth Amendment. Although the federal common law remedy fashioned in *Bivens* dealt with the Fourth Amendment, the Supreme Court has since made Bivens-type remedies available against federal officers for other constitutional invasions.[60] The common law constitutional accountability of federal law enforcement officers today closely resembles the statutory liability of state officers under section 1983.[61] Doctrines developed in section 1983 litigation are often ap-

---

[58] Bivens v. Six Unknown Agents of the Federal Bureau of Narcotics, 403 U.S. 388, 91 S. Ct. 1999, 29 L. Ed. 2d 619 (1971).

[59] *Id.*

[60] Carlson v. Green, 446 U.S. 14, 100 S. Ct. 1468, 64 L. Ed. 2d 15 (1980).

[61] Paton v. LaPrade, 524 F.2d 862 (3d Cir. 1975) (First Amendment); Wounded Knee Legal Defense/Offense Comm. v. Federal Bureau of Investigation, 507 F.2d 1281, 1284 (8th Cir. 1974) (Sixth Amendment); States Marine Lines, Inc. v. Shultz, 498 F.2d 1146, 1157 (4th Cir. 1974) (Fifth Amendment). *But see* Bush v. Lucas, 462 U.S. 367, 103 S. Ct. 2404, 76 L. Ed. 2d 648 (1983).

plied by analogy in *Bivens*-type actions.[62] No longer are citizens without a federal remedy for vindicating constitutional injuries inflicted by agents acting "under color of" federal authority.

3. *Section 1983 liability of private citizens*

Section 1983 is grounded on the Fourteenth Amendment.[63] Like the Amendment on which it is based, it reaches only "state action" or action "under color of" state legal authority, two phrases which mean the same thing.[64] Private individuals do not act "under color of" state legal authority even when they make citizens' arrests or engage in other acts similar to the acts of a police officer.[65] Moreover, they are not subject to suit under section 1983 even when they impersonate a police officer.[66]

There are, nevertheless, limited instances in which private parties may become "state actors" liable under section 1983. While a lengthy discourse on "state action" goes beyond this textbook's practical goals, a brief investigation is necessary. State action has been found in a variety of contexts, but two are especially pertinent.

(a) State concert theory

Private parties are subject to suit under section 1983 when they act in concert with, conspire with or participate with state officials in acts the officials are constitutionally forbidden to perform.[67] In *Fine v. City of New York*,[68] a private citizen assisted police officers in breaking into and conducting a warrantless search of the plaintiff's apartment. Because the search and

---

62 Mark v. Groff, 521 F.2d 1376, 1380 (9th Cir. 1975); Brubaker v. King, 505 F.2d 534, 537 (7th Cir. 1974).

63 District of Columbia v. Carter, 409 U.S. 418, 93 S. Ct. 602, 34 L. Ed. 2d 613 (1973).

64 United States v. Price, 383 U.S. 787, 86 S. Ct. 1152, 16 L. Ed. 2d 276 (1966); Lugar v. Edmondson Oil Co. Inc., 457 U.S. 922, 102 S. Ct. 2744, 73 L. Ed. 2d 482 (1982).

65 Lee v. Town of Estes Park, 820 F.2d 1112, (10th Cir. 1987); Carey v. Continental Airlines, Inc., 823 F.2d 1402 (10th Cir. 1987); Gibson v. City of Chicago, 701 F. Supp. 666, 669 (N.D. Ill. 1988).

66 Gibson v. City of Chicago, *supra* note 65.

67 United States v. Price, 383 U.S. 787, 86 S. Ct. 1152, 16 L. Ed. 2d 276 (1966); Lugar v. Edmondson Oil Co., 457 U.S. 922, 102 S. Ct. 2744, 73 L. Ed. 2d 482 (1982); Tower v. Glover, 467 U.S. 914, 104 S. Ct. 2820, 81 L. Ed. 2d 758 (1984).

68 529 F.2d 70 (2d Cir. 1975).

seizure was a joint enterprise, the court held that the private party could be sued under section 1983 along with the police officers he collaborated with.

Whether the state-concert theory will justify imposing section 1983 liability on a private individual when he makes a groundless complaint which then causes the police to falsely arrest is a question for which there are no easy answers. Simply reporting suspected criminal activity to state officials who then take whatever action they believe the facts warrant does not constitute joint action "under color of" state law so as to impose Section 1983 liability on the citizen making the complaint.[69] Where, however, the arrest results from conspiracy, prearrangement or a policy of substituting the judgment of a private party for that of the police, the rule is otherwise.[70] A local police department policy of routinely arresting suspected shoplifters on the store proprietor's word alone without independent inquiry has been found to make the shopkeeper's action "state action" and to subject him to section 1983 liability.[71]

(b) Public function theory

Where the state delegates to a private individual powers that are sovereign or governmental in nature, the requirement of "state action" is satisfied and when the private actor exercises those powers, he must conform to the same constitutional responsibilities as are imposed upon the state.[72] The Supreme Court has employed the "public function" theory in several cases where the Court has found private detectives to be acting "under color of" state law.[73] However, only where a private detective is licensed by the state and endowed with powers comparable to those vested in police officers does his action become action "under color of" legal authority with the result that he is subject to suit under section 1983.[74]

In many jurisdictions there are shoplifting statutes authorizing proprietors to detain those reasonably suspected of shoplifting. Falsely detained shoppers have occasionally attempted to hold shop owners liable under sec-

---

69 Lee v. Town of Estes Park, *supra* note 65; Carey v. Continental Airlines, Inc., *supra* note 65; Chiles v. Crooks, 708 F. Supp. 127 (D.S.C. 1989).

70 Carey v. Continental Airlines, Inc., 823 F.2d 1402, 1405 (10th Cir. 1987).

71 El Fundi v. Deroche, 625 F.2d 195 (8th Cir. 1980); Smith v. Brookshire Bros., Inc., 519 F.2d 93 (5th Cir. 1975), *cert. denied*, 424 U.S. 915, 96 S. Ct. 1115, 47 L. Ed. 2d 320 (1976).

72 Evans v. Newton, 382 U.S. 296, 86 S. Ct. 486, 15 L. Ed. 2d 373 (1966).

73 Griffin v. Maryland, 378 U.S. 130, 84 S. Ct. 1770, 12 L. Ed. 2d 754 (1964); Williams v. United States, 341 U.S. 97, 71 S. Ct. 576, 95 L. Ed. 2d 774 (1951).

74 Chiles v. Crooks, 708 F. Supp. 127, 131 (D.S.C. 1989).

tion 1983 on the theory that state law has vested in shopkeepers powers similar to police officers, making their actions of detaining citizens "state action." Courts have not looked with favor on this argument.[75] They have pointed out that proprietors, unlike police officers, act in their own self-interest rather than in the interest of the public. Consequently, while their acts may resemble police acts, they are not performing a public function. Falsely arrested citizens have had better success in reaching shopkeepers under the state concert theory if they can show a prearrangement between the store proprietor and the police to automatically arrest those the shopkeeper accuses.[76]

§ 11.7 – Section 1983 liability of state and local governments and of supervisory personnel

Respondeat superior, a Latin phrase which translates "let the master respond," is a common law doctrine that places liability on an employer for the misdeeds of his employees. The justifications for imposing *vicarious* liability (liability without fault) on innocent employers for the wrongs of their employees are that employers benefit from their employees' acts, misfortunes to third parties are inevitable, and employers, as a class, are better able to absorb the liability and to respond in damages. *Respondeat superior* is, in short, an outgrowth of deep-pocket thinking.

Forty-two U.S.C. §1983 reads, in relevant part, that "*every person* who, under color of any statute, ordinance, regulation, custom or usage...*subjects, or causes to be subjected*, any citizen...to the deprivation of any rights, privileges, or immunities secured by the Constitution and laws of the United States" is liable to the injured party in an appropriate proceeding for redress. In *Monell v. Department of Social Services*,[77] the Supreme Court, on the basis of the italicized language read in light of Section 1983's legislative history, concluded that Congress had no intent to impose vicarious liability on municipalities for constitutional wrongs committed by their employees. However, *municipalities* were 'persons" under Section 1983 and could be sued for their own wrongs whenever municipal policy or custom was the moving force behind the constitutional injury. In the *Monell* Court's words:

---

75 Ouzts v. Maryland Nat'l Ins. Co., 505 F.2d 547 (9th Cir. 1974), *cert. denied*, 421 U.S. 949, 95 S. Ct. 1681, 44 L. Ed. 103 (1975); Battle v. Dayton-Hudson Corp., 399 F. Supp. 900 (D. Minn. 1975); Warren v. Cummings, 303 F. Supp. 803 (D. Colo. 1969).

76 *See* cases note 71 *supra*.

77 436 U.S. 658, 98 S. Ct. 2018, 56 L. Ed. 2d 11 (1978).

> A local government may not be sued for an injury inflicted *solely* by its employees or agents. Instead, it is when execution of a government's policy or custom, whether made by its lawmakers or by those whose edicts or acts may fairly be said to represent official policy, inflicts the injury that the government as an entity is responsible under § 1983.[78]

Monell's official policy or custom requirement is designed to separate acts of the *municipality* for which it is liable from the acts of its *employees* for which it is not.[79] Duly promulgated statutes, ordinances, rules and departmental regulations are familiar sources of government policy. When a police officer or other local government employee implements an unconstitutional law, the government is responsible under Section 1983 for the harm it has caused.[80] However, legislative pronouncements are not the only source of municipal policy. Official policy can also grow out of the decision of an official responsible for establishing final policy on a particular matter to adopt a course of action, even though the policy is tailored to a single situation and the action is to be taken only once.[81] A municipal government, for example, would be liable if, in a jurisdiction where the prosecutor had ultimate authority to advise the police department on legal matters, the prosecutor advised the police department to take specific action that turned out to be unconstitutional and as a result, the plaintiff's rights were violated.[82] The acts of the prosecutor may fairly be attributed to the city if he acts as the city's authorized policymaker in rendering advice that causes constitutional injury.

Only high-level officials with final policy-making authority may by their actions fasten section 1983 liability on the municipal entities they represent.[83] Whether a particular official has final policy-making authority about a given matter depends on local law rather than federal law.[84] There is a difference between authority to make final policy and authority to make discretionary decisions applying policy established elsewhere. The Supreme Court in

---

78 *Id.* 436 U.S. at 694, 98 S. Ct. at 2038, 56 L. Ed. 2d at 638.

79 Pembaur v. City of Cincinnati, 475 U.S. 469, 106 S. Ct. 1292, 1296, 89 L. Ed. 2d 452 (1986).

80 Whether a police officer is *personally* liable when he enforces a law in ignorance of its unconstitutionality is covered in §§ 11.9 and 11.10 *infra*.

81 Pembaur v. City of Cincinnati, *supra* note 79.

82 *Id.*

83 City of St. Louis v. Praprotnik, 485 U.S. 112, 108 S. Ct. 915, 99 L. Ed. 2d 107 (1988).

84 *Id.*

Pembaur v. Cincinnati[85] gave the following example to illustrate this distinction.

> [F]or example, the County Sheriff may have discretion to hire and fire employees without also being the county official responsible for establishing county employment policy. If this were the case, the Sheriff's decisions respecting employment would not give rise to municipal liability, although similar decisions with respect to law enforcement practices, over which the Sheriff *is* the official policymaker, *would* give rise to municipal liability. Instead, if county employment policy was set by the Board of County Commissioners, only that body's decisions would provide a basis for county liability. This would be true even if the Board left the Sheriff discretion to hire and fire employees and the Sheriff exercised that discretion in an unconstitutional manner; the decision to act unlawfully would not be a decision of the Board. However, if the Board delegated its power to establish final employment policy to the Sheriff, the Sheriff's decision *would* represent county policy and could give rise to municipal liability.[86]

In summation, a municipality is liable under Section 1983 when an employee with final policy-making authority about a given matter adopts an unconstitutional policy, but it is not liable when an employee who has authority to apply, but not to make, government policy, applies constitutional policies in an unconstitutional way.

Official policy can also grow out of government inaction, such as a failure to properly train or discipline police officers. In *City of Canton v. Harris*,[87] the Supreme Court held that failure to adequately train and discipline police officers can serve as the basis for placing section 1983 liability on a municipality if the municipality's failure is so extreme as to reflect conscious indifference to the rights of persons with whom the police come into contact. The Court gave two examples where the "need for more or different training is so obvious, and the inadequacy so likely to result in the violation of constitutional rights, that the policymakers of the city can reasonably be said to have been deliberately indifferent to the need."[88]

---

85 *Supra* note 79.

86 475 U.S. at 483, n. 12, 106 S. Ct. at 1300 n. 12, 89 L. Ed. 2d at 465.

87 ___ U.S. ___, 109 S. Ct. 1197, 103 L. Ed. 2d 412 (1989).

88 109 S. Ct. at 1205, 103 L. Ed. 2d at 427.

> First, a municipality could fail to train its employees concerning a clear constitutional duty implicated in recurrent situations that a particular employee is certain to face...[T]he constitutional limitations established by this Court on the use of deadly force by police officers present one such situation. The constitutional duty of the individual officer is clear, and it is equally clear that failure to inform city personnel of that duty will create an extremely high risk that constitutional violations will ensue....
>
> Second,...municipal liability for failure to train may be proper when it can be shown that policymakers are aware of, and acquiesce in, a pattern of constitutional violations involving the exercise of police discretion. In such cases, the need for training may not be obvious from the outset, but a pattern of constitutional violations could put the municipality on notice that its officers confront the particular situation on a regular basis, and that they often react in a manner contrary to the constitutional requirements....[89]

It should be pointed out, however, that proof of only one instance of police brutality[90] or even several sporadic instances occurring over an extended period of time,[91] is not sufficient to establish an unconstitutional municipal policy of inadequately training or supervising police officers.

While municipalities are liable under Section 1983 for constitutional injuries inflicted pursuant to municipal policy or custom, the same does not hold true for state governments when the injury is inflicted pursuant to state policy or custom.

In *Will v. Michigan Department of State Police*,[92] the Supreme Court ruled that state governments are not "persons" subject to suit for damages under Section 1983. The Court gave several reasons for this conclusion. First, it pointed out that the statutory language "every person who, under color of any statute, ordinance, regulation, custom, or usage, of any State...," was awkward language if Congress intended to include the States themselves. Next and more important, the Court was concerned with state sovereignty. To read this language as creating a federal cause of action against the states themselves would significantly alter the balance of power between the States and the federal government. The Court felt that if Congress had intended to

---

89 109 S. Ct. at 1209, 103 L. Ed. 2d at 431-432 (O'Connor, J., concurring).

90 City of Oklahoma City v. Tuttle, 471 U.S. 808, 105 S. Ct. 2427, 85 L. Ed. 2d 791 (1985).

91 Ramos v. City of Chicago, 707 F. Supp. 345 (N.D. Ill. 1989).

92 ___ U.S. ___, 109 S. Ct. 2304, 105 L. Ed. 2d 45 (1989).

disturb State sovereignty, it would have used language more clearly placing liability on state governments than Section 1983 does. The Supreme Court's ruling in *Will v. Michigan Department of State Police* applies only to suits brought against the state itself. State government employees, like municipal employees, can be sued under Section 1983 when they cause a constitutional injury while acting under the color of their legal authority.

Like municipalities, state and local supervisory personnel are not liable solely because a subordinate within their department commits a constitutional wrong.[93] They are, however, liable for constitutional violations they themselves have *caused*. Causation sufficient to impose damages have been found when the supervisor authorizes or directs his subordinate to take unconstitutional action;[94] when he is present when his subordinate performs the unconstitutional acts and fails to intervene;[95] and when the supervisor's failure to train or oversee his subordinates is so egregious that it reflects a conscious indifference to the constitutional rights of members of the public with whom his subordinates come into contact.[96]

§ 11.8 – Deprivation of federal civil rights

In addition to establishing that the defendant was acting under color of state law when he committed the conduct complained of, the plaintiff must prove that the defendant deprived him of some right guaranteed by the Constitution or laws of the United States. Section 1983 does not create any substantive federal rights; it merely operates to provide a remedy for vindicating federal rights elsewhere conferred.[97] Rights for the violation of which the plaintiff can seek damages under section 1983 include all rights secured by

---

93 Bowen v. Watkin, 669 F.2d 979, 988 (4th Cir. 1982); Jennings v. Davis, 476 F.2d 1271 (8th Cir. 1973); White v. Taylor, 677 F. Supp. 882 (S.D. Miss. 1988), *aff'd*, 877 F.2d 971 (5th Cir. 1989).

94 Martinez v. Mancusi, 443 F.2d 921 (2d Cir. 1970), *cert. denied*, 401 U.S. 983, 91 S. Ct. 1202, 28 L. Ed. 2d 335 (1971).

95 Taylor v. Kveton, 684 F. Supp. 179 (N.D. Ill. 1988); Masel v. Barrett, 707 F. Supp. 4 (D.C. Cir. 1989).

96 Harris v. City of Pagedale, 821 F.2d 499 (8th Cir.), *cert. denied*, 484 U.S. 986, 108 S. Ct. 504, 98 L. Ed. 2d 502 (1987); Haynesworth v. Miller, 820 F.2d 1245 (D.C. Cir. 1987); Harrera v. Valentine, 653 F.2d 1220 (8th Cir. 1981); Eng v. Coughlin, 684 F. Supp. 56 (S.D.N.Y. 1988); White v. Taylor, 677 F. Supp. 882 (S.D. Miss. 1988), *aff'd*, 877 F.2d 971 (5th Cir. 1989).

97 Chapman v. Houston Welfare Rights Org., 441 U.S. 600, 99 S. Ct. 1905, 60 L. Ed. 2d 509 (1979).

the United States Constitution and the decisions interpreting it, as well as all rights secured by federal statutory law, regardless of their nature.[98]

The first step in analyzing a section 1983 claim is to identify the specific constitutional or statutory right infringed upon by the behavior that constitutes the subject matter of the suit. Police conduct can be wrongful and injurious without necessarily and inevitably violating federal rights. In *Baker v. McCollan*,[99] the police, acting under a validly issued warrant, arrested the wrong man. The plaintiff was detained in jail for eight days over his repeated protestations that he had been the victim of a mistaken identity. The authorities eventually compared his appearance with a photograph of the wanted man and, recognizing their mistake, released him. The plaintiff sued under section 1983, alleging that he had been "illegally detained." The United States Court of Appeals characterized his complaint as a "§ 1983 false imprisonment action" and upheld it without seeking to identify the claim's constitutional basis. The Supreme Court reversed and remanded on the grounds that the proper inquiry should have been whether the plaintiff's detention on the facts here deprived him of liberty without due process in violation of the Fourteenth Amendment and not whether he had a state tort law claim for false imprisonment. Having cast the inquiry into appropriate constitutional terms, the Supreme Court concluded that where a person is arrested pursuant to a facially valid warrant, a due process deprivation does not automatically result from brief detentions, even though the party arrested is innocent and repeatedly demands release. The plaintiff, therefore, had no section 1983 constitutional claim, though he may have had a state tort claim for the wrongs he had suffered at the hands of the police.

Because section 1983 claims require the court to determine whether the Constitution protects the plaintiff against the conduct he is complaining of and because novel facts continually arise, some of the most important constitutional pronouncements affecting police officers in recent years have arisen in the context of section 1983 litigation.[100] There has been a recent avalanche of section 1983 suits brought by battered women and children against police departments and social welfare agencies, charging that the defendants deprived them of due process when they failed, despite notice of abuse, to provide protective services.[101] In *DeShaney v. Winnebago County*

---

98 Maine v. Thiboutot, 448 U.S. 1, 100 S. Ct. 2502, 65 L. Ed. 2d 555 (1980).

99 443 U.S. 137, 99 S. Ct. 2689, 61 L. Ed. 2d 433 (1980).

100 The leading cases affecting police officers are discussed in other chapters in this text where the relevant constitutional provisions are covered.

101 *See, e.g.*, Balistreri v. Pacific Police Dept., 855 F.2d 1421 (9th Cir. 1988); *see also*, Archie v. City of Racine, 847 F.2d 1211 (7th Cir. 1988), *cert. denied*, ___ U.S. ___, 109 S. Ct. 1338, 103 L. Ed. 2d 80 (1989) (alleging failure of fire department

Department of Social Services,[102] the Supreme Court seized the opportunity to clarify whether the Fourteenth Amendment, which forbids states from depriving individuals of life, liberty or property without due process of law, creates liability for failing to protect victims known to be at risk of abuse. The case involved the suit of a severely beaten and permanently injured child against social workers and others who had received earlier complaints that he was being abused, but had taken no steps to remove him from his father's custody. He claimed that their failure to do so deprived him of liberty without due process in violation of the Fourteenth Amendment. The Supreme Court disagreed that the Fourteenth Amendment casts on the government an affirmative duty to protect the life, liberty or property of its citizens against harms inflicted by persons other than its own employees. Pointing out that the Due Process Clause was phrased as a "limitation on the State's power to act" and not as a "guarantee of certain minimal levels of safety and security," the court concluded that the Fourteenth Amendment's "language cannot fairly be extended to impose an affirmative obligation on the State to insure that" the life, liberty and property of its citizens do not come to harm from outside dangers.

In *Tennessee v. Garner*,[103] the Supreme Court turned its attention to whether a police officer's use of unnecessary deadly force in making an arrest triggers a constitutional claim for which he is liable in damages. Here, the father of an unarmed youth who had been shot and killed by an officer while fleeing a burglary, claimed the officer had violated his son's Fourth Amendment rights and sued for damages under section 1983. The Supreme Court ruled that the use of deadly force to halt a suspect's flight was a seizure and, therefore, was subject to the Fourth Amendment standard of reasonableness. Lethal force is reasonable, the Court stated, only if the officer has probable cause to believe that his suspect poses a threat of serious physical harm to the officer or to others. This standard could be met if the suspect threatened the officer with a weapon or if the officer had probable cause to believe that the suspect had committed a crime involving the infliction of serious physical harm and that lethal force was necessary to prevent his escape. It is constitutionally unreasonable, however, to employ deadly force to halt the flight of an unarmed, nondangerous suspect. The court cautioned that, even when

---

to provide rescue services in response to request of woman who subsequently died); Burgos v. Camareno, 708 F. Supp. 25 (D. Puerto Rico 1989) (alleging failure to provide adequate police protection for business repeatedly burglarized).

102 ___ U.S. ___, 109 S. Ct. 998, 103 L. Ed. 2d 249 (1989).

103 Tennessee v. Garner, 471 U.S. 1, 105 S. Ct. 1694, 85 L. Ed. 2d 1 (1985).

Fourth - freedom from unreasonable search + seizures

lethal force is justified, the officer should, if possible, first give warning before opening fire.

The Supreme Court's announcement of new constitutional rights causes a corresponding expansion of a police officer's potential § 1983 damage liability. It is no coincidence that the number of damage suits filed in federal courts rose sharply during recent decades when there has been a rapid federalization of numerous specific Bill of Rights guarantees through Fourteenth Amendment incorporation. Damages have been recovered against police officers for: infringing upon the First Amendment right of orderly protest,[104] arresting without a warrant or probable cause,[105] applying unreasonable force in making arrests,[106] conducting illegal searches,[107] coercively extracting confessions,[108] denying suspects their *Escobedo* stationhouse counsel rights,[109] and for varied untold other constitutional invasions.

§ 11.9 –Required mental state for section 1983 liability

Unlike its criminal counterpart,[110] section 1983 makes no mention of the mental state required before an actor will incur liability for damages caused by his unconstitutional behavior. The reason is that no single mental state is necessary, or even sufficient, to establish the differing constitutional invasions for which section 1983 provides a remedy. The required mental state or standard of culpability varies with the particular underlying constitutional violation that the plaintiff alleges as his basis for recovery.[111] For some con-

---

104 Glasson v. City of Louisville, 518 F.2d 899 (6th Cir.), *cert. denied*, 423 U.S. 930, 96 S. Ct. 280, 46 L. Ed. 2d 258 (1975).

105 Monroe v. Pape, 365 U.S. 167, 81 S. Ct. 473, 5 L. Ed. 2d 492 (1961), *partially overruled*, Monell v. Department of Social Serv., 436 U.S. 658, 98 S. Ct. 2018, 56 L. Ed. 2d 611 (1978).

106 Brower v. County of Inyo, ___ U.S. ___, 109 S. Ct. 1378, 103 L. Ed. 2d 628 (1989).

107 Monroe v. Pape, *supra* note 105.

108 Hardwick v. Hurley, 289 F.2d 529 (9th Cir. 1971).

109 Ney v. California, 439 F.2d 1285 (9th Cir. 1971).

110 18 U.S.C. § 242, the criminal counterpart to 28 U.S.C. § 1983, imposes criminal accountability on those who act under color of law in invading constitutional rights only when the invasion is *willful*. Section 242 of the criminal code is analyzed in detail in § 11.12 *infra*.

111 Parratt v. Taylor, 451 U.S. 527, 101 S. Ct. 1908, 68 L. Ed. 2d 420 (1981).

stitutional violations, intentional misbehavior is necessary,[112] while for others, a lesser standard of culpability, such as willful or reckless indifference,[113] or sometimes even objective unreasonableness,[114] will suffice.

In a series of recent cases, the Supreme Court has painstakingly analyzed and defined the behavior and accompanying mental states necessary to work a violation of a large range of constitutional rights that section 1983 protects. The Court has attempted to answer such questions as what conduct and accompanying mental state is necessary to cause a Fourth Amendment "seizure,"[115] a Fourteenth Amendment "deprivation" of life, liberty or property without due process,[116] or an Eighth Amendment infliction of "cruel" punishment.[117]

The Fourteenth Amendment forbids state actors from depriving persons of life, liberty, or property without due process of law. Because this Amendment is the most generalized of the various constitutional procedural safeguards available to injured parties, it is the initial source most parties turn to when they are unable to fit their claims under one of the more specific constitutional guarantees. Several recent Supreme Court decisions discussing what an injured party must establish to state a claim against a public official for "depriving" him of due process in violation of the Fourteenth Amendment offer police officers welcome relief from the threat of federal civil damage li-

---

112 *See e.g.*, Village of Arlington Heights v. Metropolitan Housing Dev. Corp., 429 U.S. 252, 97 S. Ct. 555, 50 L. Ed. 2d 450 (1977) (proof of racially discriminatory intent necessary for a violation of the Equal Protection Clause).

113 *See e.g.*, Estelle v. Gamble, 429 U.S. 97, 97 S. Ct. 285, 50 L. Ed. 2d 251 (1976) (proof of deliberate indifference necessary to establish prisoner's claim under the Eighth Amendment for failure to provide adequate medical care).

114 *See e.g.*, Graham v. Connor, 490 U.S. ___, 109 S. Ct. 1865, 104 L. Ed. 2d 443 (1989) (proof of objective unreasonableness necessary for Fourth Amendment claim charging excessive force in the context of an arrest or investigatory stop).

115 Brower v. County of Inyo, 489 U.S. ___, 109 S. Ct. 1378, 103 L. Ed. 2d 628 (1989) ("seizure" requires a "governmental termination of freedom of movement through means intentionally applied").

116 Daniels v. Williams, 474 U.S. 327, 106 S. Ct. 662, 88 L. Ed. 2d 662 (1986) (public official's negligent acts causing unintended loss of life, liberty or property insufficient to work a "deprivation" under the Fourteenth Amendment Due Process Clause); Davidson v. Cannon, 474 U.S. 344, 106 S. Ct. 668, 88 L. Ed. 2d 677 (1986) (same).

117 Whitley v. Albers, 475 U.S. 312, 106 S. Ct. 1078, 89 L. Ed. 2d 251 (1986) (proof that prison authorities acted with a malicious and sadistic purpose of causing harm necessary to establish violation of Eighth Amendment rights where an inmate is injured during prison riot).

ability for negligently-caused personal injury or property damage. In the companion cases of *Daniels v. Williams*[118] and *Davidson v. Cannon*,[119] the Court ruled that negligent acts which cause the unintentional loss of life, liberty or property do not constitute "deprivations" so as to allow the injured party to bring a section 1983 action grounded on the Fourteenth Amendment.

In *Daniels*, a prisoner sued prison officials under §1983, alleging that he was injured when he slipped on a pillow negligently left on a staircase by a correctional deputy. In *Davidson*, a prisoner sued prison officials for negligently failing to protect him from attack by a fellow prisoner. In both cases, the Supreme Court ruled that the Fourteenth Amendment Due Process Clause was not implicated. The Court pointed out that the Due Process Clause has historically been designed to deter abusive exercises of power by state officials and had been applied only to "*deliberate* decisions...to deprive a person of life, liberty or property."[120] The Court reasoned that to permit recovery for negligent injuries caused by public officials would "trivialize" constitutional claims provided for in section 1983 and ultimately reduce this statute to a substitute vehicle for litigating state tort claims in federal court in those cases where the defendant, by happy coincidence, happened to be a public official. The Supreme Court's holdings in *Daniels* and *Davidson* insulate police officers from federal civil liability for personal injuries and property damage arising out of such circumstances as the negligent driving of police vehicles,[121] careless discharge of firearms,[122] and similar mishaps.

When the plaintiff is complaining about injuries suffered through a public official's application of excessive force in capturing or subduing him, there are two relevant constitutional theories. Each theory presents a different standard of culpability. If the injured party is a free citizen who complains he was subjected to excessive force during an arrest or an investigatory stop, his claim derives from the Fourth Amendment right to be free from unreasonable seizures of the person. Fourth Amendment claims are tested by a stan-

---

118 *Supra* note 116.

119 *Id*.

120 Daniels v. Williams, 474 U.S. at 331, 106 S. Ct. at 665, 88 L. Ed. 2d at 668 (emphasis added).

121 Checki v. Webb, 785 F.2d 534 (5th Cir. 1986); Canon v. Taylor, 782 F.2d 947, 950 (11th Cir. 1986); Timko v. City of Hazleton, 665 F. Supp. 1130 (M.D. Pa. 1986).

122 Dodd v. City of Norwich, 827 F.2d 1 (2d Cir. 1987), *cert. denied*, 484 U.S. 1007, 108 S. Ct. 701, 98 L. Ed. 2d 653 (1988). Nor does unintentional shooting act as a "seizure" for purposes of stating a Fourth Amendment claim. *See* Brower v. County of Inyo, *supra* note 115.

dard of *objective reasonableness* under the totality of the circumstances.[123] If, on the other hand, the injured party is an inmate who has been convicted and imprisoned, his primary safeguard against excessive force inside the prison environment is found in the Eighth Amendment right to be free from cruel and unusual punishments.[124] Fourth and Eighth Amendment claims invoke different standards of culpability.

In *Graham v. Conner*,[125] a diabetic sued several police officers to recover for injuries suffered when the officers allegedly used excessive force in the course of an investigatory stop. The plaintiff had been stopped for behavior the officers had mistaken as drunkenness, but which in fact was caused by an insulin reaction. The Supreme Court noted that this plaintiff's claim for excessive force arose out of the Fourth Amendment right of citizens to be secure in their persons against *unreasonable* seizures. Whether an officer's behavior is *unreasonable* calls for an objective inquiry into the facts and circumstances confronting him; the officer's subjective mental state is irrelevant. The relevant circumstances include "the severity of the crime at issue, whether the suspect poses an immediate threat to the safety of the officers or others, and whether he is actively resisting arrest, or attempting to evade arrest by flight."[126] The Court, however, cautioned that in evaluating whether the force used in stopping or arresting a person is *objectively unreasonable*, due allowance must be made "for the fact that police officers are often forced to make split-second judgments -- in circumstances that are tense, uncertain, and rapidly evolving -- about the amount of force that is necessary in a particular situation."[127]

In *Whitley v. Albers*,[128] a prison guard mistook a prisoner for a rioter and shot him in the leg during a prison riot. The injured party brought a section 1983 action alleging that the force applied was excessive and unjustified. The Supreme Court held that claims of excessive force brought by incarcerated prisoners must be analyzed under the Eighth rather than the Fourth Amendment. The Eighth Amendment prohibition against "cruel" punishments incorporates a standard of culpability governing the use of excessive force entirely different from that found in the Fourth Amendment. Whether behavior is *cruel* calls for an inquiry into the actor's subjective motivations. Excessive force in quelling a prison riot inflicts a *cruel* punishment only if the force is maliciously and sadistically applied without belief that this force is

---

[123] Graham v. Connor, ___ U.S. ___, 109 S. Ct. 1865, 104 L. Ed. 2d 443 (1989).

[124] Whitley v. Albers, 475 U.S. 312, 106 S. Ct. 1078, 89 L. Ed. 2d 251 (1986).

[125] *Supra* note 123.

[126] *Id*. at ___ 109 S. Ct. at 1872, 104 L. Ed. 2d at 455.

[127] *Id*.

[128] Whitley v. Albers, *supra* note 124.

necessary to maintain or restore order. Unlike the *objective reasonableness* standard of the Fourth Amendment, the Eighth Amendment protects prisoners only when unnecessary and unreasonable force is applied in bad faith. The Supreme Court justified reading a subjective and less protective standard into the Eighth Amendment both because this inquiry was suggested by the term *cruel* and because the added dangers inside prison settings made a broader margin for errors necessary.[129]

The Supreme Court has not yet had occasion to express its views on the behavior and mental state needed to establish claims under section 1983 for several other important constitutional safeguards. Nevertheless, under the law as it appears to be evolving, a standard of culpability more serious than negligence will be required before those operating under color of state legal authority are subject to damage liability under section 1983.

§ 11.10 – Defenses against section 1983 liability

Section 1983 contains sweeping language which provides that every person who acts under color of state law in depriving another of his federal civil rights shall be liable to the party injured. The text of the statute makes no mention of any defenses against liability. The Supreme Court, however, has ruled that Congress intended to incorporate into section 1983 immunity defenses that had developed over the centuries in analogous common law tort actions.[130]

Public officials performing legislative, judicial and prosecutorial functions have historically enjoyed absolute immunity from tort liability for their official acts.[131] Immunity was believed necessary to encourage public officials to vigorously exercise their public responsibilities. The Supreme Court has incorporated the historic treatment of lawmakers, judges and prosecutors into section 1983 and government officials performing these three functions are absolutely immune from liability for acts within the scope of their official duties.[132]

The duties police officers perform are of an executive or administrative nature. Unlike legislators, judges and prosecutors, members of the executive

---

129 Graham v. Connor, 109 S. Ct. at 1873, 104 L. Ed. 2d at 457.

130 City of Newport v. Facts Concert, 453 U.S. 247, 258, 101 S. Ct. 2748, 2755, 69 L. Ed. 2d 616 (1981).

131 Tenney v. Brandhove, 341 U.S. 367, 71 S. Ct. 783, 95 L. Ed. 1019 (1951), Stump v. Sparkman, 435 U.S. 349, 98 S. Ct. 1099, 55 L. Ed. 2d 331 (1978); Imbler v. Pachtman, 424 U.S. 409, 96 S. Ct. 984, 47 L. Ed. 2d 128 (1976).

132 *See* cases cited in note 131 *supra*.

branch of government historically have enjoyed only a partial or qualified immunity from tort liability for their official wrongs. Qualified, as distinguished from absolute, immunity can be claimed by a member of the executive branch only if, based on the law and the facts in his possession, a reasonable official could have believed that the actions he took were lawful.[133] The function of qualified immunity is to excuse an official who makes a reasonable mistake in the exercise of his official duties. In *Anderson v. Creighton*,[134] the Supreme Court gave the following explanation for qualified immunity for members of the executive branch:

> When government officials abuse their offices, 'action[s] for damages may offer the only realistic avenue for vindication of constitutional guarantees.' On the other hand, permitting damage suits against government officials can entail substantial social costs, including the risk that fear of personal liability and harassing litigation will unduly inhibit officials in the discharge of their duties. Our cases have accommodated these conflicting concerns by generally providing government officials performing discretionary functions with a qualified immunity, shielding them from civil damage liability so long as their actions could reasonably have been thought consistent with the rights they are alleged to have violated....[135]

The qualified immunity defense for police officers under section 1983 has undergone several major shifts and changes over the years.[136] Under the contemporary standard or test, a police officer is entitled to qualified immunity if:

> a reasonable officer could have believed [his conduct] to be lawful, in light of clearly established law and the information...the officer possessed.[137]

---

133 Anderson v. Creighton, 483 U.S. 635, 107 S. Ct. 3034, 97 L. Ed. 2d 523 (1987).

134 *Id.*

135 *Id.* at 638, 107 U.S. at 3040, 97 L. Ed. 2d at 529-530.

136 Wood v. Strickland, 420 U.S. 308, 95 S. Ct. 993, 43 L. Ed. 2d 214 (1975); Scheuer v. Rhodes, 416 U.S. 232, 94 S. Ct. 1683, 40 L. Ed. 2d 90 (1974); Harlow v. Fitzgerald, 457 U.S. 800, 102 S. Ct. 2727, 73 L. Ed. 2d 396 (1982); Anderson v. Creighton, 483 U.S. 635, 107 S. Ct. 3034, 97 L. Ed. 2d 523 (1987).

137 Anderson v. Creighton, *supra* note 136, 483 U.S. at 641, 107 S. Ct. at 3040, 97 L. Ed. 2d at 532.

Under this standard, a police officer who violates constitutional rights is immune from damage liability in two separate instances. First, he is immune if the constitutional or legal standards he is charged with violating were not clearly established at the time he acted. Second, even though the standards are clear, the officer will still be immune if a reasonable officer in his position could have believed that his particular behavior complied with those standards. The first grounds for immunity focuses on the state of the law at the time the officer acted, while the second grounds is fact-specific and concentrates on whether a reasonable police officer in the defendant's position should have known that *his particular conduct* violated those standards.

Police officers are shielded from liability under section 1983 if the rights they violated were not clearly established at the time they acted. In *Procunier v. Navarette*,[138] the Supreme Court affirmed the dismissal of a prisoner's claim for damages for interfering with his mail because at the time prison officials committed the acts complained of, inmate correspondence had not yet received First Amendment protection. In *Pierson v. Ray*,[139] the Supreme Court upheld a qualified immunity defense asserted by police officers sued for making an arrest under an unconstitutional statute because the statute had not yet been declared unconstitutional at the time they made the arrest.

A police officer is entitled to rely on the state of the law as it exists at the time he is called upon to act and is immune from damage liability under section 1983 if the rights he is charged with violating were not "clearly established" as of that date. To be "clearly established," "the contours of the right must be sufficiently clear that a reasonable official would understand that what he was doing would violate that right."[140] This does not necessarily mean that a police officer will be protected unless the Supreme Court has declared the very actions he took unconstitutional. It is sufficient that, based on existing legal precedents, a reasonable police officer in the defendant's position should have appreciated that his proposed course of action was unlawful.[141]

Although the applicable constitutional standards may be more or less clear, it may, nonetheless, remain unclear whether the actions the officer took in the specific situation with which he was confronted complies with or violates those standards. For instance, every well-trained police officer knows that citizens have a right to be free from warrantless searches of their homes unless the searching officer has probable cause and is faced with exi-

---

[138] 434 U.S. 555, 98 S. Ct. 855, 55 L. Ed. 2d 24 (1978).

[139] 386 U.S. 547, 87 S. Ct. 1213, 18 L. Ed. 2d 288 (1967).

[140] Anderson v. Creighton, *supra* note 136, 483 U.S. at 640, 107 S. Ct. at 3039, 97 L. Ed. 2d at 530.

[141] *Id*. at 640, 107 S. Ct. at 3039, 97 L. Ed. 2d at 530.

gent circumstances. Nevertheless, "probable cause" and "exigent circumstances" are both fact-specific. Even constitutional scholars and judges often differ over whether particular searches and seizures or particular patterns of fact comport with Fourth Amendment standards. Recognizing the unfairness of expecting police officers to make these difficult determinations at their peril, the Supreme Court has expanded qualified immunity to protect police officers who violate the Constitution from section 1983 damage liability *if a reasonable police officer, knowing the law and possessed of the facts and information the defendant possessed, could have believed that his particular acts complied with constitutional standards.*[142] In other words, it is not sufficient that the applicable legal standards were clearly established; a police officer is entitled to qualified immunity unless it also should have been clear to him that his proposed course of action violated those standards.

The qualified immunity defense, as it now exists, takes into account that reasonable mistakes are unavoidable and gives police officers adequate breathing space. In the words of the Supreme Court, this defense "protects all but the plainly incompetent or those who knowingly violate the law."[143] It should be noted that qualified immunity is inapplicable to police departments and other municipal agencies when they are sued under the *Monell* doctrine[144] for constitutional injuries inflicted pursuant to official policies or customs.[145]

Qualified immunity is not the only defense courts have recognized in section 1983 actions. Several decisions have dealt with the legal ramifications of the section 1983 claimant's criminal guilt on a police officer's damage liability. While the fact that the plaintiff was found guilty at his criminal trial does not automatically exonerate an officer from civil liability for constitutional torts committed during the investigation or aftermath,[146] it may lay a foundation for the assertion of a defense known as collateral estoppel. Under the collateral estoppel doctrine, when a matter has been raised and litigated in one judicial proceeding, the losing party is precluded from making the same contention in a subsequent proceeding.

In *Allen v. McCurry*,[147] the Supreme Court granted certiorari to consider whether the collateral estoppel defense could be raised in section 1983 ac-

---

142 *Id.* at 641, 107 S. Ct. at 3040, 97 L. Ed. 2d at 532.

143 Malley v. Briggs, 475 U.S. 335, 344-345, 106 S. Ct. 1092, 1096, 89 L. Ed. 2d 271 (1986).

144 The *Monell* doctrine is covered in § 11.7 *supra*.

145 Owen v. City of Independence, 445 U.S. 622, 100 S. Ct. 1398, 63 L. Ed. 2d 673 (1980).

146 Haring v. Prosise, 462 U.S. 306, 103 S. Ct. 2368, 76 L. Ed. 2d 595 (1983).

147 449 U.S. 90, 101 S. Ct. 411, 66 L. Ed. 2d 308 (1980).

tions. A state criminal defendant had been convicted of narcotics offenses after he had unsuccessfully opposed admission of the narcotics at a pretrial suppression hearing where he had argued that this evidence was a product of an illegal search and seizure. Following his conviction, he brought suit in a federal court under section 1983 seeking damages for what he again claimed had been an illegal search and seizure. The Supreme Court ruled that collateral estoppel was available as a defense in section 1983 actions. Because this plaintiff had previously raised the identical issues -- unsuccessfully -- at his criminal trial, the collateral estoppel doctrine barred him from again claiming that the search and seizure was illegal, this time in a section 1983 damage suit.

That a section 1983 claimant had the opportunity to litigate his constitutional claim at the criminal trial where he was found guilty is not sufficient to preclude him from seeking damages. The identical contentions must in fact have been argued and resolved against the claimant before the officer can raise a collateral estoppel defense to his section 1983 suit. In *Haring v. Prosise*,[148] a convict who had pleaded guilty to narcotics charges at his trial brought a section 1983 action contending that he had been the victim of an illegal search and seizure. He, however, unlike the *Allen v. McCurry* plaintiff, had not raised this issue at his criminal trial in a motion to suppress the evidence. The Supreme Court ruled that the plaintiff's guilty plea neither operated as an admission, for section 1983 purposes, that no constitutional rights had been violated, nor precluded him from seeking damages. Only where a section 1983 claimant has in fact raised the identical constitutional issues unsuccessfully at his trial will his conviction of the charges insulate the officer involved from civil liability.

§ 11.11 Federal criminal remedies for willful police misbehavior

Since the Reconstruction era, the U.S. Department of Justice has been empowered to criminally prosecute public officials for the willful violation of federal civil rights. The two statutes conferring this power are 18 U.S.C. §§ 241 and 242.

---

148 *Supra* note 146. *But see* Migra v. Warren City Bd. of Educ., 465 U.S. 75, 104 S. Ct. 892, 79 L. Ed. 2d 56 (1984).

§ 11.12 – 18 U.S.C. § 242

Eighteen U.S.C. § 242 is the criminal counterpart of 42 U.S.C. § 1983. It derives from section 2 of the Civil Rights Act of 1866,[149] which was later incorporated into the Enforcement Act of 1870.[150] Section 242 of the Criminal Code[151] makes it a crime for any person:

(1) who acts "under color of" legal authority to
(2) willfully subject a United States inhabitant to the deprivation of federal constitutional and statutory rights.

Its language closely parallels that of section 1983; there are, however, several important differences. First, and most obvious, section 242 is a criminal statute, while section 1983 provides civil remedies. Second, although both statutes employ the phrase "under color of," section 242's reach is broader. It condemns unconstitutional behavior by all who act "under color of" legal authority, without reference to the sovereign source from which their powers derive. Thus, while the phrase "under color of" carries the same legal meaning under both statutes,[152] the Justice Department's powers of prosecution under section 242 reach federal, as well as state and local officials, whereas section 1983 damage remedies reach only the latter two.[153] The final and most critical difference resides in the requisite mental states necessary to violate each statute. Section 1983, on its face, contains no requirement that the actor possess any particular mental state, such as a specific intent to deprive the victim of his constitutional rights. The necessary mental state or standard of culpability varies with the underlying constitutional deprivation the

---

149 Civil Rights Act of 1866, § 2, 14 Stat. 27.

150 Enforcement Act of 1870, § 17, 16 Stat. 144.

151 The full text of 18 U.S.C. § 242 reads: Whoever, under color of any law, statute, ordinance, regulation, or custom, willfully subjects any inhabitant of any State, Territory, or District to the deprivation of any rights, privileges, or immunities secured or protected by the Constitution or laws of the United States, or to different punishments, pains, or penalties, on account of such inhabitant being an alien, or by reason of his color, or race, than are prescribed for the punishment of citizens, shall be fined not more than $1,000 or imprisoned not more than one year, or both; and if death results shall be subject to imprisonment for any term of years or for life.

152 The legal meaning of "under color of" legal authority is discussed in § 11.6, *supra*.

153 Screws v. United States, 325 U.S. 91, 65 S. Ct. 1031, 89 L. Ed. 1495 (1945).

claimant alleges as his basis for recovery.[154] Procuring a criminal conviction for constitutional misbehavior under Section 242 is far more difficult because Section 242 contains a stringent standard of culpable behavior. Section 242 criminalizes unconstitutional behavior only when the wrongdoer possesses a *willful intent* to deprive the victim of his constitutional rights. The willful intent requirement, long regarded as a thorn in prosecutors' sides, proved to be section 242's salvation in *Screws v. United States*.[155]

1. Willful intent under section 242

In *Screws*, three law enforcement officers, indicted by the federal government for the blackjack murder of a prisoner, attacked section 242's constitutionality under the "void for vagueness" doctrine. They argued that deprivation of due process constituted too vague and imprecise a legal standard to hold would-be actors criminally accountable for violating. The Supreme Court found its answer to the vagueness challenge in section 242's requirement of a willful intent. "Willful," Mr. Justice Douglas wrote, imposed upon the prosecutor the burden of establishing that the accused acted with a "specific intent to deprive a person of a federal right *made definite by decision*."[156] Since no due process right could work its way into section 242 until fully crystallized and made definite by judicial decisions, the statute, in the Court's opinion, contained sufficiently clear and ascertainable standards of guilt to save it from constitutional infirmity.

Having upheld the statute, Mr. Justice Douglas attempted to explain what he meant by a "specific intent" to invade federal civil rights. In one breath, he asserted that the defendant must act with a "purpose" to deprive his victim of a clearly-defined constitutional right, while in the next breath, he admonished that the defendant need not be aware of the constitutional character of the rights invaded. This apparent inconsistency was resolved by saying that the offender must act with a conscious purpose of bringing about a result which, based on well-established precedents, is in violation of the Constitution, though the offender need not be cognizant of the constitutional basis of the claim. Purposefully bringing about a result, coupled with the fact that that result is constitutionally forbidden, makes the conduct "willful" despite the offender's ignorance of the constitutional implications of his behavior.

---

154 *See* § 11.9 *supra*.

155 *Supra* note 153.

156 *Id.* at 104, 65 S. Ct. at 1037, 89 L. Ed. at 1504.

For example, if the Justice Department were to prosecute a police officer for making an unconstitutional arrest, it must establish, under the *Screws* doctrine, that the officer consciously took his victim into custody, fully aware that he lacked probable cause for believing his victim was guilty. If the officer acts with this mental state, he has a specific intent to violate the arrested person's right to be free from unconstitutional arrests, searches and seizures of his person, though the officer may be wholly unfamiliar with the dictates of the Fourth Amendment.[157]

2. *Specific applications*

Section 242 makes the willful deprivation of federal rights by those acting "under color of" law punishable. There is no additional requirement that the acts be accompanied by physical abuse or violence. Nevertheless, because of the difficulty of establishing a willful intent, the Justice Department has concentrated its efforts on cases involving outrageous misbehavior such as torture,[158] brutal beating of prisoners,[159] and extortionate arrests,[160] relying upon state criminal prosecutions and Section 1983 damage claims to redress less serious abuses.

The Kent State University incident, in which four students died and nine others were wounded when National Guardsmen opened fire, lead to section 242 criminal prosecution. At the conclusion of the Justice Department's case, the court directed verdicts of acquittal against all eight defendants because the government's evidence was insufficient to establish a willful intent.[161] While the conduct of the Guardsmen is not to be condoned, this case was correctly decided. The Guardsmen were not motivated by a specific intent to deprive the student victims of any constitutional rights. Their use of force may have been excessive, but most were motivated by irrational fears for personal safety, exhaustion, confusion, and a mistaken belief that an order had been given. Had the Guardsmen employed excessive force, knowing it to be excessive, and with a specific intent to inflict injury, they could have been convicted for willfully denying the students their constitutional right not to be

---

157 Note, *Criminal Law: Criminal Deprivation of Another's Constitutional Rights: The Mens Rea Requirement*, 28 OKLA. L. REV. 845 (1975).

158 Williams v. United States, 341 U.S. 97, 71 S. Ct. 756, 95 L. Ed. 774 (1951).

159 Screws v. United States, 325 U.S. 91, 65 S. Ct. 1031, 89 L. Ed. 1495 (1945).

160 United States v. Lester, 363 F.2d 68 (6th Cir. 1966), *cert. denied*, 385 U.S. 1002, 875 S. Ct. 705, 17 L. Ed. 2d 542 (1967); United States v. Ramey, 336 F.2d 512 (4th Cir. 1964), *cert. denied*, 379 U.S. 972, 85 S. Ct. 649, 13 L. Ed. 2d 564 (1965).

161 United States v. Shafer, 384 F. Supp. 496 (N.D. Ohio 1974).

punished without a trial, because the Guardsmen would have possessed the mental state which *Screws* requires.

The Justice Department has successfully prosecuted several cases where constitutional deprivations resulted from willful inaction. A prisoner is entitled to protection while in a police officer's custody. If a policeman voluntarily surrenders his prisoner to a mob, he may be found by virtue of his deliberate inaction to have become a participant in the denial of federal civil rights. In *Lynch v. United States*,[162] a sheriff was convicted under section 242 for willful dereliction of duty in voluntarily turning a black prisoner over to the Ku Klux Klan. And in *Catlette v. United States*,[163] a peace officer was convicted for permitting and assisting members of the American Legion to commit sadistic acts upon several Jehovah's Witnesses who had come to his office seeking safety. Where the officer joins the ruffians in the commission of the civil rights crimes, his conduct has the additional consequence of making them criminally accountable under section 242, though they, as private citizens, could not have been prosecuted under section 242 had they acted alone. When private citizens act in concert with public officials, they too will be regarded as acting "under color of" law.[164]

§ 11.13 – 18 U.S.C. § 241 Conspiracies

Eighteen U.S.C. § 241 is a federal criminal conspiracy statute with historical antecedents tracing to the Civil Rights Act of 1870.[165] Its language reads as follows:

> If two or more persons conspire to injure, oppress, threaten, or intimidate any citizen in the free exercise or enjoyment of any right or privilege secured to him by the Constitution or laws of the United States, or because of his having so exercised the same; or
>
> If two or more persons go in disguise on the highway, or on the premises of another, with intent to prevent or hinder his free exercise or enjoyment of any right or privilege so secured--
>
> They shall be fined not more than $10,000 or imprisoned not more than ten years, or both; and if death results, they shall be subject to imprisonment for any term of years or for life.

---

162 189 F.2d 476 (5th Cir.), cert. denied, 342 U.S. 831, 72 S. Ct. 50, 96 L. Ed. 629 (1951).

163 132 F.2d 902 (4th Cir. 1943).

164 United States v. Price, 383 U.S. 787, 86 S. Ct. 1152, 16 L. Ed. 2d 267 (1966).

165 Civil Rights Act of May 31, 1870, ch. 114, 16 Stat. 140.

Prior to 1966, prosecutions under section 241 were rare because it was thought that this statute reached only *private* conspiratorial behavior designed to interfere with the narrow class of rights which Congress had the power to protect against abridgment by *private individuals*, and did not reach conspiracies implicating *public officials*.[166] Support for this view was found both in the nature of the conduct condemned -- such as going in "disguise upon the highway," activity more likely to be associated with private terrorist groups like the Ku Klux Klan than with rational public officials -- and in the lack of any explicit requirement that the violator act "under color of" law when depriving his victim of civil rights. The phrase "under color of" authority was employed by Congress in 42 U.S.C. § 1983 and 18 U.S.C. § 242 when it had official behavior in mind. Moreover, because due process and equal protection rights are, by virtue of their Fourteenth Amendment derivation, capable of being violated only when the invasion is accompanied by "state action" or action "under color of" state law, courts reasoned that section 241's omission of any reference to state action excluded both public officials and Fourteenth Amendment rights from the conspiracy statute's coverage. This left within section 241's narrow ambit a few relatively unimportant rights existing independently of the Fourteenth Amendment, rights which Congress had the power to secure against invasions by private citizens.

This remained the settled construction until 1966, when the Supreme Court in *United States v. Price*[167] took what was, for all practical purposes, a dead statute and revived it into a respectable civil-rights protection law. The *Price* case grew out of the highly-publicized murder of three civil rights activists -- James Chaney, Andrew Goodman and Michael Schwerner. A Mississippi deputy sheriff detained these three men and released them late at night in order that he and seventeen others, mostly private citizens, might intercept and murder them on a dark road. All eighteen men were indicted under section 241 for conspiring to "injure, oppress, threaten, and intimidate" the three victims "in the free exercise and enjoyment of the right...not to be deprived of life or liberty without due process of law." The district court dismissed the indictments on the ground that section 241 did not embrace conspiracies to deprive an individual of due process of law. The government appealed, and the issue of section 241's breadth was brought squarely before the Supreme Court. The Supreme Court ruled that the trial court had construed section 241 too narrowly and that the section *did* embrace conspiracies to interfere with Fourteenth Amendment rights where public officials are implicated or where "state action" is otherwise present.

---

166 United States v. Williams, 341 U.S. 70, 71 S. Ct. 581, 95 L. Ed. 758 (1951).

167 383 U.S. 787, 86 S. Ct. 1152, 16 L. Ed. 2d 267 (1966).

The primary significance of *Price* is not that it gives the Justice Department power to prosecute conduct formerly beyond its reach. The identical misbehavior was and is indictable under section 242. Nor will the government's election to proceed under section 241 ease its path to conviction because courts have read into Section 241 conspiracy law a requirement of willfulness identical to section 242.[168] *Price*'s primary importance relates to the punishment that can now be imposed upon conviction for conspiring to deny due process and equal protection rights. Under section 242, the maximum punishment that the Justice Department can secure upon a conviction, unless death has resulted, is a one-year prison sentence; under section 241, however, a ten-year prison sentence is authorized. As a result of *Price*, the threat of prosecution for conspiratorial deprivations of due process and equal protection rights now has some force behind it. *Price* restyled a moribund statute into a serviceable civil rights protection measure.

§ 11.14 Summary

The Reconstruction era altered the nature of the federal union. The Fourteenth Amendment conferred broad powers on Congress to protect individual civil rights against state governments and those acting "under color of" state legal authority. The Thirteenth Amendment gave Congress power to legislate against racially discriminatory practices of private parties. The Congress which met after the Civil War enacted numerous civil rights measures designed to give legal protection to the newly-freed slaves. The first Reconstruction was hampered, however, by conservative judges. A century passed during which the black citizens of the nation were denied equal rights under the law. A new era was ushered in, in 1954 when *Brown v. Board of Education* integrated the schools. During the decade of the 1960s, Congress passed measures prohibiting discrimination in places of public accommodations, in employment, and in housing markets. The second Reconstruction was climaxed by *Jones v. Alfred H. Mayer Co.*, where the Supreme Court declared that the Thirteenth Amendment's impact extended beyond abolishing slavery and that skepticism concerning Congress's power to ban racial discrimination by private citizens was wholly unfounded.

Three statutes surviving from the Reconstruction period have a direct impact upon the professional liability of law enforcement officers. The first, 42 U.S.C. § 1983, creates a civil cause of action against those who violate federal constitutional or statutory rights while acting "under color of" state

---

168 Anderson v. United States, 417 U.S. 211, 94 S. Ct. 2253, 41 L. Ed. 2d 20 (1974).

law. A state or local police officer acts "under color of" his legal authority and is subject to section 1983 damage liability when:

(1) he intends or purports to act in the line of duty in performing the acts that constitute the subject of suit, or when
(2) the fact that he is a police officer aids him in perpetrating the wrong.

Local municipal bodies, including police departments, are not *vicariously* liable under section 1983 for the constitutional injuries their employees cause but they are liable where official policy or custom is the moving force behind the constitutional violation. The failure to adequately train and discipline police officers can serve as the basis for recovering section 1983 damages against a municipal agency if the failure to train or supervise is so egregious that it reflects conscious indifference to the rights of persons whom the police come into contact with.

The plaintiff, as the second element of his section 1983 damage claim, must establish that the defendant's conduct deprived him of some right secured by the Constitution or laws of the United States. The mental state an actor must possess for section 1983 liability varies with the underlying constitutional violation constituting the subject matter of the section 1983 claim. For some constitutional violations, the plaintiff must establish intentional misbehavior, while for others, lesser standards of culpability such as reckless indifference or sometimes objective unreasonableness will suffice.

Even though the plaintiff demonstrates that the defendant violated his federal constitutional or statutory rights, the defendant is entitled to qualified immunity from damage liability under section 1983 if:

(1) the constitutional standards he is charged with violating were not clearly established at the time he acted, or if
(2) a reasonable police officer, knowing the law and possessed of the facts the defendant possessed, could have believed that his particular acts complied with those legal standards.

Where a police officer *willfully* deprives his victim of federal civil rights, he is subject, in addition, to federal criminal liability. The Justice Department has two statutes for prosecuting willful invasions by public officials of due process and equal protection rights -- 18 U.S.C. § 241 and 18 U.S.C. § 242.

Chapter 12
PERSONNEL REGULATIONS AND THE CONSTITUTION*

> *Twentieth Century America has a right to demand for itself, and the obligation to secure for its citizens, law enforcement personnel whose conduct is above and beyond reproach. The police officer is expected to conduct himself lawfully and properly to bring honor and respect to the law which he is sworn and bound to uphold. He who fails to so comport brings upon the law grave shadows of public distrust. We demand from our law enforcement officers, and properly so, adherence to demanding standards which are higher than those applied in many other professions. It is a standard which demands more than forbearance from overt and indictable illegal conduct. It demands that in both an officer's private and official lives he do nothing to bring dishonor upon his noble calling and in no way contribute to a weakening of the public confidence and trust.*
>
> *Cerceo v. Darby*,
> 281 A(2d) 251,
> 255 (Pa. 1971)

Section

---

* *by Jacqueline R. Kanovitz*

§ 12.1 Introduction

Justice personnel are commonly subjected to regulations and restrictions that differ both in kind and degree from those found in other branches of the civil service: height, weight, grooming and personal appearance are commonly regulated;[1] officers are frequently prohibited from supplementing their income by holding off-duty moonlighting jobs;[2] and their ability to participate in partisan political activities is severely curtailed.[3] Even their off-duty associations and private lives can be subjected to departmental scrutiny when job performance or the department's public image is affected. Courts have sustained regulations imposing comprehensive and substantial restrictions on the personal liberty of justice personnel. Recognizing that local legislative and administrative bodies are better situated than courts to judge what is necessary for efficient operation of a justice agency, courts have given these public bodies broad latitude in formulating departmental regulations.[4] Except when fundamental rights are at stake, departmental regulations which affect organization, structure, discipline and related matters are treated by courts as presumptively valid, and will be struck down only if the challenging party can demonstrate that the regulation fails to serve any legitimate governmental purpose or is so irrational as to be arbitrary.[5]

Justification for intensified regulation of justice personnel is found in the unique service that uniformed civil servants perform in our society, a service that sets them apart from the general population and from other branches of the civil service. As one court has observed:

> Traditionally, the policeman has been a highly trained officer who is entrusted with a responsible and oftentimes dangerous role as a public servant. His work habits on active duty require disciplined conduct, regimentation and frequent strict adherence to regulation and authorized detail....It is essential that a policeman's training be such that he is taught to obey strict disciplinary procedures and

---

1 *See* § 12.5 *infra*.

2 *See* § 12.7 *infra*.

3 Civil Service Comm'n v. National Ass'n of Letter Carriers, 413 U.S. 548, 93 S. Ct. 2880, 37 L.Ed. 2d 796 (1973); Broadrick v. Oklahoma, 413 U.S. 601, 93 S. Ct. 2908, 37 L. Ed. 2d 830 (1973).

4 RHYNE, POLICE AND FIREFIGHTERS LAW 8 (1982).

5 Kelley v. Johnson, 425 U.S. 238, 96 S. Ct. 1440, 47 L. Ed. 2d 708 (1976).

> rules in order to lend practical assurance that he will follow command and not abuse his awesome authority.[6]

These considerations have prompted courts to strike the constitutional balance in favor of allowing certain forms of restriction on a uniformed civil servant's personal liberty that would be wholly unconstitutional if levied on the population as a whole or on non-uniformed branches of the civil service. This Chapter investigates the legal status of common employment restrictions placed upon the liberty of justice personnel, as well as certain employment rights such employees enjoy under recent federal civil rights laws.

§ 12.2 Public employment and the First Amendment

The First Amendment protects freedom of speech, press, religion, assembly, and the right of the people to petition government for a redress of grievances. Under the constitutional thinking which prevailed during the early part of this century, government employees were second-class citizens with respect to their First Amendment rights. Courts, adopting the position that government employment was a special grant or privilege, allowed the government to annex any conditions it desired to public employment, including restrictions arbitrarily curtailing the employee's freedom of expression.[7] The public employee took the position on the terms offered, or not at all. This philosophy is reflected in Mr. Justice Holmes' caustic quip: "A policeman may have a constitutional right to talk politics, but he has no constitutional right to be a policeman."[8]

Under contemporary First Amendment interpretation, the government may no longer use the absence of a "right" to government employment as a justification for arbitrarily and unnecessarily limiting a public servant's freedom of expression.[9] Nevertheless, the First Amendment does not absolutely prohibit regulation of a public servant's speech. Courts have recognized that the government in its capacity as employer has an interest in regulating the behavior and speech of employees that is significantly different from its inter-

---

6 Stradley v. Anderson, 349 F. Supp. 1120 (D. Neb. 1971), *aff'd*, 478 F.2d 188, 190 (8th Cir. 1973).

7 Connick v. Myers, 461 U.S. 138, 103 S. Ct. 1684, 1689, 75 L. Ed. 2d 708 (1983).

8 McAuliffe v. Mayor of New Bedford, 29 N.E. 517 (Mass. 1892).

9 Keyishian v. Board of Regents, 385 U.S. 589, 605, 87 S. Ct. 675, 684-685, 17 L. Ed. 2d 629 (1967).

est in regulating the speech and behavior of citizens generally.[10] The government's interest as employer stems from its paramount responsibility for the efficient operations of government. It may regulate employee speech only when its interests as employer are significantly implicated. An employee's speech, conduct, and personal associations away from work become subject to government scrutiny only when, because of the context or content, these activities have a serious adverse impact on the government's operations or on the employee's job effectiveness.[11] The reconciliation of a public servant's free speech rights with the interest of his government employer requires a delicate balancing of the employee's interest as a citizen in expressing himself against his employer's concern for efficiency in the public service it performs.[12] The next section investigates the scope of First Amendment protection for speech critical of departmental policies or supervisory personnel. An understanding of the First Amendment rights of public employees also calls for investigation of the overbreadth and void-for-vagueness doctrines because even when the Constitution allows regulation of a public servant's speech, the Constitution demands that such regulations be drafted with a high degree of clarity and precision. The overbreadth and vagueness doctrines are explored in Section 12.4.

§ 12.3 – Criticism of departmental policies and supervisory personnel

The architects of the First Amendment were primarily concerned with safeguarding the free flow of information about public issues and affairs -- information necessary to enable citizens of a free society to make informed decisions about the workings of their government.[13] Those employed by government agencies are unquestionably the best informed and thus the most qualified to evaluate how their departments are or should be operated. In speaking out about public issues relating to his department's operations, an employee makes a valuable contribution to informed public opinion. However, the employee's interest in contributing to public affairs, and the public's

---

10 Pickering v. Board of Education, 391 U.S. 563, 568, 88 S. Ct. 1731, 1734, 20 L. Ed. 2d 811 (1968).

11 Shuman v. City of Philadelphia, 470 F. Supp. 449 (E.D. Pa. 1979); Waters v. Chaffin, 684 F.2d 833 (11th Cir. 1982); Flanagan v. Munges, 890 F.2d 1557 (10th Cir. 1989).

12 Pickering v. Board of Education, *supra* note 10.

13 MIEKLEJOHN, FREE SPEECH AND ITS RELATIONSHIP TO SELF-GOVERNMENT, pp. 22-27 (1948).

interest in securing his information are not the sole interests at stake when an employee voices public criticism of policies, practices and personnel within the agency where he works. Public criticism by a member of a department can undermine the authority of supervisors, create morale problems, impair harmonious working relationships, or in other ways disrupt his department's normal routine.

In *Pickering v. Board of Education*,[14] the Supreme Court focused upon the right of a government employee to address the public about problems that he perceives within the agency where he works. Pickering, a school teacher, was dismissed for "conduct detrimental to the efficient operation" of his school district after he sent a letter to the local newspaper criticizing the Board of Education's handling of a proposed tax increase and its allocation of revenues between athletic and educational programs. Adopting a balancing approach, the Supreme Court ruled that government employees can be disciplined for speech only where the government's interest as employer in the efficiency of the service it performs outweighs the employee's interest as a citizen in informing the public about problems in his department. The factors that *Pickering* and other cases have weighed in the balance include: the importance of the subject commented upon to the political and social affairs of the community; the employer's need for confidentiality; whether the employee's speech was critical of an immediate superior and thus was likely to impair harmonious working relationships; whether the speech undermined rank-and-file confidence in departmental leadership, created morale problems, or fomented internal controversy; and whether the employee's speech revealed incompetence.

The Supreme Court weighed these factors in reaching its conclusion that Pickering's dismissal for criticizing the Board of Education was unwarranted. Of particular importance to the Court was the fact that Pickering's statements had concerned information "vital to informed decision-making by the electorate."[15] Moreover, his criticism had not been "directed toward any person with whom [he] would normally be in contact in the course of his daily work as a teacher," and thus posed "no question of maintaining either discipline by immediate superiors or harmony among co-workers."[16] Finally, there was no showing that his statements had in any way "either impeded [his] performance of his daily duties in the classroom or to have interfered with the regular operation of the school generally."[17] Thus, weighing Pickering's interest as a citizen in informing the electorate about matters of cur-

---

14 *Supra* note 10.

15 *Id.* 391 U.S. at 572, 88 S. Ct. at 1736, 20 L. Ed. 2d at 819.

16 *Id.* 391 U.S. at 569-570, 88 S. Ct. at 1735, 20 L. Ed. 2d at 818.

17 *Id.* 391 U.S. at 572-573, 88 S. Ct. at 1737, 20 L. Ed. 2d at 819-820.

rent political importance against the school district's interest as his employer, the Supreme Court concluded that Pickering's interest was paramount and that his dismissal was unwarranted.

1. Speech must relate to matters of public importance

A government employee demoted or fired for criticizing his department's policies, practices or supervisory personnel must establish that his speech touched on a matter of public concern before he can claim First Amendment protection for it. The Supreme Court has refused to constitutionalize every employment controversy sparked by speech simply because the employer is a public agency. A government employee enjoys no special First Amendment protection when he engages in a heated debate concerning private grievances and internal office matters. In *Connick v. Meyers*,[18] an assistant district attorney, disgruntled over news that she was scheduled to be transferred, circulated a questionnaire among co-workers soliciting their views on department transfer policies, the level of office morale, the need for departmental grievance procedures, their confidence in their immediate supervisor, and whether they felt pressured to work in campaigns. She was fired for insubordination. The Supreme Court characterized this controversy as an internal office dispute and stated:

> [W]hen a public employee speaks not as a citizen upon matters of public concern, but instead as an employee upon matters only of personal interest, absent the most unusual circumstances, a federal court is not the appropriate forum in which to review the wisdom of personnel decisions taken by a public agency allegedly in reaction to the employee's behavior.[19]

Whether an employee's speech relates to matters of importance to the community or instead touches on private office matters depends on its content, form and context.[20] At one pole is speech concerning work assignments, unfavorable employment evaluations or other private grievances that have no relevance to the community's perception of the department's per-

---

18 461 U.S. 138, 103 S. Ct. 1684, 75 L. Ed. 2d 708 (1983).

19 461 U.S. at 147, 103 S. Ct. at 1690, 75 L. Ed. 2d at 720.

20 Allred, *From Connick to Confusion: The Struggle to Define Speech on Matters of Public Concern*, 64 IND. L.J. 43 (1988).

formance.[21] Speech concerning matters of internal office administration falls beneath First Amendment concern. At the other pole is speech which discloses information necessary to assist citizens in evaluating the performance and integrity of their government[22] and speech on newsworthy topics that have already captured the public limelight.[23] Speech on these topics is central to the First Amendment. Between these extremes there is a vast area where it is difficult to predict whether the court will find that a subject relates to issues of public concern, on the one hand, or to the purely private affairs of the government, on the other.

The fact that the fired employee has a personal stake in the controversy is a factor, although not a controlling factor, in assessing the public or private character of the employee's speech.[24] In *Rode v. Dellaciprete*,[25] a civilian employee in the state police department told a news reporter that she had been harassed and mistreated because of her involvement in a prior racial discrimination suit brought against her employer. She received a two-day suspension for participating in the interview. The court held that the employee's comment during her news interview, while motivated by self-interest, nonetheless touched on a matter of public concern because it charged a government agency with racially discriminatory employment practices.

The forum the employee selects to air his views presents another relevant consideration. The victorious *Rode v. Dellaciprete* and *Pickering* plaintiffs both selected the newspaper, a highly public vehicle, to air their views, while the unsuccessful plaintiff in *Connick v. Meyers* used an internal office questionnaire addressed to her co-workers. While a government employee is not beyond First Amendment protection when he addresses matters of unmistakable public concern during private conferences with supervisors,[26] in official reports,[27] or in other internal office communications,[28] if his subject

---

21 Huber v. Leis, 704 F. Supp. 131, 134 (S.D. Ohio 1989), *aff'd*, 884 F.2d 579 (6th Cir. 1989), *cert. denied*, ___ U.S. ___, 110 S. Ct. 721 (1990).

22 Brawner v. City of Richardson, 855 F.2d 187 (5th Cir. 1988); Solomon v. Royal Oak Township, 842 F.2d 862, 865 (6th Cir. 1988); Matulin v. Village of Lodi, 862 F.2d 609 (6th Cir. 1988).

23 *See* Allred *supra* note 20 at pp. 50-55.

24 Zamboni v. Stamler, 847 F.2d 73, 78 (3d Cir.), *cert. denied*, ___ U.S. ___, 109 S. Ct. 245, 102 L. Ed. 2d 233 (1988).

25 845 F.2d 1195 (3d Cir. 1988).

26 Givan v. Western Line Consol. School Dist., 439 U.S. 410, 99 S. Ct. 693, 58 L. Ed. 2d 619 (1978).

27 Koch v. City of Hutchinson, 847 F.2d 1436 (10th Cir.), *cert. denied*, ___ U.S. ___, 109 S. Ct. 262, 102 L. Ed. 2d 250 (1988).

28 Connick v. Meyer, *supra* note 18.

is less clearly of general importance, an employee who excessively criticizes departmental practices, policies or supervisors in an institutional setting may place his job on the line. In *Steinberg v. Thomas*,[29] a legal staff attorney with the administrative office of the state courts criticized his supervisor for being unwilling to consider input with which he disagreed and for denying democratic processes in departmental planning. His criticism was spoken during a private staff meeting in the presence of ten other co-workers. He lost his job. The court held that the legal officer's critical assessment of his supervisor's management style made during a private staff meeting, both because of its content and context, raised an internal office matter. The court denied free speech protection both because it regarded the speech as dealing with internal office administration and because it found that criticism of the plaintiff's supervisor in the presence of co-workers damaged his department's efficiency.

2. *Factors considered in Pickering balancing*

If the fired employee's speech touches on a matter of public concern, the discharge raises a potential First Amendment claim. Resolution of the controversy then requires the court to balance the department's and employee's interests following the guidelines established in *Pickering v. Board of Education*.[30] The government, to justify a speech-related discharge, must establish that its interest in promoting efficiency outweighs the employee's interest in expressing his views on a matter of public concern. Among those considerations which courts have focused upon in assessing whether the employee's speech has injured his department's efficiency are the following:

1. Whether the disclosure breaches the department's need for confidentiality;[31]
2. Whether the employee's statements damaged working relationships with an immediate superior;[32]

---

29 659 F. Supp. 789 (D. Colo. 1987).

30 *Supra* note 10.

31 Pickering v. Board of Education, *supra* note 10; Ely v. Honaker, 451 F. Supp. 16 (W.D. Va. 1977), *aff'd*, 588 F.2d 1348 (4th Cir. 1978); Hanneman v. Breier, 528 F.2d 750 (7th Cir. 1976).

32 Rankin v. McPherson, 483 U.S. 378, 107 S. Ct. 2891, 97 L. Ed. 2d 315 (1987); Pickering v. Board of Education, *supra* note 10; Sprague v. Fitzpatrick, 546 F.2d 560, (3d Cir. 1976), *cert. denied*, 431 U.S. 937, 97 S. Ct. 2649, 53 L. Ed. 2d 255 (1977); Kannisto v. County of San Francisco, 541 F.2d 841 (9th Cir. 1976), *cert.*

3. Whether the employee's statements threatened to undermine the authority of high-level department superiors, foment controversy, create disharmony among co-workers, or adversely affect departmental morale or discipline;[33] and
4. Whether the content of the employee's speech reflected incompetence to perform his public responsibilities.

Breach of departmental confidentiality rules

When the subject of an employee's public commentary relates to sensitive matters that his employer has a legitimate interest in preserving as confidential, an officer's imprudent public disclosure can lead to the loss of his job. Most police departments have rules prohibiting employees from making premature disclosures of the results of pending investigations or from divulging other confidential business of the department. In *Ely v. Honnaker*,[34] a police officer was discharged for discussing the substance of an ongoing investigation into a suspected prostitute ring with a television reporter before formal charges had been brought. In upholding his discharge for violating departmental confidentiality rules, the court stated:

> A police department could scarcely perform in an efficient and productive manner if its individual officers were at liberty to freely discuss specific persons and matters under investigation with members of the public at large. Aside from the obvious tort considerations, the potential for abuse is abundant. The court is simply unable to conclude that the First Amendment must be interpreted so as to protect an individual police officer's publication of substantive elements of a pending criminal investigation.[35]

The existence of a departmental confidentiality rule, nevertheless, does not eliminate the department's need to establish that its interest in preserving confidentiality of the particular matters disclosed outweighs the disciplined

---

denied, 430 U.S. 931, 97 S. Ct. 1552, 51 L. Ed. 2d 775 (1977); Hosford v. California State Personnel Board, 74 Cal. App. 3d 302, 141 Cal. Rptr. 354 (1977).

33 Rankin v. McPherson, *supra* note 32; Magri v. Giarrusso, 379 F. Supp. 353 (E.D. La. 1974); Brukiewa v. Police Commissioner, 257 Md. 36, 263 A.2d 210 (Md. 1970).

34 451 F. Supp. 16 (W.D. Va. 1977), *aff'd*, 588 F.2d 1348 (4th Cir. 1978).

35 *Id.* at 21.

employee's interest in informing the public. In cases like *Ely v. Honnaker*, where the employee's disclosure relates to the results of an ongoing investigation, the employee's interest in making a premature public disclosure is minimal in relationship to the damage to his department's efficient operations. In *Hanneman v. Brier*,[36] on the other hand, a lower federal court found that the police department had unconstitutionally applied its confidentiality rules in disciplining an officer for publicly confirming the existence of an internal investigation into possible police improprieties where, at the time the officer spoke, the investigation had ceased to be secret, where the chief himself had publicly acknowledged the previous day that it was in progress, and where the officer's disclosure contained no factual information not already publicized. The balance was struck in the employee's favor in the *Hanneman* case both because investigation into possible police improprieties is information that the public has a right to hear and because the department suffered no demonstrable injury from the repetition of information already made public.

Impairment of superior-subordinate working relationships

The Supreme Court in *Pickering v. Board of Education*[37] repeatedly emphasized the fact that the teacher's criticism had been directed at the school board and the superintendent rather than an immediate superior or person with whom he had to work in close daily association. The Court further noted that Pickering's speech was not shown to have had any adverse effects on the school system's operations. Where the target of an employee's criticism is his immediate superior, and where their working relationship requires a high degree of personal loyalty and confidence, harmonious interaction thereafter may become impossible. If their relationship is badly damaged, the subordinate's usefulness to his department is impaired and he is subject to discharge. In *Kannisto v. City & County of San Francisco*,[38] a lower federal court upheld disciplinary measures imposed on a lieutenant who, while addressing his subordinates during a morning inspection, described his immediate superior as an " 'unreasonable, contrary, vindictive individual,' whose behavior was 'unreasonable, belligerent, arrogant, contrary and unpleasant.' " In *Hosford v. California State Personnel Board*,[39] a state highway patrolman

---

36 528 F.2d 750 (7th Cir. 1976).

37 *Supra* note 10.

38 541 F.2d 841 (9th Cir. 1976), *cert. denied*, 430 U.S. 931, 97 S. Ct. 1552, 51 L. Ed. 2d 775 (1977).

39 74 Cal. App. 3d 302, 141 Cal. Rptr. 354 (1977).

who committed similar indiscretions also lost his appeal. The court there stated:

> We...find that the conduct complained of may be appropriately characterized as... 'insubordination'.... We think it reasonable to conclude that, to the extent that Hosford's misbehavior impaired relations between himself and those with whom he worked, it necessarily rendered him less efficient in his job performance. To the extent he created a moral [sic] problem among other men, his efficiency...was certainly impaired.[40]

Nevertheless, it is by no means true that whenever an officer voices any criticism about his immediate superior, he places his job on the line. Not every superior-subordinate relationship is of such a close and intimate nature as to be incapable of surviving some forms of public criticism, particularly where the remarks are temperate and respectful. For example, while the mayor normally appoints the police chief and supervises the police chief, the relationship between them is not of such a personal and intimate nature that no public criticism of the mayor can be tolerated.[41] Moreover, when the focal point of the employee's derogatory comments is his superior's policies or practices rather than his integrity or competence, the discharged employee's chances of prevailing in court are increased.[42]

The critical employee's position in the department is another factor. Low-level, nonsupervisory employees enjoy greater latitude for critical commentary concerning department leaders than do persons who themselves occupy supervisory or policymaking roles.[43] The Supreme Court has remarked:

> The burden of caution employees bear with respect to the words they speak will vary with the extent of authority and public accountability the employee's role entails. Where...an employee serves no confidential, policymaking role, the danger to the agency's successful function from that employee's private speech is minimal.[44]

---

40 *Id*. at 360.

41 Hoopes v. City of Chester, 473 F. Supp. 1214 (E.D. Pa. 1973).

42 RHYNE, POLICE AND FIREFIGHTER LAW pp. 91-92 (1982).

43 Rankin v. McPherson, 483 U.S. 378, 107 S. Ct. 2891, 97 L. Ed. 2d 315 (1987).

44 *Id*. at 390-391, 107 S. Ct. at 2900, 97 L. Ed. 2d at 328.

This view is sensible because a rank-and-file officer's critical remarks about the chief of police are far less likely to adversely impact the police department than similar remarks uttered by high level employees.[45]

Damage to departmental morale, discipline or harmony

Occasionally speech directed at high-level superiors with whom an officer has no regular personal contact will undermine discipline or stir departmental controversy. In *Magri v. Giarrusso*,[46] a police sergeant, who was head of the local policemen's union and an outspoken critic of the superintendent of his department, became embroiled in a bitter public debate over pay raises and overtime compensation. During this controversy, he made a series of public statements in which he charged that the superintendent was a "coward" and a "liar," and made repeated public demands for his resignation. The court refused to set aside the sergeant's dismissal. While conceding that union spokesmen were entitled to broader latitude for voicing public criticism of departmental policies and leaders than rank-and-file officers, the court felt that this sergeant's inflammatory and vitriolic attacks on the integrity and leadership ability of his department's chief exceeded the limits of freedom of speech. Pointing out that a department chief requires the confidence and loyalty of the men who serve under him to run a well-organized and disciplined force, the court found that the sergeant's insubordinate remarks threatened working relationships vital to the successful administration of a police department. The officer's dismissal was therefore justified.

Must the department demonstrate that the officer's remarks *actually* damaged the department's efficient operations before taking disciplinary action against an officer for his speech or may the department act on the basis of its reasonable apprehension that damage is likely to result? In *Connick v. Meyers*,[47] the Supreme Court suggested a flexible approach that varies with First Amendment importance of the subject addressed. Where the subjects addressed are of marginal free speech concern, the department need not wait until "disruption of the office and...destruction of working relationships is manifest before taking action." The department may act in response to a reasonable perception that the potential for disruption exists. If, on the other hand, the employee's speech covers matters of central First Amendment concern, the department bears a heavier burden of justification and may retaliate against an employee for his speech only when serious harm is imminent.

---

45 Pierson v. Gondles, 693 F. Supp. 408 (E.D. Va. 1988).

46 379 F. Supp. 353 (E.D. La. 1974).

47 *Supra* note 18.

§ 12.4 – Clarity and precision of regulation

An employee who has been disciplined for statements critical of departmental actions, policies, or leaders may have a second ground for seeking review of disciplinary action taken against him. Even when his speech lacks First Amendment protection, he may object to disciplinary action if the departmental regulations invoked against him were not drafted with the rigorous standards of clarity and precision demanded by the Constitution when regulations are addressed at speech. Two closely related doctrines have been devised by courts for scrutinizing regulations that impact speech -- the overbreadth and the void-for-vagueness doctrines.

Overbreadth

Regulations which sweep within their prohibition constitutionally privileged behavior as well as conduct that can be banned are candidates for overbreadth challenges. Departments face a formidable task in drafting regulations that are sufficiently general to cover a broad spectrum of potentially disruptive behavior while, at the same time, sufficiently narrow to exclude constitutionally privileged speech. Courts, in policing regulations for overbreadth, have taken this problem into account. Judges have been reluctant to strike down regulations as unconstitutionally overbroad, thereby preventing the government from applying the regulations to conduct they are entitled to punish, when the regulation is primarily aimed at *conduct* other than speech.[48] Before an officer can successfully challenge regulations aimed primarily at conduct, the regulation's overbreadth must not only be "real, but substantial as well, judged in relation to the regulation's plainly legitimate sweep."[49] This explains why departmental regulations prohibiting "conduct unbecoming an officer,"[50] sanctioning behavior that will "bring discredit on the department,"[51] or authorizing dismissal "for such cause as will promote the efficiency of the service"[52] have been able to withstand overbreadth chal-

48 Broadrick v. Oklahoma, 413 U.S. 601, 93 S. Ct. 2908, 37 L. Ed. 2d 830 (1973); Rode v. Dellaciprette, 845 F.2d 1195 (3d Cir. 1988); Aiello v. City of Wilmington, 623 F.2d 845 (3d Cir. 1980); Hayes v. City of Wilmington, 451 F. Supp. 696 (D. Del. 1978).

49 Broadrick v. Oklahoma, *supra* note 48, 413 U.S. at 615, 93 S. Ct. at 2818, 37 L. Ed. 2d at ___.

50 See cases cited in note 48 *supra*.

51 *Id.*

52 Arnette v. Kennedy, 416 U.S. 134, 94 S. Ct. 1633, 40 L. Ed. 2d 15 (1974).

lenges. Even though elastic provisions like these are capable of being used by departments to punish employees for their speech, these regulations are primarily directed against nonspeech behavior. The danger that these measures will be misapplied against speech is slight when compared to their broad range of legitimate applications. In *Aiello v. City of Wilmington*,[53] a federal court rejected an overbreadth challenge made by a fireman against department regulations authorizing disciplinary action for "conduct unbecoming a fireman and a gentleman" and for failure to abide by "customary rules of good behavior observed by law-abiding and self-respecting citizens." This officer had been suspended after he was found lying intoxicated on the floor of a retail establishment that he had unlawfully entered. Observing that Aiello had engaged in conduct appropriately subject to discipline and not speech, the court refused to overturn the challenged regulations on grounds of unconstitutional overbreadth.

When the regulation's thrust is *speech* rather than conduct, courts, on the other hand, have employed more rigorous overbreadth scrutiny. Departmental regulations condemning public criticism of departmental policies, practices and supervisory personnel have been before the courts many times, and with few exceptions, reviewing courts have found such regulations unconstitutionally overbroad and void on their face.[54] In *Gasparinetti v. Kerr*,[55] the United States Court of Appeals for the Third Circuit invalidated three Newark police department regulations curtailing criticism. These regulations provided:

> Police officers...shall not by manner, gesture, or speech criticize or make derogatory references to Department orders or instructions either to the police or to members of the Department.
>
> Unless in accord with official duties, police officers...shall not, either in writing or discussion, censure other Department members concerning official transactions within the Department.

---

53 *Supra* note 48.

54 Muller v. Conlisk, 429 F.2d 901 (7th Cir. 1970); Gasparinetti v. Kerr, 568 F.2d 311 (3d Cir. 1977), *cert. denied*, 436 U.S. 903, 98 S. Ct. 2232, 56 L. Ed. 2d 401 (1978); Pierson v. Gondles, 693 F. Supp. 408 (E.D. Va. 1988); Haurilak v. Kelley, 425 F. Supp. 626 (D. Conn. 1977); Flynn v. Giarrusso, 321 F. Supp. 1295 (E.D. La. 1971). *But see* Hall v. Mayor & Director of Public Safety, 170 N.J. Super. 306, 406 A.2d 317 (1979), *rev'd*, 176 N.J. Super. 229, 422 A.2d 797 (A.D. 1980).

55 *Supra* note 54.

> Department members shall not publicly disparage or comment unfavorably or disrespectfully on the official action of a superior officer, nor on the Rules, Regulations, Procedures or Orders of the Police Department.

These regulations outlawed all critical speech whether or not it had an adverse effect on the Department, and in so doing, went significantly beyond the constitutional boundaries the Supreme Court established in *Pickering v. Board of Education*.[56] As we have earlier seen, the fact that an employee has made public statements critical of the agency where he is employed does not automatically cast him outside First Amendment protection. If his speech concerns matters of public importance, if the target of criticism is not an immediate superior or one with whom he works in close daily contact, and if his speech is not shown to have had any injurious effects on his department's operations, the employee's interest in commenting as a citizen prevails and he is not subject to discipline. Finding the Newark Police Department's unqualified ban on all unfavorable commentary dramatically over-inclusive, the *Gasparinetti v. Kerr* court stated:

> We recognize that the Newark Police Department has important interests in regulating some speech of its members. Ch. 6:7, however, indiscriminately casts its net so as to catch, along with that speech which the Department may properly regulate, much speech in which the Department's legitimate interest is minimal. Given the substantial encroachment on the first amendment-protected areas of police officers' speech, the lack of interpretative guidance in construing the regulation, the failure to differentiate between criticism of immediate superiors, which might result in disruption, and criticism of remote superiors, where disruption is unlikely, and the public's strong interest in open debate and access to information about its police, we hold that Ch. 6:7 is overbroad and therefore invalid on its face.[57]

In *Flynn v. Giarrusso*,[58] a federal district court struck down as facially overbroad a departmental regulation which provided that officers should not "unjustly criticize or ridicule, or express hatred or contempt toward, or indulge in remarks which may be detrimental to...any person." In *Muller v.*

---

56 *Supra* note 10.

57 568 F.2d 311, 317 (3d Cir. 1977), *cert. denied*, 436 U.S. 903, 98 S. Ct. 2232, 56 L. Ed. 2d 401 (1978).

58 *Supra* note 54.

Conlisk,[59] another federal court invalidated a measure which prohibited officers from engaging in "any activity, conversation, deliberation, or discussion which is derogatory to the Department or any member." These precedents immediately raise concern whether it is possible to draft departmental regulations controlling critical speech with sufficient precision that they can withstand First Amendment overbreadth challenges. The only safe drafting technique for avoiding a successful overbreadth challenge is to incorporate the *Pickering v. Board of Education* test for differentiating between protected and unprotected expression directly into the regulation's text. The New Orleans police department did this after its regulation on derogatory speech had been struck down in a federal suit.[60] The current regulation, held constitutional in *Magri v. Giarrusso*,[61] reads:

> Members...shall not publicly criticize or ridicule the department, its policies or other employees...*where [their] talking, writing or other expression...tends to impair the operation of the department by interfering with its efficiency; interfering with the ability of supervisors to maintain discipline; or having been made with reckless disregard for truth or falsity.*

The italicized language prevents this regulation from being overly broad because it limits the regulation's application to that speech for which *Pickering v. Board of Education*[62] allows departmental discipline.

Void-for-vagueness doctrine

When the department regulates the speech of its employees, the regulation also must be drafted with sufficient clarity and precision that persons of ordinary imytelligence exercising ordinary common sense can understand its meaning and comply with its dictates.[63] This requirement promotes several constitutional policies.[64] First, due process requires that

---

59 *Supra* note 54.

60 Flynn v. Giarrusso, *supra* note 54.

61 379 F. Supp. 353, 357 (E.D. La. 1974).

62 *Supra* note 10.

63 Civil Serv. Comm'n v. National Ass'n of Letter Carriers, 413 U.S. 548, 578, 93 S. Ct. 2880, 2897, 37 L. Ed. 2d 796 (1973); Broadrick v. Oklahoma, 413 U.S. 601, 608, 93 S. Ct. 2908, 2914, 37 L. Ed. 2d 830 (1973); Arnette v. Kennedy, 416 U.S. 134, 161, 94 S. Ct. 1633, 1647, 40 L. Ed. 2d 15 (1974).

64 Grayned v. City of Rockford, 408 U.S. 104, 92 S. Ct. 2294, 33 L. Ed. 2d 222 (1972).

would-be actors be given fair notice of what conduct is forbidden before punishment is allowed. Second, departmental regulations must give supervisors and administrative boards standards adequate to guide their decisions when they are called upon to apply them. Finally, regulations applying to speech must be clear enough to avoid unnecessarily suppressing more speech than was intended.

The void-for-vagueness doctrine is closely related to overbreadth and courts often confuse the two concepts. A regulation, however, can lack clarity without possessing an unconstitutional sweep. In assessing vagueness challenges, the Supreme Court has recognized the practical difficulties confronting government agencies in drafting regulations general enough to cover a broad range of employment-related misbehavior while at the same time specific enough to afford employees fair notice of what behavior is to be avoided.[65] In evaluating a regulation for vagueness, courts do not scrutinize its language in a vacuum; rather, they consider long-standing applications and authoritative judicial interpretations. In *Arnett v. Kennedy*,[66] the Supreme Court upheld a regulation authorizing dismissal from federal employment "for such cause as will promote the efficiency of the service" because this phrase had acquired content and meaning through applications, administrative regulations, and judicial interpretation. In the course of its opinion, the Court observed:

> [I]t is not feasible or necessary for the Government to spell out in detail all that conduct which will result in retaliation. The most conscientious of codes that defines prohibited conduct of employees includes catchall clauses prohibiting employee 'misconduct,' 'immorality,' or 'conduct unbecoming.'[67]

To challenge a regulation for vagueness, a litigant must do more than show that the regulation's language is vague at its outermost boundaries or that it fails to give fair warning with respect to hypothetical behavior not before the court. At the core of the void-for-vagueness doctrine is fair notice. A litigant must demonstrate that the regulation was vague and failed to give fair notice with respect to the conduct in which he was engaged.[68] One to whom a regulation clearly applies lacks standing to challenge a regulation's

65 Arnett v. Kennedy, *supra* note 63.

66 *Id.*

67 *Id.* at 161, 94 S. Ct. at 1648, 40 L. Ed. 2d at 37.

68 Arnett v. Kennedy, *supra* note 63; Civil Serv. Comm'n v. National Ass'n of Letter Carriers, *supra* note 63; Aiello v. City of Wilmington, *supra* note 48.

language as vague when applied in other contexts.[69] In *Kannisto v. City & County of San Francisco*,[70] a lieutenant remarked to his subordinates during morning inspection that his immediate superior was a most "unreasonable, belligerent, arrogant, contrary and unpleasant" person. He was suspended pursuant to departmental rules treating "any conduct...which tends to subvert the good order, efficiency or discipline" of or "to bring discredit upon" the department as grounds for disciplinary action. The court conceded that this regulation was vague at its fringes, but ruled that any uncertainty or imprecision in the regulation was irrelevant in this case because there could have been no reasonable doubt in the lieutenant's mind that his disrespectful attack on his superior during an official inspection was "unofficerlike" behavior which tended "to subvert the good order, efficiency or discipline" of his department. In *Aiello v. City of Wilmington*,[71] the United States Court of Appeals for the Third Circuit smilarly refused to treat as unconstitutionally vague a regulation requiring officers to abide by "customary rules of good behavior observed by law-abiding and self-respecting citizens" and to refrain from conduct "that will bring discredit to themselves or to the Department" when applied to an officer who illegally broke into a retail establishment while in a drunken state. The court characterized this as "hard core" conduct that any reasonable person should have appreciated would be grounds for disciplinary action.

When a court upholds a broadly-worded regulation, such as one prohibiting "conduct unbecoming an officer," or authorizing dismissal for "such cause as will promote the efficiency of the service," the court does not place an unconditional constitutional stamp of approval on this language as fair notice of all conceivable behavior that the department may later seek to punish. While such broad catch-all language might suffice to convey notice in advance that an officer should refrain from raucous, lewd, or drunken behavior or from making defamatory and vitriolic remarks about his immediate superior, such language has been regarded as inadequate in warning that he should refrain from writing letters to city officials complaining about or seeking redress for wrongs he perceives within his department.[72] Thus, departmental regulations banning unofficerlike behavior may be sufficient to give fair notice in some factual settings but unconstitutionally vague in others.

---

69 Parker v. Levy, 417 U.S. 733, 94 S. C.t 2547, 41 L. Ed. 2d 439 (1974).

70 541 F.2d 841 (9th Cir. 1976), *cert. denied*, 430 U.S. 931, 95 S. Ct. 804, 42 L. Ed. 2d 821 (1978).

71 *Supra* note 48.

72 Bence v. Brier, 501 F.2d 1185 (7th Cir. 1974), *cert. denied*, 419 U.S. 1121, 95 S. Ct. 804, 42 L. Ed. 2d 743 (1973).

§ 12.5 Height, weight, grooming, and personal appearance

Uniformed civil servants do not enjoy the same First Amendment liberty to control matters of personal appearance and grooming while on the job that nonuniformed government employees and citizens generally enjoy.[73] Officers can be compelled to wear standard uniforms meeting specified details and to be neat and clean in appearance. Many departments and local governments, however, have gone beyond general grooming and dress standards and have imposed comprehensive regulations on height, weight, hairstyles and other aspects of an officer's personal appearance. Though the government is without power to dictate what private citizens may wear or to impose personal grooming codes generally, when a citizen accepts employment as a member of the uniformed civil service, he surrenders a large measure of his personal liberty and autonomy in matters of his personal appearance.

In *Kelley v. Johnson*,[74] a Patrolmen's Benevolent Association waged an unsuccessful battle to the Supreme Court challenging departmental grooming standards regulating hair length, sideburns and mustaches and prohibiting beards and goatees. The regulation was attacked as an unconstitutional interference with the First and Fourteenth Amendment rights of policemen. Holding that the challengers had failed to sustain their burden of demonstrating the lack of rational connection between this regulation and the promotion of health and safety considerations, the Court noted:

> The overwhelming majority of state and local police of the present day are uniformed. This fact itself testifies to the recognition by those who direct those operations...that similarity in appearance of police officers is desirable. This choice may be based on a desire to make police officers readily recognizable to members of the public, or a desire for the esprit de corps which such similarity is felt to inculcate within the police force itself. Either one is a sufficient rational justification for regulations so as to defeat the respondent's claim based on the liberty guarantee of the Fourteenth Amendment.[75]

While it is unnecessary for the department to establish a compelling reason for promulgating grooming codes, few would question that an officer's

---

73 Kelley v. Johnson, 425 U.S. 238, 96 S. Ct. 1440, 47 L. Ed. 2d 708 (1976).

74 *Supra* note 73.

75 *Id*. at 248, 96 S. Ct. at 1446, 47 L. Ed. 2d at 716.

physical appearance has a direct bearing on his ability to command public respect and confidence. Restrictions on hair length and beards are also justifiable as safety precautions because long hair and beards may increase an officer's vulnerability in hand-to-hand combat and thus may jeopardize his life. Even when an officer's religious convictions cause him to object to departmental grooming regulations his interest in upholding those convictions has been found to be inferior to the interest of his department.[76]

Challenges against departmental regulations which establish an officer's maximum allowable weight have fared little better in the courts.[77] The government has a legitimate interest in the physical fitness as well as the physical appearance of uniformed justice personnel. Obese officers may find it more difficult to perform physically strenuous activities required by their jobs. Furthermore, overweight employees are far more likely to encounter illnesses leading to excessive absenteeism and in extreme cases, to costly disabilities and untimely retirements, all to the public's detriment. Because of these and other job-related considerations, suits by obese justice employees attacking restrictions on maximum weight have made little headway in the courts.

In contrast to regulations which establish maximum allowable weight for uniformed civil servants, regulations which establish *minimum* height and weight standards for entry into the profession are presently under attack in suits around the nation as violating Title VII of the Civil Rights Act of 1964.[78] Title VII prohibits employers from discriminating against employees or job applicants on the basis of race, color, religion, sex or national origin.[79] Because minimum height and weight qualifications have a disproportionate impact on women applicants and certain ethnic minorities, when a member of one of the protected groups is disqualified from employment on the basis of such restrictions, a Title VII suit may result. While comprehensive treatment of the Title VII implications of minimum height and weight standards is beyond the scope of this work, it should be mentioned that in numerous cases, the Title VII challenge has been successful.[80] In *Dothard v.*

---

76 Goldman v. Weinberger, 475 U.S. 503, 106 S. Ct. 1310, 89 L. Ed. 2d 478 (1986).

77 *See e.g.* Metropolitan Dade County v. Wolf, 274 So. 2d 584 (Fla. 1973), *cert. denied*, 414 U.S. 1116, 94 S. Ct. 849, 38 L. Ed. 2d 743 (1973); Gray v. City of Florissant, 588 S.W.2d 722 (Mo. 1979).

78 Evans, *Height, Weight and Physical Agility Requirements – Title VII and Public Safety Employment*, 8 J. POL. SCI. & ADMIN. 414 (1980).

79 Title VII is discussed in greater detail in § 12.11 *infra*.

80 *See e.g.* Blake v. City of Los Angeles, 595 F.2d 1367 (9th Cir. 1979), *cert. denied*, 446 U.S. 928, 100 S. Ct. 1865, 64 L. Ed. 2d 281 (1980).

Rawlinson,[81] the Supreme Court invalidated the use of a 5'2" height and 120-pound weight requirement for the position of correctional counselor (prison guard) where this standard had worked to disqualify a disproportionate number of woman applicants and where the employing agency failed to establish a direct link between its standards and the amount of strength essential to efficient job performance.

§ 12.6 Citizenship and residency requirements

A majority of states require that uniformed justice employees be citizens of the United States. In *Foley v. Connelie*,[82] a resident alien who was turned down for a position as a New York state trooper was turned down challenged the New York statute which imposed a citizenship requirement on the grounds that it denied resident aliens equal protection of the laws. The Supreme Court disagreed. Applying the rational relationship test, the Court determined that citizenship was rationally related to the special demands made on police officers. Police officers, as the Court pointed out, are authorized to enter dwellings, stop vehicles, make arrests and searches without prior judicial authority, carry weapons, apply lethal force where necessary, and to make other difficult and delicate judgments affecting the privacy, liberty and security of every member of the community. Because police officers are vested with broad discretionary powers that operate "in the most sensitive areas of daily life," the states may legitimately confine employment to those who it "may reasonably presume to be more familiar with and sympathetic to American traditions."[83]

Residency in or near the employing political subdivision is also a common requirement for continuing employment as a criminal justice officer. Because restrictions on where an officer can live strike deep at his personal liberty, residency requirements have repeatedly been singled out for constitutional attacks under the Due Process and Equal Protection Clauses as well as under miscellaneous constitutional provisions.[84] Any lingering doubt as to the constitutional validity of residency requirements was laid to rest by the Supreme Court in *McCarthy v. Philadelphia Civil Service Commission*,[85]

---

81 433 U.S. 321, 97 S. Ct. 2720, 53 L. Ed. 2d 786 (1977).

82 435 U.S. 291, 98 S. Ct. 1067, 55 L. Ed. 2d 287 (1978).

83 *Id*. at 299-300, 98 S. Ct. at 1072, 55 L. Ed. 2d at 294.

84 Annotation, *Validity, Construction, & Application of Enactments Relating to Requirement of Residency Within or Near Specified Government Unit as Condition of Continued Employment for Policemen or Firemen* 4 A.L.R. 4th 380 (1981).

85 424 U.S. 645, 96 S. Ct. 1154, 47 L. Ed. 2d 366 (1976).

where the Supreme Court upheld a residency requirement over the Fourteenth Amendment challenge of a fireman who was terminated by the Philadelphia Fire Department when he established his permanent residence in New Jersey.

Residency requirements for continuing employment have been found to be rationally related to a number of legitimate governmental concerns.[86] Requiring justice officers to be residents of the community enhances job effectiveness by increasing the officer's knowledge of local geography and problems of the local community, as well as his personal stake in the community's progress. Other claimed benefits include decreased tardiness and absenteeism, ready availability of trained manpower in emergency situations, and benefits to the local economy from the expenditures of salaries within the local community. Where residency requirements have been imposed, a justice employee must give up the right to live where he pleases and must locate in the hiring community.

§ 12.7 Restrictions on outside employment

Legislative and administrative regulations curtailing the freedom of justice employees to hold outside employment during their off-duty hours are relatively common. Despite hard economic times, courts have shown little sympathy to suits challenging restrictions on moonlighting activities.[87] In rejecting constitutional challenges, courts have found restrictions on off-duty employment to be rationally related to several legitimate municipal concerns.[88] First, uniformed officers are required to make decisions and take actions that tax their mental and physical capabilities to the limits. The department may rightfully insist that its employees forego outside employment that may lead to fatigue and impair efficiency. Furthermore, unforeseen emergencies requiring extra manpower can arise; the department has an in-

---

86 Ector v. City of Torrance, 28 Cal. App. 3d 293, 104 Cal. Rptr. 594 (1972); *see also* *Rhyne, Police and Firefighter Law* ch. 4 (1982).

87 Reichelderfer v. Ihrie, 59 F.2d 873 (D.C. Cir. 1932), *cert. denied*, 287 U.S. 631, 53 S. Ct. 82, 77 L. Ed. 2d 547 (1932); Hayes v. Civil Service Comm'n, 348 Ill. App. 346, 108 N.E.2d 505 (1952); Hopwood v. Paducah, 424 S.W.2d 134 (Ky. 1968); Isola v. Belmar, 112 A.2d 738 (N.J. 1955); Flood v. Kennedy, 12 N.Y.2d 345, 239 N.Y.S.2d 665, 190 N.E.2d 13 (1963). *But see* Firemen v. City of Crowley, 280 So. 2d 897 (La. 1973).

88 Annotation, *Validity, Construction, and Application of Regulation Regarding Outside Employment of Governmental Employees or Officers*, 94 A.L.R.3D 1240 (1979).

terest in assuring that rank-and-file members are available to assist in extraordinary situations where their services are necessary. Finally, the department has a right to insist upon an officer's undivided loyalty and allegiance to his public calling. Private employment may create potential conflicts of interest, and even where it does not, the department has an interest in avoiding public appearances of impropriety on the part of uniformed civil servants. For these and other reasons, courts have subordinated the justice department employee's interest in supplementing his income through outside employment to the interest of his department and the public.

§ 12.8 Smoking and substance abuse in the workplace

Substance abuse in the workplace has become an increasingly serious national concern. No one questions the right of government employers to demand that workers in safety-sensitive jobs refrain while on duty from using substances that might alter their perception, motor skills or judgment and cause them to become a danger to themselves, fellow workers or the public. The current controversy centers, not on whether substance abuse can be prohibited in the government workplace, but on procedures the government can employ to detect drug and alcohol impaired employees.

Blood and urinalysis testing are common drug screening techniques. More than two decades ago, the Supreme Court ruled that the involuntary extraction of blood for chemical analysis constituted a search.[89] The Court has recently ruled that compulsion to produce a urine sample also entails a search because the process of collecting the specimen and its subsequent laboratory analysis both intrude on the subject's reasonable expectation of privacy.[90] Because searches are involved, drug screening programs which require government employees to furnish blood or urine samples for chemical testing are subject to Fourth Amendment reasonableness requirements.

There are limited instances when a search can be reasonable even though a warrant and probable cause are lacking. Courts have held that a police department's interest in identifying substance-impaired officers justifies the department in compelling a police officer to submit to urinalysis testing whenever the department has a reasonable basis for suspecting him of using or being under the influence of alcohol or narcotic substances while on

---

89 Schmerber v. California, 384 U.S. 757, 87 S. Ct. 1826, 16 L. Ed. 2d 908 (1966).

90 National Treasury Employees Union v. Von Raab, ___ U.S. ___, 109 S. Ct. 1384, 103 L. Ed. 2d 685 (1989); Skinner v. Railway Labor Executives' Ass'n, ___ U.S. ___, 109 S. Ct. 1402, 103 L. Ed. 2d 639 (1989).

duty.[91] Reasonable individualized suspicion may be linked to a combination of objective factors such as deficient job performance, unexplained excessive absenteeism, apparent substance-related physical or mental impairments, and aberrant behavior coupled with financial difficulties. With few exceptions, however, lower federal courts have drawn the line at reasonable individualized suspicion and have found suspicionless mass random drug testing of police department employees to be an unconstitutional invasion of their Fourth Amendment rights.[92]

Two cases handed down by the Supreme Court during the 1988 Term[93] promise public safety employers broader powers to engage in drug testing than lower federal courts have thought. How much broader remains problematic since neither case involved sporadic, random drug-testing without a warrant and without reasonable suspicion. In *National Treasurer Employees Union v. Von Raab*[94] the Supreme Court, in a sharply divided opinion, upheld the constitutionality of a United States Custom Service drug screening program which required urinalysis testing of employees who applied for promotions to drug enforcement positions or to positions requiring them to carry a deadly weapon. The majority ruled that where a government-initiated employee drug-testing program is adopted to serve needs unrelated to crime detection, a search resulting from drug screening tests may be reasonable although individualized suspicion is lacking if the intrusion on the tested employee's privacy interest is minimal as compared to the government's need to conduct a suspicionless search.

The majority gave several rasons why they regarded the intrusion on privacy under the Custom Service program to be slight in comparison with what they regarded as the Service's overriding need to determine whether applicants for promotion to "front-line [drug] interdiction"[95] and weapon carrying positions were drug users. They pointed out that job applicants have "diminished expectations of privacy"[96] with regard to information bearing on

---

91 Fraternal Order of Police Lodge No. 5 v. Tucker, 868 F.2d 74 (3d Cir. 1989); Copeland v. Philadelphia Police Department, 840 F.2d 1139 (3d Cir. 1988), *cert. denied*, ___ U.S. ___ 109 S. Ct. 1636, 104 L. Ed. 2d 153 (1989).

92 Penny v. Kennedy, 846 F.2d 1536 (6th Cir. 1988); Feliciano v. City of Cleveland, 661 F. Supp. 578, 590 (N.D. Ohio 1987); Capua v. City of Plainfield, 643 F. Supp. 1507 (D.N.J. 1986) (fire fighters); Lovvorn v. City of Chattanooga, 647 F. Supp. 875 (E.D. Tenn. 1986). *But see* McDonell v. Hunter, 809 F.2d 1302 (8th Cir. 1987) (corrections institution worker).

93 *See* cases note 90 *supra*.

94 ___ U.S. ___, 109 S. Ct. 1384, 103 L. Ed. 2d 685 (1989).

95 *Id.* at ___, 109 S. Ct. at 1393, 103 L. Ed. 2d at 705.

96 *Id.* at ___, 109 S. Ct. at 1394-1395, 103 L. Ed. 2d 706.

their job fitness. The Court also emphasized the many features of the Custom Service's particular program that minimized the potential for the types of arbitrariness that the Fourth Amendment was designed to deter. In this regard, the Court stressed the fact that only those employees who applied for and were accepted for promotion to covered jobs were subject to testing and that these applicants knew when they sought these jobs that drug testing would be required. The Court also pointed out that since the test administered was a standard test and since those charged with administering the program had no discretion in selecting the employees who would be required to submit to a urinalysis test, the requirement of a search warrant would have added nothing to the privacy protection this program already assured.

In *Skinner v. Railway Labor Executives Association*,[97] handed down the same day as *National Treasurer Employees Union v. Von Raab*, the Supreme Court ruled that the government's interest in regulating the conduct of railroad employees engaged in safety-sensitive jobs justified prohibiting those employees from using drugs or alcohol and in monitoring their compliance by requiring employees involved in major train accidents to immediately undergo urinalysis testing. Though accident involvement, by itself, may have been insufficient to trigger a reasonable suspicion of substance abuse, this event served to identify those employees who were subject to testing and to remove unbridled discretion from those administering the program to arbitrarily select.

National Treasurer Employees Union v. Von Raab and *Skinner v. Railway Labor Executives Association* leave little doubt that criminal justice agencies can make drug testing part of their application process for safety-sensitive positions. Whether these cases reach and sanction suspicionless drug testing at will thereafter, however, is questionable. There are significant differences between subjecting employees to drug testing when they apply to be hired or promoted or when they are involved in a serious accident that might have been caused by substance abuse, on the one hand, and subjecting them daily to the continuing risk of suspicionless drug testing at the whim of their employer, on the other hand. Dragnet, suspicionless drug testing as a means of spot checking on whether departmental substance abuse regulations are being obeyed creates a serious risk of arbitrariness of the type the Fourth Amendment was designed to deter. This writer believes it unlikely that a majority of the Court would approve suspicionless drug-testing of randomly selected employees to determine whether they are complying with departmental drug regulations.

---

97 *Supra* note 90.

As society has become increasingly more health conscious, employers have responded by adopting smoking regulations. In *Grusendorf v. City of Oklahoma City*,[98] a firefighter trainee unsuccessfully challenged a departmental regulation prohibiting smoking either on or off duty for a period of a year after a firefighter trainee commenced employment. The court found the nonsmoking rule to be rationally related to the department's legitimate concerns with the health and fitness of its employees. Citing *Kelley v. Johnson*[99] for the proposition that departmental regulations offend due process only when they are arbitrary and irrational, the court declined to find a violation of the officer's liberty, privacy or due process rights. The Court pointed out that smoking is hazardous to health, and found the regulation to be rationally related to legitimate employment concerns even though it extended to the employee's off-duty activities. This case shows once more that public safety employers may adopt regulations that strike deeply into their employees' liberty when the regulations are rationally related to health and job fitness.

§ 12.9 Homosexuality and sexual misbehavior

Whether a government employee can be subjected to employment discrimination or discharged because he or she is a homosexual or lesbian remains a controversial topic. Title VII of the Civil Rights Act[100] does not protect a person who is discriminated against because of sexual preference rather than gender.[101] Because of this, the gay community has been forced to structure legal arguments either around a claimed constitutional right to privacy or under the Fourteenth Amendment Equal Protection Clause.

The Supreme Court, in a legal context unrelated to employment, has determined that the constitutional right to privacy does not reach private homosexual behavior even between two consenting adults. Though *Bowers v. Hardwick*[102] concerned the constitutionality of a state sodomy statute, this case has had negative repercussions for the gay community in government employment disputes.[103]

---

98 816 F.2d 539 (10th Cir. 1987).

99 425 U.S. 238, 96 S. Ct. 1440, 47 L. Ed. 2d 708 (1976), discussed in § 12.5 *infra*.

100 For a discussion of Title VII, *see* § 12.11 *infra*.

101 De Santis v. Pacific Tel. & Tel. Co., 608 F.2d 327 (9th Cir. 1979); Holloway v. Arthur Andersen & Co., 566 F.2d 659 (9th Cir. 1977); Todd v. Navarro, 698 F. Supp. 871 (S.D. Fla. 1988).

102 478 U.S. 186, 106 S. Ct. 2841, 92 L. Ed. 2d 140 (1986).

103 Padula v. Webster, 822 F.2d 97 (D.C. Cir. 1987); Todd v. Navarro, *supra* note 101.

The prevailing view today is that homosexuality is not a "suspect class" entitled to strict scrutiny under the Equal Protection Clause. This means that a lesbian or homosexual can complain of discrimination in government employment only if he or she can convince the court that the government's consideration of his or her homosexual lifestyle in its employment decision was arbitrary, irrational and lacking in any legitimate governmental purposes. Where police department hiring practices are involved, homosexuals have rarely succeeded in convincing courts that the government acted irrationally in taking their sexual preferences into account in employment decisions.[104] This is particularly true concerning homosexuals who openly acknowledge their lifestyles because, as courts have noted, public acknowledgment may embarrass the department or provoke hostility in co-workers.[105]

It goes without saying that officers should refrain from seeking to promote *any* type of sexual activity while on duty. There are special reasons for guarding against improper sexual remarks and advances directed toward female co-workers. Not only is inappropriate sexual behavior grounds for disciplinary action,[106] unwelcome sexual overtures in extreme cases constitute a form of sexual harassment in violation of Title VII of the Civil Rights Act,[107] subjecting the officer and possibly even his department to suit.[108] In one recent case, the court affirmed the suspension of a police officer for conductng a private, off-duty sexual relationship with a probationary patrolwoman who consented because the court felt that such behavior created a sufficient potential for sexual harassment and abuse of authority that departments should discourage it.[109]

There is little agreement whether an officer's off-duty heterosexual relations with prostitutes, minors or simply persons other than his wife, can afford grounds for disciplinary action. While older cases tended to view police officers as role models for the entire community and to place them on moral pedestals,[110] recent cases show greater sensitivity for their rights of

---

104 Dronenburg v. Zech, 741 F.2d 1388 (D.C. Cir. 1984); Childers v. Dallas Police Dept., 513 F. Supp. 134 (N.D. Tex. 1982); Todd v. Navarro, *supra* note 101.

105 Singer v. United States Civil Service Comm'n, 530 F.2d 247 (9th Cir. 1976), *vacated by* 429 U.S. 1034, 97 S. Ct. 725, 50 L. Ed. 2d 744 (1977).

106 Puzick v. Colorado Springs, 680 P.2d 1283 (Colo. App. 1983); Altman v. Board of Fire & Police Comm'rs, 110 Ill. App. 3d 282, 442 N.E.2d 305 (1982).

107 For a discussion of Title VII, *see* § 12.11 *infra*.

108 Meritor Savings Bank v. Vinson, 477 U.S. 57, 106 S. Ct. 2399, 91 L. Ed. 2d 49 (1986); Watts v. New York City Police Dept., 724 F. Supp. 99 (S.D.N.Y. 1989).

109 Puzick v. Colorado Springs, *supra* note 106.

110 Steward v. Leary, 57 Misc. 2d 792, 293 N.Y.S.2d 573 (1968); Waseman v. Roman, 153 W. Va. 320, 168 S.E.2d 548 (1969).

privacy and freedom of association and will not allow discipline for private, off-duty sexual behavior if the officer conducts himself appropriately in public and his job performance is unaffected.[111]

§ 12.10 Mandatory retirement

Mandatory retirement laws requiring public safety workers to retire at some pre-established age, often between the ages of 55 and 65, have been around for a long time.[112] While public safety work is physically demanding and age eventually takes its toll, enormous individual differences exist with the effects of aging. Many officers reaching the mandatory retirement age remain physically and mentally alert, vigorous and capable of performing the duties of their job. In *Massachusetts Board of Retirement v. Murgia*,[113] the Supreme Court rejected the argument that forcing public safety workers to retire at 50 pursuant to state law was so arbitrary and irrational as to violate the Fourteenth Amendment.

Research conducted in the last few decades has exploded the popular belief that job performance inevitably declines with age. In 1967, Congress enacted the Age Discrimination in Employment Act (ADEA)[114] to protect older workers from arbitrary discrimination based on considerations of chronological age alone. The Age Discrimination in Employment Act protects covered workers against discrimination based on age in decisions affecting hiring, promotion, discharge, compensation and other terms and conditions of employment.[115] Though originally workers were protected against age discrimination only until they reached 65, the upper age limit was subsequently extended to 70 and more recently removed entirely. There is no longer any upper age limitation on protection under the Act.[116]

The Act makes it unlawful for employers to involuntarily retire employees when they reach some pre-established retirement age[117] unless

---

111 Smith v. Price, 616 F.2d 1371 (5th Cir. 1980); Briggs v. North Muskegon Police Dept., 563 F. Supp. 585 (W.D. Mich. 1983), *aff'd*, 746 F.2d 1475 (6th Cir. 1984), *cert. denied*, 473 U.S. 909, 105 S. Ct. 3535, 87 L. Ed. 2d 659 (1985).

112 Nelson, Age Discrimination in Police Employment, 9 J. POL. SCI. & ADMIN. 428, 434 (1981).

113 427 U.S. 307, 49 L. Ed. 2d 520, 96 S. Ct. 2562, 49 L. Ed. 2d 520 (1976).

114 29 U.S.C. § 621 *et seq*.

115 29 U.S.C. § 623 (a) (1).

116 29 U.S.C. § 631, as amended by Age Discrimination in Employment Act Amendments of 1986, 100 Stat. 171 (1989 Supp.).

117 29 U.S.C. § 623 (a) (1).

the employer can demonstrate that age is a bona fide occupational qualification (BFOQ) reasonably necessary for the operation of the employer's business.[118] In other words, unless the employer can establish that age is a BFOQ, the employer must make retirement decisions on the basis of individualized assessments of the particular worker's health capabilities and the demands of his job.[119] An employee can be forced to retire if, because of age-related disabilities, he is no longer capable of performing in a competent manner.[120] However, unless the BFOQ exception applies, he cannot be retired because of chronological age alone.

Congress, nevertheless, recognized that in some jobs with unusually high demands age may be a bona fide occupational qualification reasonably necessary for the operation of an employers business and contained an exemption for such businesses known as he BFOQ exception.[121] The BFOQ exception permits an employer to establish a mandatory retirement age for his employees if the employer can demonstrate that: (1) particular physical traits or job characteristics are reasonably necessary to the proper performance of his business; and *either* that (2) he has a clear factual basis for believing that all or substantially all persons above the established retirement age would be unable to safely and efficiently perform the duties of the job *or* that (3) it is impossible or impracticable to make retirement decisions affecting older employees on an individual basis.[122]

Prior to the 1967 Age Discrimination in Employment Act, it was rare to find state and local jurisdictions without mandatory retirement laws forcing public safety workers into early retirement usually around age 55.[123] Immediately after the enactment of 1967 law, state and local governments became embroiled in expensive and time-consuming litigation all over the nation challenging the validity of mandatory retirement laws for firefighters and police officers. The issue in all of these suits was whether the physical rigors of public safety work and the limitations upon individualized screening were such as to make age a bona fide occupational qualification (BFOQ) for public safety employees. Courts repeatedly listened to testimony whether

---

118 29 U.S.C. § 623 (f) (1).

119 EEOC v. Elrod, 674 F.2d 601, 605 (7th Cir. 1982); Orzel v. City of Wauwatosa Fire Department, 697 F.2d 743 (7th Cir.), *cert. denied*, 464 U.S. 992, 104 S. Ct. 484, 78 L. Ed. 2d 680 (1983).

120 29 U.S.C. § 623 (f) (3).

121 29 U.S.C. § 623 (f) (1).

122 Western Airlines, Inc. v. Criswell, 472 U.S. 400, 105 S. Ct. 2743, 86 L. Ed. 2d 321 (1985); Usery v. Tamiami Trail Tours, Inc., 531 F.2d 224 (5th Cir. 1976).

123 Nelson, *Age Discrimination in Police Employment*, 9 J. POL. SCI. & ADMIN. 428 (1981).

physical and cardiovascular fitness were traits reasonably necessary for the performance of various public safety jobs, whether these traits invariably decline with age, and whether substantially all persons below the government's mandatory retirement age lacked the ability to safely and efficiently perform the duties of the job. While the decisions split, public safety agencies lost more cases than they won.[124] Courts gave many reasons for their reluctance to treat mandatory retirement laws as BFOQs for public safety workers. Where public safety departments lacked regular programs calling for periodic testing and evaluation of the cardiovascular and physical fitness of rank-and-file employees, courts often refused to give serious consideration to their claims that these characteristics were necessary traits for the job.[125] Even when departments succeeded in convincing courts that these characteristics were necessary, they often failed to muster medical, scientific or statistical proof to support their further claims that substantially all workers above their mandatory retirement age lacked the necessary fitness or that individualized screening was not feasible.

The Age Discrimination in Employment Act, as originally enacted, did not cover federal workers. When federal workers were eventually brought within the Act, Congress left standing a former law requiring federal fire-fighters and law enforcement officers to retire at age 55. An outcry by state and local governments was sparked in 1985 after the Supreme Court rejected the argument that the existence of a federal statute requiring federal public

---

124 For cases involving high-level public safety officials, *see* EEOC v. Minneapolis, 537 F. Supp. 750 (D. Minn. 1982); Aaron v. Davis, 424 F. Supp. 1238 (E.D. Ark. 1976); Adams v. James, 526 F. Supp. 80 (N.D. Ala. 1981); EEOC v. St. Paul, 500 F. Supp. 1135 (D. Minn.), *aff'd*, 691 F.2d 1162 (8th Cir. 1982). For cases involving rank-and-file public safety officers, *see* EEOC v. Tennessee Wildlife Resources Agency, 859 F.2d 24 (6th Cir. 1987), *cert. denied*, ___ U.S. ___, 109 S. Ct. 1342, 103 L. Ed. 2d ___ (1989); EEOC v. Kentucky State Police Dept., 860 F.2d 665 (6th Cir. 1988), *cert. denied*, 109 S. Ct. 2066, 104 L. Ed. 2d 631 (1989); EEOC v. State Department of Highway Safety, 660 F. Supp. 1104 (N.D. Fla. 1987); Johnson v. Mayor and City Council of Baltimore, 515 F. Supp. 1287 (D. Md. 1981), *rev'd*, 731 F.2d 209 (4th Cir. 1989); EEOC v. Missouri State Highway Dept., 555 F. Supp. 97 (W.D. Mo. 1982), *aff'd in part, rev'd in part*, 748 F.2d 447, *cert. denied*, Price v. Wilmer, 474 U.S. 828, 88 L. Ed. 2d 72, 106 S. Ct. 88 (1985).

125 EEOC v. Pennsylvania, 829 F.2d 392 (3d Cir. 1987), *cert. denied*, 485 U.S. 935, 108 S. Ct. 1109, 99 L. Ed. 2d 271 (1988); EEOC v. Tennessee Wildlife Resources Agency, *supra* note 124; EEOC V. Kentucky State Police Dept., *supra* note 124; Heiar v. Crawford County, 746 F.2d 1190 (7th Cir. 1984), *cert. denied*, 472 U.S. 1027, 105 S. Ct. 3500, 87 L. Ed. 2d 631 (1985); EEOC v. State Dept. of Highway Safety, *supra* note 124.

safety workers to retire at 55 caused age to be a BFOQ for state and local public safety officers.[126] Shortly thereafter, Congress recognized the inequity of this dual standard and temporarily lifted the ban against enforcement by State and local governments of their existing mandatory retirement programs. State and local governments remain free until the end of 1993 to continue enforcing existing bona fide mandatory retirement programs for public safety workers.[127] At the same time, Congress directed the Secretary of Labor and the Equal Employment Opportunity Commission to study whether physical and mental fitness tests are valid measures of the ability and competency of police officers and fire fighters to perform their jobs and if so, to determine which particular tests are most effective.[128] What Congress intends to do about the validity of police and firefighter mandatory retirement laws after 1993 remains to be seen.

§ 12.11 Racial and sexual discrimination in employment

As part of the Civil Rights Act of 1964, Congress enacted a comprehensive law designed to protect women and minorities against discrimination in employment practices. The 1964 Equal Employment Opportunities Act,[129] better known as Title VII, makes it unlawful for employers to refuse to hire, discharge, or otherwise discriminate against applicants or existing employees with respect to compensation, classifications, promotions, or other terms and conditions of employment because of their race, color, religion, gender, or national origin.[130] In 1972, the employment practices of state and local government agencies were brought within Title VII's coverage.[131] Public safety agencies, long criticized for their dramatic underemployment of women and minorities, are with alarming frequency in recent years being called upon to defend Title VII discrimination suits. This section highlights the more important obligations public safety employers must meet to bring their employment practices into compliance with Title VII requirements.

---

126 Johnson v. Mayor & City Council of Baltimore, 472 U.S. 353, 86 L. Ed. 2d 300, 105 S. Ct. 2712 (1985).

127 29 U.S.C. § 623 (i), as amended by the Age Discrimination in Employment Act of 1986, 100 Stat. 171 (1989 Supp.). Pub. L. No. 99-592, § 3 (b) provides for the repeal of 29 U.S.C. § 623 (i) as of December 31, 1993.

128 29 U.S.C. § 622, as amended by Pub. L. No. 99-592, § 5, Oct. 31, 1986, 100 Stat. 3343 (1989 Supp.).

129 42 U.S.C. § 2000(e) *et seq.*

130 42 U.S.C. § 2000(e)-(2) (a).

131 42 U.S.C. § 2000(e) (a) (1964), as amended by Equal Employment Opportunity Act of 1972, Pub. L. No. 92-261 (1972).

Most public safety agencies have long ago ceased deliberately treating applicants for jobs or promotions unequally because of their race, color, sex, religion or national origin. However, Title VII compliance places a duty on public safety agencies that extends beyond eliminating racial and sexual job classifications and beyond cleansing their hiring and promotional practices of *intentional* discrimination. In the landmark case of *Griggs v. Duke Power Company*,[132] the Supreme Court articulated the concept of "disparate impact discrimination," a concept that has measurably increased the employer's burdens of Title VII compliance. At stake in *Griggs v. Duke Power Co.* was a private industry's job eligibility requirement of a high school diploma and satisfactory scores on two professionally administered aptitude tests. Though this corporate employer had no intent to discriminate and was seeking only to assure the qualifications of those hired, the selection criteria disproportionately eliminated black applicants. Furthermore, neither aptitude test was specially designed to measure knowledge, traits, or skills necessary for the particular jobs for which applicants were being evaluated. Denouncing these selection requirements as discriminatory, the Supreme Court wrote:

> [G]ood intent or absence of discriminatory intent does not redeem employment procedures or testing mechanisms that operate as 'built-in headwinds' for minority groups and are unrelated to measuring job capability.[133]

The form of discrimination recognized in *Griggs* has become known as *disparate impact* discrimination to differentiate it from *disparate treatment* which occurs when an individual is *deliberately treated unequally* because of his or her race or gender. Disparate impact discrimination, in contrast, occurs when an employer utilizes employee selection requirements or procedures that disproportionately eliminate women and minorities from employment opportunities but lack the redeeming justification of being valid predictors of the knowledge, skills or traits necessary for the successful performance of the job for which the applicant is being evaluated.[134] Elimination of disparate impact discrimination requires that employers study the job-relatedness of their hiring and promotional requirements to assure that their

---

132 401 U.S. 424, 91 S. Ct. 849, 28 L. Ed. 2d 158 (1971).

133 *Id.* at 432, 91 S. Ct. at 854, 28 L. Ed. 2d at 165.

134 *See, e.g.*, Horace v. City of Pontiac, 624 F.2d 765 (6th Cir. 1980); Blake v. City of Los Angeles, 595 F.2d 1367 (9th Cir. 1979).

requirements "measure the person for the job and not the persons in the abstract."[135]

A Title VII claimant establishes a prima facie case of disparate impact discrimination once he demonstrates through statistical analysis that the adverse results of the challenged selection procedure fall more heavily on women or minorities, i.e., that women or minorities have significantly lower pass rates or are more likely to be eliminated than others to whom these standards are applied. Once a discriminatory impact has been demonstrated, the employer must justify his use of the challenged selection requirements. Title VII does not preclude employers from giving and acting upon the results of professionally developed abilities tests;[136] nor does it prevent employers from seeking to assure that those hired are qualified for the position. Furthermore, the Act does not compel employers to pass over more qualified applicants for the sake of hiring less qualified women or minorities.[137] What the Act does require, however, is that whenever an employer uses selection procedures that produce a discriminatory end result, the employer must be capable of demonstrating that his selection requirements operate as valid predictors of the knowledge, skills or traits necessary for successful performance of the particular jobs for which applicants are being evaluated.[138]

The Equal Employment Opportunities Commission (E.E.O.C.) has promulgated detailed technical guidelines for the conduction of validation studies of selection criteria to determine whether the particular test or employment procedure being utilized is sufficiently job-related to survive a Title VII disparate impact challenge.[139] However, even when job-relatedness can be established, if alternative screening techniques exist which minimize the discriminatory impact without sacrificing the employer's legitimate concern that employees hired are qualified for the job, Title VII requires employers to adopt these alternative techniques.[140]

Because statistically significant discrepancies continue to exist between the representation of minorities and women on public safety employment rosters and their representation in the relevant labor markets, justice agen-

---

135 Griggs v. Duke Power Co., 401 U.S. 432, 436, 91 S. Ct. 849, 856, 28 L. Ed. 2d 158 (1971).

136 42 U.S.C. § 2000(e)-(2) (h).

137 Griggs v. Duke Power Co., *supra* note 132.

138 Albemarle Paper Co. v. Moody, 422 U.S. 405, 95 S. Ct. 2362, 45 L. Ed. 2d 280 (1975); Dothard v. Rawlinson, 433 U.S. 321, 97 S. Ct. 2720, 53 L. Ed. 2d 786 (1977).

139 Uniform Guidelines on Employee Selection Procedures, 29 C.F.R. § 1607 *et seq.* (1978).

140 *See* cases cited in note 138 *supra; see also* 29 C.F.R. § 1607.3(b).

cies have frequently been targeted for Title VII suits. Such diverse selection procedures as educational requirements,[141] standardized written entrance and promotional exams,[142] minimum height and weight requirements,[143] physical fitness and agility tests,[144] as well as subjective selection criteria such as supervisory evaluations and oral interviews[145] have and are being challenged on disparate impact theories -- often with successful results.

Because minimum height and weight requirements for public safety jobs disproportionately eliminate women applicants, these selection criteria have formed the nucleus of several sex discrimination suits.[146] In *Dothard v. Rawlinson*,[147] the Supreme Court tossed out a 5 feet 2 inches, 120 pound minimum height and weight qualification for prison guard positions, a requirement that disproportionally excluded women applicants. The *Dothard v. Rawlinson* employer lost because it failed to demonstrate to the Court's satisfaction that its minimum height and weight requirement accurately measured strength essential to successful performance of this particular job. One investigator, noting the poor record that public safety employers have shown in Title VII suits challenging minimum height and weight requirements, has observed:

> Unsupported and unilluminating statements to the effect that shorter individuals would be unlikely to perform adequately...or that those of smaller stature would probably precipitate disturbances within prisons have been universally ignored by courts re-

---

141 Castro v. Beecher, 459 F.2d 725 (1st Cir. 1972); United States v. City of Buffalo, 457 F. Supp. 612 (W.D.N.Y. 1978).

142 United States v. City of Buffalo, *supra* note 141; Ensley Branch of NAACP v. Seibels, 616 F.2d 812 (5th Cir. 1980), *cert. denied*, 449 U.S. 1061, 101 S. Ct. 783, 66 L. Ed. 2d 603 (1980); Guardians Ass'n of New York City v. Civil Service Comm'n, 630 F.2d 79 (2d Cir. 1980).

143 Dothard v. Rawlinson, *supra* note 138; United States v. City of Buffalo, *supra* note 141; Horace v. City of Pontiac, *supra* note 134; Blake v. City of Los Angeles, *supra* note 134; Costa v. Markey, 706 F.2d 1 (1st Cir. 1982), *cert. denied*, 464 U.S. 1017, 104 S. Ct. 547, 78 L. Ed. 2d 722 (1983).

144 Harless v. Duck, 619 F.2d 611 (6th Cir. 1980), *cert. denied*, 449 U.S. 872, 101 S. Ct. 212, 66 L. Ed. 2d 92 (1980); Blake v. City of Los Angeles, 595 F.2d 1367 (9th Cir. 1979).

145 Watson v. Ft. Worth Bank & Trust, 487 U.S. 977, 108 S. Ct. 2777, 101 L. Ed. 2d 827 (1988); Harless v. Duck, *supra* note 144; Harrison v. Lewis, 559 F. Supp. 943 (D.C. Cir. 1983).

146 *See* cases cited in note 143 *supra*.

147 *Supra* note 138.

viewing Title VII claims, even though common sense indicates that public safety employees occasionally encounter life-threatening situations requiring exertion of strength, the ability to see over crowds, and the capacity to command respect. This is due primarily to the fact that public safety employers have relied upon assumptions about the nature of such employment and the capabilities of shorter individuals rather than seeking to validate the use of these screening techniques by means of thorough and professionally acceptable methods.[148]

Even when the challenge has been leveled at such clearly relevant screening devices as physical fitness and agility tests, courts have held public safety employers to scientific standards of validation and have refused to accept conclusory assertions that passing a fitness test calling for 15 push-ups, 25 sit-ups, a 6-foot standing broad jump, and a 25-second obstacle course or the like accurately predicts physical strength and agility necessary for public safety employment.[149] When their selection requirements are questioned, public safety employers must be prepared to demonstrate, based on professionally accepted methods backed up by hard empirical data, that their requirements are "predictive of or significantly correlated with important elements of work behavior which comprise or are relevant to the job or jobs for which candidates are being evaluated."[150]

Federal courts, employing disparate impact discrimination theories, have frequently required public safety agencies to revise written entrance and promotion exams,[151] to restructure oral interviews,[152] or to change methods of supervisory evaluations.[153] The disappointing record of public safety employers in Title VII disparate impact suits highlights the need for departments to hire qualified experts to conduct job analyses identifying important elements of work behavior for each position and to conduct validation studies designed to determine whether existing selection criteria are predictive of skills, traits or knowledge necessary for effective job performance. As one court has aptly observed:

---

148 Evans, *Height, Weight, and Physical Agility Requirements – Title VII and Public Safety Employment*, 9 J. POL. SCI. & ADMIN. 414, 426 (1980).

149 Harless v. Duck, *supra* note 144; Blake v. City of Los Angeles, *supra* note 144.

150 29 C.F.R. § 1604.7(c), *see also* Zamlen v. City of Cleveland, 686 F. Supp. 631 (N.D. Ohio 1988); Evans v. City of Evanston, 695 F. Supp. 922 (N.D. Ill. 1988), *vacated*, 881 F.2d 382 (9th Cir. 1989).

151 *See* cases cited in note 142, *supra*.

152 Harless v. Duck, *supra* note 144.

153 Harrison v. Lewis, *supra* note 145.

> It may intuitively seem that college training, a good driving record, and absence of criminal activity or drug use are related to good justice performance, but the court cannot take judicial notice that they are manifestly related to the hiring of qualified law enforcement personnel.[154]

Racial[155] and sexual[156] harassment in the workplace constitutes another rapidly developing area of Title VII litigation. The Supreme Court has ruled that harassment by co-workers and supervisors is actionable under Title VII when it becomes so severe or pervasive as to unreasonably interfere with the victim's work performance and creates a hostile or offensive working environment.[157] While the Court has not yet addressed the circumstances in which an employer becomes liable for sexual or racial harassment committed by its supervisors and other employees, the Court has indicated that it will look to agency principles for guidance. Lower courts have held that the police department is liable under Title VII if commanding officers are aware of repeated instances of racial slurs, jokes and derogatory comments against black officers and the department does nothing to correct this hostile atmosphere.[158]

§ 12.12 Affirmative action programs

Affirmative action programs are programs voluntarily adopted by employers to overcome the present effects of past discrimination and to hasten realization of the national policy of equal employment opportunity. Affirmative action programs normally include one or more of the following features:[159]

---

154 Davis v. City of Dallas, 487 F. Supp. 389, 392 (N.D. Tex 1980), *aff'd*, 777 F.2d 205 (5th Cir. 1985), *cert. denied*, 476 U.S. 1116, 106 S. Ct. 1973, 90 L. Ed. 2d 656 (1989).

155 Ways v. City of Lincoln, 705 F. Supp. 1420 (D. Neb. 1988), *aff'd in part, rev'd in part*, 871 F.2d 750 (8th Cir. 1989).

156 Meritor Savings Bank v. Vinson, 477 U.S. 57, 106 S. Ct. 2399, 91 L. Ed. 2d 49 (1986).

157 *Id.*

158 Ways v. City of Lincoln, *supra* note 155.

159 Policy Statement on Affirmative Action Programs for State and Local Government Agencies, 29 C.F.R. § 1607.17 (1978).

1. Recruitment programs designed to attract qualified minority or women applicants.
2. Systematic efforts to promote career advancement for minority or women employees through on-the-job or other training programs.
3. Long and short-range goals for correcting racial and sexual imbalances in the employer's work force by granting preference in hiring and promotion to qualified women and minorities.

Nothing in Title VII requires *any* employer to take affirmative action to eliminate existing racial or sexual imbalances in the work place by granting preferential treatment to minorities or women.[160] Employers can comply with Title VII by eliminating discriminatory barriers to equal employment opportunity and by treating men and women of all races equally. However, experience has shown that removal of barriers, without more, represents a painfully slow process for integrating women and minorities into the work force on a parity with more-skilled men and nonminorities who have been competing successfully in the market place for centuries. While Title VII does not *require* affirmative action, the federal government has adopted a strong national policy of encouraging *voluntary* efforts by private employers and government agencies to assist women and minorities in gaining entry into the mainstream.

Preferential treatment for women and minorities in allocating scarce employment opportunities inevitably causes resentment in nonminorities disadvantaged by the operation of affirmative action programs. Leveling charges of "reverse discrimination," nonminorities who have suffered career setbacks and disappointments are today waging legal battles in court challenging the constitutional and statutory legitimacy of disadvantaging white males for the sake of creating opportunities for women and minorities.[161] In *United States Steel Workers v. Weber*,[162] the Supreme Court for the first time confronted whether an employer's adoption of an affirmative action plan granting preferential treatment to women and minorities was itself a violation of Title VII's ban against consideration of sex and race in employment deci-

---

160 42 U.S.C. § 2000(e) (2) (j).

161 United States Steel Workers v. Weber, 443 U.S. 193, 99 S. Ct. 2721, 61 L. Ed. 2d 480 (1979); Wygant v. Jackson Board of Education, 476 U.S. 267, 106 S. Ct. 1842, 90 L. Ed. 2d 260 (1986); Johnson v. Transportation Agency, Santa Clara County, 480 U.S. 616, 107 S. Ct. 1442, 94 L. Ed. 2d 615 (1987).

162 *Supra* note 161.

sions. The Court firmly rejected the argument that Title VII absolutely prohibits private employers from voluntarily adopting any special programs to benefit the very groups for whose protection the anti-discrimination law was enacted. *Weber* interprets Title VII to permit the voluntary adoption of affirmative action plans in industries where there is a "manifest imbalance" reflecting underrepresentation of women or minorities in the work force. To withstand a Title VII challenge, the plan adopted, however, may not unnecessarily burden or disadvantage nonminorities. In particular, the plan may not

(1) require the discharge of existing employees and their replacement with women or minorities,

(2) completely foreclose all opportunities of advancement for nonminorities,

(3) authorize hiring or promotion of *unqualified* women or minorities, or

(4) remain in effect, once the plan's goals have been realized, freezing and artificially perpetuating the existence of a racially and sexually balanced work force.[163]

Employers may, nonetheless, without violating Title VII, take a candidate's race or sex into consideration as a "plus" factor in choosing among *otherwise qualified* applicants and may select a qualified female or minority in preference to a white male whose test scores or other credentials may cause him to "rank" higher.[164]

United States Steel Workers v. Weber[165] established the right of private industries to adopt suitably limited affirmative action programs without violating Title VII. When state or local government agencies adopt affirmative action plans, however, the concomitant unequal treatment for white males must be reconciled, as well, with the constitutional mandate of the Equal Protection Clause. The Supreme Court in a series of recent cases has struggled with defining the conditions under which state and local government employers may grant preferences based on race or gender to women and minorities without violating the dictates of the Equal Protection

---

163 United States Steel Workers v. Weber, *supra* note 161; Johnson v. Transportation Agency, *supra* note 161; Ledoux v. District of Columbia, 820 F.2d 1293 (D.C. Cir.), *reh'g granted*, 833 F.2d 868 (1987), *opinion vacated*, 841 F.2d 400 (1988).

164 Johnson v. Transportation Agency, Santa Clara County, *supra* note 161.

165 *Supra* note 161.

Clause.[166] This controversial topic has sharply divided the Court. Consensus, nevertheless, seems to exist that this constitutional determination calls for a multi-factor inquiry. First, the court must decide whether the government had an adequate factual predicate for adopting an affirmative action plan. If the court determines that remedial efforts were justified, the court must next examine whether the plan adopted complies with constitutional standards.[167]

1. *Necessity for remedial purpose of affirmative action plan*

Under the Equal Protection Clause of the Fourteenth Amendment, state and local governments may not, without compelling justification, treat individuals differently on the basis of race or gender. Preferential treatment for women and minorities in state employment is justified when this remedy is adopted to correct the effects of past discrimination practiced by the government unit involved. A suitably crafted affirmative action plan will be upheld if the underrepresentation of women or minorities on the department's employment rolls resulted from the department's own prior discriminatory practices.[168] A gross statistical disparity between the racial and sexual composition of the department and the percentage of qualified women and minorities in the local labor market may, in some instances, justify an inference of discrimination, though direct evidence of illegal employment practices is lacking.[169]

Whether affirmative action programs within state government are proper to achieve purposes other than remedying the government's past illegal behavior remains one of the most hotly debated issues before the Supreme Court today. The Supreme Court has roundly rejected the notion that state governments can disadvantage innocent nonminorities to redress the consequences of discriminatory treatment by society as a whole. Gov-

---

166 Wygant v. Jackson Board of Education, *supra* note 161; United States v. Paradise, 480 U.S. 149, 107 S. Ct. 1053, 94 L. Ed. 2d 203 (1987); City of Richmond v. J.A. Croson Co., ___ U.S. ___, 109 S. Ct. 706, 102 L. Ed. 2d 854 (1989).

167 Wygant v. Jackson Board of Education, *supra* note 161; Ledoux v. District of Columbia, *supra* note 163; Fountain v. City of Waycross, 701 F. Supp. 1570 (S.D. Ga. 1988).

168 *See* cases note 166 *supra*.

169 City of Richmond v. J.A. Croson Co., *supra* note 166; Ledoux v. District of Columbia, *supra* note 163.

ernment agencies may not grant women and minorities job preferences to compensate them because society has given them inferior opportunities.[170]

Mr. Justice Stevens believes that race-conscious remedies are sometimes justifiable for reasons other than to correct past government wrongs.[171] For instance, he takes the position that, in a community troubled by racial unrest, the superintendent of police would be justified in taking active steps to increase minority representation on the police force because "an integrated police force could develop better relationships with the community and thereby do a more effective job of maintaining law and order than a force composed only of white officers."[172]

2. *Consideration of legitimate interests of nonminorities*

Not only must the department possess adequate justification for adopting an affirmative action plan, the plan adopted must be carefully crafted to minimize the harm suffered by innocent nonminorities.[173] While some "sharing of the burden by innocent parties"[174] is permissible, the means chosen to remedy prior discrimination may not excessively or unnecessarily burden innocent third parties. The Supreme Court has pointed out several features that it regards as placing unacceptable burdens on innocent nonminorities and consequently as objectionable in affirmative action plans. First, plans which adopt quotas or which set aside a fixed number or percentage of openings for women or minorities are much more objectionable than plans which establish flexible goals and authorize consideration of race or sex as a "plus" factor when evaluating candidates qualified for jobs in which members of their race or gender are poorly represented.[175] Set-asides and quotas are more drastic than hiring goals and preferences because they completely deny nonminorities the opportunity to compete for job opportunities and advancements earmarked for women and minorities. Blatant past discriminatory practices, however, may justify the

---

170 Wygant v. Jackson Board of Education, *supra* note 161; City of Richmond v. J.A. Croson Co., *supra* note 166.

171 Wygant v. Jackson Board of Education, 476 U.S. at 313-315, 106 S. Ct. at 1867-1868 (Stevens, J., dissenting).

172 *Id.*

173 *See* cases note 167 *supra*.

174 Wygant v. Jackson Board of Education, *supra* note 161.

175 Johnson v. Transportation Agency, Santa Clara County, *supra* note 161; Ledoux v. District of Columbia, *supra* note 163; Fountain v. City of Waycross, *supra* note 167. *But see* United States v. Paradise, *supra* note 166.

establishment of quotas. In *United States v. Paradise,*[176] the Supreme Court approved a lower federal court order requiring the Alabama Department of Public Safety to promote black troopers on a one-for-one basis with whites until 25 percent black representation was reached in the upper ranks of the Department or until the Department devised a promotional plan that complied with the law. The Court pointed out that the long-term and pervasive discrimination practiced by the Alabama Department of Public Safety demonstrated a need for more stringent corrective measures than ordinarily imposed. Although the one-for-one promotional requirement burdened innocent white candidates for promotion, the Supreme Court did not regard this burden constitutionally unacceptable here because it was temporary and no other alternative appeared available to bring the Alabama Department of Public Safety's employment practices in line with Title VII and the Constitution.

Affirmative action plans which seek to correct racial or sexual imbalances in the work force by laying off innocent nonminorities in order to create vacancies are also objectionable.[177] Nor may plans prefer women and minorities by requiring that nonminorities with greater seniority be laid off first when a reduction in force becomes necessary.[178] The laying off of innocent parties is a more objectionable method for removing imbalances than the establishment of hiring goals and preferences in promotions because, while promotional preferences and hiring goals may burden innocent individuals, the denial of a future employment opportunity is not nearly so disruptive of the affected individual's life as a layoff would be.

Plans are also onjectionable if they give preferences to women or minorities who are *unqualified* for the vacancy or promotion they receive. "If a nonminority or male employee 'loses out' on an available job or promotion in favor of another qualified candidate, he or she has in a very real sense suffered a less severe injury than if passed over in favor of an unqualified candidate."[179] Nonminorities possess legitimate expectations of receiving government jobs or promotions if no other candidates are qualified.

Finally, affirmative action plans must be temporary measures and must end once the underrepresentation of women and minorities in the work force has been corrected.[180] A plan designed to permanently and artificially

---

176 *Supra* note 166.

177 Wygant v. Jackson Board of Education, *supra* note 161; Ledoux v. District of Columbia, *supra* note 163.

178 Wygant v. Jackson Board of Education, *supra* note 161.

179 Ledoux v. District of Columbia, 820 F.2d 1293, 1301 (D.C. Cir), *reh'g granted*, 833 F.2d 368 (1987), *opinion vacated*, 841 F.2d 400 (1988).

180 *Id*. at 1302.

maintain a racially and sexually balanced work force after equal employment opportunity has been realized would unnecessarily encroach upon the rights of nonminorities.

While the existence of affirmative action programs may cause white male public safety employees temporary career setbacks and disappointments, correction of racial and sexual imbalances within public safety organizations will in the long run lead to better relations with the minority community and to an increase in public respect and confidence that will be vital to law enforcement in the decades to come.[181]

§ 12.13 Summary

Public safety professionals have traditionally been subjected to regulations that differ both in kind and degree from those found in other branches of public service. Except where fundamental rights are at stake, courts have been unwilling to strike departmental regulations down on constitutional grounds unless the challenging party can demonstrate that they serve no legitimate government purpose and are so irrational as to be arbitrary. Public safety employees have repeatedly waged unsuccessful attacks on citizenship and residency requirements, grooming and personal appearance codes, and restrictions on their outside employment.

Regulations restricting a public safety employee's First Amendment freedoms stand on a different legal footing. Government employees can be disciplined for speaking out on matters of public concern about affairs within their department only where the speech:

(1) violates the department's legitimate interest in confidentiality;
(2) damages working relations with immediate superiors;
(3) creates problems of morale or discipline; or
(4) in other ways disrupts the department's efficient operations.

Moreover, when a department regulates speech, the regulations must be drafted with a high degree of clarity and precision to withstand overbreadth and void-for-vagueness challenges.

The employment practices of state and local public safety organizations are now subject to two federal anti-discrimination laws -- one dealing with

---

181 Detroit Police Officers Ass'n v. Young, 608 F.2d 671, 695-696 (6th Cir. 1979), *cert. denied*, 452 U.S. 938, 101 S. Ct. 3079, 69 L. Ed. 2d 951 (1980), *appeal after remand*, 824 F.2d 512 (6th Cir. 1987).

age discrimination while the other with discrimination on the basis of race and sex. The federal Age Discrimination in Employment Act prohibits employers from discriminating against employees or applicants because of their age unless age is a "bona fide occupational qualification reasonably necessary to the normal operations of the particular business...." Because of sharp controversy among courts whether mandatory retirement laws for state and local public safety workers could be sustained under the BFOQ exception Congress lifted the ban on enforcement of these laws until the end of 1993, pending the outcome of a study be the Secretary of Labor and the EEOC.

The Equal Employment Opportunities Act, popularly known as Title VII, prohibits discrimination against women and minorities in hiring, promotion, discharge and other employment decisions. Even though a public safety employer has no intent to discriminate but is seeking only to assure that applicants are qualified, use of selection requirements that exclude members of classes protected by Title VII with greater frequency than others, is a violation of the law unless the employer can demonstrate by professionally acceptable methods that the selection requirements employed constitute valid predictors of traits, skills or knowledge necessary for successful performance of the jobs for which the requirements are being applied. The poor showing of public safety employers in Title VII suits challenging minimum height and weight qualifications, written entrance and promotional examinations, and the like is often attributable to the employers' over-reliance on intuition and hunch rather than hard empirical data to establish the essential job-relatedness that Title VII requires.

Efforts to remedy past discriminatory practices and to increase representation by women and minorities in the ranks of public safety agencies have prompted many departments voluntarily to adopt affirmative action programs with hiring and promotional quotas. If the department has adequate justification for adopting a plan and if the plan does not unnecessarily disadvantage white males, nonminorities passed up for openings and promotions cannot complain about preferences given to qualified women and minority candidates.

PART II:

JUDICIAL DECISIONS RELATING TO PART I

The judicial decisions in this part of the book have been edited and reprinted in order to make the textual discussion in Part I more meaningful. For maximum benefit, they should be read immediately following the chapters they accompany.

Several of the cases cut across chapter lines. For example, *Miranda* v. *United States*, one of the leading modern cases on self-incrimination, contains some very pertinent and timely comments on the right to counsel as well as on confessions. Consequently, it is mentioned and discussed in all three chapters.

It is not enough to learn the decision or rule of law of a case. To fully appreciate the significance of a rule and to be capable of applying the rule intelligently, the reasoning of the court in reaching the decision must also be considered. Although a court decides only the case which is before it, the decision rendered would be of little use if it did not serve as a guideline for future cases in which similar factual patterns arise. Therefore, the facts are of importance and careful attention must be paid to them in reading the cases.

Cases which follow have been selected primarily for their importance as precedents. Most of the cases interpret constitutional provisions and demonstrate the judicial processes followed when the United States Supreme Court reaches a decision involving a constitutional question. Due to space limitations, some editing has been necessary. However, every effort has been made not to delete those parts of the case which bear directly on the points discussed.

For the reader who desires to acquire the full text of these cases or to research the cases cited in Part I, this material is available in law schools and courthouse libraries. If this book is used as a text, it is recommended that selected cases be assigned to the students and that they be required to report on the cases.

PART II.

JUDICIAL DECISIONS RELATING TO PART I.

TABLE OF CASES IN PART II

(For complete table of cases, see p. 923)

Cases relating to **Chapter 1**

HISTORY AND GENERAL APPLICATION OF CONSTITUTIONAL PROVISIONS

M'CULLOCH v. MARYLAND

17 U.S. (4 Wheat.) 316, 4 L.Ed. 579 (1819)

This was an action of debt, brought by the defendant in error, John James, who sued as well for himself as for the State of Maryland, in the county court of Baltimore county, in the said State, against the plaintiff in error, M'Culloch, to recover certain penalties under the act of the legislature of Maryland, hereafter mentioned. Judgment being rendered against the plaintiff in error, upon the following statement of facts, agreed and submitted to the court by the parties, was affirmed by the court of appeals of the State of Maryland, the highest court of law of said State, and the cause was brought, by writ of error, to this court.

It is admitted by the parties in this cause, by their counsel, that there was passed, on the 10th day of April, 1816, by the congress of the United States, an act, entitled, "An act to incorporate the subscribers to the Bank of the United States"; and that there was passed, on the 11th day of February, 1818, by the general assembly of Maryland, an act, entitled, "An act to impose a tax on all banks, or branches thereof, in the State of Maryland, not chartered by the legislature," which said acts are made part of this statement, and it is agreed may be read from the statute books in which they are respectively printed. It is further admitted, that the president, directors, and company of the bank of the United States, incorporated by the act of congress aforesaid, did organize themselves, and go into full operation in the city of Philadelphia, in the State of Pennsylvania, in pursuance of the said act, and that they did on the . . . day of . . . eighteen hundred and seventeen, establish a branch of the said bank, or an office of discount and deposit, in the city of Baltimore, in the State of Maryland, which has from that time, until the first day of May, eighteen hundred and eighteen, ever since transacted and carried on business as a bank, or office of discount and deposit, and as a branch of the said bank of the United States, by issuing bank notes and discounting promissory notes, and performing other operations usual and customary for banks to do and perform, under the authority and by the direction of the said president, directors, and company of the bank of the United States, established at Philadelphia, as aforesaid. It is further admitted, that the said president, directors, and company of the said bank, had no authority to establish the said branch, or office of discount and deposit, at the city of Baltimore, from the State of Maryland, otherwise than the said State having adopted the constitution of the United States, and composing one of the States of the Union. It is further admitted, that James William M'Culloch, the defendant below, being the cashier of the said branch, or office of discount and deposit, did, on the several days set forth in the declaration in this cause, issue the said respective bank-notes therein described, from the said branch, or office, to a certain George Williams, in the city of Baltimore, in part payment of a promissory note of the said Williams, discounted by the said branch or office, which said respective bank-notes were not, nor was either of them, so issued on stamped paper, in the manner prescribed by the act of assembly aforesaid. It is further admitted, that the said president, directors, and company of the bank of the United States, and the said branch or office of discount and deposit, have not, nor has either of them, paid in advance, or otherwise, the sum of fifteen thousand dollars, to the treasurer of the Western Shore, for the use of the State of Maryland, before the issuing of the said notes, or any of them, nor since those periods. And it is further admitted, that the treasurer of the Western Shore of Maryland, under the direction of the governor and council of the said State, was ready, and offered to deliver to the said president, directors, and company of the said bank, and to the said branch, or office of discount and deposit, stamped paper of the kind and denomination required and described in the said act of assembly.

The question submitted to the court for their decision in this case, is as to the validity of the said act of the general assembly of Maryland, on the ground of its being repugnant to the constitution of the United States, and the act of congress aforesaid, or to one of them.

Upon the foregoing statement of facts, and the pleadings in this cause (all errors in which are hereby agreed to be mutually released), if the court should be of opinion that the plaintiffs are entitled to recover, then judgment, it is agreed, shall be entered for the plaintiffs, for twenty-five hundred dollars, and costs of suit. But if the court should be of opinion that the plaintiffs are not entitled to recover upon the statement and pleadings aforesaid, then judgment of *non pros* shall be entered, with costs, to the defendant.

It is agreed that either party may appeal from the decision of the county court to the court of appeals, and from the decision of the court of appeals to the supreme court of the United States, according to the modes and usages of law, and have the same benefit of this statement of facts, in the same manner as could be had if a jury had been sworn and impanelled in this cause, and a special verdict had been found, or these facts had appeared and been stated in an exception taken to the opinion of the court, and the court's direction to the jury thereon.

. . . .

MARSHALL, C. J., delivered the opinion of the court.

In the case now to be determined, the defendant, a sovereign state, denies the obligation of a law enacted by the legislature of the Union; and the plaintiff, on his part, contests the validity of an act which has been passed by the legislature of that State. The constitution of our country, in its most interesting and vital parts, is to be considered; the conflicting powers of the government of the Union and of its members, as marked in that constitution, are to be discussed; and an opinion given, which may essentially influence the great operations of the government. No tribunal can approach such a question without a deep sense of its importance, and of the awful responsibility involved in its decision. But it must be decided peacefully, or remain a source of hostile legislation, perhaps of hostility of a still more serious nature; and if it is to be so decided, by this tribunal alone can the decision be made. On the supreme court of the United States has the constitution of our country devolved this important duty.

The first question made in the cause is, has congress power to incorporate a bank?

It has been truly said, that this can scarcely be considered as an open question, entirely unprejudiced by the former proceedings of the nation respecting it. The principle now contested was introduced at a very early period of our history, has been recognized by many successive legislatures, and has been acted upon by the judicial department, in cases of peculiar delicacy, as a law of undoubted obligation.

It will not be denied that a bold and daring usurpation might be resisted, after an acquiescence still longer and more complete than this. But it is conceived that a doubtful question, one on which human reason may pause, and the human judgment be suspended, in the decision of which the great principles of liberty are not concerned, but the respective powers of those who are equally the representatives of the people, are to be adjusted, if not put at rest by the practice of the government, ought to receive a considerable impression from that practice. An exposition of the constitution, deliberately established by legislative acts, on the faith of which an immense property has been advanced, ought not to be lightly disregarded.

The power now contested was exercised by the first congress elected under the present constitution. The bill for incorporating the Bank of the United States did not steal upon an unsuspecting legislature, and pass unobserved. Its principle was completely understood, and was opposed with equal zeal and ability. After being resisted, first in the fair and open field of debate, and afterwards in the executive cabinet, with as much persevering talent as any measure has ever experienced, and being supported by arguments which convinced minds as pure and as intelligent as this country can boast, it became a law. The original act was permitted to expire; but a short experience of the embarrassments to which the refusal to revive it exposed the government, convinced those who were most prejudiced against the measure of its necessity, and induced the passage of the present law. It would require no ordinary share of intrepidity to assert that a measure adopted under these circumstances was a bold and plain usurpation, to which the constitution gave no countenance.

These observations belong to the cause: but they are not made under the impression that, were the question entirely new, the law would be found irreconcilable with the constitution.

In discussing this question, the counsel for the State of Maryland have deemed it of some importance, in the construction of the constitution, to consider that instrument not as emanating from the people, but as the act of sovereign and independent States. The powers of the general government, it has been said, are delegated by the States, who alone are truly sovereign; and must be exercised in subordination to the States, who alone possess supreme dominion.

It would be difficult to sustain this proposition. The convention which framed the constitution was, indeed, elected by the state legislatures. But the instrument, when it came from their hands, was a mere proposal, without obligation, or pretensions to it. It was reported to the then existing congress of the United States, with a request that it might "be submitted to a convention of delegates, chosen in each State, by the people thereof, under the recommendation of its legislature, for their assent and ratification." This mode of proceeding was adopted; and by the convention, by congress, and by the State legislatures, the instrument was submitted to the people. They acted upon it, in the only manner in which they can act safely, effectively, and wisely, on such a subject, by assembling in convention. It is true, they assembled in their several States; and where else should they have assembled? No political dreamer was ever wild enough to think of breaking down the lines which separate the States, and of compounding the American people into one common mass. Of consequence, when they act, they act in their States. But the measures they adopt do not, on that account, cease to be the measures of the people themselves, or become the measures of the State governments.

From these conventions the constitution derives its whole authority. The government proceeds directly from the people; is "ordained and established" in the name of the people; and is declared to be ordained, "in order to form a more perfect union, establish justice, insure domestic tranquility, and secure the blessings of liberty to themselves and to their posterity."

The assent of the States, in their sovereign capacity, is implied in calling a convention, and thus submitting that instrument to the people. But the people were at perfect liberty to accept or reject it; and their act was final. It required not the affirmance, and could not be negatived, by the State governments. The constitution, when thus adopted, was of complete obligation, and bound the State sovereignties.

It has been said, that the people had already surrendered all their powers to the State sovereignties, and had nothing more to give. But, surely, the question whether they may resume and modify the powers granted to government, does not remain to be settled in this country. Much more might the legitimacy of the general government be doubted, had it been created by the States. The powers delegated to the State sovereignties were to be exercised by themselves, not by a distinct and independent sovereignty, created by themselves. To the formation of a league, such as was the confederation, the State sovereignties were certainly competent. But when, "in order to form a more perfect union," it was deemed necessary to change this alliance into an effective government, possessing great and sovereign powers, and acting directly on the people, the necessity of referring it to the people, and of deriving its powers directly from them, was felt and acknowledged by all.

The government of the Union, then, (whatever may be the influence of this fact on the case,) is, emphatically and truly, a government of the people. In form and in substance it emanates from them. Its powers are granted by them, and are to be exercised directly on them, and for their benefit.

This government is acknowledged by all to be one of enumerated powers. The principle, that it can exercise only the powers granted to it, would seem too apparent to have required to be enforced by all those arguments which its enlightened friends, while it was depending before the people, found it necessary to urge. That principle is now universally admitted. But the question respecting the extent of the powers actually granted, is perpetually arising, and will probably continue to arise, as long as our system shall exist.

In discussing these questions, the conflicting powers of the general and State governments must be brought into view, and the supremacy of their respective laws, when they are in opposition, must be settled.

If any one proposition could command the universal assent of mankind, we might expect it would be this: that the government of the Union, though limited in its powers, is supreme within its sphere of action. This would seem to result necessarily from its nature. It is the government of all; its powers are delegated by all; it represents all and acts for all. Though any one State may be willing to control its operations, no State is willing to allow others to control them. The nation, on those subjects on which it can act, must necessarily bind its component parts. But this question is not left to mere reason: the people have, in express terms, decided it, by saying, "this constitution, and the laws of the United States, which shall be made in pursuance thereof," "shall be the supreme law of the land," and by requiring that the members of the State legislatures, and the officers of the executive and judicial departments of the States, shall take the oath of fidelity to it.

The government of the United States, then, though limited in its powers, is supreme; and its laws, when made in pursuance of the constitution, form the supreme law of the land, "any thing in the constitution or laws of any State, to the contrary notwithstanding."

Among the enumerated powers, we do not find that of establishing a bank or creating a corporation. But there is no phrase in the instrument which, like the articles of confederation, excludes incidental or implied powers; and which requires that every thing granted shall be expressly and minutely described. Even the 10th amendment, which was framed for the purpose of quieting the excessive jealousies which had been excited, omits the word "expressly," and declares only that the powers "not delegated to the United States, nor prohibited to the States, are reserved to the States or to the people"; thus leaving the question, whether the particular power which may become the subject of contest, has been delegated to the one government, or prohibited to the other, to depend on a fair construction of the whole instrument. The men who drew and adopted this amendment, had experienced the embarrassments resulting from the insertion of this word in the articles of confederation, and probably omitted it to avoid those embarrassments. A constitution, to contain an accurate detail of all the subdivisions of which its great powers will admit, and of all the means by which they may be carried into execution, would partake of the prolixity of a legal code, and could scarcely be embraced by the human mind. It would probably never be understood by the public. Its nature, therefore, requires, that only its great outlines should be marked, its important objects designated, and the minor ingredients which compose those objects be deduced from the nature of the objects themselves. That this idea was entertained by the framers of the American constitution, is not only to be inferred from the nature of the instrument, but from the language. Why else were some of the limitations, found in the 9th section of the 1st article, introduced? It is also, in some degree, warranted by their having omitted to use any restrictive term which might prevent its receiving a fair and just interpretation. In considering this question, then, we must never forget, that it is a constitution we are expounding.

Although, among the enumerated powers of government, we do not find the word "bank" or "incorporation," we find the great powers to lay and collect taxes; to borrow money; to regulate commerce; to declare and conduct a war; and to raise and support armies and navies. The sword and the purse, all the external relations, and no inconsiderable portion of the industry of the nation, are intrusted to its government. It can never be pretended that these vast powers draw after them others of inferior importance, merely because they are inferior. Such an idea can never be advanced. But it may, with great reason, be contended, that a government, intrusted with such ample powers, on the due execution of which the happiness and prosperity of the nation so vitally depends, must also be intrusted with ample means for their execution. The power being given, it is the interest of the nation to facilitate its execution. It can never be their interest, and cannot be presumed to have been their intention, to clog and embarrass its execution by withholding the most appropriate means. Throughout this vast republic, from the St. Croix to the Gulf of Mexico, from the Atlantic to the Pacific, revenue is to be collected and expended, armies are to be marched and supported. The exigencies of the nation may require, that the treasure raised in the North should be transported to the South, that raised in the East conveyed to the West, or that this order should be reversed. Is that construction of the constitution to be preferred which would render these operations difficult, hazardous, and expensive? Can we adopt that construction, (unless the words imperiously require it,) which would impute to the framers of that instrument, when granting these powers for the public good, the intention of impeding their exercise by withholding a choice of means? If, indeed, such be the mandate of the constitution, we have only to obey; but that instrument does not profess to enumerate the means by which the powers it confers may be executed; nor does it prohibit the creation of a corporation, if the existence of such a being be essential to the beneficial exercise of those powers. It is, then, the subject of fair inquiry, how far such means may be employed.

It is not denied, that the powers given to the government imply the ordinary means of execution. That, for example, of raising revenue, and applying it to national purposes, is admitted to imply the power of conveying money from place to place, as the exigencies of the nation may require, and of employing the usual means of conveyance. But it is denied that the government has its choice of means; or, that it may employ the most convenient means, if, to employ them, it be necessary to erect a corporation.

On what foundation does this argument rest? On this alone: The power of creating a corporation, is one appertaining to sovereignty, and is not expressly conferred on Congress. This is true. But all legislative powers appertain to sovereignty. The original power of giving the law on any subject whatever, is a sovereign power;

and if the government of the Union is restrained from creating a corporation, as a means for performing its functions, on the single reason that the creation of a corporation is an act of sovereignty; if the sufficiency of this reason be acknowledged, there would be some difficulty in sustaining the authority of congress to pass other laws for the accomplishment of the same objects.

The government which has a right to do an act, and has imposed on it the duty of performing that act, must, according to the dictates of reason, be allowed to select the means; and those who contend that it may not select any appropriate means, that one particular mode of effecting the object is excepted, take upon themselves the burden of establishing that exception.

The creation of a corporation, it is said, appertains to sovereignty. This is admitted. But to what portion of sovereignty does it appertain? Does it belong to one more than to another? In America, the powers of sovereignty are divided between the government of the Union, and those of the States. They are each sovereign, with respect to the objects committed to it, and neither sovereign with respect to the objects committed to the other. We cannot comprehend that train of reasoning which would maintain, that the extent of power granted by the people is to be ascertained, not by the nature and terms of the grant, but by its date. Some state constitutions were formed before, some since that of the United States. We cannot believe that their relation to each other is in any degree dependent upon this circumstance. Their respective powers must, we think, be precisely the same as if they had been formed at the same time. Had they been formed at the same time, and had the people conferred on the general government the power contained in the constitution, and on the States the whole residuum of power, would it have been asserted that the government of the Union was not sovereign with respect to those objects which were intrusted to it, in relation to which its laws were declared to be supreme? If this could not have been asserted, we cannot well comprehend the process of reasoning which maintains, that a power appertaining to sovereignty cannot be connected with that vast portion of it which is granted to the general government, so far as it is calculated to subserve the legitimate objects of that government. The power of creating a corporation, though appertaining to sovereignty, is not like the power of making war, or levying taxes, or of regulating commerce, a great substantive and independent power, which cannot be implied as incidental to other powers, or used as a means of executing them. It is never the end for which other powers are exercised, but a means by which other objects are accomplished. No contributions are made to charity for the sake of an incorporation, but a corporation is created to administer the charity; no seminary of learning is instituted in order to be incorporated, but the corporated character is conferred to subserve the purposes of education. No city was ever built with the sole object of being incorporated, but is incorporated as affording the best means of being well governed. The power of creating a corporation is never used for its own sake, but for the purpose of effecting something else. No sufficient reason is, therefore, perceived, why it may not pass as incidental to those powers which are expressly given, if it be a direct mode of executing them.

But the constitution of the United States has not left the right of congress to employ the necessary means, for the execution of the powers conferred on the government, to general reasoning. To its enumeration of powers is added that of making "all laws which shall be necessary and proper, for carrying into execution the foregoing powers, and all other powers vested by this constitution, in the government of the United States, or in any department thereof."

The counsel for the State of Maryland have urged various arguments, to prove that this clause, though in terms a grant of power, is not so in effect; but is really restrictive of the general right, which might otherwise be implied, of selecting means for executing the enumerated powers.

In support of this proposition, they have found it necessary to contend, that this clause was inserted for the purpose of conferring on congress the power of making laws. That, without it, doubts might be entertained, whether congress could exercise its powers in the form of legislation.

But could this be the object for which it was inserted? A government is created by the people, having legislative, executive, and judicial powers. Its legislative powers are vested in a congress, which is to consist of a senate and house of representatives. Each house may determine the rule of its proceedings; and it is declared that every bill which shall have passed both houses, shall, before it becomes a law, be presented to the President of the United States. The 7th section describes the course of proceedings, by which a bill shall become a law; and, then, the 8th section enumerates the powers of congress. Could it be necessary to say, that a legislature should exercise legislative powers, in the shape of legislation? After allowing each house to prescribe its own course of proceeding, after describing the manner in which a bill should become a law, would it have entered into the mind of a single member of the convention, that an express power to make laws was necessary to enable the legislature to make them? That a legislature, endowed with legislative powers, can legislate, is a proposition too self-evident to have been questioned.

. . . .

But the argument which most conclusively demonstrates the error of the construction contended for by the counsel for the State of Maryland, is founded on the intention of the convention, as manifested in the whole clause. To waste time and argument in proving that, without it, congress might carry its powers into execution, would be not much less idle than to hold a lighted taper to the sun. As little can it be required to prove, that in the absence of this clause, congress would have some choice of means. That it might employ those which, in its judgment, would most advantageously effect the object to be accomplished. That any means adapted to the end, any means which tended directly to the execution of the constitutional powers of the government, were in themselves constitutional. This clause, as construed by the State of Maryland, would abridge and almost annihilate this useful and necessary right of the legislature to select its means. That this could not be intended, is, we should think, had it not been already controverted, too apparent for controversy. We think so for the following reasons:—

1. The clause is placed among the powers of congress, not among the limitations on those powers.

2. Its terms purport to enlarge, not to diminish the powers vested in the government. It purports to be an additional power, not a restriction on those already granted. No reason has been or can be assigned, for thus concealing an intention to narrow the discretion of the national legislature, under words which purport to enlarge it. The framers of the constitution wished its adoption, and well knew that it would be endangered by its strength, not by its weakness. Had they been capable of using language which would convey to the eye one idea, and after deep reflection, impress on the mind another, they would rather have disguised the grant of power, than its limitation. If then, their intention had been, by this clause, to restrain the free use of means which might otherwise have been implied, that intention would have been inserted in another place, and would have been expressed in terms resembling these: "In carrying into execution the foregoing powers, and all others," &c., "no laws shall be passed but such as are necessary and proper." Had the intention been to make this clause restrictive, it would unquestionably have been so in form as well as in effect.

The result of the most careful and attentive consideration bestowed upon this clause is, that if it does not enlarge, it cannot be construed to restrain the powers of congress, or to impair the right of the legislature to exercise its best judgment in the selection of measures, to carry into execution the constitutional powers of the government. If no other motive for its insertion can be suggested, a sufficient one is found in the desire to remove all doubts respecting the right to legislate on that vast mass of incidental powers which must be involved in the constitution, if that instrument be not a splendid bauble.

. . . .

After the most deliberate consideration, it is the unanimous and decided opinion of this court, that the act to incorporate the Bank of the United States is a law made in pursuance of the constitution, and is a part of the supreme law of the land.

The branches, proceeding from the same stock, and being conducive to the complete accomplishment of the object, are equally constitutional. It would have been unwise to locate them in the charter, and it would be unnecessarily inconvenient to employ the legislative power in making those subordinate arrangements. The great duties of the bank are prescribed; those duties require branches, and the bank itself may, we think, be safely trusted with the selection of places where those branches shall be fixed; reserving always to the government the right to require that a branch shall be located where it may be deemed necessary.

It being the opinion of the court, that the act incorporating the bank is constitutional; and that the power of establishing a branch in the State of Maryland might be properly exercised by the bank itself, we proceed to inquire:—

[The second part of the decision concerned the right of the State of Maryland to tax the Bank of the United States and has been omitted. The Court concluded the opinion with:]

We are unanimously of opinion, that the law passed by the legislature of Maryland, imposing a tax on the Bank of the United States, is unconstitutional and void.

This opinion does not deprive the States of any resources which they originally possessed. It does not extend to a tax paid by the real property of the bank, in common with the other real property within the State, nor to a tax imposed on the interest which the citizens of Maryland may hold in this institution, in common with other property of the same description throughout the State. But this is a tax on the operations of the bank, and is, consequently, a tax on the operation of an instrument employed by the government of the Union to carry its powers into execution. Such a tax must be unconstitutional.

JUDGMENT. This cause came on to be heard on the transcript of the record of the court of appeals of the State of Maryland, and was argued by counsel. On consideration whereof, it is the opinion of this court, that the act of the legislature of Maryland is contrary to the constitution of the United States, and void; and therefore, that the said court of appeals of the State of Maryland erred in affirming the judgment of the Baltimore county court, in which judgment was rendered against James W. M'Culloch, but that the said court of appeals of Maryland ought to have reversed the said judgment of the said Baltimore county court, and ought to have given judgment for the said appellant, M'Culloch. It is therefore adjudged and ordered, that the said judgment of the said court of appeals of the State of Maryland, in this case, be, and the same hereby is, reversed and annulled. And this court, proceeding to render such judgment as the said court of appeals should have rendered, it is further adjudged and ordered, that the judgment of the said Baltimore county court be reversed and annulled, and that judgment be entered in the said Baltimore county court for the said James W. M'Culloch.

EQUAL EMPLOYMENT OPPORTUNITY COMMISSION v. WYOMING

460 U.S. 226, 103 S. Ct. 1054, 75 L.Ed. 2d 18 (1983)
[Syllabus only]

The Age Discrimination in Employment Act of 1967 makes it unlawful for an employer to discriminate against any employee or potential employee between the ages of 40 and 70 on the basis of age, except "where age is a bona fide occupational qualification reasonably necessary to the normal operation of the particular business, or where the differentiation is based on reasonable factors other than age." In 1974, the definition of "employer" under § 11(b) of the Act was extended to include state and local governments. After a supervisor for the Wyoming Game and Fish Department was involuntarily retired at age 55 pursuant to a Wyoming statute, he filed a complaint with the Equal Employment Opportunity Commission, alleging violation of the Act. The Commission ultimately filed suit in Federal District Court against appellees, the State and various state officials, seeking relief on behalf of the supervisor and others similarly situated. The District Court dismissed the suit, holding that insofar as the Act regulated Wyoming's employment relationship with its game wardens and other law enforcement officials, it violated the doctrine of Tenth Amendment immunity articulated in *National League of Cities v. Usery,* 426 U.S. 833, 96 S.Ct. 2465, 49 L.Ed.2d 245, which struck down Congress' attempt to extend the wage and hour provisions of the Fair Labor Standards Act to state and local governments.

Held: The extension of the Age Discrimination in Employment Act to cover state and local governments is a valid exercise of Congress' powers under the Commerce Clause, both on its face and as applied in this case, and is not precluded by virtue of external constraints imposed on Congress' commerce powers by the Tenth Amendment.

(a) The purpose of the doctrine of Tenth Amendment immunity articulated in *National League of Cities, supra,* is to protect States from federal intrusions that might threaten their "separate and independent existence." A claim that congressional commerce power legislation is invalid can succeed only if (1) the challenged statute regulates the States as States, (2) the federal regulation addresses matters that are indisputably attributes of state sovereignty, and (3) the States' compliance with the federal law would "directly impair their ability 'to structure integral operations in areas of traditional governmental functions' " *Hodel v. Virginia Surface Mining & Reclamation Assn.,* 452 U.S. 264, 287–288, 101 S.Ct. 2352, 2365–66,

69 L.Ed.2d 1. The first requirement is met in this case, but even assuming, *arguendo*, that the second requirement is met, the Act does not "directly impair" the State's ability to "structure integral operations in areas of traditional governmental functions."

(b) In this case, the degree of federal intrusion on the States' ability to structure their integral operations is not sufficient to override Congress' choice to extend its regulatory authority to the States. Appellees claim no substantial stake in their retirement policy other than assuring the physical preparedness of Wyoming game wardens to perform their duties. The Act does not require the State to abandon those goals, or the public policy decisions underlying them. Under the Act, the State may assess the fitness of its game wardens on an individualized basis and may dismiss those wardens whom it reasonably finds to be unfit. Moreover, appellees remain free under the Act to continue to do precisely what they are doing now, if they can demonstrate that age is a "bona fide occupational qualification" for the job of game warden. And nothing in the nature of the Act suggests that it will have substantial and unintended consequential effects on state decisionmaking in other areas, such as the allocation of state financial resources or the pursuit of broad social and economic policies. *National League of Cities, supra*, distinguished.

514 F.Supp. 595, reversed and remanded.

MACKEY v. MONTRYM

443 U.S. 1, 61 L.Ed.2d 321, 99 S.Ct. 2612 (1979)
[Syllabus only]

A Massachusetts statute mandates suspension of a driver's license for refusing to take a breathalyzer test upon arrest for operating a motor vehicle while under the influence of intoxicating liquor. The Registrar of Motor Vehicles must order a 90-day suspension upon receipt of the police report of the licensee's refusal to take such test; the licensee, after surrendering his license, is entitled to an immediate hearing before the Registrar. Appellee, whose license was suspended under the statute, brought a class action in Federal District Court alleging that the Massachusetts statute was unconstitutional on its face and as applied in that it authorized the suspension of his license without affording him a presuspension hearing. The District Court held that appellee was entitled as a matter of due process to some sort of presuspension hearing, declared the statute unconstitutional on its face as violative of the Due Process Clause of the Fourteenth Amendment, and granted injunctive relief.

Held: The Massachusetts statute is not void on its face as violative of the Due Process Clause. Cf. *Dixon* v. *Love*, 431 U.S. 105, 97 S.Ct. 1723, 52 L.Ed.2d 172. Pp. 2617-2621.

(a) Suspension of a driver's license for statutorily defined cause implicates a property interest protected by the Due Process Clause. Resolution of the question of what process is due to protect against an erroneous deprivation of a protectible property interest requires consideration of (i) the nature and weight of the private interest affected by the official action challenged; (ii) the risk of an erroneous deprivation of such interest as a consequence of the summary procedures used; and (iii) the governmental function involved and state interests served by such procedures, as well as the administrative and fiscal burdens, if any, that would result from the substitute procedures sought. *Mathews* v. *Eldridge,* 424 U.S. 319, 96 S.Ct. 893, 47 L.Ed.2d 18. Pp. 2617-2618.

(b) Here, neither the nature of the private interest involved—the licensee's interest in the continued possession and use of his license pending the outcome of the hearing due him—nor its weight compels a conclusion that the summary suspension procedures are unconstitutional, particularly in view of the post-suspension hearing immediately available and of the fact that the suspension is for a maximum of only 90 days. Pp. 2617-2618.

(c) Nor is the risk of error inherent in the presuspension procedure so substantial in itself as to require a departure from the "ordinary principle" that "something less than an evidentiary hearing is sufficient prior to adverse administrative action." *Dixon* v. *Love, supra,* 431 U.S., at 113, 97 S.Ct., at 1728 .The risk of erroneous observation or deliberate misrepresentation by the reporting police officer of the facts forming the basis for the suspension is insubstantial. When there are disputed facts, the risk of error inherent in the statute's initial reliance on the reporting officer's representations is not so substantial in itself as to require the Commonwealth to stay its hand pending the outcome of any evidentiary hearing necessary to resolve questions of credibility or conflicts in the evidence. Pp. 2618-2620.

(d) Finally, the compelling interest in highway safety justifies Massachusetts in making a summary suspension effective pending the outcome of the available prompt post-suspension hearing. Such interest is substantially served by the summary suspension because (i) it acts as a deterrent to drunk driving; (ii) provides an inducement to take the breathalyzer test, permitting the Commonwealth to obtain a reliable form of evidence for use in subsequent criminal proceedings; and (iii) summarily removes from the road licensees arrested for drunk driving who refuse to take the test. Conversely, a presuspension hearing would substantially undermine the Commonwealth's interest in public safety by giving drivers an incentive to refuse the breathalyzer test and demand such a hearing as a dilatory tactic, which in turn would cause a sharp increase in the number of hearings sought and thus impose a substantial fiscal and administrative burden on the Commonwealth. Nor is it any answer to the Commonwealth's interest in public safety promoted by the summary sanction that such interest could be served as well in other ways. A state has the right to offer incentives for taking the breathalyzer test, and, in exercising its police powers, is not required by the Due Process Clause to adopt an "all or nothing" approach to the acute safety hazard posed by drunk drivers. Pp. 2620—2621.

Reversed and remanded.

OREGON v. HASS

420 U.S. 714, 95 S. Ct. 1215, 43 L. Ed. 2d 570 (1975)

Defendant was convicted before the Circuit Court, Klamath County, Oregon, of first-degree burglary, and he appealed. The Court of Appeals of Oregon, 510 P.2d 852, reversed and remanded, and review was granted. The Oregon Supreme Court, 267 Ore. 489, 517 P.2d 671, affirmed the Court of Appeals, and certiorari was granted. The Supreme Court, MR. JUSTICE BLACKMUN, held that State may not impose greater restrictions on police activity as a matter of federal constitutional law than those which the United States Supreme Court holds to be necessary under federal constitutional standards; that for purposes of review, State was aggrieved by holding that, for constitutional reasons, prosecution could not utilize otherwise relevant evidence; and that where defendant, who was in the custody of a state police officer, had been given full *Miranda* warnings and accepted them and later stated that he would like to telephone a lawyer but was told that he could not do so until officer and defendant reached station, and defendant then provided inculpatory information, that information was admissible in evidence solely for impeachment purposes after defendant had taken the stand and testified contrary to the inculpatory information, knowing such information had been ruled inadmissible for the prosecution's case in chief.

Reversed.

MR. JUSTICE BRENNAN, with whom MR. JUSTICE MARSHALL joined, filed a dissenting opinion.

MR. JUSTICE MARSHALL, with whom MR. JUSTICE BRENNAN joined, filed a dissenting opinion.

MR. JUSTICE DOUGLAS took no part in consideration or decision of the case.

MR. JUSTICE BLACKMUN delivered the opinion of the Court.

This case presents a variation of the fact situation encountered by the Court in *Harris* v. *New York*, 401 U.S. 222 (1971): When a suspect, who is in the custody of a state police officer, has been given full *Miranda* warnings and accepts them, and then later states that he would like to telephone a lawyer but is told that this cannot be done until the officer and the suspect reach the station, and the suspect then provides inculpatory information, is that information admissible in evidence solely for impeachment purposes after the suspect has taken the stand and testified contrarily to the inculpatory information, or is it inadmissible under the Fifth and Fourteenth Amendments?

I

The facts are not in dispute. In August 1972, bicycles were taken from two residential garages in the

Moyina Heights area of Klamath Falls, Ore. Respondent Hass, in due course, was indicted for burglary in the first degree, in violation of Ore. Rev. Stat. § 164.225, with respect to the bicycle taken from the garage attached to one of the residences, a house occupied by a family named Lehman. He was not charged with the other burglary.

On the day of the thefts, Officer Osterholme of the Oregon State Police traced an automobile license number to the place where Hass lived. The officer met Hass there and placed him under arrest. At Hass' trial Osterholme testified *in camera* that, after giving Hass the warnings prescribed by *Miranda* v. *Arizona*, 384 U.S. 436, 467–473 (1966), he asked Hass about the theft of the bicycle taken from the Lehman residence. Hass admitted that he had taken two bicycles but stated that he was not sure, at first, which one Osterholme was talking about. He further said that he had returned one of them and that the other was where he had left it. Osterholme and Hass then departed in a patrol car for the site. On the way Hass opined that he "was in a lot of trouble," and would like to telephone his attorney. Osterholme replied that he could telephone the lawyer "as soon as we got to the office." Thereafter, respondent pointed out a place in the brush where the bicycle was found.

The court ruled that statements made by Hass after he said he wanted to see an attorney, and his identification of the bicycle's location, were not admissible. The prosecution then elicited from Osterholme, in its case in chief before the jury, that Hass had admitted to the witness that he had taken two bicycles that day because he needed money, that he had given one back, and that the other had been recovered.

Later in the trial Hass took the stand. He testified that he and two friends, Walker and Lee, were "just riding around" in his Volkswagen truck; that the other two got out and respondent drove slowly down the street; that Lee suddenly reappeared, tossed a bicycle into the truck, and "ducked down" on the floor of the vehicle; that respondent did not know that Lee "stole it at first"; that it was his own intention to get rid of the bike; that they were overtaken by a jeep occupied by Mr. Lehman and his son; that the son pointed out Lee as "that's the guy"; that Lee then returned the bike to the Lehmans; that respondent drove on and came upon Walker "sitting down there and he had this other bicycle by him," and threw it into the truck; that he, respondent, went "out by Washburn Way and I threw it as far as I could"; that later he told police he had stolen two bicycles; that he had had no idea what Lee and Walker were going to do; and that he did not see any of the bikes being taken and did not know "where those residences were located."

The prosecution then recalled Officer Osterholme in rebuttal. He testified that Hass had pointed out the two houses from which the bicycles were taken. On cross-examination, the officer testified that, prior to so doing, Hass had told Osterholme "that he knew where the bicycles came from, however, he didn't know the exact street address." Osterholme also stated that Lee was along at the time but that Lee "had some difficulty" in identifying the residences "until Mr. Hass actually pointed them" and then "he recognized it."

The trial court, at the request of the defense, then advised the jury that the portion of Officer Osterholme's testimony describing the statement made by Hass to him "may not be used by you as proof of the Defendant's guilt . . . but you may consider that testimony only as it bears on the [credibility] of the Defendant as a witness when he testified on the witness stand."

Respondent again took the stand and said that Osterholme's testimony that he took him out to the residences and that respondent pointed out the houses was "wrong."

The jury returned a verdict of guilty. Hass received a sentence of two years' probation and a $250 fine. The Oregon Court of Appeals, feeling itself bound by the earlier Oregon decision in *State* v. *Brewton*, 247 Ore. 241, 422 P.2d 581 (1967), a pre-*Harris* case, reversed on the ground that Hass' statements were improperly used to impeach his testimony. 13 Ore. App. 368, 374, 510 P.2d 852 (1973). On petition for review, the Supreme Court of Oregon, by a 4-to-3 vote, affirmed. 267 Ore. 489, 517 P.2d 671 (1973). The court reasoned that in a situation of proper *Miranda* warnings, as here, the police have nothing to lose, and perhaps could gain something, for impeachment purposes, by continuing their interrogation after the warnings; thus, there is no deterrence. In contrast, the court said, where warnings are yet to be given, there is an element of deterrence, for the police "will not take the chance of losing incriminating evidence for their case in chief by not giving adequate warnings." The three dissenters perceived no difference between the two situations. Because the result was in conflict with that reached by the North Carolina court in *State* v. *Bryant*, 280 N.C. 551, 554–556, 187 S.E.2d 111 (1972), and because it bore upon the reach of our decision in *Harris* v. *New York*, 401 U.S. 222 (1971), we granted certiorari. We reverse.

II

The respondent raises some preliminary arguments. We mention them in passing:

1. Hass suggests that "when state law is more restrictive against the prosecution than federal law," this Court has no power "to compel a state to conform to federal law." Brief for Respondent 1. This, apparently, is proffered as a reference to our expressions that a State is free *as a matter of its own law* to impose greater restrictions on police activity than those this Court holds to be necessary upon federal constitutional standards. See, *e.g.*, *Cooper* v. *California*, 386 U.S. 58, 62 (1967); *Sibron* v. *New*

York, 392 U.S. 40, 60–61 (1968). See also *State* v. *Kaluna,* 55 Haw. 361, 368–369, 520 P.2d 51 (1974). But, of course, a State may not impose such greater restrictions as a matter of *federal constitutional law* when this Court specifically refrains from imposing them. See *Smayda* v. *United States,* 352 F.2d 251, 253 (CA9 1965), cert. denied, 382 U.S. 981 (1966); *Aftanase* v. *Economy Baler Co.,* 343 F.2d 187, 193 (CA8 1965).

Although Oregon has a constitutional provision against compulsory self-incrimination in any criminal prosecution, Ore. Const., Art. 1, § 12, the present case was decided by the Oregon courts on Fifth and Fourteenth Amendment grounds. The decision did not rest on the Oregon Constitution or state law; neither was cited. The fact that the Oregon courts found it necessary to attempt to distinguish *Harris* v. *New York, supra,* reveals the federal basis.

2. Hass suggests that a decision by a State's highest court in favor of a criminal defendant is not reviewable here. This, we assume, is a standing argument advanced on the theory that the State is not aggrieved by the Oregon judgment. Surely, a holding that, for constitutional reasons, the prosecution may not utilize otherwise relevant evidence makes the State an aggrieved party for purposes of review. This should be self-evident, but cases such as *California* v. *Green,* 399 U.S. 149 (1970), manifest its validity.

3. *State* v. *Brewton,* 247 Ore. 241, 422 P.2d 581 (1967), by which the Oregon Court of Appeals in the present case felt itself bound, merits comment. There the Oregon court, again by a 4-to-3 vote, held that statements, elicited from a murder defendant, that were inadmissible in the State's case in chief because they had not been preceded by adequate warnings, could not be used to impeach the defendant's own testimony even though the statements had been voluntarily made.

In the present case the Supreme Court of Oregon stated that it took review "for the purpose of deciding whether we wished to overrule *Brewton.*" It found it "not necessary to make that determination" because, in the majority view, *Brewton* and *Harris* were distinguishable. As set forth below, we are unable so to distinguish the two cases. Furthermore, *Brewton* is pre-*Harris.* * * *

We therefore hold that the Oregon appellate courts were in error when they ruled that Officer Osterholme's testimony on rebuttal was inadmissible on Fifth and Fourteenth Amendment grounds for purposes of Hass' impeachment. The judgment of the Supreme Court of Oregon is reversed.

It is so ordered.

MR. JUSTICE DOUGLAS took no part in the consideration or decision of this case.

* * *

MR. JUSTICE MARSHALL, with whom MR. JUSTICE BRENNAN joins, dissenting.

. . . .

In my view, we have too often

rushed to correct state courts in their view of federal constitutional questions without sufficiently considering the risk that we will be drawn into rendering a purely advisory opinion. Plainly, if the Oregon Supreme Court had expressly decided that Hass' statement was inadmissible as a matter of state as well as federal law, this Court could not upset that judgment. [Citations omitted.] The sound policy behind this rule was well articulated by Mr. Justice Jackson in *Herb* v. *Pitcairn*, 324 U.S. 117 (1945):

> This Court from the time of its foundation has adhered to the principle that it will not review judgments of state courts that rest on adequate and independent state grounds. The reason is so obvious that it has rarely been thought to warrant statement. It is found in the partitioning of power between the state and federal judicial systems and in the limitations of our own jurisdiction. Our only power over state judgments is to correct them to the extent that they incorrectly adjudge federal rights. And our power is to correct wrong judgments, not to revise opinions. We are not permitted to render an advisory opinion, and if the same judgment would be rendered by the state court after we corrected its views of federal laws, our review could amount to nothing more than an advisory opinion. *Id.*, at 125–126 (citations omitted).

Where we have been unable to say with certainty that the judgment rested solely on federal law grounds, we have refused to rule on the federal issue in the case; the proper course is then either to dismiss the writ as improvidently granted or to remand the case to the state court to clarify the basis of its decision. *California* v. *Krivda*, 409 U.S. 33 (1972); *Mental Hygiene Dept.* v. *Kirchner*, 380 U.S. 194 (1965). Of course, it may often be unclear whether a state court has relied in part on state law in reaching its decision. As the Court said in *Herb* v. *Pitcairn*, *supra*, however, where the answer does not appear "of record" and is not "clear and decisive,"

> it seems consistent with the respect due the highest courts of states of the Union that they be asked rather than told what they have intended. If this imposes an unwelcome burden it should be mitigated by the knowledge that it is to protect their jurisdiction from unwitting interference as well as to protect our own from unwitting renunciation. 324 U.S., at 128.

From a perusal of the Oregon Supreme Court's opinion it is evident that these exacting standards were not met in this case. The Constitution of Oregon contains an independent prohibition against compulsory self-incrimination, and there is a distinct possibility that the state court intended to express its view of state as well as federal constitutional law. The majority flatly states that the case was decided below solely on federal constitutional grounds, but I am not so certain. Although the state court did not expressly cite state law in support of its judgment, its opinion suggests that it may well have considered the matter one of state as well as federal law. The court stated that it had initially viewed the issue of the case as whether it should overrule one of its prior precedents in light of this Court's opinion in *Harris* v. *New York*, 401 U.S. 222 (1971). It concluded that it was not required to consider whether to overrule the earlier state case, however, since upon examination it determined that *Harris* did not reach this fact situation. In view of the court's suggestion that the federal constitutional rule in *Harris* would be regarded as merely a persuasive authority even if it were deemed to be squarely in conflict with the state rule, it seems quite possible that the state court intended its decision to rest at least in part on independent state grounds. In any event, I agree with Mr. Justice Jackson that state courts should be "asked rather than told what they have intended."

In addition to the importance of avoiding jurisdictional difficulties, it seems much the better policy to permit the state court the freedom to strike its own balance between individual rights and police practices, at least where the state court's ruling violates no constitutional prohibitions. It is peculiarly within the competence of the highest court of a State to determine that in its jurisdiction the police should be subject to more stringent rules than are required as a federal constitutional minimum.

The Oregon court's decision in this case was not premised on a reluctant adherence to what it deemed federal law to require, but was based on its independent conclusion that admitting evidence such as that held admissible today will encourage police misconduct in violation of the right against compulsory self-incrimination. This is precisely the setting in which it seems most likely that the state court would apply the State's self-incrimination clause to lessen what it perceives as an intolerable risk of abuse. Accordingly, in my view the Court should not review a state-court decision reversing a conviction unless it is quite clear that the state court has resolved all applicable state-law questions adversely to the defendant and that it feels compelled by its view of the federal constitutional issue to reverse the conviction at hand.

Even if the majority is correct that the Oregon Supreme Court did not intend to express a view of state as well as federal law, this Court should, at the very least, remand the case for such further proceedings as the state court deems appropriate. I can see absolutely no reason for departing from the usual course of remanding the case to permit the state court to consider any other claims, including the possible applicability of state law to the issue treated here. [Citation omitted.] Surely the majority does not mean to suggest that the Oregon Supreme Court is foreclosed from considering the respondent's state-law claims or even ruling *sua sponte* that the statement in question is not admissible as a matter of state law. If so, then I should think this unprecedented assumption of authority will be as much a surprise to the Supreme Court of Oregon as it is to me.

I dissent.

Cases relating to **Chapter 2**

FREE SPEECH, PRESS AND ASSEMBLY

TEXAS v. JOHNSON

__ U.S. __, 109 S. Ct. 2533, 105 L. Ed. 2d 342 (1989)

[The Court's footnotes have been omitted.]

* * *

JUSTICE BRENNAN delivered the opinion of the Court.

After publicly burning an American flag as a means of political protest, Gregory Lee Johnson was convicted of desecrating a flag in violation of Texas law. This case presents the question whether his conviction is consistent with the First Amendment. We hold that it is not.

I

While the Republican National Convention was taking place in Dallas in 1984, respondent Johnson participated in a political demonstration dubbed the "Republican War Chest Tour." As explained in literature distributed by the demonstrators and in speeches made by them, the purpose of this event was to protest the policies of the Reagan administration and of certain Dallas-based corporations. The demonstrators marched through the Dallas streets, chanting political slogans and stopping at several corporate locations to stage "die-ins" intended to dramatize the consequences of nuclear war. On several occasions they spray-painted the walls of buildings and overturned potted plants, but Johnson himself took no part in such activities. He did, however, accept an American flag handed to him by a fellow protestor who had taken it from a flag pole outside one of the targeted buildings.

The demonstration ended in front of Dallas City Hall, where Johnson unfurled the American flag, doused it with kerosene, and set it on fire. While the flag burned, the protestors chanted, "America, the red, white, and blue, we spit on you." After the demonstrators dispersed, a witness to the flag-burning collected the flag's remains and buried them in his backyard. No one was physically injured or threatened with injury, though several witnesses testified that they had been seriously offended by the flag-burning.

Of the approximately 100 demonstrators, Johnson alone was charged with a crime. The only criminal offense with which he was charged was the desecration of a venerated object in violation of Tex. Penal Code Ann. § 42.09 (a)(3) (1989). After a trial, he was convicted, sentenced to one year in prison, and fined $2,000. The Court of Appeals for the Fifth District of Texas at Dallas affirmed Johnson's conviction, 706 S.W.2d 120 (1986), but the Texas Court of Criminal Appeals reversed, 755 S.W.2d 92 (1988), holding that the State could not, consistent with the First Amendment, punish Johnson for burning the flag in these circumstances.

* * *

The First Amendment literally forbids the abridgement only of "speech," but we have long recognized that its protection does not end at the spoken or written word. While we have rejected "the view that an apparently limitless variety of conduct can be labeled 'speech' whenever the person engaging in the conduct intends thereby to express an idea," *United States v. O'Brien, supra,* at 376, we have acknowledged that conduct may be "sufficiently imbued with elements of communication to fall within the scope of the First and Fourteenth Amendments." *Spence, supra,* at 409.

In deciding whether particular conduct possesses sufficient communicative elements to bring the First Amendment into play, we have asked whether "[a]n intent to convey a particularized message was present, and [whether] the likelihood was great that the message would be understood by those who viewed it." 418 U.S., at 410-411. Hence, we have recognized the expressive nature of students' wearing of black armbands to protest American military involvement in Vietnam, *Tinker v. Des Moines Independent Community School Dist.,* 393 U.S. 503, 505 (1969); of a sit-in by blacks in a "whites only" area to protest segregation, *Brown v. Louisiana*, 383 U.S. 131, 141-142 (1966); of the wearing of American military uniforms in a dramatic presentation criticizing American military involvement in Vietnam, *Schacht v. United States,* 398 U.S. 58 (1970); and of picketing about a wide variety of causes, see *e.g., Food Employees v. Logan Valley Plaza, Inc.,* 391 U.S. 308, 313-314 (1968); *United States v. Grace,* 461 U.S. 171, 176 (1983).

* * *

The State of Texas conceded for purposes of its oral argument in this case that Johnson's conduct was expressive conduct, Tr. of Oral Arg. 4, and this concession seems to us as prudent as was Washington's in *Spence*. Johnson burned an American flag as part -- indeed, as the culmination -- of a political demonstration that coincided with the convening of the Republican Party and its renomination of Ronald Reagan for President. The expressive, overtly political nature of this conduct was both intentional and overwhelmingly apparent. At his trial, Johnson explained his reasons for burning the flag as follows: "The American Flag was burned as Ronald Reagan was being renominated as President. And a more powerful statement of symbolic speech, whether you agree with or not, couldn't have been made at that time. It's quite a just position [juxtaposition]. We had new patriotism and no patriotism." 5 Record 656. In these circumstances, Johnson's burning of the flag was conduct "sufficiently imbued with elements of communication," *Spence,* 418 U.S., at 409, to implicate the First Amendment.

III

The Government generally has a freer hand in restricting expressive conduct than it has in restricting the written or spoken word. See *O'Brien*, 391 U.S. at 376-377; *Clark v. Community for Creative Non-Violence,* 468 U.S. 288, 293 (1984); *Dallas v. Stanglin,* 490 U.S. __, __ (1989) (slip op., at 5-6). It may not, however, proscribe particular conduct *because* it has expressive elements. "[W]hat might be termed the more generalized guarantee of freedom of ex-

The government may not Regulate ideas
ex: people sleeping in park vs. people protesting for Homeless in Park

pression makes the communicative nature of conduct an inadequate *basis* for singling out that conduct for proscription. A law *directed at* the communicative nature of conduct must, like a law directed at speech itself, be justified by the substantial showing of need that the First Amendment requires." *Community for Creative Non-Violence v. Watt,* 227 U.S. App. D.C. 19, 55-56, 703 F.2d 586, 622-623 (1983) (Scalia, J., dissenting), rev'd *sub nom. Clark v. Community for Creative Non-Violence,* 468 U.S. 288 (1984) (emphasis in original). It is, in short, not simply the verbal or nonverbal nature of the expression, but the governmental interest at stake, that helps to determine whether a restriction on that expression is valid.

Thus, although we have recognized that where "'speech' and 'nonspeech' elements are combined in the same course of conduct, a sufficiently important governmental interest in regulating the nonspeech element can justify incidental limitations on First Amendment freedoms," *O'Brien, supra,* at 376, we have limited the applicability of *O'Brien's* relatively lenient standard to those cases in which "the governmental interest is unrelated to the suppression of free expression." *Id.,* at 377; see also *Spence,* 418 U.S., at 414, n. 8. ***

In order to decide whether *O'Brien's* test applies here, therefore, we must decide whether Texas has asserted an interest in support of Johnson's conviction that is unrelated to the suppression of expression. *** The State offers two separate interests to justify this conviction: preventing breaches of the peace, and preserving the flag as a symbol of nationhood and national unity. We hold that the first interest is not implicated on this record and that the second is related to the suppression of expression.

A

Texas claims that its interest in preventing breaches of the peace justifies Johnson's conviction for flag desecration. However, no disturbance of the peace actually occurred or threatened to occur because of Johnson's burning of the flag. *** The only evidence offered by the State at trial to show the reaction to Johnson's actions was the testimony of several persons who had been seriously offended by the flag-burning. *Id.,* at 6-7.

The State's position, therefore, amounts to a claim that an audience that takes serious offense at particular expression is necessarily likely to disturb the peace and that the expression may be prohibited on this basis. Our precedents do not countenance such a presumption. On the contrary, they recognize that a principal "function of free speech under our system of government is to invite dispute. It may indeed best serve its high purpose when it induces a condition of unrest, creates dissatisfaction with conditions as they are, or even stirs people to anger." *Terminiello v. Chicago,* 337 U.S. 1, 4 (1949). See also *Cox v. Louisiana,* 379 U.S. 536, 551 (1965); *Tinker v. Des Moines Independent School Dist.* 393 U.S., at 508-509; *Coates v. Cincinnati,* 402 U.S. 611, 615 (1971); *Hustler Magazine, Inc. v. Falwell,* 485 U.S. 46, 55-56 (1988). ***

Thus, we have not permitted the Government to assume that every expression of a provocative idea will incite a riot, but have instead required careful consideration of the actual circumstances surrounding such expression, asking whether the expression "is directed to inciting or producing imminent lawless action and is likely to incite or produce such action." *Brandenburg v. Ohio,* 395 U.S. 444, 447 (1969) (reviewing circumstances surrounding rally and speeches by Ku Klux Klan). To accept Texas' arguments that it need only demonstrate "the potential for a breach of the peace," Brief for Petitioner 37, and that every flag-burning necessarily possesses that potential, would be to eviscerate our holding in *Brandenburg*. This we decline to do.

Nor does Johnson's expressive conduct fall within that small class of "fighting words" that are "likely to provoke the average person to retaliation, and thereby cause a breach of the peace." *Chaplinsky v. New Hampshire,* 315 U.S. 568, 574 (1942). No reasonable onlooker would have regarded Johnson's generalized expression of dissatisfaction with the policies of the Federal Government as a direct personal insult or an invitation to exchange fisticuffs. See *id.*, at 572-573; *Cantwell v. Connecticut,* 310 U.S. 296, 309 (1940); *FCC v. Pacifica Foundation, supra*, at 745 (opinion of STEVENS, J.).

We thus conclude that the State's interest in maintaining order is not implicated on these facts. The State need not worry that our holding will disable it from preserving the peace. We do not suggest that the First Amendment forbids a State to prevent "imminent lawless action." *Brandenburg, supra,* at 447. And, in fact, Texas already has a statute specifically prohibiting breaches of the peace, Tex. Penal Code Ann. § 42.01 (1989), which tends to confirm that Texas need not punish this flag desecration in order to keep the peace. See *Boos v. Barry,* 485 U.S., at 327-329.

B

The State also asserts an interest in preserving the flag as a symbol of nationhood and national unity. In *Spence,* we acknowledged that the Government's interest in preserving the flag's special symbolic value "is directly related to expression in the context of activity" such as affixing a peace symbol to a flag. 418 U.S., at 414, n. 8. We are equally persuaded that this interest is related to expression in the case of Johnson's burning of the flag. The State, apparently, is concerned that such conduct will lead people to believe either that the flag does not stand for nationhood and national unity, but instead reflects other, less positive concepts, or that the concepts reflected in the flag do not in fact exist, that is, we do not enjoy unity as a Nation. These concerns blossom only when a person's treatment of the flag communicates some message, and thus are related "to the suppression of free expression" within the meaning of *O'Brien.* We are thus outside of *O'Brien's* test altogether.

IV

It remains to consider whether the State's interest in preserving the flag as a symbol of nationhood and national unity justifies Johnson's conviction.

As in *Spence,* "[w]e are confronted with a case of prosecution for the expression of an idea through activity," and "[a]ccordingly, we must examine with particular care the interests advanced by [petitioner] to support its prosecution." 418 U.S., at 411. Johnson was not, we add, prosecuted for the expression of just any idea; he was prosecuted for his expression of dissatisfaction with the policies of this country, expression situated at the core of our First Amendment values. See, e.g., *Boos v. Barry, supra,* at 318; *Frisby v. Schultz*, 487 U.S.__, __ (1988).

* * *

If there is a bedrock principle underlying the First Amendment, it is that the Government may not prohibit the expression of an idea simply because society finds the idea itself offensive or disagreeable. See, *e.g., Hustler Maga-*

zine v. Falwell, 485 U.S., at 55-56; *City Council of Los Angeles v. Taxpayers for Vincent,* 466 U.S. 789, 804 (1984); *Bolger v. Youngs Drug Products Corp.,* 463 U.S. 60, 65, 72 (1983); *Carey v. Brown,* 447 U.S. 455, 462-463 (1980); *FCC v. Pacifica Foundation,* 438 U.S., at 745-746; *Young v. American Mini Theatres, Inc.,* 427 U.S. 50, 63-65, 67-68 (1976) (plurality opinion); *Buckley v. Valeo,* 424 U.S. 1, 16-17 (1976); Grayned v. Rockford, 408 U.S. 104, 115 (1972); Police Dept. of Chicago v. Mosley, 408 U.S. 92, 95 (1972); Bachellar v. Maryland, 397 U.S. 564, 567 (1970); O'Brien, 391 U.S., at 382; *Brown v. Louisiana,* 383 U.S., at 142-143; *Stromberg v. California,* 283 U.S., at 368-369.

We have not recognized an exception to this principle even where our flag has been involved. In *Street v. New York,* 394 U.S. 576 (1969), we held that a State may not criminally punish a person for uttering words critical of the flag. Rejecting the argument that the conviction could be sustained on the ground that Street had "failed to show the respect for our national symbol which may properly be demanded of every citizen," we concluded that "the constitutionally guaranteed 'freedom to be intellectually...diverse or even contrary,' and the 'right to differ as to things that touch the heart of the existing order,' encompass the freedom to express publicly one's opinions about our flag, including those opinions which are defiant or contemptuous." *Id.,* at 593, quoting *Barnette,* 319 U.S., at 642. Nor may the Government, we have held, compel conduct that would evince respect for the flag. "To sustain the compulsory flag salute we are required to say that a Bill of Rights which guards the individual's right to speak his own mind, left it open to public authorities to compel him to utter what is not in his mind." *Id.,* at 634.

In holding in *Barnette* that the Constitution did not leave this course open to the Government, Justice Jackson described one of our society's defining principles in words deserving of their frequent repetition: "If there is any fixed star in our constitutional constellation, it is that no official, high or petty, can prescribe what shall be orthodox in politics, nationalism, religion, or other matters of opinion or force citizens to confess by word or act their faith therein." *Id.,* at 642. In *Spence,* we held that the same interest asserted by Texas here was insufficient to support a criminal conviction under a flag-misuse statute for the taping of a peace sign to an American flag. "Given the protected character of [Spence's] expression and in light of the fact that no interest the State may have in preserving the physical integrity of a privately owned flag was significantly impaired on these facts," we held, "the conviction must be invalidated." 418 U.S., at 415. See also *Goguen,* 415 U.S., at 588 (WHITE, J., concurring in judgment) (to convict person who had sewn a flag onto the seat of his pants for "contemptuous" treatment of the flag would be "[t]o convict not to protect the physical integrity or to protect against acts interfering with the proper use of the flag, but to punish for communicating ideas unacceptable to the controlling majority in the legislature").

In short, nothing in our precedents suggests that a State may foster its own view of the flag by prohibiting expressive conduct relating to it. To bring its argument outside our precedents, Texas attempts to convince us that even if its interest in preserving the flag's symbolic role does not allow it to prohibit words or some expressive conduct critical of the flag, it does permit it to forbid the outright destruction of the flag. The State's argument cannot depend here on the distinction between written or spoken words and nonverbal conduct. That distinction, we have shown, is of no moment where the nonverbal conduct is expressive, as it is here, and where the regulation of that conduct is related to expression, as it is here. See *supra*, at 4-5. In addition, both *Barnette* and *Spence* involved expressive conduct, not only verbal communication, and both found that conduct protected.

* * *

We are fortified in today's conclusion by our conviction that forbidding criminal punishment for conduct such as Johnson's will not endanger the special role played by our flag or the feelings it inspires. To paraphrase Justice Holmes, we submit that nobody can suppose that this one gesture of an unknown man will change our Nation's attitude towards its flag. See *Abrams v. United States,* 250 U.S. 616, 628 (1919) (Holmes, J., dissenting). Indeed, Texas' argument that the burning of an American flag "'is an act having a high likelihood to cause a breach of the peace,'" Brief for Petitioner 31, quoting *Sutherland v. DeWulf,* 323 F.Supp. 740, 745 (SD Ill. 1971) (citation omitted), and its statute's implicit assumption that physical mistreatment of the flag will lead to "serious offense," tend to confirm that the flag's special role is not in danger; if it were, no one would riot or take offense because a flag had been burned.

We are tempted to say, in fact, that the flag's deservedly cherished place in our community will be strengthened, not weakened, by our holding today. Our decision is a reaffirmation of the principles of freedom and inclusiveness that the flag best reflects, and of the conviction that our toleration of criticism such as Johnson's is a sign and source of our strength. Indeed, one of the proudest images of our flag, the one immortalized in our own national anthem, is of the bombardment it survived at Fort McHenry. It is the Nation's resilience, not its rigidity, that Texas sees reflected in the flag--and it is that resilience that we reassert today.

The way to preserve the flag's special rule is not to punish those who feel differently about these matters. It is to persuade them that they are wrong. "To courageous, self-reliant men, with confidence in the power of free and fearless reasoning applied through the processes of popular government, no danger flowing from speech can be deemed clear and present, unless the incidence of the evil apprehended is so imminent that it may befall before there is opportunity for full discussion. If there be time to expose through discussion the falsehood and fallacies, to avert the evil by the processes of education, the remedy to be applied is more speech, not enforced silence." *Whitney v. California,* 274 U.S. 357, 377 (1927) (Brandeis, J., concurring). And, precisely because it is our flag that is involved, one's response to the flag-burner may exploit the uniquely persuasive power of the flag itself. We can imagine no more appropriate response to burning a flag than waving one's own, no better way to counter a flag-burner's message than by saluting the flag that burns, no surer means of preserving the dignity even of the flag that burned than by--as one witness here did--according its remains a respectful burial. We do not consecrate the flag by punishing its desecration, for in doing so we dilute the freedom that this cherished emblem represents.

V

Johnson was convicted for engaging in expressive conduct. The State's interest in preventing breaches of the peace does not support his conviction because Johnson's conduct did not threaten to disturb the peace. Nor does the State's interest in preserving the flag as a symbol of nationhood and national unity justify his criminal conviction for engaging in political expression. The judgment of the Texas Court of Criminal Appeals is therefore

Affirmed.

CITY OF HOUSTON v. HILL

482 U.S. __, 107 S. Ct. 2502, 96 L. Ed. 2d 398 (1987)
[No. 86-243]

Argued March 23, 1987. Decided June 15, 1987.

[The Court's footnotes have been omitted.]

OPINION OF THE COURT

Justice **Brennan** delivered the opinion of the Court.

[1a] This case presents the question whether a municipal ordinance that makes it unlawful to interrupt a police officer in the performance of his or her duties is unconstitutionally overbroad under the First Amendment.

I

Appellee Raymond Wayne Hill is a lifelong resident of Houston, Texas. At the time this lawsuit began, he worked as a paralegal and as executive director of the Houston Human Rights League. A member of the Board of the Gay Political Caucus, which he helped found in 1975, Hill was also affiliated with a Houston radio station, and had carried city and county press passes since 1975. He lived in Montrose, a "diverse and eclectic neighborhood" that is the center of gay political and social life in Houston. App. 26-27.

The incident that sparked this lawsuit occurred in the Montrose area on February 14, 1982. Hill observed a friend, Charles Hill, intentionally stopping traffic on a busy street, evidently to enable a vehicle to enter traffic. Two Houston police officers, one of whom was named Kelley, approached Charles and began speaking with him. According to the District Court, "shortly thereafter" Hill began shouting at the officers "in an admitted attempt to divert Kelley's attention from Charles Hill." App. to Juris Statement B-2. Hill first shouted "Why don't you pick on somebody your own size?" After Officer Kelley responded "[A]re you interrupting me in my official capacity as a Houston police officer?" Hill then shouted, "Yes, why don't you pick on somebody my size?" App. 40-41, 58, 71-74. Hill was arrested under Houston Municipal Code § 34-11(a) for "wilfully or intentionally interrupt[ing] a city policeman...by verbal challenge during an investigation." App. 2. Charles Hill was not arrested. Hill was then acquitted after a nonjury trial in Municipal Court.

* * *

[4a] The City's principal argument is that the ordinance does not inhibit the exposition of ideas, and that it bans "core criminal conduct" not protected by the First Amendment. Brief for Appellant 12. In its view, the application of the ordinance to Hill illustrates that the police employ it only to prohibit such conduct, and not "as a subterfuge to control or dissuade free expression." Ibid. Since the ordinance is "content-neutral," and since there is no evidence that the City has applied the ordinance to chill particular speakers or ideas, the City concludes that the ordinance is not substantially overbroad.

* * *

[7a 8] [C]ontrary to the City's contention, the First Amendment protects a significant amount of verbal criticism and challenge directed at police officers. "Speech is often provocative and challenging...[But it] is nevertheless protected against censorship or punishment, unless shown likely to produce a clear and present danger of a serious substantive evil that rises far above public inconvenience, annoyance or unrest." *Terminiello v. Chicago,* 337 U.S. 1, 4, 93 L.Ed. 1131, 69 S.Ct. 894 (1949). In *Lewis v. City of New Orleans,* 415 U.S. 130, 39 L.Ed.2d 214, 94 S.Ct. 970 (1974), for example, the appellant was found to have yelled obscenities and threats at an officer who had asked appellant's husband to produce his driver's license. Appellant was convicted under a municipal ordinance that made it a crime "'for any person wantonly to curse or revile or to use obscene or opprobrious language toward or with reference to any member of the city police while in the actual performance of his duty.'" Id., at 132, 39 L.Ed.2d 214, 94 S.Ct. 970 (citation omitted). We vacated the conviction and invalidated the ordinance as facially overbroad. Critical to our decision was the fact that the ordinance "punishe[d] only spoken words" and was not limited in scope to fighting words that "'by their very utterance inflict injury or tend to incite an immediate breach of the peace.'" Id., at 133, 39 L.Ed.2d 214, 94 S.Ct. 970, quoting Gooding v. Wilson, 405 U.S. 518, 525, 31 L.Ed.2d 408, 92 S.Ct. 1103 (1972); see also *ibid.* (Georgia breach-of-peace statute not limited to fighting words held facially invalid). Moreover, in a concurring opinion in Lewis, Justice Powell suggested that even the "fighting words" exception recognized in Chaplinsky v. New Hampshire, 315 U.S. 568, 86 L.Ed 1031, 62 S.Ct. 766 (1942), might require a narrower application in cases involving words addressed to a police officer, because "a properly trained officer may reasonably be expected to 'exercise a higher degree of restraint' than the average citizen and thus be less likely to respond belligerently to 'fighting words.'" 415 U.S. at 135, 39 L.Ed.2d 214, 94 S.Ct. 970 (citation omitted).

[1c, 7b, 9a, 10a, 11a] The Houston ordinance is much more sweeping than the municipal ordinance struck down in Lewis. It is not limited to fighting words nor even to obscene or opprobrious language, but prohibits speech that "in any manner...interrupt[s]" an officer. The Constitution does not allow such speech to be made a crime. The freedom of individuals verbally to oppose or challenge police action without thereby risking arrest is one of the principal characteristics by which we distinguish a free nation from a police state.

The city argues, however, that even if the ordinance emcompasses some protected speech, its sweeping nature is both inevitable and essential to maintain public order. The City recalls this Court's observation in *Smith v. Goguen,* 415 U.S. 566, 581, 39 L.Ed.2d 605, 94 S.Ct. 1242 (1974):

> "There are areas of human conduct where, by the nature of the problems presented, legislatures simply cannot establish standards with great precision. Control of the broad range of disorderly conduct that may inhibit a policeman in the performance of his official duties may be one such area requiring as it does an on-the-spot assessment of the need to keep order."

The City further suggests that its ordinance is comparable to the disorderly conduct statute upheld against a facial challenge in *Colten v. Kentucky,* 407 U.S. 104, 32 L.Ed.2d 584, 92 S.Ct. 1953 (1972).

[1d, 12a] This Houston ordinance, however, is not narrowly tailored to prohibit only disorderly conduct or fighting words, and in no way resembles the law upheld in Colten. Although we appreciate the difficulties of drafting precise laws, we have repeatedly invalidated laws that provide the police with unfettered discretion to arrest individuals for words or conduct that annoy or offend them. As the Court observed over a century ago, "[i]t would certainly be dangerous if the legislature could set a net large enough to catch all possible offenders, and leave it to the courts to step inside and say who could be rightfully detained, and who should be set at large." *United States v. Reese,* 92 U.S. 214, 221, 23 L.Ed. 563 (1876). In Lewis, Justice Powell elaborated the basis for our concern with such sweeping, dragnet laws:

"This ordinance, as construed by the Louisiana Supreme Court, confers on police a virtually unrestrained power to arrest and charge persons with a violation. Many arrests are made in "one-on-one" situations where the only witnesses are the arresting officer and the person charged. All that is required for conviction is that the court accept the testimony of the officer that obscene or approbrious language had been used toward him while in the performance of his duties...Contrary to the city's argument, it is unlikely that limiting the ordinance's application to genuine 'fighting words' would be incompatible with the full and adequate performance of an officer's duties....[I]t is usually unnecessary [to charge a person] with the less serious offense of addressing obscene words to the officer. The present type of ordinance tends to be invoked only where there is no other valid basis for arresting an objectionable or suspicious person. The opportunity for abuse, especially where a statute has received a virtually open-ended interpretation, is self-evident.

[1e] Houston's ordinance criminalizes a substantial amount of constitutionally protected speech, and accords the police unconstitutional discretion in enforcement. The ordinance's plain language is admittedly violated scores of times daily, App. 77, yet only some individuals --those chosen by the police in their unguided discretion-- are arrested. Far from providing the "breathing space" that "First Amendment freedoms need...to survive," NAACP v. Button, 371 U.S. 415, 433, 9 L.Ed.2d 405, 83 S.Ct. 328 (1963), the ordinance is susceptible of regular application to protected expression. We conclude that the ordinance is substantially overbroad, and that the Court of Appeals did not err in holding it facially invalid.

***

IV

Today's decision reflects the constitutional requirement that, in the face of verbal challenges to police action, officers and municipalities must respond with restraint. We are mindful that the preservation of liberty depends in part upon the maintenance of social order. Cf. *Terminiello v. Chicago,* 337 U.S., at 37, 93 L.Ed. 1131, 69 S.Ct. 894 (dissenting opinion). But the First Amendment recognizes, wisely we think, that a certain amount of expressive disorder not only is inevitable in a society committed to individual freedom, but must itself be protected if that freedom would survive. We therefore affirm the judgment of the Court of Appeals.

It is so ordered.

HESS v. INDIANA

414 U.S. 105, 94 S. Ct. 326, 38 L.Ed. 2d 303 (1973)

PER CURIAM.

Gregory Hess appeals from his conviction in the Indiana courts for violating the State's disorderly conduct statute.[1] Appellant contends that his conviction should be reversed because the statute is unconstitutionally vague, *Connally* v. *General Construction Co.,* 269 U.S. 385 (1926), because the statute is overbroad in that it forbids activity that is protected under the First and Fourteenth Amendments, *Gooding* v. *Wilson,* 405 U.S. 518 (1972), and because the statute, as applied here, abridged his constitutionally protected freedom of speech, *Terminiello* v. *Chicago,* 337 U.S. 1 (1949). These contentions were rejected in the City Court, where Hess was convicted, and in the Superior Court, which reviewed his conviction. The Supreme Court of Indiana, with one dissent, considered and rejected each of Hess' constitutional contentions, and accordingly affirmed his conviction.

The events leading to Hess' conviction began with an antiwar demonstration on the campus of Indiana University. In the course of the demonstration, approximately 100 to 150 of the demonstrators moved onto a public street and blocked the passage of vehicles. When the demonstrators did not respond to verbal directions from the sheriff to clear the street, the sheriff and his deputies began walking up the street, and the demonstrators in their path moved to the curbs on either side, joining a large number of spectators who had gathered. Hess was standing off the street as the sheriff passed him. The sheriff heard Hess utter the word "fuck" in what he later described as a loud voice and immediately arrested him on the dis-

---

[1] "Whoever shall act in a loud, boisterous or disorderly manner so as to disturb the peace and quiet of any neighborhood or family, by loud or unusual noise, or by tumultuous or offensive behavior, threatening, traducing, quarreling, challenging to fight or fighting, shall be deemed guilty of disorderly conduct, and upon conviction, shall be fined in any sum not exceeding five hundred dollars [$500] to which may be added imprisonment for not to exceed one hundred eighty [180] days." Ind. Code 35–27–2–1 (1971), Ind. Ann. Stat. § 10–1510 (Supp. 1972).

orderly conduct charge. It was later stipulated that what appellant had said was "We'll take the fucking street later," or "We'll take the fucking street again." Two witnesses who were in the immediate vicinity testified, apparently without contradiction, that they heard Hess' words and witnessed his arrest. They indicated that Hess did not appear to be exhorting the crowd to go back into the street, that he was facing the crowd and not the street when he uttered the statement, that his statement did not appear to be addressed to any particular person or group, and that his tone, although loud, was no louder than that of the other people in the area.

Indiana's disorderly conduct statute was applied in this case to punish only spoken words. It hardly needs repeating that "[t]he constitutional guarantees of freedom of speech forbid the States to punish the use of words or language not within 'narrowly limited classes of speech.'" *Gooding* v. *Wilson, supra,* at 521–522. The words here did not fall within any of these "limited classes." In the first place, it is clear that the Indiana court specifically abjured any suggestion that Hess' words could be punished as obscene under *Roth* v. *United States,* 354 U.S. 476 (1957), and its progeny. Indeed, after *Cohen* v. *California,* 403 U.S. 15 (1971), such a contention with regard to the language at issue would not be tenable. By the same token, any suggestion that Hess' speech amounted to "fighting words," *Chaplinsky* v. *New Hampshire,* 315 U.S. 568 (1942), could not withstand scrutiny. Even if under other circumstances this language could be regarded as a personal insult, the evidence is undisputed that Hess' statement was not directed to any person or group in particular. Although the sheriff testified that he was offended by the language, he also stated that he did not interpret the expression as being directed personally at him, and the evidence is clear that appellant had his back to the sheriff at the time. Thus, under our decisions, the State could not punish this speech as "fighting words." *Cantwell* v. *Connecticut,* 310 U.S. 296, 309 (1940); *Cohen* v. *California, supra,* at 20.

In addition, there was no evidence to indicate that Hess' speech amounted to a public nuisance in that privacy interests were being invaded. "The ability of government, consonant with the Constitution, to shut off discourse solely to protect others from hearing it is . . . dependent upon a showing that substantial privacy interests are being invaded in an essentially intolerable manner." *Cohen* v. *California, supra,* at 21. The prosecution made no such showing in this case.

The Indiana Supreme Court placed primary reliance on the trial court's finding that Hess' statement "was intended to incite further lawless action on the part of the crowd in the vicinity of appellant and was likely to produce such action." 260 Ind. 427, 297 N.E.2d 413, 415 (1973). At best, however, the statement could be taken as counsel for present moderation; at worst, it amounted to nothing more than advocacy of illegal action at some indefinite future time. This is not sufficient to permit the State to punish Hess' speech. Under our decisions, "the constitutional guarantees of free speech and free press do not permit a State to forbid or proscribe advocacy of the use of force or of law violation except where such advocacy is directed to inciting or producing *imminent* lawless action and is likely to incite or produce such action." *Brandenburg* v. *Ohio,* 395 U.S. 444, 447 (1969). (Emphasis added.) See also *Terminiello* v. *Chicago,* 337 U.S., at 4. Since the uncontroverted evidence showed that Hess' statement was not directed to any person or group of persons, it cannot be said that he was advocating, in the normal sense, any action. And since there was no evidence, or rational inference from the import of the language, that his words were intended to produce, and likely to produce, *imminent* disorder, those words could not be punished by the State on the ground that they had "a 'tendency to lead to violence.'" 260 Ind., at 427, 297 N.E.2d, at 415.

Accordingly, the motion to proceed *in forma pauperis* is granted and the judgment of the Supreme Court of Indiana is reversed.

[The opinion of MR. JUSTICE REHNQUIST, with whom THE CHIEF JUSTICE and MR. JUSTICE BLACKMUN join, dissenting, has been omitted.]

UNITED STATES v. GRACE

461 U.S. 171, 75 L.Ed.2d 736, 103 S.Ct. 1702
(1983)

Title forty U.S.C. § 13k made it "unlawful to parade, stand, or move in processions or assemblages in the Supreme Court building or grounds, or to display therein any flag, banner or device designed or adapted to bring into public notice any party, organization, or movement." Supreme Court grounds, as defined for purposes of this statute, included the public sidewalks adjacent to the Supreme Court in addition to the building, lawn area and plaza in and on which this nation's highest court is housed. Appellees Zywicki and Grace on several occasions were stopped by Court police officers while they were distributing leaflets and displaying picket signs on the sidewalks in front of the Supreme Court. They were advised, accurately, that Title 40 of the United States Code prohibited their conduct and were threatened with arrest if they did not move on. They filed suit in the United States District Court for the District of Columbia seeking a declaratory judgment that 40 U.S.C. § 13k was unconstitutional and an injunction against continued enforcement. The District Court dismissed their complaint. The Court of Appeals overturned the dismissal and struck the statute down as an unconstitutional restriction on First Amendment rights in a public place. The Government appealed this ruling to the Supreme Court.

JUSTICE WHITE delivered the opinion of the Court.

In this case we must determine whether 40 U.S.C. § 13k, which prohibits, among other things, the "display [of]...any flag, banner, or device designed or adapted to bring into public notice any party, organization, or movement" in the United States Supreme Court building and on its grounds, violates the First Amendment.

* * *

The First Amendment provides that "Congress shall make no law...abridging the freedom of speech.... " There is no doubt that as a general matter peaceful picketing and leafletting are expressive activities involving "speech" protected by the First Amendment. *E.g., Carey v. Brown*, 447 U.S. 455, 460, 100 S.Ct. 2286, 2290, 65 L.E.2d 263 (1980): *Gregory v. Chicago*, 394 U.S. 111, 112, 89 S.Ct. 946, 947, 22 L.Ed.2d 134 (1969)....

It is also true that "public places "historically associated with the free exercise of expressive activities, such as streets, sidewalks, and parks, are considered, without more, to be "public forums." See *Perry Education Assn. v. Perry Local Educator's Assn.*, 460 U.S. 37, 45, 103 S.Ct. 948, 955, 74 L.Ed.2d 794 (1983); *Carey v. Brown*, 447 U.S. 455, 460, 100 S.Ct. 2286, 2290, 65 L.Ed.2d 263 (1980)....In such places, the government's ability to permissibly restrict expressive conduct is very limited: the government may enforce reasonable time, place, and manner restrictions as long as the restrictions "are content-neutral, are narrowly tailored to serve a significant government interest, and leave open ample alternative channels of communication." *Perry Education Assn., supra,* at 45, 103 S.Ct., at 955....

Publicly owned or operated property does not become a "public forum" simply because members of the public are permitted to come and go at will. See *Greer v. Spock,* 424 U.S. 828, 836, 96 S.Ct. 1211, 1216, 47 L.Ed.2d 505 (1976). Although whether the property has been "generally opened to the public" is a factor to consider in determining whether the government has opened its property to the use of the people for communicative purposes, it is not determinative of the question. We have regularly rejected the assertion that people who wish "to propagandize protests or views have a constitutional right to do so whenever and however and wherever they please." *Adderly v. Florida,* 385 U.S. 39, 47-48, 87 S.Ct. 242, 247, 17 L.Ed.2d 149 (1966).... There is little doubt that in some circumstances the government may ban the entry on to public property that is not a "public forum" of all persons except those who have legitimate business on the premises. The Government, "no less than a private owner of property, has the power to preserve the property under its control for the use to which it is lawfully dedicated." *Adderly v. Florida,* 385 U.S., at 47, 87 S.Ct., at 247. See Cox II, 379 U.S., at 563-564, 85 S.Ct., at 480.

It is argued that the Supreme Court building and grounds fit neatly within the description of non-public forum property....We need not make that judgment at this time, however, because § 13k covers the public sidewalks as well as the building and grounds inside the sidewalks. As will become evident, we hold that § 13k may not be applied to the public sidewalks.

...Sidewalks, of course, are among those areas of public property that traditionally have been held open to the public for expressive activities and are clearly within those areas of public property that may be considered, generally without further inquiry, to be public forum property.... Traditional public forum property occupies a special position in terms of First Amendment protection and will not lose its historically recognized character for the reason that it abuts government property that has been dedicated to a use other than as a forum for public expression. Nor may the government transform the character of the property by the expedient of including it within the statutory definition of what might be considered a non-public forum parcel of property. The public sidewalks forming the perimeter of the Supreme Court grounds, in our view, are public forums and should be treated as such for First Amendment purposes.

The government submits that § 13k qualifies as a reasonable time, place, and manner restriction which may be imposed to restrict communicative activities on public-forum property such as sidewalks.... We are convinced, however, that the section, which totally bans the specified communicative activity on the public sidewalks around the Court grounds, cannot be justified as a reasonable place restriction primarily because it has an insufficient nexus with any of the public interests that may be thought to undergird § 13k....

* * *

We do not denigrate the necessity to protect persons and property and to maintain proper order and decorum within the Supreme Court's grounds, but we do question whether a total ban on carrying a flag, banner or device on the public sidewalks substantially serves these purposes. There is no suggestion, for example, that appellees' activities in any way obstructed the sidewalks or access to the Building, threatened injury to any person or property, or in any way interfered with the orderly administration of the building or other parts of the grounds. As we have said, the building's perimeter sidewalks are indistinguishable from other public sidewalks in the city that are normally open to the conduct that is at issue here and that § 13k forbids. A total ban on that conduct is no more necessary for the maintenance of peace and tranquility on the public sidewalks surrounding the building than on any other sidewalks in the city. Accordingly, § 13k cannot be justified on this basis.

* * *

The judgment below is accordingly affirmed to the extent indicated by this opinion and is otherwise vacated.

* * *

So ordered.

Cases relating to **Chapter 3**

AUTHORITY TO DETAIN AND ARREST

PAYTON v. NEW YORK

445 U.S. 573, 100 S. Ct. 1371, 63 L. Ed. 2d 639 (1980)

MR. JUSTICE STEVENS delivered the opinion of the Court.

These appeals challenge the constitutionality of New York statutes that authorize police officers to enter a private residence without a warrant and with force, if necessary, to make a routine felony arrest.

The important constitutional question presented by this challenge has been expressly left open in a number of our prior opinions. In *United States* v. *Watson*, 423 U.S. 411, 96 S.Ct. 820, 46 L.Ed.2d 598, we upheld a warrantless "midday public arrest," expressly noting that the case did not pose "the still unsettled question . . . whether and under what circumstances an officer may enter a suspect's home to make a warrantless arrest." The question has been answered in different ways by other appellate courts. The Supreme Court of Florida rejected the constitutional attack as did the New York Court of Appeals, 45 N.Y.2d 300, 408 N.Y.S.2d 395, 380 N.E.2d 224 in this case. The courts of last resort in 10 other States, however, have held that unless special circumstances are present, warrantless arrests in the home are unconstitutional. Of the seven United States Courts of Appeals that have considered the question, five have expressed the opinion that such arrests are unconstitutional.

Last Term we noted probable jurisdiction of these appeals in order to address that question. After hearing oral argument, we set the case for reargument this Term. We now reverse the New York Court of Appeals and hold that the Fourth Amendment to the United States Constitution, made applicable to the States by the Fourteenth Amendment, *Mapp* v. *Ohio*, 367 U.S. 643, 81 S.Ct. 1684, 6 L.Ed.2d 1081; *Wolf* v. *Colorado*, 338 U.S. 25, 69 S.Ct. 1359, 93 L.Ed. 1782, prohibits the police from making a warrantless and nonconsensual entry into a suspect's home in order to make a routine felony arrest.

We first state the facts of both cases in some detail and put to one side certain related questions that are not presented by these records. We then explain why the New York statutes are not consistent with the Fourth Amendment and why the reasons for upholding warrantless arrests in a public place do not apply to warrantless invasions of the privacy of the home.

On January 14, 1970, after two days of intensive investigation, New York detectives had assembled evidence sufficient to establish probable cause to believe that Theodore Payton had murdered the manager of a gas station two days earlier. At about 7:30 a.m. on January 15, six officers went to Payton's apartment in the Bronx, intending to arrest him. They had not obtained a warrant. Although light and music emanated from the apartment, there was no response to their knock on the metal door. They summoned emergency assistance and, about 30 minutes later, used crowbars to break open the door and enter the apartment. No one was there. In plain view, however, was a 30-caliber shell casing that was seized and later admitted into evidence at Payton's murder trial.

In due course Payton surrendered to the police, was indicted for murder, and moved to suppress the evidence taken from his apartment. The trial judge held that the warrantless and forcible entry was authorized by the New York Code of Criminal Procedure, and that the evidence in plain view was properly seized. He found that exigent circumstances justified the officers' failure to announce their purpose before entering the apartment as required by the statute. He had no occasion, however, to decide whether those circumstances also would have justified the failure to obtain a warrant, because he concluded that the warrantless entry was adequately supported by the statute without regard to the circumstances. The Appellate Division, First Department, summarily affirmed.

On March 14, 1974, Obie Riddick was arrested for the commission of two armed robberies that had occurred in 1971. He had been identified by the victims in June of 1973 and in January 1974 the police had learned his address. They did not obtain a warrant for his arrest. At about noon on March 14, a detective, accompanied by three other officers, knocked on the door of the Queens house where Riddick was living. When his young son opened the door, they could see Riddick sitting in bed covered by a sheet. They entered the house and placed him under arrest. Before permitting him to dress, they opened a chest of drawers two feet from the bed in search of weapons and found narcotics and related paraphernalia. Riddick was subsequently indicted on narcotics charges. At a suppression hearing, the trial judge held that the warrantless entry into his home was authorized by the revised New York statute, and that the search of the immediate area was reasonable under *Chimel* v. *California*, 395 U.S. 752, 89 S.Ct. 2034, 23 L.Ed.2d 685. The Appellate Division, Second Department, affirmed the denial of the suppression motion.

The New York Court of Appeals, in a single opinion, affirmed the convictions of both Payton and Riddick. The court recognized that the question whether and under what circumstances an officer may enter a suspect's home to make a warrantless arrest had not been settled either by that court or by this Court. In answering that question, the majority of four judges relied primarily on its perception that there is a

> ". . . substantial difference between the intrusion which attends an entry for the purpose of searching the premises and that which results from an entry for the purpose of making an arrest, and on the significant difference in the governmental interest in achieving the objective of the intrusion in the two instances." 45 N.Y.2d, at 310, 408 N.Y.S.2d, at 399, 380 N.E.2d, at 228–229.

The majority supported its holding by noting the "apparent historical acceptance" of warrantless entries to make felony arrests, both in the English common law and in the practice of many American States.

Three members of the New York Court of Appeals dissented on this issue because they believed that the Constitution requires the police to obtain a "warrant to enter a home to arrest or seize a person, unless there are exigent circumstances." Starting from the premise that, except in carefully circumscribed instances, "the Fourth Amendment forbids police entry into a private home to search for and seize an object without a warrant," the dissenters reasoned that an arrest of the person involves an even greater invasion of privacy and should therefore be attended with at least as great a measure of constitutional protection. The dissenters noted "the existence of statutes and the American Law Institute imprimatur codifying the common-law rule authorizing warrantless arrests in private homes" and acknowledged that "the statutory authority of a police officer to make a warrantless arrest in this State has been in effect for almost 100 years," but concluded that "neither antiquity nor legislative unanimity can be determinative of the grave constitutional question presented" and "can never be a substitute for reasoned analysis."

Before addressing the narrow question presented by these appeals, we put to one side other related problems that are *not* presented today. Although it is arguable that the warrantless entry to effect Payton's arrest might have been justified by exigent circumstances, none of the New York courts relied on any such justification. The Court of Appeals majority treated both *Payton's* and *Riddick's* cases as involving routine arrests in which there was ample time to obtain a warrant, and we will do the same. Accordingly, we have no occasion to consider the sort of emergency or dangerous situation, described in our cases as "exigent circumstances," that would justify a warrantless entry into a home for the purpose of either arrest or search.

Nor do these cases raise any question concerning the authority of the police, without either a search or arrest warrant, to enter a third party's home to arrest a suspect. The police broke into Payton's apartment intending to arrest Payton and they arrested Riddick in his own dwelling. We also note that in neither case is it argued that the police lacked probable cause to believe that the suspect was at home when they entered. Finally, in both cases we are dealing with entries into homes made without the consent of any occupant. In *Payton*, the police used crowbars to break down the door and in *Riddick*, although his three-year-old son answered the door, the police entered before Riddick had an opportunity either to object or to consent.

It is familiar history that indiscriminate searches and seizures conducted under the authority of "general warrants" were the immediate evils that motivated the framing and adoption of the Fourth Amendment. Indeed, as originally proposed in the House of Representatives, the draft contained only one clause, which directly imposed limitations on the issuance of warrants, but imposed no express restrictions on warrantless searches or seizures. As it was ultimately adopted, however, the Amendment contained two separate clauses, the first protecting the basic right to be free from unreasonable searches and seizures and the second requiring that warrants be particular and supported by probable cause. The Amendment provides:

> "The right of the people to be secure in their persons, houses, papers, and effects, against unreasonable searches and seizures, shall not be violated, and no Warrants

> shall issue, but upon probable cause, supported by Oath or affirmation and particularly describing the place to be searched, and the persons or things to be seized."

It is thus perfectly clear that the evil the Amendment was designed to prevent was broader than the abuse of a general warrant. Unreasonable searches or seizures conducted without any warrant at all are condemned by the plain language of the first clause of the Amendment. Almost a century ago the Court stated in resounding terms that the principles reflected in the Amendment "reached farther than the concrete form" of the specific cases that gave it birth, and "apply to all invasions on the part of the government and its employes of the sanctity of a man's home and the privacies of life." *Boyd* v. *United States*, 116 U.S. 616, 630, 6 S.Ct. 524, 532, 29 L.Ed.2d 746. Without pausing to consider whether that broad language may require some qualification, it is sufficient to note that the warrantless arrest of a person is a species of seizure required by the Amendment to be reasonable. Indeed, as MR. JUSTICE POWELL noted in his concurrence in *United States* v. *Watson, supra*, the arrest of a person is "quintessentially a seizure."

The simple language of the Amendment applies equally to seizures of persons and to seizures of property. Our analysis in this case may therefore properly commence with rules that have been well established in Fourth Amendment litigation involving tangible items. As the Court unanimously reiterated just a few years ago, the "physical entry of the home is the chief evil against which the wording of the Fourth Amendment is directed." And we have long adhered to the view that the warrant procedure minimizes the danger of needless intrusions of that sort.

It is a "basic principle of Fourth Amendment law" that searches and seizures inside a home without a warrant are presumptively unreasonable. Yet it is also well-settled that objects such as weapons or contraband found in a public place may be seized by the police without a warrant. The seizure of property in plain view involves no invasion of privacy and is presumptively reasonable, assuming that there is probable cause to associate the property with criminal activity. The distinction between a warrantless seizure in an open area and such a seizure on private premises was plainly stated in *G. M. Leasing Corp.* v. *United States*, 429 U.S. 338, 354, 97 S.Ct. 619, 629, 50 L.Ed.2d 530:

> "It is one thing to seize without a warrant property resting in an open area or seizable by levy without an intrusion into privacy, and it is quite another thing to effect a warrantless seizure of property, even that owned by a corporation, situated on private premises to which access is not otherwise available for the seizing officer."

As the late Judge Leventhal recognized, this distinction has equal force when the seizure of a person is involved. Writing on the constitutional issue now before us for the United States Court of Appeals for the District of Columbia Circuit sitting en banc, *Dorman* v. *United States*, 140 U.S. App.D.C. 313, 435 F.2d 385 (1969), Judge Leventhal first noted the settled rule that warrantless arrrests in public places are valid. He immediately recognized, however, that

> "[a] greater burden is placed [ ] on

officials who enter a home or dwelling without consent. Freedom from intrusion into the home or dwelling is the archetype of the privacy protection secured by the Fourth Amendment."

His analysis of this question then focused on the long-settled premise that, absent exigent circumstances, a warrantless entry to search for weapons or contraband is unconstitutional even when a felony has been committed and there is probable cause to believe that incriminating evidence will be found within. He reasoned that the constitutional protection afforded to the individual's interest in the privacy of his own home is equally applicable to a warrantless entry for the purpose of arresting a resident of the house; for it is inherent in such an entry that a search for the suspect may be required before he can be apprehended. Judge Leventhal concluded that an entry to arrest and an entry to search for and to seize property implicate the same interest in preserving the privacy and the sanctity of the home, and justify the same level of constitutional protection.

This reasoning has been followed in other circuits. Thus, the Second Circuit recently summarized its position:

> "To be arrested in the home involves not only the invasion attendant to all arrests but also an invasion of the sanctity of the home. This is simply too substantial an invasion to allow without a warrant, at least in the absence of exigent circumstances, even when it is accomplished under statutory authority and when probable cause is clearly present." *United States* v. *Reed,* 572 F.2d 412, 423 (CA2 1978).

We find this reasoning to be persuasive and in accord with this Court's Fourth Amendment decisions.

The majority of the New York Court of Appeals, however, suggested that there is a substantial difference in the relative intrusiveness of an entry to search for property and an entry to search for a person. It is true that the area that may legally be searched is broader when executing a search warrant than when executing an arrest warrant in the home. See *Chimel* v. *California, supra.* This difference may be more theoretical than real, however, because the police may need to check the entire premises for safety reasons, and sometimes they ignore the restrictions on searches incident to arrest.

But the critical point is that any differences in the intrusiveness of entries to search and entries to arrest are merely ones of degree rather than kind. The two intrusions share this fundamental characteristic: the breach of the entrance to an individual's home. The Fourth Amendment protects the individual's privacy in a variety of settings. In none is the zone of privacy more clearly defined than when bounded by the unambiguous physical dimensions of an individual's home—a zone that finds its roots in clear and specific constitutional terms: "The right of the people to be secure in their . . . houses . . . shall not be violated." That language unequivocally establishes the proposition that "[a]t the very core [of the Fourth Amendment] stands the right of a man to retreat into his own home and there be free from unreasonable government intrusion." *Silverman* v. *United States,* 365 U.S. 505, 511, 81 S.Ct. 679, 683, 5 L.Ed. 2d 734. In terms that apply equally to seizures of property and to seizures of persons, the Fourth Amendment has drawn a firm line at the entrance to the house. Absent exigent circumstances, that threshold may not reasonably be crossed without a warrant.

* * *

It is obvious that the common-law rule on warrantless home arrests was not as clear as the rule on arrests in public places. Indeed, particularly considering the prominence of Lord Coke, the weight of authority as it appeared to the Framers was to the effect that a warrant was required, or at the minimum that there were substantial risks in proceeding without one. The common-law sources display a sensitivity to privacy interests that could not have been lost on the Framers. The zealous and frequent repetition of the adage that a "man's house is his castle," made it abundantly clear that both in England and in the Colonies "the freedom of one's house" was one of the most vital elements of English liberty.

Thus, our study of the relevant common law does not provide the same guidance that was present in *Watson*. Whereas the rule concerning the validity of an arrest in a public place was supported by cases directly in point and by the unanimous views of the commentators, we have found no direct authority supporting forcible entries into a home to make a routine arrest and the weight of the scholarly opinion is somewhat to the contrary. Indeed, the absence of any Seventeenth or Eighteenth Century English cases directly in point, together with the unequivocal endorsement of the tenet that "a man's house is his castle," strongly suggest that the prevailing practice was not to make such arrests except in hot pursuit or when authorized by a warrant. In all events, the issue is not one that can be said to have been definitively settled by the common law at the time the Fourth Amendment was adopted.

A majority of the States that have taken a position on the question permit warrantless entry into the home to arrest even in the absence of exigent circumstances. At this time, 24 States permit such warrantless entries; 15 States clearly prohibit them, though three States do so on federal constitutional grounds alone; and 11 States have apparently taken no position on the question.

But these current figures reflect a significant decline during the last decade in the number of States permitting warrantless entries for arrest. Recent dicta in this Court raising questions about the practice, have led state courts to focus on the issue. Virtually all of the state courts that have had to confront the constitutional issue directly have held warrantless entries into the home to arrest to be invalid in the absence of exigent circumstances. Three state courts have relied on Fourth Amendment grounds alone, while seven have squarely placed their decisions on both federal and state constitutional grounds. A number of other state courts, though not having had to confront the issue directly, have recognized the serious nature of the constitutional question. Apparently, only the Supreme Court of Florida and the New York Court of Appeals in this case have expressly upheld warrantless entries to arrest in the face of a constitutional challenge.

A longstanding, widespread practice is not immune from constitutional scrutiny. But neither is it to be lightly brushed aside. This is particularly so when the constitutional standard is as amorphous as the word "reasonable," and when custom and contemporary norms necessarily play such a large role in the constitutional analysis. In this case, although the weight of state-law authority is clear, there is by no means the kind of virtual unanimity on this question that was present in *United States* v. *Watson, supra,* with regard to warrantless arrests in public places. See 423 U.S., at 422-423, 96 S.Ct., at 827-828. Only 24 of the 50 States currently sanction warrantless entries into the home to arrest, see nn. 46-48, *supra,* and there is an obvious declining trend. Further, the strength of the trend is greater than the numbers alone indicate. Seven state courts have recently held that warrantless home arrests violate their respective *state* constitutions. That is significant because by invoking a state constitutional provision, a state court immunizes its decision from review by this Court. This heightened degree of immutability underscores the depth of the principle underlying the result.

No congressional determination that warrantless entries into the home are "reasonable" has been called to our attention. None of the federal statutes cited in the *Watson* opinion reflects any such legislative judgment. Thus, that support for the *Watson* holding finds no counterpart in this case.

MR. JUSTICE POWELL, concurring in *United States* v. *Watson, supra,* stated:

> "But logic sometimes must defer to history and experience. The Court's opinion emphasizes the historical sanction accorded warrantless felony arrests [in public places]."

In this case, however, neither history nor this Nation's experience requires us to disregard the overriding respect for the sanctity of the home that has been embedded in our traditions since the origins of the Republic.

The parties have argued at some length about the practical consequences of a warrant requirement as a precondition to a felony arrest in the home. In the absence of any evidence that effective law enforcement has suffered in those States that already have such a requirement, we are inclined to view such arguments with skepticism. More fundamentally, however, such arguments of policy, must give way to a constitutional command that we consider to be unequivocal.

Finally, we note the State's suggestion that only a search warrant based on probable cause to believe the suspect is at home at a given time can adequately protect the privacy interests at stake, and since such a warrant requirement is manifestly impractical, there need be no warrant of any kind. We find this ingenious argument unpersuasive. It is true that an arrest warrant requirement may afford less protection than a search warrant requirement, but it will suffice to interpose the magistrate's determination of probable cause between the zealous officer and the citizen. If there is sufficient evidence of a citizen's participation in a felony to persuade a judicial officer that his arrest is justified, it is constitutionally reasonable to require him to open his doors to the officers of the law. Thus, for Fourth Amendment purposes, an arrest warrant founded on probable cause implicitly carries with it the limited authority to enter a dwelling in which the suspect lives when there is reason to believe the suspect is within.

Because no arrest warrant was obtained in either of these cases, the judgments must be reversed and the cases remanded to the New York Court of Appeals for further proceedings not inconsistent with this opinion.

It is so ordered.

MR. JUSTICE BLACKMUN, concurring.

I joined the Court's opinion in *United States* v. *Watson*, 423 U.S. 411, 96 S.Ct. 820, 46 L.Ed.2d 598 (1976), upholding, on probable cause, the warrantless arrest in a public place. I, of course, am still of the view that the decision in *Watson* is correct. The Court's balancing of the competing governmental and individual interests properly occasioned that result. Where, however, the warrantless arrest is in the suspect's home, that same balancing requires that, absent exigent circumstances, the result be the other way. The suspect's interest in the sanctity of his home then outweighs the governmental interests.

I therefore join the Court's opinion, firm in the conviction that the result in *Watson* and the result here, although opposite, are fully justified by history and by the Fourth Amendment.

MR. JUSTICE WHITE, with whom THE CHIEF JUSTICE and MR. JUSTICE REHNQUIST join, dissenting.

The Court today holds that absent exigent circumstances officers may never enter a home during the daytime to arrest for a dangerous felony unless they have first obtained a warrant. This hard-and-fast rule, founded on erroneous assumptions concerning the intrusiveness of home arrest entries, finds little or no support in the common law or in the text and history of the Fourth Amendment. I respectfully dissent.

* * *

[Part of dissenting opinions omitted]

Today's decision ignores the carefully crafted restrictions on the common-law power of arrest entry and thereby overestimates the dangers inherent in that practice. At common law, absent exigent circumstances, entries to arrest could be made only for felony. Even in cases of felony, the officers were required to announce their presence, demand admission, and be refused entry before they were entitled to break doors. Further, it seems generally accepted that entries could be made only during daylight hours. And, in my view, the officer entering to arrest must have reasonable grounds to believe, not only that the arrestee has committed a crime, but also that the person suspected is present in the house at the time of the entry.

These four restrictions on home arrests—felony, knock and announce, daytime, and stringent probable cause—constitute powerful and complementary protections for the privacy interests associated with the home. The felony requirement guards against abusive or arbitrary enforcement and ensures that invasions of the home occur only in case of the most serious crimes. The knock and announce and daytime requirement protect individuals against the fear, humiliation and embarrassment of being aroused from the beds in states of partial or complete undress. And these requirements allow the arrestee to surrender at his front door, thereby maintaining his dignity and preventing the officers from entering other rooms of the dwelling. The stringent probable cause requirement would help ensure against the possibility that the police would enter when the suspect was not home, and, in searching for him, frighten members of the family or ransack parts of the house, seizing items in plain view. In short, these requirements, taken together, permit an individual suspected of a serious crime to surrender at the front door of his dwelling and thereby avoid most of the humiliation and indignity that the Court seems to believe necessarily accompany a house arrest entry. Such a front door arrest, in my view, is no more intrusive on personal privacy than the public warrantless arrests which we found to pass constitutional muster in *Watson*.

All of these limitations on warrantless arrest entries are satisfied on the facts of the present cases. The arrests here were for serious felonies—murder and armed robbery—and both occurred during daylight hours. The authorizing statutes required that the police announce their business and demand entry; neither Payton nor Riddick makes any contention that these statutory requirements were not fulfilled. And it is not argued that the police had no probable cause to believe that both Payton and Riddick were in their dwellings at the time of the entries. Today's decision, therefore, sweeps away any possibility that warrantless home entries might be permitted in some limited situations other than those in which exigent circumstances are present. The Court substitutes, in one sweeping decision, a rigid constitutional rule in place of the common-law approach, evolved over hundreds of years, which achieved a flexible accommodation between the demands of personal privacy and the legitimate needs of law enforcement.

A rule permitting warrantless arrest entries would not pose a danger that officers would use their entry power as a pretext to justify an otherwise invalid warrantless search. A search pursuant to a warrantless arrest entry will rarely, if ever, be as complete as one under authority of a search warrant. If the suspect surrenders at the door, the officers may not enter other rooms. Of course, the suspect may flee or hide, or may not be at home, but the officers cannot anticipate the first two of these possibilities and the last is unlikely given the requirement of probable cause to believe that the suspect is at home. Even when officers are justified in searching other rooms, they may seize only items within the arrestee's position or immediate control or items in plain view discovered during the course of a search reasonably directed at discovering a hiding suspect. Hence a warrantless home entry is likely to uncover far less evidence than a search conducted under authority of a search warrant. Furthermore, an arrest entry will inevitably tip off the suspects and likely result in destruction or removal of evidence not uncovered during the arrest. I therefore cannot believe that the police would take the risk of losing valuable evidence through a pretextual arrest entry rather than applying to a magistrate for a search warrant.

* * *

Further, police officers will often face the difficult task of deciding whether the circumstances are sufficiently exigent to justify their entry to arrest without a warrant. This is a decision that must be made quickly in the most trying of circumstances. If the officers mistakenly decide that the circumstances are exigent, the arrest will be invalid and any evidence seized incident to the arrest or in plain view will be excluded at trial. On the other hand, if the officers mistakenly determine that exigent circumstances are lacking, they may refrain from making the arrest, thus creating the possibility that a dangerous criminal will escape into the community. The police could reduce the likelihood of escape by staking out all possible exits until the circumstances become clearly exigent or a warrant is obtained. But the costs of such a stakeout seem excessive in an era of rising crime and scarce police resources.

The uncertainty inherent in the exigent circumstances determination burdens the judicial system as well. In the case of searches, exigent circumstances are sufficiently unusual that this Court has determined that the benefits of a warrant outweigh the burdens imposed, including the burdens on the judicial system. In contrast, arrests recurringly involve exigent circumstances, and this Court has heretofore held that a warrant can be dispensed with without undue sacrifice in Fourth Amendment values. The situation should be no different with respect to arrests in the home. Under today's decision, whenever the police have made a warrantless home arrest there will be the possibility of "endless litigation with respect to the existence of exigent circumstances, whether it was practicable to get a warrant, whether the suspect was about to flee, and the like."

Our cases establish that the ultimate test under the Fourth Amendment is one of "reasonableness." I cannot join the Court in declaring unreasonable a practice which has been thought entirely reasonable by so many for so long. It would be far preferable to adopt a clear and simple rule: after knocking and announcing their presence, police may enter the home to make a daytime arrest without a warrant when there is probable cause to believe that the person to be arrested committed a felony and is present in the house. This rule would best comport with the common-law background, with the traditional practice in the States, and with the history and policies of the Fourth Amendment. Accordingly, I respectfully dissent.

MR. JUSTICE REHNQUIST, dissenting.

The Court today refers to both *Payton* and *Riddick* as "routine felony arrests." I have no reason to dispute the Court's characterization of these arrests, but cannot refrain from commenting on the social implications of the result reached by the Court. Payton was arrested for the murder of the manager of a gas station; Riddick was arrested for two armed robberies. If these are indeed "routine felony arrests," which culminated in convictions after trial upheld by the state courts on appeal, surely something is amiss in the process of the administration of criminal justice whereby these convictions are now set aside by this Court under the exclusionary rule which we have imposed upon the States under the Fourth and Fourteenth Amendments to the United States Constitution.

I fully concur and join the dissenting opinion of MR. JUSTICE WHITE. There is significant historical evidence that we have over the years misread the history of the Fourth Amendment in connection with searches, elevating the warrant requirement over the necessity for probable cause in a way which the Framers of that Amendment did not intend. See Taylor, "Two Studies in Constitutional Interpretation," (1969), pp. 38-50. But one may accept all of that as *stare decisis,* and still feel deeply troubled by the transposition of these same errors into the area of actual arrests of felons within their houses with respect to whom there is probable cause to suspect guilt of the offense in question.

TENNESSEE v. GARNER

471 U.S. 1, 105 S.Ct. 1694, 85 L.Ed. 2d 1 (1985)

***

Justice WHITE delivered the opinion of the Court.

This case requires us to determine the constitutionality of the use of deadly force to prevent the escape of an apparently unarmed suspected felon. We conclude that such force may not be used unless it is necessary to prevent the escape and the officer has probable cause to believe that the suspect poses a significant threat of death or serious physical injury to the officer or others.

I

At about 10:45 p.m. on October 3, 1974, Memphis Police Officers Elton Hymon and Leslie Wright were dispatched to answer a "prowler inside call." Upon arriving at the scene they saw a woman standing on her porch and gesturing toward the adjacent house.[1] She told them she had heard glass breaking and that "they" or "someone" was breaking in next door. While Wright radioed the dispatcher to say that they were on the scene, Hymon went behind the house. He heard a door slam and saw someone run across the backyard. The fleeing suspect, who was appellee-respondent's decendent, Edward Garner, stopped at a 6-feet-high chain link fence at the edge of the yard. With the aid of a flashlight, Hymon was able to see Garner's face and hands. He saw no sign of a weapon, and, though not certain, was "reasonably sure" and "figured" that Garner was unarmed. App. 41, 56; Record 219. He thought Garner was 17 or 18 years old and about 5'5" or 5'7" tall.[2] While Garner was crouched at the base of fence, Hymon called out "police, halt" and took a few steps toward him. Garner then began to climb over the fence. Convinced that if Garner made it over the fence he would elude capture,[3] Hymon shot him. The

1 The owner of the house testified that no lights were on in the house, but that a back door light was on. Record 160. Officer Hymon, though uncertain, stated in his deposition that there were lights on in the house. Record 209.

2 In fact, Garner, an eighth-grader, was 15. He was 5'4" tall and weighed somewhere around 100 or 110 pounds. App. to Pet. for Cert. A5.

3 When asked at trial why he fired, Hymon stated:

> "Well, first of all it was apparent to me from the little bit that I knew about the area at the time that he was going to get away because, number 1, I couldn't get to him. My partner then couldn't find where he was because, you know, he was late coming around. He didn't know where I was talking about. I couldn't get to him because of the fence here, I couldn't have jumped this fence and come up, consequently jumped this fence and caught him before he got away because he was already up on the fence, just one leap and he was already over the fence, and so there is no way that I could have caught him." App. 52.

bullet hit Garner in the back of the head. Garner was taken by ambulance to a hospital, where he died on the operating table. Ten dollars and a purse taken from the house were found on his body.[4]

In using deadly force to prevent the escape, Hymon was acting under the authority of a Tennessee statute and pursuant to Police Department policy. The statute provides that "[i]f, after notice of the intention to arrest the defendant, he either flee or forcibly resist, the officer may use all the necessary means to effect the arrest." Tenn. Code Ann. § 40-7-108 (1982).[5] The department policy was slightly more restrictive than the statute, but still allowed the use of deadly force in cases of burglary. App. 140-144. The incident was reviewed by the Memphis Police Firearm's Review Board and presented to a grand jury. Neither took any action. App. 57.

Garner's father then brought this action in the Federal District Court for the Western District of Tennessee, seeking damages under 42 U.S.C. § 1983 for asserted violations of Garner's constitutional rights. The complaint alleged that the shooting violated the Fourth, Fifth, Sixth, Eighth, and Fourteenth Amendments of the United States Constitution. It named as defendants Officer Hymon, the Police Department, its Director, and the Mayor and city of Memphis. After a 3-day bench trial, the District Court entered judgment for all defendants. It dismissed the claims against the Mayor and the Director for lack of evidence. It then concluded that Hymon's actions were authorized by the Tennessee statute, which in turn was constitutional. Hymon had employed the only reasonable and practicable means of preventing Garner's escape. Garner had "recklessly and heedlessly attempted to vault over the fence to escape, thereby assuming the risk of being fired upon." App. to Pet. for Cert. A10.

The Court of Appeals for the Sixth Circuit affirmed with regard to Hymon, find that he had acted in good-faith reliance on the Tennessee statute and was therefore within the scope of his qualified immunity. 600 F.2d 52 (1979). It remanded for reconsideration of the possible liability of the city, however, in light of *Monell v. New York City Dept. of Social Services,* 436 U.S. 658, 98 S.Ct. 2018, 56 L.Ed.2d 611 (1978), which had come down after the District Court's decision. The District Court was directed to consider whether a city enjoyed a qualified immunity, whether the use of deadly force and hollow point bullets in these circumstances was constitutional, and whether any unconstitutional municipal conduct flowed from a "policy or custom" as required for liability under *Monell*. 600 F.2d, at 54-55.

The District Court concluded that *Monell* did not affect its decision. While acknowledging some doubt as to

---

He also stated that the area beyond the fence was dark, that he could not have gotten over the fence easily because he was carrying a lot of equipment and wearing heavy boots, and that Garner, being younger and more energetic, could have outrun him. *Id*., at 53-54.

4 Garner had rummaged through one room in the house, in which, in the woods of the owner, "[a]ll the stuff was out on the floors, all the drawers was pulled out, and stuff was scattered all over." App. 34. The owner testified that his valuables were untouched but that, in addition to the purse and the 10 dollars, one of his wife's rings was mising. The ring was not recovered. App. 34-35.

5 Although the statute does not say so explicitly, Tennessee law forbids the use of deadly force in the arrest of a misdemeanant. See *Johnson v. State,* 173 Tenn. 134, 114 S.W.2d 819 (1938).

the possible immunity of the city, it found that the statute, and Hymon's actions, were constitutional. Given this conclusion, it declined to consider the "policy or custom" question. App. to Pet. for Cert. A37-A39.

The Court of Appeals reversed and remanded. 710 F.2d 240 (CA6 1983). It reasoned that the killing of a fleeing suspect is a "seizure" under the Fourth Amendment[6] and is therefore constitutional only if "reasonable." The Tennessee statute failed as applied to this case because it did not adequately limit the use of deadly force by distinguishing between felonies of different magnitudes-- "the facts, as found, did not justify the use of deadly force under the Fourth Amendment." *Id.*, at 246. Officers cannot resort to deadly force unless they "have probable cause...to believe that the suspect [has committed a felony and] poses a threat to the safety of the officers or a danger to the community if left at large." *Ibid*.

The State of Tennessee, which had intervened to defend the statute, see 28 U.S.C. § 2403(b), appealed to this Court. No. 83-1035. The city filed a petition for certiorari. No. 83-1070. We noted probable jurisdiction in the appeal and granted the petition. 465 U.S. __, 104 S.Ct. 1589, 80 L.Ed.2d 122 (1984).

II

Whenever an officer restrains the freedom of a person to walk away, he has seized that person. *United States v. Brignoni-Ponce,* 422 U.S. 873, 878, 95 S.Ct. 2574, 2578, 45 L.Ed.2d 607 (1975). While it is not always clear just when minimal police interference becomes a seizure, see *United Sates v. Mendenhall,* 446 U.S. 544, 100 S.Ct. 1870, 64 L.Ed.2d 497 (1980), there can be no question that apprehension by the use of deadly force is a seizure subject to the reasonableness requirement of the Fourth Amendment.

A

A police officer may arrest a person if he has probable cause to believe that person committed a crime. *E.g., United Sates v. Watson,* 423 U.S. 411, 96 S.Ct. 820, 46 L.Ed.2d 598 (1976). Petitioners and appellant argue that if this requirement is satisfied the Fourth Amendment has nothing to say about *how* that seizure is made. To determine the constitutionality of a seizure "[w]e must balance the nature and quality of the intrusion on the individual's Fourth Amendment interests against the importance of the governmental interests alleged to justify the intrusion." *United States v. Place,* 462 U.S. 696, 703, 103 S.Ct. 2637, 2642, 77 L.Ed.2d 110 (1983); see *Delaware v. Prouse,* 440 U.S. 648, 654, 99 S.Ct. 1391, 1396, 59 L.Ed.2d 660 (1979); *United States v. Martinez-Fuerte,* 428 U.S. 543, 555, 96 S.Ct. 3074, 3081, 49 L.Ed.2d 1116 (1976). We have described "the balancing of competing interests" as "the key principle of the Fourth Amendment." *Michigan v. Summers,* 452 U.S. 692, 700, n. 12, 101 S.Ct. 2587, 2593, n. 12, 60 L.Ed.2d 340 (1981). See also *Camara v. Municipal Court,* 387 U.S. 523, 536-537, 87 S.Ct. 1727, 1734-1735, 18 L.Ed.2d 930 (1967). Because one of the factors is the extent of the intrusion, it is plain that reasonableness depends on not only when a seizure is made, but also how it is carried out. *United States v. Ortiz,* 422 U.S. 891, 895, 95 S.Ct. 2585, 2588, 45

---

6 "The right of the people to be secure in their persons...against unreasonable searches and seizures, shall not be violated...." U.S. Const, Amdt. 4.

L.Ed.2d 623 (1975); *Terry v. Ohio,* 392 U.S. 1, 28-29, 88 S.Ct. 1868, 1883-1884, 20 L.Ed.2d 889 (1968).

Applying these principles to particular facts, the Court has held that governmental interests did not support a lengthy detention of luggage, *United States v. Place, supra,* an airport seizure not "carefully tailored to its underlying justification," *Florida v. Royer,* 460 U.S. 491, 500, 103 S.Ct. 1319, 1325, 75 L.Ed.2d 229 (1983) (plurality opinion), surgery under general anesthesia to obtain evidence, *Winston v. Lee,* __U.S.__, 105 S.Ct.__, 83 L.Ed.2d__ (1985), or detention for fingerprinting without probable cause, *Davis v. Mississippi,* 394 U.S. 721; 89 S.Ct. 1394, 22 L.Ed.2d 676 (1969); *Hayes v. Florida,* __U.S.__, 105 S.Ct.__, 83 L.Ed.2d__ (1985). On the other hand, under the same approach it has upheld the taking of fingernail scrapings from a suspect, *Cupp v. Murphy,* 412 U.S. 391, 93 S.Ct. 2000, 36 L.Ed.2d 900 (1973), an unannounced entry into a home to prevent the destruction of evidence, *Ker v. California,* 374 U.S. 23, 83 S.Ct. 1623, 10 L.Ed.2d 726 (1963), administrative housing inspections without probable cause to believe that a code violation will be found, *Camara v. Municipal Court, supra*, and a blood test of a drunk-driving suspect, *Schmerber v. California,* 384 U.S 757, 86 S.Ct. 1826, 16 L.Ed.2d 908 (1966). In each of these cases, the question was whether the totality of the circumstances justified a particular sort of search or seizure.

B

The same balancing process applied in the cases cited above demonstrates that, notwithstanding probable cause to seize a suspect, an officer may not always do so by killing him. The intrusiveness of a seizure by means of deadly force is unmatched. The suspect's fundamental interest in his own life need not be elaborated upon. The use of deadly force also frustrates the interest of the individual, and of society, in judicial determination of guilt and punishment. Against these interests are ranged governmental interests in effective law enforcement. It is argued that overall violence will be reduced by encouraging the peaceful submission of suspects who know that they may be shot if they flee. Effectiveness in making arrests requires the resort to deadly force, or at least the meaningful threat thereof. "Being able to arrest such individuals is a condition precedent to the state's entire system of law enforcement." Brief for Petitioners 14.

Without in any way disparaging the importance of these goals, we are not convinced that the use of deadly force is a sufficiently productive means of accomplishing them to justify the killing of non-violent suspects. Cf. *Delaware v. Prouse, supra,* 440 U.S., at 659, 99 S.Ct., at 1399. The use of deadly force is a self-defeating way of apprehending a suspect and so setting the criminal justice mechanism in motion. If successful, it guarantees that that mechanism will not be set in motion. And while the meaningful threat of deadly force might be thought to lead to the arrest of more live suspects by discouraging escape attempts, the presently available evidence does not support this thesis. The fact is that a majority of police departments in this country have forbidden the use of deadly force against nonviolent suspects. See *infra*, at 1704-1705. If those charged with the enforcement of the criminal law have abjured the use of deadly force in arresting nondangerous felons, there is a substantial basis for doubting that the use of such force is an essential attribute of the arrest power in all felony cases. See *Schumann v. McGinn,* 307 Minn. 446, 472, 240 N.W.2d 525, 540 (1976) (Rogosheske, J., dissenting in part). Petitioners and appellant have not persuaded us that shooting nondangerous fleeing suspects is so vital as to outweigh the suspects interest in his own life.

The use of deadly force to prevent the escape of all felony suspects, whatever the circumstances, is constitutionally unreasonable. It is not better that all felony suspects die than that they escape. Where the suspect poses no immediate threat to the officer and no threat to others, the harm resulting from failing to apprehend him does not justify the use of deadly force to do so. It is no doubt unfortunate when a suspect who is in sight escapes, but the fact that the police arrive a little late or are a little slower afoot does not always justify killing the suspect. A police officer may not seize an unarmed, nondangerous suspect by shooting him dead. The Tennessee statute is unconstitutional insofar as it authorizes the use of deadly force against such fleeing suspects.

It is not, however, unconstitutional on its face. Where the officer has probable cause to believe that the suspect poses a threat of serious physical harm, either to the officer or to others, it is not constitutionally unreasonable to prevent escape by using deadly force. Thus, if the suspect threatens the officer with a weapon or there is probable cause to believe that he has committed a crime involving the infliction or threatened infliction of serious physical harm, deadly force may be used if necessary to prevent escape, and if, where feasible, some warning has been given. As applied in such circumstances, the Tennessee statute would pass constitutional muster.

III

A

It is insisted that the Fourth Amendment must be construed in light of the common-law rule, which allowed the use of whatever force was necessary to effect the arrest of a fleeing felon, though not a misdemeanant. As stated in Hale's posthumously published Pleas of the Crown:

> "[I]f persons that are pursued by these officers for felony or the just suspicion thereof...shall not yield themselves to these officers, but shall either resist or fly before they are apprehended or being apprehended shall rescue themselves and resist or fly, so that they cannot be otherwise apprehended, and are upon necessity slain therein, because they cannot be otherwise taken, it is no felony." 2M. Hale, Historia Placitorum Coronae 85 (1736). See also 4 W. Blackstone, Commentaries *289.

Most American jurisdictions also imposed a flat prohibition against the use of deadly force to stop a fleeing misdemeanant, coupled with a general privilege to use such force to stop a fleeing felon. *E.g., Holloway v. Moser,* 193 N.C. 185, 136 S.E. 375 (1927); *State v. Smith,* 127 Iowa 534, 535, 103 N.W. 944, 945 (1905); *Reneau v. State,* 70 Tenn. 720 (1879); *Brooks v. Commonwealth,* 61 Pa. 352 (1869); *Roberts v. State,* 14 Mo. 138 (1851); see generally R. Perkins & R. Boyce, Criminal Law 1098-1102 (3d ed. 1982); Day, Shooting the Fleeing Felon: State of the Law, 14 Crim.L.Bull. 285, 286-287 (1978); Wilgus, Arrest Without a Warrant, 22 Mich.L.Rev. 798, 807-816 (1924). But see *Storey v. State,* 71 Ala. 329 (1882); *State v. Bryant,* 65 N.C. 327,

328 (1871); *Caldwell v. State,* 41 Tex. 86 (1874).

The State and city argue that because this was the prevailing rule at the time of the adoption of the Fourth Amendment and for some time thereafter, and is still in force in some States, use of deadly force against a fleeing felon must be "reasonable." It is true that this Court has often looked to the common law in evaluating the reasonableness, for Fourth Amendment purposes, of police activity. See, *e.g.*, *United Sates v. Watson*, 423 U.S. 411, 418-419, 96 S.Ct. 820, 825-826, 46 L.Ed.2d 598 (1976); *Gerstein v. Pugh*, 420 U.S. 103, 111, 114, 95 S.Ct. 854, 861, 863, 43 L.Ed.2d 54 (1975); *Carroll v. United States*, 267 U.S. 132, 149-153, 45 S.Ct. 280, 283-285, 69 L.Ed. 543 (1925). On the other hand, it "has not simply frozen into constitutional law those law enforcement practices that existed at the time of the Fourth Amendment's passage." *Payton v. New York*, 445 U.S. 573, 591, n. 33, 100 S.Ct. 1371, 1382, n. 33, 63 L.Ed.2d 639 (1980). Because of sweeping change in the legal and technological context, reliance on the common-law rule in this case would be a mistaken literalism that ignores the purposes of a historical inquiry.

B

It has been pointed out many times that the common-law rule is best understood in light of the fact that it arose at a time when virtually all felonies were punishable by death. "Though effected without the protections and formalities of an orderly trial and conviction, the killing of a resisting or fleeing felon resulted in no greater consequences than those authorized for punishment of the felony of which the individual was charged or suspected." American Law Institute, Model Penal Code § 3.07, Comment 3, p. 56 (Tentative Draft No. 8, 1958) (hereinafter Model Penal Code Comment). Courts have also justified the common-law rule by emphasizing the relative dangerousness of felons. See, *e.g.*, *Schumann v. McGinn,* 307 Minn., at 458, 240 N.W.2d at 533; *Holloway v. Moser, supra,* 193 N.C., at 187, 136 S.E., at 376 (1927).

Neither of these justifications makes sense today. Almost all crimes formerly punishable by death no longer are or can be. See *e.g.*, *Enmund v. Florida,* 458 U.S. 782, 102 S.Ct. 3368, 73 L.Ed.2d 1140 (1982); *Coker v. Georgia,* 433 U.S. 584, 97 S.Ct. 2861, 53 L.Ed.2d 982 (1977). And while in earlier times "the gulf between the felonies and the minor offenses was broad and deep," 2 Pollock & Maitland 467, n. 3; *Carroll v. United States,* 267 U.S. 132, 158, 45 S.Ct. 280, 287, 69 L.Ed. 543 (1925), today the distinction is minor and often arbitrary. Many crimes classified as misdemeanors, or nonexistent, at common law are now felonies. Wilgus, 22 Mich.L.Rev., at 572-573. These changes have undermined the concept, which was questionable to begin with, that use of deadly force against a fleeing felon is merely a speedier execution of someone who has already forfeited his life. They have also made the assumption that a "felon" is more dangerous than a misdemeanant untenable. Indeed, numerous misdemeanors involve conduct more dangerous than many felonies.

There is an additional reason why the common-law rule cannot be directly translated to the present day. The common-law rule developed at a time when weapons were rudimentary. Deadly force could be inflicted almost solely in a hand-to-hand struggle during which, necessarily, the safety of the arresting officer was at risk. Handguns were not carried by police officers until the latter half of the last century. L. Kennett & J. Anderson, The Gun in America 150-151 (1975). Only then did it become possible to use deadly force from a distance as a means of apprehension. As a practical matter, the use of deadly force under the standard articulation of the common-law rule has an altogether different meaning --and harsher consequences-- now than in past centuries. See Wechsler & Michael, A Rationale for the Law of Homicide: I, 37 Colum.L.Rev. 701, 741 (1937).

One other aspect of the common-law rule bears emphasis. It forbids the use of deadly force to apprehend a misdemeanant, condemning such action as disproportionately severe. See *Holloway v. Moser,* 193 N.C., at 187, 136 S.E., at 376; *State v. Smith,* 127 Iowa, at 535, 103 N.W., at 945. See generally Annot., 83 A.L.R.3d 238 (1978).

In short, though the common law pedigree of Tennessee's rule is pure on its face, changes in the legal and technological context mean the rule is distorted almost beyond recognition when literally applied.

B

In evaluating the reasonableness of police procedures under the Fourth Amendment, we have also looked to prevailing rules in individual jurisdictions. See, *e.g., United States v. Watson,* 423 U.S., at 421-422, 96 S.Ct., at 826-827. The rules in the States are varied. See generally Comment, 18 Ga.L.Rev. 137, 140-144 (1983). Some 19 States have codified the common-law rule, though in two of these the courts have significantly limited the statute. Four States, though without a relevant statute, apparently retain the common-law rule. Two States have adopted the Model Penal Code's provision verbatim. Eighteen others allow, in slightly varying language, the use of deadly force only if the suspect has committed a felony involving the use or threat of physical or deadly force, or is escaping with a deadly weapon, or is likely to endanger life or inflict serious physical injury if not arrested. Louisiana and Vermont, though without statutes or case law on point, do forbid the use of deadly force to prevent any but violent felonies. The remaining States either have no relevant statute or case-law, or have positions that are unclear.

It cannot be said that there is a constant or overwhelming trend away from the common-law rule. In recent years, some States have reviewed their laws and expressly rejected abandonment of the common-law rule. Nonetheless, the long-term movement has been away from the rule that deadly force may be used against any fleeing felon, and that remains the rule in less than half the States.

This trend is more evident and impressive when viewed in light of the policies adopted by the police departments themselves. Overwhelmingly, these are more restrictive than the common-law rule. C. Milton, J. Halleck, J. Lardner, & G. Abrecht, Police Use of Deadly Force 45-46 (1977). The Federal Bureau of Investigation and the New York City Police Department, for example, both forbid the use of firearms except when necessary to prevent death or grievous bodily harm. *Id.*, at 40-41; App. 83. For accreditation by the Commission on Accreditation for Law Enforcement Agencies, a department must restrict the use of deadly force to situations where "the officer reasonably believes that the action is in defense of human life...or in defense of any person in immediate danger of serious physical injury." Commission on Accreditation for Law Enforcement Agencies, Inc., Standards for Law Enforcement Agencies 1-2 (1983) (italics deleted). A 1974 study reported that the police department regulations in a majority of the large cities of the United States allowed the firing of a weapon only when a felon presented a threat of death of serious bodily harm. Boston Police Department, Planning & Research Division, The Use of Deadly Force by Boston Police Personnel (1974), cited in *Mattis v. Schnarr,* 547 F.2d 1007, 1016, n.19 (CA8 1976), vacated as moot *sub nom. Ashcroft v. Mattis,* 431 U.S. 171, 97 S.Ct. 1739, 52 L.Ed.2d 219 (1977). Overall, only 7.5% of departmental and municipal policies explicitly permit the use of deadly force against any felon; 86.8% explicitly do not. K. Matulia, A Balance of Forces: A Report of the International Association of Chiefs of Police 161 (1982) (table). See also Record 1108-1368 (written policies of 44 departments). See generally W. Geller & K. Karales, Split-Second Decisions 33-42 (1981); Brief for Police Foundation et al. as *Amici Curiae*. In light of the rules adopted by those who must actually administer them, the older and fading common-law view is a dubious indicium of the constitutionality of the Tennessee statute now before us.

C

Actual departmental policies are important for an additional reason. We would hesitate to declare a police practice of long standing "unreasonable" if doing so would severely hamper effective law enforcement. But the indications are to the contrary. There has been no suggestion that crime has worsened in any way in jurisdictions that have adopted, by legislation or departmental policy, rules similar to that announced today. *Amici* noted that "[a]fter extensive research and consideration, [they] have concluded that laws permitting police officers to use deadly force to apprehend unarmed, non-violent fleeing felony suspects actually do not protect citizens or law enforcement officers, do not deter crime or alleviate problems caused by crime, and do not improve the crime-fighting ability of law enforcement agencies." Brief for Police Foundation et al. as *Amici Curiae* 11. The submission is that the obvious state interests in apprehension are not sufficiently served to warrant the use of lethal weapons against all fleeing felons. See *supra*, at 1700-1701, and n.10.

Nor do we agree with petitioners and appellant that the rule we have adopted requires the police to make impossible, split-second evaluations of unknowable facts. See Brief for Petitioners 25; Brief for Appellant 11. We do not deny the practical difficulties of attempting to assess the suspect's dangerousness. However, similarly difficult judgments must be made by the police in equally uncertain circumstances. See, *e.g., Terry v. Ohio,* 392 U.S., at 20, 27, 88 S.Ct., at 1879, 1883. Nor is there any indication that in States that allow the use of deadly force only against dangerous suspects, see *supra*, nn. 15, 17-19, the standard has been difficult to apply or has led to a rash of litigation involving inappropriate second-guessing of police officers' split-second decisions. Moreover, the highly technical felony/misdemeanor distinction is equally, if not more, difficult to apply in the field. An officer is in no position to know, for example, the precise value of property stolen, or whether the crime was a first or second offense. Finally, as noted above, this claim must be viewed with suspicion in light of the similar self-imposed limitations of so many police departments.

IV

The District Court concluded that Hymon was justified in shooting Garner because state law allows, and the Federal Constitutional does not forbid, the use of deadly force to prevent the escape of a fleeing felony suspect if no alternative means of apprehension is available. See App. to Pet. for Cert. A9-A11, A38. This conclusion made a determination of Garner's apparent dangerousness unnecessary. The court did find, however, that Garner appeared to be unarmed, though Hymon could not be certain that was the case. *Id.*, at A4, A23. See also App. 41, 56; Record 219. Restated in Fourth Amendment terms, this means Hymon had no articulable basis to think Garner was armed.

In reversing, the Court of Appeals accepted the District Court's factual conclusions and held that "the facts, as found, did not justify the use of deadly force." 710 F.2d, at 246. We agree. Officer Hymon could not reasonably have believed that Garner--young, slight, and unarmed--posed any threat. Indeed, Hymon never attempted to justify his actions on any basis other than the need to prevent an escape. The District Court stated in passing that "[t]he facts of this case did not indicate to Officer Hymon that Garner was 'nondangerous.'" App to Pet. for Cert. A34. This conclusion is not explained, and seems to be based solely on the fact that Garner had broken into a house at night. However, the fact that Garner was a suspected burglar could not, without regard to the other circumstances, automatically justify the use of deadly force. Hymon did not have probable cause to believe that Garner, whom he correctly believed to be unarmed, posed any physical danger to himself or others.

The dissent argues that the shooting was justified by the fact that Officer Hymon had probable cause to believe that Garner had committed a nighttime burglary. *Post*, at 1711, 1712. While we agree that burglary is a serious crime, we cannot agree that it is so dangerous as automatically to justify the use of deadly force. The FBI classifies burglary as a "property" rather than a "violent" crime. See Federal Bureau of Investigation, Uniform Crime Reports, Crime in the United States 1 (1984). Although the armed burglar would present a different situation, the fact that an unarmed suspect has broken into a dwelling at night does not automatically mean he is physically dangerous. This case demonstrates as much. See also *Solem v. Helm,* 463 U.S. 277, 296-297, and nn. 22-23, 103 S.Ct. 3001, __, __, nn. 22-23, 77 L.Ed.2d 637 (1983). In fact, the available statistics demonstrate that burglaries only rarely involve physical violence. During the 10-year period from 1973-1982, only 3.8% of all burglaries involved violent crime. Bureau of Justice Statistics, Household Burglary, p. 4 (1985). See also T. Reppetto, Residential Crime 17, 105 (1974); Conklin & Bittner, Burglary in a Suburb, 11 Criminology 208, 214 (1973).

V

We wish to make clear what our holding means in the context of this case. The complaint has been dismissed as to all the individual defendants. The State is a party only by virtue of 28 U.S.C. § 2403(b) and is not subject to liability. The possible liability of the remaining defendants-- the Police Department and the city of Memphis -- hinges on *Monell v. New York City Dept. of Social Services*, 436 U.S. 658, 98 S.Ct. 2018, 56 L.Ed.2d 611 (1978), and is left for remand. We hold that the statute is invalid insofar as it purported to give Hymon the authority to act as he did. As for the policy of the Police Department, the absence of any discussion of this issue by the courts below, and the uncertain state of the record, preclude any consideration of its validity.

The judgment of the Court of Appeals is affirmed, and the case is remanded for further proceedings consistent with this opinion.

So ordered.

The dissenting opinion is not included.

TERRY v. OHIO

392 U.S. 1, 88 S. Ct. 1868, 20 L. Ed. 2d 889 (1968)

MR. CHIEF JUSTICE WARREN delivered the opinion of the Court.

This case presents serious questions concerning the role of the Fourth Amendment in the confrontation on the street between the citizen and the policeman investigating suspicious circumstances.

Petitioner Terry was convicted of carrying a concealed weapon and sentenced to the statutorily prescribed term of one to three years in the penitentiary. Following the denial of a pretrial motion to suppress, the prosecution introduced in evidence two revolvers and a number of bullets seized from Terry and a codefendant, Richard Chilton, by Cleveland Police Detective Martin McFadden. At the hearing on the motion to suppress this evidence, Officer McFadden testified that while he was patrolling in plain clothes in downtown Cleveland at approximately 2:30 in the afternoon of October 31, 1963, his attention was attracted by two men, Chilton and Terry, standing on the corner of Huron Road and Euclid Avenue. He had never seen the two men before, and he was unable to say precisely what first drew his eye to them. However, he testified that he had been a policeman for 39 years and a detective for 35 and that he had been assigned to patrol this vicinity of downtown Cleveland for shoplifters and pickpockets for 30 years. He explained that he had developed routine habits of observation over the years and that he would "stand and watch people or walk and watch people at many intervals of the day." He added: "Now, in this case when I looked over they didn't look right to me at the time."

His interest aroused, Officer McFadden took up a post of observation in the entrance to a store 300 to 400 feet away from the two men. "I get more purpose to watch them when I seen their movements," he testified. He saw one of the men leave the other one and walk southwest on Huron Road, past some stores. The man paused for a moment and looked in a store window, then walked on a short distance, turned around and walked back toward the corner, pausing once again to look in the same store window. He rejoined his companion at the corner, and the two conferred briefly. Then the second man went through the same series of motions, strolling down Huron Road, looking in the same window, walking on a short distance, turning back, peering in the store window again, and returning to confer with the first man at the corner. The two men repeated this ritual alternately between five and six times apiece—in all, roughly a dozen trips. At one point, while the two men were standing together on the corner, a third man approached them and engaged them briefly in conversation. This man then left the two others and walked west on Euclid Avenue. Chilton and Terry resumed their measured pacing, peering, and conferring. After this had gone on for 10 to 12 minutes, the two men walked off together, heading west on Euclid Avenue, following the path taken earlier by the third man.

By this time Officer McFadden had become thoroughly suspicious. He testified that after observing their elaborately casual and oft-repeated reconnaissance of the store window on Huron Road, he suspected the two men of "casing a job, a stick-up," and that he considered it his duty as a police officer to investigate further. He added that he feared "they may have a gun." Thus, Officer McFadden followed Chilton and Terry and saw them stop in front of Zucker's store to talk to the same man who had conferred with them earlier on the street corner. Deciding that the situation was ripe for direct action, Officer McFadden approached the three men, identified himself as a police officer and asked for their names. At this point his knowledge was confined to what he had observed. He was not acquainted with any of the three men by name or by sight, and he had received no information concerning them from any other source. When the men "mumbled something" in response to his inquiries, Officer McFadden grabbed petitioner Terry, spun him around so they were facing the other two, with Terry between McFadden and the others, and patted down the outside of his clothing. In the left breast pocket of Terry's overcoat Officer McFadden felt a pistol. He reached inside the overcoat pocket, but was unable to remove the gun. At this point, keeping Terry between himself and the others, the officer ordered all three men to enter Zucker's store. As they went in, he removed Terry's overcoat completely, retrieved a .38 caliber revolver from the pocket and ordered all three men to face the wall with their hands raised. Officer McFadden proceeded to pat down the outer clothing of Chilton and the third man, Katz. He discovered another revolver in the outer pocket of Chilton's overcoat, but no weapons were found on Katz. The officer testified that he only patted the men down to see whether they had weapons, and that he did not put his hands beneath the outer garments of either Terry or Chilton until he felt their guns. So far as appears from the record, he never placed his hands beneath Katz's outer garments. Officer McFadden seized Chilton's gun, asked the proprietor of the store to call a police wagon, and took all three men to the station, where Chilton and Terry were formally charged with carrying concealed weapons.

On the motion to suppress the guns the prosecution took the position that they had been seized following a search incident to a lawful arrest. The trial court rejected this theory, stating that it "would be stretching the facts beyond reasonable comprehension" to find that Officer McFadden had had probable cause to arrest the men before he patted them down for weapons. However, the court denied the defendant's motion on he ground that Officer McFadden, on the basis of his experience, "had reasonable cause to believe . . . that the defendants were conducting themselves suspiciously, and some interrogation should be made of their action." Purely for his own protection, the court held, the officer had the right to pat down the outer clothing of these men, whom he had reasonable cause to believe might be armed. The court distinguished between an investigatory "stop" and an arrest, and between a "frisk" of the outer clothing for weapons and a full-blown search for evidence of crime. The frisk, it held, was essential to the proper performance of the officer's investigatory duties, for without it "the answer to the police officer may be a bullet, and a loaded pistol discovered during the frisk is admissible."

After the court denied their motion to suppress, Chilton and Terry waived jury trial and pleaded not guilty. The court adjudged them guilty, and the Court of Appeals for the Eighth Judicial District, Cuyahoga County, affirmed. *State* v. *Terry*, 5 OhioApp.2d 122, 214 N.E.2d 114 (1966). The Supreme Court of Ohio dismissed petitioner's appeal on the ground that no "substantial constitutional question" was involved. We granted certiorari, 387 U.S. 929 (1967), to determine whether the admission of the revolvers in evidence violated petitioner's rights under the Fourth Amendment, made applicable to the States by the Fourteenth. *Mapp* v. *Ohio*, 367 U.S. 643 (1961). We affirm the conviction.

I.

The Fourth Amendment provides that "the right of the people to be secure in their persons, houses, papers, and effects, against unreasonable searches and seizures, shall not be violated. . . ." This inestimable right of personal security belongs as much to the citizen on the streets of our cities as to the homeowner closeted in his study to dispose of his secret affairs. For as this Court has always recognized,

> No right is held more sacred, or is more carefully guarded, by the common law, than the right of every individual to the possession and control of his own person, free from all restraint or interference, unless by clear and unquestionable authority of law. *Union Pac. R. Co.* v. *Botsford,* 141 U.S. 250, 251 (1891).

. . . .

We would be less than candid if we did not acknowledge that this question thrusts to the fore difficult and troublesome issues regarding a sensitive area of police activity—issues which have never been before squarely presented to this Court. Reflective of the tensions involved are the practical and constitutional arguments pressed with great vigor on both sides of the public debate over the power of the police to "stop and frisk"—as it is sometimes euphemistically termed—suspicious persons.

On the one hand, it is frequently argued that in dealing with the rapidly unfolding and often dangerous situations on city streets the police are in need of an escalating set of flexible responses, graduated in relation to the amount of information they possess. For this purpose it is urged that distinctions should be made between a "stop" and an "arrest" (or a "seizure" of a person), and between a "frisk" and a "search." Thus, it is argued, the police should be allowed to "stop" a person and detain him briefly for questioning upon suspicion that he may be connected with criminal activity. Upon suspicion that the person may be armed, the police should have the power to "frisk" him for weapons. If the "stop" and the "frisk" give rise to probable cause to believe that the suspect has committed a crime, then the police should be empowered to make a formal "arrest," and a full incident "search" of the person. This scheme is justified in part upon the notion that a "stop" and a "frisk" amount to a mere "minor inconvenience and petty indignity," which can be properly imposed upon the citizen in the interest of effective law enforcement on the basis of a police officer's suspicion.

On the other side the argument is made that the authority of the police must be strictly circumscribed by the law of arrest and search as it has developed to date in the traditional jurisprudence of the Fourth Amendment. It is contended with some force that there is not—and cannot be—a variety of police activity which does not depend solely upon the voluntary cooperation of the citizen and yet which stops short of an arrest based upon probable cause to make such an arrest. The heart of the Fourth Amendment, the argument runs, is a severe requirement of specific justification for any intrusion upon protected personal security, coupled with a highly developed system of judicial controls to enforce upon the agents of the State the commands of the Constitution. Acquiescence by the courts in the compulsion inherent in the field interrogation practices at issue here, it is urged, would constitute an abdication of, substantial interference with liberty and personal security by police officers whose judgment is necessarily colored by their primary involvement in "the often competitive enterprise of ferreting out crime." *Johnson* v. *United States*, 333 U.S. 10, 14 (1948). This, it is argued, can only serve to exacerbate police-community tensions in the crowded centers of our Nation's cities.

In this context we approach the issues in this case mindful of the limitations of the judicial function in controlling the myriad daily situations in which policemen and citizens confront each other on the street. The State has characterized the issue here as "the right of a police officer . . . to make an on-the-street stop, interrogate and pat down for weapons (known in the street vernacular as 'stop and frisk')." But this is only partly accurate. For the issue is not the abstract propriety of the police conduct, but the admissibility against petitioner of the evidence uncovered by the search and seizure. Ever since its inception, the rule excluding evidence seized in violation of the Fourth Amendment has been recognized as a principal mode of discouraging lawless police conduct. . . . Thus its major thrust is a deterrent one, . . . and experience has taught that it is the only effective deterrent to police misconduct in the criminal context, and that without it the constitutional guarantee against unreasonable searches and seizures would be a mere "form of words." . . . The rule also serves another vital function—"the imperative of judicial integrity." . . . Courts which sit under our Constitution cannot and will not be made party to lawless invasions of the constitutional rights of citizens by permitting unhindered governmental use of the fruits of such invasions. Thus in our system evidentiary rulings provide the context in which the judicial process of inclusion and exclusion approves some conduct as comporting with constitutional guarantees and disapproves other actions by state agents. A ruling admitting evidence in a criminal trial, we recognize, has the necessary effect of legitimizing the conduct which produced the evidence, while an application of the exclusionary rule withholds the constitutional imprimatur.

The exclusionary rule has its limitations, however, as a tool of judicial control. It cannot properly be invoked to exclude the products of legitimate police investigative techniques on the ground that much conduct which is closely similar involves unwarranted intrusions upon constitutional protections. Moreover, in some contexts the rule is effective as a deterrent. Street encounters between citizens and police officers are incredibly rich in diversity. They range from wholly friendly exchanges of pleasantries or mutually useful information to hostile confrontations of armed men involving arrests, or injuries, or loss of life. Moreover, hostile confrontations are not all of a piece. Some of them begin in a friendly enough manner, only to take a different turn upon the injection of some unexpected element into the conversation. Encounters are initiated by the police for a wide variety of purposes, some of which are wholly unrelated to a desire to prosecute for crime. Doubtless some police "field interrogation" conduct violates the Fourth Amendment. But a stern refusal by this Court to condone such activity does not necessarily render it responsive to the exclusionary rule. Regardless of how effective the rule may be where obtaining convictions is an important objective of the police, it is powerless to deter invasions of constitutionally guaranteed rights where the police either have no interest in prosecuting or are willing to forego successful prosecution in the interest of serving some other goal.

. . . .

Having thus roughly sketched the perimeters of the constitutional debate over the limits on police investigative conduct in general and the background against which this case presents itself, we turn our attention to the quite narrow question posed by the facts before us: whether it is always unreasonable for a policeman to seize a person and subject him to a limited search for weapons unless there is probable cause for an arrest. Given the narrowness of this question, we have no occasion to canvass in detail the constitutional limitations upon the scope of a policeman's power when he confronts a citizen without probable cause to arrest him.

II.

Our first task is to establish at what point in this encounter the Fourth Amendment becomes relevant. That is, we must decide whether and when Officer McFadden "seized" Terry and whether and when he conducted a "search." There is some suggestion in the use of such terms as "stop" and "frisk" that such police conduct is outside the purview of the Fourth Amendment because neither action rises to the level of a "search" or "seizure" within the meaning of the Constitution. We emphatically reject this notion. It is quite plain that the Fourth Amendment governs "seizures" of the person which do not eventuate in a trip to the station house and prosecution for crime—"arrests" in traditional terminology. It must be recognized that whenever a police officer accosts an individual and restrains his freedom to walk away, he has "seized" that person. And it is nothing less than sheer torture of the English language to suggest that a careful exploration of the outer surfaces of a person's clothing all over his or her body in an attempt to find weapons is not a "search." Moreover, it is simply fantastic to urge that such a procedure performed in public by a policeman while the citizen stands helpless, perhaps facing a wall with his hands raised, is a "petty indignity." It is a serious intrusion upon the sanctity of the person, which may inflict great indignity and arouse strong resentment, and it is not to be undertaken lightly.

The danger in the logic which proceeds upon distinctions between a "stop" and an "arrest," or "seizure" of the person, and between a "frisk" and a "search" is two-fold. It seeks to isolate from constitutional scrutiny the initial stages of the contact between the policeman and the citizen. And by suggesting a rigid all-or-nothing model of justification and regulation under the Amendment, it obscures the utility of limitations upon the scope, as well as the initiation, of police action as a means of constitutional regulation. This Court has held in the past that a search which is reasonable at its inception may violate the Fourth Amendment by virtue of its intolerable intensity and scope. [Citations omitted.] The scope of the search must be "strictly tied to and justified by" the circumstances which rendered its initiation permissible. [Citations omitted.]

The distinctions of classical "stop-and-frisk" theory thus serve to divert attention from the central inquiry under the Fourth Amendment—the reasonableness in all the circumstances of the particular governmental invasion of a citizen's personal security. "Search" and "seizure" are not talismans. We therefore reject the notions that the Fourth Amendment does not come into play at all as a limitation upon police conduct if the officers stop short of something called a "technical arrest" or a "full-blown search."

In this case there can be no question, then, that Officer McFadden "seized" petitioner and subjected him to a "search" when he took hold of him and patted down the outer surfaces of his clothing. We must decide whether at that point it was reasonable for Officer McFadden to have interfered with petitioner's personal security as he did. And in determining whether the seizure and search were "unreasonable" our inquiry is a dual one—whether the officer's action was justified at its inception, and whether it was reasonably related in scope to the circumstances which justified the interference in the first place.

III.

If this case involved police conduct subject to the Warrant Clause of the Fourth Amendment, we would have to ascertain whether "probable cause" existed to justify the search and seizure which took place. However, this is not the case. We do not retreat from our holdings that the police must, whenever practicable, obtain advance judicial approval of searches and seizures through the warrant procedure, [citations omitted], or that in most instances failure to comply with the warrant requirement can only be excused by exigent circumstances, [citations omitted]. But we deal here with an entire rubric of police conduct—necessarily swift action predicated upon the on-the-spot observations of the officer on the beat—which historically has not been, and as a practical matter could not be, subjected to the warrant procedure. Instead, the conduct involved in this case must be tested by the Fourth Amendment's general proscription against unreasonable searches and seizures.

Nonetheless, the notions which underlie both the warrant procedure and the requirement of probable cause remain fully relevant in this context. In order to assess the reasonableness of Officer McFadden's conduct as a general proposition, it is necessary "first to focus upon the governmental interest which allegedly justifies official intrusion upon the constitutionally protected interests of the private citizen," for there is "no ready test for determining reasonableness other than by balancing the need to search [or seize] against the invasion which the search [or seizure] entails." *Camara* v. *Municipal Court,* 387 U.S. 523–535, 536–537 (1967). And in justifying the particular intrusion the police officer must be able to point to specific and articulable facts which, taken together with rational inferences from those facts, reasonably warrant that intrusion. The scheme of the Fourth Amendment becomes meaningful only when it is assured that at some point the conduct of those charged with enforcing the laws can be subjected to the more detached, general scrutiny of a judge who must evaluate the reasonableness of a particular search or seizure in light of the particular circumstances. And in making that assessment it is imperative that the facts be judged against an objective standard: would the facts available to the officer at the moment of the seizure or the search "warrant a man of reasonable caution in the belief" that the action taken was appropriate? [Citations omitted.] Anything less would invite intrusion upon constitutionally guaranteed rights based on nothing more substantial than inarticulate hunches, a result this Court has consistently refused to sanction. [Citations omitted.] And simple " 'good faith on the part of the arresting officer is not enough.' . . . If subjective good faith alone were the test, the protections of the Fourth Amendment would evaporate, and the people would be 'secure in their persons, houses, papers and effects,' only in the discretion of the police." *Beck* v. *Ohio, supra* at 97.

Applying these principles to this case, we consider first the nature and extent of the governmental interests involved. One general interest is of course that of effective crime prevention and detection; it is this interest which underlies the recognition that a police officer may in appropriate circumstances and in an appropriate manner approach a person for purposes of investigating possibly criminal behavior even though there is no probable cause to make an arrest. It was this legitimate investigative function Officer McFadden was discharging when he decided to approach petitioner and his companions. He had observed Terry, Chilton, and Katz go through a series of acts, each of them perhaps innocent in itself, but which taken together warranted further investigation. There is nothing unusual in two men standing together on a street corner, perhaps waiting for someone. Nor is there anything suspicious about people in such circumstances strolling up and down the street, singly or in pairs. Store windows, moreover, are made to be looked in. But the story is quite different where, as here, two men hover about a street corner for an extended period of time, at the end of which it becomes apparent that they are not waiting for anyone or anything; where these men pace alternately along an identical route, pausing to stare in the same window roughly 24 times; where each completion of this route is followed immediately by a conference between the two men on the corner; where they are joined in one of these conferences by a third man who leaves swiftly and where the two men finally follow the third and rejoin him a couple of blocks away. It would have been poor police work indeed for an officer of 30 years' experience in the detection of thievery from stores in this same neighborhood to have failed to investigate this behavior further.

The crux of the case, however, is not the propriety of Officer McFadden's taking steps to investigate petitioner's suspicious behavior, but rather, whether there was justification for McFadden's invasion of Terry's personal security by searching him for weapons in the course of that investigation. We are now concerned with more than the governmental interest in investigating crime; in addition, there is the more immediate interest of the police officer in taking steps to assure himself that the person with whom he is dealing is not armed with a weapon that could unexpectedly and fatally be used against him. Certainly it would be unreasonable to require that police officers take unnecessary risks in the performance of their duties. American criminals have a long tradition of armed violence, and every year in this country many law enforcement officers are killed in the line of duty, and thousands more are wounded. Virtually all of these deaths and a substantial portion of the injuries are inflicted with guns and knives.

In view of these facts, we cannot blind ourselves to the need for law enforcement officers to protect themselves and other prospective victims of violence in situations where they may lack probable cause for an arrest. When an officer is justified in believing that the individual whose suspicious behavior he is investigating at close range is armed and presently dangerous to the officer or to others, it could appear to be clearly unreasonable to deny the officer the power to take necessary measures to determine whether the person is in fact carrying a weapon and to neutralize the threat of physical harm.

We must still consider, however, the nature and quality of the intrusion on individual rights which must be accepted if police officers are to be conceded the right to search for weapons in situations where probable cause to arrest for crime is lacking. Even a limited search of the outer clothing for weapons constitutes a severe, though brief, intrusion upon cherished personal security, and it must surely be an annoying, frightening, and perhaps humiliating experience. Petitioner contends that such an intrusion is permissible only incident to a lawful arrest, either for a crime involving the possession of weapons or for a crime the commission of which led the officer to investigate in the first place. However, this argument must be closely examined.

Petitioner does not argue that a police officer should refrain from making any investigation of suspicious circumstances until such time as he has probable cause to make an arrest; nor does he deny that police officers in properly discharging their investigative function may find themselves confronting persons who might well be armed and dangerous. Moreover, he does not say that an officer is always unjustified in searching a suspect to discover weapons. Rather, he says it is unreasonable for the policeman to take that step until such time as the situation evolves to a point where there is probable cause to make an arrest. When that point has been reached, petitioner would concede the officer's right to conduct a search of the suspect for weapons, fruits or instrumentalities of the crime, or "mere" evidence, incident to the arrest.

There are two weaknesses in this line of reasoning, however. First, it fails to take account of traditional limitations upon the scope of searches, and thus recognizes no distinction in purpose, character, and extent between a search incident to an arrest and a limited search for weapons. The former, although justified in part by the acknowledged necessity to protect the arresting officer from assault with a concealed weapon, *Preston* v. *United States*, 376 U.S. 364, 367 (1964), is also justified on other grounds, *ibid.*, and can therefore involve a relatively extensive exploration of the person. A search for weapons in the absence of probable cause to arrest, however, must, like any other search, be strictly circumscribed by the exigencies which justify its initiation. *Warden* v. *Hayden*, 387 U.S. 294, 310 (1967) (MR. JUSTICE FORTAS, concurring). Thus it must be limited to that which is necessary for the discovery of weapons which might be used to harm the officer or others nearby, and may realistically be characterized as something less than a "full" search, even though it remains a serious intrusion.

A second, and related, objection to petitioner's argument is that it assumes that the law of arrest has already worked out the balance between the particular interests involved here—the neutralization of danger to the policeman in the investigative circumstance and the sanctity of the individual. But this is not so. An arrest is a wholly different kind of intrusion upon individual freedom from a limited search for weapons, and the interests each is designed to serve are likewise quite different. An arrest is the initial stage of a criminal prosecution. It is intended to vindicate society's interest in having its laws obeyed, and it is inevitably accompanied by future interference with the individual's freedom of movement, whether or not trial or conviction ultimately follows. The protective search for weapons, on the other hand, constitutes a brief, though far from inconsiderable, intrusion upon the sanctity of the person. It does not follow that because an officer may lawfully arrest a person only when he is apprised of facts sufficient to warrant a belief that the person has committed or is committing a crime, the officer is equally unjustified, absent that kind of evidence, in making any intrusions short of an arrest. Moreover, a perfectly reasonable apprehension of danger may arise long before the officer is possessed of adequate information to justify taking a person into custody for the purpose of prosecuting him for a crime. Petitioner's reliance on cases which have worked out standards of reasonableness with regard to "seizures" constituting arrests and searches incident thereto is thus misplaced. It assumes that the interests sought to be vindicated and the invasions of personal security may be equated in the two cases, and thereby ignores a vital aspect of the analysis of the reasonableness of particular type of conduct under the Fourth Amendment. See *Camara* v. *Municipal Court, supra.*

Our evaluation of the proper balance that has to be struck in this type of case leads us to conclude that there must be a narrowly drawn authority to permit a reasonable search for weapons for the protection of the police officer, where he has reason to believe that he is dealing with an armed and dangerous individual, regardless of whether he has probable cause to arrest the individual for a crime. The officer need not be absolutely certain that the individual is armed; the issue is whether a reasonably prudent man in the circumstances would be warranted in the belief that his safety or that of others was in danger. [Citations omitted.] And in determining whether the officer acted reasonably in such circumstances, due weight must be given, not to his inchoate and unparticularized suspicion or "hunch," but to the specific reasonable inferences which he is entitled to draw from the facts in light of his experience. Cf. *Brinegar* v. *United States, supra.*

IV.

We must now examine the conduct of Officer McFadden in this case to determine whether his search and seizure of petitioner were reasonable, both at their inception and as conducted. He had observed Terry, together with Chilton and another man, acting in a manner he took to be preface to a "stick-up." We think on the facts and circumstances Officer McFadden detailed before the trial judge a reasonably prudent man would have been warranted in believing petitioner was armed and thus presented a threat to the officer's safety while he was investigating his suspicious behavior. The actions of Terry and Chilton were consistent with McFadden's hypothesis that these men were contemplating a daylight robbery—which, it is reasonable to assume, would be likely to involve the use of weapons—and nothing in their conduct from the time he first noticed them until the time he confronted them and identified himself as a police officer gave him sufficient reason to negate that hypothesis. Although the trio had departed the original scene, there was nothing to indicate abandonment of an intent to commit a robbery at some point. Thus, when Officer McFadden approached the three men gathered before the display window at Zucker's store he had observed enough to make it quite reasonable to fear that they were armed; and nothing in their response to hailing them, identifying himself as a police officer, and asking their names served to dispel that reasonable belief. We cannot say his decision at that point to seize Terry and pat his clothing for weapons was the product of a volatile or inventive imagination, or was undertaken simply as an act of harassment; the record evidences the tempered act of a policeman who in the course of an investigation had to make a quick decision as to how to protect himself and others from possible danger, and took limited steps to do so.

The manner in which the seizure and search were conducted is, of course, as vital a part of the inquiry as whether they were warranted at all. The Fourth Amendment proceeds as much by limitations upon the scope of governmental action as by imposing preconditions upon its initiation. Compare *Katz* v. *United States,* 389 U.S. 347, 354–356 (1967). The entire deterrent purpose of the rule excluding evidence seized in violation of the Fourth Amendment rest on the assumption that "limitations upon the fruit to be gathered tend to limit the quest itself." [Citations omitted.] Thus, evidence may not be introduced if it was discovered by means of a seizure and search which were not reasonably related in scope to the justification for their initiation. [Citations omitted.]

We need not develop at length in this case, however, the limitations which the Fourth Amendment places upon a protective seizure and search for weapons. These limitations will have to be developed in the concrete factual circumstances of individual cases. See *Sibron* v. *New York,* 392 U.S. 40, decided today. Suffice it to note that such a search, unlike a search without a warrant incident to a lawful arrest, is not justified by any need to prevent the disappearance or destruction of evidence of crime. See *Preston* v. *United States,* 376 U.S. 364, 367 (1964). The sole justification of the search in the present situation is the protection of the police officer and others nearby, and it must therefore be confined in scope to an intrusion reasonably designed to discover guns, knives, clubs, or other hidden instruments for the assault of the police officer.

The scope of the search in this case presents no serious problem in light of these standards. Officer McFadden patted down the outer clothing of petitioner and his two companions. He did not place his hands in their pockets or under the outer surface of their garments until he had felt weapons, and then he merely reached for and removed the guns. He never did invade Katz's person beyond the outer surfaces of his clothes, since he discovered nothing in his pat-down which might have been a weapon. Officer McFadden confined his search strictly to what was minimally necessary to learn whether the men were armed and to disarm them once he discovered the weapons. He did not conduct a general exploratory search for whatever evidence of criminal activity he might find.

V.

We conclude that the revolver seized from Terry was properly admitted in evidence against him. At the time he seized petitioner and searched him for weapons, Officer McFadden had reasonable grounds to believe that petitioner was armed and dangerous, and it was necessary for the protection of himself and others to take swift measures to discover the true facts and neutralize the threat of harm if it materialized. The policeman carefully restricted his search to what was appropriate to the discovery of the particular items which he sought. Each case of this sort will, of course, have to be decided on its own facts. We merely hold today that where a police officer observed unusual conduct which leads him reasonably to conclude in light of his experience that criminal activity may be afoot and that the persons with whom he is dealing may be armed and presently dangerous, where in the course of investigating this behavior he identifies himself as a policeman and makes reasonable inquiries, and where nothing in the initial stages of the encounter serves to dispel his reasonable fear for his own or others' safety, he is entitled for the protection of himself and others in the area to conduct a carefully limited search of the outer clothing of such persons in an attempt to discover weapons which might be used to assault him. Such a search is a reasonable search under the Fourth Amendment, and any weapons seized may properly be introduced in evidence against the person from whom they were taken.

Affirmed.

[The concurring opinions of MR. JUSTICE BLACK, MR. JUSTICE HARLAN and MR. JUSTICE WHITE, as well as the dissenting opinion of MR. JUSTICE DOUGLAS, have been omitted.]

UNITED STATES v. SOKOLOW

109 S. Ct. 2022 (1989)

Syllabus

Drug Enforcement Administration (DEA) agents stopped respondent upon his arrival at Honolulu International Airport. The agents found 1,063 grams of cocaine in his carry-on luggage. When respondent was stopped, the agents knew, *inter alia*, that (1) he paid $2,100 for two round-trip plane tickets from a roll of $20 bills; (2) he traveled under a name that did not match the name under which his telephone number was listed; (3) his original destination was Miami, a source city for illicit drugs; (4) he stayed in Miami for only 48 hours, even though a round-trip flight from Honolulu to Miami takes 20 hours; (5) he appeared nervous during his trip, and (6) he checked none of his luggage. Respondent was indicted for possession with intent to distribute cocaine. The District Court denied his motion to suppress the evidence, finding that the stop was justified by a reasonable suspicion that he was engaged in criminal activity, as required by the Fourth Amendment. The Court of Appeals disagreed and reversed respondent's conviction, applying a two-part test for determining reasonable suspicion. First, ruled the court, at least one fact describing "ongoing criminal activity"--such as the use of an alias or evasive movement through an airport--was always necessary to support a reasonable suspicion finding. Second, "probabilistic" facts describing "personal characteristics" of drug couriers--such as the cash payment for tickets, a short trip to a major source city for drugs, nervousness, type of attire, and unchecked luggage--were only relevant if there was evidence of "ongoing criminal activity" and the Government offered "[e]mpirical documentation" that the combination of facts at issue did not describe the behavior of "significant numbers of innocent persons." The Court of Appeals held the agents' stop impermissible, because there was no evidence of ongoing criminal behavior in this case.

Held: The DEA agents had a reasonable suspicion that respondent was transporting illegal drugs when they stopped him on the facts of this case. Pp. 1585-87.

(a) Under *Terry v. Ohio,* 392 U.S. 1, 30, 88 S.Ct. 1868, 1884-85, 20 L.Ed.2d 889, the police can stop and briefly detain a person for investigative purposes if they have a reasonable suspicion supported by articulable facts that criminal activity "may be afoot," even if they lack probable cause under the Fourth Amendment. Reasonable suspicion entails some minimal level of objective justification for making a stop-- that is, something more than an inchoate and unparticularized suspicion or "hunch," but less than the level of suspicion required for probable cause. P. 1585.

(b) The Court of Appeals' two-part test creates unnecessary difficulty in dealing with one of the relatively simple concepts embodied in the Fourth Amendment. Under this Court's decisions, the totality of the circumstances must be evaluated to determine the probability, rather than the certainty, of criminal conduct. *United States v. Cortez,* 449 U.S. 411, 417, 101 S.Ct. 690, 694-95, 66 L.Ed.2d 621. The Court of Appeal's test draws an unnecessarily sharp line between types of evidence, the probative value of which varies only in degree. While traveling under an alias or taking an evasive path through an airport may be highly probative, neither type of evidence has the sort of ironclad significance attributed to it by the Court of Appeals, because there are instances in which neither factor would reflect ongoing criminal activity. On the other hand, the test's "probablistic" factors also have probative significance. Paying $2,100 in cash for airline tickets from a roll of $20 bills containing nearly twice that amount is not ordinary conduct for most business travelers or vacationers. The evidence that respondent was traveling under an alias, although not conclusive, was sufficient to warrant consideration. Of similar effect is the probability that few Honolulu residents travel for 20 hours to spend 48 hours in Miami during July. Thus, although each of these factors is not by itself proof of illegal conduct and is quite consistent with innocent travel, taken together, they amount to reasonable suspicion that criminal conduct was afoot. Pp. 1585-86.

(c) The fact that the agents believed that respondent's behavior was consistent with one of the DEA's "drug courier profiles" does not alter this analysis, because the factors in question have evidentiary significance regardless of whether they are set forth in a "profile." P. 1587.

(d) The reasonableness of the decision to stop does not, as respondent contends, turn upon whether the police used the least intrusive means available to verify or dispel their suspicions. Such a rule would unduly hamper the officers' ability to make on-the-spot decisions--here, respondent was about to enter a taxicab--and would require courts to indulge in unrealistic second-guessing. *Florida v. Royer,* 460 U.S. 491, 495, 103 S.Ct. 1319, 1322-23, 75 L.Ed.2d 229, distinguished. P. 1587.

831 F.2d 1413 (CA9 1987), reversed and remanded.

***

Cases relating to **Chapter 4**

SEARCH AND SEIZURE

MAPP v. OHIO

367 U.S. 643, 81 S. Ct. 1684, 6 L. Ed. 2d 1081 (1961)

MR. JUSTICE CLARK delivered the opinion of the Court.

Appellant stands convicted of knowingly having had in her possession and under her control certain lewd and lascivious books, pictures, and photographs in violation of § 2905.34 of Ohio's Revised Code. As officially stated in the syllabus to its opinion, the Supreme Court of Ohio found that her conviction was valid though "based primarily upon the introduction in evidence of lewd and lascivious books and pictures unlawfully seized during an unlawful search of defendant's home. . . ." 170 Ohio St. 427–428, 166 N.E.2d 387, 388.

On May 23, 1957, three Cleveland police officers arrived at appellant's residence in that city pursuant to information that "a person [was] hiding out in the home, who was wanted for questioning in connection with a recent bombing, and that there was a large amount of policy paraphernalia being hidden in the home." Miss Mapp and her daughter by a former marriage lived on the top floor of the two-family dwelling. Upon their arrival at that house, the officers knocked on the door and demanded entrance but appellant, after telephoning her attorney, refused to admit them without a search warrant. They advised their headquarters of the situation and undertook a surveillance of the house.

The officers again sought entrance some three hours later when four or more additional officers arrived on the scene. When Miss Mapp did not come to the door immediately, at least one of the several doors to the house was forcibly opened and the policemen gained admittance. Meanwhile Miss Mapp's attorney arrived, but the officers, having secured their own entry, and continuing in their defiance of the law, would permit him neither to see Miss Mapp nor to enter the house. It appears that Miss Mapp was halfway down the stairs from the upper floor to the front door when the officers, in this highhanded manner, broke into the hall. She demanded to see the search warrant. A paper, claimed to be a warrant, was held up by one of the officers. She grabbed the "warrant" and placed it in her bosom. A struggle ensued in which the officers recovered the piece of paper and as a result of which they handcuffed appellant because she had been "belligerent" in resisting their official rescue of the "warrant" from her person. Running roughshod over appellant, a policeman "grabbed" her, "twisted [her] hand," and she "yelled [and] pleaded with him" because "it was hurting." Appellant, in handcuffs, was then forcibly taken upstairs to her bedroom where the officers searched a dresser, a chest of drawers, a closet and some suitcases. They also looked into a photo album and through personal papers belonging to the appellant. The search spread to the rest of the second floor including the child's bedroom, the living room, the kitchen and a dinette. The basement of the building and a trunk found therein were also searched. The obscene materials for possession of which she was ultimately convicted were discovered in the course of that widespread search.

At the trial no search warrant was produced by the prosecution, nor was the failure to produce one explained or accounted for. At best, "There is, in the record, considerable doubt as to whether there ever was any warrant for the search of defendant's home." 170 Ohio St., at 430. The Ohio Supreme Court believed a "reasonable argument" could be made that the conviction should be reversed "because the 'methods' employed to obtain the [evidence] . . . were such as to 'offend "a sense of justice,"' " but the court found determinative the fact that the evidence had not been taken "from defendant's person by the use of brutal or offensive physical force against defendant." 170 Ohio St., at 431.

The State says that even if the search were made without authority, or otherwise unreasonably, it is not prevented from using the unconstitutionally seized evidence at trial, citing *Wolf* v. *Colorado*, 338 U.S. 25 (1949), in which this Court did indeed hold "that in a prosecution in a State court for a State crime the Fourteenth Amendment does not forbid the admission of evidence obtained by an unreasonable search and seizure." At p. 33. On this appeal, of which we have noted probable jurisdiction, 364 U.S. 868, it is urged once again that we review that holding.

I.

Seventy-five years ago, in *Boyd* v. *United States*, 116 U.S. 616, 630 (1886), considering the Fourth and Fifth Amendments as running "almost into each other" on the facts before it, this Court held that the doctrines of those Amendments

> apply to all invasions on the part of the government and its employés of the sanctity of a man's home and the privacies of life. It is not the breaking of his doors, and the rummaging of his drawers, that constitutes the essence of the offence; but it is the invasion of his indefeasible right of personal security, personal liberty and private property . . . . Breaking into a house and opening boxes and drawers are circumstances of aggravation; but any forcible and compulsory extortion of a man's own testimony or of his private papers to be used as evidence to convict him of crime or to forfeit his goods, is within the condemnation . . . [of those Amendments].

The Court noted that

> constitutional provisions for the security of person and property should be liberally construed. . . . It is the duty of courts to be watchful for the constitutional rights of the citizen, and against any stealthy encroachments thereon. At p. 635.

In this jealous regard for maintaining the integrity of individual rights, the Court gave life to Madison's prediction that "independent tribunals of justice . . . will be naturally led to resist every encroachment upon rights expressly stipulated for in the Constitution by the declaration of rights." I Annals of Cong. 439 (1789). Concluding, the Court specifically referred to the use of the evidence there seized as "unconstitutional." At p. 638.

Less than 30 years after *Boyd*, this Court, in *Weeks* v. *United States*, 232 U.S. 383 (1914), stated that

> the Fourth Amendment . . . put the courts of the United States and Federal officials, in the exercise of their power and authority, under limitations and restraints [and] . . . forever secure[d] the people, their persons, houses, papers and effects against all unreasonable searches and seizures under the guise of law . . . and the duty of giving to it force and effect is obligatory upon all entrusted under our Federal system with the enforcement of the laws. At pp. 391, 392.

Specifically dealing with the use of the evidence unconstitutionally seized, the Court concluded:

> If letters and private documents can thus be seized and held and used in evidence against a citizen accused of an offense, the protection of the Fourth Amendment declaring his right to be secure against such searches and seizures is of no value, and, so far as those thus placed are concerned, might as well be stricken from the Constitution. The efforts of the courts and their officials to bring the guilty to punishment, praiseworthy as they are, are not to be aided by the sacrifice of those great principles established by years of endeavor and suffering which have resulted in their embodiment in the fundamental law of the land. At p. 393.

Finally, the Court in that case clearly stated that use of the seized evidence involved "a denial of the constitutional rights of the accused." At p. 398. Thus, in the year 1914, in the *Weeks* case, this Court "for the first time" held that "in a federal prosecution the Fourth Amendment barred the use of evidence secured through an illegal search and seizure." *Wolf* v. *Colorado, supra*, at 28. This Court has ever since required of federal law officers a strict adherence to that command which this Court has held to be a clear, specific, and constitutionally required —even if judicially implied—deterrent safeguard without insistence upon which the Fourth Amendment would have been reduced to "a form of words." HOLMES J., *Silverthorne Lumber Co.* v. *United States*, 251 U.S. 385, 392 (1920). It meant, quite simply, that "conviction by means of unlawful seizures and enforced confessions . . . should find no sanction in the judgments of the courts . . . ," *Weeks* v. *United States, supra,* at 392, and that such evidence "shall not be used at all." *Silverthorne Lumber Co.* v. *United States, supra,* at 392.

There are in the cases of this Court some passing references to the *Weeks* rule as being one of evidence. But the plain and unequivocal language of *Weeks*—and its later paraphrase in *Wolf*—to the effect that the *Weeks* rule is of constitutional origin, remains entirely undisturbed. In *Byars* v. *United States,* 273 U.S. 28 (1927), a unanimous Court declared that "the doctrine [cannot] . . . be tolerated *under our constitutional system,* that evidences of crime discovered by a federal officer in making a search without lawful warrant may be used against the victim of the unlawful search where a timely challenge has been interposed." At pp. 29, 30 (emphasis added). The Court, in *Olmstead* v. *United States,* 277 U.S. 438 (1928), in unmistakable language restated the *Weeks* rule:

> The striking outcome of the *Weeks* case and those which followed it was the sweeping declaration that the Fourth Amendment, although not referring to or limiting the use of evidence in courts, really forbade its introduction if obtained by government officers through a violation of the Amendment. At p. 462.

In *McNabb* v. *United States,* 318 U.S. 332 (1943), we note this statement:

> [A] conviction in the federal courts, the foundation of which is evidence obtained in disregard of liberties deemed fundamental by the Constitution, cannot stand. *Boyd* v. *United States* . . . *Weeks* v. *United States*. . . . And this Court has, on Constitutional grounds, set aside convictions, both in the federal and state courts, which were based upon confessions "secured by protracted and repeated questioning of ignorant and untutored persons, in whose minds the power of officers was greatly magnified" . . . or "who have been unlawfully held incommunicado without advice of friends or counsel". . . . At pp. 339, 340.

Significantly, in *McNabb,* the Court did then pass on to formulate a rule of evidence, saying, "[i]n the view we take of the case, however, it becomes unnecessary to reach the Constitutional issue [for] . . . [t]he principles governing the admissibility of evidence in federal criminal trials have not been restricted . . . to those derived solely from the Constitution." At pp. 340, 341.

II.

In 1949, 35 years after *Weeks* was announced, this Court, in *Wolf*

v. *Colorado, supra,* again for the first time, discussed the effect of the Fourth Amendment upon the States through the operation of the Due Process Clause of the Fourteenth Amendment. It said:

> [W]e have no hesitation in saying that were a State affirmatively to sanction such police incursion into privacy it would run counter to the guaranty of the Fourteenth Amendment. At p. 28.

Nevertheless, after declaring that the "security of one's privacy against arbitrary intrusion by the police" is "implicit in 'the concept of ordered liberty' and as such enforceable against the States through the Due Process Clause," cf. *Palko v. Connecticut,* 302 U.S. 319 (1937), and announcing that it "stoutly adhere[d]" to the *Weeks* decision, the Court decided that the *Weeks* exclusionary rule would not then be imposed upon the States as "an essential ingredient of the right." 338 U.S., at 27–29. The Court's reasons for not considering essential to the right to privacy, as a curb imposed upon the States by the Due Process Clause, that which decades before had been posited as part and parcel of the Fourth Amendment's limitation upon federal encroachment of individual privacy, were bottomed on factual considerations.

While they are not basically relevant to a decision that the exclusionary rule is an essential ingredient of the Fourth Amendment as the right it embodies is vouchsafed against the States by the Due Process Clause, we will consider the current validity of the factual grounds upon which *Wolf* was based.

The Court in *Wolf* first stated that "[t]he contrariety of views of the States" on the adoption of the exclusionary rule of *Weeks* was "particularly impressive" (at p. 29); and, in this connection, that it could not "brush aside the experience of States which deem the incidence of such conduct by the police too slight to call for a deterrent remedy . . . by overriding the [States'] relevant rules of evidence." At pp. 31, 32. While in 1949, prior to the *Wolf* case, almost two-thirds of the States were opposed to the use of the exclusionary rule, now, despite the *Wolf* case, more than half of those since passing upon it, by their own legislative or judicial decision, have wholly or partly adopted or adhered to the *Weeks* rule. See *Elkins v. United States,* 364 U.S. 206, Appendix, pp. 224–232 (1960). Significantly, among those now following the rule is California, which, according to its highest court, was "compelled to reach that conclusion because other remedies have completely failed to secure compliance with the constitutional provisions . . . ." [Citation omitted.] In connection with this California case, we note that the second basis elaborated in *Wolf* in support of its failure to enforce the exclusionary doctrine against the States was that "other means of protection" have been afforded "the right to privacy." 338 U.S. at 30. The experience of California that such other remedies have been worthless and futile is buttressed by the experience of other States. The obvious futility of relegating the Fourth Amendment to the protection of other remedies has, moreover, been recognized by this Court since *Wolf*. See *Irvine* v. *California*, 347 U.S. 128, 137 (1954).

Likewise, time has set its face against what *Wolf* called the "weighty testimony" of *People* v. *Defore*, 242 N.Y. 13, 150 N.E. 585 (1926). There Justice (then Judge) Cardozo, rejecting adoption of the *Weeks* exclusionary rule in New York, had said that "[t]he Federal rule as it stands is either too strict or too lax." 242 N.Y., at 22. However, the force of that reasoning has been largely vitiated by later decisions of this Court. These include the recent discarding of the "silver platter" doctrine which allowed federal judicial use of evidence seized in violation of the Constitution by state agents, *Elkins* v. *United States*, *supra*; the relaxation of the formerly strict requirements as to standing to challenge the use of evidence thus seized, so that now the procedure of exclusion, "ultimately referable to constitutional safeguards," is available to anyone even "legitimately on [the] premises" unlawfully searched, *Jones* v. *United States*, 362 U.S. 257, 266, 267 (1960); and, finally, the formulation of a method to prevent state use of evidence unconstitutionally seized by federal agents, *Rea* v. *United States*, 350 U.S. 214 (1956). Because there can be no fixed formula, we are admittedly met with "recurring questions of the reasonableness of searches," but less is not to be expected when dealing with a Constitution, and, at any rate, "[r]easonableness is in the first instance for the [trial court] . . . to determine." *United States* v. *Rabinowitz*, 339 U.S. 56, 63 (1950).

It, therefore, plainly appears that the factual considerations supporting the failure of the *Wolf* Court to include the *Weeks* exclusionary rule when it recognized the enforceability of the right to privacy against the States in 1949, while not basically relevant to the constitutional consideration, could not, in any analysis, now be deemed controlling.

. . . .

V.

. . . .

The ignoble shortcut to conviction left open to the State tends to destroy the entire system of constitutional restraints on which the liberties of the people rest. Having once recognized that the right to privacy embodied in the Fourth Amendment is enforceable against the States, and that the right to be secure against rude invasions of privacy by state officers is, therefore, constitutional in origin, we can no longer permit that right to remain an empty promise. Because it is enforceable in the same manner and to like effect as other basic rights secured by the Due Process Clause, we can no longer permit it to be revocable at the whim of any police officer who, in the name of law enforcement itself, chooses to suspend its enjoyment. Our decision, founded on reason and truth, gives to the individual no more than that which the Constitution guarantees him, to the police officer no less than that to which honest law enforcement is entitled, and, to the courts, that judicial integrity so necessary in the true administration of justice.

The judgment of the Supreme Court of Ohio is reversed and the cause remanded for further proceedings not inconsistent with this opinion.

Reversed and remanded.

[The concurring opinions of MR. JUSTICE BLACK and MR. JUSTICE DOUGLAS have been omitted.]

MR. JUSTICE HARLAN, whom MR. JUSTICE FRANKFURTER and MR. JUSTICE WHITTAKER join, dissenting.

In overruling the *Wolf* case the Court, in my opinion, has forgotten the sense of judicial restraint which, with due regard for *stare decisis,* is one element that should enter into deciding whether a past decision of this Court should be overruled. Apart from that I also believe that the *Wolf* rule represents sounder Constitutional doctrine than the new rule which now replaces it.

I.

From the Court's statement of the case one would gather that the central, if not controlling, issue on this appeal is whether illegally state-seized evidence is Constitutionally admissible in a state prosecution, an issue which would of course face us with the need for re-examining *Wolf*. However, such is not the situation. For, although that question was indeed raised here and below among appellant's subordinate points, the new and pivotal issue brought to the Court by this appeal is whether § 2905.34 of the Ohio Revised Code making criminal the *mere* knowing possession or control of obsence material, and under which appellant has been convicted, is consistent with the rights of free thought and expression assured against state action by the Fourteenth Amendment. That was the principal issue which was decided by the Ohio Supreme Court, which was tendered by appellant's Jurisdictional Statement, and which was briefed and argued in this Court.

In this posture of things, I think it fair to say that five members of this Court have simply "reached out" to overrule *Wolf*. With all respect for the views of the majority, and recognizing that *stare decisis* carries different weight in Constitutional adjudication than it does in nonconstitutional decision, I can perceive no justification for regarding this case as an appropriate occasion for re-examining *Wolf*.

The action of the Court finds no support in the rule that decision of Constitutional issues should be avoided wherever possible. For in overruling *Wolf* the Court, instead of passing upon the validity of Ohio's § 2905.34, has simply chosen between two Constitutional questions. Moreover, I submit that it has chosen the more difficult and less appropriate of the two questions. The Ohio statute which, as construed by the State Supreme Court, punishes knowing possession or control of obscene material, irrespective of the purposes of such possession or control (with exceptions not here applicable) and irrespective of whether the accused had any reasonable opportunity to rid himself of the material after discovering that it was obscene, surely presents a Constitutional question which is both simpler and less far-reaching than the question which the Court decides today. It seems to me that justice might well have been done in this case without overturning a decision on which the administration of criminal law in many of the States has long justifiably relied.

Since the demands of the case before us do not require us to reach the question of the validity of *Wolf*, I think this case furnishes a singularly inappropriate occasion for reconsideration of that decision, if reconsideration is indeed warranted. Even the most cursory examination will reveal that the doctrine of the *Wolf* case has been of continuing importance in the administration of state criminal law. Indeed, certainly as regards its "nonexclusionary" aspect, *Wolf* did no more than articulate the then existing assumption among the States that the federal cases enforcing the exclusionary rule "do not bind [the States], for they construe provisions of the Federal Constitution, the Fourth and Fifth Amendments, not applicable to the States." [Citation omitted.] Though, of course, not reflecting the full measure of this continuing reliance, I find that during the last three Terms, for instance, the issue of the inadmissibility of illegally state-obtained evidence appears on an average of about fifteen times per Term just in the *in forma pauperis* cases summarily disposed of by us. This would indicate both that the issue which is now being decided may well have untoward practical ramifications respecting state cases long since disposed of in reliance on *Wolf*, and that were we determined to re-examine that doctrine we would not lack future opportunity.

The occasion which the Court has taken here is in the context of a case where the question was briefed not at all and argued only extremely tangentially. The unwisdom of overruling *Wolf* without full-dress argument is aggravated by the circumstance that that decision is a comparatively recent one (1949) to which three members of the present majority have at one time or other expressly subscribed, one to be sure with explicit misgivings. I would think that our obligation to the States, on whom we impose this new rule, as well as the obligation of orderly adherence to our own processes would demand that we seek that aid which adequate briefing and argument lends to the determination of an important issue. It certainly has never been a postulate of judicial power that mere altered disposition, or subsequent membership on the Court, is sufficient warrant for overturning a deliberately decided rule of Constitutional law.

Thus, if the Court were bent on reconsidering *Wolf*, I think that there would soon have presented itself an appropriate opportunity in which we could have had the benefit of full briefing and argument. In any event, at the very least, the present case should have been set down for reargument, in view of the inadequate briefing and argument we have received on the *Wolf* point. To all intents and purposes the Court's present action amounts to a summary reversal of *Wolf*, without argument.

I am bound to say that what has been done is not likely to promote respect either for the Court's adjudicatory process or for the stability of its decisions. Having been unable, however, to persuade any of the majority to a different procedural course, I now turn to the merits of the present decision.

[Part II of the dissenting opinion is omitted.]

ILLINOIS v. GATES

462 U.S. 213, 103 S. Ct. 2317, 76 L. Ed. 2d 527 (1983)
[Syllabus only]

On May 3, 1978, the Police Department of Bloomingdale, Ill., received an anonymous letter which included statements that respondents, husband and wife, were engaged in selling drugs; that the wife would drive their car to Florida on May 3 to be loaded with drugs, and the husband would fly down in a few days to drive the car back; that the car's trunk would be loaded with drugs; and that respondents presently had over $100,000 worth of drugs in their basement. Acting on the tip, a police officer determined respondents' address and learned that the husband made a reservation on a May 5 flight to Florida. Arrangements for surveillance for the flight were made with an agent of the Drug Enforcement Administration (DEA), and the surveillance disclosed that the husband took the flight, stayed overnight in a motel room registered in the wife's name, and left the following morning with a woman in a car bearing an Illinois license plate issued to the husband, heading north on an interstate highway used by travelers to the Bloomingdale area. A search warrant for respondents' residence and automobile was then obtained from an Illinois state-court judge, based on the Bloomingdale police officer's affidavit setting forth the foregoing facts and a copy of the anonymous letter. When respondents arrived at their home, the police were waiting and discovered marihuana and other contraband in respondents' car trunk and home. Prior to respondents' trial on charges of violating state drug laws, the trial court ordered suppression of all the items seized, and the Illinois Appellate Court affirmed. The Illinois Supreme Court also affirmed, holding that the letter and affidavit were inadequate to sustain a determination of probable cause for issuance of the search warrant under *Aguilar v. Texas*, 378 U.S. 108, 84 S.Ct. 1509, 12 L.Ed.2d 723, and *Spinelli v.*

United States, 393 U.S. 410, 89 S.Ct. 584, 21 L.Ed.2d 637, since they failed to satisfy the "two pronged test" of (1) revealing the informant's "basis of knowledge" and (2) providing sufficient facts to establish either the informant's "veracity" or the "reliability" of the informant's report.

Held:

1. The question–which this Court requested the parties to address–whether the rule requiring the exclusion at a criminal trial of evidence obtained in violation of the Fourth Amendment should be modified so as, for example, not to require exclusion of evidence obtained in the reasonable belief that the search and seizure at issue was consistent with the Fourth Amendment will not be decided in this case, since it was not presented to or decided by the Illinois courts. Although prior decisions interpreting the "not pressed or passed on below" rule have not involved a State's failure to raise a defense to a federal right or remedy asserted below, the purposes underlying the rule are, for the most part, as applicable in such a case as in one where a party fails to assert a federal right. The fact that the Illinois courts affirmatively applied the federal exclusionary rule does not affect the application of the "not pressed or passed on below" rule. Nor does the State's repeated opposition to respondents' substantive Fourth Amendment claims suffice to have raised the separate question whether the exclusionary rule should be modified. The extent of the continued vitality of the rule is an issue of unusual significance, and adhering scrupulously to the customary limitations on this Court's discretion promotes respect for its adjudicatory process and the stability of its decisions, and lessens the threat of untoward practical ramifications not forseen at the time of decision.

2. The rigid "two-pronged test" under *Aguilar* and *Spinelli* for determining whether an informant's tip establishes probable cause for issuance of a warrant is abandoned, and the "totality of the circumstances" approach that traditionally has informed probable-cause determinations is substituted in its place. The elements under the "two-pronged test" concerning the informant's "veracity," "reliability," and "basis of knowledge" should be understood simply as closely intertwined issues that may usefully illuminate the common-sense, practical question whether there is "probable cause" to believe that contraband or evidence is located in a particular place. The task of the issuing magistrate is simply to make a practical, common-sense decision whether, given all the circumstances set forth in the affidavit before him, there is a fair probability that contraband or evidence of a crime will be found in a particular place. And the duty of a reviewing court is simply to ensure that the magistrate had a substantial basis for concluding that probable cause existed. This flexible, easily applied standard will better achieve the accomodation of public and private interests that the Fourth Amendment requires than does the approach that has developed from *Aguilar* and *Spinelli.*

3. The judge issuing the warrant had a substantial basis for concluding that probable cause to search respondents' home and car existed.

Under the "totality of the circumstances" analysis, corroboration by details of an informant's tip by independent police work is of significant value. Here, even standing alone, the facts obtained through the independent investigation of the Bloomingdale police officer and the DEA at least suggested that respondents were involved in drug trafficking. In addition, the judge could rely on the anonymous letter, which had been corroborated in major part by the police officer's efforts.

85 Ill.2d 376, 53 Ill.Dec. 218, 423 N.E.2d 887 (1981), reversed.

CHIMEL v. CALIFORNIA

395 U.S. 752, 89 S. Ct. 2034, 23 L. Ed. 2d 685 (1969)

MR. JUSTICE STEWART delivered the opinion of the Court.

This case raises basic questions concerning the permissible scope under the Fourth Amendment of a search incident to a lawful arrest.

The relevant facts are essentially undisputed. Late in the afternoon of September 13, 1965, three police officers arrived at the Santa Ana, California, home of the petitioner with a warrant authorizing his arrest for the burglary of a coin shop. The officers knocked on the door, identified themselves to the petitioner's wife, and asked if they might come inside. She ushered them into the house, where they waited 10 or 15 minutes until the petitioner returned home from work. When the petitioner entered the house, one of the officers handed him the arrest warrant and asked for permission to "look around." The petitioner objected, but was advised that "on the basis of the lawful arrest," the officers would nonetheless conduct a search. No search warrant had been issued.

Accompanied by the petitioner's wife, the officers then looked through the entire three-bedroom house, including the attic, the garage, and a small workshop. In some rooms the search was relatively cursory. In the master bedroom and sewing room, however, the officers directed the petitioner's wife to open drawers and "to physically move contents of the drawers from side to side so that [they] might view any items that would have come from [the] burglary." After completing the search, they seized numerous items—primarily coins, but also several medals, tokens, and a few other objects. The entire search took between 45 minutes and an hour.

At the petitioner's subsequent state trial on two charges of burglary, the items taken from his house were admitted into evidence against him, over his objection that they had been unconstitutionally seized. He was convicted, and the judgments of conviction were affirmed by both the California District Court of Appeal, 61 Cal.Rptr. 714, and the California Supreme Court, 68 Cal.2d 436, 439 P.2d 333, 67 Cal.Rptr. 421. Both courts accepted the petitioner's contention that the arrest warrant was invalid because the supporting affidavit was set out in conclusory terms, but held that since the arresting officers had procured the warrant "in good faith," and since in any event they had had sufficient information to constitute probable cause for the petitioner's arrest, the arrest had been lawful. From this conclusion the appellate courts went on to hold that the search of the petitioner's home had been justified, despite the absence of a search warrant, on the ground that it had been incident to a valid arrest. We granted certiorari in order to consider the petitioner's substantial constitutional claims.

Without deciding the question, we proceed on the hypothesis that the California courts were correct in holding that the arrest of the petitioner was valid under the Constitution. This brings us directly to the question whether the warrantless search on the petitioner's entire house can be constitutionally justified as incident to that arrest. The decisions of this Court bearing upon that question have been far from consistent, as even the most cursory review makes evident.

Approval of a warrantless search incident to a lawful arrest seems first to have been articulated by the Court in 1914 as dictum in *Weeks* v. *United States*, 232 U.S. 383, in which the Court stated:

> What then is the present case? Before answering that inquiry specifically, it may be well by a process of exclusion to state what it was not. It is not an assertion of the right on the part of the Government, always recognized under English and American law, to search the person of the accused when legally arrested to discover and seize the fruits or evidences of crime. *Id.*, at 392.

That statement made no reference to any right to search the *place* where an arrest occurs, but was limited to a right to search the "person." Eleven years later the case of *Carroll* v. *United States*, 267 U.S. 132, brought the following embellishment of the *Weeks* statement:

> When a man is legally arrested for an offense, whatever is found upon his person *or in his control* which it is unlawful for him to have and which may be used to prove the offense may be seized and held as evidence in the prosecution. *Id.*, at 158 (Emphasis added.)

Still, that assertion too was far from a claim that the "place" where one is arrested may be searched so long as the arrest is valid. Without explanation, however, the principle emerged in expanded form a few months later in *Agnello* v. *United States,* 269 U.S. 20—although still by way of dictum:

> The right without a search warrant contemporaneously to search persons lawfully arrested while committing crime and to search the place where the arrest is made in order to find and seize things connected with the crime as its fruits or as the means by which it was committed, as well as weapons and other things to effect an escape from custody, is not to be doubted. [Citations omitted.]

In 1950, two years after *Trupiano,* came *United States* v. *Rabinowitz,* 339 U.S. 56, the decision upon which California primarily relies in the case now before us. In *Rabinowitz,* federal authorities had been informed that the defendant was dealing in stamps bearing forged overprints. On the basis of that information they secured a warrant for his arrest, which they executed at his one-room business office. At the time of the arrest, the officers "searched the desk, safe, and file cabinets in the office for about an hour and a half," *id.,* at 59, and seized 573 stamps with forged overprints. The stamps were admitted into evidence at the defendant's trial, and this Court affirmed his conviction, rejecting the contention that the warrantless search had been unlawful. The Court held that the search in its entirety fell within the principle giving law enforcement authorities "[t]he right 'to search the place where the arrest is made in order to find and seize things connected with the crime. . . .' " *Id.,* at 61. *Harris* was regarded as "ample authority" for that conclusion. *Id.,* at 63. The opinion rejected the rule of *Trupiano* that "in seizing goods and articles, law enforcement agents must secure and use search warrants wherever reasonably practicable." The test, said the Court, "is not whether it is reasonable to procure a search warrant, but whether the search was reasonable." *Id.,* at 66.

Rabinowitz has come to stand for the proposition, *inter alia,* that a warrantless search "incident to a lawful arrest" may generally extend to the area that is considered to be in the "possession" or under the "control" of the person arrested. And it was on the basis of that proposition that the California courts upheld the search of the petitioner's entire house in this case. That doctrine, however, at least in the broad sense in which it was applied by the California courts in this case, can withstand neither historical nor rational analysis.

Even limited to its own facts, the *Rabinowitz* decision was, as we have seen, hardly founded on an unimpeachable line of authority. As MR. JUSTICE FRANKFURTER commented in dissent in that case, the "hint" contained in *Weeks* was, without persuasive justification, "loosely turned into dictum and finally elevated to a decision." 339 U.S., at 75. And the approach taken in cases such as *Go-Bart, Lefkowitz,* and *Trupiano* was essentially disregarded by the *Rabinowitz* Court.

Nor is the rationale by which the State seeks here to sustain the search of the petitioner's house supported by a reasoned view of the background and purpose of the Fourth Amendment. MR. JUSTICE FRANKFURTER wisely pointed out in his *Rabinowitz* dissent that the Amendment's proscription of "unreasonable searches and seizures" must be read in light of "the history that gave rise to the words"—a history of "abuses so deeply felt by the Colonies as to be one of the potent causes of the Revolution. . . ." 339 U.S., at 69. The Amendment was in large part a reaction to the general warrants and warrantless searches that had so alienated the colonists and had helped speed the movement for independence. In the scheme of the Amendment, therefore, the requirement that "no Warrants shall issue, but upon probable cause," plays a crucial part. As the Court put it in *McDonald* v. *United States,* 335 U.S. 451:

> We are not dealing with formalities. The presence of a search warrant serves a high function. Absent some grave emergency, the Fourth Amendment has interposed a magistrate between the citizen and the police. This was done not to shield criminals nor to make the home a safe haven for illegal activities. It was done so that an objective mind might weigh the need to invade that privacy in order to enforce the law. The right of privacy was deemed too precious to entrust to the discretion of those whose job is the detection of crime and the arrest of criminals. . . . And so the Constitution requires a magistrate to pass on the desires of the police before they violate the privacy of the home. We cannot be true to that constitutional requirement and excuse the absence of a search warrant without a showing by those who seek exemption from the constitutional mandate that the exigencies of the situation made that course imperative.

Even in the *Agnello* case the Court relied upon the rule that "[b]elief, however well founded, that an article sought is concealed in a dwelling house furnishes no justification for a search of that place without a warrant. And such searches are held unlawful notwithstanding facts unquestionably showing probable cause." 269 U.S., at 33. Clearly, the general requirement that a search warrant be obtained is not lightly to be dispensed with, and "the burden is on those seeking [an] exemption [from the requirement] to show the need for it. . . ." *United States* v. *Jeffers,* 342 U.S. 48, 51.

Only last Term in *Terry* v. *Ohio,* 392 U.S. 1, we emphasized that "the police must, whenever practicable, obtain advance judicial approval of searches and seizures through the warrant procedure," *id.*, at 20, and that "[t]he scope of [a] search must be 'strictly tied to and justified by' the circumstances which rendered its initiation permissible." *Id.*, at 19. The search undertaken by the officer in that "stop and frisk" case was sustained under that test, because it was no more than a "protective . . . search for weapons." *Id.*, at 29. But in a companion case, *Sibron* v. *New York*, 392 U.S. 40, we applied the same standard to another set of facts and reached a contrary result, holding that a policeman's action in thrusting his hand into a suspect's pocket had been neither motivated by nor limited to the objective of protection. Rather, the search had been made in order to find narcotics, which were in fact found.

A similar analysis underlies the "search incident to arrest" principle, and marks its proper extent. When an arrest is made, it is reasonable for the arresting officer to search the person arrested in order to remove any weapons that the latter might seek to use in order to resist arrest or effect his escape. Otherwise, the officer's safety might well be endangered, and the arrest itself frustrated. In addition, it is entirely reasonable for the arresting officer to search for and seize any evidence on the arrestee's person in order to prevent its concealment or destruction. And the area into which an arrestee might reach in order to grab a weapon or evidentiary items must, of course, be governed by a like rule. A gun on a table or in a drawer in front of one who is arrested can be as dangerous to the arresting officer as one concealed in the clothing of the person arrested. There is ample justification, therefore, for a search of the arrestee's person and the area "within his immediate control"—construing that phrase to mean the area from within which he might gain possession of a weapon or destructible evidence.

There is no comparable justification, however, for routinely searching any room other than that in which an arrest occurs—or, for that matter, for searching through all the desk drawers or other closed or concealed areas in that room itself. Such searches, in the absence of well-recognized exceptions, may be made only under the authority of a search warrant. The "adherence to judicial processes" mandated by the Fourth Amendment requires no less.

. . . .

Rabinowitz and *Harris* have been the subject of critical commentary for many years, and have been relied upon less and less in our own decisions. It is time, for the reasons we have stated, to hold that on their own facts, and insofar as the principles they stand for are inconsistent with those that we have endorsed today, they are no longer to be followed.

Application of sound Fourth Amendment principles to the facts of this case produces a clear result. The search here went far beyond the petitioner's person and the area from within which he might have obtained either a weapon or something that could have been used as evidence against him. There was no constitutional justification, in the absence of a search warrant, for extending the search beyond that area. The scope of the search was, therefore, "unreasonable" under the Fourth and Fourteenth Amendments, and the petitioner's conviction cannot stand.

Reversed.

MR. JUSTICE HARLAN, concurring.

I join the Court's opinion with these remarks concerning a factor to which the Court has not alluded. The only thing that has given me pause in voting to overrule *Harris* and *Rabinowitz* is that as a result of *Mapp* v. *Ohio,* 367 U.S. 643 (1961), and *Ker* v. *California,* 374 U.S. 23 (1963), every change in Fourth Amendment law must now be obeyed by state officials facing widely different problems of local law enforcement. We simply do not know the extent to which cities and towns across the Nation are prepared to administer the greatly expanded warrant system which will be required by today's decision; nor can we say with assurance that in each and every local situation, the warrant requirement plays an essential role in the protection of those fundamental liberties protected against state infringement by the Fourth Amendment.

Thus, one is now faced with the dilemma, envisioned in my separate opinion in *Ker,* 374 U.S. 23, at 45–46, of choosing between vindicating sound Fourth Amendment principles at the possible expense of state concerns, long recognized to be consonant with the Fourteenth Amendment before *Mapp* and *Ker* came on the books, or diluting the Federal Bill of Rights in the interest of leaving the States at least some elbow room in their methods of criminal law enforcement. No comparable dilemma exists, of course, with respect to the impact of today's decision within the federal system itself.

This federal-state factor has not been an easy one for me to resolve, but in the last analysis I cannot in good conscience vote to perpetuate bad Fourth Amendment law.

I add only that this case, together with *Benton* v. *Maryland,* *Pearce* v. *North Carolina,* and *Simpson* v. *Rice,* all decided today, serve to point up, as few other cases have, the profound changes that the "incorporation doctrine" has wrought both in the workings of our federal system and upon the adjudicative processes of this Court.

MR. JUSTICE WHITE, with whom MR. JUSTICE BLACK joins, dissenting.

Few areas of the law have been as subject to shifting constitutional standards over the last 50 years as that of the search "incident to an arrest." There has been a remarkable instability in this whole area, which has seen at least four major shifts in emphasis. Today's opinion makes an untimely fifth. In my view, the Court should not now abandon the old rule.

I.

The modern odyssey of doctrine in this field is detailed in the majority opinion. It began with *Weeks* v. *United States*, 232 U.S. 383 (1914), where the Court paused to note what the case before it was not. "It is not an assertion of the right on the part of the Government, always recognized under English and American law, to search the person of the accused when legally arrested to discover and seize the fruits or evidences of crime. This right has been uniformly maintained in many cases. . . . Nor is it the case of burglar's tools or other proofs of guilt found upon his arrest *within the control of the accused.*" *Id.*, at 392. This scope of search incident to arrest, extending to all items under the suspect's "control," was reaffirmed in a dictum in *Carroll* v. *United States*, 267 U.S. 132, 158 (1925). Accord, *Agnello* v. *United States*, 269 U.S. 20, 30 (1925) (holding that "the place where the arrest is made" may be searched "is not to be doubted"). The rule was reaffirmed in *Marron* v. *United States*, 275 U.S. 192, 199 (1927), where the Court asserted that authority to search incident to an arrest "extended to all parts of the premises used for the unlawful purpose."

Within four years, this rule was qualified by two Prohibition Act cases, *Go-Bart Importing Co.* v. *United States*, 282 U.S. 344, 356–358 (1931), and *United States* v. *Lefkowitz*, 285 U.S. 452, 463–467 (1932).

If *Go-Bart* and *Lefkowitz* represented a retreat from the rule of *Weeks, Carroll, Agnello*, and *Marron*, the vigor of the earlier rule was reaffirmed in *Harris* v. *United States*, 331 U.S. 145 (1947) which has, but for one brief interlude, clearly been the law until today. The very next Term after *Harris*, in *Trupiano* v. *United States*, 334 U.S. 699 (1948), the Court held unjustifiable the seizure of a still incident to the arrest of a man at the still site, even though the still was contraband, had been visible through an open door before entering the premises to be "searched," and although a crime was being committed in the officers' presence. Accord, that year, *McDonald* v. *United States*, 335 U.S. 451 (1948) (gambling game seen through transom before entry). Two years later, however, the Court returned to the *Harris* rule in *United States* v. *Rabinowitz*, 339 U.S. 56 (1950), where the Court held that the reasonableness of a search does not depend upon the practicability of obtaining a search warrant, and that the fact of a valid arrest is relevant to reasonableness. *Trupiano* was *pro tanto* overruled.

Such rapid reversals had occurred before, but they are rare. Here there had been two about-faces, one following hard upon the other. JUSTICE FRANKFURTER objected in this language: "Especially ought the Court not reenforce needlessly the instabilities of our day by giving fair ground for the belief that Law is the expression of chance—for instance, of unexpected changes in the Court's composition and the contingencies in the choice of successors." 339 U.S., at 86. Since that time, the rule of *Weeks, Marron, Harris,* and *Rabinowitz* has clearly been the law. [Citations omitted.]

II.

The rule which has prevailed, but for very brief or doubtful periods of aberration, is that a search incident to an arrest may extend to those areas under the control of the defendant and where items subject to constitutional seizure may be found. The justification for this rule must, under the language of the Fourth Amendment, lie in the reasonableness of the rule. [Citations omitted.] The Amendment provides:

> The right of the people to be secure in their persons, houses, papers, and effects, against unreasonable searches and seizures, shall not be violated, and no Warrants shall issue, but upon probable cause, supported by Oath or affirmation, and particularly describing the place to be searched, and the persons or things to be seized.

In terms, then, the Court must decide whether a given search is reasonable. The Amendment does not proscribe "warrantless searches" but instead it proscribes "unreasonable searches" and this Court has never held nor does the majority today assert that warrantless searches are necessarily unreasonable.

Applying this reasonableness test to the area of searches incident to arrests, one thing is clear at the outset. Search of an arrested man and of the items within his immediate reach must in almost every case be reasonable. There is always a danger that the suspect will try to escape, seizing concealed weapons with which to overpower and injure the arresting officers, and there is a danger that he may destroy evidence vital to the prosecution. Circumstances in which these justifications would not apply are sufficiently rare that inquiry is not made into searches of this scope, which have been considered reasonable throughout.

. . . .

IV.

. . . .

An arrested man, by definition conscious of the police interest in him, and provided almost immediately with a lawyer and a judge, is in an excellent position to dispute the reasonableness of his arrest and contemporaneous search in a full adversary proceeding. I would uphold the constitutionality of this search contemporaneous with an arrest since there was probable cause both for the search and for the arrest, exigent circumstances involving the removal or destruction of evidence, and a satisfactory opportunity to dispute the issues of probable cause shortly thereafter. In this case, the search was reasonable.

UNITED STATES v. ALBERT ROSS, JR.

456 U.S. 798, 102 S. Ct. 2157, 72 L. Ed. 2d 572 (1982)

MR. JUSTICE STEVENS delivered the opinion of the Court.

In *Carroll v. United States,* 267 U.S. 132, 45 S.Ct. 280, 69 L.Ed. 543, the Court held that a warrantless search of an automobile stopped by police officers who had probable cause to believe the vehicle contained contraband was not unreasonable within the meaning of the Fourth Amendment. The Court in *Carroll* did not explicitly address the scope of the search that is permissible. In this case, we consider the extent to which police officers—who have legitimately stopped an automobile and who have probable cause to believe that contraband is concealed somewhere within it—may conduct a probing search of compartments and containers within the vehicle whose contents are not in plain view. We hold that they may conduct a search of the vehicle that is as thorough as a magistrate could authorize in a warrant "particularly describing the place to be searched."

I

In the evening of November 27, 1978, an informant who had previously proved to be reliable telephoned Detective Marcum of the District of Columbia Police Department and told him that an individual known as "Bandit" was selling narcotics kept in the trunk of a car parked at 439 Ridge Street. The informant stated that he had just observed "Bandit" complete a sale and that "Bandit" had told him that additional narcotics were in the trunk. The informant gave Marcum a detailed description of "Bandit" and stated that the car was a "purplish maroon" Chevrolet Malibu with District of Columbia license plates.

Accompanied by Detective Cassidy and Sergeant Gonzales, Marcum immediately drove to the area and found a maroon Malibu parked in front of 439 Ridge Street. A license check disclosed that the car was registered to Albert Ross; a computer check on Ross revealed that he fit the informant's description and used the alias "Bandit." In two passes through the neighborhood the officers did not observe anyone matching the informant's description. To avoid alerting persons on the street, they left the area.

The officers returned five minutes later and observed the maroon Malibu turning off Ridge Street onto Fourth Street. They pulled alongside the Malibu, noticed that the driver matched the informant's description, and stopped the car. Marcum and Cassidy told the driver—later identified as Albert Ross, the respondent in this action—to get out of the vehicle. While they searched Ross, Sergeant Gonzales discovered a bullet on the car's front seat. He searched the interior of the car and found a pistol in the glove compartment. Ross then was arrested and handcuffed. Detective Cassidy took Ross' keys and opened the trunk, where he found a closed brown paper bag. He opened the bag and discovered a number of glassine bags containing a white powder. Cassidy replaced the bag, closed the trunk, and drove the car to Headquarters.

At the police station Cassidy thoroughly searched the car. In addition to the "lunchtype" brown paper bag, Cassidy found in the trunk a zippered red leather pouch. He unzipped the pouch and discovered $3,200 in cash. The police laboratory later determined that the powder in the paper bag was heroin. No warrant was obtained.

Ross was charged with possession of heroin with intent to distribute, in violation of 21 U.S.C. § 841(a). Prior to trial, he moved to suppress the heroin found in the paper bag and the currency found in the leather pouch. After an evidentiary hearing, the District Court denied the motion to suppress. The heroin and currency were introduced in evidence at trial and Ross was convicted.

A three-judge panel of the Court of Appeals reversed the conviction. It held that the police had probable cause to stop and search Ross' car and that, under *Carroll v. United States, supra,* and *Chambers v. Maroney,* 399 U.S. 42, 90 S.Ct. 1975, 26 L.Ed.2d 419, the officers lawfully could search the automobile—including its trunk—without a warrant. The court considered separately, however, the warrantless search of the two containers found in the trunk. On the basis of *Arkansas v. Sanders,* 442 U.S. 753, 99 S.Ct. 2586, 61 L.Ed.2d 235, the court concluded that the constitutionality of a warrantless search of a container found in an automobile depends on whether the owner possesses a reasonable expectation of privacy in its contents. Applying that test, the court held that the warrantless search of the paper bag was valid but the search of the leather pouch was not. The court remanded for a new trial at which the items taken from the paper bag, but not those from the leather pouch, could be admitted.

The entire Court of Appeals then voted to rehear the case en banc. A majority of the court rejected the panel's conclusion that a distinction of constitutional significance existed between the two containers found in the respondent's trunk; it held that the police should not have opened either container without first obtaining a warrant. The court reasoned:

> "No specific, well-delineated exception called to our attention permits the police to dispense with a warrant to open and search 'unworthy' containers. Moreover, we believe that a rule under which the validity of a warrantless search would turn on judgments about the durability of a container would impose an unreasonable and unmanageable burden on police and courts. For these reasons, and because the Fourth Amendment protects all persons, not just those with the resources or fastidiousness to place their effects in containers that would rank in the luggage line, we hold that the Fourth Amendment warrant requirement forbids the warrantless opening of a closed, opaque paper bag to the same extent that it forbids the warrantless opening of a small unlocked suitcase or a zippered leather pouch." 655 F.2d 1159, 1161 (CADC 1981) (footnote omitted).

The en banc Court of Appeals considered, and rejected, the argument that it was reasonable for the police to open both the paper bag and the leather pouch because they were entitled to conduct a warrantless search of the entire vehicle in which the two containers were found. The majority concluded that this argument was foreclosed by *Sanders.*

Three dissenting judges interpreted *Sanders* differently. Other courts also have read the *Sanders* opinion in different ways. Moreover, disagreement concerning the proper interpretation of *Sanders* was at least partially responsible for the fact that *Robbins v. California,* 453 U.S. 420, 101 S.Ct. 2841, 69 L.Ed.2d 744, was decided last Term without a Court opinion.

There is, however, no dispute among judges about the importance of striving for clarification in this area of the law. For countless vehicles are stopped on highways and public streets every day and our cases demonstrate that it is not uncommon for police officers to have probable cause to believe that contraband may be found in a stopped vehicle. In every such case a conflict is presented between the individual's constitutionally protected interest in privacy and the public interest in effective law enforcement. No single rule of law can resolve every conflict, but our conviction that clarification is feasible led us to grant the Government's petition for certiorari in this case and to invite the parties to address this question whether the decision in *Robbins* should be reconsidered.

II

We begin with a review of the decision in *Carroll* itself. In the fall of 1921, federal prohibition agents obtained evidence that George Carroll and John Kiro were "bootleggers" who frequently traveled between Grand rapids and Detroit in an Oldsmobile Roadster.[5] On December 15, 1921, the agents unexpectedly encountered Carroll and Kiro driving west on that route in that car. The officers gave pursuit, stopped the roadster on the highway, and directed Carroll and Kiro to get out of the car.

No contraband was visible in the front seat of the Oldsmobile and the rear portion of the roadster was closed. One of the agents raised the rumble seat but found no liquor. He raised the seat cushion and again found nothing. The officer then struck at the "lazyback" of the seat and noticed that it was "harder than upholstery ordinarily is in those backs." 267 U.S., at 174, 45 S.Ct., at 292. He tore open the seat cushion and discovered 68 bottles of gin and whiskey concealed inside. No warrant had been obtained for the search.

Carroll and Kiro were convicted of transporting intoxicating liquor in violation of the National Prohibition Act. On review of those convictions, this Court ruled that the warrantless search of the roadster was reasonable within the meaning of the Fourth Amendment. In an extensive opinion written by Chief Justice Taft, the Court held:

> "On reason and authority the true rule is that if the search and seizure without a warrant are made upon probable cause, that is, upon a belief, reasonably arising out of circumstances known to the seizing officer, that an automobile or other vehicle contains that which by law is subject to seizure and destruction, the search and seizure are valid. The Fourth Amendment is to be construed in the light of what was deemed an unreasonable search and seizure when it was adopted, and in a man-

> ner which will conserve public interests as well as the interests and rights of individual citizens." *Id.*, at 149, 45 S.Ct., at 283.

The Court explained at length the basis for this rule. The Court noted that historically warrantless searches of vessels, wagons, and carriages—as opposed to fixed premises such as a home or other building—had been considered reasonable by Congress. After reviewing legislation enacted by Congress between 1789 and 1799, the Court stated:

> "Thus contemporaneously with the adoption of the Fourth Amendment we find in the first Congress, and in the following Second and Fourth Congresses, a difference made as to the necessity for a search warrant between goods subject to forfeiture, when concealed in a dwelling house or similar place, and like goods in course of transportation and concealed in a movable vessel where they readily could be put out of reach of a search warrant."

The Court reviewed additional legislation passed by Congress and again noted that

> "the guaranty of freedom from unreasonable searches and seizures by the Fourth Amendment has been construed, practically since the beginning of the Government, as recognizing a necessary difference between a search of a store, dwelling house or other structure in respect of which a proper official warrant readily may be obtained, and a search of a ship, motor boat, wagon or automobile, for contraband goods, where it is not practicable to secure a warrant because the vehicle can be quickly moved out of the locality or jurisdiction in which the warrant must be sought."

Thus, since its earliest days Congress had recognized the impracticability of securing a warrant in cases involving the transportation of contraband goods. It is this impracticability, viewed in historical perspective, that provided the basis for the *Carroll* decision. Given the nature of an automobile in transit, the Court recognized that an immediate intrusion is necessary if police officers are to secure the illicit substance. In this class of cases, the Court held that a warrantless search of an automobile is not unreasonable.

In defining the nature of this "exception" to the general rule that "[i]n cases where the securing of a warrant is reasonably practicable, it must be used," the Court in *Carroll* emphasized the importance of the requirement that officers have probable cause to believe that the vehicle contains contraband.

> "Having thus established that contraband goods concealed and illegally transported in an automobile or other vehicle may be searched for without a warrant, we come now to consider under what circumstances such search may be made. It would be intolerable and unreasonable if a prohibition agent were authorized to stop every automobile on the chance of finding liquor and thus subject all persons lawfully using the highways to the inconvenience and indignity of such a search. Travellers may be so stopped in crossing an international boundary because of national self protection reasonably requiring one entering the country

> to identify himself as entitled to come in, and his belongings as effects which may be lawfully brought in. But those lawfully within the country, entitled to use the public highways, have a right to free passage without interruption or search unless there is known to a competent official authorized to search, probable cause for believing that their vehicles are carrying contraband or illegal merchandise."

Moreover, the probable cause determination must be based on objective facts that could justify the issuance of a warrant by a magistrate and not merely on the subjective good faith of the police officers. " '[A]s we have seen, good faith is not enough to constitute probable cause. That faith must be grounded on facts within knowledge of the [officer], which in the judgment of the court would make his faith reasonable.' "

In short, the exception to the warrant requirement established in *Carroll*—the scope of which we consider in this case—applies only to searches of vehicles that are supported by probable cause.[11] In this class of cases, a search is not unreasonable if based on facts that would justify the issuance of a warrant, even though a warrant has not actually been obtained....

III

* * *

The parties in *Robbins* had not pressed that argument, however, and Justice Powell concluded that institutional constraints made it inappropriate to re-examine basic doctrine without full adversary presentation. He concurred in the judgment, since it was supported—although not compelled—by the Court's opinion in *Sanders,* and stated that a future case might present a better opportunity for thorough consideration of the basic principles in this troubled area.

That case has arrived. Unlike *Chadwick* and *Sanders,* in this case police officers had probable cause to search respondent's entire vehicle. Unlike *Robbins,* in this case the parties have squarely addressed the question whether, in the course of a legitimate warrantless search of an automobile, police are entitled to open containers found within the vehicle. We now address that question. Its answer is determined by the scope of the search that is authorized by the exception to the warrant requirement set forth in *Carroll.*

IV

In *Carroll* itself, the whiskey that the prohibition agents seized was not in plain view. It was discovered only after an officer opened the rumble seat and tore open the upholstery of the lazyback. The Court did not find the scope of the search unreasonable. Having stopped Carroll and Kiro on a public road and subjected them to the indignity of a vehicle search—which the Court found to be a reasonable intrusion on their privacy because it was based on probable cause that their vehicle was transporting contraband—prohibition agents were entitled to tear open a portion of the roadster itself. The scope of the search was no greater than a magistrate could have authorized by issuing a warrant based on the probable cause that justified the search. Since such a warrant could have authorized the agents to open the rear portion of the roadster and to rip the upholstery in their search for concealed whiskey, the search was constitutionally permissible.

In *Chambers v. Maroney* the police found weapons and stolen property "concealed in a compartment under the dashboard." No suggestion was made that the scope of the search was impermissible. It would be illogical to assume that the outcome of *Chambers* —or the outcome of *Carroll* itself— would have been different if the police had found the secreted contraband enclosed within a secondary container and had opened that container without a warrant. If it was reasonable for prohibition agents to rip open the upholstery in *Carroll,* it certainly would have been reasonable for them to look into a burlap sack stashed inside; if it was reasonable to open the concealed compartment in *Chambers,* it would have been equally reasonable to open a paper bag crumpled within it. A contrary rule could produce absurd results inconsistent with the decision in *Carroll* itself.

* * *

A lawful search of fixed premises generally extends to the entire area in which the object of the search may be found and is not limited by the possibility that separate acts of entry or opening may be required to complete the search. Thus, a warrant that authorizes an officer to search a home for illegal weapons also provides authority to open closets, chests, drawers, and containers in which the weapon might be found. A warrant to open a footlocker to search for marijuana would also authorize the opening of packages found inside. A warrant to search a vehicle would support a search of every part of the vehicle that might contain the object of the search. When a legitimate search is under way, and when its purpose and its limits have been precisely defined, nice distinctions between closets, drawers, and containers, in the case of a home, or between glove compartments, upholstered seats, trunks, and wrapped packages, in the case of a vehicle, must give way to the interest in the prompt and efficient completion of the task at hand.

This rule applies equally to all containers, as indeed we believe it must. One point on which the Court was in virtually unanimous agreement in *Robbins* was that a constitutional distinction between "worthy" and "unworthy" containers would be improper. Even though such a distinction perhaps could evolve in a series of cases in which paper bags, locked trunks, lunch buckets, and orange crates were placed on one side of the line or the other, the central purpose of the Fourth Amendment forecloses such a distinction. For just as the most frail cottage in the kingdom is absolutely entitled to the same guarantees of privacy as the most majestic mansion, so also may a traveler who carries a toothbrush and a few articles of clothing in a paper bag or knotted scarf claim an equal right to conceal his possessions from official inspection as the sophisticated executive with the locked attaché case.

As Justice Stewart stated in *Robbins,* the Fourth Amendment provides protection to the owner of every container that conceals its contents from plain view. But the protection afforded by the Amendment varies in different settings. The luggage carried by a traveler entering the country may be searched at random by a customs officer; the luggage may be searched no matter how great the traveler's desire to conceal the contents may be. A container carried at the time of arrest often may be searched without a warrant and even without any specific suspicion concerning its contents. A container that may conceal the object of a search authorized by a warrant may be opened immediately; the individual's interest in privacy must give way to the magistrate's official determination of probable cause.

In the same manner, an individual's expectation of privacy in a vehicle and its contents may not survive if probable cause is given to believe that the vehicle is transporting contraband. Certainly the privacy interests in a car's trunk or glove compartment may be no less than those in a movable container. An individual undoubtedly has a significant interest that the upholstery of his automobile will not be ripped or a hidden compartment within it opened. These interests must yield to the authority of a search, however, which—in light of *Carroll*—does not itself require the prior approval of a magistrate. The scope of a warrantless search based on probable cause is no narrower—and no broader—than the scope of a search authorized by a warrant supported by probable cause. Only the prior approval of the magistrate is waived; the search otherwise is as the magistrate could authorize.

The scope of a warrantless search of an automobile thus is not defined by the nature of the container in which the contraband is secreted. Rather, it is defined by the object of the search and the places in which there is probable cause to believe that it may be found. Just as probable cause to believe that a stolen lawnmower may be found in a garage will not support a warrant to search an upstairs bedroom, probable cause to believe that undocumented aliens are being transported in a van will not justify a warrantless search of a suitcase. Probable cause to believe that a container placed in the trunk of a taxi contains contraband or evidence does not justify a search of the entire cab.

V

Our decision today is inconsistent with the disposition in *Robbins v. California* and with the portion of the opinion in *Arkansas v. Sanders* on which the plurality in *Robbins* relied. Nevertheless, the doctrine of *stare decisis* does not preclude this action. Although we have rejected some of the reasoning in *Sanders,* we adhere to our holding in that case; although we reject the precise holding in *Robbins,* there was no Court opinion supporting a single rationale for its judgment and the reasoning we adopt today was not presented by the parties in that case. Moreover, it is clear that no legitimate reliance interest can be frustrated by our decision today. Of greatest importance, we are convinced that the rule we apply in this case is faithful to the interpretation of the Fourth Amendment that the Court has followed with substantial consistency throughout our history.

We reaffirm the basic rule of Fourth Amendment jurisprudence stated by Justice Stewart for a unanimous Court in *Mincey v. Arizona,* 437 U.S. 385, 390, 98 S.Ct. 2408, 2412, 57 L.Ed.2d 290:

> "The Fourth Amendment proscribes all unreasonable searches and seizures, and it is a cardinal principle that 'searches conducted outside the judicial process, without prior approval by judge or magistrate, are *per se* unreasonable under the Fourth Amendment—subject only to a few specifically established and well-delineated exceptions.' "

The exception recognized in *Carroll* is unquestionably one that is "specifically established and well-delineated." We hold that the scope of the warrantless search authorized by that exception is no broader and no narrower than a magistrate could legitimately authorize by warrant. If probable cause justifies the search of a lawfully stopped vehicle, it justifies the search of every part of the vehicle and its contents that may conceal the object of the search.

The judgment of the Court of Appeals is reversed. The case is remanded for further proceedings consistent with this opinion.

It is so ordered.

MR. JUSTICE BLACKMUN, concurring.

My dissents in prior cases have indicated my continuing dissatisfaction and discomfort with the Court's vacillation in what is rightly described as "this troubled area."

I adhere to the views expressed in those dissents. It is important, however, not only for the Court as an institution, but also for law enforcement officials and defendants, that the applicable legal rules be clearly established. JUSTICE STEVENS' opinion for the Court now accomplishes much in this respect, and it should clarify a good bit of the confusion that has existed. In order to have an authoritative ruling, I join the Court's opinion and judgment.

MR. JUSTICE POWELL concurring.

In my opinion in *Robbins v. California,* 453 U.S. 420, 429, 101 S.Ct. 2841, 2847, 69 L.Ed.2d 744 (1981), concurring in the judgment, I stated that the judgment was justified, though not compelled, by the Court's opinion in *Arkansas v. Sanders,* 442 U.S. 753, 99 S.Ct. 2586, 61 L.Ed.2d 235 (1979). I did not agree, however, with the "bright line" rule articulated by the plurality opinion. Rather, I repeated the view I long have held that one's "reasonable expectation of privacy" is a particularly relevant factor in determining the validity of a warrantless search. I have recognized, that with respect to automobiles in general, this expectation can be only a limited one. I continue to think that in many situations one's reasonable expectation of privacy may be a decisive factor in a search case.

It became evident last Term, however, from the five opinions written in *Robbins*—in none of which THE CHIEF JUSTICE joined—that it is essential to have a Court opinion in *automobile* search cases that provides "specific guidance to police and courts in this reoccurring situation." *Robbins v. California,* 453 U.S., at 435, 101 S.Ct., at 2850 (POWELL, J., concurring). The Court's opinion today, written by Justice STEVENS and now joined by four other Justices, will afford this needed guidance. It is fair also to say that, given *Carroll v. United States,* 267 U.S. 132, 45 S.Ct. 280, 69 L.Ed. 543 (1925) and *Chambers v. Maroney,* 399 U.S. 42, 90 S.Ct. 1975, 26 L.Ed.2d 419 (1970), the Court's decision does not depart substantially from Fourth Amendment doctrine in automobile cases. Moreover, in enunciating a readily understood and applied rule, today's decision is consistent with the similar step taken last Term in *New York v. Belton,* 453 U.S. 454, 101 S.Ct. 2860, 69 L.Ed.2d 768 (1981).

I join the Court's opinion.

MR. JUSTICE WHITE, dissenting:

I would not overrule *Robbins v. California,* 453 U.S. 420, 101 S.Ct. 2841, 69 L.Ed.2d 744 (1981). For the reasons stated by Justice Stewart in that case, I would affirm the judgment of the Court of Appeals. I also agree with much of Justice Marshall's dissent in this case.

MR. JUSTICE MARSHALL, with whom MR. JUSTICE BRENNAN joins, dissenting.

The majority today not only repeals all realistic limits on warrantless automobile searches, it repeals the Fourth Amendment warrant requirement itself. By equating a police officer's estimation of probable cause with a magistrate's, the Court utterly disregards the value of a neutral and detached magistrate.

[Parts of dissenting opinions are not included.]

ARIZONA v. HICKS

__U.S.__, 107 S. Ct. 1149, 94 L.Ed.2d 347 (1987)

* * *

Justice SCALIA delivered the opinion of the Court.

In *Coolidge v. New Hampshire,* 403 U.S. 443, 91 S.Ct. 2022, 29 L.Ed.2d 564 (1971), we said that in certain circumstances a warrantless seizure by police of an item that comes within plain view during their lawful search of a private area may be reasonable under the Fourth Amendment. See *id.,* at 465-471, 91 S.Ct. at 2037-2041 (plurality opinion); *id.,* at 505-506, 91 S.Ct. at 2057-2058 (Black, J., concurring and dissenting).; *id.* at 521-522, 91 S.Ct. at 2065-2066 (WHITE, J., concurring and dissenting). We granted certiorari, 475 U.S. __, 106 S.Ct. 1512, 89 L.Ed.2d 912 (1986), in the present case to decide whether this "plain view" doctrine may be invoked when the police have less than probable cause to believe that the item in question is evidence of a crime or is contraband.

I

On April 18, 1984, a bullet was fired through the floor of respondent's apartment, striking and injuring a man in the apartment below. Police officers arrived and entered respondent's apartment to search for the shooter, for other victims, and for weapons. They found and seized three weapons, including a sawed-off rifle, and in the course of their search also discovered a stocking-cap mask.

One of the policemen, Officer Nelson, noticed two sets of expensive stereo components, which seemed out of place in the squalid and otherwise ill-appointed four-room apartment. Suspecting that they were stolen, he read and recorded their serial numbers--moving some of the components, including a Bang and Olufsen turntable, in order to do so--which he then reported by phone to his headquarters. On being advised that the turntable had been taken in an armed robbery, he seized it immediately. It was later determined that some of the other serial numbers matched those on other stereo equipment taken in the same armed robbery, and a warrant was obtained and executed to seize that equipment as well. Respondent was subsequently indicted for the robbery.

The state trial court granted respondent's motion to suppress the evidence that had been seized. The Court of Appeals of Arizona affirmed. It was conceded that the initial entry and search, although warrantless, were justified by the exigent circumstance of the shooting. The Court of Appeals viewed the obtaining of the serial numbers, however, as an additional search, unrelated to that exigency. Relying upon a statement in *Mincey v. Arizona,* 437 U.S. 385, 98 S.Ct. 2408, 57 L.Ed.2d 290 (1978), that a "warrantless search must be 'strictly circumscribed by the exigencies which justify its initiation,'" *id.,* at 393, 98 S.Ct. at 2413 (citation omitted), the Court of Appeals held that the police conduct violated the Fourth Amendment, requiring the evidence derived from that conduct to be excluded. Both courts--the trial court explicitly and the Court of Appeals by necessary implication--rejected the State's contention that Officer Nelson's actions were justified under the "plain view" doctrine of *Coolidge v. New Hampshire, supra*. The Arizona Supreme Court denied review, and the State filed this petition.

II

As an initial matter, the State argues that Officer Nelson's actions constituted neither a "search" nor a "seizure" within the meaning of the Fourth Amendment. We agree that the mere recording of the serial numbers did not constitute a seizure. To be sure, that was the first step in a process by which respondent was eventually deprived of the stereo equipment. In and of itself, however, it did not "meaningfully interfere" with respondent's possessory interest in either the serial numbers or the equipment, and therefore did not amount to a seizure. See *Maryland v. Macon,* 472 U.S. 463, 469, 105 S.Ct. 2778, 2782, 86 L.Ed.2d 370 (1985).

Officer Nelson's moving of the equipment, however, did constitute a "search" separate and apart from the search for the shooter, victims, and weapons that was the lawful objective of his entry into the apartment. Merely inspecting those parts of the turntable that came into view during the latter search would not have constituted an independent search, because it would have produced no additional invasion of respondent's privacy interest. See *Illinois v. Andreas,* 463 U.S. 765, 771, 103 S.Ct. 3319, 3324, 77 L.Ed.2d 1003 (1983). But taking action, unrelated to the objectives of the authorized intrusion, which exposed to view concealed portions of the apartment or its contents, did produce a new invasion of respondent's privacy unjustified by the exigent circumstance that validated the entry. This is why, contrary to Justice POWELL's suggestion, *post,* at 1156, the "distinction between 'looking' at a suspicious object in plain view and 'moving' it even a few inches" is much more than trivial for purposes of the

Fourth Amendment. It matters not that the search uncovered nothing of any great personal value to the respondent--serial numbers rather than (what might conceivably have been hidden behind or under the equipment) letters or photographs. A search is a search, even if it happens to disclose nothing but the bottom of a turntable.

III

The remaining question is whether the search was "reasonable" under the Fourth Amendment.

On this aspect of the case we reject, at the outset, the apparent position of the Arizona Court of Appeals that because the officers' action directed to the stereo equipment was unrelated to the justification for their entry into respondent's apartment, it was *ipso facto* unreasonable. That lack of relationship *always* exists with regard to action validated under the "plain view" doctrine; where action is taken for the purpose justifying the entry, invocation of the doctrine is superfluous. *Mincey v. Arizona, supra,* in saying that a warrantless search must be "strictly circumscribed by the exigencies which justify its initiation," 437 U.S., at 393, 98 S.Ct. at 2413 (citation omitted) was addressing only the scope of the primary search itself, and was not overruling by implication the many cases acknowledging that the "plain view" doctrine can legitimate action beyond that scope.

We turn, then, to application of the doctrine to the facts of this case. "It is well established that under certain circumstances the police may *seize* evidence in plain view without a warrant," *Coolidge v. New Hampshire*, 403 U.S., at 465, 91 S.Ct. at 2037 (plurality) (emphasis added). Those circumstances include situations "[w]here the initial intrusion that brings the police within plain view of such [evidence] is supported...by one of the recognized exceptions to the warrant requirement," *ibid.,* such as the exigent-circumstances intrusion here. It would be absurd to say that an object could lawfully be seized and taken from the premises, but could not be moved for closer examination. It is clear, therefore, that the search here was valid if the "plain view" doctrine would have sustained a seizure of the equipment.

There is no doubt it would have done so if Officer Nelson had probable cause to believe that the equipment was stolen. The State has conceded, however, that he had only a "reasonable suspicion," by which it means something less than probable cause. *** We have not ruled on the question whether probable cause is required in order to invoke the "plain view" doctrine. Dicta in *Payton v. New York,* 445 U.S. 573, 587, 100 S.Ct. 1371, 1380, 63 L.Ed.2d 639 (1980), suggested that the standard of probable cause must be met, but our later opinions in *Texas v. Brown,* 460 U.S. 730, 103 S.Ct. 1535, 75 L.Ed.2d 502 (1983), explicitly regarded the issue as unresolved ***.

We now hold that probable cause is required. To say otherwise would be to cut the "plain view" doctrine loose from its theoretical and practical moorings. The theory of that doctrine consists of extending to nonpublic places such as the home, where searches and seizures without a warrant are presumptively unreasonable, the police's longstanding authority to make warrantless seizures in public places of such objects as weapons and contraband. See *Payton v. New York, supra,* at 586-587, 100 S.Ct. at 1380. And the practical justification for that extension is the desirability of sparing police, whose viewing of the object in the course of a lawful search is as legitimate as it would have been in a public place, the inconvenience and the risk--to themselves or to preservation of the evidence--of going to obtain a warrant. See *Coolidge v. New Hampshire, supra,* at 468, 91 S.Ct. at 2039 (plurality). Dispensing with the need for a warrant is worlds apart from permitting a lesser standard of *cause* for the seizure than a warrant would require, *i.e.,* the standard of probable cause. No reason is apparent why an object should routinely by seizable on lesser grounds, during an unrelated search and seizure, than would have been needed to obtain a warrant for that same object if it had been known to be on the premises.

We do not say, of course, that a seizure can never be justified on less than probable cause. We have held that it can --where, for example, the seizure is minimally intrusive and operational necessities render it the only practicable means of detecting certain types of crime. *** No special operational necessities are relied on here, however --but rather than mere fact that the items in question came lawfully within the officers plain view. That alone cannot supplant the requirement of probable cause.

The same considerations preclude us from holding that, even though probable cause would have been necessary for a *seizure*, the *search* of objects in plain view that occurred here could be sustained on lesser grounds. A dwelling-place search, no less than a dwelling-place seizure, requires probable cause, and there is no reason in theory or practicality why application of the plain-view doctrine would supplant that requirement. Although the interest protected by the Fourth Amendment injunction against unreasonable searches is quite different from that protected by its injunction against unreasonable seizures, *** (STEVENS, J., concurring in judgment), neither the one nor the other is of inferior worth or necessarily requires only lesser protection. We have not elsewhere drawn a categorical distinction between the two insofar as concerns the degree of justification needed to establish the reasonableness of police action, and we see no reason for a distinction in the particular circumstances before us here. Indeed, to treat searches more liberally would especially erode the plurality's warning in Coolidge that "the 'plain view' doctrine may not be used to extend a general exploratory search from one object to another until something incriminating at last emerges." 403 U.S., at 466, 91 S.Ct. at 2038. In short, whether legal authority to move the equipment could be found only as an inevitable concomitant of the authority to seize it, or also as a consequence of some independent power to search certain objects in plain view, probable cause to believe the equipment was stolen was required.

Justice O'CONNER's dissent suggests that we uphold the action here on the ground that it was a "cursory inspection" rather than a "full-blown search," and could therefore be justified by reasonable suspicion instead of probable cause. As already noted, a truly cursory inspection --one that involves merely looking at what is already exposed to view, without disturbing it-- is not a "search" for Fourth Amendment purposes, and therefore does not even require reasonable suspicion. We are unwilling to send police and judges into a new thicket of Fourth Amendment law, to seek a creature of uncertain description that is neither a plain-view inspection nor yet a "full-blown search." Nothing in the prior opinions of this Court supports such a distinction, not even the dictum from Justice Stewart's concurrence in *Stanley v. Georgia,* 394 U.S. 557, 571, 89 S.Ct. 1243, 1251, 22 L.Ed.2d 542 (1969), whose reference to a "mere inspection" describes, in our view, close observation of what lies in plain sight.

Justice POWELL's dissent reasonably asks what it is we would have had Officer Nelson do in these circumstances. *** The answer depends, of course, upon whether he had probable cause to conduct a search, a question that was not preserved in this case. If he had, then he should have done precisely what he did. If not, then he should have followed up his suspicions, if possible, by means other than a search --just as he would have had to do if, while walking along the street, he had noticed the same suspicious stereo equipment sitting inside a house a few feet away from him, beneath an open window. It may well be that, in such circumstances, no effective means short of a search exist. But there is nothing new in the realization that the Constitution sometimes insulates the criminality of a few in order to protect the privacy of us all. Our disagreement with the dissenters pertains to where the proper balance should be struck; we choose to adhere to the textual and traditional standard of probable cause.

The State contends that, even if Officer Nelson's search violated the Fourth Amendment, the court below should have admitted the evidence thus obtained under the "good faith" exception to the exclusionary rule. That was not the question on which certiorari was granted, and we decline to consider it.

For the reasons stated, the judgment of the Court of Appeals of Arizona is

Affirmed.

The concurring and dissenting opinions are not included.

* * *

Cases relating to **Chapter 5**

WIRETAPPING AND EAVESDROPPING

BERGER v. NEW YORK

388 U.S. 41, 87 S. Ct. 1873, 18 L. Ed. 2d 1040 (1967)

Defendant was convicted in the Supreme Court, Special and Trial Term, New York County, on two counts of conspiracy to bribe public officer attached to New York State Liquor Authority and the Supreme Court, Appellate Division, First Department, 25 A.D.2d 718, 269 N.Y.S.2d 368 affirmed and on appeal the Court of Appeals, 18 N.Y.2d 638, 272 N.Y.S.2d 782, 219 N.E.2d 295 affirmed, and certiorari was granted. The Supreme Court, Mr. Justice Clark, held that statute authorizing any justice of Supreme Court or judge of county court or of court of general sessions of New York county to issue *ex parte* order for eavesdropping upon oath or affirmation of district attorney or of attorney general or officer above rank of sergeant of any police department or political subdivision thereof that there is reasonable ground to believe that evidence of crime may be thus obtained, containing no requirement for particularity as to what specific crime has been or is being committed or place to be searched or conversations sought as required by Fourth Amendment, and requiring no showing of exigent circumstances, is too broad in its sweep, resulting in trespassory intrusion into constitutionally protected area and is violative of Fourth and Fourteenth Amendments.

Reversed.

MR. JUSTICE BLACK, MR. JUSTICE HARLAN and MR. JUSTICE WHITE dissented.

MR. JUSTICE CLARK delivered the opinion of the Court.

This writ tests the validity of New York's permissive eavesdrop statute, N.Y. Code Crim.Proc. § 813–a, under the Fourth, Fifth, Ninth, and Fourteenth Amendments. The claim is that the statute sets up a system of surveillance which involves trespassory intrusions into private, constitutionally protected premises, authorizes "general searches" for "mere evidence," and is an invasion of the privilege against self-incrimination. The trial court upheld the statute, the Appellate Division affirmed without opinion, and the Court of Appeals did likewise by a divided vote. We granted certiorari. We have concluded that the language of New York's statute is too broad in its sweep resulting in a trespassory intrusion into a constitutionally protected area and is, therefore, violative of the Fourth and Fourteenth Amendments. This disposition obviates the necessity for any discussion of the other points raised.

I.

Berger, the petitioner, was convicted on two counts of conspiracy to bribe the Chairman of the New York State Liquor Authority. The case arose out of the complaint of one Ralph Pansini to the District Attorney's office that agents of the State Liquor Authority had entered his bar and grill and without cause seized his books and records. Pansini asserted that the raid was in reprisal for his failure to pay a bribe for a liquor license. Numerous complaints had been filed with the District Attorney's office charging the payment of bribes by applicants for liquor licenses. On the direction of that office, Pansini, while equipped with a "minifon" recording device, interviewed an employee of the Authority. The employee advised Pansini that the price for a license was $10,000 and suggested that he contact attorney Harry Neyer. Neyer subsequently told Pansini that he worked with the Authority employee before and that the latter was aware of the going rate on liquor licenses downtown.

On the basis of this evidence an eavesdrop order was obtained from a Justice of the State Supreme Court, as provided by § 813–a. The order permitted the installation, for a period of 60 days, of a recording device in Neyer's office. On the basis of leads obtained from this eavesdrop a second order permitting the installation, for a like period, of a recording device in the office of one Harry Steinman was obtained. After some two weeks of eavesdropping a conspiracy was uncovered involving the issuance of liquor licenses for the Playboy and Tenement Clubs, both of New York City. Petitioner was indicted as "a go-between" for the principal conspirators, who though not named in the indictment were disclosed in a bill of particulars. Relevant portions of the recordings were received in evidence at the trial and were played to the jury, all over the objection of the petitioner. The parties have stipulated that the District Attorney "had no information upon which to proceed to present a case to the Grand Jury, or on the basis of which to prosecute" the petitioner except by the use of the eavesdrop evidence.

II.

Eavesdropping is an ancient practice which at common law was condemned as a nuisance. 4 Blackstone, COMMENTARIES 168. At one time the eavesdropper listened by naked ear under the eaves of houses or their windows, or beyond their walls seeking out private discourse. The awkwardness and undignified manner of this method as well as its susceptibility to abuse was immediately recognized. Electricity, however, provided a better vehicle and with the advent of the telegraph surreptitious interception of messages began. As early as 1862 California found it necessary to prohibit the practice by statute. Statutes of

California 1862, p. 288, CCLX II. During the Civil War General J. E. B. Stuart is reputed to have had his own eavesdropper along with him in the field whose job it was to intercept military communications of the opposing forces. Subsequently newspapers reportedly raided one another's news gathering lines to save energy, time, and money. Racing news was likewise intercepted and flashed to bettors before the official result arrived.

The telephone brought on a new and more modern eavesdropper known as the "wiretapper." Interception was made by a connection with a telephone line. This activity has been with us for three-quarters of a century. Like its cousins, wiretapping proved to be a commercial as well as a police technique. Illinois outlawed it in 1895 and in 1905 California extended its telegraph interception prohibition to the telephone. Some 50 years ago a New York legislative committee found that police, in cooperation with the telephone company, had been tapping telephone lines in New York despite an Act passed in 1895 prohibiting it. During prohibition days wiretaps were the principal source of information relied upon by the police as the basis for prosecutions. In 1934 the Congress outlawed the interception without authorization, and the divulging or publishing of the contents of wiretaps by passing § 605 of the Communications Act of 1934. New York, in 1938, declared by constitutional amendment that "[t]he right of the people to be secured against unreasonable interception of telephone and telegraph communications shall not be violated," but permitted by *ex parte* order of the Supreme Court of the State the interception of communications on a showing of "reasonable ground to believe that evidence of crime" might be obtained. N.Y.Const. Art. I, § 12.

Sophisticated electronic devices have now been developed (commonly known as "bugs") which are capable of eavesdropping on anyone in most any given situation. They are to be distinguished from "wiretaps" which are confined to the interception of telegraphic and telephonic communications. Miniature in size (3/8" x 3/8" x 1/8")—no larger than a postage stamp—these gadgets pick up whispers within a room and broadcast them half a block away to a receiver. It is said that certain types of electronic rays beamed at walls or glass windows are capable of catching voice vibrations as they are bounced off the surfaces. Since 1940 eavesdropping has become a big business. Manufacturing concerns offer complete detection systems which automatically record voices under almost any conditions by remote control. A microphone concealed in a book, a lamp, or other unsuspected place in a room, or made into a fountain pen, tie clasp, lapel button, or cuff link increases the range of these powerful wireless transmitters to a half mile. Receivers pick up the transmission with interference-free reception on a special wave frequency. And, of late, a combination mirror transmitter has been developed which permits not only sight but voice transmission up to 300 feet. Likewise, parabolic microphones, which can overhear conversations without being placed within the premises monitored, have been developed. See Westin, *Science, Privacy, and Freedom: Issues and Proposals for the 1970's*, 66 Col.L.Rev. 1003, 1005–1010.

As science developed these detection techniques, law makers, sensing the resulting invasion of individual privacy, have provided some statutory protection for the public. Seven states, California, Illinois, Maryland, Massachusetts, Nevada, New York, and Oregon, prohibit surreptitious eavesdropping by mechanical or electronic device. However, all save Illinois permit official court-ordered eavesdropping. Some 36 states prohibit wiretapping. But of these, 27 permit "authorized" interception of some type. Federal law, as we have seen, prohibits interception and divulging or publishing of the content of wiretaps without exception. In sum, it is fair to say that wiretapping on the whole is outlawed, except for permissive use by law enforcement officials in some states; while electronic eavesdropping is —same for seven states—permitted both officially and privately. And, in six of the seven states, electronic eavesdropping ("bugging") is permissible on court order.

III.

The law, though jealous of individual privacy, has not kept pace with these advances in scientific knowledge. This is not to say that individual privacy has been relegated to a second-class position for it has been held since Lord Camden's day that intrusions into it are "subversive of all the comforts of society." *Entick* v. *Carrington*, 19 How.St.Tr. 1029, 1066 (1765). And the Founders so decided a quarter of a century later when they declared in the Fourth Amendment that the people had a right "to be secure in their persons, houses, papers, and effects, against unreasonable searches and seizures. . . ." Indeed, that right, they wrote, "shall not be violated, and no Warrants shall issue, but upon probable cause, supported by Oath or affirmation, and particularly describing the place to be searched, and the persons or things to be seized." Almost a century thereafter this Court took specific and lengthy notice of *Entick* v. *Carrington, supra,* finding that its holding was undoubtedly familiar in the minds of those who framed the fourth amendment. . . ." *Boyd* v. *United States,* 116 U.S. 616, 626–627, (1886). And after quoting from Lord Camden's opinion at some length, Mr. Justice Bradley characterized it thus:

> The principles laid down in this opinion affect the very essence of constitutional liberty and security. They reach farther than the concrete form of the case . . . they apply to all invasions on the part of the government and its employés of the sanctity of a man's home and the privacies of life.

Boyd held unconstitutional an Act of the Congress authorizing a court of the United States to require a defendant in a revenue case to produce in court his private books, invoices, and papers or else the allegations of the Government were to be taken as confessed. The Court found that "the essence of the offense . . . [was] the invasion of this sacred right which underlies and constitutes the essence of Lord Camden's judgment." *Ibid.* The Act—the Court found—violated the Fourth Amendment in that it authorized a general search contrary to the Amendment's guarantee.

The Amendment, however, carried no criminal sanction, and the federal statutes not affording one, the Court in 1914 formulated and pronounced the federal exclusionary rule in *Weeks* v. *United States,* 232 U.S. 383. Prohibiting the use in federal courts of any evidence seized in violation of the Amendment, the Court held:

> The effect of the 4th Amendment is to put the courts of the United States . . . under limitations and restraints as to the exercise of such power . . . and to forever secure the people . . . against all unreasonable searches and seizures under the guise of law. This protection reaches all alike, whether accused of crime or not, and the duty of giving to it force and effect is obligatory upon all. . . . The tendency of those who execute the criminal laws of the country to obtain conviction by means of unlawful seizures . . . should find no sanction in the judgments of the courts, which are charged at all times with the support of the Constitution, and to which people of all conditions have a right to appeal for the maintenance of such fundamental rights.

IV.

The Court was faced with its first wiretap case in 1928, *Olmstead* v. *United States,* 277 U.S. 438. There the interception of Olmstead's telephone line was accomplished without entry upon his premises and was, therefore, found not to be proscribed by the Fourth Amendment. The basis of the decision was that the Constitution did not forbid the obtaining of evidence by wiretapping unless it involved actual unlawful entry into the house. Statements in the opinion that a conversation passing over a telephone wire cannot be said to come within the Fourth Amendment's enumeration of "persons, houses, papers, and effects" have been negated by our subsequent cases as hereinafter noted. They found "conversation" was within the Fourth Amendment's protections, and that the use of electronic devices to capture it was a "search" within the meaning of the Amendment, and we so hold. In any event, Congress soon thereafter, and some say in answer to *Olmstead,* specifically prohibited the interception without authorization and the divulging or publishing of the contents of telephonic communications. And the *Nardone* cases (*Nardone* v. *United States*),

302 U.S. 379, (1937) and 308 U.S. 338 (1939), extended the exclusionary rule to wiretap evidence offered in federal prosecutions.

The first "bugging" case reached the Court in 1942 in *Goldman* v. *United States,* 316 U.S. 129. There the Court found that the use of a detectaphone placed against an office wall in order to hear private conversations in the office next door did not violate the Fourth Amendment because there was no physical trespass in connection with the relevant interception. And in *On Lee* v. *United States,* 343 U.S. 747 (1952), we found that since "no trespass was committed" a conversation between Lee and a federal agent, occurring in the former's laundry and electronically recorded, was not condemned by the Fourth Amendment. Thereafter in *Silverman* v. *United States,* 365 U.S. 505 (1961), the Court found "that the eavesdropping was accomplished by means of an unauthorized physical penetration into the premises occupied by the petitioners." A spike a foot long with a microphone attached to it was inserted under a baseboard into a party wall until it made contact with the heating duct that ran through the entire house occupied by Silverman, making a perfect sounding board through which the conversations in question were overheard. Significantly, the Court held that its decision did "not turn upon the technicality of a trespass upon a party wall as a matter of local law. It is based upon the reality of an actual intrusion into a constitutionally protected area."

In *Wong Sun* v. *United States,* 371 U.S. 471 (1963), the Court for the first time specifically held that verbal evidence may be the fruit of official illegality under the Fourth Amendment along with the more common tangible fruits of unwarranted intrusion. It used these words:

> The exclusionary rule has traditionally barred from trial physical, tangible materials obtained either during or as a direct result of an unlawful invasion. It follows from our holding in *Silverman* v. *United States,* 365 U.S. 505, that the Fourth Amendment may protect against the overhearing of verbal statements as well as against the more traditional seizure of "papers and effects."

And in *Lopez* v. *United States,* 373 U.S. 427 (1963), the Court confirmed that it had "in the past sustained instances of 'electronic eavesdropping' against constitutional challenge, when devices have been used to enable government agents to overhear conversations which would have been beyond the reach of the human ear. . . . It has been insisted only that the electronic device not be planted by an unlawful physical invasion of a constitutionally protected area." In this case a recording of a conversation between a federal agent and the petitioner in which the latter offered the agent a bribe was admitted in evidence. Rather than constituting "eavesdropping" the Court found that the recording "was used only to obtain the most reliable evidence possible of a conversation in which the Government's own agent was a participant and which that agent was fully entitled to disclose."

V.

It is now well settled that "the Fourth Amendment's right of privacy has been declared enforceable against the States through the Due Process Clause of the Fourteenth" Amendment. *Mapp* v. *Ohio*, 367 U.S. 643, 655 (1961). "The security of one's privacy against arbitrary intrusion by the police—which is at the core of the Fourth Amendment—is basic to a free society." *Wolf* v. *Colorado*, 338 U.S. 25, 27 (1949). And its "fundamental protections . . . are guaranteed . . . against invasion by the States." *Stanford* v. *Texas*, 379 U.S. 476, 481 (1965). This right has most recently received enunciation in *Camara* v. *Municipal Court*, 387 U.S. 523 (1967). "The basic purpose of this Amendment, as recognized in countless decisions of this Court, is to safeguard the privacy and security of individuals against arbitrary invasions by governmental officials." Likewise the Court has decided that while the "standards of reasonableness" required under the Fourth Amendment are the same under the Fourteenth, they "are not susceptible of Procrustean application. . . ." *Ker* v. *California*, 374 U.S. 23, 33 (1963). We said there that "the reasonableness of a search is . . . [to be determined] by the trial court from the facts and circumstances of the case and in the light of the 'fundamental criteria' laid down by the Fourth Amendment and in opinions of this Court applying that Amendment." *Ibid.*

We, therefore, turn to New York's statute to determine the basis of the search and seizure authorized by it upon the order of a state supreme court justice, a county judge or general sessions judge of New York County. Section 813–a authorizes the issuance of an "ex parte order for eavesdropping" upon "oath or affirmation of a district attorney, or of the attorney-general or of an officer above the rank of sergeant of any police department of the state or of any political subdivision thereof. . . ." The oath must state "that there is reasonable ground to believe that evidence of crime may be thus obtained, and particularly describing the person or persons whose communications, conversations or discussions are to be overheard or recorded and the purpose thereof, and . . . identifying the particular telephone number or telegraph line involved." The judge "may examine on oath the applicant and any other witness he may produce and shall satisfy himself of the existence of reasonable grounds for the granting of such application." The order must specify the duration of the eavesdrop—not exceeding two months unless extended—and "[a]ny such order together with the papers upon which the application was based, shall be delivered to and retained by the applicant as authority for the eavesdropping authorized therein."

While New York's statute satisfies the Fourth Amendment's requirement that a neutral and detached authority be interposed between the police and the public, or *Johnson* v. *United States,* 333 U.S. 10, 14 (1948), the broad sweep of the statute is immediately observable. It permits the issuance of the order, or warrant for eavesdropping, upon the oath of the attorney general, the district attorney or any police officer above the rank of sergeant stating that "there is reasonable ground to believe that evidence of crime may be thus obtained. . . ." Such a requirement raises a serious probable-cause question under the Fourth Amendment. Under it warrants may only issue "but upon probable cause, supported by Oath or affirmation, and particularly describing the place to be searched, and the persons or things to be seized." Probable cause under the Fourth Amendment exists where the facts and circumstances within the affiant's knowledge, and of which he has reasonably trustworthy information, are sufficient unto themselves to warrant a man of reasonable caution to believe that an offense has been or is being committed. *Carroll* v. *United States,* 267 U.S. 132, 162 (1925); *Husty* v. *United States,* 282 U.S. 694, 700–701 (1931); *Brinegar* v. *United States,* 338 U.S. 160, 175–176 (1949).

It is said, however, by the petitioner, and the State agrees, that the "reasonable ground" requirement of § 813-a "is undisputedly equivalent to the probable cause requirement of the Fourth Amendment." This is indicated by *People* v. *Grossman,* 45 Misc.2d 557, 257 N.Y.S.2d 266, reversed on other grounds, 27 A.D.2d 572, 276 N.Y.S.2d 168 Also see *People* v. *Beshany,* 43 Misc.2d 521, 252 N.Y.S.2d 110. While we have found no case on the point by New York's highest court, we need not pursue the question further because we have concluded that the statute is deficient on its face in other respects. Since petition clearly has standing to challenge the statute, being indisputably affected by it, we need not consider either the sufficiency of the affidavits upon which the eavesdrop orders were based, or the standing of petitioner to attack the search and seizure made thereunder.

The Fourth Amendment commands that a warrant issue not only upon probable cause supported by oath or affirmation, but also "particularly describing the place to be searched, and the persons or things to be seized." New York's statute lacks this particularization. It merely says that a warrant may issue on reasonable ground to believe that evidence of crime may be obtained by the eavesdrop. It lays down no requirement for particularity in the warrant as to what specific crime has been or is being committed, nor "the place to be searched," or "the persons or things to be seized" as specifically required by the Fourth Amendment. The need for particularity and evidence of reliability in the showing required when judicial authorization of a search is sought is especially great in the case of eavesdropping. By its very nature eavesdropping involves an intrusion on privacy that is broad in scope. As was said in *Osborn* v. *United States*, 385 U.S. 323 (1966), the "indiscriminate use of such devices in law enforcement raises grave constitutional questions under the Fourth and Fifth Amendments," and imposes "a heavier responsibility on this Court in its supervision of the fairness of procedures. . . ." There, two judges acting jointly authorized the installation of a device on the person of a prospective witness to record conversations between him and an attorney for a defendant then on trial in the United States District Court. The judicial authorization was based on an affidavit of the witness setting out in detail previous conversations between the witness and the attorney concerning the bribery of jurors in the case. The recording device was, as the Court said, authorized "under the most precise and discriminate circumstances, circumstances which fully met the 'requirement of particularity' " of the Fourth Amendment. The Court was asked to exclude the evidence of the recording of the conversations seized pursuant to the order on constitutional grounds, *Weeks* v. *United States*, *supra*, or in the exercise of supervisory power, *McNabb* v. *United States*, 318 U.S. 332 (1943). The Court refused to do so finding that the recording, although an invasion of the privacy protected by the Fourth Amendment, was admissible because of the authorization of the judges, based upon "a detailed factual affidavit alleging the commission of a specific criminal offense directly and immediately affecting the administration of justice . . . for the narrow and particularized purpose of ascertaining the truth of the affidavit's allegations." The invasion was lawful because there was sufficient proof to obtain a search warrant to make the search for the limited purpose outlined in the order of the judges. Through these "precise and discriminate" procedures the order authorizing the use of the electronic device afforded similar protections to those that are present in the use of conventional warrants authorizing the seizure of tangible evidence. Among other safeguards, the order described the type of conversation sought with particularity, thus indicating the specific objective of the Government in entering the constitutionally protected area and the limitations placed upon the officer executing the warrant. Under it the officer could not search unauthorized areas; likewise, once the property sought, and for which the order was issued, was found the officer could not use the order as a passkey to further search. In addition, the order authorized one limited intrusion rather than a series or a continuous surveillance. And, we note that a new order was issued when the officer sought to resume the search and probable cause was shown for the succeeding one. Moreover, the order was executed by the officer with dispatch, not over a prolonged and extended period. In this manner no greater invasion of privacy was permitted than was necessary under the circumstances. Finally the officer was required to and did make a return on the order showing how it was executed and what was seized. Through these strict precautions the danger of an unlawful search and seizure was minimized.

By contrast, New York's statute lays down no such "precise and discriminate" requirements. Indeed, it authorizes the "indiscriminate use" of electronic devices as specifically condemned in *Osborn.* "The proceeding by search warrant is a drastic one," *Sgro* v. *United States,* 287 U.S. 206, 210 (1932), and must be carefully circumscribed so as to prevent unauthorized invasions of "the sanctity of a man's home and the privacies of life." *Boyd* v. *United States,* 116 U.S. 616, 630. New York's broadside authorization rather than being "carefully circumscribed" so as to prevent unauthorized invasions of privacy actually permits general searches by electronic devices, the truly offensive character of which was first condemned in *Entick* v. *Carrington,* 19 How.St.Tr. 1029, and which were then known as "general warrants." The use of the latter was a motivating factor behind the Declaration of Independence. In view of the many cases commenting on the practice it is sufficient here to point out that under these "general warrants" customs officials were given blanket authority to conduct general searches for goods imported to the Colonies in violation of the tax laws of the Crown. The Fourth Amendment's requirement that a warrant "particularly describ[e] the place to be searched, and the persons or things to be seized," repudiated these general warrants and "makes general searches . . . impossible and prevents the seizure of one thing under a warrant describing another. As to what is to be taken, nothing is left to the discretion of the officer executing the warrant." *Marron* v. *United States,* 275 U.S. 192, 196 (1927); *Stanford* v. *Texas, supra.*

We believe the statute here is equally offensive. First, as we have mentioned, eavesdropping is authorized without requiring belief that any particular offense has been or is being committed; nor that the "property" sought, the conversations, be particularly described. The purpose of the probable-cause requirement of the Fourth Amendment, to keep the state out of constitutionally protected areas until it has reason to believe that a specific crime has been or is being committed, is thereby wholly aborted. Likewise the statute's failure to describe with particularity the conversations sought gives the officer a roving commission to "seize" any and all conversations. It is true that the statute requires the naming of "the person or persons whose communications, conversations or discussions are to be overheard or recorded. . . ." But this does no more than identify the person whose constitutionally protected area is to be invaded rather than "particularly describing" the communications, conversations, or discussions to be seized. As with general warrants this leaves too much to the discretion of the officer executing the order. Secondly, authorization of eavesdropping for a two-month period is the equivalent of a series of intrusions, searches, and seizures pursuant to a single showing of probable cause. Prompt execution is also avoided. During such a long and continuous (24 hours a day) period the conversations of any and all persons coming into the area covered by the device will be seized indiscriminately and without regard to their connection with the crime under investigation. Moreover, the statute permits, and there were authorized here, extensions of the original two-month period — presumably for two months each—on a mere showing that such extension is "in the public interest." Apparently the original grounds on which the eavesdrop order was initially issued also form the basis of the renewal. This we believe insufficient without a showing of present probable cause for the continuance of the eavesdrop. Third, the statute places no termination date on the eavesdrop once the conversation sought is seized. This is left entirely in the discretion of the officer. Finally, the statute's procedure, necessarily because its success depends on secrecy, has no requirement for notice as do conventional warrants, nor does it overcome this defect by requiring some showing of special facts. On the contrary, it permits uncontested entry without any showing of exigent circumstances. Such a showing of exigency, in order to avoid notice would appear more important in eavesdropping, with its inherent dangers, than that required when conventional procedures of search and seizure are utilized. Nor does the statute provide for a return on the warrant thereby leaving full discretion in the officer as to the use of seized conversations of innocent as well as guilty parties. In short, the statute's blanket grant of permission to eavesdrop is without adequate judicial supervision or protective procedures.

VI.

It is said with fervor that electronic eavesdropping is a most important technique of law enforcement and that outlawing it will severely cripple crime detection. The monumental report of the President's Commission on Law Enforcement and Administration of Justice entitled "The Challenge of Crime in a Free Society" informs us that the majority of law enforcement officials say that this is especially true in the detection of organized crime. As the Commission reports, there can be no question about the serious proportions of professional criminal activity in this country. However, we have found no empirical statistics on the use of electronic devices (bugging) in the fight against organized crime. Indeed, there are even figures available in the wiretap category which indicate to the contrary. See District Attorney Silver's Poll of New York Prosecutors, in

Dash, Schwartz & Knowlton, THE EAVESDROPPERS 105, 117–119 (1959). Also see Semerjian, *Proposals on Wiretapping in Light of Recent Senate Hearings*, 45 B.U.L. Rev 217, 229. As the Commission points out, "[w]iretapping was the mainstay of the New York attack against organized crime until Federal court decisions intervened. Recently chief reliance in some offices has been placed on bugging, where the information is to be used in court. Law enforcement officials believe that the successes achieved in some parts of the State are attributable primarily to a combination of dedicated and competent personnel and adequate legal tools; and that the failure to do more in New York has resulted primarily from the failure to commit additional resources of time and men," rather than electronic devices. Moreover, Brooklyn's District Attorney Silver's poll of the State of New York indicates that during the 12-year period (1942–1954) duly authorized wiretaps in bribery and corruption cases constituted only a small percentage of the whole. It indicates that this category involved only 10% of the total wiretaps. The overwhelming majority were in the categories of larceny, extortion, coercion, and blackmail, accounting for almost 50%. Organized gambling was about 11%. Statistics are not available on subsequent years. Dash, Schwartz & Knowlton, *supra*, at 40.

An often repeated statement of District Attorney Hogan of New York County was made at a hearing before the Senate Judiciary Committee at which he advocated the amendment of the Communications Act of 1934, supra, so as to permit "telephonic interception" of conversations. As he testified, "Federal statutory law [the 1934 Act] has been interpreted in such a way as to bar us from divulging wiretap evidence, even in the courtroom in the course of criminal prosecution." Mr. Hogan then said that "[w]ithout it [wiretaps] my own office could not have convicted" "top figures in the underworld." He then named nine persons his office had convicted and one on whom he had furnished "leads" secured from wiretaps to the authorities of New Jersey. Evidence secured from wiretaps, as Mr. Hogan said, was not admissible in "criminal prosecutions." He was advocating that the Congress adopt a measure that would make it admissible; Hearings on S. 2813 and S. 1495, before the Senate Committee on the Judiciary, 87 Cong., 2d Sess., pp. 173, 174 (1962). The President's Commission also emphasizes in its report the need for wiretapping in the investigation of organized crime because of the telephone's "relatively free use" by those engaged in the business and the difficulty of infiltrating their organizations. P. 201. The Congress, though long importuned, has not amended the 1934 Act to permit it.

We are also advised by the Solicitor General of the United States that the Federal Government has abandoned the use of electronic eavesdropping for "prosecutorial purposes." [Citations omitted.] Despite these actions of the Federal Government there has been no failure of law enforcement in that field.

As The Chief Justice said in concurring in the result in *Lopez* v. *United States,* 373 U.S. 427, "the fantastic advances in the field of electronic communications constitute a great danger to the privacy of the individual; . . . indiscriminate use of such devices in law enforcement raises grave constitutional questions under the Fourth and Fifth Amendments. . . ."

In any event we cannot forgive the requirements of the Fourth Amendment in the name of law enforcement. This is no formality that we require today but a fundamental rule that has long been recognized as basic to the privacy of every home in America. While "[t]he requirements of the Fourth Amendment are not inflexible, or obtusely unyielding to the legitimate needs of law enforcement," *Lopez* v. *United States, supra,* at 464, 83 S.Ct. at 1404 (dissenting opinion of BRENNAN, J.), it is not asking too much that officers be required to comply with the basic command of the Fourth Amendment before the innermost secrets of one's home or office are invaded. Few threats to liberty exist which are greater than that posed by the use of eavesdropping devices. Some may claim that without the use of such devices crime detection in certain areas may suffer some delays since eavesdropping is quicker, easier, and more certain. However, techniques and practices may well be developed that will operate just as speedily and certainly and—what is more important—without attending illegality.

It is said that neither a warrant nor a statute authorizing eavesdropping can be drawn so as to meet the Fourth Amendment's requirements. If that be true then the "fruits" of eavesdropping devices are barred under the Amendment. On the other hand this Court has in the past, under specific conditions and circumstances, sustained the use of eavesdropping devices. See *Goldman* v. *United States,* 316 U.S. 129; *On Lee* v. *United States,* 343 U.S. 747; *Lopez* v. *United States, supra;* and *Osborn* v. *United States, supra.* In the latter case the eavesdropping device was permitted where the "commission of a specific offense" was charged, its use was "under the most precise and discriminate circumstances" and the effective administration of justice in a federal court was at stake. The States are under no greater restrictions. The Fourth Amendment does not make the "precincts of the home or the office . . . sanctuaries where the law can never reach," DOUGLAS, J., dissenting in *Warden, Maryland Penitentiary* v. *Hayden,* 387 U.S. 294, 321, but it does prescribe a constitutional standard that must be met before official invasion is permissible. Our concern with the statute here is whether its language permits a trespassory invasion of the home or office, by general warrant, contrary to the command of the Fourth Amendment. As it is written, we believe that it does.

Reversed.

MR. JUSTICE DOUGLAS, concurring.

I join the opinion of the Court because at long last it overrules *sub silentio Olmstead* v. *United States*, 277 U.S. 438, and its offspring and brings wiretapping and other electronic eavesdropping fully within the purview of the Fourth Amendment. I also join the opinion because it condemns electronic surveillance, for its similarity to the general warrants out of which our Revolution sprang and allows a discreet surveillance only on a showing of "probable cause." These safeguards are minimal if we are to live under a regime of wiretapping and other electronic surveillance.

. . . .

That is the essence of my dissent in *Hayden*. In short, I do not see how any electronic surveillance that collects evidence or provides leads to evidence is or can be constitutional under the Fourth and Fifth Amendments. We could amend the Constitution and so provide—a step that would take us closer to the ideological group we profess to despise. Until the amending process ushers us into that kind of totalitarian regime, I would adhere to the protection of privacy with the Fourth Amendment, fashioned in Congress and submitted to the people, was designed to afford the individual. And unlike my BROTHER BLACK, I would adhere to *Mapp* v. *Ohio*, 367 U.S. 643, 81 S.Ct. 1684, 6 L.Ed.2d 1081, and apply the exclusionary rule in state as well as federal trials—a rule fashioned out of the Fourth Amendment and constituting a high constitutional barricade against the intrusion of Big Brother into the lives of all of us.

MR. JUSTICE STEWART, concurring in the result.

I fully agree with MR. JUSTICE BLACK, MR. JUSTICE HARLAN, and MR. JUSTICE WHITE that this New York law is entirely constitutional. In short, I think that "electronic eavesdropping, as *such* or as it is permitted by this statute, is not an unreasonable search and seizure." The statute contains many provisions more stringent than the Fourth Amendment generally requires, as MR. JUSTICE BLACK has so forcefully pointed out. And the petitioner himself has told us that the law's "reasonable grounds" requirement "is undisputedly equivalent to the probable cause requirement of the Fourth Amendment." This is confirmed by decisions of the New York courts. *People* v. *Cohen*, 42 Misc.2d 403, 248 N.Y.S. 2d 339; *People* v. *Beshany*, 43 Misc.2d 521, 252 N.Y.S.2d 110; *People* v. *Grossman*, 45 Misc.2d 557, 257 N.Y.S.2d 266. Of course, a state court's construction of a state statute is binding upon us.

In order to hold this statute unconstitutional, therefore, we would have to either rewrite the statute or rewrite the Constitution. I can only conclude that the Court today seems to have rewritten both.

The issue before us, as MR. JUSTICE WHITE says, is "whether *this* search complied with Fourth Amendment standards." For me that issue is an extremely close one in the circumstances of this case. It certainly cannot be resolved by incantation of ritual phrases like "general warrant." Its resolution involves "the unavoidable task in any search and seizure case: was the particular search and seizure reasonable or not?"

I would hold that the affidavits on which the judicial order issued in this case did not constitute a showing of probable cause adequate to justify the authorizing order. The need for particularity and evidence of reliability in the showing required when judicial authorization is sought for the kind of electronic eavesdropping involved in this case is especially great. The standard of reasonableness embodied in the Fourth Amendment demands that the showing of justification match the degree of intrusion. By its very nature electronic eavesdropping for a 60-day period, even of a specified office, involves a broad invasion of a constitutionally protected area. Only the most precise and rigorous standard of probable cause should justify an intrusion of this sort. I think the affidavits presented to the judge who authorized the electronic surveillance of the Steinman office failed to meet such a standard.

So far as the record shows, the only basis for the Steinman order consisted of two affidavits. One of them contained factual allegations supported only by bare, unexplained references to "evidence" in the district attorney's office and "evidence" obtained by the Neyer eavesdrop. No underlying facts were presented on the basis of which the judge could evaluate these general allegations. The second affidavit was no more than a statement of another assistant district attorney that he had read his associate's affidavit and was satisfied on that basis alone that proper grounds were presented for the issuance of an authorizing order.

This might be enough to satisfy the standards of the Fourth Amendment for a conventional search or arrest. Cf. *Aguilar* v. *Texas,* 378 U.S. 108, 116 (dissenting opinion). But I think it was constitutionally insufficient to constitute probable cause to justify an intrusion of the scope and duration that was permitted in this case.

Accordingly, I would reverse the judgment.

MR. JUSTICE BLACK, dissenting.

There is yet another reason why I would adhere to the holding of *Olmstead* that the Fourth Amendment does not apply to eavesdropping. Since the Framers in the first clause of the Amendment specified that only persons, houses, and things were to be protected, they obviously wrote the second clause, regulating search warrants, in reference only to such tangible things. To hold, as the Court does, that the first clause protects words, necessitates either a virtual rewriting of the particularity requirements of the Warrant Clause or a literal application of that clause's requirements and our cases construing them to situations they were never designed to cover. I am convinced that the Framers of the Amendment never intended this Court to do either, and yet it seems to me clear that the Court here does a little of both.

V.

Both the States and the National Government are at present confronted with a crime problem that threatens the peace, order, and tranquility of the people. There are, as I have pointed out, some constitutional commands that leave no room for doubt—certain procedures must be followed by courts regardless of how much more difficult they make it to convict and punish for crime. These commands we should enforce firmly and to the letter. But my objection to what the Court does today is the picking out of a broad general provision against unreasonable searches and seizures and the erecting out of it a constitutional obstacle against electronic eavesdropping that makes it impossible for lawmakers to overcome. Honest men may rightly differ on the potential dangers or benefits inherent in electronic eavesdropping and wiretapping. See *Lopez* v. *United States, supra*. But that is the very reason that legislatures, like New York's should be left free to pass laws about the subject, rather than be told that the Constitution forbids it on grounds no more forceful than the Court has been able to muster in this case.

MR. JUSTICE HARLAN, dissenting.

The Court in recent years has more and more taken to itself sole responsibility for setting the pattern of criminal law enforcement throughout the country. Time-honored distinctions between the constitutional protections afforded against federal authority by the Bill of Rights and those provided against state action by the Fourteenth Amendment have been obliterated, thus increasingly subjecting state criminal law enforcement policies to oversight by this Court. See, e.g., *Mapp* v. *Ohio*, 367 U.S. 643; *Ker* v. *California*, 374 U.S. 23; *Malloy* v. *Hogan*, 378 U.S. 1; *Murphy* v. *Waterfront Commission*, 378 U.S. 52. Newly contrived constitutional rights have been established without any apparent concern for the empirical process that goes with legislative reform. See, e.g., *Miranda* v. *Arizona*, 384 U.S. 436. And overlying the particular decisions to which this course has given rise is the fact that, short of future action by this Court, their impact can only be undone or modified by the slow and uncertain process of constitutional amendment.

Today's decision is in this mold. Despite the fact that the use of electronic eavesdropping devices as instruments of criminal law enforcement is currently being comprehensively addressed by the Congress and various other bodies in the country, the Court has chosen, quite unnecessarily, to decide this case in a manner which will seriously restrict, if not entirely thwart, such efforts, and will freeze further progress in this field, except as the Court may itself act or a constitutional amendment may set things right.

In my opinion what the Court is

doing is very wrong, and I must respectfully dissent.

. . . .

MR. JUSTICE WHITE, dissenting.

With all due respect, I dissent from the majority's decision which unjustifiably strikes down "on its face" a 1938 New York statute applied by state officials in securing petitioner's conviction. In addition, I find no violation of petitioner's constitutional rights and I would affirm.

. . . .

[MR. JUSTICE WHITE's opinion includes a complete discussion of previous cases and a reprint of the President's Commission report.]

OMNIBUS CRIME CONTROL AND SAFE STREETS ACT OF 1968
as amended by
ELECTRONIC COMMUNICATIONS PRIVACY ACT OF 1986

Codified at United States Code Title 18, Sections 2510-2521

Chapter 119 -- WIRE AND ELECTRONIC COMMUNICATIONS INTERCEPTION AND INTERCEPTION OF ORAL COMMUNICATIONS

§2510. Definitions

As used in this chapter--

(1) "wire communication" means any aural transfer made in whole or in part through the use of facilities for the transmission of communications by the aid of wire, cable, or other like connection between the point of origin and the point of reception (including the use of such connection in a switching station) furnished or operated by any person engaged in providing or operating such facilities for the transmission of interstate or foreign communications or communications affecting interstate or foreign commerce and such term includes any electronic storage of such communication, but such term does not include the radio portion of a cordless telephone communication that

is transmitted between the cordless telephone handset and the base unit;

(2) "oral communication" means any oral communication uttered by a person exhibiting an expectation that such communication is not subject to interception under circumstances justifying such expectation, but such term does not include any electronic communication;

(3) "State" means any State of the United States, the District of Columbia, the Commonwealth of Puerto Rico, and any territory or possession of the United States;

(4) "intercept" means the aural or other acquisition of the contents of any wire, electronic, or oral communication through the use of any electronic, mechanical, or other device.

(5) "electronic, mechanical, or other device" means any device or apparatus which can be used to intercept a wire, oral, or electronic communication other than--

(a) any telephone or telegraph instrument, equipment or facility, or any component thereof,

(i) furnished to the subscriber or user by a provider of wire or electronic communication service in the ordinary course of its business and being used by the subscriber or user in the ordinary course of its business or furnished by such subscriber or user for connection to the facilities of such service and used in the ordinary course of its business; or

(ii) being used by a provider of wire or electronic communication service in the ordinary course of its business, or by an investigative or law enforcement officer in the ordinary course of his duties;

(6) "person" means any employee, or agent of the United States or any State or political subdivision thereof, and any individual, partnership, association, joint stock company, trust, or corporation;

(7) "Investigative or law enforcement officer" means any officer of the United States or of a State or political subdivision thereof, who is empowered by law to conduct investigations of or to make arrests for offenses enumerated in this chapter, and any attorney authorized by law to prosecute or participate in the prosecution of such offenses;

(8) "contents", when used with respect to any wire, oral, or electronic communication, includes any information concerning the substance, purport, or meaning of that communication;

(9) "Judge of competent jurisdiction" means--

(a) a judge of a United States district court or a United States court of appeals; and

(b) a judge of any court of general criminal jurisdiction of a State who is authorized by a statute of that State to enter orders authorizing interceptions of wire, oral, or electronic communications.

(10) "communication common carrier" shall have the same meaning which is given the term "common carrier" by section 153(h) of title 47 of the United States Code;

(11) "aggrieved person" means a person who was a party to any intercepted wire, oral, or electronic communication or a person against whom the interception was directed;

(12) "electronic communication" means any transfer of signs, signals, writing, images, sounds, data, or intelligence or any nature transmitted in whole or in part by a wire, radio, elec-

tromagnetic, photoelectronic or photooptical system that affects interstate or foreign commerce, but does not include--

(A) the radio portion of a cordless telephone communication that is transmitted between the cordless telephone handset and the base unit;

(B) any wire or oral communication;

(C) any communication made through a tone-only paging device; or

(D) any communication from a tracking device (as defined in section 3117 of this title);

(13) "user" means any person or entity who--

(A) uses an electronic communication service; and

(B) is duly authorized by the provider of such service to engage in such use;

(14) "electronic communications system" means any wire, radio, electromagnetic, photooptical or photoelectronic facilities for the transmission of electronic communications, and any computer facilities or related electronic equipment for the electronic storage of such communications;

(15) "electronic communication service" means any service which provides to users thereof the ability to send or receive wire or electronic communications;

(16) "readily accessible to the general public" means, with respect to a radio communication, that such communication is not--

(A) scrambled or encrypted;

(B) transmitted using modulation techniques whose essential parameters have been withheld from the public with the intention of preserving the privacy of such communication;

(C) carried on a subcarrier or other signal subsidiary to a radio transmission;

(D) transmitted over a communication system provided by a common carrier, unless the communication is a tone only paging system communication; or

(E) transmitted on frequencies allocated under part 25, subpart D, E, or F of part 74 or part 94 of the Rules of the Federal Communications Commission, unless, in the case of a communication transmitted on a frequency allocated under part 74 that is not exclusively allocated to broadcast auxiliary services, the communication is a two-way voice communication by radio;

(17) "electronic storage" means--

(A) any temporary, intermediate storage of a wire or electronic communication incidental to the electronic transmission thereof; and

(B) any storage of such communication by an electronic communication service for purposes of backup protection of such communication; and

(18) "aural transfer" means a transfer containing the human voice at any point between and including the point of origin and the point of reception.

§2511. Interception and disclosure of wire, oral, or electronic communications prohibited

(1) Except as otherwise specifically provided in this chapter any person who--

(a) Intentionally intercepts, endeavors to intercept, or procures any other person to intercept or endeavor to intercept, any wire, oral, or electronic communication;

(b) intentionally uses, endeavors to use, or procures any other person to use or endeavor to use any electronic, mechanical, or other device to intercept any oral communication when--

(i) such device is affixed to, or otherwise transmits a signal through, a wire, cable, or other like connection used in wire communication; or

(ii) such device transmits communications by radio, or interferes with the transmission of such communications; or

(iii) such person knows, or has reason to know, that such device or any component thereof has been sent through the mail or transported in interstate or foreign commerce; or

(iv) such use or endeavor to use (A) takes place on the premises of any business or other commercial establishment the operations of which affect interstate or foreign commerce; or (B) obtains or is for the purpose of obtaining information relating to the operations of any business or other commercial establishment the operations of which affect interstate or foreign commerce; or

(v) such person acts in the District of Columbia, the Commonwealth of Puerto Rico, or any territory or possession of the United States;

(c) intentionally discloses, or endeavors to disclose to any other person the contents of any wire, oral, or electronic communication, knowing or having reason to know that the information was obtained through the interception of a wire, oral, or electronic communication in violation of this subsection;

(d) intentionally uses, or endeavors to use, the contents of any wire, oral, or electronic communication, knowing or having reason to know that the information was obtained through the interception of a wire, oral, or electronic communication in violation of this subsection;

shall be punished as provided in subsection (4) or shall be subject to suit as provided in subsection (5).

(2)(a)(i) It shall not be unlawful under this chapter for an operator of a switchboard, or an officer, employee, or agent of a provider of wire or electronic communication service, whose facilities are used in the transmission of a wire communication, to intercept, disclose, or use that communication in the normal course of his employment while engaged in any activity which is a necessary incident to the rendition of his service or to the protection of the rights or property of the provider of that service, except that a provider of wire communication service to the public shall not utilize service observing or random monitoring except for mechanical or service quality control checks.

(ii) Notwithstanding any other law, providers of wire or electronic communication service, their officers, employees, and agents, landlords, custodians, or other persons, are authorized to provide information, facilities, or technical assistance to persons authorized by law to intercept wire, oral, or electronic communications or to conduct electronic surveillance, as defined in section 101 of the Foreign Intelligence Surveillance Act of 1978, if such provider, its officers, employees, or agents, landlord, custodian, or other specified person, has been provided with--

(A) a court order directing such assistance signed by the authorizing judge, or

(B) a certification in writing by a person specified in section 2518(7) of this title or the Attorney General of the United States that no warrant or court order is required by law, that all statutory requirements have been met, and that the specified assistance is required,

setting forth the period of time during which the provision of the information, facilities, or technical assistance is authorized and specifying the information, facilities, or technical assistance required. No provider of wire or electronic communication service, officer, employee, or agent thereof, or landlord, custodian, or other specified person shall disclose the existence of any interception or surveillance or the device used to accomplish the interception or surveillance with respect to which the person has been furnished a court order or certification under this chapter, except as may otherwise be required by legal process and then only after prior notification to the Attorney General or to the principal prosecuting attorney of a State or any political subdivision of a State, as may be appropriate. Any such disclosure, shall render such person liable for the civil damages provided for in section 2520. No cause of action shall lie in any court against any provider of wire or electronic communication service, its officers, employees, or agents, landlord, custodian, or other specified person for providing information, facilities, or assistance in accordance with the terms of a court order or certification under this chapter.

(b) It shall not be unlawful under this chapter for an officer, employee, or agent of the Federal Communications Commission, in the normal course of his employment and in discharge of the monitoring responsibilities exercised by the Commission in the enforcement of chapter 5 of title 47 of the United States Code, to intercept a wire or electronic communication, or oral communication transmitted by radio, or to disclose or use the information thereby obtained.

(c) It shall not be unlawful under this chapter for a person acting under color of law to intercept a wire, oral, or electronic communication, where such person is a party to the communication or one of the parties to the communication has given prior consent to such interception.

(d) It shall not be unlawful under this chapter for a person not acting under color of law to intercept a wire, oral, or electronic communication where one of the parties to the communication has given prior consent to such interception unless such communication is intercepted for the purpose of committing any criminal or tortious act in violation of the Constitution or laws of the United States or of any State.

(e) Notwithstanding any other provision of this title or section 705 or 706 of the Communications Act of 1934, it shall not be unlawful for an officer, employee, or agent of the United States in the normal course of his official duty to conduct electronic surveillance, as defined in section 101 of the

Foreign Intelligence Surveillance Act of 1978, as authorized by that Act.

(f) Nothing contained in this chapter or chapter 121, or section 705 of the Communications Act of 1934, shall be deemed to affect the acquisition by the United States Government of foreign intelligence information from international or foreign communications, or foreign intelligence activities conducted in accordance with otherwise applicable Federal law involving a foreign electronic communications system, utilizing a means other than electronic surveillance as defined in section 101 of the Foreign Intelligence Surveillance Act of 1978, and procedures in this chapter or chapter 121 and the Foreign Intelligence Surveillance Act of 1978 shall be exclusive means by which electronic surveillance, as defined in section 101 of such Act, and the interception of domestic wire and oral communications may be conducted.

(g) It shall not be unlawful under this chapter or chapter 121 of this title for any person--

(i) to intercept or access an electronic communication made through an electronic communication system that is configured so that such electronic communication is readily accessible to the general public;

(ii) to intercept any radio communication which is transmitted--

(I) by any station for the use of the general public, or that related to ships, aircraft, vehicles, or persons in distress;

(II) by any governmental, law enforcement, civil defense, private land mobile, or public safety communications system, including police and fire, readily accessible to the general public;

(III) by a station operating on an authorized frequency within the bands allocated to the amateur, citizens band, or general mobile radio services; or

(IV) by any marine or aeronautical communications system;

(iii) to engage in any conduct which--

(I) is prohibited by section 633 of the Communications Act of 1934; or

(II) is excepted from the application of section 705(a) of the Communications Act of 1934 by section 705(b) of that Act;

(iv) to intercept any wire or electronic communication the transmission of which is causing harmful interference to any lawfully operating station or consumer electronic equipment, to the extent necessary to identify the source of such interference; or

(v) for other users of the same frequency to intercept any radio communication made through a system that utilizes frequencies monitored by individuals engaged in the provision or the use of such system, if such communication is not scrambled or encrypted.

(h) It shall not be unlawful under this chapter--

(i) to use a pen register or a trap and trace device (as those terms are defined for the purposes of chapter 206 (relating to pen registers and trap and trace devices) of this title); or

(ii) for a provider of electronic communication service to record the fact that a wire or electronic communication was initiated or completed in order to protect such provider, another provider furnishing service toward the completion of the wire or electronic communication, or a user of that service, from fraudulent, unlawful or abusive use of such service.

(3)(a) Except as provided in paragraph (b) of this subsection, a person or entity providing an electronic communication service to the public shall not intentionally divulge the contents of any communication (other than one to such person or entity, or an agent thereof) while in transmission on that service to any person or entity other than an addressee or intended recipient of such communication or an agent of such addressee or intended recipient.

(b) A person or entity providing electronic communication service to the public may divulge the contents of any such communication--

(i) as otherwise authorized in section 2511(2)(a) or 2517 of this title;

(ii) with the lawful consent of the originator or any addressee or intended recipient of such communication;

(iii) to a person employed or authorized, or whose facilities are used, to forward such communication to its destination; or

(iv) which were inadvertently obtained by the service provider and which appear to pertain to the commission of a crime, if such divulgence is made to a law enforcement agency.

(4)(a) Except as provided in paragraph (b) of this subsection or in subsection (5), whoever violates subsection (1) of this section shall be fined under this title or imprisoned not more than five years, or both.

(b) If the offense is a first offense under paragraph (a) of this subsection and is not for a tortious or illegal purpose or for purposes of direct or indirect commercial advantage or private commercial gain, and the wire or electronic communication with respect to which the offense under paragraph (a) is a radio communication that is not scrambled or encrypted, then--

(i) if the communication is not the radio portion of a cellular telephone communication, a public land mobile radio service communication or a paging service communication, and the conduct is not that described in subsection (5), the offender shall be fined under this title or imprisoned not more than one year, or both; and

(ii) if the communication is the radio portion of a cellular telephone communication, a public land mobile radio service communication or a paging service communication, the offender shall be fined not more than $500.

(c) Conduct otherwise an offense under this subsection that consists of or relates to the interception of a satellite transmission that is not encrypted or scrambled and that is transmitted--

(i) to a broadcasting station for purposes of retransmission to the general public; or

(ii) as an audio subcarrier intended for redistribution to facilities open to the public, but not including data transmissions or telephone calls, is not an offense under this subsection unless the conduct is for the purposes of direct or indirect commercial advantage or private financial gain.

(5)(a)(i) If the communication is--

(A) a private satellite video communication that is not scrambled or encrypted and the conduct in violation of this chapter is the private viewing of that communication and is not for a tortious or illegal purpose or for purposes of direct or indirect commercial advantage or private commercial gain; or

(B) a radio communication that is transmitted on frequencies allocated under subpart D of part 74 of the rules of the Federal Communications Commission that is not scrambled or encrypted and the conduct in violation of this chapter is not for a tortious or illegal purpose or for purposes of direct or indirect commercial advantage or private commercial gain,

then the person who engages in such conduct shall be subject to suit by the Federal Government in a court of competent jurisdiction.

(ii) In an action under this subsection--

(A) if the violation of this chapter is a first offense for the person under paragraph (a) of subsection (4) or such person has not been found liable in a civil action under section 2520 of this title, the Federal Government shall be entitled to appropriate injunctive relief; and

(B) if the violation of this chapter is a second or subsequent offense under paragraph (a) of subsection (4) or such person has been found liable in any prior civil action under section 2520, the person shall be subject to a mandatory $500 civil fine.

(b) The court may use any means within its authority to enforce an injunction issued under paragraph (ii)(A), and shall impose a civil fine of not less than $500 for each violation of such an injunction.

***

§ 2512. Manufacture, distribution, possession, and advertising of wire, oral, or electronic communication intercepting devices prohibited

(1) Except as otherwise specifically provided in this chapter, any person who intentionally--

(a) sends through the mail, or sends or carries in interstate or foreign commerce, any electronic, mechanical, or other device, knowing or having reason to know that the design of such device renders it primarily useful for the purpose of the surreptitious interception of wire, oral, or electronic communications;

(b) manufactures, assembles, possesses, or sells any electronic, mechanical, or other device, knowing or having reason to know that the design of such device renders it primarily useful for the purpose of the surreptitious interception of wire, oral, or electronic communications, and that such device or any component thereof has been or will be sent through the mail or transported in interstate or foreign commerce; or

(c) places in any newspaper, magazine, handbill, or other

publication any advertisement of--

(i) any electronic, mechanical, or other device knowing or having reason to know that the design of such device renders it primarily useful for the purpose of the surreptitious interception of wire, oral, or electronic communications; or

(ii) any other electronic, mechanical, or other device, where such advertisement promotes the use of such device for the purpose of the surreptitious interception of wire, oral, or electronic communications,

knowing or having reason to know that such advertisement will be sent through the mail or transported in interstate or foreign commerce,

shall be fined not more than $10,000 or imprisoned not more than five years, or both.

(2) It shall not be unlawful under this section for--

(a) a provider of wire or electronic communication service or an officer, agent, or employee of, or a person under contract with, such a provider, in the normal course of the business of providing that wire or electronic communication service, or

(b) an officer, agent, or employee of, or a person under contract with, the United States, a State, or a political subdivision thereof, in the normal course of the activities of the United States, a State or a political subdivision thereof, to send through the mail, send or carry in interstate or foreign commerce, or manufacture, assemble, possess, or sell any electronic, mechanical, or other device knowing or having reason to know that the design of such device renders it primarily useful for the purpose of the surreptitious interception of wire, oral, or electronic communications.

§2513. Confiscation of wire or oral communication intercepting devices

Any electronic, mechanical, or other device used, sent, carried, manufactured, assembled, possessed, sold, or advertised in violation of section 2511 or section 2512 of this chapter may be seized and forfeited to the United States. All provisions of law relating to (1) the seizure, summary and judicial forfeiture, and condemnation of vessels, vehicles, merchandise, and baggage for violations of the customs laws contained in title 19 of the United States Code, (2) the disposition of such vessels, vehicles, merchandise, and baggage or the proceeds from the sale thereof, (3) the remission or mitigation of such forfeiture, (4) the compromise of claims, and (5) the award of compensation to informers in respect of such forfeitures, shall apply to seizures and forfeitures incurred, or alleged to have been incurred, under the provisions of this section, insofar as applicable and not inconsistent with the provisions of this section; except that such duties as are imposed upon the collector of customs or any other person with respect to the seizure and forfeiture of vessels, vehicles, merchandise, and baggage under the provisions of the customs laws contained in title 19 of the United States Code shall be performed with respect to seizure and forfeiture of electronic, mechanical, or other intercepting devices under this section by such officers, agents, or other persons as may be authorized or designated for that purpose by the Attorney General.

[§ 2514. Repealed. Pub. L. 91-452, title II, § 227(a), Oct. 15, 1970, 84 Stat. 930]

Section, Pub. L. 90-351, title II, § 802, June 19, 1968, 82 Stat. 216, provided for immunity of witnesses giving testimony or producing evidence under compulsion in Federal grand jury or court proceedings.

§2515. Prohibition of use as evidence of intercepted wire or oral communications

Whenever any wire or oral communication has been intercepted, no part of the contents of such communication and no evidence derived therefrom may be received in evidence in any trial, hearing, or other proceeding in or before any court, grand jury, department, officer, agency, regulatory body, legislative committee, or other authority of the United States, a State, or a political subdivision thereof if the disclosure of that information would be in violation of this chapter.
(Added Pub. L. 90-351, title III, § 802, June 19, 1968, 82 Stat. 216.)

§2516. Authorization for interception of wire, oral, or electronic communications

(1) The Attorney General, Deputy Attorney General, Associate Attorney General, any Assistant Attorney General, any acting Assistant Attorney General, or any Deputy Assistant Attorney General in the Criminal Division, specially designated by the Attorney General, may authorize an application to a Federal judge of competent jurisdiction for, and such judge may grant in conformity with section 2518 of this chapter an order authorizing or approving the interception of wire or oral communications by the Federal Bureau of Investigation, or a Federal agency having responsibility for the investigation of the offense as to which the application is made, when such interception may provide or has provided evidence of--

(a) any offense punishable by death or by imprisonment for more than one year under sections 2274 through 2277 of title 42 of the United States Code (relating to the enforcement of the Atomic Energy Act of 1954), section 2284 of title 42 of the United States Code (relating to sabotage of nuclear facilities or fuel), or under the following chapters of this title: chapter 37 (relating to espionage), chapter 105 (relating to sabotage), chapter 115 (relating to treason), chapter 102 (relating to riots), chapter 65 (relating to malicious mischief), chapter 111 (relating to destruction of vessels), or chapter 81 (relating to privacy);

(b) a violation of section 186 or section 501(c) of title 29, United States Code (dealing with restrictions on payments and loans to labor organizations), or any offense which involves murder, kidnapping, robbery, or extortion, and which is punishable under this title;

(c) any offense which is punishable under the following sections of this title: section 201 (bribery of public officials and witnesses), section 224 (bribery in sporting contests), subsection (d), (e), (f), (g), (h), or (i) of section 844 (unlawful use of explosives), section 1084 (transmission of wagering information), section 751 (relating to escape), section 1503, 1512, and 1513 (influencing or injuring an officer, juror, or witness generally), section 1510 (obstruction of criminal investigations), section 1511 (obstruction of State or local law enforcement), section 1751, (Presidential and Presidential staff assassination, kidnaping, and assault), section 1951 (interference with commerce by threats or violence), section 1952 (interstate and foreign travel or transportation in aid of racketeering enterprises), section 1952A (relating to use of interstate commerce facilities in the commission of murder for hire), section 1952B (relating to violent crimes in aid of racketeering activity), section 1954 (offer, acceptance, or solicitation to influence operations of employee benefit plan), section 1955 (prohibition of business enterprises of gambling), section 1956 (laundering of monetary instruments), section 1957 (relating to engaging in monetary transactions in property derived from specified unlawful activity), section 659 (theft from interstate shipment), section 664 (embezzlement from pension and welfare funds), section 1343 (fraud by wire, radio, or television), section 2252 or 2253 (sexual exploitation of children), sections 2251 and 2252 (sexual exploitation of children), sections 2312, 2313, 2314, and 2315 (interstate transportation of stolen property), the second section 2320 (relating to trafficking in certain motor vehicles or motor vehicle parts), section 1203 (relating to hostage taking), section 1029 (relating to fraud and related activity in connection with access devices), section 3146 (relating to penalty for failure to appear), section 3521(b)(3) (relating to witness relocation and assistance), section 32 (relating to destruction of aircraft or aircraft facilities), section 1963 (violations with respect to racketeer influenced and corrupt organizations), section 115 (relating to threatening or retaliating against a Federal Official), the section in chapter 65 relating to destruction of an energy facility, and section 1341 (relating to mail fraud), section 351 (violations with respect to congressional, Cabinet, or Supreme Court assassinations, kidnaping, and assault), section 831 (relating to prohibited transactions involving nuclear materials), section 33 (relating to destruction of motor vehicles or motor vehicle facilities), or section 1992 (relating to wrecking trains);

(d) any offense involving counterfeiting punishable under section 471, 472, or 473 of this title;

(e) any offense involving fraud connected with a case under title 11 or the manufacture, importation, receiving, concealment, buying, selling, or otherwise dealing in narcotic drugs, marihuana, or other dangerous drugs, punishable under any law of the United States;

(f) any offense including extortionate credit transactions under sections 892, 893, of 894 of this title;

(g) a violation of section 5322 of title 31. United States Code (dealing with the reporting of currency transactions);

(h) any felony violation of sections 2511 and 2512 (relating to interception and disclosure of certain communications and to certain intercepting devices) of this title;

(i) any violation of section 1679a(c)(2) (relating to destruction of a natural gas pipeline) or subsection (i) or (n) of section 1472 (relating to aircraft piracy) of title 49 of the United States Code;

(j) any criminal violation of section 2778 of title 22 (relating to the Arms Export Control Act); or

(k) the location of any fugitive from justice from an offense described in this section;

(l) any conspiracy to commit any of the foregoing offenses.

(2) The principal prosecuting attorney of any State, or the principal prosecuting attorney of any political subdivision thereof, if such attorney is authorized by a statute of that State to make application to a State court judge of competent jurisdiction for an order authorizing or approving the interception of wire, oral, or electronic communications, may apply to such judge for, and such judge may grant in conformity with section 2518 of this chapter and with the applicable State statute an order authorizing, or approving the interception of wire, oral, or electronic communications by investigative or law enforcement officers having responsibility for the investigation of the offense as to which the application is made, when such interception may provide or has provided evidence of the commission of the offense of murder, kidnapping, gambling, robbery, bribery, extortion, or dealing in narcotic drugs, marihuana or other dangerous drugs, or other crime dangerous to life, limb, or property, and punishable by imprisonment for more than one year, designated in any applicable State statute authorizing such interception, or any conspiracy to commit any of the of foregoing offenses.

(3) Any attorney for the Government (as such term is defined for the purposes of the Federal Rules of Criminal Procedure) may authorize an application to a Federal judge of competent jurisdiction for, and such judge may grant, in conformity with section 2518 of this title, an order authorizing or approving the interception of electronic communications by an investigative or law enforcement officer having responsibility for the investigation of the offense as to which the application is made, when such interception may provide or has provided evidence of any Federal felony.

§ 2517. Authorization for disclosure and use of intercepted wire, oral, or electronic communications

(1) Any investigative or law enforcement officer who, by any means authorized by this chapter, has obtained knowledge of the contents of any wire, oral, or electronic communication, or evidence derived therefrom, may disclose such contents to another investigative or law enforcement officer to the extent that such disclosure is appropriate to the proper performance of the official duties of the officer making or receiving the disclosure.

(2) Any investigative or law enforcement officer who, by any means authorized by this chapter, has ob-

tained knowledge of the contents of any wire, oral, or electronic communication or evidence derived therefrom may use such contents to the extent such use is appropriate to the proper performance of his official duties.

(3) Any person who has received, by any means authorized by this chapter, any information concerning a wire, oral, or electronic communication, or evidence derived therefrom intercepted in accordance with the provisions of this chapter may disclose the contents of that communication or such derivative evidence while giving testimony under oath or affirmation in any proceeding held under the authority of the United States or of any State or political subdivision thereof.

(4) No otherwise privileged wire, oral, or electronic communication intercepted in accordance with, or in violation of, the provisions of this chapter shall lose its privileged character.

(5) When an investigative or law enforcement officer, while engaged in intercepting wire, oral, or electronic communications in the manner authorized herein, intercepts wire, oral, or electronic communications relating to offenses other than those specified in the order of authorization or approval, the contents thereof, and evidence derived therefrom may be disclosed or used as provided in subsections (1) and (2) of this section. Such contents and any evidence derived therefrom may be used under subsection (3) of this section when authorized or approved by a judge of competent jurisdiction where such judge finds on subsequent application that the contents were otherwise intercepted in accordance with the provisions of this chapter. Such application shall be made as soon as practicable.

§2518. Procedure for interception of wire, oral, or electronic communications

(1) Each application for an order authorizing or approving the interception of a wire, oral, or electronic communication under this chapter shall be made in writing upon oath or affirmation to a judge of competent jurisdiction and shall state the applicant's authority to make such application. Each application shall include the following information:

(a) the identity of the investigative or law enforcement officer making the application, and the officer authorizing the application;

(b) a full and complete statement of the facts and circumstances relied upon by the applicant, to justify his belief that an order should be issued, including (i) details as to the particular offense that has been, is being, or is about to be committed, (ii) except as provided in subsection (11), a particular description of the nature and location of the facilities from which or the place where the communication is to be intercepted (iii) a particular description of the type of communications sought to be intercepted, (iv) the identity of the person, if known, committing the offense and whose communications are to be intercepted;

(c) a full and complete statement as to whether or not other investigative procedures have been tried and failed or why they reasonably appear to be unlikely to succeed if tried or to be too dangerous;

(d) a statement of the period of time for which the interception is required to be maintained. If the nature of the investigation is such that the authorization for interception should not automatically terminate when the described type of communication has been first obtained, a particular description of facts establishing probable cause to believe that additional communications of the same type will occur thereafter;

(e) a full and complete statement of the facts concerning all previous applications known to the individual authorizing and making the application, made to any judge for authorization to intercept, or for approval of interceptions of wire, oral, or electronic communications involving any of the same persons, facilities or places specified in the application, and the action taken by the judge on each such application; and

(f) where the application is for the extension of an order, a statement setting forth the results thus far obtained from the interception, or a reasonable explanation of the failure to obtain such results.

(2) The judge may require the applicant to furnish additional testimony or documentary evidence in support of the application.

(3) Upon such application the judge may enter an ex parte order, as requested or as modified, authorizing or approving interception of wire, oral, or electronic communications within the territorial jurisdiction of the court in which the judge is sitting (and outside that jurisdiction but within the United States in the case of a mobile interception device authorized by a Federal court within such jurisdiction), if the judge determines on the basis of the facts submitted by the applicant that--

(a) there is probable cause for belief that an individual is committing, has committed, or is about to commit a particular offense enumerated in section 2516 of this chapter;

(b) there is probable cause for belief that particular communications concerning that offense will be obtained through such interception;

(c) normal investigative procedures have been tried and have failed or reasonably appear to be unlikely to succeed if tried or to be too dangerous;

(d) except as provided in subsection (11), there is probable cause for belief that the facilities from which, or the place where, the wire, oral, or electronic communications are to be intercepted are being used, or are about to be used, in connection with the commission of such offense, or are leased to, listed in the name of, or commonly used by such person.

(4) Each order authorizing or approving the interception of any wire, oral, or electronic communication under this chapter shall specify:

(a) the identity of the person, if known, whose communications are to be intercepted;

(b) the nature and location of the communications facilities as to which, or the place where, authority to intercept is granted;

(c) a particular description of the type of communication sought to be intercepted, and a statement of the particular offense to which it relates;

(d) the identity of the agency authorized to intercept the communications, and of the person authorizing the application; and

(e) the period of time during which such interception is authorized, including a statement as to whether or not the interception shall automatically terminate when the described communication has been first obtained.

An order authorizing the interception of a wire, oral, or electronic communication under this chapter shall, upon request of the applicant, direct that a provider of wire or electronic communication service, landlord, custodian or other person shall furnish the applicant forthwith all information, facilities, and technical assistance necessary to accomplish the interception unobtrusively and with a minimum of interference with the services that such service provider, landlord, custodian, or person is according the person whose communications are to be intercepted. Any provider of wire or electronic communications, service, landlord, custodian or other person furnishing such facilities or technical assistance shall be compensated therefor by the applicant for reasonable expenses incurred in providing such facilities or assistance.

(5) No order entered under this section may authorize or approve the interception of any wire, oral, or electronic communication for any period longer than is necessary to achieve the objective of the authorization, nor in any event longer than thirty days. Such thirty-day period begins on the earlier of the day on which the investigative or law enforcement officer first begins to conduct an interception under the order or ten days after the order is entered. Extensions of an order may be granted, but only upon application for an extension made in accordance with subsection (1) of this section and the court making the findings required by subsection (3) of this section. The period of extension shall be no longer than the authorizing judge deems necessary to achieve the purposes for which it was granted and in no event for longer than thirty days. Every order and extension thereof shall contain a provision that the authorization to intercept shall be executed as soon as practicable, shall be conducted in such a way as to minimize the interception of communications not otherwise subject to interception under this chapter, and must terminate upon attainment of the authorized objective, or in any event in thirty days. In the event the intercepted communication is in a code or foreign language, and an expert in that foreign language or code is not reasonably available during the interception period, minimization may be accomplished as soon as practicable after such interception. An interception under this chapter may be conducted in whole or in part by Government personnel, or by an individual operating under a contract with the Government, acting under the supervision of an investigative or law enforcement officer authorized to conduct the interception.

(6) Whenever an order authorizing interception is entered pursuant to this chapter, the order may require reports to be made to the judge who issued the order showing what progress has been made toward achievement of the authorized objective and the need for continued interception. Such reports shall be made at such intervals as the judge may require.

(7) Notwithstanding any other provision of this chapter, any investigative or law enforcement officer, specially designated by the Attorney General, the Deputy Attorney General, the

Associate Attorney, or by the principal prosecuting attorney of any State or subdivision thereof acting pursuant to a statute of that State, who reasonably determines that--

(a) an emergency situation exists that involves--

(i) immediate danger of death or serious physical injury to any person,

(ii) conspiratorial activities threatening the national security interest, or

(iii) conspiratorial activities characteristic of organized crime,

that requires a wire, oral, or electronic communication to be intercepted before an order authorizing such interception can, with due diligence, be obtained, and

(b) there are grounds upon which an order could be entered under this chapter to authorize such interception,

may intercept such wire, oral, or electronic communication if an application for an order approving the interception is made in accordance with this section within forty-eight hours after the interception has occurred, or begins to occur. In the absence of an order, such interception shall immediately terminate when the communication sought is obtained or when the application for the order is denied, whichever is earlier. In the event such application for approval is denied, or in any other case where the interception is terminated without an order having been issued, the contents of any wire, oral, or electronic communication intercepted shall be treated as having been obtained in violation of this chapter, and an inventory shall be served as provided for in subsection (d) of this section on the person named in the application.

(8)(a) The contents of any wire, oral, or electronic communication intercepted by any means authorized by this chapter shall, if possible, be recorded on tape or wire or other comparable device. The recording of the contents of any wire, oral, or electronic communication under this subsection shall be done in such a way as will protect the recording from editing or other alterations. Immediately upon the expiration of the period of the order, or extensions thereof, such recordings shall be made available to the judge issuing such order and sealed under his directions. Custody of the recordings shall be wherever the judge orders. They shall not be destroyed except upon an order of the issuing or denying judge and in any event shall be kept for ten years. Duplicate recordings may be made for use or disclosure pursuant to the provisions of subsections (1) and (2) of section 2517 of this chapter for investigations. The presence of the seal provided for by this subsection, or a satisfactory explanation for the absence thereof, shall be a prerequisite for the use or disclosure of the contents of any wire, oral, or electronic communication or evidence derived therefrom under subsection (3) of section 2517.

(b) Applications made and orders granted under this chapter shall be sealed by the judge. Custody of the applications and orders shall be wherever the judge directs. Such applications and orders shall be disclosed only upon a showing of good cause before a judge of competent jurisdiction and shall not be destroyed except on order of the issuing or denying judge, and in any event shall be kept for ten years.

(c) Any violation of the provisions of this subsection may be punished as contempt of the issuing or denying judge.

(d) Within a reasonable time but not later than ninety days after the filing of an application for an order of approval under section 2518(7)(b) which is denied or the termination of the period of an order or extensions thereof, the issuing or denying judge shall cause to be served, on the persons named in the order of the application, and such other parties to intercepted communications as the judge may determine in his discretion that is in the interest of justice, an inventory which shall include notice of--

(1) the fact of the entry of the order or the application;

(2) the date of the entry and the period of authorized, approved or disapproved interception, or the denial of the application; and

(3) the fact that during the period, wire, oral, or electronic communications were or were not intercepted.

The judge upon the filing of a motion, may in his discretion make available to such person or his counsel for inspection such portions of the intercepted communications, applications and orders as the judge determines to be in the interest of justice. On an ex parte showing of good cause to a judge of competent jurisdiction the serving of the inventory required by this subsection may be postponed.

(9) The contents of any wire, oral, or electronic communication intercepted pursuant to this chapter or evidence derived therefrom shall not be received in evidence or otherwise disclosed in any trial, hearing, or other proceeding in a Federal or State court unless each party, not less than ten days before the trial, hearing, or proceeding, has been furnished with a copy of the court order, and accompanying application, under which the interception was authorized or approved. This ten-day period may be waived by the judge if he finds that it was not possible to furnish the party with the above information ten days before the trial, hearing, or proceeding and that the party will not be the prejudiced by the delay in receiving such information.

(10)(a) Any aggrieved person in any trial, hearing, or proceeding in or before any court, department, officer, agency, regulatory body, or other authority of the United States, a State or political subdivision thereof, may move to suppress the contents of any wire or oral communication intercepted pursuant to this chapter, or evidence derived therefrom, on the grounds that--

(i) the communication was unlawfully intercepted;

(ii) the order of authorization or approval under which it was intercepted is insufficient on its face; or

(iii) the interception was not made in conformity with the order of authorization or approval.

Such motion shall be made before the trial, hearing, or proceeding unless there was no opportunity to make such motion or the person was not aware of the grounds of the motion. If the motion is granted, the contents of the intercepted wire or oral communication, or evidence derived therefrom, shall be treated as having been obtained in violation of this chapter. The judge, upon the filing of such motion by the aggrieved person, may in his discretion make available to the aggrieved person or his counsel for inspection such portions of the intercepted communication or evidence derived therefrom as the judge determines to be in the interests of justice.

(b) In addition to any other right to appeal, the United States shall have the right to appeal from an order granting a motion to suppress made under paragraph (a) of this subsection, or the denial of an application for an order of approval, if the United States attorney shall certify to the judge or other official granting such motion or denying such application that the appeal is not taken for purposes of delay. Such appeal shall be taken within thirty days after the date the order was entered and shall be diligently prosecuted.

(c) The remedies and sanctions described in this chapter with respect to the interception of electronic communications are the only judicial remedies and sanctions for nonconstitutional violations of this chapter involving such communications.

(11) The requirements of subsections (1)(b)(ii) and (3)(d) of this section relating to the specification of the facilities from which, or the place where, the communication is to be intercepted do not apply if--

(a) in the case of an application with respect to the interception of an oral communication--

(i) the application is by a Federal investigative or law enforcement officer and is approved by the Attorney General, the Deputy Attorney General, the Associate Attorney General, and Assistant Attorney General, or an acting Assistant Attorney General;

(ii) the application contains a full and complete statement as to why such specification is not practical and identifies the person committing the offense and whose communications are to be intercepted; and

(iii) the judge finds that such specification is not practical; and

(b) in the case of an application with respect to a wire or electronic communication--

(i) the application is by a Federal investigative or law enforcement officer and is approved by the Attorney General, the Deputy Attorney General, the Associate Attorney General, an Assistant Attorney General, or an acting Assistant Attorney General;

(ii) the application identifies the person believed to be committing the offense and whose communications are to be intercepted and the applicant makes a showing of a purpose, on the part of that person, to thwart interception by changing facilities; and

(iii) the judge finds that such purpose has been adequately shown.

(12) An interception of a communication under an order with respect to which the requirements of subsections (1)(b)(ii) and (3)(d) of this section do not apply by reason of subsection (11) shall not begin until the facilities from which, or the place where, the communication is to be intercepted is ascertained by the person implementing the interception order. A provider of wire or electronic communications service that has received an order as provided for in subsection (11)(b) may move the court to modify or quash the order on the ground that its assistance with respect to the interception cannot be performed in a timely or reasonable fashion. The court, upon notice to the government, shall decide such a motion expeditiously.

§2519. Reports concerning intercepted wire, oral, or electronic communications

(1) Within thirty days after the expiration of an order (or each extension thereof) entered under Section 2518, or the denial of an order approving an interception, the issuing or denying judge shall report to the Administrative Office of the United States Courts--

(a) the fact that an order or extension was applied for;

(b) the kind of order or extension applied for (including whether or not the order was an order with respect to which the requirements of sections 2518(1)(b)(ii) and 2518(3)(d) of this title did not apply by reason of section 2518(11) of this title);

(c) the fact that the order or extension was granted as applied for, was modified, or was denied;

(d) the period of interceptions authorized by the order, and the number and duration of any extensions of the order;

(e) the offense specified in the order or application, or extension of an order;

(f) the identity of the applying investigative or law enforcement officer and agency making the application and the person authorizing the application; and

(g) the nature of the facilities from which or the place where communications were to be intercepted.

(2) In January of each year the Attorney General, an Assistant Attorney General specially designated by the Attorney General, or the principal prosecuting attorney of a State, or the principal prosecuting attorney for any political subdivision of a State, shall report to the Administrative Office of the United States Courts--

(a) the information required by paragraphs (a) through (g) of subsection (1) of this section with respect to each application for an order or extension made during the preceding calendar year;

(b) a general description of the interceptions made under such order or extension, including (i) the approximate nature and frequency of incriminating communications intercepted, (ii) the approximate nature and frequency of other communications intercepted, (iii) the approximate number of persons whose communications were intercepted, and (iv) the approximate nature, amount, and cost of the manpower and other resources used in the interceptions;

(c) the number of arrests resulting from interceptions made under such order or extension, and the offenses for which arrests were made;

(d) the number of trials resulting from such interceptions;

(e) the number of motions to suppress made with respect to such interceptions, and the number granted or denied;

(f) the number of convictions resulting from such interceptions and the offenses for which the convictions were obtained and a general assessment of the importance of the interceptions; and

(g) the information required by paragraphs (b) through (f) of this subsection with respect to orders or extensions obtained in a preceding calendar year.

(3) In April of each year the Director of the Administrative Office of the

United States Courts shall transmit to the Congress a full and complete report concerning the number of applications for orders authorizing or approving the interception of wire, oral, or electronic communications pursuant to this chapter and the number of orders and extensions granted or denied pursuant to this chapter during the preceding calendar year. Such report shall include a summary and analysis of the data required to be filed with the Administrative Office by subsections (1) and (2) of this section. The Director of the Administrative Office of the United States Courts is authorized to issue binding regulations dealing with the content and form of the reports required to be filed by subsections (1) and (2) of this section.

§2520. Recovery of civil damages authorized

(a) In general

Except as provided in section 2511(2)(a)(ii), any person whose wire, oral, or electronic communication is intercepted, disclosed, or intentionally used in violation of this chapter may in a civil action recover from the person or entity which engaged in that violation such relief as may be appropriate.

(b) Relief

In an action under this section, appropriate relief includes--

(1) such preliminary and other equitable or declaratory relief as may be appropriate;

(2) damages under subsection (c) and punitive damages in appropriate cases; and

(3) a reasonable attorney's fee and other litigation costs reasonably incurred.

(c) Computation of damages

(1) In an action under this section, if the conduct in violation of this chapter is the private viewing of a private satellite video communication that is not scrambled or encrypted or if the communication is a radio communication that is transmitted on frequencies allocated under subpart D of part 74 of the rules of the Federal Communications Commission that is not scrambled or encrypted and the conduct is not for a tortious or illegal purpose or for purposes of direct or indirect commercial advantage or private commercial gain, then the court shall assess damages as follows:

(A) If the person who engaged in that conduct has not previously been enjoined under section 2511(5) and has not been found liable in a prior civil action under this section, the court shall assess the greater of the sum of actual damages suffered by the plaintiff, or statutory damages of not less than $50 and not more than $500.

(B) If, on one prior occasion, the person who engaged in that conduct has been enjoined under section 2511(5) or has been found liable in a civil action under this section, the court shall assess the greater of the sum of actual damages suffered by the plaintiff, or statutory damages of not less than $100 and not more than $1000.

(2) In any other action under this section, the court may assess as damages whichever is the greater of--

(A) the sum of the actual damages suffered by the plaintiff and any profits made by the violator as a result of the violation; or

(B) statutory damages of whichever is the greater of $100 a

day for each day of violation or $10,000.

(d) Defense

A good faith reliance on--

(1) a court warrant or order, a grand jury subpoena, a legislative authorization, or a statutory authorization;

(2) a request of an investigative or law enforcement officer under section 2518(7) of this title; or

(3) a good faith determination that section 2511(3) of this title permitted the conduct complained of;

is a complete defense against any civil or criminal action brought under this chapter or any other law.

(e) Limitation

A civil action under this section may not be commenced later than two years after the date upon which the claimant first has a reasonable opportunity to discover the violation.

§2521. Injunction against illegal interception

Whenever it shall appear that any person is engaged or is about to engage in any act which constitutes or will constitute a felony violation of this chapter, the Attorney General may initiate a civil action in a district court of the United States to enjoin such violation. The court shall proceed as soon as practicable to the hearing and determination of such an action, and may, at any time before final determination, enter such a restraining order or prohibition, or take such other action, as is warranted to prevent a continuing and substantial injury to the United States or to any person or class of persons for whose protection the action is brought. A proceeding under this section is governed by the Federal Rules of Civil Procedure, except that, if an indictment has been returned against the respondent, discovery is governed by the Federal Rules of Criminal Procedure.

UNITED STATES v. WILLOUGHBY

860 F.2d 15 (2d Cir. 1988)
United States Court of Appeals, Second Circuit.
Argued June 21, 1988. Decided Oct. 6, 1988.
860 F.2d 15

***

Before NEWMAN, KEARSE and CARDAMONE, Circuit Judges.

KEARSE, Circuit Judge:

Defendants Richard Willoughby, Quintin Prioleau ("Quintin"), Arthur Prioleau ("Arthur"), and Carleton Montgomery appeal from judgments entered after a jury trial in the United States District Court for the Southern District of New York before Morris E. Lasker, *Judge,* convicting them of conspiracy to obstruct justice, in violation of 18 U.S.C. § 371 (1982), in connection with an impending trial of Quintin, Arthur, and Montgomery for armed robbery; and convicting Quintin of witness tampering, in violation of 18 U.S.C. § 1512(b)(2)(D) (1982 & Supp. IV 1986). Arthur and Montgomery were sentenced to one-year prison terms; Quintin was sentenced to concurrent one-year prison terms on each of the two counts on which he was convicted. Each of these sentences was to run consecutively to sentences previously imposed on Arthur, Montgomery, and Quintin for convictions of bank robbery. Willoughby was given a suspended sentence and placed on three years' probation. Each defendant was assessed $50 for each count on which he was convicted, under 18 U.S.C. § 3013(a)(2)(A) (1982 & Supp. IV 1986).

On appeal, defendants contend principally that the trial court erred in admitting into evidence tape recordings of conversations held in June 1987 between Quintin and Willoughby, Quintin and Montgomery, and Arthur and a government witness. For the reasons below, we affirm the judgments of conviction.

I. BACKGROUND

In July 1987, Arthur, his brother Quintin, and Montgomery were convicted of the armed robbery of the City College branch of Chemical Bank ("Chemical branch") in New York City. The present prosecution arises out of their efforts, with Willoughby, to prevent certain witnesses from testifying at the trial of the bank robbery charges. The record in the present case includes the following.

A. *The Events of June 1987*

In the spring of 1987, Arthur, Quintin, and Montgomery were inmates at the New York Metropolitan Correctional Center ("MCC"), awaiting trial, scheduled for July of that year, on the charges that they and one Cornel Everett ("Cornel") had robbed the Chemical branch in March 1982. In June 1987, Arthur sent word to Sabrina Johnson, who had been one of his girlfriends in early 1982, that he wanted her to visit him at MCC on June 11.

During the investigation of the robbery, Johnson had been in contact with Agent Paul Harvey of the Federal Bureau of Investigation. On June 10, 1987, she informed Harvey and Assistant United States Attorney Joan McPhee of Arthur's request that she visit him at MCC. Johnson, after being advised that it was solely her decision whether or not to visit Arthur, stated that she probably would visit him. The government was aware that Arthur and Johnson had been largely out of contact for several years, that he had recently made repeated efforts to contact her, and that in 1982 he had conversed with Johnson about the Chemical branch robbery and had then told her he might marry her in order to prevent her from testifying against him. Recognizing that the government's case on the robbery charges consisted primarily of the testimony of defendants' friends such as Johnson and one Patricia White, another of Arthur's girlfriends in early 1982, McPhee was concerned that Arthur would attempt to intimidate Johnson or to influence her testimony at the robbery trial and therefore asked Johnson if she would be willing to wear a concealed recording device during the visit. Johnson agreed to do so, and her June 11 conversation with Arthur was thus taped.

During the June 11 visit, Arthur and Johnson discussed the 1982 robbery and the evidence available to the government to prove that Arthur, Quintin, and others had perpetrated it. Arthur stated that he had gotten the idea for the robbery from "Pat" (Patricia White testified in the present case that she had mentioned to Arthur in early 1982 that the Chemical branch would be easy to rob) and that he had passed the idea along to Quintin and others. He said the government would have had no evidence against him and Quintin but for the fact that "Ina and Pat snitched on us." He stated, "Ina and Pat snitched. They did a lot of talking...That's what happened. Other than that, they didn't have no case." (Ellipsis in tape transcript.) He predicted that the robbery trial would end in acquittal "because they don't have no evidence. It's alot [*sic*] of hearsay. Nobody from the bank identified nobody. It's just Ina and, um, Pat's testimony, that's holdin' us."

Arthur indicated that defendants had sent threats to Ina and had attempted to locate Pat to prevent their "stand[ing] in our way." He stated, "we sent a few people around there [to Ina] to tell her, if Ina comes, they'll have to move her mother out of the block, anybody who's part of her family..." but stated that they had not "been able to locate" Pat. Arthur advised Johnson that, if she were questioned again by law enforcement officers, she should "[t]ell 'em that you don't know nothing, just leave it at that." He said, "You watch enough TV to know what happens to snitches."

On June 22, 1987, with Montgomery at his side, Quintin called Willoughby at his home, using an MCC telephone that was available to inmates. Pursuant to MCC policy, of which inmates were advised upon their arrival at MCC, and notice of which they were requested to acknowledge in writing (*see* Part II.A.1. below), all inmate calls from MCC institutional telephones, except properly placed calls to attorneys, were automatically recorded and were monitored on a random basis. Quintin's call to Willoughby was thus recorded. In addition, the call was monitored, and an MCC official visually observed Quintin and Montgomery from a distance of 15-20 feet.

During the telephone conversation, Quintin and Willoughby discussed preventing testimony be someone referred to as "the person." Quintin stated that "we need somebody to take care of that," and that "Cornel" would make arrangements to have "his man...do it," but that Cornel's man did not know what "the person" looked like. Willoughby stated that he could "pick out the person" for Cornel's man.

Quintin promised to call Willoughby the next day with the telephone number of Cornel's man. He urged Willoughby to make arrangements quickly, stating that "we gotta do it this week," because in the following week the government would serve defendants with its list of prospective witnesses, and after Cornel's man "hit 'em," defendants wanted to be able to say, "we never knew who they was."

Upon completing his call to Willoughby, Quintin attempted to dial another number, and as he did so, Montgomery asked him, "What's the plan?" After Quintin's response, which was unintelligible on the tape, Montgomery said, "You blew the whole plan..." Quintin replied that they had no one to do the job, asking, "who do you want to do it?" and stating that Willoughby would "go up there with the guy" to identify "her...I didn't want to mention the name on the phone or nothin'..." Montgomery asked, "He said he wanna do it?" Quintin assured him that Willoughby had said he knew where to go and what to do. Montgomery walked away in apparent anger.

Because this conversation took place while Quintin was holding the MCC telephone's handset off the hook, the conversation was automatically recorded.

B. *The Indictments and the Verdicts*

On the basis of these events, defendants were indicted in a five-count indictment. Count one charged all four defendants with conspiracy to tamper with witnesses White and Johnson and to obstruct justice, in violation of 18 U.S.C. § 371; count two charged Quintin with obstruction of justice by endeavoring to influence or prevent the testimony of "certain witnesses," in violation of 18 U.S.C. § 1503 (1982); count three charged Arthur with witness tampering, to wit, threatening Johnson with physical harm if she testified at the robbery trial, in violation of 18 U.S.C. § 1512(b)(2)(A) (1982 & Supp. IV 1986); count four charged Quintin with witness tampering, to wit, attempting to prevent the appearance of White at trial, in violation of 18 U.S.C. § 1512(b)(2)(D); and count five charged Arthur with witness tampering, to wit, directing Johnson to withhold evidence relating to the robbery, in violation of 18 U.S.C. § 1512(b)(3) (1982 & Supp. IV 1986).

Prior to trial, defendants moved to suppress the tape recordings of the June 11 and June 22 conversations on various grounds. To the extent pertinent here, Quintin, Willoughby, and Montgomery moved to suppress the June 22 conversations on the grounds that the taping of those conversations violated their rights under Title III of the Omnibus Crime Control and Safe Streets Act ("Title III"), 18 U.S.C. §§ 2510-21 (1982 & Supp. IV 1986), and their rights under the Fourth Amendment to the Constitution to be free from unreasonable searches and seizures; Arthur moved to suppress the tape of his June 11 conversation with Johnson on the ground that the taping violated his Fifth Amendment privilege against compulsory self-incrimination because he was not given *Miranda* (*Miranda v. Arizona,* 384 U.S. 436, 86 S.Ct. 1602, 86 L.Ed.2d 694 (1964) warnings. In a published opinion, *United States v. Montgomery,* 675 F.Supp. 164 (1987), the district court denied the motions to suppress. Relying on *United States v. Amen,* 831 F.2d 373 (2d Cir. 1987), *cert. denied,* __U.S.__, 108 S.Ct. 1573, 99 L.Ed.2d 889 (1988), the court held that the taping of the June 22 conversations was permissible under the "consent" exception to Title III; it rejected the Fourth

Amendment argument on the ground that the government's interest in prison security outweighed any expectation defendants might have had of privacy in their conversations, especially in light of the notice given that telephone conversations would be intercepted. The court rejected Arthur's *Miranda* claim on the ground that his June 11 conversation with Johnson was voluntary rather than the product of coercion.

Accordingly, the government's evidence at trial included the tape recordings of the June 11 conversation and both June 22 conversations. In addition, there was testimony from several witnesses, including MCC officials, Johnson, and White.

The jury found all four defendants guilty of conspiracy (count one) and found Quintin guilty of witness tampering (count four). Count two against Quintin was dismissed at the close of the government's case; Arthur was acquitted on counts three and five. Defendants were sentenced as indicated above, and these appeals followed.

II. DISCUSSION

On appeal, Willoughby, Quintin, and Montgomery contend principally that the government's taping of the June 22 conversations violated their rights under Title III and the Fourth Amendment; Arthur contends principally that the use of his June 11 conversation with Johnson violated his *Miranda* rights. In addition, defendants contend that evidence that Quintin, Arthur and Montgomery participated in the 1982 bank robbery should have been excluded pursuant to Fed.R.Evid. 403 and 404(b), and Montgomery contends that the evidence was insufficient to support an inference that he participated in the conspiracy to obstruct justice. We have considered all of defendants' contentions on these appeals and have found them to be without merit.

A. *The Quintin-Willoughby Telephone Conversation*

The contentions that the taping of Quintin's telephone call to Willoughby violated Title III and the Fourth Amendment are, as the district court ruled, largely foreclosed by our decision in *United States v. Amen,* 831 F.2d 373.

1. *Title III*

Title III generally prohibits the intentional interception of wire communications, including telephone conversations, in the absence of authorization by court order. 18 U.S.C. §§ 2510-2521; *see id.* § 2510(1) ("wire communication" includes any communication "made in whole or in part through the use of facilities for the transmission of communications by the aid of wire, cable, or other like connection" furnished or operated by an interstate common carrier). The prohibition against interception does not apply, however, when "one of the parties to the communication has given prior consent to such interception." *Id.* § 2511(2)(c). Such consent may be express or implied. *United States v. Amen,* 831 F.2d at 378; S.Rep. No. 1097, 90th Cong., 2d Sess., *reprinted in* 1968 U.S. Code Cong. & Admin. News 2112, 2182. In the prison setting, when the institution has advised inmates that their telephone calls will be monitored and has prominently posted a notice that their "use of institutional telephones constitutes consent to this monitoring," the inmates' use of those telephones constitutes implied consent to the monitoring within the meaning of Title III. *United States v. Amen,* 831 F.2d at 379.

In the present case, the record established that MCC had a policy and practice of automatically recording and randomly monitoring all inmate calls, other than those properly placed to an attorney, made on institutional telephones. Inmates received ample notice of this practice. First, they were advised of the practice at orientation lectures upon their arrival at MCC; Quintin attended such a lecture in March 1987. In addition, MCC posted above each telephone available to inmates a bilingual sign, the English version of which read:

> NOTICE
>
> The Bureau of Prisons reserves the authority to monitor conversations on this telephone. Your use of institutional telephones constitutes consent to this monitoring. A properly placed telephone call to an attorney is not monitored.

In these circumstances the district court could properly find that Quintin impliedly consented to the monitoring and taping of his call to Willoughby. *See Amen.*

Finally, Quintin was given a form that stated as follows:

> The Bureau of Prisons reserves the authority to monitor (this includes recording) conversations on any telephone located within its institutions, said monitoring to be done to preserve the security and orderly management of the institution and to protect the public. An inmate's use of institutional telephones constitutes consent to this monitoring.

Just above a line for the signature of the inmate, the form included the statement, "I understand that telephone calls I make from institution telephones may be monitored and recorded." Quintin signed the form on March 5, 1987. This sufficed to support a finding that Quintin expressly consented to the taping. We conclude that the court properly rejected Quintin's Title III contention.

The court also properly rejected the Title III arguments made on behalf of Willoughby. Whether or not Willoughby himself consented to the interception, the consent of Quintin alone, as a party to the conversation, sufficed to avoid the prohibitions of Title III. 18 U.S.C. § 2511(2)(c) (interception not prohibited when "one" of the parties to the communication has consented).

2. *The Fourth Amendment Arguments*

In *Amen*, we rejected a Fourth Amendment attack on the interception of telephone calls made by certain convicted prisoners, ruling that they had no reasonable expectation of privacy in their calls to nonattorneys on institutional telephones. 831 F.2d at 379-80. Quintin, Montgomery, and Willoughby, suggesting that pretrial detainees have greater privacy rights than do convicted inmates, claim that the interception of Quintin's telephone conversation with Willoughby therefore violated their Fourth Amendment rights. We find no merit in this claim.

Preliminarily, we note that defendants' brief merely asserts the principle that pretrial detainees have greater rights than convicted inmates, without ever stating that either Quintin or Montgomery in June 1987 was only a pretrial detainee and not a convicted prisoner. The government's brief on appeal states that neither Quintin nor Montgomery was simply a pretrial detainee, though they were awaiting trial on the robbery charges; rather, both had been convicted of state crimes and had been brought from state prisons to MCC for purposes of the robbery trial. Thus, the government argues that they were convicted prisoners to whom the *Amen* rule squarely applies. If the record before us clearly substantiated the government's factual premise, we would agree that Amen foreclosed the constitutional arguments. Unfortunately, the record is opaque. While revealing that Quintin had previously been convicted of attempted murder and that both he and Montgomery had been brought to MCC from state prisons, the record does not exclude the possibility that Quintin had completed his prior sentence and that both he and Montgomery had been in state facilities as pretrial detainees on new charges.

Even if Quintin and Montgomery were merely pretrial detainees, however, the Fourth Amendment challenge to the interception of Quintin's telephone call to Willoughby must be rejected. Although pretrial detainees may have some residual privacy interests that are protected by the Fourth Amendment, see *United States v. Cohen,* 796 F.2d 20, 23-24 (2d Cir. 1986), *cert. denied,* 479 U.S. 1055, 107 S.Ct. 932, 93 L.Ed.2d 982 (1987), the maintenance of prison security and the preservation of institutional order and discipline are "essential goals that may require limitation or retraction of the retained constitutional rights of both convicted prisoners and pretrial detainees." *Bell v. Wolfish,* 441 U.S. 520, 546, 99 S.Ct. 1861, 1878, 60 L.Ed.2d 447 (1979) (footnote omitted). The *Bell* Court noted that:

> [t]here is no basis for concluding that pretrial detainees pose any lesser security risk than convicted inmates. Indeed, it may be that in certain circumstances they present a greater risk to jail security and order... In the federal system, a detainee is committed to the detention facility only because no other less drastic means can reasonably assure his presence at trial... As a result, those who are detained prior to trial may in many cases be individuals who are charged with serious crimes or who have prior records. They also may pose a greater risk of escape than convicted inmates... This may be particularly true at facilities like the MCC, where the resident convicted inmates have been sentenced to only short terms of incarceration and many of the detainees face the possibility of lengthy imprisonment if convicted.

Id. at 546 n. 28, 99 S.Ct. at 1878 n. 28 (citations omitted). Given the difficulties inherent in prison administration, prison administrators are to be "accorded wide-ranging deference in the adoption and execution of policies and practices that in their judgment are needed to preserve internal order and discipline and to maintain institutional security." *Id.* at 547, 99 S.Ct. at 1878. Accordingly, whatever Fourth Amendment rights pretrial detainees retain have been held uninfringed by such security measures as strip and body-cavity searches, *see id.* at 558-60, 99 S.Ct. at 1884-85, and the monitoring of their conversations with visitors, *see Christman v. Skinner,* 468 F.2d 723, 726 (2d Cir. 1972).

The telephone interception practices at MCC are among several security procedures (including for example, the search of handbags carried by visitors, the continuous surveillance of visiting rooms, and the random examination of nonattorney mail) in effect at that institution. The telephone taping system, which is triggered automatically by the lifting of the telephone's handset, is considered by prison officials to be an extremely effective tool in helping to maintain internal security. The recording system and the random live monitoring of telephone conversations have assisted, for example, in the detection of escape plans of schemes to smuggle controlled substances into the facility, and of inmate identification of another inmate as an informant in the government's Witness Protection Program.

In all the circumstances, including the fact that inmates receive ample notice that such interceptions will occur, *see* Part II.A.1. above, we conclude that MCC's practice of automatically taping and randomly monitoring telephone calls of inmates in the interest of institutional security is not an unreasonable invasion of the privacy rights of pretrial detainees.

Nor do we find merit in Willoughby's contention that his own privacy rights were entitled to greater protection than those of Quintin because he received Quintin's call in his home. Contacts between inmates and noninmates may justify otherwise impermissible intrusions into the noninmates privacy. Thus, noninmate mail to prisoners may be subject to inspection, *see generally Procunier v. Martinez,* 416 U.S. 396, 408-09, 412-14, 94 S.Ct. 1800, 1808-09, 1810-12, 40 L.Ed.2d 224 (1974); and noninmate visitors may have their conversations with inmates monitored, *see United States v. Harrelson,* 754 F.2d 1153, 1169-70 (5th Cir.), *cert. denied,* 474 U.S. 908 & 1034, 106 S.Ct. 277 & 599, 88 L.Ed.2d 241 & 578 (1985), or be subject, based upon reasonable suspicion, to strip searches, see *Hunter v. Auger,* 672 F.2d 668, 673-75 (8th Cir. 1982). With respect to telephone communications, the public is on notice pursuant to regulations published in 28 C.F.R. §§ 540.100 and 540.101 (1987) that prison officials are required to establish procedures for monitoring inmates' calls to noninmates. Given the institution's strong interest in preserving security, we conclude that the interception of calls from inmates to noninmates does not violate the privacy rights of the noninmates.

B. *The Quintin-Montgomery Conversation*

Quintin and Montgomery contend also that the recording of their conversation, following the conclusion of Quintin's call to Willoughby, violated their rights under Title III and the Fourth Amendment. We reject the Fourth Amendment argument essentially for the reasons discussed in Part II.A above. We reject the Title III argument on somewhat different grounds.

Whereas the Quintin-Willoughby conversation was a telephone communication, the interception of which plainly was consented to by Quintin, the ensuing conversation between Quintin and Montgomery was not "made in whole or in part through the use of" telephone wires, *see* 18 U.S.C. § 2510(1) (defining "wire" communication). Rather, it was a face-to-face conversation adventitiously picked up by the recording system because Quintin was in the process of trying to make another telephone call at the time he was conversing with Montgomery. Since Title III also forbids the interception, without prior court authorization, of certain nonwire "oral" conversations, *see* 18 U.S.C. § 2511(1), we are skeptical of the government's contention that Quintin's consent to the interception of his telephone calls also constituted consent to the interception of his in-person conversation with Montgomery.

Rather, the basis for our rejection of the statutory challenge to the recording of the Quintin-Montgomery conversation is that the communication simply was not one of those protected by Title III. The statute defines an "oral" conversation, in pertinent part, as "any oral communication uttered by a person exhibiting an expectation that such communication is not subject to interception under circumstances justifying such expectation." 18 U.S.C. § 2510(2). Thus, to be an oral communication that is protected by Title III, the speaker must have had a subjective expectation that the communication was not subject to interception, and this expectation must have been objectively reasonable. *United States v. Harrelson,* 754 F.2d at 1169-70; *United States v. Pui Kan Lam,* 483 F.2d 1202, 1206 (2d Cir. 1973), *cert. denied,* 415 U.S. 984, 94 S.Ct. 1578, 39 L.Ed.2d 881 (1974). We conclude that the requisite conditions were not met.

It is questionable whether Quintin and Montgomery had even a subjective belief that their conversation could not be overheard. The words of their conversation appeared to be deliberately cryptic, as was the telephone conversation with Willoughby. Thus, Quintin said to Montgomery afterwards, "I didn't want to mention the name on the phone or nothin'"; and so far as appears from the tape, Quintin similarly took care not to mention the name of the targeted person in his conversation with Montgomery.

Further, the conversation was conducted at one of the telephones available to inmates at MCC. These telephones were located in a multipurpose area which included dining tables, pool tables, and chairs. At the time of the conversation, there were some 35 people in the area, many of them milling around. Some four or five people were within 10 feet of the spot at which Quintin and Montgomery stood. Their conversation was thus conducted in a public area.

Finally, Quintin and Montgomery conversed while Quintin was in the process of using the telephone to make another call, and they knew the telephones were linked to a recording system. They had no basis for assuming that conversations next to an open telephone would not be overheard. "Mistaking the degree of intrusion of which probable eavesdroppers are capable is not at all the same thing as believing there are no eavesdroppers." *United State v. Harrelson,* 754 F.2d at 1170. We doubt that in all the circumstances Quintin and Montgomery had a subjective belief that they could not be overheard, and we conclude that even if they did have such a belief, the circumstances did not justify it. Accordingly, the conversation between Quintin and Montgomery was not an "oral" communication protected by Title III.

***

CONCLUSION

The judgments of conviction are affirmed.

[Note: Parts of this case dealing with the admissibility of the confession and the sufficiency of the evidence are not included.]

Cases relating to **Chapter 6**

INTERROGATIONS AND CONFESSIONS

CULOMBE v. CONNECTICUT

367 U.S. 568, 81 S. Ct. 1860, 6 L. Ed. 2d 1037 (1961)

MR. JUSTICE FRANKFURTER announced the judgment of the Court and an opinion in which MR. JUSTICE STEWART joins.

Once again the Court is confronted with the painful duty of sitting in judgment on a State's conviction for murder, after a jury's verdict was found flawless by the State's highest court, in order to determine whether the defendant's confessions, decisive for the conviction, were admitted into evidence in accordance with the standards for admissibility demanded by the Due Process Clause of the Fourteenth Amendment. This recurring problem touching the administration of criminal justice by the States presents in an aggravated form in this case the anxious task of reconciling the responsibility of the police for ferreting out crime with the right of the criminal defendant, however guilty, to be tried according to constitutional requirements.

On December 15, 1956, the dead bodies of two men where found in Kurp's Gasoline Station in New Britain, Connecticut. Edward J. Kurpiewski, the proprietor, was found in the boiler room with a bullet in his head. Daniel J. Janowski, a customer, was found in the men's toilet room shot twice in the head. Parked at the pumps in front of the station was Janowski's car. In it was Janowski's daughter, physically unharmed. She was the only surviving eyewitness of what had happened at the station. She was eighteen months old.

The Kurp's affair was one in a series of holdups and holdup killings that terrified the operators of gasoline stations, package stores and small shops throughout the environing Connecticut area. Newspapers and radio and television broadcasters reported each fresh depredation of the "mad killers." At Hartford, the State Police were at work investigating the crimes, apparently with little evidence to go on. At the scene of the killings of Kurpiewski and Janowski no physical clues were discovered. The bullet slugs removed from the brains of the two victims were split and damaged.

In the last week of February 1957, for reasons which do not appear in this record, suspicion in connection with at least two of the holdups under investigation, holdups of a country store in Coventry and of a package store in Rocky Hill, focused on two friends, Arthur Culombe and Joseph Taborsky. On the afternoon of February 23, the two were accosted by teams of officers and asked to come to

State Police Headquarters. They were never again out of police custody. In the Headquarters interrogation room and elsewhere, they were questioned about the Coventry and Rocky Hill holdups, Kurp's, and other matters. Within ten days Culombe had five times confessed orally to participation in the Kurp's Gasoline Station affair—once reenacting the holdup for the police—and had signed three typed statements incriminating himself and Taborsky in the Kurp's killings. Taborsky also confessed.

The two were indicted and tried jointly for murder in the first degree before a jury in the Superior Court at Hartford. Certain of their oral and written statements were permitted to go to the jury over their timely objections that these had been extracted from them by police methods which made the confessions inadmissible consistently with the Fourteenth Amendment. Both men were convicted of first-degree murder and their convictions affirmed by the Supreme Court of Errors. 147 Conn. 194, 158 A.2d 239. Only Culombe sought review by this Court. Because his petition for certiorari presented serious questions concerning the limitations imposed by the Federal Due Process Clause upon the investigative activities of state criminal law enforcement officials, we issued the writ. 363 U.S. 826.

The occasion which in December 1956 confronted the Connecticut State Police with two corpses and an infant as their sole informants to a crime of community-disturbing violence is not a rare one. Despite modern advances in the technology of crime detection, offenses frequently occur about which things cannot be made to speak. And where there cannot be found innocent human witnesses to such offenses, nothing remains—if police investigation is not to be balked before it has fairly begun—but to seek out possibly guilty witnesses and ask them questions, witnesses, that is, who are suspected of knowing something about the offense precisely because they are suspected of implication in it.

The questions which these suspected witnesses are asked may serve to clear them. They may serve, directly or indirectly, to lead the police to other suspects than the persons questioned. Or they may become the means by which the persons questioned are themselves made to furnish proofs which will eventually send them to prison or death. In any event, whatever its outcome, such questioning is often indispensable to crime detection. Its compelling necessity has been judicially recognized as its sufficient justification, even in a society which, like ours, stands strongly and constitutionally committed to the principle that persons accused of crime cannot be made to convict themselves out of their own mouths.

But persons who are suspected of crime will not always be unreluctant to answer questions put by the police. Since under the procedures of Anglo-American criminal justice they cannot be constrained by legal process to give answers which incriminate them, the police have resorted to other means to unbend their reluctance, lest criminal investigation founder. Kindness, cajolery, entreaty, deception, persistent cross-questioning, even physical brutality have been used to this end. In the United States, "interrogation" has become a police technique, and detention for purposes of interrogation a common, although generally unlawful, practice. Crime detection officials, finding that if their suspects are kept under tight police control during questioning they are less likely to be distracted, less likely to be recalcitrant and, of course, less likely to make off and escape entirely, not infrequently take such suspects into custody for "investigation."

This practice has its manifest evils and dangers. Persons subjected to it are torn from the reliances of their daily existence and held at the mercy of those whose job it is—if such persons have committed crimes, as it is supposed they have—to prosecute them. They are deprived of freedom without a proper judicial tribunal having found them guilty, without a proper judicial tribunal having found even that there is probable cause to believe that they may be guilty. What actually happens to them behind the closed door of the interrogation room is difficult if not impossible to ascertain. Certainly, if through excess of zeal or aggressive impatience or flaring up of temper in the face of obstinate silence a prisoner is abused, he is faced with the task of overcoming, by his lone testimony, solemn official denials. The prisoner knows this—knows that no friendly or disinterested witness is present—and the knowledge may itself induce fear. But, in any case, the risk is great that the police will accomplish behind their closed door precisely what the demands of our legal order forbid: make a suspect the unwilling collaborator in establishing his guilt. This they may accomplish not only with ropes and a rubber hose, not only by relay questioning persistently, insistently subjugating a tired mind, but by subtler devices.

In the police station a prisoner is surrounded by known hostile forces. He is disoriented from the world he knows and in which he finds support. He is subject to coercing impingements, undermining even if not obvious pressures of every variety. In such an atmosphere, questioning that is long continued—even if it is only repeated at intervals, never protracted to the point of physical exhaustion—inevitably suggests that the questioner has a right to, and expects, an answer. This is so, certainly, when the prisoner has never been told that he need not answer and when, because his commitment to custody seems to be at the will of his questioners, he has every reason to believe that he will be held and interrogated until he speaks.

However, a confession made by a person in custody is not always the result of an overborne will. The police may be midwife to a declaration naturally born of remorse, or relief, or desperation, or calculation. If that is so, if the "suction process" has not been at the prisoner and drained his capacity for freedom of choice, does not the awful responsibility of the police for maintaining the peaceful order of society justify the means which they have employed? It will not do to forget, as Sir Patrick (now Lord Justice) Devlin has put it, that "The least criticism of police methods of interrogation deserves to be most carefully weighed because the evidence which such interrogation produces is often decisive; the high degree of proof which the English law requires—proof beyond reasonable doubt—often could not be achieved by the prosecution without the assistance of the accused's own statement." Yet even if one cannot adopt "an undiscriminating hostility to mere interrogation . . . without unduly fettering the States in protecting society from the criminal," there remain the questions: When, applied to what practices, is a judgment of impermissibility drawn from the fundamental conceptions of Anglo-American accusatorial process "undiscriminating"? What are the characteristics of the "mere interrogation" which is allowable consistently with those conceptions?

. . . . [Parts of this case have been omitted. These parts should be read for a history of the rules concerning confessions.]

Each of these factors, in company with all of the surrounding circumstances—the duration and conditions of detention (if the confessor has been detained), the manifest attitude of the police toward him, his physical and mental state, the diverse pressures which sap or sustain his powers of resistance and self-control—is relevant. The ultimate test remains that which has been the only clearly established test in Anglo-American courts for two hundred years: the test of voluntariness. Is the confession the product of an essentially free and unconstrained choice by its maker? If it is, if he has willed to confess, it may be used against him. If it is not, if his will has been overborne and his capacity for self-determination critically impaired, the use of his confession offends due process. *Rogers* v. *Richmond*, 365 U.S. 534. The line of distinction is that at which governing self-direction is lost and compulsion, of whatever nature or however infused, propels or helps to propel the confession.

IV.

The inquiry whether, in a particular case, a confession was voluntarily or involuntarily made involves, at the least, a three-phased process. First, there is the business of finding the crude historical facts, the external, "phenomenological" occurrences and events surrounding the confession. Second, because the concept of "voluntariness" is one which concerns a mental state, there is the imaginative re[-]creation, largely inferential, of internal, "psychological" fact. Third, there is the application to this psychological fact of standards for judgment informed by the larger legal conceptions ordinarily characterized as rules of law but which, also, comprehend both induction from, and anticipation of, factual circumstances.

. . . .

VI.

In the view we take of this case, only the Wednesday confessions need be discussed. If these were coerced, Culombe's conviction, however convincingly supported by other evidence, cannot stand. *Malinski* v. *New York*, 324 U.S. 401; *Stroble* v. *California*, 343 U.S. 181; *Payne* v. *Arkansas*, 356 U.S. 560. On all the circumstances of this record we are compelled to conclude that these confessions were not voluntary. By their use petitioner was deprived of due process of law.

Consideration of the body of this Court's prior decisions which have found confessions coerced informs this conclusion. For although the question whether a particular criminal defendant's will has been overborne and broken is one, it deserves repetition, that must be decided on the peculiar, individual set of facts of his case, it is only by a close, relevant comparison of situations that standards which are solid and effectively enforceable—not doctrinaire or abstract—can be evolved. In approaching these decisions, we may put aside at the outset cases involving physical brutality, threats of physical brutality, and such convincingly terror-arousing, and otherwise unexplainable, incidents of interrogation as the removal of prisoners from jail at night for questioning in secluded places, the shuttling of prisoners from jail to jail, at distances from their homes, for questioning, the keeping of prisoners unclothed or standing on their feet for long periods during questioning. No such obvious, crude devices appear in this record. We may put aside also cases where deprivation of sleep has been used to sap a prisoner's strength and drug him or where bald disregard of his rudimentary need for food is a factor that adds to enfeeblement. Culombe was not subjected to wakes or starvation. We may put aside cases stamped with the overhanging threat of the lynch mob, for although it is true that Culombe saw crowds of people gathered to witness his booking and presentation in New Britain, this circumstance must be accounted of small significance here. There were no mobs at Hartford where he was held securely imprisoned at State Police Headquarters. Finally, we may put aside cases of gruelling, intensely unrelaxing questioning over protracted periods. Culombe's most extended session prior to his first confession ran three and a half hours with substantial respites. Because all of his questioning concerned not one but several offenses, it does not present an aspect of relentless, constantly repeated probing designed to break concentrated resistance. Particularly, the sustained four-and-a-half-hour interview that preceded the Wednesday-midnight confession was almost wholly taken up with matters other than

Kurp's, and at that time, far from resisting, Culombe was wholly cooperating with the police.

. . . .

What appears in this case, then, is this. Culombe was taken by the police and held in the carefully controlled environment of police custody for more than four days before he confessed. During that time he was questioned—questioned every day about the Kurp's affair—and with the avowed intention, not merely to check his story to ascertain whether there was cause to charge him, but to obtain a confession if a confession was obtainable.

All means found fit were employed to this end. Culombe was not told that he had a right to remain silent. Although he said that he wanted a lawyer, the police made no attempt to give him the help he needed to get one. Instead of bringing him before a magistrate with reasonable promptness, as Connecticut law requires, to be duly presented for the grave crimes of which he was in fact suspected (and for which he had been arrested under the felony-arrest statute), he was taken before the New Britain Police Court on the palpable ruse of a breach-of-the-peace charge concocted to give the police time to pursue their investigation. This device is admitted. It had a two-fold effect. First, it kept Culombe in police hands without any of the protections that a proper magistrate's hearing would have assured him. Certainly, had he been brought before it charged with murder instead of an insignificant misdemeanor, no court would have failed to warn Culombe of his rights and arrange for appointment of counsel. Second, every circumstance of the Police Court's procedure was, in itself, potentially intimidating. Culombe had been told that morning that he would be presented in a court of law and would be able to consult counsel. Instead, he was led into a crowded room, penned in a corner, and, without ever being brought before the bench or given a chance to participate in any way, his case was disposed of. Culombe had been convicted of crimes before and presumably was not ignorant of the way in which justice is regularly done. It would deny the impact of experience to believe that the impression which even his limited mind drew from this appearance before a court which did not even hear him, a court which may well have appeared a mere tool in the hands of the police, was not intimidating.

That same evening, by arrangement of the State Police, Culombe's wife and daughter appeared at Headquarters for the interview that left him sobbing in his cell. The next morning, although the mittimus of the New Britain Police Court had committed Culombe to the Hartford Jail until released by due course of law, the police "borrowed" him, and later the questioning resumed. There can be no doubt of its purpose at this time. For Paige then "knew"—if he was ever to know—that Culombe was guilty. Paige opened by telling Culombe to stop lying and to say instead that he did not want to answer. But when Culombe said that he did not want to answer, Detective Murphy took over and repeated the same questions that Paige had asked.

It is clear that this man's will was broken Wednesday afternoon. It is no less clear that his will was broken Wednesday night when, after several hours in a car with four policemen, two interviews with his wife and his apparently ill child, further inquiries made of him in the presence of the Police Commissioner, and a four-and-a-half-hour session which left him (by police testimony) "tired," he agreed to the composition of a statement that was not even cast in his own words. We do not overlook the fact that Culombe told his wife at their apartment that he wanted to cleanse his conscience and make a clean breast of things. This item, in the total context, does not overbalance the significance of all else, particularly since it was his wife who the day before, at the request of Lieutenant Rome, had asked him to confess. Neither the Wednesday-afternoon nor the Wednesday-midnight statement may be proved against Culombe, and [nor] he [be] convicted by their use, consistently with the Constitution.

VII.

Regardful as one must be of the problems of crime detection confronting the States, one does not reach the result here as an easy decision. In the case of such unwitnessed crimes as the Kurp's killings, the trials of detection challenge the most imaginative capacities of law enforcement officers. Often there is little else the police can do than interrogate suspects as an indispensable part of criminal investigation. But when interrogation of a prisoner is so long continued, with such a purpose, and under such circumstances, as to make the whole proceeding an effective instrument for extorting an unwilling admission of guilt, due process precludes the use of the confession thus obtained. Under our accusatorial system, such an exploitation of interrogation, whatever its usefulness, is not a permissible substitute for judicial trial.

Reversed.

.... [Additional concurring opinions have been omitted.]

MR. JUSTICE HARLAN, whom MR. JUSTICE CLARK and MR. JUSTICE WHITTAKER join, dissenting.

I agree to what my Brother FRANKFURTER has written in delineation of the general principles governing police interrogation of those suspected of, or under investigation in connection with, the commission of crime, and as to the factors which should guide federal judicial review of state action in this field. I think, however, that upon this record, which contains few of the hallmarks usually found in "coerced confession" cases, such considerations find their proper reflection in affirmance of this judgment.

With due regard to the medical and other evidence as to petitioner's history and subnormal mentality, I am unable to consider that it was constitutionally impermissible for the State to conclude that petitioner's "Wednesday" confessions were the product of a deliberate choice on his part to try to ameliorate his fate by making a clean breast of things, and not the consequence of improper police activity. To me, petitioner's supplemental confession on the following Saturday night, which as depicted by the record bears all the *indicia* of spontaneity, is especially persuasive against this Court's contrary view.

I should also add that I find no constitutional infirmity in the standards used by the Connecticut courts in evaluating the voluntariness of petitioner's confessions. Cf. *Rogers* v. *Richmond*, 365 U.S. 534.

I would affirm.

MALLORY v. UNITED STATES

354 U.S. 449, 77 S. Ct. 1356, 1 L. Ed. 2d 1479 (1957)

MR. JUSTICE FRANKFURTER delivered the opinion of the Court.

Petitioner was convicted of rape in the United States District Court for the District of Columbia, and, as authorized by the District Code, the jury imposed a death sentence. The Court of Appeals affirmed, one judge dissenting. 98 U.S.App.D.C. 406, 236 F.2d 701. Since an important question involving the interpretation of the Federal Rules of Criminal Procedure was involved in this capital case, we granted the petition for certiorari. 352 U.S. 877.

The rape occurred at six p.m. on April 7, 1954, in the basement of the apartment house inhabited by the victim. She had descended to the basement a few minutes previous to wash some laundry. Experiencing some difficulty in detaching a hose in the sink, she sought help from the janitor, who lived in a basement apartment with his wife, two grown sons, a younger son and the petitioner, his nineteen-year-old half-brother. Petitioner was alone in the apartment at the time. He detached the hose and returned to his quarters. Very shortly thereafter, a masked man, whose general features were identified to resemble those of petitioner and his two grown nephews, attacked the woman. She had heard no one descend the wooden steps that furnished the only means of entering the basement from above.

Petitioner and one of his grown nephews disappeared from the apartment house shortly after the crime was committed. The former was apprehended the following afternoon between two and two-thirty p.m. and was taken, along with his older nephews, also suspects, to police headquarters. At least four officers questioned him there in the presence of other officers for thirty to forty-five minutes, beginning the examination by telling him, according to his testimony, that his brother had said that he was the assailant. Petitioner strenuously denied his guilt. He spent the rest of the afternoon at headquarters, in the company of the other two suspects and his brother a good part of the time. About four p.m. the three suspects were asked to submit to "lie detector" tests, and they agreed. The officer in charge of the polygraph machine was not located for almost two hours, during which time the suspects received food and drink. The nephews were then examined first. Questioning of petitioner began just after eight p.m. Only he and the polygraph operator were present in a small room, the door to which was closed.

Following almost an hour and one-half of steady interrogation, he "first stated that he could have done this crime, or that he might have done it. He finally stated that he was responsible. . . ." (Testimony of polygraph operator, R. 70.) Not until ten p.m., after petitioner had repeated his confession to other officers, did the police attempt to reach a United States Commissioner for the purpose of arraignment. Failing in this, they obtained petitioner's consent to examination by the deputy coroner, who noted no *indicia* of physical or psychological coercion. Petitioner was then confronted by the complaining witness and "[p]ractically every man in the Sex Squad," and in response to questioning by three officers, he repeated the confession. Between eleven-thirty p.m. and twelve-thirty a.m. he dictated the confession to a typist. The next morning he was brought before a Commissioner. At the trial, which was delayed for a year because of doubt about petitioner's capacity to understand the proceedings against him, the signed confession was introduced in evidence.

The case calls for the proper application of Rule 5(a) of the Federal Rules of Criminal Procedure, promulgated in 1946, 327 U.S. 821. That Rule provides:

> (a) APPEARANCE BEFORE THE COMMISSIONER. An officer making an arrest under a warrant issued upon a complaint or any person making an arrest without a warrant shall take the arrested person without unnecessary delay before the nearest available commissioner or before any other nearby officer empowered to commit persons charged with offenses against the laws of the United States. When a person arrested without a warrant is brought before a commissioner or other officer, a complaint shall be filed forthwith.

This provision has both statutory and judicial antecedents for guidance in applying it. The requirement that arraignment be "without unnecessary delay" is a compendious restatement, without substantive change, of several prior specific federal statutory provisions. [Citations omitted.] Nearly all the States have similar enactments.

In *McNabb* v. *United States*, 318 U.S. 332, 343–344, we spelled out the important reasons of policy behind this body of legislation:

> The purpose of this impressively pervasive requirement of criminal procedure is plain. . . . The awful instruments of the criminal law cannot be entrusted to a single functionary. The complicated process of criminal justice is therefore divided into different parts, responsibility for which is separately vested in the various participants upon whom the criminal law relies for its vindication. Legislation such as this, requiring that the police must with reasonable promptness show legal cause for detaining arrested persons, constitutes an important safeguard —not only in assuring protection for the innocent but also in securing conviction of the guilty by methods that commend themselves to a progressive and self-confident society. For this procedural requirement checks resort to those reprehensible practices known as the 'third degree' which, though universally rejected as indefensible, still find their way into use. It aims to avoid all the evil implications of secret interrogation of persons accused of crime.

Since such unwarranted detention led to tempting utilization of intensive interrogation, easily gliding into the evils of "the third degree," the Court held that police detention of defendants beyond the time when a committing magistrate was readily accessible constituted "willful disobedience of law." In order adequately to enforce the congressional requirement of prompt arraignment, it was deemed necessary to render inadmissible incriminating statements elicited from defendants during a period of unlawful detention.

In *Upshaw* v. *United States*, 335 U.S. 410, which came here after the Federal Rules of Criminal Procedure had been in operation, the Court made it clear that Rule 5(a)'s standard of "without unnecessary delay" implied no relaxation of the *McNabb* doctrine.

The requirement of Rule 5(a) is part of the procedure devised by Congress for safeguarding individual rights without hampering effective and intelligent law enforcement. Provisions related to Rule 5(a) contemplate a procedure that allows arresting officers little more leeway than the interval between arrest and the ordinary administrative steps required to bring a suspect before the nearest available magistrate. Rule 4(a) provides: "If it appears from the complaint that there is probable cause to believe that an offense has been committed and that the defendant has committed it, a warrant for the arrest of the defendant shall issue. . . ." Rule 4(b) requires that the warrant "shall command that the defendant be arrested and brought before the nearest available commissioner." And Rules 5(b) and (c) reveal the function of the requirement of prompt arraignment:

> (b) STATEMENT BY THE COMMISSIONER. The commissioner shall inform the defendant of the

complaint against him, of his right to retain counsel and of his right to have a preliminary examination. He shall also inform the defendant that he is not required to make a statement and that any statement made by him may be used against him. The commissioner shall allow the defendant reasonable time and opportunity to consult counsel and shall admit the defendant to bail as provided in these rules.

(c) PRELIMINARY EXAMINATION. The defendant shall not be called upon to plead. If the defendant waives preliminary examination, the commissioner shall forthwith hold him to answer in the district court. If the defendant does not waive examination, the commissioner shall hear the evidence within a reasonable time. The defendant may cross-examine witnesses against him and may introduce evidence in his own behalf. If from the evidence it appears to the commissioner that there is probable cause to believe that an offense has been committed and that the defendant has committed it, the commissioner shall forthwith hold him to answer in the district court; otherwise the commissioner shall discharge him. The commissioner shall admit the defendant to bail as provided in these rules.

The scheme for initiating a federal prosecution is plainly defined. The police may not arrest upon mere suspicion but only on "probable cause." The next step in the proceeding is to arraign the arrested person before a judicial officer as quickly as possible so that he may be advised of his rights and so that the issue of probable cause may be promptly determined. The arrested person may, of course, be "booked" by the police. But he is not to be taken to police headquarters in order to carry out a process of inquiry that lends itself, even if not so designed, to eliciting damaging statements to support the arrest and ultimately his guilt.

The duty enjoined upon arresting officers to arraign "without unnecessary delay" indicates that the command does not call for mechanical or automatic obedience. Circumstances may justify a brief delay between arrest and arraignment, as for instance, where the story volunteered by the accused is susceptible of quick verification through third parties. But the delay must not be of a nature to give opportunity for the extraction of a confession.

The circumstances of this case preclude a holding that arraignment was "without unnecessary delay." Petitioner was arrested in the early afternoon and was detained at headquarters within the vicinity of numerous committing magistrates. Even though the police had ample evidence from other sources than the petitioner for regarding the petitioner as the chief suspect, they first questioned him for approximately a half hour. When this inquiry of a nineteen-year-old lad of limited intelligence produced no confession, the police asked him to submit to a "lie-detector" test. He was not told of his rights to counsel or to a preliminary examination before a magistrate, nor was he warned that he might keep silent and "that any statement made by him may be used against him." After four hours of further detention at headquarters, during which arraignment could easily have been made in the same building in which the police headquarters were housed, petitioner was examined by the lie-detector operator for another hour and a half before his story began to waiver. Not until he had confessed, when any judicial caution had lost its purpose, did the police arraign him.

We cannot sanction this extended delay, resulting in confession, without subordinating the general rule of prompt arraignment to the discretion of arresting officers in finding exceptional circumstances for its disregard. In every case where the police resort to interrogation of an arrested person and secure a confession, they may well claim, and quite sincerely, that they were merely trying to check on the information given by him. Against such a claim and the evil potentialities of the practice for which it is urged stands Rule 5(a) as a barrier. Nor is there an escape from the constraint laid upon the police by that Rule in that two other suspects were involved for the same crime. Presumably, whomever the police arrest they must arrest on "probable cause." It is not the function of the police to arrest, as it were, at large and to use an interrogating process at police headquarters in order to determine whom they should charge before a committing magistrate on "probable cause."

Reversed and remanded.

MIRANDA v. ARIZONA

384 U.S. 436, 86 S. Ct. 1602, 16 L. Ed. 2d 694 (1966)

MR. CHIEF JUSTICE WARREN delivered the opinion of the Court.

The cases before us raise questions which go to the roots of our concepts of American criminal jurisprudence: the restraints society must observe consistent with the Federal Constitution in prosecuting individuals for crime. More specifically, we deal with the admissibility of statements obtained from an individual who is subjected to custodial police interrogation and the necessity for procedures which assure that the individual is accorded his privilege under the Fifth Amendment to the Constitution not to be compelled to incriminate himself.

We dealt with certain phases of this problem recently in *Escobedo v. Illinois,* 378 U.S. 478 (1964). There, as in the four cases before us, the law enforcement officials took the defendant into custody and interrogated him in a police station for the purpose of obtaining a confession. The police did not effectively advise him of his right to remain silent or of his right to consult with his attorney. Rather, they confronted him with an alleged accomplice who accused him of having perpetrated a murder. When the defendant denied the accusation and said "I didn't shoot Manuel, you did it," they handcuffed him and took him to an interrogation room. There, while handcuffed and standing, he was questioned for four hours until he confessed. During this interrogation, the police denied his request to speak to his attorney, and they prevented his retained attorney, who had come to the police station, from consulting with him. At his trial, the State, over his objection, introduced the confession against him. We held that the statements thus made were constitutionally inadmissible.

This case has been the subject of judicial interpretation and spirited legal debate since it was decided two years ago. Both state and federal courts, in assessing its implications, have arrived at varying conclusions. A wealth of scholarly material has been written tracing its ramifications and underpinnings. Police and prosecutor have speculated on its range and desirability. We granted certiorari in these cases [discussed *infra*] in order further to explore some facets of the problems, thus exposed, of applying the privilege against self-incrimination to in-custody interrogation, and to give concrete constitutional guidelines for law enforcement agencies and courts to follow.

We start here, as we did in *Escobedo*, with the premise that our holding is not an innovation in our jurisprudence, but is an application of principles long recognized and applied in other settings. We have undertaken a thorough re-examination of the *Escobedo* decision and the principles it announced, and we reaffirm it. That case was but an explication of basic rights that are enshrined in our Constitution—that "No person . . . shall be compelled in any criminal case to be a witness against himself," and that "the accused shall . . . have the Assistance of Counsel"—rights which were put in jeopardy in that case through official overbearing. These precious rights were fixed in our Constitution only after centuries of persecution and struggle. And in the words of CHIEF JUSTICE MARSHALL, they were secured "for ages to come, and . . . designed to approach immortality as nearly as human institutions can approach it," *Cohens* v. *Virginia*, 19 U.S. (6 Wheat.) 264, 387 (1821).

Over 70 years ago, our predecessors on this Court eloquently stated:

> The maxim *'Nemo tenetur seipsum accusare,'* had its origin in a protest against the inquisitorial and manifestly unjust methods of interrogating accused persons, which [have] long obtained in the continental system, and, until the expulsion of the Stuarts from the British throne in 1688, and the erection of additional barriers for the protection of the people against the exercise of arbitrary power,

[were] not uncommon even in England. While the admissions or confessions of the prisoner, when voluntarily and freely made, have always ranked high in the scale of incriminating evidence, if an accused person be asked to explain his apparent connection with a crime under investigation, the ease with which the questions put to him may assume an inquisitorial character, the temptation to press the witness unduly, to browbeat him if he be timid or reluctant, to push him into a corner, and to entrap him into fatal contradictions, which is so painfully evident in many of these earlier state trials, notably in those of Sir Nicholas Throckmorton, and Udal, the Puritan minister, made the system so odious as to give rise to a demand for its total abolition. The change in the English criminal procedure in that particular seems to be founded upon no statute and no judicial opinion, but upon a general and silent acquiescence of the courts in a popular demand. But, however adopted, it has become firmly embedded in English, as well as in American jurisprudence. So deeply did the iniquities of the ancient system impress themselves upon the minds of the American colonists that the States, with one accord, made a denial of the right to question an accused person a part of their fundamental law, so that a maxim, which in England was a mere rule of evidence, became clothed in this country with the impregnability of a constitutional enactment. *Brown* v. *Walker*, 161 U.S. 591, 596–597 (1896).

. . . .

Our holding will be spelled out with some specificity in the pages which follow but briefly stated it is this: the prosecution may not use statements, whether exculpatory or inculpatory, stemming from custodial interrogation of the defendant unless it demonstrates the use of procedural safeguards effective to secure the privilege against self-incrimination. By custodial interrogation, we mean questioning initiated by law enforcement officers after a person has been taken into custody or otherwise deprived of his freedom of action in any significant way. As for the procedural safeguards to be employed, unless other fully effective means are devised to inform accused persons of their right of silence and to assure a continuous opportunity to exercise it, the following measures are required. Prior to any questioning, the person must be warned that he has a right to remain silent, that any statement he does make may be used as evidence against him, and that he has a right to the presence of an attorney, either retained or appointed. The defendant may waive effectuation of these rights, provided the waiver is made voluntarily, knowingly and intelligently. If, however, he indicates in any manner, and at any stage of the process, that he wishes to consult with an attorney before speaking there can be no questioning. Likewise, if the individual is alone and indicates in any manner that he does not wish to be interrogated, the police may not question him. The mere fact that he may have answered some questions or volunteered some statements on his own does not deprive him of the right to refrain from answering any further inquiries until he has consulted with an attorney and thereafter consents to be questioned.

I.

The constitutional issue we decide in each of these cases is the admissibility of statements obtained from a defendant questioned while in custody or otherwise deprived of his freedom of action in any significant way. In each, the defendant was questioned by police officers, detectives, or a prosecuting attorney in a room in which he was cut off from the outside world. In none of these cases was the defendant given a full and effective warning of his rights at the outset of the interrogation process. In all the cases, the questioning elicited oral admissions, and in three of them, signed statements as well which were admitted at their trials. They all thus share salient features—incommunicado interrogation of individuals in a police-dominated atmosphere, resulting in self-incriminating statements without full warnings of constitutional rights.

An understanding of the nature and setting of this in-custody interrogation is essential to our decisions today. The difficulty in depicting what transpires at such interrogations stems from the fact that in this country they have largely taken place incommunicado. From extensive factual studies undertaken in the early 1930's, including the famous Wickersham Report to Congress by a Presidential Commission, it is clear that police violence and the "third degree" flourished at that time. In a series of cases decided by this Court long after these studies, the police resorted to physical brutality—beatings, hanging, whipping—and to sustained and protracted questioning incommunicado in order to extort confessions. The Commission on Civil Rights in 1961 found much evidence to indicate that "some policemen still resort to physical force to obtain confessions," 1961 Comm'n on Civil Rights Rep., Justice, pt. 5, 17. The use of physical brutality and violence is not, unfortunately, relegated to the past or to any part of the country. Only recently in Kings County, New York, the police brutally beat, kicked and placed lighted cigarette butts on the back of a potential witness under interrogation for the purpose of securing a statement incriminating a third party. *People* v. *Portelli*, 15 N.Y.2d 235, 257 N.Y.S.2d 931, 205 N.E.2d 857 (1965).

The examples given above are undoubtedly the exception now, but they are sufficiently widespread to be the object of concern. Unless a proper limitation upon custodial interrogation is achieved—such as these decisions will advance—there can be no assurance that practices of this nature will be eradicated in the foreseeable future. . . .

Again we stress that the modern practice of in-custody interrogation is psychologically rather than physically oriented. As we have stated before, "Since *Chambers* v. *Florida,* 309 U.S. 227, this Court has recognized that coercion can be mental as well as physical, and that the blood of the accused is not the only hallmark of an unconstitutional inquisition." *Blackburn* v. *Alabama,* 361 U.S. 199, 206 (1960). Interrogation still takes place in privacy. Privacy results in secrecy and this in turn results in a gap in our knowledge as to what in fact goes on in the interrogation rooms. A valuable source of information about present police practices, however, may be found in various police manuals and texts which document procedures employed with success in the past, and which recommend various other effective tactics. These texts are used by law enforcement agencies themselves as guides. It should be noted that these texts professedly present the most enlightened and effective means presently used to obtain statements through custodial interrogation. By considering these texts and other data, it is possible to describe procedures observed and noted around the country.

. . . . [Here the court includes a detailed description of techniques and procedures advocated in texts and manuals. This description should be read to understand the Court's conception of police investigation techniques.]

From these representative samples of interrogation techniques, the setting prescribed by the manuals and observed in practice becomes clear. In essence, it is this: To be alone with the subject is essential to prevent distraction and to deprive him of any outside support. The aura of confidence in his guilt undermines his will to resist. He merely confirms the preconceived story the police seek to have him describe. Patience and persistence, at times relentless questioning, are employed. To obtain a confession, the interrogator must "patiently maneuver himself or his quarry into a position from which the desired object may be obtained." When normal procedures fail to produce the needed result, the police may resort to deceptive stratagems such as giving false legal advice. It is important to keep the subject off balance, for example, by trading on his insecurity about himself or his surroundings. The police then persuade, trick, or cajole him out of exercising his constitutional rights.

. . . .

In the cases before us today, given this background, we concern ourselves primarily with this interrogation atmosphere and the evils it can bring. In *Miranda* v. *Arizona,* the police arrested the defendant and took him to a special interrogation room where they secured a confession. In *Vignera* v. *New York,* the defendant made oral admissions to the police after interrogation in the afternoon, and then signed an inculpatory statement upon being questioned by an assistant district attorney later the same evening. In *Westover* v. *United States*, the defendant was handed over to the Federal Bureau of Investigation by local authorities after they had detained and interrogated him for a lengthy period, both at night and the following morning. After some two hours of questioning, the federal officers had obtained signed statements from the defendant. Lastly, in *California* v. *Stewart*, the local police held the defendant five days in the station and interrogated him on nine separate occasions before they secured his inculpatory statement.

In these cases, we might find the defendants' statements to have been involuntary in traditional terms. Our concern for adequate safeguards to protect precious Fifth Amendment rights is, of course, not lessened in the slightest. In each of the cases, the defendant was thrust into an unfamiliar atmosphere and run through menacing police interrogation procedures. The potentiality for compulsion is forcefully apparent, for example in *Miranda*, where the indigent Mexican defendant was a seriously disturbed individual with pronounced sexual fantasies, and in *Stewart*, in which the defendant was an indigent Los Angeles Negro who had dropped out of school in the sixth grade. To be sure, the records do not evince overt physical coercion or patent psychological ploys. The fact remains that in none of these cases did the officers undertake to afford appropriate safeguards at the outset of the interrogation to insure that the statements were truly the product of free choice.

It is obvious that such an interrogation environment is created for no purpose other than to subjugate the individual to the will of his examiner. This atmosphere carries its own badge of intimidation. To be sure, this is not physical intimidation, but it is equally destructive of human dignity. The current practice of incommunicado interrogation is at odds with one of our Nation's most cherished principles —that the individual may not be compelled to incriminate himself. Unless adequate protective devices are employed to dispel the compulsion inherent in custodial surroundings, no statement obtained from the defendant can truly be the product of his free choice.

From the foregoing, we can readily perceive an intimate connection between the privilege against self-incrimination and police custodial questioning. It is fitting to turn to history and precedent underlying the Self-Incrimination Clause to determine its applicability in this situation.

. . . .

II.

The question in these cases is whether the privilege is fully applicable during a period of custodial interrogation. In this Court, the privilege has consistently been accorded a liberal construction. [Citations omitted.] We are satisfied that all the principles embodied in the privilege apply to informal compulsion exerted by law-enforcement officers during in-custody questioning. An individual swept from familiar surroundings into police custody, surrounded by antagonistic forces, and subjected to the techniques of persuasion described above cannot be otherwise than under compulsion to speak. As a practical matter, the compulsion to speak in the isolated setting of the police station may well be greater than in courts or other official investigations, where there are often impartial observers to guard against intimidation or trickery.

. . . .

In addition to the expansive historical development of the privilege and the sound policies which have nurtured its evolution, judicial precedent thus clearly establishes its application to incommunicado interrogation. In fact, the Government concedes this point as well established in *Westover* v. *United States*, stating: "We have no doubt . . . that it is possible for a suspect's Fifth Amendment right to be violated during in-custody questioning by a law-enforcement officer."

Because of the adoption by Congress of Rule 5(a) of the Federal Rules of Criminal Procedure, and this Court's effectuation of that Rule in *McNabb* v. *United States*, 318 U.S. 332 (1943), and *Mallory* v. *United States*, 354 U.S. 449 (1957), we have had little occasion in the past quarter century to reach the constitutional issues in dealing with federal interrogations. These supervisory rules, requiring production of an arrested person before a commissioner "without unnecessary delay" and excluding evidence obtained in default of that statutory obligation, were nonetheless responsive to the same considerations of Fifth Amendment policy that unavoidably face us now as to the States. In *McNabb*, 318 U.S., at 343–344, and in *Mallory*, 354 U.S., at 455–456, we recognized both the dangers of interrogation and the appropriateness of prophylaxis stemming from the very fact of interrogation itself.

Our decision in *Malloy* v. *Hogan*, 378 U.S. 1 (1964), necessitates an examination of the scope of the privilege in state cases as well. In *Malloy*, we squarely held the privilege applicable to the States, and held that the substantive standards underlying the privilege applied with full force to state court proceedings. There, as in *Murphy* v. *Waterfront Comm'n* and *Griffin* v. *California*, we applied the existing Fifth Amendment standards to the case before us. Aside from the holding itself, the reasoning in *Malloy* made clear what had already became apparent—that the substantive and procedural safeguards surrounding admissibility of confessions in state cases had become exceedingly exacting, reflecting all the policies embedded in the privilege. The voluntariness doctrine in the state cases, as *Malloy* indicates, encompasses all interrogation practices which are likely to exert such pressure upon an individual as to disable him from making a free and rational choice. The implications of this proposition were elaborated in our decision in *Escobedo* v. *Illinois*, decided one week after *Malloy* applied the privilege to the States.

. . . .

III.

Today, then, there can be no doubt that the Fifth Amendment privilege is available outside of criminal court proceedings and serves to protect persons in all settings in which their freedom of action is curtailed in any significant way from being compelled to incriminate themselves. We have concluded that without proper safeguards the process of in-custody interrogation of persons suspected or accused of crime contains inherently compelling pressures which work to undermine the individual's will to resist and to compel him to speak where he would not otherwise do so freely. In order to combat these pressures and to permit a full opportunity to exercise the privilege against self-incrimination, the accused must be adequately and effectively apprised of his rights and the exercise of those rights must be fully honored.

It is impossible for us to foresee the potential alternatives for protecting the privilege which might be devised by Congress or the States in the exercise of their creative rule-making capacities. Therefore we cannot say that the constitution necessarily requires adherence to any particular solution for the inherent compulsions of the interrogation process as it is presently conducted. Our decision in no way creates a constitutional strait-jacket which will handicap sound efforts at reform, nor is it intended to have this effect. We encourage Congress and the States to continue their laudable search for increasingly effective ways of protecting the rights of the individual while promoting efficient enforcement of our criminal laws. However, unless we are shown other procedures which are at least as effective in apprising accused persons of their right of silence and in assuring a continuous opportunity to exercise it, the following safeguards must be observed.

At the outset, if a person in custody is to be subjected to interrogation, he must first be informed in clear and unequivocal terms that he has the right to remain silent. For those unaware of the privilege, the warning is needed simply to make them aware of it—the threshold requirement for an intelligent decision as to its exercise. More important, such a warning is an absolute prerequisite in overcoming the inherent pressures of the interrogation atmosphere. It is not just the subnormal or woefully ignorant who succumb to an interrogator's imprecations, whether implied or expressly stated, that the interrogation will continue until a confession is obtained or that silence in the face of accusation is itself damning and will bode ill when presented to a jury. Further, the warning will show the individual that his interrogators are prepared to recognize his privilege should he choose to exercise it.

The Fifth Amendment privilege is so fundamental to our system of constitutional rule and the expedient of giving an adequate warning as to the availability of the privilege so simple, we will not pause to inquire in individual cases whether the defendant was aware of his rights without a warning being given. Assessments of the knowledge the defendant possessed, based on information as to his age, education, intelligence, or prior contact with authorities, can never be more than speculation; a warning is a clearcut fact. More important, whatever the background of the person interrogated, a warning at the time of the interrogation is indispensable to overcome its pressures and to insure that the individual knows he is free to exercise the privilege at that point in time.

The warning of the right to remain silent must be accompanied by the explanation that anything said can and will be used against the individual in court. This warning is needed in order to make him aware not only of the privilege, but also of the consequences of foregoing it. It is only through an awareness of these consequences that there can be any assurance of real understanding and intelligent exercise of the privilege. Moreover, this warning may serve to make the individual more acutely aware that he is faced with a phase of the adversary system—that he is not in the presence of persons acting solely in his interest.

The circumstances surrounding in-custody interrogation can operate very quickly to overbear the will of one merely made aware of his privilege by his interrogators. Therefore, the right to have counsel present at the interrogation is indispensable to the protection of the Fifth Amendment privilege under the system we delineate today. Our aim is to assure that the individual's right to choose between silence and speech remains unfettered throughout the interrogation process. A once-stated warning, delivered by those who will conduct the interrogation, cannot itself suffice to that end among those who most require knowledge of their rights. A mere warning given by the interrogators is not alone sufficient to accomplish that end. Prosecutors themselves claim that the admonishment of the right to remain silent without more "will benefit only the recidivist and the professional." . . . Even preliminary advice given to the accused by his own attorney can be swifty overcome by the secret interrogation process. . . . Thus, the need for counsel to protect the Fifth Amendment privilege comprehends not merely a right to consult with counsel prior to questioning, but also to have counsel present during any questioning if the defendant so desires.

The presence of counsel at the interrogation may serve several significant subsidiary functions as well. If the accused decides to talk to his interrogators, the assistance of counsel can mitigate the dangers of untrustworthiness. With a lawyer present the likelihood that the police will practice coercion is reduced, and if coercion is nevertheless exercised the lawyer can testify to it in court. The presence of a lawyer can also help to guarantee that the accused gives a fully accurate statement to the police and that the statement is rightly reported by the prosecution at trial. [Citation omitted.]

An individual need not make a pre-interrogation request for a lawyer. While such request affirmatively secures his right to have one, his failure to ask for a lawyer does not constitute a waiver. No effective waiver of the right to counsel during interrogation can be recognized unless specifically made after the warnings we here delineate have been given. The accused who does not know his rights and therefore does not make a request may be the person who most needs counsel. . . .

In *Carnley* v. *Cochran*, 369 U.S. 506, 513 (1962), we stated: "[I]t is settled that where, the assistance of counsel is a constitutional requisite, the right to be furnished counsel does not depend on a request." This proposition applies with equal force in the context of providing counsel to protect an accused's Fifth Amendment privilege in the face of interrogation. Although the role of counsel at trial differs from the role during interrogation, the differences are not relevant to the question whether a request is a prerequisite.

Accordingly, we hold that an individual held for interrogation must be clearly informed that he has the right to consult with a lawyer and to have the lawyer with him during interrogation under the system for protecting the privilege we delineate today. As with the warnings of the right to remain silent and that anything stated can be used in evidence against him, this warning is an absolute prerequisite to interrogation. No amount of circumstantial evidence that the person may have been aware of this right will suffice to stand in its stead. Only through such a warning is there ascertainable assurance that the accused was aware of this right.

If an individual indicates that he wishes the assistance of counsel before any interrogation occurs, the authorities cannot rationally ignore or deny his request on the basis that the individual does not have or cannot afford a retained attorney. The financial ability of the individual has no relationship to the scope of the rights involved here. The privilege against self-incrimination secured by the Constitution applies to all individuals. The need for counsel in order to protect the privilege exists for the indigent as well as the affluent. In fact, were we to limit these constitutional rights to those who can retain an attorney, our decisions today would be of little significance. The cases before us as well as the vast majority of confession cases with which we have dealt in the past involve those unable to retain counsel. While authorities are not required to relieve the accused of his poverty, they have the obligation not to take advantage of indigence in the administration of justice. Denial of counsel to the indigent at the time of interrogation while allowing an attorney to those who can afford one would be no more supportable by reason or logic than the similar situation at trial and on appeal struck down in *Gideon* v. *Wainwright* and *Douglas* v. *California*.

In order to fully apprise a person interrogated of the extent of his rights under this system then, it is necessary to warn him not only that he has the right to consult with an attorney, but also that if he is indigent a lawyer will be appointed to represent him. Without this additional warning, the admonition of the right to consult with counsel would often be understood as meaning only that he can consult with a lawyer if he has one or has the funds to obtain one. The warning of a right to counsel would be hollow if not couched in terms that would convey to the indigent—the person most often subjected to interrogation—the knowledge that he too has a right to have counsel present. As with the warnings of the right to remain silent and of the general right to counsel, only by effective and express explanation to the indigent of this right can there be assurance that he was truly in a position to exercise it.

Once warnings have been given, the subsequent procedure is clear. If the individual indicates in any manner, at any time prior to or during questioning, that he wishes to remain silent, the interrogation must cease. At this point he has shown that he intends to exercise his Fifth Amendment privilege; any statement taken after the person invokes his privilege cannot be other than the product of compulsion, subtle or otherwise. Without the right to cut off questioning, the setting of in-custody interrogation operates on the individual to overcome free choice in producing a statement after the privilege has been once invoked. If the individual states that he wants an attorney, the interrogation must cease until an attorney is present. At that time, the individual must have an opportunity to confer with the attorney and to have him present during any subsequent questioning. If the individual cannot obtain an attorney and he indicates that he wants one before speaking to police, they must respect his decision to remain silent.

This does not mean, as some have suggested, that each police station must have a "station house lawyer" present at all times to advise prisoners. It does mean, however, that if police propose to interrogate a person they must make known to him that he is entitled to a lawyer and that if he cannot afford one, a lawyer will be provided for him prior to any interrogation. If authorities conclude that they will not provide counsel during a reasonable period of time in which investigation in the field is carried out, they may do so without violating the person's Fifth Amendment privilege so long as they do not question him during that time.

If the interrogation continues

without the presence of an attorney and a statement is taken, a heavy burden rests on the government to demonstrate that the defendant knowingly and intelligently waived his privilege against self-incrimination and his right to retained or appointed counsel. . . . This Court has always set high standards of proof for the waiver of constitutional rights, . . . and we reassert these standards as applied to in-custody interrogation. Since the State is responsible for establishing the isolated circumstances under which the interrogation takes place and has the only means of making available corroborated evidence of warnings given during incommunicado interrogation, the burden is rightly on its shoulders.

An express statement that the individual is willing to make a statement and does not want an attorney followed closely by a statement could constitute a waiver. But a valid waiver will not be presumed simply from the silence of the accused after warnings are given or simply from the fact that a confession was in fact eventually obtained. A statement we made in *Carnley* v. *Cochran*, 369 U.S. 506, 516 (1962), is applicable here:

> Presuming waiver from a silent record is impermissible. The record must show, or there must be an allegation and evidence which show, that an accused was offered counsel but intelligently and understandingly rejected the offer. Anything less is not waiver.

. . . Moreover, where in-custody interrogation is involved, there is no room for the contention that the privilege is waived if the individual answers some questions or gives some information on his own prior to invoking his right to remain silent when interrogated.

Whatever the testimony of the authorities as to waiver of rights by an accused, the fact of lengthy interrogation or incommunicado incarceration before a statement is made is strong evidence that the accused did not validly waive his rights. In these circumstances the fact that the individual eventually made a statement is consistent with the conclusion that the compelling influence of the interrogation finally forced him to do so. It is inconsistent with any notion of a voluntary relinquishment of the privilege. Moreover, any evidence that the accused was threatened, tricked, or cajoled into a waiver will, of course, show that the defendant did not voluntarily waive his privilege. The requirement of warnings and waiver of rights is a fundamental with respect to the Fifth Amendment privilege and not simply a preliminary ritual to existing methods of interrogation.

The warnings required and the waiver necessary in accordance with our opinion today are, in the absence of a fully effective equivalent, prerequisites to the admissibility of any statement made by a defendant. No distinction can be drawn between statements which are direct confessions and statements which amount to "admissions" of part or all of an offense.

The privilege against self-incrimination protects the individual from being compelled to incriminate himself in any manner; it does not distinguish degrees of incrimination. Similarly, for precisely the same reason, no distinction may be drawn between inculpatory statements and statements alleged to be merely "exculpatory." If a statement made were in fact truly exculpatory it would, of course, never be used by the prosecution. In fact, statements merely intended to be exculpatory by the defendant are often used to impeach his testimony at trial or to demonstrate untruths in the statement given under interrogation and thus to prove guilt by implication. These statements are incriminating in any meaningful sense of the word and may not be used without the full warnings and effective waiver required for any other statement. In *Escobedo* itself, the defendant fully intended his accusation of another as the slayer to be exculpatory as to himself.

The principles announced today deal with the protection which must be given to the privilege against self-incrimination when the individual is first subjected to police interrogation while in custody at the station or otherwise deprived of his freedom of action in any way. It is at this point that our adversary system of criminal proceedings commences, distinguishing itself at the outset from the inquisitorial system recognized in some countries. Under the system of warnings we delineate today or under any other system which may be devised and found effective, the safeguards to be erected about the privilege must come into play at this point.

Our decision is not intended to hamper the traditional function of police officers in investigating crime. . . . When an individual is in custody on probable cause, the police may, of course, seek out evidence in the field to be used at trial against him. Such investigation may include inquiry of persons not under restraint. General on-the-scene questioning as to facts surrounding a crime or other general questioning of citizens in the fact-finding process is not affected by our holding. It is an act of responsible citizenship for individuals to give whatever information they may have to aid in law enforcement. In such situations the compelling atmosphere inherent in the process of in-custody interrogation is not necessarily present.

In dealing with statements obtained through interrogation, we do not purport to find all confessions inadmissible. Confessions remain a proper element in law enforcement. Any statement given freely and voluntarily without any compelling influences is, of course, admissible in evidence. The fundamental import of the privilege while an individual is in custody is not whether he is allowed to talk to the police without the benefit of warnings and counsel, but whether he can be interrogated. There is no requirement that police stop a person who enters a police station and states that he wishes to confess to a crime, or a person who calls the police to offer a confession or any other statement he desires to make. Volunteered statements of any kind are not barred by the Fifth Amendment and their admissibility is not affected by our holding today.

To summarize, we hold that when an individual is taken into custody or otherwise deprived of his freedom by the authorities and is subjected to questioning, the privilege against self-incrimination is jeopardized. Procedural safeguards must be employed to protect the privilege, and unless other fully effective means are adopted to notify the person of his right of silence and to assure that the exercise of the right will be scrupulously honored, the following measures are required. He must be warned prior to any questioning that he has the right to remain silent, that anything he says can be used against him in a court of law, that he has the right to the presence of an attorney, and that if he cannot afford an attorney one will be appointed for him prior to any questioning if he so desires. Opportunity to exercise these rights must be afforded to him throughout the interrogation. After such warnings have been given, and such opportunity afforded him, the individual may knowingly and intelligently waive these rights and agree to answer questions or make a statement. But unless and until such warnings and waiver are demonstrated by the prosecution at trial, no evidence obtained as a result of interrogation can be used against him.

IV.

A recurrent argument made in these cases is that society's need for interrogation outweighs the privilege. This argument is not unfamiliar to this Court. [Citation omitted.] The whole thrust of our foregoing discussion demonstrates that the Constitution has prescribed the rights of the individual when confronted with the power of government when it provided in the Fifth Amendment that an individual cannot be compelled to be a witness against himself. That right cannot be abridged. As MR. JUSTICE BRANDEIS once observed:

> Decency, security, and liberty alike demand that government officials shall be subjected to the same rules of conduct that are commands to the citizen. In a government of laws, existence of the government will be imperilled if it fails to observe the law scrupulously. Our government is the potent, the omnipresent teacher. For good or for ill, it teaches the whole people by its example. Crime is contagious. If the government becomes a lawbreaker, it breeds contempt for law; it invites every man to become a law unto himself; it invites anarchy. To declare that in the administration of the criminal law the end justifies the means . . . would bring terrible retribution. Against that pernicious doctrine this court should resolutely set its face. *Olmstead v. United States*, 277 U.S. 438, 485 (1928) (dissenting opinion).

In this connection, one of our

country's distinguished jurists has pointed out: "The quality of a nation's civilization can be largely measured by the methods it uses in the enforcement of its criminal law."

If the individual desires to exercise his privilege, he has the right to do so. This is not for the authorities to decide. An attorney may advise his client not to talk to police until he has had an opportunity to investigate the case, or he may wish to be present with his client during any police questioning. In doing so an attorney is merely exercising the good professional judgment he has been taught. This is not cause for considering the attorney a menace to law enforcement. He is merely carrying out what he is sworn to do under oath—to protect to the extent of his ability the rights of his client. In fulfilling this responsibility the attorney plays a vital role in the administration of criminal justice under our Constitution.

In announcing these principles, we are not unmindful of the burdens which law enforcement officials must bear, often under trying circumstances. We also fully recognize the obligation of all citizens to aid in enforcing the criminal laws. This Court, while protecting individual rights, has always given ample latitude to law enforcement agencies in the legitimate exercise of their duties. The limits we have placed on the interrogation process should not constitute an undue interference with a proper system of law enforcement. As we have noted, our decision does not in any way preclude police from carrying our their traditional investigatory functions. Although confessions may play an important role in some convictions, the cases before us present graphic examples of the overstatement of the "need" for confessions. In each case authorities conducted interrogations ranging up to five days in duration despite the presence, through standard investigating practices, of considerable evidence against each defendant. [Citations omitted.]

It is also urged that an unfettered right to detention for interrogation should be allowed because it will often redound to the benefit of the person questioned. When police inquiry determines that there is no reason to believe that the person has committed any crime, it is said, he will be released without need for further formal procedures. The person who has committed no offense, however, will be better able to clear himself after warnings with counsel present than without. It can be assumed that in such circumstances a lawyer would advise his client to talk freely to police in order to clear himself.

Custodial interrogation, by contrast, does not necessarily afford the innocent an opportunity to clear themselves. A serious consequence of the present practice of the interrogation alleged to be beneficial for the innocent is that many arrests "for investigation" subject large numbers of innocent persons to detention and interrogation. In one of the cases before us, *California* v. *Stewart,* police held four persons, who were in the defendant's house at the time of the arrest, in jail for five days until defendant confessed. At that time they were finally released. Police stated that there was "no evidence to connect them with any crime." Available statistics on the extent of this practice where it is condoned indicate that these four are far from alone in being subjected to arrest, prolonged detention, and interrogation without the requisite probable cause.

. . . .

It is also urged upon us that we withhold decision on this issue until state legislative bodies and advisory groups have had an opportunity to deal with these problems by rule making. We have already pointed out that the Constitution does not require any specific code of procedures for protecting the privilege against self-incrimination during custodial interrogation. Congress and the States are free to develop their own safeguards for the privilege, so long as they are fully as effective as those described above in informing accused persons of their right of silence and in affording a continuous opportunity to exercise it. In any event, however, the issues presented are of constitutional dimensions and must be determined by the courts. The admissibility of a statement in the face of a claim that it was obtained in violation of the defendant's constitutional rights is an issue the resolution of which has long since been undertaken by this Court. . . . Judicial solutions to problems of constitutional dimension have evolved decade by decade. As courts have been presented with the need to enforce constitutional rights, they have found means of doing so. That was our responsibility when *Escobedo* was before us and it is our responsibility today. Where rights secured by the Constitution are involved, there can be no rule making or legislation which would abrogate them.

V.

Because of the nature of the problem and because of its recurrent significance in numerous cases, we have to this point discussed the relationship of the Fifth Amendment privilege to police interrogation without specific concentration on the facts of the cases before us. We turn now to these facts to consider the application to these cases of the constitutional principles discussed above. In each instance, we have concluded that statements were obtained from the defendant under circumstances that did not meet constitutional standards for protection of the privilege.

No. 759. *Miranda* v. *Arizona*

On March 13, 1963, petitioner, Ernesto Miranda, was arrested at his home and taken in custody to a Phoenix police station. He was there identified by the complaining witness. The police then took him to "Interrogation Room No. 2" of the detective bureau. There he was questioned by two police officers. The officers admitted at trial that Miranda was not advised that he had a right to have an attorney present. Two hours later, the officers emerged from the interrogation room with a written confession signed by Miranda. At the top of the statement was a typed paragraph stating that the confession was made voluntarily, without threats or promises of immunity and "with full knowledge of my legal rights, understanding any statement I make may be used against me."

At his trial before a jury, the written confession was admitted into evidence over the objection of defense counsel, and the officers testified to the prior oral confession made by Miranda during the interrogation. Miranda was found guilty of kidnapping and rape. He was sentenced to 20 to 30 years' imprisonment on each count, the sentences to run concurrently. On appeal, the Supreme Court of Arizona held that Miranda's constitutional rights were not violated in obtaining the confession and affirmed the conviction. In reaching its decision, the court emphasized heavily the fact that Miranda did not specifically request counsel.

We reverse. From the testimony of the officers and by the admission of respondent, it is clear that Miranda was not in any way apprised of his right to consult with an attorney and to have one present during the interrogation, nor was his right not to be compelled to incriminate himself effectively protected in any other manner. Without these warnings the statements were inadmissible. The mere fact that he signed a statement which contained a typed-in clause stating that he had "full knowledge" of his "legal rights" does not approach the knowing and intelligent waiver required to relinquish constitutional rights. [Citations omitted.]

No. 760. *Vignera* v. *New York*.

Petitioner, Michael Vignera, was picked up by New York police on October 14, 1960, in connection with the robbery three days earlier of a Brooklyn dress shop. They took him to the 17th Detective Squad headquarters in Manhattan. Sometime thereafter he was taken to the 66th Detective Squad. There a detective questioned Vignera with respect to the robbery. Vignera orally admitted the robbery to the detective. The detective was asked on cross-examination at trial by defense counsel whether Vignera was warned of his right to counsel before being interrogated. The prosecution objected to the question and the trial judge sustained the objection. Thus, the defense was precluded from making any showing that warnings had not been given. While at the 66th Detective Squad, Vignera was identified by the store owner and a saleslady as the man who robbed the dress shop. At about 3:00 p.m. he was formally arrested. The police then transported him to still another station, the 70th Precinct in Brooklyn, "for detention." At 11:00 p.m. Vignera was questioned by an assistant district attorney in the presence of a hearing reporter who transcribed the questions and Vignera's answers. This verbatim account of these proceedings contains no statement of any warnings given by the assistant district attorney. At Vignera's trial on a charge of first degree robbery, the detective testified as to the oral confession. The transcription of the statement taken was also introduced in evidence. At the conclusion of the testimony, the trial judge charged the jury in part as follows:

> The law doesn't say that the confession is void or invalidated because the police officer didn't advise the defendant as to his rights. Did you hear what I said? I am telling you what the law of the State of New York is.

Vignera was found guilty of first degree robbery. He was subsequently adjudged a third-felony offender and sentenced to 30 to 60 years' imprisonment. The conviction was affirmed without opinion by the Appellate Division, Second Department, and by the Court of Appeals, also without opinion. In argument to the Court of Appeals, the State contended that Vignera had no constitutional right to be advised of his right to counsel or his privilege against self-incrimination.

We reverse. The foregoing indicates that Vignera was not warned of any of his rights before the questioning by the detective and by the assistant district attorney. No other steps were taken to protect these rights. Thus he was not effectively apprised of his Fifth Amendment privilege or of his right to have counsel present and his statements are inadmissible.

No. 761. *Westover* v. *United States.*

At approximately 9:45 p.m. on March 20, 1963, petitioner, Carl Calvin Westover, was arrested by local police in Kansas City as a suspect in two Kansas City robberies. A report was also received from the FBI that he was wanted on a felony charge in California. The local authorities took him to a police station and placed him in a line-up on the local charges, and at about 11:45 p.m. he was booked. Kansas City police interrogated Westover on the night of his arrest. He denied any knowledge of criminal activities. The next day local officers interrogated him again throughout the morning. Shortly before noon they informed the FBI that they were through interrogating Westover and that the FBI could proceed to interrogate him. There is nothing in the record to indicate that Westover was ever given any warning as to his rights by local police. At noon, three special agents of the FBI continued the interrogation in a private interview room of the Kansas City Police Department, this time with respect to the robbery of a savings and loan association and a bank in Sacramento, California. After two or two and one-half hours, Westover signed separate confessions to each of these two robberies which had been prepared by one of the agents during the interrogation. At trial one of the agents testified, and a paragraph on each of the statements states, that the agents advised Westover that he did not have to make a statement, that any statement he made could be used against him, and that he had the right to see an attorney.

Westover was tried by a jury in federal court and convicted of the California robberies. His statements were introduced at trial. He was sentenced to 15 years' imprisonment on each count, the sentences to run consecutively. On appeal, the conviction was affirmed by the Court of Appeals for the Ninth Circuit. 342 F.2d 684.

We reverse. On the facts of this case we cannot find that Westover knowingly and intelligently waived his right to remain silent and his right to consult with counsel prior to the time he made the statement. At the time the FBI agents began questioning Westover, he had been in custody for over 14 hours and had been interrogated at length during that period. The FBI interrogation began immediately upon the conclusion of the interrogation by Kansas City police and was conducted in local police headquarters. Although the two law enforcement authorities are legally distinct and the crimes for which they interrogated Westover were different, the impact on him was that of a continuous period of questioning. There is no evidence of any warning given prior to the FBI interrogation nor is there any evidence of an articulated waiver of rights after the FBI commenced its interrogation. The record simply shows that the defendant did in fact confess a short time after being turned over to the FBI following interrogation by local police. Despite the fact that the FBI agents gave warnings at the outset of their interview, from Westover's point of view the warnings came at the end of the interrogation process. In these circumstances an intelligent waiver of constitutional rights cannot be assumed.

We do not suggest that law enforcement authorities are precluded from questioning any individual who has been held for a period of time by other authorities and interrogated by them without appropriate warnings. A different case would be presented if an accused were taken into custody by the second authority, removed both in time and place from his original surroundings, and then adequately advised of his rights and given an opportunity to exercise them. But here the FBI interrogation was conducted immediately following the state interrogation in the same police station—in the same compelling surroundings. Thus, in obtaining a confession from Westover the federal authorities were the beneficiaries of the pressure applied by the local in-custody interrogation. In these circumstances the giving of warnings alone was not sufficient to protect the privilege.

No. 584. *California* v. *Stewart*

In the course of investigating a series of purse-snatch robberies in which one of the victims had died of injuries inflicted by her assailant, respondent, Roy Allen Stewart, was pointed out to Los Angeles police as the endorser of dividend checks taken in one of the robberies. At about 7:15 p.m.,

January 31, 1963, police officers went to Stewart's house and arrested him. One of the officers asked Stewart if they could search the house to which he replied, "Go ahead." The search turned up various items taken from the five robbery victims. At the time of Stewart's arrest police also arrested Stewart's wife and three other persons who were visiting him. These four were jailed along with Stewart and were interrogated. Stewart was taken to the University Station of the Los Angeles Police Department where he was placed in a cell. During the next five days, police interrogated Stewart on nine different occasions. Except during the first interrogation session, when he was confronted with an accusing witness, Stewart was isolated with his interrogators.

During the ninth interrogation session, Stewart admitted that he had robbed the deceased and stated that he had not meant to hurt her. Police then brought Stewart before a magistrate for the first time. Since there was no evidence to connect them with any crime, the police then released the other four persons arrested with him.

Nothing in the record specifically indicates whether Stewart was or was not advised of his right to remain silent or his right to counsel. In a number of instances, however, the interrogating officers were asked to recount everything that was said during the interrogations. None indicated that Stewart was ever advised of his rights.

Stewart was charged with kidnapping to commit robbery, rape, and murder. At his trial, transcripts of the first interrogation and the confession at the last interrogation were introduced in evidence. The jury found Stewart guilty of robbery and first degree murder and fixed the penalty at death. On appeal, the Supreme Court of California reversed. 62 Cal.2d 571, 43 Cal.Reptr. 201, 400 P.2d 97. It held that under this Court's decision in *Escobedo,* Stewart should have been advised of his right to remain silent and of his right to counsel and that it would not presume, in the face of a silent record, that the police advised Stewart of his rights.

We affirm. In dealing with custodial interrogation, we will not presume that a defendant has been effectively apprised of his rights and that his privilege against self-incrimination has been adequately safeguarded on a record that does not show that any warnings have been given or that any effective alternative has been employed. Nor can a knowing and intelligent waiver of these rights be assumed on a silent record. Furthermore, Stewart's steadfast denial of the alleged offenses through eight of the nine interrogations over a period of five days is subject to no other construction than that he was compelled by persistent interrogation to forego his Fifth Amendment privilege.

Therefore, in accordance with the foregoing, the judgments of the Supreme Court of Arizona in No. 759 of the New York Court of Appeals in No. 760, and of the Court of Appeals for the Ninth

Circuit in No. 761 are reversed. The judgment of the Supreme Court of California in No. 584 is affirmed.

It is so ordered.

MR. JUSTICE CLARK, dissenting in Nos. 759, 760, and 761 and concurring in the result in No. 584.

It is with regret that I find it necessary to write in these cases. However, I am unable to join the majority because its opinion goes too far on too little, while my dissenting brethren do not go quite far enough. Nor can I join in the Court's criticism of the present practices of police and investigatory agencies as to custodial interrogation. The materials it refers to as "police manuals" are, as I read them, merely writings in this field by professors and some police officers. Not one is shown by the record here to be the official manual of any police department, much less in universal use in crime detection. Moreover, the examples of police brutality mentioned by the Court are rare exceptions to the thousands of cases that appear every year in the law reports. The police agencies—all the way from municipal and state forces to the federal bureaus—are responsible for law enforcement and public safety in this country. I am proud of their efforts, which in my view are not fairly characterized by the Court's opinion.

I.

The *ipse dixit* of the majority has no support in our cases. Indeed, the Court admits that "we might not find the defendants' statements [here] to have been involuntary in traditional terms." *Ante.* In short, the Court has added more to the requirements that the accused is entitled to consult with his lawyer and that he must be given the traditional warning that he may remain silent and that anything that he says may be used against him. [Citation omitted.] Now, the Court fashions a constitutional rule that the police may engage in no custodial interrogation without additionally advising the accused that he has a right under the Fifth Amendment to the presence of counsel during interrogation and that, if he is without funds, that counsel will be furnished him. When at any point during an interrogation the accused seeks affirmatively or impliedly to invoke his rights to silence or counsel, interrogation must be foregone or postponed. The Court further holds that failure to follow the new procedures requires inexorably the exclusion of any statement by the accused, as well as the fruits thereof. Such a strict constitutional specific inserted at the nerve center of crime detection may well kill the patient. Since there is at this time a paucity of information and an almost total lack of empirical knowledge on the practical operations of requirements truly comparable to those announced by the majority, I would be more restrained lest we go too far too fast.

II.

Custodial interrogation has long been recognized as "undoubtedly an essential tool in effective law enforcement." [Citation omitted.]

Recognition of this fact should put us on guard against the promulgation of doctrinaire rules. Especially is this true where the Court finds that "the Constitution has prescribed" its holding and where the light of our past cases, from *Hopt* v. *Utah*, 110 U.S. 574 (1884), down to *Haynes* v. *Washington*, *supra*, are to the contrary. Indeed, even in *Escobedo* the Court never hinted that an affirmative "waiver" was a prerequisite to questioning; that the burden of proof as to waiver was on the prosecution; that the presence of counsel—absent a waiver—during interrogation was required; that a waiver can be withdrawn at the will of the accused; that counsel must be furnished during an accusatory stage to those unable to pay; nor that admissions and exculpatory statements are "confessions." To require all those things at one gulp should cause the Court to choke over more cases than *Crooker* v. *California* and *Cicenia* v. *La Gay*, which it expressly overrules today.

The rule prior to today—as MR. JUSTICE GOLDBERG, the author of the Court's opinion in *Escobedo*, stated it in *Haynes* v. *Washington* —depended upon "a totality of circumstances evidencing an involuntary . . . admission of guilt." And he concluded:

> Of course, detection and solution of crime is, at best, a difficult and arduous task requiring determination and persistence on the part of all responsible officers charged with the duty of law enforcement. And, certainly, we do not mean to suggest that all interrogation of witnesses and suspects is impermissible. Such questioning is undoubtedly an essential tool in effective law enforcement. The line between proper and permissible police conduct and techniques and methods offensive to due process is, at best, a difficult one to draw, particularly in cases such as this where it is necessary to make fine judgments as to the effect of psychologically coercive pressures and inducements on the mind and will of an accused. . . . We are here impelled to the conclusion, from all of the facts presented, that the bounds of due process have been exceeded." *Id.*, at 515.

III.

I would continue to follow that rule. Under the "totality of circumstances" rule of which my BROTHER GOLDBERG spoke in *Haynes*, I would consider in each case whether the police officer prior to custodial interrogation added the warning that the suspect might have counsel present at the interrogation and, further, that a court would appoint one at his request if he was too poor to employ counsel. In the absence of warnings, the burden would be on the State to prove that counsel was knowingly and intelligently waived or that in the totality of the circumstances, including the failure to give the necessary warnings, the confession was clearly voluntary.

Rather than employing the arbitrary Fifth Amendment rule which the Court lays down I would follow the more pliable dictates of Due Process Clauses of the Fifth and Fourteenth Amendments which we are accustomed to administering and which we know from our cases are effective instruments in protecting persons in police custody. In this way we would not be acting in the dark nor in one full sweep changing the traditional rules of custodial interrogation which this Court has for so long recognized as a justifiable and proper tool in balancing individual rights against the rights of society. It will be soon enough to go further when we are able to appraise with somewhat better accuracy the effect of such a holding.

I would affirm the convictions in *Miranda* v. *Arizona,* No. 759; *Vignera* v. *New York,* No. 760; and *Westover* v. *United States,* No. 761. In each of those cases I find from the circumstances no warrant for reversal. In *California* v. *Stewart,* No. 584, I would dismiss the writ of certiorari for want of a final judgment, 28 U.S.C. § 1257(3) (1964); but if the merits are to be reached I would affirm on the ground that the State failed to fulfill its burden, in the absence of a showing that appropriate warnings were given, of proving a waiver or a totality of circumstances showing voluntariness. Should there be a retrial, I would leave the State free to attempt to prove these elements.

[MR. JUSTICE HARLAN also wrote a dissenting opinion in which JUSTICES STEWART and WHITE joined, and MR. JUSTICE WHITE wrote a dissenting opinion in which JUSTICES HARLAN and STEWART joined. These have been omitted. However, the opinion of MR. JUSTICE WHITE is especially good as it traces the history of the confession rules and the self-incrimination clause.]

DUCKWORTH v. EAGAN

No. 88-317.

Argued March 29, 1989. Decided June 26, 1989.

_U.S._, 109 S.Ct. 2875, _L.Ed.2d_ (1989).

* * *

Syllabus

Respondent, when first questioned by Indiana police in connection with a stabbing, made an exculpatory statement after being read and signing a waiver form that provided, *inter alia,* that if he could not afford a lawyer, one would be appointed for him "if and when you go to court." However, 29 hours later, he was interviewed again, signed a different waiver form, confessed to the stabbing, and led officers to a site where they recovered relevant physical evidence. Over respondent's objection, his two statements were admitted into evidence at trial. After the Indiana Supreme Court upheld his conviction for attempted murder, respondent sought a writ of habeas corpus in the District Court claiming, among other things, that his confession was inadmissible because the first waiver form did not comply with the requirements of *Miranda v. Arizona,* 384 U.S. 436, 86 S.Ct. 1602, 16 L.Ed.2d 694. The District Court denied the petition, holding that the record clearly manifested adherence to *Miranda*. The Court of Appeals reversed on the ground that the advice that counsel will be appointed "if and when you go to court" was constitutionally defective because it denied the indigent accused a clear and unequivocal warning of the right to appointed counsel before interrogation and linked that right to a future event.

Held: Informing a suspect that an attorney would be appointed for him "if and when you go to court" does not render *Miranda* warnings inadequate. Pp. 2878-2881.

(a) *Miranda* warnings need not be given in the exact form described in *Miranda* but simply must reasonably convey to a suspect his rights. The initial warnings given to respondent--that he had a right to remain silent, that anything he said could be used against him in court, that he had the right to speak to an attorney before and during questioning even if he could not afford to hire one, that he had the right to stop answering questions at any time until he talked to a lawyer, and that the police could not provide him with a lawyer but one would be appointed "if and when you go to court"--touched all of the bases required by *Miranda*. Pp. 2879-2880.

(b) The Court of Appeals misapprehended the effect of the "if and when you go to court" language. This instruction accurately reflects Indiana's procedure for appointment of counsel, which does not occur until a defendant's first court appearance, and it anticipates a suspect's question as to when he will obtain counsel. P. 2880.

(c) *Miranda* does not require that attorneys be producible on call, but only that the suspect be informed of his right to an attorney and to appointed counsel, and that if the police cannot provide appointed counsel, they will not question him until he waives, as respondent did, his right to counsel. P. 2880.

(d) Respondent's reliance on *California v. Prysock,* 453 U.S. 355, 101 S.Ct. 2806, 69 L.Ed.2d 696--which held that *Miranda* warnings would not be sufficient "if the reference to the right to appointed counsel was linked [to a] future point in time *after* police interrogation" --is misplaced since *Prysock* involved warnings that did not apprise the accused of his right to have an attorney present if he chose to answer questions. However, of the eight sentences in respondent's first warning, one described his right to counsel "before [the police] ask[ed] [him] questions," while another stated his right "to stop answering at any time until [he] talk[ed] to a lawyer." Pp. 2880-2881.

843 F.2d 1554 (CA7 1988), reversed and remanded.

REHNQUIST, C.J., delivered the opinion of the Court, in which WHITE, O'CONNOR, SCALIA, and KENNEDY, JJ., joined. O'CONNOR, J., filed a concurring opinion, in which SCALIA, J., joined. MARSHALL, J., filed a dissenting opinion, in which BRENNAN, J., joined, and in Part I of which BLACKMUN and STEVENS, J.J., joined.

* * *

Cases relating to **Chapter 7**

SELF-INCRIMINATION AND RELATED ISSUES*

SCHMERBER v. CALIFORNIA

384 U.S. 757, 86 S. Ct. 1826, 16 L. Ed. 2d 908 (1966)

MR. JUSTICE BRENNAN delivered the opinion of the Court.

Petitioner was convicted in Los Angeles Municipal Court of the criminal offense of driving an automobile while under the influence of intoxicating liquor. He had been arrested at a hospital while receiving treatment for injuries suffered in an accident involving the automobile that he had apparently been driving. At the direction of a police officer, a blood sample was then withdrawn from petitioner's body by a physician at the hospital. The chemical analysis of this sample revealed a percent by weight of alcohol in his blood at the time of the offense which indicated intoxication, and the report of this analysis was admitted in evidence at the trial. Petitioner objected to receipt of this evidence of the analysis on the ground that the blood had been withdrawn despite his refusal, on the advice of his counsel, to consent to the test. He contended that in that circumstance the withdrawal of the blood and the admission of the analysis in evidence denied him due process of law under the Fourteenth Amendment, as well as specific guarantees of the Bill of Rights secured against the States by that Amendment: his privilege against self-incrimination under the Fifth Amendment; his right to counsel under the Sixth Amendment; and his right not to be subjected to unreasonable searches and seizures in violation of the Fourth Amendment. The Appellate Department of the California Superior Court rejected these contentions and affirmed the conviction. In view of constitutional decisions since we last considered these issues in *Breithaupt* v. *Abram,* [citations omitted] we granted certiorari. We affirm.

I.

THE DUE PROCESS CLAUSE CLAIM

Breithaupt was also a case in which police officers caused blood to be withdrawn from the driver of an automobile involved in an accident, and in which there was ample justification for the officer's conclusion that the driver was under the influence of alcohol. There, as here, the extraction was made by a physician in a simple, medically acceptable manner in a hospital environment. There, however, the driver was unconscious at the time the blood was withdrawn and hence had no opportunity to object to the procedure. We affirmed the conviction there resulting from the use of the test in evidence, holding

* See also *Miranda* v. *Arizona, supra.*

that under such circumstances the withdrawal did not offend "that 'sense of justice' of which we spoke in *Rochin* v. *California*, 342 U.S. 165." 352 U.S., at 435. *Breithaupt* thus requires the rejection of petitioner's due process argument, and nothing in the circumstances of this case or in supervening events persuades us that this aspect of *Breithaupt* should be overruled.

II.

THE PRIVILEGE AGAINST SELF-INCRIMINATION CLAIM

Breithaupt summarily rejected an argument that the withdrawal of blood and the admission of the analysis report involved in that state case violated the Fifth Amendment privilege of any person not to "be compelled in any criminal case to be a witness against himself," citing *Twining* v. *New Jersey*, 211 U.S. 78. But that case, holding that the protections of the Fourteenth Amendment do not embrace this Fifth Amendment privilege, has been succeeded by *Malloy* v. *Hogan*, 378 U.S. 1. We there held that "[t]he Fourteenth Amendment secures against state invasion the same privilege that the Fifth Amendment guarantees against federal infringement—the right of a person to remain silent unless he chooses to speak in the unfettered exercise of his own will, and to suffer no penalty . . . for such silence." We therefore must now decide whether the withdrawal of the blood and admission in evidence of the analysis involved in this case violated petitioner's privilege. We hold that the privilege protects an accused only from being compelled to testify against himself, or otherwise provide the State with evidence of a testimonial or communicative nature, and that the withdrawal of blood and use of the analysis in question in this case did not involve compulsion to these ends.

It could not be denied that in requiring petitioner to submit to the withdrawal and chemical analysis of his blood the State compelled him to submit to an attempt to discover evidence that might be used to prosecute him for a criminal offense. He submitted only after the police officer rejected his objection and directed the physician to proceed. The officer's direction to the physician to administer the test over petitioner's objection constituted compulsion for the purposes of the privilege. The critical question, then, is whether petitioner was thus compelled "to be a witness against himself."

If the scope of the privilege coincided with the complex of values it helps to protect, we might be obliged to conclude that the privilege was violated. In *Miranda* v. *Arizona*, the Court said of the interests protected by the privilege: "All these policies point to one overriding thought: the constitutional foundation underlying the privilege is the respect a government—state or federal—must accord to the dignity and integrity of its citizens. To maintain a 'fair state-individual balance,' to require the government 'to shoulder the entire load,' . . . to respect the inviolability of the human personality, our accusatory system of criminal justice demands that the government seeking to punish an individual produce the evidence against him by its own independent labors, rather than by the cruel, simple expedient of compelling it from his own mouth." The withdrawal of blood necessarily involves puncturing the skin for extraction, and the percent by weight of alcohol in that blood, as established by chemical analysis, is evidence of criminal guilt. Compelled submission fails on one view to respect the "inviolability of the human personality." Moreover, since it enables the State to rely on evidence forced from the accused, the compulsion violates at least one meaning of the requirement that the State procure the evidence against an accused "by its own independent labors."

As the passage in *Miranda* implicitly recognizes, however, the privilege has never been given the full scope which the values it helps to protect suggest. History and a long line of authorities in lower courts have consistently limited its protection to situations in which the State seeks to submerge those values by obtaining the evidence against an accused through "the cruel, simple expedient of compelling it from his own mouth. . . . In sum, the privilege is fulfilled only when the person is guaranteed the right 'to remain silent unless he chooses to speak in the unfettered exercise of his own will.'" *Ibid.* The leading case in this Court is *Holt* v. *United States,* 218 U.S. 245. There the question was whether evidence was admissible that the accused, prior to trial and over his protest, put on a blouse that fitted him. It was contended that compelling the accused to submit to the demand that he model the blouse violated the privilege. MR. JUSTICE HOLMES, speaking for the Court, rejected the argument as "based upon an extravagant extension of the Fifth Amendment," and went on to say:

> [T]he prohibition of compelling a man in a criminal court to be witness against himself is a prohibition of the use of physical or moral compulsion to extort communications from him, not an exclusion of his body as evidence when it may be material. The objection in principle would forbid a jury to look at a prisoner and compare his features with a photograph in proof. 218 U.S., at 252–253.

It is clear that the protection of the privilege reaches an accused's communications, whatever form they might take, and the compulsion of responses which are also communications, for example, compliance with a subpoena to produce one's papers. *Boyd* v. *United States,* 116 U.S. 616. On the other hand, both federal and state courts have usually held that it offers no protection against compulsion to submit to fingerprinting, photographing, or measurements, to write or speak for identification, to appear in court, to stand, to assume a stance, to walk, or to make a particular gesture. The distinction which has emerged, often expressed in different ways, is that the privilege is a bar against compelling "communications" or "testimony," but that compulsion which makes a suspect or accused the source of "real or physical evidence" does not violate it.

Although we agree that this distinction is a helpful framework for analysis, we are not to be understood to agree with past applications in all instances. There will be many cases in which such a distinction is not readily drawn. Some tests seemingly directed to obtain "physical evidence," for example, lie detector tests measuring changes in body function during interrogation, may actually be directed to eliciting responses which are essentially testimonial. To compel a person to submit to testing in which an effort will be made to determine his guilt or innocence on the basis of physiological responses, whether willed or not, is to evoke the spirit and history of the Fifth Amendment. Such situations call to mind the principle that the protection of the privilege "is as broad as the mischief against which it seeks to guard." [Citation omitted.]

In the present case, however, no such problem of application is presented. Not even a shadow of testimonial compulsion upon or enforced communication by the accused was involved either in the extraction or in the chemical analysis. Petitioner's testimonial capacities were in no way implicated; indeed, his participation, except as a donor, was irrelevant to the results of the test, which depend on chemical analysis and on that alone. Since the blood test evidence, although an incriminating product of compulsion, was neither petitioner's testimony nor evidence relating to some communicative act or writing by the petitioner, it was not inadmissable on privilege grounds.

III.

THE RIGHT TO COUNSEL CLAIM

This conclusion also answers petitioner's claim that in compelling him to submit to the test in face of the fact that his objection was made on the advice of counsel, he was denied his Sixth Amendment right to the assistance of counsel. Since petitioner was not entitled to assert the privilege, he has no greater right because counsel erroneously advised him that he could assert it. His claim is strictly limited to the failure of the police to respect his wish, reinforced by counsel's advice, to be left inviolate. No issue of counsel's ability to assist petitioner in respect of any rights he did possess is presented. The limited claim thus made must be rejected.

IV.

THE SEARCH AND SEIZURE CLAIM

In *Breithaupt*, as here, it was also contended that the chemical analysis should be excluded from evidence as the product of an unlawful search and seizure in violation of the Fourth and Fourteenth Amendments. The Court did not decide whether the extraction of blood in that case was unlawful, but rejected the claim on the basis of *Wolf* v. *Colorado*, 338 U.S. 25. That case had held that the Constitution did not require, in state prosecutions for state crimes, the exclusion of evidence obtained in violation of the Fourth Amendment's provisions. We have since overruled *Wolf* in that respect, holding in *Mapp* v. *Ohio* that the exclusionary rule adopted for federal prosecutions in *Weeks* v. *United States* must also be applied in criminal prosecutions in state courts. The question is squarely presented therefore, whether the chemical analysis introduced in evidence in this case should have been excluded as the product of an unconstitutional search and seizure.

. . . .

Because we are dealing with intrusions into the human body rather than with state interferences with property relationships or private papers—"houses, papers, and effects"—we write on a clean slate. Limitations on the kinds of property which may be seized under warrant, as distinct from the procedures for search and the permissible scope of search, are not instructive in this context. We begin with the assumption that once the privilege against self-incrimination has been found not to bar compelled intrusions into the body for blood to be analyzed for alcohol content, the Fourth Amendment's proper function is to constrain, not against all intrusions as such, but against intrusions which are not justified in the circumstances, or which are made in an improper manner. In other words, the questions we must decide in this case are whether the police were justified in requiring petitioner to submit to the blood test, and whether the means and procedures employed in taking his blood respected relevant Fourth Amendment standards of reasonableness.

In this case, as will often be true when charges of driving under the influence of alcohol are pressed, these questions arise in the context of an arrest made by an officer without a warrant. Here, there was plainly probable cause for the officer to arrest petitioner and charge him with driving an automobile while under the influence of intoxicating liquor. The police officer who arrived at the scene shortly after the accident smelled liquor on petitioner's breath, and testified that petitioner's eyes were "bloodshot, watery, sort of a glassy appearance." The officer saw petitioner again at the hospital, within two hours of the accident. There he noticed similar symptoms of drunkenness. He thereupon informed petitioner "that he was under arrest and that he was entitled to the services of an attorney, and that he could remain silent and that anything that he told me would be used against him in evidence."

While early cases suggest that there is an unrestricted "right on the part of the government always recognized under English and American law, to search the person of the accused when legally arrested to discover and seize the fruits or evidences of crime," . . . the mere fact of a lawful arrest does not end our inquiry. The suggestion of these cases apparently rests on two factors—first, there may be more immediate danger of concealed weapons or of destruction of evidence under the direct control of the accused, [citation omitted]; second, once a search of the arrested person for weapons is permitted, it would be both impractical and unnecessary to enforcement of the Fourth Amendment's purpose to attempt to confine the search to those objects alone [citation omitted]. Whatever the validity of these considerations in general, they have little applicability with respect to searches involving intrusions beyond the body's surface. The interests in human dignity and privacy which the Fourth Amendment protects forbid any such intrusions on the mere chance that desired evidence might be obtained. In the absence of a clear indication that in fact such evidence will be found, these fundamental human interests require law officers to suffer the risk that such evidence may disappear unless there is an immediate search.

Although the facts which established probable cause to arrest in this case also suggested the required relevance and likely success of a test of petitioner's blood for alcohol, the question remains whether the arresting officer was permitted to draw these inferences himself, or was required instead to procure a warrant before proceeding with the test. Search warrants are ordinarily required for searches of dwellings, and absent an emergency, no less could be required where intrusions into the human body are concerned. The requirement that a warrant be obtained is a requirement that inferences to support the search "be drawn by a neutral and detached magistrate instead of being judged by an officer engaged in the often competitive enterprise of ferreting out crime." [Citations omitted.] The importance of informed, detached and deliberate determinations of the issue whether or not to invade another's body in search of evidence of guilt is indisputable and great.

The officer in the present case, however, might reasonably have believed that he was confronted with an emergency, in which the delay necessary to obtain a warrant, under the circumstances, threatened "the destruction of evidence." . . . We are told that the percentage of alcohol in the blood begins to diminish shortly after drinking stops, as the body functions to eliminate it from the system. Particularly in a case such as this, where time had to be taken to bring the accused to a hospital and to investigate the scene of the accident, there was no time to seek out a magistrate and secure a warrant. Given these special facts, we conclude that the attempt to secure evidence of blood-alcohol content in this case was an appropriate incident to petitioner's arrest.

Similarly, we are satisfied that the test chosen to measure petitioner's blood-alcohol level was a reasonable one. Extraction of blood samples for testing is a highly effective means of determining the degree to which a person is under the influence of alcohol. . . . Such tests are commonplace in these days of periodic physical examinations and experience with them teaches that the quantity of blood extracted is minimal, and that for most people the procedure involves virtually no risk, trauma, or pain. Petitioner is not one of the few who on grounds of fear, concern for health, or religious scruple might prefer some other means of testing, such as the "breathalyzer" test petitioner refused. We need not decide whether such wishes would have to be respected.

Finally, the record shows that the test was performed in a reasonable manner. Petitioner's blood was taken by a physician in a hospital environment according to accepted medical practices. We are thus not presented with the serious questions which would arise if a search involving use of medical technique, even of the most rudimentary sort, were made by other than medical personnel or in other than a medical environment—for example, if it were administered by police in the privacy of the stationhouse. To tolerate searches under these conditions might be to invite an unjustified element of personal risk of infection and pain.

We thus conclude that the present record shows no violation of petitioner's right under the Fourth and Fourteenth Amendments to be free of unreasonable searches and seizures. It bears repeating, however, that we reach this judgment only on the facts of the present record. The integrity of an individual's person is a cherished value of our society. That we today hold that the Constitution does not forbid the States minor intrusions into an individual's body under stringently limited conditions in no way indicates that it permits more substantial intrusions, or intrusions under other conditions.

Affirmed.

MR. JUSTICE HARLAN, whom MR. JUSTICE STEWART joins, concurring.

In joining the Court's opinion I desire to add the following comment. While agreeing with the Court that the taking of this blood test involved no testimonial compulsion, I would go further and hold that apart from this consideration the case in no way implicates the Fifth Amendment. Cf. my dissenting opinion and that of MR. JUSTICE WHITE in *Miranda* v. *Arizona*, 384 U.S. 436, 526.

MR. CHIEF JUSTICE WARREN, dissenting.

While there are other important constitutional issues in this case, I believe it is sufficient for me to reiterate my dissenting opinion in *Breithaupt* v. *Abram*, 352 U.S. 432, 440, as the basis on which to reverse this conviction.

MR. JUSTICE BLACK with whom MR. JUSTICE DOUGLAS joins, dissenting.

I would reverse petitioner's conviction. I agree with the Court that the Fourteenth Amendment made applicable to the States the Fifth Amendment's provision that "No person . . . shall be compelled in any criminal case to be a witness against himself. . . ." But I disagree with the Court's holding that California did not violate petitioner's constitutional right against self-incrimination when it compelled him, against his will, to allow a doctor to puncture his blood vessels in order to extract a sample of blood and analyze it for alcoholic content, and then used that analysis as evidence to convict petitioner of a crime.

The Court admits that "the State compelled [petitioner] to submit to an attempt to discover evidence [in his blood] that might be [and was] used to prosecute him for a criminal offense." To reach the conclusion that compelling a person to give his blood to help the State convict him is not equivalent to compelling him to be a witness against himself strikes me as quite an extraordinary feat. The Court, however, overcomes what had seemed to me to be an insuperable obstacle to its conclusion by holding that

> . . . the privilege protects an accused only from being compelled to testify against himself, or otherwise provide the State with evidence of a testimonial or communicative nature, and that the withdrawal of blood and use of the analysis in question in this case did not involve compulsion to these ends. (Footnote omitted.)

I cannot agree that this distinction and reasoning of the Court justify denying petitioner his Bill of Rights' guarantee that he must not be compelled to be a witness against himself.

In the first place it seems to me that the compulsory extraction of petitioner's blood for analysis so that the person who analyzed it could give evidence to convict him had both a "testimonial" and a "communicative nature." The sole purpose of this project which proved to be successful was to obtain "testimony" from some person to prove that petitioner had alcohol in his blood at the time he was arrested. And the purpose of the project was certainly "communicative" in that the analysis of the blood was to supply information to enable a witness to communicate to the court and jury that petitioner was more or less drunk.

I think it unfortunate that the Court rests so heavily for its very restrictive reading of the Fifth Amendment's privilege against self-incrimination on the words "testimonial" and "communicative." These words are not models of clarity and precision as the Court's rather labored explication shows. Nor can the Court, so far as I know, find precedent in the former opinions of this Court for using these particular words to limit the scope of the Fifth Amendment's protection. . . .

. . . .

How can it reasonably be doubted that the blood test evidence was not in all respects the actual equivalent of "testimony" taken from petitioner when the result of the test was offered as testimony, was considered by the jury as testimony, and the jury's verdict of guilt rests in part on that testimony? The refined, subtle reasoning and balancing process used here to narrow the scope of the Bill of Rights' safeguard against self-incrimination provides a handy instrument for further narrowing of that constitutional protection, as well as others, in the future. Believing with the Framers that these constitutional safeguards broadly construed by independent tribunals of justice provide our best hope for keeping our people free from governmental oppression, I deeply regret the Court's holding. For the foregoing reasons as well as those set out in concurring opinions of BLACK and DOUGLAS, JJ., in *Rochin* v. *California*, and my concurring opinion in *Mapp* v. *Ohio*, and the dissenting opinions in *Breithaupt* v. *Abram*, I dissent from the Court's holding and opinion in this case.

MR. JUSTICE DOUGLAS, dissenting.

I adhere to the views of THE CHIEF JUSTICE in his dissent in *Breithaupt* v. *Abrams*, and to the views I stated in my dissent in that case and add only a word.

We are dealing with the right of privacy which, since the *Breithaupt* case, we have held to be within the penumbra of some specific guarantees of the Bill of Rights. *Griswold* v. *Connecticut*, 381 U.S. 479. Thus, the Fifth Amendment marks "a zone of privacy" which the Government may not force a person to surrender. Likewise the Fourth Amendment recognizes that right when it guarantees the right of the people to be secure "in their persons." *Ibid.* No clearer invasion of this right of privacy can be imagined than forcible blood-letting of the kind involved here.

MR. JUSTICE FORTAS, dissenting.

I would reverse. In my view, petitioner's privilege against self-incrimination applies. I would add that, under the Due Process Clause, the State, in its role as prosecutor, has no right to extract blood from an accused or anyone else, over his protest. As prosecutor, the State has no right to commit any kind of violence upon the person, or to utilize the results of such a tort, and the extraction of blood, over protest, is an act of violence. [Citation omitted.]

NEIL v. BIGGERS

409 U.S. 188, 93 S. Ct. 375, 43 L. Ed 2d 401 (1972)

Habeas corpus proceeding by state prisoner. The United States District Court for the Middle District of Tennessee, Nashville Division, entered judgment granting writ, and the state appealed. The

Court of Appeals, 448 F.2d 91, affirmed, and certiorari was granted. The Supreme Court, MR. JUSTICE POWELL, held that United States Supreme Court's equally divided affirmance of petitioner's state court conviction was not an "actual adjudication" barring subsequent consideration on habeas corpus. The Court further held that even though station house showup may have been suggestive, and notwithstanding lapse of seven months between crime and the confrontation, there was no substantial likelihood of misidentification and evidence concerning the out-of-court identification by victim was admissible, where victim spent up to half an hour with her assailant, victim was with assailant under adequate artificial light in her house and under a full moon outdoors and at least twice faced him directly and intimately, victim's description to police included her assailant's approximate age, height, weight, complexion, skin texture, build, and voice, victim had "no doubt" that defendant was person who raped her, and victim made no previous identification at any of the showups, lineups, or photographic showings.

Affirmed in part, reversed in part, and remanded.

MR. JUSTICE MARSHALL took no part in consideration or decision of case.

MR. JUSTICE BRENNAN concurred in part and dissented in part and filed opinion in which MR. JUSTICE DOUGLAS and MR. JUSTICE STEWART concurred.

MR. JUSTICE POWELL delivered the opinion of the Court.

In 1965, after a jury trial in a Tennessee court, respondent was convicted of rape and was sentenced to 20 years' imprisonment. The State's evidence consisted in part of testimony concerning a station-house identification of respondent by the victim. The Tennessee Supreme Court affirmed. *Biggers* v. *State*, 219 Tenn. 553, 411 S.W.2d 696 (1967). On certiorari, the judgment of the Tennessee Supreme Court was affirmed by an equally divided Court. *Biggers* v. *Tennessee*, 390 U.S. 404, 88 S.Ct. 979, 19 L.Ed.2d 1267 (1968) (MARSHALL, J., not participating). Respondent then brought a federal habeas corpus action raising several claims. . . .

[That part of the decision dealing with the question of whether an affirmance by an equally divided court is an actual adjudication barring subsequent consideration on habeas corpus is not included.]

II.

We proceed, then, to consider respondent's due process claim. As the claim turns upon the facts, we must first review the relevant testimony at the jury trial and at the habeas corpus hearing regarding the rape and the identification. The victim testified at trial that on the evening of January 22, 1965, a youth with a butcher knife grabbed her in the doorway to her kitchen:

A. [H]e grabbed me from behind, and grappled—twisted me

on the floor. Threw me down on the floor.

Q. And there was no light in that kitchen?

A. Not in the kitchen.

Q. So you couldn't have seen him then?

A. Yes, I could see him, when I looked up in his face.

Q. In the dark?

A. He was right in the doorway—it was enough light from the bedroom shining through. Yes, I could see who he was.

Q. You could see? No light? And you could see him and know him then?

A. Yes.

When the victim screamed, her 12-year-old daughter came out of her bedroom and also began to scream. The assailant directed the victim to "tell her [the daughter] to shut up, or I'll kill you both." She did so, and was then walked at knifepoint about two blocks along a railroad track, taken into a woods, and raped there. She testified that "the moon was shining brightly, full moon." After the rape, the assailant ran off, and she returned home, the whole incident having taken between 15 minutes and half an hour.

She then gave the police what the Federal District Court characterized as "only a very general description," describing him as "being fat and flabby with smooth skin, bushy hair and a youthful voice." Additionally, though not mentioned by the District Court, she testified at the habeas corpus hearing that she had described her assailant as being between 16 and 18 years old and between five feet ten inches and six feet tall, as weighing between 180 and 200 pounds, and as having a dark brown complexion. This testimony was substantially corroborated by that of a police officer who was testifying from his notes.

On several occasions over the course of the next seven months, she viewed suspects in her home or at the police station, some in lineups and others in showups, and was shown between 30 and 40 photographs. She told the police that a man pictured in one of the photographs had features similar to those of her assailant, but identified none of the suspects. On August 17, the police called her to the station to view respondent, who was being detained on another charge. In an effort to construct a suitable lineup, the police checked the city jail and the city juvenile home. Finding no one at either place fitting respondent's unusual physical description, they conducted a showup instead.

The showup itself consisted of two detectives walking respondent past the victim. At the victim's request, the police directed respondent to say "shut up or I'll kill you." The testimony at trial was not altogether clear as to whether the victim first identified him and then asked that he repeat the words or made her identification after he had spoken. In any event, the victim testified that she had "no doubt" about her identification. At the habeas corpus hearing, she elaborated in response to questioning.

A. That I have no doubt, I mean that I am sure that when I—see, when I first laid eyes on him, I knew that it was the individual, because his face—well, there was just something that I don't think I could ever forget. I believe—

Q. You say when you first laid eyes on him, which time are you referring to?

A. When I identified him—when I seen him in the courthouse when I was took up to view the suspect.

We must decide whether, as the courts below held, this identification and the circumstances surrounding it failed to comport with due process requirements.

III.

We have considered on four occasions the scope of due process protection against the admission of evidence deriving from suggestive identification procedures. In *Stovall* v. *Denno*, 388 U.S. 293 (1967), the Court held that the defendant could claim that "the confrontation conducted . . . was so unnecessarily suggestive and conducive to irreparable mistaken identification that he was denied due process of law." This we held, must be determined "on the totality of the circumstances." We went on to find that on the facts of the case then before us, due process was not violated, emphasizing that the critical condition of the injured witness justified a showup in her hospital room. At trial, the witness, whose view of the suspect at the time of the crime was brief, testified to the out-of-court identification, as did several police officers present in her hospital room, and also made an in-court identification.

Subsequently, in a case where the witnesses made in-court identifications arguably stemming from previous exposure to a suggestive photographic array, the Court restated the governing test:

> [W]e hold that each case must be considered on its own facts, and that convictions based on eye-witness identification at trial following a pretrial identification by photograph will be set aside on that ground only if the photographic identification procedure was so impermissibly suggestive as to give rise to a very substantial likelihood of irreparable misidentification. *Simmons* v. *United States*, 390 U.S. 377, 384 (1968).

Again we found the identification procedure to be supportable, relying both on the need for prompt utilization of other investigative leads and on the likelihood that the photographic identifications were reliable, the witnesses having viewed the bank robbers for periods of up to five minutes under good lighting conditions at the time of the robbery.

The only case to date in which this Court has found identification procedures to be violative of due process is *Foster* v. *California*, 394 U.S. 440, 442 (1969). There, the witness failed to identify Foster the first time he confronted him, despite a suggestive lineup. The police then arranged a showup, at which the witness could make only a tentative identification. Ultimately, at yet another confrontation, this time a lineup, the witness was able to muster a definite identification. We held all of the identifications inadmissible, observing that the identifications were "all but inevitable" under the circumstances. *Id.*, at 443.

In the most recent case of *Coleman* v. *Alabama*, 399 U.S. 1 (1970), we held admissible an in-court identification by a witness who had a fleeting but "real good look" at his assailant in the headlights of a passing car. The witness testified at a pretrial suppression hearing that he identified one of the petitioners among the participants in the lineup before the police placed the participants in a formal line. MR. JUSTICE BRENNAN for four members of the Court stated that this evidence could support a finding that the in-court identification was "entirely based upon observations at the time of the assault and not at all induced by the conduct of the lineup."

Some general guidelines emerge from these cases as to the relationship between suggestiveness and misidentification. It is, first of all, apparent that the primary evil to be avoided is "a very substantial likelihood of irreparable misidentification." *Simmons* v. *United States*, 390 U.S., at 384. While the phrase was coined as a standard for determining whether an in-court identification would be admissible in the wake of a suggestive out-of-court identification, with the deletion of "irreparable" it serves equally well as a standard for the admissibility of testimony concerning the out-of-court identification itself. It is the likelihood of misidentification which violates a defendant's right to due process, and it is this which was the basis of the exclusion of evidence in *Foster*. Suggestive confrontations are disapproved because they increase the likelihood of misidentification, and unnecessarily suggestive ones are condemned for the further reason that the increased chance of misidentification is gratuitous. But as *Stovall* makes clear, the admission of evidence of a showup without more does not violate due process.

What is less clear from our cases is whether, as intimated by the District Court, unnecessary suggestiveness alone requires the exclusion of evidence. While we are inclined to agree with the courts below that the police did not exhaust all possibilities in seeking persons physically comparable to respondent, we do not think that the evidence must therefore be excluded. The purpose of a strict rule barring evidence of unnecessarily suggestive confrontations would be to deter the police from using a less reliable procedure where a more reliable one may be available, and would not be based on the assumption that in every instance the admission of evidence of such a confrontation offends due process. *Clemons* v. *United States*, 133 U.S.AppD.C. 27, 48, 408 F.2d 1230,

1251 (1968) (Leventhal, J., concurring); cf. *Gilbert* v. *California*, 388 U.S. 263, 273 (1967); *Mapp* v. *Ohio*, 367 U.S. 643 (1961). Such a rule would have no place in the present case, since both the confrontation and the trial preceded *Stovall* v. *Denno, supra,* when we first gave notice that the suggestiveness of confrontation procedures was anything other than a matter to be argued to the jury.

We turn, then, to the central question, whether under the "totality of circumstances" the identification was reliable even though the confrontation procedure was suggestive. As indicated by our cases, the factors to be considered in evaluating the likelihood of misidentification include the opportunity of the witness to view the criminal at the time of the crime, the witness' degree of attention, the accuracy of the witness' prior description of the criminal, the level of certainty demonstrated by the witness at the confrontation, and the length of time between the crime and the confrontation. Applying these factors, we disagree with the District Court's conclusion.

In part, as discussed above, we think the District Court focused unduly on the relative reliability of a lineup as opposed to a showup, the issue on which expert testimony was taken at the evidentiary hearing. It must be kept in mind also that the trial was conducted before *Stovall* and that therefore the incentive was lacking for the parties to make a record at trial of facts corroborating or undermining the identification. The testimony was addressed to the jury, and the jury apparently found the identification reliable. Some of the State's testimony at the federal evidentiary hearing may well have been self-serving in that it too neatly fit the case law, but it surely does nothing to undermine the state record, which itself fully corroborated the identification.

We find that the District Court's conclusions on the critical facts are unsupported by the record and clearly erroneous. The victim spent a considerable period of time with her assailant, up to half an hour. She was with him under adequate artificial light in her house and under a full moon outdoors, and at least twice, once in the house and later in the woods, faced him directly and intimately. She was no casual observer, but rather the victim of one of the most personally humiliating of all crimes. Her description to the police, which included the assailant's approximate age, height, weight, complexion, skin texture, build, and voice, might not have satisfied Proust but was more than ordinarily thorough. She had "no doubt" that respondent was the person who raped her. In the nature of the crime, there are rarely witnesses to a rape other than the victim, who often has a limited opportunity of observation. The victim here, a practical nurse by profession, had an unusual opportunity to observe and identify her assailant. She testified at the habeas corpus hearing that there was something about his face "I don't think I could ever forget." App. 127.

There was, to be sure, a lapse of seven months between the rape and the confrontation. This would be a seriously negative factor in most cases. Here, however, the testimony is undisputed that the victim made no previous identification at any of the showups, lineups, or photographic showings. Her record for reliability was thus a good one, as she had previously resisted whatever suggestiveness inheres in a showup. Weighing all the factors, we find no substantial likelihood of misidentification. The evidence was properly allowed to go to the jury.

Affirmed in part, reversed in part, and remanded.

MR. JUSTICE MARSHALL took no part in the consideration or decision of this case.

MR. JUSTICE BRENNAN, with whom MR. JUSTICE DOUGLAS and MR. JUSTICE STEWART concur, concurring in part and dissenting in part. [That opinion has been omitted.]

SOUTH DAKOTA v. NEVILLE
459 U.S. 553, 103 S. Ct. 916, 74 L. Ed. 2d 748 (1983)
[Syllabus only]

A South Dakota statute permits a person suspected of driving while intoxicated to refuse to submit to a blood-alcohol test, but authorizes revocation of the driver's license of a person so refusing the test and permits such refusal to be used against him at a trial. When respondent was arrested by police officers in South Dakota for driving while intoxicated, the officers asked him to submit to a blood-alcohol test and warned him that he could lose his license if he refused but did not warn him that the refusal could be used against him at trial. Respondent refused to take the test. The South Dakota trial court granted respondent's motion to suppress all evidence of his refusal to take the blood-alcohol test. The South Dakota Supreme Court affirmed on the ground that the statute allowing introduction of evidence of the refusal violated the privilege against self-incrimination.

Held:

1. The admission into evidence of a defendant's refusal to submit to a blood-alcohol test does not offend his Fifth Amendment right against self-incrimination. A refusal to take such a test, after a police officer has lawfully requested it, is not an act coerced by the officer, and thus is not protected by the privilege against self-incrimination. The offer of taking the test is clearly legitimate and becomes no *less* legitimate when the State offers a second option of refusing the test, with the attendant penalties for making that choice.

2. It would not be fundamentally unfair in violation of due process to use respondent's refusal to take the blood-alcohol test as evidence of

guilt, even though the police failed to warn him that the refusal could be used against him at trial. *Doyle v. Ohio,* 426 U.S. 610, 96 S.Ct. 2240, 49 L.Ed.2d 91, distinguished. Such failure to warn was not the sort of implicit promise to forego use of evidence that would unfairly "trick" respondent if the evidence were later offered against him at trial.

312 N.W.2d 723 (S.D. 1981) reversed and remanded.

Cases relating to **Chapter 8**

ASSISTANCE OF COUNSEL*

PATTERSON v. ILLINOIS

No. 88-7059

Argued March 22, 1988. Decided June 24, 1988.

__U.S.__, 108 S.Ct. 2389, __L.Ed.2d__ (1988)

Justice WHITE delivered the opinion of the Court.

In this case, we are called on to determine whether the interrogation of petitioner after his indictment violated his Sixth Amendment right to counsel.

I

Before dawn on August 21, 1983, petitioner and other members of the "Vice Lords" street gang became involved in a fight with members of a rival gang, the "Black Mobsters." Some time after the fight, a former member of the Black Mobsters, James Jackson, went to the home where the Vice Lords had fled. A second fight broke out there, with petitioner and three other Vice Lords beating Jackson severely. The Vice Lords then put Jackson into a car, drove to the end of a nearby street, and left him face down in a puddle of water. Later that morning, police discovered Jackson, dead, where he had been left.

That afternoon, local police officers obtained warrants for the arrest of the Vice Lords, on charges of battery and mob action, in connection with the first fight. One of the gang members who was arrested gave the police a statement concerning the first fight; the statement also implicated several of the Vice Lords (including petitioner) in Jackson's murder. A few hours later, petitioner was apprehended. Petitioner was informed of his rights under *Miranda v. Arizona,* 384 U.S. 436, 86 S.Ct. 1602, 16 L.Ed.2d 694 (1966), and volunteered to answer questions put to him by the police. Petitioner gave a statement concerning the initial fight between the rival gangs, but denied knowing anything about Jackson's death. Petitioner was held in custody the following day, August 22, as law enforcement authorities completed their investigation of the Jackson murder.

On August 23, a Cook County grand jury indicted petitioner and two other gang members for the murder of James Jackson. Police officer Michael Gresham, who had questioned petitioner earlier, removed him from the lockup where he was being held, and told petitioner that because he had been indicted he was being transferred to the Cook County jail. Petitioner asked Gresham which of the gang members had been charged with Jackson's murder, and upon learning that one particular Vice Lord had been omitted from the indictments, asked: "[W]hy wasn't he indicted, he did everything." App. 7. Petitioner also began to

* Also see *Miranda v. Arizona* for further comments on assistance of counsel.

explain that there was a witness who would support his account of the crime.

At this point, Gresham interrupted petitioner, and handed him a *Miranda* waiver form. The form contained five specific warnings, as suggested by this Court's *Miranda* decision, to make petitioner aware of his right to counsel and of the consequences of any statement he might make to police. Gresham read the warnings aloud, as petitioner read along with him. Petitioner initialed each of the five warnings, and signed the waiver form. Petitioner then gave a lengthy statement to police officers concerning the Jackson murder; petitioner's statement described in detail the role of each of the Vice Lords--including himself--in the murder of James Jackson.

Later that day, petitioner confessed involvement in the murder for a second time. This confession came in an interview with Assistant State's Attorney (ASA) George Smith. At the outset of the interview, Smith reviewed with petitioner the *Miranda* waiver he had previously signed, and petitioner confirmed that he had signed the waiver and understood his rights. Smith went through the waiver procedure once again: reading petitioner his rights, having petitioner initial each one, and sign a waiver form. In addition, Smith informed petitioner that he was a lawyer working with the police investigating the Jackson case. Petitioner then gave another inculpatory statement concerning the crime.

Before trial, petitioner moved to suppress his statements, arguing that they were obtained in a manner at odds with various constitutional guarantees. The trial court denied these motions, and the statements were used against petitioner at his trial. The jury found petitioner guilty of murder, and petitioner was sentenced to a 24-year prison term.

On appeal, petitioner argued that he had not "knowingly and intelligently" waived his Sixth Amendment right to counsel before he gave his uncounseled postindictment confessions. Petitioner contended that the warnings he received, while adequate for the purposes of protecting his *Fifth* Amendment rights as guaranteed by *Miranda*, did not adequately inform him of his *Sixth* Amendment right to counsel. The Illinois Supreme Court, however, rejected this theory, applying its previous decision in *People v. Owens,* 102 Ill.2d 88, 79 Ill.Dec. 663, 464 N.Ed.2d 261, *cert. denied*, 469 U.S. 963, 105 S.Ct. 362, 83 L.Ed.2d 297 (1984), which he had held that *Miranda* warnings were sufficient to make a defendant aware of his Sixth Amendment right to counsel during postindictment questioning.***

In reaching this conclusion, the Illinois Supreme Court noted that this Court had reserved decision on this question on several previous occasions and that the lower courts are divided on the issue. *** We granted this petition for certiorari, 484 U.S. __, 108 S.Ct. 227, 98 L.Ed.2d 186 (1987), to resolve this split of authority and to address the issues we had previously left open.

II

There can be no doubt that petitioner had the right to have the assistance of counsel at his postindictment interviews with law enforcement authorities. Our cases make it plain that the Sixth Amendment guarantees this right to criminal defendants. *Michigan v. Jackson,* 475 U.S. 625, 629-630, 106 S.Ct. 1404, 1407-1408, 89 L.Ed.2d 631 (1986); *Brewer v. Williams,* 430 U.S. 387, 398-401, 97 S.Ct. 1232, 1239-1241, 51 L.Ed.2d 424 (1977); *Massiah v. United States,* 377 U.S. 201, 205-207, 84 S.Ct.

1199, 1202-1204, 12 L.Ed.2d 246 (1964). Petitioner asserts that the questioning that produced his incriminating statements violated his Sixth Amendment right to counsel in two ways.

A

Petitioner's first claim is that because his Sixth Amendment right to counsel arose with his indictment, the police were there after barred from initiating a meeting with him. *** He equates himself with a preindictment suspect who, while being interrogated, asserts his Fifth Amendment right to counsel; under *Edwards v. Arizona*, 451 U.S. 477, 101 S.Ct. 1880, 68 L.Ed.2d 378 (1981), such a suspect may not be questioned again unless he initiates the meeting.

Petitioner, however, at no time sought to exercise his right to have counsel present. The fact that petitioner's Sixth Amendment right came into existence with his indictment, *i.e.,* that he had such a right at the time of his questioning, does not distinguish him from the preindictment interrogatee whose right to counsel is in existence and available for his exercise while he is questioned. Had petitioner indicated he wanted the assistance of counsel, the authorities' interview with him would have stopped, and further questioning would have been forbidden (unless petitioner called for such a meeting). This was our holding in *Michigan v. Jackson, supra*, which applied *Edwards* to the Sixth Amendment context. We observe that the analysis in *Jackson* is rendered wholly unnecessary if petitioner's position is correct: under petitioner's theory, the officers in *Jackson* would have been completely barred from approaching the accused in that case unless he called for them. Our decision in *Jackson*, however, turned on the fact that the accused "ha[d] asked for the help of a lawyer" in dealing with the police. ***

At bottom, petitioner's theory cannot be squared with our rationale in *Edwards,* the case he relies on for support. *Edwards* rested on the view that once "an accused...ha[s] expressed his desire to deal with the police only through counsel" he should "not [be] subject to further interrogation by the authorities until counsel has been made available to him, unless the accused himself initiates further communication." *** Preserving the integrity of an accused's choice to communicate with police only through counsel is the essence of *Edwards* and its progeny--not barring an accused from making an *initial* election as to whether he will face the State's officers during questioning with the aid of counsel, or go it alone. If an accused "knowingly and intelligently" pursues the latter course, we see no reason why the uncounseled statements he then makes must be excluded at his trial.

B

Petitioner's principal and more substantial claim is that questioning him without counsel present violated the Sixth Amendment because he did not validly waive his right to have counsel present during the interviews. Since it is clear that after the *Miranda* warnings were given to petitioner, he not only voluntarily answered questions without claiming his right to silence or his right to have a lawyer present to advise him but also executed a written waiver of his right to counsel during questioning, the specific issue posed here is whether this waiver was a "knowing and intelligent" waiver of his Sixth Amendment right.***

In the past, this Court has held that a waiver of the Sixth Amendment right to counsel is valid only when it reflects "an intentional relinquishment or abandonment of a known right or privilege." *Johnson v. Zerbst, supra,* at 464, 58 S.Ct. at 1023. In other words, the accused must "kno[w] what he is doing" so that "his choice is made with eyes open." *Adams v. United States ex rel. McCann,* 317 U.S. 269, 279, 63 S.Ct. 236, 87 L.Ed. 268 (1942). In a case arising under the Fifth Amendment, we described this requirement as "a full awareness [of] both the nature of the right being abandoned and the consequences of the decision to abandon it." *Moran v. Burbine*, 475 U.S. 412, 421, 106 S.Ct. 1135, 1141, 89 L.Ed.2d 410 (1986). Whichever of these formulations is used, the key inquiry in a case such as this one must be: Was the accused, who waived his Sixth Amendment rights during postindictment questioning, made sufficiently aware of his right to have counsel present during the questioning, and of the possible consequences of a decision to forgo the aid of counsel? In this case, we are convinced that by admonishing petitioner with the *Miranda* warnings, respondent has met this burden and that petitioner's waiver of his right to counsel at the questioning was valid.

First, the *Miranda* warnings given petitioner made him aware of his right to have counsel present during the questioning. By telling petitioner that he had a right to consult with an attorney, to have a lawyer present while he was questioned, and even to have a lawyer appointed for him if he could not afford to retain one on his own, Officer Gresham and ASA Smith conveyed to petitioner the sum and substance of the rights that the Sixth Amendment provided him. "Indeed, it seems self-evident that one who is told he "has such rights to counsel "is in a curious posture to later complain" that his waiver of these rights was unknowing. Cf. *United States v. Washington,* 431 U.S. 181, 188, 97 S.Ct. 1814, 1819, 52 L.Ed.2d 238 (1977). There is little more petitioner could have possibly been told in an effort to satisfy this portion of the waiver inquiry.

Second, the *Miranda* warnings also served to make petitioner aware of the consequences of a decision by him to waive his Sixth Amendment rights during postindictment questioning. Petitioner knew that any statement that he made could be used against him in subsequent criminal proceedings. This is the ultimate adverse consequence petitioner could have suffered by virtue of his choice to make uncounseled admissions to the authorities. This warning also sufficed--contrary to petitioner's claim here, *** --to let petitioner know what a lawyer could "do for him" during the postindictment questioning: namely, advise petitioner to refrain from making any such statements. By knowing what could be done with any statements he might make, and therefore, what benefit could be obtained by having the aid of counsel while making such statements, petitioner was essentially informed of the possible consequences of going without counsel during questioning. If petitioner nonetheless lacked "a full and complete appreciation of all of the consequences flowing" from his waiver, it does not defeat the State's showing that the information it provided to him satisfied the constitutional minimum. *Cf. Oregon v. Elstad,* 470 U.S. 298, 316-317, 105 S.Ct. 1285, 1296-1297, 84 L.Ed.2d 222 (1985).

Our conclusion is supported by petitioner's inability, in the proceedings before this Court, to articulate with precision what additional information should have been provided to him before he would have been competent to waive his right to counsel. All that petitioner's brief and reply brief suggest is petitioner should have been made aware of his "right under the Sixth Amendment to the broad protection of counsel"--a rather nebulous suggestion--and the "gravity of [his] situation." Reply Brief for Petitioner 13; see Brief for Petitioner 30-31. But surely this latter "requirement" (if it is one) was met when Officer Gresham informed petitioner that he had been formally charged with the murder of James Jackson. *** Under close questioning on this same point at argument, petitioner likewise failed to suggest any meaningful additional information that he should have been, but was not, provided in advance of his decision to waive his right to counsel. The discussions found in favorable court decisions, on which petitioner relies, are similarly lacking.

As a general matter, then, an accused who is admonished with the warnings prescribed by this Court in *Miranda,* 384 U.S., at 479, 86 S.Ct., at 1630, has been sufficiently apprised of the nature of his Sixth Amendment rights, and of the consequences of abandoning those rights, so that his waiver on this basis will be considered a knowing and intelligent one. We feel that our conclusion in a recent Fifth Amendment case is equally apposite here: "Once it is determined that a suspect's decision not to rely on his rights was uncoerced, that he at all times knew he could stand mute and request a lawyer, and that he was aware of the State's intention to use his statements to secure a conviction, the analysis is complete and the waiver is valid as a matter of law." See *Moran v. Burbine,* 475 U.S., at 422-423, 106 S.Ct. at 1142.

C

We consequently reject petitioner's argument, which has some acceptance from courts and commentators that since "the sixth amendment right [to counsel] is far superior to that of the fifth amendment right" and since "[t]he greater the right the greater the loss from a waiver of that right," waiver of an accused's Sixth Amendment right to counsel should be "more difficult" to effectuate than waiver of a suspect's Fifth Amendment rights. *** While our cases have recognized a "difference" between the Fifth Amendment and Sixth Amendment rights to counsel, and the "policies" behind these Constitutional guarantees, we have never suggested that one right is "superior" or "greater" than the other, nor is there any support in our cases for the notion that because a Sixth Amendment right may be involved, it is more difficult to waive than the Fifth Amendment counterpart.

Instead, we have taken a more pragmatic approach to the waiver question--asking what purposes a lawyer can serve at the particular stage of the proceedings in question, and what assistance he could provide to an accused at that stage--to determine the scope of the Sixth Amendment right to counsel, and the type of warnings and procedures that should be required before a waiver of that right will be recognized.

At one end of the spectrum, we have concluded there is no Sixth Amendment right to counsel whatsoever at a postindictment photographic display identification, because this procedure is not one at which the accused "require[s] aid in coping with legal problems or assistance in meeting his adversary." See *United States v. Ash,* 413 U.S. 300, 313-320, 93 S.Ct. 2568, 2575, 37 L.Ed.2d 619 (1973). At the other extreme, recognizing the enormous importance and role that an attorney plays at a criminal trial, we have imposed the most rigorous restrictions on the information that must be conveyed to a defendant, and the procedures that must be observed, before permitting him waive his right to counsel at trial. See *Faretta v. Calfornia,* 422 U.S. 806, 835-836, 95 S.Ct. 2525, 2541-2542, 45 L.Ed.2d 562 (1975); cf. *Von Moltke v. Gillies,* 332 U.S. 708, 723-724, 68 S.Ct. 316, 323-324, 92 L.Ed. 309 (1948). In these extreme cases, and in others that fall between these two poles, we have defined the scope of the right to counsel by a pragmatic assessment of the usefulness of counsel to the accused at the particular proceeding, and the dangers to the accused of proceeding without counsel. An accused's waiver of his right to counsel is "knowing" when he is made aware of these basic facts.

Applying this approach, it is our view that whatever warnings suffice for *Miranda's* purposes will also be sufficient in the context of postindictment questioning. The State's decision to take an additional step and commence formal adversarial proceedings against the accused does not substantially increase the value of counsel to the accused at questioning, or expand the limited purpose that an attorney serves when the accused is questioned by authorities. With respect to this inquiry, we do not discern a substantial difference between the usefulness of a lawyer to a suspect during custodial interrogation, and his value to an accused at postindictment questioning.

Thus, we require a more searching or formal inquiry before permitting an accused to waive his right to counsel at trial than we require for a Sixth Amendment waiver during postindictment questioning--*not* because postindictment questioning is "less important" than a trial (the analysis that petitioner's "hierarchical" approach would suggest)--but because the full "dangers and disadvantages of self-representation," *Faretta, supra,* 422 U.S. at 835, 95 S.Ct., at 2541, during questioning are less substantial and more obvious to an accused than they are at trial. Because the role of counsel at questioning is relatively simple and limited, we see no problem in having a waiver procedure at that stage which is likewise simple and limited. So long as the accused is made aware of the "dangers and disadvantages of self-representation" during postindictment questioning, by use of the *Miranda* warnings, his waiver of his Sixth Amendment right to counsel at such questioning is "knowing and intelligent."

III

Before confessing to the murder of James Jackson, petitioner was meticulously informed by authorities of his right to counsel, and of the consequences of any choice not to exercise that right. On two separate occasions, petitioner elected to forgo the assistance of counsel, and speak directly to officials concerning his role in the murder. Because we believe that petitioner's waiver of his Sixth Amendment rights was "knowing and intelligent," we find no error in the decision of the trial court to permit petitioner's confessions to be used against him. Consequently, the judgment of the Illinois Supreme Court is

Affirmed.

Justice BLACKMUN, dissenting.

I agree with most of what Justice STEVENS says in his dissenting opinion, *post.* I, however, merely would hold that after formal adversary proceedings against a defendant have been commenced, the Sixth Amendment mandates that the defendant not be "'subject to further interrogation by the authorities until counsel has been made available to him, unless the accused himself initiates further communication, exchanges, or conversation with the police.'" *Michigan v. Jackson,* 475 U.S. 625, 626, 106 S.Ct. 1404, 1406, 89 L.Ed.2d 631 (1986), quoting *Edwards v. Arizona,* 451 U.S. 477, 484-485, 101 S.Ct. 1880, 1884-1885, 68 L.Ed.2d 378 (1981).

The Court's majority concludes, *ante,* at 2394: "The fact that petitioner's Sixth Amendment right came into existence with his indictment...does not distinguish him from the preindictment interrogatee whose right to counsel is in existence and available for his exercise while he is questioned." I must disagree. "[W]hen the Constitution grants protection against criminal proceedings without the assistance of counsel, counsel must be furnished whether or not the accused requested the appointment of counsel." *Carnley v. Cochran,* 369 U.S. 506, 513, 82 S.Ct. 884, 889, 8 L.Ed.2d 70 (1962) (internal quotations omitted). In my view, the Sixth Amendment does not allow the prosecution to take undue advantage of any gap between the commencement of the adversary process and the time at which counsel is appointed for a defendant.

[The dissenting opinions of Justices Stevens, Brennan, and Marshall are not included.]

EDWARDS v. ARIZONA

451 U.S. 477, 101 S. Ct. 1880, 68 L. Ed. 2d 378 (1981)

[Syllabus only]

Defendant was convicted in an Arizona state court of robbery, burglary and first-degree murder, and he appealed. The Arizona Supreme Court, 122 Ariz. 206, 594 P.2d 72, affirmed and defendant petitioned for writ of certiorari. The United States Supreme Court, Justice White, held that: (1) state courts applied an erroneous standard for determining waiver of right to counsel by focusing on voluntariness of confession rather than on whether defendant understood his right to counsel and intelligently and knowingly relinquished it, and (2) where defendant had invoked his right to have counsel present during custodial interrogation, valid waiver of that right could not be established by showing only that he responded to police-initiated interrogation after being again advised of his rights; thus, use of defendant's confession against him at his trial violated his rights under Fifth and Fourteenth Amendments to have counsel present during custodial interrogation.

Reversed.

CHIEF JUSTICE BURGER filed separate opinion concurring in the judgment.

JUSTICE POWELL filed separate opinion concurring in the result and in which JUSTICE REHNQUIST joined.

JUSTICE WHITE delivered the opinion of the Court.

We granted certiorari in this case, 446 U.S. 950, 100 S.Ct. 2915, 64 L.Ed.2d 807 (1980), limited to Q 1 presented in the petition, which in relevant part was "whether the Fifth, Sixth, and Fourteenth Amendments require suppression of a post-arrest confession, which was obtained after Edwards had invoked his right to consult counsel before further interrogation...."

I

On January 19, 1976, a sworn complaint was filed against Edwards in Arizona state court charging him with robbery, burglary, and first-degree murder. An arrest warrant was issued pursuant to the complaint, and Edwards was arrested at his home later that same day. At the police station, he was informed of his rights as required by *Miranda v. Arizona*, 384 U.S. 436, 86 S.Ct. 1602, 16 L.Ed.2d 694 (1966). Petitioner stated that he understood his rights, and was willing to submit to questioning. After being told that another suspect already in custody had implicated him in the crime, Ewards denied involvement and gave a taped statement presenting an alibi defense. He then sought to "make a deal." The interrogating officer told him that he wanted a statement, but that he did not have the authority to negotiate a deal. The officer provided Edwards with the telephone number of a county attorney. Petitioner made the call, but hung up after a few moments. Edwards then said: "I want an attorney before making a deal." At that point, questioning ceased and Edwards was taken to county jail.

At 9:15 the next morning, two detectives, colleagues of the officer who had interrogated Edwards the previous night, came to the jail and asked to see Edwards. When the detention officer informed Edwards that the detectives wished to speak with him, he replied that he did not want to talk to anyone. The guard told him that "he had" to talk and then took him to meet with the detectives. The officers identified themselves, stated they wanted to talk to him, and informed him of his *Miranda* rights. Edwards was willing to talk, but he first wanted to hear the taped statement of the alleged accomplice who had implicated him. After listening to the tape for several minutes, petitioner said that he would make a statement so long as it was not tape-recorded. The detectives informed him that the recording was irrelevant since they could testify in court concerning whatever he said. Edwards replied: "I'll tell you anything you want to know, but I don't want it on tape." He thereupon implicated himself in the crime.

Prior to trial, Edwards moved to suppress his confession on the ground that his *Miranda* rights had been violated when the officers returned to question him after he had invoked his right to counsel. The trial court initially granted the motion to suppress, but reversed its ruling when presented with a supposedly controlling decision of a higher Arizona court. The court stated without explanation that it found Edwards' statement to be voluntary. Edwards was tried twice and convicted. Evidence concerning his confession was admitted at both trials.

On appeal, the Arizona Supreme Court held that Edwards had invoked both his right to remain silent and his right to counsel during the interrogation conducted on the night of January 19. The court then went on to determine, however, that Edwards had waived both rights during the January 20 meeting when he voluntarily gave his statement to the detectives after again being informed that he need not answer questions and that he need not answer without the advice of counsel: "The trial court's finding that the waiver and confession were voluntarily and knowingly made is upheld."

Because the use of Edwards' confession against him at his trial violated his rights under the Fifth and Fourteenth Amendments as construed in *Miranda v. Arizona, supra,* we reverse the judgement of the Arizona Supreme Court.

II

In *Miranda v. Arizona,* the Court determined that the Fifth and Fourteenth Amendments' prohibition against compelled self-incrimination required that custodial interrogation be preceded by advice to the putative defendant that he has the right to remain silent and also the right to the presence of an attorney. 384 U.S., at 479, 86 S.Ct., at 1630. The Court also indicated the procedures to be followed subsequent to the warnings. If the accused indicates that he wishes to remain silent, "the interrogation must cease." If he requests counsel, "the interrogation must cease until an attorney is present." *Id.,* at 474, 86 S.Ct., at 1627.

Miranda thus declared that an accused has a Fifth and Fourteenth Amendment right to have counsel present during custodial interrogation. Here, the critical facts as found by the Arizona Supreme Court are that Edwards asserted his right to counsel and his right to remain silent on January 19, but that the police, without furnishing him counsel, returned the next morning to confront him and as a result of the meeting secured incriminating oral admissions. Contrary to the holdings of the state courts, Edwards insists that having exercised his right on the 19th to have counsel present during interrogation, he did not validly waive that right on the 20th. For the following reasons, we agree.

First, the Arizona Supreme Court applied an erroneous standard for determining waiver where the accused has specifically invoked his right to counsel. It is reasonably clear under our cases that waivers of counsel must not only be voluntary, but must also constitute a knowing and intelligent relinquishment or abandonment of a known right or privilege, a matter which depends in each case "upon the particular facts and circumstances surrounding that case, including the background, experience, and conduct of the accused." *Johnson v. Zerbst,* 304 U.S. 458, 464, 58 S.Ct. 1019, 1023, 82 L.Ed. 1461 (1938). See *Faretta v. California,* 422 U.S. 806, 835, 95 S.Ct. 2525, 2541, 45 L.Ed.2d 562 (1975); *North Carolina v. Butler,* 441 U.S. 369, 374–375, 99 S.Ct. 1755, 1758, 60 L.Ed.2d 286 (1979); *Brewer v. Williams,* 430 U.S. 387, 404, 97 S.Ct. 1232, 1242, 51 L.Ed.2d 424 (1977); *Fare v. Michael C.,* 442 U.S. 707, 724–725, 99 S.Ct. 2560, 2571-2572, 61 L.Ed.2d 197 (1979).

Considering the proceedings in the state courts in the light of this standard, we note that in denying petitioner's motion to suppress, the trial court found the admission to have been "voluntary," App. 3, 95, without separately focusing on whether Edwards had knowingly and intelligently relinquished his right to counsel. The Arizona Supreme Court, in a section of its opinion entitled "Voluntariness of Waiver," stated that in Arizona, confessions are prima facie involuntary and that the State had the burden of showing by a preponderance of the evidence that the confession was freely and voluntarily made. The court stated that the issue of voluntariness should be determined based on the totality of the circumstances as it related to whether an accused's action was "knowing and intelligent and whether his will [was] overborne." 122 Ariz., at 212, 594 P.2d, at 78. Once the trial court determines that "the confession is voluntary, the finding will not be upset on appeal absent clear and manifest error." *Ibid.* The court then upheld the trial court's finding that the "waiver and confession were voluntarily and knowingly made." *Ibid.*

In referring to the necessity to find Edwards' confession knowing and intelligent, the State Supreme Court cited *Schneckloth v. Bustamonte,* 412 U.S. 218, 226, 93 S.Ct. 2041, 2047, 36 L.Ed.2d 854 (1973). Yet, it is clear that *Schneckloth* does not control the issue presented in this case. The issue in *Schneckloth* was under what conditions an individual could be found to have consented to a search and thereby waived his Fourth Amendment rights. The Court declined to impose the "intentional relinquishment or abandonment of a known right or privilege" standard and required only that the consent be voluntary under the totality of the circumstances. The Court specifically noted that the right to counsel was a prime example of those rights requiring the special protection of the knowing and intelligent waiver standard, *id.,* at 241, 93 S.Ct., at 2055, but held that "[t]he considerations that informed the Court's holding in *Miranda* are simply inapplicable in the present case." *Id.,* at 246, 93 S.Ct., at 2057. *Schneckloth* itself thus emphasized that the voluntariness of a consent or an admission on the one hand, and a knowing and intelligent waiver on the other, are discrete inquiries. Here, however sound the conclusion of the state courts as to the voluntariness of Edwards' admission may be, neither the trial court nor the Arizona Supreme Court undertook to focus on whether Edwards understood his right to counsel and intelligently and knowingly relinquished it. It is thus apparent that the decision below misunderstood the requirement for finding a valid waiver of the right to counsel, once invoked.

Second, although we have held that after initially being advised of his *Miranda* rights, the accused may himself validly waive his rights and respond to interrogation, see *North Carolina v. Butler, supra,* 441 U.S., at 372-376, 99 S.Ct., at 1757-1759, the Court has strongly indicated that additional safeguards are necessary when the accused asks for counsel; and we now hold that when an accused has invoked his right to have counsel present during custodial interrogation, a valid waiver of that right cannot be established by showing only that he responded to further police-initiated custodial interrogation even if he has been advised of his rights. We further hold that an accused, such as Edwards, having expressed his desire to deal with the police only through counsel, is not subject to further interrogation by the authorities until counsel has been made available to him, unless the accused himself initiates further communication, exchanges, or conversations with the police.

Miranda itself indicated that the assertion of the right to counsel was a significant event and that once exercised by the accused, "the interrogation must cease until an attorney is present." 384 U.S., at 474, 86 S.Ct., at 1627. Our later cases have not abandoned that view. In *Michigan v. Mosley,* 423 U.S. 96, 96 S.Ct. 321, 46 L.Ed.2d 313 (1975), the Court noted that *Miranda* had distinguished between the procedural safeguards triggered by a request to remain silent and a request for an attorney and had required that interrogation cease until an attorney was present only if the individual stated that he wanted counsel. 423 U.S., at 104, n. 10, 96 S.Ct., at 326, n. 10; see also *id.,* at 109–111, 96 S.Ct., at 329–330 (White, J., concurring). In *Fare v. Michael C., supra,* 442 U.S., at 719, 99 S.Ct., at 2569, the Court referred to *Miranda's* "rigid rule that an accused's request for an attorney is *per se* an invocation of his Fifth Amendment rights, requiring that all interrogation cease." And just last Term, in a case where a suspect in custody had invoked his *Miranda* right to counsel, the Court again referred to the "undisputed right" under *Miranda* to remain silent and to be free of interrogation "until he had consulted with a lawyer." *Rhode Island v. Innis,* 446 U.S. 291, 298, 100 S.Ct. 1682, 1688, 64 L.Ed.2d 297 (1980). We reconfirm these views and, to lend them substance, emphasize that it is inconsistent with *Miranda* and its progeny for the authorities, at their instance, to reinterrogate an accused in custody if he has clearly asserted his right to counsel.

In concluding that the fruits of the interrogation initiated by the police on January 20 could not be used against Edwards, we do not hold or imply that Edwards was powerless to countermand his election or that the authorities could in no event use any incriminating statements made by Edwards prior to his having access to counsel. Had Edwards initiated the meeting on Janaury 20, nothing in the Fifth and Fourteenth Amendments would prohibit the police from merely listening to his voluntary, volunteered statements and using them against him at the trial. The Fifth Amendment right identified in *Miranda* is the right to have counsel present at any custodial interrogation. Absent such interrogation, there would have been no infringement of the right that Edwards invoked and there would be no occasion to determine whether there had been a valid waiver. *Rhode Island v. Innis, supra,* makes this sufficiently clear. 446 U.S., at 298, n. 2, 100 S.Ct., at 1688, n. 2.

But this is not what the facts of this case show. Here, the officers conducting the interrogation on the evening of January 19 ceased interrogation when Edwards requested counsel as he had been advised he had the right to do. The Arizona Supreme Court was of the opinion that this was a sufficient invocation of his *Miranda* rights, and we are in accord. It is also clear that without making counsel available to Edwards, the police returned to him the next day. This was not at his suggestion or request. Indeed, Edwards informed the detention office that he did not want to talk to anyone. At the meeting the detectives told Edwards that they wanted to talk to him and again advised him of his *Miranda* rights. Edwards stated that he would talk, but what prompted this action does not appear. He listened at his own request to part of the taped statement made by one of his alleged accomplices and then made an incriminating statement, which was used against him at his trial. We think it is clear that Edwards was subjected to custodial interrogation on January 20 within the meaning of *Rhode Island v. Innis, supra,* and that this occurred at the instance of the authorities. His statement made without having had access to counsel, did not amount to a valid waiver and hence was inadmissible.

Accordingly, the holding of the Arizona Supreme Court that Edwards had waived his right to counsel was infirm, and the judgment of that court is reversed.

So ordered.

(Concurring opinions not included.)

ARGERSINGER v. HAMLIN

407 U.S. 25, 92 S. Ct. 2006, 32 L. Ed. 2d 530 (1972)

A state prisoner brought an original habeas corpus proceeding in the Florida Supreme Court, which discharged the writ, 236 So.2d 442. Certiorari was granted. The Supreme Court, MR. JUSTICE DOUGLAS, held that absent knowing and intelligent waiver, no person may be imprisoned for any offense, whether classified as petty, misdemeanor or felony, unless he was represented by counsel at his trial.

Reversed.

MR. CHIEF JUSTICE BURGER concurred in result and filed opinion.

MR. JUSTICE BRENNAN filed a concurring opinion in which MR. JUSTICE DOUGLAS and MR. JUSTICE STEWART joined.

MR. JUSTICE POWELL concurred in result and filed opinion in which MR. JUSTICE REHNQUIST joined.

MR. JUSTICE DOUGLAS delivered the opinion of the Court.

Petitioner, an indigent, was charged in Florida with carrying a concealed weapon, an offense punishable by imprisonment up to six months, a $1,000 fine, or both.

The trial was to [before] a judge, and petitioner was unrepresented by counsel. He was sentenced to serve 90 days in jail, and brought this habeas corpus action in the Florida Supreme Court, alleging that, being deprived of his right to counsel, he was unable as an indigent layman properly to raise and present to the trial court good and sufficient defenses to the charge for which he stands convicted. The Florida Supreme Court by a four-to-three decision, in ruling on the right to counsel, followed the line we marked out in *Duncan* v. *Louisiana,* 391 U.S. 145, 159, as respects the right to trial by jury and held that the right to court-appointed counsel extends only to trials "for non-petty offenses punishable by more than six months imprisonment." 236 So.2d 442, 443.

The case is here on a petition for certiorari, which we granted. We reverse.

The Sixth Amendment, which in enumerated situations has been made applicable to the States by reason of the Fourteenth Amendment (see *Duncan* v. *Louisiana, supra; Washington* v. *Texas,* 388 U.S. 14; *Klopfer* v. *North Carolina,* 386 U.S. 213; *Pointer* v. *Texas,* 380 U.S. 400; *Gideon* v. *Wainwright,* 372 U.S. 335; and *In re Oliver,* 333 U.S. 257), provides specified standards for "all criminal prosecutions."

* * *

While there is historical support for limiting the "deep commitment" to trial by jury to "serious criminal cases," there is no such support for a similar limitation on the right to assistance of counsel:

> Originally, in England, a person charged with treason or felony was denied the aid of counsel, except in respect of legal questions which the accused himself might suggest. At the same time parties in civil cases and persons accused of misdemeanors were entitled to the full assistance of counsel. . . .
>
> . . . .
>
> [It] appears that in at least twelve of the thirteen colonies the rule of the English common law, in the respect now under consideration, had been definitely rejected and the right to counsel fully recognized in all criminal prosecutions, save that in one or two instances the right was limited to capital offenses or to the more serious crimes . . . *Powell* v. *Alabama,* 287 U.S. 45, 60, 64–65.

The Sixth Amendment thus extended the right to counsel beyond its common-law dimensions. But there is nothing in the language of the Amendment, its history, or in the decisions of this Court, to indicate that it was intended to embody a retraction of the right in petty offenses wherein the common law previously did require that counsel be provided.

We reject, therefore, the premise that since prosecutions for crimes punishable by imprisonment for less than six months may be tried without a jury, they may also be tried without a lawyer.

The assistance of counsel is often a requisite to the very existence of a fair trial. The Court in *Powell* v. *Alabama, supra*—a capital case—said:

> The right to be heard would be, in many cases, of little avail if it did not comprehend the right to be heard by counsel. Even the intelligent and educated layman has small and sometimes no skill in the science of law. If charged with crime, he is incapable, generally, of determining for himself whether the indictment is good or bad. He is unfamiliar with the rules of evidence. Left without the aid of counsel he may be put on trial without a proper charge, and convicted upon incompetent evidence, or evidence irrelevant to the issue or otherwise inadmissible. He lacks both the skill and knowledge adequately to prepare his defense, even though he have a perfect one. He requires the guiding hand of counsel at every step in the proceedings against him. Without it, though he be not guilty, he faces the danger of conviction because he does not know how to establish his innocence. If that be true of men of intelligence, how much more true is it of the ignorant and illiterate, or those of feeble intellect.

The requirement of counsel may well be necessary for a fair trial even in a petty-offense prosecution. We are by no means convinced that legal and constitutional questions involved in a case that actually leads to imprisonment even for a brief period are any less complex than when a person can be sent off for six months or more. See, *e.g., Powell* v. *Texas,* 392 U.S. 514; *Thompson* v. *Louisville,* 362 U.S. 199; *Shuttlesworth* v. *Birmingham,* 382 U.S. 87.

The trial of vagrancy cases is illustrative. While only brief sentences of imprisonment may be imposed, the cases often bristle with thorny constitutional questions. See *Papachristou* v. *Jacksonville,* 405 U.S. 156.

In re Gault, 387 U.S. 1, dealt with juvenile delinquency and an offense, which, if committed by an adult, would have carried a fine of $5 to $50 or imprisonment in jail for not more than two months, but which when committed by a juvenile might lead to his detention in a state institution until he reached the age of 21. We said that "[t]he juvenile needs the assistance of counsel to cope with problems of law, to make skilled inquiry into the facts, to insist upon regularity of the proceedings, and to ascertain whether he has a defense and to prepare and submit it. The child 'requires the guiding hand of counsel at every step in the proceedings against him,'" citing *Powell* v. *Alabama, supra.* The premise of *Gault* is that even in prosecutions for offenses less serious than felonies, a fair trial may require the presence of a lawyer.

Beyond the problem of trials and appeals is that of the guilty plea, a problem which looms large in misdemeanor as well as in felony cases. Counsel is needed so that the accused may know precisely what he is doing, so that he is fully aware of the prospect of going to jail or prison, and so that he is treated fairly by the prosecution.

. . . .

We must conclude, therefore, that the problems associated with misdemeanor and petty offenses often require the presence of counsel to insure the accused a fair trial. MR. JUSTICE POWELL suggests that these problems are raised even in situations where there is no prospect of imprisonment. We need not consider the requirements of the Sixth Amendment as regards the right to counsel where loss of liberty is not involved, however, for here petitioner was in fact sentenced to jail. And, as we said in *Baldwin* v. *New York, supra,* "the prospect of imprisonment for however short a time will seldom be viewed by the accused as a trivial or 'petty' matter and may well result in quite serious repercussions affecting his career and his reputation."

We hold, therefore, that absent a knowing and intelligent waiver, no person may be imprisoned for any offense, whether classified as petty, misdemeanor, or felony, unless he was represented by counsel at his trial.

That is the view of the Supreme Court of Oregon, with which we agree. It said in *Stevenson* v. *Holzman,* 254 Or. 94, 102, 458 P.2d 414, 418:

> We hold that no person may be deprived of his liberty who has been denied the assistance of counsel as guaranteed by the Sixth Amendment. This holding is applicable to all criminal prosecutions, including prosecutions for violations of municipal ordinances. The denial of the assistance of counsel will preclude the imposition of a jail sentence.

We do not sit as an ombudsman to direct state courts how to manage their affairs but only to make clear the federal constitutional requirement. How crimes should be classified is largely a state matter. The fact that traffic charges technically fall within the category of "criminal prosecutions" does not necessarily mean that many of them will be brought into the class where imprisonment actually occurs.

. . . .

Under the rule we announce today, every judge will know when the trial of a misdemeanor starts that no imprisonment may be imposed, even though local law permits it, unless the accused is represented by counsel. He will have a measure of the seriousness and gravity of the offense and therefore know when to name a lawyer to represent the accused before the trial starts.

The run of misdemeanors will not be affected by today's ruling. But in those that end up in the actual deprivation of a person's liberty, the accused will receive the benefit of "the guiding hand of counsel" so necessary when one's liberty is in jeopardy.

Reversed.

Case relating to **Chapter 9**

DOUBLE JEOPARDY

ASHE v. SWENSON

397 U.S. 436, 90 S. Ct. 1189, 25 L. Ed. 2d 469 (1970)

MR. JUSTICE STEWART delivered the opinion of the Court.

In *Benton* v. *Maryland*, 395 U.S. 784, the Court held that the Fifth Amendment guarantee against double jeopardy is enforceable against the States through the Fourteenth Amendment. The question in this case is whether the State of Missouri violated that guarantee when it prosecuted the petitioner a second time for armed robbery in the circumstances here presented.

Sometime in the early hours of the morning of January 10, 1960, six men were engaged in a poker game in the basement of the home of John Gladson at Lee's Summit, Missouri. Suddenly three or four masked men, armed with a shotgun and pistols, broke into the basement and robbed each of the poker players of money and various articles of personal property. The robbers—and it has never been clear whether there were three or four of them—then fled in a car belonging to one of the victims of the robbery. Shortly thereafter the stolen car was discovered in a field, and later that morning three men were arrested by a state trooper while they were walking on a highway not far from where the abandoned car had been found. The petitioner was arrested by another officer some distance away.

The four were subsequently charged with seven separate offenses—the armed robbery of each of the six poker players and the theft of the car. In May 1960 the petitioner went to trial on the charge of robbing Donald Knight, one of the participants in the poker game. At the trial the State called Knight and three of his fellow poker players as prosecution witnesses. Each of them described the circumstances of the holdup and itemized his own individual losses. The proof that an armed robbery had occurred and that personal property had been taken from Knight as well as from each of the others was unassailable. The testimony of the four victims in this regard was consistent both internally and with that of the others. But the State's evidence that the petitioner had been one of the robbers was weak. Two of the witnesses thought that there had been only three robbers altogether, and could not identify the petitioner as one of them. Another of the victims, who was the petitioner's uncle by marriage, said that at the "patrol station" he had positively identified each of the other three men accused of the holdup, but could say only the petitioner's voice "sounded very much like" that of one of the robbers. The fourth participant in the poker game did identify the petitioner, but only by his "size and height, and his actions."

The cross-examination of these witnesses was brief, and it was aimed primarily at exposing the weakness of their identification testimony. Defense counsel made no attempt to question their testimony regarding the holdup itself or their claims as to their losses. Knight testified without contradiction that the robbers had stolen from him his watch, $250 in cash, and about $500 in checks. His billfold, which had been found by the police in the possession of one of the three other men accused of the robbery, was admitted in evidence. The defense offered no testimony and waived final argument.

The trial judge instructed the jury that if it found that the petitioner was one of the participants in the armed robbery, the theft of "any money" from Knight would sustain a conviction. He also instructed the jury that if the petitioner was one of the robbers, he was guilty under the law even if he had not personally robbed Knight. The jury—though not instructed to elaborate upon its verdict—found the petitioner "not guilty due to insufficient evidence."

Six weeks later the petitioner was brought to trial again, this time for the robbery of another participant in the poker game, a man named Roberts. The petitioner filed a motion to dismiss, based on his previous acquittal. The motion was overruled, and the second trial began. The witnesses were for the most part the same, though this time their testimony was substantially stronger on the issue of the petitioner's identity. For example, two witnesses who at the first trial had been wholly unable to identify the petitioner as one of the robbers, now testified that his features, size, and mannerisms matched those of one of their assailants. Another witness who before had identified the petitioner only by his size and actions now also remembered him by the unusual sound of his voice. The State further refined its case at the second trial by declining to call one of the participants in the poker game whose identification testimony at the first trial had been conspicuously negative. The case went to the jury on instructions virtually identical to those given at the first trial. This time the jury found the petitioner guilty, and he was sentenced to a 35-year term in the state penitentiary.

The Supreme Court of Missouri affirmed the conviction, holding that the "plea of former jeopardy must be denied." *State* v. *Ashe*, 350 S.W.2d 768, at 771. . . .

. . .

The doctrine of *Benton* v. *Maryland*, 395 U.S. 784, puts the issues in the present case in a perspective quite different from that in which the issues were perceived in *Hoag* v. *New Jersey*, [356 U.S. 464]. The question is no longer whether collateral estoppel is a requirement of due process, but whether it is a part of the Fifth Amendment's guarantee against double jeopardy. And if collateral estoppel is embodied in that guarantee, then its applicability in a particular case is no longer a matter to be left for state court determination within the broad bounds of "fundamental fairness," but a matter of constitutional fact we must decide through an examination of the entire record. Cf. *New York Times Co.* v. *Sullivan*, 376 U.S. 254, 285; *Niemotko* v. *Maryland*, 340 U.S. 268, 271; *Watts* v. *Indiana*, 338 U.S. 49, 51; *Chambers* v. *Florida*, 309 U.S. 227, 229; *Norris* v. *Alabama*, 294 U.S. 587, 590.

"Collateral estoppel" is an awkward phrase, but it stands for an extremely important principle in our adversary system of justice. It means simply that when an issue of ultimate fact has once been determined by a valid and final judgment, that issue cannot again be litigated between the same parties in any future lawsuit. Although first developed in civil litigation, collateral estoppel has been an established rule of federal criminal law at least since this Court's decision more than 50 years ago in *United States* v. *Oppenheimer*, 242 U.S. 85. As MR. JUSTICE HOLMES put the matter in that case, "It cannot be that the safeguards of the person, so often and so rightly mentioned with solemn reverence, are less than those that protect from a liability in debt." 242 U.S., at 87. As a rule of federal law, therefore, "[i]t is much too late to suggest that this principle is not fully applicable to a former judgment in a criminal case, either because of lack of 'mutuality' or because the judgment may reflect only a belief that the Government had not met the higher burden of proof exacted in such cases for the Government's evidence as a whole although not necessarily as to every link in the chain." *United States* v. *Kramer*, 289 F.2d 909, at 913.

The federal decisions have made clear that the rule of collateral estoppel in criminal cases is not to be applied with the hypertechnical and archaic approach of a 19th century pleading book, but with realism and rationality. Where a previous judment of acquittal was based upon a general verdict, as is usually the case, this approach requires a court to "examine the record of a prior proceeding, taking into account the pleadings, evidence, charge, and other relevant matter, and conclude whether a rational jury could have grounded its verdict upon an issue other than that which the defendant seeks to foreclose from consideration." The inquiry "must be set in a practical frame, and viewed with an eye to all the circumstances of the proceedings." *Sealfon* v. *United States*, 332 U.S. 575, 579. Any test more technically restrictive would, of course, simply amount to a rejection of the rule of collateral estoppel in criminal proceedings, at least in every case where the first judgment was based upon a general verdict of acquittal.

Straightforward application of the federal rule to the present case can lead to but one conclusion. For the record is utterly devoid of any indication that the first jury could rationally have found that an armed robbery had not occurred, or that Knight had not been a victim of that robbery. The single rationally conceivable issue in dispute before the jury was whether the petitioner had been one of the robbers. And the jury by its verdict found that he had not. The federal rule of law, therefore, would make a second prosecution for the robbery of Roberts wholly impermissible.

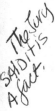

The ultimate question to be determined, then, in the light of *Benton* v. *Maryland, supra,* is whether this established rule of federal law is embodied in the Fifth Amendment guarantee against double jeopardy. We do not hesitate to hold that it is. For whatever else that constitutional guarantee may embrace, *North Carolina* v. *Pearce,* 395 U.S. 711, 717, it surely protects a man who has been acquitted from having to "run the gantlet" a second time. *Green* v. *United States,* 355 U.S. 184, 190.

The question is not whether Missouri could validly charge the petitioner with six separate offenses for the robbery of the six poker players. It is not whether he could have received a total of six punishments if he had been convicted in a single trial of robbing the six victims. It is simply whether, after a jury determined by its verdict that the petitioner was not one of the robbers, the State could constitutionally hale him before a new jury to litigate that issue again.

After the first jury had acquitted the petitioner of robbing Knight, Missouri could certainly not have brought him to trial again upon that charge. Once a jury had determined upon conflicting testimony that there was at least a reasonable doubt that the petitioner was one of the robbers, the State could not present the same or different identification evidence in a second prosecution for the robbery of Knight in the hope that a different jury might find that evidence more convincing. The situation is constitutionally no different here, even though the second trial related to another victim of the same robbery. For the name of the victim, in the circumstances of this case, had no bearing whatever upon the issue of whether the petitioner was one of the robbers.

In this case the State in its brief has frankly conceded that following the petitioner's acquittal, it treated the first trial as no more than a dry run for the second prosecution: "No doubt the prosecutor felt the state had a provable case on the first charge, and, when he lost, he did what every good attorney would do—he refined his presentation in light of the turn of events at the first trial." But this is precisely what the constitutional guarantee forbids.

The judgment is reversed, and the case is remanded to the Court of Appeals for the Eighth Circuit for further proceedings consistent with this opinion.

It is so ordered.

[The concurring opinions of MR.

JUSTICE BLACK and of MR. JUSTICE HARLAN are not included.]

MR. JUSTICE BRENNAN, whom MR. JUSTICE DOUGLAS and MR. JUSTICE MARSHALL join, concurring.

I agree that the Double Jeopardy Clause incorporates collateral estoppel as a constitutional requirement and therefore join the Court's opinion. However, even if the rule of collateral estoppel had been inapplicable to the facts of this case, it is my view that the Double Jeopardy Clause nevertheless bars the prosecution of petitioner a second time for armed robbery. The two prosecutions, the first for the robbery of Knight and the second for the robbery of Roberts, grew out of one criminal episode, and therefore I think it clear on the facts of this case that the Double Jeopardy Clause prohibited Missouri from prosecuting petitioner for each robbery at a different trial. *Abbate* v. *United States*, 359 U.S. 187, 196–201 (1959) (separate opinion).

. . . .

The Double Jeopardy Clause is a guarantee "that the State with all its resources and power [shall] not be allowed to make repeated attempts to convict an individual for an alleged offense, thereby subjecting him to embarrassment, expense and ordeal and compelling him to live in a continuing state of anxiety and insecurity. . . ." *Green* v. *United States*, 355 U.S. 184, 187 (1957). This guarantee is expressed as a prohibition against multiple prosecutions for the "same offence." Although the phrase "same offence" appeared in most of the early common-law articulations of the double-jeopardy principle, questions of its precise meaning rarely arose prior to the 18th century, and by the time the Bill of Rights was adopted it had not been authoritatively defined.

When the common law did finally attempt a definition, in *Rex* v. *Vandercomb & Abbott*, 2 Leach 708, 720, 168 Eng. Rep. 455, 461 (Crown 1796), it adopted the "same evidence" test, which provided little protection from multiple prosecution:

> [U]nless the first indictment were such as the prisoner might have been convicted upon by proof of the facts contained in the second indictment, an acquittal on the first indictment can be no bar to the second.

The "same evidence" test of "same offence" was soon followed by a majority of American jurisdictions, but its deficiencies are obvious. It does not enforce but virtually annuls the constitutional guarantee. For example, where a single criminal episode involves several victims, under the "same evidence" test a separate prosecution may be brought as to each. E.g., *State* v. *Hoag*, 21 N.J. 496, 122 A.2d 628, (1956), aff'd, 356 U.S. 464 (1958). The "same evidence" test permits multiple prosecutions where a single transaction is divisible into chronologically discrete crimes. E.g., *Johnson* v. *Commonwealth*, 201 Ky. 314, 256 S.W. 388 (1923) (each of 75 poker hands a separate "offense"). Even a single criminal act may lead to multiple prosecutions if it is viewed from the perspectives of different statutes. E.g., *State* v. *Elder,* 65 Ind. 282 (1879). Given the tendency of modern criminal legislation to divide the phases of criminal transaction into numerous separate crimes, the opportunities for multiple prosecutions for an essentially unitary criminal episode are frightening. And given our tradition of virtually unreviewable prosecutorial discretion concerning the initiation and scope of a criminal prosecution, the potentialities for abuse inherent in the "same evidence" test are simply intolerable.

. . . .

In my view, the Double Jeopardy Clause requires the prosecution, except in most limited circumstances, to join at one trial all the charges against a defendant which grow out of a single criminal act, occurrence, episode, or transaction. This "same transaction" test of "same offence" not only enforces the ancient prohibition against vexatious multiple prosecutions embodied in the Double Jeopardy Clause, but responds as well to the increasingly widespread recognition that the consolidation in one lawsuit of all issues arising out of a single transaction or occurrence best promotes justice, economy, and convenience. Modern rules of criminal and civil procedure reflect this recognition. See *UMW* v. *Gibbs,* 383 U.S. 715, 724–726 (1966). Although in 1935 the American Law Institute adopted the "same evidence" test, it has since replaced it with the "same transaction" test. England, too, has abandoned its surviving rules against joinder of charges and has adopted the "same transaction" test. . . .

. . . .

The present case highlights the hazards of abuse of the criminal process inherent in the "same evidence" test and demonstrates the necessity for the "same transaction" test. The robbery of the poker game involved six players—Gladson, Knight, Freeman, Goodwin, McClendon, and Roberts. The robbers also stole a car. Seven separate informations were filed against the petitioner, one covering each of the robbery victims, and the seventh covering the theft of the car. Petitioner's first trial was under the information charging the robbery of Knight. Since Missouri has offered no justification for not trying the other informations at that trial, it is reasonable to infer that the other informations were held in reserve to be tried if the State failed to obtain a conviction on the charge of robbing Knight. Indeed, the State virtually concedes as much since it argues that the "same evidence" test is consistent with such an exercise of prosecutorial discretion.

Four of the robbery victims testified at the trial. Their testimony conflicted as to whether there were three or four robbers. Gladson testified that he saw four robbers, but could identify only one, a man named Brown. McClendon testified that he saw only three men at any one time during the course of the robbery, and he positively identified Brown, Larson, and Johnson; he also thought he heard petitioner's voice during the robbery, but said he was not sure. Knight thought only three men participated in the robbery, and he could not identify anyone. Roberts said he saw four different men and he identified them as Brown, Larson, Johnson, and petitioner. Under cross-examination, he conceded that he did not recognize petitioner's voice, and that he did not see his face or his hands. He maintained that he could identify him by his "size and height" even though all the robbers had worn outsized clothing, and even though he could not connect petitioner with the actions of any of the robbers. On this evidence the jury acquitted petitioner.

At the second trial, for the robbery of Roberts, McClendon was not called as a witness. Gladson, who previously had been able to identify only one man—Brown—now was able to identify three—Brown, Larson, and petitioner. On a number of details his memory was much more vivid than it had been at the first trial. Knight's testimony was substantially the same as at the first trial—he still was unable to identify any of the robbers. Roberts, who previously had identified petitioner only by his size and height, now identified him by his size, actions, voice, and a peculiar movement of his mouth. As might be expected, this far stronger identification evidence brought a virtually inevitable conviction.

The prosecution plainly organized its case for the second trial to provide the links missing in the chain of identification evidence that was offered at the first trial. McClendon, who was an unhelpful witness at the first trial was not called at the second trial. The hesitant and uncertain evidence of Gladson and Roberts at the first trial became detailed, positive, and expansive at the second trial. One must experience a sense of uneasiness with any double jeopardy standard that would allow the State this second chance to plug up the holes in its case. The constitutional protection against double jeopardy is empty of meaning if the State may make "repeated attempts" to touch up its case by forcing the accused to "run the gantlet" as many times as there are victims of a single episode.

Fortunately for petitioner, the conviction at the second trial can be reversed under the doctrine of collateral estoppel, since the jury at the first trial clearly resolved in his favor the only contested issue at that trial, which was the identification of him as one of the robbers. There is at least doubt whether collateral estoppel would have aided him had the jury been required to resolve additional contested issues on conflicting evidence. But correction of the abuse of criminal process should not in any event be made to depend on the availability of collateral estoppel. Abuse of the criminal process is foremost among the feared evils which led to the inclusion of the Double Jeopardy Clause in the Bill of Rights. That evil will be most effectively avoided, and the Clause can thus best serve its worthy ends, if "same offence" is construed to embody the "same transaction" standard. Then both federal and state prosecutors will be prohibited from mounting successive prosecutions for offenses growing out of the same criminal episode, at least in the absence of a showing of unavoidable necessity for successive prosecutions in the particular case.

MR. CHIEF JUSTICE BURGER, dissenting.

. . . .

III.

The essence of MR. JUSTICE BRENNAN'S concurrence is that this was all one transaction, one episode, or, if I may so characterize it, one frolic, and, hence, only one crime. His approach, like that taken by the Court, totally overlooks the significance of there being *six entirely separate charges of robbery* against six individuals.

This "single transaction" concept is not a novel notion; it has been urged in various courts including this Court. One of the theses underlying the "single transaction" notion is that the criminal episode is "indivisible." The short answer to that is that to the victims, the criminal conduct is readily divisible and intensely personal; each offense is an offense against *a person.* For me it demeans the dignity of the human personality and individuality to talk of "a single transaction" in the context of six separate assaults on six individuals.

No court which elevates the individual rights and human dignity of the accused to a high place—as we should—ought to be so casual as to treat the victims as a single homogenized lump of human clay. I would grant the dignity of individual status to the victims as much as to those accused, not more but surely no less.

If it be suggested that multiple crimes can be separately punished but must be collectively tried, one can point to the firm trend in the law to allow severance of defendants and offenses into separate trials so as to avoid possible prejudice of one criminal act or of the conduct of one defendant to "spill over" on another.

What the Court holds today must be related to its impact on crimes more serious than ordinary housebreaking, followed by physical assault on six men and robbery of all of them. To understand its full impact we must view the holding in the context of four men who break and enter, rob and then kill six victims. The concurrence tells us that unless all the crimes are joined in one trial the alleged killers cannot be tried for more than one of the killings even if the evidence is that they personally killed two, three or more of the victims. Or alter the crime to four men breaking into a college dormitory and assaulting six girls. What the Court is holding is, in effect, that the second and third and fourth criminal acts are "free," unless the accused is tried for the multiple crimes in a single trial—something defendants frantically use every legal device to avoid, and often succeed in avoiding. This is the reality of what the Court holds today; it does not make good sense and it cannot make good law.

I therefore join with the four courts which have found no double jeopardy in this case.

To borrow some wise words from MR. JUSTICE BLACK in his [separate opinion] in *Jackson* v. *Denno*, 378 U.S. 368, 401, 407–408 (1964), the conviction struck down in this case "is in full accord with all the guarantees of the Federal Constitution and . . . should not be held invalid by this Court because of a belief that the Court can improve on the Constitution."

Cases relating to Chapter 10

FAIR TRIAL AND HUMANE PUNISHMENT

ARIZONA v. YOUNGBLOOD

488 U.S. __, 109 S. Ct. 333, 102 L. Ed. 2d 281 (1988)

Argued October 11, 1988. Decided November 29, 1988.

[The Court's footnotes have been omitted.]

SYLLABUS BY REPORTER OF DECISIONS

The victim, a 10-year-old boy, was molested and sodomized by a middle-aged man for 1 1/2 hours. After the assault, the boy was taken to a hospital where a physician used a swab from a "sexual assault kit" to collect semen samples from the boy's rectum. The police also collected the boy's clothing, which they failed to refrigerate. A police criminologist later performed some tests on the rectal swab and the boy's clothing, but he was unable to obtain information about the identity of the boy's assailant. At trial, expert witnesses testified that respondent might have been completely exonerated by timely performance of tests on properly preserved semen samples. Respondent was convicted of child molestation, sexual assault, and kidnapping in an Arizona state court. The Arizona Court of Appeals reversed the conviction on the ground that the State had breached a constitutional duty to preserve the semen samples from the victim's body and clothing.

* * *

OPINION OF THE COURT

Chief Justice **Rehnquist** delivered the opinion of the Court.

* * *

Decision of this case requires us to again consider "what might loosely be called the area of constitutionally-guaranteed access to evidence." United States v. Valenzuela-Bernal, 458 U.S. 858, 867, 73 L.Ed.2d 1193, 102 S.Ct. 3440 (1982). In Brady v. Maryland, 373 U.S. 83, 10 L.Ed.2d 215, 83 S.Ct. 1194 (1963), we held "that the suppression by the prosecution of evidence favorable to the accused upon request violates due process where the evidence is material either to guilt or to punishment, irrespective of the good faith or bad faith of the prosecution." Id., at 87, 10 L.Ed.2d 215, 83 S.Ct. 1194. In United States v. Agurs, 427 U.S. 97, 49 L.Ed.2d 342, 96 S.Ct. 2392 (1976), we held that the prosecution had a duty to disclose some evidence of this description even though no requests were made for it, but at the same time we rejected the notion that a "prosecutor has a constitutional duty routinely to deliver his entire file to defense counsel." Id., at 111, 49 L.Ed.2d 342, 96 S.Ct. 2392; see also Moore v. Illinois, 408 U.S. 786, 795, 33 L.Ed.2d 706, 92 S.Ct. 2562 (1972) ("We know of no constitutional requirement that the prosecution make a complete and detailed accounting to the defense of all police investigatory work on a case").

There is no question but that the State complied with Brady and Agurs here. The State disclosed relevant police reports to respondent, which contained information about the existence of the swab and the clothing, and the boy's examination at the hospital. The State provided respondent's expert with the laboratory reports and notes prepared by the police criminologist, and respondent's expert had access to the swab and to the clothing.

[2a] If respondent is to prevail on federal constitutional grounds, then, it must be because of some constitutional duty over and above that imposed by cases such as Brady and Agurs. Our most recent decision in this area of the law, California v. Trombetta, 467 U.S. 479, 81 L.Ed.2d 413, 104 S.Ct. 2528 (1984), arose out of a drunk driving prosecution in which the State had introduced test results indicating the concentration of alcohol in the blood of two motorists. The defendants sought to suppress the test results on the ground that the State had failed to preserve the breath samples used in the test. We rejected this argument for several reasons: first, "the officers here were acting in 'good faith and in accord with their normal practice.'" Id., at 488, 81 L.Ed.2d 413, 104 S.Ct. 2528, quoting Killian v. United States, 368 U.S. 231, 242, 7 L.Ed.2d 256, 82 S.Ct. 302 (1961); second, in the light of the procedures actually used the chances that preserved samples would have exculpated the defendants were slim, 467 U.S., at 489, 81 L.Ed.2d 413, 104 S.Ct. 2528; and, third, even if the samples might have shown inaccuracy in the tests, the defendants had "alternative means of demonstrating their innocence." Id., at 490, 81 L.Ed.2d 413, 104 S.Ct. 2528. In the present case, the likelihood that the preserved materials would have enabled the defendant to exonerate himself appears to be greater than it was in *Trombetta,* but here, unlike in *Trombetta,* the State did not attempt to make any use of the materials in its own case in chief.

* * *

[1b, 3] The Due Process Clause of the Fourteenth Amendment, as interpreted in Brady, makes the good or bad faith of the State irrelevant when the State fails to disclose to the defendant material exculpatory evidence. But we think the Due Process Clause requires a different result when we deal with the failure of the State to preserve evidentiary material of which no more can be said than that it could have been subjected to tests, the results of which might have exonerated the defendant. Part of the reason for the difference in treatment is found in the observation made by the Court in Trombetta, supra, at 486, 81 L.Ed.2d 413, 104 S.Ct. 2528, that "[w]henever potentially exculpatory evidence is permanently lost, courts face the treacherous task of divining the import of materials whose contents are unknown and, very often, disputed." Part of it stems from our unwillingness to read the "fundamental fairness" requirement of the Due Process Clause, see Lisenba v. California, 314 U.S. 219, 236, 86 L.Ed. 166, 62 S.Ct. 280 (1941), as imposing on the police an undifferentiated and absolute duty to retain and to preserve all material that might be of conceivable evidentiary significance in a particular prosecution. We think that requiring a defendant to show bad faith on the part of the police both limits the extent of the police's obligation to preserve evidence to reasonable bounds and confines it to that class of cases where the interests of justice most clearly require it, i.e., those cases in which the police themselves by their conduct indicate that the evidence could form a basis for exonerating the defendant. We therefore hold that unless a criminal defendant can show bad faith on the part of the police, failure to preserve potentially useful evidence does not constitute a denial of due process of law.

[1c] In this case, the police collected the rectal swab and clothing on the night of the crime: respondent was not taken into custody until six weeks later. The failure of the police to refrigerate the clothing and to perform tests on the semen samples can at worst be described as negligent. None of this information was concealed from respondent at trial, and the evidence--such as it was--was made available to respondent's expert who declined to perform any tests on the samples. The Arizona Court of Appeals noted in its opinion--and we agree--that there was no suggestion of bad faith on the part of the police. It follows, therefore, from what we have said, that there was no violation of the Due Process Clause.

[4] The Arizona Court of Appeals also referred somewhat obliquely to the State's "inability to quantitatively test" certain semen samples with the newer P-30 test. 153 Ariz., at 54, 734 P.2d, at 596. If the court meant by this statement that the Due Process Clause is violated when the police fail to use a particular investigatory tool, we strongly disagree. The situation here is no different than a prosecution for drunk driving that rests on police observation alone; the defendant is free to argue to the finder of the fact that a breathalizer [sic] test might have been exculpatory, but the police do not have a constitutional duty to perform any particular tests.

The judgment of the Arizona Court of Appeals is reversed and the case remanded for further proceedings not inconsistent with this opinion.

Reversed.

COKER v. GEORGIA

433 U.S. 584, 97 S. Ct. 2861, 53 L. Ed. 2d 982 (1977)

[Footnotes omitted]

MR. JUSTICE WHITE announced the judgment of the Court and filed an opinion in which MR. JUSTICE STEWART, MR. JUSTICE BLACKMUN, and MR. JUSTICE STEVENS, joined.

Georgia Code Ann. § 26-2001 (1972) provides that "[a] person convicted of rape shall be punished by death or by imprisonment for life, or by imprisonment for not less than one nor more than 20 years." Punishment is determined by a jury in a separate sentencing proceeding in which at least one of the statutory aggravating circumstances must be found before the death penalty may be imposed. Petitioner Coker was convicted of rape and sentenced to death. Both the conviction and the sentence were affirmed by the Georgia Supreme Court. Coker was granted a writ of certiorari, 429 U.S. 815, limited to the single claim, rejected by the Georgia court, that the punishment of death for rape violates the Eighth Amendment, which proscribes "cruel and unusual punishments" and which must be observed by the States as well as the Federal Government. *Robinson* v. *California*, 370 U.S. 660 (1962).

I

While serving various sentences for murder, rape, kidnaping, and aggravated assault, petitioner escaped from the Ware Correctional Institution near Waycross, Ga., on September 2, 1974. At approximately 11 o'clock that night, petitioner entered the house of Allen and Elnita Carver through an unlocked kitchen door. Threatening the couple with a "board," he tied up Mr. Carver in the bathroom, obtained a knife from the kitchen, and took Mr. Carver's money and the keys to the family car. Brandishing the knife and saying "you know what's going to happen to you if you try anything, don't you," Coker then raped Mrs. Carver. Soon thereafter, petitioner drove away in the Carver car, taking Mrs. Carver with him. Mr. Carver, freeing himself, notified the police; and not long thereafter petitioner was apprehended. Mrs. Carver was unharmed.

Petitioner was charged with escape, armed robbery, motor vehicle theft, kidnaping, and rape. Counsel was appointed to represent him. Having been found competent to stand trial, he was tried. The jury returned a verdict of guilty, rejecting his general plea of insanity. A sentencing hearing was then conducted in accordance with the procedures dealt with at length in *Gregg* v. *Georgia*, 428 U.S. 153 (1976), where this Court sustained the death penalty for murder when imposed pursuant to the statutory procedures. The jury was instructed that it could consider as aggravating circumstances whether the rape had been committed by a person with a prior record of conviction for a capital felony and whether the rape had been committed in the course of committing another capital felony, namely, the armed robbery of Allen Carver. The court also instructed, pursuant to statute, that even if aggravating circumstances were present, the death penalty need not be imposed if the jury found they were outweighed by mitigating circumstances, that is, circumstances not constituting justification or excuse for the offense in question, "but which, in fairness and mercy, may be considered as extenuating or reducing the degree" of moral culpability or punishment. App. 300. The jury's verdict on the rape count was death by electrocution. Both aggravating circumstances on which the court instructed were found to be present by the jury.

II

Furman v. *Georgia*, 408 U.S. 238 (1972), and the Court's decisions last Term in *Gregg* v. *Georgia*, 428 U.S. 153 (1976); *Proffitt* v. *Florida*, 428 U.S. 242 (1976); *Jurek* v. *Texas*, 428 U.S. 262 (1976); *Woodson* v. *North Carolina*, 428 U.S. 280 (1976); and *Roberts* v. *Louisiana*, 428 U.S. 325 (1976), make unnecessary the recanvassing of certain critical aspects of the controversy about the constitutionality of capital punishment. It is now settled that the death penalty is not invariably cruel and unusual punishment within the meaning of the Eighth Amendment; it is not inherently barbaric or an unacceptable mode of punishment for crime; neither is it always disproportionate to the crime for which it is imposed. It is also established that imposing capital punishment, at least for murder, in accordance with the procedures provided under the Georgia statutes saves the sentence from the infirmities which led the Court to invalidate the prior Georgia capital punisment statute in *Furman* v. *Georgia, supra.*

In sustaining the imposition of the death penalty in *Gregg,* however, the Court firmly embraced the holdings and dicta from prior cases, *Furman* v. *Georgia, supra; Robinson* v. *California,* 370 U.S. 660 (1962); *Trop* v. *Dulles,* 356 U.S. 86 (1958); and *Weems* v. *United States,* 217 U.S. 349 (1910), to the effect that the Eighth Amendment bars not only those punishments that are "barbaric" but also those that are "excessive" in relation to the crime committed. Under *Gregg,* a punishment is "excessive" and unconstitutional if it (1) makes no measurable contribution to acceptable goals of punishment and hence is nothing more than the purposeless and needless imposition of pain and suffering; or (2) is grossly out of proportion to the severity of the crime. A punishment might fail the test on either ground. Furthermore, these Eighth Amendment judgments should not be, or appear to be, merely the subjective views of individual Justices; judgment should be informed by objective factors to the maximum possible extent. To this end, attention must be given to the public attitudes concerning a particular sentence—history and precedent, legislative attitudes, and the response of juries reflected in their sentencing decisions are to be consulted. In *Gregg,* after giving due regard to such sources, the Court's judgment was that the death penalty for deliberate murder was neither the purposeless imposition of severe punishment nor a punishment grossly disproportionate to the crime. But the Court reserved the question of the constitutionality of the death penalty when imposed for other crimes. 428 U.S., at 187 n. 95.

III

That question, with respect to rape of an adult woman, is now before us. We have concluded that a sentence of death is grossly disproportionate and excessive punishment for the crime of rape and is therefore forbidden by the Eighth Amendment as cruel and unusual punishment.

As advised by recent cases, we seek guidance in history and from the objective evidence of the country's present judgment concerning the acceptability of death as a penalty for rape of an adult woman. At no time in the last 50 years have a majority of the States authorized death as a punishment for rape. In 1925, 18 States, the District of Columbia, and the Federal Government authorized capital punishment for the rape of an adult female. By 1971 just prior to the decision in *Furman* v. *Georgia,* that number had declined, but not substantially, to 16 States plus the Federal Government. *Furman* then invalidated most of the capital punishment statutes in this country, including the rape statutes, because, among other reasons, of the manner in which the death penalty was imposed and utilized under those laws.

With their death penalty statutes for the most part invalidated, the States were faced with the choice of enacting modified capital punishment laws in an attempt to satisfy the requirements of *Furman* or of being satisfied with life imprisonment as the ultimate punishment for *any* offense. Thirty-five States immediately reinstituted the death penalty for at least limited kinds of crime. *Gregg* v. *Georgia,* 428 U.S., at 179 n. 23. This public judgment as to the acceptability of capital punishment, evidenced by the immediate, post-*Furman* legislative reaction in a large majority of the States, heavily influenced the Court to sustain the death penalty for murder in *Gregg* v. *Georgia, supra,* at 179-182.

But if the "most marked indication of society's endorsement of the death penalty for murder is the legislative response to *Furman,*" *Gregg* v. *Georgia, supra,* at 179-180, it should also be a telling datum that the public judgment with respect to rape, as reflected in the statutes providing the punishment for that crime, has been dramatically different. In reviving death penalty laws to satisfy *Furman's* mandate, none of the States that had not previously authorized death for rape chose to include rape among capital felonies. Of the 16 States in which rape had been a capital offense, only three provided the death penalty for rape of an adult woman in their revised statutes—Georgia, North Carolina, and Louisiana. In the latter two States, the death penalty was mandatory for those found guilty, and those laws were invalidated by *Woodson* and *Roberts.* When Louisiana and North Carolina, responding to those decisions, again revised their capital punishment laws, they re-enacted the death penalty for murder but not for rape; none of the seven other legislatures that to our knowledge have amended or replaced their death penalty statutes since July 2, 1976, including four States (in addition to Louisiana and North Carolina) that had authorized the death sentence for rape prior to 1972 and had reacted to *Furman* with mandatory statutes, included rape among the crimes for which death was an authorized punishment.

* * *

It should be noted that Florida, Mississippi, and Tennessee also authorized the death penalty in some rape cases, but only where the victim was a child and the rapist an adult. The Tennessee statute has since been invalidated because the death sentence was mandatory. *Collins* v. *State,* 550 S. W. 2d 643 (Tenn. 1977). The upshot is that Georgia is the sole jurisdiction in the United States at the present time that authorizes a sentence of death when the rape victim is an adult woman, and only two other jurisdictions provide capital punishment when the victim is a child.

The current judgment with respect to the death penalty for rape is not wholly unanimous among state legislatures, but it obviously weighs very heavily on the side of rejecting capital punishment as a suitable penalty for raping an adult woman.

* * *

IV

These recent events evidencing the attitude of state legislatures . . . do not wholly determine this controversy, for the Constitution contemplates that in the end our own judgment will be brought to bear on the question of the acceptability of the death penalty under the Eighth Amendment. Nevertheless, the legislative rejection of capital punishment for rape strongly confirms our own judgment, which is that death is indeed a disproportionate penalty for the crime of raping an adult woman.

We do not discount the seriousness of rape as a crime. It is highly reprehensible, both in a moral sense and in its almost total contempt for the personal integrity and autonomy of the female victim and for the latter's privilege of choosing those with whom intimate relationships are to be established. Short of homicide, it is the "ultimate violation of self."

* * *

Rape is without doubt deserving of serious punishment; but in terms of moral depravity and of the injury to the person and to the public, it does not compare with murder, which does involve the unjustified taking of human life. Although it may be accompanied by another crime, rape by definition does not include the death of or even the serious injury to another person. The murderer kills; the rapist, if no more than that, does not. Life is over for the victim of the murderer; for the rape victim, life may not be nearly so happy as it was, but it is not over and normally is not beyond repair. We have the abiding conviction that the death penalty, which "is unique in its severity and irrevocability," *Gregg* v. *Georgia,* 428 U.S., at 187, is an excessive penalty for the rapist who, as such, does not take human life.

* * *

The judgment of the Georgia Supreme Court upholding the death sentence is reversed, and the case is remanded to that court for further proceedings not inconsistent with this opinion.

So ordered.

Cases relating to **Chapter 11**

CIVIL RIGHTS AND CIVIL RIGHTS LEGISLATION

GRAHAM v. CONNOR

490 U.S. __, 109 S. Ct. 1865, 104 L. Ed. 2d 443 (1989)

Argued Feb. 21, 1989. Decided May 15, 1989.

[Some of the Court's footnotes have been deleted. The remaining footnotes have been renumbered.]

***

Syllabus

Petitioner Graham, a diabetic, asked his friend, Berry, to drive him to a convenience store to purchase orange juice to counteract the onset of an insulin reaction. Upon entering the store and seeing the number of people ahead of him, Graham hurried out and asked Berry to drive him to a friend's house instead. Respondent Connor, a city police officer, became suspicious after seeing Graham hastily enter and leave the store, followed Berry's car, and made an investigative stop, ordering the pair to wait while he found out what had happened in the store. Respondent backup police officers arrived on the scene, handcuffed Graham, and ignored or rebuffed attempts to explain and treat Graham's condition. During the encounter, Graham sustained multiple injuries. He was released when Conner learned that nothing had happened in the store. Graham filed suit in the District Court under 42 U.S.C. § 1983 against respondents, alleging that they had used excessive force in making the stop, in violation of "rights secured to him under the Fourteenth Amendment to the United States Constitution and 42 U.S.C. § 1983." The District Court granted respondents' motion for a directed verdict at the close of Graham's evidence, applying a four-factor test for determining when excessive use of force gives rise to a § 1983 cause of action, which inquires, *inter alia,* whether the force was applied in a good faith effort to maintain and restore discipline or maliciously and sadistically for the very purpose of causing harm. *Johnson v. Glick,* 481 F.2d 1028. The Court of Appeals affirmed, endorsing this test as generally applicable to all claims of constitutionally excessive force brought against government officials, rejecting Graham's argument that it was error to require him to prove that the allegedly excessive force was applied maliciously and sadistically to cause harm, and holding that a reasonable jury applying the *Johnson v. Glick* test to his evidence could not find that the force applied was constitutionally excessive.

***

Chief Justice REHNQUIST delivered the opinion of the Court.

[1] This case requires us to decide what constitutional standard governs a free citizen's claim that law enforcement officials used excessive force in the course of making an arrest, investigatory stop, or other "seizure" of his person. We hold that such claims are properly analyzed under the Fourth Amendment's "objective reasonableness" standard, rather than under a substantive due process standard.

* * *

[2] We reject this notion that all excessive force claims brought under § 1983 are governed by a single generic standard. As we have said many times, § 1983 "is not itself a source of substantive rights," but merely provides "a method for vindicating federal rights elsewhere conferred." *Baker v. McCollan,* 443 U.S. 137, 144, n. 3, 99 S.Ct. 2689, 2694, n. 3, 61 L.Ed.2d 433 (1979). In addressing an excessive force claim brought under § 1983, analysis begins by identifying the specific constitutional right allegedly infringed by the challenged application of force. See *id.,* at 140, 99 S.Ct., at 2692 ("The first inquiry in any § 1983 suit" is "to isolate the precise constitutional violation with which [the defendant] is charged"). In most instances, that will be either the Fourth Amendment's prohibition against unreasonable seizures of the person, or the Eighth Amendment's ban on cruel and unusual punishments, which are the two primary sources of constitutional protection against physically abusive governmental conduct. The validity of the claim must then be judged by reference to the specific constitutional standard which governs that right, rather than to some generalized "excessive force" standard. See *Tennessee v. Garner, supra,* 471 U.S., at 7-22, 105 S.Ct., at 1699-1707 (claim of excessive force to effect arrest analyzed under a Fourth Amendment standard); *Whitley v. Albers,* 475 U.S. 312, 318-326, 106 S.Ct. 1078, 1083-1088, 89 L.Ed.2d 251 (1986) (claim of excessive force to subdue convicted prisoner analyzed under an Eighth Amendment standard).

Where, as here, the excessive force claim arises in the context of an arrest or investigatory stop of a free citizen, it is most properly characterized as one invoking the protections of the Fourth Amendment, which guarantees citizens the right "to be secure in their persons...against unreasonable ...seizures" of the person. This much is clear from our decision in *Tennessee v. Garner, supra.* In *Garner,* we addressed a claim that the use of deadly force to apprehend a fleeing suspect who did not appear to be armed or otherwise dangerous violated the suspect's constitutional rights, notwithstanding the existence of probable cause to arrest. Though the complaint alleged violations of both the Fourth Amendment and the Due Process Clause, see 471 U.S., at 5, 105 S.Ct., at 1698, we analyzed the constitutionality of the challenged application of force solely by reference to the Fourth Amendment's prohibition against unreasonable seizures of the person, holding that that the "reasonableness" of a particular seizure depends not only on *when* it is made, but also *how* it is carried out. *Id.,* at 7-8, 105 S.Ct., at 1699-1700. Today we make explicit what was implicit in *Garner's* analysis and hold that *all* claims that law enforcement officers have used excessive force--deadly or not--in the course of an arrest, investigatory stop, or other "seizure" of a free citizen should be analyzed under the Fourth Amendment and its "reasonableness" standard, rather than under a "substantive due process" approach. Because the Fourth Amendment provides an explicit textual source of constitutional protection against this sort of physically intrusive governmental conduct, that Amendment, not the more generalized notion of "substantive due process," must be the guide for analyzing these claims.[1]

[3] Determining whether the force used to effect a particular seizure is "reasonable" under the Fourth Amendment requires a careful balancing of "'the nature and quality of the intrusion on the individual's Fourth Amendment interests'" against the countervailing governmental interests at stake. *Id.*, at 8, 105 S.Ct., at 1699, quoting *United States v. Place,* 462 U.S. 696, 703, 103 S.Ct. 2637, 2642, 77 L.Ed.2d 110 (1983). Our Fourth Amendment jurisprudence has long recognized that the right to make an arrest or investigatory stop necessarily carries with it the right to use some degree of physical coercion or threat thereof to effect it. See *Terry v. Ohio,* 392 U.S., at 22-27, 88 S.Ct., at 1880-1883. Because "[t]he test of reasonableness under the Fourth Amendment is not capable of precise definition or mechanical application," *Bell v. Wolfish,* 441 U.S. 520, 559, 99 S.Ct. 1861, 1884, 60 L.Ed.2d 447 (1979), however, its proper application requires careful attention to the facts and circumstances of each particular case, including the severity of the crime at issue, whether the suspect poses an immediate threat to the safety of the officers or others, and whether he is actively resisting arrest or attempting to evade arrest by flight. See *Tennessee v. Garner,* 471 U.S., at 8-9, 105 S.Ct., at 1699-1700 (the question is "whether the totality of the circumstances justifie[s] a particular sort of...seizure").

[4] The "reasonableness" of particular use of force must be judged from the perspective of a reasonable officer on the scene, rather than with the 20/20 vision of hindsight. See *Terry v. Ohio, supra,* 392 U.S., at 20-22, 88 S.Ct., at 1879-1881. The Fourth Amendment is not violated by an arrest based on probable cause, even though the wrong person is arrested, *Hill v. California,* 401

---

1 A "seizure" triggering the Fourth Amendment's protections occurs only when government actors have, "by means of physical force or show of authority, ...in some way restrained the liberty of a citizen," *Terry v. Ohio,* 392 U.S. 1, 19, n. 16, 88 S.Ct. 1868, 1879, n. 16, 20 L.Ed.2d 889 (1968); see *Brower v. County of Inyo,* 489 U.S. __, __, 109 S.Ct. 1378, __, 103 L.Ed.2d 628 (1989).

Our cases have not resolved the question whether the Fourth Amendment continues to provide individuals with protection against the deliberate use of excessive physical force beyond the point at which arrest ends and pretrial detention begins, and we do not attempt to answer that question today. It is clear, however, that the Due Process Clause protects a pretrial detainee from the use of excessive force that amounts to punishment. See *Bell v. Wolfish,* 441 U.S. 520, 535-539, 99 S.Ct. 1861, 1871-1874, 60 L.Ed.2d 447 (1979). After conviction, the Eighth Amendment "serves as the primary source of substantive protection...in cases...where the deliberate use of force is challenged as excessive and unjustified." *Whitley v. Albers,* 475 U.S., at 327, 106 S.Ct., at 1088. Any protection that "substantive due process" affords convicted prisoners against excessive force is, we have held, at best redundant of that provided by the Eighth Amendment. *Ibid.*

U.S. 797, 91 S.Ct. 1106, 28 L.Ed.2d 484 (1971), nor by the mistaken execution of a valid search warrant on the wrong premises, *Maryland v. Garrison,* 480 U.S. 79, 107 S.Ct. 1013, 94 L.Ed.2d 72 (1987). With respect to a claim of excessive force, the same standard of reasonableness at the moment applies: "Not every push or shove, even if it may later seem unnecessary in the peace of a judge's chambers," *Johnson v. Glick,* 481 F.2d, at 1033, violates the Fourth Amendment. The calculus of reasonableness must embody allowance for the fact that police officers are often forced to make split-second judgments --in circumstances that are tense, uncertain, and rapidly evolving-- about the amount of force that is necessary in a particular situation.

[5] As in other Fourth Amendment contexts, however, the "reasonableness" inquiry in an excessive force case is an objective one: the question is whether the officers' actions are "objectively reasonable" in light of the facts and circumstances confronting them, without regard to their underlying intent or motivation. See *Scott v. United States,* 436 U.S. 128, 137-139, 98 S.Ct. 1717, 1723-1724, 56 L.Ed.2d 168 (1978); see also *Terry v. Ohio, supra,* 392 U.S., at 21, 88 S.Ct., at 1879 (in analyzing the reasonableness of a particular search or seizure, "it is imperative that the facts be judged against an objective standard"). An officer's evil intentions will not make a Fourth Amendment violation out of an objectively reasonable use of force; nor will an officer's good intentions make an objectively unreasonable use of force constitutional. See *Scott v. United States, supra,* 436 U.S., at 138, 98 S.Ct., at 1723, citing *United States v. Robinson,* 414 U.S. 218, 94 S.Ct. 467, 38 L.Ed.2d 427 (1973).

Because petitioner's excessive force claim is one arising under the Fourth Amendment, the Court of Appeals erred in analyzing it under the four-part *Johnson v. Glick* test. That test, which requires consideration of whether the individual officers acted in "good faith" or "maliciously and sadistically for the very purpose of causing harm," is incompatible with a proper Fourth Amendment analysis. We do not agree with the Court of Appeals' suggestion, see 827 F.2d, at 948, that the "malicious and sadistic" inquiry is merely another way of describing conduct that is objectively unreasonable under the circumstances. Whatever the empirical correlations between "malicious and sadistic" factor puts in issue the subjective motivations of the individual officers, which our prior cases make clear has no bearing on whether a particular seizure is "unreasonable" under the Fourth Amendment. Nor do we agree with the Court of Appeals' conclusion, see *id.,* at 948, n. 3, that because the subjective motivations of the individual officers are of central importance in deciding whether force used against a convicted prisoner violates the Eighth Amendment, see *Whitley v. Albers,* 475 U.S., at 320-321, 106 S.Ct., at 1084-1085,[2] it cannot be reversible error to

2 In *Whitley,* we addressed a § 1983 claim brought by a convicted prisoner, who claimed that prison officials had violated his Eighth Amendment rights by shooting him in the knee during a prison riot. We began our Eighth Amendment analysis by reiterating the long-established maxim that an Eighth Amendment violation requires proof of the "'"unnecessary and wanton infliction of pain."'" 475 U.S., at 319, 106 S.Ct., at 1084, quoting *Ingraham v. Wright,* 430 U.S., at 670, 97 S.Ct., at 1412, quoting *Estelle v. Gamble,* 429 U.S. 97, 103, 97 S.Ct. 285, 290, 50 L.Ed.2d 251 (1976). We went on to say that when prison offi-

inquire into them in deciding whether force used against a suspect or arrestee violates the Fourth Amendment. Differing standards under the Fourth and Eighth Amendments are hardly surprising: the terms "cruel" and "punishment" clearly suggest some inquiry into subjective state of mind, whereas the term "unreasonable" does not. Moreover, the less protective Eighth Amendment standard applies "only after the State has complied with the constitutional guarantees traditionally associated with criminal prosecutions." *Ingraham v. Wright,* 430 U.S. 651, 671, n. 40, 97 S.Ct. 1401, 1412, n. 40, 51 L.Ed.2d 711 (1977). The Fourth Amendment inquiry is one of "objective reasonableness" under the circumstances, and subjective concepts like "malice" and "sadism" have no proper place in that inquiry.

Because the Court of Appeals reviewed the District court's ruling on the motion for directed verdict under an erroneous view of the governing substantive law, its judgment must be vacated and the case remanded to that court for reconsideration of that issues under the proper Fourth Amendment standard.

It is so ordered.

***

cials use physical force against an inmate "to restore order in the face of a prison disturbance, ...the question whether the measure taken inflicted unnecessary and wanton pain...*ultimately turns* on 'whether the force was applied in a good faith effort to maintain or restore discipline or maliciously and sadistically for the very purpose of causing harm.'" 475 U.S., at 320-321, 106 S.Ct., at 1084-1085 (emphasis added), quoting *Johnson v. Glick*, 481 F.2d, at 1033. We also suggested that the other prongs of the *Johnson v. Glick* test might be useful in analyzing excessive force claims brought under the Eighth Amendment. 475 U.S., at 321, 106 S.Ct., at 1085. But we made clear that this was so *not* because Judge Friendly's four-part test is some talismanic formula generally applicable to all excessive force claims, but because its four factors help to focus the central inquiry in the Eighth Amendment context, which is whether the particular use of force amounts to the "unnecessary and wanton infliction of pain." See *id.*, at 320-321, 106 S.Ct., at 1084-1085. Our endorsement of the *Johnson v. Glick* test in *Whitley* thus had no implications beyond the Eighth Amendment context.

CITY OF CANTON v. HARRIS

489 U.S. __, 109 S. Ct. 1197, 103 L. Ed. 2d 412 (1989)

[No. 86-1088]

Argued November 8, 1988. Decided February 28, 1989.

[Some of the Court's footnotes have been deleted.
The remaining footnotes have been renumbered.]

***

Although respondent fell down several times and was incoherent following her arrest by officers of petitioner city's police department, the officers summoned no medical assistance for her. After her release, she was diagnosed as suffering from several emotional ailments requiring hospitalization and subsequent outpatient treatment. Some time later, she filed suit seeking, inter alia, to hold the city liable under 42 U.S.C. § 1983 [42 U.S.C.S. § 1983] for its violation of her right, under the Due Process Clause of the Fourteenth Amendment, to receive necessary medical attention while in police custody. The jury ruled in her favor on this claim upon the basis of evidence indicating that a city regulation gave shift commanders sole discretion to determine whether a detainee required medical care, and suggesting that commanders were not provided with any special training to make a determination as to when to summon such care for an injured detainee. Both the District Court, in rejecting the city's motion for judgment notwithstanding the verdict, and the Court of Appeals, in ruling that there had been no error in submitting the "failure to train" claim to the jury, held that, under Circuit precedent, a municipality is liable for failure to train its police force, where the plaintiff proves that the municipality acted recklessly, intentionally, or with gross negligence, and that the lack of training was so reckless or grossly negligent that deprivation of persons' constitutional rights was substantially certain to result. However, upon finding that certain aspects of the District Court's jury instructions might have led the jury to believe that it could find against the city on a mere respondeat superior theory, and that the jury's verdict did not state the basis on which it had ruled for respondent, the Court of Appeals reversed the judgment in her favor and remanded the case for a new trial.

***

Justice **White** delivered the opinion of the Court.

[1a] In this case, we are asked to determine if a municipality can ever be liable under 42 U.S.C. § 1983 [42 U.S.C.S. § 1983][1] for constitutional violations resulting from its failure to train municipal employees. We hold that, under certain circumstances, such liability is permitted by the statute.

***

III

[6] In Monell v. New York City Dept. of Social Services, 436 U.S. 658, 56 L.Ed.2d 611, 98 S.Ct. 2018 (1978), we decided that a municipality can be found liable under § 1983 only where the municipality *itself* causes the constitutional violation at issue. Respondent superior or vicarious liability will not attach under § 1983. Id., at 694-695, 56 L.Ed.2d 611, 98 S.Ct. 2018. "It is only when the 'execution of the government's policy or custom...inflicts the injury' that the municipality may be held liable under § 1983." Springfield, Mass. v. Kibbe, 480 U.S. 257, 267, 94 L.Ed.2d 293, 107 S.Ct. 1114 (1987) (O'Connor, J., dissenting) (quoting Monnell, supra, at 694, 56 L.Ed.2d 611, 98 S.Ct. 2018).

Thus, our first inquiry in any case alleging municipal liability under § 1983 is the question of whether there is a direct causal link between a municipal policy or custom, and the alleged constitutional deprivation. The inquiry is a

---

1 Title 42 U.S.C. § 1983 [42 U.S.C.S. § 1983] provides, in relevant part, that:

"Every person who, under color of any statute, ordinance, regulation, custom, or usage...subjects, or causes to be subjected, any citizen of the United States or other person within the jurisdiction thereof to the deprivation of any rights, privileges, or immunities secured by the Constitution and laws, shall be liable to the party injured in an action at law, suit in equity, or other proper proceeding for redress...." 42 U.S.C. § 1983 [42 U.S.C.S. § 1983].

difficult one; one that has left this Court deeply divided in a series of cases that have followed Monnell; one that is the principal focus of our decision again today.

A

[2c, 7a, 8a] Based on the difficulty that this Court has had defining the contours of municipal liability in these circumstances, petitioner urges us to adopt the rule that a municipality can be found liable under § 1983 only where "the policy in question [is] itself unconstitutional." Brief for Petitioner 15. Whether such a rule is a valid construction of § 1983 is a question the Court has left unresolved. See e.g., St. Louis v. Praprotnik, 485 U.S. at, __, 99 L.Ed.2d 107, 108 S.Ct. 915 (Brennan, J., concurring in judgment); Oklahoma City v. Tuttle, 471 U.S., at 824, n. 7, 85 L.Ed.2d 791, 105 S.Ct. 2427. Under such an approach, the outcome here would be rather clear: we would have to reverse and remand the case with instructions that judgment be entered for petitioner. There can be little doubt that on its face the city's policy regarding medical treatment for detainees is constitutional. The policy states that the City Jailer "shall...have [a person needing medical care] taken to a hospital for medical treatment, with permission of his supervisor..." App. 33. It is difficult to see what constitutional guarantees are violated by such a policy.

[1b, 3c, 8b] Nor, without more, would a city automatically be liable under § 1983 if one of its employees happened to apply the policy in an unconstitutional manner, for liability would then rest on respondeat superior. The claim in this case, however, is that if a concededly valid policy is unconstitutionally applied by a municipal employee, the city is liable if the employee has not been adequately trained and the constitutional wrong has been caused by that failure to train. For reasons explained below, we conclude, as have all the Courts of Appeals that have addressed this issue, that there are limited circumstances in which an allegation of a "failure to train" can be the basis for liability under § 1983. Thus, we reject petitioner's contention that only unconstitutional policies are actionable under the statute.

B

[1c, 9a, 10] Though we agree with the court below that a city can be liable under § 1983 for inadequate training of its employees, we cannot agree that the District Court's jury instructions on this issue were proper, for we conclude that the Court of Appeals provided an overly broad rule for when a municipality can be held liable under the "failure to train" theory. Unlike the question of whether a municipality's failure to train employees can ever be a basis for § 1983 liability --on which the Courts of Appeals have all agreed, see n. 6, supra-- there is substantial division among the lower courts as to what *degree of fault* must be evidenced by the municipality's inaction before liability will be permitted. We hold today that the inadequacy of police training may serve as the basis for § 1983 liability only where the failure to train amounts to deliberate indifference to the rights of persons with whom the police come into contact. This rule is most consistent with our admonition in Monell, 436 U.S., at 694, 56 L.Ed.2d 611, 98 S.Ct. 2018, and Polk County v. Dodson, 454 U.S. 312, 326, 70 L.Ed.2d 509, 102 S.Ct. 445 (1981), that a municipality can be liable under § 1983 only where its policies are the "moving force [behind] the constitutional violation." Only where a municipality's failure to train its employees in a relevant respect evidences a "deliberate indifference" to the rights of its inhabitants can such a shortcoming be properly thought of as a city "policy or custom" that is actionable under § 1983. As Justice Brennan's opinion in Pembaur v. Cincinnati, 475 U.S. 469, 483-484, 89 L.Ed.2d 452, 106 S.Ct. 1292 (1986) (plurality) put it: "[M]unicipal liability under § 1983 attaches where--and only where--a deliberate choice to follow a course of action is made from among various alternatives" by city policymakers. See also Oklahoma City v. Tuttle, 471 U.S. at 823, 85 L.Ed.2d 791, 105 S.Ct. 2427. (opinion of Rehnquist, J.) Only where a failure to train reflects a "deliberate" or "conscious" choice by a municipality--a "policy" as defined by our prior cases--can a city be liable for such a failure under § 1983.

[1e, 11a] Monell's rule that a city is not liable under § 1983 unless a municipal policy causes a constitutional deprivation will not be satisfied by merely alleging that the existing training program for a class of employees, such as police officers, represents a policy for which the city is responsible. That much may be true. The issue in a case like this one, however, is whether that training program is adequate; and if it is not, the question becomes whether such inadequate training can justifiably be said to represent "city policy." It may seem contrary to common sense to assert that a municipality will actually have a policy of not taking reasonable steps to train its employees. But it may happen that in light of the duties assigned to specific officers or employees the need for more or different training is so obvious, and the inadequacy so likely to result in the violation of constitutional rights, that the policymakers of the city can reasonably be said to have been deliberately indifferent to the need.[2] In that event, the failure to provide proper training may fairly be said to represent a policy for which the city is responsible, and for which the city may be held liable if it actually causes injury.

[1g, 12] In resolving the issue of a city's liability, the focus must be on adequacy of the training program in relation to the tasks the particular officers must perform. That a particular officer may be unsatisfactorily trained will not alone suffice to fasten liability on the city, for the officer's shortcomings may have resulted from factors other than a faulty training program. See Springfield v. Kibbe, 480 U.S. at 268, 94 L.Ed.2d 293, 107 S.Ct. 1114 (O'Connor, J., dissenting); Oklahoma City v. Tuttle, supra, at 821, 85 L.Ed.2d 791, 105 S.Ct. 2427 (opinion of Rehnquist, J.). It may be, for example, that an otherwise sound program has occasionally been negligently administered. Neither will it

---

2 **[1f]** For example, city policy makers know to a moral certainty that their police officers will be required to arrest fleeing felons. The city has armed its officers with firearms, in part to allow them to accomplish this task. Thus, the need to train officers in the constitutional limitations on the use of deadly force, see Tennessee v. Garner, 471 US 1, 85 L Ed 2d 1, 105 S Ct 1694 (1985), can be said to be "so obvious," that failure to do so could properly be characterized as "deliberate indifference" to constitutional rights.

It could also be that the police, in exercising their discretion, so often violate constitutional rights that the need for further training must have been plainly obvious to the city policy makers, who, nevertheless, are "deliberately indifferent" to the need.

suffice to prove that an injury or accident could have been avoided if an officer had had better or more training, sufficient to equip him to avoid the particular injury-causing conduct. Such a claim could be made about almost any encounter resulting in injury, yet not condemn the adequacy of the program to enable officers to respond properly to the usual and recurring situations with which they must deal. And plainly, adequately trained officers occasionally make mistakes; the fact that they do says little about the training program or the legal basis for holding the city liable.

***

[1h] Consequently, while claims such as respondent's--alleging that the city's failure to provide training to municipal employees resulted in the constitutional deprivation she suffered--are cognizable under § 1983, they can only yield liability against a municipality where that city's failure to train reflects deliberate indifference to the constitutional rights of its inhabitants.

***

V

Consequently, for the reasons given above, we vacate the judgment of the Court of Appeals and remand this case for further proceedings consistent with this opinion.

It is so ordered.

SEPARATE OPINIONS

Justice **O'Connor**, with whom Justice **Scalia** and Justice **Kennedy** join, concurring in part and dissenting in part.

*** I thus agree that where municipal policymakers are confronted with an obvious need to train city personnel to avoid the violation of constitutional rights and they are deliberately indifferent to that need, the lack of necessary training may be appropriately considered a city "policy" subjecting the city itself under our decision in Monell v. New York City Dept. of Social Services, 436 U.S. 658, 56 L.Ed.2d 611, 98 S.Ct. 2018 (1978). As the Court observes, "[o]nly where a failure to train reflects a 'deliberate' or 'conscious' choice by a municipality--a 'policy' as defined by our prior cases--can a city be liable for such a failure under § 1983." ***

* * *

*** [T]he Court's opinion correctly requires a high degree of fault on the part of city officials before an omission that is not in itself unconstitutional can support liability as a municipal policy under Monell. As the Court indicates, "it may happen that...the need for more or different training is so obvious, and the inadequacy so likely to result in the violation of constitutional rights, that the policymakers of the city can reasonably be said to have been deliberately indifferent to the need." Ante, at ___, 103 L.Ed.2d 427. Where a § 1983 plaintiff can establish that the facts available to city policymakers put them on actual or constructive notice that the particular omission is substantially certain to result in the violation of the constitutional rights of their citizens, the dictates of Monell are satisfied. Only then can it be said that the municipality has made "'a deliberate choice to follow a course of action... from among various alternatives.'" Ante, at __, 103 L.Ed.2d 427, quoting Pembaur v. Cincinnati, 475 U.S. 469, 483-484, 89 L.Ed.2d 452, 106 S.Ct. 1292 (1986).

In my view, it could be shown that the need for training was obvious in one of two ways. First, a municipality could fail to train its employees concerning a clear constitutional duty implicated in recurrent situations that a particular employee is certain to face. As the majority notes, see ante, at __, n. 10, 103 L.Ed.2d 427, the constitutional limitations established by this Court on the use of deadly force by police officers present one such situation. The constitutional duty of the individual officer is clear, and it is equally clear that failure to inform city personnel of that duty will create an extremely high risk that constitutional violations will ensue.

***

Second, I think municipal liability for failure to train may be proper where it can be shown that policymakers were aware of, and acquiesced in, a pattern of constitutional violations involving the exercise of police discretion. In such cases, the need for training may not be obvious from the outset, but a pattern of constitutional violations could put the municipality on notice that its officers confront the particular situation on a regular basis, and that they often react in a manner contrary to constitutional requirements. The lower courts that have applied the "deliberate indifference" standard we adopt today have required a showing of a pattern of violations from which a kind of "tacit authorization" by city policymakers can be inferred. See, e.g., Fiacco v. City of Rensselaer, 783 F.2d 319, 327 (CA2 1986) (multiple incidents required for finding of deliberate indifference); Patzner v. Burkett, 779 F.2d 1363, 1367 (CA8 1985) ("[A] municipality may be liable if it had notice of prior misbehavior by its officers and failed to take remedial steps amounting to deliberate indifference to the offensive acts"); Languirand v. Hayden, 717 F.2d 220, 227-228 (CA5 1983) (municipal liability for failure to train requires "evidence at least of a pattern of similar incidents in which citizens were injured or endangered"); Wellington v. Daniels, 717 F.2d 932, 936 (CA4 1983) ("[A] failure to supervise gives rise to § 1983 liability, however, only in those situations where there is a history of widespread abuse. Only then may knowledge be imputed to the supervisory personnel").

ANDERSON v. CREIGHTON

483 U.S. 635, 107 S. Ct. 3034, 97 L. Ed. 2d 523 (1987)

[No. 85-1520]

Argued February 23, 1987. Decided June 25, 1987.

[The Court's footnotes have been deleted.]

***

Petitioner, a Federal Bureau of Investigation agent, participated with other law enforcement officers in a warrantless search of respondent's home. The search was conducted because petitioner believed that one Dixon, who was suspected of a bank robbery committed earlier that day, might be found there, but he was not. Respondents filed a state-court action against petitioner, asserting a claim for damages under the Fourth Amendment. Petitioner removed the suit to Federal District Court and then filed a motion for dismissal or summary judgment, arguing that the Fourth Amendment claim was barred by his qualified immunity from civil damages liability. Before any discovery occurred, the court granted summary judgment on the ground that the search was lawful. The Court of Appeals reversed, holding that the search's lawfulness could not be determined on summary judgment, because factual disputes precluded deciding as a matter of law that the search was supported by probable cause and exigent circumstances. The court also held that petitioner was not entitled to summary judgment on qualified immunity grounds, since the right he allegedly violated -- the right of persons to be protected from warrantless searches of their homes unless the searching officers have probable cause and there are exigent circumstances--was clearly established.

***

OPINION OF THE COURT

Justice **Scalia** delivered the opinion of the Court.

[1a] The question presented is whether a federal law enforcement officer who participates in a search that violates the Fourth Amendment may be held personally liable for money damages if a reasonable officer could have believed that the search comported with the Fourth Amendment.

***

II

[2a, 3a] When government officials abuse their offices, "action[s] for damages may offer the only realistic avenue for vindiction of constitutional guarantees." Harlow v. Fitzgerald, 457 U.S., at 814, 73 L.Ed.2d 396, 102 S.Ct. 2727. On the other hand, permitting damage suits against government officials can entail substantial social costs, including the risk that fear of personal monetary liability and harassing litigation will unduly inhibit officials in the discharge of their duties. Ibid. Our cases have accommodated these conflicting concerns by generally providing government officials performing discretionary functions with a qualified immunity, shielding them from civil damages liability as long as their actions could reasonably have been thought consistent with the rights they are alleged to have violated. See, e.g., Malley v. Briggs, 475 U.S. 335, 341, 89 L.Ed.2d 271, 106 S.Ct. 1092 (1986) (qualified immunity protects "all but the plainly incompetent or those who knowingly violate the law"); id., at 344-345, 89 L.Ed.2d 271, 106 S.Ct. 1092 (police officers applying for warrants are immune if a reasonable officer could have believed that there was probable cause to support the application); Mitchell v. Forsyth, 472 U.S. 511, 528, 86 L.Ed.2d 411, 105 S.Ct. 2806 (1985) (officials are immune unless "the law clearly proscribed the actions" they took); Davis v. Scherer, 468 U.S. 183, 191, 82 L.Ed.2d 139, 104 S.Ct. 3012 (1984); id., at 198, 82 L.Ed.2d 139, 104 S.Ct. 3012. (Brennan, J., concurring in part and dissenting in part); Harlow v. Fitzgerald, supra, at 819, 73 L.Ed.2d 396, 102 S.Ct. 2727. Cf., e.g., Procunier v. Navarette, 434 U.S. 555, 562, 55 L.Ed.2d 24, 98 S.Ct. 855 (1978). Somewhat more concretely, whether an official protected by qualified immunity may be held personally liable for an allegedly unlawful official action generally turns on the "objective legal reasonableness" of the action, Harlow, 457 U.S., at 819, 73 L.Ed.2d 396, 102 S.Ct. 2727, assessed in light of the legal rules that were "clearly established" at the time it was taken, id., at 818, 73 L.Ed.2d 396, 102 S.Ct. 2727.

[2b] The operation of this standard, however, depends substantially upon the level of generality at which the relevant "legal rule" is to be identified. For example, the right to due process of law is quite clearly established by the Due Process Clause, and thus there is a sense in which any action that violates that Clause (no matter how unclear it may be that the particular action is a violation) violates a clearly established right. Much the same could be said of any other constitutional or statutory violation. But if the test of "clearly established law" were to be applied at this level of generality, it would bear no relationship to the "objective legal reasonableness" that is the touchstone of Harlow. *** It should not be surprising, therefore, that our cases establish that the right the official is alleged to have violated must have been "clearly established" in a more particularized, and hence more relevant, sense: The contours of the right must be sufficiently clear that a reasonable official would understand that what he is doing violates that right. This is not to say that an official action is protected by qualified immunity unless the very action in question has previously been held unlawful, see Mitchell, 472 U.S., at 535, n. 12, 86 L.Ed.2d 411, 105 S.Ct. 2806; but it is to say that in the light of preexisting law the unlawfulness must be apparent. See, e.g., Malley, supra, at 344-345, 89 L.Ed.2d 271, 106 S.Ct. 1092; Mitchell, supra, at 528, 86 L.Ed.2d 411, 105 S.Ct. 2806; Davis, supra, at 191, 195, 82 L.Ed.2d 139, 104 S.Ct. 3012.

[1b, 3b] Anderson contends that the Court of Appeals misapplied these principles. We agree. The Court of Appeals' brief discussion of qualified immunity consisted of little more than an assertion that a general right Anderson was alleged to have violated--the right to be free from warrantless searches of one's home unless the searching officers have probable cause and there are exigent circumstances--was clearly established. The Court of Appeals specifically refused to consider the argument that it was *not* clearly established that the circumstances with which Anderson was confronted did not constitute probable cause and exigent circumstances. The previous discussion should make clear that this refusal was erroneous. It simply does not follow immediately from the conclusion that it was firmly established that warrantless searches not supported by probable cause and exigent circumstances violate the Fourth Amendment that Anderson's search was objectively legally unreasonable. We have recognized that it is inevitable that law enforcement officials will in some cases reasonably but mistakenly conclude that probable cause is present, and we have indicated that in such cases those officials --like other officials who act in ways they reasonably believe to be lawful-- should not be held personally liable. See Malley, supra, at 344-345, 89 L.Ed.2d 271, 106 S.Ct. 1092. The same is true of their conclusions regarding exigent circumstances.

It follows from what we have said that the determination whether it was objectively legally reasonable to conclude that a given search was supported by probable cause or exigent circumstances will often require examination of the information possessed by the searching officials. But contrary to the Creightons' assertion, this does not reintroduce into qualified immunity analysis the inquiry into officials' subjective intent that Harlow sought to minimize. See Harlow, supra, at 815-820, 73 L.Ed.2d 396, 102 S.Ct. 2727. The relevant question in this case, for example, is the objective (albeit fact-specific) question whether a reasonable officer could have believed Anderson's warrantless search to be lawful, in light of clearly established law and the information the searching officers possessed. Anderson's subjective beliefs about the search are irrelevant.

The principles of qualified immunity that we reaffirm today require that Anderson be permitted to argue that he is entitled to summary judgment on the ground that, in light of the clearly established principles governing warrantless searches, he could, as a matter of law, reasonably have believed that the search of the Creightons' home was lawful.

III

***

[5c, 6a] The general rule of qualified immunity is intended to provide government officials with the ability "reasonably [to] anticipate when their conduct may give rise to liability for damages." Davis, 468 U.S., at 195, 82 L.Ed.2d 139, 104 S.Ct. 3012. Where that rule is applicable, officials can know that they will not be held personally liable as long as their actions are reasonable in light of current American law. That security would be utterly defeated if officials were unable to determine whether they were protected by the rule without entangling themselves in the vagaries of the English and American common law. We are unwilling to Balkanize the rule of qualified immunity by carving exceptions at the level of detail the Creightons propose. We therefore decline to make an exception to the general rule of qualified immunity for cases involving allegedly unlawful warrantless searches of innocent third parties' homes in search of fugitives.

[6b, 7a] For the reason stated, we vacate the judgment of the Court of Appeals and remand the case for further proceedings consistent with this opinion.

It is so ordered.

Cases relating to Chapter 12

DEPARTMENTAL REGULATIONS AND THE CONSTITUTION

KELLEY v. JOHNSON,

425 U.S. 238, 96 S. Ct. 1440, 47 L. Ed. 2d 708 (1976)
[Judicial footnotes other than the first have been omitted.]

MR. JUSTICE REHNQUIST delivered the opinion of the Court.

* * *

In 1971 respondent's predecessor, individually and as president of the Suffolk County Patrolmen's Benevolent Association, brought this action under the Civil Rights Act of 1871, 42 U.S.C. § 1983, against petitioner's predecessor, the Commissioner of the Suffolk County Police Department. The Commissioner had promulgated Order No. 71–1, which established hair-grooming standards applicable to male members of the police force.[1] The regulation was directed at the style and length of hair, sideburns, and mustaches; beards and goatees were prohibited, except for medical reasons; and wigs conforming to the regulation could be worn for cosmetic

[1] Order No. 71–1 (1971), amending Chapter 2 of the Rules and Procedures, Police Department, County of Suffolk, N.Y., provided:

"2/75.0 Members of the Force and Department shall be neat and clean at all times while on duty. Male personnel shall comply with the following grooming standards unless excluded by the Police Commissioner due to special assignment:

"2/75.1 HAIR: Hair shall be neat, clean, trimmed, and present a groomed appearance. Hair will not touch the ears or the collar except the closely cut hair on the back of the neck. Hair in front will be groomed so that it does not fall below the band of properly worn headgear. In no case will the bulk or length of the hair interfere with the proper wear of any authorized headgear. The acceptability of a member's hair style will be based upon the criteria in this paragraph and not upon the style in which he chooses to wear his hair.

"2/75.2 SIDEBURNS: If an individual chooses to wear sideburns, they will be neatly trimmed and tapered in the same manner as his haircut. Sideburns will not extend below the lowest part of the exterior ear opening, will be of even width (not flared), and will end with a clean-shaven horizontal line.

"2/75.3 MUSTACHES: A short and neatly trimmed mustache may be worn, but shall not extend over the top of the upper lip or beyond the corners of the mouth.

"2/75.4 BEARDS & GOATEES: The face will be clean-shaven other than the wearing of the acceptable mustache or sideburns. Beards and goatees are prohibited, except that a Police Surgeon may grant a waiver for the wearing of a beard for medical reasons with the approval of the Police Commissioner. When a Surgeon prescribes that a member not shave, the beard will be kept trimmed symmetrically and all beard hairs will be kept trimmed so that they do not protrude more than one-half inch from the skin surface of the face.

"2/75.5 WIGS: Wigs or hair pieces will not be worn on duty in uniform except for cosmetic reasons to cover natural baldness or physical disfiguration. If under these conditions, a wig or hair piece is worn, it will conform to department standards." App. 57–58.

reasons. The regulation was attacked as violative of respondent patrolman's right of free expression under the First Amendment and his guarantees of due process and equal protection under the Fourteenth Amendment, in that it was "not based upon the generally accepted standard of grooming in the community" and placed "an undue restriction" upon his activities therein.

* * *

Respondent has sought the protection of the Fourteenth Amendment, not as a member of the citizenry at large, but on the contrary as an employee of the police department of Suffolk County, a subdivision of the State of New York. While the Court of Appeals made passing reference to this distinction, it was thereafter apparently ignored. We think, however, it is highly significant. In *Pickering v. Board of Education,* 391 U.S. 563, 568, 88 S.Ct. 1731, 1734, 20 L.Ed.2d 811, 817 (1968), after noting that state employment may not be conditioned on the relinquishment of First Amendment rights, the Court stated that "[a]t the same time it cannot be gainsaid that the State has interests as an employer in regulating the speech of its employees that differ significantly from those it possesses in connection with regulation of the speech of the citizenry in general." More recently, we have sustained comprehensive and substantial restrictions upon activities of both federal and state employees lying at the core of the First Amendment. *CSC v. Letter Carriers,* 413 U.S. 548, 93 S.Ct. 2880, 37 L.Ed.2d 796 (1973); *Broadrick v. Oklahoma,* 413 U.S. 601, 93 S.Ct. 2908, 37 L.Ed.2d 830 (1973). If such state regulations may survive challenges based on the explicit language of the First Amendment, there is surely even more room for restrictive regulations of state employees where the claim implicates only the more general contours of the substantive liberty interest protected by the Fourteenth Amendment.

The hair-length regulation here touches respondent as an employee of the county and, more particularly, as a policeman. Respondent's employer has, in accordance with its well-established duty to keep the peace, placed myriad demands upon the members of the police force, duties which have no counterpart with respect to the public at large. Respondent must wear a standard uniform, specific in each detail. When in uniform he must salute the flag. He may not take an active role in local political affairs by way of being a party delegate or contributing or soliciting political contributions. He may not smoke in public. All of these and other regulations of the Suffolk County Police Department infringe on respondent's freedom of choice in personal matters, and it was apparently the view of the Court of Appeals that the burden is on the State to prove a "genuine public need" for each and every one of these regulations.

This view was based upon the Court of Appeals' reasoning that the "unique judicial deference" accorded by the judiciary to regulation of members of the military was inapplicable because there was no historical or functional justification for the characterization of the police as "para-military." But the conclusion that such cases are inapposite, however correct, in no way detracts from the deference due Suffolk County's choice of an organizational structure for its police force. Here the county has chosen a mode of organization which it undoubtedly deems the most efficient in enabling its police to carry out the duties assigned to them under state and local law. Such a choice necessarily gives weight to the overall need for discipline, esprit de corps, and uniformity.

The county's choice of an organizational structure, therefore, does not depend for its constitutional validity on any doctrine of historical prescription. Nor, indeed has respondent made any such claim. His argument does not challenge the constitutionality of the organizational structure, but merely asserts that the present hair-length regulation infringes his asserted liberty interest under the Fourteenth Amendment. We believe, however, that the hair-length regulation cannot be viewed in isolation, but must be rather considered in the context of the county's chosen mode of organization for its police force.

The promotion of safety of persons and property is unquestionably at the core of the State's police power, and virtually all state and local governments employ a uniform police force to aid in the accomplishment of that purpose. Choice of organization, dress, and equipment for law enforcement personnel is a decision entitled to the same sort of presumption of legislative validity as are state choices designed to promote other aims within the cognizance of the State's police power. *Day-Brite Lighting, Inc. v. Missouri,* 342 U.S. 421, 423, 72 S.Ct. 405, 407, 96 L.Ed. 469, 472 (1952); *Prince v. Massachusetts,* 321 U.S. 158, 168–170, 64 S.Ct. 438, 443–44, 88 L.Ed. 645, 653, 654–655 (1944); *Olsen v. Nebraska,* 313 U.S. 236, 246–247, 61 S.Ct. 862, 865–66, 85 L.Ed. 1305, 1309, 1310 (1941). Having recognized in other contexts the wide latitude accorded the government in the "dispatch of its own internal affairs," *Cafeteria Workers v. McElroy,* 367 U.S. 886, 896, 81 S.Ct. 1743, 1749, 6 L.Ed.2d 1230, 1237 (1961), we think Suffolk County's police regulations involved here are entitled to similar weight. Thus the question is not, as the Court of Appeals conceived it to be, whether the State can "establish" a "genuine public need" for the specific regulation. It is whether respondent can demonstrate that there is no rational connection between the regulation, based as it is on the county's method of organizing its police force, and the promotion of safety of persons and property. *United Public Workers v. Mitchell,* 330 U.S. 75, 100–101, 67 S.Ct. 556, 569–570, 91 L.Ed. 754, 773–774 (1947); *Jacobson v. Massachusetts,* 197 U.S. 11, 30–31, 35–37, 25 S.Ct. 358, 363, 365–366, 49 L.Ed. 643, 651–652, 653–654 (1905).

We think the answer here is so clear that the District Court was quite right in the first instance to have dismissed respondent's complaint. Neither this Court, the Court of Appeals, nor the District Court is in a position to weigh the policy arguments in favor of and against a rule regulating hairstyles as a part of regulations governing a uniformed civilian service. The constitutional issue to be decided by these courts is whether petitioner's determination that such regulations should be enacted is so irrational that it may be branded "arbitrary," and therefore a deprivation of respondent's "liberty" interest in freedom to choose his own hairstyle. *Williamson v. Lee Optical Co.*, 348 U.S. 483, 487–488, 75 S.Ct. 461, 464–465, 99 L.Ed. 563, 571–572 (1955). The overwhelming majority of state and local police of the present day are uniformed. This fact itself testifies to the recognition by those who direct those operations, and by the people of the States and localities who directly or indirectly choose such persons, that similarity in appearance of police officers is desirable. This choice may be based on a desire to make police officers readily recognizable to the members of the public, or a desire for the esprit de corps which such similarity is felt to inculcate within the police force itself. Either one is a sufficiently rational justification for regulations so as to defeat respondent's claim based on the liberty guarantee of the Fourteenth Amendment.

The Court of Appeals relied on *Garrity v. New Jersey*, 385 U.S. 493, 87 S.Ct. 616, 17 L.Ed.2d 562 (1967), and *amicus* in its brief in support of respondent elaborates an argument based on the language in *Garrity* that "policemen, like teachers and lawyers, are not relegated to a watered-down version of consititutional rights." *Id.*, at 500, 87 S.Ct. at 620, 17 L.Ed.2d at 567. *Garrity*, of course, involved the protections afforded by the Fifth Amendment to the United States Consitution as made applicable to the States by the Fourteenth Amendment. *Malloy v. Hogan*, 378 U.S. 1, 84 S.Ct. 1489, 12 L.Ed.2d 653 (1964). Certainly its language cannot be taken to suggest that the claim of a member of a uniformed civilian service based on the "liberty" interest protected by the Fourteenth Amendment must necessarily be treated for constitutional purposes the same as a similar claim by a member of the general public.

The regulation challenged here did not violate any right guaranteed respondent by the Fourteenth Amendment to the United States Constitution, and the Court of Appeals was therefore wrong in reversing the District Court's original judgment dismissing the action. The judgment of the Court of Appeals is

Reversed.

GERMANN v. CITY OF KANSAS CITY

776 F.2d 761 (8th Cir. 1985)

United States Court of Appeals, Eighth Circuit.

Submitted Jan. 16, 1985. Decided Nov. 6, 1985.

Rehearing and Rehearing En Banc
Denied Dec. 27, 1985.

Before HEANEY, ROSS and McMILLIAN, Circuit Judges.

McMILLIAN, Circuit Judge.

John Germann appeals from a final judgment entered in the District Court for the Western District of Missouri in favor of the City of Kansas City, Missouri, Edward Wilson and John Waas. *Germann v. City of Kansas City*, 579 F.Supp. 180 (W.D.Mo. 1984). For reversal appellant argues that the district court erred in failing to find that appellees violated his federal constitutional and state statutory rights by denying him promotions to the rank of battalion chief in the City of Kansas City, Missouri, fire department between September 1977 and September 1979. Appellant alleged that appellees had denied him promotions because of protected first amendment activities. For the reasons discussed below, we affirm the judgment of the district court.

Appellant has been employed by the fire department since 1961. In July 1971 he was promoted to the rank of fire captain. In addition, from 1976 until 1981, appellant was president of the firefighters' union, International Association of Firefighters, AFL-CIO, Local No. 42.

The fire department is part of the municipal government of the City of Kansas City and is supervised by the director of fire and the fire chief. Appellee John Waas was fire chief at all times relevant to this action. Since Waas's retirement in 1980, Edward Wilson has been fire chief.

Below the rank of fire chief in order of command are deputy fire chiefs, battalion fire chiefs, fire captains, fire apparatus operators, and firefighters. Battalion chief is the lowest level management position. Promotion from fire captain to battalion chief is regulated by the city charter, administrative code, and personnel regulations. Candidates are ranked on a promotion eligibility list on the basis of written test results. Whenever a vacancy occurs, the deputy fire chiefs conduct personal interviews of the first five candidates on the list. The fire chief then appoints the battalion chief from the five candidates.

During the time period relevant to this action, the fire department experienced great turmoil and received much media attention. In October 1975 the union conducted a four-day strike. At this time all management level employees except for fire chief were members of the union; thus, during the strike Chief Waas was the only professionally trained firefighter on duty for the city.

Following the strike, in 1976 the union and the city entered into a "Memorandum of Understanding," which, among other things, prohibited management level employees from belonging to the union. In the memorandum the union and the city agreed to make good faith efforts to implement a plan of reorganization of the fire department. The plan included a work schedule change which caused a great deal of friction between the union and the city. In an attempt to resolve conflict in implementing the plan and the memorandum, appellant, as president of the union, and Waas, as fire chief, served as cochairpersons of the Labor/Management Committee. From July 1976 until May 1979, appellant frequently and vigorously opposed Waas, contending that the manner in which Waas was implementing the plan violated union members' rights.

On May 6, 1977, Waas wrote the following letter to appellant in his capacity as union president:

> This is to register my objection to the officers of Local #42 of the firefighters' union making frequent visits to the Deputy Chief's Office at Fire Station #10 to obstruct and try to alter the operation of the Fire Department.
>
> This practice is in direct violation of the Memorandum of Understanding, which sets forth a Labor/Management Committee to review procedures. I respectfully request that you refrain from any further such practice.

Copies of the letter were mailed to certain city and fire department officials.

On May 11, 1977, appellant responded to Waas by the following letter, which provided in part:

> In answer to your letter of May 6, how dare anyone who has done as much as you to tear the Kansas City fire department to shreds accuse someone else of attempted obstruction or alteration. With your hand at the controls, the Kansas City Fire Department could not possibly be more completely obstructed by anyone else on the face of the earth.
>
> Nothing would suit me better than to have a Fire Chief who would read and understand his own rules, give his word on an issue and then not violate his own word by his every action as you have....
>
> ...
>
> If you are really interested in seeing the Memorandum upheld, I suggest some study courses for yourself and the rest of the chief officers under the direction of someone who does not carry such a pitifully twisted outlook toward the employees of the department as you seem to have developed.

Appellant mailed copies of his letter to the officials who had received Waas's letter and to the attorneys for the city and the union.

During the period from September 1977 until September 1979, appellant was ranked first on the promotion eligibility list for battalion chief. It is undisputed that appellant was qualified for the position. Waas, however, did not appoint appellant to any of the seven vacancies that occurred during this period.

Appellant then filed an action in district court pursuant to 42 U.S.C. § 1983, alleging that appellees violated his rights under the first and fourteenth amendments by denying him promotions in retaliation for protected union activities. In addition, appellant asserted as a pendent state claim a violation of Mo.Rev.Stat. § 105.510 (1978), which prohibits discrimination against public employees because of certain permitted union activities.

At the bench trial Waas testified that he had not promoted appellant to battalion chief because he questioned appellant's loyalty and whether appellant would work under him to implement his policies. Waas believed that discipline, morale, and efficiency in the fire department depended upon respect being shown to rank. In addition, Waas stated that he relied on management employees to implement his policies on a day-to-day basis in the field.

In support of his belief that appellant would be unsuitable as a management employee, Waas cited appellant's May 11 letter. Waas found the letter personally insulting and an inappropriate response to his letter of May 6. In addition, Waas testified to a 1979 incident which confirmed his belief that appellant did not respect and would therefore not support him as fire chief. The district court credited Waas's testimony that in 1979 appellant came to Waas's office to inquire why he had not been promoted. After Waas did not respond, appellant became hostile and called Waas a "chicken shit." Waas also testified that he believed that appellant had not wanted a promotion to battalion chief. The district court credited Waas's testimony about a 1978 telephone conversation in which appellant indicated he did not want a promotion at that time because he would have to resign as union president. The district court noted that appellant's testimony concerning the conversation revealed hostility toward and suspicion of Waas.

The district court found that appellees had not discriminated against appellant because of union activities. The district court believed that after receipt of appellant's May 11 letter, Waas was justified in not promoting appellant to battalion chief. Applying the balancing test set forth in *Pickering v. Board of Education,* 391 U.S. 563, 88 S.Ct. 1731, 20 L.Ed.2d 811 (1968), the district court held that governmental interests in promoting the efficiency and morale of a department with a crucial public safety mission outweigh [appellant's] interest in speaking in the manner, time, and place which he chose." *Germann v. City of Kansas City,* 579 F.Supp. at 187. Because the district court found that appellees had not discriminated against appellant on the basis of union activity, the district court dismissed his pendent state claim.

This court has recently stated that "'the first amendment is violated by state action whose purpose is...to intimidate public employees...from taking an active part in [union] affairs or to retaliate against those who do.'" *Roberts v. Van Buren Public Schools,* 773 F.2d 949, 957 (8th Cir. 1985) (Roberts), *citing Professional Ass'n of College Educators v. El Paso County Community College District,* 730 F.2d 258, 262, (5th Cir.), *cert. denied,* __U.S.__, 105 S.Ct. 248, 83 L.Ed.2d 186 (1984). However, the court went on to state that "[a]s in the case of speech...an associational right [to join and participate in a union] must be balanced against, and may be overriden by, the government's interest as an employer in efficiency." Roberts, 773 F.2d at 957 (relying on *Pickering v. Board of Education,* 391 U.S. at 567, 88 S.Ct. at 1734).

[1, 2] In applying the *Pickering* balance, courts should consider the following factors:

> (1) the need for harmony in the office or work place; (2) whether the government's responsibilities require a close working relationship to exist between the plaintiff and co-workers when the speech in question has caused or could cause the relationship to deteriorate; (3) the time, manner, and place of the speech; (4) the context in which the dispute arose; (5) the degree of public interest in the speech; and (6) whether the speech impeded the employee's ability to perform his or her duties.

Bowman v. Pulaski County Special School District, 723 F.2d 640, 644 (8th Cir. 1983). It must be kept in mind, however, that the *Pickering* balance is flexible and the weight to be given to any factor varies depending on the circumstances of the case. *Egger v. Phillips,* 710 F.2d 292, 319 (7th Cir.), *cert. denied,* 464 U.S. 918, 104 S.Ct. 284, 78 L.Ed.2d 262 (1983). Resolution of the *Pickering* balance is a question of law dependent on underlying factual findings. *Brockell v. Norton,* 732 F.2d 664, 667 (8th Cir.1984).

For reversal appellant contends that the district court erred in accepting Waas's reliance on the May 11 letter as a lawful basis on which to deny promotion. Appellant maintains that under *Pickering* the letter was protected first amendment activity because the letter addressed a matter of public concern, did not create disharmony in the working place or impede his performance of his duties. Based on our independent consideration of the relevant facts as found by the district court, we disagree.

Although we agree that the May 11 letter addressed a matter of public concern, we nonetheless must consider the tone of the letter. "When a government employee personally confronts his... supervisor, the employing agency's institutional efficiency may be threatened not only by the content of the employee's message but also in the manner, time or place in which it is delivered." *Givhan v. Western Line Consolidated School District,* 439 U.S. 410, 415 n. 4, 99 S.Ct. 693, 969 n. 4, 58 L.Ed.2d 619 (1979). Appellant's May 11 letter accused Waas of being a liar, tearing the department to "shreds," having a "pitifully twisted outlook," and obstructing the department "more completely [than] anyone else on the face of the earth." After receipt of the May 11 letter, Waas understandably felt personally insulted and reasonably questioned appellant's loyalty and respect for him as fire chief and whether appellant would promote and implement department policy. The May 11 letter expressed a degree of personal animosity and distrust beyond the sharp conflict which could be expected as a consequence of forceful representation of opposing interests. *Compare Hickman v. Valley Local School District Board of Education,* 619 F.2d 606, 609 (6th Cir.1980) (personality conflict between president of teacher's union and school principal resulting from union negotiations did not justify teacher's dismissal).

Appellant argues that the fact that the letter was personally insulting to Waas is irrelevant because of the absence of a close working relationship between a battalion chief and the fire chief. The evidence was that personal contact was limited to a two-hour weekly staff meeting. Although in other cases the presence of a close working relationship was critical, *e.g., Connick v. Myers,* 461 U.S. 138, 151, 103 S.Ct. 1684, 1692, 75 L.Ed.2d 708 (1983), "blind insistence upon the presence of an intimate working relationship gives to *Pickering* precisely that rigidity and formalistic structure that the Court so recently denied in *Connick.*" *Gonzales v. Benavides,* 712 F.2d 142, 148 (5th Cir.1983). Here, as the district court noted, because close supervision of a battalion chief by the fire chief was impossible, personal loyalty to the chief was critical to the management structure of the fire department. As was recently stated by the Federal Circuit, "'[c]ohesive operation of management is dependent on the loyalty of inferior management... For management to countenance disloyalty ... would be for management to render itself impotent.'" *Brown v. Department of Transportation,* 735 F.2d 543, 547 (Fed.Cir.1984) (Brown), citing *Brousseau v. United States,* 226 Ct.Cl. 199, 640 F.2d 1235, 1249 (1981).

Appellant also argues that the *Pickering* balance favors him because of the absence of evidence that the May 11 letter caused actual disruption in the work place or impeded his ability to perform his duties. On the facts of this case, appellant "place[s] too great a burden on the agency to show harm." *Brown,* 735 F.2d at 547-48. Although in other cases evidence demonstrating actual disruption of work, *e.g., Hughes v. Whitmer,* 714 F.2d 1407, 1424 (8th Cir. 1983), *cert. denied,* 465 U.S. 1023, 104 S.Ct. 1275, 79 L.Ed.2d 680 (1984), or impaired performance, *Nathanson v. United States,* 702 F.2d 162 (8th Cir.), *cert. denied,* 464 U.S. 939, 104 S.Ct. 352, 78 L.Ed.2d 316 (1983), was significant, the absence of such evidence in this case is not critical. It is not necessary "for an employer to allow events to unfold to the extend that the disruption of the office and the destruction or working relationships is manifest before taking action." *Connick v. Myers,* 461

U.S. at 152, 103 S.Ct. 1693. Appellant's comments were made after a firefighters' strike and amidst great turmoil in the fire department. *See Brown,* 735 F.2d at 547-48 (despite absence of evidence demonstrating substantial harm or interference, nonunion supervisory air traffic controllers' comments encouraging an illegal strike were not protected given timing of comments and agency's interest in insuring safety during an emergency situation resulting from strike). Furthermore, we defer to the district court's finding that at trial appellant continued to demonstrate a great deal of personal hostility and suspicion of Waas. "In this state of affairs it would be folly [for an appellate court] to presume," *Janusaitis v. Middlebury Volunteer Fire Department,* 607 F.2d 17, 27 (2d Cir.1979), that appellant as battalion chief would respect Waas and work diligently to implement and promote his policies.

[3, 4] Our finding that after receiving appellant's May 11 letter Waas was justified in not promoting appellant to battalion chief makes unnecessary a separate *Pickering* analysis of the 1978 telephone conversation and 1979 name calling incident. We note, however, that these instances are indicative of appellant's continuing hostility and disrespect for Waas. Our holding that the May 11 letter was unprotected under *Pickering* also makes it unnecessary to address appellant's contentions that he was discriminated against because he was a named plaintiff in a state lawsuit challenging the exclusion of management employees from the union and had criticized public officials and that the city had a policy of discriminating against union leadership. *See Mt. Healthy City School District Board of Education v. Doyle,* 429 U.S. 274, 287, 97 S.Ct. 568, 576, 50 L.Ed.2d 471 (1977) (an employer can defeat an employee's first amendment claim by demonstrating that the same employment decision would have been made in the absence of protected conduct). Because appellant was not discriminated against on the basis of protected union activities, the district court correctly dismissed appellant's pendent state claim.

Accordingly, the judgment of the district court is affirmed.

NATIONAL TREASURY EMPLOYEES UNION v. VON RAAB

__ U.S. __, 109 S. Ct. 1384, 103 L. Ed. 2d 685 (1989)

Argued Nov. 2, 1988. Decided March 21, 1989.

***

The United States Customs Service, which has as its primary enforcement mission the interdiction and seizure of illegal drugs smuggled into the country, has implemented a drug-screening program requiring urinalysis tests from Service employees seeking transfer or promotion to positions having a direct involvement in drug interdiction or requiring the incumbent to carry firearms or to handle "classified" material. Among other things, the program requires that an applicant be notified that his selection is contingent upon successful completion of drug screening, sets forth procedures for collection and analysis of the requisite samples and procedures designed both to ensure against adulteration or substitution of specimens and to limit the intrusion on employee privacy, and provides that test results may not be turned over to any other agency, including criminal prosecutors, without the employee's written consent. Petitioner's, a federal employees' union and one of its officials, filed suit on behalf of Service employees seeking covered positions, alleging that the drug-testing program violated, *inter alia,* the Fourth Amendment. The District court agreed and enjoined the program. The Court of Appeals vacated the injunction, holding that, although the program effects a search within the meaning of the Fourth Amendment, such searches are reasonable in light of their limited scope and the Service's strong interest in detecting drug use among employees in covered positions.

***

Justice KENNEDY delivered the opinion of the Court.

We granted certiorari to decide whether it violates the Fourth Amendment for the United States Customs Service to require a urinalysis test from employees who seek transfer or promotion to certain positions.

***

II

[1, 2] In *Skinner v. Railway Labor Executives Assn.,* __ U.S. __, __ __, 10̶ S.Ct. 1402, 1412-1413, __ L.Ed.2d __, decided today, we hold that federal regulations requiring employees of private railroads to produce urine samples for chemical testing implicate the Fourth Amendment, as those tests invade reasonable expectations of privacy. Our earlier cases have settled that the Fourth Amendment protects individuals from unreasonable searches conducted by the Government, even when the Government acts as an employer, *O'Connor v. Ortega,* 480 U.S. 709, 717, 107 S.Ct. 1492, 1498, 94 L.Ed.2d 714 (1987) (plurality opinion); see *id.,* at 731, 107 S.Ct., at 1505 (SCALIA, J., concurring in judgment), and, in view of our holding in *Railway Labor Executives* that urine tests are searches, it follows that the Custom Service's drug testing program must meet the reasonableness requirement of the Fourth Amendment.

[3] While we have often emphasized, and reiterate today, that a search must be supported, as a general matter, by a warrant issued upon probable cause, see, *e.g., Griffin v. Wisconsin,* 483 U.S. 868, __, 107 S.Ct. 3164, 3167, 97 L.Ed.2d 709 (1987); *United States v. Karo,* 468 U.S. 705, 717, 104 S.Ct. 3296, 3304, 82 L.Ed.2d 530 (1984), our decision in *Railway Labor Executives* reaffirms the longstanding principle that neither a warrant nor probable cause, nor, indeed, any measure of individualized suspicion, is an indispensable component of reasonableness in every circumstance. *Ante,* at 1413-1416. See also *New Jersey v. T.L.O.,* 469 U.S. 325, 342, n. 8, 105 S.Ct. 733, 743, n. 8, 83 L.Ed.2d 720 (1985); United States v. Martinez-Fuerte, 428 U.S. 543, 556-561, 96 S.Ct. 3074, 3082-3085, 49 L.Ed.2d 1116 (1976). As we note in *Railway Labor Executives,* our cases establish that where a Fourth Amendment intrusion serves special governmental needs, beyond the normal need for law enforcement, it is necessary to balance the individual's privacy expectations against the Government's interests to determine whether it is impractical to require a warrant or some level of individualized suspicion in the particular context. *Ante,* at 1413-1414.

It is clear that the Customs Service's drug testing program is not designed to serve the ordinary needs of law enforcement. Test results may not be used in a criminal prosecution of the employee without the employees consent. The purposes of the program are to deter drug use among those eligible for promotion to sensitive positions within the Service and to prevent the promotion of drug users to those positions. These substantial interests, no less than the Government's concern for safe trail transportation at issue in *Railway Labor Executives,* present a special need that may justify departure from the ordinary warrant and probable cause requirements.

A

[4] Petitioners do not contend that a warrant is required by the balance of privacy and governmental interests in this context, nor could any such contention withstand scrutiny. We have recognized before that requiring the Government to procure a warrant for every work-related intrusion "would conflict with 'the common-sense realization that government offices could not function if every employment decision became a constitutional matter.'" *O'Connor v. Ortega, supra,* 480 U.S., at 722, 107 S.Ct., at 1500, quoting *Connick v. Myers,* 461 U.S. 138, 143, 103 S.Ct. 1684, 1688, 75 L.Ed.2d 708 (1983). *** Even if Customs Service employees are more likely to be familiar with the procedures required to obtain a warrant than most other government workers, requiring a warrant in this context would serve only to divert valuable agency resources from the Service's primary mission. The Customs Service has been entrusted with pressing responsibilities, and its mission would be compromised if it were required to seek search warrants in connection with routine, yet sensitive, employment decisions.

Furthermore, a warrant would provide little or nothing in the way of additional protection of personal privacy. A warrant serves primarily to advise the citizen that an intrusion is authorized by law and limited in its permissible scope and to interpose a neutral magistrate between the citizen and the law enforcement officer "engaged in the often competitive enterprise of ferreting out crime." *Johnson v. United States*, 333 U.S. 10, 14, 68 S.Ct. 367, 369, 92 L.Ed. 436 (1948). But in the present context, "the circumstances justifying toxicological testing and the permissible limits of such intrusions are defined narrowly and specifically..., and doubtless are well known to covered employees." *Ante,* at 1415. Under the Customs program, every employee who seeks a transfer to a covered position knows that he must take a drug test, and is likewise aware of the procedures the Service must follow in administering the test. A covered employee is simply not subject "to the discretion of the official in the field." *Camara v. Municipal Court,* 387 U.S. 523, 532, 87 S.Ct. 1727, 1732, 18 L.Ed.2d 930 (1967). The process becomes automatic when the employee elects to apply for, and thereafter pursue, a covered position. Because the Service does not make a discretionary determination to search based on a judgment that certain conditions are present, there are simply "no special facts for a neutral magistrate to evaluate." *South Dakota v. Opperman,* 428 U.S. 364, 383, 96 S.Ct. 3092, 3104, 49 L.Ed.2d 1000 (1976) (Powell, J., concurring).

B

[5] Even where it is reasonable to dispense with the warrant requirement in the particular circumstances, a search ordinarily must be based on probable cause. *Ante,* at 1416. Our cases teach, however, that the probable-cause standard "'is peculiarly related to criminal investigations.'" *Colorado v. Bertine,* 479 U.S. 367, 371, 107 S.Ct. 738, 741, 93 L.Ed.2d 739 (1987), quoting *South Dakota v. Opperman,* 428 U.S. 364, 370, n. 5, 96 S.Ct. 3092, 3097, n. 5, 49 L.Ed.2d 1000 (1976). In particular, the traditional probable-cause standard may be unhelpful in analyzing the reasonableness of routine administrative functions, *Colorado v. Bertine, supra,* 479 U.S., at 371, 107 S.Ct., at 741; see also *O'Connor v. Ortega,* 480 U.S., at 723, 107 S.Ct., at 1501, especially where the Government seeks to *prevent* the development of hazardous conditions or to detect violations that rarely generate articulable grounds for searching any particular place or person. *** Our precedents have settled that, in certain limited circumstances, the Government's need to discover such latent or hidden conditions, or to prevent their development, is sufficiently compelling to justify the intrusion on privacy entailed by conducting such searches without any measure of individualized suspicion. *E.g., ante,* at 1416-1417. We think the Government's need to conduct the suspicionless searches required by the Customs program outweighs the privacy interests of employees engaged directly in drug interdiction, and of those who otherwise are required to carry firearms.

The Customs Service is our Nation's first line of defense against one of the greatest problems affecting the health and welfare of our population. We have adverted before to "the veritable national crisis in law enforcement caused by smuggling of illicit narcotics." ***

Many of the Service's employees are often exposed to this criminal element and to the controlled substances they seek to smuggle into the country. *Ibid.* Cf. *United States v. Montoya de Hernandez, supra,* 473 U.S., at 543, 105 S.Ct., at 3311. The physical safety of these employees may be threatened, and many may be tempted not only by bribes from the traffickers with whom they deal, but also by their own access to vast sources of valuable contraband seized and controlled by the Service. ***

It is readily apparent that the Government has a compelling interest in ensuring that front-line interdiction personnel are physically fit, and have unimpeachable integrity and judgment. *** This national interest in self protection could be irreparably damaged if those charged with safeguarding it were, because of their own drug use, unsympathetic to their mission of interdicting narcotics. A drug user's indifference to the Service's basic mission or, even worse, his active complicity with the malefactors, can facilitate importation of sizable drug shipments or block apprehension of dangerous criminals. The public interest demands effective measures to bar drug users from positions directly involving the interdiction of illegal drugs.

The public interest likewise demands effective measures to prevent the promotion of drug users to positions that require the incumbent to carry a firearm, even if the incumbent is not engaged directly in the interdiction of drugs. Customs employees who may use deadly force plainly "discharge duties fraught with such risks of injury to others that even a momentary lapse of attention can have disastrous consequences." *Ante,* at 1419. We agree with the Government that the public should not bear the risk that employees who may suffer from impaired perception and judgment will be promoted to positions where they may need to employ deadly force. Indeed, ensuring against the creation of this dangerous risk will itself further Fourth Amendment values, as the use of deadly force may violate the Fourth Amendment in certain circumstances. See *Tennessee v. Garner,* 471 U.S. 1, 7-12, 105 S.Ct. 1694, 1699-1701, 85 L.Ed.2d 1 (1985).

Against these valid public interests we must weigh the interference with individual liberty that results from requiring these classes of employees to undergo a urine test. The interference with individual privacy that results from the collection of a urine sample for subsequent chemical analysis could be substantial in some circumstances. *Ante,* at 1418. We have recognized, however, that the "operational realities of the workplace" may render entirely reasonable certain work-related intrusions by supervisors and co-workers that might be viewed as unreasonable in other contexts. See *O'Conner v. Ortega,* 480 U.S., at 717, 107 S.Ct., at 1498; *id.,* at 732, 107 S.Ct., at 1506 (SCALIA, J., concurring in judgment). While these operational realities will rarely affect an employee's expectations of privacy with respect to searches of his person, or of personal effects that the employee may bring to the workplace, *id.,* at 716, 725, 107 S.Ct., at 1498, 1502, it is plain that certain forms of public employment may diminish privacy expectations even with respect to such personal searches. Employees of the United States Mint, for example, should expect to be subject to certain routine personal searches when they leave the workplace every day. Similarly, those who join our military or intelligence services may not only be required to give what in other contexts might be viewed as extraordinary assurances of trustworthiness and probity, but also may expect intrusive inquiries into their physical fitness for those special positions. Cf. *Snepp v. United States,* 444 U.S. 507, 509, n. 3, 100 S.Ct. 763, 765, n. 3, 62 L.Ed.2d 704 (1980); *Parker v. Levy,* 417 U.S. 733, 758, 94 S.Ct. 2547, 2562, 41 L.Ed.2d 439 (1974); *Committee for GI Rights v. Callaway,* 171 U.S.App.D.C. 73, 84, 518 F.2d 466, 477 (1975).

We think Customs employees who are directly involved in the interdiction of illegal drugs or who are required to carry firearms in the line of duty likewise have a diminished expectation of privacy in respect to the intrusions occasioned by a urine test. Unlike most private citizens or government employees in general, employees involved in drug interdiction reasonably should expect effective inquiry into their fitness and probity. Much the same is true of employees who are required to carry firearms. Because successful performance of their duties depends uniquely on their judgment and dexterity, these employees cannot reasonably expect to keep from the Service personal information that bears directly on their fitness. Cf. In re *Caruso v. Ward,* 72 N.Y.2d 433, 441, 534 N.Y.S.2d 142, 146-148, 530 N.E.2d 850, 854-855 (1988). While reasonable tests designed to elicit this information doubtless infringe some privacy expectations, we do not believe these expectations outweigh the Government's compelling interests in safety and in the integrity of our borders.

***

In sum, we believe the Government has demonstrated that its compelling interests in safeguarding our borders and the public safety outweigh the privacy expectations of employees who seek to be promoted to positions that directly involve the interdiction of illegal drugs or that require the incumbent to carry a firearm. We hold that the testing of these employees is reasonable under the Fourth Amendment.

***

The judgment of the Court of Appeals for the Fifth Circuit is affirmed in part and vacated in part, and the case is remanded for further proceedings consistent with this opinion.

It is so ordered.

***

Justice SCALIA, with whom Justice STEVENS joins, dissenting.

The issue in this case is not whether Customs Service employees can constitutionally be denied promotion, or even dismissed, for a single instance of unlawful drug use, at home or at work. They assuredly can. The issue here is what steps can constitutionally be taken to *detect* such drug use. The Government asserts it can demand that employees perform "an excretory function traditionally shielded by great privacy," *Skinner v. Railway Labor Executives' Assn.*, __ U.S., at __, 109 S.Ct., at 1418, while "a monitor of the same sex...remains close at hand to listen for the normal sounds," *ante*, at 1388, and that the excretion thus produced be turned over to the Government for chemical analysis. The Court agrees that this constitutes a search for purposes of the Fourth Amendment--and I think it obvious that it is a type of search particularly destructive of privacy and offensive to personal dignity.

***

Today's decision would be wrong, but at least of more limited effect, if its approval of drug testing were confined to that category of employees assigned specifically to drug interdiction duties. Relatively few public employees fit that description. But in extending approval of drug testing to that category consisting of employees who carry firearms, the Court exposes vast numbers of public employees to this needless indignity. Logically, of course, if those who carry guns can be treated in this fashion, so can all others whose work, if performed under the influence of drugs, may endanger others--automobile drivers, operators of other potentially dangerous equipment, construction workers, school crossing guards. A similarly broad scope attaches to the Court's approval of drug testing for those with access to "sensitive information." Since this category is not limited to Service employees with drug interdiction duties, nor to "sensitive information" specifically relating to drug traffic, today's holding apparently approves drug testing for all federal employees with security clearances--or, indeed, for all federal employees with valuable confidential information to impart. Since drug use is not a particular problem in the Customs Service, employees throughout the government are no less likely to violate the public trust by taking bribes to feed their drug habit, or by yielding to blackmail. Moreover, there is no reason why this super-protection against harms arising from drug use must be limited to public employees; a law requiring similar testing of private citizens who use dangerous instruments such as guns or cars, or who have access to classified information would also be constitutional.

There is only one apparent basis that sets the testing at issue here apart from all these other situations--but it is not a basis upon which the Court is willing to rely. I do not believe for a minute that the driving force behind these drug-testing rules was any of the feeble justifications put forward by counsel here and accepted by the Court. The only plausible explanation, in my view, is what the Commissioner himself offered in the concluding sentence of his memorandum to Customs Service employees announcing the program: "Implementation of the drug screening program would set an important example in our country's struggle with this most serious threat to our national health and security." App. 12. Or as respondent's brief to this Court asserted: "if a law enforcement agency and its employees do not take the law seriously, neither will the public on which the agency's effectiveness depends." Brief for United States 36. What better way to show that the Government is serious about its "war on drugs" than to subject its employees on the front line of that war to this invasion of their privacy and affront to their dignity? To be sure, there is only a slight chance that it will prevent some serious public harm resulting from Service employee drug use, but it will show to the world that the Service is "clean," and--most important of all--will demonstrate the determination of the Government to eliminate this scourge of our society! I think it obvious that this justification is unacceptable; that the impairment of individual liberties cannot be the means of making a point; that symbolism, even symbolism for so worthy a cause as the abolition of unlawful drugs, cannot validate an otherwise unreasonable search.

There is irony in the Government's citation, in support of its position, of Justice Brandeis's statement in *Olmstead v. United States,* 277 U.S. 438, 485, 48 S.Ct. 564, 575, 72 L.Ed. 944 (1928) that "[f]or good or for ill, [our Government] teaches the whole people by its example." Brief for United States 36. Brandeis was there *dissenting* from the Court's admission of evidence obtained through an unlawful Government wiretap. He was not praising the Government's example of vigor and enthusiasm in combatting crime, but condemning its example that "the end justifies the means," 277 U.S., at 485, 48 S.Ct., at 575. An even more apt quotation from that famous Brandeis dissent would have been the following:

> "[I]t is...immaterial that the intrusion was in aid of law enforcement. Experience should teach us to be most of our guard to protect liberty when the Government's purposes are beneficent. Men born to freedom are naturally alert to repel invasion of their liberty by evil-minded rulers. The greatest dangers to liberty lurk in insidious encroachment by men of zeal, well-meaning but without understanding." *Id.,* at 479, 48 S.Ct., at 572.

Those who lose because of the lack of understanding that begot the present exercise in symbolism are not just the Customs Service employees, whose dignity is thus offended, but all of us--who suffer a coarsening of our national manners that ultimately give the Fourth Amendment its content, and who become subject to the administration of federal officials whose respect for our privacy can hardly be greater than the small respect they have been taught to have for their own.

***

EQUAL EMPLOYMENT OPPORTUNITIES ACT

Publ.L. 88-352, Title VII, § 703, July 2, 1964, 78 Stat. 253 *et seq*. Codified and amended, this Act appears as 42 United States Code § 2000e *et seq*.

Sec.2000e-2(a) It shall be an unlawful employment practice for an employer—

(1) to fail or refuse to hire or to discharge any individual, or otherwise to discriminate against any individual with respect to his compensation, terms, conditions, or privileges of employment, because of such individual's race, color, religion, sex, or national origin; or

(2) to limit, segregate, or classify his employees or applicants for employment in any way which would deprive or tend to deprive any individual of employment opportunities or otherwise adversely affect his status as an employee, because of such individual's race, color, religion, sex, or national origin.

Sec 2000e-2(h) Notwithstanding any other provision of this subchapter, it shall not be an unlawful employment practice for an employer to apply different standards of compensation, or different terms, conditions, or privileges of employment pursuant to a bona fide seniority or merit system,... provided that such differences are not the result of intention to discriminate because of race, color, religion, sex, or national origin, nor shall it be an unlawful employment practice for an employer to give and to act upon the results of any professionally developed ability test provided that such test, its administration and action upon the results is not designed, intended or used to discriminate because of race, color, religion, sex or national origin....

Sec. 2000e-2(j) Nothing contained in this subchapter shall be interpreted to require any employer... subject to this subchapter to grant preferential treatment... because of race, color, religion, sex, or national origin... on account of an imbalance which may exist with respect to the total number or percentage of persons of any race, color, religion, sex, or national origin employed by any employer... in comparison with the total number or percentage of persons of such race, color, religion, sex, or national origin in any community, State, section, or other area, or in the available work force in any community, State, section, or other area.

DOTHARD v. RAWLINSON

433 U.S. 321, 97 S. Ct. 2720, 53 L. Ed. 2d 786 (1977)*

MR. JUSTICE STEWART delivered the opinion of the Court.

Appellee Dianne Rawlinson sought employment with the Alabama Board of Corrections as a prison guard, called in Alabama a "correctional counselor." After her application was rejected, she brought this class suit

*[Some of the Court's footnotes have been omitted and others renumbered.]

under Title VII of the Civil Rights Act of 1964, 78 Stat. 253, as amended, 42 U.S.C. § 2000e *et seq.* (1970 ed. and Supp. V), and under 42 U.S.C. § 1983, alleging that she had been denied employment because of her sex in violation of federal law. A three-judge Federal District Court for the Middle District of Alabama decided in her favor. *Mieth v. Dothard,* 418 F.Supp. 1169. We noted probable jurisdiction of this appeal from the District Court's judgment. 429 U.S. 976, 97 S.Ct. 483, 50 L.Ed.2d 583.

At the time she applied for a position as correctional counselor trainee, Rawlinson was a 22-year-old college graduate whose major course of study had been correctional psychology. She was refused employment because she failed to meet the minimum 120-pound weight requirement established by an Alabama statute. The statute also establishes a height minimum of 5 feet 2 inches.[1]

After her application was rejected because of her weight, Rawlinson filed a charge with the Equal Employment Opportunity Commission, and ultimately received a right-to-sue letter. She then filed a complaint in the District Court on behalf of herself and other similarly situated women, challenging the statutory height and weight minima as violative of Title VII and the Equal Protection Clause of the Fourteenth Amendment. A three-judge court was convened. While the suit was pending, the Alabama Board of Corrections adopted Administrative Regulation 204, establishing gender criteria for assigning correctional counselors to maximum-security institutions for "contact positions," that is, positions requiring continual close physical proximity to inmates of the institution. Rawlinson amended her class-action complaint by adding a challenge to regulation 204 as also violative of Title VII and the Fourteenth Amendment.

Like most correctional facilities in the United States, Alabama's prisons are segregated on the basis of sex. Currently the Alabama Board of Corrections operates four major all-male penitentiaries—Holman Prison, Kilby Corrections Facility, G. K. Fountain Correction Center, and Draper Correctional Center. The Board also operates the Julia Tutwiler Prison for Women, the Frank Lee Youth Center, the Number Four Honor Camp, the State Cattle Ranch, and nine Work Release Centers, one of which is for women. The Julia Tutwiler Prison for Women and the four male penitentiaries are maximum-security institutions. Their inmate living quarters are for the most part large dormitories, with communal showers and toilets that are open to the dormitories and hallways. The Draper and Fountain penitentiaries carry on extensive farming operations, making neces-

[1] The statute establishes minimum physical standards for all law enforcement officers. In pertinent part, it provides:

"(d) *Physical qualifications.*—The applicant shall be not less than five feet two inches nor more than six feet ten inches in height, shall weigh not less than 120 pounds nor more than 300 pounds and shall be certified by a licensed physician designated as satisfactory by the appointing authority as in good health and physically fit for the performance of his duties as a law-enforcement officer. The commission may for good cause shown permit variances from the physical qualifications prescribed in this subdivision." Ala. Code, Tit. 55, § 373(109) (Supp. 1973).

sary a large number of strip searches for contraband when prisoners reenter the prison buildings.

A correctional counselor's primary duty within these institutions is to maintain security and control of the inmates by continually supervising and observing their activities. To be eligible for consideration as a correctional counselor, an applicant must possess a valid Alabama driver's license, have a high school education or its equivalent, be free from physical defects, be between the ages of 20½ years and 45 years at the time of appointment, and fall between the minimum height and weight requirements of 5 feet 2 inches, and 120 pounds, and the maximum of 6 feet 10 inches, and 300 pounds. Appointment is by merit, with a grade assigned each applicant based on experience and education. No written examination is given.

At the time this litigation was in the District Court, the Board of Corrections employed a total of 435 people in various correctional counselor positions, 56 of whom were women. Of those 56 women, 21 were employed at the Julia Tutwiler Prison for Women, 13 were employed in noncontact positions at the four male maximum-security institutions, and the remaining 22 were employed at the other institutions operated by the Alabama Board of Corrections. Because most of Alabama's prisoners are held at the four maximum-security male penitentiaries, 336 of the 435 correctional counselor jobs were in those institutions, a majority of them concededly in the "contact" classification. Thus, even though meeting the statutory height and weight requirements, women applicants could under Regulation 204 compete equally with men for only about 25% of the correctional counselor jobs available in the Alabama prison system.

In enacting Title VII, Congress required "the removal of artificial, arbitrary, and unnecessary barriers to employment when the barriers operate invidiously to discriminate on the basis of racial or other impermissible classification." *Griggs v. Duke Power Co.*, 401 U.S. 424, 431, 91 S.Ct. 849, 853, 28 L.Ed.2d 158. The District Court found that the minimum statutory height and weight requirements that applicants for employment as correctional counselors must meet constitute the sort of arbitrary barrier to equal employment opportunity that Title VII forbids.[2] The appellants assert that the District Court erred both in finding that the height and weight standards discriminate against women, and in its refusal to find that, even if they do, these standards are justified as "job related."

[2] Section 703(a) of Title VII, 42 U.S.C. § 2000e-2(a) (1970 ed. and Supp. V), provides:

"(a) Employer practices. It shall be an unlawful employment practice for an employer—

"(1) to fail or refuse to hire or to discharge any individual, or otherwise to discriminate against any individual with respect to his compensation, terms, conditions, or privileges of employment, because of such individual's race, color, religion, sex, or national origin; or

"(2) to limit, segregate, or classify his employees or applicants for employment in any way which would deprive or tend to deprive any individual of employment opportunities or otherwise adversely affect his status as an employee, because of such individual's race, color, religion, sex, or national origin."

The gist of the claim that the statutory height and weight requirements discriminate against women does not involve an assertion of purposeful discriminatory motive. It is asserted, rather, that these facially neutral qualification standards work in fact disproportionately to exclude women from eligibility for employment by the Alabama Board of Corrections. We dealt in *Griggs v. Duke Power Co., supra* and *Albemarle Paper Co. v. Moody,* 422 U.S. 405, 95 S.Ct. 2362, 45 L.Ed.2d 280, with similar allegations that facially neutral employment standards disproportionately excluded Negroes from employment, and those cases guide our approach here.

Those cases make clear that to establish a prima facie case of discrimination, a plaintiff need only show that the facially neutral standards in question select applicants for hire in a significantly discriminatory pattern. Once it is thus shown that the employment standards are discriminatory in effect, the employer must meet "the burden of showing that any given requirement [has]...a manifest relationship to the employment in question." *Griggs v. Duke Power Co., supra,* at 432, 91 S.Ct., at 854. If the employer proves that the challenged requirements are job related, the plaintiff may then show that other selection devices without a similar discriminatory effect would also "serve the employer's legitimate interest in 'efficient and trustworthy workmanship.'" *Albemarle Paper Co. v. Moody, supra,* at 425, 95 S.Ct., at 2375, quoting *McDonnell Douglas Corp. v. Green,* 411 U.S. 792, 801, 93 S.Ct. 1817, 1823, 36 L.Ed.2d 668.

Although women 14 years of age or older compose 52.75% of the Alabama population and 36.89% of its total labor force, they hold only 12.9% of its correctional counselor positions. In considering the effect of the minimum height and weight standards on this disparity in rate of hiring between the sexes, the District Court found that the 5′2″ requirement would operate to exclude 33.29% of the women in the United States between the ages of 18–79, while excluding only 1.28% of men between the same ages. The 120-pound weight restriction would exclude 22.29% of the women and 2.35% of the men in this age group. When the height and weight restrictions are combined, Alabama's statutory standards would exclude 41.13% of the female population while excluding less than 1% of the male population.[3] Accordingly, the District Court found that Rawlinson had made out a prima facie case of unlawful sex discrimination.

The appellants argue that a showing of disproportionate impact on women based on generalized national

[3] Affirmatively stated, approximately 99.76% of the men and 58.87% of the women meet both these physical qualifications. From the separate statistics on height and weight of males it would appear that after adding the two together and allowing for some overlap the result would be to exclude between 2.35% and 3.63% of males from meeting Alabama's statutory height and weight minima. None of the parties has challenged the accuracy of the District Court's computations on this score, however, and the discrepancy is in any event insignificant in light of the gross disparity between the female and male exclusions. Even under revised computations the disparity would greatly exceed the 34% to 12% disparity that served to invalidate the high school diploma requirement in the *Griggs* case. 401 U.S., at 430, 91 S.Ct., at 853.

statistics should not suffice to establish a prima facie case. They point in particular to Rawlinson's failure to adduce comparative statistics concerning actual applicants for correctional counselor positions in Alabama. There is no requirement, however, that a statistical showing of disproportionate impact must always be based on analysis of the characteristics of actual applicants. See *Griggs v. Duke Power Co., supra,* 401 U.S., at 430, 91 S.Ct., at 853. The application process might itself not adequately reflect the actual potential applicant pool, since otherwise qualified people might be discouraged from applying because of a self-recognized inability to meet the very standards challenged as being discriminatory. See *International Brotherhood of Teamsters v. United States,* 431, U.S. 324, 365–367, 97 S.Ct. 1843, 1869–1871, 52 L.Ed.2d 396. A potential applicant could easily determine her height and weight and conclude that to make an application would be futile. Moreover, reliance on general population demographic data was not misplaced where there was no reason to suppose that physical height and weight characteristics of Alabama men and women differ markedly from those of the national population.

For these reasons, we cannot say that the District Court was wrong in holding that the statutory height and weight standards had a discriminatory impact on women applicants. The plaintiffs in a case such as this are not required to exhaust every possible source of evidence, if the evidence actually presented on its face conspicuously demonstrates a job requirement's grossly discriminatory impact. If the employer discerns fallacies or deficiencies in the data offered by the plaintiff, he is free to adduce countervailing evidence of his own. In this case no such effort was made.

We turn, therefore, to the appellants' argument that they have rebutted the prima facie case of discrimination by showing that the height and weight requirements are job related. These requirements, they say, have a relationship to strength, a sufficient but unspecified amount of which is essential to effective job performance as a correctional counselor. In the District Court, however, the appellants produced no evidence correlating the height and weight requirements with the requisite amount of strength thought essential to good job performance. Indeed, they failed to offer evidence of any kind in specific justification of the statutory standards.

If the job-related quality that the appellants identify is bona fide, their purpose could be achieved by adopting and validating a test for applicants that measures strength directly. Such a test, fairly administered, would fully satisfy the standards of Title VII because it would be one that "measure[s] the person for the job and not the person in the abstract." *Griggs v. Duke Power Co.,* 401 U.S., at 436, 91 S.Ct., at 856. But nothing in the present record even approaches such a measurement.

For the reasons we have discussed, the District Court was not in error in holding that Title VII of the Civil Rights Act of 1964, as amended, prohibits application of the statutory height and weight rquirements to Rawlinson and the class she represents.

Unlike the statutory height and weight requirements, Regulation 204 explicitly discriminates against women on the basis of their sex. In defense of this overt discrimination, the appellants rely on § 703(e) of Title VII, 42 U.S.C. § 2000e–2(e), which permits sex-based discrimination "in those certain instances where... sex ... is a bona fide occupational qualification reasonably necessary to the normal operation of that particular business or enterprise."

The District Court rejected the bona-fide-occupational-qualification (bfoq) defense, relying on the virtually uniform view of the federal courts that § 703(e) provides only the narrowest of exceptions to the general rule requiring equality of employment opportunities. This view has been variously formulated. In *Diaz v. Pan American World Airways,* 442 F.2d 385, 388, the Court of Appeals for the Fifth Circuit held that "discrimination based on sex is valid only when the *essence* of the business operation would be undermined by not hiring members of one sex exclusively." (Emphasis in original.) In an earlier case, *Weeks v. Southern Bell Telephone and Telegraph Co.,* 5 Cir., 408 F.2d 228, 235, the same court said that an employer could rely on the bfoq exception only by proving "that he had reasonable cause to believe, that is, a factual basis for believing, that all or substantially all women would be unable to perform safely and efficiently the duties of the job involved." See also *Phillips v. Martin Marietta Corp.,* 400 U.S. 542, 91 S.Ct. 496, 27 L.Ed.2d 613. But whatever the verbal formulation, the federal courts have agreed that it is impermissible under Title VII to refuse to hire an individual woman or man on the basis of stereotyped characterizations of the sexes, and the District Court in the present case held in effect that Regulation 204 is based on just such stereotypical assumptions.

We are persuaded—by the restrictive language of § 703(e), the relevant legislative history, and the consistent interpretation of the Equal Employment Opportunity Commission—that the bfoq exception was in fact meant to be an extremely narrow exception to the general prohibition of discrimination on the basis of sex. In the particular factual circumstances of this case, however, we conclude that the District Court erred in rejecting the State's contention that Regulation 204 falls within the narrow ambit of the bfoq exception.

The environment in Alabama's penitentiaries is a peculiarly inhospitable one for human beings of whatever sex. Indeed, a Federal District Court has held that the conditions of confinement in the prisons of the State, characterized by "rampant violence" and a "jungle atmosphere," are constitutionally intolerable. *Pugh v. Locke,* 406 F.Supp. 318, 325 (MD Ala.). The record in the present case shows that because of inadequate staff and facilities, no attempt is made in the four maximum-security male penitentiaries to classify or segregate inmates according to their offense or level of dangerousness—a procedure that, according to expert testimony, is essential to effective penological administration. Consequently, the estimated 20% of the male prisoners who are sex offenders are scattered throughout the penitentiaries' dormitory facilities.

In this environment of violence and

disorganization, it would be an oversimplification to characterize Regulation 204 as an exercise in "romantic paternalism." Cf. *Frontiero v. Richardson*, 411 U.S. 677, 684, 93 S.Ct. 1764, 1769, 36 L.Ed.2d 583. In the usual case, the argument that a particular job is too dangerous for women may appropriately be met by the rejoinder that it is the purpose of the Title VII to allow the individual woman to make that choice for herself. More is at stake in this case, however, than an individual woman's decision to weigh and accept the risks of employment in a "contact" position in a maximum-security male prison.

The essence of a correctional counselor's job is to maintain prison security. A woman's relative ability to maintain order in a male, maximum-security, unclassified penitentiary of the type Alabama now runs could be directly reduced by her womanhood. There is a basis in fact for expecting that sex offenders who have criminally assaulted women in the past would be moved to do so again if access to women were established within the prison. There would also be a real risk that other inmates, deprived of a normal heterosexual environment, would assault women guards because they were women. In a prison system where violence is the order of the day, where inmates access to guards is facilitated by dormitory living arrangements, where every institution is understaffed, and where a substantial portion of the inmate population is composed of sex offenders mixed at random with other prisoners, there are few visible deterrents to inmate assaults on women custodians.

Appellee Rawlinson's own expert testified that dormitory housing for aggressive inmates poses a greater security problem than single-cell lockups, and further testified that it would be unwise to use women as guards in a prison where even 10% of the inmates had been convicted of sex crimes and were not segregated from the other prisoners. The likelihood that inmates would assault a woman because she was a woman would pose a real threat not only to the victim of the assault but also to the basic control of the penitentiary and protection of its inmates and the other security personnel. The employee's very womanhood would thus directly undermine her capacity to provide the security that is the essence of a correctional counselor's responsibility.

There was substantial testimony from experts on both sides of this litigation that the use of women as guards in "contact" positions under the existing conditions in Alabama maximum-security male penitentiaries would pose a substantial security problem, directly linked to the sex of the prison guard. On the basis of that evidence, we conclude that the District Court was in error in ruling that being male is not a bona fide occupational qualification for the job of correctional counselor in a "contact" position in an Alabama male maximum-security penitentiary.

The judgment is accordingly affirmed in part and reversed in part, and the case is remanded to the District Court for further proceedings consistent with this opinon.

It is so ordered.

PART III: APPENDIX

THE CONSTITUTION OF THE UNITED STATES OF AMERICA

WE THE PEOPLE of the United States, in Order to form a more perfect Union, establish Justice, insure domestic Tranquility, provide for the common defence, promote the general Welfare, and secure the Blessings of Liberty to ourselves and our Posterity, do ordain and establish this CONSTITUTION for the United States of America.

ARTICLE I.

SECTION 1. All legislative Powers herein granted shall be vested in a Congress of the United States, which shall consist of a Senate and House of Representatives.

SECTION 2. The House of Representatives shall be composed of Members chosen every second Year by the People of the several States, and the Electors in each State shall have the Qualifications requisite for Electors of the most numerous Branch of the State Legislature.

No Person shall be a Representative who shall not have attained to the Age of twenty-five Years, and been seven Years a Citizen of the United States, and who shall not, when elected, be an Inhabitant of that State in which he shall be chosen.

[1] Representatives and direct Taxes shall be apportioned among the several States which may be included within this Union, according to their respective Numbers, which shall be determined by adding to the whole Number of free Persons, including those bound to Service for a Term of Years, and excluding Indians not taxed, three fifths of all other Persons. The actual Enumeration shall be made within three Years after the first Meeting of the Congress of the United States, and within every subsequent Term of ten Years, in such Manner as they shall by Law direct. The Number of Rep-

[1] This clause has been affected by the Fourteenth and Sixteenth Amendments.

resentatives shall not exceed one for every thirty Thousand, but each State shall have at Least one Representative; and until such enumeration shall be made, the State of New Hampshire shall be entitled to chuse three, Massachusetts eight, Rhode-Island and Providence Plantations one, Connecticut five, New-York six, New Jersey four, Pennsylvania eight, Delaware one, Maryland six, Virginia ten, North Carolina five, South Carolina five, and Georgia three.

When vacancies happen in the Representation from any State, the Executive Authority thereof shall issue Writs of Election to fill such Vacancies.

The House of Representatives shall chuse their Speaker and other Officers; and shall have the sole Power of Impeachment.

[2] SECTION 3. The Senate of the United States shall be composed of two Senators from each State, chosen by the Legislature thereof for six Years; and each Senator shall have one Vote.

Immediately after they shall be assembled in Consequence of the first Election, they shall be divided as equally as may be into three Classes. The Seats of the Senators of the first Class shall be vacated at the Expiration of the second Year, of the second Class at the Expiration of the fourth Year, and of the third Class at the Expiration of the sixth Year, so that one third may be chosen every second Year; and if Vacancies happen by Resignation, or otherwise, during the Recess of the Legislature of any State, the Executive thereof may make temporary Appointments until the next Meeting of the Legislature, which shall then fill such Vacancies.

No Person shall be a Senator who shall not have attained to the Age of thirty Years, and been nine Years a Citizen of the United States, and who shall not, when elected, be an Inhabitant of that State for which he shall be chosen.

The Vice President of the United States shall be President of the Senate, but shall have no Vote, unless they be equally divided.

The Senate shall chuse their other Officers, and also a

[2] This section has been affected by the Seventeenth Amendment.

President pro tempore, in the absence of the Vice President, or when he shall exercise the Office of President of the United States.

The Senate shall have the sole Power to try all Impeachments. When sitting for that Purpose, they shall be on Oath or Affirmation. When the President of the United States is tried, the Chief Justice shall preside: And no Person shall be convicted without the Concurrence of two thirds of the Members present.

Judgment in Cases of Impeachment shall not extend further than to removal from Office, and disqualification to hold and enjoy any Office of honor, Trust or Profit under the United States: but the Party convicted shall nevertheless be liable and subject to Indictment, Trial, Judgment and Punishment, according to Law.

[3] SECTION 4. The Times, Places and Manner of holding Elections for Senators and Representatives, shall be prescribed in each State by the Legislature thereof; but the Congress may at any time by Law make or alter such Regulations, except as to the Place of chusing Senators.

The Congress shall assemble at least once in every Year, and such Meeting shall be on the first Monday in December, unless they shall by Law appoint a different Day.

SECTION 5. Each House shall be the Judge of the Elections, Returns and Qualifications of its own Members, and a Majority of each shall constitute a Quorum to do Business; but a smaller Number may adjourn from day to day, and may be authorized to compel the Attendance of absent Members, in such Manner, and under such Penalties as each House may provide.

Each House may determine the Rules of its Proceedings, punish its Members for disorderly Behaviour, and, with the Concurrence of two thirds, expel a Member.

Each House shall keep a Journal of its Proceedings, and from time to time publish the same, excepting such Parts as may in their Judgment require Secrecy; and the Yeas and Nays

[3] This section has been affected by the Twentieth Amendment.

of the Members of either House on any question shall, at the Desire of one fifth of those Present, be entered on the Journal.

Neither House, during the Session of Congress, shall, without the Consent of the other, adjourn for more than three days, nor to any other Place than that in which the two Houses shall be sitting.

SECTION 6. The Senators and Representatives shall receive a Compensation for their Services, to be ascertained by Law, and paid out of the Treasury of the United States. They shall in all Cases, except Treason, Felony and Breach of the Peace, be privileged from Arrest during their Attendance at the Session of their respective Houses, and in going to and returning from the same; and for any Speech or Debate in either House, they shall not be questioned in any other Place.

No Senator or Representative shall, during the Time for which he was elected, be appointed to any civil Office under the Authority of the United States, which shall have been created, or the Emoluments whereof shall have been encreased during such time; and no Person holding any Office under the United States, shall be a Member of either House during his Continuance in Office.

SECTION 7. All Bills for raising Revenue shall originate in the House of Representatives; but the Senate may propose or concur with Amendments as on other Bills.

Every Bill which shall have passed the House of Representatives and the Senate, shall, before it become a Law, be presented to the President of the United States; If he approve he shall sign it, but if not he shall return it, with his Objections to that House in which it shall have originated, who shall enter the Objections at large on their Journal, and proceed to reconsider it. If after such Reconsideration two thirds of that House shall agree to pass the Bill, it shall be sent, together with the Objections, to the other House, by which it shall likewise be reconsidered, and if approved by two thirds of that House, it shall become a Law. But in all such Cases the Votes of both Houses shall be determined by Yeas and Nays, and the Names of the Persons voting for and against the Bill shall be entered on the Journal of each House respectively. If any

Bill shall not be returned by the President within ten Days (Sundays excepted) after it shall have been presented to him, the Same shall be a Law, in like Manner as if he had signed it, unless the Congress by their Adjournment prevent its Return, in which Case it shall not be a Law.

Every Order, Resolution, or Vote to which the Concurrence of the Senate and House of Representatives may be necessary (except on a question of Adjournment) shall be presented to the President of the United States; and before the Same shall take Effect, shall be approved by him, or being disapproved by him, shall be repassed by two thirds of the Senate and House of Representatives, according to the Rules and Limitations prescribed in the Case of a Bill.

SECTION 8. The Congress shall have Power To lay and collect Taxes, Duties, Imposts and Excises, to pay the Debts and provide for the common Defence and general Welfare of the United States; but all Duties, Imposts and Excises shall be uniform throughout the United States;

To borrow Money on the credit of the United States;

To regulate Commerce with foreign Nations, and among the several States, and with the Indian Tribes;

To establish an uniform Rule of Naturalization, and uniform Laws on the subject of Bankruptcies throughout the United States;

To coin Money, regulate the Value thereof, and of foreign Coin, and fix the Standard of Weights and Measures;

To provide for the Punishment of counterfeiting the Securities and current Coin of the United States;

To establish Post Offices and post Roads;

To promote the Progress of Science and useful Arts, by securing for limited Times to Authors and Inventors the exclusive Right to their respective Writings and Discoveries;

To constitute Tribunals inferior to the supreme Court;

To define and punish Piracies and Felonies committed on the high Seas, and Offences against the Law of Nations;

To declare War, grant Letters of Marque and Reprisal, and make Rules concerning Captures on Land and Water;

To raise and support Armies, but no Appropriation of

Money to that Use shall be for a longer Term than two Years;

To provide and maintain a Navy;

To make Rules for the Government and Regulation of the land and naval Forces;

To provide for calling forth the Militia to execute the Laws of the Union, suppress Insurrections and repel Invasions;

To provide for organizing, arming, and disciplining the Militia, and for governing such Part of them as may be employed in the Service of the United States, reserving to the States respectively, the Appointment of the Officers, and the Authority of training the Militia according to the discipline prescribed by Congress;

To exercise exclusive Legislation in all Cases whatsoever, over such District (not exceeding ten Miles square) as may, by Cession of particular States, and the Acceptance of Congress, become the Seat of the Government of the United States, and to exercise like Authority over all Places purchased by the Consent of the Legislature of the State in which the Same shall be, for the Erection of Forts, Magazines, Arsenals, dock-Yards, and other needful Buildings;—And

To make all Laws which shall be necessary and proper for carrying into Execution the foregoing Powers, and all other Powers vested by this Constitution in the Government of the United States, or in any Department or Officer thereof.

SECTION 9. The Migration or Importation of such Persons as any of the States now existing shall think proper to admit, shall not be prohibited by the Congress prior to the Year one thousand eight hundred and eight, but a Tax or duty may be imposed on such Importation, not exceeding ten dollars for each Person.

The privilege of the Writ of Habeas Corpus shall not be suspended, unless when in Cases of Rebellion or Invasion the public Safety may require it.

No Bill of Attainder or ex post facto Law shall be passed.

[4] No Capitation, or other direct, Tax shall be laid, unless in Proportion to the Census or Enumeration herein before directed to be taken.

[4] This clause has been affected by the Sixteenth Amendment.

No Tax or Duty shall be laid on Articles exported from any State.

No Preference shall be given by any Regulation of Commerce or Revenue to the Ports of one State over those of another: nor shall Vessels bound to, or from, one State, be obliged to enter, clear, or pay Duties in another.

No Money shall be drawn from the Treasury, but in Consequence of Appropriations made by Law; and a regular Statement and Account of the Receipts and Expenditures of all public Money shall be published from time to time.

No Title of Nobility shall be granted by the United States: And no Person holding any Office of Profit or Trust under them, shall, without the Consent of the Congress, accept of any present, Emolument, Office, or Title, of any kind whatever, from any King, Prince, or foreign State.

SECTION 10. No State shall enter into any Treaty, Alliance, or Confederation; grant Letters of Marque and Reprisal; coin Money; emit Bills of Credit; make any Thing but gold and silver Coin a Tender in Payment of Debts; pass any Bill of Attainder, ex post facto Law, or Law impairing the Obligation of Contracts, or grant any Title of Nobility.

No State shall, without the Consent of the Congress, lay any Imposts or Duties on Imports or Exports, except what may be absolutely necessary for executing it's inspection Laws: and the net Produce of all Duties and Imposts, laid by any State on Imports or Exports, shall be for the Use of the Treasury of the United States; and all such Laws shall be subject to the Revision and Controul of the Congress.

No State shall, without the Consent of Congress, lay any Duty of Tonnage, keep Troops, or Ships of War in time of Peace, enter into any Agreement or Compact with another State, or with a foreign Power, or engage in War, unless actually invaded, or in such imminent Danger as will not admit of delay.

ARTICLE II.

SECTION 1. The executive Power shall be vested in a President of the United States of America. He shall hold his Office during the Term of four Years, and, together with the Vice President, chosen for the same Term, be elected, as follows

Each State shall appoint, in such Manner as the Legislature thereof may direct, a Number of Electors, equal to the whole Number of Senators and Representatives to which the State may be entitled in the Congress: but no Senator or Representative, or Person holding an Office of Trust or Profit under the United States, shall be appointed an Elector.

[5] The Electors shall meet in their respective States, and vote by Ballot for two persons, of whom one at least shall not be an Inhabitant of the same State with themselves. And they shall make a List of all the Persons voted for, and of the Number of Votes for each; which List they shall sign and certify, and transmit sealed to the Seat of the Government of the United States, directed to the President of the Senate. The President of the Senate shall, in the Presence of the Senate and House of Representatives, open all the Certificates, and the Votes shall then be counted. The Person having the greatest Number of Votes shall be the President, if such Number be a Majority of the whole Number of Electors appointed; and if there be more than one who have such Majority, and have an equal Number of Votes, then the House of Representatives shall immediately chuse by Ballot one of them for President; and if no Person have a Majority, then from the five highest on the List the said House shall in like Manner chuse the President. But in chusing the President, the Votes shall be taken by States, the Representation from each State having one Vote; A quorum for this Purpose shall consist of a Member or Members from two thirds of the States, and a Majority of all the States shall be necessary to a Choice. In every Case, after the Choice of the President, the Person having the greatest Number of Votes of the Electors shall be the Vice President. But if there should remain two or more who have equal Votes, the Senate shall chuse from them by Ballot the Vice President.

The Congress may determine the Time of chusing the

[5] This clause has been affected by the Twelfth Amendment.

Electors, and the Day on which they shall give their Votes; which Day shall be the same throughout the United States.

No person except a natural born Citizen, or a Citizen of the United States, at the time of the Adoption of this Constitution, shall be eligible to the Office of President; neither shall any Person be eligible to that Office who shall not have attained to the Age of thirty five Years, and been fourteen Years a Resident within the United States.

In Case of the Removal of the President from Office, or of his Death, Resignation, or Inability to discharge the Powers and Duties of the said Office, the same shall devolve on the Vice President, and the Congress may by Law provide for the Case of Removal, Death, Resignation or Inability, both of the President and Vice President, declaring what Officer shall then act as President, and such Officer shall act accordingly, until the Disability be removed, or a President shall be elected.

The President shall, at stated Times, receive for his Services, a Compensation, which shall neither be encreased nor diminished during the Period for which he shall have been elected, and he shall not receive within that Period any other Emolument from the United States, or any of them.

Before he enter on the Execution of his Office, he shall take the following Oath or Affirmation:—"I do solemnly swear (or affirm) that I will faithfully execute the Office of President of the United States, and will to the best of my Ability, preserve, protect and defend the Constitution of the United States."

SECTION 2. The President shall be Commander in Chief of the Army and Navy of the United States, and of the Militia of the several States, when called into the actual Service of the United States; he may require the Opinion in writing, of the principal Officer in each of the executive Departments, upon any subject relating to the Duties of their respective Offices, and he shall have Power to grant Reprieves and Pardons for Offenses against the United States, except in Cases of Impeachment.

He shall have Power, by and with the Advice and Consent of the Senate, to make Treaties, provided two thirds of the

Senators present concur; and he shall nominate, and by and with the Advice and Consent of the Senate, shall appoint Ambassadors, other public Ministers and Consuls, Judges of the supreme Court, and all other Officers of the United States, whose Appointments are not herein otherwise provided for, and which shall be established by Law: but the Congress may by Law vest the Appointment of such inferior Officers, as they think proper, in the President alone, in the Courts of Law, or in the Heads of Departments.

The President shall have Power to fill up all Vacancies that may happen during the Recess of the Senate, by granting Commissions which shall expire at the End of their next Session.

SECTION 3. He shall from time to time give to the Congress Information of the State of the Union, and recommend to their Consideration such Measures as he shall judge necessary and expedient; he may, on extraordinary Occasions, convene both Houses, or either of them, and in Case of Disagreement between them, with Respect to the Time of Adjournment, he may adjourn them to such Time as he shall think proper; he shall receive Ambassadors and other public Ministers; he shall take Care that the Laws be faithfully executed, and Shall Commission all the Officers of the United States.

SECTION 4. The President, Vice President and all civil Officers of the United States, shall be removed from Office on Impeachment for, and Conviction of, Treason, Bribery, or other high Crimes and Misdemeanors.

ARTICLE III.

SECTION 1. The judicial Power of the United States, shall be vested in one supreme Court, and in such inferior Courts as the Congress may from time to time ordain and establish. The Judges, both of the supreme and inferior Courts, shall hold their Offices during good Behaviour, and shall, at stated Times, receive for their Services, a Compensation, which shall not be diminished during their Continuance in Office.

[6] SECTION 2. The judicial Power shall extend to all Cases, in Law and Equity, arising under this Constitution, the Laws of the United States, and Treaties made, or which shall be made, under their Authority;—to all Cases affecting Ambassadors, other public Ministers and Consuls;—to all Cases of admiralty and maritime Jurisdiction;—to Controversies to which the United States shall be a Party;—to Controversies between two or more States;—between a State and Citizens of another State;—between citizens of different States;—between Citizens of the same State claiming Lands under Grants of different States, and between a State, or the Citizens thereof, and foreign States, Citizens or Subjects.

In all Cases affecting Ambassadors, other public Ministers and Consuls, and those in which a State shall be Party, the supreme Court shall have original Jurisdiction. In all the other Cases before mentioned, the supreme Court shall have appellate Jurisdiction, both as to Law and Fact, with such Exceptions, and under such Regulations as the Congress shall make.

The Trial of all Crimes, except in Cases of Impeachment, shall be by Jury; and such Trial shall be held in the State where the said Crimes shall have been committed; but when not committed within any State, the Trial shall be at such Place or Places as the Congress may by Law have directed.

SECTION 3. Treason against the United States, shall consist only in levying War against them, or in adhering to their Enemies, giving them Aid and Comfort. No Person shall be convicted of Treason unless on the Testimony of two Witnesses to the same overt Act, or on Confession in open Court.

The Congress shall have Power to declare the Punishment of Treason, but no Attainder of Treason shall work Corruption of Blood, or Forfeiture except during the Life of the Person attainted.

ARTICLE IV.

SECTION 1. Full Faith and Credit shall be given in each State to the public Acts, Records, and judicial Proceedings of every

[6] This section has been affected by the Eleventh Amendment.

other State. And the Congress may by general Laws prescribe the Manner in which such Acts, Records and Proceedings shall be proved, and the Effect thereof.

SECTION 2. The Citizens of each State shall be entitled to all Privileges and Immunities of Citizens in the several States.

A Person charged in any State with Treason, Felony, or other Crime, who shall flee from Justice, and be found in another State, shall on Demand of the executive Authority of the State from which he fled, be delivered up, to be removed to the State having Jurisdiction of the Crime.

[7] No Person held to Service or Labour in one State, under the Laws thereof, escaping into another, shall, in Consequence of any Law or Regulation therein, be discharged from such Service or Labour, but shall be delivered up on Claim of the Party to whom such Service or Labour may be due.

SECTION 3. New States may be admitted by the Congress into this Union; but no new State shall be formed or erected within the Jurisdiction of any other State; nor any State be formed by the Junction of two or more States, or parts of States, without the Consent of the Legislatures of the States concerned as well as of the Congress.

The Congress shall have Power to dispose of and make all needful Rules and Regulations respecting the Territory or other Property belonging to the United States; and nothing in this Constitution shall be so construed as to Prejudice any Claims of the United States, or of any particular State.

SECTION 4. The United States shall guarantee to every State in this Union a Republican Form of Government, and shall protect each of them against Invasion; and on Application of the Legislature, or of the Executive (when the Legislature cannot be convened) against domestic Violence.

ARTICLE V.

The Congress, whenever two thirds of both Houses shall deem it necessary, shall propose Amendments to this Constitution, or, on the Application of the Legislatures of two

[7] This clause was affected by the Thirteenth Amendment.

thirds of the several States, shall call a Convention for proposing Amendments, which, in either Case, shall be valid to all Intents and Purposes, as Part of this Constitution, when ratified by the Legislatures of three fourths of the several States, or by Conventions in three fourths thereof, as the one or the other Mode of Ratification may be proposed by the Congress; Provided that no Amendment which may be made prior to the Year One thousand eight hundred and eight shall in any Manner affect the first and fourth Clauses in the Ninth Section of the first Article; and that no State, without its Consent, shall be deprived of its equal Suffrage in the Senate.

ARTICLE VI.

All Debts contracted and Engagements entered into, before the Adoption of this Constitution, shall be as valid against the United States under this Constitution, as under the Confederation.

This Constitution, and the Laws of the United States which shall be made in Pursuance thereof; and all Treaties made, or which shall be made, under the Authority of the United States, shall be the supreme Law of the Land; and the Judges in every State shall be bound thereby; any Thing in the Constitution or Laws of any State to the Contrary notwithstanding.

The Senators and Representatives before mentioned, and the Members of the several State Legislatures, and all executive and judicial Officers, both of the United States and of the several States, shall be bound by Oath or Affirmation, to support this Constitution; but no religious Test shall ever be required as a Qualification to any Office or public Trust under the United States.

ARTICLE VII.

The Ratification of the Conventions of nine States shall be sufficient for the Establishment of this Constitution between the States so ratifying the Same.

DONE in Convention by the Unanimous Consent of the States present the Seventeenth Day of September in the Year of our Lord one thousand seven hundred and Eighty seven and of the Independence of the United States of America the Twelfth. IN WITNESS whereof We have hereunto subscribed our Names,

Go. WASHINGTON—*Presidt. and deputy from Virginia*

New Hampshire

JOHN LANGDON
NICHOLAS GILMAN

Massachusetts

NATHANIEL GORHAM
RUFUS KING

Connecticut

WM. SAML. JOHNSON
ROGER SHERMAN

New York

ALEXANDER HAMILTON

New Jersey

WIL: LIVINGSTON
DAVID BREARLEY
WM. PATERSON
JONA: DAYTON

Pennsylvania

B. FRANKLIN
THOMAS MIFFLIN
ROBT. MORRIS
GEO. CLYMER
THOS. FITZSIMONS
JARED INGERSOLL
JAMES WILSON
GOUV MORRIS

Delaware

GEO: READ
GUNNING BEDFORD jun
JOHN DICKINSON
RICHARD BASSETT
JACO: BROOM

Maryland

JAMES MCHENRY
DAN OF ST THOS JENIFER
DANL. CARROLL

Virginia

JOHN BLAIR
JAMES MADISON, JR.

North Carolina

WM. BLOUNT
RICHD. DOBBS SPAIGHT
HU WILLIAMSON

South Carolina

J. RUTLEDGE
CHARLES COTESWORTH PINCKNEY
CHARLES PINCKNEY
PIERCE BUTLER

Georgia

WILLIAM FEW
ABR BALDWIN

Attest
WILLIAM JACKSON
Secretary

Articles in Addition To, and Amendment Of, the Constitution of the United States of America, Proposed by Congress, and Ratified by the Legislatures of the Several States, Pursuant to the Fifth Article of the Original Constitution.

AMENDMENT I. (1791)

Congress shall make no law respecting an establishment of religion, or prohibiting the free exercise thereof; or abridging the freedom of speech, or of the press; or the right of the people peaceably to assemble, and to petition the Government for a redress of grievances.

AMENDMENT II. (1791)

A well regulated Militia, being necessary to the security of a free State, the right of the people to keep and bear Arms, shall not be infringed.

AMENDMENT III. (1791)

No Soldier shall, in time of peace be quartered in any house, without the consent of the Owner, nor in time of war, but in a manner to be prescribed by law.

AMENDMENT IV. (1791)

The right of the people to be secure in their persons, houses, papers, and effects, against unreasonable searches and seizures, shall not be violated, and no Warrants shall issue, but upon probable cause, supported by Oath or affirmation, and particularly describing the place to be searched, and the persons or things to be seized.

AMENDMENT V. (1791)

No person shall be held to answer for a capital, or otherwise infamous crime, unless on a presentment or indictment of a Grand Jury, except in cases arising in the land or naval forces, or in the Militia, when in actual service in time of War or public danger; nor shall any person be subject for the same offence to be twice put in jeopardy of life or limb; nor shall be compelled in any criminal case to be a witness against himself, nor be deprived of life, liberty, or property, without due process of law; nor shall private property be taken for public use, without just compensation.

AMENDMENT VI. (1791)

In all criminal prosecutions, the accused shall enjoy the right to a speedy and public trial, by an impartial jury of the State and district wherein the crime shall have been committed, which district shall have been previously ascertained by law, and to be informed of the nature and cause of the accusation; to be confronted with the witnesses against him; to have compulsory process for obtaining Witnesses in his favor, and to have the Assistance of Counsel for his defence.

AMENDMENT VII. (1791)

In Suits at common law, where the value in controversy shall exceed twenty dollars, the right of trial by jury shall be preserved, and no fact tried by a jury, shall be otherwise reexamined in any Court of the United States, than according to the rules of the common law.

AMENDMENT VIII. (1791)

Excessive bail shall not be required, nor excessive fines imposed, nor cruel and unusual punishments inflicted.

AMENDMENT IX. (1791)

The enumeration of the Constitution, of certain rights, shall not be construed to deny or deparage others retained by the people.

AMENDMENT X. (1791)

The powers not delegated to the United States by the Constitution, nor prohibited by it to the States, are reserved to the States respectively, or to the people.

AMENDMENT XI. (1798)

The Judicial power of the United States shall not be construed to extend to any suit in law or equity, commenced or prosecuted against one of the United States by Citizens of another State, or by Citizens or Subjects of any Foreign State.

AMENDMENT XII.[S] (1804)

The Electors shall meet in their respective states and vote by ballot for President and Vice-President, one of whom, at least, shall not be an inhabitant of the same state with themselves; they shall name in their ballots the person voted for as President, and in distinct ballots the person voted for as Vice-President, and they shall make distinct lists of all persons voted for as President, and of all persons voted for as Vice-President, and of the number of votes for each, which lists they shall sign and certify, and transmit sealed to the seat of the government of the United States, directed to the President of the Senate;—The President of the Senate shall, in the presence of the Senate and House of Representatives, open all the certificates and the votes shall then be counted; —The person having the greatest number of votes for President, shall be the President, if such number be a majority of the whole number of Electors appointed; and if no person have such majority, then from the persons having the highest numbers not exceeding three on the list of those voted for as President, the House of Representatives shall choose immediately, by ballot, the President. But in choosing the President, the votes shall be taken by states, the representation from each state having one vote; a quorum for this purpose shall consist of a member or members from two-thirds of the states, and a majority of all the states shall be necessary to a choice.

[S] This amendment was affected by the Twentieth Amendment, section 3.

And if the House of Representatives shall not choose a President whenever the right of choice shall devolve upon them, before the fourth day of March next following, then the Vice-President shall act as President, as in the case of the death or other constitutional disability of the President. The person having the greatest number of votes as Vice-President, shall be the Vice-President, if such number be a majority of the whole number of Electors appointed, and if no person have a majority, then from the two highest numbers on the list, the Senate shall choose the Vice-President; a quorum for the purpose shall consist of two-thirds of the whole number of Senators, and a majority of the whole number shall be necessary to a choice. But no person constitutionally ineligible to the office of President shall be eligible to that of Vice-President of the United States.

AMENDMENT XIII. (1865)

SECTION 1. Neither slavery nor involuntary servitude, except as a punishment for crime whereof the party shall have been duly convicted, shall exist within the United States, or any place subject to their jurisdiction.

SECTION 2. Congress shall have power to enforce this article by appropriate legislation.

AMENDMENT XIV. (1868)

SECTION 1. All persons born or naturalized in the United States, and subject to the jurisdiction thereof, are citizens of the United States and of the State wherein they reside. No State shall make or enforce any law which shall abridge the privileges or immunities of citizens of the United States; nor shall any State deprive any person of life, liberty, or property, without due process of law; nor deny to any person within its jurisdiction the equal protection of the laws.

SECTION 2. Representatives shall be apportioned among the several States according to their respective numbers, counting the whole number of persons in each State, excluding Indians not taxed. But when the right to vote at any election for the choice of electors for President and Vice-President of the

United States, Representatives in Congress, the Executive and Judicial officers of a State, or the members of the Legislature thereof, is denied to any of the male inhabitants of such State, being twenty-one years of age, and citizens of the United States, or in any way abridged, except for participation in rebellion, or other crime, the basis of representation therein shall be reduced in the proportion which the number of such male citizens shall bear to the whole number of male citizens twenty-one years of age in such State.

SECTION 3. No person shall be a Senator or Representative in Congress, or elector of President and Vice-President, or hold any office, civil or military, under the United States, or under any State, who, having previously taken an oath, as a member of Congress, or as an officer of the United States, or as a member of any State legislature, or as an executive or judicial officer of any State, to support the Constitution of the United States, shall have engaged in insurrection or rebellion against the same, or given aid or comfort to the enemies thereof. But Congress may by a vote of two-thirds of each House, remove such disability.

SECTION 4. The validity of the public debt of the United States, authorized by law, including debts incurred for payment of pensions and bounties for services in suppressing insurrection or rebellion, shall not be questioned. But neither the United States nor any State shall assume or pay any debt or obligation incurred in aid of insurrection or rebellion against the United States, or any claim for the loss or emancipation of any slave; but all such debts, obligations and claims shall be held illegal and void.

SECTION 5. The Congress shall have power to enforce, by appropriate legislation, the provisions of this article.

AMENDMENT XV. (1870)

SECTION 1. The right of citizens of the United States to vote shall not be denied or abridged by the United States or by any State on account of race, color, or previous condition of servitude.

SECTION 2. The Congress shall have power to enforce this article by appropriate legislation.

AMENDMENT XVI. (1913)

The Congress shall have power to lay and collect taxes on incomes, from whatever source derived, without apportionment among the several States, and without regard to any census or enumeration.

AMENDMENT XVII. (1913)

The Senate of the United States shall be composed of two Senators from each State, elected by the people thereof, for six years; and each Senator shall have one vote. The electors in each State shall have the qualifications requisite for electors of the most numerous branch of the State legislatures.

When vacancies happen in the representation of any State in the Senate, the executive authority of such State shall issue writs of election to fill such vacancies: *Provided,* That the legislature of any State may empower the executive thereof to make temporary appointments until the people fill the vacancies by election as the legislature may direct.

This amendment shall not be so construed as to affect the election or term of any Senator chosen before it becomes valid as part of the Constitution.

AMENDMENT XVIII.[9] (1919)

SECTION 1. After one year from the ratification of this article the manufacture, sale, or transportation of intoxicating liquors within, the importation thereof into, or the exportation thereof from the United States and all territory subject to the jurisdiction thereof for beverage purposes is hereby prohibited.

SECTION 2. The Congress and the several States shall have concurrent power to enforce this article by appropriate legislation.

SECTION 3. This article shall be inoperative unless it shall have been ratified as an amendment to the Constitution by the legislatures of the several States, as provided in the Constitution, within seven years from the date of the submission hereof to the States by the Congress.

[9] Repealed. See the Twenty-first Amendment.

AMENDMENT XIX. (1920)

The right of citizens of the United States to vote shall not be denied or abridged by the United States or by any State on account of sex.

Congress shall have power to enforce this article by appropriate legislation.

AMENDMENT XX. (1933)

SECTION 1. The terms of the President and Vice President shall end at noon on the 20th day of January, and the terms of Senators and Representatives at noon on the 3d day of January, of the years in which such terms would have ended if this article had not been ratified; and the terms of their successors shall then begin.

SECTION 2. The Congress shall assemble at least once in every year, and such meeting shall begin at noon on the 3d day of January, unless they shall by law appoint a different day.

SECTION 3. If, at the time fixed for the beginning of the term of the President, the President elect shall have died, the Vice President elect shall become President. If a President shall not have been chosen before the time fixed for the beginning of his term, or if the President elect shall have failed to qualify, then the Vice President elect shall act as President until a President shall have qualified; and the Congress may by law provide for the case wherein neither a President elect nor a Vice President elect shall have qualified, declaring who shall then act as President, or the manner in which one who is to act shall be selected, and such person shall act accordingly until a President or Vice President shall have qualified.

SECTION 4. The Congress may by law provide for the case of the death of any of the persons from whom the House of Representatives may choose a President whenever the right of choice shall have devolved upon them, and for the case of the death of any of the persons from whom the Senate may choose a Vice President whenever the right of choice shall have devolved upon them.

SECTION 5. Sections 1 and 2 shall take effect on the 15th day of October following the ratification of this article.

SECTION 6. This article shall be inoperative unless it shall have been ratified as an amendment to the Constitution by the legislatures of three-fourths of the several States within seven years from the date of its submission.

AMENDMENT XXI. (1933)

SECTION 1. The eighteenth article of amendment to the Constitution of the United States is hereby repealed.

SECTION 2. The transportation or importation into any State, Territory, or possession of the United States for delivery or use therein of intoxicating liquors, in violation of the laws thereof, is hereby prohibited.

SECTION 3. This article shall be inoperative unless it shall have been ratified as an amendment to the Constitution by conventions in the several States, as provided in the Constitution, within seven years from the date of the submission hereof to the States by the Congress.

AMENDMENT XXII. (1951)

SECTION 1. No person shall be elected to the office of the President more than twice, and no person who has held the office of President, or acted as President, for more than two years of a term to which some other person was elected President shall be elected to the office of the President more than once. But this Article shall not apply to any person holding the office of President when this Article was proposed by the Congress, and shall not prevent any person who may be holding the office of President, or acting as President, during the term within which this Article becomes operative from holding the office of President or acting as President during the remainder of such term.

SECTION 2. This article shall be inoperative unless it shall have been ratified as an amendment to the Constitution by the legislatures of three-fourths of the several States within seven years from the date of its submission to the States by the Congress.

AMENDMENT XXIII. (1961)

SECTION 1. The District constituting the seat of Government of the United States shall appoint in such manner as the Congress may direct:

A number of electors of President and Vice President equal to the whole number of Senators and Representatives in Congress to which the District would be entitled if it were a State, but in no event more than the least populous State; they shall be in addition to those appointed by the States, but they shall be considered, for the purposes of the election of President and Vice President, to be electors appointed by a State; and they shall meet in the District and perform such duties as provided by the twelfth article of amendment.

SECTION 2. The Congress shall have power to enforce this article by appropriate legislation.

AMENDMENT XXIV. (1964)

SECTION 1. The right of citizens of the United States to vote in any primary or other election for President or Vice President, for electors for President or Vice President, or for Senator or Representative in Congress, shall not be denied or abridged by the United States or any State by reason of failure to pay any poll tax or other tax.

SECTION 2. The Congress shall have power to enforce this article by appropriate legislation.

AMENDMENT XXV. (1967)

SECTION 1. In case of the removal of the President from office or of his death or resignation, the Vice President shall become President.

SECTION 2. Whenever there is a vacancy in the office of the Vice President, the President shall nominate a Vice President who shall take office upon confirmation by a majority vote of both Houses of Congress.

SECTION 3. Whenever the President transmits to the President pro tempore of the Senate and the Speaker of the House of Representatives his written declaration that he is unable to discharge the powers and duties of his office, and until he transmits to them a written declaration to the contrary, such powers and duties shall be discharged by the Vice President as Acting President.

SECTION 4. Whenever the Vice President and a majority of either the principal officers of the executive departments or of such other body as Congress may by law provide, transmit to the President pro tempore of the Senate and the Speaker of the House of Representatives their written declaration that the President is unable to discharge the powers and duties of his office, the Vice President shall immediately assume the powers and duties of the office as Acting President.

Thereafter, when the President transmits to the President pro tempore of the Senate and the Speaker of the House of Representatives his written declaration that no inability exists, he shall resume the powers and duties of his office unless the Vice President and a majority of either the principal officers of the executive department or of such other body as Congress may by law provide, transmit within four days to the President pro tempore of the Senate and the Speaker of the House of Representatives their written declaration that the President is unable to discharge the powers and duties of his office. Thereupon Congress shall decide the issue, assembling within forty-eight hours for that purpose if not in session. If the Congress, within twenty-one days after receipt of the latter written declaration, or, if Congress is not in session, within twenty-one days after Congress is required to assemble, determines by two-thirds vote of both Houses that the President is unable to discharge the powers and duties of his office, the Vice President shall continue to discharge the same as Acting President; otherwise, the President shall resume the powers and duties of his office.

AMENDMENT XXVI. (1971)

SECTION 1. The right of citizens of the United States, who are eighteen years of age or older, to vote shall not be denied or abridged by the United States or by any State on account of age.

SECTION 2. The Congress shall have power to enforce this article by appropriate legislation.

TABLE OF CASES

This listing includes all cases cited in the textual material in Part I. Those cases which appear in **bold face type** are also reprinted in Part II. For those select cases, see the *Table of Cases for Part II*, which appears on page 631.

References are to section numbers

Flood v. Kennedy, 12 N.Y.2d 345, 239 N.Y.S.2d 665, 190 N.E.2d 13 (1963) **12.7**
The Florida Star v. BJF, 109 S. Ct, 2603 (1989) **10.13**
Flynn v. Giarrusso, 321 F. Supp. 1295 (E.D. La. 1971) **12.4**
Folie v. Connelie, 435 U.S. 291 (1978) **12.6**
Fong Foo v. United States, 369 U.S. 141 (1962) **9.6**
Ford v. Childers, 650 F. Supp. 110 (C.D. Ill. 1986) **3.14**
Ford v. Wainwright, 477 U.S. 399 (1986) **10.17**
Foster v. California, 394 U.S. 440 (1969) **7.14**
Fountain v. City of Waycross, 701 F. Supp. 1570 (S.D. Ga. 1988) **12.12**
Frank v. United States, 395 U.S. 147 (1969) **10.7**
Franks v. Delaware, 438 U.S. 154 (1978) **4.7**
Fraternal Order of Police Lodge No. 5 v. Tucker, 868 F.2d 74 (3d Cir. 1989) **12.8**
Freeman v. United States, 237 F.2d 815 (2d Cir. 1916) **9.5**
Frisbie v. Collins, 342 U.S. 519 (1952) **3.3**
Frisby v. Schultz, 108 S. Ct. 2495 (1988) **2.15**
Furman v. Georgia, 408 U.S. 238 (1972) **10.16, 10.17**

Gagnon v. Scarpelli, 411 U.S. 778 (1973) **8.14**
Gandy v. State, 42 Ala. App. 215, 159 So. 2d 71, *cert. denied*, 276 Ala. 704, 159 So. 2d 73 (1963) **9.8**
Gannett Co. v. DePasquale, 443 U.S. 368 (1979) **10.5, 10.13**
Garcia v. San Antonio Metropolitan Transit Authority, 469 U.S. 528 (1985) **1.11**
Gardner v. Broderick, 392 U.S. 273 (1968) **7.10**
Garrett v. United States, 471 U.S. 773 (1985) **9.8**
Garrity v. New Jersey, 385 U.S. 493 (1967) **6.2, 7.10**
Gasparinetti v. Kerr, 568 F.2d 311 (3d Cir. 1977), *cert. denied*, 436 U.S. 903 (1978) **12.4**
Gavieres v. United States, 220 U.S. 338 (1911) **9.8, 9.9**
Geary v. Commonwealth, 503 S.W.2d 505 (Ky. 1972) **4.14**
Gelbard v. United States, 408 U.S. 41 (1972) **5.11**
Gerstein v. Pugh, 420 U.S. 103 (1975) **3.8**
Gibson v. City of Chicago, 701 F. Supp. 666 (N.D. Ill. 1988) **11.6**
Gideon v. Wainwright, 372 U.S. 335 (1963) **1.14, 1.16, 8.5, 8.8**
Giglio v. United States, 405 U.S. 150 (1972) **10.15**

INDEX

References are to section numbers